The
Papers
of
James Monroe

The Papers of James Monroe

A Comprehensive Catalogue of the Correspondence and Papers of James Monroe
2 volumes

The Papers of James Monroe, Volume 1:
A Documentary History of the Presidential tours of James Monroe,
1817, 1818, 1819

The Papers of James Monroe, Volume 2:
Selected Correspondence and Papers,
1776-1794

The Papers of James Monroe, Volume 3:
Selected Correspondence and Papers,
1794-1796

The
Papers
of
James Monroe

Selected Correspondence and Papers, 1794–1796

VOLUME 3

WITHDRAWN

Daniel Preston, Editor

Marlena C. DeLong, Assistant Editor

Prepared under the auspices of the
James Monroe Presidential Center
The University of Mary Washington
Fredericksburg, Virginia

GREENWOOD PRESS
An Imprint of ABC-CLIO, LLC

ABC🟤CLIO

Santa Barbara, California • Denver, Colorado • Oxford, England

Copyright 2009 by Daniel Preston, Editor, Marlena C. DeLong, Assistant Editor

Cataloging-in-Publication Data is on file with the Library of Congress

ISBN: 978-0-313-31980-8

13 12 11 10 9   1   2   3   4   5

This book is also available on the World Wide Web as an eBook.
Visit www.abc-clio.com for details.

ABC-CLIO, LLC
130 Cremona Drive, P.O. Box 1911
Santa Barbara, California 93116-1911

This book is printed on acid-free paper ∞

Manufactured in the United States of America

Permission Acknowledgments

The editor and publisher gratefully acknowledge permission to reprint the following material.

Excerpts from archival material:

Adams Family Papers. Letter from John Quincy Adams, 12 March 1795, pg. 269–271. Adams family papers, 1639-1889, microfilm edition, 608 reels (Boston: Massachusetts Historical Society, 1954-1959), reel 127, Massachusetts Historical Society. Letter to John Quincy Adams, 2 April 1795, pg. 284–285. Adams family papers, 1639-1889, microfilm edition, 608 reels (Boston: Massachusetts Historical Society, 1954-1959), reel 379, Massachusetts Historical Society. Letter to John Quincy Adams, 6 May 1795, pg. 304–305. Adams family papers, 1639-1889, microfilm edition, 608 reels (Boston: Massachusetts Historical Society, 1954-1959), reel 379, Massachusetts Historical Society. Letter to John Quincy Adams, 14 June 1795, pg. 355. Adams family papers, 1639-1889, microfilm edition, 608 reels (Boston: Massachusetts Historical Society, 1954-1959), reel 379, Massachusetts Historical Society. Letter from Willink, Van Staphorst & Hubbard, 17 Dec 1795, pg. 543. Adams family papers, 1639-1889, microfilm edition, 608 reels (Boston: Massachusetts Historical Society, 1954-1959), reel 380, Massachusetts Historical Society.

American Philosophical Society. Letter from William Short, 26 Aug 1794, pg. 42–43. Courtesy of the American Philosophical Society. Letter from Willhemina Mosheim Golofkin, 4 Oct 1794, pg. 96–97. Courtesy of the American Philosophical Society.

Connecticut Historical Society. Letter from Thomas B Adams 4 Dec 1795, pg. 530. Courtesy of the Connecticut Historical Society. Letter to Thomas B Adams, 11 Dec 1795, pg. 537. Courtesy of the Connecticut Historical Society. Letter to Thomas B Adams, 28 Dec 1795, pg. 555. Courtesy of the American Philosophical Society. Letter from Thomas B Adams 29 Dec 1795, pg. 555–556. Courtesy of the Connecticut Historical Society.

Cornell University Library. Letter from Aaron Burr. Courtesy of the Division of Rare and Manuscript Collections, Cornell University Library.

Duke University Library. List of toasts, 4 July 1795, pg. 395–396. Purviance Family Papers, Duke University Rare Book, Manuscript, and Special Collections Library.

Haverford College Library. Letter To Robert R. Livingston. Courtesy of the Haverford College Library, Haverford, PA, Special Collections, Charles Roberts Autograph Letters Collection, Coll. No. 722.

Historical Society of Pennsylvania. Letter from William Short, 30 Sept 1794, pg. 90–91. The Historical Society of Pennsylvania, Gilpin Collection: Short Papers. Letter to William Short, 19 Nov 1794, pg. 149–150. The Historical Society of Pennsylvania, Gilpin Collection: Short Papers. Letter from William Short, 10 Jan 1795, pg. 201. The Historical Society of Pennsylvania, Gilpin Collection: Short Papers. Letter from William Short, 28 July 1795, pg. 407. The Historical Society of Pennsylvania, Gilpin Collection: Short Papers. Letter from Edmund Randolph, 8 Mar 1795, pg. 257–259. The Historical Society of Pennsylvania, Gilpin Collection: Short Papers. Letter to Robert R. Livingston, 23 June 1795, pg. 372–373. The Historical Society of Pennsylvania, Gilpin Collection: Short Papers. Letter to Samuel Bayard, 18 Sept 1795, pg. 457–458. The Historical Society of Pennsylvania, Gilpin Collection: Short Papers. Letter to Charles Delacroix, 19 Dec 1795, pg. 544. The Historical Society of Pennsylvania, Gilpin Collection: Short Papers. Letter from George Clinton, 8 Sept 1794, pg. 60. The Historical Society of Pennsylvania, Dreer Collection. Letter from Enoch Edwards, 2 Oct 1795, pg. 473–474. The Historical Society of Pennsylvania, Provincial Delegates Collection. Letter to Samuel Bayard, 17 Dec 1795, pg. 542–543. The Historical Society of Pennsylvania, Society Collection.

Houghton Library. Letter to Ralph Izard, Aug 1795, pg. 431–432. Courtesy of the Houghton Library, Harvard University. Call number MS AM.

James S. Copley Library. Letter to Edmund Randolph, 17 Au 1795, pg. 419–421. From the collection of The James S. Copley Library.

Lilly Library. Letter to Thomas Pinckney, 23 Sept 1795, pg. 466. Courtesy Lilly Library, Indiana University, Bloomington IN.

Massachusetts Historical Society. Letter from Edmund Randolph, 2 May, pg. 299–300. Charles Edward French Autograph Collection, Massachusetts Historical Society. Letter to John Beckley, 23 June 1795, pg. 368–372. Alexander Calvin and Ellen Morton Washburn Autograph Collection, Massachusetts Historical Society. Letter to Philibert Buchot, 22 Aug 1794, pg. 37. R.C. Waterston Autograph Collection, Massachusetts Historical Society.

Morristown National History Park. Letter to Henry Tazewll, 6 June 1794, pg. 6. Courtesy of Morristown National Historical Park. Letter to Henry Tazewell, 22 June 1794, pg. 18–19. Courtesy of Morristown National Historical Park. Letter from Ralph Izard, 29 Jan 1795, pg. 211–213. Courtesy of Morristown National Historical Park. Letter to Madame Lafayette, 11 March 1795, pg. 267–268. Courtesy of Morristown National Historical Park. Letter to Jean-Victor Colchen, 27 July 1795, pg. 380–381. Courtesy of Morristown National Historical Park.

New-York Historical Society. Letter to Edmund Randolph, 7 Nov 1794, pg. 141–144. Courtesy of the Gilder Lehrman Collection at the New-York Historical SocietyLetter to John Jay, 17 Jan 1795, pg. 207. Courtesy of the Gilder Lehrman Collection at the New-York Historical Society.

Pierpont Morgan Library. Letter from John Jay, 19 Feb 1795, pg. 222. The Pierpont Morgan Library, New York.

Princeton University Library. Four letters of James Monroe and one letter of Thomas Pinckney. Courtesy of Manuscripts Division, Department of Rare Books and Special Collections, Princeton University Library.

Rosenbach Museum & Library. Letter from Stephen Cathalan, 4 Oct 1794, pg. 94–95. Courtesy of the Rosenbach Museum & Library.

South Carolina Historical Society. Letter from William Allen Deas, 7 Nov 1795, pg. 508–509. Courtesy of the South Carolina Historical Society.

Special Collections & University Archives, The University of Iowa. Letter from Melancton Smith, 1796, pg. 577–578. Courtesy of Special Collections & University Archives, The University of Iowa.

Virginia Historical Society. Letter To William A Deas, 30 Sept 1795, pg. 470–471. Courtesy of the Virginia Historical Society.

CONTENTS

Acknowledgements   xix
Introduction: Notes on the Documents   xxi
Editorial Method   xxiii
Abbreviations and Short Titles   xxv

1794

To James Madison, 26 May   1
To Thomas Jefferson, 27 May   1
Commission as Minister to France, 28 May   2
Credence as Minister to France, 28 May   3
From Aaron Burr, 30 May   3
To George Washington, 1 June   4
From Aaron Burr, 5 June   5
To Thomas Jefferson, 6 June   5
To Henry Tazewell, 6 June   6
From Edmund Randolph, 10 June   6
From Pierre de Rieux, 12 June   12
To Henry Lee, 12 June   14
To Joseph J. Monroe, 16 June   14
To Thomas Jefferson, 17 June   16
To Fulwar Skipwith, before 19 June   17
From John Francis Mercer, June   17
To George Clinton, 19 June   18
Journal, 19 June   18
To Henry Tazewell, 22 June   18
To St. George Tucker, 22 June   19
From John Langdon, 24 July   19
From Edmund Randolph, 30 July   20
Journal, 31 July   22
To Philippe Merlin de Douai, 13 August   24
To Edmund Randolph, 15 August   24
To the French Convention, 15 August   30
From Philippe Merlin de Douai, 15 August   31
Journal, 15 August   32
From Thomas Paine, 16 August   33
From Thomas Paine, 17 August   34
From La Société Populaire de Billom, 19 August   36

To Philibert Buchot, 22 August   37
From John Jay, 24 August   37
From Thomas Paine, 25 August   38
To Edmund Randolph, 25 August   39
From William Short, 26 August   42
From Adrienne Lafayette, 27 August   44
From Gouverneur Morris, 31 August   46
To La Société Populaire de Billom, August   47
To James Madison, 2 September   47
To the Committee of Public Safety, 3 September   49
To Joseph Jones, 4 September   52
From Philibert Buchot, 6 September   56
To Thomas Jefferson, 7 September   58
From George Clinton, 8 September   60
From Joseph Fenwick, 8 September   61
From Diego de Gardoqui, 9 September   63
To André-Antoine Bernard, 10 September   63
To Philibert Buchot, 13 September   64
From Philibert Buchot, 14 September   64
From M. G. Hector St. John Crèvecoeur, 14 September   66
From Thomas Paine, 14 September   67
To Edmund Randolph, 15 September   73
From Etienne-Solomon Reybez, 15 September   77
To Etienne-Solomon Reybez, September   77
From Adrienne Lafayette, 18 September   78
From Robert R. Livingston, 18 September   79
To Thomas Paine, 18 September   81
From Thomas Pinckney, 18 September   82
To Thomas Pinckney, 19 September   83
To Philibert Buchot, 20 September   84
To Philibert Buchot, 22 September   84
     Enclosures: From Henry Preble, 22 September   85
                  From Jared Goodrich, September   86
To J. Hector St. John de Crèvecoeur, 22 September   86
From Edmund Randolph, 25 September   87
From William Short, 30 September   90
From William Short, 30 September   91
From Adrienne Lafayette, 3 October   92
From Stephen Cathalan, 4 October   94
From Wilhelmina Mosheim Golofkin, 4 October   96
From Thomas Paine, 4 October   97
From Edmund Randolph, 4 October   98
To James C. Mountflorence, 5 October   99
From James Anderson, 6 October   100
From Diego de Gardoqui, 7 October   102

To Louis-Guillaume Otto, 9 October   102
From Gouverneur Morris, 10 October   103
From James Swan, 11 October   103
To Jacques LeRay de Chaumont, 13 October   104
From Thomas Paine, 13 October   104
To Edmund Randolph, 16 October   109
From Thomas Pinckney, 17 October   116
From Fulwar Skipwith, 17 October   117
To the Committee of Public Safety, 18 October   122
From Adrienne Lafayette, 18 October   126
From the Committee of Public Safety, 21 October   127
From Thomas Paine, 21 October   128
From Philip Filicchy, 22 October   134
From Mr. Cibon, 26 October   135
From John Jay, 31 October   136
Journal, October   136
To the Committee of General Security, 1 November   138
From Thomas Paine, 2 November   139
From Thomas Pinckney, 3 November   140
To Edmund Randolph, 7 November   141
To David Humphreys, 11 November   145
To the Committee of Public Safety, 13 November   145
From Edmund Randolph, 17 November   146
To Diego de Gardoqui, 18 November   147
Observations Submitted to the Consideration of the Diplomatic
    Members of the Committee of Public Safety, 19 November   148
To William Short, 19 November   149
From William Short, 19 November   150
To George Washington, 19 November   151
To Edmund Randolph, 20 November   153
From John Quincy Adams, 22 November   156
To Mr. Cibon, 22 November   157
From John Jay, 24 November   158
From André-François Miot, 24 November   158
From John Jay, 25 November   160
From André-François Miot, 26 November   160
To James Madison, 30 November   161
From Adrienne Lafayette, [November]   165
To the Committee of Public Safety, 1 December   171
From Edmund Randolph, 2 December   172
To Edmund Randolph, 2 December   174
From James Madison, 4 December   179
From John Brown, 5 December   182
From John Langdon, 5 December   185
From Edmund Randolph, 5 December   186

From Edmund Randolph, 5 December   186
From P. Feuty, 8 December   187
To James Madison, 18 December   187
To Edmund Randolph, 18 December   188
From the Committee of Public Safety, 26 December   191
To the Committee of Public Safety, 27 December   192
To the Committee of Public Safety, 27 December   193
From Edmund Randolph, 30 December   193
To the Société Populaire de Nevers, 1794   194
To Unknown, [1794-1795]   194

1795

To the Committee of Public Safety, 4 January   195
From the Committee of Public Safety, 5 January   196
From the Committee of Public Safety, 7 January   197
To Thomas Pinckney, 7 January   199
From Jeanne-Louise-Henriette Genet Campan, 9 January   199
To the Committee of Public Safety, 10 January   200
From William Short, 10 January   201
From Joseph Fenwick, 11 January   202
To Edmund Randolph, 13 January   202
To John Jay, 17 January   207
From Pierce Butler, 19 January   207
To the Committee of Public Safety, 28 January   209
From Ralph Izard, 29 January   211
From Benjamin Vaughan, 29 January   213
To Joseph Jones, 1 February   216
To Edmund Randolph, 1 February   218
From the Committee of Public Safety, 5 February   221
From John Jay, 5 February   222
From Robert Brooke, 6 February   223
From Fulwar Skipwith, 10 February   223
To Edmund Randolph, 12 February   224
From Edmund Randolph, 15 February   229
To James Madison, 18 February   230
From Thomas Pinckney, 18 February   232
To Edmund Randolph, 18 February   234
From William Short, 18 February   235
To the Committee of Public Safety, 19 February   237
From John Jay, 19 February   237
From Robert R. Livingston, 19 February   238
To John Brown, 20 February   239
From James C. Mountflorence, 22 February   240
From John Quincy Adams, 23 February   241

To Robert R. Livingston, 23 February 242
From William Short, 23 February 244
To James Madison, 25 February 245
From Adrienne Lafayette, [February] 247
From James C. Mountflorence, [February] 249
From James C. Mountflorence, 1 March 250
To the Committee of Public Safety, 2 March 251
From Thomas Pinckney, 6 March 252
To Edmund Randolph, 6 March 253
From Edmund Randolph, 8 March 257
From St. George Tucker, 8 March 259
From James C. Mountflorence, 9 March 263
From Henry Tazewell, 9 March 264
To Adrienne Lafayette, 11 March 267
From James Madison, 11 March 268
From John Quincy Adams, 12 March 269
To Edmund Randolph, 17 March 271
From John Quincy Adams, 23 March 273
From David Gelston, 24 March 274
From Joseph Jones, 26 March 275
From James Madison, 26 March 276
From Emmanuel Sieyès, 26 March 278
From James Madison, 27 March 280
From John Quincy Adams, 30 March 281
From Benjamin Hichborn, 31 March 282
To Fulwar Skipwith, [March] 283
To John Quincy Adams, 2 April 284
From Jean-Victor Colchen, 4 April 285
To Jean-Victor Colchen, 7 April 286
From Edmund Randolph, 7 April 287
From William Short, 11 April 288
To Edmund Randolph, 14 April 290
From Timothy Pickering, 27 April 297
To Fulwar Skipwith, 1 May 299
From Edmund Randolph, 2 May 299
From William Short, 4 May 300
To William Short, 4 May 302
To John Quincy Adams, 6 May 304
From Joseph Fenwick, 15 May 305
From John Quincy Adams, 16 May 305
To Edmund Randolph, 17 May 307
From Thomas Jefferson, 26 May 311
To Francis Coffyn, Jr., 28 May 314
From Claude-Adam Delamotte, 28 May 315
To William Short, 30 May 316

From Edmund Randolph, 31 May   317
From John Beckley, 1 June   318
From Edmund Randolph, 1 June   321
To Jean Victor Colchen, 3 June   339
From George Washington, 5 June   339
Notes on a Constitution, 7 June   340
From Edmund Randolph, 7 June   350
From Stephen Rochefontaine, 10 June   350
From Joseph Fenwick, 11 June   351
From Joseph Jones, 12 June   352
To James Madison, 13 June   353
To John Quincy Adams, 14 June   355
To Edmund Randolph, 14 June   356
From Thomas Pinckney, 15 June   363
To the U.S. Consuls in France, 17 June   363
From David Gelston, 18 June   365
To Joseph Jones, 20 June   366
To John Beckley, 23 June   368
To Robert R. Livingston, 23 June   372
From Oliver Wolcott, 23 June   374
From John Langdon, 24 June   375
To George Logan, 24 June   375
From Edmé Mauduit, 24 June   377
To Edmund Randolph, 26 June   378
From Jean-Victor Colchen, 27 June   380
To Thomas Jefferson, 27 June   381
From Henry Tazewell, 27 June   382
To James Madison, 28 June   383
From Stevens Thomson Mason, 29 June   384
To James Madison, 30 June   385
To Fulwar Skipwith, 30 June   386
From Baron Staël-Holstein, 30 June   386
To Joseph Jones, 2 July   389
From Edmund Randolph, 2 July   390
To Jean-Victor Colchen, 3 July   390
To Thomas Jefferson, 3 July   391
To Edmund Randolph, 4 July   392
Independence Day Toasts, 4 July   395
From Aaron Burr, 5 July   397
To the Committee of Public Safety, 5 July   397
From John Quincy Adams, 8 July   398
To Fulwar Skipwith, 8 July   399
To the Committee of Public Safety, 10 July   399
From Robert R. Livingston, 10 July   400
From Edmund Randolph, 14 July   401

To the Committee of Public Safety, 15 July 402
To Jean-Claude Redon, 20 July 403
From Edmund Randolph, 21 July 403
From Jean Delmas and Jean-Baptiste Treilhard, 23 July 404
To James Madison, 26 July 405
To Jean-Victor Colchen, 27 July 406
To the Committee of Public Safety, 28 July 406
From William Short, 28 July 407
From Edmund Randolph, 29 July 408
From Edmund Randolph, 30 July 409
To Edmund Randolph, 1 August 410
From Aaron Burr, 2 August 413
From Joseph Fenwick, 3 August 414
To Joseph Jones, 4 August 414
To James Madison, 5 August 415
From Melancton Smith, 6 August 416
From Joseph Fenwick, 8 August 416
From David Gelston, 15 August 417
From Benjamin Vaughan, 15 August 418
To Edmund Randolph, 17 August 419
To Robert Brooke, 20 August 421
From Samuel Bayard, 21 August 421
From Joseph Fenwick, 22 August 422
To James Madison, 22 August 423
From William Short, 22 August 425
From Robert R. Livingston, 25 August 426
To Fulwar Skipwith, 26 August 427
From Thomas Pinckney, 27 August 427
From Janet Montgomery, 29 August 428
To Jean-Claude Redon, 30 August 429
From Joseph Fenwick, 31 August 430
To Ralph Izard, August 431
To Jean-Victor Colchen, 1 September 432
From Thomas Jefferson, 6 September 433
From Thomas Pinckney, 7 September 435
To James Madison, 8 September 436
To the Secretary of State, 10 September 441
From William Short, September 10 444
To Oliver Wolcott, 10 September 445
From Aaron Burr, 11 September 446
From Timothy Pickering, 12 September 447
To Thomas Pinckney, 13 September 452
From Timothy Pickering, 14 September 453
To Joseph Jones, 15 September 455
To Samuel Bayard, 18 September 457

From Benjamin Vaughan, 18 September   459
To Jean-Claude Redon, 19 September   463
From John Beckley, 23 September   464
To Thomas Pinckney, 23 September   466
From Stephen Cathalan, 26 September   467
From François Barbé-Marbois, 28 September   468
From William Short, 28 September   469
To William Allen Deas, 30 September   470
To Timothy Pickering, 30 September   471
To Stephen Rochefontaine, 30 September   472
From Jeanne-Louise Campan, [September-October]   473
From Enoch Edwards, 2 October   473
To David Humphreys, 2 October   474
To David Humphreys, 3 October   475
To Mr. Cibon, 4 October   475
To the Secretary of State, 4 October   476
From David Humphreys, 5 October   478
To Jean-Victor Colchen, 7 October   480
From Timothy Pickering, 9 October   481
From Samuel Bayard, 18 October   481
To Thomas Pinckney, 19 October   483
To the Secretary of State, 20 October   484
From Claude-Adam Delamotte, 21 October   493
To James Madison, 23 October   494
From John Quincy Adams, 24 October   496
To James Madison, 24 October   497
To Fulwar Skipwith, 26 October   500
From Joseph Fenwick, 28 October   500
To James Madison, 29 October   502
To Joseph Rayneval, 30 October   504
From Elbridge Gerry, 2 November   505
To Timothy Pickering, 5 November   505
From Fulwar Skipwith, 5 November   507
From William Allen Deas, 7 November   508
From Charles Delacroix, 7 November   509
From Timothy Pickering, 7 November   509
To James Madison, 8 November   511
From Constantin Volney, 8 November   512
To Charles Delacroix, 10 November   514
To Benjamin Vaughan, 11 November   514
From Charles Delacroix, 15 November   514
To Adrienne Lafayette, 16 November   516
To Thomas Jefferson, 18 November   516
To Fulwar Skipwith, 19 November   521
From Timothy Pickering, 23 November   522

To Fulwar Skipwith, 25 November   522
To Charles Delacroix, 2 December   523
To Charles Delacroix, 3 December   524
From William Hull, 3 December   526
Account With Gabriel Thouin, 3 December   526
From Thomas B. Adams, 4 December   530
From Charles Delacroix, 4 December   531
From Charles Delacroix, 4 December   531
From Andrew Masson, 6 December   533
To Timothy Pickering, 6 December   534
To Charles Delacroix, 9 December   536
To Thomas B. Adams, 11 December   537
From Robert R. Livingston, 13 December   537
From John Beckley, 14 December   538
From Charles Delacroix, 14 December   539
To Guillaume-Charles Faipoult, 14 December   540
From Thomas B. Adams, 17 December   541
From Samuel Bayard, 17 December   542
From Willink, Van Staphorst & Hubbard, 17 December   543
To Charles Delacroix, 19 December   544
From James Madison, 20 December   544
From Guillaume-Charles Faipoult, 21 December   547
To Timothy Pickering, 22 December   547
From Charles Delacroix, 23 December   550
From Aaron Burr, 24 December   550
From Willink, Van Staphorst & Hubbard, 24 December   551
From Henry Tazewell, 26 December   553
To Thomas B. Adams, 28 December   555
From Thomas B. Adams, 29 December   555

1796

From Fulwar Skipwith, 1 January   556
To George Washington, 3 January   556
From Timothy Pickering, 7 January   558
To Thomas Pinckney, 7 January   559
From John S. Eustace, 10 January   560
To James Madison, 12 January   563
To Oliver Wolcott, 14 January   566
From John Breckinridge, 15 January   566
To Charles Delacroix, 16 January   568
From Joseph Jones, 16 January   570
To James Madison, 20 January   573
From Guillaume-Charles Faipoult, 22 January   576
From David Humphreys, 23 January   576

To Melancton Smith, 25 January   577
From James Madison, 25 January   579
From James Madison, 26 January   579
To Timothy Pickering, 26 January   581
From Thomas Pinckney, 29 January   583
From Andrew Masson, 2 February   584
To Guillaume-Charles Faipoult, 4 February   586
From Jean-Jacques Cambacérès, 5 February   586
From Guillaume-Charles Faipoult, 5 February   587
From Jacob Van Staphorst, 10 February   587
From Thomas Pinckney, 15 February   588
Theobald Wolfe Tone Journal, 15 February   589
To Timothy Pickering, 16 February   590
To Charles Delacroix, 17 February   591
From Charles Delacroix, 20 February   593
To Timothy Pickering, 20 February   594
From Bartholomew Terrasson, 20 February   595
From Joel Barlow, 23 February   596
Theobald Wolfe Tone Journal, 23 February   599
From Joel Barlow, 26 February   600
From James Madison, 26 February   601
To James Madison, 27 February   604
From Fulwar Skipwith, 27 February   605
To Charles Delacroix, 28 February   605
Theobald Wolfe Tone Journal, 28 February   607
From Thomas Jefferson, 2 March   607
To Charles Delacroix, 5 March   609
Journal, 8 March   609
From Charles Delacroix, 9 March   612
From David Humphreys, 9 March   618
From Aaron Burr, 10 March   619
To Timothy Pickering, 11 March   619
To Charles Delacroix, 15 March   621
To Andrew Masson, 20 March   627
From Thomas Jefferson, 21 March   628
To Charles Delacroix, 24 March   628
To James Madison, 24 March   629
To Thomas Pinckney, 24 March   630
To George Washington, 24 March   631
To Timothy Pickering, 25 March   631
To Joseph Jones, 26 March   634
From Thomas Pinckney, 26 March   635
To Philippe Merlin de Douai, 29 March   636

Index   639

ACKNOWLEDGMENTS

We wish to extend our thanks to the many people who have lent their aid to the preparation of this volume, beginning with graphic designer Dorothy Thompson, who prepared the camera-ready copy of the text. A host of librarians and archivists at institutions across the United States has provided research assistance and copies of documents. We wish to especially thank the staff of Simpson Library here at the University of Mary Washington. Thanks also goes to our colleagues at other documentary editing projects—most notably the Jefferson Papers, Madison Papers, Washington Papers, and Jackson Papers—for their help and advice. We continue to benefit from the assistance of our student aides. Caitlin Smith, Laura Summers, and Lisa Meissner typed transcriptions and did other useful tasks. Sandra Ricks and Gisele Novak helped Assistant Editor Marlena DeLong with transcribing and translating the documents written in French. The University of Mary Washington, as always, provides a congenial home for the Monroe Papers, and we offer our thanks to everyone here—administrators, faculty, and students—who have helped us in a hundred different ways. Very special thanks goes to Richard Hurley, interim president at UMW, and Judy Hample, our new president, for their strong support of the Monroe Papers.

INTRODUCTION: NOTES ON THE DOCUMENTS

This volume covers a portion of the period of Monroe's term as U. S. minister to France, beginning with his appointment in May 1794 and ending with March 1796. The remainder of the documents for this period—from April 1796 until his departure from France in April 1797—will be presented in volume four. Much has been written about Monroe's tenure in Paris, and much of that has been critical. This volume presents a broader range of documents regarding Monroe's ministry than has been heretofore available in print, and will perhaps allow readers to formulate a more accurate and more just assessment of Monroe's performance as minister.

Monroe's correspondence with Secretaries of State Edmund Randolph and Timothy Pickering is complete and is published in its entirety except for a few letters relating to minor administrative matters. None of Monroe's original dispatches to the secretary of state survives in the records of the State Department in the National Archives; there are only letterbook copies of dubious quality made by a clerk in the State Department. Some originals of Monroe's dispatches exist in collections in other repositories, and these have been used when found. The copies in the State Department records have been used only when no other version was available.

Monroe's correspondence with the French government also appears to be complete. Documents of the greatest significance are, of course, published, as are many of those of a secondary nature. Letters of secondary importance that are not published are referenced, when appropriate, in annotations. Letters on routine matters (arrangements for meetings, for example) are not published. Letters written in French are accompanied by English translations.

France was at war with Great Britain during Monroe's ministry, and the treaty signed by the United States and Great Britain (the Jay Treaty) in November 1794 caused a storm of controversy. Much of Monroe's correspondence centers on this crisis. The war created a number of other problems that required Monroe's attention, most notably the detention of persons and the seizure of ships and other property. Monroe received numerous letters requesting his assistance in obtaining the release of persons and restitution for seized property. Only a few of these letters have been published as representative of this aspect of Monroe's duties.

Two cases relating to detained persons received special attention. Thomas Paine, the renowned pamphleteer of the American Revolutionary War, was imprisoned in Paris because of his English birth. The correspondence relating to Monroe's successful efforts to obtain his release is given in full. After his release from prison, Paine, who was seriously ill, resided with Monroe. Monroe's efforts to restrain Paine from publishing essays critical of President Washington are also documented here. Another person of renown imprisoned in Paris when Monroe arrived there was Madame Lafayette, wife of the American Revolutionary War hero, the Marquis de Lafayette. Correspondence regarding Monroe's efforts to aid her both while she was in prison and after her release is likewise given in full.

The letters and papers in this volume also document several special assignments given to Monroe: the delivery of funds to Amsterdam as payment on the American debt owed there; the acquisition of books and equipment for the War Department; and the appointment of a special emissary to negotiate a treaty with Algiers.

Monroe conducted a regular correspondence with his fellow American diplomats in Europe—especially his good friends William Short and Thomas Pinckney, but also with John Quincy Adams, John Jay, Joel Barlow, and David Humphreys. He also corresponded with the American consuls stationed in France, although this correspondence appears to be less complete than that with diplomats of higher rank.

And, of course, Monroe continued to correspond with his friends in the United States. Communications between France and the United States were bad, and many of these letters never reached their destinations and do not survive. Most of these letters dealt with public affairs, but Monroe's correspondence with his uncle, Joseph Jones, and with James Madison addressed personal matters, both in France and in the United States.

Several third-person documents are published in this volume. Theobald Wolfe Tone, the Irish nationalist, was in Paris at the same time as Monroe, and several of his diary entries recount important meetings with the American minister. Other third-person accounts of events relating to Monroe's tenure in France are presented in the annotations.

Summaries of all of Monroe's known surviving papers, both those included and omitted, can be found in *A Comprehensive Catalogue of the Correspondence and Papers of James Monroe*. Letters referred to in the text that have not been located are indicated in the annotations.

EDITORIAL METHOD

The primary objective in making transcriptions of documents for *The Papers of James Monroe* is to render an accurate but easily readable reproduction of the text. Documents are transcribed as written with the following exceptions:

Each document is preceded by a heading. The heading gives the name of the recipient if the letter was written by Monroe, the name of the author if addressed to Monroe, or the title of the document. The name of the addressee, if given on a letter, is omitted.

The date and place of writing are placed on a single line flush right at the top of the document regardless of its position in the original. Supplied, conjectured, or corrected portions of dates are placed in brackets, and an explanation of the conjecture or correction given in an annotation.

Complimentary closings are attached to the end of the last paragraph. Signatures are placed at the end flush right.

Substantial deletions (mostly in drafts) are included in the text but struck through. Routine deletions and insertions—those in which one or only a few words are deleted, inserted, or changed or where the wording of a sentence is changed—are made silently. Significant emendations are noted with an annotation.

Illegible words or letters and words or letters obscured or excised by damage to the document are noted in angle brackets; conjectural words or letters inserted by the editors are placed in square brackets. Obscure abbreviations and contractions are expanded with the added letters placed in square brackets. The deciphered text of words originally written in code is given in italics.

Superscripts are retained. Dots and lines accompanying superscripts are rendered as a line under the superscript.

Translations are rendered in modern usage. Passages of deciphered code are rendered with correct spelling and contractions are elongated.

Documents are presented in chronological sequence. Documents that cannot be dated specifically are placed at the end of the appropriate month or year.

The type of document (received copy or letterbook copy, for example) and its source is given at the end of the document.

Annotations are accompanied by a citation to the source.

ABBREVIATIONS & SHORT TITLES

CSdCo	Copley Library, La Jolla, CA
CtHi	Connecticut Historical Society, Hartford
DNA	National Archives, Washington, DC
DLC	Library of Congress, Washington, DC
GLC	Gilder Lehrman collection, New York City
ICU	University of Chicago, Chicago, IL
IaU	University of Iowa, Iowa City
InU	Indiana University, Bloomington
MCH	Houghton Library, Harvard University, Cambridge, MA
MHi	Massachusetts Historical Society, Boston
NHi	New-York Historical Society, New York City
NIC	Cornell University, Ithaca, NY
NN	New York Public Library, New York City
NNC	Columbia University, New York City
NNPM	Pierpont Morgan Library, New York City
NcD	Duke University, Durham, NC
NjP	Princeton University, Princeton, NJ
NJMoHP	Morristown National Historic Park, Morristown, NJ
PHi	Historical Society of Pennsylvania, Philadelphia
PP	Free Library of Philadelphia
PPAmP	American Philosophical Society, Philadelphia
PPL	Library Company of Philadelphia
PPRF	Rosenbach Museum and Library, Philadelphia
SCHi	South Carolina Historical Society, Charleston
ViFreJM	James Monroe Museum and Memorial Library, Fredericksburg, VA
ViHi	Virginia Historical Society, Richmond
ViMtvL	Mount Vernon, Fairfax, VA
ViU	University of Virginia, Charlottesville
ViW	College of William and Mary, Williamsburg, VA
WHi	Wisconsin Historical Society, Madison

AD	Autograph Document
Dft	Draft
FC	File Copy
LBC	Letterbook Copy
RC	Received Copy

ANB	*American National Biography*
Appletons' Cyclopedia	*Appletons' Cyclopædia of American Biography*
ASP:FR	*American State Papers: Foreign Relations*
BDAC	*Biographical Dictionary of the American Congress*
Burr Papers	Mary-Jo Kline and others, *Political Correspondence and Public Papers of Aaron Burr*
Catalogue of Monroe's Papers	Daniel Preston, *Comprehensive Catalogue of the Correspondence and Papers of James Monroe*
Correspondence of the French Ministers	Frederick Jackson Turner, ed., "Correspondence of the French Ministers, 1791-1797," *Annual Report of the American Historical Association for the Year 1903*, volume 2
DAB	*Dictionary of American Biography*
DNB	*Dictionary of National Biography*
FCP—France	Foreign Copying Project—France: Archives des Affaires Etrangères: Correspondance Politique—Etats-Unis
Hamilton Papers	Harold Syrett and others, eds., *The Papers of Alexander Hamilton*.
Jefferson Papers	Julian Boyd, Charles T. Cullen, John Catanzariti, Barbara Oberg, and others, eds., *The Papers of Thomas Jefferson*
Madison Papers	William T. Hutchinson, Robert A. Rutland, J. C. A. Stagg, and others, eds., *The Papers of James Madison*
Marshall Papers	Herbert A. Johnson, Charles T. Cullen, Charles F. Hobson, and others, eds., *The Papers of John Marshall*
View of the Conduct	James Monroe, *View of the Conduct of the Executive*
Washington Papers	William W. Abbot, Dorothy Twohig, Philander Chase, and others, eds., *The Papers of George Washington*
Writings of Monroe	Stanislaus Hamilton, ed., *The Writings of James Monroe*

The Papers of James Monroe

To James Madison

Phil^a May 26. 1794.

Dear Sir

I have been with Mr R. & have given him no final answer. The fact appears to be that the message to me was directly from the President, so that a decision settles it.[1] He has also had an interview with Mr Dayton.[2]

May I request of you to go to Mr Randolph, & settle the matter with him. I promised him you wo^d in the course of ½ an hour. If it has not the approbation of my few friends & yourself in particular & certainly will decline it. Weigh therefore all circumstances, & paying as little regard to private considerations as sho^d be, tell him for me what answer to give. I write in haste in the Senate, being engaged on the balance bill.[3] Y^r friend & serv^t

Ja^s Monroe

An answer must be given the President immediately.

RC, DLC: Madison Papers

1. Secretary of State Edmund Randolph informed JM that President Washington wished to appoint him as minister to France. Washington initially wanted John Jay, who was going to London as special envoy, to remain in London as U. S. minister to Great Britain, and Thomas Pinckney, the current minister in London, to fill the position at Paris left vacant by the recall of Gouverneur Morris. Jay rejected this arrangement, and Pinckney retained his post in London. Washington then offered the job to James Madison and to Robert R. Livingston, both of whom declined. JM and a number of other members of Congress, both Republican and Federalist, backed Aaron Burr for the appointment, but the president never gave him any consideration for the post. Washington instructed Randolph to offer the position to JM, but left no explanation for the choice (John J. Reardon, *Edmund Randolph*, 267-268).

2. Jonathan Dayton (1760-1824) represented New Jersey in the House of Representatives 1791-1799 and in the U. S. Senate 1799-1805. He was a leader of the Federalist contingent who backed Aaron Burr for the appointment as minister to France. Randolph met with Dayton to inform him that Burr was not in contention for the appointment (*BDAC*; Mary-Jo Kline, ed., *Political Correspondence and Public Papers of Aaron Burr*, 1: 181.

3. The Senate was considering a bill entitled "An act making provision for the payment of the interest on the balances due to certain states, upon a final settlement of the accounts between the United States and the individual states." JM's vote on a proposed amendment to this bill was the last ballot he cast as a U. S. Senator (*Journal of the Senate of the United States*, 2: 90).

To Thomas Jefferson

Phil^a May 27. 1794.

Dear Sir

Early yesterday morning & immediately after my last was written[1] I was called on by Mr R. to answer the question "whether I wo^d accept the legation to France?" The proposition as you will readily conceive surprised me, for I really thought I was among the last men to whom it wo^d be made, & so observed. He said the President was resolved to send a republican character to that nation; that Mr Madison & ch^r Livingston had refused, that he wo^d not appoint Col^o Burr, lest it sho^d seem as if he sought persons from that state only, & probably it wo^d not have been offered to L. but on acc^t of his having been in the department of foreign aff^rs, & under these circumstances & considerations he was desired by the President to call on me & ascertain whether I wo^d act. As I had espoused B. I told Mr R. I could not even think on the subject whilst there was a prospect of his success. He assured me he was out of the question, & if I declined, it wo^d probably be offered to Govr Paca of Maryl^d or some person not yet thought of.[2] That he would satisfy the friends of Col^o B. on this head. Before I wo^d consult my friends I requested that this be done—& in consequence the above assurance was given some of them, & I presume they were satisfied. This point of delicacy being removed, I then desired Mr Madison in conference with a few of our friends to determine what answer sho^d be given to the proposition. The result was that I sho^d accept upon the necessity of cultivating France, & the incertainty of the person upon whom it might otherwise fall. An answer was accordingly given last evening to the Presid^t to that effect, & the nomination sent in to day. I have not attended nor shall I till after that body shall be pleased to decide upon it. If approved it is wished that I embark immediately for France. I am however extremely anxious to visit albemarle before I sit out taking Mr Jones in my way. But whether I shall be able to visit either of you is incertain, & will depend in a great measure upon the practicability of getting a vessel about to sail, in a term short of the time, it will take me to perform the journey. Upon this head however I can say nothing untill the nomination is decided on, nor can I say how the decision will be, for my services in the Senate have given me but little claim to the personal regards of the reigning party there. I suspect the nomination created as great a surprize in that house as the proposition to me did, yesterday morning. As yet I have not seen the President. I shall write you more fully in my next. With great respect & esteem I am y^r affectionate friend & servant

Ja^s Monroe

Govr Mifflins movment has been suspended by the President.[3]

RC, DLC: Jefferson Papers

1. JM to Jefferson, 26 May 1794, *Monroe Papers*, 2: 724-725.

2. William Paca (1740-1799), a Maryland legislator and jurist, was a signer of the Declaration of Independence. He served as governor of Maryland 1782-1786 and was judge of the U. S. District Court for Maryland 1789-1799 (*ANB*).

3. Pennsylvania's plan to build a new settlement near Presque Isle on Lake Erie met with resistance from the Indians and the British. Governor Thomas Mifflin issued an order on May 23 calling out 1,000 militiamen to protect the state's claim to the region. On the 24th Mifflin complied with a request from President Washington and suspended the order (Kenneth Rossman, *Thomas Mifflin and the Politics of the American Revolution*, 232-248).

Commission as Minister to France

[28 May 1794]

George Washington, President of the United States of America to James Monroe—Greeting

Reposing especial trust and confidence in your integrity, prudence and ability, I have nominated, and by and with the advice and consent of the Senate, do appoint you the said James Monroe, minister Plenipotentiary for the United States of America with the Republic of France, authorizing you hereby to do and perform all such matters and things as to the said place or office doth appertain, or as may be duly given you in charge hereafter, and the said office to hold and exercise during the pleasure of the President of the United States for the time being.

In Testimony whereof I have caused the seal of the United States to be hereunto affixed. Given under my hand at the City of Philadelphia the twenty eighth day of May, in the Year of our Lord one thousand seven hundred and ninety four, and of the Independence of the United States of America, the eighteenth.

G. Washington
By the President of the United States
Edm: Randolph,
Secretary of State.

Copy, DNA: RG 59: Credences

Washington submitted the nomination on May 27 and the Senate confirmed it on May 28 (*Executive Journal of the Senate of the United States*, 1: 157).

Credence as Minister to France

[28 May 1794]

George Washington, President of the United States of America

To the Representatives of the French People, Members of the Committee of Public Safety of the French Republic, the Great and good Friend and Ally of the United States.

On the intimation of the wish of the french Republic that a new Minister should be sent from the United States, I resolved to manifest my sense of the readiness, with which my request was fulfilled, by immediately fulfilling the request of your Government.[1] It was some time before a character could be obtained, worthy of the high office of expressing the attachment of the United States to the happiness of our Allies, and drawing closer the bands of our friendship. I have now made choice of James Monroe, one of our distinguished citizens to reside near the french Republic, in the quality of minister plenipotentiary of the United States of America. He is instructed to bear to you our sincere solicitude for your welfare, and to cultivate with zeal the cordiality, so happily subsisting between us. From a knowledge of his fidelity, probity and good conduct, I have entire confidence, that he will render himself acceptable to you, and give effect to our desire of preserving and advancing on all occasions the interest and connection of the two nations. I beseech you, therefore, to give full credence to whatever he shall say to you on the part of the United States; and most of all when he shall assure you, that your prosperity is an object of our affection. And I pray God to have the french Republic in his holy keeping. Written at Philadelphia this 28 day of May 1794.

G. Washington
By the President of the United States
Edm: Randolph Sec^y of State.

Copy, DNA: RG 59: Credences

1. Washington refers to his request that France recall Edmond Genet as its minister to the United States.

From Aaron Burr

NYork 30 May 1794

My dear Sir,

I receive your obliging Letter of the 28th at the Moment of the closing of the Mail—so that I have a Moment only to acknowledge.[1]

Be assured that I receive with the most sincere pleasure the news of your appointment. You know me but little, if you imagine me capable of suspecting a friendship of which I have such frequent and substantial proofs—you would have done very wrong to have declined or embarassed the Nomination. I am satisfied that it is in every View a better arrangement than any other which could have been made. Without accusing me of personal Vanity you may conceive reasons which require my presence here.

Allow me to recommend to you my Stepson Mʳ Prevost, if you should imagine that he could be in any Way useful to you—his Manners are agreeable & easy, his Talents above common—he speaks the French—has been well educated—has some eminence in his profession (the Law) of Strict honor and truth & a Decided Democrat.[2]

In the Military arrangements I would wish you would take an occasion, if any offers, to recommend Joseph R. Yates son of our Chief Justice Yates for a <u>Company</u> in the Artillery—be assured that he is every Way deserving—but the recommendation must not appear to have been influenced by me.[3]

I hope to see you on Sunday or Monday. Sincerely & affecʸ Yʳˢ

AB

RC, DLC: Monroe Papers

1. JM's letter to Burr of 28 May 1794 has not been located.

2. John B. Prevost (1766-1825) was the son of Theodosia Prevost Burr. He was admitted to the bar in New York in 1790 and was a partner in Burr's legal practice (Mary-Jo Kline, ed., *Political Correspondence and Public Papers of Aaron Burr*, 1: lxiv, 182).

3. Joseph R. Yates (1773-1804) was nominated for appointment as a lieutenant in the artillery on 31 May 1794 and confirmed June 2 (*Political Correspondence and Public Papers of Aaron Burr*, 1: 182).

To George Washington

Philadelphia June 1. 1794.

Sir

I was presented yesterday evening by Mʳ Randolph with the commission of Minister for the French republick, which you were pleas'd with the approbation of the Senate, to confer on me. As I had previously intimated to him in consequence of a conversation I had with him the day before the nomination was presented, that I would accept this trust, I have only now to request that you will consider me as ready to embark in the discharge of its duties, as soon as I shall be honored with your commands, and a suitable passage can be procured for myself & family to that country.

In accepting this very distinguished mark of your confidence I should do injustice to my own feelings, if I did not express to you the particular obligation it has conferrd on me, and assure you of the zeal with which I shall endeavour to discharge the duties of so high a trust in a manner that may justify the executive in committing it to me. On that zeal but more especially on the councils which will direct my conduct, I rely as the resources which are to supply the inadequacy of my abilities to a station at all times important, and at the present crisis peculiarly arduous and delicate. Be assured it will be my study and will give me the highest gratification, to have it in my power to promote by my mission the interest of my country, and the honor and credit of your administration which I deem inseparably connected with it. I have the honor to be sir with sentiments of the highest respect & esteem yʳ most obᵗ & very humble servant

Jaˢ Monroe

RC: CtY: Van Sideran Collection

From Aaron Burr

5 June [94][1]

Dear Sir,

The Senate did not adjourn yesterday till near four ºClock & were so constantly engaged that I could not find time to answer your letter.[2] I should have done it in the evening, but for the expectation of seeing you at my lodgings agreeably to your verbal Message

I have communicated to Mʳ Prevost your obliging offer; not having however the <u>smallest expectation</u> that he will avail himself of this instance of your politeness. With regard to Mʳ Skipwith,[3] there is nothing more in my power than what has been already communicated. In deciding on this business, I beg you to be governed solely by the dictates of your own Judgment, uninfluenced by any Motives of personal friendship for Yʳ affec. H. S.

Aaron Burr

RC, NIC

1. Burr wrote "95" as the year.

2. JM's letter to Burr has not been located.

3. Embassies at this time had no staff members, so JM had to hire his own secretary to assist him with his duties as minister. JM initially selected Fulwar Skipwith to fill this post, but both JM and Skipwith viewed it as a temporary arrangement, for Skipwith was a candidate for appointment as U. S. consul general at Paris. JM may have suggested that John B. Prevost accompany him to France and assume the duties of secretary if and when Skipwith received the other appointment. Skipwith (1765-1839), a member of a prominent Virginia family, served as the U. S. consul at Martinique 1790-1794 (*Dictionary of Louisiana Biography*).

To Thomas Jefferson

Philᵃ June 6. 1794.

Dear Sir

Since my appointment I have been extremely occupied in a variety of respects. I had likewise flattered myself with the hope I shoᵈ see you before my departure till within a day or two past—but of this I now begin to despair. I shall sail from Bal: for which place I sit out in 4 days hence. Tis possible the vessel may not be ready altho I am advised she is. I feel extremely anxious upon the subject of a cypher. Our former one is in a small writing desk at my house, can you get & send it after me in case I do not see you before I sail?

Danton has been executed, the charge the plunder of publick money.[1] The King of Prussia withdrawn[2]—& the British driven from Corsica.[3] I will write by the several succeeding posts whilst I stay. I am yʳ affectionate friend & servᵗ

Jaˢ Monroe

RC, DLC: Jefferson Papers

Georges-Jacques Danton (1759-1794) was a Paris attorney who rose to prominence in the French Revolution during the summer of 1792. He held a number of public offices, including minister of justice, deputy to the National Convention, and member of the Committee of Public Safety. He became a leader of the moderate wing of the Revolution and opposed the more radical measures of Robespierre. Danton was arrested in March 1794 on charges of corruption (relating to a sum of money that was not accounted for during his term as minister of justice) and treason; he was guillotined on 5 April 1794 (*Encyclopedia Britannica*).

Prussia was fighting the Poles as well as the French, and during the winter of 1793-1794 King Frederick Wilhelm II decided to give ascendancy to the war in Poland. He withdrew his troops from Belgium during the spring of 1794 and took steps towards formally ending his treaty obligations to Great Britain and Austria (Sydney S. Biro, *The German Policy of Revolutionary France*, 1: 244-247; 266-273).

The British began military operations against Corsica in September 1793 and continued them sporadically over the next nine months. Reports that the British had withdrawn after the failure of their attack on the French fortress at Bastia apparently led JM to believe that the British had been driven away. The British, in fact, continued the campaign and won control of the island in May 1794. The pro-British Corsicans then created a new government that was a protectorate of Great Britain and recognized George III as its sovereign (Peter Thrasher, *Pasquale Paoli*, 281-290; [Philadelphia] *General Advertiser*, 1-12 June 1794).

To Henry Tazewell

Phil^a June 6. 1794.

Dear Sir

You will before the rec^t of this have heard of my appointment to France—an event which was only known to be in contemplation with the Ex: the day before it took place. The first intimation I had was by Mr R. from the President desiring information whether I wo^d serve.

I believe Mr Madison will be mentioned as willing to act; but on this point will write you ag^n.[1]

I sail from Bal: & sit out hence on wednesday next.

Danton was charged with peculation of publick money & executed. The king of P. has withdrawn & the British are driven from Corsica. Y^r fn^d & serv^t

Ja^s Monroe

RC, NjMoHP

1. JM's appointment as minister to France left Virginia without representation in the Senate during the final days of the first session (which ended on 9 June 1794) and the opening weeks of second session (which began on 3 November 1794) of the Third Congress, for John Taylor, the other senator, had resigned on 11 May 1794, and Tazewell, who had been elected to replace Taylor, did not take his seat until 29 December 1794. JM's seat remained vacant until June 1795 when Stevens T. Mason assumed the duties (*BDAC*).

From Edmund Randolph

Philadelphia, June 10th 1794

Sir

You have been nominated as the Successor of Mr Gouverneur Morris, in the office of Minister plenipotentiary of the United States of America to the Republic of France, from a confidence, that, while you keep steadily in view the necessity of rendering yourself acceptable to that Government, you will maintain the self-respect, due to our own. In doing the one and the other of these things, your own prudence and understanding must be the guides; after first possessing yourself of the real sentiments of the Executive relative to the French nation.

The President has been an early and decided friend of the French Revolution; and whatever reason there may have been, under our ignorance of facts, and policy, to suspend an opinion upon some of its important transactions; yet is he immutable in his wishes for its accomplishment; incapable of assenting to the right of any foreign prince to meddle with its interior arrangement; persuaded that success will attend their efforts; and particularly that union among themselves is an impregnable barrier against external assaults.

How the French government, when it shall be no longer attacked by foreign arms, will ultimately settle, is a point, not yet reduced to any absolutely certain expectation. The gradation of public opinion from the beginning of the new order of things to this day; and the fluctuation and mutual destruction of parties, forbid a minister of a foreign country to attach himself to any as such, and dictate to him not to incline to any set of men, further than they appear to go with the sense of the nation.

2. When the Executive provisory Council recalled Mr Genet, they expressed a determination to render it a matter of eclat, as you have seen; and at the same time disavowed all his offensive acts. Nothing having been forwarded to us, relative to Mr Morris, which requires a disavowal, you will, if you should be interrogated as to any particular feeling prevailing with the President upon the occasion, refer to the letter from the Secretary of State to Mr Fauchet, as explanatory of the President's promptness to comply with their demand.[1]

3. From Mr Genet and Mr Fauchet we have uniformly learned, that France did not desire us to depart from neutrality; and it would have been unwise to have asked us to do otherwise. For our ports are open to her prizes, while they are shut to those of Great Britain; and supplies of Grain could not be forwarded to France with so much certainty, were we at war, as they can even now, notwithstanding the British Instructions; and as they may be, if the demands to be made upon Great Britain should succeed. We have, therefore, pursued neutrality with faithfulness; we have paid more of our debt to France than was absolutely due, as the Secretary of the Treasury asserts; and we should have paid more, if the state of our affairs did not require us to be prepared with funds for the possible event of war. We mean to continue the same line of conduct in future; and to remove all jealousy with respect to Mr Jay's mission to London, you may say, that he is positively forbidden to weaken the engagements between this Country and France.[2] It is not improbable that you will be obliged to encounter on this head suspicions of various kinds. But you may declare the motives of that mission to be, to obtain immediate compensation for our plundered property, and restitution of the posts.[3] You may intimate, by way of argument, but without ascribing it to the Government, that if war should be necessary, the affections of the people of the United States towards it, would be better secured by a manifestation, that every step had been taken to avoid it; and that the British nation would be divided, when they found that we had been forced into it. This may be briefly touched upon as the path of prudence with respect to ourselves; and also, with respect to France, since we are unable to give her aids of men or money. To this matter you cannot be too attentive and you will be amply justified in repelling with firmness any imputation of the most distant intention to sacrifice our connexion with France to any connection with England. You may back your assertions by a late determination of the President to have it signified abroad, that he is averse to admit into his public room, which is free to all the world besides, any Frenchmen who are obnoxious to the French Republic; although perhaps it may again happen sometimes, as many go thither, whose names and characters are utterly unknown.

It is very probable that our country will become the asylum for most of the French who expatriate themselves from their native land. Our laws have never yet made a distinction of persons, nor is such a distinction very easy. Hence some of those who are perhaps attainted in France, have thrown themselves upon the protection of the United States. This will not, as it surely ought not, to be misinterpreted into any estrangement from the French cause. You will explain this, whensoever it shall be necessary.

The stories of Genet as to the Royal Medallions &c: being exhibited in the president's Room, and his giving private audiences to certain French Emigrés, are notoriously untrue. And if any insinuation should be made with regard to M. de la Fayette, so directly, as indispensably to call for an answer; it may be affirmed, that notwithstanding the warmest friendship, contracted between the president and him, in the most interesting scenes; notwithstanding the obligation of the United States to him, and the old prepossessions in his favor, the efforts of the President in his behalf have never gone further, than to express a wish to the authority which held him in confinement, that he should be liberated.[4] But even this much need not be said, without the most invincible necessity; because though what has been done is justified by every consideration, it is never well to give notice of it to those, whose extreme sensibility may see impropriety, where none exists.

4. If we may judge from what has been at different times uttered by M[r] Fauchet, he will represent the existence of two parties here, irreconcileable to each other: one Republican, and friendly to the French Revolution; the other monarchical, Aristocratic, Britannic and Antigallican; that a majority of the House of Representatives, the people, and the President, are in the first class; and a majority of the Senate in the second. If this intelligence should be used, in order to inspire a distrust of our good will to France, you will industriously obviate such an effect; and if a fair occasion should present itself, you may hint that the most effectual means of obtaining from the United States, what is desired by France, will be by a plain and candid application to the Government, and not by those insidious operations on the people, which Genet endeavored to carry on.

5. The information, which we possess of France, before and in the early stages of the Revolution, must be considerably changed at this day. You will, therefore, transmit to us, as soon as possible, an account of the Navy, the Agriculture, and the Commerce of France. It is desirable too to know, upon what footing Religion really stands. These, however, are general objects. But we are particularly concerned to understand the true state of the different sects of politics. Are there any of the old friends to the ancient regime remaining? Are any new friends created by the course of things? Are the Brissotines extinguished? Are the Dantonists overwhelmed? Is Robespierre's party firmly fixed?[5] Is he capable from talents and personal fortitude to direct the storm? Is his character free from imputation, as to money? Is he friendly to the United States? How is the Executive power administered now? What new accession of authority may have lately accrued to the Committee of public safety? What relation do the twelve Commissions of Administration, which have been lately established, bear to that Committee? What is the true cause of the various changes, which have lately taken place, by one party rising upon the ruins of another? What assurance can be had, that any party can so long maintain itself, as to promise stability to the Government? Are the people sincerely affectionate to their present Government; or are they restrained by the terror of the revolutionary Tribunal, or by the danger of having their country dismembered by the coalesced princes? What species of executive will probably be at last adopted? What characters bid fair to take the helm of affairs, after the great destruction and banishment of able men? These and many other questions of the same nature ought to be solved, to enable us to see things in a true light. For without doubting the solidity of the French cause, we ought not to be unprepared for any event. If, therefore, any very momentous turn should arise in French affairs, upon which the conduct of our Government may depend, you need not hesitate at the expense of an advice boat, if no other satisfactory opportunity should occur. But it is the wish of the President, that at the end of every week, you commit to a letter the transactions of it, and embrace every proper conveyance, by duplicates, and, in great cases, even by triplicates.

6. Should you be interrogated about the treaty of commerce, you may reply that it has never been proposed to us by Mr Fauchet. As to any thing else concerning it, you will express yourself not to be instructed, it being a subject to be negotiated with the Government here.

7. In like manner, if a treaty of alliance or if the execution of the Guarantee of the French Islands, by force of arms, should be propounded, you will refer the Republic of France to this side of the water.[6] In short, it is expected, with a sure reliance on your discretion, that you will not commit the United States by any specific declarations, except where you are particularly instructed, and except too in giving testimony of our attachment to their cause.

8. There is reason to believe, that the Embargo, when it was first laid, excited some uneasy sensations in the breast of the French minister. For it so happened, that at the moment before its operation, pretty considerable shipments of flour were made to the British west Indies, and a Snow, called La Camille, laden with flour for France, was arrested near new Castle, on the Delaware, after she had quitted the port of Philadelphia. But you know enough of the history of this business to declare that the embargo was levelled against Great Britain, and was made general merely because if it had been partial against her, it would have amounted to a cause of war; and, also, that it was not continued, merely because it was reputed to be injurious to France. My letters to Mr Fauchet will explain the case of La Camille, and all his complaints about the embargo.[7]

Should our Embargo be brought up, the way will be easy for our complaint against the Embargo of Bordeaux. At any rate, you will remonstrate against it, and urge satisfaction for the sufferers. You will receive all the papers, which have come into the department of State, relative to those matters, and you will besides open a correspondence with the Captains and persons interested at Bordeaux, in order to obtain more accurate information.[8]

But you will go farther, and insist upon compensation for the captures and spoliations of our property, and injuries to the persons of our citizens, by French cruizers. Mr Fauchet has been applied to, and promises to co-operate for the obtaining of satisfaction. The dilatoriness, with which business is transacted in France, will, if not curtailed in the adjustment of these cases, produce infinite mischief to our merchants. This must be firmly represented to the French Republic; and you may find a season for intimating how unfortunate it would be if so respectable a Body as that of our merchants should relax in their zeal for the French cause, from irritation at their losses. The papers on this head are a statement of French cases, Mr Fauchet's letter to me,[9] and the Documents themselves.

9. You know the extreme distress in which the inhabitants of Saint Domingo came hither after the disasters of the Cape. Private charity, and especially at Baltimore most liberally contributed to their support. The Congress at length advanced 15,000 Dollars with a view of reimbursement from France.[10] This subject has been broken to Mr Fauchet here, and he appears to have been roused at the idea of supporting by French money French Aristocrats and Democrats indiscriminately. Both he and his nation ought to be satisfied, that in the cause of humanity, oppressed by poverty, political opinions have nothing to do. Add to this, that none but the really indigent received a farthing. It was the duty of the French Republic to relieve their Colonists laboring under a penury so produced; and as it would have been too late to wait for their approbation before the payments were decreed, it will not be deemed an offensive disposal of french money, that we now make a claim for repayment. If Mr Fauchet has power upon the subject an attempt will be made for a settlement with him here; but that being very doubtful it will forward the retribution by discussing it in Europe.

10. You will be also charged with the demands of several American Citizens for bills of exchange drawn in the French west Indies on France. The Report of a Committee of them, Mᵣ Fauchet's letter, and the vouchers, which you will carry, leave no doubt of your success. But if there should be any difficulty, do not fail to communicate it to the Secretary of State instantaneously. The sooner, therefore, the affair is entered upon the better.

11. It is important that no public character of the United States should be in France which is not acceptable. You will inquire into the Consuls, and inform how they are approved, and whether they be deserving. Altho' the President will avoid, as much as possible, to appoint any obnoxious person, Consul, it may happen otherwise, and must be considered as accidental. Mᵣ Alexander Duvernat goes for Paris in the quality of vice Consul,[11] and Mᵣ Fauchet said that he had nothing to object to him.

Consulates are established in every port of France, where they are conceived useful. But perhaps you may find it adviseable to mark out some other places for such Officers.

12. It is recommended that no business of consequence, be carried on verbally or in writing, but in your own Language. The minister of each nation has a right to use his national Tongue; and few men can confide in their exactness when they do business in a foreign one. But great care is necessary in the choice of interpreters, when they are to be resorted to.

13. It is a practice of great utility to note down every conversation of consequence, which you hold, immediately after retirement; and the Executive will expect to receive copies of what shall be thus written.

14. A communication with our other ministers in Europe under proper caution may be advantageous.

15. Let nothing depend upon verbal communication, which can be carried on in writing.

16. To conclude. You go, Sir, to France to strengthen our Friendship with that country; and you are well acquainted with the line of freedom and ease to which you may advance, without betraying the dignity of the United States. You will shew our confidence in the French Republic, without betraying the most remote mark of undue complaisance. You will let it be seen, that in case of war with any nation on earth, we shall consider France as our first and natural Ally. You may dwell upon the sense which we entertain of past services, and for the more recent interposition in our behalf with the Dey of Algiers. Among the great events with which the world is now teeming, there may be an opening for France to become instrumental in securing to us the free navigation of the Mississippi. Spain may perhaps negotiate a peace, separate from Great Britain, with France. If she does, the Mississippi may be acquired through this channel, especially if you contrive to have our mediation in any manner solicited. With every wish for your welfare and an honorable issue to your ministry, I am, Sir, Yo mo. ob. serv.

Edm: Randolph.

Copy, DNA: RG 59: Domestic Letters

These instructions were drafted at the same time as the instructions to John Jay for his mission to London, which were dated 6 May 1794. According to Randolph, JM's instructions "were sketched about this time, to be ready for any person who shall be appointed..." (Edmund Randolph, *A Vindication of Mr. Randolph's Rsignation*, 18; *ASP: FR*, 1: 472).

1. Fauchet officially informed Randolph on 9 April 1794 that France desired the recall of Gouverneur Morris, and Randolph replied on April 21 that President Washington had complied with the request and was seeking a successor to Morris who would be acceptable to the French government (Fauchet to Randolph, 9 April 1794, DNA: RG 59: Notes from Foreign Missions, France; Randolph to Fauchet, 21 April 1794, DNA: RG 59: Domestic Letters).

2. The portion of Jay's instructions relating to France read: "That as the British ministry will doubtless be solicitous to detach us from France, and may probably make some overture of this kind, you will inform them that the Government of the United States will not derogate from our treaties and engagements with France...." (*ASP: FR*, 1: 474).

3. This sentence was misleading, for Randolph neglected to tell JM that in addition to these two charges, Jay was also authorized to negotiate a commercial treaty with Great Britain (*ASP: FR*, 1: 473).

4. After an armed mob broke into the Tuileries on 20 June 1792 and abused the king and queen, Lafayette left his troops in the north and rode to Paris to address the Assembly. He demanded that the instigators of the violence committed on June 20 be pursued and punished. But the Assembly took no action, and even the moderates in Paris refused to support him. On August 13 the king and queen were taken prisoners and moved to the Temple. Lafayette attempted to rally his troops to march on Paris, and restore the royal family, but they would not follow him. The Assembly responded with an order for Lafayette to resign his command and return to Paris. On August 19, Lafayette crossed over the border into the Austrian Netherlands, where he was arrested near Liege. In September he was handed over to the King of Prussia and taken to the fortress of Wesel in Westphalia, followed by a transfer to Magdeburg, near Berlin, where he was imprisoned for a year. Adrienne Lafayette wrote to Washington on 8 October 1793 asking his help to get her husband released. Washington drafted a letter to Emperor Frederick William II of Prussia on 15 January 1794, but it was not sent until 16 May 1796. The Prussians delivered Lafayette to the Austrians in June 1794 who imprisoned him in the fortress at Ulmutz, outside of Vienna, where he remained until 1797 (Samuel Flagg Bemis, "The United States and Lafayette," *Daughters of the American Revolution Magazine*, 58 (1924): 343-345; Jason Lane, *General and Madame de Lafayette*, 173-184; 213-214; André Maurois, *Adrienne the Life of the Marquise de Lafayette*, 207, 223, 261).

5. The Girondin Party supported constitutional reform and believed that the fall of the monarchy had brought the Revolution to an end, and that the organization of the Republic required only a minimal amount of moderate legislation. They were opposed by the deputies and municipal authorities in Paris, including the sans-culottes who had formed the Jacobin Party. Like Robespierre himself, the Jacobins felt that constitutional questions were less vital than the immediate security of the state. In the spring of 1793 France faced the combined powers of Austria, Prussia, Spain, Holland, and Great Britain. By the end of May 1793 a new period of scarcity and rising prices gave increasing power to the Jacobins who demanded that unity should be secured by the exclusion of their principal opponents from the Convention. Surrounded by the armed forces of the Sections of Paris, the Convention was compelled to agree with the arrest of 29 of its leading Girondin deputies, who were executed in October. After December 1793, the Jacobins dominated the committees of Public Safety and General Security through which they deliberately created a revolutionary despotism that became synonymous with the Terror. For a period of seven months, France became a totalitarian state defined by the predominance of a single political party, led by Robespierre. The Terror ended with the fall of Robespierre and his associates on 27 July 1794 (9 Thermidor) (M. J. Sydenham, *The First French Republic 1792-1804*, 11-25).

6. There were two treaties of 1778, the Treaty of Amity and Commerce, and the Treaty of Alliance.

Article XI of the Treaty of Alliance between the United States and France provided for a reciprocal guarantee of territory (Albert H. Bowman, *The Struggle for Neutrality*, 44).

7. British attacks on American shipping led Congress to enact a thirty-day embargo on all ships in American ports on 26 May 1794; an extension of the act for an additional thirty days passed on April 18. When French minister Fauchet complained that the embargo did more harm to France than to Great Britain, Congress allowed the law to expire at the end of the sixty days (*Madison Papers*, 15: 295, 314, 337-338). Randolph's letters to Fauchet are in DNA: RG 59: Domestic Letters.

8. The city of Bordeaux was a center of opposition to the Jacobin-controlled National Assembly, and in retaliation the Assembly placed an embargo on the city's port in August 1793. It was lifted in April 1794, but during that time 103 American ships had been detained (Melanie Miller, "I Am Not a Cautious Man: Gouverneur Morris and France," paper presented at *Columbia's Legacy: Friends and Enemies in the New Nation*, Columbia University, 10 December 2004, p. 13-14; Samuel Flagg Bemis, "Washington's Farewell Address: A Foreign Policy of Independence," *American Historical Review*, 39: 253).

9. Fauchet's letters to Randolph are in DNA: RG 59: Notes from the French Legation in the U. S. to the Department of State.

10. "An Act providing for the relief of such of the inhabitants of Saint Domingo, resident within the United States, as may be found in want of support," *U. S. Statutes at Large*, 6: 13.

11. The Senate confirmed the appointment of Alexander Duvernet as vice consul at Paris on 9 June 1794 (*Journal of the Executive Proceedings of the Senate*, 1: 162).

From Pierre De Rieux[1]

CharlotteVille ce 12. Juin 1794.

Monsieur,

C'est dans L'instant ou nous esperions avoir Le plaisir de vous voir bientôt revenir parmi nous, que nous venons d'apprendre vos préparatifs pour vous en éloigner d'avantage, et que Votre départ doit etre Si precipité que vous aurés a peine Le tems de recevoir Les temoignages de notre empressement a vous [d'exercer] et Madame, un passage aussi prompt qu'agréable, et en général toutte la Satisfaction possible.

Je Prends La Liberté, Monsieur, de vous adresser cy inclus une Lettre pour ma tante que je vous Serai très obligé de voulloir bien Lui remettre vous même, Lorsque L'embaras de vos premières affaires vous en aûra laissé Le Loisir; elle est plus fixée a St. Germain qu'à Paris, Mais comme elle y vat cependant de tems a autres, je mets Ses deux adresses a L'une des qu'élles vous La trouverés Surement.

J'ose Esperèr que vous pardonnerér cette impotunité de ma part et que vous en trouverér mon excuse dans L'interet que vous avés quelque fois eu La bonté de me temoigner, et qui m'encourage aujourd'hui de vous prier de me le continuer aupres de cette bonne parente dans les differentes occasions qui pourront S'en offrir et etre persuadé que ma reconnaissance et Celle de M^de DeRieux ne pourra Se comparer qu'à Celle très etendue que nous conservons a Mr Jefferson Sur Le même Sujet.

En apprenant votre nomination, J'avois pensé que Si vous n'aviés pas encore trouvé d'acquereur pour votre plantation au dessus de La Ville, il vous eut peut etre été agréable de La Louer pour un Terme d'années ou pour au moins celui de votre retour, et de vous demander dans ce cas La préférence. Mais, Mr Votre frère m'a dit depuis, qu'il allait y aller vivre Lui même avec Sa famille, et qu'il L'acheteroit probablement. ainsi cela detruit L'espoir que j'avois d'en faire d'abord ma demeure quelques années, et d'en devenir peut etre Le proprietaire, Lorsque mes circonstances Seroient Meilleures. J'en avois même parlé a notre ami col. Bell. Il m'a dit avoir L'intention de vous ecrire [Jeudi] prochain qu'il L'auroit fait plutot mais qu'il vous croit parti. J'espere beaucoup que vous recevrés celle-cy auparavant, et que j'aurai le plaisir d'avoir encore été asséz a tems pour Votre reponse. [Perméttés], Monsieur que Madame Monroe trouve ici Lassurance de mon respect et celui de M^de de Rieux et agréer Je vous prie Les Sentiments d'attachement avec Les quels j'ai L'honneur d'etre Monsieur Votre très Humble et très obeissant Serviteur

P. De Rieux

P. S. Mr Jefferson qui a diné chés moi aujourd'hui m'a prié de vous marquer, Monsieur, qu'il auroit eu le plaisir de vous ecrire et de vous envoyer plusieurs Lettres par ce courier, mais qu'il ne pouvoit pas etre a tems, et qu'il Le feroit certainement La premiere poste.

Editors' Translation

CharlotteVille 12 June 1794

Sir,

It was just as we were hoping to have the pleasure of seeing you soon return amongst us, that we learned of your preparations to move away even farther. We have also learned that your hasty departure will hardly leave you time to receive the expression of our intentions to wish you and Madame, a crossing as swift as it is pleasant, and, in general, all the pleasure possible.

I take the liberty, Sir, to send you here enclosed a letter for my aunt. I would be very grateful to you if you would deliver it yourself when the tribulations of your first obligations will have allowed some leisure time. She is more often settled in St. Germaine than in Paris, but since she goes to Paris from time to time, I will include her two addresses; you will surely find her at one or the other.

I dare to hope that you will forgive this imposition on my part and that you will find that my excuse is rooted in the interest that you have had the kindness of showing me, which has encouraged me today to ask that you continue in the future to show your consideration with regard to this dear relative. And, I hope that you are assured of my gratitude as well as that of Madame De Rieux, comparable only to the boundless gratitude that we reserve for Mᴿ Jefferson on the same subject.

Upon hearing of your nomination, I thought that if you hadn't found a buyer for your plantation situated above the town, you would have found it agreeable in renting it for a period of several years or at least until you return; and if so, I would like to ask that you give me first option. However, your brother[2] has told me since that he, himself, was going to live there with his family and that he would probably buy it. Thus, this ruins my hopes of making it my residence for a few years and possibly of becoming its owner once my circumstances improved. I had even spoken to our friend Col. Bell about it. He told me he had intended on writing to you Thursday next and that he would have written earlier but he thought you were away. I truly hope that you will receive this letter beforehand and that I will have the pleasure of being in time to receive your reply. Please assure, Sir, Madame Monroe hereby of my respect and that of Madame Rieux, and please accept the sentiments of attachment with which I have the honor of being, Sir, your most humble and obedient servant

P. De Rieux

P. S. Mᴿ Jefferson who dined in my home today has asked me to point out, Sir, that he would have had the pleasure of writing to you and that he would have sent you several letters by the mail, but he could not do this on time, and would most certainly send it by the first post.

RC, ViW: Monroe Papers

1. Justin-Pierre Plumard De Rieux (b. 1756) was the son of the Countess De Rieux Jaucourt who had spent all of her son's patrimony. De Rieux married Philip Mazzei's stepdaughter, Maria Margherita Martini in 1780 in France. The couple immigrated to the United States in early 1784, where they disembarked at Charleston, S. C. De Rieux had a difficult time supporting his family, and Mazzei invited them to reside at Colle, Mazzei's home in Albemarle County. (Philip Mazzei, *My Life and Wanderings*, 256, 272, 282; Mazzei, *Memoirs of the Life and Peregrinations... Philip Mazzei,* 416).

2. Joseph Jones Monroe

To Henry Lee

Philadelphia June 12. 1794.

Sir

Having accepted the appointment conferred on me by the President and Senate of the United States, of minister to the French republick, I considered my seat in the Senate as vacant of course. I deem it however my duty to communicate this event to you officially and the rather as it affords an opportunity of adding the testimony of my profound respect for the source from whence my former appointment emanated.

As I have long served, and I flatter myself been honoured with the confidence of my native State, I would not accept this appointment which places me on a new theatre and makes me responsible to other constituents, without some emotions of concern. But as the same sentiments & principles which have heretofore guided will still continue to direct my conduct, I trust they will make it acceptable to my present, as I have had reason to presume it was to my former constituents. If in any instance it may be in my power to superadd to my duty to the United States, any services that may be useful to Virginia in particular, I sincerely hope the legislature will command me, for I shall always be happy to avail myself of every opportunity to testify to my fellow citizens of that State my gratitude and esteem for the confidence they have heretofore reposed in me. I beg of you to present me in the most respectful manner to the General Assembly & to be assured of the great respect with which I have the honor to be y^r most obedient & very humble servant

Ja^s Monroe

RC, DLC: Louis Asher Autograph Collection

Henry Lee was the governor of Virginia 1791-1794 (*ANB*).

To Joseph J. Monroe

Baltimore June 16. 1794.

Dear Joseph

I was in hopes I sho^d have been able to have visited Albemarle & seen you before my departure but the earnest pressure of the Executive that I sho^d hasten my arrival in France as soon as possible deprived me of that pleasure. I have been happy to meet Mr Jones here & with whom I have made the best arrangment of my private aff^{rs} that circumstances wo^d permit. I have given him a power over all my concerns leaving it with him to authorize others to act where it may be necessary—& I have rendered an acc^t to him of whatever I owe with what is due me and he will settle & satisfy every thing as soon as possible and I doubt not in a manner agreeably to the parties concerned. I did not associate you in this business because I knew it wo^d take you from the duties of y^r profession, upon w^h y^r own & the welfare of y^r family depends. and because I have made what provision for you, my circumstances admit of without it: It being my wish to render you service & not give you trouble. but if you can in any instance aid him in whatever concerns me it is my wish and I doubt not you will do it. I have appropriated to him the use of my houses &^{c} as he is in bad health & contemplates a retreat from the low country, & by using these will be better enabled to look around him for a situation he may like to purchase. I did this with the more pleasure as I was persuaded it wo^d better suit you to reside in Charlottesville, & likewise as I well knew that his residence near you wo^d give you an opportunity of availing yourself of his most excellent council & example.

I have appropriated to you to be given up immediately, or as soon as Mr Jones moves his furniture up, the following articles—The sheets, I think there are 5 or 6 p^r—the pillow cases—the table cloths—the carpets—(such as they are) the knives & forks, (of w^h there are some ivory)—the tin bread baskets & knife box—The tea boards & waiters—The breakfast china & Queen ware—half dozen—silver table & tea spoons—The candlesticks—all my law books. My other books I beg you to collect & lock up. There may be some other matters of the kind w^h I cannot think of but w^h you will be welcome to & will be given up on being notic'd to Mr Jones. I direct also the following to be annually furnished for the time my circumstances will permit & you require it—1000 #^{s} of pork—20 barrels of corn & 30 bushells of wheat—some beef will be likewise furnished—and likewise butter—any other accomodations w^h may be required & can be rendered will, for it is very much my desire to give you every aid in my power to enable you to succeed & prosper in life. I wish however that these matters be kept private for both delicacy & propriety require it.

Respecting y^r debts in Scotland I wish you to write and apprize me how they stand—the am^t & the provision made for them; whether the bonds have been assigned to Glassell or any other person, or remain as heretofore; as likewise what has been done with Yates, the am^t due by him & in what manner, & at what time to be paid—whether it will be of any use for me to commence a correspondence with y^r creditors or the whole business had better be conducted thro' some person in Fred^{bg}.

I cannot leave the country without feeling some solicitude for the welfare of Andrew & y^{r}self & Mrs Buckner.[1] To the latter some attention shall be paid as well as to her family. To the former I shall write & request information in what line I shall be able to serve him. And to yourself I have only further to add a sincere wish that you may by y^r industry, prudence & studious attention to your business, as well as your books, make such exertions as will advance y^r fortune & reputation in the world, whereby alone y^r happiness or even tranquility can be secured. Not only the reality of these virtues must be possessed, but such an external must be observed as to satisfy the world you do possess them, otherwise you will not enjoy their confidence. You will recollect likewise that heretofore y^r youth & inexperience were an excuse for any apparent levity or irregularity. but now that you are advancing in life, have a family & children the case is altered. Solid merit & virtue alone will support & carry you with credit through the world. The principal danger to which a young man commencing under limited resources is exposed, & in which if he errs inflicts the most incurable wound on his reputation, is the abuse of pecuniary confidence. Let me therefore warn you never to use y^r clients money. No temptation is greater to a person possessed of it than that which daily arises in occurrences of a private family, to use this money, especially when the prospect of reimbursement furnishes the hope it may not be called for. But as the commenc'ment of this practice breaks down to a certain degree, that chaste and delicate refin'ment, which forms the strongest barrier for the protection of virtue, it sho^d never be commenc'd; I wo^d make it one of those sacred rules of my life w^h sho^d not be violated never to use it. I believe you have no passion for any thing of that kind, I sincerely hope you have not, I suggest this hint therefore rather to guard you agnst a danger w^h assails every young man, than that I believe you likely to suffer by it, I mean the vice of gambling. I recollect there is a billiard table near you; let me warn you agnst it. a passion of this kind will controul as it always has every other. if it seizes you, y^r clients money will not be safe in y^r hands. There is one incident more trifling w^h I beg to notice & remind you of. I have observed in the conduct of y^r causes that you have not patience to attend the bar with that close attention & regularity thro the day necessary to enable you to take notes & profit by the arguments of others, but that you cannot even wait the issue of y^r own causes. This is highly improper & let me advise to alter in that respect. Let me hear from you often. Inclose y^r letters

RC, ViFreJM; incomplete—first four pages only

1. JM's brother Andrew Monroe and his sister Elizabeth Monroe Buckner.

To Thomas Jefferson

Baltimore June 17. 1794.

Dear Sir

The urgent pressure of the Executive for my immediate departure has deprived me of the pleasure of seeing you before I sailed. I sincerely regret this for many reasons but we cannot controul impossibilities. Will you forward me a cypher, and letters for y^r friends remaining in Paris to the care of Mr R.[1] as soon as possible. They may probably reach Paris as soon as I shall. I beg you to add whatever occurs which may be useful where I am going to the cause in which I am engaged, or to myself in advocating it. Being well acquainted with the theatre on which I am to act it will be much in y^r power to give me hints of that kind which may be serviceable.

As you will shortly see Mr Madison who leaves this tomorrow or next day I decline saying any thing on the subject of the late proceedings in Phil^a in either department of the government. Indeed you know so much of them already that I can add but little.

I shall place in the hands of James Maury of Liverpool a sum of money to answer my engagment to you. I have written to Col^o Lewis and Mr Divers[2] to intreat them to value Thena[3] and her children and hope they will do it immediately. Let y^r draft be ab^t Sepr and payable at 60 days sight. Let it be accompanied with a letter of advice. The money shall certainly be deposited, unless you wo^d prefer it in France of which you will advise me & draw on myself. I beg you not to omit this as the money will be idle in his hands in case you do not direct otherwise soon.

I shall confide to Mr Madison y^{r}self and Mr Jones the fixing on a spot where my house shall be erected.[4] The doubt will be between the hill to the left of the road as you approach towards Blenheim[5] or the one where the barn stands. On which ever you place it I have given orders for an enclosure and the commencment of those improvments w^h are contemplated. Y^r advice on that head as well as the most suitable for the commencment of orchards of different kinds will be regarded.

We expect to imbark to morrow & to fall down the bay immediately. Accept my most affectionate wishes for your welfare and that of Mr Randolph and y^r daughters and be pleased likewise to unite with them those of Mrs Monroe. We contemplate a return in ab^t 3 or 4 years at farthest—perhaps sooner. In the interim I wish every preparation for our final repose, I mean from active life, be in the farm adjoining yours. To this object my attention will be turned whilst abroad & I will indeavor to bring back what will contribute [to] its comforts. I wish you to command me in all respects wherein I can serve you. Perhaps you may wish things from the quarter I shall be in not obtainable so easily elsewhere. I am dear [Sir] with the sincerest regard y^r affectionate friend & serv^t

Ja^s Monroe

RC, DLC: Jefferson Papers

1. Edmund Randolph.

2. JM's letters to Nicholas Lewis and George Divers have not been located.

3. Thena Hemings

4. JM had decided to sell his plantation near Charlottesville and establish his residence at his other farm, the present-day Ash Lawn-Highland (*Papers of James Monroe* 2: 663).

5. Blenheim was a farm owned by Colonel Edward Carter, located several miles south of JM's land (Emily St. Claire, *Beautiful and Historic Albemarle*, 73-74).

To Fulwar Skipwith

[before 19 June 1794][1]

As I pay so much for the accomodation of my family, in my opinion all those really of it sho^d be included, among which are Joseph (Mr Jones's son) y^rself & Mr Prevost in case he arrives. I beg you to attend to this & arrange it with Oliver & Thompson[2] in concert with Captn Barney.[3] It is plain this comp^y mean to accomodate themselves—I well know they wo^d rather I went in their vessel if nothing was paid. Let them not therefore make advantages improper & unauthorized. But act as from y^rself in a business confided to you, & respecting the engagments of Captn Barney. Y^rs

Ja^s Monroe

RC, NN: Monroe Papers; filed at the end of 1805

1. This letter is undated, but the contents indicates that it was written shortly before JM's departure from Baltimore on 19 June 1794.

2. Baltimore merchants Robert Oliver (1757?-1834) and Henry Thompson were partners in business 1785-1796 (MdHi: Robert Oliver Record Books, Inventory). This letter indicates that they were owners of the ship in which JM sailed to France.

3. Joshua Barney (1759-1818) was a Baltimore merchant and seaman who served as an officer in the American navy during the Revolutionary War and the War of 1812 (*ANB*).

From John Francis Mercer

[June 1794][1]

My dear Sir

Y^rs of the 2^d convey'd information that you may suppose was truly agreeable to me[2]—it has for the moment allayd by the reflection that I was cut of[f] from my friends & my pursuits which nature, education & health had most endeared to me. I have only the consolation that I discharge a duty that is the first of natures dictates. Had my family their health domestic life would be very comfortable to me— as it is it meets with too frequent interruptions.

I confess I was surprizd at y^r appointment—if it indicates a change of measures it will be still one agreeable to me—but I had formed an opinion of inflexibility a certain character that left me little hope of any alteration. I am so out of all political line—that I know nothing here—but what I do know—does not denote any great stability in our Government. I think there is a want of confidence fast generating that will probably shake it—if Jay's mission is dissatisfactory—which I can hardly hope will prove otherwise—Amidst conflicting opinions & charges—I am in hopes the progress of the European <illegible> will not encourage monarchical views—I hate monarchy more & more every day & of course any thing that smells of it. I do not wish to come into public life again on any terms during our present System.

I shall always be happy to hear from you—personally I need not assure you that your welfare is more interesting to me than that of I believe any Individual—as a public man I hope & expect salutary effects from y^r exertions to a cause that I am from principle devoted to. Y^r friend & ser^t

John F Mercer

RC, ViFreJM

1. This undated letter was written sometime in June 1794 before JM's departure for France.

2. JM's letter of 2 June 1794 to Mercer has not been located.

To George Clinton

Baltimore June 19. 1794.

Dear Sir

Being just about to sail I take the pleasure to assure you I shall always be happy to hear from you; I wished to have seen you when I was in New Y^k last winter but you were at Albany & fortune directed my departure from this port which has prevented it altogether for the present. But we act in the same cause of equal liberty, and I hope we shall meet here after when that question shall be settled in favor of that great principle, so as to preclude all further controversy. I am Dear Sir sincerely y^r friend

Ja^s Monroe

Remember me to Mr M. Smith.

RC, WHi: Signers Collection

Journal

19th June 1794.

Left Baltimore for France in the Cincinnatus under the command of capt^ns Barney & de Butts having Mrs Monroe & child with me.

Mr Skipwith accompanied me as secr^y of the mission, & M^r Le Blanc secr^y of the legation from France to the U States likewise took his passage in the same ship. He was probably charged by the minister with important dispatches for the French republick, if indeed any dispatches were necessary, where the agent was so fully & deservedly possessed of the confidence of both parties as M^r Le B certainly was.

I took with me also Joseph Jones son of J. J. of Fredericksburg Virg^a, a lad about 14 years of age, whom his father put under my care to be educated in France.[1]

From the time of my appointment to that of my departure ab^t three weeks intervened only. It was notified to me by the Secr^y of State that it was very much wished I sho^d sail as soon as possible, & I accordingly hurried all the preparations that were necessary with suitable dispatch.

AD, DLC: Monroe Papers

JM also took two servants with him, described only as Michael and Polly. They received salaries, so they were not slaves. Michael served as JM's major domo for the length of his stay in France (DLC: Monroe Papers, Series 3: Account Book, 1794-1797: 13 June 1794).

To Henry Tazewell

Chesapeake Bay June 22. 1794.

Dear Sir

I wished much to have visited Virg^a & to have taken Kingsmill in my rout: but the time taken in the details necessary to qualify me for the mission & afterwards in the arrangment of my private aff^rs rendered it impossible. I am now in the bay nearly opposit Hampton, from whence I write you to be returned by the pilot to Baltimore & forwarded thence by the post.

You will no doubt be surprized that a person of my tone of politicks sho^d have been sent to the French republick. till the proposition was made me by the President thro' Mr Randolph I thought was one of the last men in the community to whom it would be made. A consultation of my friends determined I ought to accept it, which was accordingly done, and I am now so far on the way.

I feel very anxious for a succ[essor to] me in the Senate. Tis an important po[sition &] sho^d be occupied by a firm & decided <torn>. upon the supposition that Taylor wo^d like[wise with] draw some gent^n pressed Mr Madison to <torn> his ground. I had no conversation with <torn> myself but understand from F. Strother who was in Phil^a when I was appointed, that he inferred from a conversation with him, he wo^d serve. If he will act, his being on the political theatre, and every way eminently qualified, will no doubt secure his appointment. But on this head I can say nothing. I can assure you however with certainty [that] the whole representation from Virg^a confide in you, & that without any intimation whether you are or are not inclined to act their attention is turned towards you as a person to be pressed into the service in case of emergency. Whether you remain where you are or embark on the political theatre let me hear from you fully & frequently, [as] I am with great sincerity y^r friend & serv^t

Ja^s Monroe

RC, NjMoHP. The lower right-hand corner of the first page of this letter torn off.

To St. George Tucker

Chesapeake bay June 22. 1794.

Dear Sir

I was so engaged in the arrangment of my private aff^rs, after I had dispatched those of a publick nature, that I had not a moment from the period of my appointment to that of my departure to devote to my friends. From the capes I look back to bid farewell to y^rself and a few others. How long I shall be absent is incertain, but I hope my mission will not prove altogether useless to the republican cause. I sincerely wish you well & shall always be happy to hear from you. Your information of the state of our aff^rs extended to what passes within y^r view, will be useful & highly grateful to me. I will give you what may be worth y^r attention from the other hemisphere. With great sincerity, I am dear Sir y^r friend & serv^t

Ja^s Monroe

Remember me affect^y to Mr Nelson & Mr Prentis.

RC, Pvt

From John Langdon

Portsm^o N. H. July 24th 1794

Sir

I felt myself both honor'd and gratified, in receiving your friendly favor of the 19th Ul^t from Baltimore[1] a few hours before you embarked upon your important Mission; you may be assured that you have few friends who Rejoiced more at your Appointment and it was an additional pleasure that you accepted of it, tho I sincerely Regreted the loss of you in Senate. It must be particularly greatful to our good friends and Allies the french to have a Minister sent them from United America; who so sincerely partakes in their Success prosperity and happiness; I am sure S^r we both consider the Cause of France the Cause of America.

The happiness of both I am perswaded will be your persuit. I shall at all times be very happy in make^g any Communications from this part of the U S. that may contribute to the general welfare of this Country, and the Advancement of the French Republic. Things Remain pretty near the same State as when you left us, the Choice for members of Congress is going on with Spirit, the old policy is Continued to obtain a Majority in Parliament the People stand right, and I dare say things will go well. I am almost tired, of all Courts Politics, and great men, and have Serious tho'ts of Retire^g from any Public Business.

Mrs Langdon & Eliza[2] Join me in our best Regards, to yourself, and Mrs Monroe. Wishing you both every felicity, Believe me Sincerely your Friend & H^ble Servt

John Langdon

RC, NN: Monroe Papers

1. JM's letter to Langdon of 19 June 1794 has not been located.

2. Langdon married Elizabeth Sherburne (1761-1813) in 1775. Their daughter Elizabeth (b. 1777) married Thomas Elwyn in 1797 (Lawrence Mayo, *John Langdon of New Hampshire*, 141, 171, 273, 285).

From Edmund Randolph

Philadelphia 30th July 1794

Sir

I have applied to Mr Fauchet for the adjustment of the fifteen thousand dollars, voted by Congress for the relief of the St Domingo people. His answer is not yet received; although I can be at no loss to anticipate it. For I recollect, when he first came, he felt uneasy, that Congress should be granting as he called it French money against the will of the Republic; and even after I had pressed upon him the obligation of his Government to support its indigent citizens; the heavy tax, which these unhappy fugitives had been upon us, and the impossibility of seeing them starve in our Country, no other impression was made upon him, than to narrow his objection to the disbursement of French money for the support of Aristocrats as well as Democrats. You will therefore proceed to bring this article immediately into view; and as it is short in its principle, so will it be sufficient for us to obtain a short Decree, that such parts of the fifteen thousand dollars as may have been expended upon the succour of the indigent inhabitants of St Domingo, who took refuge here after the disasters of the Cape, be credited to the United States in their account with the French Republic.

We have heard with regret, that several of our citizens have been thrown into prison in France from a suspicion of criminal attempts against the Government. If they are guilty, we are extremely sorry for it: if innocent, we must protect them. It is the desire therefore of the President, that you should without delay collect intelligence of every American citizen under confinement, and of his case, and whatsoever ought and can be done, to do promptly and decisively; taking care to see, that your path is clear, and affording no pretext for being charged with demands against the law of nations. Among these persons are Archibald Hunter and Shubael Allen; concerning both of whom papers are enclosed;[1] and who ought to be immediately assisted, as far as may be right; since their sufferings are known. I consign them to your earliest attention, and warmest activity.

Mr Macarty, whose letter is enclosed, has been lately appointed Consul for the United States in the Isle of France, from whence he dates.[2] The circumstances which he relates, are serious and important; and it is wished, that you lose no time in having every thing rectified and compensated as to past instances, and to prevent a repetition of future.

The enclosed letter from one Binard of Brest[3] speaks of his having been appointed vice-Consul of the united States there, by Mʳ Burrall Carnes our late Consul at Nantes. In this he is mistaken, as Mʳ Carnes had no right to appoint a vice-Consul under himself, and probably went no farther than to constitute him an Agent, as Consuls may lawfully do. Mʳ Dobree, having succeeded Mʳ Carnes, will probably take similar measures with respect to an Agent; but it is desireable, that you should immediately examine this matter well, and cause to be done, what shall appear beneficial to our trade.[4] If a vice-Consul should appear to be really necessary, you will inform me by the first opportunity.

Mʳ G. Morris having recommended Mʳ Francis Coffyn, to be our Consul at Dunkirk, a temporary Commission is sent to him, and will be submitted to the Senate for renewal;[5] unless from a view of all circumstances relative to his situation, (he being understood to be now in confinement for some cause or other) you should think it improper, that he should be employed in the service of the United States.

Mʳ G. Morris will have probably communicated to you the steps, which he has lately taken, to accomplish a peace with Algiers, and the liberation of our fellow citizens in captivity. But lest he may have accidentally omitted to mention them, I forward a copy of his letter which describes his measures. As he had received no particular powers upon this head, and is not minute in that letter as to the instructions which he has given, we are left to conjecture, what course has been pursued.[6] You will therefore inform the proper authority, that the President learns with great satisfaction the new testimony given by the French Republic, of attachment to the interests of the United States; not doubting at the same time, that it must prove beneficial to the supplies of France from hence: that the powers, derived from Mʳ Morris to the Agent who was to accompany on our part the French commissioner, though they are as yet unknown to us, have no doubt been judicious, and the acts in conformity with those powers will be confirmed, if they shall be found to come within the spirit of the plan, hitherto adopted: that Colº Humphreys, our minister at Lisbon has been long ago specially appointed to this business,[7] possesses a full knowledge of our views and our means, and has been particularly conversant in our attempts for peace with Algiers: that he will, if he should think it necessary, instruct the agent appointed by Mʳ Morris: that we trust the auspices of the French Republic will be continued to the efforts under the guidance of Colº Humphreys; and that as an evidence of our confidence in the French Government you are impowered, if you conceive it to be adviseable, to impart the terms, upon which we expect to buy peace; but the circumstances and consequences of such communication are to be well weighed before it be made.

The cases of spoliation and vexation from the French cruisers on our trade, I again most earnestly recommend to your anxious attention. Mʳ Fauchet has promised to forward a recommendation of them to his Government. You will do well to press the <u>principle</u> without delay; and if doubts are entertained as to facts, put the subjects into a train for the most early decision. The French Republic will surely never suffer us to be plundered by their citizens; and that we have greatly suffered by their plundering, the papers accompanying this letter if they be true, manifest. We are no less disturbed at the conduct concerning the embargo at Bordeaux. If the account, brought hither lately by one of the Captains, who were detained there be genuine, the promise of compensation has been illusory only. You are therefore again charged to make this also your special and immediate business; and to press the rights of our citizens in a manner which indicates, that we cannot waive the justice due to us. In short, Sir, it is the express instruction of the President that you diligently inquire into every inconvenience, to which our trade has been subjected; and to remonstrate strongly upon them, and represent the facts to us fully and minutely. Had not Mʳ Morris so strenuously pressed the affair of the Ship Laurens of Charleston, which is committed to your care, I would here repeat all the circumstances.[8] But these may be obtained as well from

Mr Morris as from the French archives. The Decrees, upon which the conduct of the French Republic was founded, in this case, which I note particularly on account of those Decrees, have also been remonstrated against by Mr Morris; and I question whether much matter can be added to his observations. But such of those Decrees, as tend to the condemnation of the Laurens are gross violations of our rights. You no doubt will have resumed this subject immediately on your arrival; and you are at liberty to speak in a firm and decisive tone, taking care to avoid offence, or in any degree to weaken the friendship between the two Countries. As you carried with you a statement from this department, relative to the spoliations of our trade, and copies of Mr Fauchet's letters respecting them:, I do not repeat them here. But these will assist you in the demands which you are to make on the French Government. I have the honor, sir to be with great and constant esteem and repect y^r mo. ob. ser.

Edm: Randolph

RC, WHi: Draper Collection: George Rogers Clark Manuscripts, volume 54. Written in a clerk's hand, except the closing and signature, which are Randolph's.

1. These papers have not been identified.

2. William McCarty was the American consul on the French Indian Ocean island of Ile De France (now Mauritius) (National Archives, *Pamphlet Accompanying Microcopy No. 28: Diplomatic and Consular Instructions of the Department of State, 1791-1801*, 9). His letter has not been located.

3. The letter from Mr. Binard has not been located.

4. Burrell Carnes, an American merchant, served as commerical agent and consul at Nantes from 1786 to 1793. James Anderson, another American merchant, served as commerical agent from August 1793 until May 1794, when Pierre F. Dobrée was appointed consul. Dobrée held the post until 1799 (*Jefferson Papers*, 9: 303, 11: 602, 14: 59, 233, 24: 424; National Archives, *Pamphlet Accompanying Microcopy No. 28*, 10).

5. Francis Coffyn served as American commercial agent at Dunkirk from 1776 until July 1794, when he was appointed consul, a post he held until his death in May 1795. The temporary commission, referred to here was dated 9 July 1794. President Washington signed the regular commission on 18 December 1794 (Francis Coffyn, Jr. to JM, 2 June 1795, DNA: RG 59: Despatches from Nantes; *Washington Papers: Journal of the Proceedings of the President*, 311, 323).

6. Morris wrote to Secretary of State Jefferson on 7 March 1794, informing him that the French government had offered to assist the United States in its negotiations with Algiers. Morris appointed Jacques LeRay de Chaumont, who was to travel to Algiers in the character of a French diplomat, to conduct the negotiation (DNA: RG 59: Depatches from France).

7. David Humphreys served as U. S. minister to Portugal 1791-1796. He was placed in charge of negotiations with Algiers in May 1793 (*ANB*).

8. In March 1793 the French privateer *Sans Culottes* captured the American ship *Laurens* on the justification that its cargo was English-owned. The tribunal in the French port of Havre declared the seizure illegal and ordered the ship's release, a decision that was seconded by a decree of the National Convention. Even so the owners of the *Sans Culotte* were able to delay the release, and a year later the *Laurens* was still being detained (Report of Jean Bon Saint Andre, enclosed in Gouverneur Morris to the Secretary of State, 6 March 1794, DNA: RG 59: Despatches from France).

Journal

[31 July 1794]

We were detained ab^t 8 days in the bay whose capes we passed ab^t the 27th of June & 29 days from that period we obtained soundings at the mouth of the Engl^h channel where we found 8 French frigates commanding as well the entrance into that as the Irish channel—the 31st of July we arrivd at Havre—we saw no ships of war in our passage up the channel nor more than 3 or 4. merchant ships.

The coast of Normandy attracted our attention as we passed, by the beauty of the fortifications at Cherbourg, & generally for the superior state of cultivation.

Havre occupies the Eastern point which forms the mouth of the Seine. It appears to have been almost reclaimed from the sea, being very low & protected from its inroad by art. It is walled round by immense fortifications & a basin formed in the heart of the town to admit vessels of war & others when occasion requires. At present there are　　　　　frigates ready to sail & two on the stocks better than half finished.

We were met by a pilot at the mouth of the river who informed us that another great convulsion had shaken & torn Paris to pieces—that Robertspiere & his brother were executed—& that the number of executions was immense—that the cause was, Robertspiere & his party had plotted the massacre of the Convention & that their fate was just—he added that generally those who talked most about patriotism were the greatest rascals—we were presented to the municipality who received & examined the evidence of my station with strictness but with decent respect. In one instance indeed they exceeded the bounds of propriety, having ordered my trunks to be open'd which was done, but more as a matter of form they seemed to consider themselves bound to observe than strictly to search into my papers. We heard here of an action between Lord Howe & the French fleet w^h had taken place ab^t a month before. The English force being　　　& the French　　　　& in w^h the former lost　　ships of which　　were sunk & the others taken—the latter lost 8 ships, of which　　were of the line. Tis said the French kept the field the day following & that the English withdrew—a remarkable instance of enthusiasm & magnanimity is related as having been displayed by the officers & marines of one of the French ships which was lost—finding she was about to sink they brought all the sick & wounded upon deck & continued firing untill the guns were covered with water, & sunk singing the Marseilles hymn.[1]

We heard here that the French were successful by land & had driven their enemies before them in every quarter but as ab^t 3 months had elapsed thro which we wo^d have to travel in pursuit of their fortunes we had not time for the purpose.

We heard also that the spirit of liberty began to revive in Poland & that Kuskiusco at the head of ab^t 30.000 poles had succeeded in several encounters with the Russians.[2]

On reading the paper in the chamber of the municipality giving an acc^t of the executions in Paris M^r Le Blanc observed that he had thought well of many of those who had suffered—to w^h the principal member calmly replied if they died good men it was so much the better for them as they wo^d now be at repose in the elysian fields.

AD, DLC: Monroe Papers; filed 19 June 1794

1. On 1 June 1794 the British channel fleet, numbering twenty-four ships, under Admiral Lord Howe engaged in battle with a twenty-six-ship French fleet under Admiral Louis-Thomas Villaret-Joyeuse. The British severely battered the French fleet, sinking one ship, badly damaging twelve, capturing six, and inflicting over 7000 casualties. The French were successful, however, in keeping the British fleet away from a grain convoy from America, which safely entered the port at Brest. Howe was heavily criticized for allowing the convoy and the remnants of the French fleet to escape ("Richard Howe," in *The Oxford Dictionary of National Biography*, 28: 486).

2. Tadeusz Kościuszko had been driven into exile in 1792 when Russian troops overran Poland. He returned home in 1794 and became the leader of the Polish war for independence. He won victories at Raclawice and Warsaw during the spring of 1794 (*ANB*).

To Philippe Merlin de Douai

Paris. August 13. 1794

Sir

Having arrived here a few days past, commissioned by the President of the United States of America to represent those States in character of Minister Plenipotentiary with the French Republic and not being acquainted with the competent department or forms of recognition prescribed by law, I have thought it my duty to make known my mission immediately to the Representatives of the Nation. They possess the power to affix the time and prescribe the mode by which I shall be recognized as the representative of their Ally and Sister Republic; and they will likewise have the goodness, in case such Department now exists, to cause the same to be designated to me that I may immediately present myself before it [to] be recognized in the character I bear.

I make this communication with the greater pleasure, because it affords me an opportunity of testifying to the Representatives of the free citizens of France, not only my own attachment to the cause of liberty but of assuring them at the same time and in the most decided manner of the deep concern which the Government & People of America take in the liberty, prosperity, and happiness of the French Republic. With sentiments of the highest Respect I am Sir Your mo ob and mo Hum^e Servant

Ja^s Monroe

RC (photocopy), DLC: FCP—France. In clerk's handwriting with JM's signature. A variant text of this letter, derived from the copy in DNA: RG 59: Dispatches from France, is published in *Writings of Monroe*, 2: 11.

Philippe-Antoine Merlin de Douai (1754-1838), a deputy to the National Convention from Flanders, served as president of the Convention from August 3 to August 18, 1794. He was a member of the Committee of Public Safety from September 1794 to November 1795, and held several posts under the Directory. He remained in the government under Bonaparte and helped write the Napoleanic Code (Paul R. Hanson, *Historical Dictionary of the French Revolution*, 215-216; M. J. Sydenham, *The First French Republic, 1792-1804*, 335).

To Edmund Randolph

Paris August 15th 1794[1]

Sir,

On the 31 ult^o I arrived at Havre, and, on the 2^d Instant at this place. Mr Morris was upon my arrival from town, but he came in as soon as advised of it. By him I was presented to the Commissary of Foreign Affairs, who assured me that as soon as the form of my reception should be settled, he would apprize me of it, but that this would unavoidably create a delay of some days, as well from the present derangement of their affairs on account of the late commotion of Robespiere, as from the necessity of making some general regulation in that respect it being the first instance in which a minister had been addressed to the Republic. I assured him I should wait, with pleasure, the convenience of those whom it concerned: and since which I have not seen him, but hear that the subject is under consideration of the Committee of public safety, and will probably be concluded in a day or two.

I heard at Havre of the crimes and execution of Robespiere,[2] St Just,[3] Couthon[4] and others of that party, and should have written you on the subject, from that Port, but that I knew I could give only the current report, varying perhaps in every Seaport town, and which might reach you before my letter. I hastened therefore to Paris in the hope of acquiring there immediately more correct information of facts, as well as of the causes which gave birth to them: but even yet I suspect I am on the surface only, for it will take some time to become well acquainted with the true state of things on a theatre so extensive and important.

That Robespiere and his associates merited their fate is a position to which every one assents. It was proclaimed by the countenances and voices of all whom I met and conversed with from Havre to Paris. In the latter place where the oppression was heaviest, the people seemed to be relieved from a burden which had become insupportable. It is generally agreed that from the period of Danton's fall, Robespiere had amassed in his own hands all the powers of the government, and controuled every department in all its operations. It was his spirit which ruled the Committee of Public safety, the Convention, and the Revolutionary tribunal. The Convention was soon found after the abrogation of the Constitution, to be too unwieldy and slow in its deliberations to direct the great and complicated mass of executive business: this had given birth to two Committees, the one of "salut publique," the other of "surety generale," into whose hands the whole was deposited. To the former was assigned the management of foreign affairs, the direction of the army, &c; to the latter, the interior administration, and they were respectively enjoined to render an account monthly of their transactions to the Convention. It was intended that these Committees should be independant of each other; and both under the immediate controul of the Convention; but by the distribution of their powers, this design was defeated, for such an ascendancy was thereby given to the Committee of public Safety, that the other became its instrument acting only under its authority. The principal members of the Convention were placed in these Committees, and Robespiere who was by far the most influential one, was assigned to the Committee of public Safety. It soon happened in the course of the administration, from the very extensive patronage, comparative weight of character, and immense power that this Committee gained likewise an entire ascendancy in the Convention, and controuled all its measures. Nor was the organization of the Revolutionary tribunal more favorable to the independence of that branch, and of course to public and personal liberty. It was equally dependent on, and the creature of this Committee. Robespiere therefore had become omnipotent: it was his spirit which dictated every movement, and particularly the unceasing operation of the Guillotine. Nor did a more bloody and merciless tyrant ever wield the rod of power. His acts of cruelty and oppression are perhaps without parrallel in the annals of history. It is generally conceded that for some months before his fall, the list of Prisoners was shewn him every evening, by the President of the Revolutionary tribunal, and that he marked those who were to be the victims of the succeeding day, and which order was invariably executed. many whole families, those under the age of 16 excepted, were cut off, upon the imputation of conspiracies &c. but for the sole reason that some member had been more friendly to Brissot, Danton, &c. or had expressed a Jealousy of his powers.

This oppression had in fact gained to such an height that a convulsion became unavoidable. The circumstances which immediately preceded and brought on the crisis, are differently recounted: Some make him the active party, and believe that he had arranged with the commune and the guards of the City the plan of a general massacre of his enemies in the convention: But I am of opinion that these projects, for they were certainly contemplated, proceeded from despair, and were adopted at the moment only as the means of defence. The time and manner of the explosion which was in the Convention, supports this idea. It had been intimated some days before by him or S[t] Just, that other conspiracies threatened the safety of the Republic, and which ought to be laid open. The communication was given in such a manner as to satisfy the audience that he meant Talien,[5] and Some other members of the House: And in the moment of the explosion S[t] Just had commenced a development of this pretended conspiracy, leading to a denunciation of these members. If the power of Robespiere remained, it was well known that death and denunciation went hand in hand. To repel it by a counter one, was the only remaining hope; it could in no event produce a worse effect. Talien therefore rose and interrupted St Just, demanding "how long shall we be abused with denunciations of pretended conspiracies? 'Tis time to draw the veil from before perfidy so flagrant." St Just was Silenced and driven from the tribunal. Robespiere ascended and made many efforts to speak in vain. The whole Convention rose and cried out with one voice, "down with the tyrant." He stood like one amazed and stupefied, staring at the Convention with a countenance equally bespeaking indignation and terror, deprived of the power of utterance but yet afraid to descend. As soon as the Convention saw its strength he was arrested and sent a prisoner to the Committee of public safety; but by this time his immediate coadjutors had taken the alarm, and were endeavouring to excite commotions in the City in his behalf. Henriot[6] the commander of the guard with a few followers pursued and rescued him from the Committee. He then took his station with the Commune heretofore the Theatre of his power, and began to harangue the people, and with some effect, whilst Henriot in the character of <u>General</u> was busied in assembling the guards in the place before the hall of the Convention, with intention to fire on it. There was at this moment an awful pause in the affairs of the Republic; every thing was suspended, and the public mind greatly alarmed and agitated. The situation of the Convention was truly interesting. They knew that all the appointments were conferred by Robespiere, that he had been long deemed a patriot, and still possessed by means of affection or terror, a wonderful influence over the citizens at large; and, more immediately in their presence they saw Henriot at the head of a respectable force, menacing an attack. But that body was not unmindful of its dignity or its duty upon that great occasion: on the contrary it displayed a degree of fortitude and magnanimity worthy of those who aspire to the exalted character of defenders of their Country; It calmly entered upon the Subject of defence, declared Robespiere, St Just, Couthon, Henriot and the commune without the protection of the law, appointed a Commandant of the guards, and sent deputies to the sections to admonish them of their danger, and warn them to stand at their posts in defence of their Country. A moment's reflection settled the public mind. The people beheld on the one Side the Convention labouring to save the Republic, and, on the other Robespiere and his associates in open rebellion. Hesitation was at an end; the citizens rallied immediately to the standard of their sections, and Robespiere and his associates were taken at the same time to prison, and, on the next day to execution, amidst the rejoicings and acclamations of the people.

Many believe that Robespiere aimed at despotic power, and sought to establish himself upon the throne of the Capets; in the character of Protector, or some such character and in pursuit of this idea, say that he counted upon the support of the Armies, and particularly the army of the north, and had otherwise arranged things in such order as to favour the project. What his views of ambition and carnage were, I know not: that they had been great was certain, but that he had concerted any plan of permanent establishment for himself, or been promised such support even where his influence was greatest, cannot be true, nor is it warranted by circumstances. If he was not promised the support, 'tis not probable he had such a scheme, and that it was not promised must be obvious to those who take into view all the circumstances which merit consideration. It will be observed by those who wish to form a just estimate of the future course and fortune of this Revolution, that from its commencement to the present time, no person ever raised himself to power, but by the proof he had furnished of his Attachment to the cause, by his efforts to promote it: and that from the moment doubts were entertained of the solidity and purity of his principles, did his influence begin to decline in equal degree. This was seen in the instances of La Fayette, Dumouriez,[7] Brissot, Danton, and finally Robespiere himself; two of whom, tho' popular generals, were abandoned by the armies they commanded, the former compelled to seek refuge in a foreign Country, and the latter in the Camp of the enemy; and the others tho' eminent in the civil department, were upon like charges condemned by the public voice to the same fate. In fact the current of principle and Sentiment, has been such that no character or circumstance has been able to obstruct its course: on the contrary it has swept every thing before it. Can it be presumed then, and especially at this moment, when the ardor of the nation, inflamed by conquest, is at the height that any respectable number of citizens of any description, would turn aside from the great object of the Revolution, to countenance in any individual, schemes of usurpation & tyranny? did not the late event in Paris disprove it, where he had most influence, there was no opposing force but what depended on public opinion, and every thing tended to favor his views.

From due consideration of all circumstances I am led to ascribe the sanguinary course of Robespiere's proceedings to a different cause. I consider the contest between him and Danton as a contest for power between rivals, having the same political objects in view. The one was Jealous of the other, and having gained the ascendancy, and the defective organization of the Government permitting it by means of his influence in the judiciary, he cut him off. But the arrestation and condemnation were regular according to the forms prescribed by civil authority, and were on that account submitted to. The public however saw into the oppression, and disapproved it: for, at the moment of his execution there was a general gloom upon the countenances of the Citizens. They all attended at the place in hope of hearing the explanation; they heard none and retired dissatisfied. Robespiere saw this, and in it the foreboding of his own ruin. From that moment he saw nothing but conspiracies assassinations and the like. He was surrounded by informers and had spies and emissaries in every quarter. By means of severity he sought his safety, and therefore struck at all his enemies in the hope of extirpating them. But it happened in this as it always happens in like cases, every new execution increased them ten fold. It progressed thus until it could be no longer borne, and terminated as I have already stated.

It may be asked, is there any reason to hope that the vicious operation of the Guillotine may be hereafter suspended? may not factions rise again contend with and destroy each other as heretofore? To this I can only answer that the like is not apprehended here at least to the same extent: That the Country from Havre to Paris, and Paris itself, appears to enjoy perfect tranquillity; that the same order is said to prevail in the armies, who have addressed the Convention, applauding its conduct and rejoicing at the downfal of the late conspirators. Some circumstances 'tis true have been seen indicating a suspicion that all Robespieres associates had not Suffered the fate they merited, and ought not to escape; but latterly this has abated, tho' 'tis possible it may revive again. In general it may be remarked, that until peace and a well organized Government shall be established, no sure calculation can be formed of what may happen in this respect. I am happy however to observe that the subject of a reform in the Committees & Revolutionary Tribunals (and which was taken up immediately after the late commotion subsided) is now under discussion, and that the propositions which are depending are calculated to preserve, as far as possible the controul of the Convention over the former, and promote the independence and otherwise improve the organization of the latter.

But are not the people oppressed with taxes, worn out by continual drafts to reinforce the armies, do they discover no symptoms of increasing discontent with the reigning government and of a desire to relapse again under the former tyranny? What will become of the army at the end of the War, will it retire in peace and enjoy in tranquillity that liberty it has so nobly contended for, or will it not rather turn its victorious arms against the bosom of its Country? These are great and important questions and to which my short residence here will not permit me to give satisfactory answers. Hereafter I shall be able to give you better information in these respects. At present I can only observe that I have neither seen nor heard of any symptom of discontent shewing itself among the people at large. The oppression of Robespiere had indeed created an uneasiness but which disappeared with the cause. I never saw in the countenances of men more apparent content, with the lot they enjoy, than has been shewn every where since my arrival.

In the course of the last year the Convention recommended it to the people as the surest means of support for their armies to increase the sphere of cultivation, and from what I can learn there never was more land under cultivation, nor was the country ever blessed with a more productive harvest. Many fathers of families, and a great proportion of the young men are sent to the frontier, and it was feared it would be difficult to reap and secure it: but the women the boys, and the girls, even to tender age, have supplied their places. I saw this with amazement upon my route from Havre to this place, and am told 'tis generally the case. The victories of their armies are celebrated with Joy and festivity in every quarter; and scarce a day has latterly passed without witnessing a deputation to the Convention, and often from the poorest citizens, to throw into its coffers some voluntary contribution for the Support of the War. These are not Symptoms of disgust, of discontent with the reigning Government, and of a desire to change it!

With respect to the present disposition of the army or what it may be at the end of the War, I can say less, as I have not seen it. At present the best understanding subsists between it and the Convention. It is possible in the course of service, if the war should last long, many of its members may acquire habits unfriendly to retirement. But in an army composed of the Yeomanry of the Country, as this is, that sentiment will be less apt to gain ground than in any other. Besides is it not presumable that the spirit which has raised and influenced this, will continue to produce some effect, even in its final disposition. If however there should still remain a considerable force on foot, which could not be prevailed on to retire, fond of conquest, of rapine, and of plunder, can it be supposed that its parent Country will furnish the only and most grateful theatre to act on? will no other portion of Europe present before it a more productive field whereon to gratify ambition avarice, or revenge? There must always remain in the breasts of the Soldiers some sentiment in favour of their relatives and the fortunes of the wealthy will be pretty well broken and dissipated here by the course of the revolution. The example of the Roman Empire is always before those whose apprehensions are greatest upon this ground. They see there nothing but kindred armies fighting against each other, and tearing the Commonwealth in pieces: but they make no allowance for the great difference in the state of things. The armies of the Empire were raised in the conquered provinces and composed of foreigners: they therefore had no attachment to Rome. The state of the Country and the spirit of the age are likewise different. The dissentions of Rome were the convulsions of a corrupt and worn out monarchy, verging rapidly to decline. But here the case is different, the armies are otherwise composed, and the spirit of the age that of a rational and Philosophic reform, seeking to establish the public liberty, and sweeping before it, old and corrupt institutions, which were no longer tolerable. I have thus gone into this interesting subject, from a desire to give the best view in my power of the late commotions, and present state of the internal affairs of this Country, because I well know its importance to my own. It will be my object to improve my knowledge of it, and keep you correctly informed in every particular, and as regularly as opportunities offer.

With respect to the State of the War, I can only say, in general that the armies of France have prevailed over their enemies every where. The commencement of the campaign was favorable to them but the action which took place in July near Charleroy on the plains of Fleury, between Cobourg at the head of about 100,000 men, and Jourdan with an inferior force, and which terminated after the severest conflict and great Slaughter on both Sides, in favour of the French Arms, has evidently given them the superiority ever since. This was certainly one of the most important and bloody actions which has been fought in the course of the present war. Cobourg, unwilling to retire before the Republican troops, had gathered together all his forces, with design to hazard a general action and in the hope of regaining Charleroy. He attacked them at every point about 5 in the morning; formed in the field, and ready to receive him. Three times he drove them back within their intrenchments, reluctant to yield the day: but they sallied out a fourth time, with still greater impetuosity, shouting thro' all their ranks, "we will retreat no more," and singing the Marseilles hymn, and other Patriotic songs they advanced with an ardor which was irresistible. The attack succeeded. Cobourg with his routed army fled before them leaving on the field according to the French accounts about 10,000 slain. The french it is supposed lost about 15,000 men.[8] They have taken in the course of the present campaign Ostend, Mons, Tournay, Namur, Tirlemont, Landrecy, Antwerp, Ghent, Charleroy, Brussels, Quesnoy, Louvain, Liege, Nieuport, Ratsnat,[9] (at the mouth of the Scheldt) with some other places lying in that quarter. Cobourg at present occupies the ground in the neighbourhood of Maestricht, and endeavours to cover the frontiers of Holland. 'Tis however daily expected another action will take place which may settle the fate of the lower Countries. Conde and Valenciennes you observe are left far in the rear: they are yet possessed by the combined forces, but are invested and it is thought must soon fall.

Their success in spain has likewise been great. They are at present in possession of the whole of the province of Guypuscoa, Bilboa excepted. Many prisoners, and immense parks of artillery, have been taken from the Spaniards. The detail I cannot give you with any kind of accuracy, but will endeavour to comprize it in my next.[10]

There has been but one sea action, and which was between the French and English fleets in the course of the present summer, & which began on 17 June. The french had 26 ships, and the English 28. The English having the Wind, bore down on the French and separated Seven ships from their main force. of these they took 6 and sunk the other. 'Tis said there never was a more bloody or bitter fought action on both sides. It lasted three days. On the fourth the British filed off with the ships they had taken, and sailed into port. The french having offered to renew the combat likewise returned afterwards to Brest, whither they conducted the Merchantmen convoyed from America and which was the object of the contest, safe.

I shall write you again in a few days, & I hope to inform you of my reception. For the present therefore I shall conclude with assurances of the great respect and esteem with which I am Dear Sir Your most obediant and very humble Servant

Ja⁵ Monroe.

Copy, DNA: RG 59: Dispatches from France

1. Both *ASP: FA* (1: 670-671) and *View of the Conduct* date this letter as 11 August 1794.

2. Maximilien-Marie-Isidore Robespierre (1758-1794), a lawyer from Arras, was elected to the Estates General in 1789. In Paris he joined the Jacobin Club and became popular with the Sans-culottes whose cause he championed before and after the uprising of 10 August 1792. A month later he engineered the September Massacres with Jean-Paul Marat and Georges Danton. In May 1793 Robespierre orchestrated the uprising against the Girondists. After his election to the Committee of Public Safety in July, he became involved in every action of the committee as well as being its spokesman before the Convention. His success in eliminating all potential rivals, led to his own downfall on 27 July 1794 (Hanson, *Historical Dictionary of the French Revolution*, 274-277; 295).

3. Louis-Antoine Saint-Just (1767-1794) was from 1792 onward a deputy to the Convention, a member of the Jacobin club and close ally of Robespierre. As a member of the Committee of Public Safety in 1793 he worked to bring down the Girondists. In 1794 he brought an inflexible rigor to martial law in his re-organization of the Republican Army. He was denounced with Robespierre whom he followed to the guillotine (*Histoire Universelle Larousse*; Hanson, *Historical Dictionary of the French Revolution*, 287-288).

4. Georges-Auguste Couthon (1755-1794), a lawyer from Auvergne, was elected to the National Convention in 1792 where he sat with the Montagnards and became a friend of Robespierre. He joined the Committee of Public Safety in May of 1793, and urged the final abolition of seigniorial dues without monetary compensation. In June 1794, he delivered a report to the Committee on the new Law of Suspects which caused even greater numbers to be sent to the guillotine. His alliance with Robespierre sealed his fate, and he went to the guillotine on 29 July 1794 (Paul Hanson, *Historical Dictionary of the French Revolution*, 94-95).

5. Jean-Lambert Tallien (1767-1820) was the leader of the Thermidorian Reaction, and one of the main conspirators against Robespierre. After an education in the law he began publishing in 1791 *L'Ami du Citoyen*, a Parisian newspaper modeled after Jean-Paul Marat's better known *L'ami du Peuple*. Tallien was also secretary of the Paris Commune and Jacobin deputy from Seine and Oise to the Convention (Jules Michelet, *Histoire de la Révolution Française*, 1570-1572; Paul Hanson, *Historical Dictionary of the French Revolution*, 305).

6. François Hanriot (or Henriot) (1759-1794) a sans-culottes leader in Paris, was named Commandant of the National Guard in May 1793. He tried to rescue Robespierre on 9 Thermidor, but was unsuccessful and was executed with him the following day (*L'histoire de la France edition Larousse*).

7. Following the victory at Valmy on 20 September 1792, General Charles-François Dumouriez (1739-1823) pushed the Austrians back into Belgium, defeated them at the battle of Jemappes on November 6, then overran the whole country from Namur to Antwerp within a month. The execution of the Louis XVI in January 1793, raised up a multitude of new enemies including England, Holland, Austria, Prussia, Spain, and Sardinia who formed the First Coalition. While Dumouriez was beginning his proposed invasion of Holland, Prince Josias of Saxe-Coburg, the new Austrian commander on the Lower Rhine, drove in the various detachments that Dumouriez had stationed on his right. The French general abandoned his invasion of Holland and the two armies met at Neerwinden on March 18 where Dumouriez was defeated. Dumouriez planned to set up Belgium as a separate state of which he would be the ruler. As the French forces retreated, Dumouriez fled on April 5 into Austrian lines. The leaderless French armies withdrew to Condé and Valenciennes on France's northern frontier.

During the spring and summer of 1793, the Allies blockaded a series of French fortified towns on their northern frontier to strengthen the defense of Belgium. From April to July, the town of Condé lay under siege until the French ran out of food and surrendered on July 10. British, Austrian and Hanoverian troops assaulted the fortified city of Valenciennes from May 24 to August 1 when the French surrendered. Afterward the Austrians proclaimed that French territory up to the Somme River would be annexed to Belgium (Steven T. Ross, *Historical Dictionary of the Wars of the French Revolution*, 50, 169*).*

8. In the spring of 1794 the French had more success. General Jean-Baptiste Jourdan (1762-1833), who served in America under Rochambeau, took the town of Charleroi in Belgium on June 12. Four days later an Austrian-Dutch force, drove the French back in a heavy mist across the Sambre River. Jourdan counter-attacked and began a siege of the town. The Austrian army under Saxe-Coburg arrived on June 26, only to find that Charleroi had surrendered. In spite of this, he attacked the French near the town of Fleurus, northeast of Charleroi. During the battle General Jourdan went aloft in a hot air balloon to observe the action. The Austrians broke through the French wings, but the French center held, then counterattacked, forcing Coburg to pull back, and handing victory to the French. This victory at Fleurus opened all of Belgium once again to the French (David Chandler, *Napoleon's Generals*, 161-162; 220).

9. The clerk who transcribed this letter for the State Department miscopied this word. *ASP: FR* (1: 670-671), *Writings of Monroe* (2: 16-29), and *View of the Conduct* (7-16) all give the name of this town as Cadsandt.

10. During Spain's war with the French Convention, 1793-1795, separatist sentiments were revived in the Basque provinces in northern Spain along the Atlantic. Longstanding commercial and fraternal ties to France in the Guipúzcoa province made the populace unwilling to oppose France. Some hoped to establish a free republic under French protection. Guipúzcoa officials made a treaty with the French allowing free passage of French troops. Such collaboration led to the fall of San Sebastián, the capital. French troops occupied all of Guipúzcoa from 1794 to 1795 (John F. Coverdale, *The Basque Phase of Spain's First Carlist War*, 32-33).

To the French Convention

Paris Augt 15. 1794.

Citizens President and Representatives of the French People.

My admission into this Assembly in presence of the French Nation, for all the Citizens of France are represented here, to be recognized as the Representative of the American Republic, impresses me with a degree of sensibility which I cannot express. I consider it a new proof of that friendship and regard, which the french Nation has always shown to their ally, the United States of America.

Republicks should approach near to each other. In many respects they have all the same interest. But this is more especially the case with the American and french Republicks. their Governments are similar: they both cherish the same principles and rest on the same basis, the equal and unalienable rights of man. The recollection too of common dangers and difficulties, will increase their harmony and cement their union. America had her day of oppression, difficulty, and war; but her sons were virtuous and brave, and the storm which long clouded her political horizon has passed, and left them in the enjoyment of Peace, liberty, and Independence. France our Ally and our friend and who aided in the contest has now embarked in the same noble career, and, I am happy to add that whilst the fortitude magnanimity and heroic valour of her troops command the admiration and applause of the astonished world, the wisdom and firmness of her Councils unite equally in securing the happiest result.

America is not an unfeeling spectator of y^t affairs at the present crisis. I lay before you in the declarations of every Department of our Government; declarations which are founded in the affections of the Citizens at large, the most decided proof of her sincere attachment to the liberty, prosperity, and happiness of the french Republic. Each branch of the Congress according to the course of their proceedings there, has requested the President to make this known to you, in its behalf, and in fulfilling the desires of those branches I am instructed to declare to you that he has expressed his own.[1]

In discharging the duties of the office which I am now called to execute, I promise myself the highest satisfaction, because I well know that whilst I pursue the dictates of my own heart in wishing the liberty and happiness of the french nation, and which I most sincerely do, I speak the sentiments of my own Country: and that by doing every thing in my power to preserve and perpetuate the harmony so happily subsisting between the two Republicks, I shall promote the interest of both. To this great object therefore all my efforts will be directed. If I shall be so fortunate as to succeed in such manner as to merit the approbation of both Republicks, I shall deem it the happiest event of my life, and retire hereafter with a consolation, which those who mean well and have served the cause of liberty alone can feel.

Ja^s Monroe

DS, NjP. In clerk's handwriting with JM's signature.

The French National Convention formed in September 1792 for the purpose of writing a new constitution after the overthrow of the monarchy. The Convention served as the governing body of France until November 1795. Its committees, most notably the Committee of Public Safety, managed the executive duties of the government (Samuel Scott and Barry Rothaus, *Historical Dictionary of the French Revolution*).

1. The resolutions of the Senate and the House of Representatives expressing friendship for France were conveyed in two letters addressed the Committee of Public Safety by Edmund Randolph, both dated 10 June 1794 (*ASP: FR*, 1: 674).

From Philippe Merlin de Douai

[15 August 1794]

Le peuple français n'a point oublié que c'est au peuple américain qu'il doit l'initiative de sa liberté. C'est en admirant la sublime insurrection du peuple américain contre cette albion jadis si fiere, aujourd'hui si avilie; c'est en prenant lui-meme les armes pour en seconder les courageux efforts ; c'est en en cimentant l'independance du sang de ses plus braves guerriers, que le peuple français a appris a briser à son tour le sceptre de la tyrannie, et a elever la statue de la liberté sur les ruines d'un trône basé sur quatorze siècles de corruption et de crimes.

Comment donc ne seroient-ils pas amis, comment n'associrroient-ils pas les moyens réciproques de prospérité que leur offrent le commerce et la navigation, ces deux peuples qui sont devenus libres l'un pour l'autre? Mais ce n'est point une alliance purement diplomatique, c'est la fraternite la plus douce, la plus franche qui doit les unir; c'est elle qui les unit en effet, et cette union sera à Jamais le fléau des despotes, la Sauve--garde de la liberté du monde, la conservatrice de routes les vertus sociales et philantropiques.

En nous apportant, citoyen, le gage de cette union si étroite, tu ne pouvois manquer d'être accueilli avec le plus vif intérêt. Il y a cinq ans, l'usurpateur de la souveraineté du peuple l'auroit reçu avec la morgue qui ne sied qu'au vice, et il auroit cru faire beaucoup en accordant au ministre d'une nation libre, quelques signes de son insolente protection: aujourd'hui c'est le peuple souverain lui-même, représenté par des mandataires fidèles, qui le reçoit, et tu vois de quel attendrissement, de quelle effusion de cœur est accompagnée cette cérémonie simple et touchante: il me tarde de la couronner par l'accolade fraternelle que je suis chargé de le donner au nom du peuple français; viens la recevoir au nom du peuple americain, et que ce tableau achève de détruire les dernières esperances de la coalition impie des tyrans.

Editors' Translation

[15 August 1794]

The French people have not forgotten that they owe their liberty to the initiative of the American people. It is through admiring the sublime rebellion of the American people against an erstwhile proud but now debased Albion; and through taking up arms to bolster those courageous efforts, through cementing its independence with the blood of its bravest warriors, that the French people in turn learned to overthrow tyranny's sceptre, and to erect the statue of liberty upon the ruins of a monarchy built on fourteen centuries of corruption and crime.

How then could these two nations, freed by each other, not be friends, how not join together to share the wealth offered by trade and navigation? Not simply a diplomatic alliance, but the sweetest and most honest fraternity should unite them; and does, in fact, and this union will forever be the scourge of despots, the guarantor of freedom in the world, the protector of all social and philanthropic virtues.

Citizen, by bringing us a pledge of this close union, you could not fail to be welcomed with great interest. Five years ago, the usurper of the people's sovereignty would have received this pledge with the haughtiness that comes from vice, and he would have considered it a generous act to accord to a minister of a free nation, some tokens of his arrogant protection: today, the sovereign people themselves, represented by loyal representatives, receive the pledge, and you see the tenderness and heartfelt outpourings that accompany this simple and touching ceremony: it is time for me to crown it with the fraternal embrace that I am charged with giving in the name of the French people; receive it in the name of the American people, and may this scene result in the destruction of the last hopes of the impious coalition of tyrants.

Copy, DNA: RG 59; Dispatches from France; enclosed in JM to Edmund Randolph, 25 August 1794

Journal

[15 August 1794]

1ˢᵗ Augᵗ. On this morning we sat out for Paris and arrived on the 3ᵈ in the evening. Mʳ Morris was from town but being advised that I was here he came in immediately. By him I was presented to the Secrʸ of foreign relations on the & with whom I left a copy of my credentials addressed to the Committee of publick safety. Mʳ M. observed that as soon as I was installed he shoᵈ take his departure, and as the season was now advanced the sooner this was done the more agreeable it woᵈ be to him as well as to me. The Secrʸ after promising that any regret which might be felt on accᵗ of his recall would be diminished by the recognition of his successor, & which he wo^d be happy to forward as much as in him lay; but as this was a moment of commotion occasioned by the late event which had passed Robertspiere upon the list of the Guillotined to the world of spirits, and likewise as this was the first instance in w^h a minister had been addressed to the Republick, he suspected some days wo^d unavoidably elapse before it co^d be bro^t ab^t. Mr M. said that as to any regret felt on his acc^t he presumed that that might be easily got^n over. It wo^d not wound deep.

I waited days & yet heard nothing from the committee. It was however intimated to me that I might possibly wait much longer in the same situation, and that the only means by which I co^d forward the business wo^d be by notifying my arrival to the Convention itself & desiring of that body to designate the department by which I sho^d be rec^d. After some hesitation, I adopted that mode, and in consequence, addressed, a letter to that effect, to the Presid^t of the Convention, on the   day of Ag^t & which obtained a desire for my admission on the day following.[1]

On the 15 of Augt I was admitted into the Convention & to whom I made an address in the presence of a numerous audience & which was well rec^d.

AD, DLC: Monroe Papers; filed 19 June 1794

1. JM to Merlin de Douai, 13 August 1794, above.

From Thomas Paine

Luxemburg—29th Thermidor[1] [16 August 1794]

My Dear Sir

As I believe none of the public papers have announced your name right I am unable to address you by it[2]—but a <u>new</u> minister from America is joy to me and will be so to every American in France.

Eight months I have been imprisoned, and I know not for what, except that the order says—that I am a Foreigner.[3] The Illness I have suffered in this place (and from which I am but just recovering) had nearly put an end to my existance. My life is but of little value to me in this situation tho' I have borne it with a firmness of Patience and fortitude.

I enclose you a copy of a letter (as well the translation as the English)—which I sent to the Convention after the fall of the Monster Robespierre—for I was determined not to write a line during the time of his detestable influence; I sent also a copy to the Comite of public safety—but I have not heard any thing respecting it.[4]

I have now no expectation of delivery but by your means. Morris has been my inveterate enemy, and I think he has permitted something of the national Character of America to suffer by quietly letting a Citizen of that Country remain almost eight months in prison without making every official exertion to procure him justice—for every act of violence offered to a foreigner is offered also to the nation to which he belongs.[5]

The Gentleman who will present you this, has been very friendly to me. Wishing you happiness in your appointment—I am your Affectionate Friend and Hble Servt

Thomas Paine

DLC: Monroe Papers

1. The reformers in the French Republic sought to reshape everything in the new society while at the same time making everyday life more secular. The Gregorian calendar, named for Pope Gregory XIII who introduced it in 1582, (and which is

used today) was Christian in orientation and featured holidays such as Easter and Christmas. The Convention created a calendar with no Christian allusions, whose purpose was to reflect the glory of the French Revolution. The new calendar was decreed on 5 October 1793 and began retroactively with 22 September 1792, the day the Republic was founded. The Convention renamed the months to reflect the seasons or weather. Thus Thermidor, which means "hot month" occurred during the height of summer. The Republican year contained twelve thirty-day months, which produced a surplus of five days; these were placed at the end of the year (September 17-21 of the Gregorian calendar). The Republican calendar endured until 1 January 1806, when Napoleon restored the Gregorian calendar (Samuel Scott and Barry Rothaus, *Historical Dictionary of the French Revolution*, 145-146).

2. The letter is addressed to "Le Ministre De l'Amerique."

3. Paine was arrested on 28 December 1793. The arrest order, issued on the 27th, gave no indication of the crime. Robespierre and his confederates had become suspicious of all foreigners, and Paine's birth in England apparently was a sufficient indication to them of his disloyalty to the revolution. In addition, Paine had allied himself with the Girondins, who were Robespierre's enemies. Paine was confined at the Luxemburg Palace, which had been converted to a prison (Jack Fruchtman, Jr., *Thomas Paine: Apostle of Freedom*, 313-316).

4. Paine wrote to the National Convention on 7 August 1794 asking that he be released from imprisonment (Philip Foner, ed., *The Complete Writings of Thomas Paine*, 2: 1339-1341). The copy of this letter that Paine sent to JM is in DLC: Monroe Papers.

5. Gouverneur Morris, who greatly disliked Paine, did not acknowledge Paine as an American citizen, and made no effort to obtain his release (Fruchtman, *Thomas Paine*, 323-324).

From Thomas Paine

Prison of the Luxemburg 30 Thermidor [17 August 1794]

Dear Sir

In addition to my letter of yesterday (sent to M<u>r</u> Beresford to be conveyed to you, but which is delayed on account of his being at St. Germain) I send the following mem<u>da</u>.

I was in London at the time I was elected a member of this Convention. I was elected a Deputé in four different departments without my knowing any thing of the matter, or having the least Idea of it. The intention of electing the Convention before the time of the former legislature expired, was for the purpose of reforming the Constitution or rather for forming a new one.[1]

As the former legislature shewed a disposition that I should assist in this Business of the new Constitution, they prepared the way by voting me a French Citoyen (they confered the same title on General Washington[2] and certainly I had no more Idea than he had of vacating any part of my real Citizenship of America for a nominal one in france, especially at a time when she did not know whether she would be a Nation or not, and had it not even in her power to promise me protection.

I was elected (the second person in number of Votes, the Abbé Sieyes being first) a member for forming the Constitution, and every American in Paris as well as my other acquaintance knew that it was my intention to return to America as soon as the Constitution should be established.

The violence of Party soon began to shew itself in the Convention, but it was impossible for me to see upon what principle they differed—unless it was a contention for power. I acted however as I did in America, I connected myself with no Party, but considered myself altogether a National Man—but the Case with Parties generally is that when you are not with one you are supposed to be with the other.

I was taken out of bed between three and four in the morning on the 29 of Dec<u>r</u> last, and brought to the Luxemburg—without any other accusation inserted in the order than that I was a foreigner, a motion having been made two days before in the Convention to expel Foreigners therefrom. I certainly then remained, even upon their own tactics, what I was before, a Citizen of America.

About three weeks after my imprisonment the Americans that were in Paris went to the bar of the Convention to reclaim me, but contrary to my advice, they made their address into a Petition, and it miscarried.[3] I then applied to G. Morris, to reclaim me as an official part of his duty, which he found it necessary to do, and here the matter stopt. I have not heard a single line or word from any American since, which is now seven months. I rested altogether on the hope that a new minister would arrive from America. I have escaped with life from more dangers than one. Had it not been for the fall of Roberspiere and your timely arrival I know not what fate might have yet attended me. There seemed to be a determination to destroy all the Prisoners without regard to Merit Character or any thing else. During the time I laid at the height of my illness they took, in one night only, 169 persons out of this prison and executed all but eight. The distress that I have suffered at being obliged to exist in the midst of such horrors, exclusive of my own precarious situation, suspended as it were by the single thread of accident, is greater than it is possible you can conceive—but thank God times are at last changed—and I hope that your Authority will release me from this unjust imprisonment.

Thomas Paine

On the next page are Copies of two letters of invitation to me to accept the office of Depute.[4] The first is from the department of the Pas de Calais which was brought to me at London by Achille Audibert of Calais.[5] The other from Herault Seschelles one of the deputies of the department of l'oise and at the time of writing it President of the late Nationale Assemblee.[6] He has been since executed, I knew not for what. I enclose you also my letter to the people of France on my acceptance of the office of Deputé,[7] and also a letter which I had printed here as an American letter, some copies of which I sent to Mr Jefferson.[8]

RC, DLC: Monroe Papers

1. The French National Assembly passed a resolution on 26 August 1792 conferring French citizenship on a number of foreigners, including Paine. Shortly thereafter he was elected a delegate to the new French Convention by the districts of Calais, Oise, Somme, and Puy de Dôme, and chose to accept the seat from Calais. He left London for France on September 13 (Philip Foner, ed., *The Complete Writings of Thomas Paine*, 2: 538).

2. The Assembly also conferred citizenship on James Madison and Alexander Hamilton (Jack Fruchtman Jr., *Thomas Paine, Apostle of Freedom*, 266).

3. Sixteen Americans petitioned the Convention, claiming Paine as a fellow American citizen and asking his relief. The Convention forwarded the petition to the Committee of Public Safety and the Committee of General Security, both of which rejected the plea (Fruchtman, *Thomas Paine*, 318-319).

4. The letters inviting Paine to accept election to the Convention are enclosed with this letter in DLC: Monroe Papers.

5. In addition to serving as a deputy to the Convention from Calais, Achille Audibert was also a magistrate for that city (Thomas Clio Rickman, *The Life of Thomas Paine*, 40). On 19 August 1794 Audibert wrote to JM, asking him to obtain Paine's release from prison (*Catalogue of Monroe's Papers,* 1: 32).

6. Marie-Jean Hérault de Séchelles (1759-1794) was a Paris attorney who became active in the Revolution in 1789. He was a deputy to the National Assembly in 1791 and to the National Convention 1792-1794, serving as president of the convention in 1793. He became a radical Jacobin and as such served on the Committee of Public Safety May-December 1793. Hérault was denounced as an enemy of the Revolution and was guillotined in April 1794 (*Encyclopedia Britannica*).

7. Paine's letter to the people of France, written 25 September 1792, is in Foner, *Complete Writings of Thomas Paine*, 2: 538-540).

8. The "American letter," which Paine wrote in Paris but dated as written in Philadelphia on 28 July 1793, was entitled "A Citizen of America to the Citizens of Europe." Paine enclosed a copy of this essay in a letter to Jefferson dated 20 October 1793 (Foner, *Complete Writings of Thomas Paine*, 2: 561-565, 1333-1334).

From La Société Populaire de Billom

Département Dupui-Dedôme District De Billom
Ce Deux fructidor L'an Deuxiême De la République francaise
une, indivisible et Démocratique [19 August 1794]

frere et ami

La Société populaire de Billom t'invite à témoigner à La nation dont tu[1] es L'organe, la vive et tendre émotion, La joie Sincère, et pure qu'elle a éprouvée, en apprenant que Les Deux plus grandes Républiques De L'univers, malgré L'immense océan qui Les Sépare, Se donnent mutuellement La main.

Puissent Désormais Les eaux De la Seine Se mélant à celles De La Ware adoucir, et corriger L'amertume Des mers, faire disparoitre Les teintes de Sang dont elles ont été Si Souvent Rougies.

Puissent Les tyrans De la terre Déséspérés par cette union indissoluble Reconnoitre enfin la Souveraineté Des nations, Se prosterner Devant Les droits imperscriptibles De L'homme, Briser eux mêmes et jetter Leurs Scèptres aux vents.

La Société t'invite encore à Demander avec elle à La Convention que L'océan qui Séparoit autrefois, et qui maintenant uni Les deux mondes, porte Désormais Le nom De mer De la fraternité. Salut et fraternité

Les membres Composant Le bureau De Correspondance de la
Société Républicaine Séante à billom.
Roulhac, [Teyrae], Blanchard, [Pareir]

Editors' Translation

Départment of Dômes, District of Billom
This the second Fructidor in the second year of the Republic of France,
one, indivisible and democratic [19 August 1794]

Brother and friend

The People's Society of Billom invite you to bear witness to the nation which you represent of the lively and tender feelings and of the sincere and pure joy it experienced upon learning that the two greatest Republics in the universe, despite the immense ocean that separates them, have each extended a hand to the other.

May the waters of the Seine, mixed with those of the Delaware, henceforth ease the bitterness of the seas and erase the bloodstains that have often reddened them.

May the desperate tyrants of the world finally recognize in this indissoluble union the sovereignty of nations, prostrate themselves before man's inalienable rights, and they themselves smash and throw their scepters to the winds.

The society once more invites you to join it in asking of the Convention that the ocean, which once separated and now unites the two worlds, should henceforth bear the name, Sea of Fraternity. Salutations and fraternity

Members of the office of correspondence of the
Republican Society Seated at Billom.
Roulhac, [Teyrae], Blanchard, [Pareir]

RC, NN: Monroe Papers

1. After the fraternal societies in Paris began to substitute the term *Citizen* for Sir or Mister, the Sans Culottes initiated the use of the informal *tu*. The *Mercure National* endorsed the familiar *tu* on 14 December 1790 with the article, "On the Influence of Words and the Power of Language." The revolutionaries considered vous contrary to the right of equality. The general assembly of the Directory of the Paris department on 12 December 1792 issued orders that the familiar *tu* was to be used in its correspondence. Only language suitable to the French Revolution would be the language of fraternity. Some correspondents devoutly followed this dictum while others did not (Albert Soboul, *The Sans Culottes*, 228-230).

To Philibert Buchot[1]

Paris August 22 1794

Citizen.

I was favoured yesterday with yours of that date[2] informing me that the Committee of publick safety, had authorized you in the name of the republick, to appropriate a house for my use as minister of their ally the United States of America, and in such part of the city as I should designate. I have received this communication with peculiar satisfaction, because I consider it as a proof of the sincere regard which the Committee entertain for their ally whose servant I am. But upon this occasion I am not permitted to indulge in any respect my own opinion or feelings. The constitution of my country, an extract from which is hereunto annexed, has prescribed a line of conduct to me and which it is my duty to follow. The Committee of publick safety, and you citizen, respect too highly the fundimental laws of your own country not to approve my reason for declining the kind offer you have made me. I shall however immediately communicate it to our government and doubt not it will produce there the good effect it merits.

Jaˢ Monroe

Extract from the constitution of the United States. "No title of nobility shall be granted by the United States: and no person holding any office of profit or trust under them shall without the consent of the Congress accept of any present, emolument, office or title of any kind whatsoever from any king, prince, or foreign State."

RC, MHi: Waterston Autograph Collection

1. Philibert Buchot (1749-1813) a lawyer and clerk of the court, served as the French foreign minister from 9 April to 3 November 1794 (*La Grande Encyclopédie*, 8: 910; *Dictionnaire Biographie Française*, 7: 606).

2. Buchot's letter, dated 21 August 1794, is enclosed in JM to Edmund Randolph, 25 August 1794, DNA: RG 59: Despatches from France.

From John Jay

London 24 Aug˖ 1794

Sir

It was not untill Yesterday that I heard of your safe arrival at Paris—accept my congratulations on the occasion.

At the earnest Sollicitation of the writer of the enclosed Letter I take the Liberty of transmitting it to you.[1] Similar motives of Benevolence with those which induce me to commit it to your Care, will I am persuaded induce you to forward it.

I presume M˖ˢ Munro is with you—if so, be pleased to make my Comp˖ˢ to her—and also to M˖ Morris if he be still at Paris.

If it should be in my power to be useful to you here, it will give me pleasure to render you any services. I have the honor to be Sir y^r most ob. & hble Servt

FC, NNC: John Jay Collection

1. The enclosed letter has not been identified.

From Thomas Paine

Luxembourg Fruc^r 8. Augst 25 [1794]

My Dear Sir

Having nothing to do but to sit and think I will write to pass away time, and to say that I am still here. I have received two notes from Mr Beresford which are encouraging (as the generality of notes and letters are that arrive to persons here), but they contain nothing explicit or decisive with respect to my liberation, and I shall be very glad to receive a line from yourself to inform me in what condition the matter stands. If I only glide out of prison by a sort of accident America gains no credit by my liberation, neither can my attachment to her be increased by such a circumstance. She has had the services of my best days, she has my allegiance, she receives my portion of Taxes for my house in Borden Town and my farm at New Rochelle,[1] and she owes me protection both at home and thro' her Ministers abroad, yet I remain in prison, in the face of her Minister, at the arbitrary will of a committee.

Excluded as I am from the knowledge of every thing and left to a random of Ideas, I know not what to think or how to act. Before there was any Minister here (for I consider Morris as none) and while the Robesperian faction lasted, I had nothing to do but to keep my mind tranquil and expect the fate that was every day inflicted upon my comrades not individually but by scores. Many a man whom I have passed an hour with in Conversation I have seen marching to his destruction the next hour, or heard of it the next morning, for what rendered the scene more horrible was that they were generally taken away at midnight, so that every man went to bed with the apprehension of never seeing his friends or the world again.

I wish to impress upon you, that all the changes that have taken place in Paris have been sudden. There is now a moment of calm, but if thro' any over complaisance to the persons you converse with on the subject of my liberation, you omit procuring it for me now, you may have to lament the fate of your friend when its too late. The loss of a Battle to the Northward, or other possible accident may happen to bring this about. I am not out of danger until I am out of Prison. Yours affectionately

Thomas Paine

I am now entirely without money. The Convention owes me 1800 livres salary which I know not how to get while I am here, nor do I know how to draw for money on the Rent of my farm in America. It is under the care of my good friend General Lewis Morris.[2] I have rec^d no rent since I have been in Europe.

TP

RC, DLC: Monroe Papers

1. Paine purchased a house in Bordentown, New Jersey, in 1783. He acquired the farm in New Rochelle, New York, the following year as a reward from the New York assembly for his services in the American Revolution (Jack Fruchtman, Jr., *Thomas Paine: Apostle of Liberty*, 154).

2. Lewis Morris (1726-1798), the older half-brother of Gouverneur Morris, was a New York farmer, the owner of Morrisania, an extensive estate in the Hudson Valley. Morris was active in state politics during the American Revolution and was a general in the militia. He was a member of the Continental Congress 1775-1777 and was a signer of the Declaration of Independence (*ANB*).

To Edmund Randolph

Paris, August 25. 1794.

Sir,

In my last of the 15th Instant[1] I mentioned to you that I had been presented to the Commissary of Foreign Affairs for reception, and was assured he would lay the Copy of my credentials, which I left with him, before the Committee of public Safety under whom he acted, and to whom it more particularly belonged, to appoint the time and regulate the mode. After this I waited eight or ten days without progressing an iota, and as I heard that a minister from Geneva had been here about six weeks before me, and had not yet been received I was fearful I might remain as long and perhaps much longer in the same situation. It was obvious that the public boards had been so much shocked by the late disaster, that from a variety of considerations some public, and others personal, they could scarcely move forward upon any subject. At the same time I had reason to believe it was the general desire that I should be received, as soon as possible, and with every demonstration of respect for the country I represented. Upon the most mature consideration therefore I thought it incumbent on me to make an effort to break thro' these difficulties and expedite my reception. The Convention I knew possessed the Sovereign Authority of the nation, and I presumed that by addressing myself to that body, and especially in the present state of things, I should not only avoid the censure of any subordinate department, but perhaps relieve it from an unpleasant dilemma, and at the same time make an experiment of the real disposition of this Country towards my own. The latter consideration I deemed of some importance, as it would ascertain to me a fact which might have influence upon my conduct on other occasions. I therefore addressed a Letter to the President of the Convention of which the enclosed N[o] 1, is a Copy,[2] and was happy to find it was well received, for it was immediately taken by a member present to the Committee of public safety, by whom a report was made in two hours afterwards to the Convention, and a decree adopted by the latter body of which, number 2 is a Copy, for my reception by the Convention itself, at two the following day.[3] I deemed it my duty to avail myself of this opportunity to dissipate if possible, by the documents in my possession, impressions which had been made, and were still making of the unfriendly disposition of the American Government, towards the liberty and happiness of the French nation. At the same time therefore that I presented my credentials, I laid before the Convention the declarations of the Senate, and house of Representatives, as conveyed to me by the President thro' the Secretary of State, with an assurance that I was authorized to declare that the President was actuated by similar sentiments. The communication was received in a manner very interesting, and which furnished at the same time the strongest proofs of the affection entertained by the french nation for the United States of America. The inclosed N[o] 3 is a Copy of my address to the Convention & of the President's answer.[4] Every department has since shewn the strongest disposition to prove its attachment to their ally by embracing every opportunity which the slightest incident has offered. A few stores brought for the accomodation of my family in the ship which I sailed were arrested in Havre, because no declaration was rendered of them by the Captain. This was casually heard by the Committee of public safety, and without any intimation from me by their order restored. But being desirous more formally to testify their regard, the Commissary of Foreign affairs announced to me yesterday that he was instructed in the name of the Republic to appropriate a house for my use, as minister of the United States, of such accomodations, and in such part of the City as I would designate. The inclosed N° 4 is a Copy of his letter and of my reply.[5] These latter acts, it is true may be deemed in some measure acts of ceremony: so far however as they furnish any indication of the disposition of this country towards our own it is a favourable one.

I found here many of my countrymen, Captains of vessels who were taken at sea and brought in, in derogation of the treaty. I intend immediately to make an effort, to have that order rescinded, and compensation rendered for the Injury sustained. I have written to Mʳ Fenwick[6] who is best acquainted with the affair of the Bordeaux embargo to request his attendance here or to forward such documents as will enable me to pursue with suitable information, the interest of those who were affected by it, and I shall likewise enter on the affair of the bills as soon as circumstances will permit.[7]

The Position of the armies is nearly the same as when I wrote you last. No action has been fought nor any other material change taken place since. A perfect tranquility too continues to reign throughout the Republic. The execution of Robespiere and his associates, has produced the same effect every where. Every person seems to be freed from an oppression which was really destructive and terrible, and the more so because it was sanctified by the authority of the people, and covered with the mask of patriotism. It is however said that others who have been equally guilty (for Robespiere who was a small and timid man, could not make the majority of the Committee vote against their own opinions) will probably yet be brought to Justice. Of this I shall be able to give you better information in my next.

The reform[8] which I suggested in my last contemplated in the organization of the Committees and Revolutionary tribunal, is now completed or nearly so. I will inclose you copies of the decrees in my next. A great number of prisoners have been discharged who were confined here and in other parts of the Republic in consequence of a decree that those should be liberated who were committed upon suspicion only. It was however greatly unfortunate that Robespiere was not cut off sooner, for 'tis most certain that his last days were stained with some of the most innocent blood of the Republic.

The Vice Consul has not yet arrived, & to be candid I doubt, when he does whether he will be received or not.[9] A native of this Country is at the present moment unable to render any service to our own, altho' he may have always resided here, and his political principles been unquestionable. But one who has been absent is considered if not an emigrant, at best[10] indifferent and perhaps unfriendly to the revolution and therefore odious. If this Gentleman has arrived I think it probable he is confined at the port where he landed. I deem this unfortunate for there is much business which properly belongs to the Consular department here, as all the Commercial affairs of the Republic are transacted here.

I have reason to believe that Laforest and Petri[11] are displaced, and that a frigate is dispatched to announce it with you, and that Leblanc and Fachet will be—the former for British connection, the latter as followers of the fortunes of Robespiere. With great esteem, I am, Dear sir, Very respectfully your very Humble Servant

Jaˢ Monroe

Copy, DNA: RG 59: Dispatches from France

1,. The clerk of transcribed this letter for the State Department files incorrectly wrote "Ulti°".

2. JM to Merlin de Douai, 13 August 1794, above.

3. Philibert Buchot made the following report to the Committee of Public Safety on 14 August 1794:

> The arrival of Mr. Monroe, Minister Plenipotentiary of the United States, appears to compel a decision on the ceremony to observe for the reception of foreign ministers.

It seems to be even more important that this minister be received with more interest than in the case of his predecessor Morris, who did not miss any occasion to blame the cold reception he received on our indifference toward the United States, and not on our contempt for his person and his principles.

Mr. Monroe's letters of credence are addressed to the Committee of Public Safety. This conforms to the law that gives this committee control of principal diplomatic operations.

Since the last revolution, it is still our policy that the Committee should receive these letters of credence and that it should initiate any negotiations with which this Minister Plenipotentiary may be charged.

The character with which this minister is invested, however, seems to require an added formality: that of being presented to the sovereign, or to a representative of the sovereign, in other words, the National Convention.

If the Committee approves this idea, the reception should be conducted in a manner equal to the dignity of the French People and to the ties of friendship that endure between them and the United States.

Here is the ceremony that I would propose for this occasion.

Mr. Monroe will write to the Committee of Public Safety to inform it of his arrival, and he will enclose in his letter a copy of his letters of credence.

The Committee will set a time to receive him. He will be introduced by the commissary of foreign relations.

The same day the committee will inform the Convention of the arrival of this minister and propose that it welcome him into its bosom.

On the assigned day, the commissary of foreign relations will go to Mr. Monroe's home in an official carriage, and he will introduce him, as well as his secretary of legation, into the interior of the Hall. The Americans in his retinue will remain at the bar.

The members of the Convention will be in formal attire.

The minister will be seated in an armchair across from the president. He will deliver a speech in English, whose translation he will have his secretary present to the president of the Convention. A secretary will read the translation, as well as the translation of the letters of credence.

The president will give a response to the minister's speech and will send him a copy. Here the president could give the minister the fraternal embrace, to redoubled cries, "Long Live the Two Republics."

The minister will be escorted back to his home by the commissary of foreign relations.

It may not be useless to observe that this project must not be proposed to the National Convention unless the Committee is certain that it will be accepted unanimously, for a conflicting discussion could produce a wrong impression in foreign countries.

Finally, whichever ceremony the Committee might choose, it is crucial to have it communicated in writing to the minister of the United States, so that he may agree to it or make observations on points which to him appear susceptible to interpretation. It will also be advantageous to ask the minister in advance for a copy of the speech he proposes to make, so that we may prepare a response.

The commissary of foreign relations could be authorized to have the details of the reception officially inserted in the gazettes, so that the enemies of the Republic will read it with dismay.

Should we submit again to the Committee the question of whether it would be appropriate to assign a gallery in the National Convention to the foreign officers? It would, at the same time, both honor and isolate them (Editors' translation of draft, DLC: FCP—France).

The National Convention passed the following resolution the same day:

Article 1. The Minister Plenipotentiary from the United States will be introduced into the bosom of the National Convention; he will present the object of his Mission. The President will give him the fraternal embrace as a symbol of the friendship that unites the people of America and the people of France.

Article 2. The President of the Convention will write to the President of the American Congress and send him the minutes of the session (Editors' translation, NN: Monroe Papers).

4. JM's address to the French Convention and Merlin de Douai's reply, both dated 15 August 1794, above.

5. JM to Buchot, 22 August 1794, above.

6. Joseph Fenwick (c.1749-c.1810) of Maryland was a merchant in partnership with his brother James and John Mason, the son of George Mason. Fenwick was based in Bordeaux and served as the American consul in that city 1790-1798 (*Papers of George Washington, Presidential Series*, 3: 53-55; National Archives, *Diplomatic and Consular Instructions of the Department of State*, microfilm pamphlet number 28, 6).

7. Both JM's draft in PHi: Gratz Collection and the published version in *American States Papers: Foreign Relations*, 1: 672 has a different ending for this paragraph. The final clause reads: "and I shall likewise bring forward, at the same time, the claims of others of our citizens for supplies rendered to the Government of St. Domingo."

8. The word in the draft of this letter (Phi: Gratz Collection) is "reform". The clerk incorrectly wrote "form".

9. Alexander Duvernet never assumed the duties of vice consul at Paris. President Washington replaced him with Joseph Pitcairn of New York in November 1794 (*Journal of the Executive Proceedings of the Senate of the United States*, 1: 163).

10. The word in the draft of this letter is "least". The clerk incorrectly wrote "best".

11. Antoine-René-Charles Mathurin de La Forest (1756-1846) served in the French legation in the United States under Gérard and Luzerne and was vice-consul of France in Savannah 1783-1785. He replaced Barbé-Marbois as consul-general in March 1792. La Forest was made one of the commissioners to serve with Fauchet in 1794 (*Correspondence of the French Ministers*, 717). Jean-Baptiste Pétry was appointed by the French government to serve with Fauchet (Moncure Daniel Conway, *Edmund Randolph*, 237).

From William Short

Sⁿ Yldefonse (near Madrid) Aug. 26. 1794

Dear Sir

After a very long interruption to our correspondence I hope a renewal of it under our present circumstances will not be disagreeable to you. It has been announced to me by the Sec. of State that the Presᵗ has nominated you Min. Plenipo: to the French Republick, at the same time that he has informed me that he has nominated me to reside as Minister of the United States here. You are too happy my dear Sir, in having this place, to have any need of my congratulations. How happy should I have been had I never quitted that country—I shᵈ prefer a thousand times being a private Secretary there to any place of Minister in any other part of Europe.[1]

The object of this being merely of a personal nature I shall confine it within as small a compass as possible, & as I am not certain either that you will be arrived at Paris, or that Mʳ Morris will be gone from thence, I shall address it to both of you. My intention in writing at present is to ask the favor of you to do for me an act of kindness & friendship which will excite my gratitude far beyond any thing I can express—In order to [do] this it will be necessary that I should explain to you as well as I can by means of a letter which is to pass through the posts of different countries, the nature of the case in which I wish you to serve me, reserving myself to speak more fully, when I shall hear with certainty that you have arrived at Paris—At present I will simply inform you that I have a friend in Paris under misfortune in whose fate my happiness is entirely involved—this friend my dʳ Sir is a female, & her misfortune is to have been born in that class of people which is proscribed in France without exception—I say without exception, for if there had been any exception to have been made, it would certainly have been made in her favor—She has been from her infancy the friend of the country, & by instinct as it were, the enemy to all those prejudices which dominated formerly in France—She & her family were known to Mʳ Jefferson & myself from the time of our first arrival in France—They treated us both as friends & brothers because we were Americans, & because they were always friends to that liberty & equality which existed in America.[2]

Had Mr Jefferson returned to France which a general report here had almost induced me to believe he would immediately have sollicited of the French Republic, the liberty & safety of this friend of mine, as well as of her aged grandmother confined with her because he knew them well, was connected with them by the strictest friendship, & would have answered for them—There is no accusation against them whatever, & there can be none. I would pledge my life, my reputation, my all that they have never even conceived an idea of ill to their country. They are only two helpless females, the one an aged grandmother the other my friend whose filial attachment to her grandmother, her only living parent, has rendered her inseparable from her. They were both put in a state of arrestation under the general decree for confining all personas of the heretofore nobility. I wrote to Mr Morris when I first heard of this to ask his intercession. He conceived nothing could be done by him, & as I learned he was not on good terms with the French Government I feared to put the cause of my friend, which is in fact my own cause in his hands. I did not explain to Mr Morris fully how far I was interested in the state of this friend, because it did not appear to me proper by letter conveyance. I suppose however he had an idea of it. Under my then circumstances I thought it best to postpone doing anything further, until I might be at Paris, hoping constantly that the business on which I was sent here, would soon come to such an issue as would enable me to return there. Since my late nomination here, this hope is at least postponed, & the circumstances of the U. S. here are such that it is thought I cannot dispense with accepting the appointment as Mr Carmichael is determined not to remain longer, as he has now received permission to return, so that if I were not to accept the place, our country would remain here for some time without being represented.[3] As then my dear Sir, it was my duty to our common country which has retained & still retains me here & consequently keeps me at this distance from my friend, I hope you will for that reason as well as from personal friendship to me, intercede in her favor so as to procure her liberty & safety. I must add also the liberty of her grandmother, as I know she would never consent to quit her & w^d prefer being confined, to withdrawing her filial care from her aged parent, who stands in need of her constant aid & assistance.

You will know best my dear Sir in what manner to proceed, & to whom to apply. The power for such a purpose I sh^d imagine would be vested with some branch of the government & if you ask the liberation of my friend I sh^d hope it would not be refused to you. But if any consideration should prevent your doing this, I hope for my sake, you will write to me on their subject. I have heard from my friend since her confinement, & have sometimes written to her, but do not chuse too often to repeat my letters, not knowing whether it will be allowed to persons confined to hold correspondence. My letters were received & sent by Mr Morris—my friend & her grandmother were confined in a convent. I am sure if Mr Morris should have left Paris before this letter gets to you, he will have informed you of her name & place of abode. I trust you will see enough from what I have said to be induced to do all that can be done towards restoring my friend to her liberty. What I desire of you is to protect her & prevent her being considered among the enemies of her country, & to let me know what you have done or can do. I beg you my d^r Sir to write to me on this subject—Address your letters to me, as <u>Ministre des Etats-Unis d'Amerique à Madrid</u>—& send them by duplicate, one under cover to <u>Mes^srs Aime^r Regry pere & fils à Gênes</u> (or give it to the Genoese Chargé des affaires at Paris)—& another under cover to Mr Pinckney.

I wrote some time ago to Mr Morris on hearing that Mr Jefferson was coming to Paris, to ask the favor of him to turn over to Mr Jefferson, various articles of mine, that he has been so good as to take charge of— viz. trunks with cloths & one with papers (this has my seal to it) & four large packages containing my library. Mr Morris has also in his care a carriage and harness of mine. I desired him to give it to Mr Jefferson. I will thank you to take charge of them, & still more if it sh^d suit you, to take them for your use. M. Morris can give you the history of the carriage—You may take it with the harness at

The Papers of James Monroe: Volume III

your own price, as I do not see that it can ever be of any use to me. Adieu my d^r Sir. I hope you will judge how anxious I am to hear from you. Your sincere friend & servant

W Short

RC, PPAmP: Miscellaneous Manuscript Collection.

1. Short went to Paris in 1784 as Jefferson's secretary and remained there as U. S. chargé d'affaires after Jefferson returned home in 1789. President Washington appointed him U. S. minister to the Netherlands in early 1792 and shortly afterwards named him as a commissioner to negotiate a treaty with Spain. Although still minister to the Netherlands, Short left that country for Spain in December 1792 and never returned. Washington appointed him minister to Spain in May 1794, nominating both JM and Short in the same message to the Senate (*ANB*; *Executive Journal of the Senate of the United States*, 1: 157).

2. Short, who was not married, had an affair with Charlotte Alexandrine, Duchesse de La Rochefoucauld (known as Rosalie) while in Paris. After the death of the Duc de Rochefoucauld in 1792, Short tried to protect Rosalie's interests by putting most of her property in his own name. Rosalie and her grandmother, Madame d'Enville were imprisoned in late 1793. They were released from prison in November 1794, but remained under house arrest at their country home. Short did not learn of their release until June 1795 (George G. Shackelford, *Jefferson's Adoptive Son: The Life of William Short*, 111-125).

3. William Carmichael, the U. S. chargé d'affaires at Madrid, was Short's partner in the negotiations with Spain (*ANB*).

From Adrienne Lafayette[1]

au ci devant College du plessis
Le 10 fructidor L'an 2
de L[a] R[épublique] F[rançaise] une et indivisible
[27 August 1794]

J'ai appris qu'un Ministre des Etats unis etoit recemment arrivé en france, et j'ai cru qu'arrivant investi des pouvoirs d'un peuple a L'interêt duquel j'ai des droits si chers a mon cœur, tous Les malheurs que je n'ai pas encore Soufferts, n'etoient plus a redouter pour moi, que La plus injuste captivité etoit a son terme, et que mes souffrances comparées a une conduite irréprochable, et envers Les principes, et envers Les Loix de mon pays, ma cause Seroit defendue au nom de cette nation protectrice dans un moment ou La justice fait entendre Sa voix, et ou La Convention Nationale S'occupe de delivrer Les patriotes injustement opprimés.

j'ai commence a esperer que Les vœux de mon cœur seroient remplis, mes fers brisés, et que je Serois reunie a mes enfans. je Leur Suis enlevée depuis plus de 10 mois. ils avoient au moment même de Leur naissance une seconde patrie, et ils doivent esperer d'être protegés par elle.

Des intererets plus pressans, n'ont pas permis, Sans doute a L'envoyé des Etats unis, de S'occuper encore de moi; mais je conserve au fonds de mon cœur L'esperance que Son arrivée a fait naître. Je me flatte d'en eprouver L'effet. Je differe d'employer d'autres moyens d'obtenir justice, jusqu'à ce qu'il m'ait repondu Si c'est a Lui que je devrai une prochaine delivrance. Il est aise de croire ce qu'elle est pressante, mes enfans, ma santé, tout m'oblige a demander une prompte justice—et c'est à Lui j'espere que je devrai de faire valoir mes droits. Il est aise de juger ce que je Lui devrai de reconnoissance, et combien elle me sera precieuse. Salut et fraternite

M A F Noailles Lafayette

Editors' Translation

at the former College of Plessis
10 Fructidor of the 2nd year of the French Republic,
one and indivisible [27 August 1794]

I have learned that a minister of the United States has recently arrived in France, and I believe that upon his arrival was invested with the powers of a people in whose interest I have rights so dear to my heart. All the misfortunes I have not yet suffered I no longer dread. The worst unjust captivity has reached its end and my sufferings weighed in the face of an irreproachable conduct, and in the face of the principles and laws of my country. My cause will be defended under the name and protection of this nation at a moment when the voice of justice is heard, and when the National Convention is busy liberating patriots unjustly oppressed.

I have begun to hope that my heart's wish will be fulfilled, my irons broken, and that I will be united with my children. It is now ten months since they were taken from me. They had even at the hour of their birth, a second country, and they must hope for her protection.[2]

More pressing business no doubt has not yet allowed the envoy from the United States to be bothered with me; but I keep alive deep in my heart the hope his arrival has caused to be born. I flatter myself that I will experience its reality. I am postponing other ways to obtain justice, until he has responded, if it is through him that I will owe a next deliverance. It is easy to believe deliverance is at hand, my children, my health, all that impels me to demand prompt justice—and it is through him I hope to attain my rights. It is easy to judge how much gratitude I will owe him, and how precious it will be. Salutations and Fraternity.

M A F Noailles Lafayette

RC, NN: Monroe Papers

In preparing French transcriptions for publication, the editors retained the spelling of the eighteenth century with the *oi* forms in the imperfect indicative and conditional tense endings (i.e. *avait*, *serais*, etc.), the omission of "t" and "p" in such words as *enfans, pressans, tems*, etc., *assés* for *assez*, *chés* for *chez*, etc.

1. Marie-Adrienne-Françoise de Noailles, marquise de Lafayette (1759-1807) became the wife of Gilbert du Motier, Marquis de Lafayette, in 1774. After France declared war against Austria in April 1792, Lafayette was given command of the center of the three French armies on the northern frontier. The campaign in the Austrian Netherlands (Belgium) was a disaster, and Lafayette was forced to retreat. When the king dismissed the Girondist ministry on 12 June 1792 Lafayette left his post and rode to Paris where on 28 June he denounced the Jacobins from the floor. Upon his return to his post, Lafayette tried without success to persuade his army to rally behind the king. The Assembly ordered him to turn over his command and return to Paris for trial. Instead, Lafayette deserted and fled over the border with some of his staff officers where on 19 August near Liege, Belgium, they were arrested by the Austrians. On the same day the National Assembly charged Lafayette with treason, the Committee of General Security in Paris sent an order through Jean-Marie Roland, minister of the Interior, to arrest Adrienne Lafayette, and her children, residing at Chavaniac, the Lafayette family estate in Auvergne, and escort them to Paris where they were to be confined in prison. On 10 September the local authorities at Puy assembled a body of 86 men, drawn from members of the National Guard, gendarmes, and soldiers of the line, to bring them in Puy where Judge Alphonse Aulagnier waited to arraign them before their transfer. The prison massacres in Paris of September 2 to 6, and the fact that the roads to Paris from Puy were in the hands of the *fédérés* forced Aulagnier to reconsider transporting her to the capital. On the 28 September Roland sent Aulagnier authorization to take Adrienne Lafayette back to Chavaniac and hold her there under house arrest.

There Adrienne Lafayette remained until the National Convention passed the Law of Suspects on September 17, 1793, which required prisons to be established at the major town in each district to accommodate families of émigrés. In November Adrienne was arrested and taken to a prison at Brioude. On 27 May 1794 at the height of the Terror, an order came to transfer her to Petite

Force in Paris. En route to the capital, Adrienne instructed Felix Frestel, her son's tutor, to follow behind, and when her entourage reached Melun near Fontainebleau, to turn off the main road and head toward Seine-Port, the country estate of Gouverneur Morris. Although Morris was a critic of the Marquis de Lafayette, Adrienne had warmly welcomed him as a frequent guest to their home. Upon learning of Adrienne Lafayette's predicament on June 7, the day she arrived in Paris, Morris recounted later that he had "taken steps that appeared to him most proper for preventing the catastrophe" that lay ahead. On June 29, he wrote to the French foreign minister Philibert Buchot, "that the death Madame de Lafayette, which in itself would not benefit the French Republic, could only alienate the sympathy of America for the French cause and furnish the partisans of England with means of misrepresenting events in France." During the same period, Adrienne's mother, grandmother and sister, who had been under house arrest in Paris, were removed to the Luxembourg Prison, the so-called depot for the scaffold. Summoned before the Revolutionary Tribunal on 21 July, they were guillotined the next day, five days before the fall of Robespierre on 9 Thermidor (27 July 1794). When JM arrived in Paris on 2 August, the Terror was over. Adrienne Lafayette had survived, but she was still in prison (Charles Flowers McCombs, "The Imprisonment of Madame during the Terror," New York Public Library, *Bookmen's Holiday*, 1943, pp. 3-9; Gouverneur Morris to President Washington, 25 July 1794, Fitzpatrick, *Writings of Washington*, 32: 501; "Les Prisons de Mme Lafayette," in Marquise de Lasteyrie, *Notice sur Madame de La Fayette, par Madame de Lasteyrie, sa fille*, 291-292; 461-478).

2. Adrienne Lafayette's declaration that her children had from birth a second country refers to the United States. The Marquis de Lafayette on his 1784 visit to the United States was naturalized by the states of Maryland and Virginia. A special act of the Maryland legislature declared "that the Marquis de Lafayette and his heirs . . . are deemed, adjudged and taken to be natural-born citizens." (Samuel Flagg Bemis, "The United States and Lafayette," *Daughters of the American Revolution Magazine*, 58 (1924): 341-344; *Laws of Maryland*, vol. 12; Hening, *Virginia Statutes*, 12: 30).

The Lafayette children referred to are:

Anastasie-Louise-Pauline du Motier de Lafayette (1777-1863) accompanied her mother to Austria in the fall of 1795 and shared for the next two years the imprisonment of her father at the Ulmütz fortress near Vienna. In 1798 Anastasie married Charles, comte de La Tour Maubourg (1775-1846), the younger brother of César de La Tour-Maubourg, her father's military aide (Maurois, *Adrienne*, 399-401, 556).

George-Washington Lafayette (1779-1849), the Lafayettes' only son, made two visits to the United States: the first when he was sent by his mother to avoid arrest in the fall of 1795; the second, when he accompanied his father on a tour the United States in 1824-1825. George became a French officer and served in Napoleon's army, but retired in 1807, for lack of advancement. In 1802 George married Emilie Destutt de Tracy (1780-1860) the daughter of Antoine Destutt de Tracy, the prominent liberal political theorist and his father's friend (Jason Lane, *General and Madame de Lafayette*, 259; Maurois, *Adrienne*, 554).

Marie-Antoinette-Virginie du Motier de Lafayette (1782-1849) shared a prison cell with her sister, Anastasie, at Ulmütz. She married Louis, Marquis de Lasteyrie in 1803. Virginie was the author of *Notice sur Madame de La Fayette*, a biography of her mother (Maurois, *Adrienne*, 554, 556).

From Gouverneur Morris

Paris 31 August 1794

Dear Sir

I enclose two Copies of my letter to the Bankers in Holland of the 25th Instant and the original and Duplicate of what I wrote to them this day to which you be so kind as to affix your Signature and you can transmit them when your convenience will permit or your occasions may require it.[1]

P.S. I send you also a letter from Madame de Marbois who will probably have occasion to apply for your assistance. Mr Otto can give you a full account of the Circumstances attending her case.[2]

LBC, DLC: Morris Papers: Official Letterbook

1. Morris wrote to the banking firm of Willink, Van Staphorst and Hubbard on 25 and 31 August 174 informing them that JM was succeeding him as minister to France and was entitled to draw on the American diplomatic account at their bank (DLC: Morris Papers: Letterbooks).

2. Elizabeth Moore Barbé-Marbois (1765-1834) was the daughter of William Moore, governor of Pennsylvania. She married François Barbé-Marbois in Philadelphia in June 1784, and later accompanied her husband to France. When she attempted to return to America to settle the estate of her deceased father in August 1792, she was accused of being an émigré. Her husband also was accused and thrown in prison in March 1793, while she went into hiding. Gouverneur Morris made several appeals to the French government to recognize her status as an American citizen, but the issue remained unresolved. Madame de Marbois wrote to Morris in August 1794, once again asking his help and requesting him to inform JM of her situation. It appears that there was a favorable resolution of the case around this time, but there is no indication that JM had any role in its settlement (E. Wilson Lyon, *The Man Who Sold Louisiana*, 34, 83-86). Barbé-Marbois' letter to Morris of 26 August 1794 has not been located. Morris wrote to her on 31 August acknowledging receipt of her letter (DLC: Morris Papers: Letterbooks).

To La Société Populaire de Billom

[August 1794]

Citizens, brothers & friends

I have read with great pleasure the expressions which your favor[1] contains of regard for my country, and of inviolate attachment to republican government: an attachment which does you the highest credit, and which by pervading the breasts of all your fellow citizens, will I trust secure the freedom and happiness of your country to the latest posterity.

The interval of the sea cannot prevent the close and affectionate union of the two republicks. There is a natural bond which unites to each other free citizens of every clime, however distant they may be. But France and America are on the opposit shore of the same sea; they meet on it every day; they supply each other with what they respectively want and therefore its width cannot prevent the most friendly & fraternal intercourse.

I beg of you to be assured, citizens, of the pleasure with which I shall embrace every occasion in my power of increasing by all the means which depend on me, the harmony and good understanding which now so happily subsists between the two republicks.

Dft, NN: Monroe Papers; filed at the end of 1795

1. Societé Populaire de Billom to JM, 19 August 1794.

To James Madison

Paris Sep[r] 2 [1794]

Dear Sir

To morrow will make one month since our arrival here, and such have been my ingagments that altho' I resolved that I wo[d] begin a letter to you every succeeding day yet when the day arrived it was not in power heretofore. You will readily conceive the variety of the objects to which I have been forced to attend, many of which requiring the utmost effort of my judgment, all delicate and interesting, and you will readily admit my embarrassment when you know that I have not had a single person (M[r] S.[1] excepted and who is new in this line) with whom I could confidentially confer. I wished not to write you a superficial letter, but whether I shall be forced to hurry this is what I cannot at present determine. Between Bal: & Paris, we were 45 days. The passage was free from storms & between the soundings of each coast short, being only 29 days. We enjoyed our health; none were sea sick except Joseph[2] a few days & myself an hour or two. M[rs] M & the child escaped it altogether. We landed at Havre & left it for this the day after, whither we arrived in three days, being the 3 of Aug[t]. We are yet at lodgings, but expect to be fixed in M^r M's house which I took, in less than a week.[3] I found Mr Morris from town but he came in, in two or three days after my arrival.

About a week before my arrival Robertspiere had been executed with St Just Couthon & others so that the scene upon which I had to commence was a troubled one. The publick councils were yet somewhat agitated but tranquility and joy upon acc^t of that event reigned every where else. The whole community seemed to be liberated from the most pestilent scourge that ever harrassed a country; I found I had better look on for some days, merely to inform myself of the course to be taken to obtain my recognition.

I found myself under difficulties from the commenc'ment. The fall of Roberspiere had thrown a cloud over all whom it was supposed he had any connection with, or in whose appointment he had been anywise instrumental. This included my fellow passenger,[4] so that it was not prudent to avail myself of his aid in presenting me, or even making known my arrival to the Committee of publick safety. And I was averse to taking the introduction of my predecessor for as good a reason. I did not know the ground upon which the Americans stood here, but suspected as the acquisition of wealth had been their object in coming, they must have attached themselves to some preceding party & worn out their reputations. Upon mature reflection, therefore I resolved to wait the arrival of my predecessor & present myself as a thing of course with him. I concluded it could do me no detriment as it was the official mode, and more especially as he would have to file off at the moment I took my ground. This was done. He accompanied me to the office of foreign aff^{rs}, notified his recall & my succession. I left with the commissary a copy of my credentials, & requested my recognition from the competent department as soon as possible & which was promised.

But my difficulties did not end here. Eight or ten days elapsed and I was not accepted, nor had I heard a syllable from the Committee or seen a member. And upon enquiry I was informed that a minister from Geneva had been here 6 weeks before me and was not yet rec^d. Still further to increase my embarrassment I likewise heard that the commissary to whom I was presented being of Robertspiere's party was out of favor, and that probably his letter covering my credentials had not been read by the Committee. I could not longer bear with this delay: I foresaw that the impression to be expected from the arrival of a new minister might be lost, and that by the trammel of forms and collision of parties I might while away my time here for ever without effect. I was therefore resolved to place myself if possible above these difficulties, by addressing myself immediately to the convention. I knew this would attract the publick attention and if my country had any weight here, produce a proportional effect not only upon that body, but upon every subordinate department. The result was as I had expected; my letter being read in the Convention was well rec^d, taken immediately to the committee of publick safety, reported on in two hours afterwards by that body & a decree passed the same day for my admission on the next, at two in the afternoon. It was at the same time intimated by a special messenger from the President that he sho^d be glad to have a copy of what I sho^d say an hour or two before I was presented. I had of course but little time to prepare my address. I thought it expedient to make the occasion as useful as possible, in drawing the two republicks more closely together, by the ties of affection by shewing them the interest which every department of our government took in their success & prosperity. With this view I laid before the Convention, with suitable solemnity the declarations of the Senate & H. of R., and added a similar one for the President. The effect surpassed my expectation. My reception occupied an hour and an half, of not merely interesting but distressing sensibility, for all who beheld it. It was with difficulty that I extricated myself from the House and committee of p: safety and indeed the crowd which surrounded it, after the business was over. The cordial declaration of America in favor of France and of the French revolution (for altho' I have not mentioned the word revolut[n] after the example of both houses, yet after the example of both and especially the H. of R. I have strongly implied it) in the view of all Europe, and at a time when they were torn in sunder by parties, was a gratification which overpowerd them.

I doubt not this measure will be scanned with unfriendly eyes by many in America. They will say it was intended that those things should have been smuggled in secretly and as secretly deposited afterwards. But they are deceived if they suppose me capable of being the instrument of such purposes. On the contrary I have endeavoured to take the opposit ground, with a view of producing the best effect here as well as there. And I am well satisfied that it has produc'd here a good effect. It is certain that we had lost in a great measure the confidence of the nation. Representations from all parties had agreed, and men of different characters. . .

RC, DLC: Madison Papers. Incomplete

1. Fulwar Skipwith.

2. Joseph Jones, Jr.

3. When Monroe arrived in Paris on August 2 he rented rooms at the Hotel Cusset at 95 Rue de Richelieu. On September 6 he moved his family to the house owned by Gouverneur Morris at 88 Rue de la Planche in the Faubourg St. Germain (Brian N. Morton, *Americans in Paris*, 213-216, 218; Anne Cary Morris, ed., *The Diary and Letters of Gouverneur Morris*, 1: 554; DLC: Monroe Papers: Account book, 1794-1796).

4. Georges-Pierre LeBlanc.

To the Committee of Public Safety

[3 September 1794][1]

There are some subjects to which I wish to call your attention and which I deem of equal importance to both Republicks. They have grown out of the occurrences of the present war, have pressed particularly hard upon the United States, and will I doubt not be immediately rectified in a manner becoming the character of the french nation, and of course satisfactorily to us.

The first, respects the departure on the part of France from the 23. and 24. articles of the treaty of commerce subsisting between the two Republicks.

The second, the embargo of our Vessels at Bordeaux and the injuries arising from it to those whom it concerns.

The third, respects the claims of some of our Citizens for supplies furnished to the Government of St Domingo, authenticated by bills upon the minister of the Republick in Philadelphia, by bills upon France, and by mandates and other instruments usual in such cases.

By the 23. Article of the Treaty of Amity and Commerce it is stipulated that free ships shall make free goods, and that all goods shall be free, except those which are termed contraband, and that no dispute might arise as to contraband, all those which should be deemed such on the one hand, and which should be deemed free on the other, are particularly specified in the 24th.

It is necessary for me in bringing this subject to your view, briefly to observe, that these articles have been dispensed with on your part: that our vessels, laden with merchandise not only the property of your enemies made free by these articles, but likewise of our Citizens, the latter of which was always free, have been brought into your ports, detained for a great length of time, their cargoes taken, and the captains and proprietors otherwise subjected to great embarrassments, losses, and injuries. But I will not dwell upon this subject in this view, because I frankly own to you it is painful for me thus to contemplate it. I wish to reserve my free comments for the other side of the picture, when I shall favorably explain the motives of the act, in communicating to my Country what I hope you will enable me to communicate, and upon this friendly intimation only, the ready acquiescence with which the decree was rescinded.

It may be said that Great Britain has rendered us the same injury, and that when she shall change her conduct in that respect, France will likewise follow her example. But the case is widely different. Britain may dispute the law of nations, even with respect to contraband, however clear its doctrine; but with France it is in both respects regulated by treaty. Besides, we are the allies, and, what is more interesting, the friends of France. These considerations naturally inspire in the councils of the two Countries different sentiments in regard to us, and if Britain proves true to those which belong to her situation, shall we on the other hand find France reluctant to cherish such as are friendly to us, and correspondent with hers? Will she say that the injuries of Britain furnish a justificatory example for her to render us like injuries? Will our ally contend with that nation in rivalship which shall harass our commerce most, and do us the greatest detriment? This is surely not a relation for the two Republicks to bear towards each other. Other sentiments will I hope inspire their common councils, sentiments more congenial with their mutual interests, and consonant to the dispositions of the Citizens of both nations.

If the French Republick gained the smallest benefit from the regulation, there might be some motive for adhering to it. But this cannot it is presumed be the case. The most to be derived from it is, the occasional seizure of a straggling vessel destined with provisions for the ports of Spain and Portugal, for they are excluded from the ports of England, except under particular circumstances, and which rarely happen. It must be obvious if the price was higher here, this would be their destination. Add to which the charges attending the seizure and conducting of vessels from their course must be great, and make it not only an uncertain but unprofitable mode of supply.

It may be apprehended that if this decree should be rescinded, it will open a door, thro' which under the protection of our flag, the commerce of Britain may be carried on with advantage to her, and detriment to France. But a moments reflection will demonstrate that this apprehension cannot in any degree, be well founded, for the navigation act of England, and whose great principles have been wisely adopted here, forbids almost altogether any such commerce. By this act the manufactures of the metropolis cannot be carried to the Colonies, nor can the productions of the Colonies, nor the productions of any other country be carried in our bottoms to Great Britain. This restriction must in a great degree inhibit the use of our vessels in any but the direct trade between the two nations, for it is not probable that Great Britain will use the American vessels to export her Cargoes to other countries to any amount, if at all, since not being able to return they would generally be left there empty and idle. On the contrary we know that her practice in such cases has been, not to countenance the navigation of any other Country at the expense of her own, but to protect the latter by Convoys. But if this were otherwise it is to be presumed that the fortune of the present war, in the triumphant success of the french arms, will have decisively settled itself, before this could have produced any material effect.

It must be obvious that the conduct of Great Britain and especially in regard to the articles of contraband, must depend, in a great measure upon that of France in this particular. For if France declines to rescind this decree Great Britain most probably will, unless indeed she should make a merit of receding at the expense of France. But if France should comply in the first instance she will put Great Britain in an embarrassing dilemma, for if she refuses afterwards, it will not only tend to cement our union with France but combine all America in the condemnation of the conduct of Britain: and if they should then comply, to France will the credit be given, of having forced her into it.

At the same time that I express to you a desire that this decree be rescinded, and the parties heretofore affected by it compensated for the injuries they have received, I consider it likewise my duty to add some observations upon the state of our trade in general in the Republick. When an American Vessel arrives in any port of France, it is immediately in the hands of Government. The Captain or Supercargo, cannot sell the cargo to any other person, nor can he get more for it than the Publick agents will give, nor sail elsewhere without permission. Often times it happens that great delays take place from the necessity of communicating from the seaports with the metropolis, and other inconveniencies detrimental to the parties. A regulation of this kind, in its fullest extent, must prove very injurious to both Countries and especially to France. Trade cannot exist under it. It will soon happen that not a single Adventurer will seek the french ports. No merchant will enter them but by constraint. The consequence must be, that the commerce of America so extensive and productive, and especially in those articles in greatest demand here, will be either exterminated, threwn into other channels or forced here by publick funds and under the direction of publick agents, a resource which however productive should not be the sole one, for many reasons, but more especially because the produce of our country having thus become the property of France will be liable by the law of nations, equally in yours and our Vessels, to seisure and condemnation by your enemies; and, because if we succeed in securing the respect which is due to our flag by other nations, and which would enable our Citizens in their own bottoms to supply in abundance, your markets, (and in which I trust we shall succeed) it would be of no use to you, and lastly because the competition of private adventurers would thus be destroyed, a competition which with suitable encouragment would not only supply the defect of these agents, and satisfy the demand of the market, but by making known constantly and regularly the prices in America, form a check on their conduct, and furnish the best test of their integrity.

You will observe I do not complain that the publick are the sole purchasers and regulate at pleasure what shall be exported, provided the venders are paid for their cargoes in some commodity or specie at their option, or that agents of the Publick are appointed in the United States and as many as may be thought necessary to purchase our productions on publick account and send them here. These are subjects which the legislators of the Republick will regulate according as publick exigencies may in their judgment require. What I wish is that the ports of France may be opened freely to the enterprises of my Countrymen, and which will be the case, provided they be permitted to leave them immediately if they do not like the market, and despatched without delay in case they do. To accomplish the first point a general order only will be requisite to the officers of the customs or persons in authority in the several ports, and the latter a regulation of the prices to be immediately given by these officers upon all occasions when a vessel should arrive, and which might be furnished as often as any change should be deemed necessary. This would I am satisfied banish every cause of complaint, greatly increase the competition and of course the supply of the market, and at a much less expence.

Upon the second subject of the Bordeaux embargo I find the committee has already passed an arret which secures to the persons interested an indemnity for the delay and other injuries sustained; it only remains therefore to adjust the amount of the claims and pay the parties entitled to it.

3^{d} which respects the claims for supplies rendered by our citizens to the Government of St Domingo, is likewise a matter of account and which it is earnestly hoped will be immediately adjusted and paid. A person authorized will appear in support of the claims with the evidence, before any board or tribunal which shall be appointed for that purpose.

I have to observe that I shall be happy to give every aid in my power to facilitate the adjustment and subsequent payment of these several classes of claims. So far as they are well founded I doubt not they will be allowed by the french Republick, and where this is not the case they will not be supported by me. In an aggregate view they respect the great mass of American merchants. It is of importance for France to cultivate that interest and the present is for many reasons a critical moment to make an impression on it. I hope therefore it will not be neglected.

Tis my duty to observe to you that I am under no instruction to complain of or request the repeal of the decree authorizing a departure from the 23[d] and 24 articles of the treaty of amity and commerce: on the contrary I well know that if upon consideration, after the experiment made, you should be of opinion that it produces any solid benefit to the republick, the American Government and my Countrymen in general will not only bear the departure with patience but with pleasure. It is from the confidence alone which I entertain that this departure cannot be materially beneficial to you, and that the repeal would produce the happiest effect, in removing every possible cause of uneasiness, and conciliating still more and more towards each other, the affections of the citizens of both Republicks, and thereby cementing more closely their union, that I have taken the liberty, as connected with the other concerns, to bring the subject before you. To cement that union, in other situations, has long been the object of my efforts: for I have been well satisfied that the closer and more intimate it was the happier it would be for both Countries. America and France thus united, the one the greatest Power in the European world, and the other rapidly repairing the wastes of war, and rising to the first rank in the scale of nations, both bounded by and measuring an immense space along, the Atlantic, abundant in productions suiting the demand of each other, and, above all both Republicks have nothing to fear from foreign danger, and every thing to hope from the happiest and most beneficial domestick intercourse. By a generous and liberal policy France has it at the present moment much in her power to promote this more intimate union, and in the hope she will avail herself of it I have thought proper thus to develop the subjects which I have submitted to your consideration.

Ja[s] Monroe

RC, DLC: FCP—France

JM wrote to Philibert Buchot on 2 September 1794 asking him to present this paper to the committee (DLC: FCP—France.

The date is taken from JM's draft in PHi: Gratz Collection.

The National Convention issued a decree on 9 May 1793 declaring that foodstuffs bound for any enemy port on a neutral ship or enemy merchandise found on a neutral ship, were lawful prize. Gouverneur Morris protested this decree, noting, as JM does here, that it violated the terms of the commercial treaty of 1778. The Committee of Public Safety recognized Morris's complaint, but the matter remained unresolved (*ASP: FR*, I: 364). The French responded to JM's complaint with a decree issued on 15 November 1794. See André-François Miot to JM, 24 November 1794, below.

To Joseph Jones

Paris. Sepr 4. 1794.

Dear Sir

We have been here one month, and I have been so extremely occupied that I have not written a single letter to America except to the secr[y] of State till the present opportunity & by which I hope to write likewise to M[r] Jefferson and M[r] Madison. You will readily conceive how difficult my situation was, arriving a few days after the commotion created by Robertspiere & associates, and when every thing was yet in agitation by that event and especially as it was more important it seemed for me to commence in a manner w[h] sho[d] secure me due respectability, and avoid all collision with any of the parties. Fortunately all this business has been concluded according to my wishes, and I have now a little leasure to apprize our friends on y^r side the water of our real situation.

Between Bal: & Havre we were 41 days. We were favored with good health on the passage & had the perspective of a storm without enjoying the reality of it. We reachd this in three days from Havre which was on the 3 or 4 of August. As yet we have been in lodgings but shall move into the House lately occupied by Mr Morris tomorrow: It is commodious & retired, has a garden &c. I have taken an office for the convenience of the Americans more in the center of the town where Mr Skipwith will lodge, but near enough for him to dine with me. The whole costs ab^t 4600 livres p^r an^m.

I was desirous to make the most eligible arrangment for Joe,[1] when I made any, and therefore kept him with me till ab^t 4 days past. I procured however a tutor to attend him in my family with the child &c immediately on my arrival. I have now plac'd him in the best academy in Paris under the care of Mr Lamoine whose plan &c I [now] enclose you. He lives in the house adjoining Mr Jeffersons & is personally known to him, so that you will have a better idea of his merits thro' this channel than I can possibly give you.[2] I have furnished him according to the rector of the school with a silver cup, spoon & fork, 3 p^r of sheets & cloaths: and have likewise paid the quarter in advance. I think when I say that all charges including his outfit will not exceed annually £60 our currency I speak within bounds. This however will be owing to the benefit of exchange to which I become entitled in consequence of having my funds in a foreign country. I need not tell you that I will do every thing in my power to limit his expences & finish his education in the best manner possible. I have entered into the most explicit and candid communication with the Professor relative to his past life, present disposition &c and assured him that I would do every thing in my power to support his authority & aid his operations: and as a further encour-agement have made his family acquainted with mine, shall have them with us occasionally, and pay him every suitable attention.

On the passage Joe soon discovered his independance of every person but myself, and that by com-ing here he sought rather to extricate himself from present evils, than encounter others. This spirit shewed itself in many instances, and in such a degree as to demonstrate that reproofs from me wo^d not be effectual. I threatened severe treatment and with some effect. Here I have been able to confine him pretty close to the house, but in my absence he sometimes [ga]ve a license to his temper, which rendered the authority of the tutor of no effect. Finding him disposed to be idle, obstinate & cross in two instances I thought it my duty to correct him a little. Upon inquiry I found that correction was not used in the academies here and thought it necessary he sho^d know he wo^d not be exempt from it, if he merited it, he commenced therefore under the professor with the prospect of the kindest usage, of the most assiduous attention to his advancment, if by encourag'ment, emulation, and every means w^h long practice and a knowledge of the human heart have taught the Professor, on his part, and on mine, with kind and friendly attention, with encouragement, with little complimentary presents to excite emulation &c and likewise with assurance of punishment in case he merits it: the latter of which I do not think I shall ever resort to again for he now advances to an age, when it will produce no effect, if reason does not. One thing of importance he sees and understands well, which is that if he were ever disposed, he cannot get out of the country, without my passport, but in case he left school wo^d be immediately apprehended & confined.

He is under an impression, that he will inherit, a respectable property, and may probably relax his studies, on that account. I have stated all these things, that you may be able to make the most suitable impression, in consequence, by your correspondence. It will not be necessary to notice what I have said above but inculcate attention to his books morals &c. Tell him you are happy to find he is well settled <torn> him, that if he does not leave this country, with a good character, & much improved, that he must not expect to see you or inherit any thing of consequence: and above all depress the hope, from the state of y^r aff^{ts}, after acc^{ts} being settled &c of inheriting much property from you, pointing his attention towards some profession as his principal means of support. I am happy to add that Mr Skipwith has just returned from a visit to him, & informs us, that the professor upon this short experiment speaks well of him, and that Joe on his part is very well satisfied with his situation, so that the commencment is a favorable one.

I enclose you a copy of my address &c to the Convention upon my introduction & of the Presidents reply. I thought it my duty to lay those papers before the Convention as the basis of my mission—containing the declaration of every department in favor of the French revolution, or implying it strongly. My address you will observe goes no further than the decl^{ns} of both Houses.

The French have succeeded in every enterprize. They have retaken Conde & Valenciennes with every other post heretofore lost and have in addition taken the whole of the Austrian low countries and are now pressing by Mastricht towards the Rhine. Tis thought a general action will soon take place, and which must settle the fate of the United Provinces & perhaps of some other countries. The French have between the Meuse & the Rhine ab^t 400,000 troops, the best in Europe well appointed elated with victory; suppose 250,000 effectives w^h from the best information is probable, thus exceeds Cob: & G^n W^3 by 1/2 at least, and their armies are depressed by defeats retreats &c and in addition to which these two are disputing for the command, the latter obtaining it upon acc^t of the number of Prussians in B^h pay. There can be no doubt what the issue will be.   In Sp^n the whole of the Province of Guypuscoa Bilboa excepted (& w^h tis tho^t has fallen by this time as the French were within 4 leagues by the last acc^t). Indeed a general terror appears to have seizd the combined powers & they seem to be endeavoring to defend themselves in the best manner possible till the winter when they hope to end their difficulties by negotiation: but as an attempt it is said was made of the same kind last winter, it is doubtful whether it will succeed now or not. Many think they will not treat with crowned heads, but press the war till there is no opposition, leaving it with the people to change their gov^{ts} afterwards if they think fit.

In the sea action which took place between the British & French, the latter lost 7 ships owing to their being separated in the begining of the action from the main force: but they saved the Convoy & offered battle on the 3 or 4 day (for it lasted that length of time) without having it accepted. The force was, Brit^h 28, F^h 26 in the beginning. One of the ships lost was sunk. The crew as she went down fired off the upper tier & cried "vive La Republique." many were taken up & saved. I hear of many feats of heroism surpassing any thing ever [recorded] before.

I have not heard a word from America since our arrival & am anxious to do it. I fear it will be difficult to get letters from your side, but let not this deter you; for as you will readily conceive we shall very desirous to hear often.

By this I presume you have made a final arrangment in you own affairs and have become well acquainted with mine. I hope you purchased for us Carter's land, and have fix'd on my farm. Indeed I take it for granted that this is done.[4] If you have made the purchase, advise me of it immediately as I will endeavor to have the funds to fulfill my part of the contract subject to y^r draft in Amsterdam or Hamburg, which ever may be preferable. Or so much as I shall be able. Indeed it is probable I may be able to provide money also for you if requisite, of w^h you will inform me.

I feel the deepest concern that all my debts be punctually paid or at times suited to those to whom due. And I wish also that my plantation on the side of Mr Jefferson to be forwarded in improvment as fast as possible. I instructed Mr Hogg to continue enclosing the ground by successive fields towards M^r

Jefferson till he got the whole enclosed. These to comprize a good field toward the lower end, by clearing up the ground & uniting several small ones. But whether this is the best plan or any other you will be best able to decide. I hope the whole of the corn ground & w^h I presume is in wheat will be served down in clover either this fall or next spring on the <torn>. You will be so kind as fix on the most suitable <torn> for orchards, apples, peach &c, in concert with M^r J: & have them planted this winter or next spring. Let the trees be procured where to be had of the best kind not forgetting to include some crab: for cider. The ground allotted for our houses &c on the hill east of the road, will be enclosed to the road, all the pines cut with the under wood & old trees of other kinds & sown with greensward.   I have a real desire that Mr Marks be relieved from the contract with me and with the loss on my part of ab^t £500 to be paid in favor of his wife & children. This will leave due me including the interest of last year (of w^h ab^t £15 was overp^d) £1060 & which you may take in money; slaves at their value & a <illegible> an adequate one; good bonds upon interest for one half & the residue in money, or even the whole in bonds if you think fit; or part in slaves & part in land of good quality, and which may possibly suit both parties provided the land be really good and obtainable at a proper price for I hear Birch wants the lotts & his land. If you take slaves have in view those which will suit me; we shall not want more than one female servant & her with Mr Nicholas in preference to any other from her character; three boys for servants and the rest for the field & trades. I wish <illegible> to apply to some trade, but if he declines to remain with Peter as gardener &c for the lower farm. I want a lad to be sent to the b. smith trade, one or two to the carpenters, & one the bricklayers.

Tis probable notwithstanding the product of the farm, the resource of Marks &c you may have a occasion (either for the payment of my debts, the improvement of my farm, the purchase of a suitable number of slaves for the cultivation of it, or purposes aforementioned, or for all in part) for further sums of money, I have therefore written Mr Randolph to pay to your draft one thousand dol^rs to be allowed by me here.[5] And if on finding by consulting him that he will execute my arrangment I hope if any were necessary you will certainly draw for it & I shall therefore consider this as paid.

I must repeat my wish that you fulfill all my intimations in favor of my sister & brothers. You recollect that I promised to educate a son of hers & supply her with what she might want to the amount of £15 annually or such p^t as might be useful to her; an attention due only on acc^t of the negligence of her husband, and her suffering in consequence of it, for he is rich enough.[6] You likewise remember my promise to Joseph[7] of supplies &c. I wish you to settle with him an acc^t furnished him some time since, containing a statment of all my transactions for him, advances of money, sale of slaves &c. I intend exclusive of all that has passed, & of the little supplies directed, to give him £200 or perhaps £300 to help him commence with credit & advantage. I shall be able to pay this in the course of the next year without an accident: so that without directly telling him of it you may turn y^r own & his attention to the purchase of some land where he may prefer it of that value or greater founded on his other prospects. When advanc'd if ever, let him keep it to himself & never mention it. I intend likewise to do some friendly office for Andrew,[8] by assisting him in the purchase of some land, gift of a slave, or aid in the education of a child. I hinted to him before I sailed and requested in case of necessity he would communicate with you on the subject. In fact I owe him & Mr Buckner, on acc^t of Fanny to each 1/4 of £90 with interest from the time of her sale to Benj^m Johnson in Novr 1786. This sum ought to be paid & a receipt taken for it specifying the consideration.

Sepr 6.

This being decade day[9] Joe is with us. He is well and says he is quite satisfied with M^r Le Moine. He returns tomorrow morning. I really hope every thing will mend for the future, and answer our wishes. Mʳˢ M. Joe Eliza & Mʳ Skipwith join in best wishes for yʳ health & welfare. Very sincerely I am yʳ friend & servant.

Jaˢ Monroe

Perhaps a barn may be necessary on my farm above spoken of & of wʰ you will judge & plan where adviseable having regard for the place we mean to build on.

There is among our plate a silver cream pot carved. It contains the initials of the childs name & was presented by her grandfather. If disposed of pray get it back & keep it for her.

RC, ViFreJM

1. Joseph Jones, Jr.

2. Edme-Marie-Joseph Lemoine D'Essoies (1751-1816) was a geographer and mathematician who ran a school for boys in the Rue de Berri, across the street from where Jefferson resided when he was in Paris (*Nouvelle Biographie General*," 30: 619; Howard Rice, *Thomas Jefferson's Paris*, 53).

3. Prince von Coburg and General Dagobert von Wurmser.

4. Jones purchased 4,400 acres from Colonel Charles Carter in Loudoun County, Virginia, in 1794. This became the site of Oak Hill, JM's home in Loudoun County (Gerard Gawalt, "James Monroe, Presidential Planter," *Virginia Magazine of History and Biography*, 101(1993): 255; *Madison Papers*, 15: 369-370).

5. This letter to Edmund Randolph has not been located.

6. JM's sister Elizabeth was married to William Buckner (1753-1800), A Caroline County, Virginia farmer.

7. Joseph Jones Monroe.

8. Andrew Monroe.

9. According to the French revolutionary calendar, each month was divided into three ten-day periods called décades, with the tenth day being the equivalent of Sunday (Samuel Scott and Barry Rothaus, *Historical Dictionary of the French Revolution*, 145-146).

From Philibert Buchot

Paris le. 20. Fructidor l'an 2. de la Republ. [6 September 1794]

Citoyen Ministre

J'ai reçu la lettre que tu m'as adressée concernant la demande qui t'a été faite par la famille Bingham pour obtenir des passeports en qualité de Citoyens Americains.

J'applaudis d'autant plus à la circonspection, dont tu crois devoir user à l'égard des Voyageurs, qui ont le double caractère de Citoyens Americains et Anglois, qu'il me revient que plusieurs d'entre eux ont abusé des egards que la Republique a pour Ses Alliés et ont entretenu avec le Gouvernement Anglois des liaisons très reprehensibles. Convaincu que les Etats unis Sont bien eloignés de vouloir proteger de pareils Citoyens, je pense qu'ils approuveront de même que nous ta repugnance à leur accorder des passeports.

Au reste les loix de ton pays ont Sans doute determiné cette question très importante dans les circonstances actuelles. A ne la considerer que pour les rapports généraux du Droit des gens, il paroitroit qu'à l'exception des Negocians et agens politiques et commerciaux, le Domicile et non la propriété de quelques terres devroit decider de la qualité de Citoyen des Etats unis. On Sait qu'un grand nombre d'Anglois, de Hollandois et même de François ont acheté des terres en Amerique sans y resider et qu'il y auroit une grande inconvenance à les faire passer pour Americains uniquement parce qu'ils ont placé quelques fonds dans les Etats unis.

La famille Bingham ayant residé cinq années en France doit être suffisamment connue dans sa municipalité pour obtenir des passeports par la voie ordinaire. La loi ne me permet d'en accorder qu'aux Agens exterieurs de la Republique et aux Envoyés des Puissances etrangeres.

Editors' Translation

Paris, 20 Fructidor Year 2 of the Republic [6 September 1794]

Citizen Minister,

I have received the letter that you addressed to me concerning the request from the Bingham Family to obtain passports as American Citizens.[1]

I commend even more the caution you feel you should use with respect to these travelers who have two-fold character of American citizen and British subject, since I recall that several of them abused the hospitality that the Republic has for its allies and entered into reprehensible liaisons with the British Government. Convinced that the United-States is a long way from wanting to protect such citizens, I think it will also approve, as we do, of your reluctance to grant them passports.

For the rest, the laws of your country have no doubt addressed this very important question in the actual circumstances. Even if we only consider it from the general perspective of People's Rights, it would seem that with the exception of merchants and political agents, the place of residence and not the ownership of some land should decide United States' citizenship. It is known that a great number of English, Dutch and even French citizens have bought land in America without having resided there, and that there would be a great impropriety in allowing them to pass as Americans simply because they invested a few funds in the United States.

Having resided in France for five years, the Bingham family must be sufficiently known in its municipality to obtain the passports in the usual way. The law permits me to grant them only to foreign agents of the Republic and to the envoys of foreign powers.

Dft, DLC: FCP—France

1. English-born American citizens traveling abroad had difficulty in obtaining passports due to the suspicion of their being English spies. On 4 September JM wrote to Buchot regarding passports for the British-born Bingham family, constituting the husband and his wife, and the wife's mother, Mrs. Cuniffe, who claimed that her husband owned considerable property in Virginia and that he was a citizen of that state. The Bingham family had lived for the past five years in France and desired passports to go to the United States. JM explained that he was obliged to refuse passports to all British subjects, except in unusually favorable cases, and asked Buchot to grant the passports, by reason of the family's residence in France for several years. Buchot responded on September 10, notifying JM that he had issued the passports (Both letters are in DLC: FCP—France.

To Thomas Jefferson

Paris Sep.ʳ 7. 1794.

Dear Sir

I have been here rather more than a month and so much engaged with the duties which devolved on me immediately that I have not yet been able [to] send a single private letter to America. It happened that I took my station a few days after Robertspierre had left his in the Convention, by means of the guillitin, so that every thing was in commotion, as was natural upon such an event; but it was the agitation of universal joy occasioned by a deliverance from a terrible oppression & which had pervaded every part of the Republick. After encountering some serious difficulties growing out of the existing state of things, I was presented to the Convention and recognized in the manner the enclosed paper will shew you.[1] Many incidents have since turned up to shew the pleasure with which the organized departments and the people generally have received a mission immediately from our republick to theirs, and I have every reason to believe that it will not only remove any previous existing solicitude, but tend to encrease permanently the harmony between the two countries.

After Robertsperre's exit there seemed to be an end of divisions and altercations for sometime in the convention. Even those of his own party were most probably happy in the event, for in the progress of his power a connection with him had already been of little service, and it was to be apprehended that it would prove of less hereafter. It was not only necessary to be devoted to him, but to be unpopular with the community also. The list of his oppressions, and the acts of cruelty committed by means of his influence, in the convention & in consequence the revolutionary tribunal, would amaze you. He was believed by the people at large to be the foe to kings, nobles, Priests & to be the friend of republican gov.ᵗ regardless of money and in fact devoted to their cause. Under this impression he perpetrated acts, which without perceiving the cause, had gradually spread a gloom over the whole republick. But as soon as they saw him in opposition to the Convention, the cause was known, his atrocities were understood, and the people abandoned him with demonstrations of joy rarely seen.

But it seemed improbable he sho.ᵈ have been able to carry every thing in the Committee of p: safety & by means of it in the Convention &c, without more associates than S.ᵗ Just & Couthon who were executed with him or rather this was the opinion of others, for I can readily conceive that a man may gain an influence in society powerful enough to controul everyone and every thing; as soon therefore as the preternatural calm subsided, which the Liberation from him had universally created, a spirit of inquiry began to shew itself, as to other accomplices. It terminated in the denunciation of Barrere[2] Collot D Herbois,[3] & some others. The Convention gave a hearing to the charges rejected them, & pass'd a censure upon the author as seeking to disturb the publick repose. Thus therefore that business rests, and I declare to you that I not only think hereafter they will be more free from parties of the turbulent kind heretofore known, but if they sho.ᵈ not that I am persuaded their revolution rests perfectly secure in the unanimity & affections of the people. Greater proofs of patriotism and personal sacrifice were never seen in any country than are daily shewn in this, and in acts of heroism, they have thrown a shade over the antient and modern world. The spirit of the combination is absolutely broken. In the neighbourhood of Charleroy a decisive action was fought in July between Jourdan and Cob:[4] & in which the former gained the victory with the loss of ab.ᵗ 15000 men, and at the expence to the latter of about 10,000 slain on the feild. This has eventually driven the troops of the combined powers to Mastrecht and the neighbourhood of the Rhine, & of course out of all their possessions not only in France (including Conde and Valenciennes) but likewise their proper territory in the low countries. Tis thought they are ab.ᵗ to hazard another great action, but they do it with hazard for they fight dispirited troops against those who are flushed with victory, superior numbers, & resolved to conquer, & sure in case of misfortune of immediate succour. If France succeeds and which I am led to believe from every thing I can hear & very dispassionately, the combination in the ordinary course of war will be at an end, and the several powers composing it entirely at the mercy of France, except the Islands in her neighbourhood whose safety will depend altogether on the superiority at sea, if preserved there. Tis said that these powers (the Islanders excepted & who probably prompted the others with a view of taking advantage in case of success) sounded this gov^t last winter upon the subject of peace, but without effect: that on the contrary they were treated with the utmost contempt, and I have reason to believe they will never treat with them under the gov^ts at present existing in each, press the war till no force shews itself against them, & in case the people sho^d rise in any one & organize themselves, treat such organiz'd body as the only legitimate gov^t & aid it in crushing the antient one. If France succeeds in the battle contemplated this will soon be the state of things: indeed it must be so immediately after.

That Mr Jay should easily obtain the object of his errand in Engl^d will be readily inferred. The successful battles of France have plead our cause with great effect in the councils of that humane Cabinet. He will however arrogate to himself much merit for address in negotiation, and the concession of the court will be a theme for high panegeric to many in our country. They will deem it a proof of that sincere attachment to us which has always been shewn in that quarter.

The spirit of liberty begins to shew itself in other regions. Geneva has undergone a revolution—the people have taken the gov^t into their hands, apprehended the aristocrats, and executed seven of the most wicked.[5] And in Poland under the direction of   who acted with us in America,[6] a formidable hand has been raised against Prussia & Russia. I have hopes that our trade, by mere regulation, will be plac'd on a very safe and good footing shortly: and that France will rescind the decree respecting the seizure of our vessels laden with provisions &c as heretofore. Indeed I think she will go back to the ground of the commercial treaty. I have hinted the good effect such a measure wo^d have in America, without positively requesting it to be done.

I rely upon yourself & Mr Jones in planning many little tho' very important matters for me, ab^t my farm. Such as fixing the place for my house orchards & the like. It will not be very long before we join you. We are all well. Mrs M. is with her child a pupil to a professor in the French language. They desire to be affectionately remembered to yourself and family taking it for granted you have Mr R.[7] and both your daughters with you. I am Dear Sir y^r affectionate friend & servant

Ja^s Monroe

RC, DLC: Jefferson Papers

1. The enclosed paper may have been Philibert Buchot's report of 14 August 1794 on JM's reception by the National Convention (See JM to Randolph, 25 August 1794, above).

2. Bertrand Barère (1755-1841), a lawyer from Toulouse, was among the original members of the Committee of Public Safety in which he directed foreign affairs, military affairs and the navy. He was part of the coup that brought down Robespierre, but in late December 1794, Barère was denounced by the Thermidorians and brought to trial with Billaud-Varenne and Collot d'Herbois. Sentenced to deportation, he escaped and successfully remained in hiding. Later he was elected to the Chamber of Deputies in Napoleon's final days (Paul R. Hanson, *Historical Dictionary of the French Revolution*, 26).

3. Jean-Marie Collot D'Herbois (1749-1796), was an actor and playwright when he entered the Committee of Public Safety on 6 Sept 1793. He became an advocate of extreme terror. He organized the terror in Lyons after the city surrendered, and ordered the execution of 1,900 rebels. He was tried as a terrorist and deported in May 1795 to Cayenne where he died a year

later (Bernard Gainot, *Dictionnaire des Membres du Comité de Salut Public*, 97-98; Hanson, *Historical Dictionary of the French Revolution*, 72-73; M. J. Sydenham, *The First French Republic, 1792-1804*, 329).

4. Prince von Cobourg.

5. The people of Geneva staged a revolution against the city's aristocratic rulers in 1792. Widespread unemployment and hunger led to the institution of a reign of terror against aristocrats in 1793 and the writing of a new constitution in 1794 (Helena Rosenblatt, review essay, *Journal of Modern History*, 75: 982-983).

6. Thaddeus Kościusko.

7. Thomas Mann Randolph.

From George Clinton

New York 8ᵗʰ September 1794

My dear Sir

This Letter will be delivered to you by Mʳ John M. Gelston, Son of my worthy and esteemed Friend David Gelston of this City Merchant.[1] He is a Young Man of excellent Character and possesses Civic Virtues in an eminent degree. I therefore take the Liberty of recommending him to your Friendly Notice and Attention which no consideration would induce me to do, if I had not the most perfect confidence in his Integrity and patriotism. The principal Motive of his Voyage I have reason to believe is to see a Country famous for its virtuous exertions in the cause of Liberty, and it is probable he may wish to avail himself of the Opportunity while in France of forming some commercial Connection.

Personal Friendship as well as other considerations made me very desirous of seeing you before your departing for France, and having been made to believe that you would take passage from this Place I flattered myself with that Pleasure until I was undeceived by the Receipt of your Letter dated at Baltimore the 18ᵗʰ June, and it came to Hand even to be acknowledged before you sailed.

Interested as I feel myself for your prosperity and happiness both in your public and private Capacity it will give me great Pleasure to hear from you by every Opportunity. I entreat you to present my best Respects to Mʳˢ Munroe & believe me sincerely & Affectionately your's

Geo Clinton

RC, PHi: Dreer Collection

1. David Gelston (1744-1828) was a New York City merchant who became active in state politics during the American Revolution. He was a member of the Continental Congress in 1789, and in 1801 Jefferson appointed him collector of customs for the port of New York, a post he held until 1820 (*BDAC*). JM served as guardian for Gelston's son, John (d. 1804) while he was France. Another of Gelston's sons, Maltby (ca. 1773-1860), arrived in Paris in August 1795. John later became a merchant in New Orleans and Maltby a banker in New York (*Burr Papers*, 1: 226). Both young men resided in JM's household and served as secretaries.

2. JM to Clinton, 19 June 1794, above.

From Joseph Fenwick

Bordeaux 8 Septr 1794. 22 Fructidor 2.

Sir

I have the honor of your favor of the 31 Ult.^o.[1] No effort shall be wanting in me to coopperate in all the measures that promise to cement & promote the material interests of the American & French Republics.

I will collect & bring or send forward all the Documents required relative to the late embargo here as you desire, tho I do not know what papers will be called for by the convention from hence on that business—the Comitte of public Safety will not I presume contest the existence of the embargo on all vessels indistinctly as they did prior to my going to Paris last March. The Arrette I then obtained dated 7 Germinal (27 March) establishes the date of the cessation of the embargo which comenced the 12 Aug.st preceding. It was first laid on by orders from the Comitté of the Convention, which facts the correspondence of the minister of the marine Dalberade[2] will establish, and the Registers of the proceedings of the Representatives Ysabeau[3] & Tallien deputed in this Department who continued it will prove its non interruption from the 12th Aug.st to the 10 April, the time when the arrete of 7 Germinal officially reached Bord.^x. During the embargo there were several vessels obtained special permissions to depart, particularly toward the latter part of the time, scarcely any permissions to vessels in balast were refused, but the want of resources to pay the debts unavoidably contracted during their long detention & the difficulty of obtaining provisions prevented all but a very few from profiting of this facility.

The captains left with their accounts & powers of attorney to pursue their claim for the indemnity on the principles decretted[4] in the Arreté of the 7 Germinal—these accounts I have nearly all made out fair & translated into french as soon as they are finished I will forward them on to you with what other documents you may require. These accounts with a general repport from me that will accompany them will give you the dates of the arrival & departure the owners names & residence all and the loss sustained by each Captain agreeable to their own estimates. I have received on account of the indemnity in virtue of the arreté of the 7 Germinal 400,000 Livres for all the neutral Nations of which 182,334.^{tt} came to the Americans after a division made by the Tribunal of Commerce here. Prior to that arrete (which promised an advance of 800,000) I received from the Representatives Ysabeau & Tallien here £180,000 which makes the sum of 312,334.^{tt} in all, that the Americans have received. Ysabeau now here, has given me some hope of receiving the remainder 400,000 apprised in the in the arreté of the 7 Germinal. In a few days I shall know whether he will grant it or not. Thus stands the state of things relative to that business.

In consequence of an application I made to the comitté of public safety last winter, they passed an arreté the 24 ventose (14 march) suppressing all duties on the productions of the french west Indias imported in France thro the U. States in American vessels per copy inclosed. On application here to the director of the Customs to suspend the collection of these duties (which amount to a prohibition if the maximum prevailes) he refused to admit the exemption without original Documents from the west Indias and America proving that the goods were realy from the french settlements, notwithstanding the material proofs which I exhibited here viz a certificate on oath of the Captain & mate of their being imported from the french Islands and a declaration of sworn national Brokers here corroborating with the oath of the Captain in the proof of the identity of goods. I in vain pleaded the impropriety & danger of french papers accompanying these goods during the existence of the arbitrary measures of the british against vessels loaded with that property.

This exemption Sir, is an important object to the commerce of the United States founded in justice (at least while the maximum exists) and the reciprocal interest of the two Republics—but the old sprit of the Farmers general which still reigns in the Custom House as all that are there employed were formerly clerks in the same offices to the Farmers, and they think all other form of proofs can be received there such as was formerly admitted. I think if the Comitté of public Safety or the Commission of the national Revenue would take time to hear the case plainly represented they would not hesitate a moment to admit the proofs offered. I wrote to the comitté some time past on this subject & sent the Documents to the Commission of the Revenue who has the direction of the custom Houses, where they still lay without an answer. I send you a Copy of my letter to the comitte & of the certificates it cited.[5]

The American Traders in the different ports of France meet a friendly & favorable reception but great difficulties and delays in any reclamations they have to make in bartering their goods owing more perhaps to the indifference or ignorance of the agents than a will to disappoint—these delays and difficulties I think are more disadvantageous in the present circumstance to the French than to the Americans themselves as they tend to enhance the demands of the latter & deprive the former of more frequent importations of the articles they are now in great want of & subject them to pay greater prices for what they receive.

There are now here 25 or 30 new england vessels with provisions or what they call notions, to barter off which & get on board their returns, take them more time than to go & return from America. There are also Ten or Twelve ships from the middle States with Flour contracted for by the french minister at Philad^a to be paid in specie on the delivery. Many of these vessels have been here now six weeks & there is not a farthing of the money yet arrived from Paris to pay them, nor is there any persons here that can inform when it will come. These delays & uncertainties are common to all their ports on the Atlantic (Brest I believe excepted) and extremely injurious to the importations as well as to the individuals who wait. I think the evil is in the organization of the branches of the commission of Commerce & Approvisionment who seem totally unprepared to give that facility and expedition which alone is wanting to render the intercourse between the two countries active & useful as the resources the french Republic is in possession of is certainly entirely adequate to that end and their disposition is not wanting.

I have received a number of Bills drawn by the French agents in the west Indias particularly in St Domingo on the payer general of the marine of the Republic and still more applications from Citizens of the United States to know if those Bills woud be paid which have been refused by the Treasurer since nine months past. As there are large sums of these Bills in hands of our Citizens who received them from the agents of the french Government in the west Indias in payment for supplies made them I think it becomes a national concern to know whether these holders will be reimbursed or not. When at Paris I spoke with Mr Cambon the chief of the comitte of finance on the subject.[6] He gave me no direct answer. I shall be glad to know Sir if you have got any assurances on this business. With the greatest respect & esteem I have the honor to be Sir Your most obedient Servant

Joseph Fenwick

RC, DLC: Monroe Papers

1. JM's letter to Fenwick of 31 August 1794 has not been located.

2. Jean Dalbarade (1743-1819) was a French naval officer. He served as minister and then commissioner of the marine 1793-1795 (*La Grande Encyclopédie*).

3. Claude-Alexandre Ysabeau (1754-1831), a clergyman and teacher from Tours, was elected to the Convention in 1792. In 1794 the Convention appointed him and Jean-Lambert Tallien as its agents to in Bordeaux, charging them to suppress opposi-

tion to the revolution and to administer the district. Ysabeau became a member of the Committee of General Security in 1795 and later that year was elected to the Council of Elders (*La Grande Encyclopédie*).

4. Fenwick may have meant "decreed".

5. The enclosed letter and documents have not been identified.

6. Pierre Cambon (1756-1820) was a merchant from Montpellier. He was a member of the National Assembly and the Convention. Cambon served on the Committee of Public Safety and was minister of finance 1793-1794 (Paul Hanson, *Historical Dictionary of the French Revolution*, 54).

From Diego de Gardoqui

Madrid 9ᵗʰ Sepʳ 1794.

My dear Sir

Being informed of your arrival at Paris with the character of Minister from the United States I beg leave to renew you our old friendship in America & I congratulate you on your safe arrival here & sincerely wish you all manner of happyness. Permit me Dear sir to trouble you with the enclosed letter for my friend Mʳ John Otto[1] whom we knew in Newyork as charge d'affairs from France, for I learn by Mʳ Short that he is in Paris & it regards me particularly that it comes to his hands safely. Should he however be absent I should be glad you would open it & should be extremely oblig'd to you if you could procure me the contents which I hope will be the means of reestablishing my health.

Excuse me Dʳ Sir the liberty I take in giving you their trouble, & if in my publick or private character I can render you any service you may freely command Dear sir Your assᵈ friend & most obedᵗ servᵗ

James De Gardoqui

My best respects to your worthy Mʳˢ Monroe & to Mʳ Jay if with you.

Copy, ViFreJM

1. The correct name is Louis-Guillaume Otto. Gardoqui's letter to him, dated 8 September 1794 and written in Spanish, is in NN: Monroe Papers.

To André-Antoine Bernard[1]

Paris 10 Sepʳ 1794

Citizen President

The Convention having decreed that the flag of the American & French republicks should be united together & suspended in its own hall in testimony of eternal union & friendship between the two people, I have thought I could not better evince the impression this act has made on my mind, or the grateful sense of my constituents than by causing it to be correctly made & presented in their behalf to the representatives of the French people. Having executed the office according to the model prescribed by a late act of Congress,[2] I now commit it to the care of Captⁿ Barney an officer of distinguished merit in our own revolution and who now attends for the purpose of depositing it wherever you will be pleased to direct. I pray you therefore to accept it as a proof of the sensibility with which my country receives every act of friendship from our ally, and of the pleasure with which it cherishes every incident which tends to cement & consolidate the union between the two countries.

Jaˢ Monroe

RC, DLC: FCP—France

1. André-Antoine Bernard (1751-1818) served as president of the National convention 3-22 September 1794 (*Dictionnaire de Biographie Française*).

2. A law enacted on 13 January 1794 specified that the American flag would have fifteen alternating red and white stripes and fifteen white stars on a blue field (*U. S. Statutes at Large*, 1: 341).

To Philibert Buchot

Paris 13 Septembre 1794

Citizen

I found upon my arrival in the Republick two of the Servants of the United States, the Citizen la Motte, Consul at Havre Marat[1] and le Carpentier at Rouen under arrest and who Still continue in that Situation. Tis not an agreeable Spectacle to behold in Office in this Republick anyone under our Government bearing the mark of displeasure or distrust from yours. Tis certainly not the intention of the United States to employ or continue in employment, any persons of that description. I have considered it my duty to inquire into the character and conduct of these citizens, and it is but Justice to them to observe that from every thing I have been able to obtain on the subject, they appear to be deserving the confidence of both countries. Tis however possible that circumstances unknown to me have inspired different sentiments. In either case it is incumbent on me to call the attention of the Republick to the subject and request that in case there be no cause of complaint against them, they be liberated, and that they be brought to trial as soon as possible in case there is.

Ja[s] Monroe

RC, DLC: FCP—France

1. Claude-Adam Delamotte or La Motte was a partner in the business firm of Le Mesurier & Cie. He was appointed vice-consul at Le Havre by President Washington in 1790 and held that post until 1803. When JM arrived in France, La Motte was under arrest on suspicion of being hostile to the Revolution (*Jefferson Papers*, 12: 236; 15:206; Walter B. Smith, *America's Diplomats and Consuls of 1776-1865*, 64.).

From Philibert Buchot

Paris, le 28 fructidor l'an 2e de la République une & indivisible
ou 14 Septembre 1794.

Citoyen Ministre

Quoique les témoignages d'amitié et d'attachement que le Gouvernement & les Citoyens Américains ont constamment donnés à la République française ne laissent aucun doute sur leurs dispositions, il est à craindre que quelques individus n'abusent de la confiance qui subsiste sy heureusement entre les deux nations pour entretenir avec nos ennemis les plus inveterés des liaisons nuisibles au Succès de la République. Le double caractère de Citoyen Américain et Anglais dont plusieurs voyageurs sont révetus serait Surtout & à vraisemblablement été très favorable aux trahisons que le ministere de la Grande Bretagne s'efforce de multiplier en france. J'ai lieu de croire d'après ce là que tu Mettras la plus grande circonspection à n'accorder des passeports et des certificats de Citoyen Américain qu'à ceux qui auront leur domicile en Amerique et qui par leur civisme te paraitront dignes d'appartenir aux Etats unis. tu jugeras Sans doute de même que nous qu'un Américain ne peut conspirer contre la liberté Sans conspirer contre son propre pays, qui en a été le berceau.

La réserve avec laquelle les Passeports americains seront expediés deviendra un nouveau motif pour accorder à ceux qui en auront obtenu le plus haut dégré de protection.

Je Saisis cette occasion pour te prevenir que d'après un arrété du comité de Salut public, tous les passeports pour les pays étrangers doivent lui étre presentés avant d'etre legalisés par la Commission des Relations extérieures. Pour abreger cette formalité je te prie de vouloir bien adresser directement au Bureau du Comité les porteurs de ces passeports avant de les faire remettre au Secretariat de ma Commission.

Buchot

Editors' Translation

Paris 28 fructidor Year 2 of the Republic one and indivisible
or 14 September 1794

Citizen Minister

Although the marks of friendship and high regard that the American government and its citizens have consistently given to the French Republic leave no doubt as to their allegiances, it is feared that there are a few individuals who are abusing the trust that exists so happily between the two nations, in order to maintain with our most inveterate enemies contacts that are harmful to the success of the Republic. The dual status of American and English citizenship which several travelers hold would be above all, and in all likelihood has been, very favorable to the treasons that the British Ministry endeavors to spread in France. I have reason to believe that considering this, you will place the greatest caution in granting passports and documents only to those who reside in America and who seem to you to be worthy of belonging to the United States by their civic responsibility. You will no doubt deem as we do that an American citizen cannot conspire against freedom without conspiring against his own country the cradle of its birth.

The restraint with which the American passports will be delivered should become a new incentive to approve only those who have obtained the highest degree of security.

I take this opportunity to inform you that according to a decree of the Committee of Public Safety, the passports for foreign countries must be presented to it before being authenticated by the Commission of Foreign Relations. To shorten this procedure, I ask you kindly to have the passport bearers first address the Office of the Committee before they have them forwarded to the Secretary of my Commission.

Buchot

Copy, DNA: RG 59: Dispatches from France; enclosed in JM to Edmund Randolph, 16 October 1794. A draft dated 24 Fructidor (10 September) is in DLC: FCP—France. An imperfect translation is in DLC: Monroe Papers.

From M. G. Hector St. John Crèvecoeur

Paris 14th Septre 1794

Sir

An Antient Citizen and Inhabitant of North America, who has been long naturalised, and resided in it as a Farmer and Freeholder, who has shared in its painfull Strugles for freedom and Independence, begs leave, for want of The originals to present you with The Translation of Some Sketches he published in London, as Early as The year 1780,[1] soon after his being released from The severe confinement he underwent in New York & In Ireland.

The[y] are as you'll easily perceive, The natives untutored effusions of a heart zealous for The Glory and Prosperity of a Country, to which he has been Indebted These Thirty years & upwards, for The only civil and Political existence, he ever enjoyed, as well as for the only property he ever was possess'd of, rather Than The offspring of a Literary and Informed mind, for Truely Speaking, he held his own Plough, at The Time That most of them were written.

His only delight was That of manifesting to The world, The price at which the Americans have purchased Their Freedom, some of The many enormities and Wanton Cruelties, The English were guilty of, in Their vain attempt to subdue The continent, and of giving to Europe Some faint Idea, of That rural, civil & Political happiness, which peculiarly belongs to The Inhabitants of United America.

As a sincere and well meant Testimony of his Respect and Esteem, not only for The Minister Plenipotentiary, and The Senator of the United States, but also for the Warm and Enlightened friend of American Freedom and agriculture, The Author Sollicits your acceptance of Those Three volumes; he feels Incourag'd by The favourable reception They meet with from the Publick, both in London & here, as well as by Doctor Franklin's and Mr Jefferson's approbation. The Latter even Condescended to help him in protracting, and Tracing The maps; The Former Soon after his return To Philadelphia, honoured him in 1787 with a Letter relative to Those Sketches, and with Two American Medals which he received in New York.

That after having Cimented by your Wisdom and Talents, The Closest political and Commercial union, between The Two republicks of France and America, you may withdraw To The Honourable Shades of a Sweet and Philosphical retreat, on your Estate in Virigina, and There by your example and Incouragment, promote agricultural Improvements. The True and only Source of Freedom and wealth, is The Sincere Wish of him who also Intends Ending his Career under the Locusts and Wild Vines, he has long since reared, on the Plantation he possesses in the State of New York. Your very Hble & Fellow Citizen

MG Hector St John

RC, NN: Monroe Papers

1. Crèvecoeur misremembered the initial date of publication. He sold the essays that became *Letters from an American Farmer* to the publisher at London in May 1781 when he arrived in London while enroute to France, and the book was published in 1782. A two-volume French edition was published in 1784, followed by an expanded three-volume French edition in 1787 (*ANB*; *Encyclopedia Britannica*).

From Thomas Paine

Prison of the Luxembourg Sep[r] 14th 1794

I address this Memorial to you in Consequence of a letter I received from a friend 18th Fructedor (Sep[r] 4) in which he says "M[r] Monroe has told me that he has no orders (meaning from Congress) respecting you; but I am sure he will leave nothing undone to liberate you—but from what I can learn from all the late Americans you are not considered either by the Government or by the individuals as an American Citizen—you have been made a french Citizen which you have accepted, and you have further made yourself a Servant of the french republic, and therefore it would be out of character for an American Minister to interfere in their interior concerns—you must therefore either be liberated out of complement to America, or stand your trial which you have a right to demand."

This information was so unexpected by me that I am at a loss how to answer it. I know not on what principle it originates; whether from an Idea that I had voluntarily abandoned my Citizenship of America for that of France, or from any article of the American Constitution applied to me. The first is untrue with respect to any intention on my part; and the second is without foundation as I shall shew in the course of this memorial.

The Idea of confering the honour of Citizenship upon foreigners who had distinguished themselves in propagating the principles of liberty and humanity, in opposition to despotism war and bloodshed, was first proposed by me to la Fayette at the commencement of the french Revolution when his heart appeared to be warmed with those principles. My motive in making this proposal was to render the people of different Nations more fraternal than they had been or then were.—I observed that almost every branch of Science had possessed itself of the exercise of this Right so far as it regarded its own institution. Most of the Academies and Societies in Europe and also those of America confered the rank of honorary Member upon foreigners eminent in knowledge, and made them in fact, citizens of their literary or Scientific Republic, without affecting or anyways diminishing their Rights of Citizenship in their own Country, or in other societies: and why the Science of Government should not have the Same advantages, or why the people of one Nation should not by their Representatives exercise the Right of confering the honour of Citizenship upon individuals eminent in another Nation without affecting <u>their</u> rights of Citizenship in their proper Country is a problem yet to be solved.

I now proceed to Remark on that part of the letter, in which the writer says, "that <u>from what he can learn from all the late Americans I am not considered in America, either by the Government or by the individuals as an American Citizen.</u>"

In the first place, I wish to ask, what is here meant by the Government of America? The Members who compose the Government are only individuals when in Conversation, and who most probably hold very different opinions upon the Subject.—Have Congress as a body made any declaration that they now no longer consider me as a Citizen? If they have not, any thing they may say is no more than the opinion of individuals, and consequently is not legal authority, nor any ways sufficient authority to deprive any Man of his Citizenship. Besides whether a man has forfeited his Rights of Citizenship is a question not determinable by Congress, but by a Court of Judicature and a Jury, and must depend upon evidence and the application of some Law or Article of the Constitution to the Case. No such proceeding has yet been had, and consequently I remain a Citizen untill it be had, be that decision what it may; for there can be no such thing as a Suspension of Rights in the interim.

I am very well aware and always was, of the Article of the Constitution which says, as nearly as I can recollect the words, that <u>any Citizen of the United States who shall accept any title, place, or office, from any foreign king prince or State shall forfeit and lose his right of Citizenship of the United States</u>.

Had the Article said, that <u>any Citizen of the United States who shall be Member of any foreign Convention for the purpose of forming a free Constitution shall forfeit and lose the Right of Citizen of the United States</u>," the Article had been directly applicable to me; but the Idea of such an Article never could have entered the mind of the American Convention, and the present Article is altogether foreign to the case with respect to me.—It supposes a Government in active existance, and not a Government dissolved; and it supposes a Citizen of America accepting titles and offices under that Government, and not a Citizen of America who gives his assistance in a Convention chosen by the people for the purpose of forming a Government de nouveau founded on their authority.

The late Constitution and Government of France was dissolved the 10th of August 1792. The National legislative Assembly then in being supposed itself without sufficient Authority to continue its sittings, and it proposed to the departments to elect, not another legislative Assembly, but a Convention for the express purpose of forming a New Constitution. When the Assembly were discoursing on this matter some of the Members said that they wished to gain all the assistance possible upon the subject of free constitutions, and expressed a wish to elect and invite foreigners of any Nation to the Convention who had distinguished themselves in defending, explaining and propagating the principles of Liberty. It was on this occasion that my Name was mentioned in the Assembly. After this, a deputation from a body of the people, in order to remove any objection that might be made against my assisting at the proposed Convention, requested the Assembly as their Representatives to give me the title of french Citizen; after which I was elected a Member of the Convention (in four different departments) as is already known.

The case therefore is, that I accepted nothing from any King, Prince, or State, nor from any Government, for france was without any Government except what arose from common consent and the necessity of the case. Neither "<u>did I make myself a servant of the 'french Republic'</u>" as the letter alluded to expresses, for at that time France was not a Republic not even in Name. She was altogether a people in a State of Revolution.

It was not until the Convention met that France was declared a Republic and Monarchy abolished; soon after which a Committee was elected, of which I was a Member, to form a Constitution, which was presented to the Convention the 15th & 16th of Feby following, but was not to be taken into Consideration till after the expiration of two Months, and if approved of by the Convention was then to be referred to the people for their acceptance with such additions or amendments as the Convention should make.

In thus employing myself upon the formation of a Constitution I certainly did nothing inconsistent with the American Constitution. I took no oath of allegiance to France nor any other oath whatever. I considered the Citizenship they had presented me with as an honorary Mark of respect paid to me not only as a friend to Liberty but as an American Citizen. My acceptance of that, or of the deputiship, not confered on me by any King Prince or State, but by a people in a State of revolution and contending for liberty, required no transfer of my allegiance or of my Citizenship from America to France. There I was a real Citizen paying Taxes; here, I was a voluntary friend, employing myself on a temporary service. Every American in Paris knew that it was my constant intention to return to America as soon as a Constitution should be established and that I anxiously waited for that event.

But it was not the Americans only but the Convention also that knew what my intentions were upon that subject. In my last discourse delivered at the Tribune of the Convention Jany 19. 1793 on the

Motion for suspending the execution of Louis 16th I said (the deputy Bancal read the translation in french)—"It unfortunately happens that the person who is the subject of the present discussion is considered by the Americans as having been the friend of their Revolution. His execution will be an affliction to them, and it is in your power not to wound the feelings of your Ally. Could I speak the french language I would descend to your Bar and in their name become your petitioner to respit the Execution of the sentence."—"As the Convention was elected for the express purpose of forming a Constitution its continuance cannot be longer than four or five months more at furthest; and if, after my return to America, I should employ myself in writing the history of the french Revolution, I had rather record a thousand Errors on the side of Mercy than be obliged to tell one Act of severe Justice."—"Ah Citizens! give not the Tyrant of England the triumph of seeing the Man perish on a scaffold who had aided my much-loved America." Does this look as if I had abandoned America? But if she abandons me, in the situation I am in, to gratify the enemies of humanity, let that disgrace be to herself. But I know the people of America better than to believe it, tho' I undertake not to answer for every individual.

When this discourse was pronounced Marat[1] launched himself into the middle of the Hall and said that "I voted against the punishment of death because I was a Quaker." I replied, "that I voted against it both morally and politically."

I certainly went a great way, considering the rage of the times, in endeavouring to prevent that execution. I had many reasons for so doing. I judged, and events have shewn that I judged rightly, that if they once began shedding blood there was no knowing where it would end; and as to what the world might call honour, the execution would appear like a Nation killing a Mouse; and in a political view would serve to transfer the hereditary claim to some more formidable Enemy. The Man could do no more mischief, and that which he had done was not only from the Vice of his education, but was as much the fault of the Nation in restoring him after he had absconded June 21st 1791 as it was his. I made the proposal for imprisonment until the end of the war and perpetual banishment after the war instead of the punishment of death. Upwards of three hundred deputies voted for this proposal. The sentence for absolute death (for some Members had voted the punishment of death conditionally) was carried by a Majority of twenty-five out votes out of more than seven hundred.

I return from this degression to the proper subject of my Memorial. I ever must deny that the Article of the American Constitution already mentioned can be applied either verbally, intentionally, or constructively to me. It undoubtedly was the intention of the Convention that framed it to preserve the purity of the American Republic from being debased by foreign and foppish customs; but it never could be its intention to act against the principles of liberty by forbidding its Citizens to assist in promoting those principles in foreign Countries. Neither could it be its intention to act against the principles of gratitude. France had aided America in the establishment of her Revolution when invaded and oppressed by England and her Auxiliaries; France in her turn was invaded and oppressed by a combination of foreign despots. In this situation I conceived it an Act of gratitude in me, as a Citizen of America, to render her in Return the best Services I could perform. I came to France (for I was in England when I received the invitation) not to enjoy ease, emoluments, and foppish honours as the Article supposes, but to encounter difficulties and dangers in defence of liberty: And I much question whether those who now malignantly seek (for some I believe do) to turn this to my injury would have had courage to have done the same thing. I am sure Governeur Morris would not, for he told me the second day after my arrival, that the Austrians and Prussians, who were then at Verdun, would be in Paris in a fortnight. "I have no Idea, said he, "that seventy thousand disciplined Troops can be stopt in their march by any power in France."

Besides the reasons I have already given for accepting the invitation to the Convention, I had another that has reference only to America, and which I mentioned to Mʳ Pinckney the night before I left London to come to Paris—"<u>that it was to the interest of America to change the system of European Governments and place on the same principle with herself.</u>" Mʳ Pinckney agreed fully in the same opinion. I have done my part towards it.

It is certain that Governments upon similar systems associate better together than those that are discordant, and the Same Rule holds good with respect to the people living under them. In the latter case they offend each other by Pity, or by reproach, and the discordancy carries itself to matters of Commerce. I am not an ambitious Man, but perhaps I have been an ambitious American. I have wished to see America the <u>Mother Church</u> of Governments; and I have done my utmost to exalt her character and her condition.

I have now stated sufficient matter to shew that the Article in question is not applicable to me, and that any such application to my injury, as well in circumstances as in Rights, is contrary both to the letter and intention of that Article, and is illegal and unconstitutional; Neither do I believe that any Jury in America, when they are informed of the whole of the Case, would give a Verdict to deprive me of my Rights upon that article. The Citizens of America, I believe are not very fond of permitting forced and indirect explanations to be put upon matters of this kind. I know not what were the merits of the Case with respect to the person who was prosecuted for acting as Prize Master to a french Privateer, but I know that the Jury gave a Verdict against the prosecution. The Rights I have acquired are dear to me. They have been acquired by honorable means, and by dangerous Service, in the worst of times, and I cannot passively permit them to be wrested from me. I conceive it my duty to defend them as the Case involves a Constitutional and public question, which is, how far the power of the federal Government extends in depriving any Citizen of his Rights of Citizenship, or of suspending them.

That the explanation of National Treaties belong to Congress is strictly constitutional, but not the explanation of the Constitution itself, any more than the explanation of Law, in the case of individual Citizens. These are altogether judiciary Questions. It is however worth observing that Congress in explaining the Article of the Treaty with respect to french Prizes and french Privateers confined itself strictly to the letter of the Article. Let them explain the Article of the Constitution with respect to me in the Same manner, and the decision, did it appertain to them, could not deprive me of my Rights of Citizenship nor suspend them, for I have accepted nothing from any king, prince, state, or Government.

You will please to observe, that I speak as if the federal Government had made some declaration upon the subject of my Citizenship; whereas the fact is otherwise, and your saying that you have no order respecting me is a proof of it. Those therefore who propagate the Report of my not being considered as a Citizen of America by the <u>Government</u> do it to the prolongation of my imprisonment and without authority; for Congress <u>as a Government</u> has neither decided upon it, nor taken the matter into consideration; and I request you to caution such persons against spreading such opinions.—But be these matters as they may I cannot have a doubt that you find and feel the case very different since you have heard what I have to say and known what my situation is, than you did before your arrival.

I know not what opinions have been circulated in America. It may have been supposed there that I had intentionally and voluntarily abandoned America and that my Citizenship had ceased by my own choice. I can easily conceive there are those in that Country who would take such a proceeding on my part somewhat in disgust. The Idea of forsaking old friendships for new acquaintances is not agreeable. I am a little warranted in making this supposition by a letter I received some time ago from the wife of one of the Georgia delegates, in which she says "your friends on this side the water cannot be reconciled to the Idea of your abandoning America."

I have never abandoned her in <u>Thought</u>, <u>Word</u> or <u>Deed</u>; and I feel it incumbent upon me to give this assurance to the friends I have in that Country and with whom I have always intended and am determined, if the possibility exists, to close the Scene of my Life.—It is there that I have made myself a home—It is there that I have given the services of my best days. America never saw me flinch from her cause in the most gloomy and perilous of her situations; and I know there are those in that Country who will not flinch from me. If I have enemies (and every Man has some) I leave them to the enjoyment of their ingratitude.*

It is somewhat extraordinary that the Idea of my not being a Citizen of America should have arisen only at the time that I am imprisoned in France because, or on the pretence that I am a foreigner. The case involves a Strange contradiction of Ideas. None of the Americans who came to France whilst I was in liberty had conceived any such Idea or circulated any such opinion, and why it should arise now is a matter yet to be explained. However discordant the late American Minister Governeur Morris and the late french Committee of public safety were, it suited the purpose of both that I should be continued in Arrestation. The former wished to prevent my return to America that I should not expose his misconduct, and the latter lest I should publish to the world the history of its wickedness. Whilst that Minister and the committee continued I had no expectation of liberty.—I speak here of the Committee of which Robespiere was Member.

Painful as the want of Liberty may be, it is a consolation to me to believe that my imprisonment proves to the world that I had no share in the murderous system that then reigned. That I was an Enemy to it both morally and politically is known to all who had any knowledge of me; and could I have written french as well as I can english I would publicly have exposed its wickedness and shewn the ruin with which it was pregnant. Those who have esteemed me on former occasions, whether in America or in Europe, will, I know, feel no cause to abate that esteem when they reflect, that <u>imprisonment with preservation of Character is preferable to liberty with disgrace</u>.

I here close my Memorial and proceed to offer you a proposal, that appears to me suited to all the Circumstances of the Case, which is, that you Reclaim me conditionally until the opinion of Congress can be obtained on the Subject of my Citizenship of America; and that I remain in liberty under your protection during that time.

I found this proposal upon the following grounds.

First—you say you have no orders respecting me. Consequently, you have no orders <u>not</u> to reclaim me, and in this case you are left discretionary judge whether to reclaim or not. My proposal therefore unites a consideration of your Situation with my own.

Secondly. I am put in Arrestation because I am a foreigner. It is therefore necessary to determine to what Country I belong. The Right of determining this question cannot appertain exclusively to the Committee of Public Safety or of General Surety; because I appeal to the Minister of the United States and shew that my Citizenship of that Country is good and Valid; refering at the same time through the agency of the Minister, my claim of Right to the opinion of Congress. It being a matter between two Governments.

Thirdly. France does not claim me for a Citizen; neither do I set up any claim of Citizenship in France. The question is simply is, whether I am, or am not, a Citizen of America. I am imprisoned here on the decree for imprisoning foreigners, because, say they, I was born in England. I say in answer, that though born in England, I am not a Subject of the English Government any more than any other American who was born, as they all were, under the Same government; or than the Citizens of France are Subjects of the french Monarchy under which they were born. I have twice taken the oath of Abjuration to the british king and Government and of allegiance to America: Once as a Citizen of the State of Pennsylvania in 1776, and again before Congress administered to me by the President Mr Hancock when I was appointed Secretary in the Office of foreign Affairs in 1777.

The letter before quoted in the first page of this Memorial says that "it would be out of Character for an American Minister to interfere in the internal affairs of France." This declaration goes on the Idea that I am a Citizen of France and a Member of the Convention which is not the fact. The Convention have declared me to be a foreigner and consequently the citizenship and the electon are nul and void. It also has the appearance of a decision that the article of the Constitution respecting grants made to American Citizens by foreign kings princes or States is applicable to me, which is the very point in question, and against the application of which I contend. I state evidence to the Minister to shew that I am strictly within the letter and meaning of that Article; that it cannot operate against me; and I apply to him for the protection that, I conceive, I have a right to ask and to receive. The internal affairs of France are out of the question with respect to my application or his interference. I ask it not as a Citizen of France for I am not one; I ask it not as a Member of the convention for I am not one; both these things, as before said have been rendered nul and void; I ask it not as a Man against whom there is any accusation, for there is none; I ask it not as an exile from America whose independance I have honorably and generously contributed to establish; I ask it as a Citizen of America deprived of his liberty in France under the plea of being a foreigner, and I ask it because I conceive I am entitled to it upon every principle of Constitutional Justice and National honour.

But though I thus positively assert my claim because I believe it to be my Right, it is perhaps most eligible, in the present situation of things, to put that claim upon the footing I have already mentioned, that is, that the Minister reclaims me conditionally untill the opinion of Congress can be obtained on the subject of my Citizenship of America, and that I remain in liberty under the protection of the Minister during that interval.

N. B. I should have added that as Govr Morris could not inform Congress of the Cause of my Arrestation, as he knew it not himself, it is to be supposed that Congress were not enough acquainted with the Case to give any directions respecting me when you came away.

Thomas Paine.

* I subjoin in a Note, for the sake of wasting the solitude of a prison, the answer that I gave to the part of the letter above mentioned. It is not inapplicable to the subject of this Memorial; but it contains somewhat of a melancholy Idea a little predictive that I hope is not becoming true so soon.

"You touch me on a very tender point when you say, that my friends on your side the Water cannot be reconciled to the Idea of my abandoning America. They are Right. I had rather see my horse Button eating the Grass of Borden-Town or Morrisania than see all the Pomp and shew of Europe.—A thousand Years hence (for I must indulge a few thoughts) perhaps in less, America may be what Europe now is. The innocence of her character that won the hearts of all Nations in her favour may sound like a romance and her inimitable virtue as if it had never been. The ruin of that liberty which thousands bled for, or struggled to obtain may just furnish materials for a village tale or extort a sigh from rustic sensibility, whilst the fashionable of that day, envelloped in dissipation, shall deride the principle and deny the fact.

"When we contemplate the fall of Empires and the extinction of the Nations of the ancient world, we see but little to excite our regret, than the mouldering ruins of pompous palaces, magnificent monuments, lofty pyramids and walls and Towers of the most costly workmanship; but when the empire of America shall fall, the subject for contemplative sorrow will be infinitely greater than crumbling brass and marble can inspire. It will not then be said, here stood a temple of vast antiquity; here rose a babel of invisible height; or there a palace of sumptuous extravagance:—But here, Ah, painful thought! the noblest work of human Wisdom, the grandest scene of human glory, the fair cause of Freedom rose and fell.—Read this, and then ask if I forget America."

RC, DLC: Monroe Papers

Paine published this letter as a pamphlet in Paris under the date of 10 September 1794. Both Philip Foner, *The Complete Writings of Thomas Paine* (2: 1345) and Moncure D. Conway, *The Writings of Thomas Paine* (3: 175) use this date for the letter, although Foner cites the copy of the letter in DLC: Monroe Papers as his source, which is clearly dated September 14. Conway used a copy in the British Museum, but gives no indication that it bore a different date than the LC copy, to which he refers (*Writings of Paine*, 3: 150). An abridged version of this letter printed as an appendix in Paine's *Letter to George Washington* (Philadelphia ,1796) is dated "Sept. 10th, 1796."

1. Jean-Paul Marat (1743-1793) was the publisher and editor of the newspaper *L'Ami du Peuple* and a member of the National Convention. His verbal attacks in both his newspaper and on the floor of the Convention earned him many enemies. The Girondins brought him before the Revolutionary Tribunal in April 1793, but he won acquittal. He was murdered four months later (Paul R. Hanson, *Historical Dictionary of the French Revolution*).

To Edmund Randolph

Paris 15th Septr 1794.

As soon as I could command a moment's leisure, I applied myself to the immediate duties of my station. I found many of my Countrymen here labouring under embarrassments of a serious kind, growing out of the War, and was soon furnished with like complaints from others in several of the seaports. Correct information upon every point was my first object, for unless I knew the nature & extent of the evil, I could not seek a remedy. I encouraged therefore by my letters these representations, as the only means by which I could acquire it. Nor was it difficult to be obtained, for the parties interested had been too deeply affected and long delayed, to be remiss upon the present occasion. In the course of a few weeks, I believe most of the complaints which had been occasioned by the War, and especially where the parties were present either in person or by attorney, were laid before me. By analyzing them (including those which were committed to me from your department whilst in Philadelphia) I found they might be classed under the following heads.

1. Those who were injured by the embargo at Bordeaux.

2. Those who had claims upon the Republic for supplies rendered to the Government of St Domingo.

3. Those who had brought cargoes in for Sale and were detained by delay of payment or some other cause.

4. Those who had been brought in by the Ships of the Republic in derogation of the treaty of amity and commerce, and were subjected to like detention and delay.

5. Those who had been taken at sea or elsewhere, and were confined in derogation of the treaty of amity and Commerce or rights of citizen-ship in the United States.

Upon the two first heads and indeed upon the two latter, so far as compensation to the injured parties was in question, I had no difficulty how to act. Your instructions had fully marked the course to be taken. I therefore required that compensation be made as soon as possible, and upon just principles, according to the contract where such was the case, and the fair estimated value, where it was not. But the two latter involved in them something more than the mere adjustment of existing claims, and which closed the scene when that was made. They grew out of measures which if suffered to continue might create like injuries every week, & which would require a like interposition on my part. I therefore considered it my duty not only to require a full indemnity to the claimants, as in the other instances, but to mount to the source of the evil and seek a remedy commensurate therewith.

I found that the delays above spoken of did not proceed from interest, or design on their part: from interest they could not, for they not only disgusted and often injured the claimants, but likewise exposed the Government to considerable loss, upon account of demurage.[1] And if there was no motive of interest there could be none for design. They proceeded in fact from the System of trade adopted here by which the whole commerce of the Country was taken into the hands of the republic itself. The regulation was such, that none but the Officers of Government could purchase, nor could any contract be concluded and executed in any of the Sea ports, or elsewhere than in Paris. This threw every case into the hands of a board of commerce, in this City, who were otherwise borne down with an immense weight of the most extensive and complicated duties. The defect in our arrangements too, had increased the imbarrassment; for as we had no consul here every Captain or Super-cargo became his own negotiator, and as they were generally ignorant of the City, the language and of the prices last given, they were badly calculated for the purpose. Every new cargo formed a distinct negotiation, and as there was no system on the part of the vendors, who wished, as was natural, to make the most of their voyage, they usually asked an extravagant price for it in the first instance. This occasioned a kind of traffic between the parties, and which frequently terminated in the disgust of both, and particularly of the vendors, who after they were wearied out with the clerks in the department, and whose duty it was to receive them, generally assigned the business over to some agent, and who as he was not cloathed with any public character, could neither be much respected by the French Government, nor possessed in any high degree of the confidence of his employers. Such was the state of our trade in this republic, and such the cause of the delay. As soon therefore as I understood it, I considered it my duty to bring the subject before the Government, and desire on its part a suitable remedy: and if the person lately appointed does not soon arrive, I shall deem it equally necessary to nominate some one as Consul provisionally, to take charge of the business on ours. And if he does arrive I am by no means certain it will remedy the difficulty, for reasons I shall hereafter explain.

I had more difficulty in determining how to act on the 4th point. I was not instructed to desire a repeal of the decree, and did not know but that it had been tolerated, from the soundest motives of political expedience. This Republic had declined calling on us to execute the guarantee, from a spirit of magnanimity, and a strong attachment to our welfare.

This consideration entitled it to some attention in return. An attempt to press it, within the pale of the stipulation contained in the 23[d] and 24th articles of the treaty of Amity and commerce, might give birth to sentiments of a different kind, and create a disposition to call on us to execute that of the treaty of alliance. The subject was therefore of the utmost delicacy, and I saw that I could not enter on it without the greatest care. But yet I was persuaded that France gained nothing by the departure, and had reason to believe if it were otherwise that she would at the present time concede it for our accomodation: and I knew its importance to our commerce, and especially as it would deprive the cabinet of S[t] James of the Smallest pretext for continuing the violation on its part. Upon full consideration of all these circumstances the paper presented, was drawn and I trust whatever may be its effect, it will have the approbation of the President, since it may prove a beneifcial one, and has in no respect compromitted him. My note was presented a few days past,[2] and I expect an answer as soon as circumstances will permit, paying due regard to the immense weight of business before the department.

Upon the article of Citizenship, I have as yet said nothing. I did not wish to complicate the Subjects which I presented before them too much at any one time. It is however an important one, and shall be soon attended to, as shall likewise the claim for reimbursement, of 50,000 dollars, advanced to the French Emigrants from S[t] Domingo.

Nothing of great importance has lately taken place in the public councils. The remaining spirit of ancient parties has, it is true occasionally shewn itself, but not with its former vigor, for it seems in a great measure to have withdrawn, and to lurk in the bosoms of the more inveterate only. Happily a different spirit, more congenial with the temper of the nation, and which inclines to humanity, to peace, and concord, seems to pervade the great mass of the convention. I think this latter will soon prevail so as not only to prevent, at least for the present further enormities, but to heal in some degree the wounds which have already been inflicted. Some latter circumstances authorise this expectation. Barrere, Collot D'Herbois, and Billaud Varennes,[3] of the committee of public safety, and several of the Committee of surety general, were suspected by many of having countenanced and supported the measures of Robespierre, and it was apprehended that after the perfect and preternatural calm, which ensued his execution, should subside, some discussion would take place on that subject. Accordingly they were lately denounced by le Cointre of Versailles, who brought forward a long list of charges against them.[4] But it was immediately seen, that the party in favor of the denunciation, tho' violent, was weak. The convention heard the accusation with patience, and rejected it with disdain, and le Cointre himself was eventually censured as a disturber of the public repose. Many of this party were now in their turn alike agitated and alarmed, because they thought they saw, in the rejection of the motion the invincible strength of the other party, and the certainty of their own fate. But they were superficial observers of the course of the present revolution, and of the theatre on which they acted. They did not perceive that there was a force in the convention actuated by more humane and dignified principles, able to control both, and render their extravagant and pernicious efforts abortive and harmless. This latter fact was farther demonstrated by an event which followed immediately after. Under the re-organization of the committee of public safety, it became necessary to re-elect its members; and, if the influence of those lately denounced had preponderated, they would of course have been re-chosen. But the contrary was the case, for they were every one rejected, and others preferred in their stead. I have mentioned this incident because I deem it an important one in the character of the present moment, tending to prove the certainty with which the revolution progresses towards a happy close, since the preponderance of those Councils which are equally distinguished for their Wisdom, temperance and humanity, continues to increase.

Nor is fortune less propitious to the affairs of this Republic in the field than in the cabinet. Within a few days past, Conde and Valenciennes have surrendered to its victorious arms. About 6,000 troops were taken in these garrisons and 1100 emigrants,[5] and which latter were immediately put to the sword. The rigor with which the emigrants have been pursued continues nearly the same, and seems still to be dictated equally by the sentiment of the public councils and the people at large: it will not, therefore, be easily or soon removed.

The Surrender of these garrisons has relieved from a state of inactivity about 50,000 men who were immediately added to the armies upon the Meuse and on the frontier of Holland. These armies are at present of great strength and certainly upon the ordinary rules of calculation, not to be resisted by the force now embodied against them. In point of numbers they are by far superior, and they possess the means by which this superiority may be increased at pleasure and to any amount. Their discipline too is exact, their spirits high, and enterprize astonishingly great. Whilst on the other side every thing wears a more gloomy aspect. Their troops are dispirited and daily wasting away by the events of War, and reinforcements have been for a long time past with difficulty obtained, & seem now to be exhausted, or at least at a stand. And to increase the embarrassments on their part, 'tis said a dispute has taken place between Cobourg and York[6] for the command, in case they should unite their forces: the latter having set up a claim in consequence of the great force, Prussians, &c. in British pay.

Cobourg occupies at present a position near Maestricht, and York[5] one in the neighbourhood of Bergen-op-zoom. 'Tis thought the French will direct their principal force towards those posts, since their conquest will not only lay open the whole Country to the Rhine, but likewise deprive Holland of its chief barrier. They are strong and well provided but deemed by no means impregnable to the ardor and enterprize of the French troops. 'Tis therefore probable some severe rencontres may soon take place in each quarter, for surely nothing but absolute despair will induce the combined powers to abandon them and which they must otherwise do, in case the french continue to exert themselves with their usual vigor.

You will observe I have adopted in my movements here the plan of conciliation, and that I have intimated in consideration of the alliance subsisting between the two Republics, the preference we have on that and other accounts, for France to any other country. I have done so not only in obedience to the dictates of my own Judgment, but because I thought I thereby followed the spirit of your instructions, and because I well knew I could not otherwise count upon success in any thing I undertook. In the brilliant career of victory which now attends the arms of the Republic you will readily conceive that a cordial but dignified tone, is better calculated to produce a happy effect, than one which was distant, formal, and merely diplomatic. And I was the more inclined to do it from a belief that I saw in the temper of the nation a sincere disposition to accomodate us in all cases within its power, and to cultivate the most perfect harmony between the two countries. Whether this is real or fallacious, time, and a very short one, will now disclose, since I have presented before the Government propositions which must eventually test it. I have the honor to be with great respect and esteem Your most obedient servant

Ja[s] Monroe

Copy, DNA: RG 59: Dispatches from France

1. Demurrage is compensation paid to a ship owner for the detention of a ship in port or for an unnessary delay in its departure (*Oxford English Dictionary*).

2. JM to the Committee of Public Safety, 3 September 1794, above.

3. Jacques-Nicolas Billaud de Varennes (1756-1819), an unsuccessful lawyer from LaRochelle, was one of the first members of the Committee of Public Safety, where he became known for his ruthlessness. He was condemned with Barère and Collot on 26 May 1795 and sentenced to deportation to Guyane (Guyana). He was given amnesty shortly after Napoleon's coup d'état in 1797, but refused to return to France (Bernard Gainot, *Dictionnaire des Membres du Comité de Salut Public*, 85-87; M. J. Sydenham, *The First French Republic 1792-1804*, 326).

4. Laurent Lecointre (1742-1805) was elected a deputy to the National Convention from Seine and Oise in 1792. Lecointre first attacked the terrorists, on 12 Fructidor (29 August) then again on 3 October 1794, maintaining that the members of the former committees were lying when they denied their solidarity with Robespierre, and demanding that they be indicted The Plain would not go this far fearing it might put itself on trial. (Jean Tulard, Jean–François Fayard, Alfred Fierro, *Historire et Dictionnaire de la Révolution Française, 1789-1799*).

5. The correct appellation is *émigrés*, which refers those Frenchmen who fled the country at the time of the Revolution and especially those who took up arms in the royalist cause (Samuel Scott and Barry Rothaus, *Historical Dictionary of the French Revolution*).

6. Frederick, duke of York, (1762-1827) was the second son of George III of England. In 1793 he became colonel of the 1st Regiment of Guards, and given command of English troops in Belgium. During three engagements his losses were so great as to leave but a remnant of his troops with whom he re-embarked for England. It was not until 1799 that he received another command (Jules Michelet, *Histoire de la Révolution Française*, 2: 1588).

From Etienne-Solomon Reybaz

Paris 29 Fructidor 2$\underline{d}$ year of the French republick [15 September 1794]

Citizen minister

I have the honor to inform you that the government of Geneva, upon receiving intelligence so flattering to our republick, of what passed in the sitting of the national convention of the 6$\underline{th}$ of fructidor, has suspended in its own municipal house, in sign of joy and harmony, three colours similar to those which float together in the hall of this convention; and that those united emblems of three republicks have excited with us universal applauses.

The republick of Geneva will hear with sincere pleasure that the U States of America, instructed by you of this event, has rec$\underline{d}$ favorably this testimony of fraternity.

I am happy on my own part citizen minister to have been the organ of these sentiments to you.

Reybaz

Copy (in JM's handwriting), NN: Monroe Papers

Etienne-Solomon Reybaz (1737-1804) was the minister to France from the Republic of Geneva. His reception by the National Convention on 23 August 1794 was similar to the one given JM eight days earlier. The Convention voted the same day to display the Genevan flag in its hall alongside the French and American flags (Linda Frey and Marsha Frey, "The Reign of the Charlatans Is Over: The French Revolutionary Attack on Diplomatic Practice," *Journal of Modern History*, 65 (1993): 723).

To Etienne-Solomon Reybez

[September 1794]

Citizen Minister

I have received, with great satisfaction the account you have been pleased to render me of the generous impression which the suspension of the flags of the three Republics of America, France and Geneva, in the Hall of the National Convention, has excited in the breasts of your countrymen. The standards of Republics should always be ranged together, and I am perfectly satisfied, that this event will be received with equal joy by the government and citizens of the United States, to whom I shall communicate it. I beg of you Citizen Minister to be assured of the solicitude which the government & People of America feel for the freedom, prosperity and happiness of the Republic of Geneva, and of the pleasure with which I shall at all times become the instrument of the most intimate and friendly communications between them.

Copy, NN: Monroe Papers (first page) and DLC: Monroe Papers (second page)

From Adrienne Lafayette

au plessis nº 23 5eme etage 2ᵈ Sans Culotides

L'an 2 de L[a] R[épublique] F[rançoise] [18 September 1794]

Dear Sir,

toutes Les fois que jentends parler de vous, je recois de nouvelles assurances, de L'intéret que vous voulés bien prendre a ce qui me touche, et ma confiance a droit de Saccroitre. permettes qu'aujourd'huy je vous en offre un nouveau temoignage, en vous envoyant l'homme du monde a qui je dois Le plus, et en vous demandant Le service Le plus touchant pour mon cœur. celui qui vous porte cette Lettre a constamment donne des soins a celles que je pleure, pendant tout Le tems de Leur captivité; il a ete Leur consolation dans Les derniers momens, avec un courage Sans exemple, et au dessus de toute expression. il est resté depositaire des enfans de cette dame cherie, qui partageoit tous mes Sentimens, et dont La perte est pour moi, celle de tout bonheur dans cette douloureuse vie, il est a La fois Le pere et La mere, de ces pauvres enfans, et Leur seule ressource dans tous Les genres. Sa seule ambition est de ne jamais Les abandoner, c'est Le dernier vœu de Leur tendre mere.

peutêtre, my dear Sir pourrés vous en assurer Lexecution, je vous Laisse a juger quel titre vous auriés a ma reconnoissance. Lexemple des grandes vertus, et Surtout de La generosite, est Si rare qu'on peut, ce me semble, feliciter celui qui auroit Le moyen de Connoitre, a plus forte raison de servir, un homme qui en est un modele. c'est un soulagement a tout ce qu'on voit de perversite. j'aime a croire que vous Sentirés Le prix de cette Satisfaction, et qu'elle animera votre interêt pour celui que je vous envoye. il causera avec vous, et vous jugerés par vous-même, La pureté de Ses vues. je vous reponds, de Sa Sincerite, de Sa discretion, de toutes ses vertus. et je vous demande pour mes petis neveux, Si cruellement orphelins, tous Les services qu'il peut solliciter de vous, non seulement au nom de tous mes malheurs, mais au nom de celui qu'il ne m'est permis de nommer, qui cherissoit tendrement Leur mere, dont ce dernier malheur achevera d'empoisonner La vie, j'en suis sure, et qui partagera ma reconnoissance de tout ce que vous pourrés faire pour Lui et pour eux. adieu, Lémotion de mon cœur est trop forte pour que je puisse exprimer aucun de mes sentimens. Salut et fraternité

N Lf

Editors' Translation

at Plessis no 23 fifth floor 2 Sans Culottides[1]

Year 2 of the French Republic [18 September 1794]

Dear Sir,

Every time I hear your name spoken, I am reassured by the attention you willingly assume for all that affects me, and my confidence grows. Allow me today to offer you a new testimony of it by sending you a man of society to whom I owe the most and in demanding the service from you that tugs at my heart the most. He who bears this letter to you has constantly provided care for those whom I weep during the entire length of their imprisonment. He has been their consolation during their last moments, with a courage beyond comparison. He has remained the guardian to the children of this dearest lady who shared all my affections, and whose loss is for me that of all happiness in this life full of sorrow. He has been both father and mother to these poor children, and their only means of support of any kind. His sole ambition is never to abandon them; this was the dying wish of their sweet mother.[2]

Perhaps, my dear Sir, you will be able to ensure its realization. I leave it to you Sir to judge what claim on my gratitude you would have. An example of great virtues and especially that of generosity is so rare that it seems to me one ought to congratulate anyone who serves as an example. Such a one is a consolation to all that one sees of depravity. I like to think you understand the price of this consolation, and that this will deepen your interest in him whom I send you. He will converse with you, and you will judge for yourself the purity of his convictions. I vouch for his sincerity, his discretion, and all his virtues, and I ask you for all the help he can obtain for my little nephews so cruelly orphaned, not only in the name of all my sufferings, but for one whose name I am not permitted to say,[3] who tenderly cherished their mother whose last ordeal resulted in poisoning life for him, I am sure of it, and who will share my gratitude for all you are able to do for him and for them. Adieu, the emotion of my heart is too strong for me to express any of my feelings. Salutations and fraternity

N Lf

RC, NN: Monroe Papers: Miscellaneous and Undated

1. Women prisoners were consigned to the attic (cinquieme etage) of the prison. The sans culottides were five complementary days that came at the end of the year (comprised of twelve thirty-day months) of the French revolutionary calendar (Edith Sichel, *The Household of the Lafayettes*, 199; *La Grande Encyclopédie*, 8: 910).

2. The bearer of this letter was Monsieur Grelet, the young tutor of the two sons of Adrienne Lafayette's sister, Louise Noailles (1758-1794) who married her first cousin, Louis-Marie, Vicomte de Noailles in 1773. Noailles reached England safely and expected that his wife and children would join him. Louise, however, unwilling to leave her mother, Madame d'Ayen, who was taking care of her ill father-in-law, the Maréchal de Noailles, delayed her departure until it was too late. Louise, her mother and her grandmother were arrested in October 1793. The Revolutionary Tribunal condemned them as spies, and on 22 July 1794, all three were guillotined. During their imprisonment Grelet attempted to alleviate their hardships. The Noailles children, Alexis, Alfred, and Euphémie were left in Grelet's care (La Duchesse de Duras, *Journal des Prisons*, 190-191; 268-280; Virginie de Lafayette Lasteyrie, *La Vie de Madame de Lafayette*, 159-182).

3. The name Adrienne Lafayette could not speak was the children's father, Louis de Noailles, proscribed as an émigré.

From Robert R. Livingston

New York 18ᵗʰ Sepʳ 1794

Dear Sir

Passing thro' the town in my way to ClerMont I am just informed of an opportunity of writing to France which I embrace with pleasure as well to remind you of me as to offer a hint for your consideration which may I think be improved to your honor & the advantage of our common country. You will find it in the enclosed extract of a Letter to Mʳ De Fauchette[1] which (if you approve) I write you to communicate to Mʳ Le Blank & consult together on the mode of bringing it before the national convention either on the suggestion of a member or on your application. This card well played will give weight to the friends of France in this country & ensure you the laurels which the courtiers expect to gather by humbling the American nation before the tyrants of Britain. You will hear much of a very serious riot in the western counties of Penselvania on account of the excise. Genˡ Nevels house was burnt & himself compelled to fly—the other excise Officers to resign. The State & President have sent commissioners to propose terms of accomodation. 15000 militia are also ordered out from Penselvania & the adjoining States. As two thirds of a large committee appointed by those counties & all the principal people have agreed to acceed to the terms of the commissioners I think the business will terminate without bloodshed tho the militia are actualy on their march except from Penselvania where some difficulties have arisen in getting them out.[2] This is the first chapter of the evils I predicted from the assumption instead of leaving to the several states the means of paying their own debts. I give you this information least you should not be able to contradict the exagerated accounts that you will receive of this affair thro' British or tory channels. The encroachments from Canada continue & are daily extending. Simcoe has sent a formal message to the inhabitants on the great Sodus to break up their settlement.[3] British officers have accompanied the Indians in their expedition. These matters are the subject of a long letter from M[r] Randolph to Hammond who makes no other answer than that he will transmit it to his masters ministers & gov[r] Simcoe.[4] Some discussions are also on the carpet between the president & the french minister on the subject of a french vessel made prize of & said to have been sold in one of the southern ports.

We have many reports of M[r] Jay's success in his mission. in the mean time our trade is more distressed than ever. A fine Ship belonging to Jn[o] R Livingston,[5] which had been embargoed at Bordeux some months, & valued at 56000 doll[s] was taken last week & carried to Bermuda tho there was neither french passengers or property on board. several others under similar circumstances have been taken within this few days. our ports are now closely blockaded by British ships & frigates who seem determined to confine our trade to their ports but accounts from the west Indies afford the most unexampled proofs of French gallantry & Spanish & British perfidy & cruelty. 794 persons who came in upon the Spanish proclamation were massacred in cold blood in the presence of the Spanish army in Fort Dauphine by the blacks in their pay & by their order.[6] All the inhabitants of the island of Desedea were put to the sword by the order of Jervis.[7] I send you this gazette of the day on the presumption that you are safly arrived of which however we have yet no information. Be pleased Sir to present my comp to M[r] Le Blank & to M[r] Morris if he is still with you & believe me to be dear Sir with the sincerest wishes for your prosperity & honor Your most Ob hum: serv[t]

Rob R Livingston

RC, DLC: Monroe Papers

1. The extract of the letter to Joseph Fauchet could not be identified.

2. John Neville was a revenue inspector in western Pennsylvania. An anti-excise tax mob burned his house on 17 July 1794. For a concise but thorough account of the Whiskey Rebellion, see *The Diaries of George Washington*, 6: 170-198.

3. Colonel John Graves Simcoe, the lieutenant governor of Upper Canada, wrote to Charles Williamson, an American who established a settlement at Great Sodus Bay on Lake Ontario, insisting that Williamson cease this "aggression" against Great Britain. The letter was delivered by a detachment of British soldiers (A. L. Burt, *The United States, Great Britain, and British North America*, 145-146; *ASP: FR*, 1: 484).

4. Edmund Randolph wrote to George Hammond, the British minister, on 1 September 1794 protesting Simcoe's effort to block American settlements in New York and the participation of British soldiers in an Indian attack on Fort Recovery in Ohio. Hammond responded on September 3 that he would send copies of Randolph's letter to Simcoe and to the ministry in London (William R. Manning, *Diplomatic Correspondence of the United States: Canadian Relations, 1784-1860*, 1: 81-82, 423).

5. John R. Livingston (1755-1851) was a New York merchant and the brother of Robert R. Livingston (George Dangerfield, *Chancellor Robert R. Livingston*, 323, genealogy chart following p. 516).

6. After the slave rebellion erupted in Saint-Domingue in August 1791, Spain sought an opportunity to regain the western end of Hispaniola. From the outset, Spain gave aid and encouragement to the Insurgents. In mid-1793 Spain as well as England invaded Saint-Domingue with Spain soon controlling most of the north. When the Spanish began their invasion of Saint-Domingue, they sent proclamations to many cities in the United States asking refugee planters to return. Many Spanish-held areas had received large numbers of them by early 1794, especially Fort Dauphin. The Spaniards depended heavily upon their black allies, and Jean François, an early black slave leader, had been closely attached to Spain since the start of the slave rebellion. The Spanish Commandant Don Casalola, persuaded Jean François in July 1794 to enter Fort Dauphin and slaughter the French planters (Thomas O. Ott, *The Haitian Revolution 1789-1804*, pp.47, 79, 81-82).

7. A British expeditionary force to the West Indies under the command of Admiral John Jervis (1735-1823) captured Guadeloupe and its neighboring islands, including Deseada (now Desirada), in April 1794. The French retook the islands in June and subsequent British attacks on them failed (*DNB*). An article in the (New York) *Weekly Museum* of 13 September 1794 reported that the British executed a number of residents of Deseada during an attack on that island.

To Thomas Paine

Paris, Sept. 18, 1794.

DEAR SIR,

I was favoured soon after my arrival here with several letters from you and more latterly with one in the character of memorial, upon the subject of your confinement; and should have answered them at the times they were respectively written had I not concluded you would have calculated with certainty upon the deep interest I take in your welfare and the pleasure with which I shall embrace every opportunity in my power to serve you. I should still pursue the same course, and for reasons which must obviously occur, if I did not find that you are disquieted with apprehensions upon interesting points, & which justice to you and our country equally forbid you should entertain. You mention that you have been informed you are not considered as an American citizen by the Americans, and that you have likewise heard that I had no instructions respecting you by the government. I doubt not the person who gave you the information meant well, but I suspect he did not even convey accurately his own ideas on the first point; for I presume the most he could say is that you had likewise become a French citizen and which by no means deprived you of being an American one. Even this however may be doubted, I mean the acquisition of citizenship in France, and I confess you have said much to shew that it has not been made. I really suspect that this was all that the gentleman who wrote to you, and those Americans he heard speak upon the subject, meant. It becomes my duty however to declare to you, that I consider you as an American citizen, and that you are considered universally in that character by the people of America. As such you are entitled to my attention; and so far as it can be given consistently with those obligations which are mutual between every government and even a transient passenger you shall receive it.

The Congress have never decided upon the subject of citizenship in a manner to regard the present case. By being with us through the revolution you are of our country as absolutely as if you had been born there, and you are no more of England, than every native American is. This is the true doctrine in the present case, so far as it becomes complicated with any other consideration. I have mentioned it to make you easy upon the only point which could give you any disquietude.

Is it necessary for me to tell you how much all your countrymen, I speak of the great mass of the people, are interested in your welfare? They have not forgotten the history of their own revolution and the difficult scenes through which they passed; nor do they review its several stages without reviving in their bosoms a due sensibility of the merits of those who served them in that great and arduous conflict. The crime of ingratitude has not yet stained, and I trust never will stain, our national character. You are considered by them as not only having rendered important services in our own revolution, but as being, on a more extensive scale, the friend of human rights, and a distinguished, an able, advocate in favour of public liberty. To the welfare of Thomas Paine the Americans are not, nor can they be, indifferent.

Of the sense which the President has always entertained of your merit, and of his friendly disposition towards you, you are too well assured to require any declaration of it from me. That I forward his wishes in seeking your safety is what I well know, and this will form an additional obligation on me to perform what I should otherwise consider as a duty.

You are, in my opinion, at present, menaced by no kind of danger. To liberate you will be the object of my endeavours, and as soon as possible. But you must, until that event shall be accomplished, bear your situation with patience and fortitude. You will likewise have the justice to recollect, that I am placed here upon a difficult theatre, many important objects to attend to, with few to consult. It becomes me in pursuit of those to regulate my conduct in respect to each, as to the manner and the time, as will, in my judgment, be best calculated to accomplish the whole. With great esteem and respect consider me personally your friend.

JAMES MONROE.

Thomas Paine, *Letter to George Washington, President of the United States of America, on Affairs Public and Private* (1796), 20-23. The original of this letter has not been located.

From Thomas Pinckney

London 18ᵗʰ Septʳ 1794

My dear Sir

This is the first opportunity which has presented itself of offering to you my congratulations on your appointment & arrival in Europe, & of assuring you of the satisfaction I feel in the hope that a friendship from which I have already derived so much advantage & pleasure may by your present situation continue to be productive of mutual utility. For my own part I stand much in need of the kind offices of those whom I esteem, having lately lost one whose unvaried friendship for 15 years past soothed my sorrows in adversity, & augmented the enjoyment of my happier hours. May you my dear Sir, never experience so heavy a Calamity.[1]

Our neutral position affords us opportunities of softening to some individuals the unavoidable miseries of war, without acting contrary to the interests, or indeed the inclinations of either party. I mean by conveying information concerning the existence & well being of those whom the chance of war has reduced to captivity, & whose friends have no other mode of receiving intelligence concerning them; & these good offices may be occasionally extended to transmitting pecuniary succours to such as need them, but always with the knowledge & consent of the party in whose power the person relieved may be, as in all transactions of this nature the most open & undisguised proceedings are indispensable. For matters which relate merely to our own national concerns, & which it may be expedient not to divulge, Mʳ Morris & I have a Cypher, his part of which I presume he will leave with you. Be pleased to inform me of your sentiments on these subjects in which you will undoubtedly by guided by considerations arising from your own particular situation, of which I cannot form a competent judgement. Under the idea however that you will find no impropriety in making such enquiries, I inclose a memorandum concerning some English persons in France whose friends are under anxiety on their account. If no obstacle should occur I safely trust to your feelings for expediting an answer. If there be objections with which I am not acquainted by informing of them you will prevent me from making in future similar applications.[2]

I have a nephew who has been more than two years in France & is known to Mʳ Morris, his name is Horry.[3] I cannot say I am myself acquainted with him, as he was not twelve years old when I last saw him, but he is the son of a much loved sister; may I therefore request the favor of your good offices to him? & if you find him tinctured with any failings, (of which I am not aware, but from which I know few are exempt) be pleased to consider them with an indulgent eye for the sake of him who is with sincere esteem & true respect Your faithful & obliged Servant

Thomas Pinckney

A letter addressed to you by Mr Short which I rec^d by the last mail is herewith.[4]

RC, NN: Monroe Papers

1. Pinckney married Betsey Motte of South Carolina in 1779. They had five children. She died in London on 24 August 1794 (Frances Leigh Williams, *A Founding Family: The Pinckneys of South Carolina*, 136-137, 302).

A copy of this letter in the handwriting of Pinckney's secretary, William Allen Deas, has the following memorandum attached to it:

> To obtain Information concerning a Mrs Sheldon, a nun with the Benedictine Dames at Dunkerque, who with the rest of the Convent was removed from thence about twelve months ago, since that period no Information has been received of her: she is upward of 70 years of Age; and if permission could be obtained for her to come to England, her Nephews who direct this Enquiry, would spare no Expense for her removal.

> Also Mr Sheldon a brother of the above lady residing at Nancy in Lorraine, he is likewise more than 70 years of Age and has not been heard of for eighteen months past.

> To obtain Information concerning Captn Killoe of his Britannic Majesty's Sloop l'Espion taken by some Frigates of the Republic and carried into Brest.

> The Same of Mr Temple Luttrell who was confined in the Prison of L'Abbaye at Paris but has not been heard of many months.

> Besides these there are some persons concerning whom I requested the favor of Mr Morris to make Enquiries but which I suppose he has not had time to complete, will you therefore be pleased to continue them if there be neither inconvenience nor impropriety in so doing.

> T. P.

3. Daniel Horry (1764-1828) was the son of Pinckney's sister Harriott and her husband, Daniel Horry. His parents sent him to England for schooling in 1780, and he entered the university at Cambridge in 1788. After leaving Cambridge he made his home in France, where he resided for the remainder of his life, marrying a niece of Lafayette. In later life he changed his name to Charles Lucas Pinckney Horry (Williams, *A Founding Family*, 170, 186, 238, 322, 332).

4. William Short to JM, 26 August 1794, above.

To Thomas Pinckney

Paris 19 September 1794

It is my duty to correspond occasionally with our Ministers in Europe, and I need not assure that it required not that motive to incline me to it with you. I shall therefore write you when safe opportunities offer and I have any thing worth communicating, and shall always be happy to hear from you.

I was apprized soon after my arrival here, of the jealousy entertained by the government of that description of persons, known by the twofold character of British subjects and American Citizens: and a remonstrance has been made to me against covering those persons by my passports, founded on an assurance that advantage would be taken of them to pass through the Republic and report its state to its neighbouring enemy. The subject was of delicate importance and I was much embarrassed how to act on it. When a man gains the right of citizenship in America, though it be by naturalization yet it seems doubtful how far I can look back here to his Anterior or even present priviledges in another country. And yet if France says that he is a British subject, that he was one before he came your citizen, and in that character is an object of jealousy to her Government, if the facts are true what can be said in reply? Does it not seem proper that a line should be drawn of which under certain limitations allegiance should be due and protection claimed of one government only, and should not this be the American coast? Is it suitable that the priviledges of citizenship should attend a man to this continent, after he has abandoned ours, settled again in his native country, and which he only left a few years for the purpose of trade, where his wealth and residence are, especially as they may by abuse stain our national character and embark us in unpleasant and improfitable controversies? The considerations appear to me to be weighty on both sides, and I have suggested them for your consideration. I mean, to bring them to the view of our Government. As yet I have arranged no plan, absolutely, with this, but it will be prevailed on to admit an exception in favor of residence.

Copy, NN: Monroe Papers

To Philibert Buchot

Paris 20ᵗʰ Septemʳ 1794
4ᵐᵉ Sansculotide l'an 2ᵈ R. f.

Citizen Commissary

A short experience has already demonstrated the interest which my Country has in the appointment of some person here known to your Government and responsible to ours, to take charge of the affairs of its Citizens in the commercial line. This consideration has induced me to appoint Fulwar Skipwith heretofore Secretary of Legation to the office of Consul at Paris, and who will take on himself and discharge the duties properly belonging thereto, untill the sense of our Government shall be known on the Subject. I have therefore to request you will be so obliging as to cause this to be communicated to the Several departments of your Government in such manner that he may be known and respected as such.

Jaˢ Monroe

RC, DLC: FCP—France. In clerk's handwriting and signed by JM.

To Philibert Buchot

1ˢᵗ Vendemiare the 3ᵈ year [22 September 1794.]

Citizen Commissary

I have this moment received the enclosed Memorials from the masters of two American Vessels; The Mary, commanded by Henry Preble and the Severn, by Jared Goodrich, who were boarded at Sea by the Proserpine Frigate of the Republic, and all the Passengers taken from the one Vessel, and the other, with her Cargo and Passengers brought into Brest where they are now detained. As these Cases form like Departures from the Treaty of Amity and Commerce between the two Republics, and are in that Respect analogous with those complained of in my Note lately presented to the Committee of Public Safety, I have thought it my Duty as connected with that Subject to bring them immediately before the Same Department. Independently of the propriety of accomodating the Principle to the Wishes of my Country, and which I earnestly hope for the Common Interest of both Republics will be soon done. I presume the Embarassments of virtuous men & good Patriots, as is the Case in the present Instance, will be an additional Motive for their enlargement as soon as possible.

Jaˢ Monroe

RC, DLC: FCP—France

Henry Preble (1770-1825) was the younger brother of the better known naval officer, Commodore Edward Preble (*The Preble Family of America*).

Enclosure One:
From Henry Preble

le 22 7$^{\underline{bre}}$ 94 [22 September 1794]

Le Vaisseau <u>La marie</u> parti de falmouth en angleterre le 13 aoust ayant à Son bord 14 passagers anglais, fut rencontré et pris le 17 du même mois par la frégate française <u>La Proserpine</u>, commandée par le Cap^{ne} Mamino, qui S'etant emparé du dit Vaisseau fit passer, à son bord, les 14 passagers ainsi qu'un grand nombre de boites, coffres et une quantité de provisions. Les officiers qui furent envoyés à bord de la Marie jetterent à la mer une voiture et ses harnois. Plusieurs tonneaux de vin furent enfoncés, des coffres furent ouverts sans examiner a qui ils appartenaient. après cela et l'examen des papiers ils permetent au Vaisseau de continuer sa route pour Boston.

Le Soussigné venu en France Sur la frégate la Proserpine réclame la liberté des passagers: il peut prouver qu'amis de la liberté ils allaient Se fixer en amérique: qu'ils y ont deja envoyé leurs propriétés pour pouvoir devenir Citoyens americains; qu'ils n'ont quitté leurs païs que parce qu'ils y etaient persécutés comme patriotes et amis de la cause française. Ils sont maintenant à Bord du Vaisseau La Ville de l'Orient dans le port de Brest, prisonièrs de guerre et traittés comme tels. Ils avaient acheté en amerique des terres considérables et ils avaient engagé quelques amis de la liberte à les y Suivre pour former un établissement. Si d'ici ce printems ils ne sont pas relachés cet événement causera la ruine d'un grand nombre de familles et privera les etats-unis de quelques bons citoyens.

Henri Preble

Editors' Translation

22 September 1794

The ship <u>The Mary</u> which had left Falmouth, England, on August 13 with 14 English passengers on board, was intercepted and taken on the 17th of the same month by a French frigate <u>The Proserpine,</u> commanded by the Captain Mamino, who, after having taken charge of the said vessel, made the 14 passengers board his own ship along with a large number of boxes, trunks and a quantity of provisions. The officers that were sent on board <u>The Mary</u> threw a carriage and its harness into the sea. Several barrels of wine were smashed into; trunks were opened without regard for whom they belonged; after this and the examination of the documents, they allowed the vessel to continue on its route to Boston.

The undersigned having arrived in France on the frigate the Proserpine demands the release of the passengers: he can prove that as friends of liberty they were going to settle in America; that they have already sent their possessions there with plans to become American citizens; that they only left their country because they had been persecuted as patriots and friends of the French cause. They are now on board the vessel The City of L'Orient in the port of Brest, prisoners of war and treated as such. They had purchased considerable land in America and they had convinced a few friends of liberty to follow them there and form a settlement. If between now and the spring they are not released, this event will cause the ruin of a great number of families and will deprive the United States of some good citizens.

Henri Preble

Copy, DLC: FCP—France

Preble attached a list of the names of the passengers removed from the *Mary*.

Enclosure Two:
From Jared Goodrich

[September 1794]

Mémoire de Jared Goodrich, Capitaine du bâtiment Américain <u>Le Severn</u> de New-York.

Ce Navire etait parti de Bristol pour New-York chargé de différentes marchandises appartenant à des Cit. de New-York et à leur compte et risques. Il avait à son bord vingt-huit passagers emigrans en Amérique, hommes, femmes et enfants. A 90°- 7eme de latitude et 8-10 de longitude, j'ai il a été abordé par la frégate Franç^{se} <u>Proserpine</u>, Cap^e qui m'a demandé et enlevé les papiers de mon bâtiment, mes connaissements et lettres de toute espèce, ainsi que mes passagers et leurs bagages; il a pris aussi tous les canards, volaille et cochons de mon equipage et a beaucoup endommagé mon navire par son abordage, il envoya les matelots à mon bord et a fait conduire mon bâtiment à Brest où nous Sommes arrivés le 1 Septembre 1794. Voilà le détail exact de ce qui s'est passé.

Jared Goodrïch.

Editors' Translation

[September 1794]

Memoir of Jared Goodrich, Captain of the American ship <u>The Severn</u> of New York.

This ship had left Bristol for New York loaded with various merchandise belonging to citizens of New York, at their account and risk. It had on board twenty-eight passengers immigrating to America, men, women and children. At 90° - 7th of latitude and 8-10 of longitude, I was boarded by the French frigate <u>Proserpine</u>, Captain who asked for and took my documents from the ship, my cargo receipts and letters of all kind, as well as my passengers and their baggage. He also took all the ducks, poultry and pigs from my crew and greatly damaged my ship upon boarding. He sent sailors on board and had my ship sail to Brest where we arrived the 1st September 1794. These are the exact details of what occurred.

Jared Goodrich.

Copy, DLC: FCP—France

Buchot acknowledged the receipt of these documents on 6 Vendemiaire An 3 (27 September 1794) and informed JM that he was forwarding them to the Committee of Public Safety (DLC: FCP—France.)

To J. Hector St. John de Crèvecoeur

Paris Sepr 22. 1794.

Dear Sir

I received the other day with great pleasure your favor accompanied with the present you were so kind as make me, the letters of an American farmer, and of which I have so often heard the most favorable mention, & by those whose opinions are most to be respected.

To one who knew the old world the theatre was an interesting one if the attention were confined to the mere description of our infant establishments only. But it became infinitely more so when connected with the British oppression and invasion of our country; their conduct upon that occasion sho^d never be forgotten, and especially as the revival of the scene will always bring to memory the virtues and services of those who suffered in our cause, and likewise the merits of our illustrious ally the French nation, & whose union with my own I wish further to cement.

I will peruse it with infinite pleasure and the more so because I shall see my own country in a language I wish to study. I know it will not only instruct my mind but greatly facilitate my efforts.

Accept my acknowledgments for your polite attention and be assured of the esteem & regard with which I am sincerely yours

Ja^s Monroe

FC, NN: Monroe Papers; variant, NvLG

From Edmund Randolph

Philadelphia Septr 25. 1794.

Sir,

My letter of the 30th July last having been repeated by duplicate, I shall only recommend to your particular and immediate attention the subjects of it.

The spoliations and vexations which are imputable to the French cruisers, and among them, the injuries to our rights by Treaty, in the case of the Ship Laurens, together with the severe effects of the Embargo at Bordeaux, have excited in the Individuals interested a flame, which now and then bursts forth in violent expressions, and which you therefore cannot quiet too soon by a proper adjustment. You will find in the enclosed Copy of Mr Fauchet's letter to me, of the 1st August, the strong assurances which he has given on this head.[1]

Another collection of depredation papers, conformable with the list which accompanies them, is placed under the Care of Mr Boland, who goes to seek compensation on account of the ship Fame.[2] It is a strong case, and will back your remonstrances, however pointed they may be. I do not state the minutiae, as his documents speak explicitly, and he himself will be on the spot, ready for further explanation. There is nothing in which you can render yourself so acceptable to an important part of our community as on these occasions. Indeed, I flatter myself with the expectation of hearing shortly of considerable advances towards final success on your part.

Mr James Anderson[3] has been highly recommended, and his letters have shewn him to deserve some degree of notice from our Government. He was not suggested to the President in the late appointment of French Consuls; because it was presumed from some information, which was received, that the places for which Consuls were designated at the last Session, were not suitable to his views. You will therefore take the earliest opportunity of inquiring into his character and respectability, and inform us.

A claim of Mr Cruger is also forwarded to you, in order that you may pursue the same measures relative to it, as in the others of a similar kind.[4]

Mr Boland has promised to deliver to you your quota of newspapers. From the beginning of August to this day they contain the late interesting transactions of the four western Counties of Pennsylvania. These would have been communicated to you, as they arose, if conveyances to France were not of all others, the most difficult to be obtained. You will recollect the murmurs, which have long prevailed there against the excise. At length the House of General Neville, the Inspector, was attacked by a large party of armed men in the day, and burnt to the ground, together with most, if not all, the out houses. Foreseeing that Government could not be inattentive, and mixing perhaps some preposterous views of ambition and personal aggrandisement, the Leaders, to render themselves formidable, contrived to give an appearance of an universal commotion, and association of sentiment. A large Body appeared in arms on Braddock's field, and appointed the 14th of August for the meeting of deputies from all the Townships at Parkinson's ferry, inviting the Virginia Counties to send Deputies also.[5] The President despatched Senator Ross, Judge Yeates, and our Attorney General Bradford, as Commissioners;[6] having first required 12,500 militia to be held in readiness in certain proportions in New Jersey, Pennsylvania, Maryland, and Virginia. A Committee of the insurgents were nominated to confer with them, and to report to a second meeting, to be held at Redstone at a Later day. Our commissioners unanimously prevailed upon those with whom they conferred, to agree to urge the people to peace. But the Redstone opinions were not so propitious as those of Parkinson's ferry. The people there assembled were dissatisfied with the conduct of the former Committee of conference, & appointed another, which, like the former, were unanimous for acquiescence. Still the people themselves were to be consulted, and the 11 September fixed for the taking of their votes. The result has been that every leading man has subscribed to the Terms required by the Commissioners; that near three thousand men above the age of sixteen have submitted; that there is no real danger of an opposition in the field. However the Militia having been on their march for some time, and it being certain that altho' open resistance will not be found, the laws cannot be executed unless some degree of military force be at hand to support the officers; their movements have not been countermanded. The command is intended for Governor Lee of Virginia; but the President goes on towards Carlisle on Monday, where after every proper arrangement of the Troops, destined to that place of rendezvous, he will decide whether to proceed or return. The principal information, which is to be procured from the news papers will be the first and second Proclamation, the representation of the Secretary of the Treasury to the President, and the proceedings of the Commissioners. In a day or two their report will be concluded, which will condense the whole State of this Business into a small Compass. I have not adverted to Judge M'Kean and General Irvine, two State Commissioners, who went upon the same expedition; because their functions were necessarily limited to the mere act of pardon, the great offences being against the United States, not the Individual State of Pennsylvania.[7] However you may be assured that the Insurrection will very quickly be subdued; and you cannot err in any political calculation built on this event.

The spirit, which the states have manifested, is astonishing. Throughout Virginia, to favor the insurgents would be disgrace, and actual personal danger. Some of their emissaries produced a momentary disturbance in Fredericktown, in Maryland, but it was soon hushed by the rapid approach of the militia. In Pennsylvania, from some mismanagement, the call of the militia was not hastily obeyed. But such an enthusiasm has now grown up and been raging for a considerable time, that the very Quakers have entered the ranks and marched to Pittsburg. New Jersey seems to be a nursery of warriors, determined to support the Constitution. Even the Democratic Societies have launched out into a reprobation of the Insurgents. All these circumstances combined, while they afford an ample range for speculation on the remote consequences, furnish a conviction, that the energy of the Government is, and will be, greatly increased.

I suspect that Europe will resound with the idle clamors, which circulate here, that the Yellow fever has again appeared in Philadelphia, Baltimore, and New York; and that quarantine will be again inflicted on our vessels. But the general and sincere opinion is, that if there be any examples of it within the City, they are too paltry to alarm even the old women or Children.

My anxiety to hear from you is multiplied tenfold by my knowledge, that all the sentiments of Mr Fauchet were deposited in the memory of M^r Le Blanc & not committed to writing. That which could not be hazarded upon the possibility of detection, must be of an important cast. One thing only is certain: that he supposes a British tendency to prevail in some members of our Government, and that the supposition is a copious theme with him. You are possessed of all the means of confronting this Idea. You know how Mr Jay is restricted. And I must acknowledge to you, that notwithstanding all the pompous expectations announced in the Gazettes of compensation to the merchants, the prospect of it is in my Judgment illusory, and I do not entertain distant hope of the surrender of the Western Posts. Thus the old exasperations continue; and new ones are daily added. Judge then, how indispensable it is that you should keep the French Republic in good humor with us.

Spain has, by a conduct similar to that of Great Britain towards us, imposed the necessity of sending an Envoy Extraordinary thither also. For the negotiation is at a stand, on the most unaccountable pretexts. My conviction is firm, that the Courts of Madrid and London are cordial in nothing but a hatred against the United States, and a determination to harass them through the Indians.

If however a report, which has come many ways, be true, that General Wayne on the 20th August, left between 150 and 300 Indians dead on the field near the Rapids of the Miami, their exultation might have fallen, and they will soon be sick of war.[8] I have the honor to be, with great and constant respect and esteem, Sir, Your most obedient servant

Edm: Randolph

RC, DLC: Monroe Papers

1. Fauchet's letter of 1 August 1794 has not been located.

2. The *Fame* was one of the many American ships detained in the embargo at Bordeaux (*ASP: FR*, 1: 757-758).

3. James Anderson was a merchant from Charleston, South Carolonia. He served as the U. S. commercial agent at Nantes 1793-1794 and at Brest 1794-1795. He became the commercial agent at Cette in 1802 (*The South Carolina Historical and Genealogical Magazine*, 26 (1925): 151-157; *Jefferson Papers*, 24: 424; *Madison Papers, Secretary of State Series*, 3: 70).

4. New York merchant Nicholas Cruger had claims against France for supplies purchased in the West Indies (*ASP: FR*, 1: 757).

5. On August 1-2, 1794 from 5,000 to 7,000 militiamen and farmers opposed to the whiskey tax gathered at Braddock's Field (the site east of Pittsburgh where British General Edward Braddock was ambushed in 1755). They then marched to Pittsburgh and destroyed property belonging to several revenue officers (Leland Baldwin, *Whiskey Rebels*, 139, 146-162).

6. James Ross (1762-1847) was a prominent attorney from Washington, Pennsylvania who served in the U. S. Senate 1794-1803. Being well-known in western Pennsylvania, Ross proved to be an effective member of the commission sent to meet with the Whiskey Rebels and was able to negotiate a settlement that avoided violence (*ANB*). Jasper Yeates (1745-1817) was an associate justice of the Pennsylvania supreme court 1791-1817 (*Appletons' Cyclopedia*). William Bradford (1755-1795), a Philadelphia attorney and jurist, served as attorney general 1794-1795 (*Appletons' Cyclopedia*).

7. Thomas McKean (1734-1817) was a delegate to the Continental Congress from Delaware and was a signer of the Declaration of Independence. He was chief justice of the supreme court of Pennsylvania 1777-1799 and governor of that state 1799-1807. William Irvine (1741-1804) of Pennsylvania was a brigadier general in the Continental army, a member of the Continental Congress 1786-1788, and a member of the House of Representatives 1793-1795. Irvine, along with McKean, was appointed a commissioner by the governor of Pennsylvania to try to resolve the crisis of the Whiskey Rebellion. Irvine declined an appointment to command federal troops sent against the rebels but did serve with the Pennsylvania militia that was called out in support of the national troops (*ANB*).

8. General Anthony Wayne won the Battle of Fallen Timbers, on 20 November 1794 near present-day Toledo, Ohio, which was the final battle fought between American Indians and the United States for control of the Northwest Territory (*Encyclopedia of American History*).

From William Short

Dear Sir

On receiving a notification that you were named Min. Plenipo. of the U. S. at Paris I wrote to you on the 26ᵗʰ ultᵒ without knowing that you had then arrived in France. My letter was therefore addressed as well to Mʳ Morris as yourself. I have now received information by the newpapers which have come here from England & from Italy that you had arrived at Paris & been publickly received by the convention. Allow me my dear Sir to congratulate you on the fortunate, important & agreeable appointment which you have received from your country—& to anticipate as a Citizen of the U. S. the advantages which shall result therefrom, & as your friend, the real happiness & satisfavtion you will experience therein.

Allow me now my dear Sir to turn your attention for a moment from so agreeable a perspective, & to fix it on my own situation. It is you who have it more in your power than any other person at present to diminish the pain I experience in it, which has already been of long duration, & which has hitherto been rendered supportable only from the prospect of its not continuing. I address myself to you as the representative of the U.S.—& with still more confidence & satisfaction as your friend.

If you have received my last letter you will already have been informed of the nature of this application—or if not I hope Mʳ Morris will have given you some idea of it, or at least as far as he was acquainted therewith—The present mode of conveyance will disable me from detailing to you all I could wish as my letter will go through the posts of different countries & be exposed to be opened.

The nature of my application obliges me however to mention to you which I do in the confidence of friendship that it will remain with you or be mentioned only where it may be necessary, that my heart & my affections are placed on a person who has been put in a state of arrestation in France, under the general decree for confining all persons of the class in which she had the misfortune to be born. As her patriotism & her innocence were unquestionable I have been in the constant hope that she would be released. I wrote to M. Morris in general terms respecting it without mentioning my reasons for the interest I felt therein—As I understood he was not agreeable to the French government I feared to put the cause of my friend, which is my own & on which my happiness depends, into his hands—After the report which came here some time ago of Mʳ Jefferson being appointed to come to France, I chose to wait for his arrival—my friend was well known to him as well as all her family—he coᵈ have sollicited her liberty for her own sake—& when he came to know my situation he would claimed it for mine. I now put the same cause in your hands.

I have obliterated the two lines above¹ after writing them from a recollection how many hands this letter is to pass through before it gets to yours—I will confine myself simply to ask you to sollicit the liberty of my friend² & of her aged grandmother from whom her filial piety renders her inseparable—& to take my friend under your protection, viz. to procure her the liberty of living on her estate in the country, & to be her security if necessary that she never conceived either by word or deed any thing against her country. Her duty to an aged parent, & my duty to my country which has obliged me to remain here, have kept us so long separate & so the cause of her being now in confinement. I now ask you my dear Sir in consideration thereof to sollicit & procure the liberty of my friend, to see & converse with her if her liberty cannot be procured, & which I comprehend the liberty of her aged parent if still alive, & without which I am sure she would not accept her own. I have written to & heard from my friend since her confinement. Mᴿ Morris was so good as to send our letters—I hope you will do the same & I therefore inclose one, without putting its address. I have done the same heretofore—I desired M. Morris to leave the name & abode of my friend, with Mᴿ Jefferson, when I thought he was coming to Paris—I trust he will have done the same with you—I avoid putting her name because it will be useless in that case—& as my letter goes through so many posts—I hope you will see my friend & I indulge myself in the pleasing idea that you will procure her liberty—Oh my dear Sir how happy should I be if I were with you at Paris—I beg & intreat you to let me hear from you—Send your letters by duplicate— one under cover to Mᴿ Pinckney—the other under cover to the correspondent of your banker at Leg- horn—By these two routes I shall be sure to receive one—Consider my situation & diminish the anxiety of your true & faithful friend.

W Short

RC, PHi: Gilpin Collection: William Short Letters

1. The struck lines could not be read.

2. Duchess de Rochefoucauld.

From William Short

Madrid Sep. 30. 1794

Dear Sir

I received this morning your favor of the 23. My last was of the 26ᵗʰ inst.[1] Sangro is the Prince de Castelpanco—he commands in Aragon—There is daily expectation here of the result of an attack medi- tated by de l'Union to succour Bellegarde—He has lately erected some entrenchments in advance of his former posts—& expresses his astonishment at the tranquillity with which the French allowed him to do it—Time will shew whether they intend it as a trap to take his canon after they shall have been lodged there[2]—It appears that the French have begun to execute their decree on the Spanish prisoners having killed two, as is said in a very inhuman manner—As far as we know here, there is no decision as yet to execute the convention of Colliaure, which as you know is the cause of this decree[3]—The conduct of Government in this respect astonishes everybody here, & is blamed even by their warmest friends—It is in fact so contrary to the interests of humanity, whilst the King is known to be really humane—& so contrary to the interests of Spain in every respect, that it is attributed in general to the English influ- ence—As the decree existed already against them they are glad to have it also against the Spaniards, for reasons of every kind—It is much to be regretted that the Government here have given into this snare— But the English have such an advantage in addressing themselves to the passions of King's ministers in the present view, that they will succeed in making the rest of Europe fight their battles for some time yet, in order that they may secure their conquests—After having persuaded this Government to assist them with real zeal in destroying the French marine—it is not surprizing that they should now persuade them to assist in confirming them in the possession of Corsica which gives a final stab to the Spanish influence in the Mediterranean & Italy—& also in the possession of Sᵗ Domingo &c &c. which will open to them infallibly the doors of all the Spanish possessions in America—& place the Spanish commerce at the avid mercy of the London Merchants.

The King of England by a late order of Council has modified his instructions of June 8. 1793.[4] I think with you it is surprizing some of our friends did not send it to us—or rather it wᵈ have been surprizing if any of mine had done it—The Danish Minister here received a copy of it from his colleague in London, the mail before the last. I have sent to ask him to lend it to me that I may copy it—Sh^d I receive it in time I will send it to you by way of greater caution, though you will probably receive it sooner by the English papers—This order of Council is given with a very bad grace—& predicated on the King chusing no longer to purchase the articles of meal flour &c.—My last letter from Mr Pinckney is of Aug. 12—The Spanish packet taken was called the Readea—the second of that name which has fallen into the hands of the French. We know nothing new here, or at least that can be new to you. Sh^d Col^o Longbane be with you I will thank you to inform him that the Duke de la <illegible> has declined as I mentioned to you in my last, forcing the Gov. of Cadiz to make him satisfaction. I have transmitted to Gov^t the letters which have passed on that subject—I inclose a letter for the Sec. of State—It is not a duplicate of the last I sent you—of course may go with it or not as you may judge proper—Y^{rs} faithfully

W Short

RC, PHi: Gilpin Collection: William Short Letters

1. Neither JM's letter to Short of 23 August 1794 nor Short's letter of 26 September 1794 has not been located.

2. The French launched a campaign in the spring of 1794 to drive the Spanish from the province of Pyrenees-Orientales. The Comte De La Union commanded the Spanish troops in the province, backed up by the army of Pablo de Sangro, Prince of Castelfranco across the border in Aragon. French troops captured the port town of Collioure on May 26, which the left Spanish only in control of Bellegarde, which guarded the route into Spain. La Union placed his artillery in a forward position to guard the approaches to Bellegarde, but the defense of the town failed, and it surrendered on September 17. La Union was not at Bellegarde and did not learn immediately of its surrender. He launched a counterattack several days after the surrender, but it was repulsed, and he was forced to retreat into Spain (Henri Jomini, *Histoire Critique et Militaire des Guerres de la Revolution* (1820 edition), 5: 216-229, 240-243; 6: 121-123).

3. The terms of surrender at Collioure, negotiated by the Spanish commander there, provided the parole of the garrison in exchange for the release of French prisoners held by the Spanish. La Union would not recognize the agreement made by his subordinate; he ordered the paroled Spanish troops back into the lines and refused to release the prisoners (Jomini, *Histoire Critique et Militaire des Guerres de la Revolution*, 5: 243; 6: 116).

4. The Order in Council of 8 June 1793—known as the "Provision Order"—directed British warships to seize neutral vessels carrying grain to France. The order was suspended on 6 August 1794 in response to the opening of treaty negotiations between the United States and Great Britain (Samuel F. Bemis, *Jay's Treaty*, 156, 235).

From Adrienne Lafayette

12 vendemiaire Lan 3 de L[a] R[epublique] [3 October 1794]

Sir

je ne vous ai pas importuné depuis La dernière decade, comme j'en avois pois Lengagement.

il est probable que je Sortirai La derniere de cette maison. je crois que Les Dangers diminuent pour tout Le monde, et Si Lespoir du moment Subsiste, ils sont nuls pour moy, puisque je n'ai pas Le moindre pretexte d'accusation—mais La situation de mes enfans si eloignés de moy ajoute, a La do[u]leur qui me Suivre jusqu'au tombeau, des Sollicitudes cruelles, et ce genre de tourment n'etant pas tout a fait irredemiable, je puis vous demander de Le Soulager, en m'accordant un moment de conversation avec un homme qui ait toute votre confiance. rien n'est plus facile que ce que je vous demande, et je ne puis croire que vous me refusiés. on peut venir ici, Sans etre connu et je me charge dobtenir La permission daller parler au Greffe. ne differés pas je vous prie, de m'accorder cette Legere faveur, elle ne puit vous compromettre, et Serve d'un grand poin pour moi. j'ai reellement besoin de vous entretenir des interets de mes chers enfans, auxquels je suis arrachée. ce n'est pas trop je pense, d'obtenir au bout de deux mois de Sejour dans La même Cité, un temoignage consolant d'interêt de ceux, dont j'avais quelque droit d'esperer ma delivrance au moment de leur arrivée. vous voyes, my dear sir, que je n'y mets pas de fierté car je sens que vous avés deja asses de titres a ma reconnoissance, pour que je sois prête a contracter, envers vous de nouvelles obligations mais accoutumée de me taire Lorsquil n'est pas permis d'exprimer sincerement ce que je sens. pardonnes La franchise avec Laquelle je m'explique avec vous; et ne doutés pas, que ce que Les etats unis, et Leur ministre non seulement ont fait, mais ont bien voulu desirer de faire pour moi, m'ont inspiré une très sincere reconnoissance. je vous demande en particulier den recevoir la bien sincere assurance. salut et fraternité

N. Lafayette

Editors' Translation

12 Vendemiaire Year 3 of the Republic [3 October 1794]

I have not bothered you for ten days,[1] as I have had no interview during that time.

It is likely that I will be the last to leave this place.[2] I believe that the threat of execution is subsiding and if hope persists, there is no danger for me, as I have not the least reason to be held. But the situation of my children so far away from me adds to the sorrow that will follow me to my grave. These cruel anxieties and this kind of torment not being completely without remedy, I beg you to ease my cares by allowing me a moment of conversation with a man who should have your full confidence.[3] Nothing is easier than what I am asking you, and I cannot believe that you would refuse me. One can come here without being recognized, and I am determined to obtain permission to go and speak with the jail's clerk. Please, do not delay, in granting me this small favor, it cannot compromise you, and it provides me great peace of mind. I truly need you to look after the interest of my dear children from whom I have been torn apart. It isn't too much I think after a two-month confinement in the same place, to ask for the consoling confirmation that I have some right to hope for my liberation at the moment of their arrival. You see, my dear sir, that I assume no pride in this because I sense that you have already enough assurances of my appreciation that I am ready for you to undertake new responsibilities. But, I am accustomed to remaining silent when I am not allowed to express openly what I feel. Pardon the candor with which I express myself to you; and doubt not that not only what the United States and its minister has done for me, but what they have willingly attempted to do for me, has instilled in me a very sincere appreciation. For this I ask you in particular to receive a truly sincere assurance. Salutation and brotherhood

N. Lafayette

RC: ICU

1. Adrienne Lafayette wrote to JM on 18 September 1794. In the French Revolutionary calendar, a year was not divided into weeks; rather, each month was divided into three *décades* of ten days each.

2. The person to whom Adrienne Lafayette refers may have been Père Carrichon, a non-juring priest, who was the confessor of Adrienne Lafayette and her mother, Henriette Daguesseau, Duchesse d'Ayen, whom Carrichon had attended during her final hours. Carrichon disguised himself as a carpenter and gained access to Adrienne's cell. She took advantage of his visit to make a general confession covering her entire life (Maurois, *Adrienne*, 248, 261).

From Stephen Cathalan[1]

Nismes the 4ᵗʰ October 1794.

Sir

Your honoured Favour of the 31ᵗʰ August Last[2] reached me in due time in this Place of Nismes; having Left Marseilles the 4ᵗʰ Ultᵒ with Missˢ Cathalan my wife to Pay a visit to my Father, Mother, & Daughter, who are retired here long time since.

If I have differed of answering to your Excellency, it is because I Intended to Spend here only about a forthnight, and according to Letters I should Receive from Consul Fenwick of Bordeaux, Push my Journey That way, then Go with him, to Paris to Pay you Jointly our Respects, or Return to Marseilles;—

I have Since Considered and find from the Letters of Cˢᵘˡ Fenwick who Says "that it is Possible he will go to Paris & Leave Bordeaux in two or Three Days, hence;" that if he gives me a Certitude of it, my Shortest way is to meet him at Paris—meantime I may take a Resolution I must stay here; but you may Depend on the Satisfaction I will have if Circumstances may admit me to have the honour & the Pleasure of making at Paris your Personal acquaintance; in that Case I hope I will be at Paris about the 15ᵗʰ Insᵗ.

I wish our Interview might become usefull & Contribute to Streghten the Ties of alliance, Friendship, and Trade which unites the United States & the Republick of France.

Now the National Convention has directed the Encouragment & the Protection of Foreing Trade, Then it is the moment for the Merchants of the Two Free Republicks to Supply one an other with the Superflect of their Respective Products;—

in this Part of France the Crop of wheat has been a very Bad one, and all your Exports are much wanted.

we are in deed Supplied by the Genoese but in a too small quantity for all these Southern Departments.

Then american Cargoes in a Great number Loaded with wheat, Flour, Pulse, Rice, Indian Corn, Codfish or Baccaloo,[3] Salted fish in Pickle, Pickled Salted Beef & Porks in Barrels, Gamon and Gamon of Bacon,[4] Tabacco, White Suggar, Indigo, Cotton, Pitch, Tar, (no turpentine nor Coffee yet) Potashes, Hemp, Iron, Staves, Plancks of white wood & oack wood Fish & whale oil for Tanneries & for Lamps & Reverbers,[5] Larger Masts for Men of war; at Length all your american Exports in very large quantity will be readily Sold at Great advantage; & in Return—Brandies, wines, olives, Capres, almonds, Prunes, Dryed verdigrease, Minces, Pomatum, Gloves, Fans, Silks umbrellas, Silks Stockings, and all Sorts of Manufactured articles of Luxe maybe obtained at moderate terms.

The vessels tho' appearing to be bound for Genoa & Leghorn, to prevent their been arrested by the Coalizated fleets, would be realy bound for Marseilles, & for the articles in Return that could not be procured at Marseilles, as olive oil, Levant Drugs &ᶜ they could proceed to these Italian Marketts, to compleat their outward Cargoes, where they are very abundant & very cheap. The Genoese and all the other neutral vessels are not at Marseilles Submitted to Sale to the Maximum Law's Rate, nor they Pay any Sort of Duty on their Goods; they Sale their Goods on Board Trartatively Either for hard Money or in assignats with Their Colour Standing; The People who is their Purchasers is Glad to obtain from them a kind of Comfort; and very Desirous to see American Vessels in Marseilles.

At this Moment the Genoese are Salling the New Codfish at 15 s[hillings] hard money or 45 s assignats & the old at 10 s or 30 s pᵣ lb. (1.00 lb of Marseilles are equal to lb 90 English) Rice 12 s or 35 s Bacon 45 s Gamon of Bacon £2-10 s or 15 s p^r lb. Dutch & Parmesson chease 20 s or £4-5 as^{ts} Salmon 30 s or 35 as^{ts} p^r lb. the other articles in Proportion & on the Same Rate for the Payment Calculating the hard Spanish Dollars at £15 or 16 ass^{at}.

Wheats arriving are already Purchased by the nation's agents, as well as all the other articles that the Govern^t is in want of Trartatively & paid either in effective hard money or in Goods procured at the Maximum, if the Importers preffer them. by my Letters wrote from Marseilles yesterday, wheats are now Paid to the Genoese £45 or 50 p^r Emine Measure of Genoa; 100 Emines of Genoa are equal to 72 Charge Measures of Marseilles; and 100 English quarters are equal to 175 charges of Marseilles; this Price is in effective and hard Money Paid.[6]

It is my Duty to Confirm you that in all times, I have wrote to your Predecessor and to the Secretary of State at Philadelphia, Since the French Revolution that tho' Marseilles has been Desolated by Sundry factious mobs, Seditions, & Riots, which have ruined in a Great Part it's ancient Splendour, however the Foreing Consuls, their vessels, Cargoes, the Stores in Town, & foreing People have been always Protected & Respected by the People and the authorities.

It is a Pity that war between algiers & the united States is an obstacle for the American vessels to Supply this Part of France by the Mediterrean. in winter time the Risk of the algerians is but small and I hope and wish that the united States may soon be able to protect their trade against Piratoes or Succeed in a Treaty of Peace; Tho' it appear that the English is doing every thing to Prevent it;—two years ago Such a Peace could be made more advantageously, easily and cheaper then now;—

I Beg your Refference to the Inclosed Copy of a Letter that I have Just now received from Cap^n obrien prisoner at algiers[7] & after your Perusal to forward it to the Secretary of State Edmund Randolph Esqr at Philadelphia Giving him at Same time a Copy of the Paragraphs of this Letter which you may find Proper to Communicate him for the Governance the american Trade; I have not Such Safe Channels as you may have to write him direct. I am with Respect Sir The most obedient friend of your Excellency & Devoted Servant

Stephen Cathalan

RC, PPRF

1. Stephen Cathalan, Jr., (d.1819) served as U. S. vice-consul at Marseilles 1790-1801 and as consul 1801-1819. He is writing from Nimes, France (Thomas Jefferson to JM, 17 August 1819, *Catalogue of Monroe's Papers*, 2: 764).

2. No letter from JM of 31 August 1794 to Cathalan has been located.

3. Baccaloo was Newfoundland salted cod.

4. Gammon bacon is made from the hind leg of a pig.

5. From *réverbère*, street lamp.

6. An emine was a measurement of grain used in the Mediterranean region. It was equal to seventy-five pounds (*Oxford English Dictionary*).

7. Richard O'Brien (1758-1824) served on an American privateer during the Revolutionary War and became an officer in the navy after the war's conclusion. He was captured by the Algerines in 1785 and remained a slave until 1795. During that time he gained the trust of his captors and became an adviser to the dey. He assisted Joel Barlow in negotiations with Algiers and Tripoli in 1796 and was named U. S. consul at Algiers in 1797, a post he held until 1804, when he returned to the United States (*Appletons' Cyclopedia*).

From Wilhelmina Mosheim Golofkin[1]

à Rolle, Paÿs de Vaud en Suisse Le 4 8bre 1794.

Citoÿen

Si mes intentions n'étoient pas droites et pures, je serois embarrassée comment débuter avec vous, mais lorsque je n'ai rien à me reproche, il me semble que tout le monde doit me juge, comme je me juge moi-même. Voulès vous un autre garant, Citoÿen? Ç'est l'immortel Francklin, qui de son vivant daigna me honore de son estime, me jugea digne de son amitié et voulut bien m'associe souvent à ses délassements, et me faire participer à ses instructions. Je veux donc sous Ses auspices, et comme votre concitoyenne sujette d'un Paÿs ami et allié du votre, vous demander un service dont conserverai une èternelle reconnoissance. L'amitiè, l'estime la reconnoissance m'attachent depuis long-tems à La Citoyenne Lafaÿette, ses vertus, sa bienfaisance—doivent lui mèriter l'interét de toute ame sensible, depuis très long-tems je suis priveè de ses nouvelles et bien de me servir des moÿens que l'on m'emploÿe que trop souvent en pareil cas, j'ai crû qu'il étoit plus digne et de vous et de moi de m'adresse directement à vous, pour vous en demander, Daignès m'en faire donner, je vous en conjure, comme j'ignore tout ce qui la concerne, je ne sais s'il est possible d'entretenir des relations avec elle, mais au moins—je dèsirerois lui faire savoir, que je pense à elle, que je ne l'ai point oublieè.

Puissiès vous, Citoÿen, ne pas vous tromper sur les motifs qui me guident, ècouté que Les inspirations de votre cœur qui d'après ce qu'on m'à dit est surement disposè à rendre service, et dans les besoins trouver quelqu'un qui vous ressemble, et qui m'acquitte envers vous.

Je vous salut de tout mon cœur, et attendrai votre rèponse avec la plus vive impatience.

Mosheim, Veuve Golofkin

J'ai plusieurs Thêmes, ou <u>Exercisses</u> comme les appelloit le celêbre Francklin, qu'il a fait pour apprendre le français; ils sont écrits de sa main, et l'on y retrouve partout cette douçe Philosophie, et, cet esprit penétrant qui le distingoient, je me ferai un plaisir de vous en envoÿer, si vous les dèsirès.

Editors' Translation

Rolle, Vaud, Switzerland 4 October 1794

Citizen

If my intentions were not correct and pure, I would be embarrassed as how to take the first step with you, but as I have nothing to reproach myself for, it seems to me that everyone must judge me, as I judge myself. Would you like another guarantee, Citizen? It is the immortal Franklin, who while alive gave me the honor of his esteem, judged me worthy of his friendship and often associated with me in his leisure time and made me a participant in his education. I wish therefore under his auspices, and as your fellow citizen, subject of a country friend and ally of yours, to ask a service of which I will preserve an eternal gratitude. Friendship, esteem, gratitude have for a long time attached me to Citizeness Lafayette, her virtues, her charity, must merit an interest in her in every sensitive soul. For a very long time I was privy to her news and well served to make use of methods that have helped me in a similar case. I thought it more convenient for you and for me to address myself directly to you, to ask you to have her news given to me, I beseech you, as I am uniformed of all that appertains to her, I don't know if it is possible to maintain relations with her, but at least—I would have her know, that I think of her, that I have not forgotten her.

Is it possible Citizen, that you not mistake the motives that guide me; listen to the murmur of your heart, that according to what I have been told about you, is surely disposed to render a service, and in extremity, find someone who is like you, and who is quite sure of my repaying you.

I salute you with all my heart, and await your answer with the most eager impatience.

Mosheim, Widow Golofkin

I have several written compositions or <u>Exercises</u> as they were called by the celebrated Franklin, that he made while learning French; they are written by his hand, and one rediscovers this sweet philosophy everywhere, and, this penetrating spirit that distinguished him, it will be a pleasure for me to send some of it to you, if you so desire.

RC, PPAmP: Miscellaneous Manuscript Collection

Wilhelmina, Baronne de Mosheim Golofkin, a variant of Golowskin, (d. 1824) was born in Gottingen, Germany, and married Russian diplomat Count Alexander Golofkin, who was assigned to the French court. She met Benjamin Franklin during his residence in Paris. Two months after the death in July 1794 of Adrienne Lafayette's mother, Golofkin married Jean-Paul-François, comte d'Ayen, then duc de Noailles, Adrienne's father (Claude-Anne Lopez, *Mon Cher Papa*, 195; André Maurois, *Adrienne ou La Vie de Mme de LaFayette*, 371, 492, 552).

From Thomas Paine

Luxembourg 14<u>th</u> Vender<u>aire</u> old stile Oct 4<u>th</u> [1794]

Dear Sir

I thank you for your very friendly and affectionate letter of the 18<u>th</u> Sepr which I did not receive till this morning. It has relieved my mind from a load of disquietude. You will easily suppose that if the information I received had been exact, my situation was without hope. I had in that case neither Section, department nor Country, to reclaim me; but this is not all, I felt a poinancy of Grief, in having the least reason to suppose that America had so soon forgotten me who had never forgotten her.

Mr Labonadaire,[1] in a note of yesterday directed me to write to the Convention. As I suppose this measure has been taken in Concert with you I have requested him to shew you the letter, of which he will make a translation to accompany the Original.[2]

I cannot see what motive can induce them to keep me in prison. It will gratify the English Government and afflict the friends I have in America. The supporters of the System of Terror might apprehend that if I was in liberty and in America I should publish the History of their crimes, but the present persons who have overset that immoral System ought to have no such apprehension. On the contrary they ought to consider me as one of themselves, at least as one of their friends. Had I been an insignificant character I had not been in arrestation. It was the literary and philosophical reputation I had gained in the world that made them my Enemies; and I am the Victim of the principles, and if I may be permitted to say it, of the talents, that procured me the esteem of America. My character is the <u>secret</u> of my arrestation.

If the letter I have written be not covered by other authority than my own it will have no effect, for they already know all that I can say. On what ground do they pretend to deprive America of the service of any of her Citizens without assigning a Cause or only the flimsy one of my being born in England? Gates, were he here, might be arrested on the same pretence and he and Burgoyne be confounded together.[3]

It is difficult for me to give an opinion, but among other things that occur to me I think that if you were to say that as it will be necessary to you to inform the Government of America of my situation that you require an explanation with the Committee upon that subject, that you are induced to make this proposal not only out of esteem for the character of the person who is the personal object of it that but because you know that his arrestation will distress the Americans and the more so as it will appear to them to be contrary to their Ideas of civil and national Justice it might perhaps have some effect. If the Committee do nothing it will be necessary to bring this matter openly before the Convention, for I do most sincerely assure you from the observations that I hear, and I suppose the same are made in other places, that the character of America lies under some reproach. All the world knows that I hall served her and they see that I am still in prison, and you know that when people can form a conclusion upon a simple fact, they trouble not themselves about reasons. I had rather that America cleared herself of all suspicion of ingratitude though I were to be the victim.

You advise me to have patience, but I am fully persuaded that the longer I continue in prison the more difficult will be my liberation. There are two reasons for this, the one is that the present Committee by continuing so long my imprisonment, will naturally suppose, that my mind will be soured against them, as it was against those who put me in, and they will continue my imprisonment from the same apprehensions as the former Committee did. The other reason is, that it is now about two months since your arrival and I am still in prison. They will explain this into an indifference upon my fate that will encourage them to continue my imprisonment. When I hear some people say that it is the Government of America that now keeps me in prison by not reclaiming me, and then pour forth a volley of execrations against her, I know not how to answer them otherwise than by a direct denial which they do not appear to believe. You will easily conclude that whatever relates to imprisonments and liberations makes a topic of prison conversation, and as I am now the oldest inhabitant within these walls, except two or three, I am often the subject of their remarks because from the continuance of my imprisonment they auger ill to themselves.—You see I write you every thing that occurs to me, and I conclude with thanking you again for your very friendly and affectionate letter and am with great respect your's affectionately

Thomas Paine

To day is the anniversary of the Action at Germain Town. Your letter has enabled me to contradict the observation before mentioned.

RC, DLC: Monroe Papers

1. Jean-Philippe-Gaspard Camet de la Bonardière (1769-1842) was a young Paris attorney who had been born in Martinique. He held several posts in the government after the restoration of the monarchy and was made a baron (*Dictionnaire de Biographie Française*).

2. Paine's letter to the Convention has not been located.

3. British-born American general Horatio Gates defeated John Burgoyne at the battle of Saratoga in 1777 (*ANB*).

From Edmund Randolph

Philadelphia October 4. 1794

Sir

This letter is intended to take the circuit of Hamburgh; so that it will be confined to the case of the Kensington, Cap[t] Kerr.

You will collect from the inclosed letters the circumstances of her capture; and perhaps the Captain may before this time have presented himself to you, and explained the mischief, sustained from the unwarrantable seizure. Unwarrantable it certainly was; the ship and cargo being purely American; and the trade, which she was prosecuting being justified by the law of nations and our treaty. I am persuaded, that you must have discussed with the French Republic all those principles, which have been violated by their decrees involving our shipping; and perhaps the business of the Kensington has in this respect been advanced. But be this as it may I confide, that you will labour immediately to procure Her liberation, and such compensation, as is bona fide for the detention and other injuries. I have the honor, sir, to be with sincere and constant respect and esteem yr. mo. ob. serv.

Edm: Randolph

RC, PP

Captain Walker Kerr and his ship *Kensington* were captured by the French and taken into Morlaix. Fulwar Skipwith reported on 20 November 1794 that the indemnity for the demurrage was recovered and paid (*ASP: FR*, 1: 753, 757).

To James C. Mountflorence[1]

Paris 14 Vendemaire [5 October] 1794

You will be so obliging as call upon the Committee of publick safety and intimate that since the appointment of M[r] Skipwith to the office of consul for the department of Paris and untill some person shall arrive from America to take the one or the other office, I shall be without a Secretary. That this has made it necessary to procure some present person acquainted with the French & American languages to act for me in the interim. That citizen Gouvain of Harve Marat in the department of the lower Seine, recommended to me by an American, (husband of citizen Gouvain's sister) possesses those qualifications & is willing to act with me but is under requisition on acc[t] of his age. You will mention these things & suggest if perfectly convenient & suitable that I sho[d] be glad this citizen was permitted to attend & render me those services until I sho[d] be situat'd as above.[2]

Ja[s] Monroe

RC, NN: Monroe Papers

1. Major James Cole Mountflorence (c.1745-post 1826) was a French-born attorney, educated at the University of Paris. He went to America in 1778 and served during the Revolutionary War as a supply officer for the North Carolina militia. Mountflorence was an early settler in Nashville, where he speculated in land investments with William Blount. As Blount's land agent he returned to Paris in 1792. The next year during the Terror, Mountflorence sought a consular position as protection against arrest. JM appointed him assistant to Fulwar Skipwith and in the following years Mountflorence held a variety of minor diplomatic posts. Although he retained his American citizenship, he never returned to the United States (*Dictionary of North Carolina Biography*, 4:336-337).

2. M. A. Gauvain was the son of Guillaume-Michel Gauvain, a merchant in Le Havre. He spoke English as well French and served as JM's secretary and translator. It is not know how long he held this post. The appointment was meant to be temporary, but the continued unsettled state of Skipwith's appointment as consul general extended the period of Gauvain's service, and he remained on the job at least through the end of July 1795. Gauvain's sister, Céleste-Rosalie Gauvain, was married to American merchant William Vans (Yvon Bizardel, *The First Expatriates*, 241-243; JM to Skipwith, March 1795; JM to Madison, 5 August 1795; JM to Jean-Victor Colchen, 27 July 1795; Gauvain statement, 2 April 1797, all below).

From James Anderson

Brest October 6th 1794

Sir

I have had the honor to receive this morning your most esteemed favor of the 29 ultimo.[1] Whatever depends upon me Sir, I will endeavour to execute without delay and as satisfactory as possible.

I am extremely sorry to observe to Your Excellency that I have little or no weight here, with many of our countrymen. I have more than once been grossly insulted while Mr Gauvin was with me; and within a few days past, a scene took place in my chamber, which has given me real pain. A Captain William Obrian, who is very well known to Col^o Swan in Paris,[2] and who sailed under the American flag, but whether entitled or not to that honor, I cannot determine, was denounced. The afternoon was fixed upon to hear the accusers and the accused—more than a dozen American Captains were present—the three accusers; Alexander White, John Munro, and William Warner, all masters of American Vessels, were absolutely intericated. much abuse, noise and confusion took place. with some pains, the accused was allowed to make his defence which he did to my perfect satisfaction, and I believe, to the satisfaction of every considerate man present. Captain Roger Robins of the Bacchus of Baltimore tho' a stranger to Mr Obrian, spoke more in his favour, than any one present; and the result of the meeting had proved, that Obrian's enemies have become those of Capt Robbins, for he has been denounced to the Representatives of the people, who are now here, Faur and Trehouart,[3] the 2^d instant for some improper expressions—I was sent for, and immediately attended—I found with the Representatives, Mr George Lane of Boston, his clerk, acting as interpreter, and the Captains Warner, Fernald, and Whitney—A short conversation took place, and the fore-mentioned persons left the room. I then represented to the Citizens Faur and Trehouart that I was concerned, the subject in question was not sufficiently serious to merit their notice—their answer was that it was too late, as the information was laid, and that Captain Robbins must appear. Unfortunately he was to have sailed the next morning early, and therefore no time was to be lost. Admiral Villeret,[4] commander in chief of the Naval force in Brest was sent for—It was after nine in the evening when he came; and an order was immediately signed and sent off, to secure Capt Robbins who was taken out of his bed, and carried on board the admirals Vessel, where he remained until the next morning. Capt Robbins waited on me about seven, attended by a french officer and I told him what had passed the evening before. The whole of the day, and the following one, were not sufficient for the denouncers to make their charge—at last, they were obliged to come forward—the crimes stated, were too trifling, and I should be ashamed to trouble Your Excellency with a recital of them—Capt Robbins was Honorably acquitted, and permitted to sail immediately, but the wind was, and has since continued contrary.

On my first arrival here many disputes took place between the Captains, and their seamen. Morning, noon, and night, applications were made to me for justice, but justice I could not render, for on the hearing both sides, the accusers and the accused were in fault. Should I ever have the honor to be in company in with Your Excellency, I will mention some transactions too long to be communicated by letter, and which I hope will be of service to our seamen, who are I conceive to be men, although difficult to manage, as well as their Captains. Mr Lane has said that it is not necessary for Captains to wait upon their Consuls and Agents unless they have business to transact with them, and he has given a proof of his assertions, for a ship of his own has been for arrived some weeks past from Havre, and I have never seen the Captain of Theirs but in the streets.

I have mentioned these particulars to Your Excellency, to convince You, at least I hope so, that Consuls nor agents cannot act effectually unless empowered to do so. I do not make the observation for myself, for I can assure Your Excellency with truth, that I would resign my place for Brest, with pleasure and satisfaction. Your Excellency can form no idea of the pain, intrigue and anxiety which I have experienced in this City, which of all others under heaven, I believe to be the most difficult to do business in. M͏ᴱ Gauvan who was with me near three months, will be enabled to give Your Excellency a just description of the manner of doing business here.

The government of the United States of America, allow no salarys to their Consuls, and few Men of fortune will accept of a place in that line—the fatal consequence is that more attention is paid to private than to public interest; and many of the Agents of the United States are frenchmen and foreigners who dare not at this moment, vindicate the honor of the flag they pretend to serve. I can with truth assure Your Excellency that I have ever met with here and at Nantes, a ready compliance to every just application, making allowances for the nature of Brest, which is a naval arsenal for Ships of War and not a trading [City] and the multiplicity of business in each office but the french complain, and with a little reason, that some of our Countrymen are not disposed to give them every assistance—this happened today—I went with a Captain to have his Vessel measured for the tonnage—The officer complained bitterly, that he had more than once been grossly insulted—that he was a man and a Citizen as well as another. I apologized as well as I could, and told him, that I hoped my countrymen in future, would be more accommodating. I can assure Your Excellency, that some scenes have passed here, which have given me real pain. We have had some Americans too often intoxicated, and disputes have taken place, not very honorable to themselves, and their more respectable fellow Citizens. Your Excellency will I hope pardon me for making this observation, but I am firmly persuaded of the necessity of your sending printed orders to each Consul and Agent, for their government and that of the Captains and seamen belonging to the United States of America; and more particularly so for the ports of Brest and Rouen, which are more or less, filled with Americans.

I will demand of the Brokers to favour me with the names of those Captains, Vessels and Cargoes, that are not immediately under my directions, which If I procured, will be forwarded with my own, agreeable to Your Excellency's desire, to our Consul in Paris M͏ᴱ Skipwith.

Your Excellency will I hope excuse the length of my letter, proceeding from a desire to give every possible information which may tend to the honor, interest and credit of my Country. With greatest esteem I have the honor to be Sir Your most obedient Servant

James Anderson

RC, DLC: Monroe Papers

1. JM's letter of 29 September 1794 has not been located.

2. James Swan (1754-1831) was a Scottish-born Boston merchant who established a mercantile business in France in 1787. He had good contacts in the French revolutionary government, and in 1793 he became a purchasing agent for France. In early 1794 the French appointed him as its commercial agent in the United States, a post he held until 1796. Upon his arrival in Philadelphia Swan met with Secretary of the Treasury Oliver Wolcott to negotiate the liquidation of the American debt to France. This settlement yielded some two million dollars, which Swan then used to purchase foodstuffs and other supplies that he shipped to France (Yvon Bizardel, *Les Américains a Paris sous Louis XVI et Pendant La Révolution*, 171-177).

3. Gilbert-Amable Faure-Conac (1755-1819) and Bernard-Thomas Tréhouart de Beaulieu (1754-1804) were members of the National Convention. Both served as officers in the French navy (*Dictionnaires de Députés Français de 1789-1889*).

4. Louis-Thomas Villaret de Joyeuse (1748-1812) became an officer in the French navy in 1765 and rose to the rank of admiral. He was a member of the council of 500 in 1795 and served as governor of Martinique and Santa Lucia 1802-1809 (Steven T. Ross, *Historical Dictionary of the Wars of the French Revolution*).

From Diego de Gardoqui

Madrid 7th Oct[r] 1794.

My dear Sir

On the 9th Ult[mo] I did myself the honour of writing you inclosing a letter for our friend M[r] Jn[o] Otto in which I begg'd he would procure me a permission from the French government to drink the waters of Bagneres de Luzon for a fortnight my health being very much impair'd by the constant attention of my Ministry of Finance. This letter went thro' the hands of the commander of the French army in the frontier of Catalogne but am uncertain whether it came to your hands, & am sorry for it as my health declines & wou'd be extremely obliged if you cou'd help me to get such a permission.

I have a further favor to ask of you my Dear Sir, it is, that you wou'd endeavour to procure the release of a particular friend of mine Colonel of the milicia Regim[t] of Ecija whose name is Don Antonio Alcala Galiano who was made prisoner in the garrison of Bellguarde, he is a man of honor, & will by no means forfall his word; shoud you therefore be able to get his release on parole or in a way that he may agree to, I shall esteem it in the highest degree, if at the same time he shoud require any money assistance I beg you wou'd deliver him assur'd of his receipt being punctually paid by me with any expence that you may be at on account of those troubles.

Pardon me the liberty I have taken & believe me that I shall think my self happy whever I receive any of your friendly commands being with sincere regard & esteem Dear Sir Your ass[d] friend & obed[t] serv[t]

Jam[s] Gardoqui

Pray endeavour to get my permission for you know me too well not to assure the government that I am not a man to be suspected of.

Copy, NN: Monroe Papers

1. Bagnères-des-Luchon is a thermal springs resort located in the eastern Pyrenees in the French department of Haute-Garonne.

To Louis-Guillaume Otto

18 Vend: [9 October] 1794

Dear Sir

Will you be so kind as return me by the bearer the paper given you the other day with your comments as you promised.

I find by the letter of the commissary of foreign relations that my note[1] respecting the two vessels with passengers bro[t] into Brest was referr'd to the Marine com[n] as appears by the letter of Dalbarade to him enclosed me.[2] Was it not also sent to the Committee of p: safety? For them it was intended as connected with my former note for it was a rectification of a principle only which I sought, & from whom by report to the convention only could it be obtained. On the contrary I find the marine &c are progressing in the condemnation of the cargo, whilst nothing can be obtain'd from the only source from whence a remedy can be obtained. If this note has not been sent to the Committee of p: safety what shall be done to bring it there? Y[rs] sincerely

Ja[s] Monroe

RC, ViU: Monroe Papers, 4909

1. JM to Buchot, 22 September 1794, above.

2. Philibert Buchot to JM, 7 October 1794, DLC: Monroe Papers.

From Gouverneur Morris

Paris 10 October 1794

My dear Sir

I intend going off tomorrow morning. I shall dine with a friend at Sainport in my late house.[1] If you can make it convenient to pass the day there and return the next morning, I undertake to make you welcome, both you and M[rs] Munroe or you only, as you may chuse a propos. I asked and have obtained leave to take out with me 400 louis. I shall therefore leave only from five to six hundred with M[r] Livingston[2] who will probably have occasion for your assistance to take them out. They are my property and I mention it here to prevent all doubts or difficulties. I leave some things to be fixed by him & the amount will perhaps be thereby lessened as the sums I have to pay are contingent it is not possible for me to be quite exact as to the Amount. I would have called on you but I am so occupied that it is impossible moreover the coachmaker is preparing my carriage for the route.[3]

LBC, DLC: Morris Papers: Official Letterbook

1. Morris bought a house at Seine-Port outside Paris in the spring of 1793. He spent most of his time there until he left France (William Howard Adams, *Gouverneur Morris*, 243-245).

2. Henry Walter Livingston (1768-1810), a New York attorney, was Morris's secretary 1792-1796. He held a several judicial and legislative posts after his return to the United States, serving in Congress 1803-1807 (*BDAC*).

3. Morris left Paris for Lausanne, Switzerland, where he arrived on 20 October 1794 (William Howard Adams, *Gouverneur Morris*, 255).

From James Swan

Paris 11 Oct[r] 1794

Sir

Being on the point of departing for America, I beg you to give me your certificate of being a citizen of the United States:—and as my name is marked by the British, as being an agent of this Republique, they might, in wanteness, carry me in to England, in order to baulk the business for which I am going, and this is the most likely to be done on my Voyage, as it is the Marine only that is instructed to stop vessels, which have been fitted out by me.—Your attachment to the interest & happiness of france,—and how much that depends on my safe arrival, so far as respects provisions, I trust will be sufficient apology for my praying you to put in your Certificate James Keadie (my mother's name) instead of James Swan— & will be a sufficient inducement for you to grant it. I engage to deposit it in the hands of the Secretary of State on my arriving in america, or to destroy it as you shall desire. You may rest assured that I shall make use of it, for myself only—besides my signalment would hardly fit any other person in the world. Yours very respectfully

James Swan

RC, DLC: Monroe Papers

No certificate of citizenship has been located. JM did give Swan a letter of introduction to James Madison, but in a later letter JM warned Madison that Swan was corrupt and not to trust him (JM to Madison, 20 September 1794, *Madison Papers*, 15: 358; JM to Madison, 30 June 1795, below).

To Jacques LeRay de Chaumont

Paris 13 October 1794

I was lately advised by the Secretary of State that the negociation of a Treaty with Algiers had been committed to Col° Humphreys our Minister at Lisbon, and that of course every movement having that object in view must be conducted under his care. Your agency if carried into effect must of course be in that line. I give you this information that in case you wish to render your services in that respect to the United States, you may communicate the same to Col° Humphreys who will I doubt not pay every attention to it that a sense of your merit and existing arrangements will allow of. I have also the pleasure to inform you that the President has approved of the measures taken by Mr Morris and of the confidence reposed in you by him in relation to that object.

Copy, DLC: Monroe Papers

From Thomas Paine

[13 October 1794][1]

Dear Sir

As I have not yet rec^d any ans^r to my last, I have amused myself with writing you the enclosed mem^da. Though you recommend patience to me I can not but feel very pointedly the uncomfortableness of my situation, and among other reflections that occur to me I cannot think that America receives any credit from the long imprisonment that I suffer. It has the appearance of neglecting her Citizens and her friends and of encouraging the insults of foreign Nations upon them, and upon her Commerce. My imprisonment is as well and perhaps more known in England than in France, and they (the English) will not be intimidated from molesting an American Ship when they see that one of her best Citizens (for I have a right to call myself so) can be imprisoned in another Country at the mere discretion of a Committee, because he is a foreigner.

When you first arrived every body congratulated me that I should soon, if not immediately, [be][2] in liberty. Since that time about two hundred have been set free from this prison on the applications of their sections or of individuals—and   I am continually hurt by the observations that are made—"that a section in Paris has more influence than America."

It is right that I furnish you with those circumstances.   It is the effect of my anxiety that the character of America suffer no reproach; for the world knows that I have acted a generous duty by her. I am the third American that has been imprisoned. Griffiths[3] nine weeks, Haskins about five, and myself eight[4] and yet in prison. With respect to the two former there was then no Minister, for I consider Morris as none; and they were liberated on the applications of the Americans in Paris—As to myself I had rather be publickly and honorably reclaimed, tho the reclamation was refused than remain in the uncertain situation that I am. Tho my health has suffered my Spirits are not broken. I have nothing to fear unless innocence and fortitude be crimes—America, whatever may be my fate, will have no cause to blush for me as a citizen; I hope I shall have none to blush for her as a country.

If, my dear Sir, there is anything in the perplexity of Ideas I have mistaken, only suppose yourself in my situation and you will easily find an excuse for it. I need not say how much I shall rejoice to pay my respects to you without-side the walls of this prison and to enquire after my American friends. But I know that nothing can be accomplished here but by unceasing perseverance and application. Your's affectionately.

Thomas Paine

RC, DLC: Monroe Papers.

1. This letter is undated, but the following enclosed letter from Paine, dated 13 October 1794, is most likely the memorandum referred to in the first sentence.

2. This word was omitted in the text.

3. Thomas Waters Griffith (1767-1838) was a Baltimore merchant who served as the U. S. consul at Havre 1794-1799. He was arrested on suspicion of being an English spy and was imprisoned from October 1793 until January 1794 (Elizabeth Wormeley Latimer, ed, *My Scrap-Book of the French Revolution*, 9-10, 41-55).

4. It is not clear what Paine meant here. He cannot mean eight weeks as is inferred by the length of imprisonment of the other two mentioned, nor would eight months be correct, for he had been imprisoned for almost ten months. He had, however, been imprisoned for eight months when he first wrote to JM in August 1794.

Enclosure:
From Thomas Paine

Luxembourg 22 Vend[re] Oct[r] 13 1794

Dear Sir

On the 28th of this Month (Oct[r]) I shall have suffered ten Months imprisonment to the dishonour of America as well as of myself, and I speak to you very honestly when I say that my patience is exhausted. It is only my actual liberation that can make me believe it. Had any person told me that I should remain in prison two months after the arrival of a New Minister I should have supposed that he meant to affront me as an American.—By the friendship and sympathy you express in your letter[1] you seem to consider my imprisonment as having connection only with myself, but I am certain that the inferences that follow from it have relation also to the National character of America. I already feel this in myself, for I no longer speak with pride of being a Citizen of that Country. Is it possible Sir that I should when I am suffering unjust imprisonment under the very Eye of her new Minister.

While there was no Minister here (for I consider Morris as none) nobody wondered at my imprisonment, but now every body wonders. The continuance of it, under a change of diplomatic circumstances, subjects me to the suspicion of having merited it, and also to the suspicion of having forfeited my reputation with America, and it subjects her to the same time to the suspicion of ingratitude, or to the reproach of wanting National or diplomatic importance. The language that some americans have held of my not being considered as an American Citizen, tho' contradicted by yourself, proceeds, I believe, from no other Motive, than the shame and dishonour they feel at the imprisonment of a fellow-Citizen, and they adopt this apology, at my expence, to get rid of that disgrace.—Is it not enough that I suffer imprisonment, but my mind also must be wounded and tortured with subjects of this kind. Did I reason from personal Considerations only independant of principles and pride of having practised those principles honorably, I should be tempted to curse the day I knew America. By contributing to her liberty I have lost my own and yet her Government beholds my situation in silence.

Wonder not, Sir, at the Ideas I express or the language in which I express them. If I have a heart to feel for others, I can feel also for myself; and if I have anxiety for my own honour, I have: also for a Country whose suffering infancy I endeavoured to Nourish and to which I have been enthusiastically attached. As to patience I have practiced it long—as long as it was honorable to do so, and when it goes beyond that point it becomes meaness.

I am inclined to believe that you have attended to my imprisonment more as a friend than as a Minister. As a friend I thank you for your affectionate attachment—As a Minister you have to look beyond me to the honour and reputation of your Government and your Country Men who have accustomed themselves to consider any subject in one line of thinking only, more especially if it makes a strong [impression]² upon them as I believe my situation has made upon you, do not immediately see the matters that have relation to it in another line; and it is to bring these two into one point that I offer you these observations, A Citizen and his Country, in a Case like mine, are so closely connected that the Case of one is the Case of both.

When you first arrived the path you had to pursue with respect to my liberation was simple. I was imprisoned as a foreigner; you knew that foreigner to be a citizen of America, and you knew also his character, and as such you should immediately have reclaimed him. You could lose nothing by taking strong ground but you might lose much by taking an inferior one. But instead of this, which I conceive would have been the right line of acting you left me in their hands on the lose intimation that my liberation would take place without your direct interference, and you strongly recommended it to me to wait the issue. This is more than seven weeks ago and I am still in prison. I suspect these people are trifling with you, and if they once believe they can do that, you will not easily get any business done except what they wish to have done.

When I take a review of my whole situation—my Circumstances ruined—my health half-destroyed, my person imprisoned, and the prospect of imprisonment still staring me in the face, can you wonder at the agony of my feelings.—You lie down in safety and rise to plenty; it is otherwise with me; I am deprived of more than half the common necessaries of life; I have not a candle to burn and cannot get one. Fuel can be procured only in small quantities and that with great difficulty and very dear, and to add to the rest, I am fallen into a relapse and am again on the sick list. Did you feel the whole force of what I suffer, and the disgrace put upon America by this injustice done to one of her best and most affectionate Citizens you would not, either as a friend or Minister, rest a day till you had procured my liberation. It is the work of two or three hours when you set heartily about it, that is, when you demand me as an American Citizen, or propose a conference with the Committee upon that subject, or you may make it the work of a twelve-month and not succeed. I know these people better than you do.

You desire me to believe that "you are placed here on a difficult Theatre with many important objects to attend to, and with but few to consult with, and that it becomes you in pursuit of these to regulate your conduct with respect to each, as to manner and time, as will in your judgment be best calculated to accomplish the whole."— As I know not what these objects are I can say nothing to that point. But I have always been taught to believe that the liberty of a Citizen was the first object of all free Governments and that it ought not to give preference to, or be blended with any other. It is that public object that all the world can see, and which obtains an influence upon public opinion more than any other. This is not the case with the objects you allude to.—But be those objects what they may, can you suppose you will accomplish them the easier by holding me in the background or making me only an accident in the negociation? Those with whom you confer will conclude from thence that you do not feel yourself very strong upon those points, and that you politically keep me out of sight in the meantime to make your approach the easier.

There is one part in your letter that is equally as proper should be communicated to the Committee as to me, and which I conceive you are under some diplomatic obligation to do. It is that part which you conclude by saying that <u>to the welfare of Thomas Paine the Americans are not and cannot be indifferent</u>.—As it is impossible the Americans can preserve their esteem for me and for my oppressors at the same time, the injustice done to me strikes at the popular part of the Treaty of Alliance. If it be the wish of the committees to reduce the treaty to a mere skeleton of Government forms they are taking the Right method to do it, and it is not improbable they will blame you afterwards for not informing them upon the subject. The disposition to retort has been so notorious here, that you ought to be guarded against it at all points.

You say in your letter that you doubt whether the gentleman who informed me of the language held by some Americans respecting my Citizenship of America conveyed even his own Ideas clearly upon the subject. I know not how this may be, but I believe he told me truth. I received a letter a few days ago from a friend and former Comrade of mine in which he tells me, that all the Americans he converses with say, that I should have [been] in liberty long ago if the Minister could have reclaimed me as an American Citizen. When I compare this with the counter-declarations in your letter I can explain the Case no otherwise than I have already done, that it is an apology to get rid of the Shame and dishonor they feel at the imprisonment of an American Citizen and because they are not willing it should be supposed there is want of influence in the American Embassy. But they ought to see that this language is injurious to me.

On the 2ᵈ of this Month Vendemeire I received a line from Mʳ Beresford in which he tells me I shall be in liberty in two or three days and that he has this from good authority. On the 12ᵗʰ I received a note from Mʳ Labonadeire, written at the bureau of the Concierge, in which he tells me of the interest you take in procuring my liberation and that after the steps that had been already taken that I ought to write to the Convention to demand my liberty <u>purely</u> and <u>simply</u> as a Citizen of the United States of America. He advised me to send the letter to him, and he would translate it. I sent the letter inclosing at the same time a letter to you. I have heard nothing since of the letter to the Convention.—On the 17ᵗʰ I received a letter from my former Comrade Van-huele,[3] in which he says "I am just come from Mʳ Russell who had yesterday a Conversation with your Minister and your liberation is certain—you will be in liberty tomorrow." Vanhuele also adds "I find the advice of Mʳ Labonʳᵉ good, for though you have some Enemies in the Convention the strongest and best part are in your favour." But the Case is, and I felt it whilst I was writing the letter to the Convention, that there is an awkwardness in my appearing, you being present; for every foreigner should apply thro his Minister, or rather his Minister for him.

When I thus see day after day and month after month, and promise after promise pass away without effect, what can I conclude? but that either the Committees are secretly determined not to let me go, or that the measures you take are not the right measures, or are not pursued with the vigour necessary to give them effect, or that the American National character is without sufficient importance in the french Republic. The latter will be gratifying to the English Government. In short, Sir, the Case is now arrived to that Crisis, that for the sake of your own reputation as a Minister you ought to require a positive Answer from the Committee.—As to myself, it is more agreeable to me now to contemplate an honourable destruction, and to perish in the Act of protesting against the injustice that I suffer, and to caution the people of America against confiding too much in the treaty of Alliance violated as it has been in every principle, and in my imprisonment tho' an American Citizen, than remain in the wretched condition I am. I am no longer of any use to the world or to myself.

There was a time when I beheld the revolution of the 10ᵗʰ Thermidor with enthusiasm. It was the first News my Comrade Van-huele communicated to me during my illness, and it contributed to my recovery. But there is still something rotten at the Center, and the Enemies that I have, though perhaps not numerous, are more active than my friends. If I form a wrong opinion of Men or things it is to you I must look to set me right. You are in possession of the secret. I know nothing of it.

But that I may be guarded against as many events as possible I shall set about writing a Memorial to Congress, another to the State of Pennsylvania, and an address to the people of America; but it will be difficult for me to finish these until I know from yourself what applications you have made for my liberation and what answers you have received.

Ah, Sir, you would have gotten a load of trouble and difficulties off your hands that I fear will multiply every day, had you made it a point to procure my liberty when you first arrived and not left me floating on the promises of Men whom you did not know.—You were then a New Character. You had come in Consequence of their own request that Morris should be recalled; and had you then before you opened any subject of negociation that might arise into controversy, demanded my liberty either as a Civility or as a Right I see not how they could have refused it.

I have already said that after all the promises that have been made I am still in prison. I am in the dark upon all the matters that relate to myself. I know not if it be to the Convention, to the Committee of public safety, of general surety, or to the deputies who come sometimes to the Luxembourg to examine and put persons in liberty that applications have been made for my liberation. But be it to whom it may, my earnest and pressing request to you as Minister is, that you will bring this matter to a conclusion by reclaiming me as an American Citizen imprisoned in France under the plea of his being a foreigner born in England, that I may know the result, and how to prepare the Memorials I have mentioned should there be occasion for them. The Right of determining who are American Citizens can belong only to America. The Convention have declared I am not a french Citizen because she has declared me to be a foreigner, and have by that declaration cancelled and annulled the Vote of the former assembly that confered the Title of Citizen upon Citizens or subjects of other Countries.—I should not be honest to you nor to myself were I not to express myself as I have done in this letter, and I confide and request you will accept it in that sense and in no other. I am with great respect—your suffering fellow Citizen

Thomas Paine

If my imprisonment is to continue, and I indulge very little hope to the contrary, I shall be under the absolute necessity of applying to you for a supply of several articles. Every person here have their families or friends upon the Spot who make provision for them. This is not the Case with me, I have no person I can apply to but the American Minister, and I can have no doubt that if events should prevent my repaying the expence that Congress, or the State of Pennsylvania will discharge it for me.

Today is 22^{d} Vend^{re} Monday Octr 13, but you will not receive this letter till the 14th.—I will send the bearer to you again on the 16th Wednesday—and I will be obliged to you to send me for the present, three or four Candles, a little sugar of any kind and some Soap for shaving—and I should be glad at the same time to receive a line from you—and a memorandum of the Articles.—Were I in your place I would order a Hogshead of Sugar, some boxes of Candles and Soap from America, for they will become still more scarce. perhaps the best method for you to procure them at present, is by applying to the American Consuls at Bordeaux and Havre, and have them up by the diligence.

T. P.

RC, DLC: Monroe Papers

1. JM to Paine, 18 September 1794, above.

2. This word was omitted in the text.

3. Joseph Vanhuele was a Belgian who was imprisoned with Paine in the Luxembourg. He later became mayor of Bruges (Jack Fruchtman, Jr., *Thomas Paine: Apostle of Freedom*, 322).

To Edmund Randolph

Paris Oct.[r] 16th 1794.

Sir,

I gave you, in my last[1] a sketch of the embarrassments under which our commerce laboured in the ports of this Republic, and of my efforts to emancipate it, as shewn by my letter to the Committee of public safety,[2] a copy of which was likewise forwarded. To this I have as yet received no answer altho' I have requested it more than once. To my applications however which were informal, I was informally answered that the subject was under consideration, and would be decided on as soon as possible.

But as these propositions were of extensive import, and connected with the system of commerce and supply, which had been adopted here, 'tis probable I shall not be favoured with an answer until the subject is generally reviewed. Nor shall I be surprised to find extraordinary efforts to protract a decision and even defeat the object in view. But as the opposition will not be warranted by the interest, so I am well satisfied it will not be supported by the sense of the French nation, when the subject is well understood. To make it so will be the object of my future and, I trust, not ineffectual endeavours.

You were I doubt not surprised to hear that the whole Commerce of France to the absolute exclusion of individuals was carried on by the government itself. An institution of this kind would be deemed extraordinary even in a small state: but when applied to the French Republic it must appear infinitely more so. Nor were the circumstances which gave birth to it more a proof of the calamities with which the society was inwardly convulsed, than of the zeal and energy with which it pursued its object. Thro' the channel of trade, it was found or suspected that the principles of the revolution were chiefly impaired; that thro' it, not only the property of the emigrants and the wealth of the Country were exported, but that foreign money was likewise thrown in, whereby the internal dissentions were fomented, and in other respects the intrigues of the coalesced [powers][3] promoted. For a considerable time it was believed that most of the evils to which France was a prey, proceeded from this source. many remedies were in consequence applied but still the disease continued. Finally an effort was made to eradicate the cause, by exterminating private trade altogether, & taking the whole commerce of the country into the hands of the government. A decree to this effect accordingly passed on the — day of October, 1793, and which has since continued in force.

But now many circumstances incline to a change of this system. The act itself was considered as a consummation of those measures which completed the ruin of the Girondine party, whose principal leaders had already fallen under the Guillotine. By it the commercial interest as distinct from the landed and dividing in certain respects with opposite views, the councils of the country was totally destroyed. All private mercantile intercourse with Foreign nations was cut off, and so severe were the measures, and great the odium on the mercantile character, that none were pleased to have it attached to them. But when the apprehension of danger, from that source was done away, the motive for the act itself was greatly diminished. Accordingly the public mind was seen vibrating back to its former station, and in which it was greatly aided by the fortune of the late dominant party, whose principal leaders had now likewise in their turn settled their accounts with the Republic, at the receipt of the Guillotine. Thus we find and especially in great commotions, that extraordinary measures not only bear in general the strong character of their author, but frequently share his fate. The fall of the Brissotine party extirpated private trade; the fall of Robespierre's may probably soon restore it.[4]

At present many symptons indicate that a change is not distant, tho' none seem willing so prominently to take the lead, as to make themselves responsible for the consequences. The only active interest that I can perceive against it, consists of those who have managed the public trade, and been intrusted with the public monies for that purpose. They readily foresee that a change will not only take from them the public cash, but likewise lead to an adjustment of their accounts for past transactions. Tis however generally the fortune of an opposition of this kind, to precipitate the adoption of the measure, it wishes to avert, for as every one suspects that its motive is not sound and which is proportionally increased by the degree of zeal shewn, so every one feels an interest in defeating it.

I have endeavoured in my propositions to confine them entirely to external objects, by suggesting such remedies as might be adopted without any interference with the interior general system of France. By so doing I hoped that the injuries of which we complain might be sooner redressed and not made dependent on the great events which happen here.

I soon found that the extraordinary expedient to which this Republic had had recourse, of excluding individuals from trade and conducting it themselves, would require in a great measure a correspondent regulation on our part: for if the conduct of the public servants on the one side was not in some measure supervised, and which it could not be but by public agents on the other, the impositions which might be practiced on our improvident countrymen would be endless. In every contest between a public officer here, and the citizen of another country in the purchase of supplies for the Republic, or the execution of a contract, the bias of the government & of the people would be in favor of the former. The consulate, under the Superintendance of the minister, forms their natural bulwark in the commercial line against impositions of every kind. Indeed it is the only one which can be provided for them. But to guard them against those proceeding from the source above described, it should be organized with peculiar care. I was sorry therefore upon inspecting into our establishment to find, that, whatever might be its merit in other situations, it was by no means in general endowed with sufficient strength or vigor for the present crisis. American citizens alone can furnish an adequate protection to their countrymen. In the hands of a frenchman, or other foreigner, the Consular functions lie dormant. In every litigated case the former shrinks into the citizen and trembles before the authority of his Country: and the latter especially if the subject of one of the coalesced powers, finds our commission only of sufficient force to exempt him from the decree which would otherwise doom him to a prison. I annex at the foot of this a list of our consuls and consular agents, with a note of those who have been actually under arrestation and confinement, and by which you will be better enabled to comprehend the justice of the remarks.

My situation was therefore in every view beyond measure an embarrassing one. But as there was no consul or agent of any kind or country here, where the whole business was concentrated, and every transaction closed, it became on that account, infinitely more so: for I was in consequence not only daily surrounded by many of my countrymen complaining of delays and injuries and entreating my intercession for redress, but applied to by them from every quarter and upon every difficulty. I could not settle their accounts with the departments, nor could I interfere in any other respect in particular cases, where there were more of the same description. I could not even go through the forms in the offices which were necessary to verify facts, and which if true furnished ground for complaint, nor could I demand redress of the government upon any supposititious case and which every one must be 'till verified. I remained thus for some time in expectation of the arrival of Mr Duvernat, altho' I was apprehensive such an event in consequence of the general objection above stated, and the decree which applied particularly to his case, instead of affording relief would plunge me into a new embarrassment on his account. But finding that he had not arrived and that I could make no progress in the public business here which was suffering, without the aid of a consul, I finally nominated my Secretary Mr Skipwith provisionally consul for this City on the — day of Sept^r, and notified it to this government; a copy of which and of the answer of the commissary of foreign affairs I herewith enclose you.[5] To him I have since assigned the interesting duty of developing and demonstrating the cause of these difficulties by an appeal to authentic facts, and the better to enable him to perform this service, I have instructed our consuls and agents in the several ports to render him a statement of those within their particular jurisdictions. Thus enlightened he will render a report upon the whole subject to me, and which I will immediately lay before the committee of public safety, in illustration of my former comments, and with such others as may be found necessary.[6]

At present I can say nothing decisively upon the subject of a general arrangement of the consulate. What I have said may furnish some hints that may be useful. But I wish before any thing is definitively done to give you the result of my further remarks on that head. Mr Fenwick will be here in a few days and from whom I doubt not much light will be thrown on it. In the interim Mr Skipwith will perform the duties of the office in which I have placed him: But as he undertook it without the prospect of emolument in the official line, (for in truth the duties required of him are not strictly consular, but novel and growing out of the emergency of the time) and more from a regard for the public interest and to accommodate me than himself, altho' I was thereby deprived of his services in the immediate station in which he had accompanied me, yet I could not bereave him of the appointment I had personally conferred, nor divert from him the salary, belonging to it. By permitting things to stand where they are for a few weeks longer, the public will derive no detriment and I shall be able to acquire and give, such information as will enable you to proceed with more propriety afterwards: a consideration which will induce me to bear the inconvenience to which I shall be personally subjected with pleasure.

I found, upon my first arrival that I should have much difficulty upon the subject of passports. The Jealousy of this government was immediately discovered with respect to those who being subjects of England or any other of the coalesced powers, had passed over to America since our revolution, become citizens of some one of the states and returned to their proper country, where they now resided. It was suggested to me by the Commissary of Foreign affairs, that if these people were covered by my passports, I should immediately spread thro' France, in the armies, and in presence of the public councils, a host of spies who would report the circumstances of the country to their enemies. It was likewise urged that I had no right to do it, for altho' this description of persons had acquired for the time, the right of citizenship with us, yet they were more attached to other countries since they resided and had their property there. I was likewise told of instances wherein this privilege had been abused by such persons, two of whom were said to be then confined at Dunkirk as spies. The subject was in point of principle difficult, and I was really embarrassed how to act in it, so as to satisfy this government, and do justice to the parties concerned: for if citizens of America, it seemed difficult to distinguish between such and any other citizens. And yet the argument was equally strong on the other side, for, if the subject of another power, it was equally difficult to distinguish between such and any other subject of the same power, especially in this region where the right of expatriation is generally denied. But in point of expedience there was less difficulty in the case. Citizenship is in its nature a local privilege. It implies a right within the government conferring it. And if considerations of this kind are to be regarded, I can see no reason why it should not in the present instance be construed strictly: for if a temporary emigrant, after availing himself of this benefit, for a few years and for the purposes of trade, in our indulgent country, chuses to abandon us & return from whence he came, why should we follow him on this side the Atlantic, to support in his behalf a privilege which can now only be claimed at best for private, and perhaps dishonorable purposes? can any motive be urged of sufficient force to induce us to embark here in this kind of controversy at the hazard of our national character, and the goodwill of the nation believing itself injured by it? will the refusal to grant passports to such persons check emigration to our country? I am satisfied it will not of the kind that merits encouragement, for it will rarely happen that a single member of that respectable list of Philosophers, artists, and yeomen who seek an asylum with us, from the troubled governments on this side the Atlantic, will ever recross it. These observations apply only to those who settled with, and abandoned us since the peace: for I consider those, be them of whatever country they may, and especially if of the British territory who were of course in the common character of British subjects equally members of our revolution who threw their fortunes into our scale, as being as much Americans as if they were born with us. After some discussion with the Commissary on the subject, it terminated by an assurance on my part that I should be particularly cautious as to such characters, and refuse my passports to all of that description (except in particular cases of hardship and upon which he should be previously consulted) who were not actually resident within the United States. This arrangement was satisfactory to the government as you will perceive by the Commissary's letters to me copies of which are herewith transmitted.[7] I shall however be happy to be instructed by you on this head.

The councils of this Republic still continue to present to view an interesting but by no means an alarming spectacle. Instances of animated debate, severe crimination and even of vehement denunciation sometimes take place, but they have hitherto evaporated without producing any serious effect. It is obvious that what is called the mountain party is rapidly on the decline, and equally so that if the opposite one acts with wisdom and moderation at the present crisis, it will not only complete its overthrow but destroy the existence (if possible in society) of all party whatever. The agitation which now occasionally shews itself proceeds from the pressure of this latter party on the mountaineers, and who, in their defence sometimes make a kind of incursive or offensive warfare upon their enemy: for having, since the fall of the Brissotines wielded the councils of the nation, and been accustomed to a pretty liberal use of their authority over the remaining members of that party, they bear with pain and not without apprehension of danger their present decline. The tone of the discussion therefore frequently exhibits to view the external of a violent controversy between two rival parties, nearly equally balanced, and which must terminate, under the preponderance of either, in the extirpation of the other. But this I deem only the external aspect; and upon considerations in my Judgment the most solid. I have observed generally that the first indications of warmth have proceeded from the weaker party, and from its less important members, who occasionally break thro' the restraint imposed on them by their leaders, (if when a force is broken and routed, there can be any leader) and sally forth into extravagances which provoke resentment, where they should only endeavour to excite pity, and whilst a different conduct is observed by the leaders themselves: for neither Barrere, Billaud Varrennes, nor Collot d'Herbois, ever take part in these discussions, otherwise than to explain some severe personal attack and to which they confine their comments strictly, and with all suitable respect for their opponents. I observe also it rarely happens that any very distinguished member in the preponderating party takes share in these discussions, tho' the field invites, and much might be said with truth & of course with effect. From these considerations I infer not only that the party of the plain has already acquired the complete preponderance, but also that its motive is rather to save the Republic than to persecute its enemies. There is likewise something in the origin and spirit of these debates which authorizes a belief they portend nothing alarming, for they generally proceed from a review of past enormities which most deny and few justify. But the scene thro' which they have past cannot always be covered with a veil; on the contrary it frequently breaks in upon their discussions and always excites, like the ghost of Hamlet whenever it appears, the horror of the innocent, and the terror of the wicked spectators. The debates therefore which ensue tho' violent, are more of the exculpatory than of the assailing and sanguinary kind. Each party endeavours to vindicate itself from the charges alledged against it, sometimes by absolute denial and at others by a counter crimination of its adversary. Hitherto the business has ended by a general reference of the depending motions to the committee of public safety, solely, or to it associated with the two other committees of general surety and legislation, and who have had sufficient wisdom either to keep up the subject till it was forgotten, or to report such a general essay upon the state of affairs, the views of the coalesced powers, trade, finance and the like, as always to obscure and sometimes to throw it entirely out of view.[8]

By this however I do not wish to be understood as intimating that in my opinion none of the members of the convention will in future be cut off. On the contrary I think otherwise, for it cannot be possible that some of those who have perpetrated such enormities in their missions in the several parts of the Republic, and particularly at Nantes should escape the justice of their country.[9]

In the movements of the present day the Jacobin Society has as heretofore borne its part. The history of this society from its origin to the present time, is of importance to mankind, and especially that portion upon which providence has bestowed the blessing of free government. It furnishes a lesson equally instructive to public functionaries & to private citizens. I am not yet fully possessed of the details, altho' I have endeavored to acquire them, but the outline I think, I now understand. In its History as in that of the revolution itself, there are obviously two great eras. The first commenced with the revolution, and ended with the deposition of the king. The second fills the space between that event and the present day. The former of these is still further divisible into two parts, upon each of which distinct characters are marked. The first commenced with the revolution and ended with the constituent assembly or adoption of the constitution. The second comprises the administration under the constitution. During the first of these, the Jacobin society was composed of almost all the enemies to the antient despotism: for in general those who were friends of the public liberty, and wished its establishment under any possible modification, became at this time members of and attended the debates of this society. But with the adoption of the constitution, many were satisfied and left it. After this and during the second part of this æra, it was composed only of the enemies to hereditary monarchy, comprizing the members of the three succeeding parties of Brissot, Danton, and Robespierre. During the whole of the first æra therefore, or until the deposition of the king, this society may be considered as the cradle of the revolution, for most certainly the Republic would not have been established without it. It was the organ of the public sentiment and by means of discussion and free criticism upon men and measures contributed greatly to forward that important event.

But from that period and thro' the whole of the second æra, the Society has acted a different part and merited a different character. The clergy, the nobility, and the royalty were gone: The whole government was in the hands of the people, and its whole force exerted against the enemy. There was in short nothing existing in that line which merited reprehension, or with which the popular sentiment, virtuously inclined, could take offence. But it had already gained a weight in the government and which it had now neither sufficient virtue nor inclination to abandon. From this period therefore its movements were counter-revolutionary, and we behold the same society which was heretofore so formidable to the despotism, now brandishing the same weapon against the legitimate representation of the people.

Its subsequent story is neither complicated nor various. As the revolution was complete, so far as depended on the interior order of things, it had no service of that kind to render, nor pretext' to color its movements. It was reduced to the alternative of either withdrawing from the stage, or taking part in the ordinary internal administration, and which it could not do otherwise than by becoming an instrument in the hands of some one of the parties against the other. This station therefore it immediately occupied, and has since held it to the present time. It became the creature of Robespierre and under his direction the principal agent in all those atrocities which have stained this stage of the revolution. It was by means of this society that he succeeded in cutting off the members of the two succeeding parties of Brissot & Danton, and had finally well nigh ruined the republic itself.

It is an interesting fact and very deserving of attention that in the more early and latter stages of this society, the best men of France were seeking an admittance into it, but from very different motives. In the commencement and until the establishment of the republic, it was resorted to by them for the purpose of promoting that great event. But in the latter stage, and until the fall of Robespierre it was resorted to by them merely as a shelter from danger. Virtue and talents with every other great and noble endowment were odious in the sight of that monster, and were of course the object of his persecution. Nor was any man of independent spirit possessing them secure from his wrath. The Jacobin society could alone furnish any kind of protection, and to this circumstance it was owing that many deserving characters were seen there and apparently countenancing measures, which in their souls they abhorred. It is therefore only justice that the present preponderating party in France and the world at large, should now look with indulgence and indeed with forgiveness upon the conduct of many of those who seemed at the time to abet his enormities. Unfortunately for them and for their Country, their presence secured only a personal exemption from danger: the preponderating influence had long been in the hands of those of a different description.

In the last scene which was acted by Robespierre and in which he placed himself at the <u>commune</u>[10] in open rebellion against the convention, 'tis said that this society arranged itself under his banner against that assembly. But after his fall and which was instantaneous, it immediately endeavoured to repair the error of this step, by charging it upon some who were admitted to be bad members, and others who were said to have forced themselves, at that tumultuous moment, unlicensed into the society and who were not members at all. It even went into high crimination of Robespierre himself. But the principles of the controversy were too deeply rooted in the minds of all, to be So Suddenly eradicated. It was obvious that a crisis had arrived which must eventually settle the point whether the Convention or this society should govern France, and equally so that the public mind was, and perhaps long had been, decisively settled in favour of the former. As the catastrophe was approaching, this Society as heretofore used at one time an elevated or commanding tone, and at others an humiliating one. But the convention acted with equal dignity throughout. Whether it contemplated to strike at its existence by an overt act or to seek its overthrow by contrasting the wisdom, the justice and magninamity of its own present conduct, with the past and recent enormities of this society, is uncertain. The leading members of the preponderating party seemed doubtful upon this point. But finally the rash and outrageous extremities of the society, which was secretly exciting commotions thro' the country, forced the convention into more decisive measures. By its order the Secretary of the society at Paris was arrested and all the deputies from those associated with it thro' France and who had arrived to deliberate upon the state of their affairs, were driven from the City, under a decree which exempted none, not inhabitants of Paris, except our countrymen. Of all France, Marseilles was the only district in which its efforts produced any effect; a small commotion, excited there, was immediately quelled by the ordinary police and who after having made an example of the leaders, reported it to the convention.[11]

What further measures may be adopted by the convention in regard to this society is uncertain: the subject is now under discussion, and I shall, I presume be able in my next to give you the result.

The same Success continues to attend the arms of the Republic and in every quarter. They have taken since my last in the north, Juliers, Aix la chapelle, Cologne, and Bois le Duc: and in the South Bellegarde, with immense stores of cannon, provision, &c. in each, and particularly in Juliers & Bois le duc: at both of which latter places a general action was hazarded by the opposite generals, and in which they were routed with great loss. 'Tis said indeed that the action which atchieved Juliers was among the most important of the present campaign, since they consider it as deciding eventually the fate of Maestricht, Bergen-op-zoom, and of Holland itself. Maestricht is now closely invested and must fall in the course of a few weeks, since the Austrian general has obviously abandoned it to its fate. Holland must fall immediately afterwards, for there is in truth nothing to prevent it. Indeed I think it probable they will previously detach 20 or 30,000 men to take possession of it, for it is generally believed it may be easily accomplished.[12]

What effect these events may produce in England, it is difficult for me to say. That Austria, Prussia, and Spain have been for some time past wearied with the war and have wished to withdraw from it, is certain. That they will withdraw from it soon, is more than probable, and upon the best terms they can get. England therefore will have to maintain the contest alone, for Holland will be conquered and subject to the will of the conquerors. This however is not the only danger which impends over her. Denmark and Sweden, offended at the unlawful restraint imposed by her on their trade in the arbitrary rule of contraband, have, for near three months past, united their fleet to the amount of about 30 sail for the purpose of vindicating their rights: and Spain equally unfriendly, and irritated with that power, has, I have reason to believe, serious thoughts not only of abandoning the war but of acceding to this combination: the lapse of a few weeks however will no doubt unfold these subjects more fully to view. I have the honour to be Dear Sir, with great respect and esteem, Your most obedient, and very humble Servant

Jaˢ Monroe.

Mᴿ Fenwick, Consul.

Mᴿ Cathalan, V. Consul.

Mᴿ Dobree, V. Consul—arrested but released.

Mᴿ Lamotte, V. Consul—arrested but released.

Mᴿ Coffyn, V. Consul—arrested but released.

Mᴿ Carpentier, Agent—arrested but released.

P. S. I likewise send you a copy of my application for the release of some persons, emigrating from England for America, taken in two of our vessels, and which, I presume, will experience the fate of the other question which depends on the treaty.[13]

Copy, DNA: RG 59: Despatches from France

1. JM to Edmund Randolph, 15 September 1794, above

2. JM to the Committee of Public Safety, 3 September 1794, above.

3. This word was omitted in the text.

4. The nationalized economy in France developed out of the exigencies of war in 1793 and the necessity of developing a strong army. Unregulated price controls required the Jacobin revolutionary government to pass the law of the Maximum on September 29. Following this, on October 22, the Committee of Public Safety installed the new subsistence commission and placed one of its twelve members, Robert Lindet (1746-1825), at its head. Under Lindet the commission on November 18 acquired the monopoly on imports, and on December 12 gained power to authorize exports. Lindet directed his agents to requisition luxury goods such as silks, jewelry and fine furniture throughout France to be exchanged for foreign wheat, wool, and grain. Lindet's ambition was to bring the circulation of all goods under national control. As a consequence his commission became one of the most powerful instruments of the new revolutionary dictatorship (Georges Lefebvre, *The French Revolution From 1793 to 1799*, p.76; R. R. Palmer, *Twelve Who Ruled*, 226, 232, 246).

5. JM to Philibert Buchot, 20 September 1794, above, and Buchot to JM, 23 September 1794, ViFreJM.

6. Fulwar Skipwith report, 17 October 1794, below.

7. Buchot to JM, 6 and 14 September 1794, above .

8. The Jacobins (the Mountain), having renounced Robespierre, still continued to advocate the revolutionary principles of 1793-1794. The Moderates (the Plain), led by Boissy d'Anglas, were in the majority and wanted government by men of property. The neo-Hébertistes, with Varlet and Babeuf in charge, formed the Electoral Club, attacked revolutionary government, and wanted the Constitution of 1793 restored (George Rudé, *The French Revolution*, 112-113).

9. JM refers to Jean-Baptiste Carrier. See JM to Edmund Randolph, 30 November 1794, below.

10. The Commune was the title given to the local government of Paris that appeared after the fall of the Bastille. It was often at odds with the National Convention. It faded away shortly after Thermidor and reappeared in 1848 and 1871 (George Rudé, *The Crowd in the French Revolution*, 254).

11. The Committees in Paris issued a decree on September 20 expelling from Paris all those who had not been living there on 1 Messidor (June 19), comprising all the departmental delegates (Lefebvre, 32).

12. From 1794 to 1814 Julich was a part of France under the name Juliers. Today it is located in North Rhine-Westphalia in Germany. The French scored a victory against the Austrians there on 23 October 1794. They defeated the Dutch at Bois-le-Duc, in Holland, on October 10 (Antoine-Henri Jomini, *Histoire critique et militaire des guerres de la Revolution*, 6: 34-48).

13. JM to Buchot, 22 September 1794, above.

From Thomas Pinckney

London 17th October 1794

My dear Sir,

I have to acknowledge the receipt of your favor of the 19th of September which I have not before had an opportunity of answering. Accept my Thanks for the friendly sentiments contained therein and be assured of a perfect Reciprocation of them on my part. The Embarrassment concerning naturalized Citizens of America seems to result from our very liberal mode of admitting Foreigners to those Rights and is I think very properly submitted by you to the Consideration of our government, in the mean time I do not know how we can make discriminations where our Laws have made none & refuse passports to any persons who produce to us authentic Testimonials of their being Citizens. The Duplicates of my former letters herewith shew the footing of propriety and Convenience to yourself on which I wish to place all Applications made to you through me in favor of persons residing here—and I now enclose you several Applications which you will act upon or not as you may judge right.[1] The letters are all open and upon Subjects which appear to me innocent, I therefore conceive there can be no impropriety in forwarding them to you—but I shall be glad of your Sentiments on this head. I make a memorandum on each Application of the wish of the party concerning it. Mr J. Q. Adams arrived here two days ago from Boston which he left about the 17th ulto.[2] The Disturbances in Pennsylvania were not terminated and it was feared recourse must be had to coercive measures—he brings no other late Intelligence of consequence. I beg my best Respects to Mrs Monroe and remain with sincere Respect and Esteem My dear Sir truly yours

Thomas Pinckney

RC, NN: Monroe Papers.

1. A list of enclosed papers is included with this letter.

2. John Quincy Adams, the newly appointed American minister to the Netherlands, stopped in London to deliver dispatches from the State Department for Pinckney and John Jay (Samuel Flagg Bemis, *John Quincy Adams and the Foundations of American Foreign Policy*, 47).

From Fulwar Skipwith

Paris Vendemiaire 3ᵈ year [17 October 1794]

Sir

At your request I now lay before you a statement of the innumerable embarrassments and difficulties which our commerce has for a long time and still continues to labour under in the different ports of the French Republic. It is evident if their Government does not soon remedy the incessant abuses and vexations practised daily upon our Merchants, Vessels, Captains and crews, the trade of the United States with France must cease. I cannot give you an ample detail of all the inconveniences and oppressions which have been thrown upon our commerce, many of the consuls and their agents to whom you have written to forward such documents to my Office, having not yet done it: besides it would take volumes to expose them at full length.

From the communication however already received from the different ports and from the information I have collected from the Captains present I can assure you that there are near 300 Sail of American vessels now in the ports of France; all of whom have suffered or are Suffering more or less delay and difficulties of which the examples annexed will afford you a general view—the hardships of which I have chiefly to complain and out of which there grows incalculable evils may be developed under four general heads.

1ˢᵗ. The capture indiscriminately of our vessels at sea by the vessels of War of the Republic.

2ⁿᵈˡʸ. The impossibility of Americans selling their cargoes and receiving payment at the ports to which they are conducted, or of their own accord arrive.

3ʳᵈˡʸ. The difficulties and procrastination which they find in their transactions with the boards of Marine and Commerce.

4ᵗʰˡʸ. The noncompliance, or heretofore delay in fulfilling the contracts, made by the agents of the French Republic in America, for supplies of provisions.

The seisure of our vessels at Sea often gives rise to the most serious and well founded complaints,— the stripping them of their Officers and crews who are generally replaced by boys and inexperienced hands in order to be conducted to ports, exposes them to much injury and sometimes total loss; the confinement of our Sailors taken out of those vessels, the Seals upon their cargoes, and, above all the sending the papers to the Commission of Marine at Paris involves the most unwarrantable hardships and delays, and I am sorry to add that all our vessels experience some of those difficulties; and, indeed, such as arrive with cargoes on account of the Republic, months elapsing before the Captains can get their clearances and papers, many of which are often lost or mislaid.

As to the second head, the agents of the Commissions of commerce at the different ports having no power to treat directly for cargoes, it follows that they must write to the Commission at Paris for orders, and after one or two months fruitless correspondence it often happens that the Captains are obliged to come up to Paris, where being ignorant of forms and language they have to encounter a thousand difficulties.

It would be too tedious to mention all the inconveniences resulting from the third general complaint. In the first place the delays at the Commission of Marine are incredible. The Captains whose vessels are brought into ports by the armed vessels of the Republic, cannot withdraw their papers from the hands of the Marine agents, but are forced to Paris to solicit time after time of the Marine a report upon them to the Committee of public safety (the cruel delays attending this will be illustrated in the examples annexed) the report being made before it can reach the latter body it must have the signature of the Commissaries and go through other formalities; and when it receives the Sanction of the Committee of safety, has to travel nearly the same road back.—Judge sir, of the tedious delay attending this; indeed, you will see cases where the poor Captains have been many months in arriving at the above point, and I myself after having pressed several reclamations for weeks past have not yet been able to bring one to that issue.

To sell to the Commission of Commerce is still more difficult. When a bargain is concluded with them an order is issued to the keepers of the public Magazines to receive the cargo sold; who often pretend that there is no room to receive it, and frequently they keep the Captains waiting weeks before their whim or convenience will induce them to receive it: this point gained, application must then be made at Paris to the Commission of Commerce for payment, who refer the Captain to their board of agency, they make a report to the Comptabilité of the same Commission, from thence it must go to the Committee of finance, then to the Committee of public safety from whence it returns to the Comptabilité. This labyrinth of perplexity of course throws the Captain into the hands of an agent who preys upon his distress; and when all these forms are fulfilled 'tis not always that the Captain can immediately touch his money. If in the first instance the Commission will not purchase his cargo on the terms he asks, they tell him he may depart; but on returning to his vessel is most commonly prevented from sailing by the agents at the port.—If it is mutually agreed that Merchandize shall be taken in Exchange the difficulties become greater. If Assignats with permission to export wines and Brandy the Captain finds himself taken in; for the Commission will put those very articles in requisition. If the Commission tells the Captain that they do not want his cargo and that he may sell to individuals, he finds that he cannot export the proceeds unless he gives a security that he will import afterwards into the republic the same amount in Articles of the first necessity, such as provisions &c. If the Captain is so unfortunate as to have to treat with the agents of the Commission he is certain to feel their imposition,—they frequently refuse to confirm their own agreements.—In short after every sort of delay and vexation should the Captain claim an indemnity he has to wade thro' double the difficulties heretofore stated, and, perhaps after all to leave his business incomplete in the hands of an agent.

The 4th and last general complaint is of a delicate and important import. Mr Fauchet the French Minister has made considerable purchases of provisions in America for account and in the name of the french Republic—one house has engaged to furnish 20 m. barrels of flour—thirteen vessels loaded with those provisions have already arrived; and in vain have I demanded of the Commission of Commerce their answer respecting the payment of those contracts, except that in the commencement they assured me the Committee of finance had ordered the payment of three cargoes at Bordeaux, but to my surprize, two days after I found that no report had been made by the Commission to that Committee.

You having judged Sir, the Commerce of this Country being immediately under the controul of one branch of the administration of its government, that it was necessary to adopt some corresponding measures in order to protect the rights and interests of our citizens, and, for that purpose, having provisionally named me to the place of Consul, I have accepted it as well to answer your views as in the hope of rendering some good to both republics.

Before I conclude permit me to observe that it is of indispensable importance to obtain some mode of having the claims of our citizens adjusted, for supplies furnished to the colonies of the French Republic, and, likewise the numerous claims in consequence of the late embargo at Bordeaux. I am authorised by many of the claimants to adjust them, and have many of the documents in hand but wish for further instructions from you.

I would offer to your view a statement of the immense sums already paid by this republic, and to be paid as indemnities for the extraordinary and useless delays of our vessels, but the consuls and agents have not yet furnished me with the requisite documents: it is however a fact that not a single vessel arrives from America and departs without having some such reclamation to make. I am persuaded that many millions are absorbed in this manner.

It is with real regret sir, that I find myself obliged, the duties of my station requiring it, to present to your view so many complaints of so serious a nature as in my opinion calls for your earliest attention; but in doing this I do not forget, and it will ever be my effort to cultivate as much as possible a good understanding between the Citizens of our Country and those of France. With respect I remain sir your most humble servant.

Fulwar Skipwith.

A report on some of the American vessels captured by the armed vessels of the French republic, and carried into the various ports of the Republic.

1ˢᵗ. The Ship Alexander, Captain Woodward with a cargo of flour on account of the french government, was captured on the 5ᵗʰ of August last, by the frigate agricola, and conducted to Rochefort, being stripped of all her crew, except the cabbin boy—this vessel from extreme neglect since her arrival at Rochefort, is in a condition unfit for sea, without undergoing considerable repairs and remains there deprived of her people. The demand of the freight agreeable to the charter party Signed by Mʳ Fauchet has been long since and remains with the Commission of Commerce.

2ᵈ. The Brigantine Olive Branch, Captain John Buffington taken by the frigate Semillante was conducted to L'Orient on the 30ᵗʰ of August, with a mixed and perishable cargo; the seals remain upon her hatches; and besides having been rudely insulted by having her colours hauled down by order of the Captain of a french sloop of War she was deprived of her crew, and ran many risks of being wrecked by the inexperience and negligence of those who were put on board of her.

3ᵈ. Brigantine Polly and Nancy Captain Brien was taken into Brest the 26ᵗʰ Augᵗ after being deprived of ten of Her Ships Compʸ.

4ᵗʰ. The Brigᵗ Apollo Captain Parker taken the 26ᵗʰ febʸ, and carried to Rochefort and not liberated until the beginning of September; and the Captain has not yet been able to prevail on the Commission to make a report to the Committee of Salut Public, in order that he might obtain the indemnity so justly due him.

5ᵗʰ. The Ship Robert, Captain Whippey taken by the Proserpine frigate and conducted to Brest.

6ᵗʰ. Ship James, taken by an armed vessel, and conducted to L'Orient in the month of August, after being deprived of Mate and 10 Men.

7ᵗʰ. Schooner Ruth, Captⁿ John Peter taken by the frigates the Railleuse la resolve and the Insurgent, and conducted to Rochefort, after being stripped of all her crew except the Cabbin boy, where she remains with her hatches closed, and the cargo (of fish) in a perishing state.

Vessels of the United States now detained in different ports, loaded on account of the Republic, their contracts signed by the French Minister and payments not obtained or at present likely to be obtained of Government here.

At Bordeaux since the 6ᵗʰ of august 1794

    The Ariel, Captⁿ Decator.

    Brigᵗ Mary . . . . . . .Fleming.

    Dᵒ Susanna . . . . Towers.

I have demanded payment of the cargoes of those three vessels of the Commission of Commerce, and was answered that the Committee of finance had given an order for that purpose, but on my application to that body I find they have not.

Arrived at Nantes in the month of August

    The Goddess of Liberty, Capᵗ Glad.

    Mary . . . . Puller. 2720 Barrels flour.

    Norfolk . . . . .Baron

    Bellona . . . . Brooks. 4203 dᵒ

At L'Orient 5ᵗʰ August

    The Alexander, Capt. Woodward 1595 Barrels flour

At Brest 26ᵗʰ August

    The Polly and Nancy Captⁿ Bryan loaded with flour, and three others.

At Rochefort 2ᵈ September.

    Brigᵗ Sally Capt. Grice 1638 Barrels flour.

All the above vessels are waiting, and tho' I do not get a positive denial, I can obtain no promise of payment for their cargoes.

Particular cases of American vessels.

1ˢᵗ. The Paragon, Captⁿ Gerrish & laded at Sᵗ Lucie in September, 1793, and cleared her for Amsterdam; in the month following she was stranded upon the French coast in the Depᵗ of Montagne sur mer. The Judges of the Canton of Sᵗ Jose ordered the part of the cargo damaged to be sold, and the good to be stored. The Captain after four journeys to Paris fruitless attendance on the Marine, and 12 Months detention has been forced to abandon the pursuit; and since my residence here, tho' in the quality of Proprietor as well as consul, I have not been able to obtain restitution of the property.

2ᵈ. Captain Newell arrived at Havre in the month of June '93 with a cargo 88,000ˡᵗ value, which he sold and purchased to the amount of 47,000lᵗ in Articles of Luxury. At the moment his vessel being ready to depart, a decree of the N. Assembly appeared prohibiting the exportation of all Merchandize whatever:—Newell was consequently obliged to dispatch his vessel empty,—many months however after he procured from the Commission of Commerce permission to export those goods; and at his arrival at Havre where they lay, not finding an American vessel to be hired, he chartered a Danish one and shipped the goods; but applying for a clearance at the custom house, he was required not only to give approved surety of his landing the goods at his particular port of residence in America, but likewise that he should ship them in An American vessel only—the hardship of the case compelled him of course, again to Paris, and he is now in vain soliciting that he may be relieved from giving a security that as a stranger he cannot obtain, and being allowed to export his property in other than a neutral bottom, the one he has chartered lying all the while, at his expense at £9 Sterling per day.

3$^{\underline{d}}$. The Brig$^{\underline{t}}$ Hope Capt$^{\underline{n}}$ Hooper, Captured and sent to Rochefort in March last, whose cargo was sold soon after to the Commission of Commerce, has only from that time to this been able to obtain a report from the Commission of Commerce to the Committees Salut Public and finance.

4$^{\underline{th}}$. The Ship Kensington Capt. Kerr was taken by a frigate and sent to Morlaix the 28$^{\underline{th}}$ April last the Commission of Commerce refused to purchase his cargo notwithstanding he has been detained in port ever since.

5$^{\underline{th}}$. Some time ago the Commission of Commerce purchased the cargo of the Brig$^{\underline{t}}$ Iris but finding afterwards that the articles which composed that cargo might be bought on lower terms, they refused to comply with their contract; the proprietor therefore demanded restitution of a considerable part of his cargo remaining unsold, and offered to take the price they pleased for the part that was; this was rejected and the Captain at present can get no satisfaction whatever.

6$^{\underline{th}}$. The agents of the Commission of commerce purchased at Havre the Cargo of the Ship Fabius, payable in bills on Hamburg; but after a tedious delay, they would only give him Bills on Basle, pretending they could not draw on Hamburg, tho' they gave immediately after Bills on that place to others,— however after another month's vexation and delay in this Situation, M$^{\underline{r}}$ Vans the proprietor obtained Bills on Hamburg, which have come back protested for nonpayment and the Commission refuses to allow the customary damages. M$^{\underline{r}}$ Vans likewise sold to their agent at Dunkirque a valuable cargo and the sale was ratified and approved by the representative of the people then with the northern army, and who was possessed of the power from the Convention of making unlimited purchases; still the commission of commerce oppose the fulfilment of the contract.

Vessels of the United States captured going to, and coming from different ports, and their treatment by armed vessels of the Republic.

1$^{\underline{st}}$. The Ship Mary Capt. Titcomb, on her passage from London to Boston was captured by the sloop of War the Hendrick (a prize to the French frigate the Surveillante) her passengers among whom there were three American families, were plundered of their Hats and Watches; the crew experienced no better fate, and the Cabin was entirely ransacked. The passengers tho' late at night and the Sea running extremely high were hurried into a small boat and sent at some distance on board the sloop of War. The women of whom there were several from the hardships they underwent have been indisposed ever since. The Ship entered Brest on the 1$^{\underline{st}}$ of September, the passengers remain at this time on board a prison ship, and the Commissary of Marine has not yet made a report upon the business.

2$^{\underline{nd}}$. The Ship Severn Capt$^{\underline{n}}$ Goodrich on her passage from Bristol to New York, with several families on board who were going to settle in America, was captured by the Proserpine frigate, who took out of the Severn the Passengers, crew, papers and live stock, and sent her into Brest on the first September, where the passengers remain on board the prison Ship, called the City of L'Orient, and no report can be obtained from the Commission of Marine.

3$^{\underline{d}}$. The Ship Mary Capt$^{\underline{n}}$ Preble was captured by the above mentioned frigate on the 18$^{\underline{th}}$ August on her passage from England to America with a number of Passengers and has experienced the same treatment in every respect that the Severn did.

4th. The Brig^{t} Theodosia Captn Justice was captured by a french squadron on the 14th September, and conducted to Brest with a perishable cargo, where she remains, her hatches closed; and as yet I cannot obtain a report from the Commission of Marine.

5th. The Schooner Roebuck Captn Kensman, captured by the frigates Surveillante and Fidele was carried into Brest in May last. Her bills of loading were given to the Commission of Marine at L'Orient, but not having been forwarded to the Commission here, no report can be had.

6th. The Ship Canton, Captn McGhee captured in the East Indies in the month of October 1793 by a french Privateer and sent to the isle of France.

7th. The Ship Woodrup Sims, Capt Hodgson, captured by the Jacobin and Atalanta frigates and sent to Rochefort the 12th September remains with a perishable cargo on board and no report can yet be obtained of the Commission of Marine, this vessel on her last voyage to Bordeaux was detained nine months.

8th. The Brig^{t} Peggy   taken by an armed Brig^{t} of the Republic, was conducted to Rochefort the the Captain and crew were in prison during eight days, the Seals put upon the hatches and the papers taken from the Captain.

9th. The Ship George Capt. Symes Captured by the frigate La Galathié and carried into Morlaix in January last, her papers and crew were wrested from her, and after considerable delay of the Cargo on board it was landed and stored by order of the Judge of the Peace, and not 'till some months after, was a report made to the Committeé Salut Public.

10th. The Brig^{t} Hope Capt. Hooper, taken by three frigates and conducted to Rochefort in the month of March, remains there still, and the Captain at Paris unable to close his business.

11th. The Ship union Capt Biard taken the 12th January by the frigate La Resolve.

Copy, DNA: RG 59: Dispatches from France, enclosed in JM to Edmund Randolph, 7 November 1794.

JM forwarded this report to the Committee of Public Safety on 18 October 1794 (see below), which suggests that he probably received it from Skipwith on 17 October. A variant copy is in DLC: FCP—France. Another variant in ViFreJM is dated 19 October 1794, but that is certainly an error made by the copyist.

Documents collected by Skipwith relating to French spoliation claims can be found in the Fulwar Skipwith Papers in the G. W. Blunt White Library, Mystic Seaport, CT.

To the Committee of Public Safety

Paris 27 Vendemaire [18 October] 1794

Citizens

Upon the several subjects on which I addressed you on the 17th of Fructidor[1] viz the embargo of Bourdeaux, the supplies rendered to the Government of St Domingo and the departure by France from the 23 & 24th articles of the treaty of amity and commerce subsisting between the two Republicks, I have but little to add at present. The two former were matters of account only, and could of course involve no topic for discussion, between the Committee and myself. I had only to ask for such despatch in the adjustment and payment, as the exigence of the parties and the circumstances of the Republick would admit of. Nor shall I add any thing upon the third point to change the principle upon which I rested it. The Committee will therefore be pleased to decide upon each, under the considerations which have been already urged.

I likewise stated in that note generally the embarrassments under which our commerce laboured in the ports of the Republick. A general view was all I could then give. But the appointment of a Consul for this City has since enabled me to obtain a more circumstantial and accurate statement on this head. This officer has already examined it with great attention, and reported the result to me, a Copy of which I now lay before you.[2] It presents to view a frightful picture of difficulties and losses equally injurious to both Countries, and which if suffered to continue, will unavoidably interrupt for the time, the commercial intercourse between them. I trust therefore the causes will be immediately removed, and suitable remedies adopted, and in this I am the more confident, because those which would be deemed adequate, will not in any degree interfere with the internal police or regulations of the Country. I also suggested in my former note, that however necessary it might be for France to avail herself of Agents in America at the present crisis, for the purchase and Shipment of supplies thence here, it should not be relied on as a principal resource. The more attention I have since paid to this subject, the better satisfied I have been of the justice of that remark. I have therefore thought it my duty to add some further observations on it, and which I now beg leave to submit to your consideration in the annexed paper.

You will observe the Consul has likewise comprised in his Report the cases of many Seamen & other persons citizens of the United States, taken at Sea and elsewhere, and who are now held as prisoners agreeably to the accounts transmitted to him by the Consuls and agents of the United States at the different ports of France. I hope an order will be issued for their immediate enlargement and as it is possible many others may be in like situation, that it may be made to comprehend all the citizens of the United States, not charged with any criminal offence, against the laws of France, and of which latter description, I hope there are none. The Committee I doubt not will designate such species of evidence necessary to establish the right of Citizenship, in doubtful cases, as it will be practicable for the parties to furnish.

Permit me to request an early decision upon these subjects, that I may immediately communicate it to our Government. The Congress will commence its Session in a few weeks, and it is the duty of the President to lay before that body, and at that time, the state of publick affairs, comprising as the most interesting particular the conduct and disposition of other nations towards the United States. Information upon these points will of course be expected from me, and I should be mortified not to be able to give such as would be deemed satisfactory.

Ja^s Monroe

RC, DLC: FCP—France. In clerk's handwriting, with JM's signature.

1. 3 September 1794, above.

2. Fulwar Skipwith to JM, 17 October 1794, above.

Enclosure:
Supplemental observations to the note of the 3d of September, upon the American Commerce

[18 October 1794]

That France will have occasion whatever may be the crop for the present year, for supplies of provision from foreign Countries for the next, is certain. These must be obtained from the neutral countries and chiefly from the United States of America. 'Tis of importance therefore for her to ascertain how they shall be obtained, and brought into her ports with greatest certainty, and least expence.

There are but two possible ways or modes by which these supplies, or any others, can be brought here, and which are first by public exertion, or by agents in those countries, whose duty it would be to purchase the articles in demand and send them here on public account, and secondly by the enterprize of individuals—both shall be impartially examined.

First, as to certainty, and which will depend upon prompt purchases, safe carriage and integrity of the agents.

As soon as agents arrive in America it will be known to the commercial interest in every quarter. Where ever they appoint sub-agents this will likewise be known. When it is intended to make purchases and shipments this will be known. The movement of vessels to take in cargoes will be observed. Immediately a combination will be formed among the merchants of the place who will buy up all the flour and with a view of taking advantage of the emergence and this will raise the price and create delay. A monopoly naturally revolts the society against it, and this will add a new stimulus to the otherwise sufficiently active one of private interest, to speculate and prey upon these agents, and of course upon the embarassments of their country.

But the purchase is finally made and shipped for France; the ships are at Sea: the property belongs to France and the ships tho' American give no protection by the antient law of nations, which is in force where not otherwise regulated by treaty, and of course with England. The cargo of every vessel which shall be taken, will be condemned: and will not many be taken? The movements of this agency will be well known to the British administration, and it will be employed to counteract it in the purchase and upon the Sea. It will be apprized of the ports from whence shipments will be made, and have vessels of war stationed to seize them.

'Tis the nature of an agency to be at war with every other mode of supply. The amount of its profits will depend upon the exclusion of every other; for every cargo which shall arrive from another source will take from it so much. It will therefore see with Jealousy the commencement of enterprizes of this kind, and deem each in the degree a robbery of its own recourses. It will fear that not only the amount of its profits, will be diminished, but that the funds upon which any are to be made, will be exhausted. It will therefore discourage these enterprizes by hinting that the republic does not want them, that is has no money to pay for them, that the Captains and Supercargos are ill treated in France by delay &c[a]. It will be the Interest of the agency to crush every other mode of supply, and it will accomplish it, unless the wisest precautions are used to prevent it.

These latter observations apply to the motive of interest only, supposing the agency disposed to discharge the trust as faithfully as it could, making at the same time the greatest profit for itself, and which would generally be done. But let it be supposed that it was capable of defrauding the public as much as possible, without being detected. In that case it would have an additional motive for discouraging private adventurers: because as these would flock to the market, and bid one against the other, they would keep the price at its proper level, and thus check its conduct; for if it charged more than they (allowing for the difference of Commission) it would of course be convicted of fraud, and if capable of fraud, other and numerous temptations to seduction might be counted. The chief agent would be known to the British Administration. Suppose France in great distress for bread, and without any other resource; the with-holding it might bring on a crisis in her affairs, and which might terminate in an arrangement that would applaud the agent for his perfidy. Would he not be an object for the British administration to assail, and would it be proper that France and the French revolution should be thus made dependent on agents in foreign countries?

As to the comparative expence there can be no question upon that point. The Commission itself will be a considerable thing, in addition to which the freight will be increased, for if American vessels are employed, the owners will charge more on account of the hazard, than if there was none, and which would be the case if the property was their own: not to repeat the encreased price which would be demanded of the agents, in consequence of the combination among the merchants, to take advantage of circumstances which would be known to them: nor to suggest that under any probably modification it would be the interest of the agents to give the highest price possible.

Besides funds must be raised some where to answer the drafts of these agents: will it be in the Sea ports, in Paris, Hamburgh, or some other neutral town? By the exportation of the productions or other commodities of the country, incurring thereby the expence of double commissions, storage, the hazard of the Sea, and of the enemy, together with the further inconvenience of overstocking the market and raising at the same time such Town to grandeur, by making it the entrepot of French productions, whilst her own were impoverished.

Every thing that has been said or can be said against a chief dependence on agencies forms an argument in favour of encouraging the ordinary private trade by individuals, and shews that the supply by that mode might be made more sure and cheap. If France would regulate things so that the parties bringing provisions into her ports were paid immediately and dispatched, she might command if necessary the whole produce of America. Nor Would it be necessary that the payment be always in specie: on the contrary return cargoes would more frequently be taken, of productions manufactures of the country, and of prize goods.

The above is a short sketch of the conveniences and inconveniences which attend the two modes of supply. The one which commences in a monopoly, will be attended with all the inconveniences which belong to monopolies in general, greater expence, disgust to all parties affected by it &c &c, with others which are peculiar to it—for other monopolies of foreign trade are confined to luxuries of little importance, and of countries whose citizens cannot send them to market—where as the present one is a monopoly of the necessaries of life in great demand here, to be obtained from Countries whose citizens can best supply them, and at a crisis of affairs when the failure may hazard every thing valuable to France, and when of course it should be most avoided. Whilst on the other hand the latter which is a system of free trade, will not only be free from these objections, but enjoy some benefits which are peculiar to it. It will leave commerce in the hands of individuals & under the protection of the flags of both Countries. It if was made known that France would protect the neutral commerce, the merchants would have a new encouragement to enterprize, and the neutral powers would be more decisive in vindicating their own rights. The french flag would be deemed the guardian of trade and the asserter of the freedom of the seas. The American merchants would behold it with pleasure, because they would find under its banner not only the friendly welcome of their ally, but likewise a safety from the pirates of the ocean. If the demand in France was great it would be known in the United States whose merchants would immediately supply the demand,—and if it was interrupted on the Sea by the vessels of another power what would be the obvious effect of such interruption? Might not France oppose it and conduct the vessels safe to her ports, and would it not rouse the nation injured to vindicate its rights and protect its own commerce?

Unhappily France has adopted a different policy towards us heretofore. Instead of encouraging individuals to supply her markets, she has given them every possible discouragement which could be devised. Instead of protecting our commerce at Sea and leaving us to seek reparation for the injuries which were rendered us by the other powers she has rendered us like injuries and thus embarassed our councils. But 'tis not too late to change this System of policy. The Americans have lamented it not more on their own account than that of France. It has as yet left no unkind impression behind it, and if the necessary regulations are made, Commerce will soon resume its ordinary course.

I do not by this, object to the plan of supply by agency altogether: on the contrary I deem it necessary because I think it proper for France to avail herself at the present crisis of every resource within her reach. I only wish that it be not relied on as the sole one, and which it will certainly be if the wisest measures are not adopted at home to encourage the ordinary private trade and to restrict and otherwise guard against any misconduct in the agency abroad.

Ja^s Monroe

Copy, DNA: RG 59: Dispatches from France; enclosed in JM to Randolph, 7 November 1794

From Adrienne Lafayette

[18 October 1794]

Dear Sir

graces a toutes les affaires qui depuis deux mois, retardent Le moment ou vous daigneres vous occuper de L'abandon ou je Suis, je viens de paroître devant Les deputés Commissaires. L'un m'a dit que nous avions des aides de camps a qui j'étois assés pour être insolente, et l'autre (Bourdon de Loise) m'a dit, que mon mari avoit trop evidemment trahi la Republique, que mon intimite avec lui étoit trop connue, pour qu'ils pussent s'occuper de moi qu'au reste, ç'étoit l'objet d'un rapport au Comité mais qu'ils ne se chargeoient d'aucunes pieces, et que c'etoit a moi a Les faire presenter par un de mes amis. j'ai repondu (et assurement j'ai dit vrai) que j'étois sans appuy, et ils ont repondu que cela etoit <illegible> egal.

voila ma position. vous eussiés pu m'eviter cette petite scene après 4 heures d'attente, qui ne me mene a rien—qu'a recommencer Sur nouveaux frais. je resterai probablement seule. ma position fera t'elle trouver un moment a un Citoyen des Etats unis, pour se charger de porter ce soir mes pièces au Cte au moment ou on fera le rapport de La seance de ce Soir? et un autre moment pour votre Secretaire pour me venir voir demain matin? je crois les momens chers, et il m'est Surtout necessaire de Savoir Si je serai ou non Secourue par les Etats unis, afin d'agir en consequence. Salut et fraternité

N. Lafayette

Editors' Translation

[18 October 1794]

Dear Sir

Thanks to all the business that for two months has delayed the time for you to be so good as to involve yourself with abandon in my situation, I just made an appearance before the deputy commissioners. One of them said that we used to have aides de camp and that I was insolent enough with them;[1] the other (Bourdon de Loise)[2] told me that my husband had too explicitly betrayed the Republic, and that my closeness to him too well known that they could incriminate themselves with me. As for the rest, it must be dealt with in a report for the Committee, but that they themselves were not responsible for any papers, and that it was up to me to present them through one of my friends. I answered (and it was certainly true) that I was without assistance. And then they replied that it was none of their affair.

This is where I stand. You can well imagine this little scene that after a four- hour wait has brought me nothing for my trouble but to begin again from scratch. I will probably remain <u>alone</u>. Will my situation help a citizen of the United States find the time to take my papers to the Committee at the time they give the report of tonight's session? And another moment for your secretary to come and see me tomorrow morning? I believe time to be precious, and that it is especially necessary for me to know if I shall or shall not be helped by the United States in order to act in consequence thereof. Salutation and brotherhood

N. Lafayette

RC, NN: Monroe Miscellaneous and Undated Papers

1. The Committee of General Security sent two deputies to the prison of Plessis to determine the fate of those detained there. Madame Philippine (de Noailles-Mouchy) de Duras, Adrienne Lafayette's cousin and best friend, who had shared the same prison cell, was interrogated on 18 October 1794 and set free the following day . Adrienne Lafayette evidently wrote this letter on the 18th, immediately after her own appearance before the commission. One of the men who sat in judgment over her was former Jacobin deputy, Louis Legendre (1752-1797). Although he released other prisoners, he refused to set her at liberty. He told her he hated the very name of Lafayette. Legendre had served under her husband in the National Guard, and may have been called up to face him several times for excess. (Charles Flowers McCombs, "The Imprisonment of Madame de Lafayette During the Terror," New York Public Library, *Bookmen's Holiday*, 1943; André Maurois, *Adrienne*, 260; *Notice sur Madame de La Fayette par Madame de Lasteyrie, sa fille*, 327-328; Edith Sichel, *The Household of the Lafayettes*, 218).

2. François-Louis Bourdon (1758-1798) was prosecutor of the Paris Parliament, and deputy from the department of Oise to the National Convention (*Nouvelle Biographie Universelle*).

Shortly after receiving this letter, JM purchased a carriage and "had it put in the best order, and his servants dressed in like manner." "In this carriage Mrs. Monroe drove directly to the prison in which Madame Lafayette was confined." When Elizabeth Monroe asked "as the wife of the American minister" to see Adrienne Lafayette, the prison concierge brought her to the "iron railing in which the gate was fixed." The Duchess of Duras, Adrienne Lafayette's cousin, who preceded her in arriving at Plessis prison, relates in similar detail the grill work and iron bars at the prison's gate and describes the concierge. The report of the "frantic state in which the two women met… immediately spread through Paris," according to JM's account. JM succeeded in getting Adrienne Lafayette transferred to a prison infirmary on the extreme edge of Paris at rue des Amandiers on 27 October 1794. Here she remained only briefly before being transferred on November 5 to the Maison Delmas (or Desnos) on rue Notre Dame des Champs, southwest of the Luxembourg Palace (Stuart Gerry Brown, ed., *The Autobiography of James Monroe*, 70-71; Mme. La Duchesse de Duras, *Journal des Prisons de Mon Père de Ma Mère et des Miennes*, 79-81; 83; Adrienne Lafayette to her daughters 17 Brumaire (7 November 1794) DLC: Lafayette Papers; "Sur l'instance de l'ambassadeur des ⬚tats-Unis, elle obtint par faveur de 'continuer sa détention' dans une maison de santé òu elle passa l'automne de 1794," Louis-Léon-Théodore Gosselin, (pseud. G. Lenotre), *De La Prison A L'Échafaud*, 14).

From the Committee of Public Safety

Paris le 30 Vendemiaire [21 October 1794]

Citoyen

Nous avons reçu la lettre que tu nous a adressée le 27. de ce mois, de même que les pieces qui y etoient jointes. Elles meritent toute notre attention. Nous nous empresserons d'examiner les griefs, qui y sont exposés et nous esperons que le resultat de nos deliberations sera aussi satisfaisant pour tes Concitoyens, que conforme aux principes de fraternité et d'attachement, qui ont toujours dirigé les demarches du gouvernement de la Republique Françoise envers ses bons et fideles alliés les Etats unis de l'Amerique.

Editors' Translation

Paris 30 Vendemiaire [21 October 1794]

Citizen

We have received the letter that you sent us on the 27th of this month, as well as the documents that were attached to it. They deserve all our attention. We will press ourselves to examine all the complaints which it therein exposes and we hope that the result of our deliberations will be as satisfactory for your fellow citizens as they are in keeping with the principles of fraternity and affection which have always directed the measures of the government of the French Republic toward its good and loyal allies, the United States of America.

FC, DLC: FCP—France

The version of this letter published in *ASP: FR*, 1: 685 bears the signatures of Philippe Merlin de Douai, Jean-Baptiste Treilhard, Joseph-Charles-Etienne Richard, and Jean-François-Bertrand Delmas.

From Thomas Paine

Vend.^re 30 [21 October 1794]

Dear Sir

I rec.^d your friendly letter of the 26 Vend.^re on the day it was written, & I thank you for communicating to me your opinion upon my Case.[1] Ideas serve to beget Ideas, and as it is from a review of every thing that can be said upon a subject, or is any ways connected with it, that the best judgment can be formed how to proceed, I present you with such Ideas as occur to me. I am sure of one thing, which is, that you will give them a patient and attentive perusal.

You say in your letter that "I must be sinsible that altho' I am an American Citizen yet if you interfere in my behalf as the Minister of my Country you must demand my liberation only in case there be no charge against me, and that if there is I must be brought to trial previously, since no person in a <u>private</u> character can be exempt from the laws of the Country in which he resides." This is what I have twice attempted to do. I wrote a letter on the 3.^d Sans Culottodi to the deputies, Members of the Committee of surety general who came to the Luxembourg to examine the persons detained.—The letter was as follows—"Citizen Representatives: I offer myself for examination. Justice is due to every Man. It is Justice only that I ask.—Thomas Paine"

As I was not called for examination nor heard anything in consequence of my letter the first time of sending it, I sent a duplicate of it a few days after. It was carried to them by my good friend and comrade Van-huele who was then going in liberty having been examin'd the day before. Van-huele wrote me on the next day and said—Bourdon de l'Oise (who was one of the examining deputies) is the most inveterate Enemy you can have. The answer he gave me when I presented your letter put me in such a passion with him that I expected I should be sent back again to prison. I then wrote a third letter but had not an opportunity of sending it as Bourdon did not come any more till after I received Mr Labonadaire's letter advising me to write to the Convention. The letter was as follows—"Citizens, I have twice offered myself for examination, and I chose to do this while Bourdon de l'Oise was one of the Commissioners. This deputy has said in the Convention that I intrigued with an ancient agent of the Bureau of foreign Affairs. My examination therefore while he is present will give him an opportunity of proving his charge or of convincing himself of his error. If Bourdon l'Oise is an honest Man he will examine me, but lest he should not I subjoin the following—That which B— calls an intrigue was at the request of a Member of the former Committee of Salut public last August was twelve month. I met the Member on the Boulevard. He asked me something in French which I did not understand and we went together to the Bureau of foreign Affairs which was near at hand. The agent (Otto, whom you probably knew in America) served as interpreter. The Member (it was Barrere) then asked me 1$^{\underline{st}}$ If I could furnish him with the plan of Constitution I had presented to the Committee of Constitution of which I was Member with himself because, he said, it contained several things which he wished had been adopted.—2$^{\underline{dly}}$ He asked me my opinion upon sending Commissioners to the United States of America—3$^{\underline{rdly}}$—If fifty or an hundred Ship loads of Flour could be procured from America. As verbal interpretation was tedious it was agreed that I should give him my opinion in writing and that the Agent should translate it which he did—I answered the first question by sending him the plan which he still has—To the second I replied that I thought it would be proper to send Com$^{\underline{rs}}$ because that in revolutions Circumstances change so fast that it was often necessary to send a better supply of information to an Ally than could be communicated by writing; and that Congress had done the same thing during the American War and I gave him some information that the Commissioners would find useful on their arrival. I answered the third question by sending him a list of American Exports to years before, distinguishing the several Articles by which he would see that the supply he mentioned could be obtained.—I sent him also the plan of Paul Jones, giving it as his, for procuring salt petre, which was to send a squadron (it did not require a large one) to take possession of the Island of St. Helens, to keep the English flag flying at the port that the English East India ships coming from the East Indies, and that ballast with Salt petre might be induced to enter as usual, and that it would be a considerable time before the English Government could know of what had happened at St. Helen's—See here what Bourdon de l'Oise has called an intrigue—If it was an Intrigue it was between a Member of the Committee of Salut public and myself; for the Agent was no more than the interpreter and translator, and the object of the intrigue was to furnish France with flour and Salt petre"—I suppose Bourdon had heard that the Agent and I were seen together talking English, and this was enough for <u>him</u> to found his charge upon.

You next say that "I must likewise be sensible that although I am an American Citizen that it is likewise believed there that I am become a Citizen of france, and that in consequence this latter character has so far <word missing> the former as to weaken if not destroy any claim you might have to interpose in my behalf"—I am sorry I cannot add any new Arguments to those I have already advanced on this part of the subject.—But I cannot help asking myself, and I wish you would ask the Committee, if it could possibly be the Intention of France to <u>Kidnap</u> Citizens from America under the pretence of dubbing them with the title of french Citizens, and then after inviting or rather enveigling them into France make it a pretence for detaining them. If it was, (which I am sure it was not tho' they now act as if it was) the insult was to America, tho the injury was to me, and the treachery was to both. Did they mean to kidnap General Washington M$^{\underline{r}}$ Madison and several other Americans whom they dubbed with the same title as well as me. Let any Man look at the condition of france when I arrived in it, invaded by Austrians and prussians and declared to be in danger, and then ask if any Man who had a home and a Country to go to as I had in America, would have come amongst them from any other Motive than of assisting them. If I could possibly have supposed them capable of treachery I certainly would not have trusted myself in their power. Instead therefore of your being unwilling or apprehensive of meeting the question of french Citizenship they ought to be ashamed of advancing it, and this will be the case unless you admit their arguments or objections too passively. It is a Case on their part fit only for the continuations of Robespiere to set up. As to the name of french Citizen I never considered it in any other light, so far as regarded myself, than as a token of honorary respect. I never made them any promise nor took any oath of Allegiance or of Citizenship, nor bound myself by an Act or means whatever to the performance of any thing. I acted altogether as a friend invited among them as I supposed, on honorable terms. I did not come to join myself to a Government already formed, but to assist in forming one de nouveau, which was afterwards to be submitted to the people whether they would accept it or not, and this any foreigner might do. And strictly speaking there are no Citizens before this is a government. They are all of the People. The Americans were not called Citizens till after Government was established, and not even then until they had taken the oath of Allegiance. This was the case in Pennsylvania.—But be this french Citizenship more or less the Convention have now swept it away by declaring me to be a foreigner and imprisoning me as such, and this is a short answer to all those who affect to say or to believe that I am french Citizen. A Citizen without Citizenship is a term Non-descript.

After the two preceeding paragraphs you ask—"If it be my wish that you should embark in this Controversy (meaning that of reclaiming me) and risque the Consequences with respect to myself and the good understanding subsisting between the two Countries, or, without relinquishing any point of right, and which might be insisted on in case of extremities, pursue according to your best judgment and with the lights before you, the object of my liberation?"

As I believe from the apparent obstinacy of the Committees that circumstances will grow towards the extremity you mention unless prevented before hand I will endeavour to throw into your hands all the lights I can upon the subject.

In the first place, reclamation may mean two distinct things—All the reclamations that are made by the sections in behalf of persons detained as <u>suspect</u> are made on the ground that the persons so detained are patriots, and the reclamation is good against the charge of suspect because it proves the contrary.— But my situation includes another Circumstance. I am imprisoned on the charge (if it can be called one) of being a foreigner born in England. You know that foreigner to be a Citizen of the United States of America, and that he has been such since the 4ᵗʰ of July 1776 the political birth-day of the United States and of every American Citizen, for before that period all were British subjects, and the States, then provinces, were british Dominions.—Your reclamation of me therefore as a Citizen of the United States (all other considerations apart) is good against the pretence for imprisoning me, or that pretence is equally good against every American Citizen born in England Ireland Scotland Germany or Holland, and you know this description of Men compose a very great part of the population of the three States of New-York, New-Jersey and Pennsylvania and make also a part of Congress, and the State legislatures.

Every politician ought to know, and every Civilian does know, that the Law of Treaty is superior to every other Law where it applies. Now the Treaty of Alliance and also that of Amity and Commerce knows no distinction of American Citizens on account of the place of their birth, but recognizes all to be Citizens whom the Constitution and laws of the United States of America recognize as such, and if I recollect rightly there is an Article in the Treaty of Commerce particular to this point. The law therefore which they have here to put all persons in Arrestation born in any of the Countries at war with France, is, when applied to Citizens of America born in England, Ireland, Scotland, Germany, or holland, a violation of the treaties of Alliance and of Commerce, because it assumes to make a distinction of Citizens which those Treaties and the Constitution of America know nothing of. This is a subject that officially comes under your cognizance as Minister and it would be consistent that you expostulated with them upon the Case. That foolish Old Man Vadier who was president of the Convention and of the Committee of Surety General when the Americans then in Paris went to the Bar of the Convention to reclaim me, gave them for answer that my being born in England was cause sufficient for imprisoning me. It happened that at least half those who went up with that address were in the same case with myself.

As to reclamations on the ground of Patriotism it is difficult to know what is to be understood by Patriotism here. There is not a vice, and scarcely a Virtue, that has not as the fashion of the moment suited been called by the name of Patriotism. The wretches who composed the revolutionary tribunal of Nantz were the Patriots of that day and the criminals of this. The Jacobins called themselves Patriots of the first order, Men up to the height of the Circumstances, and they are now considered as an Antidote to Patriotism. But if we give to Patriotism a fixed Idea consistent with that of a Republic it would signify a strict adherence to the principles of Moral Justice, to the equality of Civil and political Rights, to the System of representative Government, and an opposition to every hereditary claim to Govern; and of this Species of Patriotism you know my character.

But, Sir, there are Men on the Committee who have changed their Party but not their principles. Their Aim is to hold power as long as possible by preventing the establishment of a Constitution, and these Men are and will be my Enemies, and seek to hold me in prison as long as they can. I am too good a Patriot for them. It is not improbable that they have heard of the strange language held by some Americans that I am not considered in America as an American Citizen, and they may also have heard say, that you had no orders respecting me, and it is not improbable that they interpret that language and that silence into a Connivance at my imprisonment. If they had not some Ideas of this kind would they resist so long the civil efforts you make for my liberation, or would they attach so much importance to the imprisonment of an Individual as <u>to risque</u> (as you say to me) <u>the good understanding that exists between the two Countries.</u>—You also say that <u>it is impossible for any person to do more than you have done without adopting the other means</u>, meaning that of reclaiming me. How then can you account for the want of Success after so many efforts, and such a length of time, upwards of ten weeks, without supposing that they fortify themselves in the interpretation I have just mentioned? I can admit that it was not necessary to give orders, and that it was difficult to give direct orders, for I much question if Morris had informed Congress or the President of the whole of the Case, or had sent Copies of my letters to him as I had desired him to do. You would find the Case here when you came, and you could not fully understand it till you did come, and as Minister you would have authority to act upon it. But as you inform me that you know what the wishes of the President are, you will see also that his reputation is exposed to some risque, admitting there to be ground for the supposition I have made. It will not add to his popularity to have it believed in America, as I am inclined to think the Committee believe here, that he connives at my imprisonment.—You say also <u>that it is known to everybody that you wish my liberation.</u> It is, Sir, because they know your wishes that they misinterpret the means you use. They suppose that those mild Means arise from a restriction that you cannot use others, or from a consciousness of some defect on my part of which you are unwilling to provoke the enquiry.

But as you ask me if it be my wish that you should embark in this controversy and risque the Consequences with respect to myself, I will answer this part of the question by marking out precisely the part I wish you to take. What I mean is a sort of Middle line above what you have yet gone, and not up to the full extremity of the Case, which will still lie in reserve. It is to write a letter to the Committee, that shall in the first place defeat by anticipation all the objections they might make to a simple reclamation, and at the same time make the ground good for that object. But, instead of sending the letter immediately to invite some of the Committee to your house and to make that invitation the opportunity of shewing them the letter, expressing at the same time a wish that you had done this, from a hope that the business might be settled in an Amicable manner without your being forced into an Official interference, that would excite the observations of the Enemies of both Countries, and probably interrupt the harmony that subsisted between the two Republics. But as I can not convey the Ideas I wish you to use by any means so concisely or so well as to suppose myself the writer of the letter, I shall adopt this method, and you will make use of such parts or such Ideas of it as you please if you approve the plan.—Here follows the supposed letter.

Citizens

When I first arrived amongst you, as Minister from the United States of America I was given to understand that the liberation of Thomas Paine would take place without any official interference on my part. This was the more agreeable to me, as it would not only supercede the necessity of that interference, but would leave to yourselves the whole opportunity of doing justice to a Man who as far as I have been able to learn has suffered much cruel treatment under what you have denominated the System of Terror. But as I find my expectations have not been fulfilled I am under the official necessity of being more explicit upon the Subject than I have hitherto been.

Permit me, in the first place, to observe that as it is impossible for me to suppose that it could have been the intention of France to Seduce any Citizens of America from their Allegiance to their proper Country by offering them the title of french Citizen, so must I be compelled to believe, that the title of french Citizen conferred on Thomas Paine was intended only as a Mark of honorary respect towards a Man who had so eminently distinguished himself in defence of liberty, and on no occasion more so than in promoting and defending your own Revolution. For a proof of this I refer you to his two works entitled <u>Rights of Man</u>. Those works have procured to him an addition of esteem in America, and I am sorry they have been so ill rewarded in France. But be this title of french Citizen more or less, it is now entirely swept away by the vote of the Convention which declares him to be a foreigner and which supercedes the vote of the Assembly that confered that title upon him, and consequently upon the case are superceded with it.

In consequence of this vote of the Convention declaring him to be foreigner the former Committees have imprisoned him. It is therefore become my official duty to declare to you that the foreigner thus imprisoned is a Citizen of the United States of America as fully as legally and as Constitutionally as myself, and that he is moreover one of the principal founders of the American Republic.

I have been informed of a law or decree of the Convention which subjects foreigners born in any of the Countries at War with france to arrestation and imprisonment. This law when applied to Citizens of America born in England is an infraction of the Treaty of Alliance and of Amity and Commerce, which knows no distinction of American Citizens on account of the place of their birth, but recognizes all to be Citizens whom the Constitution and laws of America recognise as such. The Circumstances under which America has been peopled requires this guard on her treaties, because the Mass of her Citizens are composed not of Natives only but also of the Natives of almost all the Countries of Europe who have sought an Asylum there from the persecutions; they experienced in their own Countries. After this intimation you will without doubt see the propriety of Modelling that Law to the principles of the Treaty, because the law of Treaty in cases where it applies is the governing law to both parties alike, and it cannot be infracted without hazarding the existence of the Treaty.

Of the Patriotism of Thomas Paine I can speak fully if we agree to give to patriotism a fixed Idea consistent with that of a Republic. It would then signify a strict adherence to Moral Justice—to the equality of civil and political Rights, to the System of Representative Government—and an opposition to all hereditary claims to govern.—Admitting patriotism to consist in these principles, I know of no Man who has gone beyond Thomas Paine in promulgating and defending them and that for almost twenty years past.

I have now spoken to you on the principal matters concerned in the case of Thomas Paine—the title of french Citizen which you had conferred upon him and have since taken away by declaring him to be a foreigner and consequently this part of the subject ceases of itself.—I have declared to you that this foreigner is a Citizen of the United States of America, and have assured you of his patriotism.

I cannot help at the same time, repeating to you my wish that his liberation had taken place without my being obliged to go thus far into the subject, because it is the mutual interest of both Republics to avoid as much as possible all subjects of controversy especially such from which no possible good can flow.—I still hope that you will save me the unpleasant task of proceeding any farther by sending me an order for his liberation, and which the injured State of his health absolutely requires. I shall be happy to receive such an order from you and happy in presenting it to him, for to the welfare of Thomas Paine the Americans are not and cannot be indifferent.

This is the sort of letter I wish you to write for I have no Idea that you will succeed by any Measures that can, by any kind of Construction, be interpreted into a want of Confidence or an apprehension of Consequences.—It is themselves that ought to be apprehensive of consequences if any are to be apprehended. They, mean the Committees are not certain that the Convention or the Nation would support them in forcing any question to extremity that might interrupt the good understanding subsisting between the two Countries, and I know of no question to do this as that which involves the rights and liberty of a Citizen.

You will please to observe that I have put the case of french Citizenship in a point of view that ought not only to preclude, but to make them ashamed to advance, any thing upon this subject and this is better than to have to answer their counter-reclamation afterwards. Either the Citizenship was intended as a token of honorary respect, or it was intended to deprive America of a Citizen or to seduce him from his Allegiance to his proper Country. If it was intended as an honour they must act consistently with the principle of honour. But if they make a pretence for detaining me they convict themselves of the Act of Seduction. Had America singled out any particular french Citizen, complimented him with the title of Citizen of America, which he without suspecting any fraudulent intention might accept, and then after having invited or rather inveigled him into America made his acceptance of that Title a pretence for seducing or forcing him from his allegiance to France would not France have just cause to be offended at America? And ought not America to have the same Right to be offended at France? And will the Committees take upon themselves to answer for the dishonour they bring upon the National Character of their Country? If these Arguments are stated beforehand they will prevent the Committees going into the Subject of french Citizenship. They must be ashamed of it.—But after all the Case comes to this that this french Citizenship appertains no longer to me because the Convention as I have already said, have swept it away by declaring me to be foreigner, and it is not in the power of the Committees to reverse it. But if I am to be Citizen & foreigner, and Citizen again, just when and how and for any purpose they please they take the Government of America into their own hands or make her only a Cypher in their System.

Though these Ideas have been long with me they have been more particularly matured by reading your last communication, and I have many reasons to wish you had opened that Communication sooner.— I am best acquainted with the persons you have to deal with and the Circumstances of my own Case.— If you chuse to adopt the letter as it is I send you a translation for the sake of expediting the business.[2] I have endeavoured to conceive your own manner of expression as well as I could and the civility of language you would use, but the matter of the letter is essential to me.

If you chuse to confer with some of the Members of the Committee at your own house on the Subject of the letter it may render the sending it unnecessary; but in either case I must request and press you not to give away to evasion and delay and that you will fix positively with them that they shall give you an answer in three or four days whether they will liberate me on the representation you have made in the letter or whether you must be forced to go further into the Subject. The state of my health will not admit of delay, and besides the tortured State of my mind wears me down. If they talk of bringing me to trial (and I well know there is no accusation against me and that they can bring none) I certainly summons you as an Evidence to my Character. This you may mention to them either as what I intend to do or what you intend to do voluntarily for me.

I am anxious that you undertake this business without losing time, because if I am not liberated in the course of this decade, I intend, if in Case the seventy-one detained Deputies are liberated, to follow the same tract that they have done and publish my own Case myself. I cannot rest any longer in this state of miserable suspense, be the consequences what they may.

Thomas Paine

RC, DLC: Monroe Papers.

1. JM's letter to Paine of 25 Vendémiaire (16 October 1794) has not beeen located.

2. A translation into French of the letter suggested to JM accompanies this letter.

From Philip Filicchy[1]

Leghorn 22[d] Oct[r] 1794

Sir, Your Excellency

Having had the honor to be appointed Consul for the United States of America in Leghorn I have waited till now for my Commission before taking the liberty of addressing Your Excellency, by my friend William Seton Esq[r] of New-York,[2] who received it from the Secretary of State in order to forward it by a Ship he was then loading for my commercial house here, perceiv'd that it was directed to Peter Filicchy instead of Philip Filicchy & having returned it to be attended & waited since personally on the Secretary of State at Philadelphia in order to have it ready for another ship I am hourly expecting, he was told that it would be necessary to wait untill next session of Congress, as the mistaken name could not be alter'd without their approbations. Tho' deprived of this role to address Your Excellency, I beg leave to claim that of the personal acquaintance made at New York in the House of M[r] Kortwright, where I used to frequent, in order to ask Your Excellency's advice in case of an irruption of the French Armies into Tuscany, tho' for the present I see no prospect of it. If Your Excellency, who must have been directly informed of my election, should think proper to demand an order from the Convention, that my family & property should in any such instance meet with the same protection as any other Servants employed in the service of the United States, it might prove advantageous to me.

His Excellency William Short has wrote me from Madrid that he shall forward to me his Letters for Your Excellency, as soon as he gets my answer. I shall address him by next post. I remain most respectfully Your Excellency's most Hum[g] obedient Serv[t]

Philip Filicchy

RC, NN: Monroe Papers

1. Fillipo (Philip) Filicchy (1763-1816) was a merchant in Leghorn (Livorno), Italy with close ties to the United States. He made numerous trips to the United States and was married to Mary Cowper of Boston. He was the U. S. consul at Leghorn 1794-1798 (Joseph Dirvin, *Mrs. Seton: Foundress of the American Sisters of Charity*, 128).

2. William M. Seton (1768-1803) was a New York merchant. He met Filicchy (a trading partner) during a visit to Leghorn in 1788. After his death, Seton's widow, Elizabeth Seton, converted to Catholicism and founded the Sisters of Charity. She was the first American to be canonized as a saint (Dirvin, *Mrs. Seton*, 33-34, 126; *ANB*).

From Mr. Cibon

Paris 26 Oct^r [1794]

The chargé des aff^rs of Malta has the honor to communicate to Mr Monroe minister plenipotentiary of the U States of America, the <u>annex'd reflections,</u> and to request that he will be pleased to weigh them in his mind & give him frankly the result.

Mr Cibon seizes this occasion to renew to Mr Monroe an assurance of the respect and attachment with which he is &^c.

If there are nations who by their position, their industry, & their courage, become naturally opposed to & rivals of each other so there are other nations who with as much courage, & industry, feel a motive to esteem, approach, and unite together, to increase their mutual prosperity and to render themselves reciprocally happy, by a continual exchange of attentions, regards & services.

The U States of America and the Island of Malta notwithstanding the distance which seperates them, do not appear to be less bound to cultivate a close and friendly union between them, by motives of interest than they are by those of a benevolent amity.

It is principally towards the medeteranean, that the American sailors guided by their industry, present themselves in great numbers, forgetting the danger to which they are exposed of becoming a prey to the Algerine Corsairs who cover that sea.

The Island of Malta plac'd in the centre of the medeteranean between Africa & Sicily offers by its position to all navigors an asylum of provisions & of succour of every kind. Of what importance wo^d it not be for the American commerce to find upon this stormy sea, fine ports, provisions, and even protection agnst the Algerine pirates.

In exchange for these succours and protection, by means whereof the American vessels might navigate the medeteranean freely & without inquietude, wo^d the united States consent to grant in full right to the order of Malta, some lands in America in such quantity as might be agreed on between the two governments; placing such lands under the immediate protection and safeguard of the American loyalty?

Thus the commerce of the U States would find in the medeteranean, ports to secure it from storms, and vessels of war to protect it agnst the pirates of Algiers, in exchange for which Malta wo^d possess in America property, granted for ever, protected by the U States & guaranteed by them in a manner the most solid.

Copy (in JM's hand), NN: Monroe Papers; first page filed 26 October 1795, second page filed 26 October 1794.

Cibon's cover letter (the first two paragraphs of this version), written in French, is in DLC: Monroe Papers (filed 26 September 1794); the remainder of the original document, presumably also written in French, has not been located. A copy in French is enclosed in JM to Edmund Randolph, 20 November 1794, DLC: RG 59: Dispatches from France. The version used here is in JM's handwriting and is his English translation. *The Writings of James Monroe* (2: 128) gives the date of this letter as 26 September 1794.

Mr. Cibon (for whom there is no recorded first name) was the clerk of the embassy of Malta in Paris who assumed the title of chargé d'affaires when the Maltese ambassador fled in September 1792. Cibon, who was a commoner, was ineligible for a diplomatic appointment from Malta; he served in this unofficial capacity, without pay, until the French captured Malta in June

1798 (Frederick W. Ryan, *The House of the Temple: A Study of Malta and its Knights in the French Revolution*, 164, 211-213, 236-242, 258, 328).

Malta was ruled by the Sovereign Military Order of the Hospitallers of Saint John of Jerusalem, an order founded during the Crusades and known in the eighteenth century as the Knights of Malta. The order had extensive property holdings in France, which were seized in 1790, as was the property of the aristocratic members of the order (Ryan, *The House of the Temple*). Cibon, who apparently made this proposal to JM on his own, may have been seeking a refuge for the exiled French members of the order (see also, Edgar Erskine Hume, "A Proposed Alliance Between the Order of Malta and the United States, 1794," *William and Mary Quarterly*, second series, 16: 222-233).

From John Jay

London 31 Octr 1794

Sir

Altho' you are not personally acquainted with Benjn Vaughan Esqr, a member of Parliam^t, and amiable & a worthy Gent^n yet I am persuaded that his character and attachm^t to our Country are known to you.

In the correspondence between Mr Jefferson & Mr Hammond, his agency respecting the negociations for the Treaty of Peace, became more prominent, than could be agreable or useful to him; there is Reason to apprehend that certain Transactions in this Country, have led the Governm^t to regard him in an unfavorable Light.

He is now in   It is possible that circumstances may occur to render the good offices of his Friends expedient. Considering the Zeal of his family for the welfare of our Country, and that he has been particularly useful, I think he has a just Claim to our Friendship, and to such marks of it, as may be requisite and proper.

Mr Pinckney has written or will write to you on this Subject. I have the Honor to be with great Respect Sir Your most ob^t & hble Servt

Dft, NNC: John Jay Collection

Benjamin Vaughan (1751-1835) was a British politician and reformer who was elected to the House of Commons in 1792. He had served as a mediator between the British and American delegations during the peace negotiations at Paris in 1783, and his strong-pro-American position made him a valuable asset to Jay and the other American diplomats. His writings in support of the French Revolution led to charges of sedition in 1794; unable to get to the United States, Vaughan fled first to France (where he was briefly imprisoned) and then to Switzerland. He returned to Paris in 1796 where he resided for a year with Fulwar Skipwith. Vaughan moved to the United States in 1797 and became a permanent resident (*DNB; ANB*). An excerpt from the diary of John Adams, dated 17 November 1782, recounting some of the assistance that Vaughan was giving to the American negotiators at Paris, was included as an enclosure to Jefferson's letter to George Hammond of 29 May 1792 (*ASP: FR*, 1: 220).

Pinckney wrote to JM on 4 November 1794 (*Catalogue of Monroe's Papers*, 1: 36).

Journal

[October 1794]

On the 3^d of Sepr I addressed a letter to the Committee of publick safety upon a variety of points, particularly the infring'ment by France of the 23 & 24 articles of the treaty of amity & commerce subsisting between the two republicks, the embargo of Bordeaux, the supplies rendered by citizens of the US. to the gov^t of St. Domingo, & the general state of our trade, harrass'd by their cruisers at sea & by their agents & publick departments within the republick & requesting satisfactory arrangments on each point. This rem[d] for five or six weeks unanswered, or without my hearing a word from the committee on the subject. I requested a meeting with the committee & which was appointed to be at 8, in the evening. I attended with M[r] Otto to explain.[1] I mentioned I had something to add on the subject of my note & likewise something new to say. They replied in either case it wo[d] be better to commit to paper what I had to say as they wo[d] be better able to understand it. They promised in that case to answer me immediately. After making some general observations on the necessity of an early answer & to which positive assurances were given in the affirmative, I withdrew.

By my direction M[r] Skipwith whom I had appointed consul with M[r] Mountflorence his chancelor reported to me a list of depredations on our trade & which with my own comments I sent in on the day of   notifying[2] at the same time that the Congress wo[d] commence its Session soon & to whom the President must render an acc[t] of the state of the union comprizing in it the disposition of foreign powers towards us & how distressing it would be for me to have nothing to say in respect to that of France.

I rec[d] on the of Oct[r] a short note acknowledging the receit of these communications and assuring me they sho[d] be attended to.[3] But 10 days soon elapsed & nothing was heard from them to the point. In the interim the aggressions in our trade increased & the patience of the Americans here was more & more exhausted. It was in truth difficult to keep them within bounds. My patience was likewise nearly exhausted. The time was arrived when I must either say to the American gov[t] the French nation is unfriendly to us–for the conduct of the committee in refusing to comply with my propositions, an omission to ans[r] them being a refusal of the most contemptuous kind must be considerd as such, or upon the idea that the committee was the organ of the publick sentiment on that head, pass by them by way of appeal to the Convention. I called upon M[r] Otto & expressed this sentiment to him intimating that the latter course was the most just as well as expedient. I told him also I wo[d] not give any previous hint to the committee but proceed directly to the Convention if at all. M[r] Letombe[4] was present & heard the conversation. I had previously in the same morning seen <illegible> & to whom I gave the same intimation. At 3 the next day in the even[g] I rec[d] from the Committee an invitation to meet them at 12 on the same day in the room of their sitting. As the time was elapsed I could not. I answered them however I wo[d] meet them at 12 the next & which was accordingly done.[5]

AD, DLC: Monroe Papers, series 3

1. This meeting probably occurred on 17 October 1794 (see JM to Edmund Randolph, 7 November 1794, below).

2. JM to the Committee of Public Safety, 18 October 1794. Skipwith's report is dated 17 October 1794 (see both, above).

3. Committee of Public Safety to JM, 21 October 1794 (above).

4. Joseph-Philippe Létombe (b.1733) arrived in Boston on June 1781 and assumed the duties of French vice-consul to the United States. He served as French consul for New Hampshire, Massachusetts, and Rhode Island in 1784, and as French consul general at Philadelphia, before retiring in 1792. In 1797 Létombe became French minister to the United States (Abraham P. Nasatir and Gary Elwyn Monell, *French Consuls in the United States*, 12, 550, 563; *The Emerging Nation: A Documentary History of the Foreign Relations of the United States Under the Articles of Confederation, 1780-1789*, 2: 372).

5. The Committee's letter was dated 29 October 1794, so the meeting would have been on the 30th (NN: Monroe Papers).

To the Committee of General Security

Paris le 11 Brumaire l'an Troisième de la République française
[1 November 1794]

Citoyens

Dans tous les cas, où les Citoyens des Etats unis de L'Amérique se trouvent soumis aux loix de la République française, il est de leur devoir d'y obéir en conséquence de la protection qu'ils en reçoivent ou autrement de se soumettre aux peines qu'elles infligent. Ce principe est incontestable. Il appartient à la nature de la souveraineté & ne peut jamais en être séparé. Tout ce que mes compatriotes ont donc droit d'attendre de moi, comme leur Représentante, est de voir que justice leur soit rendue, suivant la nature de l'accusation, ou de l'offense qu'ils ont commise, par les Tribunaux qui doivent en connoitre.

J'espère qu'il se trouvera peu d'occasions où la conduite d'un Citoyen Américain deviendra un objet de discussion devant un Tribunal criminel, & dans le cas où il s'en trouveroit, je me reposerois entièrement sur la justice de ce Tribunal, bien persuadé que Sy la balance avait à pencher, il seroit dans le cœur du juge de la guider en faveur de mes compatriotes. Hater leur jugement, Sy cela devenoit necessaire, est donc le seul point sur lequel je puisse avoir quelque sollicitude.

Dans la circonstance actuelle je n'attirerois pas votre attention sur un objet de cette nature S'y je n'y étois poussé sur des considérations d'un grand poids, considérations que, je me flatte, vous gouterez, parce que chaque jour apporte de nouvelles preuves du devouement de la Nation française à la cause qui les suggere. Les grands efforts qu'elle a déjà faite & fait tous les jours pour la liberté démontre pleinement combien elle la cherit, & sa reconnoissance envers ceux qui ont servi cette cause est justement regardée comme inséparable de la vénération duë à la cause elle-même.

Les Citoyens des Etats-Unis ne peuvent jetter les yeux sur l'époque de leur propre revolution sans se rappeller, parmy les noms de leurs patriotes les plus distingués, celui de Thom⁵ Paine. Ses Services, qu'il leur a rendus dans leur lutte pour la liberté ont imprimé dans leur cœur une reconnoissance, qui ne S'effacera jamais tant qu'ils continueront de mériter le titre d'un Peuple juste & généreux.

Ce citoyen, en ce moment, languit dans les prisons affligé d'une Malaise qui s'aggrave par Sa détention. Permettez moi donc d'appeler votre attention sur Sa situation, & de vous prier de hater le moment où la loy prononcera sur Son Sorte S'il existe des griefs contre lui & S'il n'en existe pas, de vouloir bien le rendre à la liberté. Salut & fraternité

Ja⁵ Monroe

Editors' Translation

Paris 11 Brumaire Third Year of the French Republic
[1 November 1794]

Citizens

In all cases where the citizens of the United States submit themselves to the jurisdiction of the French Republic, it is their duty to obey the law, in consideration of the protection which it gives, or otherwise suffer the consequences. This principle is unquestionable; it belongs to the nature of sovereignty, it can never be separated from it. All my countrymen thus circumstanced have a right to claim me as their representative, to see that they have justice rendered them, according to the nature of the charge, and their offence, if they have committed any, by the tribunals whose duty it is to take cognizance of it.

I hope that few cases will ever happen where the conduct of an American citizen becomes the subject of discussion here before a criminal tribunal. In those cases which may happen, if any do, I shall repose entire confidence in the justice of the tribunal, being well satisfied, that if the scales of justice were tipped, the judge would restore the balance in favor of my countrymen. To expedite their trial, should it become necessary, is I am persuaded the only point upon which I shall ever feel or express any concern.

I should not at the present crisis, call your attention to any case of this kind, if I were not compelled by considerations of important weight. Considerations which I flatter myself, you will appreciate; because each day brings fresh proofs of the devotion of the French nation to the cause which gave them birth. The great efforts which she has already made and is now making in favor of liberty, fully demonstrates how highly she esteems it, and her gratitude to those who have served that cause is justly regarded inseparable from veneration for the cause itself.

The citizens of the United States can never look back to the era of their own revolution, without remembering, with those of other distinguished Patriots, the name of Thomas Paine. The services which he rendered them in their struggle for liberty have made an impression of gratitude which will never be erased whilst they continue to merit the character of a just and generous people.

He is now languishing in prison, afflicted by an illness that is aggravated by his confinement. Permit me then, to call your attention to his situation, and to kindly request that you expedite the moment when the law shall decide his fate if there are any charges against him, and if there be none, to ask you kindly to set him free. Salutations and brotherhood.

James Monroe

Copy, NN: Monroe Papers

From Thomas Paine

[2 November 1794][1]

Dear Sir.

I need not mention to you the happiness I rec^{d} from the information you sent me by Mr Beresford. I easily guess the persons you have conversed with on the subject of my liberation—but matters and even promises that pass in Conversation are not quite so strictly attended to here as in the Country you come from.

I am not, my Dear Sir, impatient from any thing in my disposition—but the State of my health requires liberty and a better air, and besides this, the rules of the prison do not permit me, tho I have all the indulgences the concierge can give, to procure the things necessary to my recovery which is slow as to strength. I have a tolerable appetite, but the allowance of provision is scanty. We are not allowed a knife to cut our Victuals with, nor a razor to shave, but they have lately allowed some barbers that are here to shave. The room where I am lodged is a ground floor level with the earth in the Garden and floored with brick, and is so wet after every rain that I cannot guard against taking colds that continually cheat my recovery. If you could without interfering with, or deranging the mode proposed for my liberation, inform the Committee that the State of my health requires liberty and Air, it would be good ground to hasten my liberation. The length of my imprisonment is also a reason, for I am now almost the oldest inhabitant of this uncomfortable mansion—and I see twenty, thirty, and sometimes forty persons a day put in liberty who have not been so long confined as myself—Their liberation is a happiness to me, but

I feel sometimes, a little mortification that I am thus left behind. I leave it entirely to you to arrange this matter—The messenger wait   Your's affectionately

T. P.

I hope & wish much to see you—I have much to say.—I have had the attendance of D.ʳ Graham[2] (Physician to Gen.ˡ O'Hara, who is prisoner here[3]) and of D.ʳ Makouski, house Physician, who has been most exceedingly kind to me.   After I am at liberty I shall be glad to introduce him to you

RC, DLC: Monroe Papers

1. This letter is undated. JM wrote "2.ᵈ Luxemburg" on the cover, which suggests the date of 2 November 1794.

2. This may possibly be William Graham, who served as a surgeon in the British army 1790-1795 (*Commissioned Officers in the Medical Services of the British Army, 1660-1960*, 66).

3. British general Charles O'Hara commanded the British forces at Toulon, where he was wounded and captured in November 1793 after which, he was imprisoned at the Luxembourg Palace until August 1795 (*DNB*).

From Thomas Pinckney

London 3.ᵈ Novem.ʳ 1794.

My dear Sir,

I take the liberty of enclosing to you Copy of a letter I wrote to you relating to M.ʳ Russell;[1] I have no doubt of this Gentleman being ere now liberated, but if any Difficulty can possibly arise in Opposition to the express terms of our Treaty I can certify to you what is the practice of this Country, in similar Cases which I conceive ought to have weight. Many Citizens of the French Republic have been captured on board of American Vessels and brought into this Kingdom during the present War, they have in general been considered as prisoners till they have made known their Situation to me, but on my Application to Government they have universally been liberated and permitted to depart the Country—a single Exception to this Rule has not come to my Knowledge, and this has been done merely upon the Suggestion of its being consonant to the modern practice of nations although you know we have no Treaty on this Subject with Great Britain. I think it necessary also to give you this official Information that his Britannic Majesty has revoked his Instruction to his Men of War to stop and detain neutral Vessels loaded with Corn Meal and Flour bound to the unblockaded Ports of France. I mention this Circumstance also because I have lately received Intelligence of several of our Vessels having been carried into the Ports of France and which may possibly be attempted to be justified by the former Conduct of Great Britain to us in this particular.

I take the liberty of inclosing to you a List of Books for which I have occasion, for the use of my Children. You will much oblige me by procuring them for me unbound and sending them as occasion may offer by any Americans coming this way who will have the goodness to take charge of part of them at a time—sending those first which stand first on the list. Have the goodness also to inform me in what manner I shall reimburse the Expense of them. I remain with great & sincere respect My dear Sir truly yours

Thomas Pinckney

I enclose some letters which if expedient you will have the goodness to forward to their Address and procure Answers to be transmitted to me.

RC, NN: Monroe Papers

1. Pinckney wrote to JM on 10 October 1794 asking his help in obtaining the release of Mr. Russell, a British subject who had been taken by the French from an American ship (*Catalogue of Monroe's Papers*, 1: 35).

To Edmund Randolph

Paris 7th of Novr 1794.

Sir

I have been favoured with yours of the 30th of July original & duplicate, and had the pleasure to receive them unopened.

In my two last letters which were of the 15 of Sep^{r} & 16 of Octr I informed you of the several subjects which I had brought before the committee of Publick Safety as also of the ill success which had attended my efforts to obtain an answer upon any one: and I am sorry to be under the necessity now to add that altho' I have pressed a decision with the utmost possible zeal, yet I have not been able to accomplish the object.

Being wearied with the delay, I notified to the committee, soon after the date of my last letter to you, that I should be glad to confer with them or some few members on the subject, provided it comported with their rules in such cases, and would otherwise be agreable. The proposition was immediately assented to, and the evening of the same day appointed for the interview. I attended in their chamber, we had some discussion and which ended in a request on their part that I would present in writing the sum of what I had said, or wished to say, either on the points depending, or any others I might find necessary to bring before them, and which I readily promised to do.[1]

By this time I had obtained from Mr Skipwith a comprehensive statment of the embarrassments attending our trade here, as well those which proceeded from the Cruizers of the Republick, and applied to what was destined or cleared out for foreign countries, as those which proceeded from the commercial System of France and applied to the direct commerce between the two Republicks. As his report to me specified not only each particular cause of complaint, but likewise furnished facts to Support it, I thought it best to make that report the basis of this my second communication on that head. I accordingly laid it before the committee with such comment as appeared to me suitable; and I now transmit to you a copy of it that you may be apprized how fully the subject is before them.[2] I was assured that it exhibited a picture which shocked them, for these evils progressing with the course of their own affairs, were long accumulating and had probably attained a height of which they had no conception.

As I had reason to suspect that the chief opposition proceeded from those who conducted the publick trade, and who were attached to that mode from motives not the most patriotic, I thought it proper to examine the question whether it were best for the Republick to encourage the competition of individuals in neutral countries, for the supply of its markets, or depend on agencies employed in or sent to countries for that purpose. This subject had been incidentaly touched in my first note, but I thought some benefit might be derived from a more thorough development of it. With this view I sent in at the same time the paper intitled, "Supplemental observations upon the American Commerce &ca."[3]

I felt extremely embarrassed how to touch again their infringment of the treaty of commerce, whether to call on them to execute it, or leave that question on the ground on which I had first plac'd it. You desired me in your last to contest with them the principle, but yet this did not amount to an instruction, nor even convey your idea that it would be adviseable to demand of them the execution of those articles. Upon full consideration therefore I concluded that it was the most safe and sound policy to leave this point where it was before, and in which I was the more confirmed by some circumstances that were afterwards disclosed.

The day after this last communication was presented I received a letter from the committee assuring me that the subject engrossed their entire attention, and that an answer should be given me as soon as possible: and a few days after this, I was favour'd with another, inviting me to a conference at 12 the next day.[4] I attended and found only the three members of the diplomatic branch of the committee present, Merlin de Douay, Thuriot and Threilliard. Merlin commenced by observing that I had advised and pressed them to execute the 23 & 24 articles of the treaty of amity and commerce; that they were pursuaded their complyance would be useful to us but very detrimental to them: it would likewise be distressing for Frenchmen to see British goods protected by our Flag, whilst it gave no protection to theirs: and after some other comments he finally came to this point "Do you insist upon our executing the treaty?" I replied I had nothing new to add to what I had already said on that head. Threilliard seemed surprized at the reply and expressed a wish that I would declare myself frankly on the subject. I told him I was surprized at his remark since I had not only declared myself frankly but liberally. We then passed from the point of demand to a more general discussion of the policy in France to execute the treaty, & in which I urged, that if she considered her own interest only she ought not to hesitate, since it gave her the command of neutral bottoms, and under the protection of their own flags to supply her wants, with other considerations which had been before press'd in my notes that were before them. I was however brought back twice again to the question "do you insist upon or demand it?" I found that a positive and formal declaration on this point was the sole object of the interview, and as I perceived that something was intended to be founded on it, either now or hereafter, if given in the affirmative, I was the more resolved to avoid it, & to adhere to the ground I had already taken. I therefore repeated my declaration & in the most explicit terms, that I was not instructed by the President to insist on it, nor did I insist it. That their complyance would certainly be highly beneficial to my country, but that in my observations I had considered the proposition merely in relation to France, & wished them to do the same, since I was satisfied that the true interest of France dictated the measure. They all expressed an attachment to us, spoke much of the difficulty of the situation, and of the peculiar delicacy in adopting in the present state of the publick mind, any measure which might be construed as eventually favoring England, and thus the conference ended.

In revolving the subject over since, I have been doubtful whether the solicitude shewn to draw from me a decisive answer to the question "whether I insisted or demanded of them to execute the articles of the treaty" was merely intended as the basis of their own act complying with it, & a justification for themselves in so doing, or as a ground to call on us hereafter, in the prosecution of the war against England, to fulfil the guarantie. I was at the moment of the discussion in the committee, of the latter opinion, but I must confess upon a more general view of all circumstances, that have passed under my observation since my arrival, that I am at present inclined to be of the former. I rather think as there is an opposition to the measure and it would commence an important change in their system, and might also be construed into a partiality for England, a nation by no means in favor here that the dread of denunciation in the course of events suggested it. Be this as it may, I am perfectly satisfied it would be impolitic to demand it, since the refusal would weaken the connection between the two countries, and the complyance upon that motive, might perhaps not only produce the same effect, but likewise excite a disposition to press us an other points, upon which it were better to avoid any discussion. I hope however soon to obtain an answer and a favorable one: if the subject was before the convention in the light it stands before the committee, I am convinced it would since have been the case. But it is difficult to get it there, for if I carried it there myself, it would be deemed a kind of denunciation of the committee. Yesterday there was a change of several of the members of that body and which I deem from my knowledge of those elected favourable to our views.[5] Be assured that I shall continue to press this business with all suitable energy & in the mode that shall appear to me most eligible, and in the interim that I will do every thing in my power to prevent abuses under the existing system.

Upon the subject of the 50,000 Dollars, advanced for the emigrants from S[t] Domingo, I have made no formal demand, because I wished the other points, which were depending, settled first, from an apprehension that if they granted several little matters, it would fortify them in a disposition to reject those that were important. I have however conferred informally upon it, and have no doubt it will be peremptorily allowed: I think therefore this shou'd be calculated on by the department of the treasury. I will certainly bring it before them shortly as I shall immediately the affair of the consul in the Isle of France,[6] upon which latter point however permit me respectfully to add that the appointment of a person not an american perhaps an Englishman to the office of consul has not only been the cause of the disrespect shewn to our authority, but even of the embarrassments to which our countrymen were exposed there.

With respect to the business with Algiers I have not known how to act. It will be difficult for France in the present state of affairs to support the measures of our resident in Portugal[7] or for them to concert any plan of cooperation. It seems however in every view, proper to rid ourselves of the person in Switzerland who I understand, has been in readiness to prosecute the business for some time past. I have, in consequence written him a letter in conformity to your idea of which I inclose you a copy & which I presume he will consider as a respectful discharge.[8] I am inclined to think France will cooperate with us upon this point, and if any plan can be adopted by which she may forward the measures of Col[o] Humphreys, I will endeavour to avail him of it. But certainly if it is expected that her aid will be efficacious or that she will embark with zeal in the business, the whole should be concerted & executed from this quarter. Perhaps, as I have heard nothing from Col[o] Humphreys, the business is now done, or he is pursuing it without calculating upon any aid from France. A letter which was presented me by M[r] Cathalan our Consul at Marseilles & who is now here (as are M[r] Fenwick, Dobree & Coffyn, a son of the consul & who came to represent his father) from cap[n] obrian & which I now inclose,[9] will shew you the state of the business in August last. Be assured I shall be happy to render my country any service in this distressing business in my power, even by visiting Algiers, if it were necessary.

I have enquired into the character of our Consuls at the several ports, I mean those who are Frenchmen for M[r] Fenwick is well known, viz: LaMotte at Havre, Dobree at Nantes, Coffin at Dunkirk & Chatalan[10] at Marseilles, and find them likewise all men of understanding & of excellent reputation, attached to our country & grateful for the confidence reposed in them. If displaced it will subject them to some censure: I do not therefore wish it, tho' I most earnestly advise that in future none but Americans be appointed.

I was extremely concerned upon my arrival here to find that our countryman M[r] Paine and likewise Madame Lafayette were in prison, the former of whom had been confined near 9 months and the latter about two. I was immediately intreated by both to endeavour to obtain their enlargement. I assured them of the interest which America had in their welfare, of the regard entertained for them by the President, and of the pleasure with which I should embrace every opportunity to serve them, but observed at the same time, that they must be sensible it would be difficult for me to take any step officially in behalf of either, & altogether impossible in behalf of madame La Fayette. This was admitted by her friend who assured me, her only wish was that I would have her situation in view & render her informally what services I might be able without compromitting the credit of our government with this. I assured him she might confide in this with certainty, and further that in case any extremity was threatened that I wou'd go beyond that line & do every thing in my power, let the consequence be what it might to myself to save her. With this he was satisfied. She still continues confined, nor do I think it probable she will be soon released. I have assured her that I would supply her with money & with whatever she wanted, but as yet, none has been accepted, tho' I think she will soon be compelled to avail herself of this resource.

The case was different with Mr Paine; he was actually a citizen of the united States, and of the united States only: for the revolution which parted us from Britain broke the allegiance which was before due to the crown of all those who took our side: he was of course not a british subject: nor was he strictly a citizen of France; for he came by invitation for the temporary purpose of assisting in the formation of their government only, and meant to withdraw to America when that should be completed: and what confirms this, is the act of convention itself arresting him by which he is declared to be a foreigner. Mr Paine pressed my interference. I told him I had hopes of getting him enlarged without it, but if I did, it could only be by requesting that he be tried in case there was any charge against him, and liberated in case there was none. This was admitted. His correspondence with me is lengthy and interesting and I may probably be able hereafter to send you a copy of it. After some time had elapsed without producing any change in his favor, as he was pressing & in ill health, I finally resolved to address the committee of surety general in his behalf, resting my application on the above principle. My letter was delivered by my secretary in the committee to the President, who assured him he would communicate its contents immediately to the committee of publick safety and give me an answer as soon as possible. The conference took place accordingly between the two committees and as I presume on that night or the succeeding day, for on the morning of the day after which was yesterday, I was presented by the secretary of the committee of surety general, with an order for his enlargement. I forwarded it immediately to the Luxembourg & had it carried into effect, and have the pleasure now to add that he is not only restored to the enjoyment of his liberty, but in good spirits. I send you a copy of my letter to the committee of surety general, and of their reply.[11]

Since my last the french have taken Coblentz & some other post in its neighbourhood, they have likewise taken Pampeluna & broken the whole of the spanish line, thro' a considerable extent of country.[12] About twenty standards taken from the routed Spaniards, were presented to the Convention a few days past.

I likewise send in the inclosed papers a decree respecting the Jacobins, by which all correspondence between the different societies is prohibited, as likewise is the presenting a petition to the convention in their character as such, with some other restraints I do not at present recollect.[12] With great respect & esteem I am Dear Sir yr most ob{t} & very humble servant

Ja{s} Monroe

RC, NHi: Gilder Lehrman Collection; marked "Duplicate 3." Text in clerk's handwriting; closing and signature in JM's handwriting.

1. This meeting with the Committee of Public Safety must have occurred on October 17, since JM's letter to Randolph was dated the 16th and his letter to the Committee was dated the 18th (see above).

2. JM to Committee of Public Safety, 18 October 1794 (above).

3. The "Supplemental Observations" were enclosed in JM's letter of October 18.

4. The Committee of Public Safety wrote to JM on October 21 (above) and 29 (NN: Monroe Papers); the meeting occurred on October 30 (Journal Entry, October 1794, above).

5. Joseph Eschasseriaux, Pierre-Antoine Lalay, and Jean-Baptiste Treilhard were replaced on the Committee of Public Safety by Jean-Jacques Cambercéres, Lazare Carnot, and Jean Pelet.

6. William McCarty was the American consul on the French Indian Ocean island of Ile De France (now Mauritius).

7. David Humphreys was the U. S. minister to Portugal.

8. JM to Jacques LeRay de Chaumont, 13 October 1794 (above).

9. The letter from Richard O'Brien has not been located; a copy is not enclosed with JM's letter to Randolph of this date in DNA: RG 59: Despatches from France.

10. The clerk tranposed the spelling of Cathalan.

11. JM to the Committee of General Security, 1 November 1794 (above). The Committee of Public Safety responded on the same day that it would look into Paine's imprisonment (*Catalogue of Monroe's Papers*, 1: 36).

12. The French captured Coblentz, Germany, an important refuge for French émigrés, on 23 October 1794 (Owen Connelly, *The Wars of the French Revolution and Napoleon, 1792-1815*, 70; (Annapolis) *Maryland Gazette*, 25 January 1795); The information that JM had received regarding the French capture of Pampelune was incorrect. The French armies scored several victories over the Spanish and drove them back to Pampelune, but the onset of winter prevented an attack on the city (Henri Jomini, *Histoire Critique et Militaire de Guerres de la Revolution*, 6: 163-166).

13. The decree suppressing the activities of the Jacobin clubs is not enclosed with JM's letter to Randolph of this date in DNA: RG 59: Despatches from France.

To David Humphreys

Paris   November 11. 1794

I have lately received a letter from the Secretary of State mentioning that the power to treat with the regency of Algiers was committed to you, and that the aid of this Republic if attainable must be thrown into that line. I was likewise apprized by Mͬ Morris of some measures taken by him in concert with the government here, relative to that object, but which were unconnected with you. As I have reason to think you possess powers flowing from the last session of Congress, I think it possible you have already progressed in the business, and therefore that the aid of this government will be useless. But if you have not, how shall a cooperation be concerted supposing this government disposed to enter into it? Will it not be necessary for you to come into some part of France and depart thence with some agent from her? Your thoughts upon this head will be useful: but until I know the state of the business in your hands it will be useless and improper for me to occupy the councils of this Republic on the subject. I therefore hope to hear from you on it as soon as possible.

FC, NN: Monroe Papers

To the Committee of Public Safety

Paris 13 November 1794.

Citizens,

I received some weeks past a letter from Mͬ Gardoqui Minister of the Spanish finances inclosing one to my care for Mͬ Otto then in the department of foreign affairs, requesting me to present it to him.[1] As I did not wish to be the channel of communication from Mͬ Gardoqui to any citizen of France, whatever might be its object, and whether of a private or public nature, I resolved neither to deliver the letter, nor give an answer for the time, to that which was addressed to me. And I was the more inclined to this from the persuasion that if of a private nature the delay could be of no great importance, and if of a public one, and especially if upon an interesting subject, that when it was found I attended only to the concerns of my own country, and did not chuse to interfere in those of Spain, that he would take some course more direct for the attainment of the object in view. As some weeks had now elapsed I took it for granted that this was the case. In this however I have been disappointed for I was favoured within a few days past with a second letter from M.ʳ Gardoqui, in which he enters more fully into the object of the first communication.² Finding therefore that he still addressed himself to me, notwithstanding the discouragement already given, I deemed it necessary not only to examine more attentively the object of this communication, but likewise to adopt definitively some plan in regard to it. Nor had I much difficulty in either respect, for when I recollected that he was a minister of Spain, and observed that his letters as well that to M.ʳ Otto, and which I have since examined, as those to me, expressed only a wish to be admitted within the government of France, to attend some baths, I could not but conclude that this was the ostensible motive whilst some other in reality existed. And in this I am the more confirmed from a recollection of the relation in which M.ʳ Gardoqui and myself formerly stood in America to each other, and which on account of my strong opposition in the Congress to his proposition for secluding the mississipi was not the most amicable one. From that consideration I do not think he would solicit a correspondence with me for a trifling object, what other then must be the motive? In my judgment there can be none other than the hope of thereby opening the door for the commencement of a negotiation for peace, and that the Spanish court has availed itself of this mode of making that wish known to you.

Presuming then that this was in truth the object, it remained for me only to decide what course I should take in regard to M.ʳ Gardoqui's communications: nor could I hesitate long upon this point, for I well knew it was of importance to you to become acquainted with the disposition of other powers towards the French republic. I have therefore deemed it consistent with that sincere friendship which the United States bear towards you, and the interest they take as your ally in whatever concerns your welfare, as well as with that candour I mean to observe in all my transactions, to lay the letters before you, knowing their contents, you will be enabled to determine how to act in regard to them. As it respects the United States whom I serve, or myself personally it can be of no importance to me to be acquainted with the result, since I doubt not that, under the wise counsels of the republic, the revolution will progress to a happy close: but permit me to assure you that if I can be of any service to the French Republic in regard to the answer to be given to this communication, it will give me the highest satisfaction to render it.

Copy, DNA: RG 59: Dispatches from France; enclosed in JM to Edmund Randolph, 2 December 1794.

1. Diego de Gardoqui to JM, 9 September 1794 (above).

2. Gardoqui to JM, 7 October 1794 (above).

From Edmund Randolph

Philadelphia November 17ᵗʰ 1794.

Dear Sir,

As I cannot doubt, that you have written to the Department of State, I the more freely inform you, that we are under great anxiety for intelligence from France. The fall of Robespierre, its cause and consequences; the present position of the guiding influence of the nation; and the real temper of the people, are indeed delivered to us through newspapers; but on them a political appetite cannot rely for genuine food. It is rumoured too, that France seizes our vessels, if insured in Britain, and in many instances, even if bound thither. God forbid, that a tenth part of this should be true; because it would discover a most serious irritation in the French Republic, and must produce serious discontents in our own. If such be the State of things, I confide, that you have made yourself heard in a proper remonstrance. But I still flatter myself, that under these circumstances, you would have employed an advice boat.

Your speech to the national Convention has been the Subject of some criticism. But what appears in the public prints has gone through so many translations, that we wait for the original from you, before the comments, which have occurred, will be forwarded to you. The mode of conveying this letter being by a vessel, of which I have just heard, and which is on the eve of sailing from some remote port of the United States, I am limited by Mr Fauchet who dispatches her, to too short an hour, and am too much restrained by other <u>possibilities,</u> to be more diffusive on this head <u>now</u>.

The principal reason of my writing is to admonish you of some dissatisfaction, which will probably be inculcated by Mr Fauchet, concerning the omission to return the salute of the Semillante at New York. My letters of the 9th & 16th Nov. copies of which are enclosed,[1] contain the measures adopted on this occasion, which the President so much regrets and disapproves. I think it unreasonable in him to press this subject, when he knows that Governor Clinton has been called upon to explain this affair, and ought to conclude from his politicks, that he would neither wilfully suffer an insult to the French nation within his jurisdiction, nor affect any delay in examining, reporting or even punishing it.

A quorum of the Senate have not yet assembled so that I can only transmit your newspapers, due since the last enclosure, and a triplicate of my letter of the 25 September last, together with Mausten Watson's case. I have the honor to be, with great respect & esteem Dr Sir, Your most obedient Servt

Edm: Randolph

RC, DLC: Monroe Papers

1. Copies of the two letters to Fauchet are in DNA: RG 59: Domestic Letters.

To Diego de Gardoqui

Paris [18 November 1794][1]

I have been favored with your two Letters lately,[2] and can assure you that the pleasure I should otherwise have derived from a renewal of our former acquaintance, was sensibly diminished by the information they contained of the decline of your health. And I am sorry to add that considerations of peculiar delicacy render it impossible for me to take that part in the means necessary in your judgment for its restoration, you have been pleased to desire. You will naturally infer what these are without my entering into them, and ascribe to these, and these only, my not aiding you in that request. I beg of you however to make your application to the Committee of Public Safety directly, and from whom I doubt not you will readily obtain an answer which will be satisfactory to you, for I am well convinced that the circumstance of an existing war will form no obstacle to your admission into the country upon an occasion so interesting to yourself. Be assured if the Officer your friend whom you speak of, falls within any reach, I will be happy to render him any service in my power being well satisfied of his merit from your commendation.

Copy, NN: Monroe Papers; filed at the end of October 1794.

1. This undated letter was written sometime between JM's letter to the Committee of Public Safety of 13 November 1794 and that to William Short of 19 November 1794. The editors have assigned 18 November 1794 as a likely date.

2. Gardoqui to JM, 9 September and 7 October 1794, above.

Observations Submitted to the Consideration of the Diplomatic Members of the Committee of Public Safety

[19 November 1794][1]

It is the wish of the French Republic to obtain by loan a sum of money from the United States of America to enable it to prosecute the War.[2]

This is to be expected from three sources, the general Government, the State Governments, and from individuals.

The French cause and the French nation are greatly regarded in America, and I am persuaded some money may be obtained, and perhaps a very respectable sum, from the three sources above mentioned. For this purpose the minister should possess power to make loans from either of the above parties and to give such security as the republic shall deem suitable.

The Committee however should advert to the situation of the United States in regard to England and Spain. Both those Countries have encroached upon our rights, the one holding the Western posts, in violation of the treaty of peace in 1783, whereby she harrasses our frontiers, by means of the Indians, and the other by shutting the Mississippi, and likewise exciting the Indians against us to the South. So that the United States are at present in a kind of hostility with both powers. There is likewise reason to believe that a Convention subsists between Britain & Spain, defensive and probably offensive against us, in support of their respective claims.

In this situation, would it be proper for France to make peace with either of those powers, whilst our claims were unsettled with either and whilst both encroach on our territory? would it not leave those powers free to attack us united, and in that situation would not France be forced again to embark in the war, or tamely look on and see our dismemberment? Could the Republic in short, deem its own peace sincere or durable, whilst these points remained unsettled between the United States and those powers, and should it not therefore seek an adjustment of the whole at the same time?

I have suggested these considerations in the hope that the Committee will give the minister, about to depart for America, full power in relation thereto, and in the confidence that a satisfactory assurance on that head would greatly facilitate the object of the Loan: for if the United States were assured that they would have no occasion for their own resources to support a War against those powers, it would of course be more in their power to lend them to the French Republic.

It must be obvious that France may not only secure these points for us with both those powers & without any difficulty, but with Spain whatever else she pleased; for I am persuaded that the Spanish Monarchy would even agree to open the islands to the world, and perhaps even South America, to end a war which endangers the crown itself.

The mode would be, by insinuating to both those powers, when France commenced her negotiation, that they must also adjust at the same time their differences with the United States.

The sum which might be raised in America from the different sources above mentioned, upon an assurance of this kind, would in my Judgment be considerable. In any event however I shall be happy to give the minister about to depart[3] every information and aid in my power in forwarding the object in view.

I submit to you however whether it would not be proper to enable me in my letters, on that subject, to declare what your sense is upon these points.

Ja[s] Monroe

Copy, DNA: RG 59: Dispatches from France; enclosed in JM to Edmund Randolph, 20 November 1794

1. This letter is undated, but JM informed Edmund Randolph in a letter dated 20 November 1794 (see below) that he had delivered it to the committee "to day," which suggests that it was probably written on the 19th.

2. Philippe Merlin de Douai and Jacques Thuriot of the Committee of Public Safety met with JM on 16 November 1794 and asked him if he thought that the United States would make a loan to France (Merlin de Douai and Thuriot to JM, 16 November 1794, NN: Monroe Papers; JM to Edmund Randolph, 20 November 1794, below).

3. For the appointment of a new French minister to the United States, see JM to George Washington, 19 November 1794 (below).

To William Short

Paris Novr 19. 1794.

Dear Sir

I rec^d lately two letters from Mr Gardoqui[1] (ag^t of Spain in his negotiation with you upon the subject of the Missisippi) requesting me to obtain permission for him of the French governm^t to visit certain baths within France, a measure advised by his phisicians upon acc^t of his declin^g health: and likewise requesting some other services of little importance.[1] I communicated his wish to the committee of publick safety & answered his letter in harmony with that body, whereby I requested him to make his application directly to the committee himself, not doubting he wo^d readily obtain the permission requested.[2] I readily concluded that the motive suggested was ostensible only, whilst the real one was to open a negotiation for peace. In this opinion the committee concur with me, and I consider the finesse the less pardonable from the consideration that he wishes to make me instrumental to a peace with Spain at the moment that he not only trifles with you upon the subject of the missisippi but his court in harmony with Engl^d is exciting the Indians upon our frontier to doing us all the detriment in their power. I conclude also that you know nothing of his application to me, for if he had not found it expedient to hide the measure from you, the application wo^d have been more regular thro' you.

Possessed of these facts I have thought it expedient to endeavor to turn the incident to some account in our favor agnst that court. Mr Gardoqui supposes the United States has some interest here & wishes to take advantage of it in pursuit of peace. I have sought rather to increase his idea of this interest & to turn it to your account. Evading an interference I have notwithstanding satisfied him by returning an answer thro' the representative with the army in Sp^n, that my answer was given in concert with this government.[2] And to excite the belief that projects striking directly at S^o America are in contemplation between America & France, & will be agreed on this winter in Phil^a, I have written you a letter to that effect[3] to accompany this to Portugal & be put in the post office there that it may pass thro' Mr Gardoqui's hands before it reaches you.[3] I omit my name but he will know my hand. I enclose you a copy of the letter intended to be seen by Mr Gardoqui, that you may perfectly understand the state of the business. Perhaps it may put it in y^r power to progress & close y^r treaty for opening the Missisippi, & that the best way to succeed will be to assume, in case you receive the letter intended to pass thro' Mr Gardoqui's hands an air of indifference upon the subject. I have arranged that this letter shall reach you thro a private channel & therefore be know to you alone.

Your female friend is in the country ab^t 30 miles from Paris in good health.[4] With real esteem & regard I am sincerely yours

Ja^s Monroe

I write you late at night & in great haste.

RC, DLC: Monroe Papers, series 4

1. Diego de Gardoqui to JM, 9 September and 7 October 1794, above.

2. JM's letter to the Committee of Public Safety was written 13 November 1794; his reply to Gardoqui is that of 18 November 1794 (both above).

3. JM's letter to Short has not been located.

4. Charlotte Alexandrine, Duchesse de La Rochefoucauld was released from prison in early November and allowed to return to her country home at LaRoche-Guyon. JM could not write this directly to Short but assumed that by saying she was in the country that Short would understand that she had been released (George G. Shackelford, *Jefferson's Adoptive Son*, 125).

From William Short

Madrid Nov 19. 94.

Dear Sir

It is so discouraging to be writing post after post without having ever the satisfaction of receiving an answer or even learning whether my letters get to your hands, that I have suspended for some time past troubling you—I should have hoped you would have written to me on receiving your honorable appointment for Paris—& still more on being installed there—I have learned these events—the first from the Sec. of State—the second through the public newspapers—As my letters formerly got safe to Mr Morris, I indulge myself in the hope that they will have been equally fortunate in being addressed to you— The last I wrote to him was of the 23 of July—he acknowledged its receipt on the 17th of Sep. & informed me he was then setting out for Switzerland.[1] As his letters here come to me yours would have also if you had written—of course I suppose that you had not written to me at that date—As you will have since received none I indulge myself in the hope you will have since done me that favor. I wrote to you Aug. 27, Sep. 30, Oct. 7 & Oct. 14.[2] These letters were all sent by duplicates viz. via England & Italy.

Until I hear from you I know not how to repeat the subject of my preceding letters—or to enter into further details respecting it. I count on your friendship & on your humanity to do all you can for the liberty & security of my friend—I hope & trust M. Morris will have informed you of her name & abode—I inclose a letter for her asking the favor of you to add the address & send it to her[3]—I hope you will have seen her or have written to her & also have heard from her—In former times she & her aged parent who is with her were the friends of all the Americans who came to Paris—& particularly so of Mr Jefferson & of me—I hope in these times my dear Sir, you will be theirs—My gratitude will be inexpressible—but I will endeavor to convince you of it in person when I shall have the happiness of meeting with you—Would to heaven that moment were near!

I beg & intreat you to write to me often—if it be only one line to let me know the receipt of my letters—& one and of my friend & her aged parent—I hope they are now both in the Country—& that you will have seen them—how happy sh^d I be to hear this from you—Send me your letters by duplicate, one to Mr Pinckney—the other by the way of Switzerland—desiring your correspondent there or that of your banker to forward it to me here—Accept my best wishes my dear Sir for your happiness & success in all your undertakings—& believe me your sincere friend & serv^t

W Short

RC, PHi: Gilpin Collection: William Short Letters

1. Short's letter to Gouverneur Morris of 23 July 1794 has not been located. Morris' letter to Short of 17 September 1794 is in DLC: Morris Papers: Letterbooks.

2. Short's letter of August 27 is probably that of 26 August 1794, above. His letter of 30 September 1794 is also given above. The letter of 7 October 1794 is in PPRF, and that of 14 October 1794 in DLC: Monroe Papers.

3. Short's letter to Charlotte Alexandrine, Duchesse de La Rochefoucauld, dated 19 November 1794, is in PPAmP: Short-LaRochefoucauld Letters.

To George Washington

Paris Novr 19. 1794.

Dear Sir

I had the pleasure some weeks past to receive your favor of the 25 of June and should have answered it sooner, had any safe private opportunity offered for Bordeaux, from whence vessels most frequently sail for America. I called the evening after its receit on Mr Morris, & put your letter for him into his hands so that he rec^d it unopened.[1] He left this about the beginning of Octr for Switzerland, from whence I understood he would probably proceed to Engl^d. His first intention was to have sailed from Havre to America, but this was afterwards declined and the latter rout preferred. As there was some delay in obtaining his passport & which gave him displeasure, and as I disliked from motives of delicacy to him to mention it in an official dispatch, I take the liberty to communicate it to you. Some weeks after my arrival, he intimated to me, that as it would take some time to pack up his baggage and he should in the interim be idle, he wished me to procure for him a passport from the Committee for the seat of John James Rosseau in Switzerland where he wo^d stay that time & return to take his departure.[2] I did so. It was in reply suggested to me that he might chuse his rout to leave France, but that they did not like to permit him to go into Switzerland, where the emigrants (his connections) were, & return back into the republick: that indeed they were surprized he had made such a request. I was asked would I take the measure on myself, and in case any censure attended it, be responsible to the publick opinion? To this I replied that I had shewn Mr Morris my letter submitting it to the Committee, and that it would be more agreeable to him as well as myself should it proceed from them. Thus the matter rested for some time; finally as Mr Morris pressed for a passport and complained much of the delay, and which I knew proceeded solely from an objection to his return, a circumstance I did not wish to mention to him, I found it indispensably necessary to send Mr Skipwith explicitly to ask whether he was anxious upon that point. He had suspected this difficulty before and immediately agreed to abandon the idea. The form of the passport then became a question. It was notified to him that if he would take one from me, visited by the Commissary of foreign aff^{rs}, what depended on them sho^d be performed immediately. But he wished one from the Committee or the gov^t independantly of me: the latter being the ordinary mode in the case of private citizens, merchants & others travelling thro France. I was of opinion this sho^d be granted him & said so to the Commissary. I was equally so that the other mode sho^d have been quietly accepted by him, or in other words that neither party should have made an object of the mode. I think it was Mr Morris's expectation I should demand a passport in the form desired by him & risque whatever consequences might result from it; he did not ask this of me but it was to be inferred from what I heard him say on the subject. I was however resolved to embark in no such discussion and especially upon a point so unimportant in itself. The passport was of course granted by me & certified by the Commissary in the usual course and under whose protection he has safely passed beyond the bounds of the republick. I do not know that this incident will ever reach you thro' any other channel but as it possibly may I have thought proper to state it to you correctly & according to my own knowledge.[3]

The successes of this republick have been most astonishingly great in every quarter. In my letters to the Sec^{ry} of State I have detailed the many victories gained and posts taken up to the 7th of this month:

since which Mastricht has fall'n with ab[t] 300 cannon & 8 or 10,000 troops:[4] for a considerable time past the combin'd powers have been able only to retard the progress of the French by defending posts; for ever since the battle of Fleury they have avoided, except where not to be avoided, a general action. And every post w[h] the French have sate down before, has yielded sooner than was expected. At present there appears to be nothing to impede their march to Amsterdam if they incline & of which there can be no doubt. Tis said the Prince of Orange has requested of the States General to overflow the country, & which is opposed & will probably be rejected. If the people rise & change the gov[t] they will be treated with as a free people, and I am inclined to think no treaty will otherwise be made with them. In Spain their success has been equally great: great part of that country has been overrun and in truth it appears to me to be within their power even to march to Madrid if it was their wish. Tis said that a treaty has already been made with Prussia, but this I do not credit, not because it is not attainable for I am convinc'd it is, but because I do not think the Committee wo[d] form a treaty without some hint of it to the Convention, & indeed their approbation. Spain and Austria both want peace & will I doubt not soon make one: and that Engl[d] likewise wants it there can be no doubt. In short it appears to me unquestionable that France can command a peace from every power & upon her own terms. Engl[d] alone can at present hesitate or talk of terms, and this she is enabled to do only by her fleet which may secure her from invasion: but I am inclined to think a storm is gathering over her more dangerous than any she has yet known: for I have reason to believe that Denmark and Sweden are ready to fall on her, and that Spain will be compelled to purchase her peace with France by uniting in a similar operation. A curious incident relative to this latter power has lately come to my knowledge, and which from the delicacy of the subject I shall put in cypher to the Sec[ry] of State, by which you will perceive how critically we are circumstanced in respect to that power, if she sho[d] close with France upon terms of neutrality, being at liberty to unite with England in case of such an event in hostility against us.

Every consideration of expedience invites us in my judgment to a close union with our ally: and believe me I have done all in my power to promote this object. But I have had to contend with many difficulties of a serious nature & which still embarrass me to a certain degree. These I cannot hazard otherwise than in cypher tho' I would with pleasure did I know that my letter would reach you unopened, speak more confidentially than I can do in an official despatch. A new minister will leave this for America in a few days: I think the change a fortunate event, for I am persuaded the successor will see cause to doubt many of the communications heretofore given. I am told the successor is a cool well-disposed & sensible man.[5]

Within a few days past Nimeughen has also been taken,[6] the hall of the Jacobin society shut up by the Convention,[7] & two members appointed by the Committee by consent of the Convention, whose names & offices are unknown—some say the object is to treat with Prussia Spain or the States Gen[l], or rather to accompany the army with power to treat with the people in case they rise—others say tis to treat with Denmark & Sweden, whose agents are said to be incog: in town. Certain however it is the Committee asked for permission to appoint such persons under such circumstances & that it was granted.

I found myself plac'd here as you will readily conceive upon a theatre new & very difficult to act on. And what has encreased my embarrassment has been the ignorance of the disposition of Engl[d] towards us as well as of the U. States towards her. I have also been destitute of all kind of council except M[r] Skipwith, & some is necessary in every situation. I have however acted as well as my judgment could dictate & I hope to y[rs] & the satisfaction of my countrymen in general. With great respect & esteem I am, Dear Sir, y[r] most ob[t] & very humble servant

Ja[s] Monroe

RC, DLC: Washington Papers

1. Washington asked JM to deliver a letter to Governeur Morris (dated 25 June 1794). Both letters are in DLC: Washington Papers.

2. William H. Adams, in his biography of Morris, suggests that the proposal to visit the home of Jean-Jacques Rousseau in Geneva was a ploy to mask his real intentions (Adams, *Gouverneur Morris*, 253).

3. Morris wrote to JM on 11 September 1794 requesting a passport, and JM forwarded this request to Philibert Buchot, the minister of foreign affairs, on September 13. Morris repeated his request on September 21. Buchot informed JM on September 23 that he would approve a passport for Morris issued by JM, provided that Morris did not return to France from Switzerland. Morris agreed to these terms, and JM issued the passport (*Catalogue of Monroe's Papers*, 1: 34; Adams, *Gouverneur Morris*, 253).

4. The French captured the Dutch town of Maastricht from the Austrians on 4 November 1794 (Owen Connelly, *The Wars of the French Revolution and Napoleon*, 70).

5. The French government appointed a Mr. Oudart in early October 1794 to replace Joseph Fauchet as minister to the United States (*Correspondence of the French Ministers*, 12, 515, 721-727).

6. The French occupied the Dutch city of Nijmegen on 8 November 1794 (Simon Schama, *Patriots and Liberators: Revolution in the Netherlands*, 1780-1813, 184).

7. The powerful Jacobin clubs began to decline after the fall of Robespierre. Mobs attacked the meeting place of the Paris Jacobins on November 9 and 11, 1794, which led the Convention to suspend the activities of the Paris club on November 12. When the Convention officially suppressed all the clubs, with it edict of 6 Fructidor an III (23 August 1795), only nineteen of the original 270 clubs were still active (Michael L. Kennedy, *The Jacobin Clubs in the French Revolution*, 263-281).

To Edmund Randolph

Paris Nov.[r] 20 1794

Sir

I was favor'd about five weeks past with a letter from M.[r] Gardoqui minister of finance in Spain, enclosing one for M.[r] Otto formerly in America, and at present chief of a bureau in the department of foreign affairs, mentioning the decline of his health & requesting my cooperation with M.[r] Otto in soliciting of this government permission for him to visit certain baths within the republick. This application surprised me. The season I knew was too far advanc'd for him to derive any benefit from the waters, and I was not apprized that those suggested were better than others within his reach; besides M.[r] G. and myself were, in consequence of a collision on the much litigated question of the missisippi, not on the best terms while in America; certainly not on such as to authorize an application of this kind to me. The disguise was therefore too thin to hide from me the true object. I immediately infer'd that it was the body politic of Spain that was disordered & not the animal one of M.[r] Gardoqui. As I did not wish to become the instrument of Sp.[n] in this business, or incur the slightest suspicion of the kind, since I well knew it would benefit Sp.[n] at the expense of the United States, I declined delivering his letter to M.[r] Otto, or answering, for the time that of M.[r] Gardoqui to me. About three weeks afterwards I rec.[d] a second letter, which confirmed me in the opinion first taken up, that the object was to open the door thro' me to the commenc'ment of a negotiation for peace.[1] I found therefore that it became my duty to take some step in regard to this business, and was in consequence resolved to shape my course in such manner as to make the incident if possible productive of some good to the U States, & of none to Spain.

When I reflected that we had interfering claims with Spain, as well in respect to the boundaries as the missisippi, and that we had a minister there negotiating upon those points; that the negotiation was closed without a satisfactory adjustment, & that Sp^n was probably in concert with Engl^d exciting the Indians against us, I was from these considerations inclined to deem this movment of Mr Gardoqui an insidious one. I was the more so from the further consideration, that he had made this application to me without the knowledge of Mr Short thro' whom it ought to have been made had the proposition been a candid one, and founded on any claim of Sp^n upon the United States. I was therefore the more resolved to suffer myself to be restrained by no unnecessary and false motives of delicacy towards Mr Gardoqui in the manner in which I sho^d treat the subject.

I was persuaded that a peace between France & Spain at the present moment whilst our claims were unsettled must be prejudicial to the United States. Such a peace would free Spain from a pressure which at present shakes her monarchy to the foundation. By continuing the war it enables the United States, in case they sho^d take decisive measures to do what they pleas'd with that power: for tis not reasonable to suppose when the French troops are overruning a great part of Spain, and her whole force is exerted for her protection at home, that she would be able to make a respectable opposition to any effort we might make on the other side of the Atlantick. But a peace with France would remove such pressure, and leave the Sp^h c^t at liberty to act with its whole force against us.

I was likewise persuaded it was the interest of France to have our accomodation in view, and to give her aid in forwarding our arrangment with Spain at the same time that she adjusted her own, for if she sho^d close a peace with that power whereby she left her at liberty to act against us singly or jointly with Engl^d in case of a war with the latter, she would not only expose us to great an unnecessary detriment, but likewise hazard the probability of being drawn into it again, in case it sho^d take an adverse course in regard to us.

Upon full consideration of all these circumstances I thought it best to lay the letters of Mr Gardoqui before the Committee with my free comments upon them. I did so, and told them explicitly that in my opinion it was the wish of the Sp^h court to commence a negotiation, & that it had addressed itself thro' me to inspire a distrust in me by creating a belief that the U States were more friendly to Sp^n & Brit^n. I explained fully our situation with both those powers assuring them that we were threatened with a war from both. I also mentioned the indelicacy and artifice of Mr G. in applying to me without the knowledge of our minister at that court, and resting it upon a ground of antient friendship which never existed to any great degree. I assured them, at the same time, that if I could be of any service in forwarding their wishes in regard to peace, in the present or any other instance, it was the wish of the U. States I sho^d be, and would personally give me great pleasure to render it. I intimated also the danger which would attend a peace between this republick and Sp^n, unless our difference should be compromised at the same time. The communication was well rec^d & the business terminated in an arrangment by which I was to answer Mr Gardoquis letters, declining any agency in the business myself, advising him at the same time to make his application directly (in case he continued indisposed) to the committee and from whom I was persuaded he would obtain a satisfactory answer. This was accordingly done, in a letter which was forwarded about 5 days past.[2]

In the close of this affair I was invited by the diplomatic members of the Committee of publick safety to a conference upon a new topic. I was informed it was their intention to press the war against England in particular, but that they were distressed for funds, & was asked could any aid be obtained from the United States. I told them I was satisfied if it was in their power, it would be rendered; that I possessed no power on the subject & could only advise of the probability &c. That with their permission I would put on paper such ideas as occurred to me in respect to that point, and upon which I wo^d afterwards more fully confer. This incident furnished me with a new opportunity of pressing more forcibly the propriety of their securing for us the points in discussion with Engl^d & Sp^n at the time their own peace should be made with those powers. I send you a copy of the paper delivered to them today & to which I have as yet rec^d no answer.[3]

Whether France will make any arrangment upon this point with us I cannot tell. When I mentioned in the Committee the danger which menac'd us of a war with Britain & Spain, and asked what reliance we might have on France in such event, I was answered, they sho^d consider ours as their own cause. ~~I plainly perceived to that in their judgment our neutrality was more beneficial to them than a participation in the war: a circumstance which satisfied me of the motive which influenc'd them in a former conference wher'in I was asked "do you demand or insist that we execute the treaty of commerce in the 23 & 24 articles."~~[2] No other arrangment can well be made, than that of lending money to France, if in our power, it being understood that she will secure at the time of her own peace the complete recognition of our rights from Brit^n & Spain, and which she may easily do in my judgment, and without prolonging the war a moment on that account.

On the other hand if the United States ever mean to assert those rights the present is of all others the most suitable moment. The fortune of France has risen to the utmost height of splendour whilst that of her enemies has declined to the lowest state of depression. Her arms are every where triumphant, whilst theirs are every where routed and broken. Spain makes no head against her but is trying as already shewn to steal a peace in obscurity. And Britain is perhaps in nearly as bad a situation. Mæstricht has lately surrendered whereby 8000 troops were yielded, with ab^t three hundred pieces of cannon, 257 of which were brass, with other warlike stores and in great abundance. Nimeughen was likewise taken a few days afterwards, with considerable am^t in stores; and tis said that commotions are taking place in 5 of the provinces, who have formally resolved to dismiss the Stadholder, reform the gov^ts by the republican standard, & ally with France. This must be felt in Engl^d & will probably excite disturbance there. In any event it will produce such effect that if America strikes the blow her own interest dictates & which every other consideration prompts, it must be decisive, and if not ruinous to the fortunes of that proud & insolent nation, will certainly secure us the objects we have in view.

If I hear further from the committee about the proposition for a loan &c I will advise you of it by the French minister who leaves this in ab^t 5 days. By the paper which I send, you will understand how far the point has been discussed, of the propriety in France to support our claims against Brit^n & Sp^n the opportunity for which was furnished by my friend Mr Gardoqui and you will soon be able to ascertain from the minister what his powers on that head are.

Within a few days past two deputies were appointed by the Committee of publick safety by consent of the Convention, to some important trust, but whose names and office are unknown. Tis supposed they are commissioned to treat on peace with some one of the powers, & which is most probable, but with which of the powers or whether this is the object, are only matters of conjecture.

I apprized you in a late letter that I had written to Col^o Humphreys[4] & was endeavouring to concert with him if possible, the mode by which the aid of this gov^t if disposed to grant it & which I presume to be the case, may be given him in the negotiation with Algiers. As yet I have not heard from him. As soon as I do, provided I find it necessary, I will apply for the support contemplated. Previous to this it will be improper. Touching this subject I send you a proposition from the gov^t of Malta presented by its chargé des aff^ts here to be forwarded for your consideration.[5] You will give me, for that gov^t such answer as shall be deemed suitable.

Within a few days past the Hall of the Jacobins was shut up, by order of the Convention. That body was constantly at work to undermine & impair the regular & constituted authority of the government.

Moderate measures to check its enormities were found only a stimulus to greater excesses. This last step was therefore taken, and there is reason to fear its dispersed members will still continue to provoke by some rash measure the indignation of the convention to such a height as to bring upon them a degree of severity it were better to avoid. ~~Of this however at present I see no cause for well founded apprehension.~~ Within a few days past also the commission to whom was referred the charge agnst Carrere formerly representative at Nantz have reported there was ground for accusation—and today it is believed the convention will approve the report & consign him over to the revolutionary tribunal, who will with equal certainty & with the general plaudit of the nation doom him to the guillotine.[6]

Dft, NN : Monroe Papers

The text of JM's draft is identical to that of the copy of this letter published in *ASP: FR*, 1: 685-686, which suggests that this is the definitive version of this letter. The copy in DNA: RG 59: Dispatches from France, varies significantly from this version: although the content is essentially the same, the wording is different, one paragraph is omitted, and another truncated.

1. Diego de Gardoqui to JM, 9 September and 7 October 1794 (above).

2. JM wrote to the Committee of Public Safety on 13 November 1794 (above); a subsequent meeting was held on November 16 (Philippe Merlin de Douai and Jacques Thuriot to JM, 16 November 1794, NN: Monroe Papers). JM wrote to Gardoqui on November 18 (above).

3. JM to the Committee of Public Safety, 19 November 1794 (above).

4. JM discussed the proposed negotiations with Algiers in letter to Randolph of November 7, but JM's letter to Humphreys was written afterwards, on November 11 (above).

5. Mr. Cibon to JM, 26 October 1794 (above).

6. Jean-Baptiste Carrier (1756-1794), a prosecutor, held no political office until his election to the National Convention in 1792. In 1793 he was sent on a mission to the cities engaged in the federalist revolt. In Nantes he ordered the execution of more than 3,000 captured rebels from the Vendée. His most execrable act was to order the drowning of around 1,900 of these men, women, and clergy in the Loire River. The victims were tagged "Noyades;" and this episode condemned as one of the most heinous of the Terror. After Thermidor, Carrier was denounced, tried for these acts, and sentenced to die on the guillotine in December 1794 (Paul Hanson, *Historical Dictionary of the French Revolution*, 56-57, 238).

From John Quincy Adams

Amsterdam November 22. 1794.

Sir

I received last evening from London, the papers which I now take the liberty to enclose, together with a letter from Mr Boylston, the Gentleman who chartered the vessel in question, and with whom I have had a long & valuable acquaintance.[1]

His letter states to me, and with obvious truth, that an early as well as a favourable decision upon this case is of vast importance to the Interest of the United States; that in consequence of this capture, an immediate rise of an hundred per Centum of the premium upon insurance of all american ships took place, although it was already before that time, double the ordinary peace premium. There are many other considerations which render any obstruction to the facility of our returning commerce from Great Britain at this time peculiarly injurious to us; and which you will certainly be able to appreciate at their proper value.[2]

Mr Boylston estimates at nearly £700,000, sterling the annual burthen of extraordinary insurance to which our Commerce is subjected by this rise of premium; his calculation I think is not much too high, and it becomes an object of the greater moment to the interest of our Country, as so large a proportion of our insurance is made in England: so that in its effects the principle of this capture, operates for the present to the detriment of the United States, for the benefit of Great Britain.

I am well assured Sir, that your zeal for the interests of the United States in general, and for the security and efficacy of their rights to all your fellow citizens individually, is too ardent and active to be susceptible of any accession from my solicitations. It would therefore be unnecessary, though I hope it will not be improper for me to add, that in the particular instance upon which I now address you my feelings of private friendship coincide with my concern for the public welfare. That the gentlemen to whom the property was addressed, and belonged are all personally known to me. That Mr Gill is Lieutenant Governor of Massachusetts,[3] and Messrs Head and Amory are among the most respectable citizens of Boston; and that in recommending the case to your attention, I follow the impulse of my incli-nation no less than the dictate of my duty.

I am happy, Sir, that this opportunity is given me to return you my best acknowledgments for your kind offer of a good understanding and correspondence between us, of which my father informed me at the time when I had the honour of being appointed to my present station. I should have notified you of my arrival here before, this but for the interruption of the Communication between France and this Country, consequent upon the present state of Affairs. When the regular intercourse shall again be restored I shall feel myself honoured by a correspondence as frequent and confidential as may consist with propriety and the public service. In the mean time, I have the honour to be with sentiments of the most respectful consideration, Sir, your very humble Servant

John Q. Adams.

RC, DLC: Monroe Papers

1. Ward N. Boylston was a Boston merchant who lived in London from 1775 to 1800 (Massachusetts Historical Society, Guide to the Boylston Family Papers). His letters to Adams of 13 and 14 November 1794 have not been located. Adams wrote to Boylston on 30 November 1794 acknowledging their receipt (MHi: Adams Family Papers: John Quincy Adams Letterbooks).

2. The ship in question was the *Mary*, which was captured by a French privateer (John Quincy Adams to JM, 30 November 1794 MHi: Adams Family Papers: JQ Adams Letterbooks).

3. Moses Gill (1734-1800) was a Boston merchant. He served on the executive council of Massachusetts 1775-1795 and was lieutenant governor of the state 1795-1799 (*Papers of George Washington: Presidential Series*, 12: 577).

To Mr. Cibon

Paris 2 frimaire an 3   22d Novr 1794.

I have received with great pleasure the considerations you were pleased to present to me, pointing out the mode by which the United States of America and the Isle of Malta may be serviceable to each other. Tis the duty of nations to cultivate by every means in their power, these relations subsisting between them which admit of reciprocal good offices, & I am persuaded the U States will omit no opportunity which may occur to testify that disposition towards the Island of Malta.

The Americans have it is true rec^d already great injury from the Algerines, and it is their intention to adopt such measures as shall prevent the like in future. The Island of Malta by its situation & maritime strength, possesses the means of yielding that protection, and your suggestion on that subject merits, in my opinion the serious consideration of our government, to whom I have already transmitted it.[1]

The United States possess at present extensive and very valuable territory. It is their intention to dispose of it by sale, by which however the right of soil only will be convey'd the jurisdiction still remaining with them. The government too of such territory is already prescribed; it must be elective or republican & forming a part of the existing national system. I have thought proper to add this information that you may know the powers of our government in relation to this object. Permit me to assure you that as soon as I shall be instructed thereon I will immediately communicate the same to you & that I am with the greatest respect & esteem yours

FC, DLC: Monroe Papers. Unsigned

1. JM enclosed an extract of Cibon's letter of 26 October 1794 in his letter to Edmund Randolph of 20 November 1794 (both above).

From John Jay

London 24 Nov.ʳ 1794

Sir

It gives me Pleasure to inform you that a Treaty between the United States and his Britannic Majesty was signed on the 19ᵗʰ Instant.

This Circumstance ought not to give any uneasiness to the Convention. The Treaty expressly declares that nothing contained in it shall be construed or operate contrary to existing Treaties between the United States and other Powers.

I flatter myself that the United States, as well as all their Ministers will upon every occasion, manifest the most scrupulous Regard to good Faith; and that those nations who wish us well, will be pleased with our preserving Peace and a good understanding with others. I have the Honor to be with great Respect Sir your most obᵗ & hble servᵗ

John Jay

RC, DLC: Monroe Papers

From André-François Miot[1]

[24 November 1794]

Citoyen Ministre, tu trouveras ci-joint une Copie d'un Arrêté pris le 25 Brumaire dernier, par le Comité de Salut Public, relativement à la conduite à tenir désormais, dans les Portes, et par les Bâtimens de la République, envers les Navires neutres et leurs cargaisons. Cet Arrêté Sert de réponse au Mémoire que tu avais remit le 17. fructidor. Tu Seras, Sans doute, Satisfait des dispositions qui S'y trouvent enoncées. Elles seront pour toi un nouveau témoignage du desir qu'a le Gouvernement, de maintenir et de fortifier la bonne intelligence et la fraternité qui règnent si heureusement

Editors' Translation

[24 November 1794]

You will find within, citizen minister, a copy of a decree taken on 25 Brumaire last, by the Committee of Public Safety, relative to the conduct which shall hereafter be observed in the ports, and by the vessels of the Republic, towards neutral vessels and their cargoes. This decree furnishes an answer to the report which you presented on 17 Fructidor.[2] You will doubtless be fully satisfied with the arrangements which are there announced. You will consider them as a new proof of the desire of our government to maintain and strengthen the good intelligence and the brotherhood which now so happily reigns [between our two republics.][3]

[Miot]

RC, NN: Monroe Papers; filed 24 November 1795. The second page of this letter, containing the last several words and signature is missing. The missing text, signature, and date are supplied from *ASP, FR*, 1: 689.

1. André-François Miot [de Melito] (1762-1841) was French Foreign Minister from 21 November 1794 to 19 February 1795. An able, experienced administrator, Miot found that all the important work was handled by the Committee of Public Safety. He remained in office until the Treaty of Tuscany, on which he had worked as an ambassador, was concluded in February 1795 (*La Grande Encyclopedie*, sous "Miot;" Albert Hall Bowman, *The Struggle for Neutrality*, 178-179).

2. JM to the Committee of Public Safety, 3 September 1794, above.

Miot enclosed the following decree:

Extract of the Register of Arréts of the Committees of Public Safety,
Finance, & Supplies

25th Brunaire (November [15], 1794) 3d year of the republic.

The Committees of Public Safety, Commerce, and Supplies, order as follows:

ARTICLE I. The vessels of the United States of America, and those of other neutral Powers, shall be permitted to enter freely into the ports of the republic, and retire from them when they please: nor shall it be permitted to any constituted authority to retard their departure, or to oblige the captains to sell their cargoes against their will.

ART. II. When the captains or owners of neutral vessels are disposed to sell their cargoes to the public, they shall be paid for them according to the bargain which they make.

ART. III. It is enjoined to all the commandants of naval armaments, fleets, divisions, and squadrons, of the republic, to respect, and cause to be respected, upon their responsibility, in favor of the neutral and allied Powers, the rights of nations and the stipulations of treaties, conforming themselves strictly to the terms of the decree of the Convention of the 27th of July, 1793.

ART. IV. In consequence, they are expressly prohibited from turning these vessels from their course; taking from on board of them their captains, sailors, or passengers, other than soldiers or sailors actually in the service of an enemy Power; or of seizing the effects of merchandise which shall be found in them.

ART. V. Are excepted from the prohibition contained in the preceding article—

1. Merchandises belonging to the enemies of the republic, until such enemy Powers shall have declared that the merchandises of the French shall be free on board neutral vessels.

2. Such merchandises of the neutral Powers also as are deemed contraband of war; and under which are comprised all arms, instruments, and mentions of war, and every kind of merchandise and other effects destined for an enemy's port, actually seized or blockaded.

(ART. VI. VII. VIII. And IX, regulate the manner of preceding where neutral vessels are brought in, upon a presumption of having enemy's goods on board.)

ART. X. The commission of marine shall present, without delay, a statement of the individuals, born subjects of the Powers with whom the republic is at war, who were taken before the present day, upon neutral vessels, that particular arretés may be taken in each case.

ART. XI. The indemnities which are due to the captains of neutral Powers who were detained by an embargo at Bordeaux, shall be liquidated without delay by the commission of marine and colonies, conformable to an arrêt of the committee of public safety of the 17th of Germinal; and this commission shall render an account, in the course of ten days, of the actual state of these demands.

ART. XII. The commission of marine is specially charged to receive and adjust the accounts which shall be presented to it by an agent of the United States, for such supplies as the Americans have furnished to the administration of St. Domingo; and it shall take the necessary measures to procure to the parties interested the most prompt justice, and shall also present to the committees of public safety, of finance, commerce, and supplies, the results of its operations in these respects.

ART. XIII. The commission of foreign relations is instructed to deliver a copy of this arreté to the minister plenipotentiary of the United States of America, in answer to his memorial of the 9th of Fructidor (September 3d) last.

Merlin
Thuriot
Cambaceres, &c.

ASP, FR, 1: 639; A complete copy of the decree, in French, is in DNA: RG 59: Dispatches from France, enclosed in JM to Edmund Randolph, 2 December 1794.

From John Jay

London 25 Nov. 1794

Sir

By a Letter written and sent a few Days ago[1] I had the pleasure of informing you that on the 19th Inst: the principal Business of my mission was concluded by a Treaty signed on that Day.

It contains a Declaration, that it shall not be construed nor operate contrary to our existing Treaties—as therefore our Engagements with other nations remain unaffected by it, there is Reason to hope that our preserving Peace and a good understanding with this Country, will not give uneasiness to any other.

As the Treaty is not yet ratified it would be improper to publish it. It appears to me to be upon the whole fair, and as equal as could be expected. In some Respects both nations will probably be pleased, and in others displeased. I have the honor to be with great Respect Sir Your most obt & hble servt

John Jay

RC, DLC: Monroe Papers

1. Jay to JM, 24 November 1794.

From André-François Miot

A Paris, le 6 frimaire de l'an 3ᵉ de la République, une et indivisible
[26 November 1794]

Citoyen, tu annonces à la Commission par ta Lettre du 4 du courant, que le Président des Etats-Unis a nommé François Coffin, consul à Dunkerque, et Pierre Fréderic Dobree vice-consul à Nantes. Les Provisions délivrées, en conséquence, à ces Citoyens, étaient jointes à ta Lettre, et tu réclames les Exequatur nécessaires à l'exercice de leurs fonctions.

La Commission va S'empresser de te remettre ces expéditions, cependant elle desirerait Savoir de quelle nation sont les individus dont il S'agit. Elle te prie donc de lui mander S'ils Sont français ou Américains. C'est un éclaircissement qui lui est nécessaire, relativement à quelques dispositions réglementaires que l'*Exequatur* doit énoncer, et qui différent Suivant que l'individu auquel on le délivre, est français ou non.

A. F. Miot

Editors' Translation

Paris, 6 Frimaire, year 3 of the Republic, one and indivisible
[26 November 1794]

Citizen, in your letter of the 4th of this month you announce to the Commission that the President of the United States has named François Coffyn Consul to Dunkirk and Pierre Fréderic Dobree Vice Consul to Nantes. The orders duly issued to them were enclosed with your letter, and you request the accreditation necessary for the exercise of their duties.

The Commission will expedite these notarized documents to you; however, it would like to know the nationalities of these individuals. Please advise the Commission as to whether they are French or American. This information is required by the regulations governing accreditation, which differ according to whether or not the individual concerned is French.

A. F. Miot

RC, NN : Monroe Papers

To James Madison

Paris Nov[r] 30th 1794.

Dear Sir

By not hearing from you before this I conclude I shall not untill after you shall have commenc'd the session in Phil[a]. Indeed I calculate upon hearing at the same time from M[r] Jefferson and M[r] Jones, for surely they will not decline writing by you to be forwarded thence with your communications. I therefore wait the lapse of sufficient time to bring y[r] letters here with that kind of patience which arises from a conviction I shall not get them sooner. You will I presume be able at the same time to give me a good idea of the prospect before you, and which I conclude has become more decisively settled, in regard to the European powers, than when I left you: for surely the publick mind has before this expressed itself, in this respect, with such a degree of force, as to have left no alternative to the representative.

I gave you in my last, w[h] contained several sheets, a detail of the incidents up to that date, with respect to the general state of aff[rs] here as well as of those which more particularly regarded myself.[1] The interval between that & the present time, presents to view a series of events favorable to France, both in her internal & external operations. The fall of Robertspiere bequeathed to the convention the remnant of a controversy, whose fortune seemed to be marked by that event. The issue at stake with him was, whether the party of the mountain and which was in truth always the minority in the convention, or in other words the Jacobins whose principal members consisted of that party, connected with the military force & commune of the city (who were likewise all of that society) sho[d] by means of terror, for as they had the force of the city in their hands they could at pleasure & legally put it in motion, or the majority in the convention sho[d] govern France. His fate settled the point in that respect, but yet it did not give entire repose to the country. As only the principal members of the party were cut off it was natural that those who were left sho[d] still be disquieted; it was likewise natural that many of those in the preponderating party, should be well disposed in gratification of private revenge, to pursue the advantage they had gained and endeavor to exterpate all their enemies. I am happy however to assure you, that no event has taken place which in any respect discredits the councils of the country: on the contrary I infer from what has passed the happiest result for the future. The mountain party in convention & more especially in the Jacobin society have done much to provoke the indignation of the convention, but the indignation of the publick mind has constantly preceded that of that body, if indeed it can be said to have shewn any. It has in no instance taken any step which was not previously marked out & called for by the publick voice. In the extremities of this society, which was exciting by all kind of practices, commotions thro' the country, it at length yeilded to solicitations from many quarters to shut its door in Paris; and to similar solicitations & denunciations from every quarter, it has likewise yeilded, after solemn discussion, & in the most formal manner, one of its members, to trial before the revolutionary tribunal; one Carrere a man infamous for every possible vice & enormity and which were perpetrated in his mission to Nantes.

There was a strong disposition in the preponderating party not to proceed to this extremity agnst the Jacobins of Paris, from the apprehension it might be deemed an incroachment upon the essential rights of men, establishing in that respect a dangerous precedent, but as it was in truth in a state of rebellion agnst the convention, and it was manifest that if it prevailed the representative body would be annihilated, and complete disorder insue, there seemed to be a necessity for that body to adopt a remedy commensurate with the evil. None would be so but that of shutting up their door and which was accordingly done, and since which things have remained in a state of tranquility.

Whether any other members of the late dominant party will be executed for I take it for granted Carrere will be is in my opinion doubtful. If any have committed enormities in their missions thro' the country like him they certainly ought to be. There was obviously a belief existing generally upon my arrival, that some of the old committee of p: safety merited the fate of Robertspiere, but it was equally obvious that a majority were of opinion it were best to cultivate the esteem of the world, by sheathing the sword of justice & suffering even villains to escape. I was therefore persuaded it would be practicable to suspend the guillotin at that point, yeilding to it only such men as Carrere, and whose punishment would tend to retrieve the injurd fame of France, and form a bright ornament in the character of the present party; and subsequent events have convinc'd me that this was then practicable: perhaps it is still so: but the members of the late dominant party have lately committed several capital blunders, and put in hazard their own safety when it might otherwise have been avoided. It was certain that the safety of these members depended upon the magnanimity, the benevolence and the patriotism of the majority of the present reigning party. To these virtues therefore sho^d the app^l have been made, nor sho^d any step have been taken to diminish the effect. The contrary however has been the case in many respects, for it is well known that some of these members & particularly Billaud Varrennes were active in stirring up the Jacobins agnst the Convention, this member having in pointed terms denounc'd the reigning party not many days before the hall was shut up, to the society. Barrere likewise presented himself forward a few days after that event, in a manner to excite the disgust of that party by seconding a motion for breaking up the Convention & putting the constitution into motion, a measure he was formerly opposed to, and perhaps would not now have thought of had the Jacobins retained the ascendancy. At this too I was the more surprised because he was noted for dexterity upon all previous occasions, in the vicisitudes of the several preceeding parties, and had likewise observed his usual circumspection in other respects since the fall of Robertspiere. These members have likewise erred in the countenance they have given to Carrere, for instead of drawing a line between themselves and him & yeilding him to the justice of their country, they appeared for sometime to consider his as a common cause, and acted accordingly. It is true in the close of the business, and when the appeal nominal, as yeas & naes were taken, of 500 members present 498 voted there was cause of accusation, & that he sho^d be sent to the tribunal revolutionary & the other two were for his trial but hesitated on some collateral point.

Upon the whole however I am of opinion that as it respects the publick councils every thing bears the happiest aspect. There may yet be some irregularities, but not of the kind heretofore experienc'd. And with respect to the state of the war the prospect is still more brilliant. Mæstricht & Nimeughen have lately surrendered and opened the road directly for Holland, upon wʰ the French troops are now pressing with an energy not to be resisted. The probability is they will take possession of it unless prevented by inundation, a resource not to be relied on in case the winter shoᵈ be severe, and which will in any event ruin the country for many years to come. This must strike terror into Englᵈ & probably shake that govᵗ. In Spⁿ their success has been equally great. The Spʰ forces have been routed in several actions, many prisoners & posts taken, & in fact the prospect of atchieving in that quarter what they please. The present is certainly the moment for our govᵗ to act with energy. They shoᵈ in my judgment put the British beyond the lakes & open the Missisippi & by so doing we shoᵈ be courted into peace by those powers rather than threaten'd with war; and merely by negotiation we know we can do nothing, on the contrary we play the game that those powers wish us to play, for we give them time to try their fortune with France reserving to themselves the right of pressing us after that contest shall be over, let the issue be as it may, even in case they shoᵈ be, as they certainly will be defeated. If we took this step at this moment France would in my opinion not make peace without us, in case they consider'd it as war, but as they find that we stand well with France they woᵈ probably not consider it in that light. One other great advantage resulting from this measure is that it woᵈ be supported by the wishes of all America & take with it in particular the suffrage of the western people. This woᵈ terminate at once the discontents in that quarter: how much more wise & benevolent is that policy which points the force of the country against the invaders of the publick rights than that which turns it against the members of the society itself. I do not by this mean to intimate that the effort to crush the mov'ment at Fort Pitt was unwise—I think otherwise for the law must be supported, but I likewise think that if the one above suggested would produce the same effect in that respect, and a very salutary one in many others it ought to be adopted. Indeed I am persuaded it has been adopted, for many reports authorize a belief that Genˡ Wayne has had a rencounter with the British & taken from them the post at the rapids of the Miamis.[2]

You will readily conceive that the mission of Mʳ Jay & his continuance in Englᵈ have greatly embarrass'd my movments here. It has been intimated in such manner as to inspire doubts that a mere reparation for injuries coᵈ not be the sole motive; and in proportion as those doubts have existed have they produc'd a repellant disposition towards me not from any real distrust in me, but from a distrust of the Ex: admⁿ. I have done all in my power to remove it and hope I have now succeeded. But I trust he will not stay there the winter for by so doing he only gives the British time, which they want, & keeps alive the ill founded suspicion here.

You will hear with surprise that I have been favᵈ with a letter from Mʳ Gardoqui and that the object was to get within the republick upon pretence of ill-health but in my judgment to begin a negotiation for peace. I laid his letters for I recᵈ two,[3] before the committee intimating what I believed to be the object & avail'd myself of the opportunity to state our situation with Spⁿ; so that instead of bringing his wishes forward in a manner to create a belief we assisted Spⁿ in her efforts for peace, as was I presume intended by writing me on the subject, I took the opportunity of urging France to make no peace with her untill the Missisippi be opened. Since in case we were involv'd in a war with her France woᵈ be forc'd to join, so that it were better compromise the whole at once. I am certain the incident has produc'd a good effect.

Soon after this it was intimated to me by the Committee of P. S. that they wanted to borrow some money of us. I then took occasion to state our situation with Englᵈ in like manner pressing them to make our dispute theirs—and whether we embarked in the war or not to aid our negotiation for the posts so as to have theirs & our dispute settled at the same time. I am convinc'd the communication has been useful.

I think it probable they will ask our aid in money—& I most sincerely wish we may give it. I sho^d suppose we might lend 40 or 50 millions of livres, by the gen^l the State gov^ts & individuals. If a loan of the latter kind was opened guarantied by the Congress the whole wo^d be loaned by foreigners if necessary and I am sure it wo^d be paid by this gov^t as they have great resources in national property.

I have nominated Mr Skipwith as Consul for Paris. If appointed I shall want some one to supply his place. I leave this to y^rself in concert with Mr R.[4] to send the suitable person. First however I wish you to communicate to Col^o Burr that if Mr Prevost will come it shall be for him. Mr Purvyance is here in trade & declines the offer in case Mr P. will not accept as in that case it wo^d be offered.[5] How wo^d Mr Dawson do if Prevost wo^d not come. I fear he is distressed and as an old acquaintance having some claim on me & which I never wish to disappoint, I confess if he wo^d be benefited by it which I doubt under any other alternative, I sho^d be glad to serve him. But this is only for y^r consideration for I leave it to you as mentioned above in concert with M^r R.

I feel extremely anxious to hear from you. My conduct here is by this time before you & the subject of criticism—and y^r measures are greatly interesting to me. I hope therefore soon to hear on these topics as well as whatever else you deem necessary to be notic'd.

We had in idea a loan here to be vested in America. I am satisfied it may be procured if desirable. Provided I established the fund in Hamburg for instance to the am^t of 5 or 10.000£ ster^g to be secur'd by landed security such as the property purchased could you draw for it so as to answer the purpose? where wo^d you vest it? answer me upon these points & in the interim I will endeavor in reply to assure you where the fund will be plac'd & to what amount. I really think it may be counted on. And in the interim if a most elegible contract offers itself you may draw on me to be paid in Hamburg at three months sight for three thousand pounds Ster^g in one two or three bills. I am sure I can borrow the money there of Van Stophort[6] of the house of V. S. of Amsterdam; this gent^n lives here but co^d place the money there for me & I think wo^d at a word.

I wrote you not long since by a Mr Swan—his character is better known to me now than it then was. be cautious of him & give the same hint to Mr R. Maj^r B & other fr^ds to whom I wrote.[7] This you may do without compromitting me except where perfectly safe.

There are many things here which I think wo^d suit you. I beg you to give me a list of what you want, Such as clocks carpets glass furniture table linnen &c—they are cheaper infinitely than with you considering I have advantage of the exchge & you might pay the am^t to Mr Jones. Tell Mr R. I shall also be glad to serve him. I beg you to command me freely for I need not tell how happy it will make me to serve you. Ask Taylor if I shall send him a good watch.

Will you be so kind as obtain from Col^o Orr[8] or if he has them not get him to bring them hereafter my patents for my western land consisting of 20.000 acres on Rock Castle & 5 or 6.000 beyond the Ohio & give to Mr Jones. Cap^tn Fowler[9] acts for me. My other items you will recollect of Vermont & New Y^k. Remember me affectionately to all friends of both houses, to Mr Beckley—to Mr Yard & Dr Stevens & families—Tell them Mrs M. & child are well & desire to be remembered—very affec^y I am Dear Sir Y^r friend & servant

Ja^s Monroe

Mr Paine who is of my family desires to be remembered to you. He will be with you in the spring. Not being able to present Mr Fauchets draft here for 3000 dol^rs on acc^t of the depreciat^n I shall return it to Mr Randolph & subject it to Mr Jones's order. Will you attend to this.

RC, DLC: Madison Papers

1. JM to Madison , 20 September 1794, above.

2. JM's information was incorrect. Anthony Wayne did not capture Fort Miami. When Wayne attacked the Indians at Fallen Timbers they fled to the protection of the British fort but were denied shelter. Wayne demanded the surrender of Fort Miami, but the British commander refused. The strategic value of the fort to the British was lost, however, for the British refusal to aid the Indians destroyed the confidence that the tribes had place in them (Richard Kohn, *Eagle and Sword: The Beginnings of the Military Establishment in America*, 156-157).

3. Diego de Gardoqui to JM, 9 September 1794 and 7 October 1794 (above).

4. Edmund Randolph.

5. John Henry Purviance (1763-1820), the son of Samuel Purviance of Baltimore, was an attorney who replaced Skipwith as JM's secretary. Purviance served as secretary of the American legation in London 1804-1810 (Internments in the Historic Congressional Cemetery, Washington, D. C., http/www.congressionalcemetery.org, accessed 21 November 2006; Stuart Hoye Purvines, *The Purviance Family* (privately printed, 1986).

6. Jacob and Nicholas Van Staphorst were bankers in Amsterdam. They made numerous loans to the United States during the Revolution and in the years following (James C. Riley, "Foreign Credit and Fiscal Stability: Dutch Investment in the United States, 1781-1794, *Journal of American History*, 65: 654-678).

7. JM sent Madison a letter of introduction for James Swan on 20 September 1794 (*Madison Papers*, 15: 358). Letters of introduction for Swan addressed to Edmund Randolph, Pierce Butler, or any other of JM's acquaintances have not been located.

8. Alexander D. Orr (1765-1835), a Kentucky attorney, served in Congress 1792-1797 (*BDAC*).

9. John Fowler (1755-1840) served in the Virginia House of Delegates in 1787. He moved to Lexington, Kentucky and represented that state in Congress 1797-1807 (*BDAC*).

From Adrienne Lafayette

[November 1794]

Si j'obtiens ma Liberté, avant de retourner dans mes montagnes, et de m'ensevelir de nouveau dans La retraite, je presente avec confiance, au Ministre des Etats unis, Les demandes suivantes, dont tous Les objets interessent ma tranquillité.

1° je Lui demande de vouloir bien se charger de mon fils. je [le] désire de finir Son education dans une maison de commerce americaine. il me paroitroit preferable de L'établir ches un Consul des Etats unis. je desire qu'il entre dans Leur marine, et S'il etoit absolument impossible, qu'il commençait sa première campagne de mer, Sur un vaisseau americain je voudroit que ce fut Sur un bâtiment Marchand françois.

je prie Le Ministre des Etats unis, de se rappeller que mon fils, et depuis 1785, adopté par L'état de Virginie; et qu'il a depuis cette année Le Diplôme, de Citoyen de cet état. Je n'entrevois donc aucune difficulté à ce qu'il entre au Service de cette Seconde patrie, amie et alliée de L[a] R[épublique] F[rançoise].

2° je prie Le Ministre des Etats unis, de vouloir bien Se charger du Depôt de mon testament, et d'une Lettre pour mon fils que je desire y joindre.

3° j'ai Recours a Ses bontés ou plutôt à celles de La Nation, dont il est L'organe, pour emporter dans ma retraite, La certitude que des engagemens bien sacrés pour moi Seront remplis, et voici 3 billets que Le Lui demande de cautionner—et je ne puis exprimer qu'elle Sera ma recconnoissance d'un tel Service. voici mes trois billets:

1er billet

je promets et m'engage a payer annuellement a La C^enne L. Ch. de Motier La fayette Ve Chavaniac tante de mon mari, pendant tout Le tems de Sa vie, en deux payemens egaux de 6 en 6 mois, La somme de 2700^lt pour interets de La Somme de 54000^lt qu'elle nous avoit prête en 1785. et dont Le billet a ete deposé, au bureau des emigrés, dans Le delai que Les decrets prescrivent. je m'engage a payer annuellement La dite somme, jusqu'a L'entiere et parfaite Liquidation, et payement du fonds principal de cette creance.

La caution qui veut bien signer avec moi Le present billet, me repond des moyens de remplir cet engagement, c'est a plusieurs titres un devoir pour moi de Le contracter, et il est necessaire a mon repos, autant que precieux a mon cœur, d'être assurer de L'acquitter avec exactitude. a Paris ce . . . .

2 billet

je promets et m'engage a payer annuellement, a La C^enne Marthe aufroy, L'institutrice et L'amie de La mere que je pleure, 7 mille Livres de pension viagere payable d'avance de 3 en 3 mois Sans aucune retenue d'impositions.

La caution qui veut bien signer avec moy Le present billet, me repond de ne pas manquer d'acquitter Le present engagement, qui n'est pas Seulement un devoir pour moi, mais qu'il m'est consolant de remplir. a P. . . .

3 billet

je promets et m'engage a payer annuellement a La C^enne Marie Anne Marin, Mon institutrice, et celle de mes Sœurs, qui depuis Leur etablissement n'a cessé de donner ses soins a mes enfans, et qui enfin, depuis mes malheurs, et pendant notre cruelle Separation, Leur a tenu Lieu de mere; La somme de quinze cent Livres de rente viagère, payable d'avance de 3 en trois mois, Sans aucune retenue d'impositions, Le tout a commencer de L'epoque a Laquelle elle seroit separée de nous. je La prie d'accepter ce temoignage de mon amitié, de ma juste et tendre recconnoissance.

La caution qui veut bien signer avec moi Le present billet, me repond de ne jamais manquer a un engagement qui est un repos necessaire, et precieux a mon cœur. a P. . . .

Ce ne peut etre qu'après avoir expliquer Les details de ma position que j'ose presenter, avec confiance ces billets, et demander de Les cautionner. j'ai comme doit le scavoir Le ministre americain des ressources plus que suffisantes, pour acquitter La 1ère année mais il importe a ma tranquillité, de Les voir assurer avant de quitter Paris, et de pouvoir en remettre un double aux personnes interessees. je scais par experience, combien mille evenemens imprevus dans une revolution, rendent Les correspondances difficiles, même dans L'interieur de L[a] R[épublique]. il y a plusieurs raisons d'esperer que Les cautions que je demande, ne seront pas une charge. je demande La permission d'entrer dans quelques details Sur la position des personnes pour qui je Les donne et Les motifs qui me [poussent] a Les donner.

Le 1er billet regarde une personne de 71 ans. C'est une tante de mon mari, que je regarde comme Sa mere. tout ce qu'elle possède, etoit placé Sur nous. Le billet de 54,000^lt forme plus de moitié, de ce qu'elle possede. c'est nous qui lui avions demandé de placer Sur nous, ce remboursement, d'une terre qu'elle vendit en 1785 a La suite d'un procès, qu'elle avoit perdu. c'étoit moy qui me mêlois des affaires, et j'ai a me reprocher, d'avoir négligé quelques formalités qui n'étoient pas fort necessaires entre nous. cependant Si L'affaire est bien suivie, j'espere que Lorsqu'on restituera Les creances des emigrés, on restituera ces 54,000^lt dont Le titre a ete deposé dans Le delai prescrit, et alors mon billet Seroit brulé.

Le second billet, est pour une personne aussi septuagenaire, excessivement infirme. si jamais Le testament de ma respectable mere, est connu, et qu'au moins Les articles qui les remunerations Soyent executés, L'objet sera rempli, et mon billet Sera aneanti.

Le troisieme, a pour objet, d'assurer Le sort d'une personne de plus de 60 ans, d'une Santé foible, accablée de nos malheurs, et qu'il m'est necessaire de Songer qui ne manque pas au moins, d'une aisance necessaire dans cet état, Si Le genre de vie penible auquel je suis destinée m'oblige a me separer d'elle.

il Seroit assurement possible, que j'employasse des fonds que m^r Morris a bien voulu nous remettre a placer quelque chose pour remplir ces objets; mais 1^{ier} tous, ces fonds à L'exception d'environ 10,000^{lt} ont ete promis en avances de remboursement de creances dont La delicatesse me faisoit un devoir.

2° il me paroitroit peu raisonnable, de placer a fonds perdu, Sur La tête de 3 personnes dont La malheureuse Situation, ne me permet pas d'esperer, une longue vie, et si vous trouvés, peutêtre, que mes Sollicitudes Sont exagerées, vous pardonnerés, au moins, La confiance avec Laquelle j'y cherche un soulagement, dans Les bontés des États unis, dont vous êtes L'organe. mes enfans et moi, nous Sommes Si indifferens, non seulement à L'opulence, mais meme aux commodités de La vie, que nous esperons, etre Le moins a charge possible, dans tout ce qui nous sera personnel. et je me pardonnerai, mon indiscretion pour d'autres dans Les momens ou il sera question de nos besoins a nous mêmes.

Le Citoyen Beauchet, et sa femme, ayant traité toutes mes affaires, pres du Ministre des Etats unis, il peut juger tout ce que je dois a Leur constante amitié pour moi. mon vœu est qu'il se rencontre des occasions de Les reunir a moi, Leur famille a La mienne, d'une maniere qui ne nuise pas a Leurs interets. je prie Le Ministre des Etats unis, d'ecouter en toute circonstance, Les idées que peuvent Leur suggerer Leur attachement pour moy, et de Les aider de Ses moyens et de Son credit. mais cet objet est naturellement ajourné jusqu'à La paix, où Les fortunes Seront plus Stables, et ou mon sort Sera fixé irrevocablement.

Si jamais La C^{enne} Beauchet avoit Le malheur de perdre Son mari et elle resteroit sans fortune, je mets elle et ses enfans, Sous La Speciale protection des Etats unis, jusqu'au moment ou nous pourrions, elle et moi, ses enfans et Les miens, partager ensemble nos maux.

je Lui commande encore une jeune personne appellée La C^{enne} Benjamin qui a partage quelques uns de mes dangers. Si jamais elle venoit a perdre elle auroit recours au ministre des Etats unis, pour Lui en fournir Les moyens d'être près de moi. je prends La Liberté de La Lui recommander pour cet objet. elle m'a montre un attachement de fille, et je Lui dois des Soins maternels, Si elle devenoit orpheline.

je ne finirai pas Sans recommander encore aux bontes du ministre americain un domestique m^r Merceir qui m'a servi 17 ans avec fidelite et zele, et qui a couru aussi avec moy des dangers et partagé avec moi un mois de prison. il est placé dans ce moment, mais je ne supporterois pas L'idée qu'il Souffrit de La misère, et j'ai besoin d'esperer qu'il ne sera pas abandonné par Les Etats unis.

une famille très pauvre dont Le fils est victime avec mon mari a des droits sacrés a Leur bontés, Le pere La mere et 5 enfans Leur fourniront de quoi [s'exercer].

ma confiance est La seule expression de ma reconnoissance et il est aise de La juger par Le prix que je mets a des services qui sont dans ce moment L'objet de mes sollicitudes.

Editors' Translation

[November 1794]^1

If I obtain my freedom, before returning to my mountains and burying myself once again in seclusion, I entrust to the minister of the United States the following requests, whose attainment will give me peace of mind.

1. I ask him kindly to look after my son. I want him to finish his education in an American house of commerce. It would appear to me preferable to set him up at the residence of a consul of the United States. I want him to join their navy, and if it is absolutely impossible for him to begin his first line of duty at sea on an American vessel, I would have him serve on a French merchant ship.

I encourage the minister of the United States to recall that my son was adopted by the state of Virginia in 1785, and that he still has his certificate as a citizen of that state.[2] I foresee therefore no difficulty in his entering the service of this second country, friend and ally of the French Republic.

2. I request that the Minister of the United States be responsible for the deposition of my will, and a letter for my son I would like to attach to it.

3. I rely on these courtesies, or rather on those of the nation whose agent he is, in order to take with me into my seclusion the certitude that these very sacred promises will be fulfilled. Here are three that I ask him to safeguard—and I cannot express how much my gratitude will be for such a service. Here are my three promissory notes:

First Promissory Note

I promise and commit myself to pay annually to Citizen L. Charlotte de <u>Motier Lafayette, Widow Chavaniac</u>,[3] my husband's aunt, for the rest of her life, two equal payments every 6 months, the sum of 2700 livres, the interest on the sum of 54,000 livres, which she loaned to us in 1785, and whose promissory note has been deposited at the Office of Émigrés, in the period of time that the decrees prescribe. I pledge myself to pay annually the said sum, until the entire liquidation and payment of the principal of this debt is complete.

The guarantor, who of his own free will signs this promissory note, answers for me as to the means to execute this contract, which has several titles. It is a burden for me to take on, but it is as necessary to my repose as it is invaluable to my heart. Be assured I will acquit it with exactitude. At Paris. . . .

Second Promissory Note

I promise and commit myself to pay annually to the Citizen Marthe Aufroy,[4] teacher and friend of the mother whom I mourn, 7 thousand livres for a life-annuity, payable in advance every three months, without any deductions.

The guarantor who kindly signs this promissory note, is in agreement with me as to the means to execute this contract, which has several titles. It is a burden for me to take on but it is as necessary to my consolation as it is precious to my heart. Be assured I will acquit it with exactitude. At P. . . .

Third Promissory Note

I promise to do my part to pay annually to Citizen Marie Anne Marin,[5] my instructor and that of my sisters, who since their growing up has never ceased to provide for their needs and who after my misfortunes and during our cruel separation, has acted as a mother to them, the sum of 1500 livres as a pension payable in advance every three months, no withdrawal for taxes, the whole to commence from the time in which she would be separated from us. I beg her to accept this testimony of my friendship, with my true and affectionate gratitude.

The guarantor who is willing to sign with me the present note tells me he will not fail to keep his promise, which is essential to my peace of mind and precious to my heart. At P. . . .

It can be only after having explained the details of my position that I dare present with confidence these directives, and ask for their security. I, with the American minister, am aware of resources more than sufficient to take care of the first year; but it affords me peace of mind to see them authenticated before leaving Paris, and the power to return double the amount to persons of vested interest. I know by experience how a thousand occurrences unforeseen in a revolution can render correspondence difficult, even in the interior of the Republic. There are several reasons to hope that the commitments I ask of you will not be an inconvenience. I request permission to enter into certain details on the status of individuals to whom I give them and the motives which drive me to give to them.

The first directive concerns a person of 71 years.[6] She is the aunt of my husband whom I regard as his mother. All that she owns was given to us. The promissory note of 54,000 livres forms more than a half of what she is worth. It was we who had asked her to grant us a reimbursement of land she sold in 1785 following a lawsuit that she lost. It was I who got involved in these affairs and I have myself to blame for having neglected some formalities which were not really necessary between us. However, if the affair proceeds well, I hope that when they provide restitution for the titles of émigrés they will return these 54,000 livres whose title has been filed for the allotted time, and then my promissory note will be burned.

The second directive is for an individual, also a septuagenarian, who is extremely infirm.[7] If ever my respected mother's will is read, and at least the articles concerning the remunerations carried out, the promise will be fulfilled and my request made void.

The third is intended to ensure the future of a person more than 60 years of age,[8] in poor health, overwhelmed by our misfortunes, and for whom it is necessary for me to be assured that she shall not lack the basic necessities to live comfortably, should the difficult life to which I am destined forces me to separate from her.

It would surely be possible that I could use the funds which Mr Morris kindly returned to us to have something for these needs; but first all the funds with the exception of about 10,000 livres have been promised in advance to repay our creditors whose consideration places an obligation on me.[9]

2. It appears to me hardly reasonable to place the loss of such money over the head of three people whose unfortunate situation does not permit me to hope for a long life. Should you find, perhaps, that my concerns are exaggerated, you will forgive at least the confidence with which I seek relief through the generosity of the United States, whose agent you are. My children and I are so indifferent not only to the luxuries of life but even to life's conveniences that we would be the least likely to charge anything personal. and I ask pardon for any indiscretion to others in instances where there will be a question of our needs to ourselves.

Citizen Beauchet and his wife[10] having dealt with all our affairs regarding the minister of the United States, he can judge all I owe to their constant friendship for me. My wish is to bring about opportunities for them to be reunited with me, their family with mine, in a manner that will be no disadvantage to their interests. I implore the minister of the United States to listen in all circumstances for ideas that could suggest their attachment to me, and to help them with his means and his credit. But this goal is naturally put off until peace or fortunes will be more stable, when my fate will be fixed irrevocably.

If ever the Citizeness Beauchet has the misfortune to lose her husband and she should be without money, I place her and her children under the special protection of the United States until the moment when we will be able, she and I, her children and mine, to share our difficulties together.

I remind him again of a young person named Citizeness Benjamin[11] who has shared some of my dangers. If she ever loses her father, she has recourse to the minister of the United States to furnish her the means to be near me. And I take the liberty to recommend her to him for this purpose. She has been like a daughter to me, and I owe her maternal care if she becomes an orphan.

I cannot finish without recommending again to the kindnesses of the American minister, Mr Mercier, a servant who has served me for seventeen years with fidelity and zeal, and who has also run risks for me and shared with me a month in prison.[12] He has a position at this moment, but I cannot bear the idea that he would suffer poverty. And I need to hope that he will not be abandoned by the United States.

A very poor family whose son is the victim with my husband also has sacred claims to their kindness, the father, the mother and five children will be furnished of what aid that will relieve them.

My confidence is the only expression of my gratitude and it is easy to judge it by the price that I place to such services that are at this moment the object of my concerns.

RC, NN: Monroe Papers: Miscellaneous and Undated Papers

1. Adrienne Lafayette remained imprisoned at Maison Delmas from 5 November 1794 until 21 January 1795, when the Committee of General Security ordered her release (Charles Flowers McCombs, "The Imprisonment of Madame de Lafayette During the Terror," New York Public Library, *Bookmen's Holiday*, 1943, 10-11). This letter was probably written sometime in November shortly after her transfer to Maison Delmas

2. The acts of naturalization passed by Connecticut and Maryland granting citizenship to the Marquis de Lafayette also granted it to his son. The Virginia act did not specifically include any of the Marquis' family, but Adrienne Lafayette apparently interpreted it as doing so (Stanley Izarda and Robert Crout, eds., *Lafayette in the Age of the American Revolution*, 5: 269, 290; Hening, *Statutes at Large*, 12: 30).

3. Louise-Charlotte de Motier Lafayette, Madame de Chavaniac (1729-1811) raised the Marquis de Lafayette. During 1792 and 1793 when Adrienne Lafayette was under house arrest, she resided with her at the Château Chavaniac in Auvergne (André Maurois, *Adrienne ou La Vie de Mme De Lafayette*, 548).

4. Marthe Aufroy was the companion and governess of Adrienne d'Ayen, Adrienne Lafayette's mother (Maurois, *Adrienne*, 557).

5. Marie-Anne Marin was the governess of Adrienne Lafayette and her sister Louise; she was later governess to Adrienne Lafayette's two daughters (McCombs, "The Imprisonment of Madame de Lafayette," 23).

6. Madame de Chavaniac, who was 65 years old, not 71.

7. Marthe Aufroy.

8. Marie-Anne Marin.

9. Gouverneur Morris had loaned Adrienne Lafayette one hundred thousand livres in November 1793 (Maurois, *Adrienne*, 229).

10. Nicolas Beauchet (1757-1816) was the husband of Marie-Josèphe Daustry Beauchet (1750-1833), former chamber maid and friend of Adrienne Lafayette (Maurois, *Adrienne*, 305, 546).

11. Mademoiselle Benjamin was one of Adrienne Lafayette's maids (McCombs, "The Imprisonment of Madame de Lafayette," 26).

12. Pierre-Louis Mercier was a servant at Chateau Chavaniac. He accompanied Adrienne Lafayette upon her first arrest to the court at Le Puy (McCombs, "The Imprisonment of Madame de Lafayette," 27).

To the Committee of Public Safety

Paris 11 frimaire l'an 3ᵉ de la République fr.
[1 December 1794]

Citoyens

J'ai été extrêmement peiné de voir que <u>mes observations sur l'Agence comerciale en Amérique</u> se trouvoient publiées dans le Journal de Tallien de hier et dans celui d'aujourd'hui, par continuation: & J'ai craint qu'elles n'y fussent été inserées par quelque personne des Départements dans lesquels elles ont été discutées: Mais d'après des informations Je viens de découvrir qu'au contraire elles y avaient été insérées par un Américain. ce qui nécessite l'explication suivante.

Ayant engagé les consuls qui se trouvèrent icy à une conférence Sur les avantages du commerce entre les deux Nations Je leur soumis mes observations comme un court exposé Sur cette matière. Ils ignoroient que les mêmes vous eussent été transmises officiellement et en conséquence ne s'y firent aucun scrupule de les communiquer dans leurs conférences, à d'autres Américains lesquels ignoroient eux-mêmes que ces observations fussent écrites par moi. C'est ainsi qu'elles se sont indiscretement & sans la moindre intention d'impropriété, livrees à l'impression.

Cette notte n'étant qu'un court exposé, je ne crois pas que cette circonstance puisse blesser aucun individu; Mais cette piece étant devant votre comité; j'ai cru devoir vous expliquer par quel accident elle se trouvoit publique.

Jaˢ Monroe

Editors' Translation

Paris 11 Frimaire, Year 3 of the French Republic
[December 1, 1794.]

Citizens

I was extremely upset to see my <u>Observations on the Commercial Agency in America</u>[1] published in Tallien's newspaper[2] of yesterday and continued in today's paper. I feared that they had been inserted by a person from the departments which had been discussed. However, according to recent information, I have discovered that on the contrary, they were inserted by an American, which demands the following explanation.

Having met with the consuls, who were here attending a conference on the advantages of commerce between the two nations, I presented them with my observations on this subject in the form of a short briefing. They did not know that the same notes were to be officially transmitted to you, and consequently had no reservations communicating them to other Americans who themselves did not realize that the observations were written by me. This is how, without the least intention of impropriety, they were sent to be printed.

This note being but a short exposé, I do not believe that this circumstance could wound any individual; but this piece being before your committee, I thought it necessary to explain to you by what accident it came to be made public.

Jᵃˢ Monroe

RC, DLC: FCP—France

1. These observations were enclosed in JM's letter to the Committee of Public Safety of 18 October 1794 (above).

2. Jean-Lambert Tallien was editor of the Paris newspaper, *L'Ami des Citoyens* (Jules Michelet, *Histoire de la Revolution Française*, 1570-1572).

From Edmund Randolph

Philadelphia, Decem.ʳ 2ᵈ 1794

Sir

On the 27ᵗʰ ultimo, I had the honor of receiving the duplicate of your letter, nº 3 of the 15ᵗʰ of September last, being the first and only official notification of your having entered upon the duties of your mission.

Alexander Duvernet, who was appointed Vice Consul of Paris, during the last session of the Senate, loitered here so long, without a suspicion being entertained of his default, that the President has superseded him by commissioning Joseph Pitcairn of New York, who goes off for his residence immediately.

With the frankness of my friendship, I must discharge the obligation of my office, by communicating to you the opinions which we entertain here concerning the speech, which you made on your introduction into the National Convention.

When you left us, we all supposed, that your reception, as the minister of the United States, would take place in the private Chamber of some Committee. Your Letter of Credence contained the degree of profession, which the government was desirous of making; and tho' the language of it would not have been cooled, even if its subsequent publicity had been foreseen; still it was natural to expect, that the remarks, with which you might accompany its delivery, would be merely oral, and therefore not exposed to the rancorous criticism of nations, at war with France.

It seems that, upon your arrival, the downfal of Robespierre, and the suspension of the usual routine of business, combined perhaps with an anxiety to demonstrate an affection for the United States, had shut up for a time the diplomatic Cabinet, and rendered the hall of the National Convention the theatre of diplomatic civilities. We should have supposed, that an introduction there would have brought to mind these ideas. "The United States are neutral: The allied powers jealous: with England we are now in treaty: by England we have been impeached for breaches of faith in favor of France: Our Citizens are notoriously Gallican in their hearts: it will be wise to hazard as little as possible on the score of good humour: and therefore in the disclosure of my feelings something is due to the possibility of fostering new suspicions." Under the influence of these sentiments we should have hoped that your address to the National Convention would have been so framed, as to leave heart-burning no where. If private affection and opinions had been the only points to be consulted, it would have been immaterial, where or how they were delivered. But the range of a public Minister's mind will go to all the relations of our country with the whole world. We do not perceive, that your instructions have imposed upon you the extreme glow of some parts of your address; and my letter in behalf of the House of Representatives, which has been considered by some Gentlemen as too strong, was not to be viewed in any other light, than as executing the task assigned by that Body.

After these remarks, which are never to be interpreted into any dereliction of the French cause, I must observe to you, that they are made principally to recommend caution, lest we should be obliged at some time or other to explain away or disavow an excess of fervor, so as to reduce it down to the cool system of neutrality. You have it still in charge to cultivate the French Republic with zeal; but without any unnecessary eclat; because the dictates of sincerity do not demand, that we should render notorious all our feelings in favor of that nation.

In your letter you say, that you have not been instructed to desire a repeal of the Decree which violated the 23$^{\underline{d}}$ and 24$^{\underline{th}}$ articles of the treaty of commerce: that you did not know, but it had been tolerated from the soundest motives of political expedience—lest the demand for the rescinding it might produce a call for the guarantee. Indeed you have gone further; having declared in your memorial, that you were under no instructions to <u>complain</u> of or request the repeal of the decree authorizing a departure from those articles; and that if upon reconsideration after the experiment made, the Committee of public safety should be of opinion that it produces any solid benefit to the French Republic, the American government and your countrymen in general would not only bear the departure with patience but with pleasure.

The fourth head of injury, stated in your letter, shews that you were possessed of cases which turned entirely upon the impropriety of the decree; and such too was certainly the fact. Now without the abrogation of the decree, so far as it respected those cases, the redress which you were instructed to demand could not be obtained. In truth, there was no cause or pretence for asking relief, but upon the ground of that decree having violated the treaty. Does not this view lead to the inevitable conclusion, that the decree, if operative in future instances, would be no less disagreeable; and consequently, that its operation in future instances ought to be prevented—a circumstance, which could be accomplished only by a total repeal. The papers of the Ship Laurens contained a reference to one or more representations of M$^{\underline{r}}$ Morris against the decree: so that the business had been actually broken to the French Government.

Neither these representations, nor yet your application appears to have suggested a requisition of the guarantee. The omission to demand its fulfilment up to this day is a proof, that their policy did not approve of such measure: and in this they were wise, since we should have been less advantageous to them by associating in the war, than we have been in our neutral character. If I am not mistaken, this sentiment has been delivered often by M$^{\underline{r}}$ Fauchet. Besides, you might have very readily repelled any serious allusion to the guarantee, by saying, as your instructions indicate, that you were directed to send that subject on this side of the water. I must add another observation: that I do not see how, if you are to be deterred by the guarantee, you can ever claim compensation for an infraction of the treaty, since you will always be in danger of having it brought up to you.

But, my good Sir, let these things be as they will, was it necessary to intimate that an indifference prevailed in our government as to these articles, by a declaration, that you were not instructed to complain of the decree? I confess, that I am unapprised of the data, upon which such an opinion could be founded: and undoubtedly the President himself would not undertake, that the people of the United States would bear with patience a departure from stipulations which are generally believed to be important to us. But if from our friendship to the French Republic we might sustain a mischief with pleasure, still we should not choose that the assumption of one of our rights, without consulting us, should become a precedent for the assumption of any other.

Let me therefore entreat you, if my letter of July 30$^{\underline{th}}$ has not already stimulated you to remonstrate against the decree, to do so without delay. We do not wish you to swerve from the line of conciliation which is marked out in the last paragraph of your letter. On the contrary, conciliation, which does not detract from the dignity of his government, its rights, and his own self-respect, is a valuable quality in a minister. We only hope, that the Committee of public Safety may not continue in the belief, that the Executive are of opinion, that it will be satisfactory to dispense with the articles.

I am extremely happy in assuring you, that many of Mr Fauchet's discontents have been removed. The documents, concerning the failure to salute the Semillante, and the supposed insult to the Favorite, are inclosed to you, that you may be able to evince our solicitude to cement our good will on every occasion, which is offered.[1]

Col^l Alexander Anderson, of this City,[2] who has a claim for compensation, and whose Agent will call upon you, requests me to forward the inclosed papers. I also transmit some imperfect preparatory information in the case of Mr A. Gracie.[3]

A fresh collection of spoliation papers is sent, according to the List subjoined.[4] The newspapers &c. accompany this letter. I have the honor, Sir, to be with great respect and esteem Y^r mo. ob. serv.

Edm: Randolph

LBC, DNA: RG 59: Diplomatic and Consular Instructions

1. The *Favorite* was a French warship that was being dismantled in New York harbor. Customs officials boarded the hulk and seized goods that they suspected were hidden there by French privateers. Fauchet complained in a letter to Randolph of 23 September 1794 that customs officers had no right to seize goods from on board a French warship; he also claimed that the customs officers had prevented the commander of the ship from raising a French flag over it. Randolph replied on November 17, saying that any insult to France was unintentional and that customs officers would be instructed not to board foreign warships (*Hamilton Papers*, 17: 398-400; *ASP: FR*, 1: 598-600).

2. Alexander Anderson was a Philadelphia merchant (*Philadelphia Directory and Register*, 1794).

3. Archibald Gracie (1755-1829) was a New York merchant who had immigrated to the United States from Scotland in 1784. He built Gracie Mansion, which is now the official residence of the mayor of New York (*Burr Papers*, 2: 768).

4. The subjoined list of spoliation papers has not been located.

To Edmund Randolph

Paris December 2nd 1794

Sir,

I have at length obtained an answer from the Committee of public safety to the several propositions heretofore presented before it: in an arrete of the 15th ult^o and which I now transmit to you.[1] By this arrete the commission of marine is ordered to adjust the amount due to such of our citizens as were injured by the Embargo of Bordeaux, and likewise to such others as have claims for supplies rendered to the government of St Domingo. By it also many embarrassments which impeded the direct trade between the two countries are removed; the arbitrary rule of contraband which authorised the seizure of our vessels laden with provisions destined for other countries is done away; and the stipulation of the treaty of commerce which gives free passage, under our flag to the subjects of any of the powers at war with the Republic, is likewise inforced. In short, every thing has [been] conceded that was desired, except the execution of that part of the treaty which gave freedom to goods, in Ships that were so.

I have in consequence notified to the commission of marine that I had impowered Mr Skipwith to take charge of these claims, and attend their adjustment on the part of our citizens, and I shall continue to give every aid in my power to obtain [for] them the justice to which they are intitled. In respect to the liquidation, unless indeed some difficulty should arise as to the mode of payment, whether in assignats or specie, I presume all difficulty is at an end. But in regard to the payment, I think it probable unless assignats are taken and which are now depreciated, further delay will be desired, owing to the great expenditures of the government at the present very important crisis of its affairs.

Upon this however, I shall be able to give you more correct information in my next.

If the treaty could have been carried into effect, by general agreement, I should have deemed it a fortunate thing, because it would have secured our commerce hereafter from the possibility of vexation, and upon any pretext whatever, by the French cruisers; and because it would have arranged the French republic and at an important period of its affairs, on the side of a principle founded in benevolence and necessary to the freedom of the Seas. But as connected with other considerations more immediately applicable to ourselves, and especially if the hope of forcing it upon other nations as a law, is abandoned, I have deemed it of but little consequence.

It certainly precludes the probability of our being called on hereafter to fulfill any stipulations whatever, and will of course gain us greater credit for any services we may render them, in case it should suit us to render them any. I am likewise pursuaded from the responsibility the arrete imposes, and the increasing partiality pervading all France towards us, and which is felt by the Americans, and observed by the subjects of other neutral powers, that the execution will not vary much from the import of the treaty itself, for I cannot think that many of our vessels will hereafter be brought in upon the suspicion of having enemies goods on board.

I informed you some time since that I was pursuaded, if the subject was before the Convention, it would readily be granted: and in this I have not only been since confirmed, but in the further belief, that a majority of the several committees was favorable to the object. The dread however of denunciation in the course of events, detered them from adopting it. It was opposed, as was likewise every other change, by a party who would not fail to take advantage of it, shoud a favorable opportunity occur. The sordid spoilers of the public wealth, never forgive those who detect and expose to view their iniquities. And this was the most vulnerable point upon which recrimination could hereafter act. For as it is contemplated when the other powers are withdrawn, to prosecute the war against England with the collected force of the republic; and this might be construed into a partiality for that nation, it was deemed too hazardous a measure, in respect to the personal safety of the members to be encountered. In this decision too it is probable they were the more confirmed, by the necessity of cultivating Denmark and Sweden at the present moment (from whence great resources are drawn in support of the war) whose councils are wielded by Burnstoff, a man believed to be well disposed to a reform in the existing governments of Europe, and whose fleets are combined with no friendly disposition towards England.[2] They would most probably have pressed to be put on the same footing, and the pressure could not easily have been resisted after the example was given. As a proof however of the disposition of the committee, upon the subject generally, I herewith transmit to you a copy of a report, drawn upon my notes, by Merlin de Douay, to whom they were referred, and which was informally given me by its diplomatic members.[3]

I apprized you in my last, of the 20th instant[4] of M[r] Gardoqui's attempt to obtain permission to attend certain baths within the Republic, ostensibly upon account of his ill health, but in my judgment to commence a negotiation for peace, (a finesse too often practised by a certain grade of politicians) and at the same time lessen any weight the United States might have upon that subject in respect to their own affairs, by inspiring a distrust in me in the outset. I likewise stated to you in what manner I had acted, upon that occasion, laying his original letters before the committee, with my free and candid comments upon them: as also the further discussion which took place between the committee and myself in regard to Spain, and to which an incident of a different kind gave birth, in which I exposed as far as the nature of the case would admit the real situation of the United States with respect to Spain and Britain, menaced with war by both, shewing how France would be affected by that event, and of course the part she should take in our affairs at the present moment. To that communication I have now nothing new to add, having since heard neither from Mr Gardoqui on the subject of his proposition, nor the committee upon that, or the one which afterwards occurred. I omitted however at that time to transmit to you a copy of my letter accompanying Mr Gardoqui's to the committee and which I now inclose, for the purpose of presenting that business more fully before you.[5]

I am convinced that this exposition of our situation with Britain and Spain, and to which the incident of Mr Gardoqui furnished the first opening, has been useful: for before that exposition, I had reason to believe that it was not only unknown, but that a very erroneous opinion was entertained by many in the committee upon that subject. I thought I had felt the effect of that opinion, created no doubt in the manner you suggest, but as it was not communicated in a way to enable me to take official notice of it, I was embarrassed how to act or what measure to adopt in regard to it. For a while, as it was circulated only in private, I thought it best to counteract it by making the necessary explination only, to those who mentioned it to me: finally as I knew the campaign was progressing towards a close, and that the winter was the season for negotiation and more especially as I feared its commencement with either of those powers with such improper opinion of our situation with each, because I well knew they would improve it with great dexterity to their advantage, I deemed it my duty to make an extraordinary effort to remove it. With this view I appointed a rendezvous with the diplomatic members of the committee, and which took place accordingly. I was resolved however not to meet the imputation as a charge supposed to exist, or which I was bound to answer in case it did. A denial of a charge might beget a suspicion where there was none. I took different ground by informing the committee, that the war in which they were engaged, like all other wars, must have a termination: that most were concluded by the friendly mediation of third powers: that I was well convinced the United States would be happy to render the French republic any service in their power in that respect, to bring the present war to a happy close: that it was not their interest to interfere even by mediation, nor, in my judgment would they otherwise than at the instance and by the request of the French republic, in the hope of promoting thereby the success of their revolution. I observed further that I wanted no answer to this, and had only given the information, that they might retain it in memory, for the purpose of availing themselves of it hereafter, in case it should be found expedient. It was received respectfully but calmly. By one of the members it was observed that having beaten their enemies completely, it belonged to those enemies to determine whether they wished peace or not, and if they did, they would no doubt be able to find a way whereby to make it known to the republic. By another I was asked whether Mr Jay was still in London, and whether he intended [to come] over to Paris as had been published in an English paper? This was the very suspicion I wished to combat and remove, tho' indeed I did not expect it would have been avowed in so abrupt a manner. I replied I could not tell whether he had returned or not, but that it was impossible the paragraph in the English paper should be true, as he was sent to England upon an especial business only, to demand reparation for injuries, and to which his authority was strictly limited. I then repeated what I had before said of the friendly disposition of the United States towards the French republic in all cases, and of the pleasure with which they would, in my judgment serve it upon the present one, if in their power. That I was pursuaded they would listen to no proposition upon the subject of mediation from any other power, for as it was a business which could not possibly benefit them, they would of course embark in it only upon account of their ally. I likewise added that I knew nothing of the disposition of any power upon the subject of peace, but presumed the success of their arms had disposed them all well towards it, and thus I left them to reflect at leisure upon what I had said, in the belief however that the communication must produce a good effect. As this took place prior to the affair of Mr Gardoqui, and which was more particularly detailed in my last, I have thought proper to communicate it to you, that you may be possessed of every the minutest circumstance relative to our affairs upon this very important theatre. The day after my remarks upon the subject of a loan were handed in, I was favored with yours of the 25<u>th</u> of September, and which I beg leave now to acknowledge. Finding that my idea of our situation with Britain and Spain was correct, I was extremely happy that I had given that representation of it.

The motive for strong union here on our part is the greater, and nothing tends so effectually to promote that object as the belief that we are not cordial with England. In consequence I waited on the committee again and told them I had received a dispatch from you since our last conference, and that our dilemma with those two Powers was even more critical than I had before intimated. Facts go further in removing doubts than any assurances I could otherwise give them.

These discussions have enabled me to examine attentively whether it was their real wish that we should embark with them in the war, and I can assure you, that whatever it may have been at any previous stage, upon which I can give no opinion, that at present I am pursuaded they would rather we would not, from an idea it might diminish their supplies from America: but such is their disposition towards us that I am inclined to think, if the point depended on them, they would leave us to act in that respect according to our own wishes. And I am likewise persuaded if we do embark in the war, that they will see us through it [&] have some hope if we do not, and especially if we aid them in the article of money, that they will support, as far as they will be able, our demands upon Spain and England.

If the subject of a loan is mentioned again here or in America, that of securing for us the points in question with these powers must likewise be; but as I have said every thing on that head that I can say, having only a right to conjecture, I am not anxious to revive it here. I am however persuaded it will be revived with you, for so vast are their armies and extensive their operations, that they must be distressed for money and forced to gain it from whence they can, and I sincerely wish we may assist them if possible, and which I presume it will be, especially if not comprized in the war, and which I think cannot be, altho' we should immediately wrest from Britain and Spain the rights they have usurped from us. The credit of the United States is such in Europe and America & their means of reimbursement so unquestionable, especially in the particular of the Western Territory, an object viewed at present with great cupidity on this side of the Atlantic, that I am persuaded the amount expected might be obtained by loan, and I am equally so, that the people would cheerfully bear a tax, the product of which was to be applied in aid of the French republic. Upon these topics however, I have only a right to conjecture, and as such you will be pleased to consider what I have said.

I intimated in my last that this was the most seasonable period that could be desired for possessing ourselves of those rights which have been long usurped by Britain and Spain, and that if it was the sense of America ever to possess them, it should be taken advantage of.[6] Britain is certainly not in a condition to embark in a war against us, tho' we [should] dispossess her of Canada: she would of course be less apt to do it if we only placed her troops beyond the lakes. Her own land force was scarcely felt in the present war against France; nor has she been otherwise regarded than on account of her fleet & pecuniary resources, by which she subsidised Prussia and other powers. But that force small as it was, is greatly diminished, & the combination in which she has been associated appears not only to be completely foiled, but in a great measure broken. The prospect now before her is, that Prussia, Austria, and all the other powers will extricate themselves from the war upon the best terms they can, and leave her singly to support it against France. And that the latter will be aided by Spain unless a particular combination against us should prevent it, and likewise by Denmark and Sweden if not directly, yet in a manner to produce a serious effect. The preponderance of her fleet & the wanton & licentious use made of it, have excited the disgust of all nations against her who would be pleased to see it reduced, and the present is considered as a favorable time to reduce it. She likewise knows or confidently believes, that it is the intention of France to prosecute the war against her for the purpose of breaking her maritime strength, and ridding the Ocean from such a tyranny. At home too she cannot be free from disquietude: the total failure of her operations in this quarter (what they are in the West Indias is better known to you) has excited some uneasiness in the public mind & proportionally lessened the weight of the court. This was lately shewn in a prosecution against a Mr. Hardy, & in which a verdict was given for the defendant. And should the French take Holland, which nothing but an inundation already commenced, can prevent, if even that can, this sensation will of course be increased. Thus circumstanced, what have we to fear from her? will she in her decline bring upon herself another enemy, who can wound her so vitally? for let her merchants and politicians boast as they will of her resources, yet it is well known that if the American demand was cut off, upon which she thrives so much, that it would greatly diminish her revenue and impair her strength. How is she enabled to support her engagments and carry on her operations but by commerce? and lessened as this already is by the war, how could she sustain such a stroke at the present crisis? From her friendship we have nothing to hope. The order of the 6th of November was war in fact, and that has since been modified according to circumstances.[7]

Be assured she is infinitely less disposed for such an event at the present than at any preceding period. On the contrary, if we only took possession of what we are intitled to, she will readily join with us in reprehending the conduct of her own officers, for having transcended their orders. With respect to Spain, I have nothing new to add, since my last, except that in two days successive actions, two complete victories have been obtained over her troops by those of this republic, unless indeed some ingenious sophist might dispute that, as they were completely routed on the first, and maintained only a straggling battle on the second, it ought to be called but one. Certain it is that in the two days' conflict, several thousands were slain, and upwards of two thousand taken prisoners, with their camp on each day, and on one, tents for fifty thousand men.

I promised you some time since my comments upon the subject of a consular arrangment for the ports of this republic: the Consuls have been here to confer with me upon the subject of trade, and I have obtained from them their ideas on that of the arrangment, which I now inclose you.[8] I will add my own comments on it in my next, & will subjoin some american names of persons now here that may be deemed worthy your attention. I think proper however now to mention, that M͏ʳ Skipwith will accept the office of Consul for this City, and that I think him worthy of it. He is in my opinion a sensible man, of strict integrity and well acquainted with the duties of the office. The duties of consul here, will be those of Consul-General, and in strictness the commission should be correspondent: they may however be performed under that of consul only, for I presume those in the ports will respect him equally in either character. I have the honor to be with great respect and esteem, your most obedient servant

Jaˢ Monroe

Copy, DNA: RG 59: Dispatches from France

1. Decree Relating To American Trade, 15 November 1794, enclosed in Andre François Miot to JM, 24 November 1794, above.

2. Andreas Peter Bernstorff (1735-1797) was Denmark's foreign minister from 1784 to 1797. When the French Revolution erupted, he condemned any interference in the domestic affairs of France, and avoided any anti-French coalition. Nevertheless, Denmark needed protection for its maritime trade from its more powerful and belligerent neighbors. Aware of this necessity, Bernstorff in March 1794 negotiated an armed treaty with Sweden. Sweden in 1795 became the first monarchy to recognize the French Republic (Byron J. Nordstrom, ed., *Dictionary of Scandinavian History*).

3. A copy of this report, dated 13 Brumaire Year 3 (3 November 1794) is enclosed with this letter in DNA: RG 59: Dispatches from France. There is also a copy in NN: Monroe Papers.

4. This should be ultimo, not instant—that is, 20 November 1794.

5. JM to the Committee of Public Safety, 13 November 1794, above.

6. The version of this letter in *ASP, FR* (1: 687-688) varies in some particulars from the one used here, especially in this sentence.

7. A British Order in Council of 6 November 1793 placed a blockade on the French islands of the Caribbean to stop American vessels, supposedly neutral, from carrying West Indian exports to French ports. The wholesale seizure and condemnation of American vessels in the West Indies which followed so enraged American merchants that Washington sent John Jay to London to obtain concessions. One year later on 6 November 1794, a British order allowed American ships to trade in the British West Indies and the East Indies and permitted direct trade from these areas to England or the United States; it also promised reimbursement for losses resulting from seizures of American ships (John D. Forbes, "European Wars and Boston Trade, 1783-1815," *New England Quarterly*, 11 (1938): 709-734).

8. The enclosure relating to consular arrangements has not been located.

From James Madison

Philadª Decr 4. 1794

Dear Sir

I did not receive your favor of Sepr 2ᵈ the only one yet come to hand, till yesterday. The account of your arrival and reception had some time ago found its way to us thro' the English Gazettes. The language of your address to the Convention was certainly very grating to the ears of many here; and would no doubt have employed the tongues and the pens too of some of them, if external as well as internal circumstances had not checked them; but more particularly, the appearance about the same time of the Presidents letter and those of the Secretary of State.[1] Malicious criticisms if now made at all are confined to the little circles which relish that kind of food. The sentiments of the P. will be best communicated by Mr R.[2] You are right in your conjecture both as to the facility given to the Envoy Extrʸ[3] by the triumphs of France, and the artifice of referring it to other causes. The prevailing idea here is that the mission will be successful, tho' it is scarcely probable that it will prove so in any degree commensurate to our rights, or even to the expectations which have been raised: Whilst no industry is spared to prepare the public mind to eccho the praises which will be rung to the address of the Negociator, and the policy of defeating the commercial retaliations proposed at the last session. It will not be easy however to hide from the view of the judicious & well disposed part of the Community, that every thing that may be obtained from G. B. will have been yielded by the fears inspired by those retaliating measures, and by the state of affairs in Europe.

You will learn from the Newspapers and official communications the unfortunate scene in the Western parts of Pennª which unfolded itself during the recess.[4] The history of its remote & immediate causes, the measures produced by it, and the manner in which it has been closed, does not fall within the compass of a letter. It is probable also that many explanatory circumstances are yet but imperfectly known. I can only refer to the printed accounts which you will receive from the Department of State, and the comments which your memory will assist you in making on them. The event was in several respects a critical one for the cause of liberty, and the real authors of it, if not in the service, were in the most effectual manner, doing the business of Despotism. You well know the general tendency of insurrections to increase the momentum of power. You will recollect the particular effect, of what happened some years ago in Massachᵗˢ.[5] Precisely the same calamity was to be dreaded on a larger scale in this Case. There were eno' as you may well suppose ready to give the same turn to the crisis, and to propagate the same impressions from it. It happened most auspiciously however that with a spirit truly republican, the people every where and of every description condemned the resistance to the will of the Majority, and obeyed with alacrity the call to vindicate the authority of the laws. You will see in the answer of the House of Rep[s] to the P's speech, that the most was made of this circumstance as an antidote to the poisonous influence to which Republicanism was exposed. If the insurrection had not been crushed in the manner it was I have no doubt that a formidable attempt would have been made to establish the principle that a standing army was necessary for <u>enforcing the laws</u>. When I first came to this City about the middle of October, this was the fashionable language. Nor am I sure that the attempt would not have been made, if the P. could have been embarked in it, and particularly if the temper of N. England had not been dreaded on this point. I hope we are over that danger for the present. You will readily understand the business detailed in the Newspapers, relating to the denunciation of the "Self created Societies." The introduction of it by the President was perhaps the greatest error of his political life. For his sake, as well as for a variety of obvious reasons, I wish'd it might be passed over in silence by the H. of Rep[s]. The answer was penned with that view; and so reported. This moderate course would not satisfy those who hoped to draw a party-advantage out [of] the P's popularity. The game was, to connect the democratic Societies with the odium of the insurrection to connect the Republicans in Cong[s] with those Societies— to put the P. ostensibly at the head of the other party, in opposition to both, and by these means prolong the illusions in the North—& try a new experiment on the South. To favor the project, the answer of the Senate was accelerated & so framed as to draw the P. into the most pointed reply on the subject of the Societies. At the same time, the answer of the H. of R. was procrastinated till the example of the Senate, & the commitment of the P. could have their full operation. You will see how nicely the House was divided, and how the matter went off. As yet the discussion has not been revived by the newspaper combatants. If it Should and equal talents be opposed, the result can not fail to wound the P's popularity more than any thing that has yet happened. It must be seen that no two principles can be either more indefensible in reason, or more dangerous in practice—than that 1. arbitrary denunciations may punish, what the law permits, & what the Legislature has no right, by law, to prohibit—and that 2. the Gov[t] may stifle all censures whatever on its misdoings; for if it be itself the Judge it will never allow any censures to be just, and if it can suppress censures flowing from one lawful source it may those flowing from any other—from the press and from individuals as well as from Societies, &c.[6]

The elections for the H. of Rep[s] are over in N. Eng[d] & P[a]. In Mass[ts] they have been contested so generally as to rouse the people compleatly from their lethargy, tho not sufficiently to eradicate the errors which have prevailed there. The principal members have been all severely pushed; several changes have taken place, rather for the better; and <u>not one</u> for the worse. In Pen[a] Republicanism claims 9 out of 13, notwithstanding the very disadvantageous circumstances under which the election was made. In N. Y. it is expected the proportion of sound men will be increased. In Maryland the choice has been much as heretofore. Virg[a] & N. C. will probably make no changes for the worse. In the former M[r] Griffin resigns his pretensions. M[r] Lee will probably either do so or be dropped by his constituents.[7] In S. Carolina the death of Gillon will probably let in M[r] Barnwell.[8] In Delaware Patten is elected in lieu of Latimer.[9] On the whole the prospect is rather improved than otherwise. The election of Swanwick as a Republican, by the commercial & political Metropolis of the U. S. in preference to Fitzimmons, is of itself of material consequence, and is so felt by the party to which the latter belongs.[10]—For what relates to the Senate, I trust to the letters which you will receive from Brown & Langdon,[11] whom I have apprized of this opportunity of answering yours. I shall observe only that Tazewell & S. Tho: Mason were elected by the most decided majorities, to fill your vacancy and that of Col. Taylor who gave in his resignation. Not a single anti-republican was started. M[r] Dawson was a candidate and got 40 votes ag[st] 122. Brooke is also Gov[r] by a pretty decided vote. He had 90 odd ag[st] 60 odd given to Wood his only competitor.

I had a letter lately from Mr Jefferson; He has been confined by the Rhematism since August, and is far from being entirely recovered.[12] Mr T. M. Randolph has also been in a ticklish situation. What it is at present I can not say. Mr Jones was well a few days ago. He was then setting out to Loudon where he has made a great purchase of land from Col. Ch^s Carter. I infer from his letters to me that you are included in it. He will no doubt write you fully on that subject, or more probably has written already.

I have not rec^d any thing from Wilkinson—nor from Vermont: nor heard any thing relating to your interests in N. York. I have given notice to Mr Yard & Doc^r Stephens of this conveyance and expect both will write.[13] Mrs Heilager is also here on her way to St Croix and will no doubt write to Mrs Monroe.[14] She tells me all friends are well in N. York. I hope her letter will give all the particulars which may be interesting.

When in Albemarle last fall I visited your farm along with Mr Jefferson; and viewed the scites out of which a choice is to be made for your House. The one preferred by us is that which we favored originally on the East side of the road, near the field not long since opened. All that could be suggested by way of preparation was, that Trees be planted promiscuously & pretty thickly (in) the field adjoining the wood. In general your farm appeared to be as well as was to be expected. Your upper farm I did not see, being limited in my stay in that quarter.

I have just seen Mr Ross, who tells me he has rec^d your letter. He would write by this opportunity, but wishes to be more full than the time will permit.[15] We expect another will offer in a few weeks when we shall all continue our communications. I should say more to you now, if I could say it in cypher.

Present my best respects to Mrs Monroe and Eliza, and tell them I shall be able on their return to present them with a new acquaintance who is prepared by my representations to receive them with all the affection which they merit, & who I flatter myself will be entitled to theirs. The event which put this in my power took place on the 15th of Sep^r.[16] We are at present inhabitants of the House which you occupied last winter & shall continue in it during the Session. With my sincerest wishes for your happiness and that of your amiable family, I remain affectionately

[James Madison][17]

Hamilton has given notice that he means to resign. Knox means to do the same[18]—It is conjectured that the former will contend for the Govr of N. York. Burr will be the competitor.

RC, DLC: Madison Papers

1. The Philadelphia newspapers published Washington's letter of credence for JM (28 May 1794, above) and Edmund Randolph's two letters to the Committee of Public Safety of 10 June 1794 (written at the behest of the Senate and the House of Representatives) expressing friendship for France (*The Aurora*, 15, 18 November 1794; *Philadelphia Gazette*, 15, 19 November 1794).

2. Edmund Randolph.

3. John Jay.

4. The Whiskey Rebellion.

5. Shays's Rebellion.

6. Most of Washington's annual message to Congress of 19 November 1794 dealt with his efforts to suppress the resistance to the whiskey tax in western Pennsylvania. In his speech, Washington claimed that resistance to the law had been fomented by "certain self-created societies," a reference to the Democratic-Republican clubs. The Senate's reply to the President's speech echoed the accusations against the clubs, but the House of Representatives, after some debate, employed more moderate language, deploring resistance to the law "either by individuals or combinations of men." The House response then went on to emphasize the desire of the "zealous friends of republican government" for the maintenance of public order (*ASP: FR*, 1: 24-27; *Madison Papers*, 15: 386-393). The Democratic-Republican clubs, which began in Pennsylvania during the spring and

summer of 1793 and quickly spread across the country, became centers of opposition to the policies of the Washington administration. Washington and other Federalist leaders saw the clubs as an illegitimate challenge to their right to govern the nation, and they equated dissent, especially in the case of the excise tax, with sedition (Philip S. Foner, The *Democratic-Republican Societies, 1790-1800*, 3-40).

7. Samuel Griffin did not run for re-election to the House of Representatives, and Richard Bland Lee was defeated in his try for another term (*Monroe Papers*, 2: 687)

8. Alexander Gillon (1741-1794) was a Dutch-born Charleston merchant. He served in the House of Representatives from March 1793 until his death in early October 1794. Robert Barnwell (1761-1814), who served in the Continental Congress 1788-1789 and the House of Representatives 1791-1793, was not elected to succeed Gillon. The post went to Charleston attorney Robert Goodloe Harper (1765-1825) who served 1794-1801 (*BDAC*).

9. John Patten (1746-1800) served in the Continental Congress with JM 1785-1786. He was elected to the House of Representatives in 1793, but lost his seat in February 1794 to Henry Latimer (1752-1819), who had successfully challenged the election. Latimer resigned from the House in February 1795 to become U. S. Senator from Delaware (serving 1795-1801), and Patten was once again elected to the seat, serving one term, 1795-1797 (*BDAC*).

10. John Swanwick (1740-1798) was a Philadelphia merchant who served in the House of Representatives from 1795 until his death in 1798. He defeated Thomas Fitzsimons, who was making a bid for a fourth term in the House (*BDAC*).

11. John Brown to JM, 5 December 1794 and John Langdon to JM, 1794 (below).

12. Jefferson to Madison, 30 October 1794 (*Madison Papers*, 15: 366).

13. No letters from James Yard nor Edward Stevens written at this time have been located.

14. No letters from Sarah Kortright Heyliger to Elizabeth Monroe have been located.

15. No letters to or from James Ross have been located.

16. Madison met Dolley Payne Todd (1768-1849), a young Philadelphia widow, in May 1794 (*ANB*).

17. Madison blacked out his signature.

18. Alexander Hamilton left his post as secretary of the treasury on 31 January 1795; Henry Knox stepped down as secretary of war on 31 December 1794 (*BDAC*).

From John Brown

Philad[a] 5th Dec[r] 1794

Dear Sir

I was this day honor'd with your very acceptable favor of the 10th Sep[r] which with its inclosures came safe to hand.[1] You have my most sincere, & grateful acknowledgments for this mark of your friendship, & kind attention; & be assured that it is with extreme pleasure I have received from you the interesting intelligence of your safe arrival at Paris, & of the friendly & generous reception given you by the National Convention. Every real American must, & will acknowledge with a most lively sensibility, & gratitude the distinguishing Honors & respect paid by that generous Nation to you as the Representative of the U. States; & will mark the day of your recognition as such, as one of the most auspicious in the annals of his Country. Your address to the August Body has been read with enthusiasm, & approbation, by every friend to the Rights of Man, as breathing the genuine sentiments of Republicanism, & as expressing the sense of nineteen twentieths of the Citizens of the Union. You are too well acquainted with the political Opinions of Individuals here, to expect that it could be equally acceptable to all. No my friend, there are some, & that too in the Senate whose names will readily occur to you, who did not relish such unequivocal declarations of friendship & regard for the New Republic, & who could not suppress their apprehensions least this transaction should offend, & irritate G. Britain, & tend to obstruct Mr Jays Negotiation. But the Smiles, & frowns of this party ever have been & I trust ever will be equally disregarded by you.

It is with great pleasure I learn that you have discovered on the part of the New Republic Dispositions so friendly to the Interests of the U. States; I am persuaded every means in your power will be exerted to cultivate & improve this good understanding to the mutual advantage of the two Countries. I have no doubt but your efforts for that purpose will be duely supported by the National Legislature, & here especially as you in so great a degree possess the confidence of all parties.

The most important event which has occurred in this Country since your departure was the Insurrection in the Western Counties of this State. The Presidents speech at the opening of the present Congress which the Sec^y of State will doubtless transmit to you will detail to you all the circumstances which attended this disgraceful Business—It has been completely suppressed & I believe will be productive of fewer ill consequences than were generally expected. The expense thereby incurred greatly exceeded the necessities of the case & will amount to about one Million & a half of Dollars. A few of the most influential of the disaffected have been brought to this City for trial & will probably be executed by way of example. Genl Wayne has been more successful against the Indians than I believe was expected by any one. On the 20th August he defeated their united forces amounting to about 1000. in sight of the British Garrison at the foot of the Rapids of the Miami, which was established last spring by Govr Simcoe. The Enemy as usual sustained an inconsiderable loss in numbers, but as the action took place in sight of a British Garrison who not only declined giving them any assistance in Battle, but refused them when flying the protection of the fort these circumstances have effectually shaken their attachment to, & dependence upon their British Allies—There is now but little doubt that a general Peace will shortly be made with all the Western & Northwestern Tribes, especially as Col^o Pickering has lately concluded a Treaty with the six Nations to the entire satisfaction of both parties.[2] Genl Wayne summoned the B. fort to surrender, the Commanding Officer refused. Some insulting letters passed between them, & as Genl W. had forgot his Cannon at Greenville he marched off to the Miami Villages where he has been engaged in erecting (to use his own expression) an impregnable Fort—[3]

Congress have as yet made so little progress in the Business of the present Session that I can give no satisfactory information respecting it. Almost three weeks elapsed before we made a Senate & it is as yet but thinly attended. Virg^a & Maryland are still unrepresented, but Mr Tazewell & S. T. Mason have been elected to fill your seat & Col^o Taylors who resigned in consequence of the indisposition of his family, & they are expected in a few days—Butler & Gunn are both absent & not expected during the Session. Thus you see I remain in a smaller Minority than ever, but I still hope to see better days. Langdon will be reelected—Bradley in consequence I believe of trimming a little last Session lost his election but his Successor (Mr Payne) is a good Republican.[4] Kings reelection is doubtful,—the death of two Members of the State Legislature (Republicans) leaves I am told a Majority of but <u>one</u> against him. Morris will not serve, but who will succeed him it is not known. A good man is expected from Delaware.[5] Macon will be chosen in place of Hawkins—Izard declines, & a man of different Sentiments is expected from that State.[6] From the Elections which have already taken place, there is reason to expect the next H. of Representatives will be more republican than the present. Dearborne, Lyman & Shearborn[7] are reelected, & three or four of similar sentiments are elected in Massachusetts—Ames has been reelected only in consequence of the most strenuous exertions in his behalf—Sedgwicks election is doubtful—<u>Wadsworth</u> & Learned of Connecticut have declined. also Bowdoin[8]. Swanwick is chosen in place of Fitzsimmons—& Gallatin of Mr Scott.[9] Patton is reelected in Delaware—Lee & Griffin will be superceded by Brent, & Meriwether Jones[10]—No unfavorable changes to the South. Thus you see the prospect is by no means discouraging—The Sec^y of War & Sec^y of the Treasury are both to resign in the course of the ensuing month. It will require some time fully to develope the views & plans in contemplation of the latter. Col^o Innis of Richmond has been sent by the President to Kentucky to inform the people of that Country fully of the Measures which have been taken by the Genl Government to obtain the Navigation of the Mississippi.[11] They are become so impatient upon this subject that I much fear his Mission will not be productive of all the conciliatory effects the President expects from it—The assurances you have given me that your friendly attention to this important Subject shall not be wanting demand my sincere acknowledgments & when known to my Constituents (& I shall take pleasure in making the communication) they cannot fail to inspire their disponding minds with fresh hopes that this object so essential to their happiness will yet be obtained.

The last Harvest did not prove so abundant as had been expected owing to the great losses occasioned by the long continued Rains which fell about that time. But there is notwithstanding a very considerable surplus on hand for exportation; & the deficiency in quantity is amply made up in price.— Wheat is now selling at 10/ Virg^a Cur^y per Bushel & Flour at eight Dollars & upwards per Barrell—

The Monied Men of this & the neighbouring Cities have been seized with a land Mania which for sometime past has raged with uncommon violence. Not a Swamp, a Sand Hill, or a Pine Barren in all the lower Country to the southw^d but has been taken up & brought to Market; Not a desert, or rocky Mountain, in all the back Country has escaped the Hand of Speculation—& all are purchased with avidity in order to be shipped to the European Market for the <u>use</u> of Foreigners who inticed by quantity, price, & fictitious descriptions may be subjected to the grossest impositions—You will readily perceive how far the American character may be affected by this traffic & you are best able to determine respecting the means which may be employed to prevent it—

I have written my dear friend to you in the most careless manner, presuming perhaps too far upon the belief that you will receive with indulgence everything which relates to your Native Country.

Present my most respectful Comp^{ts} to Mrs Monroe & be assured of the friendship & esteem with which I am Dr Sir y^r mo. Ob^t Servt

J Brown

RC, DLC: Monroe Papers

1. JM's letter to Brown of 10 September 1794 has not been located.

2. Timothy Pickering, who served as postmaster general from 1791 to 1795, conducted negotiations with the Iroquois on five different occasions between 1790 and 1794. The treaty signed in November 1794 adjusted boundaries to the satisfaction of both the Iroquois and the United States (Gerard Clarfield, *Timothy Pickering and the American Republic*, 116-152).

3. Although Wayne demanded the evacuation of the British fort, neither he nor the commander of the British post wanted to take any action that would precipitate a war between the two countries. Leaving the British in control of the post, Wayne strengthened his own position at nearby Fort Defiance and then marched west to the headwaters of the Wabash River, where he built Fort Wayne. The construction of this bastion at the site of the principal Indian town in the region confirmed the complete defeat of the tribes in Ohio (Paul David Nelson, *Anthony Wayne*, 267-270),

4. Elijah Paine (1757-1842) was an attorney and jurist who was U. S. Senator from Vermont 1795-1801. Brown was mistaken about his political affiliation—Paine was a Federalist (*BDAC*).

5. Rufus King won re-election to the Senate from New York. William Bingham succeeded Robert Morris as senator from Pennsylvania. Henry Latimer was the new senator from Delaware (*BDAC*).

6. Nathaniel Macon (1757-1837) was a long-time member of Congress from North Carolina, serving in the House of Representatives 1791-1815 and in the Senate 1815-1828. Timothy Bloodworth (1736-1814) succeeded Benjamin Hawkins as

senator, serving 1795-1801. Jacob Read (1751-1816) succeeded Ralph Izard as senator from South Carolina and served 1795-1801. He was U. S. district judge for South Carolina 1801-1816 (*BDAC*).

7. William Lyman (1755-1811) was a member of the House of Representatives from Massachusetts 1793-1797. JM later knew Lyman when JM was minister to Great Britain and Lyman was U. S. consul at London. John Sherburne (1757-1830) served as representative from New Hampshire 1793-1797. He was U. S. attorney for New Hampshire 1801-1804 and U. S. district judge for the same state 1804-1830 (*BDAC*).

8. Theodore Sedgwick was re-elected to the House of Representatives from Massachusetts. New London attorney Amasa Learned (1750-1825) served in the House of Representatives 1791-1795. James Bowdoin (1752-1811) was a Boston merchant and member of the Massachusetts assembly. Although he did not run for election to the House of Representatives in 1794, he was a candidate in 1796 but was defeated. Jefferson appointed Bowdoin as minister to Spain in 1804, but Bowdoin never assumed the duties of the office in Madrid and officially resigned in 1808 (*BDAC*; *ANB*).

9. Thomas Scott (1739-1796) served two terms in the House of Representatives as a member from Pennsylvania, 1789-1791, 1793-1795. Albert Gallatin was a representative from Pennsylvania 1795-1801 (*BDAC*).

10. Richard Brent (1757-1814) was a member of the House of Representatives from Virginia 1795-1799, 1801-1803 and senator from Virginia 1809-1814. Meriwether Jones (d. 1806) was a member of the House of Delegates. In 1798 he became the editor of the (Richmond) *Examiner* and the state printer for Virginia. He was not elected to Congress—Samuel Griffin's seat in the House of Representatives went to John Clopton (1756-1816), who served in the House 1795-1799, 1801-1816 (*BDAC*; Jeffrey Pasley, *The Tyranny of Printers*, 159-161).

11. Westerners were becoming increasingly dissatisfied with the Washington administration because of its failure to obtain a guarantee of navigation rights on the Mississippi. Washington, hoping to defuse this growing discontent, gave James Innes of Virginia copies of papers relating to negotiations with Spain and instructed him to show them to the governor and assembly of Kentucky (Samuel Flagg Bemis, *Pinckney's Treaty*, 210-211).

From John Langdon

Philad.ª 5ᵗʰ Decm.ʳ 1794

Dear Sʳ

It is with Infinite satisfaction I hear the generous and kind Reception, you have met with from the National Assembly of France. The Intrepidity, Justice and Magnanimity of that great Nation Astonishes the Universe; I pray God they may finally prevail, over all their enemies, and establish such a government as shall conduce to their lasting happiness, and an example to the Rest of the World—Our Congress now in Session, are going on as usual. Mʳ Hamilton has Signified to the House of Representatives his Intention of Resignᵍ the Next month. The Magnanimity and Justice of Great Britain, is not <u>now</u> much Spoken of. I wish to be more particular but prudence forbids it, you are sensible of the feelings of my soul. We are every day entertained, and gratified with the Amazing Successes of France in which the great Body of the people of their Country, most Righteously Rejoice and I most Religiously wish our Government would do more, than barely to Rejoice however. I believe it is Intended by good Providence that France shall have all the honor and Glory, of Saving not only themselves, But the Rest of the World from Despotism—Robertspere is gone, may his fate be a warning to all those who are entrusted with the peoples liberties, and betray their Trust. If any thing should offer in which I can be any way Serviceable, in that part of this Continent where I live, you'll please Command. Your Sincere friend and Hbl.ᵉ Serv.ᵗ

John Langdon

Pray make my kind Respects Acceptable to your Lady.

RC, DLC: Monroe Papers

From Edmund Randolph

Private

Philadelphia Dec.ʳ 5. 1794.

Dear sir

I am much indebted to you for your two favors of Sep.ʳ 11 & 12.

Your public letters of Aug: 15 & 25. have enabled me to place upon a proper footing the delicacy of your situation, and to efface any improper impressions, which may have been entertained any where.

From my occupation, you will not expect lengthy details in private communications—Summarily therefore I inform you, that Col.º Hamilton goes out of office on the last day of January, General Knox perhaps sooner, and their successors are not known. Robert Brooke is governor of Virginia; Henry Tazewell & S. T. Mason senators.

My best respects attend M.ʳˢ M. and E;[1] and you will always find me Y.ʳ sincere friend

E. R.

When Fauchet's letter returns, I shall arrange his draft, comme vous avez demande!

RC, DLC: Monroe Papers

1. Eliza Monroe.

From Edmund Randolph

Philadelphia, December 5ᵗʰ 1794

Sir

Since my letter of the 30ᵗʰ ultimo, which will be conveyed by the same vessel with this, I have had the honor of receiving your very interesting letters of August 15ᵗʰ and 25ᵗʰ. They are the more acceptable, as affording an earnest of your attention to the kind of intelligence which is to us very important.

We are fully sensible of the importance of the friendship of the French republic. Cultivate it with zeal, proportioned to the value, which we set upon it. Remember to remove every suspicion of our preferring a connection with Great Britain, or in any manner weakening our old attachment to France. The caution suggested in my letter of the 30ᵗʰ ultimo arises solely from an honorable wish to sustain our character of neutrality, in a style which may be a pattern for the morality of nations. The Republic, while they approve of the purity of our conduct, cannot but be persuaded of the purity of our affection.

The President approves your conduct as to the national house offered for your residence. Your interpretation of the Constitution is correct. But you are charged to make known his sense of this evidence of respect.

The affair of the Consul is noticed in my letter of the 30ᵗʰ ultimo. I have the honor to be, Sir with great respect and esteem &c:

Edm: Randolph.

LBC, DNA: RG 59: Diplomatic and Consular Instructions

From P. Feuty

[8 December 1794]

Le Soussigné reconnais avoir recu du Ministre Plenipotentiaire des Etats unis d'Amerique, la Somme de Mille livres pour employer aux besoins des Indigents de la Section du Bonnet rouge. fait au Comité Civil le Dix huit frimaire l'an troisieme de la Republique francoise une et indivisible.

P feuty
Tresorier du Comité de bienfaisance

Editors' Translation

[8 December 1794]

The undersigned acknowledges receipt of the sum of one thousand livres from the Minister Plenipotentiary of the United States of America, to be used for the needs of the destitute members of the Bonnet rouge section. Signed before the Civil Committee on the eighteenth Frimaire in the third year of the French Republic, one and indivisible.

P Feuty
Treasurer of the Committee for Charity

RC, NN: Monroe Papers

A note on the back of this letter in JM's handwriting reads:

Print the certificates of Mᵣ Skipwith & Mᵣ Gelston, from the report of the Committee of the last session.

Likewise the correspondence & recᵗ of the Committee of the Sectⁿ of Bonnet rouge, translating the same. The money had depreciated, but it is believd that the sum granted, would have amounted to little less than the £110. The mov'ment being thus entirely popular, & often tumultuous, donations of the kind, & to considerable amᵗ, were deem'd proper & useful.

Paris was divided into forty-eight sections for political and electoral purposes in 1790. The Bonnet Rouge section (formerly called the "Croix Rouge," later the "Bonnet de la Liberté," then "Ouest" section) was located in the Faubourg Saint-Germain on the left bank of Paris (the neighborhood in which JM resided). The left bank's western sections of the city were deemed less radical than those in the city center. In October 1794 prices began to rise to a level two thirds above that of June 1790, and bread and meat were rationed. The scarcity of food, particularly of bread began in September and continued until May 1795 (George Rudé, *The Crowd in the French Revolution*, 138, 144, 150-151, 168, 256, and Appendix I).

To James Madison

Paris Decᵣ 18. 1794.

Dear Sir

I enclose you three letters one for Mᵣ R. and the other two for whom ever you may think it best to direct them. You will in case they are delivered take a copy of one for yᵣself, for I have not had time to write you nor indeed is it necessary on that subject as I send them open to yᵣ inspection. You will know whether there is any thing in the report & act accordingly either by presenting or suppressing all. I really wish mine to Mᵣ R. to be seen by the Pr: if expedient to be delivered. As to the persons to whom to be addressed I leave it entirely to you (advising that you consult with no one on that point lest it be known they were not addressed by me) but am inclined to think that one shoᵈ be addressed to Langdon, & the other either to Burr, Butler or Ross. As you will take a copy, you will be able to shew it to our Virg[a] friends and others as by my request & which will apologize for my not writing them.

After all there is but one kind of policy which is safe, which is the <u>honest policy</u>. If it was intended to cultivate France by sending me here Jay sho[d] not have been sent to Engl[d]: but if indeed it was intended to cultivate Engl[d] it was wise to send some such person as myself here, for it was obvious that in proportion as we stood well with France sho[d] we be respected by Engl[d]. I have not time to write you further at present than to assure you that the aff[rs] of the republick are in every respect in the most flourishing condition: wise, humane, & just in its councils, & eminently successful in its armies, & also that we are well. Affec[y] I am y[r] friend & serv[t]

Ja[s] Monroe

As the letters are closed in great hurry, see that there are no inaccuracies. If M[r] Skipwith is confirmed, pray send Prevost off immediately. I repeat again that I put this business entirely under y[r] care. You will readily conclude, if the report is entirely without foundation & w[h] I most earnestly hope it is, that it will be best to suppress the whole.

RC, DLC: Madison Papers.

JM sent this letter to Madison via Havre, enclosing three copies of his letter to Edmund Randolph of 18 December 1794 (below). JM sent another copy of this letter to Madison on the same day via Bordeaux, enclosing one copy of the letter to Randolph (DLC: Madison Papers). Madison received both letters, which means that he had received four copies of the letter to Randolph, two of which are in DLC: Madison Papers. Madison probably sent one copy to Randolph, but it is not known who received the other.

To Edmund Randolph

Paris Decem[r] 18th 1794.

Dear Sir

Within a few days past English papers have been received here stating that M[r] Jay had adjusted the points in controversy between that country and the United States: in some of those papers it is stated that Canada is to be ceded with the posts, that priviledges are to be given in the west Indias and other stipulations which imply an alliance offensive & defensive as likewise a commercial treaty.[1] As this government has always felt uneasiness upon the subject of his mission, and which was greatly mitigated but not intirely done away by the solemn declarations I had made upon the authority of my instructions, that he had no power other than to demand the surrender of the posts & compensation for injuries, this recent intelligence has excited a kind of horror in the minds of those acquainted with it. And as it will probably get into the papers I fear the same sensation will be universal for a while. As it is known that this accomodating disposition in the cabinet of S[t] James, if it really exists, is owing to the successes of the French arms, the good understanding between the United States & this republick, and the decisive temper of our government as shewn in the movments and letters of Wayne, and which were previously published in the opposition papers there, it might perhaps be [expected][2] from a just and generous people that we would pursue the adjustment of our controversy with that country in concert with this: in any event that we would not bind up ourselves in relation to the present war, in any manner to prevent us from fulfilling existing stipulations if called on to execute them, or rendering other service to our ally which a recollection of past and recent good offices might incline us to render. But to take advantage of the success of the French arms, of the good understanding subsisting between this republick and our own, and which was created by the dismission of a minister odious to all France, and the frank declarations which I made in obedience to my instructions, in the presence of the Convention and in the view of Europe, of our attachment to their welfare and sollicitude for their success, to part the two countries and draw us into the bosom of our mortal foe, would be an act of perfidy the example of which was perhaps never seen before.

As yet I have not been spoken to upon this subject by the Committee nor do I expect to be, for <u>reserve</u> is the peculiar characteristic of that Department, and from which it never deviates, except in cases when the person in whose favor the deviation is, possesses their intire confidence. Notwithstanding the harmony of opinion which prevailed among all their parties here, in respect to my political principles, and attachment to their nation, for services in our revolution, yet this impenetrable cloak was for some time after my arrival, assumed even towards myself. It was laid aside by degrees only and upon their own experience of the verity of these reports: for so common are the cases of political depravity in the courts of the European world, that they act as if nothing else were to be found any where. If then this report should be entirely discredited, or if it should be credited I think I shall not be spoken to. In the former instance they will not offend me, by letting it be seen that they had even noticed it. And in the latter as they will be mortified for having given me a rank in their estimation more elevated than that of other political agents, whom they class generally or in the mass as rascals, and will consider themselves as duped, they will endeavour to hide it from me. So that in either case tis probable I shall not be spoken to on the subject. If credited it will be seen only by their relapse into the former State of reserve & which the first interview will decide.

On my part I entirely disbelieve it. I can readily conceive that the British administration under the pressure of the french arms, and the decisive tone of our government will yield the posts and pay us for our losses, or rather their piracies: and I can also readily conceive that in so doing it would be the endeavour of that administration to make us pay for it if possible by betraying us into some stipulation which would weaken our connection with France and stain our national character, for they know too well the temper of the publick mind to think it possible to connect us with them. And I can also readily conceive that our agent there would be well disposed to harmonize with that administration in an effort to weaken that connection, and that in the pursuit of this object he would not be over nice or scrupulous as to the means. But I rest with unshaken confidence in the integrity of the President and in the veracity of the instructions given me to declare that he had no such power. When I contemplate the fixed and steady character of the President, cautious in his measures, but immoveable after he has adopted them, jealous of his honor & regardful of his fame, the precious acquirement of great services and of a long and venerable life, I cannot hesitate for a moment in pronouncing that in placing me here he meant what he said, and that I should be the organ of an honest and not a double and perfidious policy. Upon this point I am perfectly at ease. The only point therefore upon which I feel any concern, is the apprehension of the dish which may be prepared for the palate of those who have particular interests with us & which tis possible may be contrived with great art by Messrs Pitt & Jay, the latter of whom would be useful in giving information how such interests might be acted on so as to make it irresistible. And what increases this apprehension is the report that several of the stipulations are provisional, to be executed hereafter whereby the hostage remains in the hands of Great Britain, it being only a project (and of course no violation of instructions in form tho' absolutely so in fact) to be offered for the approbation of the President and the Senate. By this he would keep his ground in England, harmonize with the administration and aid it in the means of attacking the integrity of our councils. Upon this point I have my fears for I knew him play the same game upon the subject of the Mississippi. He was instructed to enter into no stipulation which did not <u>open</u> that river and fix the boundaries according to our treaty with Great Britain. He should therefore not have heard a proposition on that subject: on the contrary he absolutely entered into a stipulation which shut the river up, or according to his own language <u>forbore the use of it</u> and left the boundaries to be settled by commissaries to be appointed by both countries, as I understand is the case with some of the litigated points in the present case. The analogy in the project reported to be now depending with that I have here recited (and which I have often wished the President would peruse from beginning to the end) together with my own perfect knowledge of the principles and crooked policy of the man, disguised under the appearance of great sanctity and decorum, induce me to pay more attention to those papers than I otherwise should do.

If any thing of this kind should have taken place I know the dilemma into which you will be all thrown. <u>The western posts are offered you</u>—<u>compensation for losses</u>—free <u>trade</u> to the <u>Islands</u> under the protection of the all <u>powerful British flag</u>—<u>Canada is</u> or <u>will be</u> given up, whereby the fisheries become more accessible—England will no longer Support Spain in favor of the <u>Mississippi</u> &c. This will be resounded in the publick papers, and the impudence of the british faction become intollerable. But will it not be perceived that whatever is offered cannot be deemed the amicable concession of England but is already your own, attained by the illustrious atchievments & prosperous fortunes of your ally, & the decision of your own councils? Will you take therefore in breach of plighted faith, and expense of our national character, and as an amicable concession of England what may be obtained without loss, and is in truth due to the merits of our ally? I will candidly own that I do not think it in the power of Mess.ʳˢ Pitt and Jay to succeed in any project they can contrive whereby to weaken our connection with France & put us again under the influence of England, for such would be the case, provided that connection was weakened.

I have written you freely upon this subject as well to state the report and explain the light in which such an adjustment would be received here, as to put you on your guard in relation to transactions in England, a country which will never smile upon but to deceive you. Tis impossible to be closely connected with both these countries, if no other considerations prevented it from the animosity and frequent wars that will take place between them, and which must terminate from the superior strength of this, in the ruin at least to a certain degree of the other: unless indeed we should now abandon our ally to prop the declining fortunes of hers and our adversary. I write to you in confidence that you will make no improper use of this, & that from the necessity of retaining a copy you will excuse its being dressed in the character of a friend. With great respect and esteem I am dear Sir very sincerely yours

Jaˢ Monroe

Copy, DLC: Madison Papers

JM sent this letter to Randolph through the agency of James Madison. See JM to Madison, 18 December 1794, above.

1. John Jay signed a treaty with the British on 18 November 1794, but the terms were different than those reported in the newspapers that JM saw (*Encyclopedia of American History*). JM apparently had not yet received John Jay's letters of 24 and 25 November (above) or 28 November (DLC: Monroe Papers) informing him of the treaty.

2. JM's secretary wrote "excepted".

From the Committee of Public Safety

Paris, le Six Nivose l'an 3 de la République française une et indivisible.
[26 December 1794]

Nous sommes informés, citoyen, qu'il à été tout récemment conclu à Londres un traité de commerce et d'alliance entre le Gouvernement Britannique et le citoyen Jay, envoyé extraordinaire des Etats-Unis.

Un Bruit sourd Se répand que dans ce traité le citoyen Jay à oublié ce que nos traités avec le peuple Américain et les sacrifices faites par le peuple français pour le rendre libre, nous donnaient droit d'attendre de la part du ministre d'une nation que nous avons tant de sujets de regarder comme Amie.

Il importe que nous Scachions positivement à quoi nous en tenir. Ce n'est point entre deux Peuples Libres, que doivent exister les dissimulations de la politique des Cours; et nous nous plaisons à déclarer qu'elles te répugnent personnellement autant qu'à nous.

Nous t'invitons donc à nous communiquer le plutôt possible le traité dont il S'agit. C'est le Seul moyen de Mettre la Nation française à portée d'apprécier les bruits injurieux au Gouvernement Américain, au quels ce traité donne Lieu. Salut et fraternité

Les Membres du Comité de salut Public.
Merlin (d.d), Carnot, fourcroy, L. B. Guyton,
Prieur de la Marne, A. Dumont, Cambaceres

Editors Translation

Paris, Six Nivose, year 3 of the French Republic, one and indivisible
[26 December 1794]

We are advised, citizen, that there was lately concluded at London a treaty of commerce and alliance between the British Government and Citizen Jay, envoy extraordinary of the United States.

A persistent rumor is spreading that in this treaty Citizen Jay has forgotten our treaties with the American people and the sacrifices made by the French people to render them free, that gave us the right to expect more from the minister of a nation that we have so much reason to regard as a friend.

It is most important that we know where we stand. There ought not to exist between two free peoples the dissimulation that belongs to the courts; and it gives us pleasure to declare that we consider you as much opposed personally to that kind of policy as we are ourselves.

We therefore invite you to communicate to us the treaty in question as soon as possible. This is the only way in which the French nation will be in a position to evaluate the rumors, harmful to America, that this treaty has engendered. Salutations and fraternity,

The members of the Committee of Public Safety
Merlin (d.d.) Carnot, Fourcroy, L.B. Guyton,
Prieur de la Marne, A. Dumont, Cambaceres

RC, NN: Monroe Papers; the copy of this letter enclosed to Edmund Randolph, 13 January 1795, in DNA: RG 59: Dispatches from France is dated 5 January 1795.

Lazare-Nicholas Carnot (1753-1823) was one of the most prominent leaders of the French Revolution. Due to his middle class origins his desire for a career in the military appeared limited, as he could rise no higher than a captain, the rank he obtained in 1783. Elected to the Legislative Assembly in 1791, then the National Convention in 1792, he became a dominant figure on the military committees. Soon after, he joined the Committee of Public Safety, where he was placed in charge of the citizens' armies. For eleven months he dealt with civil attacks in the Vendee and the threat of foreign invasion. Carnot is credited with having raised, equipped, transported and maintained an army of one million men for which he was awarded the title "Organizer of Victory in Year II." In the fall of 1795 Carnot became one of the five original members of the Directory (Samuel Scott & Barry Rothaus, *Historical Dictionary of the French Revolution, 1789-1799*, 154-156).

Antoine-François Fourcroy (1755-1809), a French physician, entered the world of politics in 1793 as a deputy from a department in Paris to the Convention. He was assigned to work on weapons for the national defence, and he is also credited for initiating a plan for a central school for public works which became the renowned École Polytechnique. Fourcroy became a member of the Committee of Public Safety in September 1794, a position he held (with the exception of January 1795) until June 1795 (*Dictionnaire Biographique Française*, 750-752).

Widely-known chemist, lawyer, and man of letters, Louis-Bernard Guyton-Morveau (1737-1816) became president of the Legislative Assembly in 1792, and served as a member of the Committee of Public Safety, 6 October 1794 to 3 February 1795 (Jules Michelet, *Histoire de la Revolution Française*, 2: 1437; A. Kuscinski, *Dictionnaire Des Conventionnels*, 322-323).

Pierre-Louis Prieur De La Marne (1756-1827), a lawyer from Châlons-sur-Marne, served as a deputy to the Convention from 1789 onward. Although an ally of Robespierre, Prieur De La Marne argued for democratic measures and contributed to many constitutional, administrative and judicial reforms. He served two terms on the Committee of Public Safety, his second occurring from 6 October 1794 to 3 February 1795. His harsh treatment of prisoners during his missions to the departments caused the Thermidorians to arrest him. He escaped, however, and all charges against him were dropped in the General Amnesty of October 1795 (Scott and Barry, *Historical Dictionary of the French Revolution*).

André Dumont (1765-1836) presided over the National Convention from 22 September to 7 October 1794, and served as a member of the Committee of Public Safety, 5 December 1794 to 4 April 1795. He prevailed in restoring order on three consecutive missions to the provinces, but his cruelty in doing so, sullied his reputation (Kuscinski, *Dictionnaire des Conventionnels*, 225-226).

Jean-Jacques-Regis Cambacères (1753-1824) practiced law in his native city of Montpellier and gained a reputation as a legal expert. He was elected in 1792 to a seat on the Committee of Legislation of the National Convention and served as president of the Convention from 7 to 21 October 1794. He was president of the Committee of Public Safety from 7 November 1794 to 30 October 1795 (*Dictionnaire de Biographie Française*; Kuscinski, *Dictionnaire des Conventionnels*).

To the Committee of Public Safety

Paris Decr 27. 1794.

Citizens

I was favoured this morning with yours of yesterday intimating that the report of a treaty said to have been concluded by Mr Jay envoy of the united States of America to England with that nation derogatory to the treaties of alliance and commerce subsisting between those states and this republick, had given you some disquietude and requesting information from me upon that point. I obey the invitation with pleasure because I well know that a candid policy is that alone which becomes republicks, and because it is likewise most correspondent with the wishes of the American government and my own feelings.

Having already communicated to you the limited object of Mr Jay's mission it only remains for me to inform you what I know of the result. All that I know upon this subject is comprized in a letter received yesterday from Mr Jay, of Novr 2 [5] in which he says that he had fulfilled the principal object of his mission by concluding a treaty signed the 19th of the same month, which contains a declaration that it should not be construed nor operate contrary to our existing treaties & that therefore our engagments with other nations remain unaffected by it. He adds that as the treaty is not yet ratified it would be improper to publish it. I am altogether ignorant of the particular stipulations of the treaty, but I beg leave to assure you that as soon as I shall be regularly informed I will communicate the same to you.

I take it however for granted that the report is without foundation, for I cannot believe that an american minister would ever forget the connections between the United States and France, which every day's experience demonstrates to be the interest of both republicks still further to cement.

Ja^s Monroe

RC, DLC: FCP—France

To the Committee of Public Safety

Decr 27. 1794

citizens

I consider it of great importance to y^r interest & my reputation that you apprize me of the propositions if any w^h you may contemplate to make to the american gov^t. You ~~are I presume sufficiently well acquainted with my character & principles to know~~ must be sensible that I will not only give you the best advice in this respect but aid you in obtaining y^r wishes all in my power. On the other hand if you sho^d make a proposition to the gov^t w^h it might not be able to grant, and the feeling existed that it was done by my advice, it wo^d do an essential injury to you as well as myself. I wish therefore that you wo^d commission one of y^r members to confer freely with me, upon these points, & which may be done either in some room of the committee or here as shall be agreeable to him. I think I can make myself understood without the aid of an interpreter.

Dft, DLC: Monroe Papers

From Edmund Randolph

Philadelphia [30 December 1794]

Dear Sir,

I do myself the honor of enclosing to you two records, one in the case of the Brigantine Catherine belonging to Messrs Mead and other citizens of the United States, the other in the case of the William Tell, belonging to a British Subject. You will perceive that they have been both unjustly seized by the french Ship of War L'Ambuscade and that Damages have been assessed accordingly. But there is no redress, unless the french Republic becomes responsible for the acts of its own public cruisers. You will therefore be pleased to make such representations upon this subject as the [nature] of the affair will admit, and as existing circumstances may render proper. At the same time you will observe from the enclosed letter which I wrote to Mr Hammond what the sense of our Government is with respect to the Compensation urged by him in his letter of the 9th Ultimo for the owners of the Wm Tell—but the rights of our citizens stand upon a very different footing and constitute positive claims upon the justice of the french Republic. I have the honor to be dear sir yr friend & serv^t

Edm: Randolph

RC, DLC: Monroe Papers; filed December 1794. The date is torn from this letter; date is supplied from the copy in DLC: RG 59: Diplomatic and Consular Instructions.

The case of the Brigantine *Catharine* was adjudicated in the U. S. Circuit Court for the Southern District of New York in 1794. Philadelphia merchant George Meade (1741-1808) was the owner and appellant in the case (DNA: RG 21: Appellate Case Files for the U. S. Circuit Court for the Southern District of New York, 1793-1845, Case 79).

In 1794 a British ship, the *William Tell,* was within a mile of the shore of the United States when seized by the French ship *l'Ambuscade* and brought into New York. Great Britain wanted the United States to pay the damages caused to the British ship taken within the limits and jurisdiction of the United States. A similar incident took place on 29 August 1793 involving the *William Tell,* when it was captured by the French ship of war *Cerf* less than a mile from the American coast ("Memorial from George Hammond," *Papers of Thomas Jefferson,* 27: 44-46).

The enclosed letter to British minister George Hammond could not be identified.

To the Société Populaire de Nevers

[1794]

Citizens republicans

I have received with singular satisfaction your affectionate address upon the subject of my mission from the American to the French republick, and am deeply impress'd with the propriety of those sentiments you have felt and been pleased to express upon that event. I consider the attention shewn me by your society as one among the many proofs I have witnessed since my arrival, of the devotion of the citizens of France to the cause of republican government, and of their attachment to my constituents, their friends and allies, the good people of the United States of America. The alliance which now unites the two republicks was formed at a day of difficulty to us. It was strong before your revolution, as founded upon a sentiment of gratitude, but now that you have planted the standard of republican government by our side its strength and energy have increased. That it may gain accumulated vigor every day, and be perpetual, is my sincere wish.

Ja⁵ Monroe

FC, NN: Monroe Papers; filed at the end of 1795

Nevers is a town in central France in the department of Nièvre. Local political clubs were known as *Sociétés populaires* after the summer of 1791. Generally these were centers for progressive views and independent policies. Many of these were Jacobin clubs, which were closed down after Thermidor. A few survived until the early months of 1795 (George Rudé, *The Crowd in the French Revolution,* 256).

To Unknown

[1794-1795]

It is likewise whispered that Engl^d has promised to give her support in favor of our treaty with Algiers &c and for this purpose that Mr Humphreys has gone to America most probably upon an arrangment with Mr Jay. If this is the case it is obvious that Mr Jay in harmony with the English administration has done every thing in his power to inform that governm^t of the means whereby to wound the republican interest in America, & at the expence of France.

If these things are true it shews the necessity of the closest union between the republicans in both countries for the success of republican gov^t in each depends upon its continuance in the other. The future happiness of mankind therefore every where depends at the present moment upon this union. It is most certain that Engl^d never wo^d have been disposed to render such services had not the success of France forced her into it. It is equally so that she offers them for the most insidious purposes & in the hope of producing an effect upon the American councils whereby to alienate in the degree that country from this. It were then an incident no less singular than unfortunate, if by any kind of knavish dexterity the very successes of France & which have saved the republican cause in both countries & ought to cement that union sho^d prove an instrument in the hands of Engl^d more powerful than her fleets or armies to wound that cause & weaken that union. These consequences ought to be guarded agnst.

In this dilemma there were two ways by which France might counteract this policy. The first by acts of unkindness upon the American gov^t & people. The other was by acts of liberality and Friendship. What wo^d probably be the effect of each.

Acts of unkindness co^d produce no other effect than that of irritating the Americans & favoring the views of Engl^d & the aristocratic party in America. This policy too wo^d be no less cruel than imprudent, for as the mass of the American people are on the side of France & republican gov^t, five friends wo^d be hurt by such acts of unkindness where only one enemy wo^d be affected: for it is certain that the aristocratic party does not bear a greater ratio to the republican one there than that of one to five. It's strength proceeds from its members holding offices & not from its numbers.

Acts of liberality confining them only to such points as the Missisippi Algiers &c and which France wo^d render without feeling the act wo^d gain to France the credit to which her arms entitle her. They wo^d overwhelm the aristocratic party there & defeat the intrigues of Engl^d, by shewing that what Engl^d offered with insidious views & under the pressure of necessity, France rendered from a magnanimous policy and in the moment of her greatest prosperity.

Suggestions of this kind have however been already before you. I mention them now merely as connected with the above facts hinted to me in regard to the movments of Engl^d & Mr Jay, and that being informed of every particular that comes to my knowledge, according to the evidence I have, you may do the best in y^r power to promote the course of republican gov^t in both countries.

It is possible if the arrangment between Mr Jay & Engl^d with respect to the Missisippi & the boundaries was known in Spain it wo^d seperate Spain from Engl^d & hasten her peace with France. I am willing to give every aid in my power to forward that object, in confidence France will secure our rights in that particular, and which I wish her to have the credit of.

Dft, DLC: Monroe Papers; incomplete; filed at the end of 1795.

David Humphreys left Lisbon for the United States on 27 November 1794 (Frank L. Humphreys, *The Life and Times of David Humphreys*, 2: 224). JM's reference to Humphreys going to America suggests that this letter was written in December 1794 or in the early months of 1795. The contents suggest that it was addressed either to the commissary of foreign relations or to a member of the Committee of Public Safety.

To the Committee of Public Safety

Paris 4 J^y 1795 (14 Nivôse) l'an 19e de la République Américaine

Citoyens

Le Décret qui vient de passer, portant l'exécution des articles 23 & 24 du traité d'Amitié et de commerce entre les deux Républiques est d'une telle importance à mon pays que je crois expédient de l'y envoyer officiellement par quelqu'un de confiance particuliere & personne ne m'a paru plus propre à ce message que le c^n Thomas Payne. Ayant résidé longtems en France & ayant une parfaite connaissance des vicissitudes diverses qu'a éprouvé la République, il est à même d'expliquer la comparaison du Sort heureux dont elle jouit maintenant & comme il en a éprouvé lui-même personnellement & qu'il est resté fidelle à Ses principes, les rapports qu'il en fera obtiendrons d'autant plus de créance & par la même raison produiront un meilleur effet. Mais comme le c^n Payne est membre de la Convention, J'ai cru à propos de soumettre cet objet à votre considération & Sy la chose peut s'arranger, le c^n partira immediatement pour le Amérique par voix de Bordeaux sur un N^re Américain qui Sera preparé pour lui. Comme il a des raisons a craindre la persécution du gouvernement anglais, en cas qu'il fût fait prisonnier il désireroit que son départ trés sécret

Ja^s Monroe

Editors' Translation

Paris 4 J^y 1795 (14 Nivôse)[1] Year 19 of the American Republic

Citizens

The decree that has just been passed, containing the enactment of articles 23 and 24 of the Treaty of Friendship and of Commerce between the two Republics is of such importance to my country that I find it worthwhile to send it officially with someone of exceptional trust, and no one has seemed more appropriate to me for this message than Citizen Thomas Payne. Since he has been a longtime resident of France and has a perfect understanding of the various changes the Republic has undergone, he is in a position to explain the comparison with the happy circumstance in which it now finds itself, and since he has personally suffered himself and has remained faithful to his principles, the reports that he will give will obtain even more credit and by the same principle will produce a better effect. Nevertheless, since Citizen Payne is a member of the Convention, I thought it appropriate to submit this issue for your consideration and if it can be arranged, the citizen will leave immediately for America from Bordeaux on an American ship prepared for him. Since he has reasons to fear persecution from the English government, in case he should be taken prisoner, he would desire that his departure remain very secret.

Ja^s Monroe

RC, DLC: FCP—France

1. 4 January 1795 would have been 15 Nivôse on the French revolutionary calendar.

From the Committee of Public Safety

Paris, le [16 Nivose] l'an 3 de la République française une et indivisible.
[5 January 1795]

Citoyen,

Nous Voyons avec Satisfaction [et] Sans Surprise, que Vous attachez quelque Intérêt à faire Parvenir officiellement aux Etats-unis le decret que la Convention Nationale Vient de Rendre, dans lequel elle Rappelle et Confirme les Rapports d'amitié et de Commerce qui Existent Entre les deux Républiques.

Quant au Dessein que Vous avez de Confier Ce Message au Citoyen Thomas Payne, Nous devons Vous observer Que le caractere dont il Est Revetu ne lui Permet Point de l'accepter. Salut et Fraternité.

Cambacérés
Pelet
Carnot

Editors' Translation

Paris, [16 Nivôse][1] Year 3 of the French Republic one and indivisible
[5 January 1795].

Citizen,

We note with pleasure and without surprise that you attach some interest in officially forwarding to the United States the decree just passed by the National Convention, which recalls and confirms the ties of friendship and of commerce that exist between the two republics.

As to the plan you have of entrusting this message to Citizen Thomas Payne, we should point out that the character he bears hardly allows him to accept. Salutation and fraternity,

Cambacérés
Pelet[2]
Carnot

RC, NN: Monroe Papers

1. This copy is undated. The date is supplied from the copy in DLC: FCP—France.

2. Jean Pelet (1759-1842) was a lawyer and deputy from the department of Lozère. He served on the Committee of Public Safety from 5 November 1794 to 5 March 1795, during which time he was a member of the diplomatic section. He was president of the National Convention from 24 March to 5 April 1795 (Bernard Gainot, *Dictionnaire des Membres du Comité du Salut Public*, 139; *La Grande Encyclopédie*; *Writings of Monroe*, 2: 228).

From the Committee of Public Safety

Paris, le 18 Nivose l'an 3 de la République française une et indivisible.
[7 January 1795]

Par notre empressement, Citoyen, à te communiquer Notre arrêté du 14 de ce mois tu jugeras de celui que nous mettrons toujours à t'instruire de tout ce que nous ferons constamment Pour maintenir les Rapports d'une Sincère amitié entre les Etats unis et la République française. Salut et fraternité

Cambacérés
Breard

Editors' Translation

Paris, 18 Nivose, year 3 of the French Republic, one and indivisible
[7 January 1795]

From the haste with which we communicate to you our decree of the 14th of this month, you will discern the haste with which we will always inform you of all that we are constantly doing to maintain the bonds of sincere friendship between the United States and the French Republic. Salutations and fraternity

Cambacérés
Breard[1]

RC, NN: Monroe Papers

1. Jean-Jacques Bréard (1751-1840) was elected in 1791 to the Legislative Assembly and placed in charge of the confiscation of émigré property. He became president of the National Assembly for three weeks in February 1793, and served on the Committee of Public Safety intermittently after 31 July 1794 (*Dictionnaire Biographie Française*).

Cambacérés and Breard sent JM a copy of the following decree of the Committee of Public Safety of 14 Nivôse An 3 (3 January 1795) (translated from a copy in French in NN: Monroe Papers).

The Committee for Public Safety, in reference to Article 23 of the Commercial Treaty between France and the United States of America of February 6, 1778, formally determines that, 1. French and American ships will be able to sail in all security, free of any hindrance based on the ownership of the goods, regardless of the port in which they originate and regardless of whether the power for whom they are destined is at that time, or subsequently becomes, an enemy of one or the other party; their vessels and goods will also be able to sail in safety, and call at the markets, ports, and harbors of enemy powers of the two parties, or of one of them, and conduct trade, not only from an enemy port to another, neutral port, but also from an enemy port to another enemy port. 2. Ships free to navigate will ensure the freedom of movement of goods, and all goods on board ships belonging to citizens of the two nations party to the contract will be considered free of all hindrance, even when the cargo belongs, in part or in toto, to enemies of one of the parties, with the exception of contraband. 3. This freedom of movement extends to persons found aboard, even if they are enemies of one of the two nations party to the contract; in consequence, these persons may not be removed from said ships, unless they are military personnel or in the service of the enemy at that time.

Given that England's despotic crimes have introduced into the war on liberty injustice and atrocity not yet found in the annals of history, the National Convention, observing the right of reprisal, felt obliged to decree on May 9, 1793 that warships and French corsairs could stop and bring into the ports of the Republic neutral ships that were laden, in part or in toto, with foodstuffs belonging to neutral parties and destined for enemy ports, or with merchandise belonging to enemies; but soon thereafter, on July 1, 1793, the National Convention hastened to reestablish the terms of the February 6, 1778 Treaty mentioned above. In truth it had been revoked by the treaty of the 27th of the same month; but only as regards foodstuffs and merchandise belonging to enemy powers; it thus continued in force as regards foodstuffs and goods belonging to neutral powers, with regard to which the government of France feels no embarrassment for having waited to prove its sense of justice and loyalty, until the cabinet in London revoked—as it did, a long time afterwards—the order it gave the year before to seize all neutral ships carrying neutral foodstuffs and merchandise to France.

It is established that, despite the affectation with which that cabinet continues daily to insult the rights of men, and to violate the neutrality of non-belligerent nations by seizing their ships laden with goods destined for France, the National Convention has, by means of article 7 of the Law of the 13th day of this month, charged all agents of the Republic, all army commanders, and all civilian and military officers, to enforce all the terms of the treaties which unite France with the neutral powers of the Old World and with the United States of America; and by means of the same article it is forbidden to defy these treaties, and all measures contrary to them are annulled.

Given the importance of making known to the entire world this great act of loyalty and justice, and of removing all malicious pretexts aimed either at hindering or delaying its effect, or at abusing it to the detriment of the Republic, it is decreed that:

Article 1.

The Commission for the Navy and the Colonies will without delay communicate to all commanders of naval forces, divisions, squadrons, fleets and ships, the above-mentioned article from the law of the 13th day of this month, and advise them that they must in consequence consider invalid the terms of article 5 of the decree of the Committees of Public Safety, Finance and Trade and Supply of last November 15, which authorized the seizure of goods belonging to enemy powers until such time as they declared French goods loaded on neutral ships to be free and not subject to seizure.

Article. 2.

Goods, even neutral goods, which are contraband or otherwise prohibited, will continue to be subject to seizure.

Article 3.

Included in the term prohibited or contraband goods are arms, weapons of war and munitions of any kind, horses and their tackle, and all sorts of items, foodstuff or goods destined for enemy markets which are at the time besieged, blockaded, or occupied.

Article 4.

The Commission for Foreign Relations will transmit this decree to the officials of the Republic who are assigned in allied or neutral countries with orders to transmit it to the governments of those countries.

Article 5.

This decree shall be incorporated in the legal record.

To Thomas Pinckney

Paris Jany 7. 1795.

Dear Sir

I wrote you sometime since by Mr Morris jun^r & since which I have not heard from you.[1] The importance & delicacy of that com^n make me anxious to hear you have rec^d it, & likewise to hear from you in reply. At present I have only add that the Convention have agreed to carry into full effect the treaty of commerce between the two republicks. This was checked by the report from y^r side the channel but executed afterwards upon my assurance there co^d be no foundation in the extent suggested, and if there was that it wo^d be rejected in America. I refer you to the bearer for political intelligence. I will procure the books you want & send them by the first oppr^y. I find by the American papers that the Eng^h translat^n of my address to the Convention made nonsense of it—I therefore send you a copy. I beg you to be assured of the sincerity with w^h I am dear sir y^r friend & servant

Ja^s Monroe

RC, DLC: Charles C. Pinckney Papers

1. Robert Morris, Jr., was the son of Robert Morris of Philadelphia. Robert Morris, Jr., served as a courier between JM and John Jay. He also worked on financial concerns of his father while traveling in Europe, 1791-1798 (*Hamilton Papers*, 9: 49; 18: 360-361, 368; 19: 430, 499; 20: 186-187; 21: 351; 25: 250-251; 490). JM's letter to Pinckney of 20 December 1796 has not been located. See Pinckney to JM, 18 February 1795, below.

From Jeanne-Louise-Henriette Genet Campan

20 nivose an 3e de la République [9 January 1795]

J'ai reçu cet Eté Monsieur une lettre qui etoit venue sous votre Couvert, et que vous m'avez fait remettre pour M. Tomazini ancien Chargé des affaires de Portugal en France et qui réside dans cette ville. Il a répondu plusieurs fois à la Haïe à M. D'araujo Sans qu'aucune lettre lui Soit par venue, il m'a demandé avec instance de vous prier de faire passer la réponse ci-jointe à La Haïe.

Eliza Se porte à merveille, elle a une grande amitié pour une petite pensionnaire nouvelle qui est ici et qui lit en même temps qu'elle, j'ai promis une belle bonbonniere dans un mois à celle qui lis à couramment, cela donnera j'espère de l'émulation car cette malheureuse lecture nous coute beaucoup. Je vous dirai en confidence que l'on me fait une petit Théatre et qu'Eliza apprend un rôle, mais comme vous devez être Surpris je vous demande le Secret.

mille amitiés à Madame Monroe. croyez je vous prie Monsieur à la Sincérité de tous mes Sentimens

Genet Campan

Editors' Translation

20 Nivose, Year 3 of the Republic [9 January 1795]

I received last summer, Sir, a letter under cover of your address, and which you had me forward to Mr. Tomazini, formerly the Chargé d'affaires of Portugal in France who resides in this city. He wrote several times in answer to Mr. D'Araujo at The Hague. Without receiving any reply, he has asked me insistently to ask you to forward the enclosed response to The Hague.

Eliza gets on wonderfully. She has been very friendly with a new little pensioner who is here and who reads at the same time as she. I have promised a fine box of candy in a month to the person who reads fluently. This will provide I hope some competition as this distressing reading requires a lot. I tell you in confidence that they have made me a little Theater and that Eliza is learning a role, but as you ought to be surprised, I ask you to keep it a secret.

Best wishes and regards to Madame Monroe. Sincerely yours with feeling

Genet-Campan

RC, ViW: Monroe Family Papers

Jeanne-Louise-Henriette Genêt Campan (1752-1822) was the daughter of a French interpreter in the Department of Foreign Affairs. A gifted child, given an excellent education, she was only fifteen years old when King Louis XV hired her as a "reader" for his youngest daughters. Over the next twenty-five years she participated in the life of the Court where she had the opportunity to observe world leaders and to absorb state secrets. Marie-Antoinette both as dauphine and queen played a prominent role in her life. It was due to Marie Antoinette that she married unhappily Pierre-Dominique-François Berthollet, dit Campan, a distant relation, in May 1774. In 1786 Madame Campan became the queen's "*première femme de chambre*," serving her until 1792, when Madame Campan herself became suspect to the revolutionaries. Forced into hiding with her son and mother, and later joined by her ill, insolvent husband, she added three nieces to her household, in July 1794, after her sister, summoned for arrest, committed suicide. Strapped for money, Campan established a boarding school for girls later known as the National Institution of Saint-Germain. During this desperate time following the fall of Robespierre, she was often paid in flour, as many of the parents had no money. JM was her first benefactor, paying her in cash for the instruction and boarding of his eight-year-old daughter Eliza (*Dictionnaire de Biographie Française*; Inès de Kertanguy, *Secrets de Cour: Madame Campan au Service de Marie-Antoinette et de Napoléon,* 106-108).

To Committee of Public Safety

Paris, 10 J^y 1795. (21 Nivôse) l'an 19e de la République Américaine

Citoyens

J'ai reçu avec la plus grande satisfaction votre lettre du 18 de ce mois, me portant votre arrêté du 14 du même mois, et persuadé de celle qu'il produira en Amérique je m'empresserai de le transmettre à mes constituants. Non seulement il résultera de cet arrêté des avantages considérable pour le commerce mais aussy il resserre les liens d'amitié qui unissent les deux Républiques.

Ja^s Monroe

Editors' Translation

Paris, 10 J.y 1795 (21 Nivôse) Year 19 of the American Republic.

Citizens

I have received with the greatest satisfaction your letter of the 18th of this month, which informed me of your decree of the 14th of the same month,[1] and certain that it will produce the same reaction in America I hasten to transmit it to my constituents. Not only will tremendous advantages for commerce arise from this decree but it also strengthens the ties of friendship that unite the two Republics.

Ja.s Monroe

RC, DLC: FCP—France

1. Committee of Public Safety to JM, 7 January 1794 (18 Nivôse), enclosing the decree of 3 January 1794 (14 Nivôse), above.

From William Short

Madrid Jan. 10. 1795.

Dear Sir

The present letter is sent to you by a servant who having come with me from France is now returning to his own country on my mission here being rendered permanent. It will be sent open as it could not be proper to give him a letter sealed being to pass from the Spanish to the French army on the frontier—The principal object of the letter is to desire you (in the case of M.r Morris having left with you my trunks &c, as I had desired him to do on learning he was to leave Paris) to deliver to the bearer Louis Francois Dubart, or if he should not go to Paris, to any person he may authorize to receive it, one of those trunks which contains his clothes & other effects & which he informs me is marked with the number three— This letter he will forward to you by post on his arriving in France—& I give him further a request to you written in French to deliver to him or to whoever he may entrust with that paper, the trunk abovementioned—He will be the bearer himself of the paper written in French, or will send it to his agent at Paris who will present it to you—M.r Morris wrote me some time ago after my arrival in this country that he had received into his house the effects I had left at Paris—although he did not particularize them I take it for granted, he received them all together & among them the trunk in question.

The present mode of conveyance prevents my speaking to you on any other subject. I cannot however omit repeating that no letter has come to my hands from you since your arrival at Paris, although I still flatter myself from our ancient friendship that you will have frequently written to me—I have written to you very often both by England & Italy, & requested you to write to me by the same routes—As letters from hence to Paris & vice versa come & go regularly, though slowly by that means, I still wait in the impatient expectation of hearing from you—When you write to me by Italy I will thank you to address your letters for me under cover to M.r Peter Feliechy the Consul of the United States at Leghorn—You will be the best judge of the best & surest means of sending letters at present from Paris to Leghorn—they should be put under cover to some person in Switzerland—or at Genoa to be forwarded from thence—otherwise they will be stopped in those countries for the postage—Another mode by which you might write to me might be to send your letter to the Representative or the General of the French army on this frontier, with a request to send it to the Spanish General when he should send a flag—This General would of course send it to the minister here who would give it to me—On indifferent subjects it would be best however perhaps to send your letters via

RC, PHi: Gilpin Collection: William Short Letters. Incomplete—first page only.

From Joseph Fenwick

Bord^x 22 Nivose 3. 11 Jany 1795.

Dear Sir

I sincerely congratulate you on the Decree of the Convention which Ratify's our Treaty with France—and that which suppresses the commission of Commerce—I had no doubt when I left you but what your measures & your zeal woud be crowned with this success—We have now only to hope that these Decrees may be justly estimated in America.

There has been no arrivals here from the U. States, since my last.

If you have any certain accounts of the much talked of Treaty of Mr Jay's & its conditions I shall be obliged by any information of them. I am Dear Sir Your most Obedient & H^{ble} Servant

Joseph Fenwick

RC, DLC: Monroe Papers

To Edmund Randolph

Paris January 13th 1795.

Sir,

I have the pleasure to inform you that upon the report of the United Comittes of public safety, general surety, legislation, commerce and finances, a decree has passed the Convention since my last whereby it is resolved to carry into strict execution the treaty of amity and commerce subsisting between the United States and this republic.[1] I beg leave to congratulate you upon this event, and particularly the unanimity with which it passed the convention, since it demonstrates the good disposition of that body and of the nation generally towards us. I was always satisfied as heretofore intimated, that if I could have brought the subject, in the first instance, before the convention, I should have succeeded immediately in the object in view: but as the committee was the department organized for such business, this was impossible without commencing a species of warfare upon it, and which was equally improper as it might tend to increase their own dissentions and embark me afloat upon the fortune of those dissentions. Happily by pursuing the object patiently with the comittee, removing doubts, and obviating objections, aided by occasional changes of the members, this has not only been avoided, but I have the additional pleasure to assure you that it was finally accomplished without the least difficulty, and without exciting the animosity of any one.

After my late communications to the committee of Public Safety in which were exposed freely the object of Mr Jay's mission to England and the real situation of the United States with Britain and Spain, I had reason to believe that all apprehension on those parts was done away and that the utmost cordiality had now likewise taken place in that body towards us. I considered the report above recited and upon which the decree was founded, as the unequivocal proof of that change of sentiment, and flattered myself that in every respect we had now the best prospect of the most perfect and permanent harmony between the two republics. I am very sorry however to add that latterly this prospect has been somewhat clouded by accounts from England, that Mr Jay had not only adjusted the points in controversy but concluded a treaty of commerce with that government: some of those accounts state that he had also concluded a treaty of alliance offensive and defensive. As I knew the baneful effects which these reports would produce, I deemed it my duty, by repeating what I had said before of his powers, to use my utmost endeavours informally to discredit them. This however did not arrest the progress of the report, nor remove the disquietude it had created: for I was finally applied to directly by the committee in a letter which stated what had been heard, and requested information of what I knew in regard to it.[2] As I had just before received one from Mr Jay announcing that he had concluded a treaty and which contained a declaration that our previous treaties should not be affected by it, I thought fit to make this letter the basis of my reply.[3] And as it is necessary that you should be apprized of whatever has passed here on this subject, I now transmit to you, copies of these several papers and which comprize a full statement thereof up to the present time.

I cannot admit for a moment that Mr Jay has exceeded his powers or that any thing has been done which will give just cause of complaint to this republic: I lament however that he has not thought himself at liberty to give me correct information in that respect, for untill it is known that their interest has not been wounded, the report will certainly keep alive suspicion and which always weakens the bonds of friendship. I trust therefore you will deem it expedient to advise me on this head as soon as possible.

I apprized you in my two last letters of an informal communication between the diplomatic members of the committee and myself upon an interrogatory of theirs, whether it would be possible for France to obtain aid from or within the United States for the purchase of supplies, and of my effort upon that occasion to interest this government in support of our claims with Britain and Spain, and to which I was stimulated by intelligence that Mr Jay's negotiation had failed, and that we were on the point of war or actually engaged in it with Britain, as likewise by the knowledge that Spain was covertly seeking a seperate peace. I was satisfied that if France would embark in our cause in the present state of things, and which I found her well disposed to do, and without the prospect of much aid in return, that the object in each instance would be secure. I therefore thought it eligible in that state of things, and with that view, to leave the door open for a communication with you upon the subject. But as soon as I understood that Mr Jay had adjusted the points in controversy with that Nation, the object on my part was at an end: I was aware that if the adjustment was approved we could render no such service, indeed I doubted whether <u>in peace</u> the government possessed power to render it. I called therefore immediately upon those members with whom the previous communication had been, and suggested the same to them. They had anticipated the idea and were prepared to answer it by a peremptory assurance that it was not their wish to create embarrassment in this or any other respect; on the contrary that regard should be shewn in all cases to our actual situation, and with respect to the point in question, that the minister about to depart should be instructed not even to mention it, if you forbade it. So that this business stands upon a footing as indeed it always did, whereby under a particular state of things, some benefit may be derived from it, and no detriment under any.

The operations of this government continue to progress in the same course they have done for some time past. During the time of Robespierre a period of the administration, which is emphatically called the reign of terror, much havoc was made not only on the rights of humanity, but great confusion was likewise introduced in other respects in the affairs of the government. It has been the systematic effort of the administration to repair this waste and heal the bleeding wounds of the country, and in this, great progress has been made. By the same report which proposed the execution of the violated articles of the treaty of amity and commerce with the United States, it was likewise proposed to open wide the door of commerce to every citizen (excluding them from navigation only) and which was adopted: so that at present any person bringing productions into any port in this republic, may sell them to whom he pleases, and generally with astonishing profit, the agents of the republic stand upon the ground of other persons:

they are preferred only by out-bidding them. In my judgment no region of the world presents such an opening to the enterprises of our countrymen as this does. The restraints upon their own navigation operate in the degree as a bounty to ours, and the government and citizens of France seem equally pleased to see ours preferred to that of any other nation. The restraints likewise which are imposed in other countries on account of the war upon a commerce with the french citizens produce in other respects the same effect. 'Tis the interest of the latter to employ our countrymen in ordinary mercantile transactions and especially with foreign nations, whereby they get into their hands a great proportion of the whole trade of the republic. The profits which those of the theatre have already made and continue to make surpass what you have any idea of. I sincerely wish that this was more generally known, that more might be induced to embark in it, not only for the purpose of diffusing more generally the immediate emolument, but for the more important one of gaining an interest in the commerce of this republic which may be of lasting advantage to the United States. Before the revolution the English possessed this advantage, as they did in most other countries: but now that interest is annihilated, and if the Americans step in, aided as they will be by the preference of the government and people in their favour, they may occupy the ground and retain it for ever afterwards. Permit me to add that nothing will more essentially forward this object than an extensive and numerous appointment of Consuls. In every port an agent should be placed; and I should suppose the object of sufficient importance to induce our countrymen to accept of those offices. If a prudent and creditable person, the appointment attaches to it confidence and gives him the command of capital. I am satisfied that any young man of good character having the appointment in any of the ports, might immediately connect himself advantageously with the first house there and gradually command elsewhere what capital he pleased. I have examined into this subject, and have thought proper to give you the result of my researches into it.

Nor has this wise and humane system been limited to this object alone. It has already been extended to many branches of National policy and promises to embrace the whole. A decree was not long since passed by which the seventy one members, formerly of the Brissotine or Girondine party, and who had been confined on that account, were all at liberty, and called into the convention: and a few days afterwards our countryman Mr Paine was likewise restored to his seat in that body with marks of the most respectful attention.[4] These events have given satisfaction to the community at large. A decree also which had excluded the ex-nobles and foreigners (the Americans excepted) from Paris and the Sea-ports, has likewise been repealed. This latter act though comparatively of apparant little importance has notwithstanding produced an excellent effect: for as it breathes a spirit of humanity and on that account captivates all, so it has contributed by passing in review many members of the ancient order of nobility, and who have not forgotten and never will forget old habits, to present before the public and much to the credit of the revolution, the strong and interesting contrast, between the manly character of the French nation at the present day, and the miserable effeminacy, foppery and decrepitude of former times.

A decree has likewise passed, by which a general amnesty has been proclaimed in the Vendee, and a report has been since received from the deputies who were sent to carry it into effect, that all those to whom it was announced, had laid down their arms, and arranged themselves under the banner of the republic, and that they were likewise satisfied it would terminate the war: a war heretofore beyond example, bloody and destructive, and whose origin support and means of continuance, appear even yet to be but little understood. Freed from this embarrassment, the republic will acquire new vigour in all its enterprises; it will certainly have under its command for other purposes, a considerable force which was heretofore employed there.[5]

But in retracing the ground, to repair in detail the injuries which the reign of terror had inflicted, it was impossible to behold the havoc it had made, without feeling some indignation for the authors of such great and complicated misery. This propensity however and which was equally incited by the obligations of justice and humanity was strongly opposed from the period of Robesperre's death to the present time, by a sentiment of extensive impression, that it were better to prevent the further effusion of blood, and to cover with a veil the atrocities which had passed so far as they could be covered, than to punish even the authors of those of greatest enormity; for sometime this sentiment prevailed, and though often irritated and disturbed by the remaining leaders of the opposite party, who courted danger and provoked their own fate, yet it appeared probable it would finally preponderate and confirm the administration within that limit. The trial however of the Nantais a long train of respectable citizens fromt Nantes, who were arrested under the administration of Carrier in his mission there, and brought lately before the Tribunal of Paris, opened the scene again and revived the sensation of horror which had before in some measure subsided. Such enormities were disclosed in the course of this trial, that it was impossible otherwise to appease the public mind than by submitting Carrier and his accomplices to the tribunal in their turn. Condemnation was the sure consequence of his trial, and it was expected, so clear was the case against him, that all those of that party, would now separate from and yield him to his fate. From such a line of conduct some merit might have been arrogated, and the public censure thrown in a great measure on him alone: by whose punishment the public resentment might possibly have been satisfied. But Billaud de Varennes, Collot-d'Herbois, and even Barrere, a man heretofore noted for skilful movements in critical conjunctures, acted otherwise. They obviously and from the beginning, made Carrier's cause their own, not only by supporting him in the Convention, as far as it was possible, but by exciting the Jacobins to take part in his favor, thereby attaching themselves to the declining fortunes of that club, and likewise making some unseasonable motions which bore on their face the complexion of that party. The separation required at best a dexterous managment, but by these means they presented themselves out as an object, invited the public attention and in the degree the public resentment. Whether they will finally escape is now doubtful. Le Cointre who has shewn himself sufficiently prone upon a former occasion to commence the attack, took advantage of one of these moments of indiscretion to renew it, and with better effect: his motion was sent to the commision of twenty one heretofore organized, to report whether there was just ground of accusation, and there it now is.[6]

Another signal victory was obtained over the Spaniards since my last and in which the two commanding Generals with many men were slain, and nine thousand taken prisoners: and in the north since the ice, nearer approaches are made to Holland which will most probably soon be taken. Within a few days past Deputies arrived from the Stadholderian party to negotiate a separate peace: but at the same time others came from the patriotic party to oppose it, and who pressed the committee to order forward the troops immediately to assail and enter Amsterdam, and to which effect orders were accordingly issued. I am satisfied that peace will not be granted to the Netherlands although a revolution should take place there, on any other condition than that of their uniting in the war against England.[6] It is conceived that a peace to that power on other terms, would be more favorable to England than its continuance in the war, for thereby the british troops might be withdrawn, and great advantage gained in other respects from its neutrality. This it is thought was the object of England in assenting to their peace; but in rejecting the offer, France opens a trait in her views that will add much to the weight of the ministerial argument for a continuance of the war.[5] No argument is so strong as that of necessity, and if France will not make peace it will be impossible for England to do it. In my judgment it is the determination of this republic, to pursue the war untill the maritime strength of England is broken, and when the actual state of things is regarded, with that of the comparative population, force and enterprise of the two nations, I do not see how it can be prevented. A single victory at sea accomplishes the object, and the rapidity with which Ships are built and fleets equiped here, is inconceivable. Within few weeks past the Brest fleet has been out twice (indeed it is now out) consisting of 36 ships of the line, 15 frigates, 14 sloops of war and cutters giving the defiance to its antagonist, which continues close locked to the land: more latterly however some indications were seen on that coast of a disposition to take the Sea, and hazard the fate of the Island on a battle, so that 'tis probable something decisive may take place soon.[8]

With respect to the other powers nothing definitive has yet been done in regard to peace. 'Tis certain that several wish it and particularly Spain and Prussia; but yet some difficulties have occurred in regulating the commencement and manner of the negotiation. England opposes it, because she knows she will not be included; and they on that account wish it to be private merely to avoid the imputations that would arise if it were known; and this cannot well be accomodated under the present organization of the French government. 'Tis said that a Minister from Prussia is at Basle in Switzerland, with power to treat, and that they all have agents there for the same purpose is likewise probable.[9]

I will endeavour, if possible, to forward by this opportunity a report rendered me by Mr Skipwith upon the subject of American claims.[10] Be assured that every possible attention has been and shall be paid to this subject. With great respect and esteem, I have the honor to be, dear Sir, your very humble servant.

Ja^s Monroe.

P. S. I had omitted to mention the official communication by the committee of public safety of the decree of the Convention for carrying into effect the treaty of amity and commerce between the United States and France. The polite terms however in which it is expressed merit attention.

Copy: DNA: RG 59: Dispatches from France

1. Decree of the Committee of Public Safety, 3 January 1795, enclosed in Committee of Public Safety to JM, 7 January 1795, above.

2. Committee of Public Safety to JM, 24 December 1794, above.

3. John Jay to JM, 25 November 1794; JM to the Committee of Public Safety, 27 December 1794, both above.

4. The Convention voted on 7 December 1794 to allow Thomas Paine to retake his seat. The vote on reseating the other Girondins took place the following day (A. J. Ayer, *Thomas Paine*, 132).

5. During 1794 rebels in the Vendée continued to resist in the form of guerrilla warfare. General Hoche was brought back from Germany to take overall command of troops north of the Loire, and he proclaimed amnesty and bounty for all rebels who turned in their arms. On 1 December, the Convention decreed an amnesty for all who would surrender within a month. Many complied, and by January 1795 serious negotiations began for a general cease-fire (William Doyle, *Oxford History of the French Revolution*, 288-289).

6. Laurent Lecointre, a deputy from Versailles, denounced several former members of the governing committees as allies of Robespierre on 12 Fructidor (29 August 1794). At first his condemnation was not taken seriously, but in December 1794 a commission of twenty-one was appointed to consider the charges against the accused (Alphonse Aulard, *French Revolution*, 3: 238, 245).

7. In 1787 Dutch revolutionaries attempted to overthrow the government of William V, who bore the hereditary title of Stadtholder, but Prussian intervention suppressed the movement. A group of Dutch patriots who were in exile in Paris established the Batavian Revolutionary Committee in 1792, and once again began to plot the overthrow of the Stadtholder. When it became clear that the French forces would soon conquer Holland, both the patriots and the Stadholderate factions appealed to France for support (Simon Schama, *Patriots and Liberators, Revolution in the Netherlands, 1780-1813*, 14, 158-159).

8. The Committee of Public Safety issued orders in December 1794 to Admiral Louis-Thomas Villaret de Joyeuse, commander of the Brest fleet, to sail out and attack British shipping in the English Channel. A violent gale thrust the three-decker *Républicaine* against the Mingan rock in the center of the harbor's mouth, and the huge ship was entirely lost. Due to this disaster, Villaret de

Joyeuse's fleet came to anchor, and a second attempt was not made until December 31, when the fleet stood out to sea (William James, *Naval History of Great Britain during the French Revolutionary and Napoleonic Wars*, 232-234).

9. Prussia made peace with France by signing the Treaty of Basel, 5 April 1795. The treaty required Prussia to cede the left bank of the Rhine to France (Owen Connelly, *The Wars of the French Revolution and Napoleon, 1792-1815*, 71).

10. Skipwith to JM, 17 October 1794, above. There is no record of JM sending this report to Randolph.

To John Jay

Paris Jan.ʸ 17. 1795.

Sir

Early in Dec.ʳ last English papers were rec.ᵈ here containing such acc.ᵗˢ of y.ʳ adjustment with the British adm.ⁿ as excited much uneasiness in the councils of this gov.ᵗ & I had it in contemplation to dispatch a confidential person to you for such information of what had been done as would enable me to remove it. At that moment however I was favored with yours of the 25. of Nov.ʳ intimating that the contents of the treaty could not be made known untill it was ratified, but that I might say it contained nothing derogatory to our existing treaties with other powers. Thus advised I thought it improper to make the application, because I concluded the arrangment was mutual, and not to be departed from. I proceeded therefore to make the best use in my power of the information already given.

Today however I was fav.ᵈ with y.ʳˢ of the 28.ᵗʰ of the same month by which I find you consider y.ʳself at liberty to communicate to me the contents of the treaty, and as it is of great importance to our aff.ʳˢ here to remove all doubt upon this point I have thought fit to resume my original plan of sending a person to you for the necessary information & have in consequence dispatched the bearer M.ʳ John Purveyance for that purpose. I have been the more induc'd to this from the further consideration that in case I sho.ᵈ be fav.ᵈ with the communication promised in cypher it wo.ᵈ be impossible for me to comprehend it, as M.ʳ Morris took his off with him. M.ʳ Purveyance is from Maryland, a gent.ⁿ of integrity & merit & to whom you may commit whatever you may think proper to confide, with perfect safety. Tis necessary however to observe that <u>as nothing will satisfy this government but a copy of the instrument itself</u>, and which as our ally it thinks itself <u>entitled to</u>, so it will be useless for me to make to it any new communications short of that: I mention this that you may know precisely the state of my engagments here & how I deem it my duty to act under them in relation to this object. I beg leave to refer you to M.ʳ Purveyance for whatever other information you may wish to have either on this subject or the aff.ʳˢ more generally of this republick. I have the honor to be with great respect y.ʳ most ob.ᵗ serv.ᵗ

Ja.ˢ Monroe

RC, NHi: Gilder Lehrman Collection

From Pierce Butler

Charleston S.º Carolina Jan.ʸ 19.ᵗʰ 1795

My Dear Sir

The letter that You intended favouring me with by Commodore Gillon never reached my hand till the 24.ᵗʰ of last Month. His Widow found it among His papers, and sent it to me. He departed this life in October. I had the honor of writing You a short letter from Philadelphia by a M.ʳ Forbes.[1] When I heard of Your departure for France, I felt disappointed at not hearing from You before You Sailed, because I persuaded myself, that You saw, and believed that that friendship which commenced in public life settled into a warm and sincere private friendship; if I may so express myself, I mean that it goes to the Man, as well as the Senator. In truth my Dear Sir, Mʳˢ Monroe, Yourself and Miss Eliza will ever have my good wishes for every happiness this life presents. I carry into private life those sensations, and that Attachment with which the Virtuous Conduct of the Senator inspired me. A Conduct that I so often, with heartfelt gratification, bore testimony to.

I hope You find Your new situation quite to Your mind, and that Mʳˢ Monroe and Miss Eliza are also pleased. I have no doubt that the Republic are pleased and fully satisfied in the Change of American Ministers.

You are in the Centre of the most important European transactions. In a Country that gives Existance to scenes and sentiments that astonish; and Compell Admiration. Among a Magnanimous Race, that have done more to secure, and are of course better entitled to the blessings flowing from, liberty than any People the Page of History makes Us acquainted with. Gallant French Men I bow before the Altar Ye have Erected! America You have a useful lesson given to You, but alas!

Of the existing State of Politicks in the States, You will have ample information from other of Your friends than I can give You. Two days before the meeting of Congress I sailed from Philadelphia for my Farms in the State of Georgia where in Solitude I coud converse with myself—Your change of situation and our friend Taylor's resignation left too little inducement for me to try another Session I shoud have felt myself but illy supported. A timely retreat is better than a total defeat.² I came here the 24ᵗʰ of last month I shall return to Georgia in a day or two. The Politicks of this State appear to me to be Governd by the whim or Caprice of the moment. Mʳ Wᵐ Smith, tho' openly opposed by Messʳˢ Rutledges and Pinckney, has been re-Elected.³ The Legislature of this State have Chosen Mʳ Reid to succeed Mʳ Izard. You may possibly Know something of the Genˡ Character of this Gentleman. He married a Miss Van Horn of New York. there is as little prospect of His draw[ing] with me as of Mʳ Izard's. He is decidedly AntiGallican and I think, not much of a Republican. He is said to have tried to be Chosen Governor of this State; He failed in that Attempt, And in Order to prevent mortification, they made Him a Senator.⁴ I never went near the Legislature: Indeed I remaind in Georgia during their Sitting. I have seen nothing of Genˡˢ Jackson or Gunn since I saw You—the latter is in Georgia Attending to some Land Speculations.⁵

I beg to present my best respects to Mʳˢ Monroe And to Assure You that I am with sentiments of great regard and Esteem My Dear Sir, sincerely & affectionately Yʳ friend

P. Butler

P.S. Mʳ Hary Grant a very respectable Merchᵗ and worthy Man of this City, solicits me, to ask of You, in Case any French Merchˢ shoud inquire of You, who in Carolina may be Eligible for them to Consign their Merchandize to, to mention His name. I will thank you to do so; And if any oppʸ offers, without laying Yourself under any obligation, of serving this worthy Man You will oblige me.

RC, DLC: Monroe Papers

1. Neither JM's letter to Butler nor Butler's letter to JM has not been located.

2. Although disheartened, Butler did not resign from the Senate at this time, but served until October 1796 (*BDAC*).

3. John Rutledge, supported by his brother Edward Rutledge and by Charles Pinckney, mounted an unsuccessful challenge to William Loughton Smith for his seat in Congress (George C. Rogers, *Evolution of a Federalist*, 264-268; *ANB*).

4. Jacob Read (1752-1816) was a member of the Senate 1795-1801. He married Catherine Van Horn of New York in 1785 (*BDAC*, Rogers, *Evolution of a Federalist*, 404). Ralph Izard (1742-1804), was born in South Carolina, educated in England,

and held several minor diplomatic posts during the American Revolution. He was a senator from South Carolina 1789-1795 (*ANB*).

5. James Jackson (1757-1806) was an English-born Savannah attorney who rose to the rank of general in the Georgia service during the Revolutionary War. He was a member of the House of Representatives 1789-1791 and served two terms in the Senate 1793-1795 and 1801-1806. He was governor of Georgia 1798-1801. James Gunn (1753-1801) was also a Savannah attorney who served as a general in the Georgia militia. He was a senator from Georgia 1789-1801 (*BDAC*).

To the Committee of Public Safety

Paris 2[8]ᵗʰ Janʸ 1795.[1]

I have thought proper to present to your view in the enclosed paper the situation of the United States in relation to the river Missisipi, and respecting which a negotiation is now depending with the court of Spain. This paper opens fully this interesting subject in its relation to both republics, and which it is proper you should be correctly informed of, at the present time. France can only assist in opening the river by inviting the American Minister Mᵣ Short to act in concert with her, when she shall conclude her treaty with that power, and which by her permission I can easily accomplish: or by comprising it in her own Treaty. I have no power to treat upon this subject otherwise than by bringing it thus before you for the purpose of ascertaining what your disposition is upon it; and which with any comments you may be pleased to make I shall be happy immediately to communicate to the American Government.

Enclosure:
Notes Respecting the River Mississippi:
Communicated to the Committee of Public Safety

Paris 25 Janʸ 1795

The River Missisipi extends from about the 48 degree of Nᵒ Latitude to the 29 where it empties into the gulph of Mexico running nearly a north and south course and through a tract of the most fertile country in the world.

It bounds the United States to the west from Lat. 31. to its source, an extent pursuing the course of the river, of about 2000 miles.

Many rivers empty into the Missisipi on the East, the principal of which are the Illinois and the Ohio, and which with their branches spread thro the whole of the western interior of the United States and make it a most delightful region. Other rivers empty into it from the west of which the Missouri is the most important. This latter has never been traced to its source, altho' voyagers have passed up it, above 1500 Miles: It is however believed that it penetrates further into the bosom of the continent, than the Missisipi itself.

The whole of that portion of the United States lying westward of the Alleghany mountains, and which comprizes about one half the territory within the said states, depends upon this river for the export of its productions to foreign markets. It comprehends a portion of the territory of several of the existing states perhaps one third of Pennsylvania, Virginia, Nᵒ Carolina and Georgia; the whole of Kentucky and an immense tract of vacant territory lying between the Ohio and the Missisipi, and which has already been laid out into five separate States, and which are to be admitted into the Union with the same rights, as the old States, when they shall respectively attain a certain number of Inhabitants. Of these it is proposed to settle one only at a time, and of which the first has already been commenced.

When we examine the extent of this Territory, its fertility superior to that of the old States, the felicity of its climate lying all within the temperate zone, the kind and quality of its productions, such as hemp, flour, corn, in short every thing necessary in human life, protected in its infant settlement by the Government of the United States, and admitted as soon as it shall attain a certain degree of maturity to equal membership with them, we are compelled to appreciate it more highly, than any other vacant tract known upon the Globe.

Its settlement is of importance to all those European countries whose inhabitants are engaged in manufactures, because it will furnish in abundance rude materials for every species of manufacture: to those which have occasion at times for the supply of provisions, because it will furnish an exhaustless source of every species of provision: but it is of peculiar importance to those which have Islands in the West Indies, because it lies in the neighbourhood of those Islands, the mouth of the Missisipi being nearly in the same latitude, and will furnish every thing in demand there, such as lumber provisions &c.

But the Commerce of this country when settled will depend upon the navigation of the Missisipi and of course, the settlement itself will depend upon the same cause. This was secured by a treaty of Peace between the United States and Great Britain in 1783 but has hitherto been prevented by Spain, from motives equally unjust and illiberal. A negotiation, the object of which on our part is to open it, is and has been depending with that power since that time.

At the time our peace was made with England, the importance of this country was little known in her councils: it is said that her negociators did not even know on which side of the lakes and of course within whose jurisdiction the forts, which have since been the subject of contention, lay: but its importance was soon afterwards understood, and from which time it is certain that Britain has regarded it with particular attention, in hopes either of gaining it to herself, or otherwise making it subservient to her schemes of policy. With this view she refused to surrender the posts, excited the Indians to make war on our frontiers, encouraged Spain to refuse our right to the navigation of the Missisipi, and did us other injuries of the same kind.

It is certain that the western people will sooner or later open this river, either by negotiation or by force, and more than probable that England retaining as she still does her resentment against the old States for their independence, and against France for the aid given in that war, will watch the uneasiness of the Western People, on account of the obstructed navigation of the river, and improve it into an opportunity of separating the new from the old States, and connecting them with her Interest in Canada by undertaking to open the Missisipi to both countries: and with that view it is said that she has long had agents there to treat upon this subject, and that nothing has prevented her success but the attachment the people have to their bretheren in the old states, their repugnance to become the sport of foreign politics; and which would follow their separation; and the particular enmity they bear to that power. Next to conquest, separation would be the most advantageous arrangement for Britain, for in consequence, and especially if opened under her auspices, she would become the ally of the western states, and play them off against the Eastern, whereby their importance and weight in the scale of nations, would be diminished, if not destroyed. Many believe, and with this view, that she was at the bottom of the late insurrection on the frontier and which grew out of the discontents proceeding from the occlusion of the river.

But the same motive which inclines England to promote the separation of the new from the old States should dispose France to prevent it. As they now stand, the whole are the allies and the friends of France, and whilst they remain united they will continue so: by the separation therefore Britain might gain but France could not.

It is then the Interest of France to keep the whole of this territory under the same government: but this cannot be done unless the intrigues of England be defeated, and the Missisipi opened under the patronage of the United States. It is therefore the interest of France to yield her aid to her ally, to open this river and which at the present crisis would most probably produce a decisive effect. Nor would her retribution be limited to those considerations only, which have been already mentioned. Experience has shewn that those alliances are not only the most beneficial but likewise most durable, which are founded equally in the affection and the interest of the parties, and by this act of friendship France would establish a claim to the gratitude of the American people, which by pervading every quarter would reach the heart of every citizen. It would be known to the present race and remembered by posterity, that by the aid of France, the old States were enabled to gain their independence, and that likewise by her aid the new States commenced their settlement grew up to the enjoyment of their rights, and attained their maturity.

In the present state of the War with Spain it is presumed that France may obtain what is here proposed, and indeed infinitely more, either in the Islands or even in South America, and without the least difficulty. Her system is a system of freedom to the world, as well in respect to the rights of nations as of men: it is therefore hoped she will avail herself of the present opportunity not only to verify that fact, but to manifest at the same time, the pleasure with which she embraces every opportunity that occurs to promote the interest of her ally.

Copy, NN: Monroe Papers. An extract in French, dated 3 Nivose An 4 (24 December 1795) is in DLC: FCP—France.

1. The date has been written over and is difficult to read. The Committee, in its acknowledgement of the receipt of this letter on February 5 (below), gives the date as 9 Pluviose, which corresponds with January 28.

From Ralph Izard

Philadelphia Jany 29th 1795.

Dear Sir

My Son George[1] has chosen the military Profession, & it is my desire to give him the best education in that Line which can be procured, as it may at some future day enable him to render service to his Country. This business has occasioned me very great anxiety on his account; not having been able to determine what would be the best plan to obtain the object intended. I have consulted the President on the subject, & he advises me to send him directly to France, & have him placed in one of the Institutions in that Country, where he will have an opportunity of qualifying himself in every branch of his Profession, better than in any other part of the World. Feeling very sensibly the interest which the President has been so good as to take in the welfare of my Son, & having the highest confidence in his judgment, I have determined to follow his advice. I have several times conversed with Mr Randolph on the subject; he is likewise of opinion that my Son should be sent to France for his education, & assured me that you would undertake the superintendence, & direction of the business for me.[2] I felt a repugnance at giving you the trouble, to which I knew you must be subjected by undertaking such an arrangement. But the friendly part that Mr Randolph has taken in the business, has induced me to request the favor of you to be troubled with the direction of it. My Son is at present at Marbourg in Germany, where he was placed by Mr Pinckney, & where he has been pursuing such a course of studies as are necessary to qualify him for the military Profession. My desire is that he should be a good Engineer, & Artillery Officer, & that he should likewise be made as perfect as possible in the business of an Officer of the Ponts, et Chaussèes. This includes Drawing, Surveying, Dams, Water Courses, Mills, Bridges, Hydraulic & other Machines, & every sort of Architecture. This education is, in my judgment, the best that can be devised for him. If his Country should have occasion for him as an Officer, he will be able to serve her. If he should quit the military Profession, & dwindle into a Planter, he will always find those branches of knowledge highly useful to him in his retirement. Under the old Government of France, the best Institution for the education of an Engineer was at Mezières in Champagne. Probably at present, the best will be that mentioned in the enclosed Law Nº 350; & if you find it to be the best, it will be a satisfaction to me to learn that he has undergone the examination prescribed by the 2ᵈ Article, with reputation, & that he has been admitted en qualité d'eleve. I have written to Mʳ Pinckney, & desired him to have my Son sent to you in Paris early in the Spring, & I request that you will as soon as you can, take measures to have him properly placed. If the Institution is in a Garrison Town, at some distance from Paris, I think it better than in the Capital. The less my Son is in Paris, the more agreeable it will be to me. He is between 18 & 19 years old; this is too young for him to be entirely his own Master, without any restraint, or control. If therefore in the Institution, some sensible Man of good character could be engaged, to pay particular attention to him, & act the part of a Mentor, it would give me much satisfaction, & I would willingly allow him any gratuity that might be thought reasonable for his trouble. I have done everything in my power hitherto, to have him as well educated as possible, & believe he is a good Mathematician for his age. His capacity is good, & if he is placed under the direction of able Instructors, I have no doubt he will become a good Officer, & have it in his power to render essential service to his Country. This is the time of Life, at which he may be made a useful, & valuable Member of Society. But if he should neglect his business, or fall into improper company, he may give me reason to repent of my having sent him to Europe. There will not, I hope, be any objection to his being admitted into the Institution, established for the education of Engineers, on account of his not being a Citizen of France. He is a Lieutenant in the Corps of Artillerists, & Engineers, established by Congress last Session. My wish is that he should not for the present enter into actual service; but employ himself diligently in perfecting himself in the theoretic part of his Profession. It is not however my desire that he should be exempted from the contingent duty pointed out in the 16ᵗʰ Article of the enclosed Law. I do not know what will be the best mode of supplying you with money for my Son's expences. If Bills of Exchange on London were negotiable in Paris, the matter would be easy. I have written to my Merchant in London, Mʳ Henry M. Bird, & desired him to make some arrangement, by which you may be supplied with money for the use of my Son; & if it cannot be done by a direct communication with London, probably it may by way of Hamburgh. When my Son arrives in Paris & should be obliged to you if you would write to Mʳ Bird on the subject, & settle some plan with him, by which you may be regularly supplied at particular periods, as the money may be wanted for the use of my Son. What his annual expences may be I can not tell. I have recommended economy to him, & hope he will pay attention to my recommendation; not only because it will be more convenient to my Finances, but because I think that extravagance will be prejudicial to him. I should think that after he is settled at his studies, his expences, including his education, cloaths, and everything will not much exceed Two Hundred Pounds Sterling a year. Through I wish him to avoid all useless expence, yet I am desirous that he should have everything that is necessary, & which can be of service to him. You will soon be able to form a judgment respecting his expences, & will be so good as to write to me on the subject. I have delivered to Mʳ Randolph Twelve Hundred Livres in gold, & requested him to send it to you by the first opportunity for the use of my Son. This I have done, lest there should be in the beginning some difficulty in the business; & I shall be glad to learn that you have made such an arrangement with Mʳ Bird as that you shall receive from him regular supplies for the use of my Son. I think he is too young for the money to pass through his hands. If a Mentor could be found for him in the Institution who would trouble himself with the care of his expenditures, it would be more agreeable to me. He has hitherto been allowed two guineas a Month pocket money. I think that enough now but if you are of opinion a small addition might be made to this article without disadvantage, I shall have no objection to it. Perhaps it may be necessary to transmit to him a Passport, before he can be admitted into France. If so, I should be obliged to you if you would send it to him. He lives at the House of Professor de Beauclair in the University of Marbourg, in Germany. I request my Compliments may be presented to Mrs Monroe, & am, Dear Sir Your most obedient Servant

Ra. Izard.

You will direct your Letters to Mr Bird in the care of Messrs Bird, Savage, & Bird Merchants in London; & your Letters to me in Charleston, South Carolina.

I enclose a Letter for my Son, & request the favor of you to sent it to him.

RC, NjMoHP

1. George Izard (1776-1828) was born in London. He moved to South Carolina in 1783 when his parents returned home. He graduated from King's College (now Columbia University) in 1792 and then attended military academies in England, Scotland, and Germany. He was a student at École du Génie, a prestigious military school in Metz, 1795-1797. He was commissioned a lieutenant in the U. S. Army in 1794 and rose to the rank of major general during the War of 1812. He served as governor of Arkansas Territory 1825-1828. He and JM became life-long friends (*ANB*).

2. Edmund Randolph wrote to JM on 5 February 1795 asking him to assist George Izard (*Catalogue of Monroe's Papers*, 1: 41).

From Benjamin Vaughan

Basle, Jany 29, 1795.

Dear sir,

By your silence, I am inclined to think that two letters which I have had the pleasure to address to you have miscarried. I presume to send you copies of them.—A friend of mine will call upon you to concert measures with you respecting me, which I hope will be the last trouble which will be occasioned by, dear sir, Your respectful & very sincere humble serv^t

Basle, Decr 18, 1794.

Dear sir,

I am honored with your favors of the 23rd ult^o & the 4th inst^t the last arriving only a day or two ago.[1] Your silence no longer embarrasses me; I submit chearfully to necessary evils; & I claim leave to explain only a few particulars.

You were misinformed, but I trust not imposed upon, by those who stated to you M^r B's pretensions.[2] That gentleman has indeed been in America, but only to fight against it; for by birth & descent he is Irish; & the situation of his wife only resembles, but is less strong than mine. I was not out of order therefore in citing this case.

I scarcely perused Mr Pinckney's letter regarding Mr Russel, though empowered to do it; for it reached me in company, when the post was waiting.[3] Without adverting to the treaty between America & France, I thought that as between friendly powers, any person who was in the <u>act</u> of becoming an American citizen, ought by the French to be deemed as such already; at least as to his person, if not as to his property; & under this rule I felt myself comprized.

I am ready to acknowledge the diplomatic delicacies which you state.—I should ill deserve justice for myself, did I not render it to you.

I was so far from approving the doctrines respecting citizenship which I cited, that I expressly stated, that I would not pretend that what was law on this subject, was also reason.—What for example can shew less of reason, than to consider citizenship as something <u>distinctive</u>; & yet as capable of existing in the same individual towards two states? Thus the family of my wife, though known to have resolved to continue as English, are all made Danes by an act signed by the King of Denmark; merely to encourage their investments in the Danish West Indies.—Miss Laurens, the niece of my wife, as part of that family & as born in England, is English & Danish; & had she taken an oath while she resided in America, as she has property there, she would be an American also.[4] Perhaps indeed, as your American oath is an oath of abnegation towards Great Britain, there is something contradictory in this; but without difficulty, she might be French, as well as Danish & American, that is, she might belong to <u>three</u> states, all capable of being at war with each other.—What could be more contrary to sense, than the history of neutral [bur]ghership during the American war; by which so many subjects of the belligerent powers (not forgetting the Americans themselves) protected themselves against capture by sea?—The Swiss abound in instances of triplicate & other more multiplied combinations of citizenship; to say nothing of their well known privileges in France.—I have been assured also, that the Duke of Richmond remained to the last a peer of France, & even sent over his proxy against some of the early French reforms, as Duke of Aubigny; though he himself is an English legislator & a reformer.[5]—These facts therefore prove, that the <u>practice</u>, which ultimately is all that constitutes the <u>law</u> of nations, is not very rigid as to citizenship.

Jan.ʸ 12, 1795

I had designed here to introduce some English law, to do justice either to you or to myself, respecting the mode of preserving English citizenship to those born in foreign parts of English parents; but I cannot, after the search of near a month, discover Blackstone's commentaries to exist, either in French or English, in the whole republic of Basle. I once studied enough of English law to enable me not only heartily to despise it, but to be surprized that the American revolution could ever be thought compleat, while the English law made a part of American jurisprudence and, under such impressions, you will not wonder if my remembrance of the English law is imperfect.—But in passing over this subject, I beg to assure you, that when I spoke of the English law in this particular, it was not only from the impression left on my mind respecting the language of it; but from my acquaintance with persons born abroad, who are reputed as English, from having an English parentage, though not born in the house of an English minister. My friend the celebrated M.ʳ Cavendish, who was born in Italy, I conceive to be of this description;[6] as well as others of my acquaintance; & some of these, who were born in the Turkish dominions, had even a Greek mother. I never heard of any oaths of allegiance being taken by any of these persons, to heal the defect of their not being born under a diplomatic roof; & these oaths as you know, are only administered in England upon extraordinary occasions, except to persons in public situations.—As to myself, you will allow that one circumstance has been physically impossible to me; namely that I should have been born in the house of an American minister, before such ministers existed.

But if we consult what is reason, and what therefore ought to be the law, I think we shall find, that men in general ought to be allowed easily to assume, & easily to resign their citizenship; making at the same time a strong distinction between the <u>resident</u> citizen & the <u>travelling</u> citizen. A state can seldom depend upon a reciprocity of duties from the travelling citizen; & yet no citizen is more likely than himself to compromize his country, even to the extent of producing war.—Such a distinction naturally militates against my own case; but I have repeatedly intimated, that reason is against me. You add, that law is also unfavorable to me; & as I have no means of contending against this assertion, I cease to press the subject. You will certainly however forgive the notice which I have taken of it; since it has only been designed to prove, that I did not speak without consideration in my former letters.

If I understand you right, you have protected others within the influence of a given government, where you had the <u>concurrence</u> of that government, notwithstanding there was some defect in the claim of the parties, generally considered. This species of protection I may still have to ask at your hands; trusting to your flag for what regards the seas.—In the interim, if you favor me with the letters requested for Mr Ochs, the Chancellor of this republic,[7] couched in the terms proposed, which have been arranged with him, (pursuant to the suggestion received through Mr Van Staphorst;) I may probably be safe at Basle; & not impossibly be useful in that case to America, or at least to those greater interests to which no American will be insensible.

I return you many thanks for your obliging expressions towards myself & my family.

I doubt whether Dr Franklin knew as much of my proceedings in 1782-3, as Mr Jay; to insert a full account of them in his journal.

There is another diplomatic journal, that of the Vice-president Adams, an extract from which has laid me open in England to some inconvenience, which the author (who does me the honor to call himself my friend) never intended; & which the citer, Mr Jefferson, another of my friends, as little foresaw the effect of as Mr Adams. I am made to ask for materials to "<u>run down the American loyalists.</u>" (See the printed correspondence between Mr Jefferson & Mr Hammond respecting the peace of 1782.) In the war of 1756 when the letters sent from the army to London were opened, Dr Brocklesby having stated in his, that he had made some unexpected cures, the person charged with this business, by way of minute, wrote down; "<u>Dr Brocklesby is surprized with his own success.</u>"[8] My conversation has been epitomized in a like unfortunate manner. It is indeed plain that Mr Adams does not follow my own words; for he makes me call Mr Secretary Townshend, Lord Townshend; though this person was not made a peer till some time afterwards, under the title of Lord Sydney.[9] He also give me an American phrase, absolutely unknown in England, when he makes me speak of Mrs V.[10]—The truth is, that Mr Adams was principally concerned on his side, to shew what arguments he had employed respecting the American loyalists; it being only important to name me, in order to shew how those arguments came to be called for—On my side, I must frankly confess, that I was ignorant of the proceedings of some of the loyalists at that time; & as the American negotiation was partly stopped by what [related] to them, it was but fair, if it was expected that the British minister should give way with respect to them, that they should be informed of what those loyalists had done that was wrong. My conversation on this subject could have no other object. That the tenor of it was not given to lenity or insensibility, will appear from these facts; I had relations, property, & character at stake; & I had written a strong memorial to Dr Franklin in favor of these loyalists, which fortunately for me was copied by a loyalist friend then at Paris, & which induced Dr Franklin to write somewhat in favor of lenity towards them in his letters to America—Forgive this detail I pray you, Sir; believe it only intended as explanatory; & as not in the least designed to impeach our friends named in it, for whom I feel a peculiar respect & affection.

I beg permission to trouble you with a letter to forward to London when you have a good private opportunity. Mr Pinckney will convey it to the party, & it is left open to shew you how innocent is the nature of it.—I beg to trouble you also with another letter for America. I have the honor to be with great respect & great esteem, dear sir, your very sincere humble serv^t.

NB. I have to remark with respect to the above letter. 1°. That it shews, that (notwithstanding I have a mother born in the United States & a father who is a citizen of the United States,) yet that you refused to acknowledge me as a citizen; <u>which can do you no harm.</u> 2°. That although the paragraph respecting Mr Adams is rendered more superfluous, by a conversation which his son has lately had with my family; I should here suppress it; did I not think it proper, as the letter has miscarried to all appearance, that you should see that I had in nothing compromised you in it.

Mem^m. The first letter here, copied, went under cover to M^r — our common friend. The second letter went under cover to him, but was again inclosed under the cover of <u>his</u> friend.—It appears that you are therefore somewhat less confidentially considered than heretofore, on account of the treaty concluded by Mr Jay; & that our common friend is more looked after on account of the proceedings with Holland.—Letters going out of France are little examined; & you will be told how yours to me will arrive without fail.

RC: NN: Monroe Papers. Unsigned.

1. JM's letters to Benjamin Vaughan of 23 November and 4 December 1794 have not been located.

2. Mr. Bingham. See Philibert Buchot to JM, 6 September 1794, above.

3. Mr. Russell was taken prisoner from an American ship. See Thomas Pinckney to JM, 10 October 1794, above.

4. Vaughan was married to Sarah Manning, whose niece, Martha Manning, had married John Laurens of South Carolina, an American revolutionary and diplomat in London in 1776. Their daughter, to whom Vaughan refers, was Frances Eleanor "Fanny" Laurens (1777-1860) who received land holdings in South Carolina upon the death of her grandfather, Henry Laurens, in 1792 (*Papers of Henry Laurens* 15: 388).

5. Charles Richmond (1735-1806) was the Duke of Richmond in England and the Duke of Aubigny in France (*DNB*).

6. Henry Cavendish (1731-1810) was a scientist distinguished for his research into the properties of heat and atmosphere. He was born in Nice, which at the time belonged to Italy. He resided in London but visited Paris often (Alan Valentine, *The British Establishment, 1760-1784*, 158-159).

7. Peter Ochs (1752-1821) was a Swiss revolutionary who wrote most of the constitution of the Helvetian Republic in 1798 (*Encyclopedia Britannica*). Vaughan inclosed a draft of a proposed letter to Ochs asking that Vaughan be allowed to stay in Basel.

8. Richard Brocklesby (1722-1797) was a prominent London physician whose most famous patient was Samuel Johnson (*DNB*).

9. Thomas Townshend, Viscount Sydney (1732-1800) entered Parliament in 1754 as a Whig. He joined Pitt in opposition to Grenville; became lord of the treasury; then in 1767 became a member of the Privy Council. Townshend remained in opposition to the North Ministry, and spoke frequently in the House of Commons against the American War. When Shelburne became prime minister in 1782, Townshend succeeded him as secretary of state for the Home Office, and continued in the office under Pitt 1783-1789 (*DNB*).

10. Sarah Manning Vaughan.

To Joseph Jones

Paris Feby 1. 1795.

Dear Sir

I have lately been favored with yours of the   of   last. You have no doubt long since rec^d two or three of mine apprizing you of our arrival and whatever else appertained to use as well as the publick on this theatre up to their respective dates.[1] The sum of what has since followed may be comprized in a small space. Within the last week the French have actually taken Amsterdam[2] & the whole of the province of Holland, with the forts of Breda, Bergen Op-zoom &c and threaten the entire conquest of the whole of the 7. provinces. The Stadholder with his family made his escape & whither is unknown but presumed either to Engl^d or Prussia. Before this last event a minister had arrived from the States gen^l who had offered great sums, the forts the fleet &c, but he was amused & the army ordered to the advance. The extent & details of the acquisition are not fully known as yet, nor is it known how this country will be considered, but I am inclined to think that the French will ostensibly leave them to arrange their own aff^rs, (intending absolutely ultimately so to do) but confide only in the patriots & thereby favor & effect a revolution. Engl^d will most sensibly feel this event: indeed I suspect it is but the commencment of her misfortunes, for it is certainly the intention of France to crush her if possible. Nor will this be avoidable if the other powers are detach'd & the Holland fleet taken. Within a few days a minister Baron Stahl arrived from Sweden,[3] and a Count Carliti from Tuscany,[4] & tis said that Baron Golz from Prussia[5] is on the way so that these powers want no invitation (the Tuscan it is presumed comes on behalf of the Emperor) to abandon Engl^d. The eyes of the world are cast upon her & her fate is deemed almost inevitable and yet none pity her. In my next I shall be able to give more comprehensive details.

In other respects the aff^rs of the republick flourish much. The people are contented, of which the best proof in this city has lately been shewn, by the patience with which they have borne the severest winter known for many years past, altho' there was the worst possible provision made for such incident. The public councils are it is true sometimes somewhat animated, & now and then the head of a capital offender is taken off as was lately done of Carrier the infamous representative at Nantes—but yet no danger threatens from this source. With respect to our own aff^rs they may be said to be on a good footing. They have actually agreed to execute the treaty of commerce whereby our flag will protect enemy's goods. Some uneasiness is entertained upon the subject of Jay's treaty but it is hoped when it is seen it will appear that there is no cause for it: after which every thing will be right again.

I transmit by this opportunity to Mr Randolph the order for 3000 dol^rs it was intended I sho^d receive here. It was detained to be committed to the minister ab^t to depart but his delay continuing I have forwarded it to Bordeaux to be sent by some safe Captn. I have directed this money to be paid to you.

I am extremely glad to hear that you have purchased Carters land. You will of course apply this sum in that & other purposes according to y^r own judgment & knowledge of my affairs. I suspect you will not be able to apply any to the claims of Virg^a officers, tho' certainly the profit wo^d be immense, for be assured land there will soon rise greatly—surpassing what you have any idea of. And with respect to my brothers I can add nothing wishing you to do for them what you can within the limits and according to what I have heretofore intimated: as likewise my sister. Joseph[6] is well and since my last, his conduct has been much improved. He begins to understand the French which was prerequisite to every thing. He has grown very perceptibly & seems inclined to corpulent. Mrs M. & child are well & who with Joe desire to be affectionately remembered to you. You will be so kind as remember me to Mr Jefferson & family and to my other neighbours. I shall probably write to Joseph.[7] I hope my people do not suffer & particularly Peter & Thena to whom remember us.[8] With great sincerity I am yr affectionate friend & serv^t

Ja^s Monroe

RC, ViW: Monroe Papers

1. No letters from Jones to JM in Paris prior to this date have been located. JM's letter to Jones of 4 September 1794 (above) is the only letter to Jones from France in 1794 that has been located.

2. The French army under Pichegru entered Amsterdam on 20 January 1795 (Martyn Lyons, *France under the Directory*, 241).

3. Eric Magnus, Baron Staël-Holstein (d. 1802) was the Swedish ambassador to France 1783-1799. His wife, Madame de Staël was a renowned author and salonist in Paris (*Nouvelle Biographie Générale*).

4. Francesco Saverio Carletti (1740-1803) arrived in Paris as minister from Tuscany in January 1795 (*Dizionario Biographica Degli Italiani*).

5. Bernhard Wilhelm, Baron von Goltz (1730-1795) was an aide-de-camp to Prussian emperor Frederick II before embarking on his diplomatic career. He undertook missions to Paris in 1772, 1792, and 1794 (*Nouvelle Biographie Générale*).

6. Joseph Jones, Jr.

7. Joseph Jones Monroe.

8. Peter may have been the husband of Thenia Hemings. Annette Gordon-Reed says in her book *The Hemingses of Monticello* (482-483) that Thenia may have requested Jefferson to sell her to JM so that she could be united with her husband.

To Edmund Randolph

Paris 1ˢᵗ February 1795.

Sir,

I was lately informed by Mᴿ Jay that it was his intention to communicate to me the contents of his treaty with the British administration,[1] and as I knew the good effect which correct information upon that point would produce upon our affairs here, admitting it to be as heretofore represented, I thought it my duty to endeavour to avail myself of it as soon as possible. But as the communication promised was to be in cypher, and Mᴿ Morris had taken his copy with him, I knew that I should not be able to comprehend it in case it was received. I therefore deemed the acquisition of it an object of sufficient importance to authorise the expence of an especial dispatch to London to obtain it, and have in consequence committed that trust to Mᴿ Purvyance of Baltimore who left this immediately after the receipt of Mᴿ Jay's letter, and who was likewise instructed to bring me a copy of Mᴿ Pinckney's cypher for future use. By his return I hope to be enabled to remove all uneasiness upon that head, and in which I am the more confident, from a knowledge that the government here is well disposed to view it, with the utmost liberality.

I was also lately informed by a letter from Mᴿ Fenwick,[2] that he understood that Mᴿ Muscoe Livingston,[3] who had not long since arrived from Lisbon, that Colᵒ Humphreys had sailed thence for Algiers upon the business as was presumed intrusted to him with that regency, and that prior to his departure he had committed to him a message for me to be communicated in person: Mᴿ Fenwick adds that Mᴿ Livingston was taken sick, and in consequence deprived of his senses, just as he was about to set out from Bordeaux for Paris whereby he was not only rendered unable to proceed on his journey, but even to communicate to him the purport of his message for me. Thus I am left in perfect ignorance, equally of Colᵒ Humphreys' wishes, the time of his departure, and plan of operation. I intimated to you before that, although I had written to Colᵒ Humphreys for information upon that point,[4] and with the view of forwarding his wishes to the utmost of my power, yet I was fearful, in consideration of those embarrassments which were inseparable from the war, it would be difficult to concert any plan of harmonious operation, which should commence and proceed from such distant points, whereby the aid of this republic would be yeilded us in that negotiation: under present circumstances therefore you will readily perceive, that it has become altogether impossible.

The French troops have at length entered Amsterdam whereby the whole of the province of Holland was brought immediately under the power of this republic, as indeed the whole of the 7 United Provinces most probably soon will be. This was announced a few days past to the convention by a letter from the deputies in that quarter, two of whom it is said are on their way to render an account in detail, of this very important acquisition. It is reported that Breda and Bergenopzoom have surrendered: indeed the general idea is that no further opposition will be made there to the French Arms, and of course that this republic will become possessed of the fleet and immense stores of every kind. The Prince of Orange with his family, accompanied by several members of the states general, had made their escape, but by what rout, and whether for London or Berlin is unknown.

After the entry of the French into Amsterdam was certain, and in consequence the entire conquest of the seven provinces more than probable, an effort was made by the States general to yeild the same thing upon terms, for the purpose of putting this republic in possession of the country by treaty instead of conquest: and with this view an agent who arrived here about a fortnight before that event, was dispatched, and who offered as I am well assured, to surrender all the important fortifications of the country, and to provide at their own expense and for the residue of the war, quarters and provisions for such forces as should be deemed adequate to hold them, to yeild immediately 25 sail of the line, and likewise to pay at stated times, convenient for both parties, the sum of 300,000,000 of florins. But it was known by the committee that without an accident as much might be gained and perhaps more by conquest: that the latter mode which knew of no condition, freed them from fetters and of course from the possibility of any future imputation of breach of treaty, and of violated faith. The agent however who was an ancient Minister of that government here, was suffered to remain and treated with respect, whilst orders were issued to the troops to advance and which were obeyed.

There arrived about the same time a deputation from the patriots who associating with Mr Vanstaphorst[5] and one or two others of those who were banished from their country in 1787, endeavoured to counteract the movements of the agent from the States general, and to attract to that body the attention of the Convention. Before the entry into Amsterdam they wished admittance to the bar as well for that purpose as to sound the disposition of the convention in regard to the future fate of Holland. But in that stage it was evaded, perhaps from policy, perhaps from the real impropriety of expressing any opinion upon that point in the then state of affairs, or perhaps indeed from the impossibility of forming one. But since that event they were admitted and with an address founded on it, though in other respects adapted as was before intended. The answer of the President was respectful, but cautious, for whilst it breathed a spirit of patriotism, and of particular regard for the <u>ancient</u> virtues of the Belgic confederacy,[6] and of course, left them no cause of complaint, it carefully avoided all compromitment of the government itself.

What will be the future fate of those provinces is altogether uncertain, and must be in a great measure dependant on events. At present I am satisfied there is no settled plan on that head, nor indeed is it possible there should be within so short a space of time. Many members, and among those some of distinguished weight in the Convention seem disposed to extend the future boundary of the republic to the Rhine, and of course to comprehend within its limits, all that part of them lying on this side of that river. This idea was lately avowed by Boissy d'Anglas a member of the committee of public safety, in a speech delivered apparantly by authority of that body, and for the purpose equally of sounding the Convention upon the conditions of peace, to ascertain such as they would approve, and of announcing in that informal manner to the parties concerned the ultimate upon which they might expect it. In this he proposes that the Republic shall be hereafter bounded only "by the Ocean, the Mountains and the great Rivers." Be this however as it may I think it certain, unless the fortune of the war should inspire other councils, that the whole of these provinces will be retained in the hands of this republic until its termination, and be made in the progress as instrumental to that event, in its favor, as circumstances will admit of.

But even in case they be not dismembered yet a revolution in their government seems to be unavoidable. Their strong posts, their harbours, perhaps their fleet, will be under the controul of France, and of course their councils likewise will be so. Ancient forms may for a while remain, but it is not possible under circumstances of this kind, that they should be more than forms. Half the political regulations of the country, perhaps the whole, will proceed from the representatives of this republic with the army; nor will any of its inhabitants, other than those of decided patriotism, be employed by them in any office of trust or profit. Thus the weight and authority of the government will be gradually transferred to the popular scale. The people at large will soon take the admonition, and from that moment the ancient fabric which was before tottering will be levelled with the ground. The ordinary allurements of freedom are sufficiently great to the mass of mankind to require no additional recommendation in its favour, and the hand of power must be strong where it is not pursued with effect; but in the present instance the additional inducement will be great, for as it is known that this republic can repose no confidence in the existing government and especially in the house of Orange, and which might not be the case and most probably would not, with that, which would succeed a revolution, so it must be equally obvious that its continuance, will furnish a strong argument here for the dismemberment. This consideration therefore will add a new stimulus to all those, who incline rather to preserve the independence of their country, than become reduced into a few departments of France.

Before this great achievement and which resembles more an exploit of the ancient Roman empire than those of modern Princes, there was a collection of diplomatic characters, formal and informal, from several of the powers at war, and others friendly to some of them, at Basle in Switzerland, and who expected to be met there by some agent or agents from this Republic, to commence the negotiation for peace. But as soon as they heard of this event that prospect vanished, and tis said that some of them have retired home, and others arrived here to confer more directly with the government itself. Count Cartely from Florence[7] and Baron Stahl from Denmark,[8] men said to be friendly to the french revolution, are those only who are known, and the latter is supposed rather to expect than to have brought his credentials with him.

I herewith transmit to you some communications received from M̲r̲ Skipwith, and which will shew the state of the Bordeaux and S̲t̲ Domingo claims,[9] and I beg of you to be assured of the unremitted attention which I shall continue to pay to these concerns, and indeed to every other in which my country-men are interested. With great respect and esteem, I have the honor to be your most ob̲t̲ and very humble servant.

Ja̲s̲ Monroe.

Feb̲y̲ 5.

P. S. Since the above was written some details have been received of the success of the French in the U. Netherlands, and by which it appears that every thing which was predicted in that respect has been verified. Williamstadt, Breda, Gorcum, Bergen-op-zoom, the fleet held by ice in the Texel &c are all taken.[10] I enclose however the papers containing those accounts.

Copy, DNA: RG 59: Dispatches from France

1. John Jay to JM, 28 November 1794, above.

2. The letter from Joseph Fenwick has not been located.

3. Muscoe Livingston (d. 1798) was a Norfolk, Virginia, sea captain (*William & Mary Quarterly*, series 1, 13: 263).

4. JM to David Humphreys, 11 November 1794, above.

5. Jacob Van Staphorst was part of a group that represented Francophile interests in the 1780s in Amsterdam. Their ambition after the fall of the House of Orange was to become the new leaders of the Dutch provinces (Simon Schama, *Patriots and Liberators*, 121, 214).

6. The Belgic confederacy was initially a loose republican confederacy formed by the Union of Utrecht in 1579 after the expulsion of the Spanish from the Netherlands. The confederacy, known as the Seven United Provinces, was governed by the statholder as chief executive and the stats-general, a legislative body comprised of representatives of the provinces. (Simon

Schama, *Patriots and Liberators*, 46). Americans were familiar with the Belgic confederacy as an example of a republican confederation. Madison discussed its virtues and vices in *The Federalist*, number twenty.

7. Francesco Saverio Carletti.

8. Baron de Staël represented Sweden, not Denmark.

9. The Skipwith reports regarding Bordeaux and Santo Domingo have not been located.

10. After the Dutch towns of Bergen-op-Zoom, Breda, and Gorcum (Goringen) surrendered, Pichegru's troops continued north where they discovered and captured most of the Dutch fleet icebound off the coast of Texel, the island opposite the tip of the peninsula between the North Sea and the Zuiderzee. (Adolphe Thiers, *L'Histoire de la Révolution Française* 7: 22).

From the Committee of Public Safety

Paris le 17 Pluviôse l'an 3ᵉ de la
Rèpublique française une & indivisible ([5] Fevrier 1795.)[1]

Nous avons reçu avec votre lettre du 9. Pluviôse, la note instructive de la situation des Etats-Unis relativement au fleuve Mississippi.

Nous reconnaissons par l'empressement que vous mettez à ce que nous soyons pleinement informés de vos dispositions dans la négociation de cette affaire, que rien de ce qui peut resserrer les liens de l'amitié et de la bonne harmonie entre les deux premieres Republiques du monde ne vous est étranger ou indiférent.

Nous vous remercions des idées que vous nous avez communiquées: nous allons les approfondir; et nous vous ferons passer incessamment nos observations sur votre note. Nous apprécions d'avance les motifs de cette communication loyale.

Cambaceres, Pelet, Merlin (d.d.)

Editors' Translation

Paris, 17 Pluviôse year 3 of the French Republic,
one & indivisible ([5] February 1795.)

We have received with your letter of 9 Pluviose,[2] a note explanatory of the situation of United States in regard to the Mississippi River.

We recognize from your attentiveness to ensure that we are fully informed of your actions in the negotiation of this business, that nothing escapes you which might confirm the bonds of friendship and good harmony between the two leading republics of the world.

We thank you for the ideas you have communicated. We will examine them and we will forward our observations on your note very shortly. We appreciate in advance the motives for this loyal communication.

Cambaceres, Pelet, Merlin (d.d.)

Copy, DNA : RG 59 : Dispatches from France; enclosed in JM to Edmund Randolph, 6 March 1795.

1. The clerk wrote 15 Fevrier 1795.

2. JM to the Committee of Public Safety, 28 January 1795, above.

From John Jay

London 5ᵗʰ February 1795.

Sir

I have received the Letter which you did me the Honour to write on the 17ᵗʰ of last month by Mʳ Purvyance.

It is much to be regretted that any unauthorized Accounts in English Newspapers of my "Adjustment with the British Administration," should have excited much uneasiness in the Councils of the French Government;—and the more so, as it does not imply that Confidence in the Honour and good Faith of the United States, which they certainly merit.

You must be sensible that the United States as a free and independant nation, have an unquestionable Right to make any pacific Arrangements with other Powers, which mutual Convenience may dictate,—provided those Arrangements do not contradict or oppugn their prior Engagements with other States.

Whether this Adjustment was consistent with our Treaty with France, struck me as being the only Question which could demand or receive the Consideration of that Republic, and I thought it due to the Friendship subsisting between the Two Countries, that the French Government should have, without Delay, the most perfect satisfaction on that Head.—I therefore by three Letters, vizᵗ of 24ᵗʰ 25ᵗʰ and 28ᵗʰ November 1794. gave You what I hoped would be very acceptable and satisfactory Information on that point:—I am happy in this opportunity of giving you an exact and literal Extract from the treaty;—it is in these Words—Vizᵗ

"Nothing in this Treaty contained, shall, however, be construed or operate contrary to former and existing Public Treaties with other Sovereigns or States."

Considering that Events favourable to our Country could not fail to give you pleasure I did intend to communicate to you concisely some of the most interesting particulars of this Treaty, but in the most perfect Confidence:—As that Instrument has not yet been ratified, nor received the ultimate forms necessary to give it validity;—As further Questions respecting parts of it may yet arise, and give occasion to further Discussion and Negotiations, so that if finally concluded at all, it may then be different from what it now is, the Impropriety of making it Public at present is palpable and obvious;—Such a Proceeding would be inconvenient and unprecedented;—It does not belong to Ministers who negotiate Treaties, to publish them even when perfected, much less Treaties not yet compleated and remaining open to alteration or Rejection;—such Acts belong exclusively to the Governments who form them.

I cannot but flatter myself that the French Government is too enlightened and reasonable to expect that any Consideration ought to induce me to overleap the bounds of my Authority, or to be negligent of the Respect which is due to the United States:—That respect and my obligations to observe it, will not permit me to give without Permission of their Government, a Copy of the Instrument in question to any person or for any purpose; and by no means for the purpose of being submitted to the Consideration and Judgment of the Councils of a foreign Nation, however friendly.

I will, Sir, take the earliest opportunity of transmitting a Copy of your Letter to me, and of this in answer to it, to the Secretary of State;—and will immediately and punctually execute such Orders and Instructions as I may receive on the Subject. I have the Honour to be with great Respect Sir your most Obedient Humble ser[vant]

John Jay

RC, ViU: Monroe Papers.

From Robert Brooke

In Council February 6th 1795 Richmond, Virginia.

Sir

You are not now to be informed, that the Assembly of Virginia, several years ago, voted a Statue of our then late Commander in Chief, General Washington, and directed their intention to be carried into effect by the Executive.

As mr Jefferson was then in France, his known taste in the execution of designs of that kind, as well as readiness on every occasion to gratify the wishes of his Country induced the Executive to solicit him to undertake the direction of it. To this he assented and in the year 1784, a considerable sum was remitted to and applied by him to commence the Work: but as it was not finished at the time he left Paris, and we have had no information since with respect to its progress or any estimate of the ultimate expence we are unable to determine what is still incumbent upon us to carry into effect the object of the Legislature.

Permit me therefore to request you will be so obliging as to make such enquiry as will trace this business to its present stage and communicate such information respecting it as will enable the Executive both to complete mr Jefferson's contract and attain the object of it.

Trusting that the recollection of the meritorious and signal services of the person whose memory this work is intended to perpetuate will render the execution of my request rather a pleasing than disagreeable employment, I will make no apology for the liberty I take in making it. I am Sir, with the most perfect Sentiments of esteem and respect, your most obedient Servant

R. Brooke

RC, ViU: Monroe Papers (photocopy)

JM was a member of the Continental Congress in July 1785 when he received a letter from Jefferson, then minister to France, requesting his help in obtaining a commission for Jean-Antoine Houdon to make a statue of George Washington. JM's efforts obtained £3000 from the state of Virginia, and Houdon arrived at Mount Vernon in October of that year and spent two weeks making sketches and models; he then returned to Paris where he asked Gouverneur Morris, of a similar height and build as Washington, to pose for him. JM succeeded in carrying out Governor Brooke's request, for on 29 July 1796, JM wrote to Brooke hoping that the statue had arrived safely, unaware that it had already been received and erected in the state capitol rotunda on 14 May. Houdon, however, still had not received full payment when JM was once again appointed minister to France in 1802. JM's involvement ceased after he sent Houdon's last reimbursement in October 1803 (*Jefferson Papers*, 8: 288; *Papers of George Washington, Confederation Series*, 3: 306; *Catalogue of Monroe's Papers*, 1: 121,122, 145, 148, 150).

From Fulwar Skipwith

Bordeaux 22 Pluvios 3d year [10 February 1795]

My dear Sir

After a little difficulty and delay Hichburn[1] and myself arrived here in good health and spirits—we find the Inhabitants realy pinched for bread,[2] and have found them so during the latter part of our journey from Paris; but 'tis not difficult to forsee that, from the prevalent spirit of those Sons of liberty aided a little by the prospect of a more bountiful and prolific Season, they will work thro' their present distresses.

Forced by the impending displeasure of the freemen of the United States, it Seems by the last arrival from America, that their poisoned bane and Antidote, Hamilton is about to give in his resignation—'tis certain that he has anounced this intention to the Speaker of the House of Representatives—Tazewell you must have known before this, replaces you in the Senate—in Maryland, two rotton and contemptible limbs of Aristocracy, Forrest and Key[3] have been left out and Country Democrats placed in their stead. So Says our worthy and Sincere friend Fenwick—a few days more, being but a few hours on the ground, I may Say Something, if not more to this purpose, at least less in a hurry—the present being the moment of my arrival. My affectionate respects to M[rs] M., and yours mo. Sincerely

Fulwar Skipwith

RC, NN: Monroe Papers

1. Benjamin Hichborn (1746-1817), a Boston lawyer, graduated from Harvard in 1768 and went to France in 1793. He worked as an agent for the sale of land in the United States and negotiated sales for the Commission des Subsistences of France (*Sibley's Harvard Graduates*, 17: 36-44).

2. The abolition of the law of the maximum in late 1794 created a huge inflation of prices compounded by increasingly worthless assignats. Added to this, the winter of 1794-1795 was exceptionally cold with many crop failures. Meat and bread became scarce if not impossible to obtain. Lack of food and bitter cold weather added to the suffering of the population. This was particularly obvious in the south of France where goods were often scarce in winter (Georges Lefebvre, *The Thermidorians and the Directory*,105-114).

3. Federalist Uriah Forrest (1756-1805) served as a representative for Maryland in the U. S. Congress from 4 March 1793 until his resignation on 8 November 1794. Philip Key (1750-1820) was also a congressman from Maryland who served 1791-1793 (*BDAC*).

To Edmund Randolph

Paris February 12. 1795.

Sir.

I was honoured with yours of the 2nd Dec[r] three days since, and by which I find that my third letter only had then reached you, although the two preceding with duplicates were forwarded according to their respective dates and by opportunities which promised security and dispatch.

I read with equal surprise and concern the strictures you deemed it necessary to make upon some particulars of my conduct here, because I think it did not merit them and trust upon a further view of all circumstances you will entertain the same opinion. Of these by this time you will possess a general view: a more particular detail however I think proper now to communicate.

It is objected that I addressed the convention with a glow of sentiment not warranted by my instructions.—2[dly] That I made public what was intended and policy dictated should be kept private, and 3[dly] That I compromitted the government by saying it was willing to tolerate injuries, which it was not disposed to tolerate, whereby an important interest to our country was slighted or given up.

Whether my address contains a single sentiment or expression different from what my instructions and the declarations of the legislative branches contain, is to be determined by comparing the one with the other. I had them before me at the time and drew it by them: of course I thought it did not, and I now think so. The force however of this objection is I presume comprized in the second, for if the communication had been in private and not in public, the objection most probably would not have been made. Upon this point therefore a more thorough explanation is necessary, and for this purpose a full view of the circumstances and motives which influenced my conduct equally so.

Upon my first arrival I found our affairs as it was known they were before I sailed, in the worst possible situation. The treaty between the two republics was violated: our commerce was harrassed in every quarter and in every article, even that of Tobacco not excepted. Our seamen taken on board our vessels, were often abused, generally imprisoned, and treated in other respects like the subjects of the powers at war with them: our former Minister was not only without the confidence of the government, but an object of particular jealousy and distrust: in addition to which it was suspected that we were about to abandon them for a connection with England and for which purpose principally it was believed that Mr Jay had been sent there. The popular prepossession too in our favour had abated and was in some measure at a stand, for the officers of the fleets from America had brought unfavourable accounts of our disposition towards them. Thus the connection between the two countries hung as it were by a thread, and I am convinced, that if some person possessing their confidence had not been sent, it would have been broken.

My first reception was marked with circumstances which fully demonstrated these facts, and shewed how critical the ground was on which we stood, for it is unquestionably true that notwithstanding my political principles were subscribed to, the committee or the governing party in it were disposed to delay my reception, throw me intirely out of view, and destroy altogether the effect of my mission. It was said that as my principles were with them I ought on that account to be the more dreaded, for if they confided in me I should only lull them asleep, as to their true interest, in regard to the movements on foot: and under this impression I was viewed with a jealous eye and kept at the most awful distance. This deportment towards me was so observable, that it attracted the attention of the representatives of the other powers here, and was most probably communicated elsewhere.

Into what consequences this policy which was hostile to us might lead I could not readily perceive, but I was alarmed on that head, for I well knew that an avowed enmity by this government against our executive administration, and in which shape it threatened to break out, persued with passion as I had reason to apprehend it would be, would not only injure our national character, but likewise disturb our internal tranquillity and perhaps involve us in war. The interval between such a step and the existing state of things was small, and in the tide of their fortunes which were prosperous, I was fearful it would be taken. Thus circumstanced what course did policy dictate that I should pursue? Did it become me to look on as a tranquil spectator of machinations that portended so much mischief to my country and so completely defeated the object of my mission, or was it more wise, more consistent with the obligations of the trust I had accepted, to make a decisive effort to defeat them? And in adopting the latter council, in what line should that effort be directed, or by what means enabled to succeed? The doors of the committee, as already mentioned were closed against me, and had it been otherwise, knowing as I did the disposition of that body towards us, would it have been prudent to have deposited those documents under its care, since they furnished the only means by which I could counteract its views? Or was it to be presumed that the declarations of friendship which they contained, would produce in the councils of that body any change of sentiment, advised as it had been, and armed as it was, with a series of contrary evidence, and in which it would place a greater confidence? I can assure you and with great sincerity, that after taking in my mind so far as I was able, and with perfect calmness (for the imputations against me were not of a nature to inspire zeal) that range of our affairs in their general relation to those of other powers, and in which you deem my conduct defective, that the measure I adopted appeared to me not only the most eligible one, but that in the then juncture of affairs I thought it my indispensable duty to adopt it. Nor was I disappointed in any of the consequences upon which I had calculated, for by this public demonstration of our regard for this nation and its <u>revolution</u> (though indeed the word was not used) the people at large were settled on the right side: the abettors of a contrary doctrine were in a great measure confounded: and as soon as the impression upon the public mind had time to react back upon the public councils aided by the little incidents I caught at to inspire confidence, together with a change of the members of the committee, was the object even in that body, tho' slowly yet finally, completely accomplished.

But you intimate that I ought to have shunned this publicity from the fear it might injure our depending negotiations with Britain and Spain. Had I seen cause to apprehend that consequence, I should certainly have been more averse to the measure: but that there was none, on the contrary that it would produce the opposite effect, was in my opinion certain. To demonstrate this, permit me to develope, according to my idea of it, the object of Mr Jay's mission, and the contingencies upon which his success depended. This will shew the relation which mine had to his, and more satisfactorily than I can otherwise do, the motives in that respect of my conduct.

I understood that the sole object of Mr Jay's Mission was to demand the surrender of the posts and compensation for injuries, and was persuaded that his success would depend upon two primary considerations, the success of the French arms, and the continuance of a most perfect good understanding between the two republics. If [we] were disappointed in either of these events I concluded that his mission would fail, for we knew that a long and able negotiation for the first object had already proved abortive, and we saw that in the preceding year when Toulon was taken and fortune seemed to frown upon the arms of this republic, that an order was issued for those spoliations of which we so justly complain. We likewise saw afterwards when the spirit of this nation was roused and victory attended its efforts, that that order was rescinded and some respect was shewn to the United States. Thus it appeared that our fortune at least so far as depended upon Britain, and of course the success of Mr Jay's mission, depended upon that of France.

But the success of France could not redound to our advantage and especially in the negotiation with Britain without a good understanding and concert with the French government: for without which, we could neither count upon success in negotiation, nor in case it failed, upon the fortunate issue of arms if war should be appealed to. By negotiation we could not hope for success otherwise than from the apprehension in the British cabinet, that if we were not accomodated, we would join in the war against them: we could not accept it at the price of an equivalent, and thus pay again for what was already our due: nor could we expect it from the affection, the justice, or the liberality of that court; for we well knew that if it had possessed those virtues we should have had no cause of complaint. But we could not join in the war nor even avail ourselves of that argument in negotiation, without a concert with France, for without such concert, we might commence at the moment she was about to conclude, whereby we should be left alone to contend with that power who would probably be supported by Spain. If then our good understanding with France was broken or the necessary concert between us incomplete, Britain would only have to amuse us 'till the crisis had passed, and then defy us.

If this doctrine is true and it is admitted that the success of Mr Jay's mission depended upon a good understanding with the French republic, it follows that the more cordial it was and the more generally known the happier the effect would be, and of course, that by exhibiting this public proof of it, instead of retarding, I forwarded essentially the objects of that negotiation: and such indeed was my idea at the time, for I knew that the movement would be so understood on the other side of the channel, and in consequence believed it would produce a good effect, and in which I was the more confirmed by the information of several of my countrymen, who were in England when the embargo was imposed, and who assured me that if it had been continued Mr Jay's success would have been immediate.

That the English administration would complain of this movement and of me, was what I expected, but I knew that I was sent here not to subserve the views of that administration, and trusted that whilst I rested on my instructions and performed my duty with integrity, although my judgment occasionally err, as those of most men sometimes do, that no concession would be made to my discredit, in favour of that administration: on the contrary that I should be firmly supported against its attacks by those who sent me here. I trust that this has been the case in the present instance, and upon which point I am more anxious, upon public than private considerations, because I well know that if any such concession has been made, it was immediately communicated by its instruments here, and for the purpose of weakening the confidence of this government in our own, a practice systematically pursued heretofore, and with the hope of separating or at least of preventing any kind of concert between the two countries.

Had the fortunes of France been unprosperous upon my arrival the motive for greater caution would have been stronger. But the case was in every respect otherwise. Her fortunes were at the height of prosperity, those of her enemies decisively on the decline. It was obvious that nothing was wanting to preserve tranquillity at home, and to ensure success in our foreign negotiations, but the good wishes and the good offices of this republic towards us. By the measure therefore I thought that every thing was to be gained and nothing to be lost.

Upon the third point little need be said: I have some time since transmitted to you a decree which carried the treaty into effect and yielded the point in question. Satisfied I am too it was greatly forwarded if not absolutely obtained by the manner in which it was urged: for a generous policy is better calculated to produce to good effect here than a strict one. And other than in that light my declaration cannot be considered. Surely I did not [concede][1] the point nor intimate an indifference upon it: on the contrary I laboured with the greatest force of which I was capable, to demonstrate the interest we had in it as well as themselves: nor did I condescend in that or any other transaction: in general I know I am more apt to err on the other side, and I am persuaded that in the present instance, you will find upon a reperusal of the paper in question, that altho' it contains expressions of friendship, it certainly betrays none of condescention.

I have thus answered the objections contained in your strictures upon my conduct, by stating the circumstances under which I acted with my motives of action, and I presume satisfied you that I did not merit them. But I cannot dismiss the subject without observing that when I review the scenes through which I have passed, recollect the difficulties I had to encounter, the source from whence they proceeded, and my efforts to inspire confidence here in our administration, and without which nothing could be done, and much mischief was to be apprehended, I cannot but feel mortified to find that for this very service, I am censured by that administration.

You have already seen by the course of my correspondence, that however difficult it was to succeed; yet at certain times we were completely possessed of the confidence of this government, and that at those times I had the good fortune to accomplish some objects of importance to us. But it is likewise my duty to inform you, that I was at the same time enabled to penetrate more accurately into what would most probably be its policy towards us, in case we continued to possess that confidence unimpaired; and I now declare that I am of opinion, if we stood firmly upon that ground, that there is no service within the power of this republic to render that it would not render us and upon the slightest intimation. In the interval between the period of those communications which were made by me to the committee, explanatory of our situation with Britain, Spain &c, and the arrival of the intelligence of Mr Jay's treaty, the indications of this disposition were extremely strong: for at that time I had reason to believe that it contemplated, to take under its care and provide for our protection against Algiers, for the expulsion of the British from the western posts, and the establishment of our right with Spain to the free navigation of the Missisippi, to be executed in the mode we should prefer, and upon terms perfectly easy to us; terms in short which sought only the aid of our credit to obtain a loan from our own Banks, for an inconsiderable sum, to be laid out in the purchase of provisions within our own country, and to be reimbursed if possible by themselves. But by that intelligence this disposition was checked though not changed, for it is with the course of opinions as with that of bodies, and which are not easily to be forced in an opposite direction, after they have decisively taken a particular one. I mention this for your information, not indeed in relation to the passed but the future measures of the Executive, for I am still inclined to believe that if the arrangement with England or the negotiation with Spain should fail, it is possible, provided a suitable attempt be made here before a peace is closed with those powers respectively, to accomplish the whole through the means of this government, and upon terms which would perhaps require on our part no offensive movement, or other act which would rightfully subject us to the imputation of a breach of neutrality: well satisfied I am that the full weight of its fortunes might be thrown with decision into our scale, and in a manner that would enable us to turn those fortunes to the best account in negotiation.

I am happy to inform you that M⁻ˢ La Fayette was lately set at liberty,[2] and altho' I could not make a formal application in her favour, yet it was done in accomodation with that which was informally made. She attended immediately at my house to declare the obligations she owed to our country and of which she manifested the highest sensibility. Unfortunately she is and has been for some time past destitute of resource, and in consequence required aid, not only for present support but to discharge the debts that were already due, and for which she applied to me and was accordingly furnished with a sum in assignats equivalent to about 1,000 dollars in specie. I made this advance upon the principle it was my duty to make it as the representative of the U. States, and in the expectation that the like sum which should be paid to my order by our Bankers in Amsterdam, would be taken from the fund appropriated to the use of her husband, by the Congress in the course of the last year. Is this approved and may I make, upon that fund future advances, adequate to her support, and for which the interest will perhaps suffice?[3]

A treaty of peace or rather of amity with Tuscany,[4] with the progress of a revolution in Holland and which has been more rapid than I expected it would be, are the only events worthy notice that have taken place since my last, and for more particular details respecting which I beg leave to refer you to M⁻ Edet[5] to whose care the present is committed. With great respect and esteem, I have the honor to be, Dear Sir, your most ob⁻ serv⁻

Ja⁻ Monroe.

P. S. I herewith inclose you a report from M⁻ Skipwith upon some cases that were noticed in your last dispatch, as likewise upon some others upon which application will most probably be made to you, and whereby you will be enabled to give satisfactory information to the parties concerned.[6]

Copy, DNA: RG 59: Dispatches from France

1. The clerk wrote "conclude".

2. Adrienne Lafayette was released on 21 January 1795 (André Maurois, *Adrienne ou La Vie De Mme De LaFayette*, 310).

3. A law enacted on 27 March 1794 granted $25,000 to Lafayette as pay for his services as a major general in the Continental Army. Randolph informed JM in June 1795 that the government had authorized the use of $6,000 of this money for Adrienne Lafayette (*U. S. Statutes at Large*, 6: 14; Randolph to JM, 7 June 1795, below).

4. France and Tuscany signed a treaty at Paris on 19 February 1795 that affirmed Tuscany's neutrality (George Lefebvre, *The French Revolution from 1793 to 1799*, 147, 150).

5. Pierre-Auguste Adet (1763-1834) held several diplomatic positions, including one at Geneva, before being appointed France's minister to the United States. He continued to hold public office during the revolutionary period and under Napoleon. He served as minister to the United States 1795-1797 (*Correspondence of the French Ministers*, 728).

6. The enclosed report from Skipwith could not be identified.

From Edmund Randolph

Department of State. February 15ᵗʰ 1795.

Dear Sir

The last date, which I have received from you is of the 15ᵗʰ of September 1794; and it has been duly acknowledged by duplicates. It occasioned no small anxiety as to the issue of many points which you had brought before the French Republic. That anxiety has been considerably increased, by observing in the newspaper a decree, rescinding the stipulation between the United States and France, making goods free, which are found in free Ships. It has appeared only in a translation; and there is ambiguity enough in its present dress to lead us to hope, that the treaty, having been declared at the beginning of the decree to be in full force, may possibly be an exception still to the general provision for condemning hostile property in neutral bottoms.[1]

We do not doubt, that we should have obtained the most ample explanation of this and every other of our relations to France, had not the advice-boat, which was lately dispatched from thence, been captured by a British Frigate.

Acceptable as Mᵣ Fauchet has hitherto been, we read with great sensibility, that Mᵣ Oudard formerly, and Mᵣ Adet recently, have been appointed in his place. If this should be true, and Mᵣ Fauchet is, as we suppose, uncontaminated towards the French interest, it is rather an unpleasant circumstance, that upon a change of party we are to expect a change of minister. However the only thing which essentially concerns us, is, that the Representative of the French Republic in the United States, should lay aside all intrigue, and imitate ourselves in a course of plain and fair dealing.

We confide, that you have lost no opportunity of fixing the friendship of the two countries upon solid grounds. On our part, we really do all that we can; and as one instance, I will mention the legislative act, which has, within these few weeks enabled Mᵣ Fauchet to use, by anticipation the instalments of the French debt, due in September and November next, amounting to two millions and a half of livres.[2] But I am afraid, that Mᵣ Fauchet, and probably the french nation have been urged to believe, that the Treaty, said to have been concluded by Mᵣ Jay with Great Britain interferes with our engagements and attachments to France. It has not come to hand yet; and therefore I can deliver no decided opinion on it. But so far is this from any instruction to Mᵣ Jay, that I am persuaded that he could not think of a treaty having such an object. In the principal heads of the negotiation, the surrender of the posts, the vexations and spoliations of our commerce, and the payment of British debts, France can have no possible concern. If we choose to modify them ever so capriciously, we are the true and only Arbiters of the question. It is probable, indeed, that our commercial intercourse has been also regulated. Say, if you please, that a treaty has been concluded for commerce, also. France will enjoy all the advantages of the most favored nation; and we have been long ready to discuss and settle new commercial arrangements with France. But none have been ever proposed during my connection with the Administration. It may well be supposed that the access to the West Indies, with as few restrictions as possible, must be desireable to us. But let the possession of them ultimately center in France or England, we shall, I presume, be unfettered by our contracts with the one, so as to be at perfect liberty to contract with the other.

I shall give you no comments upon the proceedings of Congress, until they rise, which will be in a fortnight hence. At present you will receive by the French Ship which Mᵣ Fauchet dispatches, your quota of news-papers

The conduct of Spain towards us is unaccountable and injurious. Mᵣ Pinckney is by this time gone over to Madrid, as our Envoy Extraordinary, to bring matters to a conclusion some way or other.[3] But you will seize any favorable moment to execute, what has been entrusted to you respecting the Mississippi.

Col⁰ Humphreys, our Minister for Lisbon, being disappointed in the Loan, which was to be opened for the relief of our captive brethren in Algiers, has come over to press the subject. He will return in a few days, full-handed; and altho' we have heard nothing of late concerning the friendly interposition of France with the Dey, we beg that the influence of our Ally may be exerted in this great cause of humanity. I have the honor to be, Dear Sir, with constant and sincere respect and esteem Yr. mo. ob. serv.

Edm: Randolph.

LBC, DNA: RG 59: Diplomatic and Consular Instructions

1. Decree of 15 November 1794, enclosed in Miot to JM, 24 November 1794, above.

2. "An act providing for the payment of certain instalments of the foreign Debts, and of the third instalment due on a Loan made of the Bank of the United States," enacted on 8 January 1795 authorized the president to make payments on the French loan. Fauchet had asked Randolph for an advance payment of $40,000 on the loan (*U. S. Statutes at Large*, 1: 409; *Hamilton Papers*, 18: 8, 16-17, 159-160).

3. The United States had several outstanding issues with Spain, most notably access to the Mississippi River and the delineation of the boundary between the United States and the Spanish possessions along the Gulf coast. William Short, as minister to Spain, was charged with resolving these matters. During the summer of 1794 Spain requested that a diplomat of greater rank and prestige be sent to finish the negotiations. President Washington responded by appointing Thomas Pinckney as envoy extraordinary and gave him sole authority to negotiate the treaty. Washington made the appointment in November 1794, but Pinckney's commission and instructions did not arrive in London until 23 February 1795. He left for Spain in mid-May (Samuel Flagg Bemis, *Pinckney's Treaty*, 280-291).

To James Madison

Paris Feby 18. 1795.

Dear Sir

I was yesterday favored with yours of the 4th of Decr the only one yet rec^d. I had perfectly ancipated the secret causes & motives of the western business, and was extremely happy to find that the patriotism of the people in every quarter, left to its own voluntary impulse and without any information that was calculated to stimulate it, was sufficient to triumph over the schemes of wicked and designing men. I have been always convinced that this was a resource to be counted on with certainty upon any emergency, & that the more frequent these were, the sooner wo^d the possibility of success in such schemes be destroyed, & our gov^t assume a secure and solid form. I likewise perfectly comprehended the motive and tendency of the discussion upon the subject of the societies, but was persuaded that the conduct of the societies themselves upon that occasion, together with the knowledge diffused every where of the principle upon which they were formed, would give that business likewise a happy termination. This was the case in one house and will I doubt not likewise be so in the publick mind if the discussion sho^d be provoked. The fact is, such societies cannot exist in an enlightened country, unless there is some cause for them: their continuance depends upon that cause. for whenever you test them by the exigence and it is found inadequate they will fall: and if there is one an attack upon them will encrease it, for they are not even to be put down by law. I was fearful the conduct of the Jacobin society here would injure the cause of republicanism every where, by discrediting popular complaints and inclining men on the side of government however great its oppressions might be. But that society was different from those that ever existed before; it was in fact the government of France, and the principal means of retarding the revolution itself; by it all those atrocities which now stain & always will stain certain stages of the revolution were committed: and it had obviously become the last pivot upon which the hopes of the coalisd powers depended. This society was therefore the greatest enemy of the revolution, and so clear was this that all France called for its overthrow by some act of violence. It is easy for designing men to turn the vices of one society somewhat similar in its origin, and which became such only in the course of events by degenerating and losing sight of the object which gave birth to them, agnst all others, altho' the parellel may go no further than that stage in which they all had merit. As the conduct of the Jacobin society made such an impression upon aff^{ts} here it became my duty to notice it in my official dispatches: I accordingly did so by giving an historic view of its origin progress & decline,[1] truely & of course under the above impression, & which I think will be found marked upon the statment to an observant reader: for in one stage viz from the deposition of the king I say that the danger was from confusion alone, since the old government was overset & the new one entirely in the hands & exerted virtuously for the sole benefit of the people, and it is intimated in the close that however enormous the vices may be provided treasonable practices be not discovered, that its overthrow must be left to publick opinion only. It became my duty to notice this subject & I think I have done it with propriety; however examine it & write me what you think of it.

I rec^d some days past a letter from Mr Randolph containing a severe criticism upon my address to the Convention & the publication of the papers committed to my care,[2] and which justified that address & makes its defense agnst the attacks of that party with you. I was hurt at the criticism & equally surprised, for I did not expect it would be avowed that it was wished I sho^d make a <u>secret</u> use of them, giving them weight by any opinion which might be entertained of my own political principles, or in other words that I would become the instrument of that party here thereby putting in its hands my own reputation, to be impeached hereafter in the course of events. They were deceived if they supposed I was such a person. On the contrary I was happy in the opportunity furnish'd not only on acc^t of the good effects I knew it would produce in other respects, but likewise as it furnishd me with one of presenting to the eyes of the world the covenant which subsisted between them and me: by the publication they are bound to the French nation & to me to observe a particular line of conduct. If they deviate from it they are censurable, and the judicious part of our countrymen as well as posterity will reward them accordingly. The fact is I would not upon my own authority make those declarations of their sentiments, & therefore I was glad to embrace the opportunity to let them speak for themselves. I felt some concern for Mr Randolph because I feared it would expose him to some attacks, but I concluded he would despise them: for in truth I do not apply to him the above comments. I have answered those criticisms with suitable respect but as becomes a free and independant citizen whose pride is to do his duty but who will not yeild when he is undeservedly attacked.[3] I have reviewed the state of things upon my arrival & shewed the necessity of some bold measure to retrieve it. What I have stated in my reply is true; I have many documents to prove it in each particular. Tis possible this business may end here, for I have since rec^d a letter in answer to my 2. first[4] & which were not then rec^d by Mr Randolph, in a different style; and to which latter I shall likewise write a suitable answer: but it is also possible it may not. I have therefore tho^t proper to transmit to you a copy of it, that you may perfectly comprehend the state of this business with the ground upon which I rest. Perhaps it may be proper for you to shew it in confidence to others but this is entirely submitted to you. I wish it seen by Mr Jefferson & Mr Jones.

The state of parties in America is as well known by the Committee of publick safety & other leading members as it is there. It was mentioned by some person to Merlin Doui that Hamilton & Knox were going out of office, & he instantly replied he would have it inserted in the Bulletin & communicated to the departments, as an event auspicious to France as well as America. This however was prevented, because the comm$^{\underline{n}}$ had been rec$^{\underline{d}}$ by one person only.

Fortunately the successes of this republick have been great even beyond the expectation of everyone. The entire conquest of the 7 U. provinces closed in the midst of winter for a few months the last campaign: indeed so great has the success been that they have scarcely an enemy before them, and I believe they may march whither they please in the course of the next. Their conduct in Holland too in other respects has done as much service to the cause of liberty, almost as their arms. A revolution which was immediately commenc'd has made a rapid progress there & will no doubt be soon completed. I think if our sage negotiator in London[5] had waited a little longer till the victories of France were more complete (& it was certain they would be so), he might have gained terms satisfactory to all of his countrymen: but perhaps being a <u>conciliating</u> negotiator, he could not take advantage of that argument—perhaps he wished for the honor of Engl$^{\underline{d}}$ to deprive the republican party in America of the opportunity of saying <u>his success</u> was owing in any degree to <u>that cause</u>.

I think upon the whole y$^{\underline{r}}$ prospects independant of foreign causes are much better than heretofore; the elections have been favorable: but with the aid of foreign causes they are infinitely so. We are well—our child is at school in a French family, & already speaks the language tolerably well. Joe[6] is also at school & rather in a line of improv'ment. I have little leasure & of course am but little improved in the language. We desire to be affec$^{\underline{y}}$ remembered to y$^{\underline{r}}$ lady whose esteem we shall certainly cultivate by all the means in our power. If a loan is obtained can it be laid out to advantage? inform on this head—remember me to M$^{\underline{r}}$ Beckley, to Tazewell, Mason & all my friends & believe me sincerely y$^{\underline{rs}}$

Ja$^{\underline{s}}$ Monroe

PS. Pinckney is ab$^{\underline{t}}$ sitting out for Sp$^{\underline{n}}$—suppose the peace with France is made before his arrival what success will he have?

RC, DLC: Madison Papers

1. JM to Edmund Randolph, 16 October 1794, above.

2. Randolph to Monroe, 2 December 1795, above.

3. JM to Randolph, 12 February 1795, above.

4. Randolph to JM, 5 December 1794, above.

5. John Jay.

6. Joseph Jones, Jr.

From Thomas Pinckney

London 18$^{\underline{th}}$ February 1795.

My dear Sir,

I have now before me your several Favors of 20$^{\underline{th}}$ December 1794. and 7$^{\underline{th}}$ and 17$^{\underline{th}}$ of January 1795.[1] and in answer thereto I have to assure you that it would afford me great Satisfaction, were it in my power to give you the Information for which you appear solicitous, concerning what has taken place in consequence of M$^{\underline{r}}$ Jay's Mission to this Court; but my Wish to impart this Intelligence to you is founded entirely upon the desire I have to quiet your Alarm on a Subject interesting to every American, and to keep up between us that Communication of Intelligence upon important Subjects, which may frequently be of utility, and will at all times fully accord with my Sentiments. The want of a common Cypher and the uncertainty even of the present mode of Conveyance however preclude me from entering fully into this Subject; and I must repeat that I regret this merely on your own account, because I conceive you are furnished with sufficient Information to satisfy all the reasonable Expectations of the French Government on this head; Mr Jay having informed me that he has forwarded to you a Copy of the Article of the Treaty where in it is expressly agreed that nothing contained in that Instrument should in any degree derogate from the Stipulations contained in our former Treaties. And this I conceive ought to give full Satisfaction to the French Government, as it shews an anxious Wish to perpetuate our Friendship with them; though they have avowedly continued during a considerable period in the non-Execution of their part of the Treaty respecting us, and though they even now appear from what you write to consider their Compliance therewith as an Act of favor. It ought also I conceive to be satisfactory to them, when they recollect the good Faith with which we have hitherto performed our part of the Treaty, although our Government has been thereby at times placed in Situations of Delicacy and Embarassment. It ought especially I think to be satisfactory to them when they consider the nature of our Government, and the State in which the Treaty is; as they must know that it can have no Validity till ratified by the President with the Concurrence of two thirds of the Senate. This Circumstance alone I conceive ought to have prevented any Application to you to impart to them the Treaty in its present State; for the Object of this desire could not be a mere gratification of Curiosity, or I am sure you would not have given it your Attention: the Demand must therefore have been made with a View of acting upon the Information to be received: let us only imagine then for a Moment, that the Treaty had been imparted to them, and that they had taken any Measure in consequence thereof, (and acting as you think they do from their Feelings only it is not improbable that those Measures would be prompt and decisive) let us further imagine that our Government on Deliberation should reject this Treaty, how premature must this Communication then appear! and it would not in this Event much matter in which way they might have acted, for should they, in consequence of the Impression made on them by the View of the Treaty; adopt hostile Measures, such Animosity might arise and such real Injury be done, as we might deplore, but could not repair after it should be known that the Treaty had not been ratified: or if pleased with the purport they should extend to us some extraordinary Favors, would not the Species of Delusion under which they had acted, and the mortification arising from disappointed Hope, produce Consequences, tho' perhaps not so immediately lending to a Rupture, yet in the End highly prejudicial to that Friendship between us, which it is our Wish to cultivate? These are only a part of the Inconveniences which it appears to me would arise from the present Communication of the Treaty to the French Government, but the Compass of a Letter in this form will not allow me to enlarge. We may however consider for a moment what Advantages would arise from a Compliance with their Request, providing the Treaty be ratified; and I must own I do not see any of moment; on the one Side should their View of the Subject induce them to act with Hostility, we should have to meet that Calamity sooner than otherwise, or should they be thereby induced to grant us additional Favors, I know of none, the Anticipation of which for a month or Six Weeks ought to be put in competition with the Risques I have before described.—For your own Satisfaction however I can add that I have perused the Treaty and that you may rest assured that it contains nothing like a Treaty of Alliance offensive and defensive; and indeed I do not recollect any Article of a political nature in it, unless a Composition of our former Disputes, and some temporary Regulations concerning our Neutral Rights should be so construed; but these could not be satisfactorily detailed to you unless the whole could be at the same time submitted to your Consideration. After all I should not be surprized to find this Treaty reprobated in America as not being sufficiently favorable to us and condemned in France on account of its holding out to us too many Favors from this Country.

There is one part of your Letter to me of the 20ᵗʰ of December which I own has impressed my Mind with much Astonishment, and that is what you relate as contained in your Instructions concerning this Business. It is a matter of too delicate a nature to discuss in this mode of writing—but knowing as I do the Instructions given here it conveys Results of an alarming nature and more particularly to us who are on foreign Missions. It may not perhaps be amiss to let you know that the Treaty was sent to the United States by two different Conveyances early in the month of December last, hence we may reasonably expect its return in the begining of April, so that you will have but a short time to resist the Importunity for a promulgation previous to its being made public after its Ratification.

Mʳ Purvyance having called upon me for Fifty Guineas I have according to your desire furnished him therewith and I beg you to retain that Sum in your hands until I shall have an opportunity of directing its Expenditure on my account.

I have lately received the Appointment of Envoy Extraordinary to the Court of Spain but I shall not be able to leave this Country within three weeks from this time. I have not yet determined upon my Route and other Arrangements. as soon as that shall be done I will impart it to you.

Receive, my dear Sir, my best Acknowledgments for the friendly Sentiments contained in your favor by Mʳ Morris. be pleased to make the Expression of my Respect acceptable to Mʳˢ Monroe and believe me to be Your Friend and Servant,

Thomas Pinckney

RC, NN: Monroe Papers

1. JM's letters to Pinckney of 20 December 1794 and 17 January 1795 have not been located.

To Edmund Randolph

Paris February 18ᵗʰ 1795.

Sir,

I have just been honoured with your favour of the 5ᵗʰ of Decʳ and am much gratified by its contents. The preceding one of the 2ⁿᵈ had given me great uneasiness, but this has removed it. I sincerely wish my two first letters had reached you in the order they were written, as they would have prevented yours of the 2ⁿᵈ of Decʳ by preventing the impression which gave birth to it.

Be assured I shall continue to forward by all the means in my power, the objects of my mission, and I am persuaded with the success which might be expected from those efforts, addressed to the councils of a nation well disposed favourably to receive them. The object of this is to acknowledge the receipt of your last letter, and in the expectation that it will accompany, under the care of Mʳ Edet,[1] my last dispatch which was in answer to the preceding one. With great respect and esteem, I have the honor to be your most obᵗ and very humble servant.

Jaˢ Monroe.

Copy, DNA: RG 59: Dispatches from France

1. Pierre Adet.

From William Short

Madrid Feb. 18. 1795

Dear Sir

I had this morning the pleasure of receiving your letter of Nov. 19. 1794. It is the first & only one I have received from you since your being charged with the mission at Paris. Mr Church[1] forwarded [it] from Lisbon on the 20th ul^{to} by an inhabitant of that city whom he sent here for the purpose—Unfortunately this person set out without a passport—the consequence was that on his arrival in Spain he was thrown into prison at Badajoz where he remained twelve days during which time his letters remained in the hands of the Governor of that place—At the expiration thereof, viz. after as they said they had written to Lisbon on the subject, they set him at liberty & gave him permission to proceed with his letters which they then returned to him—To judge from the appearance of the seals it might be supposed they had been untouched as they do not bear evident marks of a [lt]eration—to judge however from the circumstances it is difficult to suppose the letters should not have been opened & examined—The case must be considered at least as a doubtful one—I have thought it right to give you this idea of the reception of your letter before proceeding to answer it—which I do in great haste in order that the poor Portuguese may set out in company with some persons who depart in the course of the night, & who may serve him as a guide on his route & prevent his being stopped for the purpose of examining the letters he carries.

I am extremely obliged to you for the information you gave me as to M. de G's application to you.[2] It is a new proof of the extreme duplicity & infidelity of that Gentleman—At the time he wrote to you & long before, he had been in a kind of negotiation with me in order to the taking of some step that might open the way to peace between France & Spain through the U. S. Long since his application to you (which he had totally concealed from me) he has been aiming at the same thing—& particularly wished me to obtain permission from the committee of publick safety for him to go to Bareges (the waters you speak of) on the condition also of my accompanying him—his object as he expressed to me without scruple was to open a negotiation for peace, & aim at a close connexion between France Spain & the U. S. &c. &c. &c.—I have rendered a full & particular account of all that has passed between M. de G. & myself to our Government & should have communicated it to you if I had had a proper conveyance.— In order to give you a general idea of the subject—our negotiation & conversations were founded on M. de G's idea that the U. S. would have weight with France in obtaining a peace for Spain—my own was that this Gov^t should begin by yielding us our rights as to the Misisipi & Limits—so as that the U. S. might have a real interest in seeing that peace effected—M. de G's desire was that peace should be first attempted as being more pressing—& that we should receive the appearances of the good will of Spain as a proof that everything would be settled to our satisfaction—In this way there were several ebbs & flows between us—in proportion as dangers pressed here or subsided he was more or less intent on the subject—As he found he could not get me for a long time to count sufficiently on the good will of this Government he applied to you, as it would seem, in the hopes of finding you more confiding.—As far as I can judge he has either not made the application himself to the Committee of public safety (as advised by you) or not obtained it—for he is still here as Minister of finance. Should he apply for or obtain this permission it will be well for you to warn the committee of the little reliance to be placed in this Gentleman personally in order that they may be prepared for him—There is nothing within the circle of deception, dissimulation & duplicity, of which he is not capable—For a long time he has been incapable of deceiving any body here because there is no body who would rely on him for anything—Should he go to Bareges he would go with his usual arms & would endeavor to make use of them there.

I should notice to you that his receiving the permission to go (if he should make use of it) might be attended with one good effect to the U. S.—Such a journey by one of the King's ministers would immediately shew the English its real object, & would certainly increase the distrust already existing & every day augmenting between them & Spain—It might indeed carry that distrust to real ill-blood—& perhaps hostility—& the true interest of the U. S. must ever be to see their two land neighbors in different scales.

As to the peace between France & Spain it would seem under that point of view to be a point to be desired for the U. S. provided their just grounds of complaint against Spain were removed, so as to remove the possibility of a war between them (Spain & the U. S.)—On the subject of these complaints nothing satisfactory has been as yet obtained; although within a short time back the most positive appearances have been given me that they shall be entirely removed—Having received a notification from the Sec. of State that Mr Pinckney is to be sent here things will be naturally delayed for his arrival[3]—The letter you send me without name will previously have come here & have taken its chance for producing the effect you desire.

M. de G. has been for a long time desirous of peace with France—he feels the impossibility of providing funds—People in general here desire peace also—the fear of France & hatred of England both conspire to that end—Those most desirous of continuing the war are the King Queen & first Minister—& the will of all others here is null—The misfortune of the war however & the conduct of England has made the first minister think seriously of the means of obtaining peace—he is anxious to know on what terms France would grant it—but has been probably embarassed as to the means of ascertaining this, without risking to commit himself with England—I suspect there is some kind of negotiation however on foot—If so you will certainly know it long before this letter gets to you—Yours has been three months coming—mine will perhaps be nearly as long going—I therefore avoid troubling you more particularly at present—Should the war continue between France & Spain—& you should see any means of procuring peace for the latter on the conditions the U. S. might desire, you might write to me through the two armies—asking the Representative of the people to send it to the Spanish General, who would of course address it to the first Minister—In this case the letter must of course be considered as liable to inspection though it is possible such a mark of confidence, if the letter were carefully sealed, might determine him to give it to me without risking to break the seal—Should the case be such an one as to induce you to send a messenger here he would certainly be allowed to pass without being molested—& should any American have business at Lisbon, as happened with Mr Strobel[4] & Mr Hitchbourne, he would be allowed to pass through Spain in safety & might bring your letters.

In the course of the last month a servant who had come with me here returned to France—I procured a passport from the first minister, which carried him without obstacle to the French army at Tolosa—I wrote to you by him—& mentioned at the same time that you might write to me through the frontiers—Should anything occur on the subject of peace which I should think necessary to communicate to you, I will write to you by that route asking the Minister here to send my letter to the Spanish General to be forwarded by a flag.—The conveyance of the present letter although not altogether a sure one, I consider less liable to inspection than one sent through the frontiers—but the uncertainty of the time of its getting to you & the certainty of a great delay at best, deter me from examining with some length the various aspects of a peace between France and Spain as relative to the U. S.—& the line which we as their agents ought to observe.

Accept my dear Sir my most grateful thanks for the information you gave me as to my friend in the country[5]—how much would you have added to it if you had informed me whether you had received &

forwarded my letters at different times inclosed to you—Your letter does not acknowlege expressly the receipt of any letter from me—I infer however you must have received some of them from the mention you make of my friend—I hope the day will come when I shall have the pleasure of seeing you acquainted—With real esteem & regard I am sincerely yours

W. Short

RC, NN: Monroe Papers

1. Edward Church (1740-1816) was born in the Azores to American parents who took him to Boston when he was an infant. He graduated from Harvard in 1759 and joined his father's mercantile business. President Washington appointed him as consul at Bilboa, Spain, but he never assumed the duties of the post. Washington then appointed him as consul at Lisbon in 1792. Church assumed his duties there during the summer of 1793 and held the post until 1796. He died in London in 1816 (*Sibley's Harvard Graduates*, 16: 389-393).

2. Diego de Gardoqui. See JM's letter to Short of 19 November 1794.

3. Short learned in January that the State Department was sending Thomas Pinckney to supplant him in negotiations with Spain, negotiations in which Short had been deeply involved for nearly two years. When Short sought an explanation, he learned that Jaudenes, minister to the United States from Spain, had made a complaint against him for having written a memorial during the time Short was chargé d'affaires at Paris which Jaudenes considered unfriendly to Spain (Myrna Boyce, "The Diplomatic Career of William Short," *The Journal Of Modern History*, Vol. XV, (June 1943), 115-119).

4. Daniel Stroebel.

5. Duchess de Rochefoucauld.

To the Committee of Public Safety

Paris Feb^{ry} 19. 1795. (1 Ventôse)

It is with infinite pleasure that I communicate to you the grateful impression which the kind and fraternal reception given me upon my arrival here by the National Convention, as the representative of your ally and sister republick the United States of America, has made upon our Government and my compatriots in general: You, Citizens of France! who have proved to the world by a series of the most illustrious exploits, how highly you estimate the blessings of liberty, can well conceive with what a degree of sensibility [the] account of this reception was welcomed by a free governm^t & a free people. I hasten therefore in obedience to my instructions to make this communication, and which I do with the greater pleasure, because it furnishes me with an additional opportunity of declaring to you the affectionate interest which the United States take in whatever concerns the liberty prosperity & happiness of the French republick

Ja^s Monroe

RC, DLC: FCP—France

From John Jay

London 19th February 1795.

Sir

On the 5th of this month I had the honor of writing to you a Letter in answer to yours of the 17 ult: by Mr Purviance, who is still here waiting for an opportunity to return, and who will be the Bearer of that Letter.

You will receive this by Col. Trumbull, who for some time past has been waiting for an opportunity to go, thro' Paris, to Stutgard, on private business of his own. He did me the favor to accompany me to this Country as my Secretary. He has been privy to the negociation of the Treaty between the United States & Great Britain, which I have signed; and having copied it, is perfectly acquainted with its Contents. He is a Gentleman of Honor understanding and accuracy, and able to give you satisfactory Information relative to it.[1]

I have thought it more adviseable to authorize and request him to give you this Information personally than to send you written Extracts from the Treaty, which might not be so satisfactory. But he is to give you this Information in perfect confidence that you will not impart it to any Person whatever for as the Treaty is not yet ratified, and may not be finally concluded in its present Form and Tenor, the Inconveniences which a premature Publication of its Contents might produce, can only be obviated by Secrecy in the mean Time. I think myself justifiable in giving you the Information in Question, because you are an american minister, and because it may not only be agreable, but perhaps useful. I have the Honor to be with great Respect Sir your most obed[t] & h'ble Serv[t]

John Jay

RC, NNPM

1. John Trumbull (1756-1843) was the pre-eminent painter of scenes from the American Revolution and a prominent portraitist. He accompanied John Jay to London as secretary in 1794 and remained in Europe for the next ten years where he held a number of minor diplomatic posts (*ANB*).

From Robert R. Livingston

New York 19th Feby 1795

Dear Sir

I have not yet been favor'd with answers to three Letter that I have writen to you since you departure.[1] You are troubled with this at the request of capt Barré whose case is here considered by myself & others who are well satisfied of his patriotizm as extreamly hard if upon examining his memorial which is inclosed you can render him any service you will much oblige his numerous friends here & serve his country by restoring to it a firm republican as an officer capable by his knowledge in his profession of advancing its interests[2]

We have not yet rec[d] the treaty concluded by M[r] Jay on the 19th Nov[r] tho we have had arrivals as late as the 14th of Jan[y] from England—Every thing is tranquil here   M[r] Wolcot has replaced M[r] Hamilton & M[r] Pickering Gen[l] Knox[3]—There are many changes in Congress—My brother Edward has succeeded in this city M[r] Watts[4]—Col Hathorne M[r] Van Gaasebeck[5] The republican interest in this place has gained six members out of ten—Be pleased to present my comp[s] to M[rs] Monroe & inform her that I saw her brother[6] this day in good health—I am Dear Sir with much esteem & regard Your most Ob hum. Ser[t]

Rob R Livingston

RC, DLC: Monroe Papers

1. Livingston wrote to JM on 18 September 1794 (above), and JM acknowledged receipt of this letter on 23 February 1795 (below). The other two letters from Livingston have not been located, and there is no indication that JM received them.

2. Jean-Baptiste-Henri Barré (1763-1830) was an officer on the frigate *Le Perdrix*, which was part of the French squadron

cruising off the coast of the United States. Claiming that he had been mistreated by the ship's captain, Barré resigned his commission and sought asylum in New York. The French accused him of desertion and, citing the consular treaty between the United States and France, demanded that he be arrested and returned to his ship. When federal district judge John Laurence rejected the French plea, U. S. attorney general William Bradford asked the Supreme Court to issue a writ of mandamus forcing Laurence to comply. The request came before the court on 18 February 1795, and on March 3 it declined to issue the order. Barré later regretted his resignation and hoped to regain his commission in the French navy (*Documentary History of the Supreme Court*, 6: 522-527; Horatio Gates to JM, 5 September 1795, ViFreJM). Barré's memorial has not been located.

3. Oliver Wolcott, Jr. served as comptroller of the treasury, before he succeeded Alexander Hamilton as Secretary of the Treasury on 2 February 1795 (*ANB*). Postmaster General Timothy Pickering became the head of the War Department on 2 January 1795 (*BDAC*).

4. Edward Livingston (1764-1836), a New York city attorney won election to the House of Representatives and served 1795-1801. He later moved to Louisiana and was representative (1823-1829) and senator (1829-1831) from that state. He served as secretary of state under Andrew Jackson 1831-1833 and minister to France 1833-1835 (*ANB*). John Watts (1749-1836) was a member of Congress from New York 1793-1795.

5. John Hathorn (1749-1825), a New York Federalist, served two terms in Congress 1789-1791 and 1795-1797. He replaced one-term Congressman Peter Van Gaasbeck (1754-1797) who served 1793-1795 (*BDAC*).

6. John Kortright.

To John Brown

Paris Feby 20. 1795.

Dear Sir

I have just been favored with yours of the 5th of Decr last and was extremely gratified by the details which it contained. This, with the letters rec^d by the same opportunity are the first that have reached me of the kind since my arrival. I rejoice to find that my conduct upon my admission in the convention was satisfactory to my republican friends & of course to the great mass of my constituents. That it would prove otherwise to those of an opposit description was what I expected. The address which would have pleased them, would have obtained to the representative of their country the censure & not the plaudit of this nation. My object was to repair the injuries that our character had sustained, by declarations (which altho' they could not be complained of on the other side of the channel, as a breach of neutrality, unless they have a right to regulate our language at an official ceremonial), that would make known to them and to the world the solicitude we had for their welfare. Had my address been weaker it would have produc'd no effect; on the contrary credit wo^d have been given to reports that were circulated, that we were about to abandon France & unite with Engl^d, and whilst the object of Jay's mission was to accomplish that point, mine was to lull this gov^t asleep untill it sho^d be accomplished. By my own declarations w^h respected myself only supported however by the documents laid before them this imputation was refuted & the basis of my mission exposed to the view not only of France but the world at large. Believe me you have but an imperfect idea of the state in which things were upon my arrival: it required then but little to part us—an effort to keep us together was necessary; I made that effort at that time and my conduct since has been correspondent with the decl^ns which were made, & will continue to be so whilst I stay here.

The success of this republick has surpassed the expectation of every one. The campaign was closed a few weeks past by the entire conquest of the 7. United Provinces, and by which the fleet and every thing else have come under the power of this republick. The extent of this acquisition you will readily conceive. I am assured that those entrusted with the gov^t in Holland have announced it the rep^s of Fr. there that they will have equippd for sea in the spring 10. ships of the Line & 12. frigates to act with the forces of this republick: and in every other line aid will be derived from that source.

Spain, Prussia, and indeed all the powers wished peace but it was early seen that it would not be granted to Engl^d & in consequence great efforts were made by her to disappoint the negotiations with the other powers. As yet a peace has been made by Tuscany only. a negotiation which was depending at Basle in Switzerland with Prussia and with promising expectations of a speedy conclusion was suddenly interrupted by the death of Baron Goltz taken off as some suspect by poison. This report however sho^d not be mentioned as from me for reasons that will occur.

I can assure you in confidence that I have done all in my power to embark this gov^t in favor of the missisippi, and that I have reason to expect with effect. and I have likewise taken measures to make this known to Mr Short at Madrid. You know my solicitude upon this point. It was one of those which occupied my first political efforts, and it will continue to do so till it is accomplished.

Captn Fowler promised to forward to Mr Madison for me my patent for the 20.000 acres of land on Rockcastle. I am only anxious for its safety for I mean not to dispose of any land there whilst in a publick station here. Will you be so kind as procure it when in y^r power & deliver it to him. You will make my best respects to Tazewell & Mason as likewise to my other friends in both houses & believe me very sincerely yours

Ja^s Monroe

Let me hear from you often.

RC, CtY

From James C. Mountflorence

4th Vintes [22 February 1795]

Sir

With Some Satisfaction I transmit to you the enclosed friendly & private Note of Merlin de Douai[1] in Answer to the one I wrote at his office of the Committee on decade last, when I waited on him in that Business & that of the Passengers made prisoners on board Our Vessels.

I take the Liberty to remark to You, Sir, My Observations to him on the Mississipi, were general ones, Such as you had suggested to me, or more properly your own, but without any Signature. His answer [coin]cides with the Hour's Conversation I had last night with Col. Pelet, <torn> morally certain that the Issue of their Interference by Way of Negociation [resp]ecting the free trade of the Mississippi will depend entirely on the Conduct of our Administration on the Subject of Mr Jay's Treaty. With very great Respect I have the Honor to be Sir Y^r most Obe^d Servt

J. C. Mountflorence

I proposed doing myself the Honor of waiting personnally on You, but have had 14 Copies of the decree about our Seamen to make out & 14 Circular letters to write to all the Consuls & Agents, besides a letter to Van dorsten,[2] his Certificate, one to the Commissary of Prisoners at Auxern all which went off by this Day's post with Seven others about the Business of the office & am now employed in making up the Report on the Lanrine Capt. White, which you will have this Evening, being obliged to attend Mr Taylor at 4 o Clock to the Committee of public Safety.

RC, NN: Monroe Papers

A copy of Merlin de Douai's letter (in French), addressed to Fulwar Skipwith and dated 3 Ventôse An 3 (21 February 1795), is enclosed in JM to Edmund Randolph, 6 March 1795, DNA: RG 59: Dispatches from France. JM's translation (NN: Monroe Papers) reads:

"I have rec^d citizen the observations you have addressed to me upon the navigation of the missisippi. The ideas which they present are not new to me nor the committee of public safety, and I have reason to think they will be taken into profound consideration in suitable time and place. I ought not dissemble however that this may depend much upon the conduct which the American gov^t will observe in regard to the treaty which its minister Jay has concluded with Engl^d. You know in effect that there ought to be a reciprocity of services and of obligations between nations as individuals. I speak however here as an individual."

2. Rudolph Van Dorsten wrote to JM on 1 October 1794 from the army barracks of Napoleon's artillery college at Auxonne (near Dijon) seeking help in getting out of French custody (*Catalogue of Monroe's Papers*, 1: 35)

From John Quincy Adams

The Hague February 23. 1795.

Dear Sir

The Representatives of the french People sent me some days since your favour of January 28.[1] Please to accept my thanks for the communications it contains. The gradual renewal of favourable dispositions since your arrival, the final establishment of the principle stipulated in our Treaty, and the hopes of obtaining redress for antecedent causes of complaint, are all circumstances so important and so pleasing that the information of them gives me the highest gratification. A conciliating disposition seldom fails of having its effect, and from the Conversation of the Representatives here I have had reason to conclude that on your first arrival, there were impressions to be removed as well as claims of Justice to be presented.

As it is doubtless known to you, that in the course of the Events which have recently taken place in this Country, the persons and property even of the subjects of the powers at War with the french Republic, have not been molested or injured by the victorious Army, it is needless to mention that those of our fellow citizens have invariably been respected. But as it is declared that the Conquest is not to affect the Sovereignty and Independance of this Republic, and as an internal Revolution has introduced new Men, and new Measures to the Administration of Government here, it is perhaps proper to mention to you that the United States have the strongest assurances of a cordial disposition to continue and promote the Harmony and friendship between the two Nations.

A solemn deputation from the States-General to the Representatives of the french people has asked for an alliance with the french Republic, "in the closest fraternity of which the annals of the world make mention."—What will be the terms of this Treaty?—what the boundaries between the two Republics?— what the mutual obligations relative to their common warfare?—what the state of fortresses to be stipulated for the future?—what are to be the concessions of generosity and what the indemnities of Justice are perhaps better known to you than to me.

I have written to the agent of the Gentleman interested in the property, relative to which I had the honour of writing you some time since, informing him that the issue of the demand is delayed by a deficiency of evidence. Accepts my thanks Sir for your attention to this affair, as those of all our fellow citizens will be due to your exertions for obtaining commercial Justice for them from one of the belligerent sides.

As the late occurrences have produced a very material alteration in the aspect of the <u>maritime</u> affairs of Europe, and the prospects of a <u>naval</u> scene of action more frequently contested than the present war has hitherto exhibited, appear to increase in probability, the commercial interests of our Country, and the operation upon them of the policy which will in future be pursued by the powers at War, seem to require the particular attention of her servants in Europe. The maintenance and cultivation of a good disposition is perhaps all that is proper or even practicable, but if even the way can be prepared for <u>arrangements</u>, in case they should become necessary, I am well assured the opportunity will not be neglected.

The Necessities of this Republic have induced the Assembly of Holland, to permit the importation of flour into the ports of the Province <u>during the course of the present year</u>.—As this circumstance may be of importance in the United States I have enclosed a translation of the Laws in the packet which I send herewith, and take the liberty of recommending to you for as early transmission as possible. I am with great Respect, Dear Sir, your very humble & obedient Serv[t]

John Q. Adams

RC, DLC: Monroe Papers

1. JM's letter to Adams of 28 January 1795 has not been located. For possible misdating of this letter, see Adams to JM, 12 March 1795, below.

2. Adams to JM, 22 November 1794, above.

To Robert R. Livingston

Paris Feb[y] 23. 1795.

Dear Sir

I was lately fav[d] with yours of the 18. of Sep[r] and much gratified by its contents. The idea suggested in the enclosed paper had occurred to me from the moment of my appointment. I well knew that a decl[aratio]n to that effect by the convention, would have given to France the credit she merited, and completely overwhelmed the B[ritis]h faction with us. But unhappily I found her councils upon my arrival in such a state of irritation agnst us, that I was fearful they wo[d] make one of a different kind. Instead of announcing a determination to support our depending negotiations with Brit[n] & Sp[n], I had reason to apprehend, that by publickly avowing her dissatisfaction with our conduct, she would actually defeat those negotiations, and which would have infallibly insured such an avowal. A stroke of refined policy is to be expected from the cabinet council of few only, no way affected by the impulse of the heart. But here the disposition was rather to gratify that impulse by indulging a resentment, which in the committee was almost universal, in the convention of extensive impression, and rapidly spreading thro' the community at large. In that state of the mind a proposition for such a decl[n] would have created surprise & disgust. I found immediately that it would be impossible to embark this republick in the smallest degree in our aff[rs], or even to tolerate such an arrangm[t] as wo[d] enable us to turn its fortunes to our acc[t] in the depending negotiations, unless I sho[d] previously make some impression on the publick mind in our favor, and of which I did not despair as I knew its natural bias was most affectionate towards us, and thought the documents in my possession were of sufficient strength for the purpose. With this view my first mov'ment was taken in the convention, and in a manner you have no doubt seen by the publick papers. Nor was I disappointed in any of the consequences upon which I had calculated, for the publick mind was not only immediately arrested, but an opposit bias given to it in the course of few weeks, and which was gradually communicated to the publick councils, last of all to the committee of p: safety (the executive of the republick) where counter documents, gathering for sometime before, were deposited.

You will observe that I submitted to the Convention the decl^n of each department to speak for itself. It would have been improper for me to have added to or extenuated from it. I spoke for myself only.

Upon this basis of esteem considerable progress was made in the course of a few months in retrieving our aff^{rs}; those articles of the treaty securing freedom to goods in ships that were so, heretofore violated were executed, and sundry other injuries redressed. In short from a state of actual hostility we were plac'd upon the antient footing of real amity, and I had just commencd and with the most favorable prospect of success, to open the subject to w^h y^r note alludes. At this moment however acc^{ts} were rec^d that Mr Jay had closed a treaty with Engl^d derogating from our connection with France. The impression which these made you will readily conceive, and the more readily when you consider that the greatest jealousy was always entertained of the objects of that mission, created in a great measure by their knowledge of the political character & principles of the man. In general I can assure you that it was not only practicable but easy to gain in support of our claims upon Brit^n & Sp^n the full fortunes of this republick, and without embarking in the war unless we chose to embark in it, provided concert was sought with this government in a manner to inspire its confidence. I can also assure you that this is still practicable in case that arrang'ment be rejected (of the contents of w^h however I am yet ignorant), and suitable measures in other respects adopted.

You will have heard before this reaches you that the last campaign was closed on the part of the French by the entire conquest of the 7. united provinces, and that under their auspices a revolution as complete as their own was immediately commenc'd there, and w^h I have the pleasure to add is at present in great forwardness. The probability is the antient provincial establishments will be annulled, and a constitution completely prevailing the whole founded on the sovereignty of the people, substituted in its stead. In the convention too great tranquility prevails, for the inquiry into the conduct of a few remaining members of the antient committee & who are charged with being accomplices of Robertspiere, is conducted like a similar inquiry wo^d be with us. It attracts the publick attention but in a manner not to influence the decision. If they are condemned it will be in my opinion as the result of a fair trial. Nor is there any danger of the revolution being impeded by a famine: provision is in some quarters scarce, but the patience & fortitude of the people able to surmount much greater difficulties than are like to threaten them.

Tis probable a peace will be concluded before the commencment of the campaign, with Sp^n & Prussia, a negotiation was progressing with the latter & was lately interrupted by the death of Baron Gotz, at Basle in Switzerland—it will probably soon be revived. The war will be prosecuted with great vigor agnst Engl^d & in which the Dutch will be the associate. Tis probable an incursion will be made towards Hanover & in other directions bey^d the Rhine. Tis said the Dutch will add to the French fleet 10. ships of the line & 12. frigates. I beg of you to present our respects to Mrs L. Mrs Montg:[1] & others of your family & believe me sincerely y^r fn^d & serv^t

Ja^s Monroe

RC, PHC, Roberts Autograph Collection

1. Mary Livingston and Janet Montgomery.

From William Short

Madrid Feb 23. 1795

Dear Sir

After a silence which had forced on me an idea, which I had struggled against as long as possible, namely that you had forborne to write to me, I was agreeably relieved by the reception the 18ᵗʰ inst of your letter of the 19ᵗʰ of Nov.—I answered it the same day & rendered you an account of the manner which it had come to my hands—I expected to receive in a few days the other to which you allude in that received—I am extremely sorry your letter had been so long on the way & I fear mine which I sent by the same route will likewise have a long passage—I informed you of the accident with which your letter met on its way from the seaport to this place—I have long lamented that the communication between us was of a nature to forbid saying many things to you which I wished—had I received from you an acknowlegement of my letters sent via Italy & Switzerland, I should however have entered on some subjects of importance in such a manner as to have made them intelligible to you & as little so as possible to the inspectors of the post office—But as I have hitherto remained without receiving a sign of life from you since your arrival at Paris I thought it would be both useless & improper to trouble you—And even now I know not whether any of my letters have got to your hands, your letter received not mentioning any of them—I infer however from the sentence you are so good as to add at the end of your letter respecting my friend¹ that some of my letters must have got to your hands, although this is only an inference, & leaves me equally ignorant whether they were those sent via Italy & Switzerland, or those via England— By this latter route I could not venture to go into the subjects I wished to treat of with you—If my letters to you via Italy have miscarried it must have been between Genoa or Leghorn & Paris, as I have long ago & regularly received advice of their having arrived at those two ports & been forwarded from thence— Latterly I have addressed my letters for you to our Consul at Leghorn Mʳ P. Filiechy—though for sometime past I have written to you only seldom in consequence of your silence.—Before that of the 18 inst which I wrote to acknowlege yours of the 19ᵗʰ of Nov. the last I had written was of the 10ᵗʰ of Janʸ by my servant who set out from hence to return to his own country—As he was to pass from one army to another I sent the letter open of course—& only mentioned on public matters, that in the case you should hereafter have any thing to communicate to me that might concern the French Republic & Spain & the U. S. you might write to me by means of the Representative of the people who might send your letter to the Spanish General & who would of course send it to the Minister from whom I should receive it—In this case you would of course consider the letter as liable to inspection—On other subjects you might write to me regularly by the way of Switzerland, addressing your letters for me to some person there, to be sent to our Consul at Leghorn, from whence to this Country there is a regular Spanish Packet—But it is in vain that I trouble you with so often repeating the same thing—for it cannot be from not having a regular conveyance that letters have not come to me from you, as others here receive there's regularly though slowly from their friends at Paris.

I mentioned to you in my last of the 18ᵗʰ that I had been informed by Mʳ Randolph that it was the President's intention to send Mʳ Pinckney here as Env. Extr: on a special commission, as soon as the Senate should meet—Notwithstanding he assures me that this does not proceed from any want of confidence in me, & desires me on the contrary to continue prosecuting the negotiation, yet it must be evident from a slight observation, that such a notification from him, & the knowlege this Government had of another being to be sent here, would render inevitable a suspension until his arrival, especially as the policy of this Government in the whole of the negotiation with us has been delay & nothing but delay—

I hope however M.ʳ Pinckney will soon arrive here, & that thus the delay will be the shortest & the least prejudicial possible—All the service I can render him it will be both my duty & my inclination to render him—As to myself I have been now so long absent from my native country that my presence there becomes every day more indispensable to myself & I shall make use of every means of recovering that greatest of human blessings, liberty & the enjoyment of my natal air & friends—from which I have been already too long absent, much longer than I should have been if an imperious duty to my country's service, had not tied me down in this climate where my health & constitution have already experienced considerable decline—I have written a long time ago to ask leave to go & pass the ensuing summer in France—as I have since learned the intention of sending M.ʳ Pinckney here, I hope it will remove any difficulty which might have existed, from my presence being thought necessary at this place—The late Charge des affaires here (M.ʳ Carmichael) died in this city on the 9.ᵗʰ inst—I have no doubt that a very few summers passed here would carry me the same road.

We have just heard here by reports which coming different ways, leave us no doubt that Amsterdam has been taken by the French army, & that the allies have abandoned Holland—How happy are you my dear Sir, to be the spectator as it were of these great & momentous events which are deciding the fate & future destiny of Europe!—My last accounts from our Government are of the 9.ᵗʰ of Nov.—Judge of the pain of being in these times so long without hearing from one's country.

I take the liberty of enclosing you a letter for my friend—Yours of the 19.ᵗʰ of Nov. mentioned she was well & in the country—& of course shewed me or made me believe you co.ᵈ have received her letters for me & sent mine to her—although in the last she wrote me, by M.ʳ Livingston in the month of October she informed me as also in her preceding one, that you did not chuse to forward her letters to me—I wrote her that she must be mistaken—that you were one of my best & oldest friends & that she might rely you would receive & forward her letters—I own my dear Sir that the long silence which afterwards followed, made me sometimes reflect on what I had at first considered as a real error on the part of my friend—If you should have any difficulty in giving me this most inestimable mark of your friendship it can proceed only from your not being acquainted with the sentiments of my friend—I have to add therefore 1.ˢᵗ that she is as much & as sincerely attached to her country & its liberty as any person can be—& 2.ᵈˡʸ that our letters contain nothing absolutely nothing but of a private & personal nature as relative to ourselves—I beg & entreat you my dear Sir, to send me a letter if it be only one line to say which of my letters have got to your hand—Yours sincerely

W. Short

RC, NN: Monroe Papers

1. Duchess de Rochefoucauld.

To James Madison

Paris Feb.ʸ 25. 1795.

Dear Sir

Being under the necessity of explaining the motives of my conduct upon my arrival, to the Executive, & in consequence of presenting a statm.ᵗ of the circumstances under which I acted, I have thought I could not better convey my ideas to you on that head than by enclosing a copy of the paper.[1] This will of course be kept from M.ʳ R.[2] because of his official station, & all others from whom it ought to be kept. I have sent a copy under the care of the minister M.ʳ Edet[3] who was to depart some days since: but as he did not & probably will not in some days I have deemed it expedient to send a duplicate to the executive & likewise to y^{r}self by Bordeaux to be forwarded by some American vessel. Three days after the letter above referred to was written, a second was likewise, & in a different tone: But being on the Executive journal, my vindication ought to be there too. It is proper to observe that my first & second letters were intermediately rec^d by Mr Randolph.[4]

The revolution in Holland progresses with great rapidity & will most probably comprize the 7. provinces under a single gov^t founded of course on the sovereignty of the people. Here great tranquility continues to reign—Indeed it has never been otherwise since my arrival, than during the same space I presume it was in Phil^a. Bread is scarce in some quarters but the people are beyond example patient under it. I do not think a real distress is to be apprehended, but if such were to happen, I am convinc'd the yeomanry wo^d emulate by their fortitude, the bravery of their compatriots in the army.

Nothing is yet done with Prussia. The death of Goltz in Switzerland interrupted a negotiation which was depending. Tis reported that France demanded of that power the abandonment of Poland, & for which she proposed to give Hanover.

With Sp^n a negotiation is said to be depending. I am persuaded if Jay's treaty is rejected provided it contains any thing improper that we can not only get a decision of this gov^t to supp^t our claims there but with Sp^n. Tis possible this latter point may be aided from this quarter independ^t of the contents of that project, provided they are not very exceptionable—but the thing wo^d be certain in the opposit view of the case.

I trust he has gaind all that we claimed, for that nothing could be refused in the present state of things, or indeed when the treaty was formed, must be certain, provided he did not convince the adm^n, that as he had adopted the conciliatory plan he would in no possible event change it.

We had some idea of procuring a loan in Holland to a moderate am^t to be vested in land, is this still y^r wish? I am persuaded it may be done; inform me therefore whether it is desirable, to what am^t, and whether it would suit you to draw for it on such persons as I sho^d designate. What I intimated sometime since is not meant to be derogated from here: for I can by loans, answer y^r drafts upon three months sight for one two & even three thousand pounds str^g payable in Hamburg or Holl^d. I have rec^d but one letter from you to the present time. I wish the paper enclosed to be shewn Mr Jones & Mr Jefferson. we are happy to hear you have added a particular associate to the circle of our friends & to whom you will make our best respects.[5] Sincerely I am y^r friend & servant

Ja^s Monroe

Col^o Orr promised to procure my patent for a tract of land on Rock Castle, Kentuckey, of Captn Fowler for me. Will you be so kind as remind him of this & endeavor to get it to be deposited with Mr Jones, or sent here, as I mean to sell it after I shall have quitted this station. The latter is prefered.

I have written by Edet to Burr, Langdon, Brown & some others.[6]

The liberation of our country from the councils of H. & K.[7] had like to have been announc'd in the Bulletin. Be assured characters are well understood here.

RC, DLC: Madison Papers

1. JM to Edmund Randolph, 12 February 1795, above.

2. Edmund Randolph.

3. Pierre Adet.

4. Randolph wrote to JM on 2 December and 5 December 1794. Randolph received JM's letters of 15 and 25 August 1794 after he had written his letter of December 2 but before that of December 5 (all above).

5. Dolley Madison.

6. JM wrote to John Brown on 20 February 1795 and to Robert R. Livingston on 23 February 1795 (both above). No letters from JM to Aaron Burr or John Langdon written at this time have been located.

7. Alexander Hamilton and Henry Knox.

From Adrienne Lafayette

[February 1795]

je prends La liberté de présenter à Mr Monroë, Les trois billets qu'il a bien voulu me promettre de cautionner. L'age et Les infirmités de ceux qu'ils regardent ne me Laissent pas L'espoir, que ces pensions ayent a se payer Longtems. je demande encore a Mr Monroë La permission d'en ajouter un de 300 [livres] de pension viagere pour ma pauvre nourrice, aussi vieille et infirme.

je prends La Liberté de Lui recommander aussi, pierre Louis mercier, qui m'a servi pendant 17 ans, et a couru pour moy des dangers, depuis mes malheurs. je Le prie de me permettre de Le Lui adresser s'il avoit quelques besoins. et je Lui demande La protection pour Lui dans toutes Les occasions ou il pourroit avoir à La reclamer.

je Lui recommande encore une famille, très pauvre, et tres nombreuse, félix, notre ancien Cocher, Sa femme et Ses enfans, Son fils aîne partage la persecution qu'eprouve mon mari; il est prisonnier comme Lui, et a cause de Lui, je demande des bontés des américains, de preserver cette famille de La misere.

je Lui demande encore La permission de Lui recommander Desmanges, et sa famille s'ils avoient besoin de Lui en quoique ce soit, et de me permettre dans ce cas La, de L'encourager a recourir a ses bontés.

hennequin, et Surtout sa femme, quoiqu'ayant été bien peu de tems chés moi, m'ont donne des preuves d'attachement d'une maniere si courageuse que je serois coupable de ne pas Les mettre L'un et L'autre, Sous La protection d'une Nation, a qui je dois La consolation de montrer que je ne suis pas ingrate. je Les engagerai donc, a recourir en toute occasion au ministre des etats unis, comme ils eussent fait a moi-même.

une jeune personne qui a aussi partagé des dangers avec moi, La C^{enne} Benjamin, a un billet de moi dont elle ne veut pas faire usage. je Lui ai fait promettre que si quelque circonstance ou d'etablissement pour elle, ou quelqu'autre qui Lui rendissent cette petite somme utile elle auroit aussi recours a Mr Monroë. je m'interesse vivement a cette jeune personne.

Le C^{en} felix frestel, qui a ete Le second pere de mon fils et L'appuy de sa mere dans tous ses malheurs, ne me permet pas de m'occupper de Lui, mais je me borne a demander que sa bibliotheque qui est sous Le scellé dans Le Logement qu'il occuppoit avec mon fils, soit rachetée, Si jamais elle est vendue, et qu'elle Lui soit remise.

je finis en vous demandant, de regarder La famille de C^{en} Beauchet, et de sa femme, comme ma propre famille, de me renvoyer Leurs enfans ou je Serai, Si jamais ils avoient Le malheur de perdre Leurs parens, ou L'un d'eux, et que L'autre Le desiroit.

Après vous avoir confié mes vœux, my dear sir, et que vous avés bien voulu vous charger d'acquitter mes obligations, je pars pour retrouver mes enfans dans nos montagnes, et en interrompant toute communication avec cette ville ou j'ai ete si malheureuse, et contre Laquelle pourtant je remporte aucun sentiment de vengeance, mais seulement des vœux pour son bonheur, je vous Laisse La consolation de m'avoir donne une de celles que je suis Le plus capable de gouter celle de ne pas manquer a des devoirs precieux a mon cœur, et sacrés pour moi.—en est une aussi que d'eprouver Le sentiment de La reconnoissance que je vous dois et que je conserverai toute ma vie.

N Lafayette

Editors' Translation

[February 1795][1]

I take the liberty to present to Mr. Monroe the three promissory notes he willingly promised me to insure. The age and infirmities of those whom these regard leave me without hope that these pensions will be delivered more than for a short time. I ask Mr. Monroe again to add 300 [livres] of a life's pension for my poor nurse, also old and infirm.[2]

I take the liberty also to recommend to him Pierre-Louis Mercier who has served me for seventeen years, and who has put himself in jeopardy since the beginning of my misfortunes. Please allow me to ascertain whether he is in need of anything, and I ask for his protection on any occasion in which he would need to claim it.

Once again I consign to him a family very poor, and very numerous, Felix, our former coachman, his wife and children. His eldest son[3] shares the persecution that my husband has experienced; he is a prisoner like him, and because of him. I solicit the kindness of Americans to preserve this family from misery.

I request permission to commend him to Desmanges and his family if they have need of him in whatever it be, and to allow me in such a situation to encourage them to have recourse to his charity.

Hennequin and especially his wife, although they have spent little time at my home, have given me proof of their attachment in such a courageous manner that I would be guilty of not placing them, one and the other, under the protection of a nation to which I have the consolation of showing I am not an ingrate. I advise them therefore to avail themselves of the minister of the United States on any occasion as they would have done to me.

A young person who has also shared danger with me, the Citizeness Benjamin, has a note from me that she does not want to use. I have made her promise that if some circumstance or institution or whatever, renders this small sum useful, she will have recourse also to Mr. Monroe. I am keenly interested in this young person.

Citizen Felix Frestel, who has been a second father to my son, and the support of his mother in all her difficulties, does not permit me to take care of him. I would merely like to ask that his library which is under the affixed seal in the lodging he occupies with my son may be repurchased, if ever it is sold, and that it be turned over to him.

I finish by appealing to you to regard the family of Citizen Beauchet, and his wife, as if they were my own family, to send me their children wherever I shall be, if they ever have the misfortune to lose their parents, or one of them, and the other should desire it.

After you have been confided with my commitments, my dear sir, and you have willingly bound yourself to carry out my obligations, I leave to rejoin my children in our mountains, and thereby interrupting all communication with this city where I have been so misfortunate, and against which however I carry with me no feeling of vengeance, but only wishes for her welfare. I leave you with the consolation of having given me the sweetest taste of happiness, which was not failing to fulfill your promises so dear and sacred to me—from which is also to savor the feeling of gratitude I owe you, and that I shall retain all my life.

N Lafayette

RC, NN: Monroe Papers: Miscellaneous and Undated

1. This letter was probably written sometime in early February 1795 shortly before Adrienne Lafayette left Paris for Auvergne (Charles Flowers McCombs, "Imprisonment of Madame de Lafayette during the Terror," *Bookman's Holiday*, 1942: 27).

2. Marie-Anne Marin.

3. Félix Frestel was the tutor and companion of George W. Lafayette. He was secretary to the Marquis de Lafayette, and was captured and imprisoned with him, but escaped. Frestel accompanied George Lafayette to the United States in 1795 (André Maurois, *Adrienne, The Life of the Marquise de Lafayette*, 315-316).

From James Mountflorence

[February 1795][1]

Sir

As Mme La Fayette is to be with You to day at Twelve o Clock, at which Hour I shall wait upon You, I think it proper to inform you of the Amount of the Annuities she wishes you to become her Security for.

Widow Chavaniac...	2700^tt payable One half every six months & always 6 months before hand
Widow Bendin...	300^tt payable in the said manner
Citz Aufroy...	1000^tt from the 4th Thermidor last one half every six months & always 6 months before hand
Cit Morin ...	2400^tt payable as the 2 first 6400^tt Annum in assignats now

If you do agree to the following Redaction to be added at the Bottom of Mme laf-te's obligations please to inform me thereof that they may be ready for 12 o Clock.

Le Soussigné James Monroe Ministre plenipotentiare des Etats unis de l'amerique près la Republique francaise, promets et m'oblige pendant mon Sejour en france dans la qualité surdite, de faire paier exactement la Surdite Pension, et je promets de soliciter aupres des Etats unis L'Etablissement de la dite Pension sur les Fonds du Gouvernement des dits Etats. En foi de quoi J'ai signé &c.[2]

Very Respectfully, Sir, your most obedient Humble Servt

J^s C Mountflorence

RC, NN : Monroe Papers

1. This letter was probably written at about the same time as the preceding letter from Adrienne Lafayette.

2. The translation of this paragraph reads:

> I, the undersigned James Monroe, Minister plenipotentiary of the United States of America near the French Republic, promise and oblige myself during my stay in France in the position above mentioned to pay exactly the above mentioned pension, and I promise to solicit the United States in the establishment of the said pension from the funds of the government of the said States. In good faith of what I have signed, etc.

From James C. Mountflorence

Consular Office Paris 1ˢᵗ March 1795.

Sir

You have ordered me to give you a circumstantial account of the present situation of our commercial intercourse with this country & in obedience thereto I must inform you that I have constantly found in the Committees of Government & in each member thereof of the most friendly disposition towards us but in the several subordinate Departments, Delays & Difficulties equally injurious to our Trade & to the true interest of France; for although the Committees take arretés to order the payment of our just claims, yet as the executive Commissioners of the Government are charged with the execution of these arretés it follows that they have it in their power to defeat the whole views of the Government by suggesting difficulties & thereby procrastinating the conclusion of each business. Of this we have but too many daily instances, out of which I will only enumerate a few in order to elucidate more fully this matter:— The Committee had taken a resolve that the Commission of Marine should adjust our claims respecting the embargo at Bourdeaux & report thereon in a short limited time. The Commission complied with that order reporting that they had sent the claim down to Bordeaux to be reexamined & adjusted by the naval officer. Permit me to remark that all those accounts which I delivered myself to the Commissary had been previously made up at Bordeaux by our Consul Mʳ Fenwick under the eyes of the aforesaid naval officer & are very clear & well stated—When I delivered [to] the same Commission, the papers that came from America respecting the claims of our Countrymen for supplies they had furnished the island of Sᵗ Domingo & other of the West Indies & for depredations committed in America &c &c having previously sorted the papers, drawn a short but clear statement of the narrative of each case & annexed to it an account fairly stated with my remarks on each separate claim in the french language, I informed the Commissary that as great number of the papers such as affidavits, Protests &c &c were in our language in order to expedite the business & spare him trouble I would willingly translate the whole for his accommodation, or such only as he would deem the most important: He thanked me but told me he had interpreters belonging to the commission whose business it was to do that work yet upon my pressing at some of his offices a report on those claims I was told they were delayed by the papers in the American language which were not yet translated & so that business must still suffer unavoidable delays.—There is a positive arreté to comply with Mʳ Fauchets Contracts & to pay immediately the freights of the vessels he has sent with flour & the Cargoes likewise when it is to be paid here, notwithstanding which there are among others two of our vessels, the Recovery & the Friendship at Rochfort since several months, which brought flour to the Government & are upon demurrage to the great injury of the Republic who can reap no kind of advantage by it, whilst it creates disgust & detriment to the American Merchants.—Mʳ Taylor of Baltimore is here since upwards of five months with Bills to the amount of £30,000. Sterling drawn in favor of his House by the acknowledged Agents of the Republic sent over to the United States to purchase supplies. The Committees of Government had ordered in the first Instance the payment of one half of those Bills, with which Mʳ Taylor was then satisfied for the moment, agreing to wait some time for the other Half. but about two months ago as he was about to receive his payment, the Commission of Supplies or rather the Commissary thereof started some fresh difficulties entirely unknown both to Mʳ Taylor & myself which have suspended the payment.—I could wish that the executive Committees were made sensible that as to a Merchant a delay of payment or a suspension of it has in most every instance the same effect as a positive refusal of payment. Such delays may totally ruin him & his connexions. a merchant requires the most strict regularity in the coming in of his funds, he calculates upon it, directs his operations in consequence, takes engagements, draws Bills, accepts others & if in all these transactions so closely connected & depending entirely upon each other he meets with an unforeseen delay all his Projects are thwarted & the consequence of that delay may brake him up & cause many other banckruptcies among his Connections. No indemnity for detention or demurrage of a vessel & for the delay of payment of a cargo can compensate fully in some cases the injuries a merchant may suffer by these events.—I have seen a letter from Phil^a of 16th Jan^ry which mentioned that the merchants of that city are much alarmed at the accounts they have received from this Country respecting the delays & difficulties the Captains & Supercargoes meet with in receiving their payment & complaining of the long retention of their vessels; this is so much the case says the letter that it is difficult even to freight a vessel for France unless the freight be paid before sailing.—Indeed it must unavoidably follow if the Commissions by their delays & other embarrassments continue to defeat the intentions of the Government, as in the case of the two vessels at Rochfort & that of Mr Taylor, that all your efforts to promote our trade with this country may be frustrated.—I conclude Sir by suggesting that in my humble opinion the French Republic is much interested at this Juncture to accomodate all the just demands of our Merchants, to liquidate finally their claims & to prevent by every means in their Power, the delays of Payment, which subjects this Government, to pay immense & unnecessary demurrage—if they were to adopt such policy their ports would be full of our sails whilst an opposite line of conduct will most certainly drive our Trade from their Country. I have the honor to be with great Respect Sir Y^r most Obed^t & most Humble Servt

J^s C Mountflorence

RC, DLC: Monroe Papers

To the Committee of Public Safety

Le 12 Ventes An 3eme [2 March 1795]

Citoyens

Si dans le Cours des Negociations de L'Espagne auprès de la République pour en obtenir la Paix, il se trouvait une Circonstance favorable aux justes Réclamations du Gouvernement des Etats unis contre cette Puissance, je presume <u>Tout</u> des Dispositions fraternelles de la France, et je crois devoir vous rappeller quelle est la Somme de nos Demandes à cet Egard.

1e. La Libre Navigation du fleuve Mississippi, et les limites territoriales suivant le Traité définitif avec l'Angleterre de 1783.

2e. La Franchise de la Nouvelle Orleans pour nos Batiments, ou un autre Port également commode sur le territoire Espagnol.

Il est à presumer que les Mêmes motifs qui porteraient L'Espagne à ceder la Navigation de ce fleuve, lui feraient acquiescer au Reste qui n'en est que la Consequence, et de cette manière ce serait probablement entendu; mais afin d'éviter toute difficulté à L'avenir et de rassembler tous les Objets qui font le Sujet des Négociations actuelles du Gouvernement des Etats unis à Madrid, il serait essentiel de le bien expliquer. Salut et Fraternité

Ja^s Monroe

Editors' Translation

12 Ventôse Year 3 [2 March 1795]

Citizens

If during the course of the peace negotiations between Spain and the Republic an appropriate circumstance should arise to discuss the legitimate claims of the United States government against this power, I count on <u>all</u> fraternal assistance from France, and I believe I should remind you of the sum of our claims in this matter.

1ˢᵗ. The free navigation of the Mississippi River and the territorial limits according to the treaty with England of 1783.

2ⁿᵈ. The exemption from duties for our ships in New Orleans or in another equally convenient port in the Spanish Territory.

It is assumed that the same motives that would lead Spain to concede the free navigation of this river would also lead her to acquiesce to the rest, which is merely the consequence of it, and in this manner there would probably be accord; however, in order to avoid any difficulty in the future, and to include all the issues that are the subject of the United States' current negotiations at Madrid, it would be essential to state it specifically.

Jaˢ Monroe

RC, DLC : FCP—France. The copy of this letter enclosed in JM to Randolph, 6 March 1795 in DNA: RG 59: Dispatches from France as well as the copy in DLC: Monroe Papers is misdated 8 March 1795.

From Thomas Pinckney

London 6ᵗʰ March 1795.

My dear Sir,

As there is a possibility that my Letter by Mʳ Purvyance may miscarry I send a duplicate by Colonel Trumbull with whose Character and Merit you are sufficiently acquainted to render any Introduction of mine unnecessary, but I send this duplicate as I think it important that you should know that Mʳ Jay's Instructions were not what you conceived them to be and that you may thereby prevent any ill Impression which might otherwise result from the want of this Information. The French Government may I think rely with Confidence on ours for a strict performance of our Engagements with their Nation and a cordial Reciprocation of the friendly Conduct and good Offices which it is our mutual Interest to cultivate.

I expect to set out for Spain in a Fortnight or three Weeks and in the mean time remain with the utmost Esteem and Respect, My dear Sir, truly yours.

Thomas Pinckney

RC, NN: Monroe Papers

To Edmund Randolph

Paris 6th March 1795

Sir,

I avail myself of the opportunity by Mr Edet[1] who leaves this to succeed Mr Fauchet, of transmitting herewith some communications which have lately passed between the committee of public safety and myself, upon the subject of our interfering claims with Spain, and which will serve not only still further to illustrate my former dispatches upon that point, but likewise to shew the precise ground upon which it now rests. I had thoughts of declining any further efforts upon that head, until I was enabled to lay before the committee the project of Mr Jay's treaty with the English government, and which was and still is daily expected by the return of Mr Purvyance; but from this I was swerved by a report then current that the outlines of a treaty were nearly adjusted between the Representatives of this republic with the Army and some agent of Spain on the frontier, from the fear that the peace would be closed with that power befour our differences were compromised. Thus circumstanced I deemed it my duty, in conformity with my instructions (and the more especially as they had no right to make any inference with respect to that project other than I had stated) to bring the subject more fully before them than I had before done. Among the papers inclosed and which comprise the whole of what passed between us upon this subject you will observe a note of Merlin de Douay and which though given by a single member, and in reply to an informal application, yet as it marks a remaining solicitude upon the transaction to which it refers, I have thought it equally my duty to transmit for your information.[2]

No peace is yet made with Spain, nor indeed with any other power, Tuscany excepted, and which was before communicated: But it is still probable that one will be made with that power, and likewise with Prussia. It is however well known that England is against it, and that she exerts all the address which ingenuity, prompted by interest, can suggest to prevent it, and it is possible that those arguments which are used by the minister in the H[ouse] of C[ommons] to forward the preparations for war, may have weight in the cabinets of other powers and incline them to protract any definitive arrangement with this republic until just before the commencement of the campaign, in the hope of profiting in the interim by such events, as the chapter of accidents may throw in their way. But [I] cannot think, if the tranquillity which now reigns here should remain undisturbed, and the incidents of the internal in other respects prove favourable to the revolution, that either of them and especially Spain will hazard the probable evils of another campaign, for any benefit they can possibly expect from it. In truth the objects of the war, so far as they were ever understood, are now intirely changed: if a dismemberment of the republic was among them, that must of course be considered as abandoned: or if the restoration of the ancient monarchy was the sole one, the hope of accomplishing it by arms must now likewise be considered as gone. Nations acting intirely on the defensive never dream of conquests. The only remaining source from whence the coalised powers can derive the least hope of success is founded in the possibility of some internal commotion being excited, by the scarcity of provision, the derangment of their finances, or the divisions of their councils: calamities it is true or either of them singly, provided it attained to a certain height which it is admitted, would be sufficient to destroy any government. But whether France is threatened with real danger from this source in either of those views is the problem to be solved. Upon the two first points I do not pretend at present to be able to decide with certainty: indeed the best informed can only conjecture. Bread I know is scarce in some parts, and it is possible much distress may be experienced in those quarters, if foreign supplies are not obtained, and in great amount; but these are expected from the North and from America. 'Tis probable too that this scarcity has been increased by the speculation of individuals, and in which case it will diminish as the exigency presses. Nor am I skilled in their financial policy. When I arrived the assignats were depreciated in comparison with specie, as three to one, and now they have declined to about 5½ for one. The amount in circulation and the sums occasionally emitted are wonderfully great, and the depreciation must follow as a thing of course. What measures will be taken with the paper is yet doubtful. Formerly it had depreciated in equal or greater degree, and then it was elevated to par by striking out of circulation all the bills of a certain description, securing the payment of the liquidated amount by the mortgage of the national property; aided by the maximum law which regulated the price of every thing. Whether some measures of the like kind will be again adopted, or whether any attempt will be made to appreciate the paper is equally uncertain. Many consider the appreciation, as an evil to be avoided, preferring a gradual decline 'till it shall finally expire, and adopting then a scale suited progressively to private contracts, and redeeming the whole at the rate it passed in the last stage of circulation. I think it probable this latter policy will finally prevail, as it is advocated with ability and zeal, by some who were tutored in our school. The subject is however still under discussion and nothing absolutely decided on it. If this latter plan should be preferred, although no step be taken to appreciate the paper or even prevent its decline, a considerable time will probably elapse before the final suspension: and after this the republic will stand nearly upon the same ground on which it commenced. Its debt will be but small, and it will possess, besides the ordinary resource of taxation &c., national domains to an immense amount, equal by estimation to at least 200,000,000£ ster^g in specie, supported in its credit by Holland (from whence too other aids are to be expected) and by the reputation of its arms. I will however take a more accurate survey of this subject, and give you the results as soon as possible.

And upon the subject of those dangers which are presumed to menace the safety of this republic from the division of its councils, I have but little to add at present to the details already furnished. The papers herewith forwarded, contain the report of the commission of 21 upon the denunciation of Barrere &c and which finds cause of accusation. As soon as the report is printed, the denounced will be heard before the Convention, who will decide by what is called the appeal nominal, for their acquital or trial; and in the latter case they will, in a convenient time, be sent to the revolutionary tribunal, and in my opinion finally to the guillotine, unless they should previously abscond, as one of them (Vadier) has already done, and which it is wished even by those most active in the prosecution, they all may do. This particular incident will not be new to you, and in other respects the councils of the country bear the same aspect they have done from the time of my arrival.

In contemplating the possible effects of this prosecution, on what may be called a division of the public councils, the friends of the revolution have cause to regret that since a decision upon the conduct of these members was to be taken, it was not sooner taken. If it had followed immediately after the execution of Robespierre, it would have occasioned less noise and borne less the aspect of party collision. Its protraction too has exposed the government to dangers which would not otherwise have existed: for by the delay the twofold crisis of the trial, and of famine, or rather the scarcity of provision, will take place precisely at the same moment; than which there certainly could not be, a coincidence of events more favourable to the views of the coalised powers, or unfavourable to those of this republic. But you have already seen by the course of this transaction, that although the preponderating party has denounced, and may finally execute the[se] members, it has notwithstanding acted rather upon the defensive than otherwise. Had the prosecution been undertaken with that degree of zeal and vigour, of which so decided a majority is always capable, they must long since have been carried to the scaffold. On this side then there was obviously no plan; nor indeed is it probable there was any on the other, for I am convinced that the real object of at least 4 out of 5, on both sides, has been to complete the revolution. The coincidence therefore must be deemed one of those unlucky but fortuitous arrangements, forced by the course of events not to be controuled, and under which the friends of republican government must console themselves with the reflection, that altho' in a possible view, it may prove injurious to their cause, yet if it glides smoothly by, it will produce a correspondent benefit, by demonstrating to the world, how deeply rooted the principles of the revolution are in the hearts of the people.

But does no danger threaten the republic from this source? In my opinion, (I speak of the present moment more particularly) none: for from all those circumstances which have passed under my view since my arrival, I am satisfied that whilst the majority of the convention is on the side of the revolution, it will be supported by the people, and I am even persuaded that even if the majority was against it, although in consequence it would be able to occasion great confusion, and do in other respects much injury, yet it would not be able to restore the ancient monarchy. In advancing this position, I reason not only from recent incidents, but from past events, and by which I see that the great mass of the French nation, thro' all the vicissitudes of the war and succession of parties, was always on the side of the revolution, supporting the convention with an undeviating perseverance, not because it possessed their unbounded confidence, but because they believed it to be true to the main object, and was of course the only solid rock upon which they could rest with safety. A variety of circumstances marked in strong characters and by great events in the course of the revolution heretofore communicated (and which upon that account I forbear to repeat) tend to demonstrate the truth of this position. Nor have the citizens of this republic merited in other respects the reputation, for turbulence and licentiousness often ascribed to them in other countries: for it is unquestionably true, that the great atrocities which have stained the different stages of the revolution and particularly the massacres of the 2$^{\underline{nd}}$ and 3$^{\underline{rd}}$ September 1792 and the invasion of the Convention on the 31$^{\underline{st}}$ of May 1793, which terminated in the arrestation and destruction of the Girondine party did not proceed from a licentious commotion of the people. On the contrary it is believed that many of the immediate agents in the first, were not inhabitants of Paris, but brought from a considerable distance Marseilles and some even from Italy, put in motion by some secret cause not yet fully understood. It is also affirmed that the great mass of the people of Paris, were ignorant of what was perpetrating, at the time of the transaction, and that those who knew of it were struck with the same horror that we were when we heard of it, on the other side of the Atlantic.[3] And the movement of the 31$^{\underline{st}}$ of May when they were embodied and arranged against the Convention, was a movement on their part in obedience to the law, and for which they were regularly summoned and commanded by the ordinary Officers. 'Tis said that the great mass knew nothing of the object for which they convened, or the purpose to which they were to be made instrumental: that the secret was deposited with a few only in the Convention, such as Robespierre, Danton &c who governed the operation, and the Mayor of the City,[4] the General and some principal Officers of the guards, and who marshalled the citizens out as upon an ordinary parade. The party in the house which controuled the movement knew how to turn it to good account. The Mayor (a partizan of Robespierre Danton &c) had a few days before presented a petition demanding the arrestation of the 22 members, and it was now urged in the house by Couthon, a leading member of the same party, that the <u>present discontents</u>, and which he said occasioned the movement in question, and threatened the annihilation of the Convention, could not be satisfied unless those <u>obnoxious</u> members were arrested. And as the Girondine party did not control the movement, or know anything about it, otherwise than as appearances announced, and which were tremendous, for Henriot was then also at the head of the guards, the declarations of the other party were believed to be true, and the members in consequence arrested. Thus by mere finesse and under a dexterous management, the Girondine party was completely overwhelmed, and the mountain party as completely established on its ruins, and by means of the people, who being exhibited in dumb shew, by the latter were the object of terror, and the cause of the overthrow of the former, notwithstanding it was at the time the preponderating party in the Convention, and equally so in the public estimation.

These latter details may perhaps appear inapplicable to the subject: but as I consider them of some importance as well to enable you to judge of the future fortune of the revolution as of those dangers which are supposed by many, more immediately to threaten the welfare of the republic, I have thought proper to communicate them to you. The success of the revolution, depends of course upon the people: whatever therefore unfolds the disposition and character of the people and especially in relation to that object must be useful.

I was advised by your favour of the 2ᵈ of December that Mʳ J Pitcairn of New York was appointed Consul for this City, and upon which appointment some considerations have occurred which I have thought it my duty to suggest. Permit me to ask, is he an American citizen, and if so, whether by birth or naturalization, and in the latter case whether he became such since the revolution? If of the last description, his arrival will subject me to great embarrassment and for reasons given in my 4ᵗʰ letter of the 18ᵗʰ of October last⁵ and to which, with those from the Commissary of foreign affairs to me, transmitted at the same time, I beg leave to refer you. I candidly think if his situation is known, being a person deemed by the English law a subject of that crown, he will not be recognised or if recognised not without great reluctance. Shall I announce him then withholding a communication of the fact, admitting it to be a fact. In case I do and it is afterwards discovered, what will be the impression of the government towards myself and especially after what has passed between us on the same subject, finding that I had placed without their knowledge, in office and immediately in the presence of the public councils, a person of a description against which they had particularly objected? And that it will be discovered and immediately is most certain, for there are already letters for him here from England, and these will most probably be multiplied tenfold after his arrival: besides the character &c, of every foreign agent and of every grade being an object of systematic political inquiry is always well known. In other views this subject merits attention: admitting the acquiescence of this government in his favour, it is to be observed that a great proportion of the business of our countrymen here is transacted with the government; the adjustment frequently requires my official support: if he does not possess the confidence of the government, he will not only be unable to render that service to our countrymen which might otherwise be expected from one in his station, but as he will be brought officially into frequent and familiar communication with me, it will follow that precisely that portion of distrust to which he is subject, will attach itself to me and produce a correspondent effect, to a certain degree, upon every subject depending here in which we are interested. I know well that if my 4ᵗʰ letter had been received I should not have been placed in this dilemma: but how to act in case he arrives I do not know. I console myself under the hope he will not arrive, but by delaying his departure until that letter was received, put it in your power to reconsider the appointment. With great respect and esteem I have the honour to be Sir, Your very humble and most obᵗ servᵗ

Jaˢ Monroe.
[March] 9ᵗʰ

P. S. Since writing the above I have been explicitly assured by Mʳ Pelet a member of the Diplomatic section of the committee of public safety that, in confidence Mʳ Jay's treaty contained nothing which would give uneasiness here, they had expressly instructed their agent now negociating with Spain, to use his utmost effort to secure for us the points in controversy between the United States and that power: in consequence I thought proper to send in a short supplemental note explanatory of the several objects of that controversy. And which I likewise inclose herein with the report of Mʳ Mountflorence by whom it was delivered.[6] What the success of their endeavours in our behalf may be is uncertain: but we cannot expect the conclusion of their own treaty will be long delayed on that account.

I had forgotten to notify you officially [of] the present I had made to the Convention of our flag. It was done in consequence of the order of that body for its suspension in its hall and an intimation from the President himself that they had none and were ignorant of the model. I herewith send you a copy of my note to him accompanying it.[7]

Copy, DNA: RG 59: Dispatches from France

1. Pierre Adet.

2. JM to the Committee of Public Safety, 28 January 1795; Committee of Public Safety to JM, 5 February 1795; JM to the Committee of Public Safety, 2 March 1795 (all above). For Philippe Merlin de Douai's letter of 21 February 1795, see James C. Mountflorence to JM, 22 February 1795 (above).

3. The leaders responsible for the 1792 September Massacres in Paris were Marat and those who took over the mayor's office and established the Commune in April. Although the faltering Girondist government had hired for their own protection criminals from prisons in Marseilles, many of whom came from prisons in Corsica and Greece, it was Marat and the Commune who first met and made a contract with them when they arrived in Paris at the end of July 1792. Subsequently Marat and his Committee of Surveillance drew up "a list of suspects," who were then arrested and imprisoned in Paris. On the afternoon of September 2, drunken hired assassins with pikes, axes, and cutlasses, entered the prisons and began a savage slaughter of nearly 1500 people. The killings continued through September 5 (Stanley Loomis, *Paris in the Terror*, 74-83).

4. Jean–Nicolas Pache (1746-1823) was mayor of Paris from 14 February 1793 to 10 May 1794 (Jules Michelet, *Histoire de la Révolution Française*, 2: 1518-1519).

5. JM's letter was dated 16 October 1794 (above).

6. JM to the Committee of Public Safety, 2 March 1795 (above); James C. Mountflorence to JM, 9 March 1795 (below).

7. JM to André-Antoine Bernard, 10 September 1794 (above). The copy of this letter enclosed with JM to Randolph, 6 March 1795 in DNA : RG 59 : Dispatches from France is dated 9 September 1794.

From Edmund Randolph

Department of State March 8. 1795.

Sir

On the 15th ultimo I had the honor of writing to you at large; and on the 20th of the same month, I received your letters of October 16, November 7. and 20 1794.

Being uncertain, whether I may not be required at the next moment to close this letter, I shall not undertake to answer your dispatches fully; tho' I will proceed as far as the hurry of the opportunity will permit.

I have the pleasure to inform you, that the President much approves your attention to our commerce; and the merchants, who are immediately interested, and to whom I have communicated your measures, think them judicious.

The temporary appointment of Mr Skipwith, and his report have been also well received. But the circumstance of his being your secretary, the want of emolument to our consulates, and an ignorance of what you had done, caused a Mr. Pitcairn to be named consul for Paris, pretty early in the late session of the Senate. I shall send a general instruction to the consuls to obey the directions of the ministers of the United States. Should such a power be necessary before my general letter reaches them, you may use this as your authority upon the subject.

Your observations as to passports have for some time occurred to me. Those, which have been issued from this department lately, have been governed by strict rules; and great reproach and calumny have fallen upon the chief officer, from the mouths of foreign Aristocrats, who are a kind of half-fledged citizens of the United States, by having resided therein a few months.

Your history of the Jacobin Societies was so appropriate to the present times in our own country, that it was conceived proper to furnish the public with those useful lessons; and extracts were published, as from a letter <u>of a gentleman in Paris to his friend in this city</u>.[1]

Last night the treaty with Great Britain arrived. It will remain undivulged by the executive, until the 8ᵗʰ of June next, when the Senate will assemble, to deliberate on its ratification. I perceive, that Mʳ Fauchet is very uneasy, but upon what grounds, which are justifiable, I know not. The posts, and the spoliations of commerce will never surely be mentioned, as requiring war instead of negotiation; and if they do require war, we and no other nation are the judges. Our trade may also be regulated by any treaties, which we please; and no other government can find cause of offence, unless we derogate from its rights. You are acquainted with the restrictions on Mʳ Jay, against the weakening of our engagements with France; and as far as a cursory perusal of the treaty will enable me to speak, I have not discovered any reasonable ground for dissatisfaction in the French Republic. For it cannot be supposed, that the French nation would be displeased that our disputes with other nations should be concluded. But you will not judge from what I say, that my opinion is formed, whether the treaty will or will not be ratified. However, your idea as to Denmark and Sweden, tho' it was always attended to, grows of less importance. I shall not now answer your proposition or rather intimation, relative to a <u>certain concert</u>, until a future opportunity; and after hearing farther from you concerning it. You will have concluded from one of my late letters, that the step is viewed here, as a very strong one.

Your observations on our commercial relation to France; & your conduct as to Mʳ Gardoqui's letter, prove your judgment and assiduity. Nor are your measures as to Mʳ Paine, and the Lady of our friend[2] less approved.

Colᵒ Humphreys is here arranging the affair of Algiers.

Be so good as to bring to the earliest issue the points, which You have pressed upon the French Republic; and, particularly the <u>fifteen</u> thousand dollars, advanced to the people of Sᵗ Domingo. You have generally called them fifty thousand by mistake.

My next letter will be devoted to the two important passages in your letters, conveying intelligence of your movements respecting Spain and Great Britain.

The inclosed papers from Mʳ Vincent must be submitted to your discretion, to do with them what may be best and proper. Those of Mʳ King, relative to the ship Andrew, make a part of the business already in your hands.

Mʳ Taylor[3] will prepare for this conveyance your newspapers &c. With sincere and constant esteem and respect, I have the honor to be sir your mo. ob. serv.

Edm: Randolph

P. S. Since writing the above I have received the enclosed letter of the the 7. instant from Mʳ Fitzsimons which I beg leave to consign to your particular attention[4]

RC, PHi: Gratz Collection

1. Extracts of JM's letters to Randolph of 16 October, 7 and 20 November 1794, in which JM criticized the Jacobin clubs during the Reign of Terror, found their way into newspapers such as the *Philadelphia Gazette*, the *New York Herald*, and *Dunlap*

and Claypoole's American Daily Advertiser under the title of "Three Excerpts written by a Gentleman in Paris to his friend in this City" (*Madison Papers*, 15: 478).

2. Adrienne Lafayette.

3. George Taylor served as chief clerk of the State Department from April 1792 to January 1798 (*Jefferson Papers*, 17: 356, 358).

4. The various enclosures could not be identified.

From St. George Tucker

Williamsburg March 8ᵗʰ 1795.

If I have appeared tardy, my worthy friend, in writing to you since you left America it was by no means my Intention to be so—but I found myself at a loss into what Channel to put my Letters.—I was told indeed that I might address them to the Secretary of State: but I am not on such a footing with the Gentleman who now fills that office, as to give him the trouble even of a Letter. I have resolved to enclose them to the french Consul at Norfolk, with whom I have some Acquaintance and who will, I hope take Care to forward them.

I saw with pleasure an Account of the very cordial reception you met with from the Convention of France. I saw likewise the vote of Union of the Colours of the two republics, & your Letter on that occasion.[1] This is all that I have seen in the public prints respecting you; and as I have no political Correspondent, except Jno Page, who seldom writes, & never writes much, I have heard nothing of you through private Channels.

Your Connexion with the great number of active politicians in our Country must afford you sources of Information far superior to what a sequestered mortal, such as I am, can give you—nevertheless I mean to give you a sketch of the most remarkable Incidents, public & private, as they relate to your friends, that have happened within my knowledge or recollection since you left us; for I know by Experience that Absence renders many things interesting, which we might pass over lightly did they happen under our Eyes. My Letters therefore will resemble a Village Gazette, where the Depredations committed by Hawks & Foxes upon the neigbouring poultry will find a place with the great Atchievements of Nations.

The Storm in the west was brewing, or rather ready to burst when you left us. The Secretary of the Treasury in an extra-official Letter gave a circumstantial detail of its rise and progress to the presᵗ.—If I had the paper that contained this Letter I would enclose it, because the Secretary seems to have forgot that he had no right to advise the presᵗ to have recourse to coercive measures, & I should wish for your opinion how far I am right in this Idea.[2]—Judge MᶜKean in his report to the Executive of pennsᵃ considered the Acts of violence as amounting to nothing more than a sudden riot, which the civil arm might have punished[3]—but from the presᵗ's proclamation it appears that Judge Wilson thought otherwise,[4] and the Militia were first ordered to hold themselves in readiness and afterwards to march to the number of 15000. under the command of Govʳ Lee.—They found nobody in arms to oppose them; and after having undergone Services that might be compared to those of Cæsar's tenth Legion (as one of the papers expressed it) returned without firing a Gun: some little opposition was made to the Draft in Surry County.—Two persons, were taken up & committed to Goal on a charge of high Treason agt the U. S. by a zealous magistrate, who construed what might have been deemed a mutiny in an Army into the atrocious Offense before described. They lay in Goal six Weeks, were at length bailed by Judge Griffin, and at the succeeding Term discharged for want of prosecution.[5] One Sinclair had before this time attracted the notice of the Govᵗ towards a Vessel which he was supposed to intend for a privateer.—The Militia of

Richmond & Petersburg were ordered out under Brig.ʳ Gen. Marshall to march down to Smithfield to seize her.—She was libelled under the Act of Congress prohibiting warlike Equipment; but the Jury acquitted her, & I believe very properly. Sinclair however hath been indicted, as I understand in the fed. Court.[6]— If so the Ind.ᵗ is still depending.—Upwards of 100 people I hear were brought down from the back parts of pennsylvania to be tried in phil.ᵃ for their Crimes in the business of the Insurgency.—The Goaler refused to admit them to supply themselves with bedding &c at their own Expense, declaring that Straw was good enough for traitors to lie on. Some have been bailed—the remainder are waiting the Arrival of the Spring-circuit, in the Goal of philadelphia.[7]

The Gen. Assembly at phil.ᵃ expelled the western members chosen in October, on Account of the Insurrection. Gallatin in a most able Speech clearly proved there was nothing like Opposition to law & Gov.ᵗ after the 11ᵗʰ of Sept.ʳ He also shewed most clearly the unconstitutionality of the measure: but who can restrain the zeal of <u>good</u> men, actuated by the love of their Country! M.ʳ M___'s[8] re-election to the Seat he has occupied for six years has been supposed to be that eminently advantageous event to the public felicity, which that measure was intended to secure. Whether it hath produced the desired effect I have not yet heard.—The Appointment of our friend Innes as a Missionary to Kentucky is so immediately connected with the western Affairs that I can not omit to mention it. In what Character, or with what powers he hath gone is not known.[9]—A motion was made in the house of Delegates to declare his Office vacant. It was I believe, suggested by private Expectations, which were defeated by a large majority—An Attack was intended & made upon the Gov.ʳ for accepting the Command of the militia, but dextrously warded off, & a vote of thanks substituted for one of indirect Censure.—Brooke was chosen his Successor; his only opponent M.ʳ Wood.—Dawson, Wilson Nicholas, Stevens T. Mason & Tazewell were Candidates for supplying your place, & Taylor's who resigned—the two latter were chosen. I think Nicholas lost it by Mismanagement. Tazewell having made a vacancy in the Court of Appeals a warm opposition to our friend P_____[10] whose pretensions in the order of succession heretofore observed were indisputable, was commenced. His fellow Townsman[11] who was next on the list peremptorily declined the Contest with him.—So did some others.—When the Election came on all the Judges of the Gen. C.[12] were successively nominated by M.ʳ C. L.[13]—A Member got up & made a speech recommending M.ʳ Roan in the strongest terms—The Ballot proceeded immediately and he was chosen by a large majority.[14]—This made a vacancy in the Gen. Court—Madison of Botetourt & young Paul Carrington were opponents—the latter carried it by a single vote.[15]

I am not able to inform you what Congress have done in their late Session. The pres.ᵗ's speech you will observe indirectly censured the democratic Societies. A party in Congress heard the occasion with avidity. Ames in one of his Speeches observed, <u>That that Liberty which Poetry had exalted into a Goddess, History proved to be a Cannibal.</u>[16] A fine republican Sentiment this.—The house was nearly equally divided but the democrats at length warded off the intended Blow: the president in his reply evidently appeared dissatisfied, with the Address of the house.—A debate of one or two days took place on the substitution of the word <u>your</u> in the Address, for the particle a—The Bill for naturalization of foreigners was thought to require Amend.ᵗ and among other things it was required that foreign nobility should renounce their titles on becoming American Citizens—a debate of several days ensued, with great heat. Could we have supposed this to have happened in a really democratic republic. The clause however passed, by a considerable majority: in all the Cases the same individuals were generally found linked together. An admirable specimen of the unbiased conduct of that body.—All the late taxes, including the <u>Carriage</u> tax, have been continued to the year 1801. to form a fund for redeeming the public debt. A friend of yours in this place refused to pay the carriage tax, upon the ground that it was a direct tax, & not imposed according to the Constitution—So did Mᴿ Pendleton, Mᴿ Roan, Col. Taylor, Mᴿ Page, & some others—No steps have yet been taken to inforce it: and I suspect that it will hardly be brought to a judicial test.[17] Campbell[18] acknowledged to me that the tax was unconstitutional, but said he should insist that the <u>Courts</u> had no power to pronounce the Act void.—Smith of S. C. at the head of the Committee has made a report in favor of selling the western Lands to pay off the national Debt. Timeo Danaos, et Dona ferentes.[19] Will not those who have been so assiduous in engrossing the public debt, be equally as assiduous in engrossing the Lands?[20]—This man is re-elected for Charleston. Young Rutledge & my brother[21] were his Oponents. The latter has lost his only Son & Child, since you saw him. I have not heard from him for some months.—Griffin declines—Burwell Bassett, Miles Selden, Merriwether Jones, & another are Candidates for the Vacancy. Page, I hope will be re-elected—young Stratton, of the eastern shore will it is said oppose him.[22] Parker will be re-elected without opposition, it is said, & merely for want of an Opponent.—Madison, having married, it is said means to retire. I hope otherwise. His & your friend Jefferson has had much ill health last fall but I hear he is mending. The resignations of Hamilton & Knox made way for Wolcott, & Pickering. Mᴿ Cobb it is said will succeed the latter as post-master General.[23] Griffin was however spoken of here, for some time.

Expectation is all alive on the subject of Mᴿ Jays Treaty, which was brought to Norfolk last week by a Capt. Barney, who will probably reach philadelphia tomorrow. The treaty-mongers affect to expect very great things—if the outline given us be just I think they will be disappointed. As to the surrender of the western posts much stress I think cannot be laid on an Article which postpones for two years longer, what should have been done ten years ago.

To quit the great world & speak of our friends—our Coadjutors Prentis & Nelson are both well, except that the former has an ugly sore on his right hand, which I believe has been of more than two years standing. I have sometimes feared it would end in a Cancer. I believe it at present better than usual. Nelson is at last fixed at the Indian fields.—His neighbor Tyler was very ill the last fall but has recovered his health pretty well and is as much of a Sans-Culotte as ever. Our friends the Bishop,[24] Andrews, & Barraud,[25] with their respective families are very well. I am under much concern for my son Tudor, who has been in a very ill state of health for more than six months, almost without hope of Amendment.[26] I hope you have been so happy as to retain your own health, & to see your family in the same state, a Blessing which I now feel how to estimate; my family having been most astonishingly sick since last August.—Never was sickness more general, or more fatal in Virginia, than since that period.

My better half joins me in respectful good wishes to yourself, Mᴿˢ Monroe, & little Eliza. As you cannot mistake the writer, I shall not subscribe my name, lest this Letter should fall into improper hands— but you will at a single glance know it to be from one of your most affectionate Friends

RC, ViW: Monroe Papers

1. JM to André-Antoine Bernard, 10 September 1794, above.

2. Alexander Hamilton wrote to President Washington on 5 August 1794 and presented his case for the use of the military in suppressing the Whiskey Rebellion. The letter was published in *Dunlap and Claypoole's American Daily Advertiser*, a Philadelphia newspaper, on 21 August 1794 and widely reprinted after that (*Hamilton Papers*, 17: 24-58).

3. Tucker may be referring to a meeting that President Washington called on 2 August 1794, comprising members of his cabinet and representatives of the government of Pennsylvania, including that state's chief justice, Thomas McKean. All the cabinet members advocated military action, while the Pennsylvanians called for more restraint. McKean said that "the judiciary power was equal to the task of quelling and punishing the riots, and that employment of military force, at this period, would be as bad as anything the Rioters had done—equally unconstitutional and illegal" (Leland D. Baldwin, *Whiskey Rebels*, 183-184).

4. James Wilson, an associate justice of the U. S. Supreme Court, authorized the use of the militia when he ruled on 4 August 1794 that the evidence presented to him indicated a rebellion was underway in western Pennsylvania that could not be suppressed by normal judicial proceedings (*ANB*).

5. President Washington's call for the states to provide militia to suppress the Whiskey Rebellion met with opposition in many places. When officers mustered the militia in Surry County, Virginia, many of the men refused to serve and left the field (Thomas P. Slaughter, *The Whiskey Rebellion*, 212-214).

6. John Sinclair (1755-1820) of Smithfield, Virginia, was active as a privateer during the American Revolution. In the summer of 1794 the British consul at Norfolk accused him of fitting out a vessel as a privateer near Smithfield on the James River in support of the French. Governor Henry Lee ordered John Marshall, the future chief justice, to take a regiment of militia to Smithfield to help enforce the Neutrality Act. Sinclair was arrested but not convicted (*Marshall Papers*, 2:182-183; 275).

7. Federal officials arrested twenty men in western Pennsylvania and took them to Philadelphia for trial on charges of treason. All but two were acquitted, and those two were pardoned by President Washington (Slaughter, *Whiskey Rebellion*, 219-220).

8. Mr. M. has not been identified.

9. President Washington, worried about the rumors of a separatist plot in the west, asked James Innes, the attorney general of Virginia, to visit Kentucky and inform local officials of the government's efforts to address issues important in the west, including access to the Mississippi River. Washington entrusted Innes with copies of official documents relating to negotiations with Spain to show to the governor and members of the assembly of Kentucky (Samuel Flagg Bemis, *Pinckney's Treaty*, 210-211).

10. Joseph Prentis.

11. Tucker is referring to himself.

12. The General Court.

13. Charles Lee.

14. Spencer Roane was elected judge of the Virginia Court of Appeals on 2 December 1794 and served until his death in 1822 (*ANB*).

15. Thomas Madison (1746-1798) was commonwealth attorney for Botetourt County 1778-1787. He served in the House of Delegates 1780-1782, 1793-1796 and briefly on the Council of State in 1790 (*Journal of the Council of State of Virginia*, 5: 394-395). Paul Carrington (1764-1816) was a member of the House of Delegates 1786-1788 and the Virginia Senate 1791-1794. He was appointed as a judge of the General Court in 1794, a post he held until his death in 1816 (*Dictionary of Virginia Biography*).

16. Fisher Ames made this remark in a speech in the House of Representatives on 26 November 1794 during the debate on the response to be given to President Washington's annual message and its reference to the Democratic-Republican societies. The full sentence reads: "If we look at Greece, so famed for letters and more for misery, we shall see their ferocious liberty made their petty commonwealths wolves' dens—that liberty, which poetry represents as a goddess, history describes as a cannibal" (*Works of Fisher Ames*, 2: 1058).

17. On 5 June 1794 Congress passed a law laying duties upon carriages for the conveyance of persons. The tax was viewed in Virginia as a direct tax and therefore unconstitutional. It was contested in *Hylton v. the United States*, which came before the Supreme Court in 1796. The court upheld the law and was the first instance in which it ruled on the constitutionality of a federal law (Julius Goebel, Jr., *History of the Supreme Court of the United States*, 1: 778-782).

18. Alexander Campbell was the U. S. district attorney for Virginia (*Marshall Papers*, 2: 144)

19. "Beware of Greeks bearing gifts" (Virgil, *The Aeneid*).

20. Tucker feared that the proposed legislation for the sale of the western lands to pay off the national debt would result in the sale of the entire public domain at once to speculators. He wrote a pamphlet in 1795 entitled *Cautionary Hints to Congress Respecting the Sale of Western Lands, Belonging to the United States* (1796, *Early American Imprints*), in which he argued that the gradual sale of the western lands would be better for the country and provide a long-term and steady source of revenue for the government.

21. Thomas Tudor Tucker.

22. John Page won re-election to the House of Representatives. John Stratton, Jr. (1769-1804), his opponent, represented Northampton County in the House of Delegates 1794-1798. He was a member of the House of Representatives 1801-1803 (*BDAC*; *Register of the General Assembly of Virginia*).

23. David Cobb was a representative from Massachusetts. He did not get the post office position; rather, Joseph Habersham of Georgia was appointed on 25 February 1795 (*BDAC*).

24. Bishop James Madison.

25. Philip Barraud (1757-1830) was a Williamsburg, Virginia, physician who had served as a doctor with the Continental Army. He moved to Norfolk, Virginia, in 1799 and in 1804 became the director of the navy hospital there (E. M. Barraud, *Barraud: The Story of a Family*, 38).

26. Theodorick Tudor Tucker (1782-1795) died on April 3 (Henry Fitz Gilbert "Early Printing in Virginia," *New England Historical and Genealogical Record*, 26: 34).

From James C. Mountflorence

Paris the 9ᵉ March 1795.

Sir

I delivered your Note to Mʳ Pelet[1] at the diplomatic Room of the Committee. After he had perused it, I told him that I had it in Charge from You to explain to him the Nature of our Demands on Spain, in case at a future Period that Overture should by made that Power, the french Government should find it convenient to accomodate us. I then represented to him that the free Navigation of the Mississippi without a Port for our Vessels, would be little or No Advantage to us, there being no Ankrege in that River; & the Spaniards holding both Sides of it by the Possession of West Florida as high up as the Most Northern Extremity of the 31ˢᵗ degree of Nᵒ Latitude, we would have no place for storing our Goods or refit our Vessels, & even no Means of coming up the River from its Entrance with our Ships. He seemed to be perfectly well acquainted with the Situation of that River & to be sensible of the necessity of our Having the freedom of New-Orleans. I explained to him the Limits we claimed by the Treaty with England of 1783, & the ridiculous Pretensions of Spain respecting her territorial Rights.

He asked me the present situation of Our Government's Negotiations with Spain & whether that last Power had given us Reason to expect a favorable issue; I answered him that I was <illegible> ignorant of what had been done.

He concluded by Desiring Me to assure You, that Should a Negociation take place with Spain, France would not forget the Interest of America, & would render her ever good office in her Power.

Herewith you have, Sir, a Copy of the Circular I am writing to the 14 Ports of france.[2] I have the Honor to be very respectfully Sir Yʳ most Obedᵗ & most H. Servᵗ

Jˢ C. Mountflorence

RC, NN: Monroe Papers

1. JM to the Committee of Public Safety, 2 March 1795, above.

2. Mountflorence's circular to the American consuls in France has not been located.

From Henry Tazewell

Philadelphia 9th March 1795

Dear Sir.

I have long meditated upon the business upon which I now take into my pen—for although I have never received a line from you, since your arrival in France yet that shall not operate as a reason to prevent ye pursuit of my present determination.

My details will be rendered more interesting to you by beginning with them at the period when you left this Country. To be your successor, then, in the Senate, the Executive of our State appointed Mr P. Henry, soon after your departure. He refused to accept the appointment and that office remained unfilled until the meeting of the Assembly. General Stepⁿ T. Mason was appointed to it. The votes—for him 108—for W. C. Nicholas, about 2, for Ed: Harrison[1] about the same number. Taylor resigned before the meeting of the Assembly and at the same time Mason was appointed yours, I was chosen to be his Successor in the Senate. Votes for me, 128—for Mr Dawson, 40. This appointm^t was as unexpected, or undesired by me. But as I was called upon I came on about Xmas to this place—where ever since I have been pursuing my new political duties. Mason was taken ill, soon after his appointment & has not been here at all this winter.

I had not been long in the Senate before the Vice President asked & obtained, leave of absence for the remainder of the Session. I was chosen as unexpectedly & suddenly to be the President of the Senate, as I ever saw anything done. Being alone from Virg^a unversed in the practices of older members—and indeed not desirous of committing myself before I became better informed. I accepted the appointment. My business therefore has chiefly been since my arrival here, to observe & to understand the Conduct of those with whom It is my lot to act—and my situation well secured me from a like exposure to others.[2]

With the State of politics in the Senate you are well acquainted, as the same Members you left, are still there. It is however within your recollection that this is the time for one third of these Members, either to be discontinued, or to be reelected. The Elections have taken place, and they stand thus— Langdon—King—& Gunn—reelected—Izard out, & one Reid in his place. Hawkins out, & Bloodworth in his place. Edwards[3] out & Humphrey Marshall in his place. Morris out, and Bingham in his place. Some former member whom I did not know, out, and Latimer in his place from Delaware. Mitchell out,[4] & Trumbull in his place. Bradley from Vermont out & I know not who is in his place. These new members have not yet taken their Seats. If report can be relied on, these new elections are not favourable to Republicans—I mean a majority of them. You will easily from your own remembrance class them—and account for every Election but that of H. Marshall in Kentucky. I have not enough of the history of this to detail it to you. I believe however it may be relied on that the business was not fairly conducted.

In the House of Representatives, the last Elections have made considerable changes. All the old members from Jersey are out, except Dayton, and it is said, he only assured his election by the votes he gave at a former Session upon the subject of Madison's resolutions. In New York, Watts is discontinued—Van Courtland reelected[5]—& the returns for the next year stand 7 Republicans ag^t 3 arist^{ts}. In Massachusets—Dexter[6] is out—& altho it is not yet decided, it is believed that a Mr Varnum[7] will succeed him, a good Republican—Sedgwick & Ames, were both hard run to get in—& what is a pretty good Evidence of the temper of the people, is that all the republican Members to the Eastward of this place have been easily reelected, while those of a contrary opinion have uniformly been hard pushed. In Virg^a our elections are not yet over. Griffin has resigned—& Lee will, it is conjectured be turned out for

Richd Brent. Except in these instances we shall not have a change of politics, even if there should be a change of Members.

I suppose you have heard that Hamilton had resigned and that Wolcott was put into his place—Knox resigned, & Pickering in his place—a Mr Habersham of Georgia made Postmaster—a Mr Jos: Jackson of Massachusets Comptrouler of the Treasury[8]—so that Randolph is the only one of the old Set that remains. If these changes should produce any change in the political course of the U States, it is not yet to be discovered.

The Session of Congress which ended last Tuesday—the 3^d March—has been calm & temperate compared with the last in which you were. Very few important changes if any, have taken place in former Laws—and no new subjects have been acted upon, so as to add to the Code of Laws in any material point. In revising the Citizen bill—Giles made a proposition to exclude from Citizenship every Emigrant who bore a Title, unless he previously renounced that Title. The proposition begat lengthy and warm discussions. The Eastern members pretty generally opposed it. There was a good deal of warmth manifested on this occasion—but it is not less true, it was unexpected, that the Senate passed the act without opposition to that clause.[9] This mark of disapprobation to the idle distinction of nobility, it became necessary to give, in complyance with the general wishes of the People. If it had been believed that the thing would have passed over without much discussion, the question perhaps would have met a different fate. Those who were warmly attached to Republicanism, considered the question as an evidence necessary to be given to the French Republic, after the reception which some of their Titled orders hath met with here. Towards the latter end of the Session a circumstance turned up which has excited some unpleasant sensations—Gunn, Judge Wilson & others had so contrived to manage the Assembly of Georgia, as to procure from them a purchase of 2 thirds of their western Lands for 500,000 dollars.[10]

As soon as this was known some attempts were made to check the progress of the evil which Land speculations are begetting in the U. States—but nothing material was done. Perhaps this & other speculations of the like kind, have & will produce more serious Evils among us, than any other event which has happened except the paper system: to which this seems closely allied. Independence of Character, Virtue and I had almost said the most common principles of honesty are feeling the shock which proceeds from thence. Where these evils will end it is difficult to discover, yet my own mind suggests a remedy, which after the last session of Congress I will further dilate on to you if it takes the direction I at present expect.

We have not officially received the treaty Mr Jay has signed with England. It was signed the 21 of Novr and it is a subject of surprize that it has not yet arrived. The terms of that Treaty, are not known except from conjecture. But believing this it will reach America by the 8th of June next, the President has summoned the Senate to attend on that day in Philadelphia. The eagerness with which this connection has been solicited—and the backwardness which every application from the French republick has been received on the same subject, evidences a Spirit which is not the genuine Spirit of the People of the U. States but only of the Paper Men in the Cities, & of the Governors. I mean a majority of the Governors. If the Treaty should be objectionable in any great degree on its inspection, the temper of the People will be agitated by it discussion—& I dare say I shall not be mistaken in predicting that two thirds of the Senate would not be found to approve it. Sometimes, we have heard that a Treaty has been concluded by you, with France. I wish such an Event could take place by the 8th of June. Or at any rate that you would then, or as soon after as possible intimate to me as for as it may be proper the real state of that business.

My own believe is that if the Republic of France should make peace with her Enemies, except England, the superiority she will soon acquire at Sea would strongly invite her to play the same game on our commerce which G^r Britain has done. I should however be extremely sorry, if such a course of Conduct where adopted—unless France of obtained so decisive a superiority as to prevent the hopes of that british faction that now so much influences our Government. Perhaps if this was not the case that faction would plunge us into a war with France, forgetful of their former profession of neutrality.

The American sentiment you know is very favourable to the French republic. It is the wish of the People to preserve our Country in a state of peace. The british faction has closed in with this latter wish, and every thing friendly to the French Republic is made to look like war. The friendship of the people for a peaceful State is kept in continual Action ag^t their attachment to the French Republic. The dexterity with which this artifice is conducted, conceals from the people the true interests which ought to subsist between the U. States and France—but you know enough of these things without making any comments from me necessary. Things are precisely as you left them, except that the Successes of France has silenced in a greater degree the influence of british intrigues.

At the opening of the last session of Congress, the President brought forth the Insurrection in the western parts of Pennsylvania, as a gloomy feature in our political affairs. That insurrection was commenced by ye Excise System—it cost us the expenses of a March to the Scene of violence of 15,000 militia. It was fortunately quelled without bloodshed. But it was made the preface to a denunciation of ye democratic Societies. The Secretary of State, under the signature of Germanicus, has in the news papers been endeavoring to prop up this measure, which has excited some dissatisfaction. After exhausting in his way, his fund of arguments, he has published we believed a Letter from you relative to the Jacobin Societies in France, meaning there to shew, that our Societies ought to share the same fate.[11] I conjecture that you were written to for this history, without being apprized of the use intended to be made of it, & before the act of denunciation. Let me know, if my suspicions are well founded. The publication of your Letter by extract, with your own signature to it, is here considered as an unwarrantable Act. Mutilated diplomatic correspondence cannot be proper for the news papers, and when they are intended to answer a purpose known to be directly averse to your own opinions, that becomes less justifiable. You will have seen the history of the denunciation, and of the insurrection, in the Presidents speech. I shall not therefore trouble you with a more full recital of either.

Governor Clinton of New York, has resigned the Government & so has the Lieutenant Governor.[12] Jay is named for his Successor, and Judge Yates I believe from what I can hear, the latter will succeed.[13] Brooke is the Governor of Virginia in the place of Lee.

As far as you can consistently with you situation, I wish you would keep me well informed as to the affairs of Europe, and particularly of the French Republic. The following Characters will serve as a disguise for any communication you may choose to free from ye danger of being intercepted. I will keep its counterpart.

The undermentioned [segas] will serve for each of the Letters of the Alphabet under which they are made.

I am about to set out for Virginia, where, as well as while I am here, I shall be glad to hear from you. Remember me affectionately to Mrs Monroe & Eliza—& believe me to be Sincerely yours

Henry Tazewell

RC, DLC: Monroe Papers

1. Edmund Harrison served numerous terms in the Virginia House of Delegates. In 1794 he was a member of the council of state (*Register of the General Assembly of Virginia*; *Calendar of Virginia State Papers*, vols. 6 & 7).

2. Tazewell was elected president pro tem of the Senate on 20 February 1795 and served to the end of the session (*BDAC*).

3. John Edwards (1748-1837) represented Kentucky in the Senate 1792-1795 (BDAC).

4. Stephen Mix Mitchell (1743-1835) of Connecticut served with JM in the Continental Congress. He was a member of the Senate 1793-1795, and did not stand for re-election. He was later chief justice of Connecticut (ANB).

5. Philip Van Cortlandt (1749-1831) rose to the rank of brigadier general in the Continental army. He was a member of Congress from New York 1793-1809 (*ANB*).

6. Samuel Dexter (1761-1816) was a member of Congress from Massachusetts 1793-1795. Dexter served in the Senate from 1799 until 1800, when he resigned to accept appointment as secretary of war in the cabinet of John Adams (ANB).

7. Joseph Bradley Varnum (1750-1821), chief justice of the Massachusetts Court of General Sessions, was elected to the U. S. Congress from Massachusetts and served from 1795 to 1811 when he was elected to the U. S. Senate (*ANB*).

8. President Washington nominated Jonathan Jackson of Newburyport, Massachusetts, for appointment as comptroller of treasury. The Senate confirmed the nomination, but Jackson declined to serve (*Hamilton Papers*, 18: 195).

9. William B. Giles introduced his amendment to the naturalization bill on 31 December 1794. The House approved the amendment on January 2, after an extensive debate. The naturalization bill passed the House on January 8 and the Senate on January 26 (*Madison Papers*, 15: 430, 432-435, 440; *Journal of the U. S. Senate*, 2: 149).

10. In January 1795 the Georgia assembly passed a bill providing for the sale of a significant portion of its western lands in what is now Alabama and Mississippi to several land companies (known as the Yazoo land deal), with many members of the assembly accepting stock in the companies as inducements for their support. The following year a new assembly revoked the bill. This set off a protracted controversy. In 1810 the Supreme Court ruled that the original bill constituted a contract and could not be revoked by a subsequent act. The episode ended in 1814 when Congress voted to pay compensation to holders of Yazoo land warrants.

11. Randolph had urged President Washington to denounce the Democratic-Republican societies in his annual message of 19 November 1794. Randolph continued the attack with a series of thirteen newspaper essays written under the name of Germanicus, which were published in Philadelphia between January and April 1795. Extracts of Monroe's letters to Randolph of 16 October, 7 November, and 20 November 1794 appeared in the *Philadelphia Gazette* of 23 February 1795 under the heading "Extracts from three letters, written by a Gentleman in Paris to his friend in this City." The New York *Herald* reprinted the extracts on February 28 and identified JM as the author (John J. Reardon, *Edmund Randolph*, 280; *Madison Papers*, 15: 478).

12. George Clinton, facing rising opposition and plagued by ill-health, announced on 22 January 1795 that he would not seek re-election as governor of New York. His term ended on 1 July 1795. Lieutenant Governor Pierre Van Cortlandt (1721-1814) also stepped down. Both men had been in office for eighteen years (E. Wilder Spaulding, *His Excellency George Clinton*, 216-217; *ANB*).

13. Robert Yates (1738-1801) served as chief justice of New York 1790-1798. In 1795 he ran as the anti-federalist candidate to succeed George Clinton as governor. He lost to John Jay (*ANB*).

To Adrienne Lafayette

Paris Le 11 Mars 1795.

Madame

J'ai vu les deux Billets que vous m'avez fait presenter, et je puis vous assurer que j'avais préalablement écrit à notre Gouvernement au Sujet de L'Emploi des fonds. Je ne doute nullement que je ne reçoivé des Instructions à cet Effet avant le terme où les 2700[tt] vous seraient necessaires, et j'espere bien que je serais autorisé à remplir toutes vers Vous, même à l'égard de L'autre Billet pour la Personne qui était devenue la Caution pour la dette de 20,000[tt] contractée pour vous par la Citoyenne Chavaniac. Ainsi vous pouvez les tranquilerer tout deux à ce Sujet, sur lequel je vous prie de n'avoir aucune inquiétude. Agréer mes Salutations

Jaˢ Monroe

Editors' Translation

Paris 11 March 1795

Madame

I have looked at the two promissory notes that you gave me, and I can assure you I have written beforehand to our government on the use of these funds. I doubt not in the least that I should receive instructions regarding this matter before the period of time in which the 2700 livres shall be necessary to you, and I fully expect that I shall be authorized to satisfy you, even with regard to the other note for the person who has become the guarantor for the debt of 20,000 livres contracted by the Citizeness Chavaniac.[1] Thus you can set your mind at ease on both subjects, for which I beg you not to worry. Accepts my compliments

Jaˢ Monroe

RC, NjMoHP

1. Charlotte de La Fayette (1729-1811), the sister of Lafayette's father, Roch-Gilbert du Motier, marquis de La Fayette (1732-1759), married her cousin Guérin de Chavaniac, and lived most of her life on the Chavaniac estate in Auvergne. She raised the young Lafayette at Chavaniac after the death of his parents. After Adrienne gained her freedom, she returned to Chavaniac in an attempt to recover her husband's birthplace. Lafayette was considered an émigré and the State had confiscated his property. To buy back the estate from the new owners, Adrienne used money obtained from her sister, Rosalie Grammont, who had sold her own diamonds. Most of the funds, however, used to purchase the chateau came from a loan from JM (Jason Lane, *General and Madame de Lafayette*, 222; André Maurois, *Adrienne, the Life of the Marquise de Lafayette*, 271).

From James Madison

Philadᵃ March 11. 1795.

Dear Sir

Along with this I forward a large packet which Mʳ Beckley has been so kind as to make up for you. It will give you such information as is not contained in the newspapers, and which forms a proper supplement to them.

I have not yet recᵈ a single line from you except yours of Sepʳ 2ᵈ long since acknowledged. Your last letters of the official kind were duplicates of Ocʳ 16. Novʳ 7. & 20. You will perceive in the newspapers that the parts of them relating to the Jacobin Societies have been extracted & printed. In New York they have been republished with your name prefixed. The question agitated in consequence of the President's denunciation of the Democratic Societies, will account for this use of your observations. In N. York where party contests are running high in the choice of a Successor to Clinton who declines, I perceive the use of them is extended by adroit comments, to that subject also. It is proper you should be apprized of these circumstances, that your own judgment may be the better exercised as to the latitude or reserve of your communications.

The Treaty concluded with G. Britain did not arrive before the adjourment and dispersion of Congress. The Senators received a summons to reassemble on the 8ᵗʰ of June, on the calculation that the

Treaty could not fail to be rec^d by that time. It arrived a few days after. It is a circumstance very singular that the first knowledge of its contents as finally settled, should not have come to the Executive till more than three months after the date of it. What its contents are, the Executive alone as yet know the most impenetrable secresy being observed. You will easily guess the curiosity and disappointment of the public. Complaints however are repressed by the confidence that some adequate reasons exist for the precaution. The arrival of this Treaty and the delicate relations in which we stand to France, are beginning to turn the public attention to the prospect of meliorating the Treaty with her, and the arrangements that may have been taken on either side for the purpose. It is certainly much to be desired that the crisis should not be suffered to elapse without <u>securing</u> to this Country the precious advantages in commerce which we now enjoy from the indulgence or temporary embarrassments of that Nation, and still more that the possibility should be precluded of any collisions that may endanger the general friendship already stipulated between them.

You will receive by this conveyance a letter from Mr Jones which will inform you among other things that young Jno Mercer, son of the late Judge is about to visit you with letters from his uncle &c.[1] I am desired by his uncle to co-operate in his introduction to France, and shall of course give him a letter to you. As you know him much better than I do, and will hear from Mr Jones who now must know him better than either, my letter will be more of form than any thing else. Mr Jones will also probably inform you that he has commissioned me to try Whether your property in Kentucky could be turned at this place into the means of executing in Virg^a some arrangements in which you are interested. I have not as yet succeeded, and much question whether I shall be able to do so. I have heard not a word from Genl Wilkison, nor can I give you any better acc^t from Vermont, or N. York.

I have been detained here since the adjournment by indisposition in my family, and shall now wait till the roads get better which I hope will be the case in 8 or 10 days. Before I leave the City, I will write again. I deplore the want of a Cypher—and the cramp it puts on our Correspondence. My sincerest regards to you all. Adieu.

RC, DLC: Madison Papers

John Fenton Mercer (1773-1812) was the son of James Mercer of Stafford County, who died in 1793. His uncle was John Francis Mercer (*William & Mary Quarterly*, series 1, 17: 209; *Encyclopedia of Virginia Biography*, 2: 26). The letter of introduction from Joseph Jones has not been located.

From John Quincy Adams

The Hague March 12th 1795.

Dear Sir

I had the honor of writing you some time since by a private hand in answer to your favor of January 21[1] but I believe the gentleman to whom I delivered the letter is not yet gone from Amsterdam and it is possible that this may reach you the first of the two.

The scarcity of subsistence and especially of bread in so many parts of Europe will doubtless give great encouragement to a very important branch of Agriculture of industry and of Commerce in the United States. In this Country there is no present want suffered, but it is greatly apprehended. The importation of flour and rye meal is permitted and freed from all duties during the course of the present year, which seems to open a vent for our superfluity of the ensuing season, as well as of that which is past.

The political fate of this Country remains undecided. The interests of the two Republics cannot in every particular be the same; but where there is so much generosity on one side and so much gratitude on the other, they will probably be reconciled without difficulty.

The circulation of paper is the circumstance which interferes the most with the habits and opinions and feelings of the people. A composition has been made which enforces it in a limited degree. Still the arrangement labours.

Amsterdam is to furnish a loan of 8 Million Guilders within a month at an interest of 3% percent. The Provisional Assembly of the province have published a statement of the finances, to shew the extremities to which the Country was reduced by their former Government, and the necessity of extraordinary measures to be taken by the present. The first efforts are turning towards an improvement in the state of the Marine. Great exertions are necessary to make it an object worth any consideration. Such exertions are already making and will doubtless be continued from an intimate conviction of its being the primary interest of the Country and involving no inferior consideration to that of existence or destruction.

There are so many regulations, which result from the singular position of a Country, which is at the same time <u>conquered</u> and <u>independent</u>, that even strangers who are not to be considered in the predicament either of victor or vanquished, must suffer some inconvenience.

The exportation of Specie is prohibited and such a construction is given to the law, that American Citizens are not allowed to carry money out of the Country, which they brought into it. The navigation of our vessels within the bounds of this Republic and from thence to foreign ports is obstructed and interrupted. I have been obliged on both these points to make reclamations for obtaining the enjoyment of advantages stipulated to us by treaty. The matter remains yet unsettled. I am promised satisfaction upon both points.

There are two authorities with whom it becomes necessary to treat, the Government of the Country, and the Representatives of the victors. In the latter particular the duties of my Office have properly merged in yours. As you are not present, I have thought myself authorised to make such observations and demands, as the circumstances render necessary . And the french representatives have not raised any scruples as to my powers.

They have uniformly received my representations with civility and a disposition to accomodate, which was the more grateful to me, because I knew perfectly well what are the forms of an opposite temper. They have hitherto given every facility required. Upon the proposal I have last made, I am in expectation of an answer.

Since the Revolution here I find it extremely difficult to get a conveyance for my letters to America. There are no opportunities directly from hence. Those by the way of England, of Hamburg and of Bremen, are all precluded by the obstruction of communication. Should there be any means of sending by way of France I must recur to your goodness for information of it.

At the desire of any of my Diplomatic bretheren here I forward the enclosed letter requesting you to take the trouble of sending it to the person to whom it is addressed, and to send the answer under cover to me. I have the honour to be, with great respect Dear Sir your very humble and obedient servant

LBC, MHi: Adams Family Papers: John Quincy Adams Letterbook

1. Adams wrote to JM on 23 February 1795 (above) in response to a letter from JM dated 28 January 1795. The reference in this letter to that correspondence suggests JM's letter of January 28 is the same as the one referred to here as dated January 21.

Which date is correct cannot be determined, since neither has been located. Adams wrote in his diary that he received a letter from Monroe on February 10 and had "passed it on to Paulus, President of the Assembly of Provisional Representatives of the People of Holland.... Their object is to make a closer treaty with America" (John Quincy Adams, *Memoirs*, 1: 73-74)

To Edmund Randolph

Paris March [17] 1795.[1]

Sir

I have just received a letter from Mr Jay of the 5th of February in answer to mine of the 17 Jan^{ry} preceding and by which he declines to communicate to me the purport of his treaty with the English government altho' he had previously promised it. As he has explicitly declar'd himself to this effect, I consider the business of course closed between him & me, nor should I make a further comment upon it, were I not otherwise impelled by the style of his reply, which is obviously addressed more for your consideration than mine. To you therefore my comments upon that reply shall also be submitted.

Mr Jay says that he has no right to communicate the treaty since it belongs exclusively to the Government which form them, and by which I understand that the minister has no discretion on the subject, being bound to communicate with his government only. If this proposition is true, and which (especially if no latitude is given him by his instructions) I am willing to admit, it follows that as the injunction of secrecy applies to the whole instrument, it must of course to every part. It were absurd to say, that in the gross or as an entire thing it must be kept secret, but yet in the detail it may be divulged. How then does his conduct correspond with his own doctrine, having in his three several letters, communicated a particular article, and <u>promised</u> in the 2^d the whole?

But he likewise says that the communication was intended to be <u>confidential</u> or in other words to be kept secret, for such is the ordinary import of the word. But will his letters bear that construction? Does it appear as if the communication was intended merely to gratify on my part private curiosity, or for the benevolent purpose only of announcing to me an event favorable to our country? On the contrary does it not appear from each of his letters that he had anticipated the disquietude of this government upon the subject of his treaty and wished to remove it, & that the communication promised was intended for me in a public capacity & to be used for publick purposes? In short had I been in a private station is it probable he would have written or communicated any thing to me on the subject? Certain however it is that in no view was it possible for me to consider the communication promised, tho' termed a confidential one, as imposing on me any other restraint than that of caution, whilst it <u>exonerated him</u> and made <u>me responsible</u> for the blame of a disclosure, in case it was made, and produced any inconvenience.

As I really believed, at the time I wrote Mr Jay that he intended to make to me the communication in question, & likewise concluded from his own assurances, as well as from other circumstances, that the treaty comprized in it nothing that could give just cause of complaint here, I thought I could not better forward his own views or the interest of our country (especially as Mr Morris had taken his copy of the cypher with him) than by sending a confidential person for it. You will therefore judge of my surprize when instead of the communication expected I received his letter of the 5 of Feb^{ry} containing an absolute refusal to make it.

But in reviewing now his several letters it is difficult to ascertain what he intended to do or what his real object was in writing them: for he says in these that he was not at liberty to disclose the purport of his treaty and yet <u>promises it</u>: that he will give me the contents or principal heads to enable me to satisfy this government, but yet will give them only in <u>confidence</u> & of course under an injunction, that will put it out of my power to give the satisfaction intended; and finally when the application is made upon the basis of his own letters for the information in question, and for the purpose by him contemplated, he not only refuses to comply with what he had promised, but criminates this Government for entertaining any uneasiness or making any enquiry on the subject.

When one party offers a thing upon the principle, the other has a right to it, as was the case in the present instance, the justice of the demand on the part of the latter is of course admitted. There may indeed be some merit in offering it before the demand is made, but to make the offer and then recede from it, subjects the party thus acting to an additional proportional reproach. Had Mr Jay however chosen to place himself in this dilemma, from me he would have heard nothing more on the subject. I should have lamented, it is true, as I now do, that I was not possessed of information that might be useful to our affairs here, but there the business would have ended, for both his promise and my application were, and still are unknown to this Government. But to recede in the manner he has done, putting his refusal upon the ground of <u>national dignity</u> &c is neither consistent with candour nor the true state of things.

Had Mr Jay confided to me the information in question and in due time and which, it is obvious he thought himself in duty bound to do, I should then have become responsible for a proper use of it: and I am satisfied admitting it to be as by him represented, good use might have been made of it: for I should not only have been enabled to quiet their fears, and whose legitimacy he acknowledges by his efforts to remove them, and silence a thousand unfavourable insinuations whispered about by the enemies of both countries, but by the frankness of the communication have most probably made the incident the means of conciliating instead of weak'ning the friendly disposition of this government towards us. I am likewise persuaded that if I had been authorized to declare generally from my own knowledge (being the minister on the ground & responsible for the truth of the declaration) that the treaty did not interfere with our engagments with this republick, but that being a mere project subject to rejection &c it ought not to be published, it would have been satisfactory. And had the communication been sent to me even in this last stage, such would have been my conduct & most probably such the effect: In any event had I gone further against his request, upon me & not upon him, would the responsibility have rested. But this was not Mr Jay's object: on the contrary it is obvious that he wished me to compromit my character and thro' me that of the U. States with this nation, upon the contents of his treaty without letting me see it, or placing in this government or myself the least confidence in regard to it, and which I would not do, nor in my opinion ought not to have done.

Whether this government acted with propriety in asking for information upon the point in question is a subject with which I have nothing to do. I am responsible only for the answer given and which you have. My application to Mr Jay was certainly not founded upon theirs to me, for I had contemplated it before theirs was received. I had then gained such an insight into their councils as to satisfy me that all our great national objects, so far as they were connected with this republick,were more easily to be secured by a frank and liberal deportment than a cool and reserved one: that if we wished to preserve our neutrality with strict integrity and avail ourselves at the same time of its fortunes & without the least hazard on our part, in the negotiation with Spain, as likewise in that with England (in case Mr Jay's treaty was rejected) that this was the way to do it: in short that if it was necessary to gain the approbation of this government to any thing in that treaty, which it would otherwise disapprove, that this was the way to do it. Nor can I see any condesension in such a line of conduct: on the contrary between nations allied as we are, and especially when past and recent circumstances are considered, I deem it the most magnanimous as well as the soundest policy. Mr Jay however is <u>now</u> of a different opinion, and for the future I shall not disturb him in the enjoyment of it.

You intimated to me in your last that Mͬ Pinckney was commissioned as Envoy Extʸ for Spain upon the subject of the mississippi, and you have seen by my last how far I had succeeded in calling the attention of this government to that object. It is probable Mͬ Pinckney will pass thro' France & of course by Paris on his mission: in case he does I will most certainly open to him every thing that has taken place here on that subject, & endeavor according to the plan he shall prescribe, to render him in every respect all the services in my power. I have already intimated to Mͬ Short by a confidential messenger from Lisbon, the good understanding which subsists between this Government and our own upon that point, so that there is in every view the most favorable prospect of a successful termination of this interesting business, the completion of which will reflect so much honor upon the administration by which it is accomplished.

The vendee war is considered as completed. M. Charette the commanding General has surrendered with all the forces immediately under his command, & likewise undertaken to quell a small remaining body of about 1000 which yet holds out.² Tis said the liberty of religion granted by a late decree terminated this war. A short time however will now disclose whether this compromise or the general favorable aspect of the present moment is real or delusive, since if there is a force in the nation opposed to the revolution of sufficient strength to make head against it & which I do not think there is, I doubt not it will soon shew itself. With great respect & esteem I have the honor to be, Sir Your very Humble & obedͭ servͭ

Jaˢ Monroe

RC, ViW: Jay Johns Collection of Monroe Papers

1. The dateline gives the month and year but no day; the date is derived from the copy of this letter in DNA: RG 59: Dispatches from France.

2. François-Athanase Charette (1763-1796) was commander of the Catholic and royalist forces in the Vendée whose courage, resourcefulness, and skill in guerrilla warfare won him victories against the regular French army. When finally cornered he chose not to émigré and was captured and executed 29 March 1796 (*Dictionnaire Biographie Française*; Samuel Scott and Barry Rothaus, *Historical Dictionary of the French Revolution* I: 176-177).

From John Quincy Adams

The Hague March 23. 1795.

Dear Sir.

I received a few days since a Letter from Mͬ Johnson in London, in which he requests me to write to him, under a cover to Mͬ Skipwith. But as I understand that Gentleman is not now at Paris, I take the Liberty of requesting you to forward the enclosed Letter, which I am desirous to have transmitted as early as possible.

I had the honour of writing you on the 12ᵗʰ Instͭ by the Post; which I hope reached you in due time. The posts from Paris here are tolerably regular. I presume they are so from hence there.

The difficulties which I mentioned in my last will probably all disappear at present. In the Ports where any impediment to our Navigation had occurred, the Commandants have now had orders; to permit all American Vessels in the ports to pursue their destination, after inspecting the Sea Letters when they shall intend to sail for foreign Ports. The same orders will be notified to all the other Ports of these Provinces that I shall designate.

These measures afford the fullest proof of the friendly disposition towards the United States, which has been testified to me by all the Representatives who have been here in mission, and particularly by the Citizens Alquier,[1] Cochon[2] and Richard.[3]

The preparations for War by this Country, are not so vigorous and rapid as some persons had expected; the maritime power of the Republic had dwindled much below the general opinion. Extraordinary exertions may produce something respectable with time. For the present campaign the appearance of any <u>considerable</u> power may be questioned.—Hardly sufficient perhaps for the protection of the North Sea.

The whole World sighs for Peace; yet to all appearance it is still a distant Event. We have an arrival here from Charleston, that brings letters as late as February, but I have not heard of any intelligence whatever they contain. I have the Honour to be, with great respect, Dear Sir, your very humble & obed[t] Serv[t]

John Q. Adams.

RC, DLC: Monroe Papers

1. Charles-Jean-Marie Alquier (1752-1826) was a lawyer from La Rochelle who, after serving as a deputy of to the National Convention, began a distinguished career in the diplomatic service of France, holding posts at Tangier, Munich, Madrid, Florence, Naples, and Rome (*Dictionnaire de Biographie Française*).

2. Charles Cochon de Lapparent (1750-1825) was a provincial lawyer who became a deputy to the French Assembly in 1789 when he took the place of a dead colleague. He served on the Committee of Public Safety from September to December 1794. Cochon became minister of police in April 1796 (*Dictionnaire de Biographie Française*; J. Q. Adams, *Memoirs*, 1:92).

3. Joseph-Charles-Etienne Richard (1761-1834), an attorney, was a member of the Committee of Public Safety of the French National Convention from October 1794 to February 1795. In the spring of 1795 he negotiated a treaty with the Batavian Republic for the upkeep of 25,000 French troops (*La Grande Encyclopédie*; Bernard Gainot, *Dictionnaire des Membres du Comité du Salut Public*, 145-146).

From David Gelston

New York March 24th 1795

Dear Sir

I have just received letters from my Son[1] in which he speaks with so much Sensibility of your goodness that it fills my mind with real emotion. I am pleased to find the Child possesses a gratefull Heart. I do not wish to trespass. I have charged him not to be troublesome but I have told him to pursue your directions and advise in every particular. I cannot wish I cannot ask your attention to him any longer than he shall continue or at least endeavour to deserve your favours. I hope he will behave with propriety. our good wishes will forever attend you. our good Friend Gov Clinton has been very unwell four Months past is now very low. I saw Col[o] Burr yesterday. he is well. My friend Cap[t] Armour will hand you this. you will permit me to introduce him to your Friendship. by him I send you the late news papers. If your leizure would permit you to drop a line it would afford me very great satisfaction.

LBC, NHi: Gelston Letterbook

This letter was written with very little terminal punctuation. The editors have supplied periods at what they deem to be the proper places.

1. John M. Gelston.

From Joseph Jones

Virg[a] Fred[g] 26th Mar: 1795

D[r] S[r]

A few days past the 23[d] I think I drew a set of bills of exchange on you (four in number) for £200. st. payable 90 days after sight at Hamburg, the situation of Holland being such as to render it impracticable to draw payable in Amsterdam. I gave at the same time the Drawee M[r] Tho[s] Southcomb of this place[1] a letter of advise to accompany the bills—lest that sho[d] not reach you I think it necessary to make the communication by other channels of conveyance, that you may provide for taking it up in due time—this is the only draught I have made. I have not seen Littlepage to whose collection on acc[t] of Brakenridge[2] and Burnly C. Carter had ass[ure]d your bonds and to whom I was to have given bills for the amount but he has not called on me since and I understand the reason he had either lost or mislaid the bonds. Had I money and could with propriety take in your bonds at discount that are not due I could save 20£ in the hundred by paying the money. Your friends have reason to complain that you neglect them as I heard last three or four public letters have been rec[d] from you but none by your acquaintances. I have been favored with only one the 4th Sep[t] last and I think this is the 5th or 6th I have written to you[3] some of them no doubt you have rec[d] or I sho[d] repeat necessary <illegible> particulars in this. In general I wo[d] observe that the purchase in Loudoun has been so far complied with as to require no immediate provision, the 1500£ ready money p[d] and the bonds to near £1200 for Pendleton being ready on whom I shall call on Monday next in my way to Richmond and deliver them and obtain a release of the <illegible>. I have ord[d] four quitrents to be served on part of the Lands to try the gent[n] whether the premises under w[ch] they claim to retain possession are such as bind me. I am just ret[d] from surveying the land but Hernley[4] not having furnished me with a plats I cannot inform you of the contents. a Debt to Kerr of Dumfries of ab[t] 400£ I hear for I have not yet seen him, rather his Es[t] for he is dead, to know exact amount—the balance is divided into two annual paym[ts] so that for Kerrs demand and the 1st paym[t] provision must be made between this and 1st Jan[ry] next. I have put half dozen hands on the place on a lott that was untenanted and have since while I was up the other day purchased a lease of another lott adjoining for 84£ a single life only the quantity of land 183. so that you may judge how difficult it is to get in the leases owing to the rents being so very low—this lott rented for only £75 per ann. I am also attending to your other affairs and pay off any pressing demands as fast as I am able—there are several small debts claimed w[ch] escaped your recollection and these for any thing I know may be unjust but I use caution ab[t] them. If I draw any other bill in the course of this year it will be to pay any of your debts that press on me. What wheat was to spare at Hogs I let Col. Bell have on acc[t]—there was none where you lived and a very short crop at Hoggs. We got four hands from Marks on hire and I sent up two young men of mine to assist this year puting both places under the managem[t] of Hogg with old Peter at the home plantation. Marks has lost his wife[5] and I think the prospect of geting money from him a very unpromising one. In a former letter I mentioned my intention of leting J. M.[6] reside in the house that was unfinished when you left it. He has since moved there and will relieve him from the expence of rent and firewood. If this step does not suit it may be corrected another year. I think I ment[d] in a former letter that M[r] Randolph had advanced ab[t] £175 and agreed to accept a draught for £200 the last was drawn and I suppose paid as the period of paym[t] is now lapsed. Your public letters giving details respecting the Jacobin Society have been (extracts from them) put into the papers and in N. York with your name to them as Madison informs me and it is not improbably to serve electioneering purposes as the Sentiments cont[d] in them are thought Such as to support the attack made here on what the P. in his speech called self created societies.

such use being made of your correspondence will of course inculcate caution in your future communications beyond what official duty requires. In the Loudoun district R. Brent has outvoted Lee by a large majority—in Fred^k & Berkeley Rutherford had a majority ag^t Genl Morgan of 450. Morgan though com^r of the Troops in actual service in the 4 western counties of P^a had leave from the War departm^t to come in and attend the election—Griffin did not offer one Clopton supplies his place—one Mr Mane now a Doctor who used to be ab^t Richmond but has settled and practices the healing art in Campbel County has been elected there a member for Congress by one vote majority.⁷ I mentioned to you before you might expect to see young J. Mercer in France—he left this but whether he proceeded from the Northward to France I have not heard. Madison Giles & Nicholas have been rechosen and I expect the whole delegation the ensuing session will be of the same <illegible>. My Stable has been broken and my large young bay horse with my Saddle and bridle stolen and no acc^t of them. your old black horse is dead. I hope your family enjoy health that Joe⁸ does the same and applies to his studies. I have written two or three letters to him but as well as from you have no answer. It wo^d give me great pleasure to hear often from you. I pray you all be happy. Y^r friend

Jos: Jones

RC, NN: Monroe Papers

1. Thomas Southcomb was a Fredericksburg merchant (*Madison Papers*, 16: 194).

2. John Breckinridge.

3. JM's letter to Jones of 4 September 1794 (above) is the only letter to Jones from France in 1794 that has been located. No letters from Jones to JM prior to March 26 have been located.

4. Possibly William H. Harding, who was the county surveyor for Loudoun County, Virginia, 1795-1801 (James Bradford, "Society and Government in Loudoun County, Virginia, 1790-1800," dissertation, University if Virginia, 1976).

5. Joanna Sydnor Marks.

6. Joseph J. Monroe.

7. Jones was mistaken about this election. Isaac Coles was elected to Congress from the sixth district, which included Campbell County (Stanley Parsons, et al, *United States Congressional Districts, 1788-1841*, 172). Dr. Manes could not be identified.

8. Joseph Jones, Jr.

From James Madison

Philad^a March 26. 1795.

Dear Sir

My last was written about ten days ago¹ for a conveyance intimated to be in the view of the office of State. I have since that rec^d yours committed to Mr Swan² and two hours ago that of Decr 18 covering the private one for Mr Randolph.³ The other referred to as sent by the way of Havre is not yet come to hand.

Mr Swan is much embarrassed in his operations by the enormous price of Wheat and flour. The latter has been above ten dollars a barrel, and is now at that price. The former has been as high as 15/3. and is now very little below that. Mr S. is apprehensive that he will be compelled to direct his attention to some other quarter of the world. It is matter of double regret that such a necessity should happen. The causes of this extraordinary rate of produce are differently explained. The deficiency of the last harvest is certainly a material one. The influence of Bank Credits on mercantile enterprize and competition may be another; tho' this cause cannot at this moment operate, as the Banks are in another paroxism of distress and have for some time discontinued their discounts. The idea of <u>great </u>demands from Europe, particularly from France has no doubt contributed to the effect; tho' this can not particularly refer to the object of Mr Swan, because the high prices preceded his operation, and in fact are not peculiar to the articles he wants, or limited to articles having any relation to them. In general prices are exorbitantly high, and in this place incredibly so. The markets have been nearly 100 perC^t advanced in some, and fifty in most, instances, beyond the state of them prior to your departure. House Rents have kept the same course. These circumstances denote some general and deeply rooted cause.

From as near a view as I have yet been able to take of your letter to Mr R. I see no reason why I should hesitate to deliver it. I cannot forbear believing that the Report of stipulations offensive and defensive is quite without foundation; but your view of things on the contrary supposition involves a variety of interesting ideas; and your communications and reflections in general with regard to the Treaty, as proceeding from one in your position and of your sentiments, merit too much attention in the Executive Department to be witheld altogether from it. I mentioned in my last that the Treaty was come, but kept a profound Secret. In that state it remains. Its contents have produced conjectural comments without number. As I am as much out of the secret as others, I can say nothing that goes beyond that character. I should hope it to be impossible that any stipulation, if any should be attempted, inconsistent with the Treaties with France, can ever be pursued into effect. I cannot even believe that any such stipulation would be hazarded. The President, to say nothing of the people, would so certainly revolt at it, that more than wickedness would be requisite in the authors. At the same time it is possible that articles may be included that will be ominous to the confidence and cordiality of France towards the U. S: not to mention that any arrangements with G. B. (beyond the simple objects you mention) made at the present juncture and extorted by the known causes, must naturally appear in the light you represent. How the instructions to Jay may square with what he may have done; or both or either with the language you were authorised to hold, must await future lights. As I do not know how far official communications may or may not put you in possession of the Contents of the Treaty before this arrives, and as it appears you had no previous or contemporary knowledge of the particulars, I ought not to decline the task of giving you what appears to me to be the most probable account of them; premising that I speak without the least clue or hint from the official quarter, & what is truly to be taken for conjecture, or at most for inferences from circumstances mostly of newspaper publicity. 1. It is generally agreed that the posts are to be surrendered; but not before June 1796; and it is among ye reports, that they are afterwards to be a sort of thoroughfare for both parties. This w^d be a very disagreeable and a very unpopular ingredient. 2. The compensations for losses are supposed to be in a train primarily judicial, eventually diplomatic. The sufferers I believe are very little sanguine, but they are in general silent from causes which you will readily imagine. 3. I should have mentioned the other stipulations in the treaty of peace, besides the delivery of ye posts. On this little is said except in general that they are to be executed on both sides. Perhaps the question of interest during the war, & complaints on the British side from State laws affecting their debts may be referred along with some of the American losses from privateers & admiralty Courts, to Commissioners. This however is purely conjectural. 4. A footing of reciprocity with respect to the trade directly with G. B: so far as to put British & American vessels on the same footing in American ports—& American & British footing in the British ports. As this w^d take from our vessels the advantage they now enjoy, particularly with respect to the difference of ten perC^t in the duties, it would be injurious, and if not countervailed, unpopular. 5. An admission of American vessels to the British W. Ind^s if under 100 or perhaps 75 tons. Whether the right be renounced of reducing British vessels to the same size is a question of some consequence in relation to this point. 6. The Treaty in relation to the commerce with G. B. to continue for 12 years; to that with <u>the W. Indies for 4 years</u>. I should be led from some particular circumstances not to doubt the latter limitation, if the aspect & effect of it were not so strikingly revolting.—Having had but a few moments notice of this opp[ortunit]y I am obliged to conclude a very hasty letter with abrupt assurances of the affectionate [esteem] with which I am D͇ᴿ Sir Your friend & serv͇ᵗ

Js Madison Jr

I hope to be able to write again before I leave this which will be in 7 or 8 days.

Enclosure:

Philad͇ᵃ Mar. 26. 95

Memorandum

The wants incident to my new situation seduce me into an unwilling tax on your goodness. As it is probable that many articles of furniture at second hand, may be had in Paris, which cannot be had here of equal quality, but at a forbidding price, it has occurred to me, to ask the favor of you to have the following procured & forwarded.

1 Suit of Bed Curtains of Damask, Chints, or Dimity as the price may be
3 Corresponding Window Curtains
3 d͇ᵒ for a Parlour
2 Carpets of different sizes
1 Tea Sett of China
1 Service of d͇ᵒ

I make this request on the idea that you can have it executed with͇ᵗ personal trouble, and can conveniently make the temporary advances. I leave the particular directions entirely to your own judgment, to which I w͇ᵈ pray the addition of a hint from M͇ʳˢ Monroes better one if I were not afraid of intruding on her goodness. You will be able to judge of the stile suitable to my faculties & fashions, by the rule you mean to pursue in providing for your own future accomodation—were I sure that you could easily have effect given to this application, and that in every respect it would be consistent with your conveniency, I would ask the favor of you to go beyond the enumerated articles into others which you may know to be acceptable to a young House-Keeper.—Those which are enumerated w͇ᵈ be particularly so, if they could to got in time to arrive here for next Winter's use; but whether or not, they are desirable.

RC, DLC: Madison Papers

1. Madison to JM, 11 March 1795, above.

2. JM to Madison, 20 September 1794, *Madison Papers*, 15: 358.

3. JM to Edmund Randolph, 18 December 1794, above.

From Emmanuel Sieyès

Paris le 6 germinal l'an 3 de la République française
une et indivisible. [26 March 1795]

Notre confiance, Citoyen, dans les soins constants que tu Donnes au maintien De l'union et de l'heureuse Intelligence qui Regnent Entre les Etats unis et la france, ne nous permet pas de douter que tu ne t'empresses D'Engager ton Gouvernement à faire Droit aux plus legers Sujets De Plaintes que nous aurions à lui Adresser.

C'est donc avec toute la franchise qui convient à Des hommes chargés de veiller Sur les Interêts Respectifs Des Peuples libres que nous te Joignons ici l'extrait D'une Lettre Du Cᵉⁿ Dannery consul De la République française à Boston Dans laquelle Il Se plaint très vivement De la Défaveur qu'éprouvent nos concitoyens De la part Du gouvernement des Etats Unis. Nous Esperons, Citoyen, que tu voudras Bien Mettre sous les yeux de ses agents les [Points] Dont il est question dans cet extrait de La Lettre De notre consul à Boston, Et En obtenir une Juste et prompt Réparation.

nous attendrons ta Reponse officielle et position sur cet article avec tous les Sentiments que tu nous connais et que nous avons le plus Sincere Désir de Conserver. Salut et fraternité

Sieyès

Editors' Translation

Paris, 6 Germinal, Year 3 of the French Republic
one and indivisible. [26 March 1795]

Our confidence, Citizen, in the constant care you take to maintain the union and good understanding that prevails between the United States and France, allows us to doubt not that you would not eagerly urge your government to give attention to the most minor subjects of complaint that we might address to it.

It is therefore with all the candor befitting men in charge of safeguarding the respective interests of free people that we enclose here the excerpt from a letter from Citizen Dannery, consul of the French Republic at Boston, in which he complains vehemently of the disregard experienced by our fellow citizens on the part of the government of the United States. We hope, Citizen, that you will not mind placing before these agents the matters that are in question in this excerpt from the letter of our consul at Boston, and that you will obtain prompt and fair redress.

We await your official response and position on this matter with all the wishes that you know we have and that we would most sincerely like to preserve. Salutations and Fraternity

Sieyès

FC, DLC: FCP—France

After a life of solitude as a Vicar General at Chartres, Emmanuel-Joseph Sieyès (1748-1836) began to write political pamphlets in the 1780s, the most important of which, *What is the Third Estate?* (1789), made him one of the most important political theorists of the French Revolution. He was a member of the National Assembly and the Convention, and served on the Committee of Public Safety from March to October 1795. He devoted much of his time on the committee to the supervision of foreign relations, including the negotiation of the peace treaty with the Netherlands (Glyndon G. Van Deusen, *Sieyes: His Life and His Nationalism*, 1-35; 61-62; Jules Michelet, *Histoire de la Révolution Française*, 1564-1565).

Jean-Baptiste-Thomas Dannery (b. 1744) became the French consul at Boston in 1792. His list of complaints has not been found. The point of contention involved the *Mary Ford*, a British merchantman that was captured en route from the West Indies to London, by French frigates off the coast of Newfoundland in September 1794. The ship was later found abandoned at sea by an American trader. The Americans brought the ship into Boston, on November 3, where it was libeled in the U. S. District Court for the District of Massachusetts. Thomas MacDonogh, the British consul at Boston, filed a claim on behalf of the original owners. A month later Dannery entered a competing claim on behalf of the French. The District Court heard the case between December 1794 and March 1795. Three parties, the original British owners, the French captains, and the American rescuers, claimed the right to the proceeds of the sale of the ship and its cargo. The court granted salvage rights to the Americans and any remaining proceeds to the British owners. The U. S. Circuit Court, upon an appeal filed by Dannery, upheld the District Court's decision. The case came before the U. S. Supreme Court on 4 February 1796 as *MacDonogh v. Dannery*. A matter of diplomatic as well as legal concern, the case forced the justices to rule on a dispute between the world's two greatest powers and yet still preserve American neutrality. On February 17, the Supreme Court unanimously affirmed the circuit court's decree (Maeva Marcus, ed., The *Documentary History of the Supreme Court of the United States, 1789-1800*, Vol. 7, *Cases: 1796-1797*, pp. 11-42).

JM responded to this letter on 1 April 1795 and informed the Committee of Public Safety that he would forward their complaint to the Department of State (*Catalogue of Monroe's Papers*, 1: 43).

From James Madison

Philad^a March 27. 1795

Dear Sir

I wrote to you yesterday acknowledging yours by Mr Swan and answering that of the 18th Decr which covered your very interesting remarks in a confidential letter to Mr Randolph. The latter was sent to M^r R today, there being no good reason for witholding it as you authorised me to do. I write this cheifly on acc^t of the Bearer Mr John Mercer son of our friend the judge, who means to visit France in order to enter the school of experience under the auspices of some military character of eminence. As he carries letters to you from his uncle Jno Mercer,[1] and is personally better known to you than to myself, I can only rely on your paying him a proper friendly attention, and express my sincere wishes that he may reap all the beneficial fruits which can be afforded by the present scenes of Europe.

You will learn from Mr Mercer that the elections in Virginia are over and in part known. The only two districts in which the question turned on <u>political</u> rather than <u>personal</u> considerations, were those in which Alexandria & Winchester stand. In the former Mr Lee & Mr Brent; in the latter Mr Rutherford, and Genl Morgan were the candidates. Mr Brent was elected by a considerable, and Mr Rutherford by a greater majority. In Mr Griffin's district it is probable that Mr Clopton is the successful candidate; tho' it is possible that he may be outvoted by Mr Basset who is also well spoken of. Mr Barnwell who was elected as successor to Gillon, has resigned;[2] and Col. Hampton of very different politics has taken his place.[3] In Massachussetts several elections remain unfinished; Among which is that lately represented by Mr Dexter. There have been two trials without an effective vote. In the last Mr Varnum had more votes than Mr Dexter, and it is expected will finally prevail. Mr Ames election I am told will be contested, on account of bribery & bad votes.—For the Senate, your old friend Jacob Read Esqr succeeds Mr Izzard. His success is represented as one of those casualties which are incident to elections. Your friend Bloodworth succeeds Mr Hawkins from a like cause. Bingham is successor to Morris.—The contest in N. York for Govr lies between Yates & Jay. Of the issue it is difficult to judge. Something will depend on the return or absence of the latter, and also on the colouring which may most sucessfully be given to the Treaty with G. B.

I inclose several papers containing the publications of Lee & Brent, and a small pamphlet mentioned in a former letter, written by our friend N.[4] The 'cautionary hints' are from the pen of S. G. Tucker. You will see from the proceedings in Georgia what a scene is opened there by a landjobbing Legislature. Wilson & Pendleton the fed^l Judges, tho' not named in the law are known adventurers. The former is reprobated here by all parties. The two Senators Gun & Jackson are now pitted agst each other, and the whole State is in convulsions. It is not improbable that attempts may be made to set aside the law, either as having some flaw, or by the paramount authority of a Convention wch is to meet in the course of the summer. These dangers with the frowns of the federal Gov^t seem to have benumbed the speculations which were likely to follow on that subject, & which have attained a scrip mania on others of the territorial kind.

In my letter of yesterday I took the liberty of asking the favor of you to have procured for me a few articles of furniture, on ye supposition that they can be had at second hand, cheap; and that it will not be inconvenient to make ye requisite advances; referring the stile & the price to your own knowledge of my situation, & authorising you to go beyond the enumerated articles into any others you may judge to be desirable to me from the fashion & the price—The articles I mentioned particularly were a suit of handsome bed curtains—3 corresponding window d$^\circ$ 3 parlour d$^\circ$ 2 Carpets of different sizes—1 Tea Sett of China—1 Service of d$^\circ$. I rely on your goodness to excuse the trouble, which I impose on you. I take the liberty, you are to understand, on the belief & y^e condition that you can have the thing done without much personal attention. If I were not afraid of intruding too much on Mrs Monroe's goodness, I w^d ask the aid of her counsel in the directions you may give towards the supply of my household. My best respects wait on her. With sentiments of perfect esteem & attachment I remain Dr Sir Y^r friend & serv^t

Js Madison Jr

RC, DLC: Madison Papers

1. The letter of introduction from John Francis Mercer has not been located.

2 Robert Barnwell (1761-1814) was a member of Congress from South Carolina 1791-1793. He declined to be a candidate for re-election. He served in the South Carolina House of Representatives 1795-1797 (*BDAC*).

3. Wade Hampton (1752-1835) of South Carolina was reputed to be the wealthiest planter in the United States; in 1830 he owned 3,000 slaves. He served as an army officer during the Revolutionary War and the War of 1812. He was a member of the House of Representatives 1795-1797 (*ANB*).

4. Congressman Richard Bland Lee wrote several letters for the (Richmond) *Virginia Gazette* in November and December 1794 signed "Marcellus" in which he argued that the Federalists were not the aristocratic party. The essays were later published as a pamphlet. He followed this with a circular letter to his constituents in which he defended his record of voting with the Federalists in Congress. Richard Brent, who unseated Lee in the congressional election, attacked his opponent in a pamphlet entitled *To the Freeholders of Fairfax, Loudoun, and Prince-William* (*Madison Papers*, 15: 458-459, 470). The pamphlet by "N" could not be identified.

From John Quincy Adams

The Hague March 30. 1795.

Dear Sir.

I had the honour of writing you on the 12th and 23^d of this month by the post; but not knowing how far the Posts from hence to Paris are regular I now take advantage of a private opportunity by the Baron de Rehausen, to whom I have taken the liberty of giving a letter of introduction to you, and whom I am persuaded you will find deserving of esteem.[1]

Our Commerce and Navigation with this Country, is now altogether free from obstructions here, and will doubtless meet with the encouragement of considerable profit.

But the political fate of this Republic remains unsettled, and liable upon the supposition of different possible circumstances, to situations extremely variant from each other. The two parties are inveterate to extremity in their mutual ill-will, and all the energy of their Liberator's councils is necessary to keep them from acts of violence among themselves. Several instances have occurred of a disposition to pursue with rigour if not with injustice, those who are obnoxious, and they would have been defenceless but for the intervention of the protecting power.

Every thing however is quiet, and no one as yet has suffered any material oppression. This state of peace will be maintained while the foreign forces continue here. Whenever that restraint shall be removed it may be foreseen as inevitable, that the present tranquility will not continue undisturbed. It is hoped however that it will not be succeeded by violence.

Baron de Rehausen has undertaken to make a purchase of some books for me, at my request.—But as it is uncertain whether he will find an opportunity convenient to forward them immediately to me; I have told him I presumed you would permit the package to be deposited at your house, untill I can procure an occasion of transmitting them. If therefore he should meet with any difficulty, I must request your indulgence, in this respect. If he should meet with any conveyance, I shall not have occasion to give you this trouble. I have the honour to be with great Respect, Dear Sir, Your very humble & obed^t Servt

John Q. Adams.

RC, DLC: Monroe Papers

1. Gotthard Maurits, Baron von Rehausen (1762-1822) was the Swedish minister to the Hague 1791-1795. He later held posting in Lisbon and London (*Svenskt Biografiskt Handlexicon*, 2: 324-325). Adams's letter of introduction for him has not been located.

From Benjamin Hichborn

Paris 11 Germinal 3^d [31 March 1795]

Sir

In some free Conversation with Col^o Trumble,[1] on the Subject of the late Treaty between Great Britain & America, I coud not avoid expressing the uneasiness I felt, at the disagreeable Effects, which had already Shewn themselves, & the still more Serious Consequences, which might result from that Negotiation—and I must confess I experienced a very agreable Surprise when he assured me upon his honor—that the Treaty had for its Object, merely the adjustment of Some Matters in dispute between the two Nations—that it secured to the Americans, some rights in Commerce, which might have been doubtful by the laws of Nations, & by which their Intercourse with this Country woud be facilitated during the War—that it provided a Compensation for those of either Nation who had been injured, and finally settled all Controversy respecting the boundary-line & the Western Posts—

He further declared—that the Treaty did not contain, any Seperate or reciprocal Guarrantee of any Rights, privileges, or Territory, or an Engagement on either part to afford aid or Supplies of any kind to the other, under any Circumstances whatever—The treaty he says, Simply declares—that the Parties shall remain at peace, & points out the mode in which the matters of Controversy between them Shall be finally Settled.

If this Information can be of any Service to you in your public Capacity, you may make use of it in any Manner you may think fit—I presume the authenticity of its Contents will not be called in question—I am Sir very truly yours

Benj Hichborn

RC, NN: Monroe Papers

1. John Trumbull

To Fulwar Skipwith

[March 1795]

Dear Sir

Some circumstances have attracted my attention wch create an opinion that Mr Gouvain is not satisfied in all respects with the footing upon which he stands, and that without an adequate compensation I shall not have that controul over his conduct I ought to have over my private Secretary. Thus circumstanc'd it becomes necessary that I have some communication with him upon that point & in consequence a previous one with you.

When he commenc'd with me it was neither his nor my expectation that he would continue with me longer than a few months, no longer indeed than untill I sho^d receive an answer from the Secretary of State whether y^r nomination was or was not confirm'd for in case it was, it was his and my expectation that either Mr Prevost or some other American wo^d come out & supply y^r place: and in case it was not that you would retake it yourself. This wo^d require the lapse of a few months only & such was the calculation we all made on it. But the delay which has taken place upon that point, and which may hereafter take place protracts the time far beyond our expectation and of course alters the nature of his claim upon me. If he continues longer he ought to receive an adequate compensation, for otherwise I can say nothing to him or have any claim upon or controul over his conduct.

The same principle applies in respect to yourself. Wishing your welfare and emolument I nominated you to the office of consul giving you time to make an experiment of its profits before I made known y^r willingness to serve, and left the office with me open for y^r return to it in case you were not confirm'd, leaving it with you to adjust with Mr Gouvain as you pleas'd, what part if any of y^r compensation sho^d be given him for performing y^r duty. This was likewise upon the expectation of an early answer and in consequence a different & more regular arrangment. The delay however alters the case, for it subjects me in the interim to accept of the services of a gentⁿ without being able to compensate him, at least in the manner the law authorizes a compensation & for a much longer term than was intended whilst the salary goes to a person in a different office independant and unconnected with me.

The line of justice therefore appears to me to be this, that you sho^d receive the salary up to the time that an answer was rec^d from the Sec^{ry} of State in reply to mine, and which was contained in his last letter, making Mr Gouvain such compensation as you think fit, and that after that time the salary sho^d go to Mr Gouvain or such other person as I shall be able to get to perform the duty of Secretary, untill in consequence of y^r rejection by the gov^t you resume y^r place, or confirmation some person shall arrive to take it. If you approve of this I shall immediately confer with Mr Gouvain on the subject and apprize of the footing upon which he will for the future stand. The office with me will of course be open for you to resume it, in case y^r nomination is not confirmed. I am Dear Sir y^r friend & Servt

J^{as} Monroe

With respect to what it will be proper for you to give for the time above mentioned viz. to the time I rec^d M^r R^s letter or indeed the end of the first year of y^r appointment, I have nothing to say. He expected nothing, even according to Mr Van's[1] impression but to have the expense of his lodging &ca defrayed. this however you will regulate as you please as the sum due you up to that time, will be answerable after my next draft.

RC, NN: Monroe Papers. Undated. Filed at end of 1797.

The dating of this letter is problematic. JM informed Edmund Randolph in his letter of 18 October 1794 that he had appointed Skipwith as consul general and asked that he be confirmed in this post. Randolph informed JM in his letter of 2 December 1794 that President Washington had appointed Joseph Pitcairn as consul for Paris. This letter was written before Randolph received JM's letter of October 18, but it seems to be the letter that JM refers to below in the fourth paragraph, for no other of Randolph's letters refers to the appointment of a consul general until that of 2 July 1795, in which he inclosed Skipwith's commission as consul general. JM acknowledged receipt of Randolph's letter of December 2 in his dispatch of 6 March 1795 and questioned the wisdom of Pitcairn's appointment. Thus it seems likely that this letter to Skipwith was written in March 1795 after the receipt of Randolph's letter of December 2.

See JM to James C. Mountflorence, 5 October 1794 (above), for Gauvain's term of service as JM' secretary.

1. William Vans (1763-1840) of Salem, Massachusetts, was a partner in the mercantile firm of Freeman and Vans. Vans was married to Gauvain's sister Rosalie. Although he held the post of consul at Morlaix, he resided in Paris (Yvon Bizardel, *The First Expatriates*, 240-243; Walter B. Smith II, *America's Diplomats and Consuls of 1776-1865*, 65).

To John Quincy Adams

Paris April 2. 1795.

Dear Sir

I have been honored with your two favors of the 12 & [2]3.[1] ult^{o} and should have answered the first sooner had I known the post was established between this and Amsterdam, or had I not been disappointed by the Dutch commissaries who promised soon after its receit to make known to me the period when their next courier should be dispatched. For the future however these difficulties will not intervene.

The situation of Holland being exclusively neither an independant or conquered country, and subject in the interim in certain respects to the controul of two authorities is a novel one in the political system: nor is it easy to decide by any circumstances known to me how soon it will be changed. As it is reasonable however to presume that the spirit of harmony which you intimate now subsists, will continue to prevail reciprocally, it is likewise so to conclude that the final adjustment will be formed upon principles equally satisfactory to both parties.

It was to be expected that whilst those provinces remained in their present situation, your duties would partake of the quality of the Government and be as complicated as it might be. In removing the embarrassments to which our commerce was subjected, it became indispensably necessary that application should be made to the competent authority, and to which your powers were certainly competent whether French or Dutch; for unless that government was totally & permanently absorb'd in this, it followed that you were the party thro' all the intermediate modifications, to whom it belong'd to take cognizance of the affairs, and redress the grievances if any there be of our countrymen there. It gives me pleasure to hear that you have experienced no difficulty upon this head because thereby the interest of the United States will be greatly promoted. I take it for granted you will experience the like facility in future; but if the contrary should be the case and any arrangment on the part of this government here appear to you necessary, to facilitate your operations, and you will be pleased to communicate the same to me and point out the line in which I may be serviceable. be assured that I shall be happy to cooperate with you in obtaining it.

The trial of Barrere, Collot D'herbois & Billaud de varenne ended yesterday by a decree of banishment.[2] A party from the suburbs of the city calling itself the same which caused the revolution of the 31. of may[3] attended in the morning & entered the convention en masse with a view probably of making a like revolution on the 1st of April. But the convention was firm. The alarm was sounded thro' the city & the citizens in General commanded by Pichegru[4] attended by the Deputies, Barras & Merlin de

Thionville,[5] immediately arranged themselves in order & repaired to its Hall in defense of the national representation. By surrounding the palace, inhibiting the admission of others, and cutting off the retreat of those within, thereby shewing that punishment was certain in case they should proceed to extremities, the commotion was terminated without the effusion of blood. Several (8) of the mountain party were arrested after the Hall was cleared, upon evidence furnished in the course of the day of being accomplices in the plot. Every thing is now tranquil, and so far as it is possible to estimate the consequences of an event so recent, by the attending circumstances, it must be deemed favorable to the revolution.[6]

I beg of you to command me in all cases wherein I can be serviceable & that you will believe me to be with great respect and esteem Your very humble Servant

Ja[s] Monroe

RC, MHi: Adams Family Papers: Letters Received

1. JM's secretary wrote 13 instead of 23.

2. The Convention ordered the deportation of Billaud-Varenne, Collot d'Herbois, and Barère to Guyana (Georges Lefebvre, *The French Revolution from 1793 to 1799*, 144). JM had attended their trial (Thomas Perkins Diary, 25 March 1795, Massachusetts Historical Society).

3. On the 31 May 1793 some representatives from the sections of Paris gathered in the heart of the Cité at the Bishop's Palace and organized themselves into a committee of insurrection. Their object was to force the Convention to throw out the Girondists. The sans-culottes invaded the Convention on 31 May and 2 June and arrested twenty-nine Girondin deputies. Other Girondin deputies took flight handing victory to the Montagnards who from then on dominated the Convention (P. A. Kropotkin, The *Great French Revolution, 1789-1793*, 399-406).

4. Jean-Charles Pichegru (1761-1804) served with the French army in America. He rose through the ranks and became a major general in August 1793. In 1794 in commanded the French troops who conquered Belgium and the Netherlands. Pichegru was in command of the Paris garrison at the time of the 12 Germinal uprising (Owen Connelly, *Wars of the French Revolution and Napoleon, 1792-1815*, 60, 70, 71, 118; *Encyclopedia Britannica, "French Revolution."*).

5. Jean-Nicolas-Paul-François Barras (1755-1829) rose to prominence with his military successes in crushing the Federalist revolt in Provence and the royalist uprising in the sections. He became a member of the Executive Directory in November 1796 (Martyn Lyons, *France Under the Directory*, 22). Antoine-Christophe Merlin de Thionville (1762-1833) served as a deputy in all elected assemblies up to 1798. He was the Thermidorian leader who appeared at the head of the National Guard to restore order during the insurrection of 12 Germinal (George Rudé, The *Crowd in the French Revolution*, 149).

6. The shortage of bread and fuel throughout the harsh winter of 1794-1795 and the devaluation of the assignats by the removal of price controls in December created unbearable conditions for the people in Paris and triggered the insurrection of 12 Germinal (April 1). Unarmed sans-culottes entered the Convention and demanded bread and the return of the 1793 Constitution. An estimated 10,000 Parisians gathered outside the hall and echoed the demands. Little violence took place, but their presence delayed debate for four hours. The stand-off ended when troops of the National Guard appeared and dispersed the crowd (George Rudé, *The French Revolution*, 116-117).

From Jean-Victor Colchen

A Paris, le 15 Germinal, de l'an 3e [4 April 1795]

La commission des Relations Extérieures a reçu, Monsieur, de M. Skipwith une réclamation qui a pour objet La mise en liberté de François Louis Dubart natif de paris, actuellement détenu à Bayonne. Ce Citoyen Français S'était à ce qu'il puvait, attaché au Service de William Short, qu'il a Suivi en Hollande et en Angleterre, et qu'il a eu dernier lieu accompagné à Madrid. Il a depuis quitté ce Ministre Américain, et revenait en France Sans autre papier qu'un Certificat de probité Soussigné de M. Short, lorsqu'il a été arrêté à Son passage à Bayonne.

La Commission des Relations Extérieures, Monsieur, doit en référer au Comité de Salut public. Cependant elle n'a pas cru devoir lui Soumettre la demande de M. Skipwith, Sans vous l'avoir communiquée. Elle vous prie de lui donner quelques éclaircissemens Sur cette affaire. Elle observe au Surplus, qu'elle ne pourra faire Son rapport au Comité de Salut public que lorsqu'elle aura l'original, ou au moins une Copie certifiée du Certificat délivré par M. Short. Ce Certificat doit exister entre les mains de M. Skipwith qui l'a transmit littéralement dans Sa lettre.

Colchen

Editors' Translation

Paris 15 Germinal Year 3 [4 April 1795]

The Commission for Foreign Relations has received a complaint from Mr. Skipwith whose purpose is to set at liberty François-Louis Dubart, a native of Paris now detained at Bayonne. This French resident was in the service of William Short whom he accompanied to Holland and England, and finally to Madrid. He has since left this American minister, without any paper certificate of proof signed by Mr. Short, and was returning to France, when he was arrested on his passage to Bayonne.

The Commission for Foreign Relations, Sir, must refer to the Committee for Public Safety. However, the Commission did not feel it should submit to the Committee Mr. Skipwith's request without communicating it to you. The Commission requests that you provide some elucidation on the matter. In addition, it will not be able to report to the Committee for Public Safety without having in possession the original, or at least a certified copy of the certificate delivered by Mr. Short. This certificate must be in the hands of Mr. Skipwith who rendered it word for word in his letter.

Colchen

RC, NN: Monroe Papers; filed 8 April 1795

Jean-Victor Colchen (1751-1830), a lawyer, was Commissioner of Foreign Affairs from 24 February 1795 to 5 November 1796 (*Dictionnaire Biographie Française*, 9: 211).

To Jean-Victor Colchen

Paris 7 Avril 1795 (18 Germinal l'an 3)

Citoyen

Conformement à votre lettre du 15. du present mois, relative à François Louis Dubart actuellement détenu à Bayonne; Je vous transmets cy-joint copie certifiée d'un certificat qui lui fut donné par le cⁿ William Short, Ministre Américain en Espagne. Ce certificat m'a été envoyé de Bayonne par le dit Louis Dubart en même tems que des lettres dont le Cⁿ William Short l'avoit chargé pour moi. Voicy toutes les informations qu'il est en mon pouvoir de vous donner à ce Sujet. Salut et fraternité.

Jaˢ Monroe

Editors' Translation

Paris 7 April 1795 (18 Germinal year 3)

Citizen

In accordance with your letter of the 15th of this month[1] concerning François Louis Dubart, currently detained in Bayonne; I enclose a certified copy of a certificate given to him by Citizen William Short, American Minister in Spain. This certificate was sent to me from Bayonne by the above-mentioned Louis Dubart, along with letters that Citizen William Short had charged him to convey to me. This is all the information that I am able to give on this subject. Salutations and fraternity

Ja^s Monroe

RC, DLC : FCP—France

1. 15 Germinal (4 April 1795, above).

From Edmund Randolph

Department of State, April 7th 1795

Sir,

My last letter of March 8th 1795, has been forwarded to you by duplicates. It will have anticipated the subject of your private letter of December 18th. 1794, tho' it is by no means so extensive as one, which I should have concluded before this time, but for a constant round of interruptions, which I have not yet been able to repel. I am resolved, however, to seclude myself from all, except the most indispensable business; that I may devote my attention to such a review of our relation to France, as may ascertain the fact, which is so firmly impressed upon me, that we have behaved to her fairly and honorably. For the present I shall say no more respecting the source of discontent, the treaty made by Mr Jay, than this: that as far as I have any definite ideas of treaties offensive and defensive, there is no ground for charging that treaty, as being offensive or defensive: that the obligation of all prior treaties is <u>expressly</u> saved; that France, from the circumstance of being the most favored nation, immediately inherits, upon equal terms, the concessions, indulgences or conditions, made to other nations; and that the confining of its contents to the President and the Secretary of State is not from any thing sinister towards France, but from the usages in such cases; not from an unwillingness, that the Executive conduct should be canvassed; but from a certain fitness and expectation, arising from such a diplomatic act.

The dispatches, which you are understood to have intrusted to Mr Smith, of this City, not having yet arrived, our anxiety continues to learn the issue of the <u>concert</u>, which you have suggested. You will have been informed by my letter of the 8th ultimo, that "<u>the step is viewed here as a very strong one</u>;" and notwithstanding the rapid successes, which have attended the arms of our Ally, we steadily direct our course to the character of neutrality, which we profess, and therefore the more it is examined, the stronger it appears. You will hear from me shortly in a more particular manner concerning it, and the style, which in our negotiations at Paris ought, in our judgment, to be observed. But I must be permitted to remark, that the <u>invariable</u> policy of the President, is to be as independent as <u>possible</u>, of every nation upon earth; and this policy is not assumed now for the first time, when perhaps it may be insidiously preached by some, who lean to Great Britain, to prevent a tendency to France; but it is wise at all times, and, if steadily pursued, will protect our country from the effects of commotion in Europe. France is at this day in the eye of the President, as she has always been, cordially embraced, and no event could be more afflicting to him, than a suspicion of the purity of our motives in regard to that Republic. But without a steady adherence to <u>principles</u> no Government can defend itself against the animadversions of the world, nor procure a permanent benefit to its own Citizens.

Cases of spoliation and injury, according to the list subjoined, will accompany this letter, as subjects to which your attention and zeal are requested.[1]

The prints, which have not been hitherto sent, are also prepared by Mr Taylor.

Until a few days hence, I must beg you to accept this letter, as the forerunner only of a more copious one upon our affairs in France. I have the honor to be, Sir with sincere respect & esteem &c.

Edm: Randolph.

LBC, DNA: RG 59: Diplomatic and Consular Instructions

1. The subjoined list reads:

List of French spoliation papers sent by Mr Mitchell 7th April 1795.

1. Bring Mary (Titcomb)
2. Schooner President. addit.
3. Brig Brothers (Smith)
4. Ship Laurens addit.
5. Schooner Lucy addit.
6. Barque John (Simond, owner.)
7. Schooner Lark. (Lovett.)
8. Schooner Deborah.
9. Schooner Polly (Willis)
10. Danish Ship Kragerve
11. Sloop Mary Ann (Brentnall.)

The papers relating to these cases have not been located.

From William Short

Aranjuez (near Madrid) April 11. 1795.

Dear Sir

The principal object of this letter is to inform you that I have not had the pleasure of receiving any letters from you since that you wrote me on the 6th of Feb^{ry} which was sent here by the Genl of the Spanish army in Catalonia & given to me by the Minister of foreign affairs. I answered it immediately on the same day (the 25th of feb^{ry})[1] & sent my letter to the same minister who promised to have it forwarded by a flag to the French camp—from whence it will certainly have been sent safely to you—As this shewed that we might correspond with safety through that chanel, I have been waiting in expectation of again having the pleasure of hearing from you—I have conceived that a communication opened between you & myself might lead to consequences of a very important nature for the two countries where we respectively reside—& which might also be interesting to our common country. With this view I proposed it to you in my letter of Jany last[2] sent by my servant who returned to France—I have heard of his safe arrival on the 21st of Jany at the French camp at Tolosa & take it therefore for granted you must long ago have received my letter sent by him; although I have not from you any express acknowledgement of it. This has been cause of some embarassment to me as I wished to hear from you again before entering more fully on the subject alluded to in that letter—I did indeed intend soon after my letter to you of the

25$\underline{th}$ of Feb$\underline{ry}$ to write to you more fully—but particular considerations induced me to think it might be best to hear from you again—& I then conceived a very short delay w$\underline{d}$ suffice so thought daily I might receive something from you in consequence of my letter of Jan$\underline{y}$ or in a short time afterwards in consequence of that of Feb$\underline{y}$ 25$\underline{th}$ sent through the two armies—as I suppose by this route my letter would go & come quickly as before the war.

I had been for some time also then in the daily expectation of M$\underline{r}$ Pinckney's arrival here in consequence of the time when I conceived he should have received his commission & orders to repair here in haste as Envoy Extra. When last he wrote to me he was to have set out in the latter part of March only—this extreme & long delay it was not possible for me at that time to have contemplated. I take it for granted he will come through France & from you will learn the state of the business here as to the US & the object of his mission. It may not be improper for me however to observe to you that as yet this Government has signed no treaty with U. S. respecting their several claims. As far as the most positive assurances however [may] go, they will make no future difficulty notwithstanding the great delay which has hitherto taken place on their side—As you are acquainted with past circumstances I need say nothing more to give you a competent idea of this matter—So much I thought it necessary to say for your guidance. I wished for some written declaration on the part of this Government upon those points of the Navigation of the Misisipi, Limits & damages for spoliations on their part during the present war. This has been evaded rather than refused on account of the business <illegible> now pending either immediately with the President, in consequence of instructions sent to their charge des affairs at Philadelphia—or transferred to M$\underline{r}$ Pinckney in consequence of his new commission—Under my circumstances I avoided for several reasons at a time to press this point—& determined therefore to postpone either until M$\underline{r}$ Pinckneys arrival or until I should hear further from you to enter on the main object which I intended to open to you—After so long a delay I have conceived it proper to give you this statement of the business, leaving you to judge whether under present circumstances it be proper for us to take any step relative to the business existing between the countries where we respectively reside.

The close friendship which exists between France & the U. S. will naturally put you in such a situation as to form a more proper judgment on the subject than I can, as the fondness of their two governments & mode of doing business will make you fully acquainted with the views & wishes of that where you reside—& thus you may see what would be conformable to their wishes concurrent with those of the U. S. I can judge also with some degree of accuracy of the wishes of the Government from a more candid & friendly communication of sentiments in general lately than what formerly existed—yet on the whole I have thought it right that the business with the U. S. should be placed on a fixed & permanent ground—not least that our rights should be clearly acknowledged before taking any measures in the line I have hinted to you. Under this view the delay arising from M$\underline{r}$ Pinckney's nomination may be considered an object of regret

As I mentioned in the beginning of this letter its principal object is simply to inform you of the state of our letters & to induce you not to wait longer to let me hear from you through the two armies—On this side you may be sure there will be no obstacles—I have involuntarily extended this letter further than was my intention from the object first announced. I will thank you immediately in the receipt of it to write to me to let me know which of my letters since your arrival at Paris have got safe to your hands—& particularly whether that sent to you by M$\underline{r}$ Church has been received.[3]—I will thank you also to state a little more fully your reasons for conceiving as mentioned in your letter of Feb. 6$\underline{th}$ that it might be useful for me to go to Paris—Early in November last I wrote to ask the permission of the President in consequence of my state of health in this climate to go & pass the summer at Paris—I have not yet received his answer although I am expecting it daily & As the Sec. of State has in his <illegible>

informed me of his wish that I should co-operate with Mᴿ Pinckney I fear this may prevent the answer coming as soon as I first expected—although as Mᴿ Pinckney stands alone in the commission I hope a very short time will suffice for all the co-operation that may be necessary on my part—I count therefore on going soon to Paris—do not let this prevent your writing to me as I will always give you timely notice before my departure.

I have been much surprized at having never received any letter from you by the way of Italy although I have written several to you which have been forwarded both from Genoa & Leghorn—I desired you to send your letters to M Feleachy our Consul at Leghorn—Letters go regularly from Paris to that place & from thence here—My last from him was the 20ᵗʰ ultᵒ—at that time he had received no letter from you, although he had long before written to you, both through Switzerland & by Genoa.⁴

Be so good as to inform my friend to whom I think it best not to write by this conveyance until I receive a letter from you by the same, that I am <illegible> & well—that since October last, the letter by Mᴿ Livingston, none has been received by me—& that those I have written have been sent either under cover to you or through our Consul at Leghorn to his correspondent in Switzerland—I am therefore ignorant of every thing respecting that friend⁵ since Oct. last, except the few words mentioned in your letters of Nov. 19ᵗʰ & Feb. 6ᵗʰ—I beg you to take the trouble of writing a line merely to repeat this & to offer to forward letters to me, as the idea was taken up, as I have often mentioned to you, that you had an objection thereto—Persuaded that objection never existed & was quite mistaken, I have repeated this several times—but know not whether my letters ever got to hand—My long desire to return to my country is increasing daily with the early prospect of it in consequence of what has lately taken place. Before my return I shall visit the country which I love next to my own—& of course see you as you are happy enough to inhabit. That you may long enjoy that blessing my dear Sir to the material interests of that country & our own & to your personal satisfaction is the sincere wish of your friend & servᵗ

W Short

FC, DLC: Short Papers

1. JM's letter to Short of 6 February 1795 has not been located. Nor has a letter from Short dated 25 February 1795 been located; Short may have meant his letter of 23 February 1795 (above).

2. Short to JM, 10 January 1795 (above).

3. The letter sent via Edward Church at Lisbon may have been Short to JM, 18 February 1795 (above).

4. Philip Filicchy to JM, 22 October 1794 (above).

5. Duchess de Rochefoucauld.

To Edmund Randolph

Paris April 14ᵗʰ 1795

Sir,

I was lately favoured with a letter from Mᴿ Jay of the 5ᵗʰ of February by which I was informed that the bearer Colᵒ Trumbull who had copied and knew the contents of his treaty with the English government was instructed to communicate the same to me, because I was an <u>American Minister</u>, and in which character it might be <u>useful</u> to me, but that I must receive it in <u>strict confidence</u> and under an injunction to impart it to no other person whatever. As I had explicitly stated to Mᴿ Jay in my letter by Mᴿ Purvyance the only terms upon which I could receive the communication, and which I had done as well for the purpose of covering my engagement with the Committee, formed after the receipt of his first letter and when I expected no further information from him on the subject, as of preventing the transmission of it in case it contained the slightest circumstance which might be objectionable here, I could not otherwise than be surprised by the contents of this letter. To withold the communication at the moment when it was presumable the report of the contents of that treaty would excite a ferment here, and offer it after the expiration of some months, and when it was expected from America, and upon terms upon which I had assured him I could not receive it (to say nothing of the impossibility of comprehending how it could be useful if it was to be kept a profound secret) was unexpected: it was the more so since it was obvious that whilst the condition insisted on precluded the possibility of enabling me to promote thereby the public interest, it would unavoidably tend in some respects, to subject me to additional embarrassment in my situation here.

I was likewise soon apprized that Colonel Trumbull did not consider himself at liberty to make the communication in question unless I asked for it, and by which it was understood that I bound myself to accept it on the terms proposed, adding thereby to the injunctions of Mr Jay the additional obligation of private stipulation. The dilemma therefore with which I was threatened was of a peculiar kind: for if I accepted and withheld the communication from the Committee I should violate my engagement with that body, and if I gave it, I subjected myself not only to the probable imputation of indiscretion but likewise certainly to that of breach of promise. The line of propriety however appeared to me to be a plain one. I was bound to use such information as Mr Jay might think fit to give me in the best manner possible, according to my discretion, to promote the public interest, but I was not bound to use any artifice in obtaining that information, or to violate any engagement by the use of it. My duty to the public did not require this of me, and I had no other object to answer. As soon therefore as I had made a decision on the subject, I apprized Col^o Trumbull that I could not receive the communication proposed, upon the terms on which it was offered.

But the mission of this gentleman here though according to my information of him, a worthy and a prudent man, produced an effect of a more serious kind. I was soon advised by a person friendly to the United States and heretofore friendly and useful to me, that his arrival had excited uneasiness in the public councils, and would probably eventually injure my standing with the government, especially if I should be able to give the committee in consequence no account of the contents of that treaty; for it would hardly be credited after this, considering the relation between Mr Jay and myself, that I knew nothing of those contents. Upon what other motive it would be asked could the Secretary of Mr Jay come here, since the pretence of private business in Germany, which lay in another direction, would be deemed a falacious one? He added that the wisest precautions were necessary on my part to guard me against any unjust imputation, since through that the interests of my country might at the present crisis be essentially wounded. As I had anticipated in some measure the effect, I was mortified but not surprised by the intimation. It became me however to profit by it, and as well from the delicate regard which was due to my private as my public character, to place the integrity of my own conduct upon ground which could not be questioned. There appeared to me to be but one mode by which this could be done and which was by making known to the committee what had passed between Mr Jay and myself, to state the terms upon which he had offered the communication and my refusal to accept it on those terms, with my reason for such refusal. This you will readily conceive was a painful task: but as I had no other alternative left, but that of exposing myself to the suspicion of having known from the beginning the purport of Mr Jay's treaty, and uniting with him in withholding it from them, whilst I was using all the means in my power to impress them with a contrary belief, I was forced to undertake it. In consequence I waited on the diplomatic section of the committee and made the representation as above, repeating Mr Jay's motive for withholding the communication as urged by himself, "that it belonged to the sovereign power alone to make it" &c.   It was replied that it could not otherwise than excite uneasiness in the councils of his government, when it was observed that in the height of their war with the coalesced powers and with England in particular, America had stept forward and made a treaty with that power, the contents of which were so carefully and strictly withheld from this government, for if the treaty was not injurious to France why was it withheld from her? Was it prudent for one ally to act in such manner in regard to another, and especially under the present circumstances and at the present time, as to excite suspicions of the kind in question? I assured them generally as I had done before, that I was satisfied the treaty contained in it nothing which could give them uneasiness, but if it did and especially if it weakened our connection with France, it would certainly be disapproved in America. They thanked me for the communication, assured me they wished me to put myself in no dilemma which would be embarrassing, and thus the conference ended.

A few days after this I was favoured with a letter from Mᴿ Hitchborn an American gentleman of character here (from Massachusetts) of which I inclose you a copy, stating the contents or outlines of the treaty in question, as communicated to him by Colᵒ Trumbull, and with a view that he might communicate the same to me for the information of this government.[1] I was surprised at this incident, because I could not suppose that Colᵒ Trumbull would take this step, or any other without the instructions of Mᴿ Jay, and it seemed to me extraordinary that Mᴿ Jay should give such an instruction or mark to him such a line of conduct. I was not surprised that Colᵒ Trumbull should confide the purport of the treaty to Mᴿ Hitchborn, for he merited the confidence, but I was surprised that Mᴿ Jay should write me it was to be communicated to me only as a public minister &c to be imparted to no one else, and that Colᵒ Trumbull however deeply impressed he might be after his arrival here, with the propriety of removing the doubts of this government upon that point, should consider himself at liberty to communicate the same to a third person, to be communicated to me under no injunction whatever. I was however possessed of the paper in question and it was my duty to turn it to the best account for the public interest that circumstances would now admit of. It was it is true the most informal of all informal communications, and one of course upon which no official measure could be taken: yet the character of the parties intitled it to attention. Upon mature reflection therefore and the more especially as I did not wish to meet the committee again on that point until I heard from you, lest I should be questioned why this new mode of diplomatic proceeding was adopted, I thought it best to send the paper in by my secretary Mᴿ Gauvain (a young gentleman who has acted with me since the provisional nomination of Mᴿ Skipwith to the Consulate) instructing him to assure the members on my part, that they might confide in the credibility of the parties. The paper was presented to Merlin de Douay with the comments suggested and since which I have neither heard from the committee, Colᵒ Trumbull, nor Mᴿ Jay on the subject.

I intimated to you in my last that I was persuaded if there was a force here able and willing to make head against the revolution it would soon shew itself, but that I was of opinion none such existed. This presage has been since verified by a great and interesting example. The storm which I thought I then saw gathering, after rising to its height and expending its force, has past, and without doing any mischief. On the contrary I am inclined to believe from present appearances, it will be productive of good.

It was natural to expect that the trial of Barrere, Collot d'Herbois and B. Varennes, three men who were, in the early stages associates, and in the latter in some degree the rivals of Robespierre's power, and who were after his fall unquestionably at the head of the mountain party, would excite some ferment. It was equally so to presume that if that party was not so completely crushed, as to preclude all hope of success, it would in some stage of the proceeding, make an extraordinary effort to save them. The epoch of this trial was therefore deemed by all an important one to France, and its several stages were marked by circumstances which were calculated rather to increase than diminish the general solicitude.

Under the banner of this party and apparantly in favour of the acquital of these members, the discontented of every description were seen rallying, forming in the whole an extraordinary assemblage, being gathered from the various and heretofore opposite classes of society, but united now for the common purpose of disturbing the public tranquility. The prisons which were filled in the time of Robespierre, and opened under the more humane administration of the present day, had discharged upon the City an immense crowd of the ancient aristocracy, and who soon gave proof that the severe discipline they had undergone, had not eradicated the propensities that were acquired under the reign of the ancient court. As the present administration had rescued them from the guillottine, and to which they were otherwise inevitably doomed, it was at least intitled to their gratitude. This slight tribute however was not paid for that important service. On the contrary they were among the most active in fomenting the present discontents. Another group not less numerous or turbulent, composed of the refuse of the lately disfranchised or rather routed Jacobins, and their adherents, was seen marshalled by its side, and acting in harmony with it. These two classes of people and who were heretofore at endless war with each other now combined, formed a force of some strength, and excited in the minds of many well disposed persons, serious apprehensions for the public safety.

The increasing scarcity of bread, and which menaced an unavoidable diminution of the ordinary allowance, contributed much to increase the apprehension of danger. A deficiency in this article in Paris under the ancient government generally excited a tumult. It was therefore a primary object in every reign, and with every administration, to guard against such deficiency, as the greatest of public calamities. Abundant stores were in consequence always provided, when it was possible to provide them, and let the scarcity or price be what it might in other quarters, the ordinary allowance and nearly at the ordinary price, was distributed, as in times of greatest plenty, among the inhabitants of this City. Such likewise had been the practice since the change of government, so that a state of affairs which announced the approach of a deficiency, announced likewise that of a crisis extremely important in the history of the revolution. The most firm knew it was an experiment yet to be made, and from which whilst they counted upon no possible benefit, they had many reasons to apprehend some real inconvenience.

It was foreseen that if any movement was set on foot, the deficiency of bread if that was the fact, would be made the pretext, and as the complaint, being addressed to the wants of all, would excite a general sympathy, it was feared that such deficiency would tend much to increase the strength of the insurgent party. In every view therefore the crisis which approached was an interesting one: it was however at hand and no other alternative remained for those whose duty it was to sustain it, than that of yielding under or meeting it with firmness and passing through it as well as possible.

As soon as it was known that a diminution of the ordinary allowance was unavoidable it was resolved to make it known likewise to the people, that they might not be taken by surprise, and for this purpose Boissy d'Anglas[2] of the section of subsistence in the committee of public safety, appeared at the tribune some days before it took effect. His discourse which was short but explicit, began by exposing freely the enormities and vicious arrangement of the ancient committees whereby he said France had already been visited with many calamities and was still threatened with others, and concluded by observing that even famine was likewise one proceeding from that source, which neither the wisdom nor the industry of the present councils had been able altogether to avert: that he was happy however to assure the convention that as the most prudent measures were long since taken to correct the abuses of that administration, the distress of Paris would be for a short term only. The communication was received by Barrere, Billaud de

Varennes &c, and by the members of the mountain party in general, with a smile of approbation. It was obvious they considered Boissy as a welcome messenger, announcing to them joyful tydings. A few days afterwards the deficiency so much dreaded took place, and at the same time the intrigues of the discontented, began more fully to unfold themselves.

The movement was commenced by about 400 citizens, from a section heretofore noted for its turbulence, and who, appearing without the hall demanded admission to the bar of the convention. A deputation from the party consisting of 20 members was admitted and who addressed that body in a style unusual, complaining of the want of bread, and declaring also that they were upon the point of regretting the sacrifices they had made to the revolution. The answer of the President (Thibodaut)[3] was firm and decisive. To that part of the address which complained of the scarcity of bread he replied, by stating the measures of the government to remedy it: and to that which exposed the temper of the party in regard to the revolution he answered explicitly that he knew the disaffected were at work to excite trouble but that their efforts would be fruitless: for enlightened by experience and strong in the power of the whole nation, the convention would be able to controul their movements; and in closing he addressed himself more particularly to the memorialists, saying that the efforts of the people to recover their liberty would not be lost, whilst good citizens seconded the labours of their representatives; that despair belonged only to slaves; freemen never regretted the sacrifices they had made in such a cause. The answer which was received with general applause, checked for a while the turbulent spirit of the disaffected.

But this party had too much at stake and its measures were probably too far advanced to be abandoned in this stage. About a week after this and which was on the 1st of April (12 Germinal) a more numerous body, consisting principally of workmen from the faubourg of S[t] Antoine, presented itself likewise before the hall demanding admission to the bar of the convention and upon some pretext and in violation of the usual forms immediately forced its way into the hall of that assembly. The crowd increased so that in the course of a few hours there were in the hall perhaps 3 or 4,000, and in the vacant external place around it, as many more. The proceedings of the convention were suspended: the President however and the members kept their seats, declaring that as their sitting was violated they would do no business; indeed it was now impossible to do any had they been so disposed, for the general and tumultuous cries that were raised by the invaders "for bread" for "liberty to the patriots" meaning some of the accomplices of Robespierre, could alone be heard. They continued thus in the hall about 4 hours, from two to six in the evening, offering in the interim no violence to any of the members, but behaving in other respects with the utmost possible indecorum. When they first entered some circumstances were seen which caused a suspicion that a good understanding subsisted between the leaders of the mob and some members of the mountain party, and it was likewise observed that their final retreat was made upon a suggestion from that quarter for as soon as an admonition to that effect was given from that quarter it was obeyed. Many believe it was intended to lay violent hands upon all the leading members of the preponderating party and either murder them in their places, or send them to prison to be murdered afterwards, under the form of a trial, as was the case in the time of Robespierre, whereby the preponderating scale would be shifted to the other side, and the reign of terror revived again for a while. Be the plan however what it might it was soon frustrated: for as the movement was that of a mob against the civil authority, its operations were irregular and disorderly: it had no chief to lead it on to acts of violence. The time was therefore whiled away in senseless uproar, till at length the putative authors of the movement were as uneasy about the issue, and as anxious to get rid of it as those at whom it was supposed to be pointed. In the interim too the means that were adopted without, tended not only to secure the general tranquillity of the City, but most probably to influence in a great measure the proceedings within. By order of the committees the tocsin was sounded, and the citizens in every section called to arms, so that the appeal was fairly made to the people of Paris whether they would support the republic, or rally under the standard of those who were for a change. Nor was the question long undecided: for as soon as the government acted in its various functions it was obeyed; the lapse of a few hours gave it the preponderance, and the lapse of a few more not only freed the hall of the Convention from the invasion with which it had been seized, but dispersed the crowd from its vicinity. At six in the evening the convention resumed its deliberations, beginning by declaring its sitting permanent, and progressing by a review of the movement of the day, which were well understood and freely discussed. By this time too it was fortified by accounts from every quarter, that the sense of the City was decisively pronounced in its favour, and against the rioters, and that the inhabitants of those sections whence the disorder proceeded were returning to their duty. The sitting continued till six in the morning, in the course whereof a decree of banishment was passed against the accused members, and of arrestation against 8 or 9 of the mountain party, which latter list was afterwards increased to about 18, and both of which decrees have since been carried into effect, by sending the former to the Isle of Oleron and the latter to the castle of Ham in the department of Somme:[4] and thus ended the commotion which was so long gathering, and which menaced at one time, not to arrest the progress of the revolution (at least such was my opinion) but to occasion much trouble, and stain its page with new atrocities.

In the course of this day, the services of General Pichegru who happened to be in Paris and was appointed commandant of the national guard, were of great importance to his country. His activity was great, for he was always on horse, and passing from one quarter of the City to another: and his arrangements in disposing of the cannon and military force, were wise. His name too was of great utility, for it tended equally to elevate the hopes of the friends, and depress those of the enemies of the public tranquillity. I do not think if he had been absent, the event would have been different, but I am satisfied that his presence contributed much to hasten the restoration of order and to preserve it afterwards.

By this event which is called the complement of the 9th of Thermidor, and which forms the catastrophe of the mountain party, tranquillity appears to be established not only in this city, but throughout the Republic in general. The scarcity of bread it is true still continues, but yet no murmering has been since heard on that subject. The moderate party, and which in principle I deem the same with that which was overwhelmed on the 31st of May, will therefore commence its career under auspices extremely favourable to its own reputation, and to the liberty and prosperity of France. The fate of its late antagonist, if there was no other motive, and which was precipitated by the general wish of France, and of all other nations not in league against the French republic, must furnish a solemn and lasting admonition to shun its example. The opposite principles too upon which it is founded, being the avowed patron of humanity justice and law, and equally at variance with the opposite extremes of aristocracy and anarchy, whose partizans were lately combined in an effort to crush it, promise to secure in its measures, some stability in the observance of those just and honourable principles which it professes.

For some time past the views of this party have been directed towards the establishment of the constitution, and some motions to that effect are now depending before select committees appointed to prepare the several organic laws necessary to introduce it. An opinion is likewise entertained by many that the constitution in question is very defective and ought to be amended before it is put in force. A discourse to this effect was lately delivered by Pelet, a respectable and well informed member, and the same sentiment was then avowed by others. But whether an attempt of this kind, should it formally be made, will succeed, or whether the general solicitude to put the constitution in force however defective it may be, in the hope of amending it afterwards, will prevail is yet uncertain.

Since the fortunate issue of the late commotion a treaty of peace was concluded with Prussia at Basle, in Switzerland, of which I inclose you a copy. The import of the 4th and 5th articles give cause to suspect that some stipulations exist which have not been communicated, and it is believed by many that it is agreed between the parties that France shall retain the Prussian territory on the left of the Rhine, in lieu whereof she is to take and cede Hanover.[5] Should this be the case, it is probable if the war continues another campaign, that Prussia will be seen arranged as a party in it on the side of France. The latter considers the old connection with Austria as broken and wishes to supply it by one with Prussia, and provided satisfactory arrangements are, or shall be hereafter formed for that purpose, will become interested in raising the latter power at the expence of the former, as well as that of England. The negotiation with Spain is also said to be far advanced and will most probably soon be closed. 'Tis likewise reported that a person or more than one from England, is now in Paris upon the pretext of treating for an exchange of prisoners, but in truth for the more substantial one of treating or at least of sounding the disposition of this government for peace. Upon this point however I hope to be able to give you in the course of a few days more correct information than I now can. I have the honor to be Sir, with great respect and esteem your very humble serv[t]

Ja[s] Monroe.

Copy, DNA: RG 59: Dispatches from France

1. Benjamin Hichborn to JM, 31 March 1795 (above).

2. François-Antoine Boissy d'Anglas (1756-1826), along with Sieyès and Cambacérès, dominated the Committee of Public Safety from 28 July 1794 to 4 November 1795. He was born into a Protestant family in the Ardèche region of south-central France; pursued a legal career and secured a position as avocat before the Parlement of Paris in the late 1780s. He played a key role in drafting the Constitution of 1795. Boissy d'Anglas was faulted for his refusal to reintroduce the law of the maximum in the face of food shortages in 1795 (Samuel Scott and Barry Rothaus, *Historical Dictionary of the French Revolution, 1789-1799*, 213-214; Paul R. Hanson, *Historical Dictionary of the French Revolution*, 37; *Dictionnaire de Biographie Française*).

3. Antoine-Claire Thibaudeau (1765-1854) was president of the National Convention, 6-24 March and a member of the Committee of Public Safety, 7 October to 4 November 1795 (WWW.Rulers.org, accessed 22 April 2007; *Encyclopedia Britannica*).

4. Montagnards Amar, Duhem, and Choudieu were arrested and sent to Ham, a castle used as a prison in the Department of the Somme; Cambon managed to escape to Lausanne. Levasseur, Le Cointre, Thuriot, and Maignet were sent to the Isle of Oléron off the western coast near Rochelle. None was deported or executed (Roger Caratini, *Dictionnaire des personnages de la Révolution*).

5. Article four of the Treaty of Basle between France and Prussia, signed on 5 April 1795, required the French Republic to evacuate their troops from the Prussian right bank, and the Prussian king to reduce his troops on the right bank to prewar numbers. Article five declared that France would continue to occupy the left bank of the Rhine. Prussia feared that France would hold these left bank territories indefinitely. The Treaty of Basle made no mention of Hanover, but the subsequent Convention of May 17 contained a secret article in which Prussia promised to occupy Hanover in case the electorate rejected neutrality (M. De Clercq, *Recueil des Traités de la France*, 1: 232-236; Sydney Seymour Biro, *The German Policy of Revolutionary France*, 1: 334-345; 337, 343, 348, 367).

From Timothy Pickering

[27 April 1795][1]

Return of Books and Mathematical instruments to be procured for the instruction and for the Use of the Corps of Artillerists and Engineers of the United States.

Books—Elemens de fortifications d'attaque et de deffenses des places par

Trincano 2ᵈ Edition . . avec planches[2] ....15 livres
Oeuvres completes . . de Vauban[3]
   ditto............de le Blond[4]
   ditto............de Besou[5]
Manuel de l'artilleur par d'urturbie[6]—<u>Six exemplaires à acheter</u>
ditto des mineralogists par Bergman . . 2 vol. broché[7]
Architecture de Vignoles[8]
Stereotomie de Fresier[9]
Fortification de Campagne par Latour de Foissac[10]
L'Architecture Militaire par un Offᵉʳ de distinction[11]
Ordonnances d artillerie du Genie et des Mineurs[12]
Traite sur Les mines[13]
Traite de Charpente[14]
Oeuvres completes de l'Abé Bosout examinateur des Ingenieurs[15]
Traité des Canaux par Dubuat[16]
Architecture hidraulique de Prosny[17]
Partie Militaire de l'anciclopedie par ordre de Matieres[18]
Tables de Logaritmes—Deux exemplaires[19]
Traite de duplain pour la Levee des cartes[20]
Travail sur les cartes de France par Cassini et Pienel[21]

Instruments—Une Planchette complete

Une equerre d'arpenteur[22]
le cercle de Borda par la longitude[23]
Six fusils complets avec leur bayonnetes, du Modile de 1776[24]
Six Gibernes completes du dernier Modele et Six Sabres des Sergents[25]

RC, NN: Monroe Papers; filed 27 April 1795

1. This undated list had been enclosed in an unlocated letter that Pickering sent JM on 27 April 1795 (JM to Pickering, 30 September 1795, below).

2. Didier-Grégoire Trincano (1719-1792) first published his *Élémens de fortification, de l'attaque et de la défense des places* in 1768, followed by a second edition in 1786 (*National Union Catalogue*).

3. Sebastien Le Prestre Vauban (1633-1707) was a French military engineer whom Voltaire called "le Premier des ingenieurs et le meilleur de citoyens." Vauban designed and built star-shaped forts with straight sided moats. After having directed fifty-three sieges under Louis XIV, Vauban developed a keen eye for "blind spots" in which an attacker could hide. Vauban was a prolific author, and JM himself owned four books written by him: *L'Art de la* Guerre (1740); *De l'Attacque et de la Défense des Places* (1739); *Mémoire pour Servir d'Instruction dans la Conduite des Sièges* (1740); and *New Method of Fortification* (1748) (*La Grande Encyclopédié* ; Gordon W. Jones, *The Library of James Monroe*, 21).

4. Guillaume Le Blond (1704-1781) wrote extensively on mathematics and military subjects (*National Union Catalogue*).

5. Etienne Bézout (1730-1773) was a French mathematician whose books on the practical application of mathematics remained in print as late as 1845 (*La Grande Encyclopédie*; *National Union Catalogue*).

6. Théodore-Bernard-Simon D'Urtubie (d. 1807) authored *Manuel de L'Artilleur*; it was published in German in 1788 and in French in 1794 (*National Union Catalogue*).

7. Torbern Olof Bergman (1735-1784) was a Swedish chemist and mathematician. A two-volume edition of his *Manuel du Mineralogiste* was published in Paris in 1792 (*Dictionary of Scientific Biography*; *National Union Catalogue*).

8. *Regola delli cinque ordini di archittura* by the Italian Renaissance architect Giocomo Barrozzio Vignola (1507-1573) was translated in many languages and remained in print into the twentieth century (*National Union Catalogue*; *Encyclopedia Britannica*).

9. Amedée-François Frézier (1682-1773), a French army engineer, authored the two-volume work, *Eléments de Stéréotomie* in 1760. Stereotomy dealt with the science or art of stonecutting (*Dictionnaire de Biographie Française*).

10. Philippe-François de Latour-Foissac (1750-1804) studied military engineering at Mézières and in 1770 left with the rank of lieutenant. After participating in the American Revolution he became chief engineer at Phalsboug, where he wrote on the utility of fortified positions and entrenchment in 1789 (*Dictionnaire de Biographie Française*).

11. *Architecture Militaire, ou L'Art de Fortifier . . .* by Louis Cormontaingne (1696-1752), a French army engineer, was published in three volumes in 1741 (*National Union Catalogue*; *Grand Larousse Encyclopédique*).

12. This may refer to a 1776 ordinance that required engineering students to serve two years in a company of miners and sappers attached to the artillery before being admitted in the Corps of Engineers ("École royale du génie de Mézières," Wikipedia, accessed 19 May 2008).

13. Philippe Francois de Latour-Foissac published a revised edition of Vauban's *Traités de Mines* (*National Union Catalogue*).

14. Matthias Mesange, *Traité de la charpenterie et des bois de toutes espèces* (Paris, 1753).

15. Abbé Charles Bossut (1730-1814), professor of mathematics and engineering at the College of Mézières, wrote extensively on mathematics and engineering (*National Union Catalogue*).

16. Pierre-Louis-Georges Du Buat (1734-1809) was a French hydraulic engineer who worked on formulas for computing the amount of water discharged from channels in order to produce results of practical value. His design for hydraulic works strongly influenced the development of experimental hydraulics in the eighteenth and nineteenth centuries. His *Principles D'Hydraulique* was published in 1779 and revised in 1786 (*Encyclopedia Britannica*; *National Union Catalogue*).

17. Gaspard Riche de Prony (1755-1839) was engineer-in-chief of the École des Ponts et Chaussés at Paris in 1791. The first volume of his *Nouvelle Architecture Hydraulique* was published in 1790, followed by a second volume in 1796 (M. M. Bradley, "Prony the Bridge Builder: the Life and Times of Gaspard de Prony, Educator and Scientist," *Centaurus*, 37 (1994): 230-268; *National Union Catalogue*).

18. "Military part of the Encyclopedia in order of contents".

19. "Logarithm Table—Two examples".

20. Benoit-Joseph Duplain (1748-1794) authored *La Carte des Traites* in 1774 (*La Biographie Française*).

21. Jean-Dominique Cassini (1748-1845) continued the work of his father César-François Cassini de Thury (1714-1784) on a new map of France. The junior Cassini used newly developed measuring instruments such as Borda's repeating circle to complete the project. Jean Perny de Villeneuve was his collaborator (*Dictionary of Scientific Biography*).

22. A planchette and an équerry d'arpenteur were surveying instruments used to measure angles. They were superceded by the theodolite (*Oxford English Dictionary*).

23. Jean-Charles de Borda (1733-1799) was a military engineer and mathematician in the army. He developed the repeating circle that had two small telescopes each fixed to rings that could rotate independently against a scale. The accuracy of Borda's repeating circle allowed distances to be found by surveying using triangulation (*Encyclopedia Britannica*).

24 "Six fusils complete with their bayonets of the 1776 model."

25. "Six complete cartridge boxes of the last model and six sabers for sergeants."

To Fulwar Skipwith

Paris May 1. 1795.

Sir

I send you herewith a statm^t of three cases, Buffenton, Law, & Snow whose vessels were taken at sea & bro^t in by the cruisers of the republick & wch are under adjustment according to the arrete of the committee with wch you are acquainted. There can be no question that the object of the com^y of marine is to create delay in this and all other cases originating in his department and it is likewise equally certain that formal applications anywhere will tend but little to promote dispatch. I co^d wish you therefore to call incessantly upon that member of the committee within whose province it particularly lies, & represent to him the time already consumed since the order of the Committee, for the adjustment of those claims, the injury to the parties arising from the delay, & in consequence the ruin which must attend the French commerce unless justice be rendered soon. Suggest to him in plain terms that many think the Com^y wishes to delay, merely to keep out of view transactions that cannot be justified. That a report must be made to the American gov^t & for this purpose one must be made to me by you within a short span of time. I sho^d suppose that in conversations with Talien, Marec[1] &c this business might be greatly forwarded or at least definitively closed soon, so that the people be in all cases dispatched & some answer given. y^{rs} respectfully

Ja^s Monroe

RC, ViW: Jay Johns Collection of Monroe Papers

This letter is not addressed; the subject matter suggests that it was written to Skipwith.

1. Jean-Lambert Tallien had become a member of the Committee of Public Safety for the second time on 4 April 1795. Pierre Marec (1759-1828) wrote a report on coastal navigation and put together the Navigation Act for the Republic in July 1793. He was a member of the Committee of Marine and Commerce, and also a member the Committee of Public Safety (August Kuscinski, *Dictionnaire des Conventionnels*).

From Edmund Randolph

Philadelphia May 2. 1795.

Sir

The letter, which I promised by Dr Edwards[1] is prepared; but the President not having returned from Mount Vernon, I cannot submit it to his correction, without which it would be improper to send it. It is long, full and perhaps an interesting review of our conduct towards France.

I have to acknowledge your letters January 13. 95. with triplicates of No 1, 2, 3, 4, 5, 6 & 7—of September 20. 94[2]—of february 1, 1795—and of a duplicate of December 2. 1794. This is the order, in which they have been received.

Mr Jay has transmitted the correspondence between you and him. When he arrives, I shall [per]haps forward the sentiments of the President as to the footing on which the business has been placed by him

Col^o Humphreys sailed six weeks ago, properly charged for the negotiation with Algiers. Before this reaches you, he will probably have had a personal interview with you; and will satisfy you, that on this and every other occassion we wish to observe delicacy towards our friends and allies. I have the honor to be sir with great respect and esteem y^r mo. ob serv.

Edm: Randolph

RC, MHi: C. E. French Papers

1. Enoch Edwards (1751-1802) was a physician who had been an apprentice of Benjamin Rush. Edwards attended the Pennsylvania convention to ratify the U. S. Constitution in 1788 and was an associate justice of the common pleas court in Philadelphia from 1791 to 1802. Edwards arrived in Paris in July 1795 and with the exception of one short interval remained until August 1796. JM described Edwards as "well-informed and very deserving of confidence." (*Letters of Benjamin Rush*, 2: 743; Benjamin Rush, *Autobiography*, 311-312; *Writings of Monroe*, 3: 51, 99).

2. A letter from JM to Randolph dated 20 September 1794 has not been located. Randolph may have meant JM's letter of 20 November 1794 (above).

From William Short

Aranjuez May 4 1795

Dear Sir

I should have waited for your answer to my late letters & particularly that of the 11ᵗʰ of April, before writing to you again, if it had not been for the particular circumstance which makes the subject of this. I have already mentioned to you the desire of this Government to open the way to a pacification with the French Commonwealth, & also my persuasion that some kind of negotiation although perhaps an unofficial one was on foot. I am confirmed in that opinion & you may consider as certain that overtures have passed between one of the persons here to whom you sent me a letter inclosed in yours of the 6ᵗʰ of Febʳʸ last[1] & the person by whom those letters were written—I have good reason to believe that this business has met with some kind of delay as to the articles of pacification—or at least that it is conceived here there would be some delay when these articles should come to be discussed—You will readily conceive from the situation of this country in respect to England that they would be afraid to enter openly on negotiation without being previously sure of its success, lest they should find themselves between two fires—The apprehension of England has certainly retained them lately & not any aversion to peace with the French Commonwealth, which on the contrary they desire most sincerely & ardently.—Under these circumstances the friendly interference of the U. S. has been wished for by this Government—I have already explained to you the difficulties which presented themselves to me from the points in litigation between the U. S & this Country having not been yet settled—& from the circumstances of Mʳ Pinckneys appointment for that purpose rendering it necessary that they should be delayed for his arrival here—Although I have the fullest assurances from this Government that all matters shall be settled to the satisfaction of the U. S.—& although present circumstances insure whatever the U. S. may now desire here, yet under my circumstances I should have chosen not taking an active interference until I should have conferred with Mʳ Pinckney & he with this Government. For a long time I had no doubt Mʳ Pinckney would have been here long ere this—I suppose he must be at present somewhere in France on his way hither—but I have received no letter from him since that of the 6ᵗʰ of March.—Things would have probably gone on in this way until his arrival viz this Government contenting themselves with the <u>pourparlers</u> on foot between the two persons mentioned above—& perhaps also between the Generals of the two armies, if nothing had occurred to make them more anxious to accelerate the business. But this has taken place in consequence of the treaty concluded between the French Commonwealth and the King of Prussia.

The Duke de la Alcudia[2] has now mentioned to me his desire that no further time should be lost & that an active negotiation should be immediately opened, declaring to me confidentially & authorizing me to mention to you, his real & sincere wish to conclude immediately a treaty with the French commonwealth, desiring however that it may be so conducted that there should be no suspicion of it on the part of England, or the least possible ground for suspicion, until the conclusion & ratification of the treaty. He has therefore requested me to communicate this to the Minister of the U. S. at Paris, & to add his desire to receive here for the purpose of concluding such a treaty, any person whom the French Government might send for that purpose & remain here in a secret way until the business should be concluded & ratified—The desire of secrecy as you will observe proceeds from the apprehension of England— This he wishes you to propose to the French Government if you find it will be acceptable to them—This is the nature of his request to me & which I have not thought it proper for several reasons to decline— Several of these reasons will naturally present themselves to you-

Having thus stated the request of the Duke in the simplest form, it is for you to decide thereon what you may think advisable to do, and in which you will of course be guided by what you conceive to be for the interest of the U. S. & conformable to the wishes of the Government where you reside, whose interests are co-incident with those of the U. S.

It may not be improper to subjoin here some incidental remarks which took place between the Minister here & myself on the above occasion. In stating to me his wish that this business should be concluded as soon as possible, he observed that if he had a person of confidence at Paris he would give him the conditions on which the king wished this treaty to be grounded—but that he had no such person there & that it would be impossible for him to send one, without its being found out here or at Paris by England—On my mentioning the probability of the same discovery being made if the French Government should send a person here, he said there would be much less difficulty if that person were charged not to discover himself—or to pass for an American—& that the communications between him & the Ministry here might pass through my hands, so as to remove all suspicion of his being a person charged with a negotiation.

Should you think it proper to communicate this desire of the Duke de la Alcudia to the French Government, you will observe that nothing in writing has passed between us—& that his request to me is made only verbally—Although I have not the smallest doubt myself of the full & unequivocal sincerity with which he has thus opened himself to me, yet I would not chuse to induce the French Government to adopt the measure proposed without at the same time stating that the ground is as yet merely verbal—If however the Republick is willing as I have no doubt to enter into negotiation for peace, & should chuse to have some written ground, I suppose it probable the Minister would not refuse to communicate to me in confidence, in writing his desire abovementioned, if he shᵈ be assured of its being complied with by sending an agent here as stated already. From the footing on which you stand of course with the French government you will be able to judge what is the mode which would be most agreeable to them in the conducting a negociation with this Country—if they do not approve that suggested by the Duke—& if they think it proper to communicate it to me, I will ascertain here the sentiments of the Minister respecting the mode that shall be proposed.

So much for the mode of the negotiation—It may not be improper to add something respecting the substance of it—It would seem natural that the Duke should have given me some intimation of the conditions on which he wished the peace to be settled with the Republick—but I did not chuse to press on this head—because it did not seem to be the proper time to be asking for particulars—& also because as he knows my attachment to France in common with that of every other American, he might chuse not to put me further in possession of his sentiments than might be absolutely necessary—From our conversation however as well on this as on preceding occasions, I find his desire would be to avoid if possible contracting any article which might force this country into an immediate war with England—He is determined to risk that event however, if the simple deviation from the Convention of May 25, 1793[3]—

& the treating separately for peace with France, should render it inevitable. He flatters himself however that Spain's making a separate peace would not induce England to declare war against her under present circumstances. He would desire therefore to conclude a peace as simple as possible—He would chuse to avoid guaranteeing to France the island of Corsica & such parts of the East & West Indies as England has taken during this war, because he conceives that would necessitate an immediate war with England—But the desire of this country is that France should reconquer those places as it is the real interest of Spain that they should belong to France rather than to England—I mention these things merely as the first desire of the Minister—how far he might be induced to deviate therefrom for the object of a pacification with the French Republick will appear in the course of the negotiation if it should be opened—The greatest difficulty will be as to the parts of Spain conquered by France—& I apprehend as I have mentioned above, that some difficulty has already shewn itself as probable, as to the place of Figueras. It is the business of negotiation of course to remove difficulties.

Should the French Government chuse to have something more certain fixed before sending an agent here, & will inform you how far they wish previously to be made acquainted with the outlines of the sentiments of this Court, it is probable the Minister would communicate them—At the same time he would probably expect an equal mark of confidence through you & myself of the sentiments on the same head of the French Government.

This letter will be forwarded by the Minister through the frontiers by a flag—You will therefore soon receive it—I will thank you immediately to acknowledge the receipt thereof—& and to let me know as soon as possible whether you have judged it proper to take any step in consequence thereof, & what shall have been the result thereof. Send your letters on this subject by the same way by which you sent that of the 6th of Febry the last I have received from you—I have as yet no answer from the President as to the absence from hence which I have asked—I hope ere long to have the pleasure of renewing to you in person the assurances of my being sincerely your friend and servt

W. Short

RC, NN: Monroe Papers

1. JM's letter to Short of 6 February has not been located.

2. Manuel Godoy, the Duke of Alcudia (1767-1851) administered foreign policy under King Charles IV of Spain (Douglas Hilt, *The Troubled Trinity: Godoy and the Spanish Monarchy*).

3. France declared war against Spain in March of 1793, which resulted in Spain forming an alliance with Great Britain in a convention signed on 25 May 1793 (*Cambridge Modern History*, 9: 254).

To William Short

Paris May 4. 1795.

Dear Sir

I have just recd yours of the 11. ulto and believe I have recd all or most of the letters you have written me by the several routes mentioned. More which covered letters to yr friend[1] came to hand, & those letters were forwarded her; two of which recd more latterly were of course sent to her but lately. She is in the country abt 20. leagues from Paris & has been in town that I have heard of but once since her enlargement & left it either before I knew of it or immediately after for when I proposed visiting her I was informed she had retired again. Her acct to you of my reluctance to be the intermediatory of yr correspondence was true. I cannot explain to you fully my motive for a decision on that point, or rather why an exception to a rule which was universal was not made in your favor untill I see you. Be satisfied however that it did not proceed from an indifference to y^r interest, or any abatment in that friendship which was formed for you in early life, & which has never ceased to attend you since. nor did it proceed from any disrespect for your friend; on the contrary I know her to be deserving of respect; on this point however I sho^d have made no question after I heard she was y^r friend. I have lately written & apprized her that the objection no longer exists,[2] & presume she will avail herself in future of my aid in facilitating her correspondence.

Yours by Mr Church & that thro' the armies[3] was rec^d & would have been sooner answered had I not expected as you have done the arrival of Mr Pinckney here and anticipated as has been the case a total suspension of y^r negotiation in consequence of his appointment. I postponed writing therefore untill his passage sho^d furnish me with an opportunity, hoping every day for his arrival, but yet I am still to hope for that event. His delay however will no longer form my excuse. Delay with us is the object of the Sp^n court and always was, and I regret that his delay sho^d harmonize so essentially with its views, for in the same degree does it disappoint ours. If it was certain that Mr Pinckney wo^d come thro' France it wo^d be well for you to meet him here. You who perfectly understand the nature of the present crisis & its importance to us, in relation to that negotiation, can fully comprehend the import & justice of this remark, so that I shall not at present enlarge upon it.

If Spain meant to do us justice the organ thro' whom it was yielded wo^d be of little importance, to her it w^d make no difference whether our boundaries and right to the navigation of the missisippi were acknowledged in a treaty signed by you or any other person: and surely whilst she violates those rights she cannot expect from us any offices of friendship. Is it not indelicate to ask it? A mere act of justice is entitled to no retribution, but to suspend the one untill the other sho^d be rendered, is rather calculated to create a doubt, that some political finesse is intended whereby her object may be gained and ours de-feated. If the points in controversy were settled with us, we sho^d have more motive to assist Spain and our weight here, being compelled by no particular interest, wo^d be the greater: for in truth I can see no reason why the closest and most friendly connection sho^d not subsist between France, Sp^n & the united States. Of France, Sp^n is the natural ally agnst Engl^d for thro' her only can she count upon a balance by sea agnst the exorbitant & tyrannous power of England; a power w^h unless it be curbed will sooner or later strike at the possessions of Sp^n in America. It likewise is equally the interest of the united States & France: in addition France is the first indeed the only and most intimate ally of the united States. Here then is the motive of common interest to all three & as soon as Spain does away her ridiculous opposition to our rights will it operate beneficially for each. What the objection on her part to yield amicably to our demands? The fear of admitting us within her territory. Does she not see that she promotes the object she wishes to counteract, for if she settled us in peace in the enjoyment of our rights, she might afterwards count upon our friendship in repressing any attempts in our citizens to transgress those of others: but by encroaching on ours she dams up a current, which will in a few years overspread her territory far to the south. The population in that country is now great, & increases rapidly. The crisis has almost arrived, when wearied out with an unprofitable negotiation & disgusted with the injuries of Sp^n, the people are ready to break the restraint hitherto imposed on them and redress themselves. Sho^d this be the case can Sp^n hope to controul such a mov'ment or to turn it to her account. Suppose 20.000. republicans sho^d pass down the missisippi does she think that a concession of the boundary contended for, or the right of the missisippi wo^d satisfy such a body, proud in its strength & contemptuous of its adversary? Indeed the patience of the American government itself is equally exhausted by the delays of Spain, and understand-ing as I think it does the merits of a former negotiation better than it formerly did, it now thinks with the people there, that no further procrastination ought to be admitted. The character of that negotiation altho you were not a member of the congress at the time, with its delusive impression on the councils of Spain, in regard to the disposition of the united States on the subject on which it touched, I know you perfectly comprehend. You will know at least I think you do, that it was an intrigue on the part of the agents on both sides, and which had it succeeded would have sown the seed of perpetual dissention between the united States & Spain. The policy of Spain was then what is now is, to make a friendly impression upon our government & people by an act of justice, and not foster sentiments of resentment which beginning with the neighbouring inhabitants in the first instance would naturally spread throughout the union and thus make enemies of those who might have been & ought to be friends. By that negotiation an essential injury was done to Spain, for altho' its views were defeated, yet by betraying a system of policy narrow, and unfriendly, as well as unjust, it left impressions of that kind not to be easily removed: the longer however the cause is suffered to remain the deeper will the impression be.[4]

By this view of the subject you will fully understand the scope of my policy in regard to Spain: if justice was rendered us I see no reason why we sho^d not be friends; on the contrary I see many why we sho^d be bound in a close and common bond, I mean the united States, France & Spain: nor can I see in the course of time, at least for ages to come any circumstance that would probably interrupt this harmony. We have territory enough & we want not colonies, and we are equally interested in checking the maritime power of a certain overbearing nation, I mean on that element, for on land she is mild & tame as others. I cannot under existing circumstances be more explicit than I have been. I see no reason why Sp^n sho^d not close with you & immediately

FC, DLC: Monroe Papers

1. Duchess de Rochefoucauld.

2. No correspondence between JM and the Duchess de Rochefoucauld has been located.

3. The letter sent via Edward Church may have been Short to JM, 18 February 1795 (above).

The letter sent "thro' the armies," was Short's letter of 23 February 1795 (above).

4. JM refers to the Jay-Gardoqui negotiations of 1785-1786 (*Encyclopedia of American History*).

To John Quincy Adams

Paris May 6, 1795.

Dear Sir

I was this moment fav^d with y^{rs} of the 13th ult^o as I was two days before with that which was some time since committed to the care of Mr Schermehorn, & w^h letter was forwarded by the post.[1] Your letters for Mr Randolph are always forwarded by the first opportunities w^h occur after their rec^t, & those for Mr Pinckney shall be delivered him in case he takes Paris in his rout for Madrid; but what must be done with them in case he does not, and which is probable since he has not intimated to me an intention of passing this way tho' much time has elapsed since his appointment was notified to him?

The scarcity of bread still continues & yet the tranquility of the city remains undisturbed. The general distress in that respect has been great since the mass of citizens were frequently allowed only 2. or 3. ounces p^r day. Some symptoms of disquietude were occasionally seen but yet they were composed without force, & thus gradually the demonstration becomes more satisfactory that the authority of the Convention founded in publick opinion requires no other aid than that of the ordinary civil police, to enforce its decrees.

Nothing definitive is yet that I know of, done with Sp^n, tho' the probability is great that something soon will be. Sr F^k Eden[2] is said to have touch'd at some port near Brest & demanded permiss^n to visit Paris. He was conducted to Dieppe where he now is under strict observance something like that of a guard. His ostensive motive is that of an exchge of prisoners, but it is thought to embrace other objects. If he means any thing else tis said he must say so explicitly & proceed afterwards as in other cases. with great respect & esteem I am dear Sir y^{rs}

Ja^s Monroe

RC, MHi: Adams Family Papers: Letters Received

1. Adams wrote to JM on 13 April 1795, enclosing letters for Thomas Pinckney (*Catalogue of Monroe's Papers*, 1: 44). The letter sent by Mr. Schermehorn could not be identified.

2. Sir Frederick Morton Eden (1766-1809) was an economist best known for his three-volume *State of the Poor* (1797). In 1794 the British forces flush with their success in the West Indies, hired transports to convey French prisoners of war to St. Maloes in France, but upon their arrival, the French seized the ships and made the British crews prisoners of war. The British government sent Sir Frederick to France in March 1795 to propose an exchange of prisoners of war. His proposal was submitted to the Committee of Public Safety but rejected (Robert Debritt, *A Collection of State Papers Relative to the War Against France Now Carrying on by Great Britain and the Several Other European Powers*, 7: 522; *DNB*).

From Joseph Fenwick

Bordeaux 15 May 1795.

Sir

By several Americans worthy of credit, lately arrived from Gersey & Guernsey, I am assured that there are a number of vessels belonging to those Islands that have forged American papers & have the names of American ports painted on their Stern, & that the papers are so well immitated that it is difficult even for an American acquainted with the signatures to distinguish the false from the real Registers & Sea Letters—by which means these English vessels sail with security as Americans, many of which have been visited by french armed Ships & let pass. I think important to communicate this information that you may make what use you think proper of it. I have the honor to be Sir your most Obed^t S^t

Joseph Fenwick

RC, DLC: Monroe Papers

From John Quincy Adams

The Hague May 16. 1795.

Dear Sir.

A few days since I received your favour of the 2^d ult^o and yesterday that of the 6th inst^t being addressed to me at Amsterdam they did not reach me so soon as they would have done had they been directed to me at this place.

The small packet which I took the liberty of addressing to Mr Pinckney under cover to you consisted principally of duplicates. I sent it to you in consequence of a Letter from him, in which he mentioned his intention to pass through Paris on his way to Spain, and desired that my Letters for him might be sent there, where he should receive them.—I understand that he has since determined to pass through this Country also, and am in daily expectation of his arrival here. If you will please to keep the packet I enclosed for him, until his arrival in Paris it will answer all the purposes. The material information it contains has probably reached him by another conveyance.

The intelligence for which I am indebted to your last Letter is equally pleasing and important. The authority of the Convention, and its possession of the public confidence, is a point so interesting to the happiness of France, and to the Peace of the World, that it is highly satisfactory to hear they are established on solid and permanent foundations.

The Citizens Syeyes and Rewbell have been here about a week together with the other members of the Convention who were previously in mission in this Country. A Deputation from the States General has had several conferences with them. It is anxiously wished that the Treaty between the two Countries may be brought to a speedy conclusion, as in the interval public and private concerns here experience a distressing and alarming stagnation.[1]

In the course of the year 1794, many American Vessels were freighted by merchants here for the Dutch Islands in the West Indies. Information has recently arrived that three of them were taken by french armed vessels on the American Coast, carried into Cayenne, the cargoes there condemned, and in two of the instances at least, the men imprisoned. The circumstance occasions great concern and some alarm to the merchants concerned in American affairs at Amsterdam.—I have been requested from them to speak upon the subject to the french Representatives here; but conceiving that would be improper, I have engaged to mention the circumstance to you, and recommended to the persons concerned in the instances alledged to address themselves with their proofs of the reality of cause to complain to you. I have likewise observed, that if those unfortunate circumstances have taken place, it might have been before the late decree of the Convention, past since your arrival in France, was made known in their Islands. That the tenor of that decree, had not since to my knowledge been infringed in Europe, and would doubtless be equally respected, as soon as it should be known in the West Indies.

It has also been represented to me that on board of a Russian Vessel, which was in the ports of this Republic at the time when the french armies arrived, there was a part of the cargo, which belonged to a Citizen of the United States. The french Representatives I understand have determined to consider as prize and sell the vessel and cargo. The persons who loaded that American property applied with the Vice Consul of the United States, to the Representative Cochon, but were informed that the Committee of Public Safety alone could admit their reclamations. At the same time the Representative Cochon as Mr Bourne[2] writes me, expressed some surprize that such a reclamation should be made.

I have not hesitated to give it as my opinion to Mr Bourne that on the supposition that the property in question be clearly proved that of an American Citizen; it is entitled to protection by the customary law of Nations, and the usual construction of Treaties.

In every other respect the property of Citizens of the United States here, has been inviolate: the object in this instance is considerable only to the proprietor of the goods, but the <u>principle</u> may be of consequence.

If the persons who made the application to me can substantiate the point of property in the American Citizen, (which they are yet unable to do, and which I have assured them is indispensable) they will doubtless address themselves hereafter to you for the purpose of obtaining restitution or indemnity, and my wishes for their success, would in that case be the stronger from the desire of seeing removed the <u>only</u> exception to the general security of American property here since the entrance of the french armies. I have the honour to be with great respect, Dear Sir, your very humble and obedt Servt

John Q. Adams.

RC, DLC: Monroe Papers

1. Dutch and French representatives reached an accord on May 13, signed it on May 15, and officially proclaimed it as the Treaty of The Hague on May 16 (Simon Schama, *Patriots and Liberators*, 206-207).

2. Sylvanus Bourne (1761-1817) was vice consul in Amsterdam from 29 May 1794 to 25 April 1801. Prior to this appointment Bourne had served as consul in Saint Domingue from 1790 to 1791. Altogether, Bourne worked as an American consul for twenty-six years, seventeen or more of these years in Amsterdam (Burt E. Powell, "Jefferson and the Consular Service," *Political Science Quarterly*, 21 (Dec. 1906): 626-638).

To Edmund Randolph

Paris 17ᵗʰ May 1795.

Sir,

I was yesterday honoured with yours of the 8ᵗʰ of March the only one received since that of the 5ᵗʰ of December last, and was at the same moment favoured with the company of Mᵣ Pitcairn who, having just arrived, had called to present his commission of V. Consul for this city to be recognized as such.

I informed you in my letter of the 6ᵗʰ of March and for reasons that were in part before explained, that the arrival of this Gentleman would subject me to an unpleasant dilemma, for if it was known that he was a British subject, although he had likewise become an American citizen, I doubted much whether he would be received: that in strict propriety I ought to communicate the fact if it were so, for after what had passed between us upon a subject analogous to this, If I announced him withholding the fact, and it was discovered afterwards, I should expose myself to the imputation of the want of candour; and that in any event if he were established, however correctly I might personally act, the circumstance of his being a British subject would not only lessen his weight and to the prejudice of our commercial affairs here, but to a certain degree and from causes that are obvious, lessen mine likewise, the ill effects of which might be felt and especially at the present moment upon concerns of more general importance. By his arrival therefore this embarrassment was realized: the commission of the President is the law to me and upon every principle it is disagreeable to suspend its force; but yet the nature of the trust reposed in a public minister, seems to imply in him, a discretionary power to controul, according to his judgment, incidents of this kind, wherever it appears that thereby he may promote the public interest and which becomes of course the stronger when necessary to prevent the public detriment. Upon mature consideration therefore I thought it best to withhold the official communication of his appointment from the government, until I should hear from you in reply to that letter, and the more especially as it might now be expected in the course of a few weeks. In consequence I communicated this decision to Mᵣ Pitcairn with the motives upon which it was founded, and was pleased to observe that he appeared to be perfectly satisfied with the propriety of it.

I observe by this letter that the treaty concluded by Mᵣ Jay with Great Britain did not arrive before the 5ᵗʰ March and in consequence would not be submitted to the Senate before the 8ᵗʰ of June, and in the interim would be kept secret. I regret equally this delay and secrecy; the delay because if it [is][1] not approved, it may become more difficult in the probable course of events on this side the Atlantic to obtain a remodification of it: and the secrecy, because the jealousy which was at first imbibed by this government of its contents will of course remain for the same space of time, and which cannot otherwise than be somewhat hurtful in the interim of our affairs depending here:[2] having too explained the object of that mission whilst its issue was incertain, they think it strange that the result should be now withheld. Upon this point however I have nothing new to add: I have already communicated to you whatever I had to communicate upon it, and waiting the issue I shall continue [by] my assurances to endeavour to inspire this government with a confidence either that the treaty in question contains in it nothing improper, or that it will not be ratified in case it does.

Your last letter gave me the first intelligence upon which I could rely that Col.º Humphreys was in America: he will of course return fully possessed of your views with respect to the piratical powers on the African coast. I assured you long since that it would be easy to obtain from this government its aid upon that point, and it is certain that its aid with each and especially Algiers, with which regency this republic is in the strictest amity, would be of great effect. Those powers hear that France is at war with Austria, Spain, England, Portugal &c and defeats them all, and in consequence conclude that she is more powerful than all united, and respect her accordingly. I have frequently been told in private conversation by the members of the committee, that they were ready to render [us] all the service in their power in that respect, and should long since have requested the government to make our peace there, in pursuit of the plan commenced by M.ʳ Morris, had I not been instructed that the business was in the hands of Col.º Humphreys, and feared by such interference I should embarrass the views and measures of our own government. I shall be ready however to act in whatever line you may think proper to direct, and shall endeavour, and without any particular compromitment on our part, to keep the committee in the same state of preparation.

In general our commercial affairs progress as well, all things considered, as could be expected. Transactions of old standing I have not lately formally pressed, because I know that the government is embarrassed at present on the score of finance: and because I think it would be better to wait the issue of the business depending with you in June next. M.ʳ Skipwith however does everything that can be done to forward those objects and perhaps with as much effect as would be possible, under any pressure that could now be made. But in the direct or current commerce our countrymen enjoy all the privileges that the government can give them, and although delays are sometimes experienced and especially in the payment of contracts that were formed in America, yet the transactions are generally closed in a manner satisfactory to the parties. The profits which some of them have made and continue to make according to report are great beyond example. In truth our countrymen are gradually planting themselves in commercial houses throughout the republic, and engaging in the commerce of France to an extent, which whilst it promises to be profitable to themselves, will likewise be of great and permanent utility to both nations, for by means thereof not only personal acquaintance and connections are formed by the citizens of each with those of the other respectively, but their common wants and common capacities will be better understood.

The claim of 15,000 dollars I mentioned long since would be admitted without a word, and that it ought to be so understood at the treasury. I omitted it in my more early applications to this government, because I wished to progress with the greater objects first, and more latterly for the reasons above suggested. I confered however on the subject with M.ʳ Edet[3] and presume he will allow it as a thing of course, but if he does not, upon notification thereof to the committee, and which I will immediately make, when so advised by you, he will certainly be instructed to do it.

Since my last, Paris and the republic in general have enjoyed a state of perfect tranquillity. Every little disturbance which ensued for a while the movement of the 2.ⁿᵈ of April[4] (12th Germinal) and there was one or two of the smaller kind which did ensue, subsided almost of itself, and in each instance without force, and of course without bloodshed. Thus the authority of the convention prevails, although it is supported by the common sense and common interest of the citizens of Paris only: a thing heretofore deemed impracticable under similar embarrassments. Certain it is that if the government had been in the hands of a King or any other description of persons than that of the people themselves, we should have seen in the course of a few weeks past, a succession of many revolutions of the ministerial kind, and which perhaps would have dethroned eventually any King that ever reigned here. The distress of the people on account of the scarcity of bread since that time, has been like that of a besieged town. They have been constantly upon allowance, and which was latterly reduced to two ounces and sometimes less per day. My family which consists of 14 persons[5] is allowed two pounds of bread per day. I mention this that you may have a just idea of the distress of others and particularly the poor, for at a great expence nearly 40 dollars specie per barrel I am supplied. The accounts which we have of the distress of the aged, the infirm, and even of children are most afflicting: yet calmness and serenity are seen every where: complaints diminish and that ferocity which was observable on the 12th of Germinal, on the part of those who forcibly entered the convention, and which was excited by the animosity of contending parties, and most probably increased by foreign influence, has intirely disappeared. In this moment they all look to America for bread, and most fervently do I join them in prayer that our countrymen may speedily bring it to them. If they can make out for 6 weeks they are safe, for by that time the rye will ripen, and from present prospects they may be in a better situation in the interim than they now are and most probably not in a worse.

In the line of negotiation nothing has been concluded since the treaty with Prussia and which was ratified by both parties soon after it was signed. Sʳ Fᵏ Eden came to Rochfort from whence he notified his arrival to the committee and requested permission to come to Paris. They had him conducted to Dieppe where he was kept under guard 'till the arrival of an Agent from the committee who was instructed to receive and report his propositions to that body, provided they embraced any other object than an exchange of prisoners, but in case they did not, to request his departure in 24 hours. The agent attended, asked his business and was answered he came to treat for an exchange of prisoners. Have you no other power? Let us settle this point first, we shall be together and may afterwards talk on what we please. But have you no other power? Your answer to this question may settle this and every other point in a word: if you have I will receive what you will be pleased to communicate: if you have not our business is at an end. Mʳ Eden replied he had none and thus they parted the agent for Paris and Mʳ Eden for London, the latter being apprized what the wish of the committee was in that respect.

The negotiation with Spain is still at a stand. The spanish court is strongly inclined to connect itself with this republic, but in so doing it foresees the necessity of an accomodation with us in respect to the boundaries and the Mississippi, and against which it thinks itself secure by adhering to England who, it is believed gives assurances to that effect. Of the views of England however Spain is and always was jealous, so that it is not improbable an accomodation will soon take place. 'Tis said that the King of Spain makes a provision for the children of the late King the object of his care; that he wishes to have them delivered up to him with the view of giving them an establishment in property somewhere in his kingdom, and to the boy the title of Duke, and that this point in some form or other will probably be agreed.[6]

'Tis said that a treaty is lately concluded with the commissioners from Holland by which the Independence of that country is acknowledged, and an alliance offensive and defensive formed upon terms which promise to be satisfactory to the parties. I will inclose a sketch of these which has been published.

General Pichegru has crossed the Rhine and with a considerable force but probably at present for the purpose only of quartering his Army in the enemies country. He is now in the neighbourhood of Mayence which is still besieged.

The campaign however cannot be considered as fairly opened: perhaps it is not definitively settled against whom in the empire the forces of the republic will be directed: for the door which was opened to receive propositions from the Provinces of the germanic body through the King of Prussia was not an idle provision. Advantage I am told has already been taken of it, and that it will most probably prove the means and to the credit and interest of the King of Prussia of promoting in the empire the views of France.

At Sea in the excursions which were made in the course of the winter, by tempest great loss was sustained, and considering that the war will hereafter be directed principally against England, less attention was for some time paid to the navy than ought to have been expected. At present however the attention of the Executive branch seems to be turned more to that object than heretofore, so that tis probable the waste of the winter will be soon repaired.

The assignats continue to depreciate, and the frequent discussions which take place upon the various propositions made to raise their credit, always produce the opposite effect of depressing them. Many however think the depreciation a blessing to the country, and that their total fall would be among the happiest of political events, especially if they can be kept up through the summer. At present their depreciation is by the standard of gold or foreign exchange as 14 to 1. The mass of wealth in national domains, is affirmed by those who ought to know, more than double than what I supposed, being after restoring the property of those who were illegally [condemned], according to a late decree, about 400,000,000 Sterling. A deputation was lately sent to Holland of Seyes and Reubell to press for money, and tis expected they will succeed, at least in such degree as to answer present exigencies.

I am happy to hear that the President approves my conduct in the instances mentioned, and I beg you to assure him that for the future I shall continue to be neither less attentive or assiduous, in the discharge of the duties of the trust reposed in me, to all its objects, that I have heretofore been. With great respect and esteem I have the honor to be, Sir, your most obedient servant.

Ja^s Monroe.

P. S. Since writing the above I was informed personally by one of the agents who attended Mr Eden at Dieppe (for there were two) that he (Mr Eden) had power to treat on other subjects than that of an exchange of prisoners, and that he not only communicated this, but likewise his propositions, and which were sent to the committee and peremptorily rejected. That the treatment given Mr Eden was polite and respectful and with which he appeared to be perfectly satisfied. what the propositions were I know not: but that they contemplated peace cannot be doubted.

Copy, DNA: RG 59: Dispatches from France

1. Words in brackets were omitted by the copyist; they are supplied from the draft in NN: Monroe Papers. Other slight errors were corrected silently.

2. The draft of this letter contains the following text at this point, which was deleted:

I informed you sometime since that a suspicion existed here upon my first arrival that I came to heal existing animosities, remove doubts and cultivate a good understanding with the french republick, whilst the real object of Mr Jay's mission to England was not merely to obtain an adjustment of antecedent controversies, by the demand of a just reparation for injuries, but to improve the impression I might make and especially if the fortunes of France were prosperous, into an opportunity of weakening our connection with this nation, by a new and more intimate one with Britain: that whilst this suspicion lasted I not only made no progress upon any of the topics upon which I touched, but was apprehensive notwithstanding the eclat of my introduction, and which was at the time in regard to the executive government a pompous ceremonial only, that it would be known abroad and produce the most mischiev

3. Pierre Adet.

4. JM meant April 1.

5. Only five members of the Monroe household can be identified for certain: James and Elizabeth Monroe, Michael and Polly (the two servants who accompanied the Monroes from the United States), and Thomas Paine. According to JM's account book (DLC: Monroe Papers), the Monroes employed at least nine and perhaps as many as twelve servants. How many of these servants (beyond Michael and Polly) resided with the Monroes is not known, nor is it known if any of the servants' family members resided with them. John and Maltby Gelston resided with them when in Paris, but it is not known when exactly they were there. JM's two secretaries, John Purviance and M. A. Gauvain presumably resided with the Monroe, but this is not known for certain. Eliza Monroe and Joseph Jones, Jr. would not have been counted as part of the household, since they resided at boarding schools outside Paris.

6. The Spanish secretly began discussions with the French in the spring of 1795 to negotiate a peace treaty. Spain's offer to grant asylum to the young Dauphin and his sister Marie-Thérèse in the newly created Kingdom of Navarre was rejected by the French who feared possible intrigues to re-establish the Bourbon monarchy in France. This issue vanished with the death of the Dauphin in June, and the decision of Marie-Thérèse to live in Austria (Douglas Hilt, *The Troubled Trinity: Godoy and the Spanish Monarchs*, 42, 44-45).

From Thomas Jefferson

Monticello May 26. 1795.

Dear Sir

I have recieved your favor of Sep. 7. from Paris, which gave us the only news we have had from you since your arrival there. on my part it would be difficult to say why this is the first time I have written to you. revising the case myself, I am sensible it has proceeded from that sort of procrastination which so often takes place when no circumstance fixes a business to a particular time. I have never thought it possible through the whole time that I should be ten days longer without writing to you, & thus more than a year has run off.

I am too much withdrawn from the scene of politics to give you any thing in that line worth your notice. the servile copyist of mr Pitt,[1] thought he too must have his alarms, his insurrections & plots against the Constitution. hence the incredible fact that the freedom of association, of conversation, & of the press, should in the 5th year of our government have been attacked under the form of a denunciation of the democratic societies, a measure which even England, as boldly as she is advancing to the establishment of an absolute monarchy, has not yet been bold enough to attempt. hence too the example of employing military force for civil purposes, when it has been impossible to produce a single fact of insurrection, unless that term be entirely confounded with occasional riots, and when the ordinary process of law had been resisted indeed in a few special cases, but by no means generally, nor had it's effect been duly tried. but it answered the favorite purposes of strengthening government and increasing the public debt; and therefore an insurrection was announced & proclaimed & armed against, & marched against, but could never be found. and all this under the sanction of a name which has done too much good not to be sufficient to cover harm also. and what is equally astonishing is, that by the pomp of reports, proclamations, armies &c the mind of the legislature itself was so fascinated as never to have asked where, when, and by whom has this insurrection been produced? the original of this scene in another country was calculated to excite the indignation of those whom it could not impose on: the mimicry of it here is too humiliating to excite any feeling but shame. our comfort is that the public sense is coming right on the general principles of republicanism, & that it's success in France puts it out of danger here. we are still uninformed what is mr Jay's treaty: but we see that the British piracies have multiplied upon us lately more than ever. they had at one time been suspended.—we will quit these subjects for our own business.

The valuation by mr Lewis & mr Divers, which had been set on foot before your departure, took place Sep. 19. 1794. it was £173. currency & exchange being then at 40. per cent, it was equivalent to

£125-11-5 sterling.[2] on the 19th of Nov. I drew on James Maury for £37-10 sterl. in favor of Wm B. Giles, & shall now immediately draw for the balance. Mr Madison & myself examined your different situations for a house. we did not think it admitted any sort of question but that that on the East side of the road, in the wood, was the best. There is a valley not far from it to the South West & on the Western side of the road which would be a fine situation for an orchard. mr Jones having purchased in Loudon we shall hardly see him here, & indeed have hardly seen him. if I can get proper orders from him I will have the ground abovementioned planted in fruit trees from my own nursery, where I have made an extra provision on your account. indeed I wish you would determine to save 500. or 1000 £ a year from your present salary, which you ought to do as a compensation for your time, and send us a plan of a house and let us be building it, drawing on you for a fixed sum annually till it be done. I would undertake to employ people in the most economical way, to superintend them and the work, and have the place in a comfortable state for your reception. if you think proper to authorize me to do this I will begin immediately on receiving your permission. I am so confident you ought to do it, & will do it that I have ventured to send a small claim or two to you, as explained in the two inclosed letters to La Motte and Froullé,[3] with an expectation that you will give me an opportunity of replacing it here to those who shall be employed for you. should you however not conclude to let us do any thing for you here, I would wish you to suppress both these letters. while speaking of Froullé, libraire, au quai des Augustins, I can assure you that after having run a severe guantlet under the Paris book-sellers, I rested at last on this old gentleman, whom I found in a long and intimate course of after dealings to be one of the most conscientiously honest men I ever had dealings with. I recommend him to you strongly, should you purchase books. I think La Motte at Havre, a very good and friendly man, and worth your forming more than an official intimacy with. should you have occasion for wines from Burgundy, apply to Monsr Parent tonnelier à Beaune, who will furnish you with the genuine wines you may call for, and at honest prices. I found him indeed very faithful in a long course of employment. he can particularly send you of the best crops of Meursault, & Goutte d'or. for fine Champagne non mousseux apply to Monsr Dorsai, or to his homme d'affaires Monsr Louis, if still in place at his Chateau at Aij near Epernay in Champagne. While recommending good subjects to you I must ask you to see for me the following persons, present my affectionate remembrance to them, & let me hear how they have weathered the storm. These are l'Abbe Arnoux place Vendome, chez M. de Ville an excellent Mentor & nd much affectioned to the Americans.[4] Monsr le Vieillard of Passy whom Dr Franklin presented to me as the honestest man in France, & a very honest & friendly one I found him.[5] Monsr & Madame Grand at Passy vastly good & friendly people also.[6] Dr Gem an old English Physician in the fauxbourgs St Germains, who practised only for his friends & would take nothing, one of the most sensible & worthy men I have ever known.[7] but I reckon he is gone to England. many others I could name of great worth, but they would be too many, and have perhaps changed their scene. if Mr Balbatre the musical preceptor of my daughters of the fauxbourg St Honore or it's neighborhood can be found, be so good as to deliver him the affectionate compliments of my family, and if he can send them any thing new & good in the musical line, I will ask you to pay him for it, & let it be packed with the books from Froullé.[8] these, if they come at all, must come before the winter, as a winter passage is inevitable ruin to books. I have bought for Mr Short the lands between yours and Blenheim, 1334. acres @ 23/6 ready money.[9] three out of seven shares (of 500 as each) of Carter's land over the mountain will be for sale soon. it is not known where these shares will lie as the partition is not yet made. should ere a one join you on the mountain, it would be worth your purchase. Collé is lately sold for £375. to a mr Catlet, a farmer, whom I do not know.[10] it is very possible it will be for sale again. should you conclude to build a house, you must decide whether of brick or stone. the latter costs about one half of the former, to wit about 8/ a perch of 25. cubic feet. I hope mr Jones will change the system of corn & wheat alternately on your land till the fields are entirely worn out, abandoned, and the new ones treated in the same manner. this is the way my lands have been ruined. yours are yet in a saveable state. but a very little time will put some of them beyond recovery. the best plan would be to divide the open grounds into 5. feilds, & tend them in this order. 1. wheat. 2 corn & potatoes. 3. rye. 4. clover. 5. clover. & then begin wheat &c. over again. by this means they would go into corn but once in 5 years. It would be still better to hire 4. or 5. men for a twelve month to clear the whole body of your tendable lands at once, that you may at once come into the use of the whole, and allow more relief to the old, & an easier service to all of it in general, instead of wearing out one half while clearing the other by little & little as we have generally done in this neighborhood. I am going to have Short's all cleared in this way. but of all this there can be no better judge than mr Jones. I have divided my farms into seven fields on this rotation. 1. wheat. 2. pease & potatoes. 3. corn & potatoes. 4. peas & potatoes till I can get the vetch from Europe. 5. rye. 6. clover. 7. clover. my lands were so worn that they require this gentle treatment to recover them. Some of yours are as far gone.——there are two or three objects which you should endeavor to enrich our country with. 1. the Alpine strawberry. 2. the skylark. 3. the red-legged partridge. I despair too much of the Nightingale to add that. we should associate mrs Monroe to you in these concerns. present to her our most affectionate esteem, not forgetting Eliza. we are all well except mr Randolph,[11] whose health is very frail indeed. it is the more discouraging as there seems to have been no founded conjecture what is the matter with him. your brother is well, but mrs Monroe rather sickly.[12] The death of D[r] Walker is the only event of that kind which has taken place in our neighborhood since you left us.[13] D[r] Gilmer still lives. His eldest daughter is to be married to a mr Wurt the day after tomorrow.[14] Frank Walker[15] has succeeded to the whole of D[r] Walker's estate, said to be worth £20,000. Sam Carr married to a daughter of Overton Carr in Maryland,[16] and probably will remove there. his mother (my sister) living at his place a little above Dr Gilmers. my budget is out. Adieu. God almighty bless you all.

P. S. If you can send us with Froullé's books a supply of 20. or 30. # of Maccaroni, they will be an agreeable addition to his bill.

RC, DLC: Monroe Papers; unsigned.

1. Alexander Hamilton

2. Nicholas Lewis and George Divers were making an evaluation of slaves that JM purchased from Jefferson (JM to Jefferson, 17 June 1794, above).

3. The letter to LaMotte has not been located. Jefferson's letter to Jean-François Froullé, dated 26 May 1795, contained a list of books sought by Jefferson, and noted: "Mr. Monroe our minister plenipotentiary at Paris will receive the books and pay you for them" (*Jefferson Papers*, 28: 357-358).

4. Abbé Arnoux lived in Passy near Benjamin Franklin. Jefferson described him as one of the "literati" (Howard C. Rice, Jr., *Thomas Jefferson's Paris*, 92).

5. Louis-Guillaume Le Veillard (1733-1794) was a physician and mayor of Passy. Nicknamed "le grand voisin," Le Veillard wrote Franklin's letters in French and translated Franklin's *Memoirs*. He died at the guillotine (*Papers of Benjamin Franklin*, 23: 542; 27: 162; *Jefferson Papers*, 29: 122).

6. Rodolphe-Ferdinand Grand, the Parisian banker, who had resided in Passy near Benjamin Franklin, died in Switzerland. Madame Grand had died before her husband (*Jefferson Papers*, 28: 318).

7. Richard Gem (1718-1800) was an English physician who divided his residence between London and Paris. He was an advocate for the French Revolution but was nevertheless arrested on several occasions by the French authorities because he was English (*Jefferson Papers*, 15: 384-387).

8. Claude-Louis Balbastre was a composer, teacher and organist of the Church of St. Roch in Paris (Edwin Morris Betts and James Adam Bear, Jr., *The Family Letters of Thomas Jefferson*, 32-33).

9. Jefferson purchased a farm named Indian Camp (present-day Morven) for Short. This property adjoined JM's farm on the south. Short never resided at this farm and sold it in 1816 (George Shackelford, *Jefferson's Adoptive Son*, 137-138, 169).

10. Kemp Catlett (ca. 1765-1813), an Albemarle county farmer, purchased Mazzei's estate, Collé. He also transacted land sales and transfers for JM between 1802 and 1806 (*Papers of Thomas Jefferson, Retirement Series*, 3: 380-381).

11. Thomas Mann Randolph, Jefferson's son-in-law.

12. Joseph Jones Monroe and Elizabeth Kerr Monroe.

13. Thomas Walker (1715-9 November 1794) was a physician, explorer, and public servant of Albemarle County. As an agent and surveyor of a land company, Walker led an expedition through the Cumberland Gap into Kentucky in 1750, which pre-dated Daniel Boone's visit by thirteen years. He served in the Virginia House of Burgesses from 1758 to 1775, and in 1778 he headed a commission to establish the border between Virginia and North Carolina (Wyndham B. Blanton, *Medicine in Virginia in the Eighteenth Century*, 244; Edgar Woods, *History of Albemarle*, 334-335).

14. George Gilmer, Jr., Jefferson's physician and friend, died on 3 December (*Jefferson Papers*, 28: 542). Attorney William Wirt (1772-1834) married Gilmer's daughter Mildred (1772-1799) (*ANB*).

15. Francis Walker (1764-1806) served in Congress 1793-1795 (*BDAC*).

16. Carr married Eleanor Carr, daughter of his uncle, John Overton Carr (*The Family Letters of Thomas Jefferson*, 32-33).

To Francis Coffyn, Jr.

Paris 28ᵗʰ May 1795.

As I am personally well acquainted with your own merit and qualification to take the place of your father, and feel at the same time the force of your claim as having been associated in that office with him, it would give me pleasure to see you gratified in that respect. It is however a justice due to you to observe, that I have reason to think our Government has come to a resolution to appoint for the future to the office of Consul, American Citizens alone, and especially in those Ports where any are willing to act who are deem'd qualified for it. if this principle is observed it will of course be admitted by you. but if it is deviated from in any case, I am persuaded it will be in yours: It is however my advice that you immedi-ately write to the Secretary of State & make Known to him the late event as well as your wish to Succeed to the vacant place, as I shall likewise do, transmitting a Copy of your letter to me & of this paragraph in reply; you will of course in the interim continue in the office to perform the requisite functions and for which I presume no other sanction is necessary having been the Chancellor of your father.

Excerpt sent to the secretary of state, DNA: RG 59: Dispatches from Nantes

Coffyn wrote to JM on 16 May 1795 informing him of the death of his father, Francis Coffyn, Sr., who was the American consul at Dunkirk, and applying for appointment as his successor (*Catalogue of Monroe's Papers*, 1: 44). He received the appointment on 27 May 1796 and held the post until 1801 (*Washington Papers: Journal of the Proceedings of the President*, 338; Walter B. Smith, *America's Diplomats and Consuls of 1776-1865*, 64).

From Claude-Adam Delamotte

Havre 9. Prairial An 3. [28 May 1795]

Monsieur,

Le navire Jane Captaine Cowell est arrivé ici de Londres avant hier. À son arrivée notre municipalité m'a communiquée qu'elle avait des ordres du comité de sureté générale de faire une visite si stricte à bord de ce navire, qu'elle serait obligée de faire arrêter, pour le tems de cette visite, le capitaine et l'équipage. Elle me taisait les motifs de ces mesûres. Je lui ai répondu que leur rigueur même me faisait penser que le motif était de nature à les justifier, mais que J'étais surpris que le comité de sureté générale ne s'en fut pas entendu avec vous, parceque alors j'aurais pu avoir vos ordres en même tems qu'elle a reçue ses instructions, que Je me bornerais à vous rendre compte de ce qui se passerait. Dépuis, et avant de rien faire, la municipalité m'a communiquée que ce navire était designé comme devant avoir à bord 150 millions de faux Assignats. On est occupé à cette visite, et je ne sçais pas qu'on ait encore rien trouvé. J'ai cru ne devoir m'opposer à rien à moins d'ordres exprès de votre part, et le cas est si grave que je suis d'opinion qu'en éffet on ne pourait y apporter aucun empêchement. S'il ne trouve rien dans le navire, je crois que le gouvernement Français devrait indemniser le capitaine. Je suis respectueusement, Monsieur, Votre très humble serviteur.

Dela Motte.

Editors' Translation

Havre 9 Prairial Year 3. [28 May 1795]

Sir,

The ship Jane, Captain Cowell, arrived here from London the day before yesterday. Upon his arrival our municipality advised me that they had orders from the Committee for Public Security to make such a thorough search of this ship that the captain and crew would need to be detained for the length of the search. I was not told the reasons for this measure. I replied that their rigor suggested to me that the reasons justified their actions, but that I was surprised that the Committee for Public Security had not conferred with you, as this would have allowed me to receive your orders at the same time as it received its instructions, and that I would limit myself to notifying you as to what would happen. Since then, and before doing anything, the municipality advised me that this ship was alleged to be carrying 150 million in forged Republican banknotes. The search is taking place, and I do not know if anything has yet been found. I felt that I should not oppose any of these actions without explicit orders from you, and the situation is so serious that I believe that we could not in fact prevent them. If nothing is found in the ship, I believe the government of France will have to indemnify the captain. With respect, I am, Sir, your very humble servant.

Dela Motte.

Copy, DNA: RG 59: Dispatches from France; enclosed in JM to Edmund Randolph, 4 July 1795

To William Short

Paris May 30. 1795

I was favored about ten days past with yours of the 4 Instant and should have answered it immediately, had I not previously done so by anticipation in some measure in one of the same date through the armies, or had I not waited for the arrival of Mᴿ Pinckney who was then on his way from Dunkirk for this place. By him this will be forwarded; indeed by him alone would I hazard what I deem it necessary to communicate to you. Previously therefore permit me to assure you that this Government will admit of no intermediate or third parties in its negotiations, but will only treat with its enemies themselves or directly. The only power whose good offices they ever thought of accepting was the United States, but the negotiation of Mᴿ Jay with England has by its manner, and particularly by withholding with such care the result, inspired such distrust in our friendship for them, that they are disposed not even to accept of ours. This is a fact of importance which I did not chuse to hazard through the route of the armies, since if it was known to the Spanish government it might lessen our weight in our negotiation with that Court, for I always knew that an opinion of a good understanding between us and this Government would greatly forward our own depending negotiations elsewhere. You must therefore (or rather Mᴿ P.) must press the object of your negotiation to a close as soon as possible, counting with certainty, that although in general, we stand well here, yet we are to have no agency in the affairs of France, and of course are to derive from that consideration, no aid to the advancement of our own.

It is proper to inform you, that just before the report of Mᴿ Jay's Treaty reached us, this government, whose attachment to us was daily increasing, had it in contemplation to extend by all the means in its power its fortunes to us in our depending negotiations elsewhere, and that even since that report upon the presumption every thing is right, they have instructed (as I am told) their Minister negotiating with Spain to secure in their Treaty the points insisted on by us.

This instruction was given just before the report of Mᴿ P.'s appointment was known, and I am inclined to think that although it was not in Mᴿ P.'s power (not being able to explain Mᴿ Jay's treaty to them without which it would have been indelicate) to ask their aid, that the instruction still continues in force. In any event Spain will have all possible proof, and from this government itself, that they wish us well, and rejoice in our prosperity, and therefore altho' they keep their own affairs to themselves, yet the Spanish Court will find, that a good understanding with France is not to be expected or preserved without a good understanding with us.

I have heard that Mᴿ Jay has stipulated something in his treaty respecting the Missisipi whereby, upon the ridiculous pretence of a guarantee to us, an extension of territory is substantially given to Britain, and she in consequence admitted to the Missisipi. The fact of a guarantee by Britain to us must excite the indignation of Spain towards her, tho' ready to yield the point to us: but the extension of her territory so as to comprehend the source of that river, and thereby intitle her to its navigation, will produce a more serious and alarming effect. I think it will tend greatly to separate Spain from England and to force the former into a more intimate connection with France and the United States the first step towards which, is an accomodation to their present demands.

Another circumstance which will facilitate this object is, that England through Sir F. Eden has absolutely and very lately attempted upon the pretext of an Exchange of Prisoners, to open a negotiation for peace with this Republic. I suspect Spain knows nothing of this, but I am assured by authority in which I confide that it is the truth. He was received at Dieppe and detained whilst his terms were sent to the Committee, and an answer received peremptorily rejecting them. If true I presume the fact will be made known to Spain, so that the latter power ought to reject all delicacy towards the former in its transactions with it.

I have one other observation to make which shews the necessity of dispatch if possible in our negotiation with Spain. Suppose her peace made with this Republic, she is of course relieved from the pressure which disposes her to accomodate us. Shall we not afterwards stand of course nearly upon the same ground that we stood in that negotiation from the epoch of the one which was conducted by Mᵣ Jay with Mᵣ Gardoqui, which had well nigh ended (tho' managed by the former with great skill and according to the rules of ancient diplomacy) in the occlusion of the river and dismemberment of the continent: which negotiation has certainly deluded the Spanish government, from that time to the present day into an opinion that half America wish it shut: at least to me who was in the Congress during the pendency of that negotiation, and who have since seen your correspondence such appeared to be the case.

The above are hints upon the real state of things here, upon which Mᵣ P. and yourself will take your measures. If I could satisfy this government that Mᵣ Jay's Treaty contained nothing with which they have a right to complain, every thing would be easy here; we might forward the views of the two countries in which we reside, which in respect to this I ardently wish to forward, making previously those of our own secure. But can any motive of Interest on the part of France induce her to accept such offers from us, until she shall receive such satisfaction? Where the Interest of our country can be advanced, or there is a possibility it may, I am willing to attempt anything in concert with you, and shall therefore be always happy to hear from you in these respects.

I inclose you a letter from a friend of yours in this country,[1] being assured it contains nothing of a treasonable nature: no intelligence of the march of Armies or preparations against Spain, which it is the Interest of this Government to keep secret.

FC. The first three paragraphs and part of the first line of the fourth paragraph are in NN: Monroe Papers. The remainder of the letter is in DLC: Monroe Papers.

1. Duchess de Rochefoucauld.

From Edmund Randolph

Private

Philadelphia May 31. 1795.

Dear Sir

You cannot conceive, what an incessant labour has employed my time, ever since I came into office. For some months past I have been quarreling with Mᵣ Hammond, who did not approve the declarations of our government against the British shipping, which frequented our waters, and Mᵣ Van Berckel, who wanted us to admit, that he was empowered at pleasure to remove Dutch Consuls, who should offend him. At the beginning of this month, Mᵣ Fauchet took up the strain of complaining, and has written an indecent letter, in which he collects all the charges, which he thinks himself qualified to maintain against the U. S. My answer, which is just finished, consists of nearly thirty pages of closely written quarto paper, and will be sent to him to morrow.[1] I am sure, that he meditates something against the treaty with G. Britain; but what I do not yet see. But I am absolutely persuaded from what I have experienced, that we must lay down some new rules with respect to foreign ministers in general, and prevent them from meddling, as they do, in our internal affairs. I confess, that I little expected from Mᵣ Fauchet the conduct, which he has pursued, and probably will pursue, before his successor arrives.

Another of my toils is a letter to you, which reviews all our conduct in general towards France. But altho' drawn it is not transcribed.[2]

In eight days the senate will meet on the British treaty. M[r] Jay arrived on the 28th instant; but he being at New-York I have heard nothing European from him. Whether it will be ratified, I cannot pronounce; but judging from the best rules in our power, unknown as the subject yet is to every body, except two, I think the vote will be a nice one.

Your letters n[o] 5. 6. & 7.[3] which came by the Pomona from Bordeaux were opened in the admiralty of Halifax. They were rendered suspicious by being inclosed in an envelope under M[r] Fenwick's seal, which was affixed on five casks of silver, called <u>paints</u>. This circumstance caused the capture of the vessel; and those five casks have been condemned. I am collecting the particulars of this case, to ascertain upon what ground we can move in it.

The President is extremely anxious to know, whether Madame Fayette ever got a sum of money, which he sent to her out of his private purse thro' Van Staphorst.[4] We shall endeavour to do some thing for her out of the Marquis's money, if it has not been absorbed.

Besides my long letter, which I have mentioned above, the treaty will furnish the necessity of being copious to you. Yrs sincerely

Edm: Randolph

RC, NN: Monroe Papers

1. Fauchet wrote to Randolph on 2 May 1795, complaining that the United States showed preference to British warships and their prizes in American ports over their French counterparts. Randolph gave a lengthy reply defending American policy in a letter dated 29 May 1795 (*ASP: FR*, 1: 608-614).

2. Randolph to JM, 1 June 1795, below.

3. JM to Randolph, 7 November 1794, 20 November 1794, 2 December 1794, above.

4. Washington wrote to Nicholas Van Staphorst in Amsterdam on 31 January 1793, enclosing a bill of exchange for 2310 guilders and asking Van Staphorst to retain the sum on account for Adrienne Lafayette. He also enclosed a letter to be forwarded to Adrienne Lafayette in which he informed her of this transaction. She never received this sum (*Papers of George Washington, Presidential Series*, 12: 75-76; JM to Washington, 3 January 1796, below).

From John Beckley

Philadelphia, 1st June 1795.

My dear Sir.

This letter will be delivered you by M[r] Cummings[1] a young Gentleman, native of Maryland, of respectable family in Frederick Town, and himself of very, amiable character & manners; permit me to recommend him to your civilities & attention—He comes out under the auspices of one of the first mercantile houses in this City, with design to settle at S[t] petersburg in Russia; his intelligence, ability and discretion, may possibly render him, <u>in some way</u>, a useful correspondent to you, but of this, you will be the better judge, after knowing and conversing with him.

I wrote you a very long letter in March and confided it to the department of State, which I hope you received, as also a number of communications & documents of a public nature, which accompanied it.[2] M[r] Cummings will hand y[o] a pamphlet by our friend Madison & a copy of Tench Coxes Book or compilation stiled 'A View of the U States', containing as usual, a great deal of useful matter blended with much Egotism and more of the clanism of a pennsylvanian.[3]

The theme of domestic politics was never so barren as at present, every thing seems suspended on the event of Jays treaty & the approaching meeting of Senate. Unfortunately, should there be any thing unsound in it, every circumstance seems to conspire in favor of the probability of its ratification—Jay arrived from England on thursday last, just in time to prepare the Government junto, and give them their previous cue, while every <u>doubtful</u> man will be kept in total ignorance until the day.⁴ The anxiety for his arrival and joy thereupon, teach me to suspect that great fears prevailed with the Executive for its final success, without his aid & presence, <u>ergo</u> there must be something rotten in it. The non arrival of Fauchetts successor,⁵ and of any communications from yᵉ later than 17ᵗʰ March, will also conduce to facilitate its adoption—Besides, my good Sir, unhappily for the interests of France, a system of Colony administration is adopted and become universal in all the French W India possessions, without a single exception, subversive at once of all treaty, Union or Connection whatsoever between the US. & France, and violative of every principle of national & neutral right, faith, justice and common honesty. The system is this, Invitations are held out to the Americans to bring their supplies of provisions &ᶜ, which being done, at no little risque and hazard, in most cases, the Cargo is taken for Government use, a prohibition to trade with the inhabitants for any part of it or for any produce of the Colony is imposed, Arbitrary prices allowed on the Cargo, greatly below what might be obtained from the inhabitants, an increased price on the produce which the administration may please to give in Exchange, tho' often it pleases them to give nothing but written acknowledgments for a sum fixed by their own arbitrary decisions, or to detain the unfortunate adventurer many months before he can obtain written acknowledgement, or produce. To the shameful abuse and monopoly on the part of the colony administrators, it is well known they add the infamous cupidity of charging the Mother Country, with fifty to a hundred per cent on the prices of the Articles thus dishonestly obtained.

You can readily conceive what effect these things are calculated to produce, and what use the Enemies of France & her glorious revolution will make of them. I will take the libery to suggest to you a mode by which this evil may be pressed to the bottom, and the villainous impositions of the Colony administrators upon the Mother Country, exposed and prevented—Suppose two Commissioners authorized for the purpose come out, first to the United States, and publish an invitation to the merchants here to furnish authentic accounts of sales of Cargoes delivered to or taken by the adminstrators of any French Colony, within a given period, and of the mode of payment and prices imposed for the same. Let them then proceed to the Colonies, and ascertain the mode, manner & amount of Supplies there, with all the administrative accounts respecting the same, and transmit the whole to France for final examination and report. The desire such a measure would manifest on the part of France to do justice to the injured Citizens of the US. and to detect & punish the infamous peculations and shameful abuses of her Colony administrators would insure to the Commissioners the most full, complete & authentic information on the part of the American merchants, and a better check could not be devised.

In respect to one of the French Colonies, Cayenne, I am possessed with the clearest information and proof, that the administrators there have imposed upon the mother Country to the amount of several millions of livres—Nor am I <u>entre nous</u> without strong suspicions that the whole business is well known to and for <u>convenient reasons</u>, connived at by Fauchett.—I mean so far as respects Cayenne.

I regret most sincerely that the friendly dispositions which the Government of France are manifesting towards us in Europe, should then be in danger of losing its effect thro' the wicked system of Colony administration at which I have glanced. My hope is that the evil will be temporary and the cure effectual.

In my first letter I gave you a full view of the complection of our next legislature, and in the late elections, except as to Virginia, where three changes only have been made, namely Cabell in room of Walker, Brent in room of Lee, and Clopton in room of Griffin.—Dexter too, has lost his election in

Massachusetts & Varnum (said to be a good republican) comes in his place on the 4th trial. Since y^{o} left us the New Hampshire Senators have both joined the republican party and zealously adhere to them—Livermore, will never forgive their giving the vacant Judgeship of N. Hampshire to another person.[6]

Randolph still continues at windy buffettings with Hammond & Van Berkel and complains much of the toilsome labors of his station, hinting now & then at retiring. Hamilton sinks fast into obscurity, he has not yet commenced his law career, nor is it believed he ever will but merely as a blind.

It is probable that Jay is elected Governor of N York—the votes are now canvassing—Burr declined, & the contest was between Yates & Jay. If the latter succeeds, a new Ch. Justice must be [chosen]—perhaps Hamilton, or Randolph.[7]

It is generally suspected that the president will decline for another election. If he does, and nothing turns up greatly to change the present temper of the public mind, Jefferson will undoubtedly succeed him.

We have strong report, by private letters from France, of a separate peace with Spain, Portugal, and Prussia, signed the 26th March, and anxiously await its confirmation or contradiction.—We are also made uneasy of accounts and appearances of great dissention in the Convention, and the fear of another concussion and massacre—Can y^{o} spare a moment to me, on the state & prospect of the internal government & the speedy and final establishment of a republican Constitution?

I shall omit, no favorable opportunity of supplying y^{o} with every information, within my limited sphere of observation. As soon as the decision of Senate is known y^{o} shall have it;

Mr Randolph writes y^{o} by another opportunity (Mr Grubb) who sails today. He transports y^{o} the newspapers of the last month, and I presume will give y^{o} a history of the manner in which your dispatches by the Pomona were intercepted, carried to Halifax, and opened by the British advocate there, as also of the unwarrantable conduct of Consul Fenwick at Bourdeaux &^{c} &^{c}.

Make my respectful compliments to your amiable lady & to friend Skipwith, and accept yourself, the best regards of, dear Sir, Your friend & Servant

John Beckley.

RC, NN: Monroe Papers

1. William Cummings, Jr. was the son of William Cummings, an attorney in Frederick, Maryland.

2. Beckley's letter of March 1795 has not been located.

3. James Madison, *Political Observations*, (*Madison Papers*, 15: 511-534, 16: 12); Tench Coxe, *A View of the United States of America, in a Series of Papers*.... (Philadelphia: 1794).

4 John Jay arrived in New York from London on 28 May 1795. President Washington submitted the treaty to the Senate, which he had called into special session, on June 8 (John J. Reardon, *Edmund Randolph*, 291-292).

5. Pierre August Adet, successor to Jean-Antoine-Joseph Fauchet as French minister to the United States, arrived in Philadelphia on June 13 (*Correspondence of the French Ministers*, 728).

6. John Langdon and Samuel Livermore. Livermore (1732-1803) was chief justuce of New Hampshire 1782-1789, a delegate to the Continental Congress 1781-1782 and 1785, and senator from New Hampshire 1793-1801 (*BDAC*).

7. Jay was elected governor of New York and resigned as chief justice on 29 June 1795. Washington offered the post to Hamilton, but he declined. Washington's next choice, John Rutledge of South Carolina, was rejected by the Senate. Several other offers were declined, and the appointment finally went to Oliver Ellsworth of Connecticut, who took office in March 1796. Edmund Randolph was not offered the post of chief justice, but Washington did consider appointing him as an associate justice of the Supreme Court (Charles Warren, *The Supreme Court in United States History*, 1: 124-141).

From Edmund Randolph

Department of State June 1ˢᵗ 1795

Sir

The uneasiness which has been discovered by the French Republic, in reference to our late Treaty with Great Britain;—the comments which you have made upon your instructions;—and the anxiety which forever leads the President to maintain an honorable interchange of Friendship between the United States and France; have determined me to review our conduct from the commencement of the present war. In it I shall unreservedly expose the policy of the Executive, as it may be collected from the documents of this Department, that the imputation of an alienation from France so systematically and unremittingly cast upon our government may lose its effect wheresoever that policy shall be known.

There never was a moment when the President hesitated upon these truths: that the antient despotism of France was degrading to human nature; that the people were the sole masters of their own fortune, free to overturn their old establishments and substitute new: and that any other nation, which should presume to dictate a letter in their constitution, was an usurper. But as an administration of ordinary prudence will not enter upon a momentous career, without combining the past and present state of things, and from a comparison of both, forming a judgment of the future; it will be necessary to follow the intelligence possessed by the Executive in relation to the great Events occurring from time to time in France.

With the fate of the King we could have no political concern, farther than as it might amount to an indication of the will of the French People. That will, it was interesting to us to understand; because being once <u>fixed</u>, whether for the Constitution of 1791, or one more democratic, it would have given us the assurance, of which we were bound by public duty to be in quest,—of a settled and stable order of things.

In this sense Louis the 16ᵗʰ attracted our notice. In him was beholden a prince fallen from the throne of his Ancestors, receiving with apparent cordiality, in lieu of absolute power, the title of restorer of Liberty—but distrusted by every man. His flight cut all confidence asunder; and it was impossible that true reconciliation should ever grow again. The revolution of the 10th August 1792, was the unavoidable sequel of what had preceded, and proclaimed abroad that the Constitution was short lived.

Immediately upon this event "only one opinion prevailed as to the badness of the Constitution."[1]— No plan of a new Constitution was even reported for a considerable time afterwards; none was adopted for many months; at this instant the proposed permanent system is locked up from operation; but what the permanent system will really be, is a difficulty which few can yet solve.

If instead of searching for the will of the people, the politics of the reigning parties had been consulted, how transitory were they? Administrations were hourly passing away. Every member of Government was engaged in the defence of himself or the attack of his neighbor. The Jacobins were busy in exciting tumults. The Convention were <u>privately</u> calling for guards to protect themselves from the people. The very ministers declared that the national assembly could be brought into no kind of consistency. A national bankruptcy and a difficulty of supplies were too much to be apprehended. Strong symptoms of anarchy; the shedding of blood; and information that the question between absolute monarchy and a Republic must be decided by force, were prophetic of some great catastrophe.

Examine next the <u>external</u> relations of France. The foreign ministers, except the minister of the United States, had fled. The alliances against her were multiplying: the enemy numerous: their object to erect a military Government: the empire of Great Britain on the sea, uncontrouled: the French army undisciplined: and the affections of the French people not decisively directed to any specific object.

If the United States had panted for war as much as antient Rome;—if their armies had been as effective as those of Prussia;—if their coffers had been full, and their debts annihilated, even then, peace was too precious to be risked for the most flattering issue of war.

As every political motive dissuaded us from war, so were we without an obligation to enter into it as a party. No casus federis had arisen upon our alliance with France: we had not, nor have we yet, been required to execute the guarantee: and therefore it was unnecessary to speak concerning it.

Had we indulged our sensibility for the crisis, hanging over France, and associated our injuries with hers, the rashness of the step would have been proverbial. An infant Country:—deep in debt—necessitated to borrow in Europe—without manufactures—without a land or naval force—without a competency of arms or ammunition—with a commerce closely connected beyond the Atlantic—with a certainty of enhancing the price of foreign productions, and diminishing that of our own;—with a Constitution little more than four years old, in a state of probation; and not exempt from foes,—such a country can have no greater curse in store for her, than war. That peace was our policy has been admitted by Congress, by the people, and by France herself: France could not have thought otherwise: for had we been active, she would have been deprived of our provisions; except by snatches,—and our payments to her must have been suspended.

The proclamation of neutrality therefore which was our first important act after the eruption of the war, deserved to be the model of our subsequent conduct.

Another public step of the President, altho' it departed not from the line prescribed by the proclamation, was no small indication of his being resolved to cultivate a friendship with the new Republic. Mr Genet came over, as minister, upon the death of Louis the 16th; he was the protegé of a party whose downfall had been predicted from Paris in August 1792; and it was not improbable, that some of the neutral powers would endeavour to inculcate an opinion, that our Treaties with France had expired with her chief magistrate, who had been the organ of the general will, when they were formed. But what said the President? Did he waiver in recognizing them as compacts with the French nation? Did he affect delays? Was he eager to seize a pretext from the disembarking of Mr Genet near the Southern extreme of our continent, his distribution of privateering Commissions, as he travelled, and his countenance of the French Consuls in arrogating a judicial authority over prizes in the United States? No, Sir. Mr Genet was received without a previous inquiry—without a qualification or condition—immediately—and with an indifference to the murmurs of the belligerent powers. For our minister had been before instructed, that "it accorded with our principles to acknowledge any Government to be rightful, which is formed by the will of the nation substantially declared."[2]

A few days brought forth a third important circumstance, in our relation to France. "He communicated the decree of the national Convention of February 19th 1793, authorizing the French Executive to propose a Treaty with us on such liberal principles, as might strengthen the bonds of good will, which unite the two nations; and informed us in a letter of May 23^d (1793) that he was authorized to treat accordingly."[3]

I really doubt whether upon this head, the French republic, if left to herself, would utter one remark. But party, which, if it be not abolished, must be the bane of the Union, fights under the popular banners of France; expecting to overthrow its adversary by propagating a belief that she has been ill treated. These calumnies cannot be more effectually faced, than by examining the commercial relations already subsisting by Treaty between the United States and France.

By Treaty the trade of the two Countries was placed, among other things, upon the following grounds.

1. Both parties "engage mutually not to grant any particular favor to other nations, in respect of commerce and navigation, which shall not <u>immediately</u> become common to the other party; who shall enjoy the same favor freely, if the concession was freely made, or on allowing the same compensation, if the concession was conditional."

2ᵈ. The French were to pay in our ports &c. no other or greater duties or imposts than those, which the nations most favored are, or shall be obliged to pay, and shall enjoy all the privileges in trade, navigation and commerce, whether in passing from one port in the United States to another, or in going to and from the same, from and to any part of the world, which the said nations do or shall enjoy.

3ᵈ. The Americans were to enjoy the same privileges in the French ports in Europe. In this is included an exemption of 100 Sols per ton, established in France on foreign Ships. Unless their Ships shall load with the merchandize of France for another port in the same dominion. They are then to pay the duty abovementioned so long as other nations, the most favored shall be obliged to pay it; the United States being at liberty to establish an equivalent duty in the same case.

4ᵗʰ. "Free ships were to give a freedom to goods."

5ᵗʰ. American or French property on board of enemy Ships was confiscable.

6ᵗʰ. Regulations were made for contraband, and the carrying on of war by either against its enemies, so as to prevent injury to the other.

7ᵗʰ. The Americans were to have one or more free ports granted to them in Europe, for bringing and disposing of their merchandize; and the free ports, which had been at the date of the Treaty (May 6ᵗʰ 1778) and were then open in the French Islands of America, were to be continued to the Americans.

Mʳ Jefferson, in his report to Congress[4] on the state of our commerce and navigation, sums up the important restrictions proceeding from France to be—

1ˢᵗ. That as far as the summer of 1792 our rice was heavily dutied in France: 2ᵈ. That our fish and salted provisions were under prohibitory duties in France: 3ᵈ. That our vessels were denied naturalization in France: 4ᵗʰ. That our salted pork and bread stuff (except maize) were received under temporary laws only in the French West Indies, and our salt fish paid there a weighty duty: and 5ᵗʰ. That our own carriage of our own Tobacco was heavily dutied in France.

The subjoined extracts from letters of this department to our minister in Paris, on the 23ᵈ of January, 10ᵗʰ of March, 28ᵗʰ of April, 16ᵗʰ of June 1792, and on the 12ᵗʰ of March 1793,[5] bespeak our earnestness for an extension of our commercial Treaty with France:

Extract from 23ᵈ January.

"I feel myself particularly bound to recommend, as the most important of your charges, the patronage of our commerce and the extension of its privileges, both in France and her Colonies; but more especially the latter."

10ᵗʰ March. "We had expected ere this, that in consequence of the recommendation of their predecessors, some overtures would have been made to us on the subject of a treaty of Commerce; an authentic copy of the recommendation was delivered, but nothing said about carrying it into effect: perhaps they expect that we should declare our readiness to meet them on the ground of Treaty; if they do, we have no hesitation to declare it: in the mean time, if the present communications produce any sensation, perhaps it may furnish a good occasion to endeavour to have matters replaced in status quo, by repealing the late innovations, as to our Ships, Tobacco, and whale oil; it is right that things should be on their antient footing at opening the Treaty."

28th April. "I hope that these manifestations of friendly dispositions towards that Country, will induce them to repeal the very obnoxious laws respecting our commerce, which were passed by the preceding national Assembly. The present Session of Congress will pass over without any other notice of them than the friendly preferences before mentioned; but if these should not produce a retaliation of good on their part, a retaliation of evil must follow on ours: it will be impossible to defer longer than the next Session of Congress, some counter regulations for the protection of our navigation and commerce. I must intreat you, therefore, to avail yourself of every occasion of friendly remonstrance on this subject. If they wish an equal and cordial treaty with us, we are ready to enter into it. We would wish that this could be the scene of negotiation, from considerations <u>suggested by the nature of our Government</u>, which will readily occur to you."

16th June. "With respect to the particular objects of commerce susceptible of being placed on a better footing, on which you ask my ideas, they will shew themselves by the enclosed Table of the situation of our commerce with France and England. That with France is stated as it stood at the time I left that Country, when the only objects whereon change was still desireable, were those of salted provisions, Tobacco, and Tar, Pitch, and Turpentine: the first was in negotiation when I came away, and was pursued by Mr Short with prospects of success till their general Tariff so unexpectedly deranged our commerce with them as to other articles. Our commerce with their West Indies had never admitted amelioration during my stay in France. The temper of that period did not allow even the essay and it was as much as we could do to hold the ground given us by the marshel de Castries' arrêt, admitting us to their Colonies with salted provisions, &c.[6] As to both these branches of commerce, to wit, with France and her Colonies, we have hoped they would pursue their own proposition of arranging them by treaty, and that we could draw that Treaty to this place. There is no other where the dependence of their Colonies on our States for their prosperity is so obvious as here, nor where their negotiator would feel it so much. But it would be imprudent to leave to the uncertain issue of such a Treaty the re-establishment of our commerce with <u>France</u> on the footing on which it was at the beginning of their revolution. That treaty may be long on the Anvil; in the mean time we cannot submit to the late innovations without taking measures to do justice to our own navigation. This object, therefore is particularly recommended to you, while you will also be availing yourself of every opportunity which may arise of benefiting our commerce in any other part. I am in hopes you will have found the moment favorable on your arrival in France when M. Claviere was in the ministry,[7] and the dispositions of the national assembly favorable to the ministers."

12th March 1793. "Mutual good offices, mutual affection and similar principles of Government, seem to destine the two nations for the most intimate communion: and I cannot too much press it on you to improve every opportunity which may occur in the changeable scenes which are passing, and to seize them as they occur for placing our commerce with that nation and its dependencies on the freest and most encouraging footing possible."

What were the corresponding efforts of our Minister relative to a treaty of commerce? In June 1792 he was intreated by Dumouriez, then minister, to defer it until he should return from the frontiers; who intimated at the same time, that France stood in need of no alliances, and that he was against all treaties, other than those of commerce. In July 1792 our Minister had "repeatedly called the minister's attention to the obnoxious acts of the (then) late assembly, and to their proposition of a new commercial treaty. The reply was that for himself he would be glad to settle every thing to our minister's satisfaction; but that his ministerial existence was too precarious to undertake any extensive plan; that the attention of Government was turned too strongly toward itself (in the present moment) to think of its <u>exterior interests,</u> and that the assembly, at open war with the Executive, would certainly reject whatever should be now presented to them."[8] The following extracts of our minister's letter to M[r] Chambonas on the 9th of July 1792 and of his answer on the 23[d] of the same month, shew the measures of our Government for the improvement of the treaty.[9]

"Je remplirai mal cependant mon devoir envers ma nation, et je ne donnerois, monsieur, qu'une foible temoignage de l'attachement que j'ai voué à la votre, depuis tant d'années si je dissimulais le malcontentément qu'ont excités en Amèrique les decréts de l'assemblée constituente qui portent atteinte au systéme de commerce etabi entre la france et les etats unis avant l'année 1789. Je m'abstiens de toute observation à cet égard parceque je m'en rapporte à vos lumières et aux sentimens de votre nation, et j'ose croire que même s'il n'etait question que de ses propres interèts l'assemblée nationale ne laisseroit plus subsister des reglemens qui pesait encore plus sur les consumateurs français qu'ils ne blessent les armateurs americains. Il est un autre objet, monsieur, auquel vous preterez surement toute l'attention qui merite son importance. L'assemblée constituante temoigne le desir que le roi fit negocier un nouveau traité de commerce avec l'amérique. La communication on a été donnée au President des etats unis par le ministre plenipotentiare de sa majesté mais jusque à present ce projet n'a point eu de suite. Je suis chargé de vous assurer, monsieur, que les etats unis se préteront avec un vrai plaisir à toute les ouvertures qui leur seront faites à ce sujet et qu'ils desirent asseoir ce traité sur des bases justes, solides, et réciproquent, utiles aux deux nations. Le ministre plenipotentiare de la france à Philadelphie est plus en etat que personne d'en apprecier les avantages, et josé vous certifier d'avance que s'il est chargé par le roi de cette negociation il eprouvera de notre part les dispositions les plus amicales. Vous me ferez un très grand plaisir, monsieur, lorsque vous voudrez bien m'autoriser à ecrire que la commission lui en été donnée."

Le 23 juillet 1792. "Je mettrai également sur leurs yeux le désir que temoigne le gouvernement Américain de cimenter l'union des deux peuples par un nouveau traité de commerce, et je prendrai incessement les ordres du roy pour entamer cette important negociation. Je ne doutte nullement qu'elle ne soit amené bientôt à une heureux conclusion puisque les deux gouvernemens ont un égal desir d'asseoir le nouveau traité sur les bases de la plus stricte justice et par consequent de l'avantage réciproque des deux peuples."

On the 13th of February we were informed by our minister, that he having been instructed to transfer the negociation of a new treaty of commerce to America, the thing wished was done, and that we may treat in America.[10]

M[r] Genet's abovementioned letter of the 23[d] of May 1793, enclosing the decree of February 19th 1793, concluded in these words. "The obstacles raised with intentions hostile to liberty, by the perfidious ministers of despotism;—the obstacles whose object was to stop the rapid progress of the commerce of the Americans, and the extension of their principles, exist no more. The French Republic, seeing in them but brothers, has opened to them, by the decrees now enclosed, all her ports in the two worlds;—has granted them all the favors which her own Citizens enjoy in her vast possessions;—has invited them to participate the benefits of her navigation, in granting to their vessels the same rights as to her own;—and has charged me to propose to your Government to establish, in a true family compact, that is in a national compact, the liberal and fraternal basis on which she wishes to see raised the commercial and political system of two people, all whose interests are confounded."

"I am invested, Sir, with the powers necessary to undertake this important negociation of which the sad annals of humanity, offer no example before the brilliant æra at length opening on it."

I find no answer to this letter from Mʳ Jefferson, and he notices the steps which were taken in consequence of it, only in his letter to Mʳ Morris, on the 23ᵈ August 1793, thus: "The Senate being then (23ᵈ May 1793) in recess, and not to meet again 'till the fall, I apprized Mʳ Genet that the <u>participation</u> in matters of treaty, given by the Constitution to that branch of our Government, would, of course, delay any <u>definitive</u> answer to his friendly proposition. As he was sensible of this circumstance, the matter has been <u>understood</u> to lie over 'till the meeting of the Senate."

Upon this conduct of Mʳ Jefferson many invidious comments have been circulated; and it has been perverted into a testimony of our evasion, and of our disaffections to France, with a design to foment dissensions between the two Republics. Your exertions will doubtless frustrate the evil purpose.

Long had we been soliciting from France a revision of the treaty of commerce; suffering in the mean time severities from her commercial regulations. Can any rational man believe, when he reads the preceding confidential letters from the Department of State to our Minister in Paris, that they were fabricated to deceive? Deception must have been gratuitous,—without an object; and therefore too absurd to be dwelt upon. Upon the supposition of sincerity on our part in the profession of a desire to improve the treaty, what culpable cause can be assigned for repelling an immediate negociation? Were we looking for an adverse stroke to the affairs of France, in order to squeeze out greater commercial indulgencies? We have been charged by Great Britain with too lively a sympathy with her successes—Were we distrustful of the issue of the contest? There were few men, who were not divided in their speculative opinions upon this occasion. But the President came to an instantaneous decision, by receiving Mʳ Genet, in the face of the war with Great Britain; recognizing the treaties, continuing to pay our debt to France, and accommodating her with money by anticipation—Had the cause of republicanism any connection with a change in the treaty of commerce? I cannot discover it; or if it had, whosoever shall deny it to be espoused by our Government, or shall insinuate a leaning towards England, is no less base, than unfounded in his calumnies. In short, it is absolutely incomprehensible why the Executive should, from a policy, which it will not avow, put off a treaty for the reforming of old <u>commercial</u> stipulations, when every melioration of our trade was so closely allied with the expectations of profits to the husbandman and merchant, created by our neutrality.

There was no such evasion; and the agreement or understanding between Mʳ Jefferson and Mʳ Genet, cannot be wrought into such a shape. Being without documents, containing the whole of their conversation, I have no other clue to it, than the letter of August 23ᵈ 1793, the nature of the subject, and the circumstances of the period, as explanatory of the postponement of the negociation.

It is of no consequence to inquire, whether it was or was not more agreeable to Mʳ Genet, that the negociation should lie over, when he heard that a <u>definitive</u> answer must be delayed, until the meeting of the Senate. Notwithstanding it has the appearance of being the voluntary act of both; especially as Mʳ Genet suffered it to rest upon an oral discourse, and never had, nor asked a written answer; yet let it be conceded to have been on the part of Mʳ Jefferson an act of the Government, and on the part of Mʳ Genet a respectful submission.

What Mʳ Jefferson asserted is true; because the President can <u>make</u> treaties <u>only</u> with the advice and consent of the Senate: a <u>definitive</u> answer was therefore necessarily deferred. He did not alledge, that <u>intermediate</u> discussions could not take place; nor indeed does it appear that either of those Gentlemen turned their attention to the <u>preliminary</u> negociation, which might have been opened before the assembling of the Senate.

But if Mʳ Genet had even pressed an immediate negociation, weighty obstacles, very different from <u>evasion</u>, or alienation from France, stood in the way. 1ˢᵗ "On the declaration of war between France and

England, the United States being at peace with both, their situation was so new and unexperienced by themselves,"[11] that it was extremely desirable to exclude any business, which would absorb much time and might be postponed; in order that the Executive might be unembarrassed in its superintendence of our neutrality. Although the labours of my predecessor from the commencement of the war to the early part of September 1793 have been seen by the world, yet cannot they judge of the perplexities and researches, which were the foundation of the documents published, and which hourly occupied not only the President himself, but those Officers also, who were around him. History had forewarned us, that, as a neutral nation, encompassed by the ministers of the belligerent powers, inflamed with a jealousy of the public functionaries, not a day would pass without a complaint, a demand, a suspicion, and a thousand temptations to irritability. Piles of papers, verifying those predictions, are now before my eyes. 2$\underline{d}$ It was not to be supposed, that a <u>new</u> treaty of commerce could be entered into without much reflection. In this view every hour gained was beneficial. 3$\underline{d}$. The power of the President to authorize the Secretary of State, or indeed any other person, to digest the matter of a treaty has been recognized in practice in several forms, one of which is barely to nominate, with the advice and consent of the Senate, and occasionally to consult them. The last was the course which was observed in the only treaty which has been negociated at the seat of Government—the treaty with the Creek Indians at New York in 1790. The Senate being on the spot and therefore convenient to the negociation, were asked, as the subject was passing, whether they would ratify certain clauses, if inserted in the treaty. In the re-adjustment of the treaty of commerce with France it was probably wished to repeat the same measure.

What would have been gained by France, by precipitating the negociation? The preliminary discussions might perhaps have been closed a few months sooner on the side of the President; but it is entirely uncertain, whether the affair would have been expedited by any step, so much as by consulting the Senate upon points of particular magnitude, before the <u>whole</u> work was submitted to them. This is among the advantages, which may be embraced in a negotiation in the United States, and is unattainable in a negotiation elsewhere. However if a commencement had been made, I question, whether from the time, which is indispensable for so grand a transaction, and the unvoidable interruption incident to the new state of things, we should not have been obliged to interrupt the progress upon a plea, similar to that of the french ministry, that we were too much employed with steering clear of the war, to attend for the present to the remoulding of the Treaty.

Had the Executive been indisposed to the Treaty, why did he in a manner pledge himself to negotiate when the Senate should meet? Why was our Minister in Paris instructed on the 23$\underline{d}$ of August 1793 "To explain to the Executive of France, this delay, which has prevented, as yet our formal accession to their proposition to treat; to assure them that the President will meet them, with the most friendly dispositions on the grounds, proposed by the national Convention, as soon as he can do it in the <u>forms of</u> the Constitution; and of course to suggest, for this purpose, that the powers of Mr Genet be renewed to his successor?"—"A <u>formal</u> accession to the proposition to treat,"—and a negotiation "in the <u>forms</u> of the constitution," appear to be still preferred to <u>informal</u> discussions, for the reasons already assigned.

It is impossible to look into this subject without remarking that other principles may be conceived upon which the Executive might have refused to treat immediately; but which do not appear to have influenced his decision.

His attention must have been arrested by the diction of Mr Genet's overtures. The President and the French Republic had hitherto agitated a change in <u>commercial</u> regulations only; when Mr Genet announces a desire to modify the <u>political</u> connection also. The precise meaning of the term <u>political</u>, was not very obvious; 'tho the most natural interpretation was, that the <u>political</u> relation, established by the treaty of alliance, was proposed to be revised.

The movements which have been noticed of Mr Genet before his arrival at Philadelphia from Charleston, were in perfect unison with this interpretation. The very decree of the 19th of february 1793, liberal as it was in its language, manifested that the recent and existing war, was a chief cause in dictating the concessions. For the French colonies could not be fed without supplies from the United States; and the <u>suspension</u> of the law of May 15th 1791; which had inhibited the Americans from introducing, selling and <u>arming</u> their vessels in France, and from enjoying all the privileges allowed to those built in the ship Yards of the Republic, was calculated to convert our Ships into French privateers.

To confirm the real views of the Executive Council of France in the regeneration of the Treaty, recollect these passages in Mr Genet's instructions:

"That the Executive Council are disposed to set on foot a negotiation upon those foundations, and that they do not know but that such a treaty admits a latitude still more extensive in becoming a national agreement, in which two <u>great</u> people shall suspend their commercial and political interests, and establish a mutual understanding to befriend the empire of liberty wherever it can be embraced, to guaranty the sovereignty of the people, and punish those powers who still keep up an exclusive colonial and commercial system, by declaring that their vessels shall not be received in the ports of contracting parties. Such a pact which the people of France will support with all the energy which distinguishes them, and of which they have already given so many proofs, will quickly contribute to the general emancipation of the new world. However vast this project may be, it will not be difficult to execute, if the Americans determine on it, and it is to convince them of its practicability that Citizen <u>Genet</u> must direct all his attention: For besides the advantages which humanity in general will draw from the success of such a negotiation, we have at this moment a particular interest in taking steps to act efficaciously against England and Spain, if, as every thing announces, these powers attack us from hatred to our principles, if the English ministers, instead of sharing in the glory of France, instead of considering that our liberty, as well as that of those people whose chains we have broken, forever establishes that of their own country, suffer themselves to be influenced by our enemies and by those to the liberty of mankind, and embark with every tyrant against the cause which we are defending. The military preparations making in Great Britain become every day more and more serious and have an intimate connection with those of Spain. The friendship which reigns between the ministers of the last power and those of St James' proves it; and in this situation of affairs we ought to excite, by all possible means, the zeal of the Americans, who are as much interested as ourselves, in disconcerting the destructive projects of <u>George</u> the third, in which they are probably an object. Their own safety still depends on ours, and, if we fail they will sooner or later fall under the iron rod of Great Britain. The Executive Council has room to believe that these reasons in addition to the great commercial advantages which we are disposed to concede to the United States, will determine their Government to adhere to all that Citizen <u>Genet</u> shall propose to them on our part. As it is possible, however, that the false representations which have been made to Congress of the situation of our internal affairs, of the state of our maritime force, of our finances, and especially of the storms with which we are threatened may make her ministers, in the negotiations which Citizen Genet is entrusted to open, adopt a timid and wavering conduct, the executive council charges him in expectation that the American Government will finally determine to make a common cause with us, to take such steps as will appear to him exigencies may require, to serve the cause of liberty and the freedom of the people."[12]

The project, therefore, of a treaty on the basis of Mr Genet's propositions ought to have been well explored, before the first advance. To assent to them, if it would not have been a departure from neutrality, would at least have magnified the suspicion of our faith, without a confidence in which, that neutrality must always be insecure. To reject them was to incur discontent, possibly a breach with our ally. The councils of nations ought to be superior to the passions, which drive individuals. <u>Permanent</u> good being the polar star of the former, they will often have to encounter the impetuosity of the latter, who substitute occasional feelings for sound policy.

Admitting that the non-establishment of a constitution, and the rapid successions in the administrative bodies, could not weaken an agreement, once fixed, even under the pressure of war, there was no probability, that the party, whose missionary Mr Genet was, would much longer tread the stage, nor any security, that his overtures would equally please those, who should rise upon the ruins of his friends. We knew from letters, that, as far back as August, 1792, the movers of the revolution on the 10th of that month, were sooner or later destined to be victims—that in January 1793, they were conscious of the downfall which awaited them: that in March 1793, an insurrection was brewing for the destruction of the Gironde: and that the revolutionary tribunal, vast and unbounded in its domination, had been erected. Was this then, a season for "modifying the <u>political</u> connection," when we might have drawn hostility upon our heads, by betraying a spirit, not impartial, and by taking measures, which amid the fluctuations in the leaders of the French politics might not have been sanctioned? And what did actually happen? The conduct of the Robesperian faction was directly the reverse of the Brissotine: the one encouraged, the other abolished private trade. For the evidence of this fact, I refer you to your own knowledge; to the vexations of our commerce; to the decrees which violated our treaty; and to the decree of October 1793, which took all trade into the hands of Government. Nor can I omit the demonstration of a general instability, as it was delivered in a late report of the five Committees.[13]

"Let us be persuaded and let us proclaim it openly; it is to that perpetual change, that all our evils are owing. Our republican annals do not yet include three years, and by the multiplicity of events 20 centuries appear required to contain them. Revolutions have followed revolutions; men, things, events and ideas, all have changed, every thing changes yet, and in this continual ebb and flow of opposite movements, in vain would the government pretend to that confidence which can only be the result of a steady and wise conduct, and of a constant attachment to principles."

"Commerce necessarily disappeared thro' this astonishing succession of contrarieties, and in a country, where individuals, incapacitated for making any sure calculations, see around them nothing but a wide prospect of changes."

"Credit is a tender plant which needs gentle and regular winds, and cannot grow in a tempestuous clime, or soil often disturbed."

"It is time we should put a period to the reign of uncertainties, and fix invariably the principles of justice, equity and loyalty, which should be the guides of our conduct. Let us hasten to subject the internal administration to a regular system: let us especially take care that no measure ever gives rise to fears concerning the solidity of the mortgage of our assignats.

"When the government, steady in its march, shall have shewn the real end they aim at; when it shall have rendered an account to itself and to others of the system it intends to adopt; when the Convention, dismissing those unfortunate bickerings which have too often impeded their progress, shall attend solely to the happiness of the people; when they shall not cease to reject with indignation all measures which can infringe in the least degree the principles of justice and good faith, which should direct them; then all alarms will be at an end, and the restoration of the finances, of credit and of commerce may be undertaken with assurance of success."

Why the subject was not resumed with Mr Genet, is well known to every body who has heard of his excesses, and our declaration to the french Republic, that we should expect his Successor to be charged with similar powers. His letter of the 30th of September 1793, written after the application for his recal, was announced to him, was prevented by the malady of Philadelphia from being received by this department, until the 5ᵗʰ of November 1793.[14] We were then counting upon a return of the vessel sent to France on that errand. Congress met in December 1793. Our minister's letter, notifying his recal, came to hand January 14ᵗʰ 1794[15] and Mʳ Fauchet actually replaced him on the 21st of February 1794. Let me observe, however, in passing from Mʳ Genet to Mʳ Fauchet, that his threat to withdraw the privileges in the decree of March 26. 1793,[16] and the decree itself, are strong symptoms of the design of the negotiation, being more than one merely commercial. For the different altercations between him and Mʳ Jefferson I refer you to the printed correspondence.

Mʳ Fauchet demanded the arrest of Mʳ Genet, for punishment. Our co-operation was refused upon reasons of law and magnanimity.

A bill passed at his instance for relief of the vessels, which had taken refuge in the ports of the United States.

We have advanced money faster than was due; and full as fast, as prudence in respect to our own wants, would permit.

The stoppage of the Camilla, a provision vessel of the French Republic, was the effect of the embargo, which operated equally on all.

Our minister was recalled as he desired. Mʳ Fauchet complained of British vessels being suffered to depart during the embargo with Frenchmen, who meant to act against their country in the West Indies. Occasional relaxations of the embargo were made in favor of all nations, French, English, &c. In the particular case complained of, the passports were supposed to be granted to American bottoms, for the humane purpose of returning to the Islands, some of the unhappy french fugitives from thence; and one of them given to a vessel, at his instance, exported a large quantity of powder, doubtless without his privity.

The Government suppressed the prosecution against Consul Juteau, of Boston, as Mʳ Fauchet desired. Whatever irritation may have been occasioned by the Attorney of the district, was owing to no instruction from the President.[17]

The demand for dismantling Cooper's vessel was inevitable, as she had been fitted out in our ports; and wheresoever, in any case, restitution of vessels was required from us, the rules of our neutrality fully justified it.[18]

We restored the Ship William of Glasgow, and the damages during her detention have been assured to the agent of the Captors.[19]

The steps adopted, and promised, for executing the Consular Convention, in the apprehension of deserters, are as much as could be done or expected.[20]

The Government has indeed differed from Mʳ Fauchet in the construction of the Treaty, not holding themselves bound to exclude British Ships of war, except when <u>they came in with prizes</u>.

The general Executive has given every instruction in his power to prevent french prizes to british vessels, coming into our ports. Mʳ Fauchet has expressly by letter approved our conduct in one instance. But this subject is fully detailed in my letter of the 29ᵗʰ ult. a copy of which is now forwarded to you.[21]

I presume, that the dissatisfaction at the arms taken from the Favorite in New York, and the omission to salute a french ship of war, have been completely expiated.

The tonnage duty was remitted to French vessels, which had been injured by the British.

It was impossible to rescue from the law Wᵐ Talbot, who was charged with being a Citizen of the United States, and accepting a privateering Commission from France.[22]

These are the most material of Mr Fauchet's transactions with the Government, except, indeed, the abolition of the embargo; the whole of which business you witnessed yourself, and can shew to have arisen from very different motives than those of disregard to France.

Altho' it was requested, that Mr Genet's Successor should be charged with commercial powers, yet is it not known or believed he brought any. No writing from him announced it: nor yet any conversation with me; unless, indeed, in November or December last, when Macpherson's blues[23] were coming into town, and he and I were together looking out at them from his eastern window. He then made some casual observations respecting Mr Jay's negotiation, and said something indefinite as to our treaty of commerce. My answer was, that I should be ready to receive his overtures. It would have been indelicate to ask him formally whether he had such powers; but a distant hint was given by me to him, two or three months after his arrival upon the subject; and from his reply I did not infer, whether he had or had not them. I am rather disposed to conclude he had them not; because he was appointed minister during the reign of Robespierre, who, as we have seen, almost extinguished commerce; and when a decree was in force assuming into the hands of Government all trade.

If Mr Fauchet had been ready, we should have proceeded sincerely and without procrastination.

If then, in the circumstances attending the proposition of a commercial treaty from Mr Genet, or in the conduct of the United States towards France since, nothing improper can be found, we ought to consider, whether in those of the late Treaty with Great Britain, a source of blame can be detected.

The message, in which the President nominated Mr Jay as Envoy Extraordinary to His Britannic Majesty was dated on the 16th of April 1794, and is the text, the examination of which will develop the total matter, previous to Mr Jay's departure.[23]

"The communications" says the message, " which I have made to you, during your present Session, from the despatches of our minister in London, contain a serious aspect of our affairs with Great Britain."

The first of these communications was to Congress on the 5th of December 1793; in which are the following passages. "The vexations and spoliation, understood to have been committed on our vessels and commerce by the Cruisers and Officers of some of the belligerent powers, appeared to require attention. The proofs of these, however, not having been brought forward, the description of Citizens supposed to have suffered were notified, that on furnishing them to the executive, due measures would be taken to obtain redress of the past, and more effectual provisions against the future. Should such documents be furnished, proper representations will be made, with a just reliance on a redress, proportioned to the exigency of the case."[25]

"The British Government having undertaken, by order to the Commanders of their armed vessels, to restrain, generally, our commerce in corn and other provisions to their own ports, and those of their friends, the instructions now communicated, were immediately forwarded to our minister at that Court.[26] In the mean time, some discussions on the subject took place, between him and them. These are also laid before you, and I may expect to learn the result of his special instructions, in time to make it known to the legislature during their present Session."

"Very early after the arrival of a British minister here, mutual explanations on the inexecution of the treaty of peace, were entered into with that minister. These are now laid before you for your information."

From the documents accompanying this message of December 5th 1793, these subjects emerge, as depending for adjustment between the United States and Great Britain:

1ˢᵗ. The inexecution of the 7ᵗʰ article of the Treaty of peace, in carrying away negroes and other property of American inhabitants, and the not withdrawing the garrisons from the posts within the United States.

2ᵈ. Regulations on the part of the British government, with respect to the commerce of the two countries, which, if reciprocally adopted, would materially injure the interests of the two nations; and an overture from Mʳ Jefferson, as far back as November 1791, to conclude, or negotiate arrangements, which might fix the commerce between the two countries on principles of reciprocal advantage.

3ᵈ. The ascertainment of the river intended by the Treaty as the river Sᵗ Croix.

4ᵗʰ. The additional instructions of the 8ᵗʰ of June 1793, which rendered provisions to a certain degree contraband, and the letter to Mʳ Pinckney from this department in consequence thereof.

5ᵗʰ. Other measures of the British government, in violation of neutral rights.

6ᵗʰ. The exposure of American seamen to impressment, and—

7ᵗʰ. The British complaints of infraction of the 4ᵗʰ 5ᵗʰ & 6ᵗʰ articles of the treaty, relative to the omissions of Congress to inforce them, the repealing of laws, which existed antecedent to the pacification, the enacting of laws subsequent to the peace, in contravention of the treaty, and the decisions of the State Courts upon questions affecting the rights of British Subjects.

The dispatches transmitted to Congress from Mʳ Pinckney on the 22ᵈ of January 1794 manifest a continuation of the same unfriendly spirit in the British Government.[27]

With the message of February 24ᵗʰ 1794 was sent to Congress a letter from Mʳ Pinckney, forwarding his conversation with Lord Grenville, concerning british agency, in fomenting the Indian war, and Algerine hostility.[28]

On the 4ᵗʰ of April 1794 was conveyed to Congress Mʳ Pinckney's letter, inclosing the instructions of the 6ᵗʰ of November 1793.[29]

In addition to this involved and injurious state of things between us and Great Britain, it had been collected and reported to Congress from the papers respecting spoliation, that "The british privateers plundered the American vessels, threw them out of their course, by forcing them upon groundless suspicion into ports other than those, to which they were destined; detained them, even after the hope of a regular confiscation was abandoned; by their negligence, while they held the possession exposed the cargoes to damage, and the vessels to destruction, and mal-treated the crews:" that our occasional trade to the British West Indies was burthened unnecessarily: that our vessels were captured in going to the french West Indies: and that the proceedings in the British vice-Admiralties were rigorous, transgressed strict judicial purity, and heaped the most intolerable and fruitless expenses upon our Citizens, who defended their property before them.[30]

It makes no part of my object to compare the various schemes which were circulating to face those public distresses; nor to prove the superiority of the policy adopted by the Executive, to commercial reprisals, sequestration, and the stoppage of intercourse. It is enough to say, that his policy is affirmed to be, to pursue peace "with unremitted zeal before the last resource, which had so often been the scourge of nations, and could not fail to check the advanced prosperity of the United States, should be contemplated."[31]

By what means did the President expect to execute the work of peace thro' the agency of Mʳ Jay? By "announcing to the world our solicitude for <u>a friendly adjustment of our complaints,</u> and a reluctance to hostility: by sending a man, who going directly from the United States, would carry with him a full knowledge of the existing temper and sensibility of our country; and would thus be taught to vindicate our rights with firmness and to <u>cultivate peace</u> with sincerity."[32]　The Senate therefore, did probably anticipate what might be the objects of this mission, when they confirmed the nomination.　For the President details no powers, and founds his nomination upon the information possessed by themselves.

It has been or may be objected 1. That the Senate did not contemplate the making of <u>any Treaty</u> whatsoever: 2. That a Treaty of Commerce, especially, was very distant from their mind: 3. That the declarations to the minister of the French republic here, and the instructions to our own minister at Paris induced a persuasion, that the President had not vested in M[r] Jay powers, as extensive as a Treaty of Commerce: and 4. That the Treaty with Great Britain, is justly offensive to France.

1. Recapitulate the several heads of intelligence in the power of the Senate, when the nomination was assented to.　Scarcely one of them could in the ordinary course of proceeding, be accommodated without an agreement.　Some expressly struck at the inexecution of the past treaty: Upon others, no treaty had ever existed, tho' overtures for that purpose had been repeated by the United States.　That a treaty would spring from such mission, and the extinction of our differences, is too clear to be in need of further elucidation.

And why should not a Treaty be concluded with Great Britain?　Was it because she had despoiled us?　The objection would lie with equal strength against even a treaty of peace.　It would forbid a Treaty of peace even with Algiers.　The fact is, that Treaties are proposed by one nation, and accepted by another, only because they can be mutually hurtful by positive enmity, or by the withholding of some benefit: We are in no danger of being corrupted by importing foreign vices, if treaties, merely, and not our own propensities should favor them.

2. A treaty of Commerce with Great Britain has for many years been anxiously pushed by the United States.　Witness the powers, given by the old Congress to M[r] Adams to negotiate it.　Witness the clamors against her for declining it.　Witness the arguments drawn from thence for a more energetic government, which should inspire a dread of reprisal.　Witness the bill which passed the House of Representatives, at an early Session, discriminating between nations, having no Commercial treaty with us, and those which had.[32]　What too was the report of the late Secretary of State, but a plan for forcing the British Government into a treaty of Commerce?　Has he not clearly unfolded this Sentiment?　What were the commercial propositions but emanations from the same system?　The want of a commercial treaty was the single circumstance, which propped up the severity of the proposed distinction of duties, and carried thro' one of the Resolutions.

Exclusively of these various acts, the facilities to our commerce, both European and West Indian, which would flow from such a treaty rendered it very desirable.

Perhaps for a treaty of commerce alone, an Envoy would not have been thought of.　But surely to include in one general arrangement, controversies as well as useful compacts, was the saving of one negotiation at least.　Some of our vexations on the water, were owing to the non-existence of the customary appendages to a commercial treaty.　Past spoliations might have been compensated without a Treaty: but a Treaty was the best assurance of the future.　In a word, the Senate must have been sensible of many particulars being comprehended by the general outlines of the nomination.

When the President nominates ministers, he may, if he pleases, restrict himself to the name, the grade, and the Prince or State.　He might, for example, have nominated M[r] Jay thus: "I nominate John Jay, as Envoy extraordinary to His Britannic Majesty."　The Senate, in their turn, might have rejected him.　But if they had approved him, the President would have been at liberty to employ him in any negotiation with that King.　Their power being ample on the completion of the Treaty, they are not a necessary constitutional party in the concoction of it, unless the President should find it expedient to request their intermediate advice. It would be superfluous to discuss how far he might have limited himself by the terms of the nomination; as I again contend and hope I have shewn, that he did not limit himself.

3. We cannot foresee the representations, which Mᴿ Fauchet is understood to be meditating to the French Republic. But as the duties of nation towards nation did not compel us to divulge to the French minister more in regard to the Treaty with Great Britain, than that our treaties with France were forbidden by the instructions of the Envoy to be infringed, so did the President approve, that the restriction should be communicated to him. This was conformable with the truth and wears no deceptive countenance.

Your own instructions speak thus "To remove all jealousy with respect to Mᴿ Jay's mission to London, you may say, that he is positively forbidden to weaken the engagements between this country and France. It is not improbable that you will be obliged to encounter on this head, suspicions of various kinds. But you may declare the <u>motives</u> of that mission to be, to obtain immediate compensation for our plundered property, and restitution of the posts. You may intimate by way of argument, but without ascribing it to the government, that if war should be necessary, the affections of the people of the United States, towards it, would be better secured by a manifestation, that every step had been taken to avoid it; and that the British nation would be divided, when they found, that we had been forced into it. This may be briefly touched upon, as the path of prudence with respect to ourselves; and also with respect to France, since we are unable to give her aids of men or money. To this matter you cannot be too attentive; and you will be amply justified in repelling with firmness any imputation of the most distant intention to sacrifice our connection with France to any connection with England."[34] When we expressed a wish "to remove all jealousy with respect to Mᴿ Jay's mission" it could not have been intended to abandon self dignity, by submitting to the pleasure or animadversions of France, any part of his instructions, with which France had no concern. A contrary conduct would have been irreconcilable also with the independence of the United States, and would have put them into leading strings. It would have been little short of trepidation under a master. 1. A treaty of commerce was altogether eventual: it was to be kept out of sight, until the posts and depredations should be so adjusted as to promise a continuance of tranquility. 2. It was eventual in another sense: being to be concluded or not, according to the degrees of advantage. 3. It was deemed important, that Mᴿ Jay should communicate or not communicate his commercial powers to the British ministry. 4. Every commercial privilege, which Great Britain should acquire would devolve on France on like conditions—what would France say, if we were to insist, that every embryo of her commercial treaties, every possibility of new commercial arrangements, should be laid before our government? Certainly this: that no fellowship between the two countries authorizes an expectation, that one will throw itself upon the discretion of the other to mar or not its negotiations; and that national honor is an ample guardian of our treaties.

Among the numberless disgusts, which nations have entertained against each other, I do not remember, that a treaty of commerce, which did not undermine the rights of some party, was ever magnified into complaint by foreigners. Let me cite only two; When Portugal, early in this century, surrendered many of her commercial advantages to Great Britain; and France not ten years ago, contracted a disadvantageous treaty with the same power; who remonstrated, but their own Subjects and people? If we are told that we ought not to draw our connection closer with Great Britain, and that France will be jealous; the answer is, that, if we can multiply the markets for our great Staples; if we can purchase our foreign goods cheaper, by having many manufacturing nations to resort to; or if even in the maintenance of neutral privileges, we can, by a stipulation, not derogatory from the rights of others, avert vexations; this is a connection unassailable by any reasonable opposition. The romantic extent, to which contrary ideas may be carried, would abolish our trade with every nation in whose institutions appeared false government, false religion, false morals, false policy, or any other political defect.

Your instructions justify you in affirming, that Mr Jay "is positively forbidden to weaken the engagements between this Country and France." After vesting a general latitude of powers in him, this case is declared to be an exception and immutable: "that as the British ministry will doubtless be solicitous to detach us from France, and may probably make some overture of this kind, you will inform them, that the Government of the United States, will not derogate from our treaties and engagements with France."

You intimate, however, that your instructions, amount to an exclusion from Mr Jay's mission of every object, except compensation for plundered property and restitution of the posts. For a moment let me entreat you to call to mind the different topics for negotiation, which were actually before the Senate at the time of Mr Jay's nomination, and which were not included in either of those points. Were not Mr Jefferson's animadversions upon the refusal of Great Britain to enter into a commercial treaty, and his plan for commercial reprisals, before you? Would it not have been extraordinary to pass by so fair an opportunity of bringing forward all our discontents? Was it not urged as an objection to the measure, that the terms of the nomination were sufficiently broad for any purpose of necotiation? But appeal to the words: "You may declare the motives of that negotiation to be" so and so. These were the motives; for if they had been away, it is probable that our minister in London would have been directed to pursue his efforts in the ordinary track, as to everything else. This was the true idea, when your instructions were prepared. "We were desirous of repelling any imputation of the most distant intention to sacrifice our connection with France, to any connection with England." It was enough to assign the leading motives of Mr Jay's errand, which were of a nature warranting the assertion, that we would not sacrifice the one connection for the other. Mr Jay was instructed to this effect: "One of the causes of your mission are the vexations and spoliations, committed on our commerce by the authority of instructions from the British government." "A second cause of your mission, but not inferior in dignity to the preceding, though subsequent in order, is to draw to a conclusion, all points of difference between the United States and Great Britain, concerning the Treaty of peace." "It is referred to your discretion, whether in case the two preceding points should be so accommodated, as to promise the continuance of tranquility between the United States and Great Britain, the subject of a commercial treaty may not be listened to by you, or even broken to the British ministry. If it should, let these be the general objects."

Your instructions therefore were commensurate with fact and propriety. 1. They were literally true, because the motives were the vexations of our commerce and the posts: 2. The declaration of two cardinal propositions does not exclude another, which is subordinate and eventual: 3. the confidential proceedings of the United States are not demandable by another nation, except where that nation is injured by them: 4. Otherwise, every modification of a direct and peremptory challenge of our rights, every compensation, but the downright payment of money—every mode of restitution, which was not instantaneous, and unqualified, ought to have been avoided by Mr Jay, because they were not stated in your instructions, as motives to his mission. But 5. to scout the suspicion of a deception on the French Republic, what manœuvre could have been more paltry, than one which a few months must certainly exhibit in open day? What emotions would the French Republic have shewn, if Mr Jay's instructions had been inspected by them? Would they have hazarded a hint, that we must have no treaty of commerce with Great Britain? We should have quoted their own example, in having repelled by arms the meddling of other nations in their internal affairs. We should have quoted our own independence, which will not tolerate the controul of any human authority. Would they have pronounced a treaty of commerce with Great Britain to be necessarily a contravention of our treaties with France? We should have searched in vain for such a provision in those treaties—Would they have argued, that a treaty of commerce with Great Britain contributed to uphold her warlike operations? Not a syllable in the instruction can be so tortured. Mercantile advantages to ourselves, and a security for neutral rights, were our aim in a commercial treaty. It remains to be disclosed, whether the contents of that treaty are inconsistent with our relation to the belligerent parties. Would the French Republic have requested us to interdict our trade with Great Britain? They could not have been gratified. Rather ought they, as friends, seriously to have reflected on the prejudicial footing of our trade with Great Britain. The British Statesmen have for many years been conscious, that Great Britain enjoys an immense harvest from its loose situation. Our own statesmen have incessantly lamented it, and sought a remedy. France was no stranger to our early opinion, that the remedy was to be found in a commercial treaty. She was no stranger to the facts already enumerated, as to Mᴿ Adams' powers, to Mᴿ Jefferson's report, to the commercial propositions in Congress; to the pressure on Mᴿ Hammond; and to the resentful speeches and motions of every Session, predicated on the reluctance of Great Britain to treat with us on commerce. And yet, that France has ever lisped a dissatisfaction on the score of injury, is hidden from me. On the contrary, some, who were privy to the French counsels, have endeavoured to rivet an odium on Great Britain, because she would not negotiate.

4ᵗʰ. You are by this time probably acquainted with the treaty with Great Britain thro' the communications of Mᴿ Trumbull; and must have determined in your own mind its probable effect upon the French Republic. Until it shall be ratified, it will be a waste of time, which I can little spare to comment upon it. If it is ratified or rejected, you shall receive an immediate and copious communication, and more particularly in relation to the 4ᵗʰ inquiry, whether the treaty with Great Britain affords just cause of offence to France. I am rather inclined to waive this inquiry for the present, in consequence of information that the French minister is concerting an attack on the ratification of the Treaty; and that sentiments, no less eccentric, than fatal to our independence, are to be scattered, at random, from a confidence in the popularity of the French cause.

Be the issue of this business, what it may, our government will neither renounce its professions and friendly conduct to the French Republic, nor ascribe to them any intemperateness, which their Agent may display. But you ought to put them on their guard. The vicissitudes in their parties have already (if newspapers may be credited) revived the old machinations and malicious stories of Genet. The fuel, which his successor may add, from considerations, and sources which I may perhaps hereafter explain, will receive a direction, best calculated to excite a flame. A late letter from him bears every symptom of an inflamed temper. My answer to it, which will accompany this letter, is our refutation.[35] We acknowledge nothing to be undone on our part, which friendship would dictate, our faculties could accomplish, and our neutrality would permit. If injuries are complained of, let us reason together, like cordial Allies; and compensate, where either may have been in fault. But let it be the last blot in the annals of the world, that the United States and France cease to be, what they ought to be—friends, who will endure no separation.

I now quit this lengthy subject; and shall in other dispatches more precisely reply to the different letters which I have lately received from you. I have the honor to be, with sentiments of the most perfect respect & esteem, Sir Yr. mo. ob. Serv.

Edm: Randolph

LBC, DNA: RG 59: Diplomatic and Consular Instructions

1. Randolph paraphrased a passage from Gouverneur Morris's letter to Thomas Jefferson of 16 August 1792 (*Jefferson Papers*, 24: 302).

2. Jefferson to Morris, 7 November 1792, *Jefferson Papers*, 24: 593.

3. Jefferson to Morris, 23 August 1793, *Jefferson Papers*, 26: 747. Genet's letter to Jefferson of 23 May 1793 is in *Jefferson Papers*, 26: 96-99).

4. Thomas Jefferson, "Report on Commerce," 16 December 1793, *Jefferson Papers*, 27: 532-581.

5. Jefferson to Morris, 23 January 1792 (*Jefferson Papers*, 23: 55-57), 10 March 1792 (*Jefferson Papers*, 23: 248-250), 28 April 1792 (*Jefferson Papers*, 23: 467-469), 16 June 1792 (*Jefferson Papers*, 24: 88-89), 12 March 1793 (*Jefferson Papers*, 25: 367-370).

6. Charles-Eugène, Marquis de Castries (1727-1801) had a distinguished military career and was awarded the rank of maréchal in 1756. He served as minister of marine 1780-1789 (*Dictionnaire de Biographie Française*). The arret referred to is: *Arret of the King's Council of State, concerning foreign commerce with the French islands in America, of the 30th of August, 1784.*

7. Étienne Clavière (1735-1793) served two separate terms as France's finance minister: 23 March-13 June 1792 and 10 August 1792-2 June 1793. His interest in the spread of liberal ideas led him to join the Girondists, and he moved up high on the list of Girondin ministers. Proscribed with other Girondist leaders, most of whom were guillotined in October, Clavière held on until December 1793, when he committed suicide (Jules Michelet, *Histoire de la Révolution Française*, 2: 1313-1314).

8. Morris to Jefferson, 10 June 1792 and 10 July 1792, *Jefferson Papers*, 24: 51, 209.

9. Scipion-Victor-Auguste La Garde, marquis de Chambonas (1750-1830) was made a general in the French army in 1791. He assumed the duties of foreign minister on 18 June 1792 (*Dictionnaire de Biographie Française*). Complete texts in English of the two letters exerpted here are printed in English in *ASP: FR*, 1: 332-333. Translations of the exceprts read:

> I should badly fulfill my duty towards my nation, and give, Sir, but a weak testimony of the attachment I have avowed to yours for so many years, were I to conceal the discontentment excited in America by the decrees of the Constituent Assembly, which operate to the injury of the commercial system established between France and the United States before the year 1789. I avoid any observation in this respect, because I report them to your understanding and to the sentiments of your nation; and I venture to believe that, even if her own interest only had been in question, the National Assembly will not allow to exist, any longer, regulations which bear much harder on the French consumer, than they injure the American merchant. There is another object, sir, to which you will certainly pay all the attention its importance merits. The Constituent Assembly testified a desire that the King should cause a new treaty of commerce to be negotiated with America. The communication of it has been made to the President of the United States by the minister plenipotentiary of his Majesty, but hitherto, this project has been stationary. I am instructed to assure you, sir, that the United States will, with true satisfaction, attend to all the overtures, which shall be made to them on this subject, and that they desire to found that treaty upon a basis just, solid, and reciprocally useful to the two nations. The minister plenipotentiary of France, at Philadelphia, is better able than any body to appreciate the advantages of it; and I venture to certify to you beforehand, that, if he is instructed by the King, for this negotiation, he will experience, on our part, the most amicable dispositions. You will give me much pleasure, sir, when you shall be pleased to authorize me to write that the commission for the purpose has been given to him (Morris to Chambonas, 9 July 1792).

> I shall also lay before them the desire testified by the American Government of cementing the union of the two people by a new treaty of commerce; and I shall immediately take the King's orders for opening this important negotiation. I have no doubt of its being soon brought to a happy conclusion, since the two Governments are equally desirous of founding the new treaty on a basis of the strictest justice, and consequently to the reciprocal advantage of the two nations (Chambonas to Morris, 23 July 1792).

10. Morris to Jefferson, 13 February 1793, *Jefferson Papers*, 25: 189-195.

11. Jefferson to Morris, 16 August 1793, *Jefferson Papers*, 26: 697.

12. A complete translation of Genet's instructions can be found in *The correspondence between Citizen Genet, minister of the French Republic to the United States of North America, and the officers of the federal government. To which are prefixed, the instructions from the constituted authorites of France to the said minister. All from authentic documents* (1794) (*Early American Imprints* #47056).

13. "Report and Project of Decree, presented in Nivose, (the latter end of Dec.) by Johannot, in the name of the Committees of Public Safety, General Security, Excise, Commerce amd Finances, on the Means of Restoring the finances and Public Credit," English translation, (Philadelphia) *Aurora*, 26, 27, 28, 30 March 1795.

14. Genet to Jefferson, 30 September 1793, *Jefferson Papers*, 27: 164-168; an English translation is in *ASP: FR*, 1: 244-245.

15. Morris to Jefferson, 18 October 1793, *ASP: FR*, 1: 374-375.

16. The decree of 26 March 1793 exempted American ships carrying provisions to the French West Indies from the payment of duties (*ASP: FR*, 1: 363.).

17. John Juttau (c. 1750-1821), the chancellor of the French consulate in Boston, was indicted in October 1793 on charges of outfitting the French privateer, *Roland*, in Boston harbor (*Jefferson Papers*, 27: 261; *Washington Papers: Presidential Series*, 13: 589-590).

18. John Cooper was captain of the French privateer, *Vanstable*, which was outfitted at Norfolk, Virginia, in April 1794. The *Vanstable* was seized at Philadelphia during the spring of 1795 for violation of American neutrality and was dismantled (*Calendar of Virginia State Papers*, 7: 107-108, 489).

19. The British ship *William* was captured by the French privateer *Citizen Genet* on 3 May 1793 (*Hamilton Papers*, 14: 548-549).

20. Article nine of the "Convention Defining and Establishing the Functions and Privileges of Consuls and Vice-Consuls," between France and the United States (1788) provided for the apprehension of deserters from ships (*Treaties, Conventions, International Acts, Protocols and Agreements between the United States of America and Other Powers* (1910), 1: 494).

21. Randolph to Joseph Fauchet, 29 May 1795, *ASP: FR*, 1: 609-614.

22. William Talbot of Virginia was the captain of a French privateer who was arrested for violation of the neutrality law when he brought a prize into Charleston. Talbot claimed that he had become a French citizen, but the U. S. Supreme Court ruled, in a civil suit filed against Talbot for the recovery of the prize, that actual expatriation required the establishment of a residence in the adopted country (*Documentary History of the Supreme Court*, 6: 650-659).

23. McPherson's Blues was a volunteer militia company in Philadelphia commanded by William McPherson. It was organized at the time of the Whiskey Rebellion (*Appletons' Cyclopedia*).

24. George Washington to the U. S. Senate, 16 April 1794, *ASP: FR*, 1: 447.

25. George Washington to Congress, 5 December 1793, *ASP: FR*, 1: 141-142.

26. The instructions of 8 June 1793 authorized British warships to intercept any ship carrying grain and bound for any port controlled by the French. The intercepted vessels were to be sent into a British port and would be released after the British purchased the cargo. Jefferson wrote to Thomas Pinckney on 7 September 1793 and instructed him to urge the British to repeal the instructions (*Jefferson Papers*, 26: 439-442; 27: 55-59).

27. George Washington to Congress, 22 January 1794, enclosing extracts of communications from Thomas Pinckney, *ASP: FR*, 1: 315.

28. Washington to Congress, 24 February 1794, enclosing papers relating to relations with Great Britain and Spain, including a letter from Thomas Pinckney to the secretary of state, 25 November 1793, *ASP: FR*, 1: 328.

29. The instructions of 6 November 1793 authorized British warships to seize ships carrying goods to or from a French colony. Thomas Pinckney enclosed a copy of the instructions in a letter to the secretary of state, dated 26 December 1793. Washington submitted these papers to Congress on 4 April 1794 (*ASP: FR*, 1: 429-430).

30. George Washington to Congress, 5 March 1794, enclosing Edmund Randolph to Washington, 2 March 1794, *ASP: FR*, 1: 423-424.

31. George Washington to the Senate, 16 April 1794 (nominating John Jay as envoy to Great Britain), *ASP: FR*, 1: 447.

32. Washington to the Senate, 16 April 1794 (paraphrase).

33. The House of Representatives passed two bills in May 1789 setting impost and tonnage duties; both discriminated between countries that had commerical treaties with the United States and those that did not. The Senate removed these provisions from the bills (*Madison Papers*, 12: 54-55).

34. Randolph to JM, 10 June 1794, above.

35. Joseph Fauchet to Randolph, 2 May 1795; Randolph to Fauchet, 29 May 1795, *ASP: FR*, 1: 608-614.

To Jean Victor Colchen

Paris 3 June 1795 (15 Prairial 3ᵈ year)
19ᵗʰ year of the American Republic.

Citizen,

I observe that there are three American citizens, William Bache (grandson of the late Dʳ Franklin),[1] William Boys and Adam Seyberts,[2] under arrest at Havre, from the circumstance I presume of their having arrived there from London on board an American Ship, which the committee of surety general,[3] for reasons doubtless of sufficient weight, ordered to be searched. These young men being students of Physic, have come into the republic for the purpose of acquiring instruction, are of course not included in the suspicions of the Committee. I have therefore thought it my duty to make known to you their real situation, hoping that an order will speedily be issued for their release.[4]

Jaˢ Monroe.

Copy, enclosed in JM to Edmund Randolph, 4 July 1795, DNA: RG 59: Dispatches from France

1. William Bache (1773-1818), a grandson of Benjamin Franklin, graduated from the University of Pennsylvania in 1794. After further study in Europe, he returned to Philadelphia and practiced medicine. JM helped Bache buy a farm in Albemarle County (which Bache named Franklin) in 1799. Bache resided there 1799-1804 (*Letters of Benjamin Rush*, 2: 652; Edgar Woods, *History of Albemarle County in Virginia*, 62; *Catalogue of Monroe's Papers*, 1: 72, 74).

2. Adam Seybert (1773-1825) graduated from the University of Pennsylvania in 1793 and then studied in Europe. He returned to Philadelphia where he became a chemist and a mineralogist. He represented Pennsylvania in the House of Representatives 1809-1815, 1817-1819 (*BDAC*).

3. The Committee of General Security, which existed from 1792 to 1795, handled matters of internal security, ranging from the issuance of passports to the prosecution of foreign agents. During the Terror its officers were charged with arresting and detaining suspected enemies of the revolution. Its powers often conflicted with those of the Committee of Public Safety (Samuel Scott and Barry Rothaus, *Historical Dictionary of the French Revolution*, 1: 209-213).

4. The Committee of Public Safety informed JM on 15 June 1795 that it had issued an order for the release of the three Americans (Committee of Public Safety to JM, 15 June 1795, enclosed in JM to Edmund Randolph, 4 July 1795, DNA: RG 59: Dispatches from France).

From George Washington

Philadelphia 5ᵗʰ June 1795.

Dear Sir,

I have to thank you for the information contained in your private letter to me, of the 19ᵗʰ of last November.

The regular & detailed accounts which you receive from the department of State of all occurrences as they arise with us, leave nothing to be added.

As a private concern, I shall take the liberty of troubling you with the enclosed;—requesting that it may be presented, or forwarded, as the case may be, to Madam la Fayette.—The papers are under a flying seal, that seeing the scope and design of them, you may (if the money therein mentioned should not have reached her hands—of which I have received no information) be enabled to assist her in obtaining it—the favor of doing which, I beg you to render us both—My best respects are presented to Mʳˢ Monroe. With esteem & regard I am—Dear Sir—Yʳ obedᵗ Servᵗ

Gᵉ Washington

RC, DLC: Monroe Papers

Washington enclosed a letter to Adrienne Lafayette, dated 5 June 1795 (DLC: Washington Papers, Series 2: Letterbooks). He also enclosed a copy of a letter that he had written to Nicholas Van Staphorst of Amsterdam on 31 January 1793, in which he had enclosed money for Adrienne Lafayette (*Papers of George Washington, Presidential Series,* 12: 75-76).

Notes on a Constitution
1: For the Committee of Public Safety

[7 June 1795]

In the United States of America, the rights of men are equal: they have no hereditary rulers of any kind or in any station. All the citizens are eligible under certain qualifications to the highest offices of the government, and these qualifications make no distinction in respect to rights every one being capable of acquiring them.

National concerns are given to the national government: local concerns are given to the State governments, & each is independant of the other in its respective sphere. The structure or organization of the national & state governments is in general the same. The power in every one is distributed into three branches, Legislative, Executive & Judicial, and each of which branches is made as independant as possible of the others: indeed it is a principle well established that in proportion as this independance is destroyed, and the ascendency given either to the Executive or legislative (for it cannot be given to the Judicial) does the government become less free.

The line of seperation between the national & State governments is drawn, in the Constitution of the former, by which it is endowed with special powers only: hence it follows that it possesses those only which are specified, & of course that the States lose those only which are likewise thus specified.

The character of the legislative, Executive & Judicial powers is well known here, so that the only object is to ascertain how that of each is distributed, or in short what the organization of each, is.

The legislative power is divided in all cases into two branches, a Senate, and house of Delegates or Representatives. Each house has a right to originate & mature bills (except that money bills or those which impose taxes must originate in the most numerous branch) & which being sent to the other, may either be rejected or passed: if rejected it is as if the subject had not been touched: if passed it is a law, except in those cases where the Executive has a qualified negative as is the case in the Constitution of some States, and in that of the U. States. And where the Executive has such qualified negative, it is then sent to that branch & subject to the like result: except that when the negative is exercised, it may still be a law independant of the Executive, in case 23$^{\underline{ds}}$ of each branch vote for it.

The term of service in the house of Delegates or representatives is in general for one year only. In the constitution of the U. States it is for two. In general any person being a citizen of the State may be elected into this branch. In general too no other qualification than that of citizenship is requisit to constitute an elector. In some instances qualifications by property, either of land or rents, is requisit in both cases.

The term of service for the Senate varies in different States. In some it is for 3. years, in others for 4. and in the constitution of the United States it is for six. The qualification for the Senator & Elector, is in general the same in each State as for the Delegate or Representative: except that in the State of Maryland the Senators are chosen by Electors who are chosen by the people, and in the Constitution of the US., they are chosen by the legislatures of each State.

The number of Delegates or Representatives & Senators in each State, is regulated either by descriptions of territory, alloting to such a county or district so many of each, let the population be what it may, or by the scale of population, alloting one rep^e or delegate to 30. 40. 50. or 100.000 & so on progressively. And the same with the senator except that as the number of Senators is in all cases smaller, that of the citizens whom each represents is proportionally increased.

The proportion in numbers between the two houses varies in different states. In none does the Senate approach in point of equality nearer, than in the ratio of 1. to 3. or perhaps 4. The principle upon which the representation in each house was form'd, was that by a very full representation in one house the interests & feelings of the people might be completely represented, & by a thin one in the other the wisdom of the country might be collected in it. The one house was designed as a popular branch, the other as a wise one or board of revision. The experiment however was shewn, that the wisest and most distinguished men generally prefer the most numerous branch, being the theatre wherein to display their talents with greater effect, and in consequence that the other branch is filled by sedate provident old men, who are more distinguished for their gravity & moderation than for their wisdom. This, it is true, is not the case in every instance, for in some instances, the Senate has been filled with men of talents, equal & perhaps superior to any in the other house. The experiment however in America makes it an object of importance, that an experiment sho^d likewise be made somewhere else, of a Senate organized upon different principles than those avowed there precisely in fact upon those of the other branch; the same in point of numbers, terms of service, and qualifications. The presumption is it wo^d possess greater talents, in a higher degree the confidence of the people, & of course that the system of legislation wo^d be wiser & the people happier.

The Executive is in all cases fill'd by a single majistrate. In some States he is allowed a council, consisting of 8. or ten members. Where the governor or <u>chief majistrate</u> has no council he alone is responsible. Where he has one, it is, in case he consults it & which it is his duty to do. In this case the council keeps a journal of its proceedings & which is laid, upon application, before the legislature. In the organization of this branch there seems to be a dilemma unavoidable & of an interesting kind. If you put in the Executive more than one member, certainly if more than 3 or 5 at most, you cannot well have a council: for when the branch is composed of several it is itself a council. It wo^d therefore be improper to have one Executive council, whose business it was simply to Execute the laws, & constituting in truth the Executive power, & another whose business it was to advise <u>this</u> how to execute the laws, & without whose advice it could not act. There seems then only to be this alternative left, either to commit the Executive power to many, 10. 15. or 20. and leave it without a council or check within the department itself, or commit it to one or very few with such council or check, and it is difficult to determine which is preferable.

The Executive Majistrate is chosen in some States by the people at large, being assembled on some day specified in their respective constitutions for that purpose, in the several districts within which they reside. In some by the legislatures of each State, & in the constitution of the U States, by Electors, chosen by the people. The qualifications to the Ch: Majistrate is in general that of citizenship by birth. In those cases wherein that of birth is dispensed with, citizenship for many years is required.

The judicial department or branch, is organized in all the States and in the Constitution of the U. States into superior and inferior tribunals. From the latter there is an appeal to the former, Whereby uniformity of decision is obtained throughout the republick. The judges in the superior courts hold their offices during good behavior, to be determined by impeachment of the house of Delegates or Rep^s, and trial by the Senate. The judgment of the Senate may go to deprivation of office & future disqualification, but to be punished criminally, they must be afterwards tried by the ordinary tribunal. The judges in the inferior courts of the U. States, hold their offices by the same tenure: but those in the inferior courts of some of the individual States hold their offices for shorter terms: in general however they stand on the same ground.

The Executive majistrates, & the Judges have fixed salaries, not to be varied whilst they respectively remain in office, the object of which is to secure and preserve their independance of the legislature.

Dft, NN: Monroe Papers

A clerk's note on the cover reads: "Note about the American constitutions the translation of which was given to M^r derros from the c. of p. s. on 7th of June 1795."

Notes on a Constitution
2: For the National Convention

[June 1795]

A bill of rights sho^d precede the constitution or form of government providing fundamental checks on the exercise of its powers.

The gov^t sho^d be founded on the sovereignty of the people, every officer ~~in every department~~ be elective, and made responsible for a faithful discharge of his duty.

The powers of the gov^t sho^d be vested in three departments, a legislative, Executive, & Judiciary, each of which sho^d be seperate distinct & independant of the other.

The legislative body sho^d be divided into two branches, a house of delegates or rep^s & senate. The first sho^d be the popular branch and have the initiative of laws, the second to be more limited in number & have the negative with the right of proposing amendments. In no case sho^d the house of rep^s exceed the number of 200. or the senate 50. members. They sho^d be elected for the same term, which sho^d be either for one or two years, & by Electors having the same qualifications.

The territory of the Commonwealth sho^d be laid off into counties or districts and the representation in both branches apportioned among them according to the number of free male inhabitants in each qualified to vote for rep^s and senators. A temporary apportionment sho^d be formed in the constitution to put the gov^t in motion, yet it sho^d be the duty of the legislature to cause a census to be taken without delay w^h sho^d be repeated once every ten years by which subsequent ~~elections~~ apportionments sho^d be made.

Every free male inhabitant of the age of 21. years being a citizen & having a fee simple interest in the soil, in such proportion as the legislature shall from time to time direct, who actually resides in the county or district, sho^d have a right to vote for rep^s & senators, and all persons qualified to vote as Electors who shall have resided one year in the district in w^h such election is made sho^d be capable of being elected members of either house, ~~except~~ of the legislature.

The legislature sho^d convene once every year at a time fixed by law.

The House of rep^s sho^d have the sole power of impeachment. The senate the sole power to try impeachments.

Each h: judge of elections &c keep a journal &c.

No member shall be appointed by President—shall be priviledged.

The Executive power sho^d be vested in a ch: majistrate who sho^d be elected annually by the legislative body, be capable of serving three years, & incapable of being elected for the next succeeding three. He sho^d administer the Executive power of the gov^t subject to the check of a council of State, which sho^d consist of not more than seven nor less than five members, to be chosen annually by the legislative body & be capable of reelection. The members of the council sho^d be taken annually from the different parts of the Commonwealth with a view to a representation of the whole. The powers of the gov^r and the council respectively sho^d be correctly defined, to make each answer the object of its institution without giving useless embarrassment to the other. It sho^d be the duty of the gov^r to act, of the council to advise only. They sho^d be distinct & independant of each other in the discharge of their respective duties. The gov^r sho^d have power to convene the council when in his judgment the publick business required it, to submit to it all measures of the department on which the council sho^d give its advice or opinion of which it sho^d keep a journal subject to the inspection of the legislature. The council sho^d not have a right to initiate any proposition, and where it was divided on any submitted to it by the gov^r, the state of the case sho^d be enterd on its journal & the vote of the members. In all cases the gov^r sho^d be a liberty on his own responsibility to act when the council was divided equally, to refuse executing the advice of the council, where his judgment disapproved it, or to act without advice of the council where it was inconvenient to obtain it: but in the latter case it sho^d be his duty to state the occassion to the council in which he thus acted without advice, who sho^d enter the same on their journal with the opinion of the several members on it, in same manner as if the measure had not been taken, for the information of the of the Genl Assembly.

He shall command the militia, communicate to the legislature &c.

shall receive a compensation.

The Govr sho^d have power to convene the legislature in case of emergency.

In case of death &c the President of the council shall act.

The Judicial power sho^d be vested in a court of appeals, and so many inferior courts of common law & ch[ancer]y jurisdiction as the legislature sho^d prescribe. The Judges sho^d be appointed by the legislative body & hold their offices during good behaviour.

Quire what becomes of the county c^ts? What the mode of appointment to office?

~~The object of a bill of rights is to mark the sphere within w^h the gov^t shall move; the boundary over which it shall not leap. All the members of the society who are parties to the social compact have the same interest in the regulations which are made for both purposes. It is a sound political maxim that the gov^t sho^d be unlimited in its power to do good & totally disabled from doing harm. Every member of society is equally interested in having its energies unimpaired for the first object,~~

~~A declaration or bill of rights should form an essential a part of every free government; indeed no gov^t can be perfectly free which does not contain one. There are certain acts which no gov^t sho^d be permitted to perform; there are certain rights which no citizen sho^d be disturbed in the enjoyment of, under any pretext whatever. There is a sphere within which while the gov^t confines itself, it fulfills the end of its institution, and the people are free. There is a hallowed ground over which it space a holy limit beyond which the gov^t must never pass or it tramples on the rights of the people & degenerates into tyranny. While it keeps within that limit the people are free, and the gov^t if wisely administered fulfills the object of its institution. It is easy to enumerate those rights or define that boundary over which the gov^t shall not leap.~~

~~A declaration or bill of rights sho^d form a part of every constitution. If drawn with care it is impossible that it ever sho^d be productive of harm, while it may serve as an useful check on the gov^t in forms a barrier in favor of liberty of the most impregnable force. Every free people have a right to such a fundimental decl^n in their favor, agnst their gov^t, nor can they consider themselves perfectly free or safe without one. Such a decl^n sho^d be confined to certain great and fundimental rights sanctioned by nature, and institutions w^h experience has shewn the utility of beyond all question, such as the liberty of conscious in his religious matters of faith, of speech and of the press, the trial by Jury, habeus corpus &c. It is impossible that any gov^t w^h sought the happiness of the people, of the most energetic kind, sho^d have occasion to infringe their rights. By imposing on it a restraint in that respect, its energy wo^d not~~

~~On what principle does the federalist say that the judiciary can~~ It is admitted in the federalist that the Judiciary can annul a law as unconstitutional but on what principle if the constitution contains no bill of rights engrafted in the instrument or seperate from it? or to what extent can the principle be carried if it applies only to the independance of each department of the other, especially if the organization be simple? what wo^d preclude the gov^t from legislating in the case of Individuals, making ex post facto laws, annulling the trial by jury &c? a simple organizat^n does not necessarily comprize in it a regulation on any of these points.

The gov^t sho^d possess power to do all the possible good in its power, & restrained from doing any harm.

~~A decl^n or bill of rights sho^d form a part of every free gov^t; indeed no gov^t can be perfectly free w^h does not contain one. This doctrine is supported by reasons the most urgent & conclusive. The arguments in favor of this doctrine appear to me to be conclusive, while not a simple object of weight can be urged agnst it.~~

Every gov^t whose powers are not thus limited or restricted may constitutionally enact such laws as those who possess the legislative power are disposed to adopt. I speak not of despotic gov^ts for they are subject to no restraint whatever, being guided by the will of the prince, and are therefore not the object of political inquiry. Free or elective gov^ts may do every thing w^h they are not prohibited doing.

~~Every gov^t whose powers are not thus limited or restricted may constitutionally enact such laws as those who possess the power of making laws are disposed to adopt. This remark is applicable to every species of elective gov^ts, even that w^h is most popular. Where the constitution itself contains no provision agnst the abuse of power, there is always danger of such abuse for w^h plausible pretext will never be wanting. The only difference between elective gov^ts which have no bill of rights the only check~~

~~the gov^t is as unlimited as if it were not elective. The quantum of power is and ought to be as great for useful purposes in elective gov^ts as in despotic. The difference between them consists in its being made subservient from the nature of the instit^n in the one to proper purposes, & in the other to improper. In those elective gov^ts w^h contain no decl^n of rights, the only check agnst the abuse of power consists in their being elective. This is, it is true, a powerful, but it might not always prove a complete one. The passions of men are the same under all gov^ts. Under those of a despotic kind Under those w^h are most free the society may occasionally be divided into parties, which might in their turn persecute each other, by trampling underfoot the soundest principles & most sacred rights. The want of such a decl^n drawn in clear & strong terms, so that every one who read ought understand it The com^n of one crime in individuals often leads to others, and so it is with gov^ts. Ingratitude for friendly offices often ends in a worse requital. The seducer of female inocence, often becomes a murderer of the unhappy victim. Thus a party in possession of the gov^t who had abused its power by every species of fraud peculation and persecution, forseeing an approaching revolution might be disposed in seeking to avoid the consequences to~~

~~go all lengths & usurp the gov.~~ ~~itself. The bill of rights well drawn directed to proper objects might~~
~~check this intemperance of party, & prevent its unhappy effects. Where the object was a sound one, the~~
~~right admitted and well defined, so that he who read might understand it, the leader of a party wo.~~ ~~not be~~
~~apt to yield to passions which wo.~~ ~~expose him to his adversaries & destroy him with his associates. Or if~~
~~the members in the rep.~~ ~~body were capable of being betrayed into such foul excess, the violation wo.~~ ~~be so~~
~~apparant to the people, that it wo.~~ ~~find its remedy in the first election w.~~ ~~ensued.~~

The doctrine of a bill of rights forming a part of free gov^{ts} has been much discussed in these States, from the earliest period of our revolution. The opponents to the doctrine have never met it with a positive denial of its utility that I have heard of. They raise objections, apparently more with a view to tranquilize its advocates, by creating doubts than with the hope or perhaps the design of establishing the contrary doctrine.

The rights which it would be proper to define & secure are not numerous. [They] are the liberty of conscience in matters of religion; the liberty of speech and of the press; the right of trial by Jury, of the habeas corpus.

It is objected that if a single right is omitted in the enumeration, it is implied that that my be trampled under foot. But that objection co^d not have much weight with those who urged it. An elective gov^t in every branch, defended agnst abuse in certain points co^d never degenerate into tyranny. If the rights of the people are protected by a few great outworks they co^d never be assailed with effect. The gov^t wo^d be forc'd to keep an efficient but a harmless course. It wo^d rest on its principles. Responsibly disarmed of the power of doing <illegible> its <illegible> when usurpat^n prevented, it wo^d never do a meanness.

Writers such <illegible>, who speak of a bill of rights seem to have no idea, of original principles or <illegible> Duty.

1. The right of equality. 2. of conscience. 3. of authorising the legislature to impose taxes for supp^t of religion, protest^t, each paying his own parson. IV. The people a right to govern themselves in a free State. 5. publick officers publick servants. VI. no man born a majistrate. 7. people alone have a right to form gov^t for themselves. 8. people a right to make offices rotative. 9. all elections to be free & all inhabitants permitted a right to vote. 10. each individual a right to equal represent^n & laws. 11. each Individual a right to obtain justice from the law &c. 12. no one to answer for crime or offense but on charge described, tried openly, be punished by fair Jury trial, in penal cases. 13. In criminal, vicanage. 14. to be secure agnst unreasonable searches or seizures of his person, houses, or papers; all warrants not supported by oath, and accompanied by special designation of persons &objects, regulated by law, contr^y to this right. 15. trial by jury in civil causes. 16. liberty of the press. 17. to keep & bear arms in common defence, armies dangerous to liberty, military power subordinate. 18. adherence to first principles. 19. The people have a right to assemble, to instruct their rep^s, petition &c. 20. The suspension of laws to be done only by the legislature or ass^y. 21. The freedom of debate in each house absolute, not to prosecute elsewhere or [suit]. 22. The legislature sho^d assemble often. 23. no subsidy &c laid without consent of legislature. 24. ex post facto laws forbidden. 25. No one ought to be declard guilty of treason or felony by the legislature. 26. excessive bail fines or punishments. 27. no soldiers in peace quartered in any house without consent of the owner &c. 28. Law martial for the army or navy only. 29. adm^n of justice to be [pure], the supreme c^ts sho^d therefore be independant. 30. Each departm^t seperate and distinct from the other.

The following are perhaps the only objects to w^h such a decl^n sho^d extend.

A decl^n in favor of equal rights; of the liberty of conscience, in matters of religious faith; of speech and of the press; of the trial by a jury of the vicanage in civil & criminal cases; of the writ of habeas corpus; to be secure agnst unreasonable searches or seizures of persons, houses or papers, agnst excessive bail, fines, or punishments; agnst ex post facto laws; to be secure in the right to keep & bear arms in the common defence, seems to me to comprise every thing that is necessary.

A declaration or bill of rights should form a part of every free government; indeed no government can be perfectly free which does not contain one. This doctrine is supported by many considerations which appear to be strong and conclusive, while not a single weighty objection can be urged agnst it. The truth of this doctrine rests on a [fact] w^h it is proper to advert to in illustration of it.

If the constitution of an elective gov^t does not contain adequate provisions against the abuse of power; it is as unlimited and unrestrained in its measures as an hereditary one. The quantum of power in all gov^ts w^h are completely sovereign, by which I mean power to do good must of necessity be the same. They must all have the power to provide for the publick welfare & be able to inforce an obedience to their laws or they do not merit the name of gov^ts. The difference between an elective and an hereditary government does not consist in the quantum of power which they severally possess, but in the use to which it becomes subservient in each, by the nature of their respective institutions. If an elective gov^t is well organised & properly checked it is harder for it to do wrong, whereas it is hardly possible for a despotic one to do right. It is supposed by many that a dependance on the people for their offices, or the elective property. The elective property alone forms it is true a strong check on the abuse of power, but is not of itself a complete one. The passions of men are the same under all gov^ts. Under those which are elective the society may be divided into parties each of which might occasionally preponderate, and persecute in its turn its adversary, by trampling under foot the soundest principles and most sacred rights. With Individuals the commission of one crime often leads to others still more atrocious. Ingratitude to a generous benefactor for friendly offices frequently ends in a worse requital. The seducer of female inocence often becomes the murderer of the unhappy victim. The same thing may occur in gov^ts. A party in power which had abused its trust by every species of malconduct, forseing an approaching revolution, and dreading its consequences, might be disposed to go to all lengths and commit the highest, last act of incomity by usurping the government itself. A <u>declaration or bill</u> of rights <u>alone</u> can check this intemperance of party, give stability to government or security to liberty. does not weaken the gov^t— but confines it to its duty.

As a declaration or bill of rights is intended only to prevent an abuse of power, it should be drawn in such manner as to answer completely that object without going beyond it. It is a sound political maxim that a gov^t should be unlimited in its power to do good, and totally destitute of the power to do harm. The declaration should be drawn with a view to that great maxim & contain such provisions ~~as [accom=plish] <illegible> object without interfering with the former~~ only as is correspondent with it. If it passed that limit it ~~wo^d counteract the end which it was intended to promote~~ might by tying up the hands of the gov^t improperly clog its motions on many important occasions, when it ought to act.

~~It is not material whether this declaration of rights be plac'd separate from the constitution, or be inserted in the body of the instrument itself. If it qualifies the power of the gov^t in the points to w^h it is intended to be applied, its object is attained and that may be done equally well in either mode.~~ Happily for mankind it is not difficult to adopt a course safe and practical for both objects. Experience has fully demonstrated that the utmost energy of gov^t is stricly compatible with the rights of individuals. that a gov^t becomes even more energetic in proportion as it pursues the legitimate object of its institution.

The following appear to be the most important objects of such an instrument. It sho^d more especially comprize a decl^n in favor of the equality of human rights; of the liberty of conscience in matters of religious faith, of speech and of the press; of the trial by a jury of the vicinage in civil & criminal cases; of the benefit of the writ of habeas corpus; of the right to keep and bear arms; to be secure agnst ex post facto laws, unreasonable searches, or seizure, of persons houses or papers; agnst excessive bail, fines or punishments. If these rights are well defind, and secured against encroachment, it is impossible that the gov^t should ever degenerate into tyranny.

The sovereign power is always an absolute one. restrain majorities. Tis their violence that oversets the State. They do not feel the law. The society loses its balance. It makes the individual, legislator, Judge & Executioner in his own behalf. Under a pretense of protecting the State, & vindicating its honor, it gives a loose to all unworthy passions, & sanctions them by law. Electing or ostracising men, is beneath the dignity of the people

provide the security within themselves, by preventing the passage of a law—gov^t offspring of society—pass its destined objects—while [in] its course it moves like a mechanic power—like the solar system but when it turns its force agnst the society like a comit irregular.

In a gov^t founded in complete sovereignty by compact

The constitution is not a metaphisical power, w^h raises those in office above the people. It is a compact between the people, in w^h each contracts with the whole, the whole with each, what the extent or power of the gov^t shall be over him.

Many are of opinion that the elective property alone forms a sufficient restraint in the abuse of power, but that cannot be supported. It is admitted that it is a great check, the greatest, perhaps the one w^h makes the others of importance, since without it they might be ineffectual: but still it is not a complete one.

gov^t is far from having attained its highest state of perfection while such things may happen under it. It is necessary to ~~controul the passions of men,~~ tie up the hands of majorities as well as of minorities, otherwise it will be impossible to check the intemperance of party, prevent the abuse of power, give stability to gov^t or security to liberty.

To illustrate the subject it will be necessary to recur to some principles

In a gov^t founded by individuals by compact in complete sovereignty, all power is granted w^h is not reserved. ~~It is incompatible with the idea of complete sovereignty~~ It wo^d be a political absurdity to say that a gov^t completely sovereign, whose powers were not checked by a bill of rights, or some other mode ~~w^h qualified the exercise of them~~ co^d not do this or that thing, because it wo^d be oppressive, was agnst principle, was unpopular or for any other reason. ~~In such a gov^t the power to do all things and in any mode that those in office think fit, is given if the contrary is not declared~~ It is inseparable to the idea of complete sovereignty not checked as above, as well in elective as hereditary gov^{ts}, to do every thing and in any mode that those in office thinks fit. Where there is no check ~~of the kind spoken of~~, the elective property forms the only difference between that & ~~an hereditary~~ a despotic gov^t. The power of each is the same except that the laws of the elective be they what they may are constitutional, ~~those of the hereditary are usurped~~ whereas those of the other are not.

~~It is a sound doctrine that the gov^t sho^d be unlimited in its power to do good; that it sho^d only be restrained from doing harm. Such provisions as effected the latter object are those only w^h sho^d be engrafted in the constitution. To carry the provision beyond that point co^d be productive of no benefit, and wo^d therefore be unnecessary. By tying up the hands of the gov^t they might possibly do harm.~~

It is not material whether these fundamental a decl^n of rights be inserted in the constitution or distinct from it. Its object is to restrain the gov^t from doing harm. If it forms a part of the constitution the object is answered.

~~As the design of a bill of rights is to protect the citizens from prevent an abuse of power by those who administer the gov⁺ the end is attained when that object is accomplished. it sho⁴ not go beyond the accomplishm⁺ of the object. It is a sound political maxim that the gov⁺ sho⁴ be unlimited in the power to do good and totally disabled from doing harm.~~

~~As a decl͟ⁿ or bill of rights is intended only to prevent an abuse of power care sho⁴ be taken in the draft to make it answer strictly and completely the object contemplated. It is a sound political maxim that a gov⁺ sho⁴ be unlimited in its power to do good, and rendered totally incapable of doing harm. The decl͟ⁿ of rights sho⁴ accomplish the latter object fully without interfering with the former. If it passed that limit it wo⁴ counteract the end w͟ʰ it was intended to promote. By tying up the hands of the gov⁺ improperly it might clog its motions on many occasions when it ought to act.~~

An organised gov⁺ not checked by a bill of rights, is not otherwise checked than by elections. It may do what any gov⁺ can, responsible to election.

In examining this question it will be proper to form determinate ideas on certain others with w͟ʰ it is connected: ~~we naturally suppose~~ there is such a vast difference between free or elective and hereditary gov͟ᵗˢ, [that] we are apt to conclude that there is no analogy between them; but nothing is more unfounded than such an idea.

If the constitution of an elective gov⁺ does not contain an adequate provision agnst the abuse of power it is as unlimited as if it were hereditary. The quantum of power in all gov͟ᵗˢ must of necessity be the same.

It is not material whether the decl͟ⁿ or bill of rights be plac'd before or after the constitution, or inserted in the body of the instrument itself. If it qualifies the power of the gov⁺ in the points to which it is intended to be applied the object is attained, and that may be equally well effected by either arrangment.

If these rights are well defined and properly secur'd agnst any encroachment of the gov⁺, it is impossible that it sho⁴ ever degenerate into tyranny.

It is the opinion of an enlighten'd writer that the press alone if free is a machine of sufficient force, to overset any despotism however firmly established.

The enjoyment of those rights is indeed the enjoyment of perfect liberty

When these rights exist oppression is unknown. It is &c.

But that is only one of the barriers which it is proposd to erect in favor of liberty. A security of the other rights above enumerated

A restraint or check must be engrafted in the instrum⁺ or there will be none. By the formation of a gov⁺ unlimited power is supposed to be given. It can only by reservations or qualifications. In the case of a federal gov⁺ what is not given remains. But in that case there is already an organized gov⁺ w͟ʰ retains the power not taken from it or transferd to another. But when a gov⁺ in complete sovereignty is formed the opposit principle is true. Then every thing is granted, checked only by election w͟ʰ is not retained.

const͟ⁿ a provision in itself—without resort to popular opposition. Hereditary a revolt.

An elective gov⁺ well checked, agnst abuse & degeneracy can not make a bad law.

Tacitus says Tiberius under the repub͟ᵏ might have been a good repub͟ⁿ.

A bill of rights directed to proper objects and drawn with care, forms the only effectual check agnst this abuse of power, the only impregnable barrier in favor of liberty. The leader of a party wo⁴ not be willing to assail an outwork

~~If the specification is judiciously made, & the right w^h it is intended to secure is well protected, & defined that he who reads may understand~~

If the right w^h it is intended to preserve be judiciously selected & well defined so that he who reads may understand it, it is not probable that any leader of a party wo^d attack an outwork w^h was so redoubtable. He wo^d be more apt to curb than to yield to passions w^h exposed him to his enimies, & destroyed him with his frds.

The object in Engl^d was to check the King—here to check the gov^t. There the gov^t can do every thing.

But sho^d those in power be capable of such intemperance & excess, it cannot be doubted under such circumstances, that the violation wo^d soon find an easy & effectual remedy. The people admonished of a breach of their constitution, by evidence the most satisfactory, wo^d prove true to themselves by remov not fail to remove from their service, at the next election those who had so deservedly lost their confidence

This doctrine has been much discussed in the U States from an early period of our revolution. It passed in review in the formation of every State constitution and in the conventions w^h ratified on the adoption of that federation constitution of the U States; many of w^h have bills of rights, in all are to be seen provisions w^h sanction it.

not material whether they be engrafted in the const^n or plac'd before it.

It is a bill of rights alone w^h can check this intemperance of party; which can controul the turbulent <illegible> oppress'd by passions of majorities, give stability to the gov^t, or safety to liberty.

W^h can controul the passions of those in power, give stability to the gov^t & security to liberty.

An elective gov^t which is well organis'd & protected agnst degeneracy & abuse by a well formed bill of rights, cannot make a bad or rather an oppressive law: whereas an hereditary one may & most probably will in respect to the interest of the great mass of the people.

Dft: NN: Monroe Papers: Miscellaneous and Undated.

JM's note on the cover of this draft reads: "Notes on the subject of a constitution &c. Being applied to by members of the convention of France, for a sketch of our constitution & my own remarks, they were furnished, & these are notes."

The note on the cover of the first document gives the date it was delivered to the Committee of Public Safety, but there is no indication when the second was written. JM makes no mention in his correspondence of being approached by either the Convention or the Committee on the subject, nor does he mention writing these drafts. The notes for the Convention are less structured than those for the Committee, which suggests that they may have been written first. But the difference in contents—the notes for the Convention place great emphasis on a bill of rights while those for the Committee focus on the structure of the government—prevents one from drawing any conclusion about the order in which they were written. They were, however, probably both written at about the same time.

The Convention had been established in September 1792 for the purpose of writing a new constitution following the overthrow of the monarchy. The Convention ratified a constitution on 24 June 1793 that placed control of the national government in the hands of a unicameral assembly that was to represent the will of the people. When the Jacobins gained control of the Convention in October 1793 they declared a national emergency, abrogated the constitution (which had not yet been implemented), and maintained the Convention as the national governing body. The moderates regained power in August 1794, and in the spring of 1795 they turned their attention to enacting a new constitution. Painfully aware of the danger of concentrating power in a single legislative body, they introduced such reforms as a bicameral legislature and a separate executive (Andrew Jainchill, "The Constitution of the Year III...," *French Historical Studies*, 2 (2003): 399-435; Samuel Scott and Barry Rothaus, *Historical Dictionary of the French Revolution*).

The Constitution of 1795 was approved by the Convention on August 22 and proclaimed as ratified by the people on September 23. It is very different from the U.S. Constitution, which defines the powers, duties, and structure of the national government.

The Constitution of 1795 went into great detail about matters of administration and security, issues that in the United States fall under the legislative authority of Congress or the administrative duties of the executive. Articles relating to the structural organization of the government were present in the Constitution of 1795, but they were so buried in the mass of detail that it is impossible to discern any influence that JM's notes may have had on the writing of the constitution. An English translation of the Constitution of 1795 is in John Hall Stewart, *A Documentary Survey of the French Revolution*, 571-612.

From Edmund Randolph

Department of State June 7. 1795

Sir.

The long letter which I have prepared,[1] is at length transmited, and goes by this opportunity. I am afraid that I shall not have time to read it over; tho' if I discover any inaccuracy, I will mention it to you hereafter.

The inclosed letter to Willinck &c[2] contains a draught from M[r] Stephen Girard[3] for forty five thousand guilders specie. Six thousand dollars have been taken from the money of M. de La Fayette and converted into this bill for the use of Madame La Fayette. You will I am sure use it with the best œconomy and judgment.

About twenty five of the Senate are upon the spot, ready for the communication of the treaty with Great Britain tomorrow. I have the honor to be Sir with sincere respect and esteem y[r] mo. ob. serv.

Edm: Randolph

RC, ViFreJM

1. Randolph to JM, 1 June 1795, above.

2. The enclosed letter to Willink and Company has not been located.

3. Stephen Girard (1750-1831) was a French sea captain who settled in Philadelphia in 1776 where he entered the mercantile and exporting trade. He became extremely wealthy. In 1810 he established Girard's Bank, which became one of the leading financial institutions in the United States (*ANB*).

From Stephen Rochefontaine[1]

Philadelphia June the 10th 1795.

Sir,

I have had the honor to inform you, that the President of the United States with the advice and Consent of the Senat, had appointed me L[t] Col. Comd[t] of the Corps of Artillerists & Engineers of the U. S., and the Secretary of war has told me that he had also given an official Notice of it to your Excellency; and requested you would, whenever I should apply to you for it, procure any thing that would be judged by you, usefull for promoting the knowledge and improvement of the Corps of artillerists & Engineers of the United States; I take the liberty Sir, to recommend to the notice of your Excellency, M[r] Vincent,[2] an Engineer of great merit, who has been temporarily employed in this country; he will perhaps be able to procure the books and instruments included in the return transmitted to your Excellency by Col[o] Pickering, thro M[r] Randolph the Secr[y] of State.[3] M[r] Vincent will perhaps give you notice also of new discoveries usefull to this country which you would chuse to procure for the corps.

I would take the liberty to observe to your Excellency, that memoirs, plans, & Models, upon the perfectionment of the artillery and the art of war in general, will be extremely usefull. we stand particularly in need of it for casting the cannon for the navy of the U S; memoirs on the means of purifying the ore; of melting it to a proper degree of heat to cast it into cannon; of the discoveries on the nature of the metal after its 1st fusion from the ore, and on its fusion from the pigs, which of the two is preferable to render the piece tougher. memoirs and models on a Small Scale, would be necessary to show the way of Casting cannon in sand. those models might be made of the same materials and metals, that they are made of, when made in great.

we have procured the plans and instructions of Mal de Castries for the artillery for the navy of France, but this was done in 1786,[4] and since the French Revolution, vast deal of improvement has been made; the newest proportions adopted for the guns and other arms, would be of an amazing advantage to the U S. I therefore beg you would procure as soon as possible, the best plans, profites, & instructions for iron <u>naval artillery</u>, with what will appear to your Excellency the most satisfactory & of the Latest date, upon founderies, and Boring of guns. I am with the greatest respect Sir, Your Excellency's most obedt humble servant

Step: Rochefontaine
Lt Col. Comdt of the corps of artillerists & Engineers

RC, NN: Monroe Papers

1. Stephen Rochefontaine (1755-1814) was born in France and was an officer in the Continental army 1778-1781. He served as commandant of the Corps of Artillerists and Engineers 1795-1798. Rochefontaine started a new military school at West Point in 1795, but the building and his material were burned the following year (Francis B. Heitman, *Historical Register of the Continental Army*; Heitman, *Historical Regiment and Dictionary of the U. S. Army*; Paul K. Walker, *Engineers of Independence: A Documentary History of the Army Engineers in the American Revolution*, 324-325, 366).

2. Charles-Humbert-Marie Vincent (1759-1831) was a French military officer, engineer and diplomat. He arrived in Saint Domingue as a brigadier general in 1786 where he served as director of fortifications. Later Vincent played a major role as military advisor and friend to Toussaint L'Ouverture. Vincent was named chief engineer for the fortification of New York in 1794, and in the spring of 1795 he visited Paris to obtain books and instruments on military subjects (Madison Smart Bell, *Toussaint L'Ouverture*, 218; *Hamilton Papers*, 17: 412-413).

3. Timothy Pickering to JM, 27 April 1795, above.

4. Charles-Eugène, Marquis de Castries, the minister of marine, issued a series of ordinances for the reorganization of the French navy in 1786. The work referred to here may have been the *Ordonnance du roi, concernant le corps-royal de l'artillerie des colonies: du 1er janvier 1786* (*Dictionnaire de Biographie Française*; *National Union Catalogue*).

From Joseph Fenwick

Bordx 11 June 1795.

Sir

By two American vessels in balast from ports in the Chanel I am creditably informed that the English Government has renewed their orders of 6 Novr 1793 to stop all neutral vessels bound to France with provision—indeed three American vessels & two Deans[1] were actually taken, in the presence of the two americans arrived here, manned & sent into England.[2]

I have communicated this information [to] Mr Pinckney who has just reached this and he seems to have no doubt of the Truth of it—as he says he learnt before leaving England indirectly that such orders were secretly issued from the Kings Council.

I shall communicate this information to the Secretary of State by several vessels about to sail for America. I have recd your letter for Mr Short which shall [be] delivered to Mr Pinckney.[3]

There are several late arrivals from America here, every thing appears tranquil there & going on as usual.

There are several letters for you arrived by the late vessels, but the Bearers of them are unwilling to trust them to the post conveyance tho I have advised that I tho^t it a safe chanel—however I am about to send a person to Paris that will depart in three days from this with the courier who will be intrusted I presume with your dispatches.

Provisions are plenty here & the crops promise to be abund^t. I have the honor to be Sir your most obed S^t

Joseph Fenwick

RC, ViFreJM

1. Fenwick probably meant Danes.

2. An order in council of 25 April 1795 authorized British warships to seize neutral vessels carrying provisions to French ports, including those of France's colonies. This measure was seen as a renewal of the orders in council of 8 June 1793 and 6 November 1793 (A. L. Burt, *The United States*, *Great Britain and British North America*, 153; *Jefferson Papers*, 28: 392).

3. Fenwick to Edmund Randolph, 12 June 1795, DNA: RG 59: Despatches from Bordeaux. JM to William Short, 30 May 1795, above.

From Joseph Jones

[12 June 1795]

. . . Taken it out, conclude it is not—the taking out the patent will be expensive and the Taxes imposed on the lands will be bothersome on large and indifferent tracts that produce no profit. there were inducements for selling, but as You think it best to reserve it until your return, I shall take no other step concerning it but inquire concerning the patent which I will get Mr Madison to do when he returns to Philadelphia. If Fowler was to obtain the patent your absence I fear will occasion its being neglected. So soon as I can get clear of my matters here I shall fix in Loudoun if I can get a tolerable house to reside in, in which case I shall pass my time alternately there and in Albemarle. At present I enjoy as good a share of health as can be expected by one of my Years and if I am blessed with a continuation of it, can be more usefull to your as well as my own affairs. I thank you for your attention to Joe,[1] and altho' I am not very anxious ab^t his being versed in greek, it is at least an ornament to be acquainted with the language yet wo^d I not employ his time to be critically nice in it. the Latin & French will be more usefull. I wish him to be improved, and cultivate his mind in usefull knowledge, but above all in moral & virtuous principles—by all means a good man, if possible a wise one. I have yet no letter from him altho' I have written several to him—he should write to me. Keep up if you please his acquaintance with the English language. Mr Swan writes me he is at an Achademy with a Son of Genl Greenes[2] and some other young Americans. If you see proper to remove him do so. The Senate are now met on the Treaty between G. B. & U.S. as yet we have no information respecting its contents or their approbation. Jay is just arrived it is said he has majority for Governor, outvoting Yates. We have reason to fear your wanting bread in France and from late News paper accounts that some great convulsion may be soon expected. It is to be hoped the violence of party will yield to those genuine sentiments and feelings that sho^d actuate the hearts of all French men who wish well to their Country—nothing can more conduce to preserve order and support authority than the establishment of a constitution and a government acting under and in support of its principles. untill this arrangement takes place there will be a continual struggle for superiority among Men who wish to rule. The system once established the constituted authorities will adhere to principles, to lives & landmarks. Adieu happiness attend you.

Jos. Jones.

RC, NN: Monroe Papers. Incomplete—last two pages only. Date written at bottom of letter in JM's hand.

1. Joseph Jones, Jr.

2. Jones's information was incorrect. George Washington Greene (1776-1793), the son of General Nathanael Greene, had been at school in Paris but had returned to the United States in 1793. He drowned shortly after his return home (John and Janet Stegeman, *Caty: A Biography of Catherine Littlefield Greene*, 24-25, 161-162).

To James Madison

Paris June 13. 1795.

Dear [Sir]

I was sometime since fav^d with yours of the 11. of March being the second since I left America. You were I presume soon after the date of that in possession of several from me, of two more especially which opened fully the state of things here under the impression of Mr Jay's treaty, and which state has not been essentially varied since: for as all communication upon the subject of that treaty has to this moment been withheld from me, it was impossible I sho^d alter the impression that was at first made by the reports concerning it. In the interim therefore the opinion of this government is suspended in regard to us. The chagrin however w^h applied in the first instance to the author of the treaty only, upon acc^t of the distrust which was shewn of this government in withholding its contents even from me, has by the continuation of the system, been extended in a great measure to the Executive itself. It is considered here even by the rep^s of the neutral powers as marking a particular harmony with Engl^d and w^h ought to excite uneasiness. You will therefore readily conceive how well disposed the minds of all are to criticise upon that transaction whenever it transpires: and you will likewise be enabled to form a just estimate of the pain & distress of my situation here, & which promises to be encreased in case that transaction is not approved.

As soon as the treaty was signed in Engl^d Mr Jay wrote me it was signed observing that it contained an article which stipulated our other engagments sho^d not be affected by it: and some time after this he wrote me that he intended to communicate to me in <u>confidence</u> the principal heads of the treaty for my use as a <u>publick minister</u>. Upon this, as I found we were losing ground in consequence of that event I sent to him for it, stating my promise to the gov^t to shew to it whatever he sent me: hoping that in case it cont^d any thing improper he wo^d not send it. Upon this application he was greatly wounded upon the score of national dignity &ca, said we were an independant people &ca, and sent nothing, but wo^d write the executive & take its orders, it being obvious that before he co^d receive which, he wo^d embark for America, as it really happened. After this again he sent Col^o Trumbull here (the Col^o having in truth some private business also in Germany) to offer a verbal communication of the contents of the treaty upon condition I wo^d not disclose it. As I had promisd the committee to communicate what I sho^d receive upon the subject & when I sho^d receive it, and which promise was made after my first letter from Mr Jay & which stated that he co^d not communicate it, and of course in the expectation that I sho^d hear nothing on the subject till I heard from America, it followed that I co^d not accept it upon the terms offered by Col. Trumbull. His mission here however excited the displeasure of this government & encreased my embarrassment, for it was suspected that he came upon some business of the Engl^h adm^n (as was published in the Engl^h papers), and was calculated to create a belief that thro him I was possess'd, if I had not been before, of the contents of M[r] Jay's treaty: so that I was plac'd in a dilemma of not only not being able to remove the doubts of the gov[t] as to the contents of this treaty, but likewise of defending my own character from the suspicion of having been acquainted with the negotiation from the beginning & of being of course in great political harmony with M[r] Jay. As I had always fortified myself agnst this very unjust suspicion by frank communications, so I deemed it equally necessary in this instance, & in consequence exposed to the Committee the proposition of M[r] Jay thro' M[r] Trumbull & my refusal to accept it. By this line of conduct together with the concurrent report of all Frenchmen who now are or have been in America, I believe I am free in the estimation of the gov[t] from unjust suspicions: and I likewise believe I shall be free from them let the issue in America (now depending) be what it may. Whether I shall have any weight in case the thing is approvd & is improper, upon the sentiment & measure of the gov[t] here is doubtful.

I find by M[r] Randolph's letter that mine of the 18th of Dec[r] has reached him: I hope you rem[d] in Phil[a] till the 8th of this month & was possess'd of the other letter alluded to above explaining more fully the impression of this gov[t] towards us, for certainly y[r] council in that interesting business wo[d] be of great use to our country, and especially as you would be confided in by many from the Eastward. I will possess you by some safe hand of the correspondence with & respecting M[r] Jay. I will now send you a letter from M[r] Short[1] shewing that if we stood well here we have every thing under our controul with respect to Sp[n] as we certainly had with respect to Engl[d] had it not been thrown away as I fear it has been. This letter is an important document, and ov[er]sets all the reasoning of those who a[re] opposed to the necessity of harmony here to give effect to our negotiations elsewhere.

The movments of the 12. of Germinal & 1st of Prarial have terminated favorably to the objects of the revolution by strengthening the hands of gov[t] & promising some change in the constitution of 1793. upon our principle, a division of the legislature into two branches, &ca which it is expected will be reported by the Committee of 11. who now have that subject under consideration.[2]

I beg of you in particular to shew my communications always to M[r] Jefferson, who I suspect declines intentionally a correspondence from a desire to enjoy free from interruption the comforts of private life: and likewise to M[r] Jones & with respect to others I leave you to Act as you please. We are well & desire to be affec[y] remembered to M[rs] M. y[r] father & his family.

The derangm[t] of Holland by the conquest puts it out of V Stophorts power to advance me money tho' I am convinc'd a loan may be obtaine[d] to purchase land if any bargain offers & of w[h] you will advise me. Sincerely I am y[r] friend & ser[t]

Ja[s] Monroe

A treaty with Holland is made whereby those states are independant, paying 100.000.000. of florins for the expences of the war &ca.

RC, DLC: Madison Papers

1. William Short to JM, 4 May 1795, above.

2. The commission of eleven, appointed on 18 April 1795, produced the Constitution of Year III. (Georges Lefebvre, *The Thermidorians and the Directory*, 176; Martyn Lyons, *France under the Directory*, 21).

To John Quincy Adams

Paris June 14. 1795.

Dear Sir

I was lately fav^d with yours of the 16th ult^o & should have answered it sooner but on acc^t of the disturbances which existed here at the time, & the necessity of preparing a communication for America immediately after they subsided.[1]

Your letters for Mr Pinckney were presented him in his rout thro' Paris for Madrid. He staid here ab^t 10. days, in the course of which he was a spectator of the interesting movement which commenc'd on the first of Prarial & ended a few days afterwards, so favorably in respect to the authority of the Convention as well as the cause of humanity. He is now perhaps at Bordeaux.

The claims you have been pleased to mention of some of our countrymen founded upon injuries rec^d in Holland from the French troops there shall be duly attended to when they are brought forward by the parties affected & with the evidence necessary to support them. A doubt may however arise upon the case of American property taken in a Russian ship, under the treaty between France & the U States, for as by it the customary law of nations, which gives security to the goods of a friend in an enemy's vessel is done away, for the superior and more important priviledge of protecting in the bottom of a friend enemies goods, I can not see and especially since the treaty has been carried into effect by this republick how the claim can be supported. I make this observation however for y^r consideration, for it will be my wish to press the claim of course provided it is bro^t forward & can be pressd with propriety.

The late movment has tended more effectually than heretofore to establish the authority of the Convention: before this event many doubted whether upon a fair experiment, (for the former one was crushed in the commenc'ment,) that body wo^d be able to sustain itself in case its authority was for awhile suspended & the confusion following such an event made complete. Many too believed that in such case the reorganization wo^d commence on other principles, than those the revolution acknowledges, & were therefore willing to hazard for awhile the reign of chaos in hope of that chance. Those speculations were however rejected by the late experiment, for it was proven, that the only way to preserve order or safety, is to support the convention & which has in consequence enlisted under its banner some who are not otherwise very friendly to that body. I commit this to the care of Captn Spring who expresses a wish that I sho^d make him known to you as an American, & to which claim to respect I can add that he served (according to what I have understood) with reputation thro' the American war as an officer in our service. With great respect & esteem I am dear Sir sincerely yours

Ja^s Monroe

I enclose you a letter from the Secr^y of State lately rec^d.

RC, MHi: Adams Family Papers: Letters Received

1. JM to Edmund Randolph, 14 June 1795, below.

To Edmund Randolph

Paris June 14$\underline{^{th}}$ 1795.

Sir,

It seemed probable after the movement of the 12. Germinal (2$\underline{^{nd}}$ of April) and which terminated in the banishment or rather deportation (for the hand of Government was never withdrawn from them) of Barrere, Billaud de Varennes and Collot d'Herbois, and the arrestation of several of the leading members in the mountain party that the convention would be left at liberty, to pursue for the future the great object of the revolution, and without further molestation. And the calm which ensued for a considerable time that movement, although the scarcity of bread continued, gave strength to this presumption. But a late event has shewn that the victory which was gained upon that occasion, by the convention, over the enemies of the present system was not so decisive as there was reason to presume it would be; for within a few days after my last, which was of the 17$\underline{^{th}}$ of May, another attempt was made upon that body, and which menaced for a while, at least in respect to the personal safety of the members, the most alarming consequences. I am happy however to be able now to assure you, that this has likewise failed, and without producing, according to present prospects and in regard to the main course of the revolution, any material effect.[1]

The circumstances which characterize this latter movement were in general the same with those of that which preceded it, except that it was attended with greater violence and its views were more completely unfolded. On the 20$\underline{^{th}}$ of May a party from the fauburgs of St Antoine and St Marceau armed and consisting of several thousands, approached the convention early in the morning, having previously circulated a paper declaring that their object was a redress of grievances, of which the scarcity of bread was the principal, and which could only be accomplished by the establishment of the constitution of 1793, and the recal of Barrere and his colleagues, or in other words the revival of the reign of terror. As these measures could not be carried into immediate effect, without the overthrow of the preponderating party, so the movement appeared to be directed unequivocally to that object. The centinels of the convention were forced upon the first approach, and in an instant the party, preceded by a legion of Women, entered and spread itself throughout the hall of that assembly. The sitting was broken and every thing in the utmost confusion. In a contest which took place between Ferraud[2]—one of the deputies, (a gallant and estimable young man) and some of the party, for the protection of the chair and person of the President, which were threatened with violation, the former was slain, and soon afterward his head was severed from his body and borne on a pike, by the perpetrator of this atrocious crime in triumph into the bosom of the convention itself. It really seemed for some time as if that body, or at least the leading members in the preponderating party, were doomed to destruction, or safety to be secured only by disguise and flight. During this conflict however the whole assembly behaved with the utmost magnanimity; no symptoms of fear were betrayed, no disposition to yield or otherwise dishonour the great theatre on which they stood: and Boissy d'Anglas, who happened to preside, not only kept his seat, but observed in his deportment a calmness and composure which became the dignified and important station which he filled. This state of confusion lasted 'till about 12. at night, when it was terminated by the decisive effort of a body gathered from the neighbouring sections, planned by the U. Committees of public safety, surety general and militaire, and led on by several deputies, among whom were most distinguished Bervelegan,[3] Anguis,[4] Mathieu,[5] Delmas,[6] Freron[7] and Legendre. They entered precipitately the hall, attacked the intruders, sabre and bayonet in hand, nor did they cease the charge until they had rescued it from the profanation. A little after 12 the convention was reestablished, and proceeded as upon the former occasion, to a review of what had passed in the course of the day.

Whilst the insurgents were in possession of the reigns of government, and after Boissy d'Anglas had retired, they placed the President, Vernier,[8] in the chair by force, and began an organization upon the principles that were first avowed. They repealed in a mass all the laws that were passed since the 9th of Thermidor; recalled Barrere, Billaud de Varennes and Collot d'Herbois; took possession of the tocsin and the telegraphe;[9] ordered the barriers of the city to be closed, and were upon the point of arresting all the members of the committees of the Executive branch, having appointed a commission of four deputies to take their places and with full power to act in their stead, so that in truth the reign of terror was nearly revived and with accumulated force. At this moment however, the plan of the committees who had continued their sitting, was ripe for execution, and fortunately the stroke was given before the system was completed.

But the commotion was not ended by the expulsion of the insurgents from the hall of the convention itself. They retreated back to the Fauburgs to which they belonged, and where for a while they opposed its authority. In the course however of the succeeding day a considerable force was collected, under the authority of the convention, from those sections who voluntarily offered their service, amounting perhaps to 20 thousand, and which being marched against them in different directions, surrounding in a great measure both fauburgs, reduced them immediately to order, and without the effusion of blood.

On the same day an insurrection took place at Toulon of the same kind and with the same objects in view, and which for several days wrested that port and its dependencies, the fleet excepted, from the authority of the government. Upon that theatre too, some outrages were committed, and fatal consequences in other respects were apprehended. But this was likewise lately suppressed by the efforts of good citizens, drawn by the representatives in mission there, from Marseilles and the neighbouring country, a report to that effect being yesterday presented to the convention by the committee of public safety: so that order may be considered as completely reestablished the authority of the convention being triumphant every where.[10]

As soon as the convention resumed its deliberations, the punishment of those who had offended in the course of the commotion was the first object which engaged its attention. Whilst the insurgents were in possession of the hall and enacting their short but comprehensive code of legislation, several members of the mountain party not only retained their seats but joined in the work. Four were appointed to the commission which was designed to supersede the Executive administration and who accepted the trust. These circumstances with many others which occurred, created a belief that the movement was in harmony with that party. It was therefore concluded that more decisive measures ought to be taken with those members and with the party generally, than had been heretofore adopted, and in consequence about 30 of them were arrested on that and the succeeding days within the course of a week, and who are to be tried, according to a late decree, in common with others charged with offences, said to be committed in the course of the commotion, by a military commission appointed at the time and invested with full power for that purpose.

It is to be observed that the character of this movement was decisively antimonarchical: its success if it had succeeded, would have revived the reign of terror and most probably carried eventually all the aristocrats with the leading members of the preponderating party to the scaffold. Bread and the constitution of 1793 were written upon the hats of many of the insurgents, and whilst the hall and its vicinity resounded in favour of the patriots meaning Barrere &c, the feeble voice of one solitary aristocrat only was heard in favor of the constitution of 1789. Indeed the aristocrats who had before the 12th of Germinal contributed much to foment the discontents which broke out on that day, in the hope that if a commotion took place and the convention was overthrown, the standard of Royalty would be erected and the monarchy reestablished and who were in the interval from the dubious character of that movement, which was crushed before it had fully unfolded itself, of neither side, for nor against the convention, were observed in the commencement of this to remain in the same state of inactivity, greatly agitated but taking no part. As soon however as the object of this latter movement was understood, and it became obvious that in case it succeeded, terrorism and not royalty would be reestablished, the disposition of this party towards the convention changed: it no longer shewed an indifference to its welfare; on the contrary it became active in its support.

But in truth the force of this party, in this City, and especially upon the late emergencies did not appear to be great. The most gallant of its members are either upon the frontiers at war against the republic, or have fallen already in the cause of royalty. These too consists of those who were of sufficient age to take their parts in the commencement, for the young men of Paris who are descended from it, or from others of the more wealthy inhabitants of the city, and who have attained their maturity during the revolution, or are now growing up, have imbibed the spirit which it was natural to expect such splendid examples of patriotism would create upon young and generous minds, and are in general on the side of the revolution.

That there should be a party of any force within the republic, or rather of sufficient force to disturb the government in the manner we have seen, disposed to subvert the present system and reestablish that of terror, must excite your surprise. You will naturally be inclined to ask of what character of citizens is it composed, what their numbers and ultimate views, since it is to be presumed that a system of terror as a permanent system of government, cannot be wished by any one? You have seen that the movement in question proceeded principally from the Faubourgs of St Antoine and Marceau. The inquiry therefore will be satisfied by exposing the character of those sections. In general I am told they are artisans and among the most industrious in Paris. Many of them are said to be foreigners, Germans, and which explains the motive of their partiality for the constitution of 1793: which naturalizes them. That they are opposed to monarchy is certain, for such has been their character from the epoch of the destruction of the bastile, in which they had a principal hand, to the present time. Indeed upon this point the late movements speak with peculiar force, for if those movements were spontaneous and commenced by the people themselves, it follows, as they cannot be suspected of any deep political finesse, and of aiming at royalty through the medium of terrorism, that the latter and not the former was the object. And if they were set on foot by foreign influence, as is believed by many, the conclusion must be the same, for as royalty is unquestionably the object of those powers who are suspected of such interference, it is to be presumed that if practicable they would have taken a more direct course to promote it, by an immediate declaration in its favour, since thereby they would rally under its standard all those who were the friends of that system: whereas by declaring in favour of terrorism the opposite effect was produced, for the royalists themselves were thereby driven into the expedient of using their utmost endeavours to save the convention, as the only means whereby they could save themselves. In every view therefore they must be deemed enemies to royalty, and as such it is natural to expect they will feel a great sensibility upon all those questions which in their judgment have a tendency to promote it. Whether any such have been agitated or contemplated, is perhaps doubtful: I have thought otherwise and still think so. But that many circumstances have presented themselves in the course of the collision of parties, that were sufficient to create a suspicion with persons, of that portion of discernment which laborious artizans usually possess, that the leading members of the preponderating party, were disposed to abandon the republican scale, and incline towards monarchy, is certain. The inhabitants of these Fauburgs, having sided always with the mountain party, have of course brought upon themselves the particular enmity of the royalists. They have therefore, or rather their leaders have been, in their turn, persecuted by the royalists. But they have likewise thought themselves persecuted by the present preponderating party with whom they were engaged in uninterrupted warfare, before and since the time of Robespierre. In this respect therefore they saw the present preponderating party and the royalists, acting apparantly in harmony together, and concluded that the former were likewise royalists. They have likewise seen under the administration of this party the royalists enlarged from prison, and other measures of that kind adopted which have probably fortified them in this belief. A report too which has been circulated through the City that under the name of organic laws, it is contemplated by the committee of 11 to introduce some important changes in the constitution of 1793, has no doubt tended in a great measure to increase their disquietude. In an attempt to explain the cause of these movements the above circumstances have appeared to me to merit attention and with that view I have presented them.

But that there was no real harmony of political views between the present preponderating party and the royalists, even with respect to the terrorists, is a fact of which I have no doubt. The reign of terror continued until it could last no longer; it was necessary to suppress it and it was suppressed. That the royalists wished this event and gave it all the aid they could, is certain: but that their efforts were of any service in that respect, is doubtful: indeed I was persuaded that for some time they produced the opposite effect, and for reasons that are obvious: for as the preponderating party sought the establishment of the republic, and knew that the mountain party had the same object in view, it was reasonable to expect that after the former had gained the ascendency, it would be disposed to exercise towards the latter some degree of moderation and humanity, and equally so to presume that the same spirit of magnanimity which inculcated this disposition towards its antagonist, chiefly from a respect for its political principles, would dispose it to reject with disdain the aid of the royalists who were enemies to both. This sentiment I think is to be traced through all the measures of the convention from the 9th of Thermidor to the 1st of Praireal: for we behold through that interval, the preponderating party rescuing from the guillotine and prison, the royalists, whilst they reprobated their principles, and terminating in other respects the reign of terror, whilst they avoided as far as was possible the punishment of those who had been the principal authors and agents under that reign. Indeed this party has appeared to me to be, and so I have often represented it to you, as equally the enemy of the opposite extremes of royalty and anarchy; as resting upon the interest and the wishes of the great mass of the French people, and who I have concluded and from those data the revolution itself has furnished, as well as from my own observations since my arrival, (the latter of which it is true has been confined to a small circle) are desirous of a free republican government: one which should be so organized as to guard them against the pernicious consequences that always attend, a degeneracy into either of those extremes.

You will likewise ask what effect have these movements had upon the public mind in regard to the present system? Is it[11] not probable they have already wearied the people out and in consequence inclined them to royalty merely from a desire of repose? That they are all wearied is most certain, and what may be the course of events in the progress of time I do not pretend to determine. These lye beyond my reach and indeed beyond the reach of all men. I only undertake to deduce immediate consequences from the facts which I witness: and when I see that these movements have produced upon the royalists themselves the opposite effect, and forced them at least for the present, to renounce their creed and cling to the convention for their safety, I cannot presume that the moderatists, who are republicans, will quit the safe ground, on which they rest, their own ground too, and become royalists. Royalty therefore, I consider at present as altogether out of the question. But that these convulsive shocks, and which proceed from the opposite extreme, may produce some effect, is probable. In my opinion they will produce a good one; for I am persuaded they will occasion, and upon the report of the committee of 11, some very important changes in the constitution of 1793, such as a division of the legislature into two branches, with an organization of the executive and judiciary upon more independent principles than that constitution admits of; upon those principles indeed which exist in the American constitutions, and are well understood there. Should this be the case the republican system will have a fair experiment here, and that it may be the case must be the wish of all those who are the friends of humanity every where.

On the day that this late commotion commenced Mr Pinckney arrived here on his way to Madrid, and was a spectator of the great scene it exhibited to the close: a few days after which he pursued his rout by the way of Bourdeaux, where before this he is probably arrived. Whilst here I presented to his view what had passed between this government and myself upon the subject of his mission, assuring him from what I had heard and seen that I was of opinion that in case he would explain himself to the committee upon that subject, and express a wish they would give what aid they conveniently could, in support of his negotiation, satisfying them at the same time that they were not injured by Mr Jay's treaty, they would do it. I likewise shewed him a letter I had just before received from Mr Short, written at the instance of the Duke de la Alcudia, to request that I would promote by certain communications to this government, a negotiation between Spain and this republic, he having previously and positively assured Mr Short, that our demands should be yielded and adjusted at the same time.[12] Mr Pinckney was sensible of the benefit which the aid of this republic would yield, in his negotiation and wished it: but upon mature consideration he was of opinion he could not request such aid without having previously exposed to view Mr Jay's treaty, and which he did not chuse to do, for considerations delicacy forbade me to inquire into. It was however equally his and my wish that his journey through the country, should be marked with all those circumstances of reciprocal civility between the government and himself, which are always due and generally paid, when the Minister of a friendly power passes through the territory of another, and in consequence I announced his arrival to the committee and obtained for him an amicable interview, with the members of its diplomatic section, and by whom he was received with the most perfect attention.

You have already seen that England and Spain are each and without the knowledge of the other, seeking a separate peace with this republic. What the motive for such secrecy on the part of the former is, remains to be hereafter unfolded: but what it is on the part of the latter is easily understood: for as she apprehends in case a peace with France is made a declaration of war from England, and of course in case the attempt to obtain a peace is known, some new pressure from that power, it follows that she must wish the arrangement to be complete, to guard her against the ill consequences which might otherwise attend such an event, before any thing upon that head transpires. As soon however as it is known to Spain that England seeks a separate peace, her jealousy of the views of England will be increased, as likewise will be the motive for an immediate accomodation with this republic. The period therefore, when a good understanding embracing perhaps the ancient connection between the two nations will be revived, cannot be considered as remote. Whether our claims upon Spain will be attended to render existing circumstances in that adjustment is a point upon which it is impossible for me to determine; for as I was not possessed of Mr Jay's treaty, and could give no other information on that head than I had before given, I have latterly forborne all further communication with the committee upon that subject. Mr Pinckney will be able soon after his arrival at Madrid, to ascertain the temper of the Spanish court in regard to our demands, and the means by which his negotiation may be forwarded; and as he likewise knows the state of things here, he will be able also to point out the line in which, if in any, I may be serviceable: and in the interim I shall not only be prepared to co-operate with him in whatever movement he may suggest but to obey with promptitude any instructions you may be pleased to give me in this or any other, respect.

Since my last the treaty with the U. Provinces has been concluded and ratified, of which I send you a copy; and the garrison of Luxembourg consisting of 12,000 men with an immense amount of military Stores cannon &c has surrendered.[13] The achievement of this post, one of the strongest in Europe, has opened the campaign on the part of France with great brilliancy: as it was taken too after a long siege, and when all possible efforts to raise it had proved abortive, it not only demonstrates the superiority of the French arms in the present stage of the war, but furnishes satisfactory ground whereon to calculate, according to the ordinary course of events, its ultimate issue.

You will perhaps have heard before this, that the British have recommenced[14] the seizure of our vessels laden with provisions destined for the ports of this republic. An American just from Hamburgh charged with other articles, informed me the other day that he was boarded on his way by two frigates whose officers informed him, they were ordered to take in all vessels thus laden.

Within a few days past the son of the late King departed this life.[15] A minute report will be published by the government of his decline, having lingered for some time past, and of the care that was taken to preserve him. They are aware of the criticisms to which this event may expose them, and suffer on that account an additional mortification. His concession to Spain as was contemplated, made his life with the government an object of interest, since it would have forwarded in some respect its views in the depending negotiation.

I have just been honoured with yours of April 7th and shall pay due attention to its contents, being with great respect and esteem your most obedient and very humble servant.

Jas Monroe.

P. S. I am sorry to inform you of the death of Mr Coffyn, Consul for the port of Dunkirk. His loss is to be regretted as he was able, diligent and faithful in the discharge of the duties of his office. His son is very desirous of succeeding him and certainly if anyone not an American is appointed, it will be impossible to find for it a more suitable person. In my opinion however Americans only should be appointed. In any event I think the merits of the Father who was distinguished for his services and attachment to our country entitle his memory to some attention and doubt not your letter of acknowledgment addressed to his Son on that head through me will be gratefully received.

Copy, DNA: RG 59: Dispatches from France

1. After the riots of Germinal (1 April 1795) involving 10,000 protestors, the Convention failed to act decisively to relieve the food shortages. Protest leaders formed a central committee of insurrection located on a street near Montmartre and made plans for a second protest. They drew up a manifest composed of eleven articles, which they had printed and distributed throughout Paris on May 19. The manifest enjoined the people living in the capital to gather enmasse at the Convention. The next day (1 Prairial) women formed the vanguard of the protestors who surrounded the hall of the Convention. The deputies, trapped inside by the hostile crowd, decided to remain through the night and continued to work. When the mob forced its way into the chamber some time after 11 p.m. Vernier, the president of the Convention, attempted to bargain with them, but his vacillating appearance had little effect. After thirty minutes of confusion, Boissy d'Anglas assumed control by rising to address the deputies and in calling for a general to occupy the President's chair. Around two in the morning some order was regained; but, when the mob broke through the doors for the third time and deputy Féraud was killed, Boissy rose from his seat, and with great self-control stared down the rioters. Legendre went out for reinforcements that finally appeared after three in the morning in the form of the National Guard (M. A Tiers, *Histoire de la Révolution Française,* 7: 202 ff; John R. Ballard, *Continuity during the Storm, Boissy d'Anglas and the Era of the French Revolution,* 100-101).

2. Jean-Bertrand Féraud (1764-1795), a deputy in the National Convention, had played a role in supplying food to the city of Paris during the month of April, when the daily distribution of bread declined to a ration of two ounces a day, producing a situation of near-famine (J. Sydenham, *The First French Republic, 1792-1804,* pp.44, 50-51).

3. Augustin-Bernard-François Kervélégan (1748-1825), after his election as a deputy from Finisterre, allied himself with the Girondists at the Convention. When the Girondists were arrested in June 1793, Kervélégan was able to escape to Brittany. He returned to Paris in March 1795, and served on the Committee of General Security from May to September and from October 7 to the end of the session (Jules Michelet, *Histoire de la Revolution Française,* 2: 1454; August Kuscinski, *Dictionnaire des Conventionnels).*

4. Pierre-Jean Baptiste Auguis (1747-1810) volunteered for military service in 1790. He represented Deux-Sèvres (near Poitiers) at the Convention in which he chose to sit with members on the political right. He entered the Committee of General Security on 3 February 1795, and was the commander of the National Guard in Paris during the insurrection of May 1795 (Kuscinski, *Dictionnaire des Conventionnels*).

5. Jean-Baptiste-Charles Mathieu (1763-1833) was a deputy from Oise and resided in Quimper. He served as a member of the Committee of Public Safety, 30 May - 22 June 1793, and was chosen to help draw up the Constitution of 1793. He served as president of the National Convention 26 May - 3 June 1795 (H. Morse Stephens' *A History of the French Revolution*, 2: 521, 535-536, 540).

6. Jean-Francois-Bertrand Delmas (1751-1798) was born in Toulouse to a bourgeois family. After a military career in which he rose to the rank of general, Delmas was elected in 1791 to the Legislative Assembly, and in 1792 elected as a member of the National Convention. He entered the Committee of Public Safety at its creation in April 1793 and returned to the same committee in early September 1794, where he sat until January 1795 (*Dictionnaire Biographie Française*).

7. Stanislas-Louis Fréron (1754-1802) was an aristocrat who threw himself into the Revolution on the side of the radical Jacobins. He entered the National Convention in 1792, after having founded the *Orateur du Peuple* in 1789, a newspaper similar in tone to Marat's *L'Ami du Peuple*. Sent with Barras to the southeast at the end of 1793, Fréron employed "terror as the order of the day," to condemn 400 people to death at Marseilles and have 800 inhabitants shot at Toulon. After Thermidor, as head of the Muscadins and *la Jeunesse dorée*, Fréron allowed Republicans to be attacked in the streets of Paris. When deputy Féraud was killed on 1 Prairial (20 May 1795) it was rumored that the mob had mistaken him for Fréron (Kuscinski, *Dictionnaire des Conventionnels*).

8. Théodore Vernier (1734-1818) was a lawyer whose primary interest was financial affairs. A deputy from the Jura to the Convention, he professed to represent no political party. He opposed the Revolutionary Tribunal, was denounced by Bourdon, and escaped to Switzerland. Recalled on 8 December 1794, he became a member of the Committee of Public Safety on 4 May 1795. The next day he was named president of the Convention (Kuscinski, *Dictionnaire des Conventionnels*).

9. The first practical telegraph system in the world was inaugurated in France by Claude Chappe on 12 July 1793 using semaphore (flag) messages. In the weeks following, the Convention authorized the creation of a French state telegraph and the construction of the first line of fifteen stations from Paris to Lille (Alexander J. Field, "French Optical Telegraphy, 1793-1855," *Technology and Culture*, 35: 315-347).

10. The Jacobins in Toulon revolted on 17 May 1795 and gained control the city for four days. They arrested returned émigrés, and subsequently marched on Marseilles to liberate other Jacobins imprisoned there. The representatives of the Convention who were on mission in Marseilles organized a force composed of the National Guard and royalists that attacked and routed the Toulonnais (Jacques Godechot, *The Counter-Revolution: Doctrine* and *Action, 1789-1804*, 253).

11. The copyist wrote "It is".

12. William Short to JM, 4 May 1795, above.

13. The siege of the city of Luxembourg took place from January to June 1795. The garrison capitulated on June 7 (Steven T. Ross, *Historical Dictionary of the Wars of the French Revolution*, 98).

14. The copyist wrote "recommended".

15. Louis-Charles (1785-1795), regarded by French royalists as Louis XVII after the death of his father, was imprisoned in Paris where he died of tuberculosis on 8 June 1795 (*La Grande Encyclopédie*).

From Thomas Pinckney

Bayonne 27 Prairial l'an 3<u>me</u> [15 June 1795]

My dear Sir

I am unwilling to leave France without once more returning my thanks to you for your attentions during my residence at Paris & for the requisition for horses which was delivered to me by M<u>r</u> Fenwick at Bordeaux[1]—I found a fine Country, well cultivated & promising a good harvest between Paris & Bordeaux, but I could not perform the journey in less than 8 days, on account of the weakness of the Post horses & the backwardness of those employed in furnishing them; who in fact at the present prices must be ruined—by paying extraordinary prices occasionally we however contrived to travel about 50 miles a day. We came at about the same rate from Bordeaux here but on this journey, in addition to high prices, we were obliged to expend a great deal of patience & to endure much fatigue; we were yesterday twenty hours in the carriage, & have, great part of the way from Bordeaux, been drawn by oxen. On Almost the whole of this last road, the adjacent Country appeared to me to be worse than the sandiest & most barren parts of the Southern States.—the inhabitants derive a scanty subsistance from their flocks of Goats & Sheep & a few of the larger Cattle.—the land only produces thin crops of Rye & the best of it some Indian Corn for which they are obliged to manure highly.—I have received every possible attention & accomodation from the Representatives of the People at this place for which, if an opportunity should offer, I beg you to express my gratitude. I am sure I have no occasion again to recommend my poor little ones to your protection and the good offices of M<u>rs</u> Monroe, but your own feelings will I know excuse me for not being able to conclude my letter without mentioning them to you[2]—Be pleased to accept & to offer to M<u>rs</u> Monroe the best wishes & sincere regards of your [torn]

Thomas Pin[ckney]

RC, ViFreJM

1. At JM's request, the Committee of Public Safety issued an order that horses be made available to Pinckney for his journey from Paris to Spain (JM to the Commissary of Foreign Relations, 31 May 1795 and Jean Victor Colchen to JM, 2 June 1795, DLC: FCP—France).

2. Pinckney left his son at his school in London, but he placed his daughters with Madame Campan in St. Germain at the school attended by Eliza Monroe. James and Elizabeth Monroe acted as guardians for the girls during Pinckney's absence (Frances Leigh Williams, *A Founding Family: The Pinckneys of South Carolina*, 305; DLC: Monroe Papers: Account Book).

To the U. S. Consuls in France

Circular

Paris 17. June 1795.

Sir

Complaint has been made to me by the commissary of foreign relations that our consuls and in some cases their agents have granted passports and certificates under the authority of which the bearers are permitted to travel thro' the interior of France and likewise into foreign countries.[1] He observed that by the law of France and of nations, no person other than the minister of a foreign power has a right to grant such passports; and that it is likewise unnecessary, since for the interior passage the passport of the municipality of the port where such persons land is sufficient, and for the exterior or to go without the Republick that of the minister alone ought to be granted, for if the party desirous of withdrawing, enters the ports of the Republick in the ordinary course of trade none is necessary to enable him to withdraw from it. And if he was brought in by the ships of the Republick taken on board those of its enemies, then his case which is always doubtful merits attention and should be examined and determined upon the evidence furnished, by the minister alone, who is more immediately responsible to the government in that respect. These observations appear to me to be just and according to the law of nations. I have therefore thought it my duty to make known to you the desire of this government upon that subject, and to request your punctual observance of it.

In those cases where our fellow citizens are permitted to depart from the Republick by existing decrees in the ordinary course of trade as above mentioned, but are improperly impeded by some circumstance or other, you will of course observe by application to the municipality or other suitable authority that the benefit of those decrees is extended to them: and in all those cases where my passports are necessary, and the parties are not able to attend here in person, you will be pleased to represent to me their pretentions, provided you think them well founded, with the evidence adduced to support those of each applicant. In such cases it will not be necessary to transmit copies of each certificate or other document laid before [you]: it will be suficient that you state in a certificate under the seal of the consulate the purport of each item of testimony, by whom furnished, and whether Americans or foreigners, the former of which are always to be preferred, because as the citizens of the United States have an interest in the character of their country, so it is to be presumed they will always be on their guard not to injure that character, by imposing on its representative here.

In describing the pretentions of those who ask for passports you will be pleased to state how they came into the Republick and what their occupation is: you will likewise observe that as there are two descriptions of persons whose claims are deemed inadmissable by the government here so it will in general be unnecessary for you to bring them forward. The first of these consists of those who having become Citizens of some state since our revolution, have left us and now reside in the country from whence they emigrated: for such persons being likewise subjects of the power where they were born, ought to be deemed here citizens of that country only to which they have given the preference by residence. The second consists of those who were refugees in the course of our revolution, and who have never returned or acquired the right of citizenship since. Such cannot be deemed citizens whether born in America or elsewhere. In all doubtful cases however you will be pleased to submit the pretentions of the parties to me that regarding principles I may pay all possible attention to them, that circumstances will admit of.

Upon ordinary commercial concerns in which my support may be deemed necessary, I shall thank you to communicate with me as heretofore through Mr Skipwith the Consul in this city: for as he is charged with those concerns and obtains redress if possible without my intervention, he is thereby enabled officially to report to me correctly, those cases in which he cannot succeed, and of course in which my interference may be useful: and which report forms generally the basis of my application. I am, Sir, respectfully Your most obed^t Servt

Ja^s Monroe

FC, NN: Monroe Papers

The recipients of this circular letter were the five American consuls in France: Joseph Fenwick at Bordeaux, Stephen Cathalan at Marsailles, Francis Coffyn at Dunkirk, Pierre Dobrée at Nantes, and Claude-Adam Delamotte at Havre.

1. Jean-Victor Colchen wrote to JM on 10 June 1795 asking him to instruct the American consuls not to issue passports (*Writings of Monroe*, 2: 320).

From David Gelston

New York June 18th 1795

Dear Sir

I am now favoured with your very obliging and Friendly Letter of 10th Feby last.[1] your very kind care and attention to my Son[2] impresses my mind with the highest sensibility and lays me under greater obligation than I ever [can] possibly discharge unless the sincerest gratitude can be accepted at least in some part as an acknowlegement. for the remainder the obligation must continue on forever. respecting the advances you have made or may make they shall be discharged immediately on your informing me the manner in which you wish me to do it. I trust however that before this reaches you my Son will have it in his power to reimburse you all the pecuniary supplies you have advansed as I have made him three different Shipments amount of the whole say 12 to 14.000 Dollars. if they all fail I have obtained Drafts on France to a considerable Amount. if these also miscarry I must then intreat you would advance the necessary sums as usual until I can be fortunate enough to succeed in a remittance.

I wrote you 24 & 27 of March 1^d of May & 5 Ins^t to all which please be refferred.[3] I have rec^d letters from my son. he feels the same sentiments of gratitude and respect for your care and attention that I have expressed. in all my letters to him I have charged him not to be troublesome but to observe with the most scrupulous exactness all your directions and advice. he writes me he does. I hope he will continue to deserve your Friendship and confidence.

The information you give me respecting the Situation of Europe is truly interesting. the communications respecting the happy Situation of the Republic of France delight my soul. may they go on and prosper is my ardent wish that they may completely humble the pride of that haughty imperious insulting tyranic plundering Nation the British. I as devoutly wish as I do that the Republic may deserve command and enjoy [respect] from and with all the world. besides in a word I wish the whole British navy totally annihilated. pardon these effusions. I would not add more to this already too long letter but I must tell you Citizen Adet has arrived. the Senate of the U. S. met on tuesday the 8th Ins^t on the Treaty. Doors are shut, the most profound secrecy is observed, not even a conjecture is hazarded. if I had not writen so long a letter I should venture some observations.

Mr Jay has arrived a few weeks since. he has been elected Governor of this State over our worthy Friend. Govr Clinton has been very ill for some more than six Months. his affections & regards to you please accept from me in the sincerest manner. Col^o Burr is at Phil^a in Senate. the Chancelor[4] is at Clermont near Albany. Mr M. Smith[5] will write you. all well. I wish you health. I wish you & your Mission & the Republic all the success all the happiness & all the prosperity that you & they are capable of enjoying.

LBC, NHi: Gelston Letterbook

This letter was written with very little punctuation. The editors have supplied periods and commas at what they deem to be the proper places.

1. JM's letter to Gelston of 10 February 1795 has not been located.

2. John M. Gelston.

3. Gelston's letter to JM of 24 March 1795 is in NHi: Gelston Letterbook. The other three letters have not been located.

4. Robert R. Livingston.

5. Melancton Smith.

To Joseph Jones

Paris June 20. 1795

Dear Sir

I have just rec^d yours of the 24. of April[1] & answer it in the moment of the rec^t—I have written you often & am surprised you have only rec^d those of the 4. 6. & 20. of sep^r last.[2] Before this I trust you have been advised that I had returned Mr Fauchets draft on this gov^t in my behalf for 3.000 dol^rs & appropriated it to your command for the payment of the sum due for my Loudon land & other purposes heretofore specified. That you wo^d likewise be paid the further sum of 150. dol^rs or thereab^ts by Mr Randolph for the like sum advanc'd by me here in fav^r of Mr Rittenhouse & by whom the money was deposited by Mr R. for you in dec^r last. If these sums have not been paid you it is an omission of which both you and I have a right to complain. you will therefore in that case press & favor the payment stating your advances for me upon my appropriations without descending to particulars.

You mention y^r drafts upon me for the sums of £185. and £200.—These were I suspect made upon the presumption that I had made no arrangment of the kind above mentioned: but you may notwithstanding be easy on the subject for they shall be punctually paid. I hope these advances will put you at ease upon the score of my aff^rs aided by my crops with what is gained from Marks, relative to which two latter items I shall thank you for some information. In the course of 6. or 8. months however if requisite I shall be able to give you further aid, of which you will likewise inform me.

I wish you not to sell my western land or any part of it, as I can easily get five times the price offered in Phil^a, & by fair & honorable bargain—I prefer however that it lay till I am ab^t to withdraw hence when I will sell it. In the interim I beg you to procure if you have not yet procured it & send me the patent here as soon as possible, as I shall probable raise money by mortgage upon it, prefering that to a sale for the present.

You mention that my brother Joseph's[3] circumstances required y^r admission of him to the use of one of my houses: my only objection to it is the fear it may incommode you, for except on that acc^t I sho^d have plac'd him there. Tis probable you may find such accomodation to him inconvenient to you. If so, do not make it, but guarding agnst that inconvenience the more he is accomodated, the more agreeable it will be to me.

I mentioned in one of my letters to you that I had been applied to by Mr Clason in favor of one Gibson & others on acc^t & for paym^t of Josephs debts in Scotland, & that I was willing to pay them if Joseph's measures co^d be suspended on that head—of which I begged y^r immediate information as likewise the transmission to me of a copy of the am^t rendered some time since by Sr Wm Forbes,[4] in possession of Joseph. I beg y^r ans^r on these points as soon as possible as I have promised one soon to his creditors. I mean to pay his debts & otherwise assist him all in my power. I wo^d even help him in addition to the above to the amt of 500. or six hundred dol^rs to be paid in 12. mo^s or sooner if possible in the purchase of a tract of land, & upon w^h I wish him to take immediate measures for land will double or treble itself in the course of a few years. But wo^d it not be better for him to settle in Loudon upon one of the farms on the land lately purchased there? I wo^d willingly give him the use of a couple of hundred acres for life, in case he cannot purchase one in fee there or elsewhere, & in w^h he may count upon my aid.

I have mentioned to you heretofore that I owed Andrew[5] his share of Fanny who sold for £90. with interest since & that I wished it paid, with something beyond if possible—make known to him my disposition to befriend him all in my power—You know my wishes with respect to my sister[6] & one of her children—upon these points be so kind as write me.

Joseph[7] is at St Germains & well—he grows fast & behaves better than heretofore—I will send you in my next an estimate of his expenses & what they probably will be for the future. The school is much superior to the one in which he commenc'd as he learns the latin & greek there (the latter but lately) & w^h was neglected at the other.

The publication of extracts from my letters respecting the Jacobins was an unbecoming & uncandid thing, as they were the only parts of my correspondence that were published. I stated the truth & therefore am not dissatisfied with the publication in that respect. But to me it appears strange that the fortunes of that misguided club sho^d be the only subject treated in my correspondence upon which it was necessary to convey the information it cont[aine]d to our countrymen. Certainly in relation to the honor & welfare of my country it was the least important of all the subjects upon which I treated. Besides that club was as unlike the patriotic societies in America, as light is to darkness, the former being a society that had absolutely annihilated all other government in France, and whose denunciations carried immediately any of the deputies to the scaffold—whereas the former are societies of enlighten'd men who discuss measures & principles, and of course whose opinions have no other weight than as they are well grounded & have reason on their side—to extirpate which is to extirpate liberty itself. You will have heard before this of the treaty with Prussia—of the taking of Luxemburg—of the attempt of Engl^d by an agent Sr F^r Eden to obtain a peace, the ostensible object being to negotiate an exchge of prisoners only—Every thing is quiet & progressing well. A Committee of 11. who have the subject of amendments to the Const^n of 1793. it is expected will report soon & propose the introduction of 2. branches in the legislature. How is Mr Jefferson & why will he not write me. We are well & all desirous to be affec^y remembered to you. Sincerely I am y^r friend & serv^t

Ja^s Monroe.

Keep clear of the low country is the wish of us all, for we know you are apt to haz[ard] y^{r}self there too much—Remember me to Col^o Taliaferro Dr Brooke & all other friends—I wish Mr Dawson wo^d come over—I have no app^t [to] confer but think he will find it useful.

RC, ViFreJM

1. Jones's letter to JM of 24 April 1795 has not been located.

2. JM to Jones, 4 September 1794 (with an addition dated 6 September), above. The letter to Jones of 20 September 1794 has not been located.

3. Joseph J. Monroe.

4. Sir William Forbes (1738-1806) was an Edinburgh banker (*DNB*).

5. Andrew Monroe.

6. Elizabeth Monroe Buckner.

7. Joseph Jones, Jr.

To John Beckley

Paris June 23. 1795

Dear Sir.

have been lately favored with yours of the 11th of March[1] (by postscript) & return you my sincere thanks for the very interesting details which it contained. I sho[d] long since have written you had I not concluded that my letters to M[r] Madison were shewn you, & had I not been always occupied so as to make it an object with me to avoid multiplying letters where it was to be avoided. Indeed I regret that I have not been able to write oftener & to many to whom I have not written: but believe me I have never been so laboriously occupied before, as since my arrival here. I will however endeavor to give you at present a concise sketch of the actual state of things upon this great and interesting theatre.

Your first inquiry will be upon what basis does the revolution rest? Has it yet weathered the storms that have beaten agnst it, and taking all circumstances into view that merit consideration, is there ground for a well founded hope that it will terminate happily for France & of course for mankind? I will give you concisely the actual state of things, by comparing which with those great events which have preceded and are known every where, you will be enabled to form as correct a judgment upon that point as can now be formed upon it.

To say that the convention maintains its authority over the whole interior of the republick, notwithstanding its late difficulties, would give you but a superficial view of the subject, without developing in some degree the nature & probable consequences of those difficulties. Internal convulsions where they happen try the strength of parties, and demonstrate what their real object is, as well as that of the society in general, in regard to the points in controversy. Fortunately such have happened here, and of a character to furnish respectable data whereon to calculate not only the strength of parties, but likewise the probable issue of the revolution itself. Fortunately, permit me to say, for as political truths depend upon experiment, so we have reason to rejoice in those experiments which prove what it is the wish and the interest of mankind to see proven.

Within less than two months past I have seen the convention twice assailed by a considerable force which was in the latter instance armed, & upon both those occasions have seen that force foiled, in the first without the effusion of blood, and in the 2[d] by the death of one man (Ferraud a deputy) only. Many circumstances too were combined to make those movments formidable and to create a belief that they would shake the revolution, if there existed in the society a force able & willing to shake it: for the first took place at the moment when the city was agitated by a twofold crisis of famine, & the trial of Billaud de Varrennes, Collot D'Herbois, & Barrere, leading members of the mountain party: and the second when the famine was at the height and the distress of the people beyond what was ever seen on our side of the Atlantick. For several hours on both days the proceedings of the Convention were interrupted, and on the last the rioters were in absolute possession of the Hall & in a great measure of the gov[t] itself; so that in truth the superiority of active force was on their side, & danger only on the side of the members & the friends of the government. At such a moment as this when the functions of the gov[t] were suspended, or exercised by the insurgents only, there was surely a fair opportunity for those who were in favor of a change to pronounce themselves on that side: and the presumption is reasonable that all those who were in favor of it, or at least who were willing to hazard any thing in support of it, did pronounce themselves on that side. It was the epoch upon w[h] foreign powers and the royalists had fixed their attention, & upon which it was understood they wo[d] unite their efforts to bring ab[t] a counter-revolution: nor was there any army at hand or other force to oppose the enterprise than the citizens of Paris itself.

Upon a fair appeal therefore to the interest & the wishes of the inhabitants of this city, the issue was put, and the experiment in both cases particularly the last proved that the strength of those who were for a counter-revolution, was comparatively with that of those agnst it like that of an infant agnst Hercules. Upon the first occasion the commotion was crushed, before the movers in it got the ascendancy, but upon the second it was otherwise so that their force was fairly ascertained & shewn to be nothing.

Nor was the issue more unfavorable to royalty, if we may judge from what appeared, than the success of the party would have been if it had succeeded: for the principle upon which the mov'ment was undertaken by the great mass of those who acted in it, was not to favor royalty but to oppose it, being impressed with an opinion that the prevailing party were disposed to reestablish that species of government, against which they declared themselves, affirming that their object was, liberty to the patriots (the members of the mountain party who were under prosecution) & the establishment of the Constitution of 1793., which certainly has in it, none of the attributes of royalty.

In the course of these commotions the royalists did not display themselves to advantage: they shewed neither enterprise nor decision. In the commencment they were active by intrigue only, fomenting by all the means in their power, the discontents of the laborious poor, which proceeded from the famine which oppressed them, contrasting their present distress with the abundant ease of former times &c &c but when the moment of danger arrived, they took no part so as to make themselves responsible in case the effort failed. And upon the latter occasion, when the party got possession of the convention & began for a while to rule, & were about to re-establish terrorism & not royalty, the royalists shifted their ground in a moment & became very vociferous against popular commotions, & equally pathetic in support of the convention & of the law, which a few hours before they disdained and endeavoured to subvert. In truth they saw that their own safety was involved in that of the convention, and in consequence became interested in the welfare of that body from the strongest of all possible motives, a regard for themselves.

Upon the whole therefore I am of opinion that these movments have tended rather to strengthen than to weaken the foundation of the revolution, for they have shewn that the mountain party which so long governed France, altho' it has latterly lost its influence, has not abandoned its principles, and that if it had recoverd its authority it would not have introduc'd royalty but on the contrary a greater degree of rigor agnst the royalists than humanity allows, or the present preponderating party is disposed to exercise. Of this truth even the avowed royalists are already admonished: is it not therefore reasonable to conclude that those who were before wavering what part to take will for the future cease to hesitate?

But you will ask is there not a party in the convention itself favorable to monarchy, are not some of the leading members in the preponderating party inclined to that system of government? If the fact were so, these late movments would have a tendency to check that bias: but I have no reason to think that the fact is so. With many I am personally acquainted, and from what I have seen of their conduct, for sometime past, in publick and in private life, can assure you that whilst I have nothing to say agnst any of these members, I consider many of them as among the most enthusiastic admirers and advocates of the publick liberty that I have ever known. I have seen them too in situations where it was impossible to dissemble. Time & circumstances it is true may produce changes, against which I do not pretend to reason: I only argue from data within my view, & deduce those consequences from them which according to the ordinary course of events are probable. So much then upon the state of parties and their respective views, by which it appears that the publick liberty will not be endangered under the auspices of either.

In other respects the prospect has become more favorable to a happy termination of the revolution than was heretofore promised. The people of France may conquer their liberties & merit to be free, but without a good government it will be impossible to preserve them. This truth has latterly been more deeply impressed upon the convention than it formerly was, and in consequence the attention of that body seems now to be principally turned to that object, a committee consisting of 11. members having been appointed for more than six weeks past to report what changes it will be necessary in their judgment to make in the existing one of 1793, & whose report is daily expected. It is believed that this committee will propose some important changes in that constitution and that the convention will adopt them, such as a division of the legislature into two branches &c after the model of the American constitutions. I have heard many deputies confer on this subject who were unanimous in favor of this change, which is certainly of greater importance to the preservation of their liberty than any other that has been spoken of. As soon as this report is presented I will transmit it to you.[2]

The external view is still more favorable. The atchievments of the last campaign surpassed every thing that the modern world has witnessed. In every quarter their arms were tryumphant, but where the greatest danger pressed, there the grandeur of their exploits was most conspicuous. Spain and Holland bear testimony in favor of this assertion, for the close of the campaign left the republick in possession of extensive territories belonging to the former, & of the whole of the latter. The armies of the Emperor too were often beaten & finally forced to abandon the field. Those of Prussia experienc'd upon several occasions the like fate and as for the British, they retreated, till they came back upon sea, where hurrying on board the ships that were prepared to receive them, they took their flight upon that element, upon which alone they could hope for safety.[3] From these successes you have already seen that France has gained the most solid and durable advantages. From an enemy Holland has become a friend and ally. In that country the government only was conquered, by whose conquest the people became free: for upon the ruins of the miserable oligarchal tyranny which reigned there, we find a sister republick reared, marshalled by the side of France, & preparing to fight with her for the common liberty of the two people. Prussia has withdrawn from the war & is now in the utmost amity with France. Spain is negotiating & will probably soon have peace: Austria is known to wish it, & Engl^d has absolutely made overtures secretly thro' the medium of Sr F^k Eden, whilst the ostensible object of his mission was an exchge of prisoners only. Exploits like these become a free people, nor are any but a free people able to perform them.

Such was the actual state of things when the campaign was lately opened on the part of France by the atchievment of Luxemburg, one of the best fortified and strongest posts in the world. The siege was closely continued for more than six months, & finally succeded after the provision was exhausted, & it was seen that the coalised powers could not raise it. At this post 12.000 men were taken with great amount in cannon & other warlike stores. Upon Mayence the whole pressure now is, nor is it probable that that garrison will long be able to sustain itself.[4] Upon Spain also some recent advantage has been gained: indeed it is well known that the troops of this republick can make what impression they please in that quarter.

Under these circumstances it is not probable that the war will be long continued upon the continent. The coalised powers have latterly plac'd their only hope, in the possibility of a counter revolution here, upon account of the dissentions in the publick councils, & the scarcity of bread: but the late events which I have already communicated, will shew how unproductive a resource the former has been & promises to be; and the revolution of a few weeks only, within which space the harvest will ripen, will I think likewise demonstrate that the latter was not less so. The war then will soon be narrowed to a contest between this republick and Engl^d, I mean such is the present prospect, & this will of course be a maritime one only, unless the former succeeds in which case, the government of Engl^d will be conquered as that of Holland was. Among the maritime powers there is not one (unless Russia forms an exception which is not absolutely certain) which does not wish to see the naval force of Engl^d broken or at least greatly diminished. Whereas on the side of France there is Holland already embarked, and Denmark & Sweden are unquestionably in the same interest; nor is it improbable that past & present injuries may force them to declare in support of it; for latterly the orders of the 6th of Novr have been revived by the C^t of St James, for seizing all neutral vessels laden with provisions for France under which many have been seized of theirs as well as ours. It is likewise probable that Spain will eventually be on the same side, for as she wishes not only to get rid of the war, but to revive with France her antient connection, which contains on the part of France a guarantee of the Spanish possessions in S^o America, and which it will otherwise be difficult to accomplish, I cannot well perceive how Spain will be able to avoid declaring herself on the side of France. Such is the external & internal state of things, upon which you will be able to form your own conjecture, of the probable issue.

But you will demand what ground does America occupy upon this great & interesting scene of affairs? How does she stand in the estimation of her generous & victorious ally? As we were never called on to bear a part in the controversy upon the issue of which ours as well as her liberty was dependant, but were left to enjoy in peace the abundant fruits of our industry, whilst she defied the storm alone, I am not surpris'd that you sho^d feel solicitous upon this point. A few lines will give the sketch you wish. Preceding unfavorable impressions, which were known to exist, were erased by the declarations of the present minister when he was introduc'd into the Convention, supported by the documents which he presented, and upon which basis the antient and close amity which had formerly subsisted was rapidly reviving & growing up. Some changes of importance were accomplished in our commercial aff^rs with this republick, and in particular the treaty of amity & commerce, which in pursuit of the policy of Engl^d had been violated, was put in activity, whereby our trade is not only free in every article (strict contraband excepted) & to every country even to Engl^d herself, altho it furnishes her with the most productive means for the supp^t of the war, but likewise the trade of Engl^d is protected under our flag, & whilst it yields no protection to that of France. Such was the actual state of things when the report of Mr Jay's treaty with the English government transpired, by which it was circulated that a new connection was formed between the U. States & that power, beneficial to the latter & probably hurtful to France. This report operated like a stroke of thunder & produc'd upon all France amazement. What the treaty really is, is not yet known, but most certainly the bias in our favor has been greatly diminished, nor is it possible that the cordiality sho^d be great under such circumstances. If the treaty is rejected, or contains in it nothing strictly objectionable, in either case we shall stand well here: but if it is adopted and does contain any thing which a just criticism can censure, be assured we shall hear from this government in terms of reproach. By this time you know what the treaty is, and therefore know according to its fate in what light we shall be considered here.

If the treaty is not precisely what we wished it to be most certainly the most favorable opportunity that was ever offered to make a good one has been thrown away: for as France was successful, & a good understanding subsisted between us & France, it was really in our power to dictate what terms we pleased, provided we could make the Engl^h government believe that in any event we would take part agnst it. Accomplishing that point every thing wo^d have been accomplished, for of all possible calamities with which they were threaten'd, a war with us is that which they most dread: not so much indeed from the fear of our maritime force, as the effect it would produce upon their commerce, by which alone they are enabled to support a war. Such was the actual state of things at the time this treaty was formed, but a new scene has since been opened which will shew how little confidence we ought to place in treaties with that power; for latterly and as I presume in violation of that treaty the same system of depredation & plunder has been recommenc'd.

By the above hasty but true picture of aff[ts] here you will perceive that this republick is rapidly rising, or rather has already obtained, a decided preponderance not only in the scale of Europe but indeed of human aff[ts]. Having combatted alone and with success all the great powers of Europe, the superiority of its strength over theirs (at least whilst that of the latter is wielded by the heavy & expensive gov[ts] which exist there), is well established. Nor is it probable that this superiority will be soon diminished, especially when it is considered that the revolution of the one is approaching fast to a happy close, under a gov[t] founded upon principles, which when completed & resting firm, must cause a similar revolution every where. To stand well with this republick is therefore now the interest of all nations; nor indeed do any of them seem at the present moment to entertain a contrary opinion; for they have all made approaches and shewn their solicitude for peace, notwithstanding the danger that will probably overwhelm them in that event, especially if France gets a good government, since they deem that danger more remote and less terrible, than the one which immediately threatens under the pressure of the French arms. Upon every principle therefore it were greatly to be regretted, if America sho[d] lose in any degree the ground upon which she hath heretofore stood, in the estimation of her ally.

Dft, MHi: Washburn Collection

JM sent copies of this letter, minus the opening paragraph, to George Logan, Robert R. Livingston, Thomas Jefferson, Aaron Burr, and possibly George Clinton (*Jefferson Papers*, 28: 397-398). For publication of this letter, see JM to Logan, 24 June 1795, below.

1. Beckley's letter to JM of 11 March 1795 has not been located.

2. The Commission of Eleven submitted its draft of the new constitution to the Convention on June 23, the day JM wrote this letter. The Convention debated the document's provisions from 4 July until 17 August and passed them on 22 August. (Jacques Godechot, *The Counter-Revolution Doctrine and Action 1789-1804*, 260-261; Andrew Jainchill, "The Constitution of the Year III… etc.," *French Historical Studies*, 2 (2003): 408).

3. After Pichegru captured Amsterdam on 20 January 1795, the British retreated into Germany and from there embarked for England (Russell F. Weigley, *The Age of Battles*, 297).

4. The French captured Mayence (Mainz) in September 795 but were forced to surrender the city in October (Steven Ross, *Historical Dictionary of the Wars of the French Revolution*, 100).

To Robert R. Livingston

Paris June 23. 1795.

Dear Sir

I give you enclosed a sketch of aff[ts] here up to the present time.[1] As I am not able to write another I have sent a copy or two of it to one or two other friends. I have rec[d] one political letter from you and which was answered[2] by M[r] Edet[3] who is no doubt with you long since.

M[r] Jay's treaty merely by the mode of managm[t] has done us infinite mischief here. The contents are not even yet known to me & of course what mischief the thing itself may do is yet to be understood. Soon after it was signed M[r] Jay wrote me he had signed it but wo[d] not tell the contents other than that it contained an article which stipulated other treaties sho[d] not be affected. The day after the receit of this letter I was applied to by the gov[t] for information what had been done in Engl[d], stating the reports & asking in what light they were to be considered [by] them, & to which I replied in the words of M[r] Jay. But at this moment it was evident that so much had been gained or rather regaind of the former amity, that if that transaction had not taken place, or co[d] be shewn not to injure them that we might command the fortunes of this republick, in our depending concerns with Engl[d] as well as in Spain, supposing that

that with the former wo^d be rejected in America, & which might be a supposeable case. Six weeks after Mr Jays first letter in which he told me he was inhibited making the communication, I rec^d a 2^d in which he promised in cypher the principal heads of the treaty. But I had no cypher & in consequence as I wished the information to satisfy the doubts of this gov^t & for the purposes above mentioned, I sent a gent^n over to him for a copy of the instrument or principal heads as he had promisd. You will observe that when Mr Jays first communication was rec^d & in which he told me he co^d give me nothing more, I concluded I sho^d get nothing more till I had it from America, & to satisfy the gov^t as well as I co^d I added after stating what he had said, that I wo^d apprize it of the contents of that treaty as soon as I sho^d know them. In consequence I told Mr Jay explicitly what use I sho^d make of the copy in case he sent it; with the further view also of preventing his sending it in case it contained any thing improper or questionable, and to which indeed a third motive may be added, I did not chuse to take the principal heads from his statment, & upon it, pledge my credit with this gov^t as to the contents of the treaty. To my application Mr Jay replied in high terms of astonishment & indeed of indignation, that his <u>doings</u> as he called them sho^d be submitted to the criticism of the councils of another country: that we were a free people &c &c, and refused to send what had been requested.[4]

It is obvious that this gent^n conducted his negotiations upon principles adverse to France: and in consequence he was greatly upon his guard agnst France & whose victories must have embarrass'd him much. Confidence with France and concert with her were out of the question, indeed what of all things he was most to avoid. He therefore acted up to the height of his principles for by his managment of his negotiation & the instrument or product of it since he has gone far in producing a reciprocal effect in the councils of this gov^t towards us.

You will have seen that the British have revived since he sailed the orders of the 6th of Novr 1793 & began anew her depredation on our trade: between 30 & 40. vessels were carried in by our last acc^ts some of the vessels immediately from the banks of N. foundland with fish. If we do not strike at them now our reputation is irretrievably gone. we hold the fortunes of that country in our hands & may overset it at pleasure: there is nothing she so much dreads as a war with us, for it cuts up her remaining resource in trade, & lets loose the whole mercantile interest ruined or upon the brink of ruin, upon the court itself. But what effect will this measure of Engl^d produce here under present discontents? formerly the example of Engl^d was followed in spoiling our commerce. will it be possible then to prevent it now? I shall do all I can but I am doubtful of the consequences.

The publication of the extracts from my letters ab^t the poor misguided Jacobins, omitting whatever I had said ab^t royalists, Jay's treaty, &c &c was an unkind something.

You mentioned to me the case of a capt^n of France[5] & to which I have attended: but yet no answer is obtained. upon this & the other private case I will write you very shortly. very sincerely I am dear sir y^rs

Ja^s Monroe

RC, PHi: Gratz Collection

1. JM enclosed a copy of his letter to John Beckley, 23 June 1795 (above), minus the opening paragraph.

2. Livingston to JM 18 September 1794 and JM to Livingston, 23 February 1795, both above.

3. Pierre Adet.

4. John Jay to JM, 24 and 25 November 1794, 5 and 19 February 1795, above.

5. Jean-Baptiste-Henri Barré.

From Oliver Wolcott

Treasury Department June 23ᵈ 1795

Sir,

The events of the War having interrupted the intercourse of this Department with our Bankers in Holland, through the usual Channels, I take the liberty to trouble you with a Negociation of importance to the credit of the United States.

For the purpose of providing funds to meet the interest which will fall due in Amsterdam on the first of September ensuing, I have entered into an arrangement with James Swan Esquire the Agent of the French Republic,[1] and now inclose his bill in your favor on Messʳˢ Dallarde[2] Swan & Company of Paris for One hundred & Twenty thousand Dollars in Specie or Bullion equivalent, which I request you to present immediately on being received.

If the bill shall be accepted & assurance of instant payment given, you will be pleased to ascertain without delay whether any regulations of the Government oppose obstacles to the transportation of Specie to Holland, & if any exist, you will endeavour to obtain a special permission for the proceeds of this bill, which I have no doubt will be readily granted as a favor to the United States.

If the bill is accepted & the transportation of the money assured you will be pleased to immediately to notify the house of Wilhem & Jan Willink, Nicholas & Jacob Van Staphorst & Hubbard of Amsterdam of what shall have been done, & you will expedite the delivery of the Funds through the house of Dallarde Swan and Company, who are to co-operate in placing the same in Amsterdam.

But if the bill on Dallarde Swan & Company will not be paid or if the permission of the Government to transport Specie cannot be obtained, you will abandon this part of the plan & notify Dallarde Swan and Company accordingly, at the same time you will return the bill on them to this Department and inform me particularly of the causes of the disappointment.

In this event you will be pleased to have recourse to another bill which you will find inclosed drawn by James Swan & Schwierer in your favor on Messʳˢ Lubbert and Dumas of Hamburgh for Three hundred thousand current florins of Holland payable in Amsterdam, which you will make payable & remit without delay to Messʳˢ Wilhem & Jan Willink Nicholas & Jacob Van Staphorst & Hubbard of Amsterdam.

It is proper for me to inform you that the proposed negociation through the house of Dallarde Swan & Company is to be preferred as being most beneficial to the United States & as requiring the least delay—in case it can be rendered successful the bill on Lubbert & Dumas may be surrendered to Dallarde Swan & Company.

I will attempt no apology for troubling you with a business which is foreign to your diplomatic duties, because I know that your zeal for the interest of the United States, will readily induce you to comply with my request, and because you will perceive that your co-operation is really necessary to the success of an interesting object. I have the honour to be with perfect respect, Sir Your Obedient Servant

Oliv: Wolcott Jr. Secrʸ of the Treasʸ

RC, NN: Monroe Papers

1. In January the French government authorized James Swan to negotiate a final liquidation of the American debt to France. Subsequently, Wolcott signed an agreement on 15 June 1795 to provide Swan with $2,024,900, the sum equal to the principal,

interest, and arrears due on the French debt (Howard C. Rice, "James Swan: Agent of the French Republic, 1794-1796," *The New England Quarterly*, 10 (1937): 477-480).

2. Pierre-Gilbert Leroy, baron d'Allarde (1749-1809) was a political economist and partner of James Swan in the firm D'Allarde, Swan, & Cie. at Paris (*Madison Papers, Secretary of State Series*, 3: 12).

From John Langdon

Philad. June 24ᵗʰ 1795

Dear Sʳ

Some time before I left home (which is three weeks since) I had the pleasure of receiving your favor of the 28ᵗʰ Janʸ ¹ I assure Sʳ it gave me great Satisfaction to have so particular account of the Situation of Affairs in Europe, which could be relied on while we have so many false reports circulating among us— The amazing Successes of the French Nation, their Magnanimous Conduct to Conquered nations, the moderation of the Convention &c; while it stops the mouth of Calumny and Slander, and Counteracts the designs of their enemies, it astonishes the world—

You'll perceive I am now in the City attending my duty in the Senate; we have under our Consideration the Treaty, made by our Envoy Mʳ Jay; <u>Secrecy is to be Observed</u>; I am sure you'll Ask for what reason; I know of no good one, that can be given; we need not we ought not, to fear the people (whose Agents we are) while their dearest rights and privilidges, are at Stake, would it not be proper and right to know their minds   Secrecy and mistary in our sort of Governmᵗ I consider as a curse—Our Country is flourishing, a good prospect of peice with the Indians, and every thing will go well, if we are wise enough, not to fetter nor tie our hands, with Treties—unless a perfect Reciprocity can be obtain'd, let us Remain as we are; it is the Interest of all the world to Trade with us, why then not Remain in such eligable Situation—I hope we shall finish our business, this week, and do as little Mischief as possible—The New French Minister, Adet has Just Arrived, but I have not heard anything from him   My whole dependance, is on the Successes of France, as I consider those have and will save us, and not our own wise conduct so much Trumpeted—

Pray make my best Regards to your Lady and Accept of my best wishes for your Welfare and happiness—I am very Respectfully Dear Sʳ your most Obdᵗ Servᵗ

John Langdon

RC, DLC: Monroe Papers

1. JM's letter to Langdon of 28 January 1795 has not been located.

To George Logan¹

PARIS, June 24, 1795

DEAR SIR,

I GIVE you within a short sketch of the actual state of things here, a copy of which I likewise send to one or two other friends of whom Mr Beckley is one. If you and Mr. Beckley, if in Philadelphia, deem it worthy the attention, I have no objection to your inserting it in Bache's paper, the first paragraph excepted,² and if you likewise approve, I will hereafter keep you regularly apprized of the course of events, whereby the community at large may be more correctly informed of the progress of the revolution than they heretofore have been or can be, from the English prints. The character will be from a gentleman in Paris to his friend in Philadelphia—occasionally varied, as from some other quarter, as Bordeaux, that it may not appear to be a regular thing: tho' in that respect act as you please, for as truths only will be communicated and with temperance, it is immaterial what the conjecture is, provided it be only conjecture.

You promised me a visit: cannot you yet make it, as we shall be very happy to see you and Mrs Logan[3] and will certainly make your time as comfortable as possible. In your absence Mr. Beckley can attend to the little object of my communications, for I wish you and him to act in concert whilst he is in that neighbourhood, and indeed if you were both absent you will arrange matters confidentially with Mr. B. himself, who likewise possesses mine.

I beg you to present my respects to Drs Writtenhouse[4] and Rush,[5] and that you believe me Sincerely, Your friend and servant

JAS. MONROE.

(Richmond) *Virginia Gazette and General Advertiser*, 3 January 1798.

The original of this letter and its enclosure that JM sent to Logan have not been found. They supposedly landed in the dead letter section of the post office and from there made their way into the hands of Timothy Pickering. There are transcriptions of these documents in MHi: Pickering Papers. A copy of the letter to Logan, in Pickering's handwriting and misdated 24 June 1796, is in DLC: Washington Papers. Pickering gave this copy to Washington as evidence of the need to recall JM as minister to France (*Jefferson Papers*, 28: 397-398). The version in *Writings of Monroe* (3: 6), which is derived from the copy in the Washington Papers, is likewise misdated.

The version of the letter reproduced here was given to the editor of *Virginia Gazette* by a critic of JM who, "having accidentally got possession of an intercepted letter in Col. Monroe's own handwriting," submitted as evidence of JM's misconduct as minister to France (*Virginia Gazette and General Advertiser*, 23 December 1797 and 3 January 1798).

1. George Logan (1753-1821) had a degree in medicine from Edinburgh, but abandoned medicine and turned his attention to the management of his farm outside Philadelphia. He was a leader of the Republicans in Pennsylvania, serving several terms in the Pennsylvania assembly and writing newspaper essays attacking the Federalists. He was a member of the U. S. Senate 1801-1807. He twice traveled to Europe on missions of private diplomacy—to France in 1798 and England in 1810 (*ANB*).

2. JM enclosed a copy of his letter to John Beckley of 23 June 1795, above. It was published in the (Philadelphia) *Aurora* on 31 August 1795 under the heading: "Extract of a letter from an American gentleman in France."

3. Deborah Norris Logan (1761-1839) married George Logan in 1781. She is noted for her extensive diaries and the publication of correspondence of her husband and of his grandfather, James Logan (Nina Baym, "Between Enlightenment and Victorian: Toward a Narrative of American Writers Writing History, *Critical Inquiry* 18 (1991): 22; Edward T. James, ed., *Notable American Women 1607-1950: A Biographical History*).

4. David Rittenhouse.

5. Benjamin Rush (1746-1813) was a Philadelphia physician and reformer. He was dedicated to humanitarian causes, providing medical treatment for the poor and the insane. As a professor of medicine at the University of Pennsylvania he sought to improve the understanding of illness and its treatment. Rush rose to prominence during the yellow fever epidemic of 1793 when he remained in the city to treat the ill; his efforts to save the lives of the afflicted by extensive bleeding was controversial but generally effective. Rush occasionally ventured in politics, and was a close friend to both Jefferson and Adams. He was a member of the Continental Congress in 1776 and signed the Declaration of Independence (*ANB*).

From Edmé Mauduit

Petersfield Le 6. Messidor an 3ᵉ de la R/que françoise—24 Juin 1795.

Monsieur,

Le 6. mai dernier j'ai eu l'honneur de vous informer qu'à mon départ de Philadelphie, j'avois été chargé par M. Randolph, d'une bourse de Cinquante Louis, que je devois vous remettre; que la Corvette Le Jean Bart sur laquelle j'étois, ayant été prise, j'ai conservé l'or et jetté à la mer la lettre qui l'accompagnoit; Enfin que j'allois demander à Monsieur le Ministre américain à Londres, la permission de déposer entre les mains, la somme, dont j'etois porteur, avec prière de vous la faire passer le plutôt et le plus sûrement possible.

M. Wᵐ Allen Deas m'a répondu qu'il regrettoit fort de ne pouvoir se rendre à mes désirs, mais que n'étant Chargé, auprès du gouvernment Anglois, que des interêts des Citoyens d'amérique, il ne Croyoit pas qu'il lui fût permis de solliciter pour moi, la permission d'aller à Londres, pour l'y voir, Comme je le demandois.

D'après cela, Monsieur, j'attendrai que vous m'indiquiez une voie sûre pour vous transmettre Vos Cinquante Louis. Peut-être Cela Seroit-il possible, si vous vouliez vous en entendre avec M. Robert Livingston, Négociant au havre, à qui j'écris et que je prie de vous envoyer ma lettre. Salut.

Edme Mauduit
Secretaire de la Commission déligués à
Cayenne par la Constitution nationale.

Editors' Translation

Petersfield[1] 6 Messidor, year 3 of the French Republic—24 June 1795.

Sir,

On May 6 last I had the honor of informing you[2] that upon my departure from Philadelphia, Mr. Randolph had charged me with bringing you the sum of fifty Louis;[3] that when the corvette, the Jean Bart,[4] on which I sailed was captured, I had retained the gold and thrown the accompanying letter into the sea; finally, that I was going to ask the American Minister in London for permission to transfer to him the money that I carried, with the request that he pass it to you as soon and as securely as possible.

Mr. Wᵐ Allen Deas[5] replied that he greatly regretted being unable to accede to my request given his position as Chargé to the British government, with responsibility for the interests of American citizens only. He believed he was not permitted to request permission on my behalf to travel to London to see him, as I requested.

This being the case, Sir, I will await your instructions regarding a secure means of transmitting your fifty Louis. Perhaps that would be possible, if you agree to it with Mr. Robert Livingston, merchant at Havre, to whom I am writing and to whom I ask you kindly to send my letter. Greetings.

Edme Mauduit
Secretary of the commission delegated at
Cayenne by the National Constitution

RC, NN : Monroe Papers

The Papers of James Monroe: Volume III

1. Maudit was writing from Petersfield, England.

2. Mauduit's letter to JM of 6 May 1795 has not been located.

3. Mauduit was carrying money that was being sent to JM by Ralph Izard for the support of his son, George, who was a student in France (Ralph Izard to JM, August 1795, below).

4. The *Jean Bart* was a French corvette taken 28 March 1795 by the *Cerberus* in the English Channel. It was the same ship whose mail pouch contained Fauchet's dispatch of 31 October 1794 compromising Secretary of State Randolph (*Dictionnaire de la flotte de guerre française de 1671 à nos jours*; Bradford Perkins, *The First Rapprochement*, 36).

5. William Allen Deas (b. 1764) was a Charleston, South Carolina, attorney who served as Thomas Pinckney's secretary while he was minister to Great Britain 1791-1796. Deas acted as U. S. chargé d'affaires in London during Pinckney's mission to Madrid in 1795 (*Biographical Dictionary of the South Carolina House of Representatives*, 4: 151-152).

To Edmund Randolph

Paris June 26th 1795.

Sir,

Since my last it is reduced to a certainty that the British government has revived its order of the 6th of November 1793, and commenced on this side the Atlantic, the same system of warfare and pillage upon our commerce that was practised on it by that government at that very calamitous Æra. Between 30 and 40 sail destined for the ports of this republic, charged with provision, have been already taken from their destination and carried into those of that Island: and as the period has arrived, when the invitation which the distresses of this country gave to our merchants here and at home to embark their fortunes in this supply, is likely to produce its effect, it is more than probable that other vessels and to a great amount will share the like fate. Among those of our merchants who are here this measure has created a kind of panic, for they think they see in its consequences little less than the ruin of their trade, and under which impression many are about to abandon it for the present and send their vessels home in ballast.

What effect this measure will produce upon this government under existing circumstances I cannot pretend to determine. Formerly it adopted the same measure for the purpose of counteracting its enemy, but the impolicy of that proceedure was afterwards discussed and demonstrated, and the measure itself in consequence abandoned. At present the distress of the country is great, and the government will no doubt be mortified to find, that whilst our flag gives no protection to its goods nor even to our goods destined for the ports of this republic, the whole of which become the spoil of its enemy, that it does protect not only our goods destined for the English ports, but likewise British goods destined equally for those and the ports of other countries. The measure has obviously excited a kind of ferment in their councils, but which I presume will be directed against their enemies only. Be assured I shall do every thing in my power to give it that direction, and to enforce those arguments which were used upon the former occasion: but should they fail in producing the desired effect, and a less amicable policy be adopted, which however I think will not be the case, I shall deem it my duty immediately to advise you of it, by a vessel (in case none other offers) to be dispatched for that purpose.

It will obviously attract your attention that this measure was so timed by the British cabinet, that it might have no influence in the decision of the Senate upon the treaty of Mr Jay: nor can the motive for such an accomodation be less doubtful, for in case it be rejected they will deem the stroke a lucky one, since thereby, they will say they had fortunately gained so much time: and if it be adopted they will probably presume that so much time will be consumed in convening the Congress, should that measure be deemed expedient, that the course of events here may render it impossible for our efforts to produce a favourable effect: and which consideration they will likewise infer will be an argument against convening the Congress. This kind of policy however shews not only the profligacy but the desparation of that government, and will probably precipitate the crisis which notwithstanding all its follies and enormities, might yet have been postponed for some time to come. I think the measure will give new vigour to the French councils, and will probably bring immediately upon its authors Denmark and Sweden. Upon this latter point however I am authorized to say nothing, for as I was not instructed to confer with the representatives of those powers here, I have carefully avoided several conferences that were sought of me by Baron Stahl from Sweden, soon after his arrival, because I knew nothing could result from them, and was fearful, as I presumed the result would be known to the committee, it might produce an ill effect there.

Your measures will no doubt be greatly influenced by the probability of the early termination or continuation of the war with this republic, and upon which some information will of course be expected from me. You will however perceive the disadvantage under which I must give any opinion upon that point and estimate it accordingly: for as I am authorized to say nothing to this government of what we will probably do in case the war continues (for the revival of the order of the 6th of November could not be foreseen) you will of course conclude it impossible for me to sound it upon that topic; indeed I was fearful that by my former communications, upon a similar occasion slight and informal as they were, I might embarrass you, and was therefore extremely uneasy on that account, after I heard of Mr Jay's treaty and until I had a conference with the committee on the subject. My judgment must therefore be formed upon general and external circumstances, and by which I perceive no prospect of an early accomodation of the war between France and England. On the contrary the preparations on both sides seem to go on with all possible activity for its continuance. The fleet of England is said to be raised to a height beyond what it ever attained before, and efforts are still making to keep it there if not to increase it. And France is exerting her utmost endeavours to increase hers, and which are the more necessary in consequence of the improvident excursions of the last winter by which it was greatly injured in the Atlantic as well as the Mediteranean Sea. Tis expected that by a continuance of those endeavours the Brest fleet will be ready to take the sea by the fall: the Miditeranean is said now to be at sea and in good order. Tis likewise expected that the Dutch fleet at least to the amount stipulated, will be in readiness in time to co-operate with that from Brest, for great efforts were latterly made and are still making by that government to equip it. Add to these the fact, and I am assured by unquestionable authority that it is one, that the overtures made by Sr F^k Eden were repulsed, and in a manner which immediately closed, under the powers possessed by the parties respectively, all further conference on the subject. From considerations therefore of these circumstances I am led to conclude that the war between these powers will be continued for some time to come, and, most probably till some change by battle or otherwise is wrought in the fortunes of one or both so as to dispose them for peace.

If Denmark and Sweden, and especially if they are joined by Spain, unite with France and Holland, they will probably have the preponderance and must bear hard upon England. In any event the enormous expence to which she is unprofitably exposed, if continued for any time, must not only exhaust her resources, but excite great discontents among the people. They have been allayed latterly, by the assurances of the minister that the people of France would be starved, and that the government must in consequence accomodate, and which were countenanced by the movements which took place here some time after those assurances were given. But when it is seen that the crisis has passed, and that the people after bearing unexampled distress, and upon the whole with unexampled patience, are quiet and in the possession of the fruits of a plentiful harvest, as promises soon to be the case, it is doubtful whether a change will not soon take place in the temper of those on the other side of the channel.

What part it becomes our country to take at this crisis belongs not to me to say. Peace is a blessing which ought not to be wantonly thrown away. But whether sufficient sacrifices have not been already made to preserve it, and the time arrived, when the duty we owe to ourselves, and the respect which is due to the opinion of the world, admonish us that the insults and injuries of Britain are to be no longer borne, and that we ought to seek redress by again appealing to arms, and putting the issue of our cause upon the event of war, is a point which will no doubt be wisely decided, by those who have a right to decide it. Permit me however to express a wish that in case any active measure is taken or likely to be taken in consequence of these aggressions, that you will immediately apprize me of it, that I may without delay begin to make a correspondent impression upon the councils of this government.

I omitted in my last to transmit to you a copy of the letter from M[r] Short,[1] which I mentioned was shewn to M[r] Pinckney, and which as it demonstrates how completely we may command success in our demands upon Spain, provided France aids us in that respect, ought not to be withheld and especially in the present state of our affairs. I make the communication with great pleasure, because at the same time that it furnishes a document of importance for you to possess, it will reflect honour on M[r] Short upon account of the able and comprehensive view he has taken of the subject.

I have the pleasure to inform you that the committee of 11, have at length reported a plan of Government of which I herewith inclose you a copy. The discussion upon the merits will commence in a few days, and as soon as the question is finally decided I will transmit to you the result. With great respect and esteem I have the honour to be, Sir, your very h[ble] and ob[t] Ser[t]

Ja[s] Monroe.

Copy, DNA: RG 59: Dispatches from France

1. William Short to JM, 4 May 1795, above

To Jean-Victor Colchen

Paris, le 27 Juin 1795. (9 Messidor An 3.) l'an 19. de la Republique Americaine.

Comme J'ai extrêmement à cœur que les droits dont jouissent içi mes compatriotes soient scrupuleusement restreints à eux seuls, ce sera avec plaisir que J'adopterai dans toutes les circonstances les mesûres nécessaires pour faire connaître à votre gouvernement ceux qui doivent être considérés comme tels. Conformément à ce principe, et au désir exprimé par votre lettre du 6. du courant, Je vous ferai parvenir chaque decade la liste de ceux qui auront obtenu des passeports. Toutes les fois que l'intérêt de cette Republique nécéssitera des mesûres dans lesquelles ma co-opération pourrait être utile, Je vous prierai de me les proposer avec la plus grande franchise, et de compter sur mon empressement à les seconder, Cet objèt etant mon plus ardent désir.

Ja[s]. Monroe

Editors' Translation

Paris, 27 June 1795 (9 Messidor Year 3) the 19th year of the American Republic.

Being extremely solicitous that the rights which my countrymen enjoy here should be strictly confined to themselves alone, I shall be happy at all times to adopt such measures as may be deemed necessary to inform your government of those who should be acknowledged as such. With this view, and the desire expressed in your letter of the 6th of this month,[1] therefore, I shall, with pleasure, arrange to furnish you each decade with a list of those to whom passports have been granted. At all times when the welfare of the Republic is at stake, I pray you to propose to me with complete frankness those measures in which my cooperation may be useful. As this object is my most ardent desire, you may always count on my determination to be of assistance.

Ja⁵. Monroe

LS, DLC: FCP—France

Colchen wrote to JM on 24 June 1795 (6 Messidor) asking him to provide a list of all Americans resident in Paris (*Writings of Monroe*, 2 : 323).

To Thomas Jefferson

Paris June 27. 1795.

Dear Sir

Of the above hasty view I have sent a copy to one or two other friends.[1] Since it was written the committee have reported a plan of govᵗ as suggested of 2. branches, the one to be called a council of 500. consisting of so many members, the other of 250. called the council of antients. The age of the 1ˢᵗ to be 30. & of the 2ᵈ 40. they are to be chosen each for 2. years but to be supplied annually by halves. The Executive to be composed of 5. members to be elected for 5. years, but so arranged that only one withdraws annually. Each member is to have a salary of abᵗ £5000 sterᵍ per annᵐ, the object whereof to receive and entertain foreign ministers &ᶜ. The Council of Antients cannot originate a bill. If possible I will procure & send you a copy of the plan.

The British have recommenc'd the seizure of our vessels as formerly under the order of the 6th of Novᵗ 1793. near 40. being carried in under by our last & which were the first accᵗˢ. This has produc'd an extreme ferment here, & it will be difficult under the irritation existing in consequence of Jay's treaty, to prevent a revival of the same practice on the part of France, and if we do nothing when it is known in America but abuse the English and drink toasts to the success of the French revolution, I do not know what step they will take in regard to us. My situation since the report of Mᵗ Jay's treaty has been painful beyond any thing ever experienc'd before, and for reasons you can readily conceive. I have however done every thing in my power to keep things where they shoᵈ be, but how long this will be practicable under existing circumstances I know not   Denmark & Sweden will I think be active.

I have just recᵈ a letter from Mᵗ Derieux with one for his aunt. if possible I will now answer it;[2] but in case I cannot, I beg you to tell him that I waited on her last fall with Mᵗˢ Monroe, having previously written her repeatedly in his behalf,[3] & after a long and earnest solicitation in his favor & returned without obtaining any thing for him. She had promised some thing before I went, & the dinner she gave us, was to pave the way for retracting & which she did. The old lady has about her (as I suspect) some persons who are poor, & who prefer their own welfare to his. By the law of France the property cannot be devised from her relatives, but tis probable these people will help to consume the annual profits; w^h latter however she says in consequence of the depreciation are nothing.

We wish most sincerely to get back & shall certainly do it, as soon as a decent respect for appearances will permit, especially if the present system of policy continues. I wish much to hear from you having written you several times but rec^d not a line since my appointment here. Is there any thing in this quarter you wish to command of books or any other article; or can I serve you in any respect whatever? you will of course command me if I can be serviceable.

I have requested Mr Madison to shew you some letters of mine to him. I wish to know much in what state my farms are. we are well: our child speaks French well and her and Mrs M. desire to be affectionately rememberd to yourself and daughters, to whom as well as to Mr R. & Mr C.[4] as likewise to my brother[5] & neighbours be so kind as remember me. with great respect & esteem I am Dear [Sir] y^r Affectionate friend

Ja^s Monroe

RC, DLC: Jefferson Papers

1. JM sent Jefferson a copy of his letter to John Beckley, 23 June 1795 (above), minus the opening paragraph.

2. Neither the letter from Peter Derieux nor JM's response has been located.

3. These letters have not been located.

4. Thomas Mann Randolph and Peter Carr.

5. Joseph J. Monroe.

From Henry Tazewell

Philadelphia 27th June 1795.

My dear Sir

I wrote you last March from this place, a full account of the political incidents that had occurred between your departure from the U States and that period[1]—I hope you have received my Letter, & I believe every day places me nearer to the receipt of your answer—

On the 8th of June I came hither in consequence of a summons from the President of the U States to deliberate with the other Senators on the late Negotiation with the british Government, conducted by Mr Jay—It has been said here that you are furnished with the result of that negotiation officially, & therefore I need not enclose you a Copy of it, nor say what is its substance—

It has undergone a discussion of 3 weeks which ended yesterday. The result is a ratification of the Treaty, conditionally. The enclosed paper n° 1, will convey the Resolution to you. By the other enclosures you will perceive the course in which the business has been conducted, as well as the names of those who have divided on the subject.[2]

I can only add to the information which these papers convey, that the proceeding has been the most uncandid & unfair proceeding I ever witnessed—What effect it will operate on the Pres^t you can imagine, as well as myself.

It is with me a question whether the form given to this ratification will not necessarily produce a new Act hereafter from the Senate—I believe the Condition suspends the whole Treaty and the manner in which the condition may be fulfilled will require it again to pass before the Senate—If so, I believe the Treaty will never be sanctified—I am sure of this, that the People of the U States will be violently opposed to it.

Mr Fouchet will leave Phila: to day, I cannot therefore lengthen my Letter, but by him I could not forbear to tell you, with what sincerity I am yours

Henry Tazewell

RC, DLC: Monroe Papers

1. Tazewell to JM, 9 March 1795, above.

2. Tazewell enclosed copies of three resolutions that were considered by the Senate. The first called for the rejection of the treaty with Great Britain, and the second proposed that negotiations be continued on certain points. Both were rejected. The third resolution, which ratified the treaty, passed. Ratification was conditional, however, and dependent upon the suspension of the twelfth article of the treaty, which related to trade between the United States and the British West Indies (DLC: Monroe Papers). The proceedings of the Senate during this special session can be found in *The Journal of the Executive Proceedings of the U. S. Senate*, 1: 177-192.

To James Madison

Paris June 28. 1795.

Dear Sir

I have rec^d from you 3. letters of which that of the sixth of April was the last.[1] Dr Edwards by whom it was sent has not yet arrived in Paris so that I am yet to receive his communications upon the state of our affairs. The cypher was rec^d in this last letter, and by which I have been highly gratified for it will greatly facilitate our future correspondence.

Since my last the committee of 11 have reported the draft of a Constitution which divides the legislature into two branches, one of which is calld the council of 500, consisting of the same number of deputies to be of the age or above 30. & the other a council of 250 not to be under 40. The first house will originate bills—they are each to be elected for 2. years, one half to be replac'd annually, & the qualifications of each to be the same—The Executive is to be composed of 5. members to be elected for 5 years, but to be replac'd by the retreat of one only annually. In fact the principle of the Senate of the U. S. is carried into the Executive branch here. Each member is to have a salary of ab^t £5000. annually to enable him to receive & entertain foreign ministers. The Judiciary will be better arranged than heretofore. The discussion will take place in a day or two, & when adopted I will forward you a copy.

The British have recommenc'd their aggressions on our commerce by a revival of the order of the 6th of Novr 1793. 40 of our vessels being carried in to the ports of Engl^d which were destined for those of this republick & charged with provision. They will I presume break up our commerce again, for the merchants of our country here, seem disposed to abandon for the present the sea. The Danes & Swedes will probably commence hostilities: Baron Stahl who is here says they will. You will readily conceive what effect this measure has produc'd in the councils of this government towards us, and how difficult it will be to prevent some indication of their resentment towards us. If they contain themselves within bounds it will verify many things that wo^d never have been otherwise admitted: but under existing circumstances it will be difficult to keep them within bounds. What shall we do in consequence? How does this measure correspond with the treaty of Mr Jay? If the Danes & Swedes act it will throw us completely under a shade & expose us in a greater degree to the censure of this gov^t—Holland has ministers &

ambassidors Extr^y here and I think that power will be in higher estimation than we shall be. Their ambassadors have been entertained by the Committee, an attention never shewn to any other power. Indeed tis not possible we sho^d preserve our ground under the circumstances that exist, & especially those that have attended the treaty of Mr Jay, the contents whereof are yet unknown to them & me. I write you in haste & am affec^y your friend & servant

Ja^s Monroe

RC, DLC: Madison Papers

1. Madison's note to JM of 6 April 1795, in which he sent a cipher, is in *Madison Papers*, 15: 507. JM received three letters that Madison had written in March: 11, 26 and 27 March 1795, all above.

From Stevens Thomson Mason

Philadelphia June 29th 1795

Dear Sir

I am this moment informed that Mr Fauchet leaves town today on his return to France. I can not let slip this opportunity of assuring you of my continued esteem and friendship, tho' I have not time to give you a detail of our politics.

Our friend Mr Tazewell tells me he has written to you, and I suppose has been pretty full on the subject of the Treaty. Whether the P__ will take the advice given him by the Senate is doubted by some, tho' not by me. The public mind is a good deal agitated at the Treaty and the proceedings repose it, having been kept in profound secrecy. it can not long remain so and coming out, under this unfavorable impression, its faults (which are abundant) will not be like to escape observation. and I think there will be a very general disapprobation of it throughout this Country. Virginia & N Carolina were the only States that united in the opposition to this measure, we were joined by Jackson, Butler, Burr, Brown, Robinson & Langdon.[1]

As I have once more entered upon the Theatre of public affairs, I feel an additional solicitude to continue our correspondence, and hope you will let me hear frequently from you. in return, I will, during our Sessions at least, give you frequent information of what is doing on this side the Water. With my respects to Mrs Monroe I am Dear Sir yours with esteem

Ste^s Tho^n Mason

PS. The British Privateers continue their depredations—two Ships belonging to this City were taken three days ago off the Capes of Delaware

RC, DLC: Monroe Papers

1. A bloc of ten senators opposed the treaty with Great Britain: Stevens T. Mason and Henry Tazewell of Virginia, Benjamin Hawkins and Alexander Martin of North Carolina, James Jackson of Georgia, Pierce Butler of South Carolina, Aaron Burr of New York, John Brown of Kentucky, Moses Robinson of Vermont, and John Langdon of New Hampshire (*The Journal of the Executive Proceedings of the U. S. Senate*, 1: 177-192).

To James Madison

Paris June 30. 1795.

Dear Sir

I send herewith a copy of the constitution reported by the committee of 11. & which will be discussed in the course of a few days. A doubt arises with many upon the propriety of the executive organiz^n, & some wish and with a view of strengthening it that the number be reduc'd to 3—but this wo^d certainly produce the opposit effect, for the annual rotation by the withdrawal of one & the speedy shift of all w^h wo^d follow the change wo^d in a great measure prevent the existence of an esprit de corps & that system of Executive operation, w^h the plan in the draft admits of: for with only three the preponderance of the legislature wo^d be comple[te], especially when it is considered that they are to be elected by the legislature. For my own part however I do not think either plan really dangerous—but I wo^d prefer having 6. members, changing 2. annually, the presiding members losing the right of voting. This wo^d be safer upon every principle. But I have no time to criticise.

You will be surprised to hear that *the only Americans whom I* found *here were a set of New England men connected with Britain and who upon British capital were trading to this country: that [they]*[1] *are hostile to the French revolution is what you well* know: but that they sho^d be, *thriving upon the credit which the efforts* of others in other quarters gain *the American name here you could not expect: that as such they should be in possession of the little confidence we had and give a tone to characters on our side of the Atlantick was still less* to be expected. *But* such was the fact. With a few exceptions *the other merchants are new made Citizens from Scotland. Swan who is a corrupt unprincipled rascal* had by virtue of being the *agent of France* and as we had no *minister* & *he being tho* (of the latter description) *the only or* most creditable *resident American here had a monopoly* of *the trade of both countries.* Indeed it is believed that he was connected with *the agents* on one side *and the minister on the other. I mention this as a trait worthy your* attention. You will confide the view to *mister Jefferson only.* But good may come from it, and especially if *the allurement here will draw them off from the other side of the channel.*

I candidly think if we bear this aggression from Engl^d without an immediate decl^n, at least by the seizure of all her property, ships, certificates &c, that our reputation is gone beyond recovery; most certainly it will be difficult & the work of time to recover it. We shall certainly lose our estimation here. If we were to take the measure suggested, of seizing British property, prohibiting the importation of her goods & which I wish was perpetual, laying hold of the posts, fitting out privateers &c we sho^d indemnify ourselves & incur but a trifling expence: for Brit^n wo^d not land a single soldier on our coast & wo^d be driven to extremities. But if we are amused we are deceived & will be despised. I am told that the most humiliating explanation & apology was made to Bernstoff for the measure at the moment the order was issued. But it is thought he will shew more decision & respect for the character of his country than to be the dupe of such finesse. Probably the same thing is done with us, but surely we are not sunk so low as to bear it. With great esteem & regard I am y^r friend & servant

Ja^s Monroe.

RC, DLC: Madison Papers. Words in italics were written in code by JM, with the deciphered text interlined by Madison.

1. JM erroneously encoded "ier".

To Fulwar Skipwith

[30 June 1795][1]

I wish you to call on Baron Stahl in my name & state to him that I am preparing dispatches for america upon the subject of B^h spoliation & wish to know what Sweden & Denmark will probably do in consequence of a like treatment. whether he is instructed to make any proposition for a concert with america. This to be delicately touched.

If he co^d be [posed] on to write me it wo^d be better letting him know I wo^d transmit his letter to america. but as Mr Murrays[2] vessel waits my dispatches by tomorrows post an immediate answer is expected.

RC, NN: Monroe Papers; undated; filed at the end of 1803.

1. The contents of this letter and Baron Staël's letter of 30 June 1795 (below) suggest that this letter was written on 30 June 1795.

2. George W. Murray was a New York merchant who was in Paris during the summer of 1795 (*Hamilton Papers*, 22: 60 and 26: 99; *Catalogue of Monroe's Papers*, 1: 46).

From Baron Staël-Holstein

Paris ce 30 Juin 1795.

Monsieur

L'Importance de la Conversation que j'ai eu avec vous il y a quelques jours, me determine, Monsieur, d'avoir l'honneur de vous donner un resumé des reflexions et des vues que j'ai eu le plaisir de vous communiquer.

Nous vivons dans une époque aussi critique qu'etonnante par les changements qu'elle a produits. Elle influera sur les siecles à venir et les politiques de nos jours ne peuvent pas être assez attentifs pour prevenir des événements, dont le resultat produiroit des grands malheurs.

Il n'est que trop prouvé que l'Angleterre nourrit le projet de s'approprier l'empire des mers et le commerce des 4 parties du monde. Toutes les puissances sont donc interessées à s'y opposer, et surtout les états unis de l'Amerique Septentrionale. L'interêt immense de leur Commerce avec l'Europe leur fait une necessité d'établir une communication facile et libre avec les differentes nations de notre hemisphère. Jusqu'ici l'Angleterre a su profiter de l'avantage que lui donne l'etroit rapport des mœurs et de la langue pour s'emparer de votre Commerce, et elle espere bien de s'en rendre tôt ou tard la maitrise absolue à l'exclusion des autres peuples. C'est pourquoi elle voit avec repugnance toutes les liaisons que l'ont cherche à cimenter avec votre patrie et porte sur tout ce que tend à detruire le commerce des autres nations la même attention qu'elle a toujours eue d'étendre le sien. Au mépris de la neutralité armée elle fit arrêter l'année dernière tous les navires neutres destinés pour la France. Afin de proteger leur navigation, la Suede et le Dannemarck se concerterent et concluerent la Convention dont l'effet heureux et prompt vous est connu. A cette occasion l'Envoyé de Suede à Londres eut ordres de temoigner au Ministre des Etats Unis le desir qu'avoit sa Cour de voir le Gouvernement Americain acceder à cette Convention. Si cette affaire n'a point eu de suite c'est probablement que le Cabinet de St James parut peu après désavouer sa premiere Conduite, en declarant que la Capture des batimens neutres n'auroit plus lieu. Actuellement qu'au mépris du droit des gens il revient à ces memes actes d'injustice et qu'il fait arrêter tous les navires destinés pour la France, soit Americains, soit danois ou suedois, il est tems qu'on se réunisse avec fermeté pour obliger l'Angleterre à rentrer dans les bornes de la justice et à ne point outrager la dignité des autres nations, ni n'attenter à leur indépendance.

Il faut encore ajouter que l'Angleterre paroit decidée à detruire leur liberté aussi bien que leur Commerce. Elle n'a pas encore oublié que l'Amerique a osé secouer son joug, elle espère bien de s'en venger un jour et le souvenir de l'appui que la France vous prêta alors augmente encore sa haine contre la République francoise. Si son projet pouvoit reussir, ce seroit fait de la liberté du Commerce de l'Europe et bientôt celle de l'Amerique Septentrionale se trouveroit exposée aux atteintes de cette formidable puissance. Elle attaqueroit votre Commerce au dehors et votre constitution au dedans. Devenue toute puissante en Europe elle Vous priveroit de toute assistance étrangère et vous serez seules à lutter contre ses flottes et ses tresors. Tachons donc, pendant qu'il en est encore tems, de detourner cet orage, et dejouons un plan qui nous menace tous. Je sais que par les circonstances actuelles ce projet harde à gagner une sorte de probabilité en ce que toutes les puissances qui pourroient l'arrêter sont enveloppées dans la combustion generalle et absorbées par les efforts qu'exige leur propre defence. Mais si cet état de crise favorise d'un coté l'ambition angloise, de l'autre il offre des moyens de la combattre. L'energie de la France, son union avec la Hollande, la probabilité que plusieurs puissances se detacheront sous peu de la Coalition, la crainte, enfin, qu'inspire l'accord inattendu et allarmant entre la Russie et la Grande Bretagne et qui obligera les autres puissances à être sur leur garde, ces differents événemens doivent servir la cause de la justice et de la liberté. Que son triomphe devienne l'objet de nos efforts communs, comme de nos vœux! Que l'Amerique se reunisse à la Suede et au Dannemarck pour proteger la neutralité! et on ne tardera pas à voir resulter de cette Union de grands avantages pour leurs Commerce et un bien incalculable pour le systeme politique des deux hemispheres.

Voilà, Monsieur, les reflexions que mon inviolable estime pour vous et mon ardent desir de pouvoir contribuer en quelque chose au bonheur et à la tranquilité des hommes m'a engagé de vous transmettre. Veuillez en faire l'usage qui Vous conviendra, car je suis bien sûr de ne jamais être compromis par un aussi galant homme que vous. Votre très humble et très obeissant Serviteur,

E: M: Stael Holstein

Editors' Translation

Paris 30 June 30 1795.

Sir

The importance of the conversation I had with you a few days ago leads me, Sir, to claim the honor of giving you a summary of the reflections and opinions that I had the pleasure of communicating to you.

We live in an era that is as critical as it is astonishing for the changes that it has produced. It will affect the centuries to come and the politicians of our day cannot be attentive enough in order to ward off events that might lead to great calamities.

It is only too clear that England harbors the intention of winning mastery of the seas and of trade in the four corners of the world. All the powers are thus concerned with opposing her, especially the United States of North America. The enormous commercial interests that they have in Europe make it essential for them to establish free and easy communications with the different nations of our hemisphere. Thus far, England has been able to take advantage of shared values and language in order to capture your trade, and she aspires sooner or later to take complete control of it to the exclusion of all other peoples. This is why she looks with repugnance upon connections that others try to establish with your nation and why she seeks to destroy other nations' commerce as assiduously as she has always sought to expand her own. Last year, in an offence against armed neutrality, she stopped all neutral ships destined for France. In order to protect their shipping, Sweden and Denmark consulted and concluded an agreement, the happy and speedy result of which you are well aware.[1] At that time, the Swedish envoy to London had orders to convey to the Minister of the United States the desire of the Swedish court to see the American government accede to this agreement. That this affair was not concluded probably results from the Court of St James' appearing soon after to disavow its previous conduct, declaring that no longer would neutral shipping be captured. Now, in contravention of the law of nations, England is repeating these same unjust acts and stopping all ships destined for France, whether they be American, Danish, or Swedish. It is time for us firmly to unite and force England to respect the rules of justice and cease attacking the dignity and independence of other nations.

It should also be added that England appears determined to destroy their freedom as well as their trade. She has not yet forgotten that America dared throw off her yoke, and she hopes to avenge herself some day, and the recollection of the support that France gave you then further increases her hatred for the Republic of France. If her plan were to succeed, it would be the end of free trade in Europe, and soon thereafter free trade in North America would be exposed to her formidable power. She would attack your trade from the exterior and your Constitution from the interior. Having become all-powerful in Europe, she would deprive you of all external aid and you would be alone in fighting her navies and her treasury. Let us, therefore, avert this storm while there is still time, and defeat a plan that threatens us all. I know that under the present circumstances such a project is hardly probable in that all the powers that could stop it are embroiled in the general conflagration and absorbed by the efforts required for their own defense. However if this state of crisis favors English ambitions on one hand, on the other it offers the means for fighting it. France's energy, her union with Holland, the likelihood that several powers will soon defect from the Coalition, and finally the fear inspired by the unexpected and alarming accord between Russia and Great Britain, which will force the other powers to be on their guard; these events must serve the cause of justice and liberty. May the victory of this cause become the object of our joint efforts and of our desires! May America join Sweden and Denmark in protecting neutrality! This great union would soon produce great benefits for their trade and an incalculable benefit for the political system of the two hemispheres.

These, Sir, are the reflections that I am led by my undying respect for you and my ardent desire to contribute in some way to the joy and tranquility of man to convey to you. You may employ them as you see fit, for I am confident of never being compromised by such a gentleman as you. Your very humble and obedient servant,

E: M: Stael Holstein

RC, NN: Monroe Papers

1. Denmark and Sweden signed a convention of armed neutrality on 27 March 1794 in which they pledged to protect each other's shipping from depredations by belligerent nations, meaning especially Great Britain. Sweden wanted the United States to join the league (the United States had been a member of a previous league of armed neutrality in the early 1780s), and the Swedish minister in London met with Thomas Pinckney on several occasions urging American participation. These queries to JM and Pinckney proved fruitless, for the Washington administration had no intention of joining any alliance (Samuel Flagg Bemis, *Jay's Treaty*, 221-225, 246-250).

To Joseph Jones

Paris July 2. 1795

Dear Sir

I have written you frequently latterly & shall therefore be very concise in the present one. I find by a letter of 8th of June from Mr Maury of Liverpool[1] that neither Mr Jefferson's nor Colo Bells bills have reached him (except one for a small sum by the former £37.10-) & in consequence the amt deposited in his hands for these gentn remains with Mr Maury every way to my disadvantage. I receive no interest from Mr Maury whilst I pay it to Colo Bell, & with respect to the case of Mr Jefferson the injury will perhaps be greater, depending on the principle adopted for the valuation of Thena[2] & children: for if the valuation is made as at present, her family have grown up and is growing up at my expence and indeed risk (for if they were to die I shod insist on paying the amt) whilst the money to pay for them is laying without bearing interest. Let me therefore entreat you to attend to these objects—settle Bell's acct (it was abt £140.) & draw for the amt for him if not yet done. and do the same with Mr Jefferson. It was intended the slaves shod be valued & it was to have been done two years since. Let them yet be valued either as of that age & upon the credit—or as at present: 'tho I can see no objection to yr agreing the price together. Indeed I think this the best mode for then both will be satisfied & there will be no dependance on the time &c of others which may still create delay.

I have heretofore mentioned that I had plac'd with Mr Randolph 3.200 dolrs or thereabts subject to yr immediate order & that I shod also pay yr orders in favr of Burnley & Southcombe when presented: that I approved yr accomodation to Joseph,[3] & wished the acct rendered by Sr Wm Forbes of his debts in Scotland that I might also pay them, & which acct Joseph has: provided however that the arrangment Joseph contemplated had not been carried too far into effect for the payment of those debts to admit my doing it.

Joseph[4] is at St Germain's abt 12. miles from this at a school where he does better than he did in Paris. Indeed his prospect of doing well there is good. He has been at the latter school abt 2. months, during which time I have formed a favorable opinion of his prospect. In the course of a few days I shall visit him & examine strictly into circumstances & apprize you immediately afterwards. Latterly I have been greatly occupied so that I have [not] been able to do it; but the measure of sending him there was adopted upon mature consideration & what I have seen & heard of the school since justifies the expectation that was formed of it. I will send you a letter from him in my next. He is perfectly well & grows fast.

I hear that the French have sustained a loss of two ships in a late accidental encounter near the mouth of Channel but in other respects things are well. Mrs M. & the child as did Joe when I heard from him, desire to be remembered to you. Affecy I am yr friend & servt

Jas Monroe

RC, ViFreJM

1. The letter from James Maury of 8 June 1795 has not been located.

2. Thenia Hemings.

3. Joseph J. Monroe.

4. Joseph Jones, Jr.

From Edmund Randolph

Department of State July 2. 1795.

Sir

I understand by a letter from Col⁰ Burr,[1] that Mᵣ John B. Prevost takes an immediate passage for France, to enter into your family. His affectation being founded on the new office of consul general, which at your instance, has been created, and given to Mᵣ Skipwith, I inclose his commission.[2]

Before this you must have seen Mᵣ Pinckney and Mᵣ Trumbull, and from them will have collected the particulars of the treaty with Great Britain. My long letter of the 4ᵗʰ June—will also have reached you within a few days from the present. Overwhelmed as I am with most urgent business, I can only communicate to you a copy of the treaty and the vote of the senate; and state to you that the President has not yet decided upon the final meausre to be adopted by himself: that a copy has been delivered to Mᵣ Adet; that he had last evening transmitted to me some remarks upon it, that this morning they will be laid before the President; and that I shall probably make explanations to Mᵣ Adet, which as far as I see into the subject ought to quiet his apprehensions.[3] I need not repeat to you how much we have at heart a pure friendship with France uninterrupted and perpetual. I have the honor to be sir with great respect and esteem yᵣ mo. ob. serv.

Edm: Randolph

PS. Mᵣ Skipwith's commission will not be completed in time for this conveyance.

RC, DLC: Monroe Papers

1. Aaron Burr's letter to Randolph has not been located.

2. President Washington nominated Fulwar Skipwith for appointment as consul general at Paris on 25 June 1795, and the Senate confirmed the appointment on the 26th (*The Journal of the Executive Proceedings of the U. S. Senate*, 1: 189, 191).

3. Pierre Adet's letter to Randolph of 30 June 1795 and Randolph's response of 6 July 1795 are in *ASP: FR*, 1: 594-597.

To Jean-Victor Colchen

Paris 3 July 1795. (15 Messidor An 3) 19 Year of the American Republick

Citizen

I have received your letter of the 13ᵗʰ Messidor[1] in answer to mine of the 27. June and to which I beg leave now to reply.

The note which I wrote to you ought to have comprised those to whom certificates are granted as well as passeports, for to many certificates are granted merely to authorize a residence in Paris and its vicinity. This change will comprize all those of whose arrival I have or can have any knowledge.

It is true that all the Americans who arrive in Paris ought to call immediately upon me and take the protection to which they are entitled from the minister of their country. But the fact is otherwise, for many never call untill they are about to depart, some of whom have thus remained for five, six and eight months. In the interim they are protected by the passports they have from the municipalities in the sea-ports and other authorities which they find adequate, for if they were not adequate, they would of course apply to me for the protection they otherwise did not enjoy. You will readily perceive that it is my business only to give protection to my countrymen entitled to it: beyond which my authority cannot extend and that it is the business of the government to see that those who are not possessed of that protection shall not be deemed such and of course be treated accordingly. I suggest this idea for your consideration, that weighing it, you may shew what step I shall take to avoid the inconvenience complained of, if possible on my part, or propose to the committee such measure as will remedy it on theirs.

In case any new regulation is adopted I beg of you to apprize me of it, that I may give the necessary notice thereof to my countrymen, that they may sustain no injury from a measure which is calculated to secure them the enjoyment of their just rights, by preventing others from imposing themselves upon this government as their compatriots, to the injury of France and the dishonor of America.

I will see that the list of those in Paris be made and furnished you as soon as possible.

Ja^s Monroe

RC, DLC : FCP—France

1. Colchen to JM, 1 July 1795 (13 Messidor), above.

To Thomas Jefferson

Paris July 3. 1795.

Dear Sir

Having written you very fully three days since[1] I have nothing to add at present to the details then given except that in an unexpected ren-counter the other day the French have lost 3. ships & by the shameful misconduct of the officers commanding them or some of them.[2] They have in consequence dismissed the Com^y of Marine which I think converts the loss of the ships into a signal victory, in such regard do I esti-mate his merits.[3]

By M^r De Rieux I learn that poor Gilmer declines & that Bell has been sick, that Mrs Marks is dead—that Miss Gilmer is about to be married—that Wardlow and Robt Jouett are.[4] This short note from Goochland which opens the interior of a place extremely dear to me contains every thing that I have heard from that quarter since my arrival here. Be so kind as forward the enclosed to him[5] and assure my neighbours I have not forgotten them, altho' they may have forgotten me. Is there any thing here you wish me to procure for you. I beg you to give me a note of it if there is. Our best respects to M^r and M^{rs} R[6] and both yours and his families. very sincerely I am y^r affectionate friend & serv^t

Ja^s Monroe

RC, DLC: Jefferson Papers

1. JM may be referring to his letter to Madison of 30 June 1795 (above), which contained information that JM asked Madison to share with Jefferson. JM's previous letter to Jefferson was that of 27 June 1795 (above).

2. A British fleet under Admiral Lord Bridport attacked a French fleet near the Ile de Groix (off L'Orient) on 23 June 1795 and captured three French ships without losing any of its own (James Rolfe, *The Naval Biography of Great Britain*, 1: 206-207).

3. Jean-Claude Redon replaced Jean Dalbarade as the minster of marine.

4. Neither the letter from Peter Derieux nor JM's response has been located.

5. William Wardlaw (1776-1829) was a Charlottesville physician who later moved to Richmond. He married Sarah Minor (1776-1808) (*Jefferson Papers*, 29: 401; Edgar Woods, *Albemarle County in Virginia*, 277). Robert Jouett (d. 1796) was a Charlottesville attorney (Woods, *Albemarle County*, 241).

6. Thomas Mann and Martha Jefferson Randolph.

To Edmund Randolph

Paris 4ᵗʰ July 1795

Sir,

About three or four weeks past one of our vessels which touched at Havre from England was taken in charge by the government and the Captain and passengers confined, upon a suspicion they had brought false assignats with them, with a view of circulating them through the country and thereby subserving the views of its enemies: complete search was made upon the vessel but no assignats were found. As I knew that the suspicion which was entertained, ought not to be extended to three young men who were passengers, I immediately applied to the commissary of foreign relations for their discharge, and obtained an order for it, though fortunately they were released by the Municipality at Havre before it reached them.[1] But as I was not acquainted with the character of the Captain or any others belonging to the vessel, and was aware of the right the government had to protect itself from injuries of every kind and from every quarter and of course to search the vessel, and as I also hoped in case the suspicion proved to be groundless it would prevent the like in future, and especially upon frivolous suggestions, I did not chuse in that stage to apply likewise in their behalf. After the search was made, and the government satisfied it had suspected without cause, the Captain was put at liberty and the vessel offered back to him. But being mortified in having been suspected, and as his vessel and cargo were somewhat injured by the search and neglect which ensued his arrestation, he seemed disposed rather to throw the whole upon government and demand an indemnity for it, and with which view he lately came here to confer with me. I advised him to gather up what he could of his own property and pursue his voyage according to the original destination, limiting his claim merely to the damage sustained and leaving that to be pursued by the consul here under my direction. As yet he waits his protest and other documents from Havre, reserving to himself the liberty of acting after their receipt as he pleases, and according as the light of preceding examples of the like kind, and whose details he will in the interim acquire, may admonish him will be most for his interest. I shall endeavour to obtain justice for him, upon sound principles, and have only mentioned the case that you may know such a one has happened, and what the circumstances of it are.

The jealousy which is entertained by this government of the commerce carried on by our countrymen between the ports of this republic and those of England has latterly shewn itself in a more unpleasant form than heretofore and I am fearful it will yet produce some more disagreeable effect. A Mʳ Eldred was lately apprehended at Marseilles and sent here under guard upon a charge of having given intelligence to the British of some movement in the French fleet. Upon enquiry I found he had my passport granted too upon the most substantial documents proving him to be an american citizen; but I likewise found that in truth he was not an American citizen: for although born in America yet he was not there in the course of our revolution but in England, nor had he been there since. From what I hear of him, he is not a person of mischievous disposition nor one who would be apt to commit the offence, charged upon him, but yet I do not see how I can officially interfere in his behalf, for when once a principle is departed from, it ceases to be a principle.[2]

More latterly I was requested by the commissary of foreign affairs to prohibit our consuls from granting passports, and which was immediately done. I was afterwards requested by him to furnish a list of the americans actually in Paris, and to render a like list every decade of those who should in the interim arrive, and which was promised and will be punctually executed. I herewith send you a copy of my instructions to the consuls and correspondence with the commissary on this subject.[3]

You will readily perceive that this jealousy proceeds from the circumstance that many of those who are actually engaged in this trade are of that description of persons, who having latterly become citizens of the United States are likewise subjects of England: nor can you be surprised when that circumstance is considered without any imputation on the character of the parties, that this jealousy should exist: they are English themselves, their connections are so, and in England their profits will ultimately settle. It is natural that a communication of this kind should draw after it suspicion, or rather it would be unnatural if it did not produce that effect. To the people of America this is an evil of serious import: for by it, it is obvious that the confidence which is due to our national character is daily diminished. Nor can the mortification which is incident to such a situation be otherwise than heightened, when it is considered that we are most a prey to this evil, at the moment when the government to which these persons belong insults our national dignity and tramples on our rights. Be assured I shall do everything in my power to guard us against injuries of this kind, by excluding all who are not, and upon the principles agreed, upon my first arrival here, strictly entitled to our protection; and by which line of conduct I hope I shall succeed, in a great measure if not altogether, in the accomplishment of an object so important to our welfare.

As connected with this subject permit me to mention another which I deem equally important and more remediable. We have at Hamburgh as Consul for the United States a Mr Parish and who has held that office for some years past.[4] This gentleman is an English subject, and was, as I am assured, never in America. All the Americans who have been at Hamburgh and who come here unite in representing him (comparatively with England) as unfriendly to America; as absolutely unfriendly to France and the French revolution, and which traits are said to be often discernible in his public conduct. It is affirmed that he is likewise an agent of England and that in particular the Prussian subsidy passed through his hands. Upon these facts you may rely and especially the latter (into which I have made more pointed enquiry) for they are agreed in by all the Americans, and I am sure have been stated to me by at least 50. Without observing how wide a door is here opened for England to benefit herself and injure France through us, even whilst its use is confined to that range, which without any imputation on the morality of this gentleman, national prejudice alone would allow, there are other considerations which at the present moment make this appointment worthy your attention. Since the commencement of the present war a great proportion of the commerce of the North and from every quarter of the world has centered at Hamburgh and will probably continue to center there, till its close, from whence it issues again in different directions France, Holland, England &c &c: that this commerce is capable of a serious impression by the public Agents of different countries there, and especially by those of the neutral powers, whose conneccion is sought with great avidity by the subjects of the powers at war, cannot be questioned: nor can it be questioned when it is considered who this gentleman is, that the impression which he makes upon it, is a British and not an American one. In addition to which it may be observed that as he resides in the dominions of an independent power and where we have no Minister, it is in some measure his duty to grant passports to Americans travelling elsewhere. This circumstance therefore and especially at the present moment increases the importance and delicacy of the trust. In justice however to this gentleman, I must add, that I do not know any instance in which he has betrayed it in this respect, and that in others I only apply to him general principles and bring to your view the complaints of our countrymen. Personally I never saw or had any communication with him. There are at present at Hamburgh several Americans worthy of this trust among whom are Joel Barlow[5] and William St John[6] son of him who by his writings is well known; but in truth so profitable is the post that there are but few American merchants in Europe who would not accept it. In general permit me to suggest for your consideration when ever a vacancy takes place, or when ever it becomes necessary to supercede an existing Consul, whether it would not be advisable to advertise the fact that candidates might offer for the post; for sure I am that it would rarely happen that suitable candidates, American citizens did not offer. In Europe such may generally be found.

Since my last the French have sustained a loss at sea of three Ships, which arose partly from accident not to be guarded against and partly from misconduct. It occasioned the immediate dismission of Dalbarade minister of marine, who gave way to a successor believed to be better quallified for the post.[7] The British have likewise landed on the French coast near Nantes about 6,000 emigrants and who being joined perhaps with some of their own troops, and since by some fanatic priests are said to make up a force of about 10,000 men. It is supposed the British government might hope, that by putting these people in the neighbourhood of the Chouans or Vendeans, they might by encouraging a rebellion there, combine a force capable of making some impression:[8] but a wish to rid themselves of these unfortunate men whose support became daily more burdensome is believed to be the more influential motive. All parties unite here in the sentiment that they are sacrificed, and consider the act of landing them as an act of barbarity excelled only by those which were formerly perpetrated in the same neighbourhood by the infatuated Carrier.

It is believed that a treaty has taken place between England and Russia in which the former has stipulated not to take the side of Poland against the latter, in consideration whereof Russia is to furnish England a certain number of ships during the residue of the war.[9] It is likewise believed that England has announced to Spain that in case the latter makes peace with France she will commence immediate hostilities upon her. This may possibly keep Spain in a state of suspence some time longer. On the other hand it is obvious that the connection between France and Holland, Denmark and Sweden becomes daily stronger, whilst Austria paralized by the peace and movements of Prussia, which threaten an entire change in the Germanic system, and such an arrangement of its parts as will give an entire preponderance to Prussia, scarcely knows what part to take, and whether to make peace or continue the war; for the pressure of France upon the Empire and which is the consequence of it, tends to favour the views of Prussia, by throwing the members of the Empire into her arms, with a view of securing their peace with France through the intercession of Prussia.

In conversation a few days past with Baron Stahl, Ambassador from Sweden, he informed me of a communication formerly made by the Court of Sweden to Mᴿ Pinckney at London for our government and upon which no answer was given although it was much wished. I desired his communication in writing that I might forward it to you and which was accordingly given and is herewith transmitted. I have no doubt that whatever he says to me is known to the committee, as I was informed by some of its members in the beginning of the winter, and before the Baron arrived, that such an application had been made to us from that quarter. It belongs to me only to forward this paper, and which I do not doubting that I shall be instructed relative thereto in the most suitable manner.[10]

Colᵒ Humphreys has just arrived and upon due consideration I presented last night a paper to the committee opening as far as was expedient the object of his visit,[11] and upon which subject generally I shall be more full in my next when I hope to be possessed of an answer to it. With great respect and esteem, I have the honor to be, Sir, your very humble servant

Jaˢ Monroe.

Copy, DNA: RG 59: Dispatches from France

1. The three young men were Adam Seybert, William Bache, and Mr. Boys. The ship was the *Jane*, commanded by a Captain Cowell (Claude-Adam Delamotte to JM, 28 May 1795 and JM to Jean-Victor Colchen, 3 June 1795, both above).

2. For more on the case of Thomas Eldred, see JM to Charles Delacroix, 28 February 1796, below.

3. JM to American Consuls, 17 June 1795 (above). JM's correspondence with Jean-Victor Colchen on this subject is reprinted in *Writings of Monroe*, 2: 320-324.

4. John Parish, a British merchant in Hamburg, was appointed American vice consul for that city in June 1790. Parish declined the appointment, telling Secretary of State Jefferson that vice consuls had little status in Hamburg. He was appointed consul in February 1793 and served until 1796 (*Jefferson Papers*, 17: 246-247, 18: 344-345, 25: 204, 208; *Washington Papers: Presidential Series*, 12: 190; William B. Smith, *America's Diplomats and Consuls of 1776-1865*, 81).

5. Joel Barlow (1754-1812) was born in Connecticut and rose to prominence in 1787 with the publication of his epic poem, *The Vision of Columbus*. He went to France in 1788 as an agent for the Scioto Associates, a company that speculated in land in Ohio. While in Europe Barlow continued his writing, both literary and, increasingly, political, in support of the French Revolution. He fled Paris in 1794 and established himself in the mercantile trade in Hamburg, which proved quite lucrative (*ANB*).

6. Guillaume-Alexandre St. John de Crèvecoeur (1772-1806) was the son of M. G. Hector St. John de Crèvecoeur. He was born in America and traveled to France with his father in 1781. In 1795 he was a partner in a mercantile business in Altona, near Hamburg (Gay Wilson Allen and Roger Asselineau, *St. John de Crèvecoeur*, 38, 177-179, 188-189, 197).

7. Count Jean-Claude Redon de Beaupréau (1738-1815) was born into an old entitled Breton family. He served in the Department of the Marine where he was employed as a commissioner in various ports and in the colonies. Incarcerated in 1793, he did not regain his freedom until after 9 Thermidor. Redon de Beaupréau returned to his post as navy commissioner and served from July to November 1795, when once again he was named minister of the Marine and Colonies, a post he maintained until July 1797. He was counselor of state under Napoléon 1799-1810 (*Nouvelle Biographie Général*).

8. The British defeat of the French fleet at the Ile de Groix cleared the way for the landing of a force of 3000 French émigrés on the Quiberon Peninsula in Brittany on 27 June 1795. They were joined there by over 5,000 Chouans, a faction that opposed the Revolution (Samuel Scott and Barry Rothaus, *Historical Dictionary of the French Revolution*).

9. The British and Russians signed a mutual assistance pact on 18 February 1795. The Russians agreed to provide troops in case England was invaded, and the British promised naval support if Russia was attacked. The Russians also agreed to send eighteen ships to cruise with a British fleet. The treaty did not require Russia to join the war against France, which left the Russians free to defend their territorial claims in Poland from the Prussians (Isabel de Madariaga, *Russia in the Age of Catherine the Great*, 449-450).

10. Baron de Staël to JM, 30 June 1795, above.

11. JM's letter to the Committee of Public Safety asking its assistance in the negotiations with Algiers is dated 5 July 1795 (below). This indicates that this last paragraph was written on July 6.

Independence Day Toasts

[4 July 1795]

1. The 4th of July.

2. The united State of America.

3. The French republick.

4. The powers in amity with the United States & the French republick—may the friendship & harmony which subsists between them never be interrupted.

5. The President of the United States & the Congress of the U. States.

6. The freedom of the seas.

7. The national Convention of France—may it end its long arduous & dangerous career, by the establishment of a constitution upon such wise, free, & equal principles as thereby to secure to the latest posterity the liberty & happiness of the French people.

8. The gallant armies of France—May those good citizens who compose them enjoy in retir'ment, & in the bosom of a grateful & munificent country, the precious fruits of that liberty which their illustrious exertions & splendid victories entitle them to.

9. The memory of those who have fought and died in defense of their country & the publick liberty. May wreaths of laurel adorn their tombs and their services be always remembered by a grateful posterity.

10. Agriculture.

11. Commerce.

12. Justice, humanity, & probity—may these great principles always form the most distinguishing characteristics of the councils of free governments.

13. Science and the arts, with those eminent men who form their brightest ornaments.

14. The fair sex in both hemispheres.

15. Those of our compatriots & their friends who are assembled in America & elsewhere to celebrate this anniversary so important in the annals of our country

Dft (in JM's handwriting), NCD: Purviance-Courtenay Family Papers

JM recorded an account of the Independence Day celebration in his autobiography:

> The 4th of July, the anniversary of our Independence, was approaching. It comported with Mr. Monroe's principles and feelings to pay a tribute of respect to that great event by celebrating it on that day. The motive for it at that period was peculiarly interesting. The revolutions of the two countries resting on the same basis, he thought that it furnished an opportunity, under a suitable arrangement, to produce a favorable effect on the councils of France towards the United States. He resolved, therefore, to avail himself of it for that purpose. With this view he took the entertainment into his own hands, provided a dinner at his own expense, and regulated it in every circumstance according to his best judgment. All the Americans then in Paris were requested to attend, and who complied therewith. He invited to the entertainment, specifying the object, the members of the government Committees, many members of the Convention, and the officers of the French government, with such as were distinguished who were then in Paris in the military and naval service and who attended. He invited also the foreign Ministers, then there, from Sweden, Tuscany, Holland, Genoa, Geneva and Malta, who likewise attended. The assemblage was, in consequence, very numerous, comprising at least 150 guests. It being impossible to entertain so great a number in his house, he asked of the Minister of War a loan of 12 marquees, which was granted, and which he arranged on a terrace, and under which the party dined. The toasts were adapted to the occasion. Due respect was paid to the Revolution of his own country and to the memory of those who had fought, bled and died in defense of it, to the President of the United States and other officers of his own government. A like respect was paid to the principles of the French Revolution, to the talent and skill of the Commander, and to the heroic bravery of their armies, and likewise to those in the public councils who braved all difficulties with firmness and sustained their stations with dignity. A tribute of respect was also paid to the Ministers then present who represented powers friendly to France. It is believed that the entertainment produced the desired effect (*Autobiography*, 102-103).

Thomas Perkins, an American visiting in Paris, also left an account of the dinner:

> This day the Anniversary of the Birth of the American Nation was celebrated by a large number of Citizens assembled by invitation of Citizen Munroe, the Minister of the U. S. of America, and in a manner which gave Satisfaction to all present. As the Company was too large to be accomodated within doors, there was an arrangment made in the garden for the purpose. the tables were Spread under a canopy formed by the tops of the Marquis, extended from one end to another of a beautiful malle of trees—this was decorated by some one of taste with wreaths of Roses & other flowers, and a most Sumptuous dinner was served to about two hundred persons amongst which were all the foreign Ministers & Consuls—the Members of Public Safety & Surety General—the President & thirty odd members of the Convention, a number of Officers of distinction both Marine & Terine and about fifty Americans. We had a Superb band of Music, which played while we were at Dinner—the toasts were patriotic, and calculated not to offend the politicks of anyone.—Citizen Cutting wrote a Song on the occasion, which was Sung to the tune of Anarion, to the Satisfaction of the Company, by Mᴿ O'Mealy & the day ended in Mirth and Glee. The french seemed much Satisfied with the good will which was Shewn towards them & every one retired at about 9 O'Clock, much gratified with the pleasures of the day (MCH: Thomas Perkins Diary, 4 July 1795).

From Aaron Burr

Nyork 5 July 1795

My dear Sir

M.ʳ Skipwith is appointed Consul general; and agreeably to your letter of the 13ᵗʰ Feb.[1] Prevost will take passage in the Course of this week to join you as your Secretary. I persuade myself that you will find him an useful and agreeable Companion.

By the Papers herewith sent you will see that the Treaty has got out, & you will now see what it is— I wish you had had an earlier knowledge of it—The public Discussion of it has scarcely commenced— The Country is considerably agitated with it—Many of the Merchants who were the Most devoted to M.ʳ Jay and to administration, express themselves decidedly & warmly against it—What the President will do, cannot be conjectured—but I do not learn that he has yet ratified it—A memorial against the ratif.ⁿ is circulating in this Town—

Your several letters in favor of Swan, Mozard & Rozier, have been delivered to me, all within a fortnight.[2] Your recommendations will always command my utmost attentions & Services

I shall write you soon by Prevost, who will sail with Fauchet in the Medusa in about eight Days[3]— This is only to advise you of his approach and to give you every chance of seeing the Treaty as early as possible—I need not apprize you of the Sensations which it has excited among the french—The Causes which excite them are too obvious & too mortifying—Yrs.

RC, DLC: Monroe. Not signed.

1. JM's letter to Burr of 13 February 1795 has not been located.

2. JM's several letters to Burr introducing James Swan, Theodore-Charles Mozard, and Jean-Antoine Rozier have not been located.

3. A British warship cruising off the coast of Rhode Island prevented the sailing of the French ship *Medusa* until 1 September 1795. Prevost did not travel on the *Medusa* and delayed his own departure until a later date (John J. Reardon, *Edmund Randolph*, 314-315; Burr to JM, 11 September 1795).

To the Committee of Public Safety

Paris. 5 July 1795. (17 Messidor 3.ᵈ year of the F. R.)
20 Year of the American Republick.

Citizens,

The injuries which the piratical powers on the African coast have rendered and continue to render to our commerce are Known to this Republick, because it takes an interest in our welfare, and because those injuries cannot otherwise than be eventually hurtful to the commerce of France likewise.

It was foreseen at the moment when we became an independant nation, that we should be exposed to the piracies of those powers, and the same spirit of amity which disposed the then councils of France, in obedience to the wishes of the people, to aid us in that struggle, disposed them likewise to assure us of their support in our negociations with each respectively. But unfortunately no treaty has yet been formed with any of those powers (Morocco excepted) and in consequence our commerce has been interrupted by their cruizers and especially those of Algiers, whereby many of our citizens were also taken and who are now detained in slavery.

'Tis the wish of the United States to make an effort at this present moment to conclude a peace with those several powers, and to pursue that object in harmony with this Republick, that its aid may be extended to them in their negociations with each, and for which purpose I have now the pleasure to inform you that Mr Humphreys minister of the United States at Lisbon has just arrived here with full power to commence and conclude such treaties. It may be necessary further to premise that suitable provision has been made for those treaties, according to our idea of what would be suitable, and so far as we were able to make it, and of course that the only aid which we wish from this Republick is that of its good offices and influence in the councils of those powers.

If the Committee is disposed to render us this aid, our future measures will be in concert with the Committee, because it best Knows how it may be most efficaciously rendered, and with least inconvenience to itself. In that view I will be happy to open to the Committee our funds &ca, that by Knowing completely our real situation the concert and harmony may be equally complete, and in consequence the best arrangements taken that circumstances will admit of, to ensure success in the negociations contemplated.

As we have reason to apprehend the interference of some other powers who would not be pleased to see us at peace with those regencies, permit me to suggest the propriety of great secrecy in respect to the present and such future communications as may take place between us, upon this interesting subject.

Ja^s Monroe

RC, DLC: FCP—France

From John Quincy Adams

The Hague July 8. 1795.

Dear Sir

I received sometime since your favour of the 14th ult^o by the Post, and last Evening that of the 24th by Baron Rehausen,[1] together with the letter from America, and the newspapers, for which be pleased to accept my best acknowledgments.

With respect to the claim of protection for American property, which was found on board a Russian Vessel in a port of this Republic, it will be unnecessary to trouble you with a detail of the reasons upon which my opinion was formed; as I have heard nothing from the claimants, since I wrote you before, and question whether they will be able to establish the fact as to the property.

I am sensible that the principle itself may be somewhat questionable, though I confess that after all the consideration I could give it there was no doubt remaining upon my mind relative to it.

I shall only observe generally that my opinion was founded upon two Reasons. The first that the property being in a Port of this Republic, was entitled to the same territorial protection, with all other neutral property then in the Country: That the capture was not maritime, neither in point of form nor of substance; and that the 14th Article of our Treaty with France relates merely to a maritime capture. The second, that even if it could be considered as a maritime capture, the case would not come within either the letter or the Spirit of that 14th Article; which makes expressly, not a <u>State of War</u>, but a <u>Declaration of War</u>, the test upon which neutral property shall be liable to confiscation on board an Enemy's vessel. And however hostile France and Russia may have been to each other there has been no Declaration of War between them on either side.

I receive with pleasure and with thanks the information of the attention paid by the Secretary of State to the supplies which might have been an occasion of embarrassment, upon the contingency of a derangement in this Country which it was natural to consider as probable, but which fortunately has not taken place. As in the actual state of affairs there was no necessity for using the bill, I am happy to hear you returned it.[2]

At the request of the Swedish Minister here, I send the letter enclosed herewith, and solicit your goodness to send to the person to whom it is addressed. I have the honour to be with great respect, Dear Sir, your very humble & obed[t] Serv[t]

John Q. Adams.

RC, DLC: Monroe Papers

1. JM to Adams, 24 June 1795, MHi: Adams Family Papers: Letter Received.

2. The United States maintained accounts with its Amsterdam bankers for the use of JM and Adams. JM informed Adams in his letter of June 24 that Secretary of State Randolph had sent a bill drawn on a Paris bank that they could use in case the war in the Netherlands prevented them from drawing on their accounts for expenses.

To Fulwar Skipwith

July 8 1795

Dear Sir

I requested of you some days past to inform me what M[r] Gelston had placd with you of flour for me or of rice if any but you have forgotten to do it. I wish to know precisely what it was because as I do not know upon what terms I get it, I wish him precisely to designate what it is to be. I wish an ans[r] by the bearer to this if convenient as I intend to send whatever I get thence if possible to day to S[t] Germains for our child: but if you cannot now send it, I hope you will let me know sometime to day. Y[rs] respectfully

Ja[s] Monroe

FC, NN: Monroe Papers

To the Committee of Public Safety

Paris July 10. 1795

I have received yours of the 20 (Messidor) requesting that I would immediately cause a list to be rendered you of my countrymen in Paris and hereafter a like list from décade to décade of those who may arrive and demand passports of me: a measure you deem it necessary to adopt to guard the Republic from danger by an accurate discrimination of your friends from your enemies.[1] I shall execute this request with pleasure being extremely anxious as well for the credit of my countrymen as the welfare of this Republic, that the most accurate line should be drawn between them and the subjects of the powers at war with France. The more accurate the line of distinction, and strict the execution the more agreeable it will be to me. I have in consequence notified to my countrymen who are in Paris, and shall cause the same to be made known to those who may hereafter arrive, that it is my wish they immediately attend at my office to enregister their names and receive passports, that I may be enabled equally to comply with your desire and extend to them the protection which is their due. I shall I presume have the pleasure to send you the list of those who are actually in Paris, on Septidi next,[2] and shall afterwards furnish a like list on the same day of every succeeding décade.

FC, NN: Monroe Papers

1. Committee of Public Safety to JM, 8 July (20 Messidor) 1795, *View of the Conduct*, 198.

2. Septidi was the seventh day of the ten-day decade (or week) of the French revolutionary calendar.

From Robert R. Livingston

ClerMont 10th July 1795.

Dear Sir

Mr Fauchette who is now here tells me that he proposes to embark in a few days for France I cannot but embrace so favourable an opportunity to acknowledge your favor of the   of Feb[y] last[1] tho my retired situation at present prevents my being able to give you so full a state of our politics as I could wish but this is the less necessary as you will learn them from M[r] Fauchette. The Senate after a months <u>secret</u> deliberation have at length agreed to advise the president to ratify the treaty on condition that the 12th article was suspended. As you will necessarily be furnished with this treaty I enter into no details. I should tell you however that it was intended to keep the secret till the ratification was exchanged, and the fetters too firmly fixed to be shaken off had not M[r] Mason contrary to their resolution given out a copy to be printed for which he is severly threatened by the Senate.[2]

It has as far as I have yet learned, been rec[d] every w[h]ere with execrations tho Hamilton has come out openly as the champion of the treaty & published a weak hasty thing in its defence[3] which has brought over a few of our tory merchants not indeed to approve but to be silent about it. By the people at large notwithstanding all their efforts it is rec[d] as it should be. For my part I know not whether to consider it as more repugnant to our interest or that of our alliance. it is evidently calculated to weaken that, to destroy our carrying trade & to continue the <illegible> the british have put upon our commerce without a possibility of shaking off our fetters.

I am fearful that it will contribute to render your situation very disagreeable unless the brave people you are with shall be willing to discriminate between our administration & our nation. The last you may be assured are firmly attached to them, whatever the first may be.

I sh[d] have told you that after the senate had passed upon the treaty the president gave M[r] Addet a copy & told him that he would not ratify it till he had his notes thereon. This delay affords him the means of knowing the sentiments of the people & pray perhaps when he sees how much they rise against it enduce him to withold his assent.

As I thought every thing was to be attempted to effect this I have written to the president on the subject. my letter will reach him this day. I have also exhorted Maddison to do the same.[4] I am preparing some observations on the treaty for the press which will come out this week under my old signature Cato.[5]

As the toasts on the 4th of July are a pretty good criterion of the sense of the people I send you those that have come to hand in the New York & Philadelphia papers least you sh[d] not have them They may be of use to shew the French nation the attachment we still feel for them.

Our last accounts from Paris being of the 20th of May represent the situation of the convention as very disagreeable. I hope the storm has blown over & that France has by this time given peace to all her enemies, one only excepted which it is her interest, & that of all mankind to see humbled first. Nothing was more fortunate for Jay than the concealm[t] of the contents of the treaty since to this alone he is endebted for his election. It will however I think deprive him of all chance for the presidents chair, which the party openly declared they designed for him on the presidents resignation which they give out is to take place on the next day of election. Sh^d this be the case, I trust that it will be better bestowed on our friend Jefferson. I am Dear Sir with the greatest esteem & regard Your Most Ob hum Servt

Rob R. Livingston

RC, DLC: Monroe Papers

1. JM to Livingston, 23 February 1795, above.

2. Senator Rufus King convinced President Washington and Secretary of State Randolph that they should terminate the secrecy surrounding the Jay Treaty and publish it, which they did on 1 July 1795 in the *Philadelphia Gazette*. Prior to this, however, the *Aurora* had obtained a copy of the treaty from Senator Stevens T. Mason and published an abstract of it on June 29. Benjamin F. Bache, the editor of the *Aurora*, then published a pamphlet containing the entire text of the treaty, which he published on July 1, followed by a second expanded edition on July 3 (Jerald Combs, *The Jay Treaty*, 162; *Hamilton Papers*, 18: 389-392).

3. Livingston seems to be mistaken here. Hamilton, together with Rufus King, wrote a series of thirty-eight essays, signed "Camillus," defending the Jay Treaty, but the first number was not published until 22 July 1795 (*Hamilton Papers*, 18: 475-479).

4. Livingston to George Washington, 8 July 1795, DLC: Washington Papers; Livingston to James Madison, 6 July 1795, *Madison Papers*, 16: 34-35.

5. Livingston wrote a series of sixteen essays over the signature "Cato." They were published in the New York *Argus* between July and September 1795 (George Dangerfield, *Chancellor Robert R. Livingston*, 272).

From Edmund Randolph

Department of State July 14. 1795.

Dear sir

My indisposition disables me from writing a long letter at this moment. But the opportune conveyance by Mr Gibson, supercargo of the ship Molly (whom I recommend to your notice and patronage, on public and private considerations) will not suffer me to omit the forwarding of the papers at foot.[1] Among them is the treaty &c. as published, and a correspondence between Mr Adet and myself upon it.[2] Since my letter to him, I have heard nothing from him.

The treaty is not yet ratified by the President; nor will it be ratified, I believe, until it returns from England; if then.[3] But I do not mean this for a public communication, or for any public body or men. I am engaged in a work, which, when finished and approved by the President, will enable me to speak precisely to you.[4] The late British order for seizing provisions is a weighty obstacle to a ratification. I do not suppose that such an attempt to starve France will be countenanced.

By Mr Prevost, who leaves the U. S. for France the day after to morrow I shall write to you again; and if possible, more at large. I have the honor to be dear [sir] with sincere respect & es[teem] yr. mo. ob. serv.

Edm: Rand[olph]

Be so good, as to protect the vessel, the description of which is enclosed.

RC, NN: Monroe Papers

1. A list of enclosures appended to this letter reads as follows:
   Dup. E. R. to James Monroe 1 June 1795

Dup. E. R. to James Monroe 7 June 1795 as to money for madame la Fayette
    dᵒ   dᵒ   8 June
    dᵒ   dᵒ   2 July
copy of the Treaty between the US & G. Britain and the newspapers including this day.
1ˢᵗ Copy of a letter from Mʳ Adet of 30 June and Mʳ Randolph's answer of 6 July relative to the Treaty between the US & G Britain.

2. Pierre Adet's letter to Randolph and Randolph's response are in *ASP: FR*, 1: 594-597.

3. Randolph was of the opinion that the Senate's conditional ratification of the Jay Treaty required the approval of the British crown to a modification of the article relating to trade with the British West Indies before the president could sign it (John J. Reardon, *Edmund Randolph*, 299-303).

4. Randolph was preparing a memorial addressed to British minister George Hammond stating President Washington's intention to sign the treaty, provided the recent Order in Council authorizing the seizure of neutral ships carrying provisions to France was revoked. Randolph hoped that this gambit would result in a revocation of the offensive order as well as a modification of the treaty to satisfy the conditions set by the Senate (Reardon, *Edmund Randolph*, 301-303).

To the Committee of Public Safety

Paris, 15 July (27 Messidor 3ʳᵈ year) 20ᵗʰ Year of the American Republick

Citizens

I sent in last night a list of my compatriots in Paris according to your request of the   instant,[1] and shall continue to furnish a like list every décade whilst you deem it necessary.

In rendering this list it becomes necessary for my future conduct that I should ask of the Committee an explanation of a decree of the Convention of the 23ʳᵈ instant upon this subject; for I observe by that decree that such citizens as are born within the jurisdiction of the powers in alliance and friendship with the French Republick, and who are acknowledged by the representatives of such powers here, are designated as entitled to protection, and by which it may be inferred, that all those who are not born there are to be excluded from such protection. Permit me to ask whether such is the import of that decree? The following considerations incline me to believe that it is not.

1ˢᵗ Because it denies the right of expatriation admitted by this Republick, and which cannot be denied without supposing a man attached to the soil where he was born, and incapable of changing his allegiance.

2ᵈˡʸ Because it denies the right to all governments to confer the priviledge of citizenship, and incorporate into their Society any person who was born elsewhere, and which is admitted and practiced every where.

3ᵈˡʸ Because as the first member of the sixth article of that decree allows even the subjects of the powers at war with this Republick who came in before the 1ˢᵗ of January 1792. to remain here, it would follow if such were the construction that many of the subjects of those powers would be put on a better footing than many of the citizens of those who are your friends and allies.

From these consideration I am inclined to think that such is not the impo[rt] of the decree and that the term birth was intended to mean political as well as natural birth, but as it is capable of a different construction I have thought it my duty to ask of you an explanation on that head for at the same time that it is my wish to extend protection to all those of my countrymen, who are deemed such by the laws of my country, it is likewise my wish to do it in such a manner and upon such principles as will be perfectly satisfactory to the French Republick.

Jaˢ Monroe

RC, DLC: FCP—France. A clerk's copy of this letter in French, dated 14 July 1795, is in this same file.

1. Committee of Public Safety to JM, 8 July (20 Messidor) 1795, *View of the Conduct*, 198.

To Jean-Claude Redon

Paris July 20. 1795

I received your favor of yesterday informing me that many of the English sailors who escaped from prison were taken From the Republic in American Vessels and particularly from the ports of Bordeaux and Dunkirk and requesting my aid to prevent a practice hurtful to France. I had also received some time before a letter of the 14 ult⁰ (Messidor) complaining of a particular case of that kind at Bordeaux and which I declined answering until I should hear from the Consul at that port on the subject.[1]

Permit me to assure you that I have already done every thing in my power to prevent this abuse, and that I shall now repeat my endeavours to accomplish that object, being equally impelled to it from a regard to the obligations of duty subsisting between the two Republics, which with me will always be held sacred, as from my attachment to the welfare of this. With this view, and that the possibility of abuses might be prevented, I have some time since not only prohibited the Consuls from granting passports to those who are Americans, but enjoined them likewise to use their utmost endeavours, to prevent the Captains of our Vessels, from taking off those who were not, and in which I am well satisfied I have their full cooperation. It is my duty however to add, that beyond this my authority within the Republic cannot extend: for to me it does not belong to Punish those who violate its laws: to inflict such punishment by making a suitable example of those who commit the aggression, lies within the province of the government itself only. I have invariably admonished my compatriots to respect the laws of our ally, to whose welfare we have so many motives to be attached, and have warned them that in case they violate those laws, I shall leave them unprotected to their penalty. To impress this however more forcibly at the present moment I will enclose a copy of your letters to me and of this my reply to all our Consuls through out the Republic.

FC, DLC: Monroe Papers

Jean-Claude Redon to JM, 2 July (14 Messidor) and 19 July 1795, *View of the Conduct*, 213.

From Edmund Randolph

Department of State July 21ˢᵗ 1795.

Sir,

By a past opportunity, I did myself the honor of sending to you a printed copy of the proposed Treaty between the United States and Great Britain. With it was bound up a copy of the act of our Senate. The want of precedent for such a mode of ratification; the doubts, whether they meant to sit in judgment again upon the article, to be added, whether the President can ratify without re-submitting the new article to them; whether he can ratify before he himself inspects the new article, after it shall have been assented to by the British King; and what effect the suspension of the 12ᵗʰ Article will have upon all those, subsequent to the 10ᵗʰ; create difficulties and delays, even independent of the <u>real merits</u> of the Treaty. The newspapers, which have been forwarded to you, will shew the unpopularity of the Treaty at Boston.[1]

The day before yesterday, New York exhibited a similar scene.[2] It will probably be re-acted in Philadelphia tomorrow; and will travel, perhaps, further. The complaints are numerous from the friends of the Treaty; that the condemnations of it have proceeded from unfair practices. Upon this I can as yet, say nothing; but will wait, until some counter-assemblies, which are said to be contemplated shall have published their appeal to the world. When I inform you, that the President has not yet ratified the Treaty; his character will convince you that nothing will deter him from doing what he thinks right; and that the final question lies open from causes, unconnected with any considerations, but the interest and duties of the United States. He is at present in Virginia; and will doubtless, very soon, take his conclusive step. If I were permitted to conjecture what that would be; I should suspect, that at any rate, he would not sign it, until it should return from England with the addition of the suspending Article; and probably not even then, if a late British Order for the capture of Provisions, going to France should have been issued as we suppose, and increase the objections, which have been lavished upon it.

The present may be well considered as a crisis, taken either upon the supposition of a ratification or rejection. In the latter case, the result with Great Britain is not so easily foreseen: in the former the result in our own Country, is involved with many delicate and hazardous topics. It is my consolation, however, that he, who guides the Helm, will by his fortitude and wisdom steer us into safe port. I have the honor to be with great respect and esteem, Sir, Your most obedient servant

Edm: Randolph

RC, DLC: Sarah Stone Autograph Collection

1. On 13 July 1795 the citizens of Boston, called together by the selectmen of the city, passed twenty resolutions condemning the treaty (Boston Selectmen to George Washington, 13 July 1795, DLC: Washington Papers: General Correspondence; Resolutions, 13 July 1795, DLC: Washington Papers: Letterbook #40).

2. Citizens of New York came together in a tumultuous and inconclusive meeting on 18 July 1795. They reconvened on the 21st and passed resolutions opposing the treaty. The chamber of commerce, meeting under the direction of Alexander Hamilton, Rufus King, and other Federalists (who had been unable to gain control of the other meetings) on July 22, passed resolutions supporting ratification. Subsequent meetings in Philadelphia, Baltimore, Charleston and many other towns condemned the treaty (Broadus Mitchell, *Alexander Hamilton: The National Adventure, 1788-1804*, 341-343).

From Jean Delmas and Jean-Baptiste Treilhard

Paris, le 5 Thermidor l'an 3 de la République
française, une et indivisible [23 July 1795]

Nous avons reçu, Citoyen plusieurs Reclamations des Marins français à Charlestown; ils Se plaignent des injustices qu'ils ont éprouvées depuis le Commencement de la guerre, des Proclamations publiées par ordre du Congrès contre les Corsaires d'Amérique, des défenses faites de laisser Sortir des Munitions de toute espèce, des Obstacles qu'ils rencontrent relativement à leurs prises toujours disputées, saisies ou rendues aux Ennemis de la Republique, des predilections a faveur des Espagnols et des Anglais. Il est Sans doute forte inutile d'observer que ces plaintes, Si elles Sont bien fondées, Sont contraires à l'esprit du traité de 1778.

Pleins de confiance dans la Loyauté de vos principes, et dans votre empressement à Prévenir toutes ce que l'œuvres à troubler l'harmonie qui règne entre les deux Républiques, nous ne doutons pas que vous ne veuillez bien nous donner une explication franche Sur le Sujet de ces plaintes, et que vous ne couderiez avec nous à soutenir dans toute leur integrité, nos intérêts repectifs.

Jean Delmas
Treilhard

Editors' Translation

Paris, 5 Thermidor Year 3 of the French Republic,
one and indivisible [23 July 1795]

We have received, Citizen, several complaints from French sailors in Charleston; they are complaining of injustices they have suffered since the beginning of the war; proclamations published by order of Congress against American privateers; orders to prohibit the transfer of any sort of munitions; obstacles encountered regarding their prizes which are always disputed, seized and returned to the enemies of the Republic; and partiality shown to the Spanish and English. It is no doubt most pointless to note that these complaints, if they are well founded, are contrary to the spirit of the Treaty of 1778.

Fully confident of your adherence to your principles, and of your eagerness to prevent all undertakings that would disturb the harmony that reigns between the two Republics, we have no doubt that you wish to give us an honest explanation on the subject of these complaints and that you would not break with us in upholding in all their integrity, our mutual interests.

Jean Delmas
Treilhard

FC, DLC: FCP—France

Charleston, South Carolina, and Savannah, Georgia, were favorite ports for French privateers and their prizes. Although the people of those cities were generally friendly towards them, the British vice-consul at Charleston, Benjamin Moodie, led an assault of British shipping interests against the privateers, filing numerous suits for the recovery of the captured vessels. The privateers usually won, but the process cost them greatly in time and money, for Moodie and his allies doggedly attacked them, appealing over a dozen of the cases to the Supreme Court (*Documentary History of the Supreme Court*, 7: 43-52, 625-633, 683-693).

To James Madison

Paris July 26. 1795.

Dear Sir

I had began a long letter to you in cypher, it appearing the British have commenc'd seizing my letters, but which not being complete I forward the enclosed by the present private opportunity, & which being on the moment of departure prohibits more being added than that the communication is intended as a friendly deposit in your hands & for the purpose of guarding my reputation from unjust attacks whether publick or private, always observing that whatever you receive is to be shewn when opportunity offers to Mᵣ Jefferson & Mᵣ Jones. we are well & desire to be affecᵞ remembered to Mᵣˢ M.

Jaˢ Monroe.

RC, DLC: Madison Papers

JM probably enclosed the first portion of his letter to Madison that was begun on July 3 (See JM to Madison, 22 August 1795, below). Madison's notation on the received copy of this letter indicates that JM also enclosed his correspondence with John Jay regarding the British treaty.

To Jean-Victor Colchen

[27 July 1795][1]

I presented sometime since a letter to the Committee of p: S: requesting the aid of this republick in favor of our negotiation with algiers, Tunis & Tripoli[2] and having yet rec^d no definitive answer to that application, permit me to desire of you to mention the subject to the committee & procure for me the answer which is sought.

As it will require in any event two voyages to Algiers &c, the first to agree the terms & the second to carry the presents, & as the season is already greatly advanc'd you will perceive how important to the United States an early decision upon that subject is. But this is further increased by the consideration that many arrangments in respect to the funds, are to be taken after this decision is obtained, and of course are now suspended, that we have many prisoners at Algiers who are exposed to the ravage of the plague which annually visits that place, as by the further consideration that Mr Humphreys our minister at Lisbon who is specially charged with that business is & has been attending here waiting this decision for near a month past. Permit me to request you to bring these circumstances to the view of the Committee, in the hope that without interfering with the concerns of this republick & whom success is of importance to mankind they may find a moment in which they may attend to those of their ally & especially in a concern which interests likewise the cause of humanity.

Dft, NjMoHP. A note on the cover in JM's handwriting reads: Mr Gauvain will immediately copy & translate this to the com^y of f: aff^rs.

1. This letter is dated on the cover.

2. JM to the Committee of Public Safety, 5 July 1795, above.

To the Committee of Public Safety

Paris 28 July. 1795

I have received your favor of the 5 Instant relative to the complaints of some corsairs of the Republic from Charleston, and in which you request me to give the necessary explication upon that subject, and so far as they are well founded to promote the just demands of the said complainants.[1] Permit me to assure you that I shall be happy to fulfill your desire in both respects, being always ready to give you the most frank and prompt explanation, according to the information I possess, and in every particular, of the conduct of our government towards our ally; and equally so to promote justice on our part, where injury has in reality been sustained, by any of the citizens of this Republic. As soon therefore as the Committee will be pleased to furnish me with an accurate detail or specification of these complaints, I promise to pay the attention to them which has been desired of me.[2]

FC, DLC: Monroe Papers

1. Jean Delmas and Jean-Baptiste Treilhard to JM, 23 July (5 Thermidor) 1795, above.

2. There is no record of the committee having provided JM with the requested information.

From William Short

Madrid July 28. 1795

Dear Sir

I had the pleasure of receiving by M[r] Pinckney your favor of the 30th of May—I intended in answering it to let you know something of the progress of his business here—but as yet it is in status quo—& this I think you should know—The circumstances you mention in your letter by him, leave of course the subject I had written to you about, out of our line for the present—of course I shall not say anything respecting it by this conveyance, as it is by the circuitous route of Italy—I make use of that route to express to you my gratitude for the letter you were so good as to convey me by M. Pinckney from my friend[1]—& your promise on that head for the future—I hope ere long I shall be in a situation to render this mark of your friendship unnecessary, as I expect with certainty to leave this country in the month of October for Paris, where I promise myself much satisfaction my dear Sir in seeing after so long a separation one of my countrymen whom I have always pleased myself in considering as my friend.—I consider it as an happy beginning of renewing my acquaintance with my country & countrymen—I anticipate in the return into the bosom of my country the only compensation I can receive for the variety of pain anxiety & trouble I have experienced in her service abroad—The important business which remained confided to me when the President named me to reside here permanently, & the peculiar state of that business at that time could alone have induced me to have accepted of a permanent appointment in a country where my health was suffering & my mind & body wearing out in a state of perpetual disgust & disorder—The combination of circumstances w[ch] has since occurred, & with which I suppose you are acquainted, having induced the President to confide this business to other hands, leaves me at liberty to withdraw from hence without waiting for its termination—I have therefore written to desire my successor may be named—& to inform the President that I shall retire from hence, under the conditional & limited congé he had granted me, as soon as Mr Pinckney shall have so far possessed himself of the business as to have no further occasion, wch will be certainly by the month of October—Don't let this prevent you from writing to me either by Italy—or the frontier—risk the loss of a few letters rather than deprive me of the chance of receiving them here, in the case of any unforeseen circumstance detaining me longer than I expect at present—I inclose a letter for my friend to w[ch] I ask your kind attention—& above all I repeat in consequence of an expression in yours of the 30th of May, that our letters relate only to ourselves—& that I hope you will never entertain a doubt on that point—Be so good as to make my compliments to M. Skipwith—He is a relation of mine—I learned accidentally by the gazettes not long ago that he was at Paris—M[r] Pinckney tells me he came there with you—Tell him I wrote to him on learning he was at Paris, by the way of Italy—I have a right to reproach him for having not written to me after his arrival there. Y[rs] truly

W Short

RC, PHi: Gilpin Collection: William Short Letters

1. Duchess de Rochefoucauld.

From Edmund Randolph

Department of State July 29ᵗʰ 1795

Sir

Notwithstanding an enfeebling disorder, which has for some days past indisposed me to business, I am induced to make an effort towards a letter, which shall go by the vessel carrying Mʳ Fauchet. It will, I am sure, be expedient that it should reach your hands, nearly at the same time with his arrival.

If it does not, you will attribute it to some forgetfulness in Mʳ Adet, who promised to inform me when Mʳ Fauchet would sail, and until last night, when I panted for rest, I never conceived, that Mʳ Adet had closed his dispatches, and that a violent hurry on my part could alone secure an opportunity, which I waited for in expectation of a leisurely notice. Even this I did not learn from him.

Most thoroughly am I now persuaded, that Mʳ Fauchet has wrapped himself round with intrigue from the first moment of his career in the United States. He found in me a temper in no manner turned towards Britain, but warm towards France. He affected a confidence in me; and often communicated to me machinations in New York against Govʳ Clinton and myself, and affirmed the authors to be Mʳ Hammond, and some of our own countrymen. He has more than once asserted his conviction that Mʳ La Forest was perfidious, and confederated with the enemies of France. He expressed his disgust and suspicions against Genet; endeavoring to inculcate an opinion that they were irreconcileable. He pretended great attachment to the President. The reverse of all this is now fixed upon my mind. His chief associates have been enemies of the Government and of the administration. His conversation has been steadily hostile to the Executive. I believe, that he has been instrumental in many of the printed attacks upon its reputation; that he has been in close league with Genet; that he has been plotting how to embroil this country with France, and that he insidiously covered with charges against the fidelity of La Forest a bait to procure information from some members of the Executive to whom he resorted. I was not one of them.[1]

Since his departure I have ample reason to suppose that he has put into the hands of Bache a declaration of my having told him, that a treaty of commerce was no part of Mʳ Jay's mission. As soon as I suspected it, I drew up a counter declaration, a copy of which is inclosed.[2] Why, when he hinted this to me, did he not write a letter, insisting on it, for I peremptorily denied it to him? I call God to witness, that I never uttered such a sentiment, and although with much better reason I might impute to him an improper motive, I will rather say more charitably, that from some cause or other he has misapprehended me.

For months before Mʳ Fauchet left this city he absented himself from the ordinary occasions of shewing respect to the President. I mean those easy attentions, now and then at his public room on Tuesday. I mention this, not on account of any stress, laid on that day, but because not visiting him on such days, Mʳ Fauchet would be presumed, as is the case, not to have visited him on any other. For myself, except for business I seldom saw him. Still, however, being anxious to impute this coldness to any thing, rather than an absolute alienation from the Government, I regretted that having no letters of recall, he could not be presented in form to the President on taking leave, as he seemed to wish. But I suggested to him, as a substitute, the waiting upon the President in an informal way, and agreed to accompany him. This was done, and he dealt out his assurances of veneration to the Chief Magistrate, and of attachment to the Secretary of State, with a lavish tongue.

To manifest, that I was not inclined to be on hostile terms, I invited him to dinner two days before his departure; and our intercourse was as free and unconstrained as ever. I had conjectured from a variety of circumstances, that he was desirous of obtaining from the Executive an exculpatory letter, which might protect him from some of those asperities, which I understood and frankly communicated to him, as threatening him, for pledging the public for purchases of flour. Being satisfied that he could not well have done otherwise, I said to his Secretary Bournonville in the evening after dinner that if I could be of service to Mr Fauchet in France, I should be happy. Some hours after the company had left my house, Mr Bournonville returned; observing that Mr Fauchet would be glad of a letter, and adding that he had expected something complimentary in answer to his letter announcing the arrival of his successor. I replied, that I would send him <u>a letter</u> with the dispatches of which he was to be the bearer for me through Mr Adet: But that the President was to be consulted. My intention was to have proposed to the President a general letter <u>officially</u> wishing him health and happiness; and to write to you <u>privately</u> my firm persuasion that the hypothecation of the public debt was an act of necessity; upon which alone the holders of flour would rely. I did slightly mention the letter to the President; but, as sufficient time appeared to be before us, and Mr Fauchet said himself that he was going upon a tour to the northward and eastward, I calculated upon the certainty of being able to settle the matter with the President, after Mr Adet should notify me, as I had grounds to hope.

The President is at Mount Vernon; and therefore the attempt would be too late. But if he were here, I should doubt whether Mr Fauchet had not forfeited his title even to a letter of ceremonious civility. My single object in stating these things to you, is to remove any impression of our failing in a point of propriety; and of his carrying with him the confidence or respect of the Government. You will use the letter as containing a collection of facts, not to be spoken of, but as supporting you in demanding that any judgment be suspended upon his representations, until we can hear from you. I have the honor to be Sir, with sincere respect & esteem your mo. ob. serv.

Edm: Randolph

LBC, DNA: RG 59: Diplomatic and Consular Instructions

1. Fauchet was convinced that the signing of the Jay treaty signaled a stronger pro-British stance on the part of the United States, despite Randolph's assurances to the contrary. Randolph's frustration turned to anger as Fauchet became more open in his criticism of the treaty (John J. Reardon, *Edmund Randolph*, 293-294).

2. Randolph refers to a passage that appeared in a letter criticizing the Jay Treaty. It read: "The French minister here was officially informed, that the mission, as set forth in the President's message to the Senate, contemplated only an adjustment of our complaints...." It was first published in the (Philadelphia) *Independent Gazetteer* on 8 July 1795 and reprinted in the *Aurora* on July 17. Randolph responded by publishing a copy of Washington's message to the Senate, along with the statement: "Every citizen of the United States who reads this communication of the PRESIDENT'S, will judge for himself—whether Mr. Jay has fulfilled the important duties of his mission as contained in the above message" (*Independent Gazetteer*, 25 July 1795).

From Edmund Randolph

Department of State July 30. 1795.

Sir

Since I closed my letter of yesterday, I have been informed by Mr Swan that Mr Adet's dispatches will not go off, until this evening, and that he purposes to notify me of the opportunity being open for a few hours longer. I hasten therefore to add, what I can in this short interval, expecting to have another conveyance next week.

I mean to send you the accusations, which have been laid before the President against Mr Fenwick our Consul at Bourdeaux. He is charged upon strong presumptive grounds with having covered French property under an American name, by virtue of his office. The proof though exparte, impresses powerfully, in the case of the Ship Pomona, on board of which he is supposed to have shipped five boxes of silver belonging to French individuals or the French Government, as verdigrise or paints, under his Consular seals; and also in the case of a Captain Allain, from whom he or some person for his use is understood to have received two and a half per centum at least for a similar service. This affair is not, and will not be prejudged. But the President thinks it proper, that M͚ Fenwick should <u>cease</u> from his Consular functions until further order, and until an inquiry can be made. I request you to communicate a copy of this paragraph of my letter to him and M͚ Skipwith, our Consul general to inform M͚ Fenwick, that it is adviseable that he should expedite to me any proofs or declarations, in opposition to these charges; to assure him that nothing less than a necessity, arising from a due respect to our national character could have induced even this provisional step: and to recommend to M͚ Skipwith to fill up by a proper agency this temporary chasm. To shew, however, that we would avoid every wound to M͚ Fenwick's feelings, it is anxiously desired, that no improper eclat be made in this business; and if you, after an accurate and extensive examination of the matter can undertake absolutely to discredit the imputations, the suspension may be withheld until some statement shall come from him.

I shall probably send you by the next vessel the final determination on the treaty. I suspect that it will not be very wide of what I wrote to you on the 14ᵗʰ instant. I have the honor to be Sir, with real regard and respect yr. mo. ob. serv.

Edm: Randolph

LBC, DNA: RG 59: Diplomatic and Consular Instructions

To Edmund Randolph

Paris August 1ˢᵗ 1795.

Sir,

I was sorry to find some days after my last that the disquietude which I intimated existed in the councils of this Republic, and to which the communication between its ports and England had given birth, assumed a form still more unpleasant in regard to us than I then apprehended it would do: for whilst the subject was under discussion between the commissary and myself and as I thought approaching towards a close, the committee interposed and taking the business out of his hands, addressed me on the same subject and to the same effect, laying at the same time the draft of a decree before the Convention, the principal object of which was to preclude all those who were not born within the jurisdiction of the neutral powers from the protection of the ministers of those powers here. The decree you will observe was made general as was the letter which preceded it from the committee: I had however seen too much of the business not to know that in regard to others it was formal only, whilst it was in reality pointed against a particular description of our own citizens and of Englishmen, who by means of American passports obtained elsewhere and no doubt by fraud sometimes passed for such. As I presumed it was not the intention of the Committee or Convention that the decree should be construed and executed strictly, because I knew upon principle it could not be supported, and because I likewise knew that many of those whom it would thereby comprehend, were resident and valuable members of our community and had been and now were by their commerce useful to France, I demanded immediately an explanation from the Committee of the decree, and soon afterwards obtained an interview with that body in which I was explicitly assured that they did not mean to call in question any principle insisted on by us: that their only wish was to exclude Englishmen and such as by their residence ought to be deemed Englishmen: and that in regard to myself they meant to impose on me no restraint in granting passports I had not already observed. Thus this business has happily terminated precisely where it ought to do, without producing any real change here or other effect any where which can be hurtful to us.

I have the pleasure to inform you that the full aid of this government will be given in support of our negotiation with Algiers &c. Upon this you may I think count with certainty as I have been assured of it by the committee and am furnished with all the light which their past negotiations with that regency enable them to give us on the subject. Difficulties however of a new kind arise and which may possibly create some serious embarrassment. The fund destined for this business is I understand in England and the english intercourse law prohibits as I hear and under the penalty of death the payment of drafts from this country in favor of any person in France or who has been in France since the commencement of the war between the two nations. Perhaps this law may not be deemed applicable to this case: perhaps if it does the inconvenience may yet be remedied some how or other so as to prevent the failure of the treaty on that account. Colº Humphreys is still here upon this business and as we devote our unremitted attention to it, you may be assured that no measure necessary to its success, will be omitted that we are capable of.

Within a few days past the emigrant army which lately landed in the Bay of Quiberon under the auspices of Great Britain, has been completely defeated, and its whole force amounting to about 10,000 men either slain or taken prisoners of which about 4,000 were slain. Many of those who composed that army are said to have been raised by compulsion from among the French prisoners and who were of course set at liberty when taken. By the law all the others are doomed to suffer capital punishment, but it is to be hoped, as many of them are weak and misguided men, its rigour will be moderated at least in regard to them.[1]

Within a few days past also a peace was concluded with Spain, whereby the whole of the Island of Sᵗ Domingo is ceded to France, the latter yielding her conquests made in this quarter since the war.[2] That there [are] some secret articles is more than probable. I herewith send you a copy of the treaty, as likewise of the details which attended the defeat and destruction of the emigrant army, according to the report thereof, rendered by Tallien who was in mission there.

You will perceive that our claims have not been provided for in this treaty with Spain, relative to which claims I have heard nothing since mine to you of the 14ᵗʰ of June last. 'Tis possible I may soon hear something on that subject either from this government or from Mʳ Pinckney and in which case I will immediately advise you of it. 'Tis likewise possible a war may soon take place in consequence of that treaty, between England and Spain and in which case it will no doubt be the wish of the former to involve us in it on her side; but this I hope will not take effect, because under existing circumstances it would not only produce many unhappy consequences, but because I am of opinion if Mʳ Pinckney finds difficulties that the object may yet be attained by the intercession of this government as soon as I am enabled to shew that Mʳ Jay's treaty stipulates nothing injurious to this republic. Doubtless France will now have great weight in the councils of Spain, and most certainly if we continue in friendship with France and of which there can be no doubt, it will be possible to avail ourselves of it in support of our claims there.

These two great events must certainly produce the most important consequences as well in securing tranquility at home as in cutting off all remaining hope of success on the part of the powers still at war with this republic. Indeed the probability is that peace will soon be made with the Italian powers and even with Austria; but with England, so peculiar is the relation between the two countries, that it is impossible to say when peace will take place between them, or even to hazard any plausible conjecture upon that point. An adjustment however with all the other powers may possibly induce an accomodation between these sooner than present circumstances authorize the expectation of.

About the time of the debarkation of the emigrant army some symptoms were seen here, which gave cause for suspicion that there was a party in Paris which <u>felt</u> at least in unison with that army. Lately a song called the "Revil du Peuple" composed in reproach of the reign of terror had become very fashionable among those who had suffered under that reign, and by some accidental circumstances was placed in a kind of rivalship, or rather of opposition to the Marseilles Hymn. The young men of Paris, the relations of many of whom had suffered under the reign of terror, formed a party who were in general in favour of the "Reveil du Peuple" often calling for it at the theatre in preference to the Marseilles Hymn, and which circumstance never failed to give uneasiness to many who were present. Light as this circumstance was yet it seemed at one time to menace some serious ill consequences; the presumption whereof was indeed so strong that the enemies of the revolution who were said to stimulate the young men on seemed to count upon it as a source from whence something in their behalf might be expected. Occasionally some excesses were committed by the young men, and in which they thought they had a right to indulge, even in contempt of the authority of the Convention itself, upon which body they presumed they had some claim, for services rendered in the late commotions. It was in truth obvious that the range which they took at this time, when tested by the standard of strict propriety, or indeed of law, could not be justified. It might on the contrary have been called an insurrection, and a little rigour would have made it one. The Convention however acted more wisely by considering it for a while as a frolic, and finally by issuing a proclamation telling them calmly the folly and impropriety of their conduct since thereby they exposed to danger the revolution and of course their own safety, neither of which could it be their interest or their intention to endanger. This mode of proceeding produced the happiest effect, for even before the reduction of the emigrant army and peace with Spain tranquility was in a great measure established; but since those events it has been completely so.[3]

The Convention is still employed upon the subject of the constitution and which will probably be gone through in the course of two weeks more. As soon as it is adopted and of which there can be no doubt and upon the principles generally proposed in the project reported by the commission, I will forward you a copy.

I have lately received a letter from a M[r] Cazeaux an unfortunate Canadian who attached himself to our cause when we invaded Canada, whose name you will find in the journals of the Congress of 1783 or 4. at Annapolis, and which letter I now transmit to you. The journal of that day explains the nature of his demand touched on in this letter: as I was of the Committee upon this memorial I am well acquainted with the nature of his claim, and think in the issue of the business that justice was not rendered to him: as the order of Congress in his behalf was not executed. He is here and I believe supported by the nation, in the expectation we will do something for him: the Minister having been instructed to patronize his claim, may I request your attention to it?[4]

I likewise inclose you a letter from M[r] Leach with one from several respectable Americans here recommending him for the consulate at Dunkirk and to which I likewise beg that attention to which you may deem it entitled.[5] My acquaintance with him is of late only; but he appears to me to be an honest and deserving citizen. I am, Sir, with sincere regard your very h[ble] & ob[t] serv[t]

Ja[s] Monroe.

Copy, DNA: RG 59: Dispatches from France

1. The French revolutionary army defeated the British-backed royalist force at Quiberon in attacks on July 16 and 21, but the casualties were not as extreme as JM reported. Six thousand royalists were captured, but about 2,000 were able to escape to British ships. Three hundred were killed in battle and another 640 were executed after capture (Ross, *Historical Dictionary of the Wars of the French Revolution*, 135-136).

2. France and Spain signed a treaty at Basel, Switzerland on 22 July 1795 (Steven T. Ross, *Historical Dictionary of the Wars of the French Revolution*, 22).

3. "La Réveil du Peuple" was the popular rallying song of the Muscadins, a pro-royalist faction in Paris. Most members of the group were young men who worked as clerks and bureaucrats, many of whom obtained their jobs as a means of avoiding military service. They were distinguished by their dandified clothing and their disdainful manner towards other people. The Muscadins played a prominent role in the suppression of the Jacobin clubs. Public reaction against the Muscadins led to the suppression of the faction beginning in the summer of 1795 (Samuel Scott and Barry Rothuas, *Historical Dictionary of the French Revolution*).

4. François Cazeau (1734-1815)was a Montreal merchant who provided supplies and money to the American army during its attack on Canada in 1775 and 1776. He petitioned Congress for compensation in 1783, and although Congress approved payment, his accounts remained unsettled. JM was on the committee that reported on his petition (*Journals of the Continental Congress*, 26 147-150; *Dictionnaire Biographique du Canada*). Cazeau, who was residing in Paris, wrote to JM on 18 July and 28 July 1795 (*Catalogue of Monroe's Papers*, 1: 47-48).

5. The letter from Mr. Leach has not been located.

From Aaron Burr

Nyork 2 Aug. 95.

Dear Sir

Our worthy friend Mr Gelston has just informed me that his second Son M. Gelston[1] is about to sail for France. I take the Liberty to request for him that protection & Countenance which you have so kindly & generously extended to his brother.[2]—The Children of such a parent cannot I think fail to merit the attention of all good Men.—Their father has made ample provision for their support while in Europe—Yet if in the Course of events those resources should fail, which you know in such Days of revolution, is possible, I beg you to give him a Credit to the am^t of a thousand Dollars if he should want it, for which your bill on his father, or on me will be paid with thanks. I am Dr Sir Y^r Affe^e H^e S^t

Aaron Burr

I have begged Mr Gelston to take out to you Greenleaf's Paper for the Month of July, which will amuse you much.[3]

RC, DLC: Monroe Papers

1. Maltby Gelston.

2. John M. Gelston.

3. Thomas Greenleaf (d. 1798) was editor and publisher of the semi-weekly newspaper, *Greenleaf's New York Journal and Patriotic Register*, which ran from 1794 until 1800. He started a second newspaper, a daily, called *The Argus, or Greenleaf's New Daily Advertiser*, in May 1795 (DLC: Newspaper and Current Periodical Collection).

From Joseph Fenwick

Bord^x 3 Augs^t 1795.

Sir

The inclosed I this day rec^d from the secretary of the Treasury at Philadel^a with directions to forward it without delay by a safe conveyance[1]—I have thought proper to comit it to the Post which I think may be considered safe.

We have two reports in Town relative to the ratification of the Treaty with great Britain, one that [it] has been rejected by 11 voices in 29—another that it is accepted by two thirds of the Senate present—Neither of these reports are to be confided in—however there is ship in the River in 29 days from Philadel^a if any account from her reaches me before the departure of the post, I will communicate it to you in the present, if not, by tomorrows courier I will do myself the honor to write you.

I have this moment procured the inclosed news paper by the vessel mentioned above extracted from the Philadel^a Gazette & universal daily advertiser by A. Brown. I am very respectfully Sir your most obed S^t

Joseph Fenwick

RC, DLC: Monroe Papers

1. Oliver Wolcott to JM, 23 June 1795, above.

To Joseph Jones

Paris Augt 4. 1795.

Dear Sir

I omitted yesterday to enclose Josephs letter:[1] I send it however by an opportunity which promises to be more secure & perhaps as quick in the passage.

You will have long since heard that I have plac'd for you in the hands of Mr Randolph 3000. dol^{rs} of what ought to have been rec^d here, & ab^t 150. on acc^t of a like sum p^d here for Mr Rittenhouse. In addition to w^h I have lately answered your bills in fav^r of Southcombe & Burnley.

A peace is concluded with Spain and the emigrant army entirely cut off amounting 10.000, of which ab^t 4000 were slain. In addition to which the constitution is nearly gone thro & which upon the whole may be considered as a very good one. It divides the legislature into two branches, gives an independant Executive composed of 5. members, of whom one only is annually displac'd. So that in every view the prospect of this country is now the best that can be. By the peace with Spⁿ the whole of St Domingo belongs to France & whereby an immense country is provided for the army when the war ends, whereby also not only justice will be rendered to those citizens who have deserved so well of the republick, but the probability of internal commotion removed.

With respect to the arrangment of my two farms in Alb: I have heretofore said so much that I have little occasion to repeat any thing here. with respect to that where I live you recollect my wish was that a fence sho^d extend in a line along the road by the house till you come to the road leading from Charlottesville & then with the latter to the lane of McKensie: that the ground inclosed sho^d continue in wood clearing out the old & ugliest trees only: that the whole of the run between the house & barn be cleared up & put in grass, planting here & there along it a weeping willow & leaving of the trees now standing here there one also.

Will it not be possible for you to pay us a visit? I think after you settle your aff^{rs} you might do it & to advantage in point of health. Suppose you did it the ensuing year. how long I shall stay is incertain provided my conduct is approved. we do not mean to stay long. but if you were to come seeing into my aff^{rs} we might fix the time positively: & the sooner we get back, the present storm being over the better: certainly the more agreeable to you. Sincerely I am y^r friend & serv^t

Ja^s Monroe

RC, ViW: Monroe Papers

1. JM's remark that he "omitted yesterday to enclose Josephs letter," suggests that JM may have meant to enclose the letter from Joseph Jones, Jr. to his father in the dispatch to Edmund Randolph of 1 August 1795. It may also infer that JM wrote to Jones on August 3, but that seems unlikely, given the content of the present letter.

To James Madison

Paris Augt 5. 1795.

Dear Sir

Soon after my arrival here last year I found it necessary to appoint some one consul provisionally & in consequence appointed Mr Skipwith to that office & announc'd him to this gov^t as well as our own: but before this step was known the President had nominated a Mr Pitcairn for that place. Mr P. being by birth a British subject & having latterly become an American citizen & in consequence being still a B^h subject, I thought it proper to suspend his introduction into the office untill I submitted to the Executive the objections which applied to the appointment & thereupon wrote Mr R.[1] that by placing such a person here, very essential injury wo^d be rendered to the U. States for if admitted & w^h w^d only be expected in case the fact above stated was withheld, he wo^d be an object of jealousy with this gov^t, & of course watched closely, and as often with me, it wo^d also unavoidably lessen any confidence they might have in me: not to mention the impolicy of putting a person with British connections capital &c at the head of our commerce in this country whereby Brit^n wo^d have the emolument at our expence. In this state the business yet rests; M^r Sk: performs the duties of the consulate & I am left to depend on providence for one to supply his place with me. In expectation his nomination wo^d be confirmed I wrote you *that I would take Prevost—but in truth I wish I could avoid it* for *I consider Burr as a man to be shunned—his friend here* & who is *mine* in every view of *his character joins me in this opinion—in short he is an unprincipled adventurer and whom it is better to get rid of at once. Can you promote* this object. I have with me at present Mr Purviance who is well qualified & a most amiable man. *And I wish Dawson could come—he is poor and sound* in principle. I write this in great haste & am affec^y y^r fn^d

Ja^s Monroe.

RC, DLC: Madison Papers. Words in italics were written in code by JM and the deciphered text interlined by Madison.

1. Edmund Randolph

From Melancton Smith

New York Aug. 6th 1795

My dear Sir

I with pleasure embrace the opportunity which offers by M[r] Gelston, the Son of our mutual friend M[r] David Gelston, to revive the memory of our former friendship—I hope you and your family enjoy health and that your situation is agreable. Our republican friends unite in the tenderest sympaty with our french bretheren in the distresses they have endured occasioned by the scarcity of provision and by the wicked machinations of their internal enemies. We do not fear but that they will surmount all the obstacles laid in the way of their freedom and independence. The enjoyment will be more pleasant when they review the dangers and difficulties they have encountered in obtaining their freedom—The Continent is agitated from end to end with Jays Treaty—No body likes it—and I believe five sixths of the people reprobate it—Persons of my political tenets and these I presume you well know, are mortified, vexed and anxious—You will doubtless receive the extraordinary instrument before this reaches you. It is not known whether the president has signed it or not, though the general opinion now is that he has not, and it is hoped will not.—A certain Secretary[1] appears to be in great distress, his popularity, as well as that of the late envoy[2] has much depreciated in the State (you know I presume the latter is Governor of the State). Our friend Gov. Clinton declined standing a Candidate, his health is much impaired. The patriotic Jefferson is blessed by all good americans—He never would have disgraced his country by putting his name to an instrument like the Treaty—I need not ask your attention to young M[r] Gelston, you know his father who continues the same unshaken friend to the rights of mankind he always was— Wishing you every felicity I am D[r] Sir with esteem your Ob. Ser[t]

Melancton Smith

RC, DLC: Monroe Papers

1. Edmund Randolph.

2. John Jay.

From Joseph Fenwick

Bord[x] 8 Augs[t] 1795. 22 Thermidor 3.

Sir

I have the honor of your Letter of the 29 July repeating your request to use every attention to prevent the evasion of English prisoners on board of American vessels.[1]—The agents of the Marine & constituted Authorities of this City can attest my exertions on this subject—as it has been by & thro' me alone that the discoveries and arrestations have been made here—I have of my own accord discovered & caused to be arrested as well on board of American vessels as on shore upwards of thirty—the very nine men mentioned in the letter of the Minister of Marine to you of the 14 Messidor, were discovered & arrested by my orders.[2]

I cannot forbear censuring the conduct of many of our Captains in this business as I have discovered in them too generally a desire to discharge their own Seamen that are on very high wages to get English Sailors for their victuals only—and I have taken every step in my power to expose and repress this conduct. It is not to be wondered where there are such a number of vessels, comanded as many of them are, that my efforts should prove ineffectual. The extreme lenity shewn the prisoners in the Country, by billetting them out in different families and the vicinity of Bordeaux (a place of great foreign resort) to the different interior entrepots account for greater abuses here than elsewhere.

You may be assured Sir no efforts on my part shall be wanting to coopperate with & execute your instructions as well as the desire of our Ally on this subject. I have the honor to be Sir your most obedient Serv[t]

Joseph Fenwick

P.S. I send you enclosed a Copy of a letter I this day wrote to the maritime agent here & to the Commissary of the District.[3]

J. F.

RC, DLC: Monroe Papers

1. JM sent a circular letter to the American consuls in France on 29 July 1795 enclosing copies of his correspondence with Jean-Claude Redon regarding escaped British prisoners leaving France on American ships (DLC: Monroe Papers).

2. Jean-Claude Redon to JM, 2 July (14 Messidor) 1795, *View of the Conduct*, 213.

3. Fenwick's letter has not been located.

From David Gelston

New York Aug[t] 15th 1795

Dear Sir

I had the pleasure of writing you 24th & 27th March 1[d] May 5. 18 & 30 June & 20 Ult[o1] telling you in all which how very sensibly I was affected with your goodness to my Son.[2] your kind[ness] and attention to him have excited emotions of grattitude which never will be effaced from my mind I trust not from his—I hope his conduct may be such as to merit both your confidence and esteem—I have made him several remittances and have ordered him to reimburse your advances unless you wish to have them paid in this Country. in which case his bills in your favour will be paid at sight my former letters have been so lengthy that I will not in this intrude upon your time—but must trespass on your Friendship— this will be handed you by my Son Maltby—his wish to be an eye witness to some of the transactions now going forward on the great Theatre of the World by the greatest nation on Earth and having finished his Education here has obtained my Permission to ask your advice to take your directions and obey your commands while in Europe he will hand you letters from our good Friends Burr and Smith—unless unforseen accidents should happen he will not trouble you for pecuniary aid. Should he however in any event have occasion for one thousand Dollars his bills on me will be paid at sight here, the Amount remitted without loss of time to you at Paris your letter of 10th Feb[y] I had the pleasure to receive[3] and acknowleged the same and told you what great satisfaction its contents gave me permit me to refer you to my Son for the news in this Country and all he can tell you will be how compleatly the Grenville Treaty is reprobated throughout the United States[4]

P. S. I saw our real Friend Gov[r] Clinton this day he was too unwell to write he told me he wished to write you he wishes you well I fear that the World will soon be deprived of that true Patriot.

LBC, NHi: David Gelston Letterbook

1. David Gelston to JM, 24 March and 18 June 1795, above; 30 June 1795, NHi: Gelston Letterbook. Gelston's letters of 27 March, 1 May, 5 June, and 20 July 1795 have not been located.

2. John M. Gelston.

3. JM's letter to Gelston of 10 February 1795 has not been located.

4. William Wyndham, Lord Grenville (1759-1834) was the British foreign minister 1791-1801. He was the British representative in the treaty negotiations with John Jay (*DNB*; Jerald Combs, *The Jay Treaty*, 137-158).

From Benjamin Vaughan

Private.

August 15 [1795][1]

My dear sir

I have seen a letter from my brother, dated July 21, which leads me to <u>suppose</u> that my wife, our seven children, my oldest sister, & the tutor of our children, were to embark in a few days for America, every thing being prepared for the voyage & their course directed for New York. They were in <u>Sussex</u> by the sea-side, & might easily take shipping where they were.—They had told me, that they should not move till I had arrived in America:—But I conjecture, that a letter which I lately took the liberty of sending through you to them (with a duplicate sent through Mr Adams at the Hague,) may have changed their determinations; & that they have taken the benefit of the season, & leave me to follow as I can. If you have intelligence, & will give it to Mr Van Staphorst, he will have the goodness to write me on the subject. My letters from England & to England appear no longer to pass via Hambourg, & therefore I am reduced to look to casual information. At the same, till the matter realizes itself, I wish as little notice taken of the affair as possible.

I am informed that Mr Jay's treaty is rejected in America. Such an event will not be wonderful, independent of the contents of the treaty, whatever they may be. America had agreed upon principles in the treaty, which were probably of a general nature; & therefore ought to have been deemed binding, as soon as they were discovered to be true; without resting upon the nice distinction between a treaty made & a treaty ratified. The principal operation of the treaty was also to have been in war; a second reason with persons of honor for not deferring its operation till the war should end.—But the English ministers seem to think, that there is but <u>one</u> interest to be consulted in the world, which is their own.—They conceive also, that America receives no injury when her corn-ships are taken, provided her corn is paid for; as if England did not by this means drive away all concurrent purchasers from the American market; thus leaving the Americans with a surplus of corn upon their hands, paying for what they take at <u>common</u> prices. They wholly overlook also not only the general inconveniences arising from a delay to <u>shipping</u> & the interruption of a circle of voyages with the disputes with insurers on these occasions but also the certainty that corn cannot go in the quantities which it otherwise ought to do, to the <u>single market left</u>, namely the British dominions if ships are delayed in the voyages. Besides, what right has an Englishman to take to task, or even to inquire into, the operations of an American: are not each <u>san juris</u>?— Such is the conduct of the English ministry, that if they are allowed to remain in place a sufficient time, they will see the coalition against France exchanged for a coalition against themselves.

The German princes are alarmed at the refusal of an armistice by the C. de S. P. and some of them shew it in their negotiations;[2] & if the French have any success in Germany, the reasons will be general.—You may judge that there are those, who will be glad to see the French beyond the Rhine. The cession of the <u>pays & entre Rhin</u> will occasion France to seek to place the temporal princes who are dispossessioned, in ecclesiastical & <u>Austrian</u> territory beyond the Rhine; where of course they will be so many <u>enemies to Austria</u> & <u>friends to Prussia</u>.

The insanity of the coalition cannot better be seen, than in the appointment of Wurmser to command the Austrians, instead of Clairfait.[3] Wurmser is old & has been beaten, & is therefore held cheap on <u>both</u> sides; while of Clairfayt there were something to be said, though that something was doubtful.—If the French pass the Rhine in force, as they mount it they will open the way for fresh forces to join them at every spot, & give themselves likewise the navigation of the river; and in the mean time, it is <u>conceived</u> that the Austrians will evacuate the Breisgau[4] & retire into posts in mountains, lest they should be cut off in the plains, & not be able to defend the more important dominions of Austria. But for this purpose, the French must have some successes.—The displacing of Clairfayt is owing to a female cabal.

The emigrants openly express their detestation of the English, & say that they belong to Austria. In truth, they are likely to make the body-guard of the Emperor, as he cannot so well rely upon his own subjects. It is not easy to explain upon other principles, why the Emperor pays such enormous sums, considered comparatively, for recruits in this rather than in other corps. I have the honor to be, dear sir, yours very sincerely & respectfully

I beg to present my respectful comp[ts] to M[rs] Monroe.

The late renewal of the captures by the British in all seas from all nations, gives great offense to neutral aristocrats.

There are parts of Alsace torn to pieces by the clergy, who enter every day by the aid of certificates given by bigotted or timid municipalities &c and expect Cardinal de Rohan[5] among them in a few days as firmly, as the Jews expect the Messiah.

RC, DLC: Monroe Papers. Not signed.

1. Vaughan was writing from Basel, Switzerland.

2. The princes of the German states wanted peace with France, and in August 1795 the Diet voted to ask Prussia to mediate a treaty that would guarantee their territorial integrity and keep the French to the west of the Rhine. The Committee of Public Safety rejected the overture (Georges Lefebvre, *The French Revolution from 1793 to 1799*, 150-159).

3. General Dogobert-Sigismund Wurmser (1724-1797) commanded the Austrian troops on the upper Rhine in 1795 (David Chandler, *Dictionary of the Napoleonic Wars*, 491).

4. The Breisgau region bordered Alsace on the east bank of the Rhine in the foothills of the Black Forest.

5. Cardinal Louis-Réné-Edouard de Rohan (1734-1803) was the royalist archbishop of Strasburg in Alsace. He resided across the Rhine from Strasburg in German territory (*Nouvelle Biographie Générale*).

To Edmund Randolph

Paris August 17. 1795.

Sir

I have not been honored with any communication from you since that of the 2[d] of May last, though doubtless others are on their way and which I shall soon receive.

Within a few days past Philadelphia papers were received as late as the 3rd of July containing M[r] Jay's treaty, together with such proceedings of the Senate upon it as were then published. As the gazettes are circulating every where I conclude some of them are in possession of the committee of public safety, and that the details they contain will likewise soon find their way into the papers of this city: indeed it is said they are already published at Havre. As yet I have heard nothing from the Committee upon the subject of this treaty, nor do I expect to hear any thing from that body upon it, let the impression be what it may, otherwise than in reply to such communication as I shall make in regard to that transaction: and in respect to which it may be proper to add that I shall take no step without your particular instruction. For as I presume that some ulterior plan is or will be adopted in regard to that treaty, and upon which, in its relation to this republick my conduct will be particularly marked out, so I deem it my indispensable duty to avoid in the interim any the slightest compromitment either of you or myself upon that subject. I mention this that you may distinctly know how completely the final result of this business, so far as it depends on me is, as indeed it ought to be, under your controul.

As I have had no communication with this government upon the subject of this treaty since its contents were known, it is of course impossible for me to say, what the impression it has made is. It is as easy for you, with the lights you have, to form a correct opinion upon that point in Philadelphia, as for me to do it here. One circumstance however I think proper to bring to your view: soon after the British government had recommenced the seizure of our vessels destined for the ports of France, was notified to the Committee by a secret agent of this government who had just returned from England that he had been advised there thro' a channel to be relied on, that the English administration had said they knew that measure would not be offensive to our government or in other words that it was a case provided for between the two governments. I treated the communication with contempt, and was happy to hear that it was considered nearly in the same light by the Committee itself. But since the arrival of the treaty I have understood that in connection with that report, the attention of many has been drawn with some degree of sollicitude to the contents of the second paragraph of the 18th article, and who say that as that article leaves the law of nations unsettled and provides payment for seizures in cases of contraband, and of course for those which are not contraband, whereby the complaints of our citizens are prevented and the British construction by implication countenanced this republick has a right to complain of it.[1] I mention this objection to you that you may be aware of it, in case it should ever be brought forward on this or your side of the water and that it will be brought forward I think probable if those seizures are not noticed in some very pointed manner. 'Tis painful for me to give you a detail of this kind, but being a fact, I do not see with what propriety it can be withheld.

It is said the Constitution will be completed in the course of a few days and of which I will immediately afterwards forward you a copy. The discussion upon this very important subject has been conducted with great temper, and the harmony of opinion greater throughout than could have been expected.

The report of Pichegru's having crossed the Rhine as heretofore intimated was without foundation: the height of the water occasioned by continual rain has hitherto prevented it: 'tis however said that he has orders to cross it and is now making the necessary movements for that purpose. The enemy are on the opposite side watchful of his measures: but from his skill, the strength of enterprize of his army, success is counted on as certain.

No indication presents itself of an approaching peace between England and France, or even of a negociation for it. The only indication to be found is in an English ministerial paper, which speaks of the Convention in very respectful terms and of peace as a desirable object. 'Tis probable however when a negociation commences it will be short: for as I presume the overture will come from England, so it is equally presumable that none will be made 'till her administration is disposed to accede to the terms of France. These I presume are in some measure known to England, at least I expect so, a consideration which I particularly suggest at present with a view of turning your attention to those symptoms which may be discoverable on the other side of the channel, as data by which you may estimate either remote or immediate approaches towards this important event. I have the honor to be, Sir, your very obedient Servant,

Ja^s Monroe

RC, CLjC

1. The paragraph referred to reads: "And whereas the difficulty of agreeing on the precise cases in which alone provisions and other articles not generally contraband may be regarded as such, renders it expedient to provide against the inconveniences and misunderstandings which might thence arise: It is further agreed that whenever such articles so becoming contraband, according to the existing laws of nations, shall for that reason be seized, the same shall not be confiscated, but the owners thereof shall be speedily and completely indemnified; and the captors, or, in their default, the Government under whose authority they act, shall pay to the masters or owners of such vessels the full value of all such articles, with a reasonable mercantile profit thereon, together with the freight, and also the demurrage incident to such detention." (Samuel Flagg Bemis, *Jay's Treaty*, 336-337).

To Robert Brooke

Paris August 20th 1795

Sir

I have lately received your favour of the 6th of February respecting the statue of General Washington, voted by the Assembly of Virginia in commemoration of the important services rendered by that citizen in the course of our revolution (the execution of which resolve was committed by the executive to the care of Mr Jefferson whilst he was minister here, but left unfinished upon his departure) and requesting my attention to that object for the purpose of forwarding the original views of the legislature. The delay of your letter on the passage is the cause that an earlier answer was not given to it. I give one at present merely for the purpose of assuring you that I will with great pleasure make the enquiries suggested, and in other respects perform every thing you have requested, and advise you afterwards of the result as soon as possible. Permit me further to assure you that I shall at all times be happy to seize every opportunity which occurs, to testify the pleasure I feel in forwarding the views of those, whom I have so many reasons to regard with sentiments of the highest gratitude and esteem, and that, I am with the most respectful consideration, Your Excellency's most obedient and very humble Servant,

Ja^s Monroe

RC, Vi-Ar: Auditor of Public Accounts: George Washington Statue

From Samuel Bayard[1]

London. 21 August 1795.

Dear Sir

I wrote you a few lines by Mr Pinckney,[2] & at the same time had the pleasure of sending you a copy of Mr Coxe's work entitled "A view of the United States" & of my friend Mr Bradfords memoir on the criminal code of Pennsylvania[3]—Whether these have been received or not I have never had the pleasure to learn.

The reason of my again taking the liberty of addressing you is merely to communicate some information relative to the state of the public mind in America since the treaty of Amity &c between the U. S. & G. B. has been published, & some reflections naturally connected with this circumstance.

All my late letters from America speak freely of the unfavourable reception the treaty has met in every part of the U. S.—The opposition to it is [by] no means confin'd to that description of our fellow citizens who were opposed to the adoption of the federal constitution & have since been generally opposed to the measures of our govern.—it is general among the merchants—who are among the most enlightened of our country, & the most quicksighted to its interest. They seem to think our negociator has been overreached, & that he has failed in effecting the most important objects of his mission.

It requires not the talent of prophecy to foresee the probable consequences of this treaty. It will do more for the French nation, than anything that has occurr[ed] since our first treaty with them in 1778. It is fast operating a change of opinion in their favour thro every part of our country, & if those great & virtuous men who at present direct the affairs of the Republic will not "be weary in well doing"[4]—will but persevere which they have hitherto done, they will establish an <u>interest</u> in the hearts of American citizens which eventually will prove advantageous to both nations.

At present the manufactures of France are not in such a state that any regulations with us could materially contribute to render them flourishing—The time however must soon arrive when the French nation will be at peace with all its neighbours—& the govern.. will have it in their power to patronize the useful arts—I trust our Country will then evince its friendly disposition to its generous allies, & that its inclination this way may not be hamper'd by any article in its treaty with another power. I have the honor to be with great respect & esteem Dear Sir your very hble Serv..

S. B.

RC, NN: Monroe Papers

1. Samuel Bayard (1767-1840) was a Philadelphia attorney. In 1795 he became the agent for presenting American claims in the British admiralty courts, a post he held until 1798. He settled in New York after his return to the United States and continued the practice of law (*DAB*; David Striling, "A Federalist Opposes the Jay Treaty: The Letters of Samuel Bayard," *William and Mary Quarterly*, 3rd series, 18 (1961): 408-424).

2. Bayard's previous letter to JM has not been located.

3. William Bradford's "An Inquiry how far the Punishment of Death is Necessary in Pennsylvania" was prepared in 1793 at the request of Governor Thomas Mifflin and was instrumental in the reform of Pennsylvania's penal code. Bradford and Bayard were law partners (*Appletons' Cyclopedia*).

4. Epistle to the Galatians, 6: 9.

From Joseph Fenwick

Bord.. 22 Aug.. 1795

Sir

I have received from Cap.. . . . of the ship General Mifflin of Philadel.. who touched at Rochfort, a Trunk of papers for you, which I shall forward on in a few days by some american to Paris—the Trunk is pretty large but light.

Two vessels just arrived from Philadel.. which they left 11 or 12 July mention that the President had not communicated any decision on the Treaty of M.. Jay—that the merchants & people in general were extremely clamerous against it, that M.. Jay & three of the Senators had been burnt in Effigy at Philadelphia & many other Towns, that M.. Langdon & M.. Mason after being threatened to be expulsed from the Senate for not consenting to secrecy, had left the House & declared they would never return to sitt again with such members—that those who voted in favor were obliged to quit Philadelphia secretly—That the people were signing petitions against the Treaty all thro' America.

Our coast was still infested with British armed vessels who continued to capture our vessels more generally than for some time before. I am very respectfully Sir your most obed Servt

Joseph Fenwick

RC, ViFreJM

To James Madison

Paris [ca. 22 August 1795]

Dear Sir

I received yours of the 26. of march and had before received those of the 4th of Decr 11 of march and 6th of April which comprize all that I have received since my arrival here.[1]   I am happy to hear that you judged it expedient to deliver my letter of the 18th of Decr to Mr R.[2] because I think it could in no view do any harm, & might possibly in a particular view do some good. I *wait* with great anxiety the *issue* of *that* [*business*][3] and which it is probable I shall *receive* in the *course* of two or three *weeks* at furthest. I send you herewith other communications on the subject & which unfold the *conduct of* another member of the *administration* on it.[4] I do it with a view that *no misrepresentation may be palmed upon the publick* in *regard* to it, and especially in respect to *myself* and which in a possible state of things might be attempted, but not in a probable one, for I do not think that that *member* will *provoke* a *publick discussion* on that point. I wish you however and those of our *friends* in *whom you confide* to be correctly *informed* of *facts* in case *he does* that *misrepresentation* may be *guarded against.*

You will be *surprised to hear* that to this *moment I know* no *more of that treaty* than I *did seven months past notwithstanding the with*holdg it *hazarded* the *confidence* and of course *the friendship* of this *country* with whatever depended on *that friendship:* and certainly *many things have depended on it* even in the line of *good offices particularly the negociations with Spain* and *Algiers* as also *eventual arrangements with this government* in regard to *England* in case *the treaty* was *rejected* or *future aggressions of the like kind* and which have actually happened, make other measures necessary and which ought always to have held in view. In these respects much was *hazarded* by this *policy* and at different *epochs* much *danger was really to* be *apprehended* from it. But this *government* has in general *acted wisely* and *generously* upon this occasion, pursuing the same *friendly policy towards us* as *if the incident had not happened.* It has in the *interim not only repaired the* injuries we had before received *as far as it was able* to *do it but interested itself* in *our behalf* in the business *with Spain* and is *now about* to do *it in that with Algiers* &c *unless indeed intelligence* from your side of the water should *prevent good* effect in both respects.

Since writing the above a peace has been concluded with Spain and the emigrant army which landed at Quiberon under the auspices of Great Britain completely destroyed, every man being either slain or taken prisoners: of which about 4000 were slain and 6000 taken prisoners.

By the treaty with Spain the whole of the Island of St Domingo is ceded to France, the latter yielding her conquests here; that there are secret articles is more than probable providing for the contingence of a war between Spain and Britain: indeed I suspect the old connection between the two countries is revived. *By this treaty no provision is made for us.* I expected it would be so. *For unless* I could *shew Jay's treaty how could we* expect it. I have long since made it known to the Executive that if that point was settled it would most certainly be done: *and I likewise told Mr. P.[5] as he went to Spain* that if *he would* shew it, *it would be done: but he did not think himself authorised to do it:* after *this I abandoned all hope: the aid* which *they* now *give us in favor of Algiers proves* this *but* an extraordinary *mission in the other case for that object through the country too took* it *out of their hands.* In case *of a war between England and Spain I should not be surprised to see an at-tempt to involve us in it* and then to see the same people who have heretofore opposed become the champions of the right *of the Missisippi embarked on the side of England our alliance with France is at an end.*

So far is a duplicate of one which has gone by the way of Bordeaux. one of the objects of this gov.^t in taking St Domingo, is to provide a settlement for those of the army who require it at the end of the war, & a very wise and benevolent object it is.

The constitution is gone thro & adopted. It is now in the press to be presented as amended & tis possible some few corrections may yet be made before it be recommended to the primary assemblies.[6] Sieyes, after it was almost gone thro, introduc'd a proposition for some changes among which what he calls a constitutional jury was one, the object of which is to create a power independant of the gov.^t to keep the several branches within their spheres. this was adopted. I will send you a copy when printed of the whole.

We will endeavor to place the furniture you wish in Phil.^a by the meeting of Congress if possible. I beg of you to have [no] reserve upon this point but to command me as you please, being assured I shall be ex-tremely gratified to serve you. we are well. sincerely I am y.^r friend

Ja.^s Monroe

RC, DLC: Madison Papers, filed 3 June 1795. *The Papers of James Madison* (16: 37-40) dates this letter as 23 July 1795.

The portions of the text rendered in italics were written in code by JM and deciphered by Madison. The first four paragraphs of the letter are in the handwriting of a clerk; the last three paragraphs are in JM's hand.

This letter was written in increments. It was dated by the clerk who copied it as "June 3.th 1795", but this is clearly a mistake and may be a misrendering of July 3, which is a more likely date for the first two paragraphs. The next two paragraphs, written at a later date, refer to events that happened on July 21 and July 22, and had to have been written after that date. These first four paragraphs, all in the clerk's handwriting, were probably sent to Madison as in enclosure to the letter of 26 July 1795 (above), although the original has not been located. The reference to the adoption of the French constitution of 1795 indicates that the last three paragraphs (which are in JM's handwriting) were written sometime around August 22, the date that the Convention approved the constitution.

1. Madison to JM, 4 December 1794, 11 March 1795, 26 March 1795, all above. Madison to JM, 6 April 1795, *Madison Papers*, 15: 507.

2. JM to Edmund Randolph, 18 December 1794, above.

3. The clerk who transcribed the letter wrote "370", which was the code for "ob". JM probably intended it to be "376", which was the code for "business".

4. JM refers to his correspondence with John Jay regarding the treaty with Great Britain.

5. Thomas Pinckney.

6. The Convention approved the new constitution on 22 August 1795 and then submitted it to a plebiscite for ratification (Samuel Scott and Barry Rothaus, *Historical Dictionary of the French Revolution*).

From William Short

Sr Yldefonso Aug. 22. 1795

Dear Sir

Since the letter which Mr Pinckney brought me & which I received on the 28th of June I have remained without having the pleasure of hearing from you[1]—As that has been already acknowleged I write to you at present merely to excite you to send me a few lines by the direct route which I trust will be opened fully before you receive this—I should indeed have imagined the letter mail between France & this country would ere this have resumed the same passage which it had before the war—but as yet it does not appear that the public send & receive letters—Since the 8th of August the day on which we received the first certain accounts of the pacification between the two countries I have been in the daily expectation of the letter post being again re-established & have therefore postponed from day to day writing to you in order to make use of it—Not to wait longer I send this notice of my existence & shall ask to have my letter sent to the French General or Representative with the army who will of course forward it to you—I beg you to send the inclosed to my friend[2] & to give Mr Skipwith that for him—I hope they will both write to me & particularly as that will render it necessary for you to do the same, as you have promised me to be so good as to send me the letters intended for me—If the letter communication with this country should not be opened at that time I beg you to send your letter to the French frontier with a request that it should be forwarded from thence to the Spanish post, from whence it will be forwarded to the Spanish Minister who will of course give it to me—

We are here in the daily expectation of the arrival of the Messenger with the ratification of the treaty exchanged, from Bale[3]—It is supposed the peace will be publickly proclaimed here on the 25th as it is a day which is celebrated by this Court every year with particular attention—& it is wished to render it as brilliant & agreeable as possible.—

Mr Pinckney purposes writing to you also. I leave to him to inform you of what may be relative to his business—as he will probably write ere long—

I have already informed you of my intention of retiring from hence & having sent in my resignation to the President—I still continue in the certain hope of setting out in the earliest part of the month of October—& I hope you will readily conceive the pleasure I anticipate in meeting with a friend of so long a standing as yourself—I have seen by the newspapers that there is a decree which renders it necessary for all foreigners entering France to remain on the frontier until their passport can be sent to the Committee of Public safety & receive their permission to continue their journey.—If this decree should still continue I will thank you to let me know it.—or if there should be any other which should render it necessary to stop on the frontier, as it would be disagreeable—When the time of my departure from hence shall be fixed with precision I shall inform you of it in order to ask you to send me a passport to the frontier, or whatever else may be necessary to prevent remaining there as above mentioned—

We have been a long time here as we generally are without hearing from our country—My last letter from the Sec. of State was of the 4th of April—It was brought by Col^{o} Humphreys to Gibraltar & sent to me from thence—I understand he proceeded to France & landed at Havre about the end of June—That is the latest intelligence I have of him—You could not confer a greater favor on me & I may say also on Mr Pinckney than by letting us know whatever you may learn from our dear & common country—Accept my dear Sir assurances of the perfect esteem & friendship with which I remain yours

W: Short

P. S. The moment of the departure of this letter does not allow me to write to Mʳ Skipwith as was my intention—Be so good as to inform him that I hope he will in this instance take the will for the deed—Let him know I have already written to him more than once & have not a line from him since his arrival in France, which I first learned by accident from the newspapers—What is your last intelligence from our good friend Mʳ Jefferson—It is an age since I have heard from him

RC, NN: Monroe Papers

1. JM to Short, 30 May 1795, above.

2. Duchess de Rochefoucauld

3. Basel, Switzerland.

From Robert R. Livingston

ClerMont 25ᵗʰ Augᵗ 1795

Dear Sir

I wrote to you by Mʳ Fauchette & was not without hopes from the general indignation which every part of this country have manifested at the treaty with Britain, to have been enabled to inform you of its final rejection by the president. But alas! that hope is frustrated, he has ratified the fatal instrument alike hostile to our Liberties & the good faith we owed to France & to our own constitution, which confines to Congress many of those powers which are bartered away by the executive. I send you the papers which will give you some Idea of what is passing here. you will find in them a full discussion of the treaty & your respect for H——n will doubtless be greatly increased by knowing that he is the author of Camillus. the papers signed Decius & Cinna are said to be B. L-v-g-n.[1] Cato you will not be at a loss to know. You need not be told that since the treaty the British have renewed their depredations on our commerce. Seamen are impressed without number from our ships not is it to be wondered at when no care has been taken of them by the treaty.

You will also have learned by them or from Mʳ Fauchette the attempt to seize him by the British ship the Affrica even in the sound & within gun shot of the shore.[2] You will also see that your dispatches have been opened by them.[3] I do not whether if the pusillanimous conduct of our government continues, we shall be secure at our firesides. You will recollect what my sentiments have been for a long time past on this subject. I am now pretty well satisfied that after all these humiliations a war will be the result of the treaty & indeed I think it is devoutly to be wished as the only means of getting rid of the trammels it imposes upon our commerce &ᶜ. This will be delivered to you by Capᵗ Barré who I recommend to your protection as he has lived a long time in my family. I am satisfied that I can answer for his attachment to the republic of France & as she is I fear deficient in good naval officers I think he will be an acquisition to his country. He will tell you all that passes here. Would it not serve the cause of the United States to let France see that whatever may be the intention of the government the people (who must ultimately direct it) are warmly attached to her. For this purpose a translation of some our papers & the resolutions of the different towns on the subject of the treaty may be advantageous. Barré will furnish you with a number that I have delivered him. I have had the pleasure of hearing but once from you since you left us & shᵈ be happy to know more frequently that you are well & successful in your views. I am Dear Sir with much esteem Your Most Ob hum. Servᵗ

Rob R Livingston

RC, DLC: Monroe Papers

1. Brockholst Livingston was the author of the essays signed "Decius" and "Cinna," which attacked the Jay Treaty. Both appeared in the (New York) *Argus*, "Decius" during July 1795 and "Cinna" during August 1795 (*Hamilton Papers*, 18: 477).

2. Fauchet left Philadelphia on 26 June 1795 for Newport, Rhode Island, where the French warship *Medusa* waited to take him to France. He boarded the packet *Peggy* at New York, but inclement weather forced him ashore at Stonington, Connecticut, and he completed his journey by land. The British ship *Africa*, which was cruising in Long Island Sound with the intention of capturing Fauchet, intercepted the *Peggy* as it neared Newport and seized Fauchet's baggage, which had remained on board. The *Medusa* remained at Newport until a heavy fog allowed it to set sail and evade the *Africa* (Albert Hall Bowman, *Struggle for Neutrality*, 215).

3. According to the (Philadelphia) *Aurora* of 11 August 1795, the British ship *Argonaut* captured an American vessel that was carrying letters from JM to Secretary of State Edmund Randolph. The captain of the *Argonaut* sent the dispatches to Halifax, but the ship carrying them was captured by a French privateer, which delivered the papers to Newport, Rhode Island.

To Fulwar Skipwith

Paris Aug.ᵗ 26. 1795.

Sir

M.ʳ Vincent is so obliging as undertake to purchase a complete collection of books for the department of war necessary for the instruction of our officers in the arts of fortification & Engineering, & for which I am authorised to draw on Col.ᵒ Pickering at Phil.ᵃ. will it suit you to advance to Col.ᵒ Vincent the am.ᵗ in assignats & specie (for a part must be paid in specie) & take my bill on Col.ᵒ Pickering for the am.ᵗ—if so you will furnish him the money as he may have occasion for it. He will have the books sent to y.ʳ office to be packed up there & sent thence for Phil.ᵃ as soon as possible. I am Sir y.ʳ most ob.ᵗ servant

Ja.ˢ Monroe

RC, NjP

From Thomas Pinckney

San Yldefonso 27 Aug.ᵗ 1795

My dear Sir

A favourable opportunity offering for France I avail myself of it to enquire after your welfare & that of your family and to request that you will forward to me some intelligence relating to my little folks, from whom I have not heard since I left you—I arrived at Arunjuez on the 29 of June, which as I left Paris on the 3.ᵈ of the same month, I consider in the present state of travelling, as a tolerably expeditious journey— The Court has changed its position twice since my arrival which added to the usual delays in business of this nature, has prevented me from being so far advanced in the business of my mission as I wished.[1] *This administration [has] proposed to our government by their charge des affaires in Philadelphia a close alliance and mutual guarantee of our territorys in America. Our secretary of state sent these proposals to M.ʳ Short but without any instructions either to him or me on the subject. I have declined acceding to the proposal and the minister has proceeded to treat with me on the subject of the Mississippi and limits in which he promises that we shall meet with little difficulty. At his desire I have proposed to him the project of a treaty on these subjects and commerce but nothing definitive is yet done. Pray let me know if any thing and what has been done by the French negotiators on this subject.*[2]

I am much pleased at the restoration of peace between the Countries we at present inhabit, as well on their own account, as for the facility of communication which it promises between us. You will greatly oblige me by subscribing for me to the best Paris newspaper & directing the publisher to forward it to me by every opportunity. If you have any American intelligence be so good also as to communicate it. We have here an American newspaper which states that Mr Jay's treaty has been ratified by our Executive.

On the 25$^{\underline{th}}$ of this month the King's brother Don Antonio was married to his niece the Infanta Doña Amelia & the hereditary Prince of Parma to Doña Maria Luisa another daughter of his Catholic Majesty: on these occasions we have had great galas and illuminations. I beg you to present my best wishes and respects to Mrs Monroe & to be assured of the sincere regard with which I am Your faithful & obed^t Servt

Thomas Pinckney

Do me the favor to forward the inclosed

RC, NN: Monroe Papers. The words in italics are written in code with the deciphered text interlined. A duplicate of this letter in NN: Monroe Papers and the copy in ScHi: Pinckney Family Papers: Thomas Pinckney Letterbook Relating to Negotiations with Spain are dated August 28.

1. Shortly after Pinckney arrived at Arunjuez, the royal court decamped to Madrid. It remained there ten days and then moved to San Ildefonso (Samuel Flagg Bemis, *Pinckney's Treaty*, 308).

2. Manuel de Godoy, the Spanish prime minister, wrote to Josef de Jaudenes, the Spanish agent in Philadelphia, on 26 July 1794, instructing him to inform President Washington that Spain was willing to negotiate a treaty that would recognize American boundary claims and grant navigation rights on the Mississippi in return for an alliance based upon a mutual guarantee of territory. Edmund Randolph enclosed a copy of the proposals presented by Jaudenes in a letter to William Short dated 5 April 1795. Pinckney informed Godoy during their first meeting that he was not authorized to make any agreement regarding a guarantee of territory. The Spanish Council of State authorized Godoy to accede to American boundary claims and navigation rights on the Mississippi on 14 April 1795; negotiations began the following day when Pinckney presented Godoy with the draft of a treaty (Bemis, *Pinckney's Treaty*, 236-237, 308-318).

From Janet Montgomery

N Y Agust 29 [1795]^1

My good friend

I have given myself the pleasure to write to you more than once as well as to Mrs Monroe but business & pleasure probably have deprived me of your answers^2—I now recomend to you both our republican friend Capt Barré and pray you to serve only as fair as he merits and you will then gratify those who have long known him as a worthy amiable Man and whose only fault in the eyes of fochet^3 and Laforest was his Nobility and perhaps he republican Ideas—

You will too soon be told of Jays infamious treaty Our family weep with thousands abt the fate of our Country you will join us Alass, but who can relieve us? Will the french no we have I fear incurr'd their vengeance—my best respects to Mrs Monroe   assure her I love her extreemly and the better for belonging to you   adieu   yours

J M

RC, DLC: Monroe Papers; filed 1796

1. Janet Montgomery is identified on the cover of this letter as the author. The contents of the letter indicates that it was written in 1795.

2. No prior correspondence between Montgomery and the Monroes has been located.

3. Fauchet.

To Jean-Claude Redon

PARIS, August 30th, 1795.

CITIZEN,

I observe by yours of the 7th Fructidor (24th August) that you complain of an intercourse which is said to be carried on by some Americans from the ports of this Republic, to those of England; whereby a correspondence by letters is kept up, money exported and English people carried out of the country: You likewise complain, that the captains of those vessels ask exhorbitant prices for the transportation or passage of French citizens from England here; whereby they subject themselves, in addition to the suspicion of intelligence with your enemies, to the charge likewise of extortion from the unfortunate; and in remedy of these evils you request of me,

1st. To instruct the consuls to prohibit the captains of our vessels from landing either men or cargoes, until a return of both is given to the maritime agents of the ports where they touch; as likewise a declaration of the port from whence they came.

2d. That I will arrange it so, that every captain shall take from me or the consuls his register, or other adequate proof of his vessel being American; by virtue of which alone, she shall be deemed such, and he entitled to the privileges of an American citizen.[1]

Permit me to assure you, that whatever regulations this Republic finds it for its interest to adopt, and which allow to my countrymen the rights of nations and of treaties, in common with the citizens of other neutral powers, I shall not only be satisfied with; but endeavour, by just and suitable representations thereof to produce a similar impression upon the American government; being persuaded, that as well in the character of nations as republics, it is the mutual interest of both to cultivate each the friendship of the other. With the same view and upon the same principle I shall be always happy to adopt, so far as depends on me, such regulations as may be calculated to promote that desirable end.

The several particulars of your complaints are comprised in that of the intercourse between the two countries; if this were done away the others would cease; no correspondence of the kind could afterwards be kept up; no money could be exported, or English subjects carried out of the country; nor could any extortion be practised upon the unfortunate French citizens, who were imprisoned there. Is it in my power to prevent this intercourse? If it is, and this government wishes it to be prevented, then I should think I merited censure if I did not. But you will admit, that this is a measure to which I am not competent, and that it belongs to the French government alone to do it, as to regulate in all other respects its commerce: Regulations of mine upon that point would be disregarded by our mariners, who would consider me as usurping a power I had no right to exercise; they might likewise be censured by this government whose interest it might be to encourage such trade.

If then I cannot prohibit this intercourse, it follows, that I can subject it to no restriction. The same power which has the right to prohibit, has likewise the power otherwise to regulate it; and this belongs of course to the French government, and to it alone. Nor have our consuls any such power; their duties are regulated by a convention between the two nations, and which excludes every authority of the kind: Indeed the exercise of such an authority by a consul of either nation, within the jurisdiction of the other, would be deemed a derogation from the sovereignty of such nation, and therefore could not be tolerated. Our consuls are placed here, as yours are placed in America, for the advantage of our citizens respectively; to see that they enjoy the benefit of treaties, and the rights of nations; not to impose on the citizens any new and oppressive regulations.

If it is the interest and wish of this Republic to prevent such intercourse, admitting that it does exist, but of which I know nothing otherwise than by your letter and the public gazettes, which latter speak equally of the vessels of other neutral powers, as of those of the United States, and it does prohibit it,— provided the prohibition be general I shall never complain of it, however decisive the regulation, or severe the penalty for infracting it. Whatever laws this government makes upon that subject, it is the duty of my countrymen to obey, and if they violate them, they must submit to the punishment such violation merits.

With respect to the two regulations which you mention; permit me to observe, that I deem the first, proceeding from your government, by arreté of the committee or decree of the convention, to be published and sent to all the ports, as a very suitable one, whether the intercourse is prohibited or not. Such a one exists in all cases with us: No vessel can land its cargo in the United States, without rendering an account thereof to the *authority* of the port; nor ought it to be done here, either in the case of cargo or passengers. With respect to the second, I have to add; that by the laws of the United States, it is already the duty of every captain of a vessel, to have a register from the government of the United States or some consul, describing his vessel, her burden, etc., and of course the object, which is herein sought, is already provided for: For you are not bound to consider any vessel as American, unless she produces some such adequate proof that she is such. I have thus answered, Citizen, the particulars of your letter with the same freedom with which it was written, and beg, likewise, to assure you, that if any further explanations are deemed necessary, I shall be happy to give them.

JAˢ MONROE.

Writings of Monroe, 2: 343-346. The original of this letter has not been located.

1. Redon to JM, 24 August 1795, NN: Monroe Papers.

From Joseph Fenwick

Bordeax 31 Augˢᵗ 1795.

Dear Sir

I have your favor of the ___ thro Mʳ Purviance covering one for Mʳ Randolph & Mʳ Tazewell, which go off tomorrow by the America Capⁿ Erving via Philadᵃ recomended to the Special care of the Capⁿ who is a steady obliging man.[1]

You perhaps have heard of several of our vessels having been taken by the Spaniards just before the Peace & carried into Sᵗ Andera many of which have been condemned at least the freight changes & Cargoes, and one ship—the Ship that was condemned belonged to New York & saild from this with a cargoe of whale oil & Cordfish principally, in perfect rule & the Cargo truly american property but on some frivolous pretext was condemned as well as the Ship—this was the more extraordinary as they were destined for Balboa before it was taken by the French. This vessel & Cargo interest some of my particular friends and I am desireous of sending on to Spain a young man that is with me to examine into the causes of the condemnation & carry on such Documents as will ground a reclamation or appeal—I have then to solicit the favor of you to be kind enough (if consistant) to procure me a passport for him from the Comittᵉ of P. Safety for which purpose I have enclosed you his description—if his being a frenchman, tho living with me, render an application from you improper pray do me the favor to ask Mʳ Skipwith to solicit this passport thro any other Chanel. I also send you a petition wrote in french in case you shoud think it necessary to accompany my application.[2]

There is a vessel arrived from Baltimore that left it the 28 July, the President had not then said anything officially of the subject of M[r] Jays Treaty—he had left Philadel[a] & passed thro' Balt[e] some days before the sailing of this vessel on his way to Mount Vernon—The Petitioners from the Town of Boston against the Treaty, not being able to meet him at Philadel[a] followed on & joind the President at Baltimore where they delivered their message[3]—Petitions, says the Capt, were duly going forward to the President against the Treaty from the different States & Town North & South & scarcely a voice lifted in its favor—what do you think of the sentiments of the Twenty Senators its advocates, tis strange they shoud be so numerous on a measure so universally obnoxious—I am told here M[r] Bingham has retracted & now thinks the Treaty improper even in the terms accepted by him & his Colleagues—a noble Representative, to hold the thirtieth part of the sovereignty of our Country! I have the honor to be Dear Sir your most obed[t] Servant

Joseph Fenwick

RC, DLC: Causten-Pickett Collection: Fulwar Skipwith Papers: General Correspondence—Fenwick.

A note at the top of this letter in Fulwar Skipwith's handwriting reads: "Deliv. me by M[r] M. 10 Sep[r] (25 Fruc[t])."

1. JM's letter to Fenwick has not been located. No letters to from JM to Edmund Randolph or Henry Tazewell written at this time have been located.

2. This issue had been resolved prior to the writing of this letter. Thomas Pinckney wrote to the Duke D'Alcudia on 6 August 1795, requesting the release of several American ships that had been captured by Spanish privateers. Among these was the *Liberty*, the ship referred to by Fenwick. Alcudia informed Pinckney on August 14 that he had issued orders for their release (*ASP: FR*, 1: 536-537). The petition enclosed with Fenwick's letter has not been located.

3. Representatives from Boston did not meet Washington in Baltimore, but the proceedings of the Boston meeting condemning the Jay Treaty were delivered to him there (James T. Flexner, *George Washington: Anguish and Farewell*, 1793-1799, 216).

To Ralph Izard

Paris Aug[t] 1795.

Dear Sir

I had the pleasure sometime since to receive y[r] favor of the 29. of Jan[y] & more latterly one from y[r] agent in London[1] relative in part to the same subject. within a month also your son has arrived here in pursuit of y[r] instructions having previously taken the rout of London with a view of seeing M[r] Pinckney, but in w[h] he was disappointed , as M[r] P. had before his arrival there sat out on his mission to Madrid.

Permit me to assure you that independant of the wishes of the President and M[r] R.[2] (whose wishes however form very interesting obligations on me) I sho[d] have been happy to render you all the services in my power in regard to the very delicate trust committed to my care. Be assured therefore that I will pay every possible attention to this trust that I shall be able to pay—that I will ascertain the most suitable place for him ultimately to sit down in for the purpose of commencing his studies, that I will find out some person the most deserving of confidence in that place & upon whom I will prevail to act as his friend & monitor in cases which may require it, that I will supply him with money in the mode you wish, & in short do every thing for him that you can wish me to do, in behalf of a son in whose welfare you are of course interested, feeling for his success in the world all the solicitude which as his parent you ought to feel.

At present he is in Paris in good lodgings with his uncle M[r] Coxe & both him & myself are making the necessary enquiries as to the place wherein it wo[d] be most eligible for him to settle. I think with you that some fortified town some distance from Paris is in many respects to be prefer'd. If such an one can be found, furnishing all the lights in the several branches you mention that Paris does, he will no doubt prefer it: but as yet no definitive opinion is formed either by him or myself on this subject. The means of information however which we have is such, that there will be no difficulty in coming soon to a decision.

I have rec^d within three days past fifty Louis from Mr R. by a Mr Maduit—this gent^n was taken prisoner in his voyage & w^h occasioned a delay in the rec^t of this money vizt what you expected. I shall draw on Mr Bird as occasion may require for the am^t you deem necessary & beyond which it will in my opinion be improper for him to go—for comparatively, as I am inform'd, it is much cheaper living in this country than in Engl^d—I shall write you several letters to make you easy upon the subject of this, & shall therefore at present confine myself simply to that object in which as a parent you are most interested. Be pleased to present our best respects to M^{rs} Iz^d [3] & y^r family & believe me Dr Sir sincerely yours

Ja^s Monroe.

RC, MCH, bMS Am 1631 (296)

1. The letter from William Bird, Izard's agent, has not been located.

2. Edmund Randolph.

3. Izard married Alice DeLancey (1745-1832) of New York in 1767 (*ANB*).

To Jean-Victor Colchen

Paris, September 1st, 1795.

Having at length completed the arrangements which appeared to us necessary, with respect to funds, presents, &c., for prosecuting our treaties with Algiers, Tunis and Tripoli, so as to be in readiness to dispatch the persons to whom the negociation with each is intrusted,—I take the liberty to communicate the same to you, that the aid of this Republic may be yielded us in our efforts to accommodate this very important object. As soon, therefore, as your instructions are prepared for your agent, or agents with those regencies, with necessary passports for the protection of those whom we send, the latter will depart hence in discharge of the trust reposed in them.

As I have heretofore mentioned to you, that the only aid we wanted from this Republic was that of its friendly mediation and influence with those powers, and have also apprized you of the extent of our funds, and the kind of treaties we wish to make; being simply treaties of peace: It only remains for me to mention the persons to whom the negociation is to be committed on our part, and with whom your agent will have to co-operate; as likewise those who must be covered by your passports. I think proper therefore now to inform you, that we have appointed Mr. Hitchborn, at present in Paris, with full powers to commence and conclude such treaties, and who will set out in discharge of that trust, as soon as he is favoured with your instructions for your agent there.[1] But as it would not be in his power to proceed further than Algiers, and it is equally necessary to form such treaties with Tunis and Tripoli, we have thought it advisable to associate with him Mr. Donaldson, who will, after the treaty with Algiers is completed, pursue the business with those other regencies alone, and who has from our government the appointment of consul to reside with the latter, in case treaties are made with them.[2] We wish you therefore, to apprize your agent accordingly, and to instruct him to co-operate with both, or either of those citizens; as both or either may be present, and circumstances require. For these two, as agents, we wish the protection of your passports, as likewise for Citizen Andrews, who will leave this in company with Citizen Hitchborn, particularly charged with the care of the presents, and for —— , who goes as servant to Citizen Hitchborn; so that we wish passports for four persons, in the characters above described.

As we are inclined to think, as well from past difficulties as more recent advices, that the success of the mission, if it does succeed, will depend principally, if not altogether, upon the friendly aid we shall derive from this Republic, so we think it advisable that the United States should appear to have as little to do in the negociation as possible; or, in other words, that they should not appear at all in it, until it be necessary to conclude: For if their agents are known to be their agents, or rather if they are not considered as your agents, with our powers, it will follow that the Dey will immediately come to them to treat with them on the part of the United States, and of course your mediation and influence will be lost. It will therefore be advisable to keep the United States as much out of view as possible; for the purpose of giving full weight to your influence and the assistance of France there. I mention this that you may give a correspondent instruction, if you approve thereof, to your agent; and particularly instruct him in rendering us all possible aid, to concert his measures in strict harmony with our agents.

It will likewise be expedient for you to leave your agent ignorant of the extent of our funds, referring him to our agents for information upon that point, and for reasons that were before explained. One other difficulty only yet remains to be provided for. Our agent will probably embark from Alicant, and of course must carry the introductory presents into Spain. It will be improper that these should be searched, or known to that government: Can you protect them by a passport or otherwise, from such search; as upon that, in some measure, will the dispatch if not the success, of the mission depend.

I have only to add, that as all the preparations on our part are complete, we shall be happy to have those on yours as soon as possible.

Writings of Monroe, 2: 375-376. The original of this letter has not been located.

1. Ill health forced Hichborn to decline the appointment (James Woodress, *A Yankee's Odyssey: The Life of Joel Barlow*, 154).

2. Joseph Donaldson, Jr. (d. 1806) of Philadelphia was appointed consul for Tunis and Tripoli on 3 April 1795, the same day that David Humphreys received his commission to negotiate with the Barbary states. Humphreys and Donaldson traveled to Europe together; Donaldson proceeded to Algiers to make preliminary arrangements for the negotiations, while Humphreys went to Paris to meet with JM (*Washington Papers: Journal of the Proceedings of the President*, 326-327; Frank Landon Humphreys, *Life and Times of David Humphreys*, 234; Elaine Forman Crane, ed., *Diary of Elizabeth Drinker*, 3: 1927).

From Thomas Jefferson

Monticello Sep. 6. 95

Dear Sir

I wrote you on the 26th of May last. since that mr. Jones has been here & mr. Madison, and have communicated to me some of your letters. mr. Jones is taking good measures for saving and improving your land, but of all this he will inform you. I inclose you a letter for M[de] Bellanger, which I leave open for your perusal as it's contents may suggest to you some service to Derieux. I also inclose you a letter from him,[1] and a draught on his uncle's executors for 4000[tt] which we must trouble you to remit in some way or other without loss if possible: and if it cannot be recieved without too sensible a loss, I think it had better lie. observe that the money is not to be remitted to Derieux, as he has conveyed it to Col[o] Gamble & Col[o] Bell to satisfy debts. I think it had better be sent to Col[o] Bell, who will pay to Gamble his part of it. if you recieve it, it may be a convenience and safety to all parties for you to apply a part of it to answer the little commissions I gave you for Froullé & La Motte, and to order me to pay their amount to Col[o] Bell which I will do on sight of your order but name the sum I am to pay in dollars to avoid all questions of depreciation. in this case I would be willing to extend my commission to the procuring me some wines from Bordeaux to be purchased & shipped for me by Mr Fenwick to Richmond, consigned to Col^o Gamble. I will note the wines at the foot of my letter. when you shall have read the letter to Madame Bellanger, be so good as to seal & send it to her.—I trouble you also with a letter to Madame de Tessé, whom I suppose to be in Switzerland.[2] pray find a safe conveyance, and recieve for me any letters she may send for me. she is a person for whom I have great friendship. Mr Gautier, banker, successor of Grand, to whom I inclose another letter,[3] can probably inform you how to address & forward that to Madame de Tessé.—nothing has happened in our neighborhood worth communication to you. mr Randolph's health was at the lowest ebb, & he determined to go to the Sweet springs, where he still is. his last letter informs me that his amendment is so great as to give him hopes of an entire recovery.—In political matters there is always something new. yet at such a distance and with such uncertain conveyances it is best to say little of them. it may be necessary however to observe to you that in all countries where parties are strongly marked, as the monocrats & republicans here, there will always be desertions from the one side to the other: and to caution you therefore in your correspondencies with *Dawson* who is now closely connected in speculations as we are told with *Harry Lee* with *Steel* become a consummate tory, and even *Innes* who has changed backwards & forwards two or three times lately.—Mr Jay's treaty has at length been made public. so general a burst of dissatisfaction never before appeared against any transaction. those who understand the particular articles of it, condemn these articles, those who do not understand them minutely, condemn it generally as wearing a hostile face to France. this last is the most numerous class, comprehending the whole body of the people, who have taken a greater interest in this transaction than they were ever known to do in any other. it has, in my opinion, completely demolished the monarchical party here. the chamber of commerce in New York, against the body of the town, the merchants in Philadelphia, against the body of their town also, and our town of Alexandria have come forward in it's support. some individual champions also appear. *Marshall, Carrington, Harvey, Bushrod Washington, Doctor Stewart.* a more powerful one is *Hamilton* under the signature of *Camillus*. Adams holds his tongue with an address above his character. we do not know whether the President has signed it or not. if he has, it is much believed the H. of representatives will oppose it as constitutionally void, and thus bring on an embarrassing & critical state in our government.—If you should recieve Derieux' money and order the wines, mr. Fenwick ought to ship them in the winter months. present my affectionate respects to mrs Monroe, and accept them yourself. no signature is necessary.

Wines to be procured & shipped by mr Fenwick from Bordeaux if it should be found advantageous to remit mr Derieux's money in that way. They will come at my risk.

> 250. bottles of the best vin rouge ordinaire used at the good tables of Bordeaux, such as mr. Fenwick sent me before.
>
> 125. bottles of Sauterne. old & ready for use.
>
> 60. bottles of Frontignan.
>
> 60. bottles of White Hermitage of the first quality, old & ready for use.

P.S. The day after writing the preceding letter, yours of June 23 & 27 came to hand.[4] I open this, therefore to acknolege the receipt & thank you for the information given. soon after that date you will have received mine of May 26. and percieve, by that & this that I had taken the liberty of asking some services from you.—yes, the treaty is now known here, by a bold act of duty in one of our Senators, and what the sentiments upon it are, our public papers will tell you, for I take for granted they are forwarded to you from the Secretary of State's office. the same post which brought your letter, brought also advice of the death of Bradford,[5] Atty Genl the resignation of E. Randolph (retiring perhaps from the storm he saw gathering)[6] and of the resolutions of the chamber of commerce of Boston in opposition to those of the town of Boston in General. P. Marks is dead within these 24. hours. His wife had died some months before. I omitted in my letter to mention that J. Rutledge was appointed Chief Justice in the room of mr Jay, and that he, Govʳ Pinckney & others of that Southern constellation had pronounced themselves more desperately than any others against the treaty.—still deliver the letters to Madᵉ Bellanger. a true state of the case, soothing and flattering terms may perhaps produce the execution of her last promise.

RC DLC: Monroe Papers; words in italics were written on code by Jefferson and deciphered by the editors.

1. Jefferson met Marie-Françoise Plumard de Bellanger in Paris in 1787. She was the aunt and patron of Peter Derieux, and over the years Jefferson acted as an intermediary between them (*Jefferson Papers*, 11: 394; 12: 124-127, 134-135). Neither Jefferson's letter to Bellanger nor Derieux's letter to JM has been located.

2. Adrienne-Catherine de Noailles de Tessé (1741-1814) was one of Jefferson's closest friends in Paris. She was the aunt of Adrienne Lafayette. She resided in Switzerland during the French Revolution (Dumas Malone, *Jefferson and the Rights of Man*, 15; *Jefferson Papers*, 10: 157-160). Jefferson's letter to her, dated 6 September 1795, is in *Jefferson Papers*, 28: 451-452.

3. Jean-Antoine Gautier was a member of the banking house of Ferdinand Grand. Gautier took over the business when Grand died in March 1795. Jefferson's letter to him is dated 7 September 1795 (*Jefferson Papers*, 28: 318-319, 452-454).

4. The letter of 23 June 1795 was the copy of JM's letter to John Beckley of that date (above).

5. Attorney General William Bradford died on 23 August 1795 (*Appletons' Cyclopedia*).

6. In May 1795 a British warship captured a French vessel carrying dispatches from Jean Fauchet to Paris. One of these dispatches implied that Randolph had made improper communications to Fauchet and had asked him for money for political purposes. The British ministry sent these papers to George Hammond, the British minister in Philadelphia, who passed them to Oliver Wolcott and Timothy Pickering. Wolcott and Pickering, recognizing this as opportunity to remove Randolph, who they considered an opponent of Federalist measures and the Jay Treaty, gave the dispatch to President Washington. When confronted by Washington, Randolph denied the charges but, dismayed that Washington doubted his loyalty, resigned as secretary of state on 19 August 1795 (Jerald Combs, *The Jay Treaty*, 166-167).

From Thomas Pinckney

San Yldefonso 7ᵗʰ Sepʳ 1795

My dear Sir

I had the pleasure of addressing you under date of the 28ᵗʰ of August and as I do not know whether the conveyances are yet certain, I inclose a duplicate of that letter to which I have only to add that I *continue to receive assurances from the minister that the limits and the navigation of the Mississippi shall be speedily arranged according to our desire.* If you have any recent accounts from our Country be pleased to communicate it, as we have had no late intelligence here. Every thing in this Country seems in a state of tranquility. The peace appears to have been agreable to all ranks of people—the paper money has received a very rapid appreciation—we have had three days of gala on the occasion and the Royal favors are now distributing in consequence of it; among others the Duke of Alcudia[1] receives the title of "Principe de la Paz"—your old acquaintance Mʳ Gardoqui has the golden key.

I shall be happy to hear from you soon and to receive any intelligence you can with propriety communicate concerning the state of the Country in which you reside, particularly with respect to the new Constitution. I beg you to present my best respects to Mʳˢ Monroe and to believe me with great sincerity Your faithful & Obedᵗ Servant

Thomas Pinckney

Do me the favor to forward the inclosed which is from the Venetian Ambassador here to his Colleague at Paris.

I have not a syllable from my children since I left them—you will much oblige me by forwarding any letters from or information concerning them.

RC, NN: Monroe Papers; the words in italics were written in code with the deciphered text interlined.

1. The Duke of Alcudia was one of the titles held by Manuel de Godoy, the Spanish prime minister (*Encyclopedia Britannica*).

To James Madison

Paris Sep[r] 8th 1795.

Dear Sir

Yours of the 2[d] of May[1] is the last with which I have been fav[d], tho most probably this is owing to the seizure of our vessels by the British & the free use I hear they make of my correspondence.

Since my last to you M[r] Masons copy of the treaty with such proceedings of the senate upon it as were published up to the 3. of July have arrived here: and since which we have seen the discussions at Charleston, Boston & New York, & which comprize all that I have seen on it.

Comments upon this instrument from me will I know be useless to you; but as they can do no harm I will suggest those that have occurred, beginning with the 9th article[2] & which not only relaxes or cheapens the character of citizenship among us & introduces a new & contradictory (at least with the existing law) principle in our law of descents, but tends in the degree to incorporate the two countries together & to the benefit of Engl[d] only; for I presume we have little land there & shall have less daily, whereas by the stock jobbing measures of many individuals among us they have much with us. The 10th disarms us of a principal weapon of our defense,[3] & perhaps the best security we have in peace agn[t] the commission of those outrages heretofore practic'd upon us: we have no fleet or other means of preventing the B[h] from robbing us at sea, than by retaliating upon land; but this deprives us of that resource: in the principle there is no difference, indeed most people had rather be robbed on land than sea, the former being a civil operation carried on like any other civil process & the latter a hostile one. Besides when plundered at sea the parties, priviteers or others, as this treaty acknowledges & provides against, may become insolvent; & which most probably wo[d] not be the case with a state. The 12th was still more extr[y],[4] for by it we sho[d] be associated with the coalised powers in the plan of starving this nation & likewise give a deep stroke to our own navigation, for it is a fact that at the present moment we are the principal carriers of W. India produce not only for France but for Holland and all the countries depending upon Hamburg & which you know are of great extent: indeed if this article was in force not a ship of ours co[d] cross the ocean without submitting to a search from the B[h] cruisers. The 13th gives nothing we do not now enjoy,[5] & which of course it is to be presumed their interest prompts them to grant. The 14. 15. & 16.[6] fetter us without a motive. The 17.[7] confirms by positive stipulation the old law of nations, & is the more odious at present on acc[t] of the opposit principles contained in our treaty with France & which is completely in force or rather activity. The 18.[8] enlarges I think in the 1st paragraph the scale of contraband & in the 2[d] by admitting the law of nations to be doubtful when provisions were so, & providing for payment of such as are seized on that principle, and of course for such as are seized agnst that principle, for it was not intended to put the latter on a worse footing than the former, and provision being made in no case agnst seizure, it seems as if the point insisted on by Engl[d] was fairly yeilded, and that she was authorized to seize when she pleased, paying us "a reasonable mercantile profit, with the freight &c"; at least I think it wo^d be difficult to resist the argument w^h this article furnishes her in fav^r of that right. It may be said, it is true, that this article authorizes seizure only according to "the existing law of nations"; but from a view of the whole, ought not this phrase to be considered as inserted rather as a palliative to silence complaints agnst the true import of the stipulation & which it required little sagacity to forsee wo^d be raised in America & here, than as controuling or forming the import itself: for if it was not intended to give the complete controul of this business to the B^h gov^t with right to seize at pleasure, & for the consideration stipulated, wo^d it not have been more correct to have begun with a specification of those cases, in which provisions either were or were not contraband, providing for such payment in cases where they were, & leaving out of the provision cases where they were not. The 19th is not worth mentioning either way.[9] The 20. serves to introduce the 21.[10] which is another stroke at France & derogates from the rights of our citizens. The 22^d is like the 10th, as it gives Engl^d time after seizing all our vessels to withdraw her property from the U S. while we are negotiating for reimbursement.[11] It will not be easy to point out any benefit we are to get from the 23. 24. & 25. articles,[12] whilst the two latter are certainly calculated to irritate if not to injure France. The priviledge given British subjects to remain with us in case of war by the 26.[13] is calculated to keep alive in that state the British party, whose influence in peace was perhaps the principal cause of the war; the 27. is not worth a remark & the 28.[14] merits one only on acc^t of the limitation given by it to the 12. & which proves that the construction insisted on above of it, was properly conceived. You will observe that in the above comments I began with the 9th article, but I will likewise add something now on those which precede. The permission to hold the posts till June 1796.[15] and as it was to be presumed till the pressure of the present war was over was a great attainment for Engl^d, for it not only secured her from any trouble on our part & on that acc^t during that time, but enabled her to refuse to surrender them afterwards upon the slightest pretext & especially if the experiment made by the other articles to weaken our connection with France sho^d prove unsuccessful. The cession of the free use of our portages to the British of Canada &c are sacrifices on our part without any consideration on theirs.[16] I was in Canada in 1784 & assured by the merchants of Montreal that if the treaty was executed & we were admitted to free use of the Lakes, they wo^d abandon the former & move within our jurisdiction, for comparatively between a commerce thro' the Hudson & the St. Lawrence the difference was at least 25. p^r cent: & w^h they wo^d not encounter. You will observe that this opinion was founded upon the idea each country was to enjoy exclusively the benefits of its own situation, & to turn them to the best acc^t for its citizens alone: for at that time all intercourse between Canada & the States was prohibited & so it was expected it wo^d remain afterwards, especially in the respect above mentioned. But by this stipulation that difficulty wo^d be at an end, & enjoying all the advantages of our situation, the B^h gov^t wo^d easily be enabled to make up for the difference to their merchants by bounties &c which the mere circumstance of residence in Canada might occasion. Indeed to the province of Canada tis difficult to estimate at present the extent of the benefit w^h wo^d be hereby gained: it wo^d however certainly be great. The extension of the line from the lake of the wood, so as to admit the B^h into the Missisippi[17] is calculated to admit her into the carriage of the immense export from our western country, by means whereof as by extending her settlements westward upon that line, she wo^d encircle us almost completely & thus communicate in some degree to our western settlements the same influence w^h she now enjoys upon our eastern. The concession in the 6th that we had violated the treaty of peace[18] & the assumption to pay for the injuries supposed to result therefrom by delay &c to be assessed by com^rs whilst the violation on her part in detaining the posts & carrying off the negroes, was unprovided for & unnotic'd was still more extraordinary. The only remaining trait to be notic'd in this project is, that by omitting to adjust principles by w^h the courts of admiralty were to be gov^d, if indeed a submission to such courts was to be tolerated at all, all reparation for spoliations seems to be abandoned. Had Mr Jay been promised that those c^{ts} sho^d decide as he wished, yet accepting a treaty without such stipulation gave it up, or precluded in case the decision was otherwise any compl^t—and even if the decision sho^d be according to his views yet the omission to stipulate it, sacrific'd our honor to preserve that of Engl^d. In examining therefore this project from the beginning to the end & impartially, I do not find one single stipulation in our favor, or which certainly improves our condition from what it was before: whilst on the other hand it most certainly contains a series of stipulations, many of which are extremely unfavorable & disgraceful, and others at best indifferent. When therefore I consider the circumstances under which the negotiation commenc'd, sometime after the battle of Fleurus when the preponderance of the French arms was established, & the troops of the coalised powers flying in every quarter before those of the republick; when the dominion of the sea was contested by the French, and after a severe contest in w^h proofs of prowess were given by the latter that struck terror into their enemies, tho' rather the superior in that contest, and when every day to the moment of the close of this negotiation, improved the fortunes of France, I must confess I think this treaty in which it terminated, one of the most extraordinary transactions of modern times. No body will I presume, attempt to vindicate the head which dictated it: the heart however may be free from taint or that pollution which is too often found among political agents: of this however the people of America, who are a just & a benevolent people, ought to be satisfied; and I doubt not will be satisfied.

If this treaty had parted us from France the views of Engl^d wo^d have been completely answered: and believe me there were moments when I had the most disquieting apprehensions upon that point, for the opinion of its contents, with a variety of other circumstances, which inspired here a belief we were about to abandon this republick for a connection with Engl^d, excited at different times a degree of irritation or rather indignation in their councils of a very menacing aspect. A single unfriendly act being committed by this gov^t towards us wo^d have led to others: this wo^d have producd recrimination from our quarter, & which might have ended in we know not what. gov^{ts} too in a course of revolution as they act much from the heart of those who fill them, are susceptible of more sensibility than in other times; this made the danger under existing circumstances the greater. Believe me that since the reports of that treaty transpired I have rested on a bed of thorns: I was often fearful the subject wo^d be taken up in the Convention, & thus progress from one thing to another. I am however happy to inform you that none of these evils have happened—on the contrary the storm appears to have passed, leaving us the prospect of a fair & durable calm. This republick has not only refrained from degenerating into the unfriendly policy formerly practic'd agnst us, but has in this interval done us some acts of service, one in particular is just on the point of being plac'd in a train hence, & which if it succeeds will be sensibly felt by all our countrymen. As this has been discussed & arranged, *I mean the business of Algiers* since the intelligence above referrd to from Phil^a arrived, it furnishes cause to hope (that notwithstanding the extreme dislike they have of the treaty) they will continue to observe the same friendly policy towards us, in the hope we will sooner or later return it.

I consider this treaty as forming an important epoch in the history of our country. It fully explains the views of its author and his political associates; views which were long known to many & charged upon him & them but denied, & by one artifice or other discredited: but this is an act which speaks for itself, & fortunately it is one in which not he alone is compromitted. This however is not the only benefit resulting from it, for having the sanction of the Senate & being presented for ratification to the President, whilst by Mr Mason it was submitted to the people at large, the opinion of the latter will be before him at the same time, whereby he will be enabled to act as the voice of his countrymen admonishes, assisted too in his reflections by the light they may throw on it. If he rejects it & which I conclude he will, the publick opinion will afterwards perhaps be pronounc'd with still greater decision on that side. This therefore will form a basis upon w$^{\underline{h}}$ our republican system & connection with France may not only rest with safety, but hereafter, in the latter instance, be greatly improved. This is a reflection which will naturally occur to you & w$^{\underline{h}}$ will doubtless be held in view in the measures of the ensuing Session.

You have seen by my past communications that *the affair of the Missisippi was lost or rather taken from this government by the mission of Pinckney—that before he past here the French minister was instructed to secure it in the treaty with Spain* & which has been since confirmed to me by the Minister himself. But *as P.* passed *through here without mentioning the subject and which he could not do without shewing the treaty above mentioned* it was concluded *their interference [would]*[19] *be deemed impertinent* & so givin up to *his care. The friendship shewn in the other instance proves it would have been in this if asked. Indeed* the manner in which *this Algerine business is conducted* is calculated to *take the aid of France without giving her the credit of it*—for altho' we pursue *her plan in everything and our agent goes* hence *with her passport and under her patronage and I am* authorised to declare *and have declared in my communications that without her aid we have no prospect of success within our resources,* yet *our agent Mr Hichborn* takes *his commission from our minister at Portugal now here* and to *whom at Portugal he will render an account of his mission if it* succeeds to be *ratified conditionally* by that *minister there subject to the approbation of the president and Senate.* Thus it will appear as if the whole *proceeded from him at Portugal* and *France will appear* to have had as little to do with it, even by circumstances *as if it had proceeded from the moon.* This however *is a piece* with all *our other European transactions: we strive to filch the aid of this government* in all cases where *we can without letting the world know it deceiving the latter by pompous missions* which appear to rest *on ourselves alone.* The *above fact however* if it *succeeds with respect to Algiers* ought to be *made known in America.* You will agree with me that *to ask a favor* under existing circumstances *and without being able to explain the contents of a certain treaty* is not a very *dignified system of policy.*

What course will be taken with respect to *England* under existing circumstances it is difficult to forsee. *I have long since made it known that in case the treaty* was *disapproved* it wo$^{\underline{d}}$ be easy *to secure the aid of this government* in *support* of *our demands upon England.* Nay I am convinced that *if our deportment was* such in *regard to England* as to inspire *confidence in France* she wo$^{\underline{d}}$ make *no peace which* did not *go hand* in *hand* with *a [proved]*[20] *ground* for *our claims and injuries. The negotiation however should be* in the hands of *a person in whom this government can confide* and be conducted *where the French negotiation was conducted either here or at Basle.* Suitable measures too sho$^{\underline{d}}$ be taken at home *by laying hold of their property vessels* &c *and by taking the posts if* not *invading Canada.* This wo$^{\underline{d}}$ be acting *like a nation and we should then be respected* as such *here and in England.* Nor wo$^{\underline{d}}$ such *a measure in my opinion lead* to *war. On the contrary I think they would promote a general peace* by forming a seasonable *diversion in favor of* and which co$^{\underline{d}}$ not be *resisted at present. If the president would adopt measures of this kind seperating himself* completely from *the advocates of the treaty everything might yet be retrieved.*

The constitution reported by the committee of 11. is finally adopted & on the principles of the report. It is now before the primary assemblies which were opened three days past & will be closed tomorrow. It will pass with almost an unanimous vote. The Convention in a decree subsequent to the constitution required that 2/3$^{\underline{ds}}$ of the existing convention sho$^{\underline{d}}$ be reelected, a principle incorporated in the constitution for the future. Tis probable this injunction will be disregarded & that in consequence some difficulty & delay may take place before the const$^{\underline{n}}$ is put in force: for if some adopt that plan and others do not it will take sometime so to arrange matters as to get them in the same line ag$^{\underline{n}}$—& w$^{\underline{h}}$ I presume will be that w$^{\underline{h}}$ the majority approve. The deliberations in Paris are conducted with calmness & perfect good temper—and every circumstance that I have heard of promises the happiest result, tho the royalists have looked to this epoch as one from which they were to hope a revolution in their favor.

The negotiation with the empire is going on & which perhaps is the cause Pichegru does not cross the Rhine. a peace is made with the Prince of Hesse whereby his troops, 6000, in Eng^h pay are withdrawn from the army of the Emperor[21]—very sincerely I am dear Sir y^r friend & servant

Ja^s Monroe.

RC, DLC: Madison Papers

JM sent Madison two copies of this letter. The first is in JM's handwriting, and portions of it are encoded; it is not deciphered. The duplicate, in a clerk's hand and signed by JM, was decoded by Madison. Both are in DLC: Madison Papers. A variant draft is in DLC: Monroe Papers. This transcription is based upon the copy in JM's handwriting. The sections in code are given as deciphered by Madison and are presented in italics.

1. Madison's letter to JM of 2 May 1795 has not been located.

2. The ninth article of the Jay Treaty protected the property rights of British subjects who owned land in the United States and American citizens who owned land in Great Britain (The treaty is printed in full in Appendix Six of Samuel Flagg Bemis, *Jay's Treaty*).

3. Article ten protected private assets from confiscation in the event of war between the two nations.

4. Article twelve granted the United States conditional commercial access to the British West Indies. It forbade American ships from carrying molasses, sugar, coffee, cocoa, or cotton from the West Indies to any country but the United States. This article was suspended at the insistence of the U. S. Senate.

5. Article Thirteen regulated American trade with the British East Indies.

6. Articles Fourteen, Fifteen, and Sixteen set the terms for trade between ports in Great Britain and ports in the United States.

7. Article Seventeen related to the capture or detention of neutral vessels carrying enemy goods or contraband.

8. Article Eighteen defined contraband articles. It also set the terms for indemnification for foodstuffs seized as contraband.

9. Article Nineteen provided for the protection seamen and passengers aboard neutral vessels.

10. Article Twenty condemned piracy. Article Twenty-one forbade citizens or subjects of one nation from engaging in hostilities against the other.

11. Article Twenty-two forbade one country from making reprisals against the other for grievances without giving the other nation an opportunity to grant satisfaction.

12. Article Twenty-three allowed the warships of each nation to use the ports of the other. It also made provision for distressed American ships to refit at any British port. Article Twenty-four forbade privateers of nations at war with one nation to use the ports of the other. Article Twenty-five allowed the warships and privateers of one nation to bring prizes into the ports of the other, but forbade nations at war with one or the other from doing so. Article Twenty-five contained the proviso frequently cited by supporters of the treaty: "Nothing in this treaty contained shall, however, be construed or operate contrary to former or existing public treaties with other sovereigns or States."

13. Article Twenty-six allowed the subjects or citizens of one nation resident in the other to remain there in case of war between the United States and Great Britain, provided they commit no offense against the host nation.

14. Article Twenty-seven provided for the extradition of fugitives. Article Twenty-eight set time limitations on the various articles of the treaty.

15. Article Two provided for the evacuation of British forts in American territory.

16. Article Three granted navigation rights on all waters in North America to British subjects and American citizens, with the exception of certain waters in British territory that were closed to Americans.

17. Article Four adjusted the boundary between the United States and British North America so that the source of the Mississippi lay in British territory, thus giving the British access to that river.

18. Article Six created a mechanism by which British merchants could be compensated for damages and losses suffered by the non-payment of pre-revolutionary debts in America.

19. Miscoded as "contest".

20. Miscoded as "pro cap".

21. France signed a peace treaty with the German states of Hesse-Cassel and Hesse-Darmstadt on 28 August 1795 (Sydney Seymour Biro, *The German Policy of Revolutionary France*, 1: 382-385).

The duplicate concludes with the following postscript, written in JM's hand: "The articles of furniture requested are ready & will leave this for Havre in a few days. I will have them insured if possible. I shall send an invoice in dol^{rs} so that you will know what duty to pay. Remember me to Mr Beckley, Maj^{r} Bulter, our senators Giles & all friends."

To the Secretary of State[1]

Paris 10th September 1795

Sir,

A private letter of the 31st of May is the last which I have been honoured with from you and as more than three months have since elapsed I am inclined to believe that some of your dispatches are carried into England and treated with the same violence that mine were by the Admiralty at Halifax.

It was doubtless an object of importance with the British government to know what were the ulterior measures of the President in regard to England after the decision of the Senate upon the treaty of Mr Jay, and as I presume you wrote me fully upon that head, and immediately after the decision was taken, so I cannot otherwise account why your letters have not yet reached me.

I sincerely wish to hear from you as soon as possible upon that subject, because if in the further pursuit of our claims upon England, it is wished to [derive][2] any aid from this republic either by harmonious co-operation or otherwise, it is obvious from a variety of considerations that the sooner an attempt is made to adjust the mode whereby such aid is to be rendered the better the prospect of success will be. You know that France viewed with anxiety the late negotiation with that power, and waited the result not without unpleasant apprehensions of the consequences; and you likewise know that the moment when that anxiety ceases and especially if there is any thing mingled in the cause producing the change, which argues an attachment for France is the moment to make a suitable impression on her councils. Oftentimes incidents of this kind in private life, increase the friendship and cement the union between the parties: and the principle is the same with nations as with individuals where the government is in the hands of the people. But the moment must be seized, otherwise the prospect diminishes and every day becomes more remote: for where a coolness which has once taken place, is suffered to remain for any time after the cause which gave birth to it ceases, that circumstance becomes a new motive for chagrin, and which and especially if afterwards increased by mutual slights often ends in mutual enmity. In addition to which it may be observed, that if such aid is wished from France, the state of the war is such as to require on our part dispatch, for it is always presumable when its substantial objects are secured on the one side and the hope of gain in a great measure abandoned on the other, as is actually now the case, that its close is not very distant.

I am still of opinion that if a timely and suitable attempt be made to engage the aid of this government in support of our claims upon England it may be accomplished and upon fair and honourable terms. But under existing circumstances, peculiar and extraordinary care becomes necessary in the arrangement to be adopted, otherwise the attempt will fail. Our negotiation must be in harmony and possess the confidence of this government or it will not support it: for no government will support a negotiation it suspects will terminate in a treaty injurious to itself. For this purpose then the person to whom we commit the trust should possess the confidence of this government, and in my opinion the negotiation should be carried on at the place where the French negotiation was carried on, either here or at Basle at which latter place it is reported Mr Eden has lately presented himself; the same person who was not long since at Dieppe for an exchange of prisoners as it was said. On the contrary, suppose any person was sent directly to England on this business what would be its effect here? It is admitted that such a person might be sent as would create no alarm here of injury to this republic from the consequence of such negotiation, but the manner would be deemed inharmonious, and would of course be considered as declining all claim upon this government for its support. England would know this and profit by it. Indeed no cooperation under such circumstances could be pursued. What are the objections to such an arrangement? I can see none. If we were at war with England none would be urged by any one, for such was the case when we were at war with her. If then, remaining at peace, against a common enemy, ought we to decline an arrangement which would be adopted in war, especially when it is considered that peace is the lot we prefer and that our success depends upon its success, unaided by any effort of our own? Would it excite disgust in England? On the contrary it would command her respect. Without compulsion we know we shall not gain from her what we are entitled to, and if this compulsion is to be procured from France will it not be more efficacious when she sees that our harmony with France is complete and beyond her reach to disturb it? But can we accomplish what we wish by the fortunes of France by any kind of negotiation we can set on foot without any effort of our own and if any such effort is to be made of what kind must it be? To this I can give no answer other than by referring you to my former letters on that head, for latterly I have had no communication with this government on it. If it can be done the above is the way to do it: but to secure success by our embarking this government with full zeal in our behalf and striking terror into England it will be necessary to lay hold of her property within the U. S. take the posts and even invade Canada. This would not only secure to us completely our claims upon Britain and especially if we likewise cut up her trade by privateers, but by making a decisive and powerful diversion in favour of France promote and very essentially a general peace.

The state of the war is the same as when I wrote you last. Pichegru is still on this side of the Rhine and the pressure upon Italy is less forcible since than it was before the peace with Spain, a circumstance which gives cause to suspect that negotiations promising a favourable issue, are depending with the powers in that quarter. A similar consideration may likewise impede the movements of Pichegru, for it is generally understood that not only the Empire as a body but several of its members separately, are negotiating for a peace with this republic, of which latter fact we have lately seen an example in a treaty with the Prince of Hesse, whereby six thousand of his troops in English pay are withdrawn from the army of the Emperor.

I lately sent you by Bordeaux a copy of the Constitution which was adopted by the convention and which is at present before the primary assemblies for ratification; and I now send you another copy of that act by Havre. The attempt which was hereby made not simply to amend but absolutely to set aside the former constitution and introduce a new one in its stead, differing too from the former in many of its great outlines and especially in the character of its legislative and executive branches under the circumstances which existed, when it was commenced being at the moment when the trial of Barrére and his associates was depending, and Paris afflicted by famine, was an enterprise you will admit of great moment. So far as it was a dangerous one it proves that such danger was encountered from motives equally benevolent and patriotic. And as the constitution which this attempt has produced, comparatively with the other, is infinitely preferable to it, and forms of course, in case it be adopted, a new bulwark in favour of republican government, it is fair to conclude that such likewise was the object of it. The primary assemblies were convened to deliberate on it five days, and this is the fifth; and in those quarters from whence accounts are already received it appears that it is adopted, in some cases unanimously and in all by great majorities. It was likewise submitted to the armies and by whom it is said to be adopted almost unanimously. In the prospect therefore, in this respect, before this republic, one circumstance only presents itself, which darkens in any degree the political horizon. In putting the new constitution in motion, the Convention wished to transfer from its own body two thirds of its members to the legislative branches of the new government, and for which a decree was passed. A [motive]³ for this was the advantage the republic would gain from keeping in office many of those in whose hands depending negotiations were, and who in other respects are acquainted with the actual state of things. There may be and doubtless are other motives for this measure and which will readily occur to you. This arrangement is however disliked by many and, particularly [by]⁴ the inhabitants of this city, and by whom it is generally rejected. The presumption is that a great majority of France will approve the decree and in which case Paris will yield: but should the majority prove to be on the other side the presumption is equally strong that the convention will yield: so that from this source I do not see cause to apprehend any serious evil. Many however are of a different opinion and count upon the division which exists upon this point as the commencement of a counter-revolution. It is well known that the royalists are active and using their utmost efforts to improve it in their favour: and it is also believed that England and some others of the coalesced powers view it with the same anxious and favourable expectation. But it is usual for the royalists and those powers to catch at every circumstance which turns up whereon to rest a hope: in general however their calculations upon the fortune of the revolution have not been verified by events, and I shall be deceived if this is not the case in the present instance. Indeed a sound reason may be given why Paris differs in this respect from the majority of the other departments and without impeaching her attachment to the republican government. All the great atrocities which have stained the different stages of the revolution were perpetrated here. Under every convulsion and change [some]⁵ of her citizens have suffered: and with the preponderating party in the Convention she is not popular as a department; so that 'tis natural she should wish a complete change of the members, who are to compose the new government.—With great respect and esteem I have the honor to be, Sir, your most obedient and very humble servant.

Jaˢ Monroe.

P. S. Respecting Algiers &c I will write you in my next.

Since writing the above it is announced in the Convention that Jourdan who commands the army of the "Sambre and the Meuse," has crossed the Rhine at the head of about 50.000 men, and in the face of about 40.000 well posted and strongly fortified on the opposite shore. It is also said that he attacked and took by storm immediately afterwards [the city and castle of Dusseldorf].⁶ Much applause is bestowed on the general and his army for this bold exploit and which under the circumstances attending it, is deemed among the most brilliant of the war.⁷

Copy, DNA: RG 59: Dispatches from France

1. JM did not yet know of Edmund Randolph's resignation as secretary of state and assumed that he would be the recipient of this dispatch.

2. The copyist wrote "desire". This and subsequent textual corrections are based upon the draft of this letter in NN: Monroe Papers.

3. The copyist wrote "motion".

4. The copyist wrote "of".

5. The copyist omitted this word.

6. The copyist omitted these words.

7. General Jean-Baptiste Jourdan crossed the Rhine on the night of September 5-6 and seized the mountainous Eichelskamp, part of the Duchy of Berg. Another French corps crossed the Rhine at Düsseldorf, which surrendered without the firing of a single shot (Sydney Seymour Biro, *The German Policy of Revolutionary France*, 1: 389).

From William Short

St Yldefonso (near Madrid) Sep. 10. 1795

Dear Sir

Since the conclusion of the peace I have been in constant expectation of having the pleasure of hearing from you—I have already mentioned that your last was that brought me by Mr Pinckney[1]—I hoped to hear from you & receive through you further accounts from yourself & my friends near you— one of them particularly[2] wrote to me that letters sh^d be sent in future regularly to your care—but I have since received nothing from either of you—I attribute it to miscarriage on the way whilst letters were sent through Italy—& to your having postponed since the pacification for the communication between France & this country being opened to the public—This consideration has also had weight with me so as to prevent my writing for some time—At length I wrote to you on the 22^d ult^o & asked the favor of the Minister to forward my letter, as the regular letter communication was not yet opened—I take it for granted you will have received that letter in the beginning of this month, & that I may soon now have an acknowlegement of it from you—for the same reason, it will be necessary for you until the communica- tion shall be opened to the public, to ask the interference of the French Minister or some person on the frontier to receive & forward your letter—It will be best perhaps that it should be under cover to the Spanish Minister—Mr Pinckney has also made use of this conveyance for writing to you twice as he informs me—As he has a cypher I leave to him to inform you of the state of his business & other points that may be interesting to you—I make use of the privilege of the private character to which I am fast tending, to confine myself to myself & my private concerns.—After a very long silence from our com- mon & incomparable friend Mr Jefferson I received a long letter from him a few days ago from Monticello[3]—He is well & so totally occupied in farming that he has postponed writing as he informs me to all his friends—He has however in the mean time purchased for me that part of Carters tract called Indian Camp—& among its other advantages he informs me that it joins your land where you propose building & settling—You may well suppose my dear Sir, how much I should value settling & ending my days near such friends as Mr Jefferson & yourself—Of this we shall talk a great deal I hope ere long— as my intention is to set out as I have already mentioned to you in the early part of the ensuing month— but dont let this prevent your writing to me—risk a few lines—send them under care to Mr Pinckney—

I have never heard from you whether & what part of my effects were put into your hands by your predecessor—I wrote to you on the subject by my servant who returned to France last January[4]—Among these effects the most valuable part is my library which to me is the apple of my eye—being formed & collected by my own care—There was a trunk also containing my papers & letters—this was sealed—I never heard from your predecessor particularly respecting it—I left also a new chariot & a pair of har- ness in his carriage house—I desired him to turn it over to his successor whom report then informed us was our friend Mr Jefferson—I shall be happy if you took it—as I afterwards wrote to you to do—& that at your own price—I fear however this has not been the case as I have never heard from you respecting it—It will be some satisfaction if you would be so good as to mention the present state of my effects as far as they have come to your knowlege—I have never learned expressly from your predecessor what he did with them, but only an acknowlegement of my letter in wch I desired him to turn them over to his successor—I have never heard from him since his first arrival in Switzerland & I know not what direction he took from thence, though I now learn from Mr Pinckney that he has either arrived in London or was expected there.

Be so good as to tell my friend & relation Mr Skipwith that I fear he has absolutely forgotten me— I have never received a single line from him since his arrival in France & I learned his being there only through the gazettes accidentally—Mr Pinckney informs me he came out with you—I have written to him, but have never received any acknowlegement thereof—I will thank you to mention this token from me—& to add that I shall be extremely happy to hear from him, & that I count with pleasure on the prospect of seeing him ere long—I hope he will write to me—& in that case I will beg you to mention to him, that until the communication shall be opened regularly it will be necessary to send his letters as I have mentioned to you—though I hope still before this gets to you that the communication will be opened—as there seems to be a willingness & desire here. In the constant expectation of hearing from you I remain my dear Sir, yours most sincerely

W: Short

RC, DLC: Monroe Papers

1. JM to Short, 30 May 1795, above.

2. Duchess de Rochefoucauld.

3. Jefferson to Short, 25 May 1795, *Jefferson Papers*, 28: 353-356.

4. Short to JM, 10 January 1795, above.

To Oliver Wolcott

Paris   10 September 1795

Sir

I have been fav^d with yours of the 23^d of June enclosing a bill from Mr Swan upon the House of Dallarde & Swan of this city for 120.000 dol^{rs} requesting of me to procure its acceptance by that house & afterwards, in case it be paid, to cause it to be transported to our bankers in Holland. I rec^d from you also at the same time a draft from the same person upon Lubbert & Dumas at Hamburg, for 300.000 current florins of Holland & which you desire me to avail myself of for the same purpose in case the other is not accepted & paid, or in case permission cannot be obtained for the transportation thereof from the country. I need not add that I undertook the trust with pleasure, or that I shall at all times be happy to render such or any other services which may be useful or acceptable to my country.

I had the bill accordingly presented to Mr Dallard by whom it was accepted on the 12. of Augt last payable according to its tenor of which I gave immediate notice to our bankers in Amsterdam. ~~Mr D. expressed a wished that it might be paid by instalments & which I communicated to the bankers, who wisely declined any such indulgence.~~ I presume the bill will be paid according to the acceptance in which case I will transmit it immediately to the Bankers as you have desired.

I have not yet asked permission of the gov^t to transport the am^t in specie out of the country, because as I had heard that some of Mr Swans drafts on Hamburg were protested & the bill on the house here was accepted, I concluded it was best to pursue the object here; & because I had hopes that the am^t might be remitted there either by bills upon Holl^d & without loss to the United States or by the acceptance of drafts thence on me here (for the transportation of such a sum in sliver under guard wo^d be expensive), & in which case it wo^d not be necessary to ask permission to transport it: and lastly because I was permission to transport it might be obtained if necessary when asked for & without delay. Thus the affair now rests. Upon the above point, however, whether drafts on Holland wo^d be suitable, or whether such can be obtained on me, I have already consulted our bankers, & to the former enquiry am answered affirmatively, & in regard to which as well as all other circumstances connected with this trust, the observance whereof is necessary to execute it according to your wishes, permit me to assure you that the strictest attention is and will be paid, untill it is completed. with great respect & esteem I have the honor to be &c

Dft, NN: Monroe Papers

From Aaron Burr

NYork 11th Septr 1795

My dear Sir,

Your letter of the 18th June, which is the latest I have had the pleasure to receive from you, came to hand about the 1st Inst.[1]—The day following that on which I received it, it appeared in our News Papers[2]—I supposed from the Copy sent to Govr Clinton—It has had a considerable effect in correcting some Mistaken Notions, and in giving just and favorable impressions respecting our allies, I am therefore glad that it has been published.

Mr Prevost will relate to you the singular disappointment and Mortification which has delayed his departure—I have now recommended to him, as he has been obliged to take passage for Hamburgh, to go thence to Basle and there wait your orders—The Place last mentioned being now the Theatre of Negociation, I have thought that it might be very desireable to you to have there a confidential & intelligent person—but in this he will be governed by circumstances upon his arrival at Hamburgh—

He will relate to you the singular events which produced M^r R—'s resignation and the influence which they had in accomplishing the final ratification of the treaty.[3]

I sincerely hope Mr Prevost will be useful to you; He has the disposition, and I think he has the talents, to be so but, on this as on all other subjects, I expect from you the most explicit Candor—You will allow me to refer you again to him, and to the News-papers which he takes, for the State of politics and parties in this Country—Affec^y Yours

AB

Why did Skipwith never attend to my small commission for Wines?—If it has been because he could not sell a bill on America, he should have advised me of the difficulty & I would forthwith have removed it by remitting the needful.

RC, DLC: Monroe Papers

1. This is the same letter that JM sent to John Beckley on 23 June 1795 (above). The copy to Burr, dated 18 June 1795, has not been located.

2. The (New York) *Argus* published the letter on 3 September 1795.

3. Shortly after the Senate ratified the Jay Treaty, word arrived in Philadelphia that the British had begun seizing American ships carrying provisions to France on authority of the Orders on Council of 25 April 1795. President Washington was outraged by this news and instructed Edmund Randolph to inform British minister George Hammond that he would not sign the

treaty until the Orders were revoked. Randolph was the only member of Washington's cabinet that supported this measure. After reading the captured Fauchet dispatch (see Jefferson to JM, 6 September 1795, above) Washington began to suspect that Randolph's support for delaying ratification was part of a conspiracy to increase the influence of France in the United States. This led Washington to change his mind and to announce in a cabinet meeting of 12 August 1795 that he intended to sign the treaty immediately, which he did on August 14 (Jerald Combs, *The Jay Treaty*, 166-169; James T. Flexner, *George Washington: Anguish and Farewell*, 1793-1799, 226-232).

From Timothy Pickering

Department of State 12 September 1795

Sir

The office of Secretary of State being at present vacant by the resignation of Mr Randolph,[1] I have it in command from the President to acknowledge your letters dated Novr 7. 1794—Jany 13. Feby 12. 18. March 6. 7. 12. 13. May 7. 17. June 14. & 26. 1795.[2] and to communicate such information as the present state of things appears to require.

You have already been furnished with a copy of the treaty lately negociated between the United States and Great Britain; but lest that should have miscarried, you will find another inclosed. This treaty has, after the most mature deliberation, been ratified by the President, on the condition proposed by the Senate, and has been transmitted to London.—On the presumption that it will receive an equivalent ratification on the part of Great Britain, and thus become a compact between the two Nations, it is proper that you should be possessed of the opinions of the Government, especially as it appears probable from your letters and from the movements of disaffected persons here, that unfavorable impressions upon the Government and people of France may be apprehended. As we have ever been most sincerely desirous of cultivating friendship with that Nation, the most prompt and candid measures were taken in every stage of the negociation, to produce tranquility and satisfaction, which the rules prescribed by custom in such cases would justify or permit: the result now made public, will evince that the rights of France, whether founded on the laws of Nations, or their treaties with us, remain unviolated and unimpaired.

It is already known to you that Mr Jay was specially instructed by the President to stipulate nothing with Great Britain contrary to the engagements of the United States to France—This part of the President's instructions was officially communicated to Mr Fauchet, the minister of the Republic; and independent of the obligation impressed upon our Envoy, the honor of the Government became pledged to refuse the ratification of any Article derogatory from our engagements to France, which might be inadvertently admitted by our negociator.

Accordingly, soon after the decision of the Senate had been given, and previous to the ratification by the President, Mr Adet, the present minister, was furnished with a copy of the treaty, and requested to communicate his observations thereon. A copy of his letter and of the reply of the Secretary of State are inclosed;[3] by which you will perceive the nature of the objections which were urged, and that such explanations were immediately given and such constructions adopted, as must have been satisfactory. We infer this no less from the explanations themselves, than from the subsequent silence of the minister.

The late conduct of Great Britain in detaining the vessels of the United States laden with provisions and bound to France, is however calculated to create inquietude;—it is therefore proper to explain the 18th Article more particularly than Mr Randolph has done; especially as this part of the treaty has been misrepresented in this Country, as being unfriendly to France.[4]

It cannot be doubted that the United States have a powerful interest in diminishing by treaty the catalogue of contraband articles as much as possible; to this they are invited no less by their pacific policy, which inclines them to cultivate and extend neutral rights, than by the operation of the law of Nations upon several valuable articles of export, the produce of our own Country. No Nation can be suspected of insincerity, in the pursuit of objects connected with its immediate interest; accordingly, the most zealous exertions have been uniformly made by the United States to establish principles favorable to free commerce. A time of war, was however most unfavorable for this purpose, especially when the object, as in the present case, was to induce a powerful maritime Nation, to make concessions in favor of a neutral and defenceless commerce.

The result of the negociation with Great Britain has therefore shewn, that she will not relax, in our favor, from the strict maxims of the law of Nations defining contraband, the principles of which are adopted in the treaty: thus though the first clause of the 18ᵗʰ Article embraces several kinds of merchandize, which the policy of modern times has by special treaties admitted to be articles of free commerce, yet it is believed that not a single one is included as contraband, which has not been ranked as such, by approved writers on the law of Nations. It is not therefore correctly said that we have <u>relinquished</u> any neutral rights, the exercise of which would have been beneficial to France; and yet this is the strongest charge which has been adduced against the treaty, with the shadow of reason. The treaty has barely recited in the list of contraband, what was before so, under a law which we could not mitigate; and though we were desirous of relaxing the rigor of this law, yet a recital of it, in the present treaty, was the best which could be done, and was necessary, in order to admonish our maritime and commercial citizens of a risque, which really existed.

The second clause of the 18ᵗʰ Article clearly refers to the doctrine asserted by Great Britain, that provisions may become contraband, when destined to places not invested or blockaded. To this pretension which is contrary to our interests, and as we are inclined to believe unwarranted by the law of Nations, especially in the extent asserted by Great Britain, we could not accede: the opinions of our Government on this subject formerly expressed, and well known to you, being amply detailed in the correspondence of Mʳ Jefferson and Mʳ Pinckney in the year 1793—though we have not been able to induce Great Britain to relinquish her construction, we have not abandoned ours; and the result has been a stipulation that whenever provisions and other articles not generally contraband shall become such and for that reason be seized, they shall not be confiscated; but paid for with a reasonable mercantile profit, including freight and the expenses incident to the detention.

It is obvious that if the British construction of the law of Nations were admitted to be just, the stipulation in the treaty would be favorable to neutral commerce; we do not however admit their construction; the contrary appears from the treaty—we have only guarded by such means as were in our power against the full effects of a doctrine which has been and which will be strenuously opposed, by all reasonable means which may offer.

Whether this pretension on the part of Great Britain was of such a nature as ought to have been resisted by force, is a question, which it pertains to the proper authorities of the United States to decide—they are the exclusive Judges and competent guardians of whatever concerns our interests, policy and honor, and, on these subjects, they will never ask the advice nor be governed by the Councils of any foreign Nation whatever. We acknowledge ourselves bound to stipulate nothing which may derogate from our prior engagements; this we have not done by the present treaty, and this we will never do; even in cases where we are not bound by treaty we will not stipulate to surrender our rights as a neutral nation to the injury of our friends, but we must be left to determine in what manner we can most beneficially obviate an evil, and when it is proper for us to repel an injury. The present situation of Europe admonishes us to avoid the calamities of war—having attained the possession of a free and happy government and having nothing left to hope or desire beyond our present internal enjoyments, our solicitudes are principally attracted to the vexations and depredations committed upon our Commerce: these are indeed great, and are inflicted upon us, by all the parties to the war; notwithstanding which, our commerce has continued to be lucrative and extensive, though unfortunately for us, as we have no means of protecting it against injustice, it is vulnerable, in the same proportion that it is extensive.

The degree of security which we enjoy is well known to depend more upon the common wants of the Nations at war, than upon any exertions which we can immediately make of an offensive nature—indeed nothing of this kind could be attempted by us, without a total sacrifice of our commerce. How preposterous is that policy which requires us to abandon and destroy the very object, for the preservation of which, we are invited to commence hostilities.

It may not be amiss to dilate on the consequences of our engaging in the war against Great Britain.

1. Seeing she has the command of the sea (and appearances strongly indicate that she will maintain that command) our commerce might in one year be annihilated; and thousands of our seamen be shut up or dying in jails and prison ships. In addition to her fleets and cruisers now in commission, Privateers would swarm, as soon as an object so alluring and so assailable as the American commerce, should present. If we look back to the two last years of our revolution war, a judgment may be formed on this point. A striking defect in her naval arrangements in preceding years, left our ports open for the entry of commerce, for the equipping of Privateers, and the introduction of prizes. A different arrangement in the latter period of that war, totally changed the scene. The small Privateers were hauled up as no longer able to cope even with their armed merchantmen; and the larger privateers were taken. Our mercantile Shipping fell at the same time a sacrifice to the vigilant operations of the British Navy. At the present moment her naval power is extended beyond all former examples; while that of her enemies is at least not increased.

2. Our landed as well as commercial interests would suffer beyond all calculation. Agriculture, above the supply of our own wants, would be suspended, or its produce perish on our hands. The value of our lands and every species of domestic property would sink.

3. The sources of revenue failing, public credit would be destroyed, and multitudes of our citizens now depending on its preservation, be involved in ruin. The people at large, from the summit of prosperity would be plunged into an abyss of misery too sudden and too severe patiently to be borne. To increase their calamities, or make them felt more sensibly, direct taxes must be levied to support the war. And it would be happy for us if we could contemplate only a foreign war in which all hearts and hands might be united.

4. Under the circumstances mentioned, a war with Great Britain would be essentially injurious to France. With our own principal ports blocked up, and her sea coast lined (as at present) with British cruisers, there would be an end to our intercourse with France. And it is by our commerce only that we can give her any valuable aid. Men she wants not; and if she did want, we could not transport them. A fruitless diversion on the side of Canada would nearly bound our efforts. But while we continue our neutrality, the benefits we may render to France and her Colonies are immense. And though the renewal of the order for capturing Neutral vessels laden with provisions, while extremely vexatious to us, adds to their distresses; yet the tenor of the 18th article of our late treaty with Great Britain, though with some a subject of clamour, will remedy, in a degree the mischievous tendency of that order. For the article, far from giving a right to Great Britain to capture our provision vessels, only prescribes the course to be taken when by the law of Nations provisions become contraband. They are not to be confiscated, but paid for with a reasonable mercantile profit. What will be the operation of this provision? Will it check or encourage adventures to France? We think the latter. For if our vessels reach the French ports, all the

expected profits of the voyage will be gained. If they are taken by the British, although there may be less profit, there can be no loss. Consequently, instead of discouraging, this article will rather promote the exportation of provisions for France: for in the event of <u>arrival</u> or <u>capture</u>, the American merchant is certain of making a <u>profitable voyage</u>.

That this article in the treaty respecting provisions has had no influence in the measures of the British Cabinet, is clear to a demonstration: for the order, so far as we are informed, extends to other neutral Nations with whom there is no similar stipulation. And before the article existed, we too well know the conduct of that Court was the same. And claiming as an independent Nation, the right of judging in such a case, it was evidently expedient for the United States to obtain from her some stipulation which, without admitting her claim, would not leave our commerce to future spoliations without any definite means of liquidation or redress.

Some men, forgetting their own professed principles, when they advert only to our relation to Great Britain—forgetting that they are the citizens of an independent State, have said, that while France with whom we have a treaty of amity and commerce was at war, we ought not to form with her enemy a similar treaty, by which our situation would be changed. But where is the principle to support this rule? and where will it find any limits? We have treaties with many other powers; one or the other of whom may be always at war; are we never then to make another treaty?

Others have said—France will be <u>displeased</u>. This we should regret for two reasons: one because we really wish to please our old and friendly allies: the other, because we desire to see, and doubt not we shall see her deportment towards us correspond with her own fundamental principle—that every independent nation has an exclusive right to manage its own affairs. All our external duties center here—that in our new engagements we violate no prior obligation.

That France should manifest a watchful jealousy of any connections we might form with her ancient and inveterate enemy, is perfectly natural. It is the same spirit which prompted her to afford us that efficient aid which was so important to the atchieving of our independence. By breaking off so large a portion of the British empire, the power of a formidable rival was essentially diminished. No wonder she should now be alive to the remotest prospect of reunion; not of Government; but of interests and good-will. But to the following positions you may give all the solemnity of truths.

1. <u>That the late negociation has not proceeded from any predilection in our Government towards Great Britain</u>. We abide by our original declaration respecting the British: "We hold them, as we hold the rest of mankind, enemies in war, in peace friends."

2. <u>That, from the remembrance of a long, bloody and distressing war, from which we were just beginning to recover, and to taste the blessings of peace, whatever even seemed to tend to a renewal of it, was seriously deprecated.</u>

3. <u>That there were many causes of difference between us and Great Britain, the adjustment of which admitted of no longer delay.</u> One was the detention of the Western Posts, under a real or affected belief that the United States were the first to infringe the peace of 1783. From this detention resulted a bloody and expensive Indian war; a loss of revenue by a suspension of the sale of lands; and a deprivation of the Fur trade. To these were added fresh excitements to a more extended Indian war, and the vexations and ruinous spoliations of our commerce. Our differences on these and other grounds had risen to a height that required an immediate remedy. War or negociation were the alternatives. We chose the latter. Had this failed, war seemed scarcely avoidable. But in that case, these good effects were counted upon. The consciousness of using the proper means of averting so great a calamity; union among ourselves, when

war should have appeared inevitable; and division among our enemies who should have refused an amicable settlement of our just demands: besides which we gained time for preparation.

4. <u>That the commercial part of the treaty, though not unimportant, was but a subordinate object, and at the same time not a new measure</u>. This is well known to every well informed Citizen of the United States. It is a fact that a Commercial treaty has been sought after ever since the peace; under the old Government; and since the establishment of the new one. It is a fact, that upon the arrival of Mr Hammond the British Minister, and an intimation that he was empowered to enter into commercial arrangements, he was met with avidity by Mr Jefferson, the Secretary of State: and when it was discovered that his powers extended only to an inconclusive discussion of this Subject, disappointment and chagrine were the result. It may be added that measures have been proposed and powerfully supported in the Legislature the sole object of which was to force Great Britain into a commercial treaty.

5. <u>That the Government of the United States is sincerely friendly to the French nation</u>. The latter doubtless believe that the body of American citizens are well affected towards them. The belief is well founded. But it is equally applicable to those in the administration of the Government. If any thing could weaken this general attachment, it would be a recurrence to such disorganizing projects, and outrages on the sovereignty and dignity of the United States, as marked and disgraced the ministry of Genet. The precipitate and, in the main, ill founded resolutions of a few small popular meetings, are not to be taken as true indications of the American sentiment. Very different is the opinion of the great body of the people. These are beyond example prosperous, contented and happy: where any symptoms of another nature have appeared, they are to be traced to ignorant or perverse misrepresentations of the treaty. This, as it becomes better understood, is more and more approved.

That the treaty would settle every point in dispute entirely to our satisfaction, and secure to us all the commercial advantages we could wish for, no reasonable man could expect. Our antagonists too had claims opinions, and wishes. And where there are opposing interests, Nations as well as individuals are likely to make erroneous estimates of their respective rights. When therefore every argument was exhausted, and found unavailing to settle the disputed points more to our advantage, the terms as we see them were adopted. The Senate after a very deliberate discussion and consideration of the treaty, in all its relations, advised its ratification on the condition stated in their resolution: and on that condition it has received the President's sanction. It now rests with the King of Great Britain to give or withhold his assent. We are disposed to think that his assent will be given: for it is the interest of Great Britain not to increase the number of her enemies, or to deprive herself of the benefits of a commercial intercourse with the United States. It is not less our interest to remain at peace. And the President, as the first minister of good to the people, is bound to take all reasonable and prudent means to preserve it. Peace is the ordinary and eligible state of our nation; and your duties as its agent abroad result from this condition of our Country. And as nothing has yet happened which renders it in any degree probable that the United States will become a party in the existing war, every intimation which may invite the expectations and enterprizes of the French Government, calculating on such an event, is therefore carefully to be avoided. With great respect, I am, Sir, your most ob^t Servant

Timothy Pickering

RC, PP. In clerk's handwriting with closing and signature in Pickering's hand.

1. President Washington appointed Pickering as acting secretary of state on 20 August 1795, the day after Randolph's resignation from that office. Unable to find anyone else willing to accept the position, Washington reluctantly appointed Pickering to the post on 10 December 1795 (James T. Flexner, *George Washington: Anguish and Farewell, 1793-1799*, 247-250; *BDAC*).

2. This list of letters is incorrect. There were no dispatches from JM dated 7 March, 12 March, 13 March or 7 May 1795. There were two, dated 17 March and 14 April 1795, that are not on the list.

3. Pierre Adet to Edmund Randolph, 30 June 1795 and Randolph to Adet, 6 July 1795, *ASP: FR*, 1: 594-597.

4. Article eighteen of the Jay Treaty defined contraband articles. It also set the terms for indemnification for foodstuffs seized as contraband (Samuel Flagg Bemis, *Jay's Treaty*, 336-337).

To Thomas Pinckney

Paris Sep.ʳ 13. 1795

Dear Sir

I have just been fav.ᵈ with yours of the 27. of Aug.ᵗ with several for Miss Nicolson & y.ʳ children at S.ᵗ Germain. They returned today hence from a visit they had lately made us, so that I can assure you with certainty as I do with pleasure they are in good health. I shall immediately send them the letters transmitted me for them.

After you left me I never inquired what this gov.ᵗ had done or meant to do respecting our claims upon Sp.ⁿ—what had pass'd before between it & me upon that subject you knew. In truth there was no ground upon which an application co.ᵈ be made & I therefore tho.ᵗ it best to leave it where it was. ~~I presume however it was inferred that an interference on its part wo.ᵈ not be acceptable to us.~~ By the treaty I saw nothing was ~~secured~~ done, and how far it had been touch'd on in the negotiation, became afterwards an object of little consequence. I am persuaded however it was touched on in the negotiation & so far as to satisfy the Sp.ʰ court that France wishes our success—If you wish the aid of France be so kind as inform me & I will endeavor to get an instruction to that effect to the minister who shall be sent to Madrid.

2/3.ᵈˢ of the Senate advised the ratification of M.ʳ Jay's treaty suspending the 12.ᵗʰ article the other 3.ᵈ being against it. An injunction of secrecy was imposed and afterwards modified by the Senate. M.ʳ Mason however thought the case of a character to authorize his presenting the instrument before his countrymen & in violation of the injunction, submitting it to them to determine who were most culpable, the majority of the Senate or himself, they for imposing such injunction or he for violating it, & from what I can hear the great mass of our fellow citizens have decided in his favor, reprobating in the strongest possible terms the treaty itself. I send you the proceedings of charleston & which were preceded by a discourse from John Rutledge upon which the proceedings or resolutions were founded.[1] I have those of Boston & which were pass'd unanimously, going rather more into detail upon the commercial part of the project, & objecting forcibly to the clause w.ʰ puts citizens & subjects in the ports of each other precisely on the same footing. The thanks of this meeting & which was numerous were given unanimously to M.ʳ M. for publishing the treaty. At New York it is said several meetings were held, & that in the last Col.ᵒ Hamilton had his head broke from some quarter or other whereby that patriotic citizen was disqualified from further debate,[2] & in consequence conducted from the field, breathing after the example of Hudebras when vanquished by the heroick Trulla, the utmost contempt of the foe, but willing for the present to retire to treat his wounds & refit his arms for a renewal of the combat, at some more seasonable moment.[3]

The object of all these proceedings is to advise the President not to ratify the treaty in question, and in which there appears to be greater unanimity among the people than has been seen upon any occasion since the decl.ⁿ of our independance. The deputies from Boston overtook the President in his way to M.ᵗ Vernon at Baltimore, & at which place they presented their address to him. It is conceived in terms very respectful & affectionate to the President expressing an appeal to that magnanimity heretofore so often displayed by him & so much to his own honor & the advantage of his country.

Beware of the commercial part of y^r treaty (if you form one) not as likely to injure us with Sp^n for we cannot be injured by her as she has no navigation &c, but as adopting a principle which being extended to others may injure us. In truth if she does not open new ports in the W. Indies or elsewhere, I wo^d not give a farthing for any treaty she can give us.

Mrs Campan has been forced to fix the board &c of y^{rs} & our child in specie, & which is at the rate of £40. p^r an^m for each—knowing her loss I requested it myself.

Dft, NN: Monroe Papers

1. *Report of the select committee, chosen by ballot of the citizens of the United States, in Charleston, South-Carolina, in pursuance of a resolution of a general meeting of the citizens, in St. Michael's Church, on Thursday, the sixteenth of July, 1795* (*Early American Imprints*, #47380). Both John Rutledge and Thomas Pinckney's cousin, Charles Pinckney, addressed the assemblage in Charleston, which met on 16, 22 and 24 July 1795. Resolutions condemning the treaty were passed on July 24 (Marty D. Matthews, *Forgotten Founder: The Life and Times of Charles Pinckney*, 89-91).

2. The meeting in New York on 18 July 1795 was a raucous affair, and reports of it are confused. When Hamilton first tried to speak he was booed off the platform. When he returned later to present resolutions supporting the treaty, members of the crowd supposedly threw rocks at him, one of which hit him on the head. Hamilton's biographer, Broadus Mitchell, dismisses the story as untrue (*Alexander Hamilton: The National Adventure, 1788-1804*, 341-343), while the *Hamilton Papers* says that "the story may be apocryphal" (28: 485). The accounts that JM read of the incident must have been written immediately after the event, which lends credence to the validity of the report.

3. Samuel Butler published his satirical poem, *Hudibras*, in three parts between 1663 and 1678. Sir Hudibras was a pompous and puritanical knight who set out on a crusade to overcome sin and moral degradation. His was repeatedly defeated and humiliated, including the time that Trulla, a female warrior, bested him in combat (A. J. Sobczak, ed., *Cyclopedia of Literary Characters*, 2: 888). At one point Hudibras suffered an insult similar to that given to Hamilton: whereas Hamilton was subjected to a volley of stones Hudibras, while trying to address a crowd, was pelted with rotten eggs.

From Timothy Pickering

Department of State Septr 14. 1795

Sir

Before this letter reaches you, inofficial information will probably get to hand, of the outrage committed by the British man of war the Africa, commanded by Captain Rodham Home, in his attempt to take Mr Fauchet and his papers, on his passage from New York down the Sound to Newport, where he was to embark for France, in the frigate Medusa. The station taken by the Africa in the waters of the State of Rhode Island, seems to have suggested to the people at Newport the idea that she intended to intercept Mr Fauchet. An express therefore was sent to Stonington in Connecticut, where the Sloop in which Mr Fauchet had embarked was detained by contrary winds, to warn him of his danger. He then quitted the Sloop, and taking his valuable papers with him, pursued his journey by land.

Captain Home made the expected attempt. The Sloop was brought to; and two officers of the Africa went on board to search and take Mr Fauchet, or his papers, or both—Captn Home, it seems, said the object was to take his papers only; and accordingly, finding that those of value had been landed with Mr Fauchet, the rest were returned unopened. The particulars of this action are stated in the deposition of Captain Thomas Bliss, the master of the Packet in which Mr Fauchet had embarked, of which a copy is inclosed.[1] You will also find inclosed the copy of an insolent letter from Captain Home for the Governor of Rhode Island,[2] to be conveyed through the British vice Consul, Mr Moore,[3] who was so indiscreet, and so little respected the dignity of our Government, as to send the Governor a copy of it.

The evidences of the outrage and insulting conduct of Captain Home, with the co-operation of Mr Moore, were communicated to the British Minister and Chargé des affaires; and the expectations of Government of reparation announced.[4] For this purpose, and to give opportunity for counter representations and explanations, time was necessary. Time accordingly was given: For justice as well as prudence required an observation of the maxim—Audi alteram partem.[5]

After a reasonable time had elapsed, and no satisfactory explanations or counter proofs being offered, the President decided on the measures he would take. These you will find in the inclosed copy of my letter of the 5th instant to Governor Fenner. Besides which, the minister of the United States in London is charged "fully to represent these outrages of Captain Home, and to press for such reparation as the nature of the case authorises the President to demand. What this should be, it was not necessary to specify. The President relies that His Britannic majesty will duly estimate the injuries and insults proved to have been committed by Captn Home against the United States, and inflict upon him such exemplary punishment as his aggravated offences deserve—as the violated rights of a sovereign State require—and as it will become the justice and honor of His Majesty's Government to impose."[6]

The letter before mentioned to Governor Fenner, was sent from Philadelphia by the post, on Saturday the 5th instant, when it bears date. On the monday following, intelligence was received that the Medusa had sailed on the first, and that the Africa in two or three hours afterwards got under way to pursue her. I am particular in stating the days when the President's orders to Governor Fenner were dispatched, and when the first information reached Philadelphia that the Medusa had sailed: because it is not improbable that the suspension of those orders may be represented as calculated to be inoperative; and it may be suggested that they were not issued finally until it was known that the Africa had left the waters of Rhode Island. But the facts are as I have stated them; and the true and only causes of the suspension are those which I have mentioned and which you will see in the letter to Governor Fenner.

The circumstances in respect to wind and weather under which the Medusa sailed, joined with her swift sailing, enabled her to escape from the Africa, which has since returned to her former station at Rhode Island. The President's orders prohibiting all intercourse with her, will now come into operation: and for her additional violation of the rights of a neutral nation, in immediately pursuing the Medusa, a new demand of satisfaction will be made on the British Government. A naval force to compel a due respect to our rights on the water you know we do not possess.

I have the pleasure to inform you, that peace with all the Indians on our frontiers is at length accomplished. Georgia and the South western Territory have for some months past enjoyed tranquillity; and the most prejudiced against the Creeks believe their pacification sincere.[7] On the third of August General Wayne concluded a treaty with all the Western Indians.[8] This fact is declared in a letter of that date from the Quarter master General at Head Quarters, to his deputy, Major Craig, at Pittsburg. So I rely upon it. I suppose Genl Wayne must have sent off the official account with the treaty by one of his aids, whose arrival I daily expect.

Quiet possession has been taken of Presqu Isle, where some works are now erecting for the protection of the inhabitants and the security of our garrison.

But for the vexatious on our commerce by the belligerent powers (for they are not confined to the British) we should enjoy perfect repose amidst unexampled prosperity. I am very respecfully Sir your obedient servant

Timothy Pickering

LBC, DNA: RG 59: Diplomatic and Consular Instructions

1. Papers relating to the *Africa* affair are in *ASP: FR*, 1: 662-663.

2. Arthur Fenner (1745-1805) served as governor of Rhode Island 1790-1805 (*ANB*).

3. Thomas W. Moore became the British vice consul at Newport in December 1793. President Washington revoked his credentials as a result of the *Africa* affair in September 1795 (*ASP: FR*, 1: 666).

4. Pickering to Phineas Bond, 2 September 1795 (Charles Upham, *The Life of Timothy Pickering*, 3: 233-237).

5. Let the other side be heard.

6. Pickering to John Quincy Adams or William Allen Deas, 12 September 1795 (DNA: RG 59: Diplomatic and Consular Instructions).

7. Victories by the Tennessee militia over hostile elements of the Cherokee and the Creeks in September 1794 brought peace to the Tennessee Valley (Gregory Dowd, *A Spirited Resistance*, 112).

8. After defeating the Indians at Fallen Timbers in August 1794, General Anthony Wayne took steps to secure his position. The tribes, acknowledging their defeat, began to sue for peace. Wayne met with representatives of twelve tribes during June and July 1795, and on 3 August 1795 they signed the Treaty of Greenville, by which they ceded most of what is now Ohio to the United States in exchange for the payment of annuities (R. Douglas Hurt, *The Ohio Frontier*, 136-141).

To Joseph Jones

Paris Sepr 15. 1795.

Dear Sir

Since my last to you I have rec^d yours of the 12. of June from Fredb^g advising me of y^r rec^t of mine of the 25. of Feb^y [1] & Mr Randolphs permission to draw on him for 2000 dol^{rs} which you presume with what you have already rec^d will am^t to the sum of 3.150. being the sum intended for you. If it is deficient I beg you to get the balance making that sum. I have already answered & paid y^r two drafts, one in fav^r of Southcombe & the other of Burnley & Co: making in the whole ab^t £390. str^g. It will I fear be difficult for me to answer any more untill next spring especially as I expect to pay the balance (between £200. & 300.) of Josephs[2] debts in Scotland, respecting which I have written you several times, requesting information whether any thing & what had been done by him on that subject, with a view if nothing had to desire that nothing might, in which case to send me the statment in his possession rendered by Sr Wm Forbes: and which I beg leave now to repeat. I find by Mr Maury's letters to me[3] that Mr Jefferson has drawn on him for £125. str^g or thereab^ts w^h was p^d—that Col^o Bell has not yet drawn for any thing & that I still have in his hands about £120. subject to y^rs or Bells draft. This possible you have adjusted with Col^o Bell by the wheat &c the balance of what I owed him—Tis also possible he kept Armsted Mr Marks's boy in w^h case the sum to be adjusted wo^d not be great. If then that fund remains so as that I may draw for it either in fav^r of Joseph's debts or any other purpose, of w^h I beg immediate information, you may draw on me payable in Hamburg or London three months after sight for ab^t 1553. dol^{rs} within a month after the rec^t of this. Indeed if really embarrassed you may do it in any event. I sho^d suppose it wo^d be easy to satisfy Carters claims (I mean Champe's & John's) w^h become due this fall by drafts on me, as they owe money in Engl^d & the House of Burnley wo^d no doubt be glad to take y^r bills. In any event I will answer (I mean in fav^r of these or other persons) y^r draft payable by Ja^s Maury of Liverpool or in London after three months sight by me here any sum not exceeding four hundred pounds our currency.

I have already in several letters given my wishes respecting the Rockcastle land & which were that the patent or a copy of it, be sent with an accurate & honest description of its quality, situation &c such an one as I co^d rely on myself, for the purchaser wo^d readily like my acc^t (if sold)—I wo^d give none however but what I might with truth. caution therefore sho^d be urged on Fowler not to err on the favorable side. He has long since had the money to pay for the patent so that all preceding expences are p^d, the taxes excepted. I intimated in my last a wish you wo^d send a person, (if the end co^d not otherwise be ans[were]d) to Kentucky for the Patent & description, but tis probable it may otherwise be ans^d in the course of the winter, with which provided I get this patent or a copy in the Spring I shall be satisfied. I wish you to obtain from the war office my patent for the 2000. acres bey^d the river, & pursue my claim to ab^t 4000 more, the warrant for w^h is in the hands of Obannon under the direction of Fowler; this & the 2000 being the am^t of my military claim.

Joe^4 is at St Germains ab^t 12. miles from Paris, under the care of a gent^n who pays great attention to him. In some respects he improves particularly in his deportment, being more manly & thoughtful: but he is lazy & without sufficient ambition to push him forward, so as to authorize a hope of his making a distinguished figure in life. In his dress too he is inclined to be expensive. I mention these things for your animadversion to him. M^r McDermot his tutor says he has genius equal to every undertaking, but adds to this observation the above comments. Be assured I shall push him forward all in my power, & the occasional visits which I make are not without their effect. As well on his acc^t as that of our child^5 who is likewise at St Germains, we had taken rooms there with intention of occupying them for a month or two in the course of the fall, but fear it will not be in our power, on acc^t of the ill health of Mr Paine who has lived in my house for ab^t 10 months past. He was upon my arrival confined in the Luxemburg & released on my application, after w^h being sick he has remained with me: for sometime the prospect of his recovery was good: his malady being an abscess in his side, the consequence of a severe fever in the Luxemb^g but more latterly the simptons have become worse, & the prospect is now that he will not be able to hold out more than a month or two at the furthest. I shall certainly pay the utmost attention to this gent^n as he is one of those whose merits in our revolution were most distinguished.

Latterly Joe's b^d & tuition have been fixed in specie & at the price of 50. guineas: his pocket money & cloaths form the only expense beyond this, so that you will be able pretty accurately to estimate the am^t.

I heretofore fully expressed what I wished in regard to Mrs Buckner & her family. I sho^d be glad to hear that one of her sons was at Carlisle or elsewhere educating at my expense. And in case neither is fit, that one of her youngest daughters was with Mrs Stv^n Chase above Fredb^g or any other person for a while untill one of her sons is fit to be put out—I perfectly approve what has been done with respect to Joseph & And^w ^{6}—If the views of the former are respectable or even decent in his profession he had better follow it. The prospect here wo^d be eligible only in case they were not, it being my wish to do him all the service in my power in this line—The accomodation in my house, with the supply of corn, wheat, pork &c is such an one as, in case he is industrious or not even negligent & remiss, to enable him to establish himself so completely as to stand alone for ever hereafter, especially when it is further considered that I leave him every farthing of his own property paying all his debts. But you wo^d do well to impress these things on him, for this accomodat^n can only last whist I am here, w^h is a term every way precarious. I wanted him to purchase somewhere a tract of land & in part whereof I wo^d engage to pay at the end of 12. months £150., for w^h you might join in a bond for me. indeed if you co^d do it out of the funds above described I sho^d be glad for that object some immediate advance might be made, as the purchase wo^d of course be better. And^w you will help as you find convenient.

Every thing is calm here—the constitution is adopted by almost all France—the minority scarcely meriting the name of an opposition—Jourdan has troops [on] the Rhine & taken Dusseldorf—the prospect of immediate peace with Engl^d—Jay's treaty surpasses all that I feared great as my fears were from his mission. Indeed it is the most shameful transaction I have ever known of the kind—y^r friend & serv^t

Ja^s Monroe

I enclose a letter for Daw[so]n. Remember me to Col^o Tal.[7] Dr Brooke Col^o Mercer Fitz[hug]h & Page & all friends.

Sepr 18. 1795.

I intended to have written Mr Dawson, Dr Brooke & Col^o Taliaferro to whom as well as to Mr Fitzhugh & Mr Page I beg you to remember me most affec^y. I will write them all soon. I have been sorry I co^d not offer Mr Dawson the place of secr^y—but in a case of this kind many things are to be considered besides inclination—If he will come over with a view of embarking in commerce or otherwise advancing his interest he may calculate on my best offices.

RC, ViFreJM

1. JM's letter to Jones of 25 February 1795 has not been located.

2. Joseph Jones Monroe.

3. No letters from James Maury to JM from this period have been located.

4. Joseph Jones, Jr.

5. Eliza Monroe.

6. Andrew Monroe.

7. John Taliaferro.

To Samuel Bayard

Paris Sepr 18. 1795

Dear Sir

I have been favored with yours of the 4th of May[1] and 21. of Aug^t & for which I beg you to accept my acknowledgments. Some considerations & which operated with peculiar force for some time after my arrival here, made it an object with me to avoid as much as possible any correspondence & even with characters the most inexceptionable, residing in the countries at war with this republick. These however have latterly been less urgent and which considerations as well as their change, you will readily ascribe to their true cause without any explanation from me: indeed I sho^d not have hinted the above but to prevent a misapprehension of the motive of my silence, for I wo^d by no means suffer you to ascribe it to an improper one.

The picture of our aff^{rs} in America is indeed a melancholy one. It furnishes in no view of it, any trait which can be grateful to those who wish the peace, the happiness or the credit of their country. Some place the happiness & glory of their country in the acquisition of wealth alone, & of course think contemptuously of national character & whatever else has been heretofore regarded by respectable & polished societies: but if we were become a sordid people, & were contented to sacrifice to the passion of avarice, all those considerations which are deemed most estimable by others, & which I trust we are not, yet the pillage to which we are subjected by the nation of w^h you speak, deprives us likewise of this, the misers delicious resource. We enjoy none of the comforts which belong to our situation, & which we might be and ought to be a happy one.

That Mr Jay has obtained nothing that he ought to have obtained, & that he has done many things which he ought upon no consideration to have done, is a position too true to admit of dispute. To pass thro' this controversy with a patient tolerance of injuries, without making one effort to vindicate our national rights, is one thing: but to legitimate these aggressions by solemn treaty & in other respects make our situation infinitely worse, is another: the latter however is the piteous dilemma to which we are reduced by Mr Jay. Where that business will end it is difficult yet to ascertain: time only will develope it.

This country is friendly to us. In the commencem^t of its revolution we were the object of its veneration; but this respect daily diminished to a certain point of time when it was in a great measure gone: an effort was made to retrieve it & the success surpassed the calculation of the party making it, for without services & by professions only of friendship, which indeed were sincere, we were rapidly regaining in the hearts of these people, the station we at first so happily held. At this moment however the acc^ts of Mr Jay's treaty transpired, & which produc'd the effect here it was natural to expect they wo^d produce any where. Acting in harmony, it was easy to rest upon the fortunes of this republick & turn them in all cases when we wished to do it, to our acc^t. It was the wish of France that this sho^d be done, and the emolument to us wo^d have been immense. This however was not done, & where the opposit policy will end, time as I have already said only will disclose. I think however I am authorised to say that this country will take no unfriendly step towards us, but will continue to act as she latterly has done, in the hope the period is not distant when we shall be disposed to make a suitable acknowledgment thereof.

I shall thank you for frequent communications of the state or our aff^rs on the theatre on which you are: the state in which the treaty is, if it is yet in negotiation & by whom if at all—whether payments are made for seizures already made, & whether seizures are continued—In short you know what is interesting of what passes where you are, to one in my place here & for communications of that kind I shall be extremely thankful to you.

Every thing is in a state of great tranquility here. The constitution is adopted every where, as is the decree by a great majority of the nation, according to present returns—the latter agnst the notions of Paris. It is certain the royalists were active here against the decree in the hope of exciting trouble: but present appearances discountenance that hope, for the inhabitants seem disposed & very quietly to follow the sense of the majority, & the principle upon w^h the decree was opposed & the opposition succeeded, being that of the right of suffrage & which right depends on that of republican gov^t, has tended essentially to diminish the hopes in other aspects of the royalists: for they saw that those principles were not only deeply rooted in the hearts of the people generally but that they understood them better than they had before believed. With great respect & esteem I am dear Sir yours

Ja^s Monroe.

RC, PHi: Gratz Collection

1. Bayard's letter to JM of 4 May 1795 has not been located.

From Benjamin Vaughan

Basle, Sept. 18, 1795.

My dear sir,

M^r De Witt, the Dutch minister here, gave me your favor of the 8th inst^t late last night,[1] & you perceive that I lose no time in answering it.

You desire me to send you "a free exposition of the view of the Marquess of Lansdown,[2] with his propositions, during the negotiation for the <u>American</u> peace; & of the grounds & motives of the American negotiators for suspecting the liberality of the French court; with regard to your boundaries, fisheries, &c; and you seem to think the suspicions of the latter excited by the address of the English negotiators, rather than by well founded causes given by the French court."—I shall reply explicitly.[3]

First, the views of Ld Lansdown were to render the two countries one & the same, as to commerce & intercourse; not as to alliance; to remove all direct cause of war to arise from the ill-will of America, and all indirect cause to arise from the intrigues of France, & thus to diminish the causes of war even with France; & by these several means to pave the way for a more liberal system of politics in Europe, & consequently for the improvement of humanity.—His steps for accomplishing this were, to remove, by the treaty of <u>peace</u>, all objects of jealousy from the mind of America, & to leave no prospect of gaining any thing by war; that is, to leave no ground either for <u>fears</u> or <u>hopes</u>, which could disturb the tranquillity of the two countries; & then to follow the treaty of peace by a generous treaty of commerce. Next, to appoint a person to negotiate with America, who had corresponding views.—The first facts are manifest on the face of the preliminary treaty of peace; & in the bill respecting the American commercial intercourse, brought into the house of commons. The second fact appeared in the nomination of Mr Oswald,[4] as negotiator, who answered the description required; & for whom, had his character been different, I alone am answerable; since he was appointed upon my recommendation, as capable of fulfilling the wishes which I was told were to preside in the negotiation. Lastly, still farther to do justice to Ld Lansdown, though to pay little compliment to any thing besides the strength of his personal attachments, I must add, that my appearance was judged eligible at Paris; in order that the long & close acquaintance with which he had honored me, might enable me to assure Dr Franklin & Mr Laurens, with whom I was connected, & thence the other gentlemen, that his views were liberal & sincere—So much for the first point.

What remains of your queries may all be comprized under a second head; since I can shew, that the American negotiators were <u>well authorized</u> to suppose, that France, on the subjects in question, took part with England. The evidence arose from the manner in which Count Vergennes recommended moderation to the American negotiators, respecting their demands on the head of boundaries, fisheries, & refugees. Perhaps the secret desire of M. Vergennes at this time, that Gibraltar should remain with the English, to perpetuate the attachment of Spain to France, seemed a case in point to the American negotiators. But, be this as it may, they were intitled to suspect that their cause was intended to be sacrificed; not only because a jealousy of England in America, seemed held synonimous to a connection with France; but because the fewer concessions were bestowed by England upon <u>America</u>, the more might be spared to <u>France</u>.—Mr Jay, observing all this, desired me to go to London to endeavor to seek a remedy.— When I arrived, I thought I saw reason to compliment Mr Jay's sagacity. Lord Lansdown however rendered all suspicion superfluous, by declaring that he thought no policy rational, but that of a permanent & affectionate peace, instead of a truce. I therefore returned joyfully to Paris.—During this treaty, no one in the British cabinet unless Mr Pitt, comprehended, & perhaps even he did not fully embrace, this policy in all its extent; so that new security was taken against the liberality of Mr Oswald, as it was necessary to conclude the treaty before the meeting of parliament, which was prepared to expect it. Mr Fitzherbert[5] (now Lord St Helens) who was at Paris negotiating with France, & Mr Strachey,[6] from London, were made his coadjutors; but his good sense was allowed to take the lead, & the preliminaries with America were signed.—Such is the beginning & conclusion of this history.—No intrigues on the part of England were known to Mr Oswald or myself, & therefore I presume that none were practiced; the system of Lord Landown did not require them; & not only his temper disdained them; but considering the confidence which prevailed between him & Count Vergennes through Mr de Raynneval,[7] he would have esteemed such dishonorable, & if he had even betrayed a confidence which had been reposed in him, it would imply that the project of Count Vergennes had previously existed.

Independent of the above evidence, I may refer you to that of Mr Genet; who, after perusing the papers of the preceding French government, drew up for himself (as I have been assured) the instructions which he carried to America as minister; & in those instructions, as published in the Moniteur, you will find many traces of the above particulars; which these instructions very severely reprobate. If I mistake not, the papers of Dr Franklin contain full confirmation of the fact, though from delicacy to the old government of France, it may never perhaps be made public.

Had Lord Lansdown possessed sufficient power, the preliminary articles would have been materially enlarged, especially in one most essential particular; & the commercial treaty would not have been left for the present day.—The systems of this statesman go to the abolition of wars, the promotion of agriculture, the unlimited freedom of trade, & the just freedom of man. He is in short against governing too much, & for reconciling the happiness of nations with that of their rulers. He is the first person in England who has ventured to espouse these principles in office & in parliament, & the experiment cost him his place, without his repining; & I am confident that he will accept of no public situation where he cannot more or less pursue them.—If his character has been mistaken, you see the source of the mistake in the subsequent conduct of a part of the Rockinghams;[8] for as they never could enter into his principles in domestic or foreign politics, it was natural that they should draw all their partisans to adopt their prejudices against him. His principles were too grand for them to comprehend, & therefore it was natural for them not to give him credit for sincerity in maintaining them. But, as time has proved their politics, it has also proved his; & if he has not rendered his own still more manifest, it is owing to the conduct & persuasion of timid friends; for his courage & disinterestedness make him, as to his own person, careless of the issue.

It is hence that I have regretted, that his proceedings have been so ill understood & requited in America; & that the Americans have enjoyed advantages which they have not referred to their proper author. The truth is, that Lord Lansdown so compleatly removed by the peace, all cause of quarrel; that it is forgotten that there was once a danger of such quarrel without it. His system, it was, which instantly calmed a struggle of near 20 years; & produced such a favorable impulse that notwithstanding it may be queried, according to Mr Jefferson, whether in the 10 years which next followed, the British ministry had at any one time given way to America; yet every thing remianed appeased, till disputes were produced by the present war.

True it is, that when Lord Lansdown was suddenly questioned in the house of Lords, he declared that the American preliminaries would have been null & of no effect had the peace not followed with France. But (to avoid other explanations & to speak frankly) what does this prove, but that he thought the Americans still bound by their engagements with France, had the treaty failed? It is no argument that he designed to take advantage of America, had America been deserted by France in consequence; for as his persuasion is, that nature must always be consulted, force being an abominable instrument of government, in such case he would probably have increased his confidence towards America, because the generosity would have been doubly valued. Any other interpretation than this, would reflect upon the feelings or judgment of him who adopted it. When we see the tranquillity & satisfaction with which Lord Lansdown becomes a private life after having twice been minister; when we find that he has never varied either in place, or out of place, respecting the necessity of a liberal conduct towards America; when he has had the good faith to declare in public debate, "that the people have rights, but that kings & princes have none"; it is needless to ask for private evidence of his sincerity towards America.—Near twenty years, however, of confidential acquaintance, with which I have been honored by him, authorize me to say, that he has never deviated from his first opinions in favor of America; yet without violating his duties to the country which he inhabits, because he conceives that both ought to stand upon a common basis. This assertion, instead of being weakened, will be fortified, when I add, that he does not confine his system to America; since he desires to see all nations viewing each other as brothers; and, in the necessity of separate governments, perceives no reason why those separate governments should become enemies. On the contrary, he thinks, that as men are happy under their domestic governments, in proportion to their union; it is the principle of union, & not of separation, which ought to form the policy between different nations.—Thus, my dear sir, you perceive that Lord Lansdown in his conduct with America has pursued not only the true policy of an Englishman, but the liberality of modern philosophers.

In like manner, when he was at one time opposed to the grant of independence to America, it was not because he sought the subjugation of America; or even altogether because he wished to reserve the cession of independence, to count for something in a treaty of peace; but because he would not throw away the chance of an affectionate reunion with America, by a wise negotiation.—In proof of this I must add, that when the American negotiators resolved not to treat in form with England, without a previous declaration of independence; & when Mr Jay had, in consequence, prevailed upon me to make a preceding journey to London, to endeavor to remove this preliminary difficulty; I found nothing more necessary in addition to my former correspondence, than to state in person, that without it, the negotiation was at an end; when the affair soon became arranged. I returned again to Paris in a few days, with the courier in my chaise, carrying the act of independence under the great seal of England; no delay occurring beyond what was necessary to procure the concurrence of the Lord Chancellor Thurlow,[9] then at a distance in the country, & who to his honor acceded without hesitation.

I may make slight mistakes in these narratives, being without a single paper or friend to aid my memory in my present situation; but the essence of every thing asserted, is correct; and it is certainly impartial, as my political connections with Lord Lansdown have wholly ceased; and Mrs Vaughan & myself have adopted the plan of settling in America, which is rendered so natural to us by inclination, & numerous family, property, & my descent from an American mother, who is herself descended from some of the first settlers in America.[10]

Before I conclude, permit me to say a word of Mr Oswald. He was born, as I have understood in the Orkney islands; and came to the south, in company with Sir Robert Strange, the celebrated engraver, in order to seek his fortune. He succeeded in acquiring one which was immense, though with a clear character; & his wealth, his qualities, & his country, had acquired him many friends. He knew America from having traded with & visited it; & he knew the operations of an army, from having been actively attached to that of Prince Ferdinand; & he therefore saw how impossible it was to render any connection with America beneficial, which was founded in force. He not only thought for himself; but was accustomed to transactions upon a large scale & of a novel nature, which both call for original ideas, & lend the experience which in time is to correct them. If he wanted the finish of a philosopher, he possessed, however, the strength & simplicity of conception, the candor, & the habits of meditation, which attach to that character; & as he was fond of retirement, even in the midst of a great city, he was a great reader. Happily, some of his friends in Scotland had written wisely upon general politics; &, though he was prior to them perhaps in many of his first notions upon these subjects, yet he must naturally have felt courage from finding himself supported in them by literary men of note. The modesty of Mr Oswald & his real ignorance of some of the small things of the world, made him sometimes appear ignorant of some of the greater things; and especially in cases where he thought that silence was wisdom: But these qualities sometimes made others dupes to him, without making him the dupe to others. He had also not only calm manners, which enabled him to listen to every body; but, although by no means deficient in sensibility, he had great patience. The last was an important qualification in the negotiation; since every new conference produced a new claim; which was rendered the more critical, as it was commonly founded upon general principles, & supported by bold language & angry documents. It was therefore not only necessary for him to hear many things without replying to them; but that in his official correspondence he should suppress much, which would have offended either his king or some of the ministry. Happily, if he was cool, he was also generous; & though his fortune was partly procured by œconomy & firmness, his temper, where it was proper; was liberal & yielding. Happily also, he was by no means insensible to the ambition of concluding a treaty, which was big with results of the first magnitude, of which few were concealed from him: At the same time, he was so little given to jealousy, that although I never communicated any of my correspondence to him, & kept him wholly ignorant of the share which I happened to have in his appointment; he never discovered any umbrage towards me; notwithstanding his age was considerably more than the double of mine; but on the contrary, he always shewed me great personal confidence & affection.—Such is a part of the character of Mr Oswald.—It was necessary to have a negotiator acquainted with mercantile & military affairs; yet few of the English merchants had seen at once America & an army; & most of them have their business, & consequently their knowledge, confined to one particular object. It was requisite to have a person versed in the world; & yet devoid of the pride of aristocracy, without being suspected of democracy. It was proper to have a man old in experience; yet with a versatility of mind & temper, capable of entering into new affairs. It was indispensable to excite confidence; & Mr Oswald was the most intimate & respected friend which Mr Laurens had in the world—Judge then, my dear sir, how often I have felicitated myself, in having been the accidental means of so fortunate a choice in so great a concern, which has led to so many subsequent events; and that Lord Lansdown had enough personal acquaintance with Mr Oswald to render him sensible of the truth of what I urged in his behalf. I have the honor to be, with great regard & respect, Dear sir, Your faithful & sincere humble servt

Benjn Vaughan

RC, DLC: Monroe Papers

1. JM's letter to Vaughan of 8 September 1795 has not been located.

2. William Petty Fitzmaurice, Lord Shelburne (1737-1805) served as British secretary of state for home and colonial affairs from March to July 1782 and first lord of the treasury and prime minister from July 1782 until March 1783. He became marquess of Lansdowne in 1784 (*DNB*).

3. Vaughan's connection with Henry Laurens and his friendship with Lord Shelburne led him into active participation in negotiations for peace between England and the United States in 1782. Although Vaughan never held any official post, his involvement in the negotiations began in March 1782 when Lord Shelburne requested him to persuade Laurens to go to Holland and meet with John Adams to ascertain the American terms for peace. During the negotiations Vaughan served as an emissary for the both the British and the Americans, working to remove obstacles to a peace settlement (*ANB*).

4. Richard Oswald (1705-1784), a native of Scotland, was a merchant in London at the time of the American Revolution. In 1781 he gave bail in the sum of £50,000 to secure the release of Henry Laurens from prison. He was the primary British commissioner in the peace negotiations with the United States (*DNB*).

5. British diplomat Alleyne Fitzherbet (1753-1839) held diplomatic posts in Brussels, St. Petersburg, and Madrid. He served as a British peace commissioner 1782-1783. He became Lord St. Helens in 1791 (*DNB*).

6. Henry Strachey (1736-1810) was undersecretary of state in the Colonial Office in 1782 when Lord Shelburne sent him to Paris to assist Richard Oswald in peace negotiations (*DNB*).

7. Joseph-Matthais-Gérard Rayneval (1736-1812) was French minister to Great Britain in early 1783 (*The Emerging Nation: A Documentary History of the Foreign Relations of the United States Under the Articles of Confederation, 1780-1789*, 2: 409).

8. Charles Watson-Wentworth, second marquess of Rockingham (1730-1782) was first lord of the treasury and prime minister 1765-1766. Although upholding the right of Parliament to legislate for the colonies, he sought reconciliation with the Americans by repealing the Stamp Act. He returned to these posts in 1782, and served briefly until his death. In the intervening years he became leader of the Whig faction known as the Rockinghams. They frequently clashed with the Whig faction led by Lord Shelburne (*DNB*).

9. Edward Thurlow (1731-1806) was a British member of Parliament 1765-1778, attorney general 1771-1778, and as Baron Thurlow, Lord Chancellor 1778-1792 (*DNB*).

10. After his sojourn in Switzerland, Vaughan went first to Boston and then to Maine, where he settled on land that he inherited from his mother (*ANB*).

To Jean-Claude Redon

Paris 19 September 1795

I was favored with yours of the 29 Ultimo (15 of sep^r)[1] and the piece inclosed which was taken on board an English Vessel and by which I understand an attempt was made to impose her on the ports of this Republic as an American one. I am by no means surprized that such attempts are made by the English, for in the degree that they do succeed in usurping the character of different nations (and in which usurpation in respect to the United States they have unfortunately a facility from the use of our language) do they enjoy the priviledges of those nations, and diminish the embarrassments of their own. I regret extremely that it is not as easy for the Citizens of France to distinguish between the Citizens of the United States and the subjects of England as it is for ourselves to do it: for to us so obvious is the difference in the Physiognomy and manners of the two people, that it is as easy to distinguish An American from an Englishman as a Frenchman from a German. It will require time however for foreigners to become acquainted with those distinguishing traits so observable to ourselves, and in the interim neither you nor we have any other means whereby to guard against such frauds, than by a vigilant superintendence of the police in our respective lines, and by severe and exemplary punishment on your part when you detect any of the English in such fraudulent attempts.

I shall repeat my instructions to our Consuls in the different ports to make known in all cases which fall within their knowledge, such vessels and their mariners as being English, [that] wish to be imposed on the officers of this Republic for Americans, so that such imposters being detected and punished as they ought to be, others may be deterred from like attempts. For other particulars upon this head permit me to refer you to my letter of the 13 Fructidor.[2]

I have also been favored with yours of the 26th Ultimo[3] and respecting which permit me to assure you that I

Copy, DLC: Monroe Papers; incomplete—second page missing.

1. Redon to JM, 15 September 1795, *View of the Conduct*, 2: 219-220.

2. JM to Redon, 30 August 1795, above.

3. Redon's letter to JM of 26 Fructidor (12 September 1795) has not been located.

From John Beckley

Philadelphia, 23ᵈ September 1795.

My dear friend,

I received and thank you for your acceptable favour of the 13ᵗʰ June[1]—all its requests were duly complied with. This letter & an accompanying packet containing Careys remembrancer[2] &ᶜ &ᶜ will be delivered you by Mᵣ LeCompte who has been in our Country a considerable time[3] and will be able to give you much useful information.

The British treaty occupies the whole attention of America—It was ratified on the 14ᵗʰ August by the president with the condition only of suspending the 12ᵗʰ Article, as recommended by the Senate, and Hammond, the British Minister, sailed with it in the Thisbe frigate from New York on the 17ᵗʰ August—It may be expected back by the meeting of Congress—Still however I do not believe it will ever become a treaty, or any thing more than a mere inexecuted instrument. The opposition is universal, and petitions from every State and district with more general signatures than ever was known, are on foot to the House of Repˢ against it. But my friend a deeper cause will finally defeat it. A wicked scene of Cabinet intrigue is just discovered, by which alone it has progressed to its present dangerous State.

Mᵣ Randolph has resigned his Office as Secretary of State—Bradford Attⁿ General is dead—both offices have now been vacant a month, and no suggestion who is to supply them. Mᵣ R's resignation—the Senate ratification, and lastly the Presidents [ratification] are the effect of this intrigue—On the 19ᵗʰ August two days after Hammond sailed, and when there was also every reason to believe that Fauchett (who had been waiting at Rhode island upwards of a month for the sailing of the Medusa) was gone, an intercepted letter of Fauchetts to the Committee of Exterior Relations, dated in October last, was communicated by the presidᵗ to Randolph. It had been made known to the President a week before. Hammond, who says it was transmitted to him by Greenville, shewed it to Woolcot, he to pickering, they two to Bradford, and the three to Washington. Its effect was this, that the president on Randolphs advice, having before made known in a formal & official manner to Hammond that he would not ratify the Treaty, without an explicit disavowal on the part of G. B. of any right or claim to seize our provision Vessels bound to France and an absolute repeal of their existing Orders of Seizure, was now influenced, without Randolph's privity, to rescind that determination & to ratify & forward the treaty by Hammond in the manner I have stated. But you are anxious for the tenor of Fauchetts letter and I hasten to give it you. Fauchett, in a confidential dispatch of ten or a dozen sheets of paper, gives to his Government a full view of parties, politics & opinion in America—in many particulars he is perfectly right, in others, as might be expected mistaken & misinformed. His view of the British party & their politics is pretty just, and the president he supposes, as we do, to be an honest man, well disposed to France, but wickedly misled & deceived. In speaking of the Republican & antiBritish party, he appears to be jealous of Randolph as not well disposed to France, and mentions Jefferson, Madison, yourself, Mifflin, Clinton & Dallas as the Republican leaders, but as honest men contrasted with their opponents—He speaks also of Randolphs previous Confessions to him, and of an overture he made to him, to employ the money of his nation thro' the uses of proper agents to procure useful intelligence of the British movements—This last circumstance is stated somewhat ambiguously, but he refers to reference papers N° 3 and 6 for more full explanation. Critically, for the views of the british faction, neither of these references accompany the intercepted letter; whether they had them & for obvious reasons withheld them, or not? is not known, tho' the president acknowledges he never saw them.[4] Sufficient however for their purposes the president was worked up into a suspicion that Randolph had either actually received, or manifested a disposition to receive French money—Accordingly on the 19ᵗʰ August he sent for him, and under all the strange circumstance I have stated, most abruptly delivered him the letter demanding an explanation of it—R. behaved very properly and Woolcot & pickering being present declined any particular answer, except signifying his determination to resign and immediately to proceed to Rhode Island in quest of Fauchett for the requisite explanation. He executed both purposes, and a few days since returned from Rh Island, the unexpected sailing of the Medusa, the day after he reached Newport, had nearly deprived him of his object—but Fauchett, with whom in presence of a third person he held a full interview the evening before, sent a dispatch from on board the Medusa, by the pilot, addressed to Mʳ Adet,[5] which covered a full & explicit explanation & exoneration of Mʳ R. added to which Adet has found the reference papers N° 3 & 6—from all which it results that there is not a shadow of suspicion agˢᵗ Randolph—The president is now absent at Mount Vernon, but on Saturday Mʳ R. published in Browns Gazette, a letter to him concerning his return & possession of proofs sufficient to satisfy every impartial mind that his resignation was dictated by considerations that ought not to have been resisted for a moment & stands upon a footing perfectly honorable to himself[6]—and further that he was digesting into order & should shortly forward him a full view of the subject. In this situation the business now stands, but that it must fully come before the public is inevitable. The attempts to assassinate R's character during his trip to Rh. island, were base and infamous to a degree—the final effect of this pretty intrigue you may readily conceive. I ought not however to omit that Fauchett declares the letter never was intercepted, but stolen from him last winter when in New York—You will probably have seen Fauchett before this reaches you, as also the letter itself, or a Copy of it.

I have endeavored to give you the outlines of this bagatelle business, and would to God, my friend, there were not better ground to suspect the application of British money in our country, than this letter or any thing else can give for a suspicion of the application of French money. In the mean time, however, the true friends of our Country, among which I may without vanity class myself, feel deeply anxious to see what will be the conduct of France respecting the treaty—Whatever step she takes, will be critically applied as it relates to the next session of Congress—that it may not be hostile I rather hope than expect—that it might be temperate, but firm & decisive I could wish, and that as far as relates to an effectual check on British intrigues in America, it should be the policy of France to repossess herself of Louisiana and the Floridas, I fervently wish as an American, a republican & a friend to Liberty. It may be satisfactory to add that the paragraphs of Fauchetts letter respecting Mʳ R's previous confessions, and the overture to apply French money, are thus explained—the previous confession was, the shewing to Fauchett so much of Jays instructions as inhibited him from agreeing to any stipulations injurious to France—the overture for applying French money was to obtain from Fauchett, without his knowing it, a concert of operation in ferretting out British machinations to foment the insurrection then at its height.

I have nothing farther to add on the State of public affairs—Every thing will remain probably in statu quo until the meeting of Congress on the 3ᵈ december. All friends in Virginia are well and that state is unanimously opposed to the treaty. Accept of what I have now written as an earnest of my purpose not to let any important occasion of possessing you of useful & necessary information, to pass away unimproved. I shall hope early in the next Session to have your acknowledgement of the receipt of this letter, with such interesting particulars as you can with propriety communicate. Make my best respects accept-able to your amiable lady, and believe me, most truly, My dear Sir, Y^r affect. friend,

John Beckley

RC, DLC: Monroe Papers

1. JM's letter to Beckley of June 13 has not been located.

2. Matthew Carey, *The American remembrancer; or, An impartial collection of essays, resolves, speeches, &c. relative, or having affinity, to the treaty with Great Britain* (Philadelphia, 1795).

3. Le Compte was secretary of the National Commission of Geneva, Switzerland. He was in the United States from 1794 to 1795 meeting political leaders such as Jefferson to give them a copy of a decree of that commission (*Jefferson Papers*, 28:196-199).

4. Fauchet's dispatch number ten, dated 31 October 1794, and excerpts of dispatches number three (4 June 1794) and six (5 September 1794) are printed in John J. Reardon, *Edmund Randolph*, 367-380.

5. Fauchet's statement, which he sent to Pierre Adet, is printed in Edmund Randolph, *A Vindication of Mr. Randolph's Resignation* (Philadelphia, 1795), 13-17.

6. Randolph's letter to Washington of 15 September 1795 was published in the *Philadelphia Gazette*, edited by Andrew Brown, on 26 September 1795. The letter is printed in Reardon, *Edmund Randolph*, 318.

To Thomas Pinckney

Paris Sepr 23. 1795.

Dear Sir

Having just written you and Mr Short by means of the Com. of p: safety,[1] I avail myself of the opportunity by c^t de Rohdes solely for the purpose of forwarding two letters lately rec^d for you, assuring you that y^r children are well, & requesting that you wo^d give such instructions to Mr Dease as will reserve for me ab^t 2500. dol^{rs} out of the money appropriated to the Marquiss of Fayette, for w^h at present I shall not draw, nor untill I see you to shew the evidence of my advances for his family—and which I suggest to you as a proper precaution in all cases, lest hereafter disputes or discontent in reg^d to the depr[eciatio]n of the assignats at the time advances were made, for I presume all advances were made in that medium. Be so kind as make my most sincere regards to Mr Short & be assured of the sincerity with which I am dear Sir y^r fn^d & servant

Ja^s Monroe

The c^t de R. is minister for Portugal from Prussia. He is a very amiable man.

RC, InU: Lafayette Manuscripts

1. JM to Pinckney 13 September 1 1795; JM to William Short 15 September 1795, both above.

From Stephen Cathalan

Marseilles the 26th September 1795.

Sir

The Agent of the Exterior Relations in this Place, has delivered me Yesterday an abstract of a Letter he has received from M. Valliere Consul General of the Republik of France at Algiers[1] as follow;

"Algier the 28 Fructidor 3d Yr

L'amerique vient de conclure La Paix avec cette Regence, elle Paye un Tribut, de 122 Milles Livres & Le prix de la Paix. Le Rachapt Des Esclaves, & les divers Presents L'eleveront a Environ 4 Millions; M. Donalson a été Le Negotiateur."[2]

He adds in his Private oppinion, that he doubted that the Americain Governt would Give its Ratification this Treaty amounting very high. A Copy of this article has been Sent to Gouvt yesterday at Paris. The Same Consul writes to the Cee of Salut Pk through the channel of the agents of Affrick in this Town; (which has been Communicated to me under Secret) the dispatchs being all open: "I don't know Exactly the whole Terms of the Treaty made by M. Donalson, but these are the principal Conditions vizt 200,000 Dollards for the Dey 100,000 Dards for the Veszil (chief Minister) 200,000 Dard for the Ransom of the 100 Slaves 26,000 Dollards in annual Tribute, a Considerable furniture of articles for the navy, Immense Presents in Bijoux & in money to the family of the Dey, to his Ministers and officers of that Regency."[3]

he adds about this Some Private Refflexions, but it appears that he presumes, that united States are not able to Support Such heavy Expences; & in that I am in a quite different opinion with him.

This Letter is to be forwarded by this Day's Post,—Then I am Sure and very Glad, that you will have received at Paris the first new of that Peace, Through my channel.[4]

it appears that the Dey is not now on Good Terms with the English, the Crew of an english Privateer has been Put in Irons, Some time ago Before a Danish Ship Loaded with Corn for Marseilles was taken and Carried by the English into Gibraltar. The dey being informed, Sent already for the English Consul, and forced him to pay already this Cargo to the Price it would have obtained in Marseilles, which was already effectuated, the Danish Consul advanced the Money.

You have now all the Informations I could obtain here on this very fortunate Event, but which appears to be as Good as if I had received officialy accounts Direct from algiers, by that Vessel.

In this negotiation the French Consul was not at all employed.

I hope now that I will See before 4 Months many American Vessels in this Harbour, with wheat, Flour, Rice, Pulse, Codfish, Salted Beef & Pork, west Indies articles, &c which will be well sold; we have now Tobacco enough for Six Months at Least. I have the honour to be with Respect Sir Your most obedient humble & Devoted Servant

Stephen Cathalan Junr

Please to Communicate this Letter to Fulwar Skipwith, as I do not write him This day, if you judge it Proper.

Messrs Cath ns & mines Compliments to you & your Respectable Family,

RC, NN: Monroe Papers

1. Césaire-Philippe Vallière (1756-1823) was the French vice consul at Algiers from 1779 to 1790, when he was appointed consul general. He held that post until November 1795 (Anne Mézin, *Les Consuls de France au Siecle de Lumieres*, 575-576).

2. The translation of this passage reads:

> "Algier 28 Fructidor 3ᵈ Yᵉ [4 September 1795]
>
> America has just concluded Peace with this Regency; she pays a tribute of 122 thousand livres and the price of the Peace. The ransom for slaves and the various gifts raises the cost to around 4 million; Mr. Donaldson has been the negotiator."

3. Joseph Donaldson, Jr., arrived in Algiers on 3 September 1795, and immediately began negotiations with the Dey for the ransom of American prisoners and for the annual tribute that would allow U. S. ships to pass unmolested on the Mediterranean. The Dey first demanded $2,247,000 in cash, two frigates, and an annual contribution of naval stores. Donaldson responded by offering a total package of $543,000. Outraged, the Dey ordered Donaldson leave Algiers. Before Donaldson departed, the Dey sent him a compromise offer of $982,000; the American countered with an offer of $585,000 in cash and naval stores, which was accepted. The U. S. Senate ratified the treaty on 2 March 1796 (Frank E. Ross, "The Mission of Joseph Donaldson, Jr., to Algiers, 1795-97," *The Journal of Modern History*, 7 (1935): 422-433; *Treaties Conventions, International Acts, Protocols and Agreements Between the United States and Other Powers*, *1776-1909*, 1: 1-6).

4. Prior to writing the current letter, Cathalan sent JM letters on 24 and 25 September 1795 informing him that he had received reports of a treaty (enclosed in JM to the Secretary of State, 4 October 1795, DNA: RG 59: Dispatches from France).

From François Barbé-Marbois

Metz 28. 7ᵗᵉ 1795. 6. Vend. 3

Monsieur,

La lettre que vous m'avéz fait l'honneur de m'écrire, le 21. m'a été remise par M. Izard. J'ai eu de la Satisfaction en revoyant le Fils d'un ancien ami. Le séjour qu'il fera ici ne peut manquer de lui être utile et il y trouvera tout ce qui est necessaire pour se perfectionner dans la profession à laquelle il se décidera. Nous nous appliquerons aussi autant qu'il dependra de nous à lui rendre agréable Sa residence en cette ville.

Nous avions quelques esperances de vous y voir: ma Femme Se felicitoit de pouvoir renouveller connaissance avec madame Monroe. Mais La Saison me parait trop avancé aujourd'hui pour que vous puissiez entreprendre un pareil voyage. Nous [ne] perdons pas l'esperance [que] ce sera dans quelques temps que vous veniez dans notre ville, une grande Satisfaction pour nous de vous y recevoir. J'ai l'honneur d'être au estime et respect, Monsieur, Votre très humble serviteur,

Barbé marbois

Editors' Translation

Metz 28 7ᵉʳ 1795 6 Vend. 3

Sir,

The letter that you paid me the honor of writing on the 21ˢᵗ was delivered by M. Izard.[1] I had the pleasure of seeing the son of an old friend. His stay here cannot fail to be useful to him; he will find all that is necessary here to perfect his skill in whichever profession he decides to pursue. We will also try as long as he is dependent on us to make his stay in this city pleasant.

We had a few hopes that we might see you here: my wife was looking forward to renewing her friendship with Madame Monroe. Nevertheless, the season seems too advanced today for you to be able to set out on such a voyage. We do not lose faith that you will come to our town in the future; it would be a great pleasure for us to welcome you here. I have the honor to be with esteem and respect, sir, Your very humble servant,

Barbé Marbois

RC, NN: Monroe Papers

1. JM's letter to Marbois of 21 September 1795 has not been located.

From William Short

Madrid Sep. 28 95

Dear Sir

This is meerly to inform you that a peace with Algiers was settled in that city on the 6th inst. by Mr Donaldson & the ransom of our unfortunate fellow citizens who have been so long captive there agreed to—I learn from Malaga that the preliminaries were brought there some days ago & forwarded to Lisbon, where it was expected they would find Col[o] Humphreys. I suppose therefore he will have left Paris on his return there, though I have not yet heard of his arrival—

The Dey of Algiers has commenced hostilities against the English flag & begun by seizing on a Privateer belonging to Gibraltar w[ch] was in the port of Algiers—The British Government will probably pay large sums to divert this storm which would be destructive to their Mediterranean navigation—But if they should not be able to procure a peace by this means, it will give an additional spring to our fisheries for the supply of the Mediterranean ports—

You have certainly learned before this that our peace with Morocco has been renewed—[1]

I have no letter from you since that by M[r] Pinckney[2]—I have written to you several times since by the chanel of the Minister—I send this to the post-office as we are told letters are now forwarded from thence to France, although as yet we have received none in that way—I am in daily hope of it, as I trust I shall then hear from you & my other friends—In the mean time, I remain my D[r] Sir yours sincerely

W Short.

RC, NN: Monroe Papers

1. George Washington wrote to the emperor of Morocco on 13 March 1795, informing him that he had appointed David Humphreys and James Simpson (the American consul at Gibraltar) as commissioners to negotiate the renewal of the treaty signed in 1787 between the United States and Morocco. Simpson had an audience with the emperor in August 1795, during which the emperor expressed friendship for the United States and said that he considered the treaty still in force. Simpson forwarded a letter from the emperor to Washington that expressed the same views (*ASP: FR*, 1: 525-527).

2. JM to Short, 30 May 1795, above.

To William Allen Deas

Paris. September 30ᵗʰ 1795

Sir

I was lately favored with yours of the 10. instant respecting a person said to have been apprehended here not long since as a spy and possessed of a passport from you, and requesting information how far that report was founded.[1] I shall always be happy to obey your commands when in my power and therefore readily comply in the present instance so far as I have any knowledge on the subject, premising however that I have none except what was gathered from publick papers and private sources (having never seen any document respecting it) but which were of a nature to command my complete confidence. By these it appeared that a man whose real name was Magget under the fictitious one of Burrows, by birth an Irishman,[2] and a Roman-catholic priest of this country, was taken in the manner you mention and under the protection of your passport. He did not pretend ever to have been in America and of course had obtained it by fraud. He was sent to the tribunal for trial as a spy, but as he was not taken near an army, and had none of the leading characteristics of such a culprit the tribunal hesitated and I believe would not condemn him. Such was the report at first & what has become of him since I know not.

Permit me in connection with this incident to call your attention to the subject of passports generally: a subject of great delicacy and importance as it respects the representative character of the United States abroad and of course their character as a nation at home. It has happened in more instances than one that persons not American citizens, but in truth British subjects have presented themselves to me under the sanction of yours and Mʳ Pinckney's passports. These I am satisfied were obtained by fraud, and against which the strictest attention will not always prove an adequate defense. Indeed it is probable that some of my own passports were the basis upon which this fraud was founded: for I am informed they are generally taken at the ports of England and particularly that of Dover, by the officers stationed there, from those Americans who pass over from those of France. Those may be sometimes transferred by design for the purpose of cloathing in our garb a suitable agent of that country for political purposes, and sometimes by negligence or accident they may become the spoil of individuals who have personal views to answer by a visit here. These passports are then presented to you, and from the respect which is due by one representative of this country to another, are admitted an adequate evidence of citizenship, and thus a man having no just claim to the title, is landed here with views hostile to France and disgraceful to us. Believe me the jealousy of this government upon this point has often been raised to such a height and particularly upon the occasion above noticed, as to give me the most disquieting apprehensions for the rights of my own passports and of course for the safety of many of those who were unquestionably American citizens. The utmost vigilance therefore has been necessary on my part to exclude from their protection all those who were [not] strictly and truly entitled to it.

The only remedy to be devised consists in the proof necessary to be adduced by the person demanding the passport, that he is an American citizen, and no other adequate rule can be adopted in that respect than to require such proof as will satisfy the mind of an impartial person that such is the fact, presuming where the contrary appeared, that the evidence adduced was obtained by fraud. To admit only of the testimony or certificates of American citizens, for they alone are interested in the character of their country and in the integrity of the protection it yields, flowing from its public functionaries; they alone too are interested upon a permanent scale, in the credit which is due to those passports. An individual of another country might skulk under that protection for a while, to serve a turn, but after the object was answered he would be more apt to boast of his dexterity in imposing on the agent from whom he had obtained it, and at the expence of the nation he represented, than to keep it a secret.

I have thus presented this subject to your consideration not only from motives of publick consideration but from a belief also that you will be equally happy to concur in those precautions that may be found best calculated to prevent the evil complained of. With great respect and esteem, I am, Sir, Your very humble Servant

Ja^s Monroe

RC, ViHi: Monroe Papers

1. Deas to JM, 10 September 1795, ScHi: Pinckney Family Papers: Thomas Pinckney Letterbook.

2. This may be the Irish nationalist Nicholas Madgett. It appears that he, like his countryman, Theobald Wolfe Tone, travelled to France on a false American passport in order to avoid detection by the British (see Wolfe Tone diary entries, 15 and 23 February 1796, below).

To Timothy Pickering

Paris Septem^r 30. 1795.

Sir

I have [lately] had the pleasure to receive from you three letters, the first of the 27. of april & the other two of the 11. of June following,[1] requesting me to procure you a supply of books suitable for our corps of artilerists & engineers, six fusees with bayonets complete after the model of those which were made in 1776. and six swords or sabres d'infantrie for the use serjeants. You intimated also that you have pressing demand for a cannon founder, & who you presume might be obtained here, upon which however you propose to take the instruction of the President & apprize me afterwards of the result, which latter communication I have not yet rec^d.

Independantly of the obligation of duty & w^h will always be a powerful one with me believe me I am otherwise sufficiently prompted by inclination to seize every opportunity which may occur to render any service in my power which may be useful and acceptable to my country. As soon therefore as those letters were rec^d I undertook the purchase of the books & instruments in question & have completed according to a list now enclosed,[2] thro the agency of Col^o Vincent, that portion of the trust reposed in me. You will observe that the list of books sent me has been greatly enlarged, that in fact a complete & very valuable collection has been obtained, and comparatively with the former price at perhaps one third the former value. Some attention is due from you to Col^o Vincent for this service for the judicious & faithful manner in which he has executed it. I have already expressed to him the sense I entertain of it. These books & instruments are already boxed up & will be forwarded under the direction of Mr Skipwith by the way of Havre to you in Phil^a so that you will probably receive them sometime in Novr next.

I sho^d have procured at the same time the other objects mentioned in y^r letters, the fusees cartridge boxes & sabres, had I not been advised by Col^o Vincent it were better to ask for these when I ask for the founder, & had I not hitherto declined an application on that head, as well in attending y^r instruction to do it, as from a belief it were better to fix my mind upon some suitable person in that line, & ask for such person, than to ask for one generally leaving the designation afterwards to casualty or favoritism. Suitable inquiry therefore has been made & is making for such a founder as you wo^d wish but as yet such an one, willing to emigrate is not found. Upon this principle a week or two more may be delayed before I shall abandon the idea of asking for a founder, after which however in case I am not authorized by you to make such demand, I shall separate the objects & endeavour to fulfill yr wishes according as they are already communicated. I have no doubt however that this government wo^d readily assent to accomodate us not only in the cases mentioned, but in all others in which its superior progress in the arts generally, or in that of war in particular, & especially some of its branches, may enable it to serve us. I mention this for y^r information in future, lest a misapprehension upon that point might prevent applications for friendly aid, in cases very essential to us & where it might be rendered by this gov^t with ease, & wo^d most probably be rendered with pleasure.

I enclose an estimate of the cost of the books & instruments[3] & will advise you in my next to whom I wish the am^t to be paid. With great respect & esteem I am y^r most ob^t & very humble servant.

PS. I shall enquire respecting the improvments mentioned in the manufacture of Gun power & apprize you of the result. I shall also be happy to facilitate the correspondence of Col^o Rochfontaine in the manner you have desired, of w^h I beg you to inform him.

Dft, NN: Monroe Papers

1. Pickering's letter to JM of 27 April 1795 and the two letters of 11 June 1795 have not been located. The list of books inclosed in the letter of April 27 is given, above, under that date.

2. The enclosed list of books has not been located.

3. The enclosed estimate of costs has not been located.

To Stephen Rochefontaine

Paris September 30. 1795.

Sir

I have rec^d with pleasure the notification of y^r appointment to the command of our corps of engineers & artilerists,[1] because I am taught to believe from y^r character that you not only possess the requisit qualifications for the trust, but that you have the attachment of a true American for our country. A person of such pretensions, merits the confidence reposed in him. I doubt not therefore that y^r future services, will do credit to those who conferred on you the appointment.

With the aid of Col^o Vincent I have procured the instruments & books which are deemed necessary at present for our corps of artilery & forwarded them by the way of Havre to the Sec^{ry} of war at Phil^a where they will probably arrive by the time this reaches you. I shall also make it my business to procure in future such memoirs and essays upon the art of war generally not herein comprized as are now extant, as well as such as may hereafter be presented by the most eminent men in each branch, for the purpose of availing my country of the experience of this, as far as that experience is to be gained from publications. I will likewise inquire whether there are any late improvments in making cannon, as well in respect of the model which is prefer'd, as in the manner of casting it, & communicate the result. As however it will be difficult for me, among the various other duties which demand my attention, to devote so much of my time to this subject as to be able to pursue it with that skill as it importance requires I must request you will always advise me of the particular objects you wish to obtain, & in which you will be greatly assisted by y^r correspondence with some professional characters here, & which correspondence I shall always be happy to facilitate. With great respect & esteem I am sir y^r most ob^t & very humble serv^t

Dft, NN: Monroe Papers

1. Rochefontaine to JM, 10 June 1795, above.

From Jeanne-Louise Campan

[September–October 1795][1]

... every thing was ready to receive you and your Lady, Dear Sir, I'm very much disappointed to See my hope differ'd and to hear of the cause; which is your worthy frien'd illness has he Seen M. Sabatier the celebrated Surgeon in Paris.[2]—I intended to procure Very pleasant walks to Mrs Monroe to lead her to a party of <u>Vendeange</u> which may be She never Saw before. I hope yet She will come, and Mr Peynne will be Soon better.—I Send you my receipt of the two hundred crowns. Eliza works prettily, She cried the first day She came back, Saying She had lost of her writing since her absence from School, her poor little innocent tears are indeed a prove of a very touching emulation, in all the child is full of Sense and with good natur' d and of an agreable Society, her levity is her only deffect. yours for life

Genet Campan

RC, ViW: Monroe Papers; incomplete—first page missing

1. JM wrote to Joseph Jones on 15 September 1795 (above) that he and Elizabeth Monroe were preparing for a visit to Eliza at Madame Campan's school in St. Germain but that Thomas Paine's illness might prevent their going. This, combined with Campan's reference to the Vendeange—the grape harvest festival, which took place in October—suggests that this letter was written in late September or early October 1795.

2. Raphael-Bienvenu Sabatier (1732-1811) was a prominent physician, educator, and public health official (*Nouvell Biographie Générale*).

From Enoch Edwards

London Octr 2. 1795—

Dear Sir—

I arrived here on Monday last and am now in very tollerable health—haveing nothing to contend with but a Cold & Weakness—

I have confered with Mr Daes on the Business you desired, & he is perfectly desirous of joining you, in promoting any Measure that shall prevent all Deceptions & accomplish the Object you have in View—respecting Passports—he is sensible of your particular Situation, & you may rely on it that independent of his Wish to do what is strictly proper—he will particularly guard against any Step that will compromitt[one] You—I mentioned the two or three Instances of Passports being surreptitiously obtained from Him—the Fault of that must lay on those who have deceived Him, for he has been particular in keeping a History of every Case when he has granted them—However he was very glad to hear what I mentioned to him—as everything of the Kind will tend to promote Caution—

I hope I have some Letters with you from Mrs Edwards[1]—if that is the Case, I beg you will have the Goodness to keep them for me—untill I arrive in Paris if ever I do, If not I will send to you for them—It is now most probable I shall stay this Winter in Europe—should that be the Case I shall be with you about the latter End of this Month—when I hope to be in such Health as to go any Journey you please—either to the Army or elsewhere—or stay quietly in Paris—The Fate of the Treaty you will have heard of before now, if not Mr Franklin can give you all the News we have here. Please to give my Compliments to Mrs Monroe & I am dear Sir your Friend &c

E. Edwards

RC, PHi: Provincial Delegates Collection

Edwards married Frances Gordon (b. 1761) of Philadelphia in 1779 (David Sellen, "A Benbridge Conversation Piece," *Philadelphia Museum of Art Bulletin*, 55 (1959): 3-9).

To David Humphreys

Paris Oct[r] 2. 1795.

Dear Sir

I have the pleasure to inform you that I have just rec[d] a letter from M[r] Cathalan our consul at Marseilles advising that intelligence is rec[d] there by a vessel which left Algiers on the 17th ult[o] that our peace is made with that regency.[1] This intelligence is rec[d] from a Jew at Algiers,[2] who has a brother in Paris & one at Marseilles, to the latter of whom it is addressed, adding further that his vessel had brought the American agent or Ambassador[3] from Alicante to Algiers to close the transaction. Two days before this arrival I was assur'd by Jean de Brie[4] that orders had gone to their Consul Hercules[5] and upon my first application on y[r] arrival, to give us all the aid in his power, a duplicate whereof to M[r] Barlow[6] was all that seemed necessary, & which were in confirmation of preceding orders given last winter, so that all circumstances consider'd I cannot hesitate to give full credit to this account. I will however send you an extract by tomorrow's post of this letter from M[r] Cathalan & after a more full communication with Jean de Brie who seems as much pleased at the intelligence as we can be, and who gives full credit also to the communication. In this state of things it appears upon every consideration adviseable to suspend all operations here untill the truth is ascertained, relative to which however I shall be happy to hear from you.

I was happy to hear from you by M[r] Church[7] & shall certainly pay him all the attention you have desired—with great respect & esteem I am Dear Sir sincerely y[r]s

Ja[s] Monroe

RC, DLC: Monroe Papers, series 4

1. Stephen Cathalan to JM, 24 September 1795 (extract, enclosed in JM to the Secretary of State, 4 October 1795, DNA: RG 59: Dispatches from France).

2. Micaiah Cohen Bacri was a merchant in Algiers and friend of the dey (Frank E. Ross, "The Mission of Joseph Donaldson, Jr., to Algiers, 1795-97," *The Journal of Modern History*, 7 (1935): 425, 432).

3. Joseph Donaldson, Jr.

4. Jean-Antoine De Bry (1760-1834) was elected to the Legislative Assembly in 1791. He was then a member of the Convention and of the Council of 500, serving briefly as president of both bodies. He was a member of the Committee of Public Safety from 3 July 1795 to 4 November 1795. He held public office during Bonaparte's reign, but was sent to exile upon the restoration of the monarchy (*Nouvelle Biographie Générale*; Aulard, *The French Revolution*, 3: 334).

5. Louis-Alexandre d'Allois d'Herculais was the newly appointed French consul to Algiers. He arrived in Algiers in April 1796 (Milton Cantor, "Joel Barlow's Mission to Algiers," *The Historian*, 25 (1963): 176-180).

6. JM and Humphreys chose Joel Barlow to serve as the diplomatic agent to Algiers after Benjamin Hichborn declined the appointment (James Woodress, *A Yankee's Odyssey: The Life of Joel Barlow*, 154).

7. Humphreys' letter introducing Edward Church has not been located.

To David Humphreys

PARIS, October 3d, 1795.

SIR,

By the inclosed extracts,[1] if what they state is correct, it seems as if Mr. Donaldson had acted from himself, and without the aid of the French consul. If this be the case, he will doubtless explain to you the cause. The price is higher than I expected it would have been. I could not call on Jean de Bry;[2] but Mr. Purviance did, the day before yesterday, on this business in my name, and was informed, that he had heard nothing from Herculais on the subject, and that the only instructions heretofore sent him (being, indeed, those only which they could send him) were, to use the influence of this Republic with the Dey, to obtain a suspension of hostilities, on his part, against the United States. However, this you will understand better when you arrive at Lisbon. I shall notify the event, or rather the report, to this government, that it may, at least for the present, take no further measure in it. With great respect and esteem, Your obedient servant,

Jaˢ Monroe.

Writings of Monroe, 2: 367. The original of this letter has not been located.

1. These extracts were probably the same ones that JM enclosed in his letter to the secretary of state of 4 October 1795 (below)—Stephen Cathalan to JM, 24 and 25 September 1795.

To Mr. Cibon[1]

Octᵒ 4 [1795]

I have just recᵈ a letter from our consul at Marseilles informing me that the U States had concluded a peace with the regency of Algiers & of which I send you an extract.[2] I hear likewise that the Committee of p. safety has recᵈ like intelligence from their consul at Algiers so that I conclude the communication is true, especially as I know that the U States have sought for some years past to make peace with those powers in preference to any other arrangment, & to which consideration it was I presume owing that our Secretary of State declined instructing me how to answer your proposition respecting those powers, untill after an attempt to obtain peace shoᵈ be made & fail. I hasten to give you the communication above in the moment and as I have recᵈ it, & shall hereafter be happy to apprize you of whatever I may hear further relative to the same. Permit me likewise to assure you that if it is the wish of yʳ govᵗ to acquire land within the US. otherwise than in the mode your last had proposed[3] I shall be happy to give you all the information & facility in my power in pursuing that object, being with sentiments of great respect & regard &c.

Dft, DLC: Monroe Papers.

1. This letter is not addressed. The Library of Congress assigns Joel Barlow as the recipient, but an attached note, addressed to John Purviance, specifically indicates that Mr. Cibon, the chargé of Malta in Paris, was the recipient.

2. Stephen Cathalan to JM, 26 September 1795, above.

3. Cibon wrote to JM on 26 October 1794 (above) offering Malta as a safe haven from Algerine corsairs in exchange for land in the United States.

The note to Purviance on the back of the letter reads:

"Mr Purviance will translate in French the enclosed to the chargè des affrs of Malta, and prepare an official note to him   he will also make the extract marked in Cathalan's letter to be annex'd at the foot in French."

To the Secretary of State[1]

Paris October 4ᵗʰ 1795.

Sir,

I herewith inclose you extracts from several letters from Mᵣ Cathalan our consul at Marseilles, and by which it appears that a treaty in behalf of the United States is made with Algiers.[2] I have likewise since conferred with Jean Debrie of the committee of public safety who is charged with the American affairs and by whom I am informed that like intelligence is received by the committee from their consul at Algiers, so that the verity of this report cannot be doubted. By these extracts as by the communications of the consul to the committee, as I am advised, it is to be inferred that the movements of Mᵣ Donaldson were unconnected with the French consul and of course that the aid of this republic was not extended to us in that negotiation. From what cause this proceeded, if such is the fact, I cannot at present divine, but presume it will be fully explained to you by Colᵒ Humphreys from Libson, where he doubtless is before this, having left Paris on his return there about three weeks since. Tis however necessary for me to state to you what took place here in that respect in consequence of Colᵒ Humphreys arrival, prior to the receipt of the above intelligence, as likewise what has been since done in consequence of that intelligence.

I was informed by Colᵒ Humphreys that you wished to obtain the aid of this government in support of our negotiations with the Barbary powers, for which purpose indeed he had come, and that you wished me to ask for it, in case I thought it attainable. From particular considerations and which will occur to you, I felt some embarrassment in making an application for aid of any kind at the present juncture, but as I was persuaded you had weighed these and deemed them no obstacle, and knew that the object was equally pressed by interest and humanity I immediately resolved to bring the subject before the government and ask for such aid, stating it was not the aid of funds that we wanted but simply the aid of the amicable mediation and interference of this government, and which was promised by our treaty of commerce but never performed. Colᵒ Humphreys and myself were agreed that as credit for the service was to be a principal motive on the part of France for embarking in it, so it would be expedient on our part to make our arrangements such, as to give full force to that motive since thereby she would engage in it with greater zeal and in consequence with proportionably greater effect. It readily occurred that the more direct our measures were from this quarter, and the more united and harmonious our councils were in this respect with those of this government, the greater its confidence in us would be and of course the better our prospect of success. Besides to give full effect to the influence of France in the councils of the Dey and thereby obtain the peace at the cheapest rate, it appeared advisable that our agent should be cloathed with a French passport, be if possible a French citizen, and even appear to be an agent of France, exhibiting ultimately our power when necessary to conclude only. By this mode it would seem as if France interfered as our friend and chiefly from motives of humanity in regard to our prisoners, whereby we should avoid inculcating any idea of wealth on our part (for wealth and imbecility are with them strong temptations for war) and which would be further supported by the long imprisonment of our people. In presenting therefore the subject before the government I left the mode or manner of the negotiation open for subsequent and less formal discussion, seeking in that step a decision only upon the first point of aid, and which I was explicitly promised by the committee and the commissary. I soon found however in touching on the other part, the execution, that our anticipation was correct, and that it was expected our agent would depart hence by the route of Marseilles, shunning the countries with which this republic was at war, and at which place the government would have a vessel provided for him to proceed to Algiers. In furtherance of the object I was furnished by the commissary with a list of such presents as would be suitable for Algiers &c a literal copy of what they had last presented themselves, with a specification of what suited the Dey and his ministers in particular, and which presents as introductory he advised us to commit to the agent, to be presented in the commencement, according to the usage of the place and as their consul should advise.

But Colᵒ Humphreys observed to me that he had left Mʳ Donaldson at Alicant with power to correspond with the French consul at Algiers and act in harmony with him, being further authorised in case he was invited over by the consul to proceed to Algiers and conclude a treaty with that power. Here then an embarrassment occurred, for it was to be feared and for the reasons above stated, that a mission from that quarter under the circumstances attending it, would be less likely to succeed than if it proceeded directly hence: and on the other hand it was likewise to be feared that if we adopted the latter plan and dispatched a person hence the two agents might interfere with and embarrass each other. Upon mature reflection therefore and especially as Colᵒ Humphreys had instructed Mʳ Donaldson not to act otherwise than in strict harmony with the French consul, nor then without an assurance of success, since he Colᵒ Humphreys was coming to Paris to secure the aid of this government, it seemed as if the two modes might be incorporated into one, or rather as if we might proceed with the business here, counting upon no interference from Mʳ Donaldson providing however in the arrangement in case he acted before Colᵒ Humphreys returned, and which we concluded he would not do, in such manner as to admit his falling in, incidentally and harmonizing with the other agent, and to admit likewise let him act as he would, provided he harmonized with the French consul, such an explanation as would be satisfactory to this government. Upon this principle therefore and with the approbation and concurrence of Colᵒ Humphreys I notified to the commissary of foreign relations that we had committed the trust to Joel Barlow who was a citizen of both republics and requested the passport of the government in his behalf, and also in behalf of Mʳ Donaldson who was eventually to be consul at Tunis and Tripoli, and whom we should associate with Mʳ Barlow to guard against accidents, in the negotiation with Algiers, requesting likewise that the committee would in the most suitable manner yield all the support in its power in favour of this negotiation. I stated also that Mʳ Barlow was here and would proceed by the most direct route in the discharge of his trust, with the presents we had bought and were buying according to the list furnished me, for the said treaty, and was promised that what I had asked should be strictly complied with: and thus stood the business when the accounts above referred to were received, and which I have thought it my duty to communicate, that you may be accurately informed of what was done here in relation thereto.

Perhaps you will ask why Mʳ Barlow or some other agent did not depart hence sooner, after the plan of sending one was agreed on? The fact is it was impossible, for owing to the state of things here at the time, about three or four weeks elapsed after I applied to the government for the aid before I obtained an answer, and after which when it appeared expedient to purchase introductory presents and for which purpose money was necessary, a doubt arose, and for reasons heretofore explained, whether Colᵒ Humphreys draft from France would be answered, and which it was thought advisable to remove in the first instance. This consumed about three weeks more, and since which every possible exertion has been made to provide the presents and forward the business that circumstances would admit of.

When the news above noticed arrived Colᵒ Humphreys was at Havre on his return to Lisbon and the first point to be decided was whether Mʳ Barlow's office should cease, and secondly what should be done in that case with the presents already purchased. We were both of opinion and for many reasons that it was advisable he should notwithstanding proceed, and take the presents with him. If any errors have been committed at Algiers, and which it is possible to rectify, we knew he would be able to do it: and we were also persuaded that in other respects a trip to that coast whereby he would be enabled to gain an insight into the policy of those powers, could not otherwise than be of great advantage to the United States. Upon this principle I have asked his permission to intimate to you his willingness to accept the office of Consul for Algiers to which he has consented, and which I now do in a confidence that no person can be found willing to accept that trust in whom it can be so happily vested, and in which opinion I doubt not Col⁰ Humphreys will readily unite.³ Mʳ Barlow leaves this upon the plan above stated in the course of a few days, and with the presents in question, and for further particulars respecting this interesting concern I beg to refer you to Col⁰ Humphreys who will doubtless be more particular in his details.

Since my last Pichegru has also crossed the Rhine and taken Manheim and in consequence whereof the siege is more closely pressed on Mayence. Since my last too the Belgic is united by a decree to this republic.⁴ In addition to which the mission of Mʳ Moneron to England ostensibly for an exchange of prisoners, but perhaps for other objects, is the only circumstance which merits attention.⁵ With great respect and esteem, I have the honor to be, Sir, your most obedient servant.

Jaˢ Monroe.

Copy, DNA: RG 59: Dispatches from France

1. JM assumed that he was writing to Edmund Randolph, not yet knowing that Randolph had resigned.

2. JM enclosed extracts of letters from Stephen Cathalan dated 24, 25, and 26 September 1795 (DNA: RG 59: Dispatches from France).

3. Joel Barlow was appointed consul general in Algiers, a post he held 1796-1797 (Walter B. Smith, *America's Diplomats and Consuls of 1776-1865*, 90).

4. The French Convention voted on 1 October 1795 to annex Belgium, Liège, and Luxemburg (Sydney Seymour Biro, *The German Policy of Revolutionary France*, 1: 438-441).

5. Louis Monneron (1742-1805) was one of four brothers of the Monneron Merchants of Paris who had had a monopoly on trade with the East India Company until the Revolution. During the Terror the revolutionary government seized their ships and goods, and imprisoned their directors, some of whom were sent to the guillotine. Louis Monneron, who had been a contributor to Diderot's *Encyclopedia*, survived (Frank A. Kafker, "A List of Contributors to Diderot's *Encyclopedia*," *French Historical Studies*, 3, (1963): 119).

From David Humphreys

Havre Octʳ 5 1795.

Dear Sir

Your letter of the 1ˢᵗ insᵗ came to hand yesterday after I had dispatched mine of that date for yourself & Mʳ Barlow.¹

You will perceive by my letter of yesterday² that the first idea which occurred to me, on hearing the news alluded to, was, that it would still be best for Mʳ Barlow to proceed to Alicant, with the Presents which had been purchased in Paris for the Barbary negotiations. Because, in case they should not be wanted for Algiers, they might notwithstanding be particularly useful in our farther negotiations with Tunis & Tripoli. Besides, if a Treaty be already concluded with Algiers (which I cannot but hope & believe is the fact) still it must have been provisional with respect to the stipulation of payments. For Mʳ

Donaldson could have recourse to the credit of no other funds, except those under my direction in England. Nor was it possible for him to know the actual state of those funds. I conceived, therefore, in all events, it would be advisable for M.ʳ Barlow, who is perfectly acquainted with the state of those funds, to go to Alicant for the purpose of assisting in making the necessary transfers. For it seemed not impossible, nor very improbable, that it might be necessary for M.ʳ Donaldson, M.ʳ Barlow, or some confidential Person, to come from Alicant to Lisbon on the business of arranging & transferring those funds.— I had it farther in idea, that M.ʳ Barlow's journey might be highly advantageous to the interests of the United States, by pressing the negotiations with Tunis & Tripoli to a conclusion. For which purpose, I imagined the articles purchased in Paris (by being somewhat multiplied in small & cheap articles, and differently arranged) might be extremely usefully applied.—Great & happy as the event is of liberating our Countrymen from bondage in Algiers, & of making a Peace with that Regency; I shall consider the Barbary business but imperfectly done, until we can really open the entire navigation of the Mediterranean to our vessels—

These were my first impressions. But should official or other authentic intelligence prove that the business is wholly concluded; or in so fair a way of being concluded, as to preclude all necessity for farther arrangements in respect to Algiers, Tunis & Tripoli, all farther preparations & expences ought certainly to cease immediately. In that case, I must desire that M.ʳ Barlow's farther Agency will forthwith terminate, & that all the property belonging to the U. S. in his possession may be deposited in your charge. Upon these subjects, I have a full confidence that M.ʳ Barlow & yourself (upon a complete view of all the circumstances according to the official or other advices you may receive) will perfectly accord in your sentiments of what will be the best & most efficacious measures for promoting the interests of the U. S.—And therefore I beg leave to recommend the ulterior deliberations & decisions on the proceedings necessary to be adopted, to your patriotic attentions.

Contrary wind has detained us yesterday & today: I hope to sail the moment it becomes favourable.— I shall expect with eagerness the pleasure of hearing from you in Lisbon, and in return will not fail of writing to you, for be assured, my dear Sir, I am with sincere regard & esteem Your most obed.ᵗ & most humble Servant

D. Humphreys

P. S. If M.ʳ Barlow should proceed on the journey originally in contemplation, I am of opinion it will be right to accelerate his proceeding as much as possible, and that he should go so light as not to be obliged to waste time on the way.—The opinion you mentioned to have heard, <u>respecting a certain Person</u>, when you proposed to me that the appointment of Agency should be confined to M.ʳ Barlow alone, may perhaps be a reason with you why M.ʳ Barlow should proceed.—But I must leave the matter absolutely discretionary, to be devised when the whole circumstances shall be known—Adieu.

RC, DLC: Monroe Papers

1. No letter from JM to Humphreys dated 1 October 1795 has been located. Humphreys may be referring to JM's letter of October 2 (above). No letter from Humphreys dated either October 1 or 2 has been located.

2. Humpreys to JM, 4 October 1795, DLC: Monroe Papers.

To Jean-Victor Colchen

Paris le 7 Octobre 1795 (15 Vendémiaire l'an 4)
l'an 20ᵉ de la République Américaine.

Je viens d'être instruit que R. B. Forbes, citoyen des Etats-Unis, arrêté à Cherbourg sur des soupçons qu'il est un emissaire employé par l'Angleterre, et envoyé par elle en France pour objet deshonorable est amené à Paris; que ses papiers lui sont pris, et qu'il est tenu sous la garde d'un gendarme.

D'après les details qui me sont parvenus il parait que Son arrestation provient de l'idée qu'on avait qu'il est Sujet d'Angleterre; mais les renseignements que J'ai pris sur son compte, fondés sur le témoignage de plusieurs Américains respectables actuellement à Paris m'assurent des contraire, et qu'il est vraiment citoyen e Américain; que sa conduite qui leur est bien connue est irréprochable, et qu'il est absolument incapable de tremper dans une tentative aussi infame que celle qu'on voudrait lui imputer. J'ai donc à vous prier, citoyen, de prendre dans le plus court délai possible les mesures qui dependent de vous pour faire mettre le dit citoyen en liberté, et aussi de lui faire Rendre les papiers; qui lui ont été pris. Salut et fraternité

Jaˢ Monroe

Editors' Translation

Paris, 7 October 1795 (15 Vendémiaire, Year 4)
Year 20 of the American Republic.

I have just been informed that R. B. Forbes, citizen of the United States, arrested in Cherbourg under suspicion that he is an emissary employed by England, and sent by her to France for a dishonorable purpose, has been brought to Paris; that his papers have been confiscated, and that he is under the surveillance of a policeman.

According to the details that have reached me, it seems his arrest results from the idea that he was an English subject; but the information that I have obtained in his case, based on the account given by several respectable Americans presently in Paris assures me of the contrary; and that he is truly an American citizen; that his conduct, which is well known to them, is impeccable, and that he is absolutely incapable of participating in an attempt as loathsome as the one of which he is accused. I must then ask you, Citizen, to take as quickly as possible the measures necessary to set at liberty the aforementioned citizen, and also that the papers taken from him be returned. Salutations and Fraternity

Jaˢ Monroe

RC, DLC : FCP—France

Ralph Bennet Forbes (1773-1824) was a Boston merchant. His son, Robert Bennet Forbes (1804-1889), made a fortune in the China trade (MHi: Guide to the Robert Bennet Forbes Correspondence; Samuel Eliot Morison, *Maritime History of Massachusetts, 1783-1860*, pp. 170-171; 241-242; 277).

There is undated letter from Forbes in DLC : Monroe Papers, filed 25 December 1794, asking JM's help in obtaining his release. JM's letter to Colchen and Colchen's response suggest that Forbes probably wrote in late September or very early October 1795.

Colchen informed JM on 8 October 1795 that he had given instructions for Forbes's release (DLC : FCP—France).

From Timothy Pickering

Department of State Oct. 9. 1795.

Sir,

This serves merely to acknowledge the receipt (on the 7ᵗʰ instant) of your letter of the 4ᵗʰ of July with its inclosures.[1]

The President is now at Mount Vernon. This forbids my saying any thing on the subject of Baron Stahl's application. Besides, I do not conceive that the Executive could ever attempt to negotiate about it until Congress should provide the means of rendering an agreement efficient. The propositions with a copy of the Convention between Sweden & Denmark I find were transmitted from London by Mʳ Pinckney in his letter of the 5ᵗʰ of last May;[2] it does not appear when they were received at this office. I have the honor to be, Sir, Your most obᵗ servant

Timothy Pickering.

Octᵒ 12ᵗʰ

This day your letter of August 17ᵗʰ came to hand.[3] What regards the late treaty between the U States & Great Britain you will find anticipated by my letter of the 12ᵗʰ of September.

RC, DLC: Monroe Papers. A duplicate of this letter, without the postscript, is in NN: Monroe Papers.

1. JM to Edmund Randolph, 4 July 1795, above.

2. Thomas Pinckney to Randolph, 5 May 1795, DNA: RG 59: Dispatches from Great Britain.

3. JM to Randolph, 17 August 1795.

From Samuel Bayard

London 18. Octʳ 1795.

Dear Sir

Your obliging favour of the 18. Septʳ reached me a few days since. I avail myself of the first opportunity that has presented, of answering it.

There is much that I would be glad to communicate to you, but which perhaps it would not be prudent to trust to paper. Would the state of the business under my direction admit, gladly would I pay a short visit to Paris, & contribute every information in my power that might be useful to yourself or to the generous & gallant nation with whom you reside. Having uniformly from the dawn of the french Revolution to the present moment been an enthusiast (& I trust a rational one) in this cause I shall ever be truly happy in hearing of their general welfare & happiness, & of serving their cause by every exertion in my power.

Sorry I am that our governmᵗ has not been more animated by this sentiment. I have no manner of doubt but "acting in harmony it was easy to rest on the fortunes of the Republic & to turn them in all cases to our accᵗ". But unfortunately there are many of our citizens who would sacrifice the national character for individual gain—who to avoid the loss of a little property, would consent to lose our reputation as a people for spirit—gratitude, & resistance to insult & oppression.

With the exception of obtaining the <u>promise</u> from the British Ministry to evacuate the Western posts, I admit, most fully with you "that Mr Jay has obtain nothing which he ought to have obtained, & that he has done many things which on no consideration he ought to have done". I find by the American papers that from those who were predetermined to praise the treaty whatever it might be, Mr J. has received applause for the footing on which he has put the American claims & appeals, now under my direction.

Never was applause more unfortunately bestowed. The footing on which they have been put compromises the interest of the American merchant, & legitimates a principle dishonorable to the Gov^t & ruinous to the Commerce of the U. S. It sanctions the principles that G. Britain or any other power, may seize on the vessels & property of American citizens by <u>an order of Gov^t</u> & then oblige the citizens in their individual capacity to seek redress by an <u>expensive</u> <u>tedious</u>, & troublesome prosecution, in a Court of justice where every prejudice & disposition is averse to the hopes & the interest of the party asking indemnity.

It is painful to reflect on the number of our fellow citizens who are thus situated. I have at present I suppose about 350 claims & appeals under my charge. The average laid expenses on <u>each</u> of them will be about £250. The time it will occupy to hear & determine the <u>whole</u> of them will I am informed be from 7 to 10 years. All this time our citizens will be deprived of the use of their vessels—& capitals & this without the payment of interest. Had Mr Jay but insisted that the Commissioners contemplated in his treaty should in <u>the first instance</u> take these spoliations into consideration, & in cases where they were of opinion there had been an improper condemnation the British gov^t should immediately compensate the American citizen, & <u>itself</u> look to the Captor, I have no doubt but he might have succeeded, & thus all the important claims under my charge been impartially & expeditiously settled.

I have <u>some</u> hopes that the business may yet be put on a footing similar to the one I have suggested. At any rate when Mr Adams arrives here,[2] if I can obtain any influence with him, it shall be used to effect an alteration in <u>that</u> part of the treaty which regards the American claims, so as to procure an early & equitable settlement of them. I have some hopes that the English Ministry will agree to reconsider this business, as they will find it gives great dissatisfaction to the people of the U. S. and as it is said & believed that they have sent dispatches to Mr Bond their Charge Des Affaires at Philad^a [3] containing assurances to our gov^t that if they wish any alteration in the treaty, no objection will be made on this side of ye water to a fair discussion of the same, & the settle^t of it on terms of reciprocity.

In regard to those vessels that have recently been brought into English ports, when laden with provisions in <u>most</u> cases our citizens cannot complain of <u>much loss</u>. The ordinary forms of law have been dispensed with—the vessels have soon been discharged with expenses, costs, & demurrage—the cargoes have mostly been paid for, according to the original invoice price, with the addition of 10 p^r cn^t profit. But they would allow nothing for commiss^{ns} of supercargo—or the Merch^t who here manages the business—the expences actually incurred were in many cases exceedingly—& very unjustly disallowed—& demurrage allow'd generally only until the <u>order for the ship's restitution</u> was obtained, when the vessel was detained in port at heavy expences, for several weeks after the order being issued, in consequence of not being unladed,—& enough money received for freight & expenses to enable the master of the vessel to leave port & commence another voyage—

You have no doubt heard from our country & received later intelligence than I can probably give you. You have no doubt heard of the resignation of Mr Randolph—& of the death of my excellent friend Mr Bradford the Att^y Genl of the U. S. The public papers will inform you of the yellow fever having made its appearance again in N. York & in Norfolk. Govr Mifflin has issued a proclamation inhibiting all intercourse between the former city & Philad͢ᵃ. The people of several parts of the U. S. particularly in N. Jersey & Pennsylᵃ have suffered heavy losses in consequence of severe rains that fell about the beginning & middle of August.

I lately rec'd a small book published by Carey in August containing the treaty, the constitution & most of the best pieces that have appeared for & against the treaty. I would now send it to you but have let a printer here have it for publication together with a number of other pieces which I have selected from our newspapers on this subject.[4] When it appears I will take care that you shall be furnish'd with a copy of it. Should any other pamphlet here make its appearance which would be interesting to you I will endeavour to convey it to you. With best regards to Mͬˢ Monroe in which Mͬˢ Bayard[5] joins me, I remain Dͬ Sir With much respect & esteem Your friend & hble servᵗ

Sam Bayard

RC, DLC: Monroe Papers

1. JM to Bayard, 18 September 1795, above. The quotations in the subsequent paragraphs are from this letter.

2. Unwilling to trust the business to William Allen Deas (who was serving as chargé during Thomas Pinckney's absence), Secretary of State Pickering instructed John Quincy Adams to go to London and execute the exchange of ratifications of the Jay Treaty. Adams was also instructed to commence negotiations for revision of the treaty if the British were willing. Adams did not arrive in London until 11 November 1795, by which time Deas had already attended to the exchange of ratifications (Samuel Flagg Bemis, *John Quincy Adams and the Foundations of American Foreign Policy*, 68-70).

3. Phineas Bond, the British consul at Philadelphia, served as British chargé from the time of George Hammond's departure in August 1795 until Robert Liston's arrival in May 1796 (William H. Masterson, *Tories and Democrats*, 27, 32).

4. An English edition of Matthew Carey's *The American remembrancer; or, An impartial collection of essays, resolves, speeches, &c. relative, or having affinity, to the treaty with Great Britain* has not been located.

5. Bayard was married to Martha Pintard of New York (*The Journal of Martha Pintard Bayard, London, 1794-1797*).

To Thomas Pinckney

Paris Octͬ 19. 1795

Dear Sir

I am very much surprised that you have heard nothing from me since yͬ arrival in Spⁿ as I have written you twice, the latter indeed not a long letter by the Cᵗ de Rohdes of Prussia who was on his rout thro' Spⁿ to Lisbon—& wͪ letter I presume you have before this recͩ—The other covͩ the proceedings of chlston on the Treaty of Mͬ Jay with some other comments on that subject & wͪ I also hope you have before this recͩ.[1]

I now enclose you the proceedings of different towns & other places on that subject & wͪ contain every thing we know of it here: except the paragraph in one of the papers stating that the President has ratified it—I have to request that you will be so kind as bring these papers with you when you return— as they contain some observations worthy notice.

I enclose you a letter from yͬ children who are well & who certainly profit greatly from the instructress under whose care they are.

You will have heard of the attempt on the convention lately & of its fate. The number in killd & wounded did not exceed abt 4. or 500. at most—at present every thing is tranquil, & the probability is that the little evaporation of the other day was an wholesome rather than an injurious incident.[2]

I put this in the post office & will write you more frequently now that that channel is opend. with great & sincere regard I am yours

Ja^s Monroe.

I enclose a letter for Mr Short & sho^d write him but presume he is on his way here.

RC: DLC: Charles Cotesworthy Pinckney Family Papers

1. JM to Pinckney, 13 and 23 September 1795, above.

2. After the passage of the Constitution of 1795 and the announcement of the two-thirds decree on 1 Vendémiaire (23 September 1795), forty-eight sections in Paris denounced the decree and challenged its ratification. Protests erupted on 13 Vendémiaire (October 5) with around 8,000 insurgents filling the streets near the Tuileries. Republican troops numbering from 5,000 to 6,000 were brought in and restored order (M. J. Sydenham, *First French Republic*, 72-81; Paul R. Hanson, *Historical Dictionary of the French Revolution*, 324-325).

To the Secretary of State[1]

Paris October 20th 179[5].[2]

Sir,

The breach which I lately intimated to you had taken place between several of the Sections of this city and the convention, respecting two decrees of the 5. and 13. Fructidor, and whose object was to transfer from the Convention so many of its members as would constitute two thirds of the legislature of the new government, continued daily to widen afterwards, 'till at length all hope of amicable compromise was gone. A final appeal therefore was made to arms, and which took place on the 5th instant 13 Vendemiaire and in which the Convention prevailed. The details of this contest though very interesting are not lengthy. In the morning of the 5th a force was marshalled out by the revolting sections, upon their respective parades, in concert, and under officers already engaged, and who led it on by different avenues towards the national palace, so that by four in the evening the Convention was nearly invested on every side. Within the garden of the Thuileries and around the national palace, were collected the troops destined for the defence of the Convention, and which were advantageously posted with cannon, to guard the several avenues by which approaches might be made. The members remained within the hall prepared to wait the issue of the day. The disposition therefore was that of beseigers against beseiged, and which grew out of the disparity of numbers on each side, for on that of the Convention taking the whole together there were not more than 6.000, whilst on the side of the sections, there were in activity at least 10.000, and a still greater body which was in arms and which was supposed to be on the same side, or at least neutral. The countenance too of the parties bespoke a strong sympathy with their respective situations, that of those without exhibited an air of cheerfulness and alacrity, and which nothing but the confidence of success could inspire whilst that of those within was dejected and melancholy. The action commenced a little after 5. in the evening, by the advance of the troops of the sections, and ended about 10 by their retreat. Wherever they approached they were repulsed, by heavy discharges of artillery and musketry which ranged and cleared the streets of their collums as soon as presented. For sometime towards the close the contest was sustained on the part of the sections, from the windows of the neighbouring houses, and from whence perhaps more of the troops were slain than from any other quarter. The loss on either side is unknown and perhaps will continue so, and the reports are so various and contradictory that they furnish but little data whereon to found a conjecture. Judging however from what I saw of the disposition of the troops, who were presented at the corner of streets, or when advancing by the head of the column only, and of the time and nature of the action, which was by intervals, I cannot think that more than 500. were killed and wounded on both sides, though some of the reports make it as many thousands. It was generally understood by the assailants, that little or no opposition would be made, and that two of the regular regiments in particular, were on their side, and would so pronounce themselves when the crisis approached. But in this they were mistaken for all those troops behaved with great bravery and integrity, acquiting themselves as they had done before on the Rhine, having been drawn from the army of the north. Indeed the probability is the report was circulated to inspire the troops of the sections with confidence, and to produce a suitable impression on the citizens of Paris in general. Many circumstances occurred in the course of the commotion to countenance this opinion, of which the strongest is that although the contest lasted 'till about 10 at night, yet by the citizens generally it was abandoned or feebly supported, after the first onset and repulse which immediately followed; and after which it was sustained principally by those who were really and truly the parties to it, for as such the greatest bulk of those who were in the ranks ought not to be considered. This opinion is likewise countenanced by a train of incidents which attended this movement from 10 at night to its close, and which was about 12 the next day. The troops of the Convention kept their ground all night, being unwilling to press as far as they might have done, the advantage gained, since it appeared that by such pressure they might slay more of their countrymen, but not gain a more complete victory. On the other hand the troops of the sections filed off gradually, in small parties, as the darkness of the night or other circumstance favoured, 'till finally none were left except those who were not properly of that description. By the morn every thing was tranquil as if nothing had happened. At the entrance of every street you saw the pavement taken up and waggons and other impediments obstructing the passage, but not a centinel was to be seen. The only armed force remaining in opposition to the Convention was of the section of Le Pelletier, consisting of a few hundred only, and which had in part retired and was retiring to its commune, as a place of retreat rather than of defense. But now the scene began to change and to exhibit to view precisely the reverse of what was seen the day before, the beseiged becoming the beseigers; for by this time the troops of the Convention were advancing towards the commune of this section, under the command of Barras who had commanded formerly on the great epoch of the 9th of Thermidor, and of Berruyer,[3] who made regular approaches and by different routs, 'till finally this corps was completely surrounded. A peremptory summons was then sent to it to surrender, and which was immediately obeyed, by laying down their arms and submitting to the will of the conquerors; and thus was this movement crushed, the authority of the Convention vindicated, and Paris restored to complete tranquillity, and within less than 24 hours after the action commenced.

Such was the order and such the issue of this contest: a contest in many respects the most interesting and critical that I have yet witnessed, and which promised had the assailants succeeded, not perhaps essentially to impede or vary the direct course of the revolution, but most probably to involve the nation in a civil war open a new scene of carnage more frightful than any yet seen, and deluge the country by kindred arms with kindred blood. In this view the character and object of the movement, on the part of the insurgents, merit some attention.

You have already seen that the decrees above noticed, were the ostensible if not the real cause of this controversy, and these you have. But to enable you to form a just estimate of its merits in other respects, and thereby of the probable views of the insurgents, it will be necessary for me to state other facts and which preceded the final appeal to arms. These decrees, as you likewise know, were submitted with the constitution to the people and according to a report of the convention by them adopted. But the verity of this report, of which I herewith send you a copy, was denied by the sections. By the report however you will perceive that the names of the departments voting for and against the decrees were published sometime since, and to which it may be added that no department or commune has since complained that the statement given of its vote was untrue. Still a doubt arises upon it, admitting that a majority of those who voted was in favour of the decrees, whether those who did vote for them, constituted a majority of French citizens entitled to vote, and upon which I cannot yet positively decide. The sections affirm the contrary, and likewise contend that all who did not vote ought to be counted against the decrees. It is probable that some of the communes, foreseeing a storm gathering from that source, did not chuse to vote for or against them, and therefore evaded the question by design: and it is certain that in others it was understood by the people that the question was taken upon the constitution and the decrees together, for latterly this was notified to the convention by several who had voted for the decrees, and particularly Nantes, to prevent a misapprehension of what their real intention was. I send you however herewith the several papers which illustrate this point, and by which you will be enabled to form as correct an opinion on it as present lights will admit: observing further that the report made by the convention respecting the decrees, was made as you will perceive at the same time with that upon the Constitution, and that another report containing a complete detail of the proceedings of every commune is making out for the satisfaction of the community at large, and which was commenced by order of the Convention immediately after the first one was rendered. It is to be wished that this had been some time since published, but when it is recollected that the publication must contain the proceedings of upwards of 7000 primary assemblies many of which are perhaps lengthy, impartial people will perceive that it could not be soon done, especially when it is also recollected, that the whole of the interval since the order was given, has been a time of unusual fermentation and trouble.[4]

Under these circumstances the electoral assemblies were to meet, and the day of meeting was not distant. The decrees and the evidence of their adoption were before France and would of course be before these assemblies: nor were the electors bound by any legal penalty to regard them if they thought they were not adopted, or even disapproved them. The presumption therefore was and especially if they discredited the report of the convention, that every assembly whose constituents voted against the decrees, would disregard them, and rejecting the two thirds of the present Convention vote for whom they pleased: leaving it to those who were elected by the several departments to the legislature of the new government, whether they were entirely new men or partly such and partly of the Convention, according to the mode that each department might adopt, to settle the point among themselves and with the Convention who should constitute the legislature of that government, or whether the whole proceeding should be declared void and a new election called for, and which in that event would most probably have been the case. But the party opposed to the Convention preferred a different series of measures whereby to forward its views, the details whereof, so far as I have any knowledge of them, I will now communicate.[5]

The primary assemblies were by law to meet on the 10. Fructidor and dissolve on the 15th. In general however those of Paris prolonged their sitting beyond the term appointed, and many of them declared their sessions permanent, and exhibited in other respects a tone of defiance and great animosity towards the existing government. Finally however the primary assemblies were dissolved, and after which the sections of Paris, to whom the same spirit was now communicated became the channel or rather the instruments of the same policy: many of whom likewise declare their sessions permanent and assume in other respects a tone equally unfriendly and menacing towards the Convention. The Section of Le Pelletier in particular, which is in the centre of Paris, and which always was and still is the theatre of its greatest gaiety and dissipation, took the lead in these councils. At one time it presented an address to the Convention copiously descanting upon the horrors of terrorism, demanding that those who were called terrorists should not only be inhibited the right of voting, but forthwith punished, and that the troops in the neighbourhood of Paris should be stationed further off, although there were then in the neighbourhood not more than 3000 foot and 600 horse and which were there for six months before. At another time it placed by its own arrêté under the safeguard of the primary assemblies all those who had delivered their opinions in those assemblies, and invited the other sections of Paris to form a meeting of 48 commissioners to declare to all France the sentiments of this commune upon the state of affairs in the present juncture. On the 10ᵗʰ of Vendémiaire this section resolved that a meeting of the electoral corps should be held at the Théâtre Français on the next day, and admonished the other sections to a like concurrence, as likewise to escort the electors to the place of rendezvous and protect the assembly whilst sitting with an armed force if necessary. A partial meeting was in consequence held there and which continued its sitting for some time after a proclamation was issued by the Convention ordering the electors to disperse: indeed it was not without great difficulty that this proclamation was read before the door of that assembly. An armed force was then ordered out under general Menou the commandant of the guard,[6] to support the proclamation, but they were gone before he arrived. On the 12ᵗʰ this section issued their inflammatory arrêtés; and on the night of the 12ᵗʰ another fruitless attempt was made by the government to surround the commune of this section and secure its members, for which failure Genˡ Menou who withdrew the troops after he had surrounded it, was degraded and the command transferred to Barras. On the 13ᵗʰ the catastrophe took place and ended as I have already stated.

That the party in question meant to subvert the revolution and restore the ancient monarchy, and that the destruction of the Convention was the first step in the train of those measures which were deemed necessary to accomplish it cannot be doubted. A slight attention only to the above facts sufficiently demonstrates the truth of the assertion in an its parts. Even in the primary assemblies a ground was taken incompatible with the present system: some free latitude, it is true, the people have a right to take in those assemblies, however limited or special the object may be, upon which they are convened to decide. But as soon as the sections took the same ground, acting in harmony with the electoral corps, in contempt of the law and in defiance of the Convention, the case was altered. From that moment rebellion was announced in form, and the sword of civil war was completely unsheathed, nor could it be restored whilst the convention survived, or without a counter-revolution, otherwise than by reducing the revolted sections to order. Fortunately the latter was the issue and in consequence whereof every thing has since progressed as the friends of the revolution have wished. The revolted sections were immediately afterwards disarmed, and without opposition, and the electoral corps is now legally convened (those of it who have not, in dread of punishment made their escape) and with a disposition to be more observant of the decrees and accomodating to the existing government.

But if this party had succeeded in its attack upon the Convention what would have followed? Would it likewise have succeeded in the other object to which this was only a step? A conjectural answer can only be given to a suppositious case. My opinion then is that although the impression would have been a deep one, yet the ultimate issue would have been the same. It is said and perhaps with truth that in case the attack succeeded, it was intended the electoral corps should immediately assemble and place itself in some measure at the head of France. The overthrow of the Convention would have left the nation without a government, or head to influence public measures, and in which case this corps being a legal one, and at the head of this great City, would have had stronger pretention to the public attention than any whatever. 'Tis not however to be presumed that it would have assumed the reins of government: but it would doubtless have undertaken to admonish, and the probability is that in such a state of things, its admonition would have been regarded. With this view it is believed that the crisis was brought on at that precise point of time, before the meeting of the electoral assemblies, to admit in the interval, the communication of the event, in case it were perpetrated, to all France, without allowing to the people sufficient time to recover from the dismay and confusion into which they would be thereby thrown. In such a state of things this corps might have made a great impression upon the whole nation, supported as it would appear to be by all Paris and as it really would be, at least to that stage, by a considerable portion. At the head of this corps was already placed the old cidevant Duke of Nivernois, a man not without some literary merit, and whose character had been so free from enormity and his temper so dormant, that although imprisoned, and in the list of those who were deemed, under what is called the reign of Robespierre, a fit subject for the guillotine, yet he survived that reign and received his life as a boon from those who were now threatened with destruction.[7] It was said he declined the presidency, but it is also believed that his modest disqualification, was more the effect of an accurate calculation of chances in the great game they were playing, than of principle, and of course that if the blow succeeded he might be prevailed on to serve. A majority of the corps, many of whom were cidevant nobles, was believed to be of the same principles. The nation would therefore have beheld on the one side the Convention over-thrown, perhaps massacred, and [w]hose[8] members were in general known to be attached to the revolu-tion, and on the other the electoral corps with this person at its head, and which it would of course conclude was decidedly of opposite political principles, the latter advanced forward upon the ruin of the former and in some sort possessed of the reins of government. Surely no opportunity more favourable to the views of the royalists could have been sought than this would have presented. How they meant to improve it, had fortune placed them in that situation, is not known, nor is it probable it will be: for it is to be presumed that whatever the plan was, admitting there was one already formed for such an event, it had been concerted by the leaders only and was not to be unfolded, until after the sections were thus far plunged into the same atrocity with themselves. There were two ways by which this opportunity might have been improved, the first by an immediate declaration in favour of royalty, the second by electing their own deputies and inviting the other departments to do the same, for the purpose of putting the constitution in motion. Had the first been adopted the nation would have doubtless been greatly con-founded, and in the moment of dismay the royalists would most probably have come forward and the patriots lain quiet. Soon however in Paris herself, symptoms of discontent would have been seen, and perhaps even in some of those sections which were foremost in the late revolt; many of whose citizens had joined the opposition from principle, in respect to the right of suffrage, some because they had been presented or censured as terrorists and only because they were patriots, and others because they doubted the political integrity of the present house and wished it changed. All of these would have been struck with consternation when they heard that a King was proclaimed, and would have looked back with horror at the scene through which they had passed. By this time too some one of the armies would have been seen advancing towards Paris, and which would most probably have had little to do, for I am persuaded that as soon as the citizens recovered from the extravagance into which they had been be-trayed, they would be among the first to fall upon their betrayers.

Had the second been adopted it is probable it would have secured the elections in favour of the royalists; the decrees would have been of course rejected, nor would any of the present members have been re-elected. Soon however this would have been seen by the people, and being seen, half the danger would have been provided against. In the memory of those who were friendly to the revolution (and the catalogue of its friends must be a long one, counting those only whose fathers and sons were slaughtered in its defense on the frontiers) the destruction of the Convention under whose banners they had bled, would form a moral cause, that would hang heavy on the shoulders of the subsequent administration. The manner of the suffrage, though in form free would be deemed an usurpation, and the slightest deviation afterwards become a signal for revolt. If they used their power with violence the same effect would be produced as if a King were immediately proclaimed, and if they used it with moderation they might perhaps prevent the calamity of another crisis, and whiling away in office the time allotted by the

Constitution, be enabled in the interim so far to efface the memory of what had passed, as to secure to themselves afterwards a retreat which would exempt them from punishment. But in neither case would they be able to restore the ancient monarchy. You will observe that my reasoning is founded upon a belief that the army is sound, that the great bulk of the citizens of Paris are so likewise, and that the farmers or cultivators in general, if not decidedly in favour of the revolution, though in my opinion they are, are at least[not][9] against it: and which belief though perhaps erroneous in the result of an attentive observation to such facts and circumstances as have appeared to me to merit attention.

But you will ask if Paris is on the side of the revolution how happened it that such a force was formed there against the Convention, whilst so small a one was marshaled on its side? Let us first establish facts and then reason from them. Paris consists of 48 sections, of which eight only were actually in arms against the Convention, three for it, and the others neutral. Of those too who were sent by the eight sections, it is presumable from the peremptory manner of their retreat, and the ease with which they were afterwards disarmed, as likewise by their uniform declarations at the time and since, that the greater number did not expect to be led against the Convention, or if they did that they went with reluctance. So that the real force which marched out for the purpose of actual hostility was in my opinion inconsiderable; and this too it is said was in part composed of adventurers from other quarters, and in some instances even of foreigners. Still however there was an actual revolt by those sections, and at best a neutrality on the part of the others, the three who declared themselves for the Convention excepted. How account for this? That the royalists had gained the preponderance in some few of the sections and particularly that of Le Pelletier is certain. But that this was not the case with many is presumable. It is well known that the inhabitants of Paris in general wished to get rid of their present deputies and for reasons heretofore explained. The opposition to the decrees may therefore be thus accounted for, and with the greater propriety, because it is certain they were opposed, and even by the royalists upon republican principles, the unalienable right of suffrage &c. and by which an impression was made in the primary assemblies upon the audience, and thence gradually extended throughout the city. In the primary assemblies too every person was allowed to speak, and it happened that among the royalists there were some good speakers, and who by taking popular ground engrossed for the time the public attention, by means whereof they were enabled to practice more extensively upon the credulity of the less enlightened of their countrymen, than they were aware of. It often happens when a collision takes place between friends, and even upon a trivial cause, that one act of irritation begets another, 'till finally the parties become irreconcileable. How much more easy was it then, for artful men at the present moment, to prevail over the ignorant and seduce them into error, especially when it is known that the latter already wished a change; that they thought they had a right to make it, and of which right they could not be deprived, without the sacrifice of their liberty in whose cause they had already so long contended and so greatly suffered?

How explain the extraordinary phenomenon why the very sections who on the fourth of Prairial were on opposite sides, should now shift their ground, so as that those who then supported the Convention should now be against it, and those who opposed should now be for it? Taking the Convention as the standard it remains only in any case, to explain the motive of such party as wanders from it, for that circumstance alone creates doubt and of course alone requires explanation. No one will ask why such a party supports the convention, because there can be no motive for such an inquiry. In some cases a party yielding such support may have less honourable motives for it than another party had. I think I have seen such myself. But in no case can the object be a counter-revolutionary one. To this inquiry then in this view I have already given a satisfactory answer, at least so far as I am able to do it, for I have already explained what I deemed in general the cause of the aberration of the sections upon the present occasion, as I did upon the former one that of the Fouxbourg St Antoine, and whose present conduct warrants the opinion then given upon that head.

But how happened it that so many of the disaffected were chosen into the electoral corps as to give the royalists a preponderance there? How could a people attached to the revolution commit the care of it to those who were its foes, especially to such as by their station and character were universally known to be such? This touches a subject extremely interesting, for it leads to facts over which a veil has been yet thrown, but to which history will doubtless do justice, and in which case it will present to view a scene of horror in some respects not perhaps less frightful than that which was exhibited under the reign of terror. Behind the curtain as it were, for it has made but little noise, in several of the departments the terrible scourge of terror has shifted hands, and latterly been wielded by the royalists, who beginning with the subaltern and perhaps wicked agents of the former reign, had persecuted and murdered many of the soundest patriots and best of men. To such a height has this evil risen, and so general was the imputation of terrorism, that in certain quarters the patriots in general were not only discouraged but in a great measure depressed. It is affirmed to be a fact by those who ought to know and who merit belief, that in some of those quarters and even where the preponderance in point of numbers was greatly in their favour, none attended the primary assemblies, and that in others a few only attended, and who took no part in the proceeding. This therefore will account why the royalists took the lead in those assemblies and why so many of them were chosen into the electoral corps.

But by what strange vicissitude of affairs was this effect produced? How could it happen under an administration unfriendly to royalty? In truth the [explanation][10] is distinctly marked by preceding events and has been in part unfolded in preceding communications. Terrorism, or what was then called so, the persecution of the royalists, had gone to such a length that it became indispensably necessary to end it. To this object therefore the whole force of the government was directed, and with effect, for it was accomplished. But in striking at terrorism, perhaps by the unguarded manner of the blow, perhaps by those consequences which are inseparable from such vibrations, and which I deem the most likely, an elevation was given for a while to the opposite extreme. The terrorism of that day was the excess of the passion for liberty, but it was countenanced by those in office as necessary in their judgment to bring about the revolution: nor were its acts displayed in private assassination: on the contrary they were sanctified by public judgments and public executions. The most culpable therefore were those who expiated for their crimes on the 9.th of Thermidor. But with others in general, and even where the excess was criminal, the intention was otherwise. At that point therefore, which discriminated between the vicious extravagances of the moment, and the spirit of patriotism itself, should the scale have been suspended. And there, by the law it was suspended, for I do not recollect any act of the Convention which passed beyond it. Special outrages were it is true specially corrected; but even in these cases, I do not know an instance, where the correction was disproportioned to the offence. But so nice was the subject upon which they had to act, and so delicate is the nerve of human sensibility, that it was perhaps impossible for the government, under existing circumstances, to moderate its rigour towards the royalists, without giving to a certain degree an encouragement to royalty. In this view therefore it is to be presumed, the late event will produce a beneficial effect, for as the views of the royalists were completely unmasked and defeated, and which were always denied to exist until they were thus unmasked, it cannot otherwise than tend to open the eyes of the community in that respect, and in the degree to repress the arrogant spirit of royalty. To your judgment however these facts and observations in respect to the late movement are respectfully submitted.

I have lately been honoured with your several favours of May 29. June the 1. and 7. and of July the 2. 8. 14. 21. 29 and 31. all of which came to hand almost at the same time and generally by the route of

England, and to which I will certainly pay the utmost attention.[11] As however this letter has already gone to an unreasonable length, and especially as I wish you to be correctly informed of the character and fate of the movement in question, I think it best to dispatch this immediately, reserving a more particular reply to those favours for a future communication. For the present however permit me to add that as yet no complaint has been made to me against the treaty, nor have I heard any thing from the Committee on the subject, since the application requesting information in what light they were to view the reports respecting it, and which was made soon after the treaty was concluded. If any thing is intended to be said I think it will not be said until after the new government is organized, nor then until after it is known that the treaty is ratified and in which case I have reason to apprehend I shall hear from them on the subject. I trust however, let the event in that respect, or the opinion which the Committee may entertain of that event, be what it may, I shall find that the same amicable and dispassionate councils still prevail towards us that have been shewn for some time past. To inculcate which disposition not only by the documents and lights derived from you, but by such others as my own imperfect experience and often too wandering judgment have supplied, has been and be assured will continue to be, equally the object of my most earnest wishes and undeviating efforts. With great respect and esteem, I have the honour to be, Sir, your very obedient and humble servant,

Ja⁵ Monroe.

October 25ᵗʰ

P. S. As the vessel by which this will be forwarded will not sail until a gentleman who is now here arrives at Havre, I have kept the letter with me for the purpose of adding to it what might intermediately happen before his departure. On the day after tomorrow the new government is to convene, and the prospect is now favourable that it will then convene and precisely on the ground stated in the preceding letter. Some symptoms were lately seen which gave cause for apprehension, that the expiring moments of the convention would be moments of great agony and convulsion. Some denunciations and counter-denunciations were made, proceeding from causes connected with the late movement, but happily they are over without producing any serious effect. A commission of 5 was appointed to make a supplemental report respecting that movement, and it was expected by many it would end in a proposal to annul the proceedings of several of the departments whose primary assemblies were said to be under constraint by the royalists, and probably also in the arrestation of several deputies, but that commission had freed every one from uneasiness on that account by a report just made, and which proposes only some new provisions for the trial of offenders in that movement and others in several of the departments who have committed atrocities of various kinds under the pretext of punishing the terrorists. Every moment must be deemed critical in the existing circumstances of this country, being at the eve of a great revolution, a transition from one government to another, and especially when it is known that there is a party not despicable in point of numbers, and less so in activity and talents, always ready to seize every incident that occurs to throw things into confusion, and which party is connected not only with the emigrants abroad, but with the surrounding powers by whom the necessary means are furnished for the purpose. But yet it seems as if the Convention would retain its strength to the last moment of its existence, and transmit its powers unimpaired to its successors. The decrees are said to be universally observed, and the leading members of both sides of the house are in general re-elected. These are to elect the others so as to make up the two thirds of the new government.

Lately Jourdan received a check on the other side of the Rhine and which occasioned his falling back to the Rhine, upon which river both his and the army of Pichegru are posted. The cause of this is not distinctly known, but certain it is that the deputy of the military section of the Committee of public safety has been since arrested upon a suspicion of treachery as are three others upon a charge of treasonable correspondence with their enemies: but with what propriety I do not pretend to determine.[12] 'Tis worthy of remark that it was known in England and [in] Basle before it happened, that there would be a movement here at the time it happened: at which time too the Count D'Artois landed from England upon the Isle-Dieu, near the French coast, opposite the Vendeé where he still is.[13]

A report was yesterday made to the Convention of an important advantage gained in a rencounter in the Mediterranean, in which the French took a ship of the line and damaged greatly two others, and likewise took 14 merchant ships richly laden and esti-mated at an enormous sum.[14] Two other advantages in other quarters are spoken of, still more signal than this, but not by authority.

Monneron is returned, but whether by order of the French government (as I suspect and in consequence of the fortunate issue of the late movement) or the failure of his mission be it what it might, is uncer-tain.

Be assured if M[r] Jay's treaty is ratified it will excite great discontent here. Of this however I shall be able to speak with more certainty after the new government is organized.

Copy, DNA: RG 59: Dispatches from France; a draft of this letter in PHi: Gratz Collection contains an additional paragraph that is crossed out; the draft does not include the P. S.

1. JM assumed that he was writing to Edmund Randolph, not yet knowing that Timothy Pickering had replaced Randolph as secretary of state.

2. The clerk who transcribed this letter misdated it 1796. The correct date is from the draft in the Gratz Collection.

3. Jean-François Berruyer (1738-1804) entered the French army in 1751 at the age of thirteen and rose to the rank of lieutenant general. He was arrested and briefly imprisoned in 1793 but was reinstated to rank in 1795 (*Dictionnaire Biographie Française*).

4. The enclosed reports have not been located.

5. At this point in JM's draft is the following deleted paragraph:

"The very first opening of the primary assemblies presented to view a scene which disquieted many & whose issue none could distinctly pronounce. It was obvious to the more intelligent observers, that there was a party in many of them disposed to subvert the revolution & restore the antient monarchy & which if not already completely organized was becoming more so daily. The characters who composed this party being avowed royalists, the free and licentious scope taken by it in debate, passing far beyond the boundary of the actual state of things together with a variety of other circumstances left little doubt even in this stage that such were its views and which every succeeding day more fully confirmed. The constitution it espoused, not however for the purpose of cherishing & supporting it, but for that of destroying it & by means thereof subverting the revolution. Whilst the present convention lasted its weight was like that of a mountain upon an infant. Royalty was in chains under it. By adopting the constitution & putting it in activity the first great obstacle of the convention would be removed: and by espousing it with unusual zeal, taking the lead in the primary assemblies, & especially if the decrees were rejected & which were opposed by this party with equal zeal, the prospect was not an unpromising one, of grasping the whole power of the government into its own hands. Thus armed its future enterprises wo[d] be more likely to succeed. To accomplish therefore this point was the first object of this party, & for the accomplishment whereof, its measures as will be seen were not illy concerted."

6. Jacques-François, Baron de Menou (1756-1810) was a major general in the French army who, although a member of the nobility, retained his rank because of his support for the revolution. He became commander of the army of the interior in 1795. The Convention ordered him on 12 Vendémiaire to suppress the growing unrest in the Lepelletier section of Paris. Hesitant to attack the section, Menou withdrew his troops after receiving false assurances from the insurgents that they would disperse. He was relieved of his command of the army of the interior, but remained in the service, later serving under Bonaparte in Egypt and Italy (Samuel Scott and Barry Rothaus, *Historical Dictionary of the French Revolution*).

7. Louis-Jules Mancini-Mazarini, duc de Nivernais (1716-1798) was a French diplomat and author. He was a minister under Louis XVI at the time of the overthrow of the monarchy and was imprisoned (*Nouvelle Biographie Générale*).

8. The clerk who transcribed this letter wrote "those" instead of "whose". The correct word here and in the following corrections is from the draft.

9. The clek omitted the word "not".

10. The clerk wrote "expectation".

11. Randolph's letters of 29 May, 1 and 7 June, and 2, 14, 21, and 29 July 1795 are given above. The letter of July 31 is probably that of July 30, above. Randolph's letter of 8 July 1795, instructing JM to present the claims of several Americans to the French government, is in DNA: RG 59: Diplomatic and Consular Instructions.

12. General Jean-Charles Pichegru grew disaffected from the revolution during the summer of 1795, feeling that his services had not been adequately acknowledged. He delayed his crossing of the Rhine until September, and although he captured Mannheim he was defeated at Heidelberg. His failure to provide adequate support to General Jean-Baptiste Jourdan forced Jourdan to withdraw back across the Rhine. The royalists, aware of Pichegru's growing disenchantment, sent agents to try to persuade him to defect to their side. He never actively did so, but he did resign from the army in March 1796 (Jacques Godechot, *The Counter-Revolution,* 263-275; *Historical Dictionary of the French Revolution*).

13. Charles-Philippe, comte d'Artois (1757-1836) was the younger brother of Louis XVI and the leader of the anti-revolutionary royalists. In September 1795 he led a British-backed expedition of 4,000 men to the Vendee. He was unable to advance beyond the coast and was forced to return to England. Artois assumed the French throne in 1824 as Charles X and ruled until he was overthrown in the revolution of 1830. He then lived in exile until his death in 1836 (*Historical Dictionary of the French Revolution*).

14. On 7 October 1795 a French squadron led by Admiral Joseph DeRichery attacked a British convoy enroute to England from Smyrna. The French captured a British warship and thirty out of thirty-one merchantmen (*Nouvelle Biographie Générale*).

From Claude-Adam Delamotte

Havre le 29 Vend^{re} an 4 [21 October 1795]

Monsieur,

J'ai reçu la lettre que vous m'avez fait L'honneur de m'écrire le 2. 8bre et vous remercie de celle que vous avez bien voulu m'acheminer, de Mr Jefferson pour me rembourser de ce que Mr Jefferson me doit. J'ai tiré sur [votre compte] 345.8 en Espéces du 27 C^t a vue à l'ordre de Delamotte & Cie. J'en previendrai Mr Jefferson en conformité quant à ce que vous me devez, vous M^r, cest si peu de chose que nous ne Compterons, si vous voulez bien, dans une autre occasion.

Vos différentes incluses ont été remises ou acheminées régulierement.

J'ai fait ce qui étoit nécessaire des différents arretés du Gouvernement françois ou autres pièces que vous m'avez fait remettre officiellement, J'en attends une de vous qui feroit grand plaisir a tous les americains, ce Sera, quand vous le jugerez convenable, de les informer officiellement de la paix avec Alger.

Veuillez me permettre d'offrir Mes Civilités respectueuses a M^{de} Monroe; Je Serai bien flaté de les lui présenter moi-même dans la belle maison que vous avez acquise, que je connais, et dont Je vous félicite, lorsque J'irai à Paris. ce pourroit bien être peu de tems après l'établissement de notre nouveau Gouvernement que je voudrois bien voir aussi agé que l'est celui des Etats-unis. J'ai L'honneur de vous Saluer respectueusement

M. Delamotte

Editors' Translation

Havre 29 Vend^re Year 4 [21 October 1795]

Sir,

I have received the letter you did me the honor of addressing to me on 2 October,[1] and I thank you for the one you were kind enough to forward to me from Mr Jefferson with repayment of the amount he owes me.[2] I have withdrawn from your account 345.8 in specie from the 27 C^t to the order of Delamotte. I will inform Mr Jefferson in the proper manner. With regard to the sum that you owe me, Sir, it is such a small amount that we will settle, if you don't mind, at another time.

Your other various insertions have been delivered or forwarded properly.

I have done what is necessary with the different orders from the French government and with the other papers that you have had officially delivered to me. I await one of these from you, but it will be a great pleasure for all Americans to be officially informed, when you deem it suitable, of the peace with Algeria.

Please allow me to offer my respectful compliments to M^de Monroe. When I come to Paris, I would be most flattered to present them to her myself in the beautiful house that you have purchased and that I know, and of which I congratulate you.[3] This could very well be shortly after the formation of our new government which I would really like to see as enduring as is the government of the United States. I have the honor of respectfully sending my regards

M. Delamotte

RC, NN : Monroe Papers

1. JM's letter to Delamotte of 2 October 1795 has not been located.

2. Jefferson's letter to Delamotte of 26 May 1795, which was enclosed in Jefferson to JM, 26 May 1795 (above), has not been located (*Jefferson Papers*, 28 : 362).

3. JM bought a house named the Folie de Bouexière during the spring of 1795 to serve as his residence during the remainder of his term as minister. The house was built in the form of a classical pavilion and decorated to represent a temple to Apollo (Lucius Wilmerding, Jr., *James Monroe: Public Claimant*, 100). Mary Pinckney, the wife of Charles Cotesworth Pinckney, who was appointed to succeed JM as minister to France, wrote a description of the house: "Their house is a little temple. It was built by a farmer general in a beautiful style of architecture, and stands in the midst of 20 arpens laid out in terraces and alleys. After ascending a high flight of steps of great length you enter a vestibule, & then, strait on, a small eating room, ornamented with large bronze statues—on each side is a beautiful octagon saloon, profuse with gilding, the finest glasses, painted ceilings, and compartments over the windows" (Charles F. McCombs, ed., *Letter Book of Mary Stead Pinckney, November 14th, 1796, to August 29th, 1797*).

To James Madison

Paris Octr 23^d 1795.

Dear Sir.

I send you herewith an invoice of the articles purchased for you according to y^r request & by w^h the duties will be paid. The price will I fear exceed what you expected, for by Dr Edwards acc^t the reports in America were very erroneous in this respect. It is however in my opinion comparatively with what is usual in America very cheap. In the bed there are ab^t 80. French ells of Damask besides the Mattrasses which we added. The window curtains are rich and good. The carpets are not entirely new, but almost so, and are good. Indeed it was impossible to get new of the kind, being of the Goblentz manufacture, & at which place none could be now obtained. Tho' if you wish one for any particular room hereafter & of any description it can be made & shall be made for you. Your china could not be forwarded by this opportunity but shall be soon & will I hope be satisfactory in the taste & price, for it will be very cheap. We beg of you to instruct us wherin we can serve you & Mⁱˢ M. for we need not tell you how happy we shall be to do it. The amount will remain in your hands till I call for it. Mʳ Paine had occasion to borrow two hundred & fifty crowns of me here & which he has instructed Mʳ Bache to pay for me to you, & tis probable I may request the payment of abᵗ 500 dolˢ by Colᵒ Pickering to you in discharge of a like sum advancd by me here in purchase of military books for the department of war at his request. In case this is done you will be so kind as receive these sums & transmit them to Mʳ Jones for me.

We are in the deepest concern respecting the treaty of Mʳ Jay: reports & which seem to be well authenticated say that it is ratified, & these I cannot contradict. If it is ratified, it may be deemed one of the most afflicting events that ever befell our country. Our connection here will certainly be weakened by it, altho the British violation be deemed a sufficient ground to set it aside & of wʰ there can be no doubt, & it be set aside. I mean by this that the pure & delicate tie of antient amity will be weakened, & wʰ was a tie of affection, of gratitude & of sentiment, deeply fix'd in the hearts of the two people, and which all the allurements of commerce &ca could not wipe away. To bear the British aggressions & spoliations without resentment was one thing, but to make this treaty is another. Denmark & Sweden did the former, but Denmark & Sweden have done no more: and yet these powers are neither of them republican, nor are they under the obligations to France which we acknowledge, or rather which the mass of our people do, notwithstanding the dishonorable efforts that are made by some individuals among us to extinguish in them a just sense of that obligation. It is impossible for me to describe the mortification I daily undergo in this respect. The opinion wʰ is gone forth to the world upon that transaction is that we are reduc'd by it to the condition of British colonies—an opinion undoubtedly untrue, abhorrent as the treaty is, but yet that is the state of things & who must be altered by time only. If on the other hand a new negotiation is opend be assured there is nothing we ask that will not be granted, & peremptorily. Tis reported that as soon as the temper of the people was seen, & the hesitation of the President, that a frigate was dispatched to offer any accomodation desired. This perhaps may not be true, but that every thing will be granted that is press'd is certain. I observe that the friends of Mʳ Jays treaty say that the alternative is between it & war: but this is false & always was. There never was danger of war after the recapture of Toulon, & a manly & able negotiation, woᵈ have made the treaty what it was wishd to be. But why have any treaty? demand that they peremptorily withdraw their troops & it will be done—do the same in respect to spoliations & they will be paid for. But if we eternally recede and avow we are afraid of war they will eternally threaten it, till to avoid it we are degraded in the dust and despised by all nations & have war likewise. Another argument equally false is always urged by that faction. When we talk of harmony & good understanding with this nation, & without which we can never take advantage of French victories, they call it putting our country under the dominion of France, & thus they keep us in what they call a state of neutrality, or what may with more propriety be called a state of universal contempt, for such is the fact. In truth such is our situation that we are menac'd with the danger of war from both these powers. We are not secure of it from Englᵈ (unless indeed we assume a bold and manly tone) and we have plac'd ourselves in such a situation with France, that we incur the like danger from that quarter. This is the more humiliating since nothing is more true than that by a more manly policy we had it in our power always to stand well here & without risking any thing & in consequence to facilitate our negotiations or rather command what we pleased elsewhere.

I intended this only to announce the few articles sent you but I have ran into other subjects which I co^d not omit touching on in writing you. Every thing here is well & the foundation of the revolution I think solid, tho' indeed the late movm^t was the most alarming I have yet seen. 4oo—or perhaps 5 were killed and wounded in an attack on the Convention but which ended most favorably for that body. In the course of 10 days the new gov^t will be organised, if nothing intervenes to prevent it. Sooner than that happens however I shall agn write you. Our best respects to Mrs M. very sincerely believe me yours.

Moneron, formerly a merch^t, is sent to Engl^d ostensibly for the exchge of prisoners, but most probably for other objects—this is the more extr^y because the same thing was done by Engl^d the other day in the case of Eden.

Enclosure:

Invoice of Two Cases containing Furniture forwarded from Paris to Havre, to be shipped from thence to Philadelphia, to the address of James Yard Merchant there, and for account of James Madison, Virginia.

1 & 2. Two Cases containing		
One Bed complete (called à la Polonaise)		
the furniture crimson Damask.		35000.
25 Ells crimson Damask		
25 Ells. green d^o	50 Ells @ 500^tt	25000.
1 Persian Carpet	12000.	
1 d^o d^o	5000.	17000.
2 Hair Mattrasses	à 2400^tt	4800.
Cases, packing &c		1500.
In Assignats		83,300.
		Liv^s Tourn^s

The intrinsic Value whereof is estimated, accord^g
to the rates of Exchange, in Specie at   £2500.

Ja^s Monroe

RC, DLC: Madison Papers. The letter is unsigned. The enclosure in a clerk's hand except for JM's signature.

From John Quincy Adams

Helvsetsluys October 24. 1795.

Dear Sir.

I understand that the Secretary of the Treasury remitted some time since to you a bill on Messrs Dallarde and Swan for 120,000 Dollars to be employed by the Bankers of the United States at Amsterdam, towards the discharge of interests due and ready to become so, on the loans of the United States in this Country and at Antwerp: and that to meet the contingency of failure in the payment of that bill, another was also remitted on the house of Lubbert and Dumas at Hamburg payable in Amsterdam.

The interest on the Antwerp loan will be payable on the first of December, and the funds to be provided for it, depend altogether upon supplies from the bankers at Amsterdam. The undertaker of the Antwerp loan, has already called on me to authorize him to draw on them for the purpose, and they have placed their compliance to my request that they would answer those drafts, upon the <u>express condition</u> that they shall previously receive in cash the 120,000 Dollars above mentioned.

Under these circumstances I take the liberty to recommend to your particular attention the measures that may be necessary to secure as speedily as possible the actual payment of the 120,000 Dollars; and in case of any probable delay in realizing the first bill, beg leave to suggest the necessity of recurring to that on the house at Hamburg.

I submit these observations to your considerations with the more solicitude because I am now upon the point of departure from this Country, in consequence of orders from the Secretary of State, and shall perhaps not have it in my power to concert with the Antwerp banker the means of being prepared for his December payment by other resources than that on which we have depended by remittances from Amsterdam.

I know not how long I shall be detained on my present tour, the destination of which is doubtless known to you. It is however very doubtful whether I shall be able to return before the first of December. I have the honour to be with the most respectful Sentiments, Sir, your very obedient humble Serv.ᵗ

John Q. Adams.

RC, DLC: Monroe Papers

To James Madison

Paris Oct.ʳ 24. 1795.

Dear Sir

I wrote you yesterday with a view of sending the letter by the same vessel which takes the articles we have purchased for you—but as an excellent opportunity, that of M.ʳ Murray a very worthy young man, offers, I shall avail myself of it not only to send the letter of yesterday but to add something to it. Perhaps these articles may likewise be sent by the same opportunity, altho the vessel sails for New York.[1]

I herewith enclose you the copy of a letter to M.ʳ R. in ans.ʳ to one of his—as likewise of my correspondence with M.ʳ Jay relative to his treaty, with such comments as I deemed it necessary to make to M.ʳ R. on that gent.ⁿˢ conduct in relation to that transaction. I sent you some considerable time since by M.ʳ Perkins of Boston a similar communication, & hope it has reached you: or rather I sent by him what respects M.ʳ Jay, having previously sent a copy of the other paper.[2] My object was and is to put in y.ʳ possession facts which may be useful in a certain view of things, perhaps to the publick & certainly to myself. So far as it respects M.ʳ R. the object is at an end for tis said he is withdrawn,[3] but if he were not I have no reason to expect an attack from that quarter—as it respects the other however it may yet be useful. In any event you will become acquainted with another instance of the duplicity & finesse of that man, and find, at least I think so, how desirous he was, of embarking my reputation here in support of his, and with a view of sacrificing it, in case his merited to be sacrific'd, and of which I had little doubt even at that time. I endeavoured to act for the best advantage of my country, under the circumstances existing, & without compromitting myself in behalf of what he had done or might do: and I now find the benefit of that policy both in respect to the state of things here & with you.

I most sincerely hope the President has not & will not ratify this treaty, for if he does, I greatly fear the consequences here. From what I can learn, we shall be deemed under it rather than otherwise in the scale of the coalisd powers: and under such an impression it will require moderation in any gov.ᵗ to withhold its resentment. How cautious therefore sho.ᵈ the President be in hazarding a step of this kind at the present moment, when the slightest circumstance is sufficient to excite indignation, & even perhaps to part the two countries for ever.

If the treaty is ratified, y^r situation is a difficult one: but even in that case do you not think the seizure on the part of Engl^d of our vessels since, a sufficient ground to declare it broken & void? Perhaps a distinction may be taken that it was ratified after the seizure began, & of course that such seizure ceased to be a cause. But this is not sound, for if the President has ratified I presume his motive was the advice of the Senate & w^h was given before the seizure was known. To that act therefore sho^d his ratification be referred & with it be dated. So that the Congress will be at liberty to act upon the seizure as a subsequent thing. In short you have a thousand grounds upon w^h you may get rid of this treaty, and I sho^d be satisfied with the slightest of these had I a vote to give in the case. But if the treaty is rejected say its advocates you have war, & to w^h I reply that if so our dilemma is an unhappy one in consequence of that treaty. To be plundered with impunity was a hard thing, but to bear this treaty also, altho we universally deem it a calamity, merely because we fear Engl^d is still worse. Surely that nation will not insist on such terms. She has too much regard for us, for Messrs Jay Hamilton & Comp^y if not for our country to push us to such an extremity, especially when she knows we are so averse to fighting. But I think the conclusion by no means a sound one: for I cannot think it possible, let her menaces, be what they may, that in the present state of things Engl^d will make war on us. We see that she is greatly exhausted, and it is the universal report of Americans & others from Engl^d, that there is no calamity yet to befall her which she dreads more than a war with us. Satisfied have I always been that, by a decent but yet determined pressure we might not only obtain what we wanted & were entitled to, but likewise do it without war: indeed I have tho^t it the surest way to avoid war. Still I am of this opinion.

The French have obtained a naval victory or rather advantage in the medeteranean, in which a ship of the line was taken, & two others greatly damaged (indeed tis said they are run on shore) & with 17 vessels, merchantmen richly laden under their convoy—Two other similar advantages yet more signal are spoken of, but not authenticated. The late commotion was a terrible one, but it ended on the next day when every thing was perfectly quiet & in w^h state it has since remained: some denunciations have followed but they have vanished in smoke, as yet—Two cases only excepted—You will be astonishd to hear that all Paris is disarmed, and by ab^t 5000 men, & you will of course conclude that the sense of its citizens are for the measure, or it co^d not be done. Indeed it was by a decree only—for under it they disarmd themselves. If they were not for it the situation of the republick wo^d be an unpleasant one, for otherwise the citizens wo^d be deemed against the revolution, & w^h is certainly (I speak of a great majority) not the case.

I write now in the evening of the 24—on the 27. the new gov^t assembles, & as every moment of the interval is of importance I take occasion to let you know that all is yet well & promises to be so: For a few days past there was a prospect of some terrible denunciations of Talien agnst Boissy d'Anglass & others upon a suspicion that the latter had fav^d the late commotion & today it was expected they wo^d be made in form, as a comn was appointed to rep^t supplementally respecting that commotion. The report was made by Talien & I attended & heard it—but it contained nothing of the kind—Indeed it was conciliatory— I know B. D'Anglass and think him true to the revolution, as I likewise think Talien, whom I also know. After this I am persuaded nothing will intervene, & that the new gov^t will commence under favorable auspices.

An American just from London tells me that Mr Pitt was at Deal & along the Eng^h coast during the late troubles here—and just before the C^t D'Artois was landed on the Isle Dieu, close by the French coast opposit the Vendee where he now is—very sincerely I am y^r friend.

PS. I think it probable an attempt may be made to vindicate Mr Jay agnst the imputations raised agnst him for his misconduct in the negotiation with Gardoqui. If such attempt is made it will be made by a publication of his reports in the office of State which contain his justification: but the true view is in the secret journal of Congress & which ought likewise to be publish'd in case the others are. There is no objection to publishing the journal (or so much as respects this topic) w^h does not apply to the publicat^n of the reports with equal force: and to publish the one and not the other will be a partizan maneuvre not very honorable to those who do it. They were in the Senate (I mean the reports) when I left it, & Mr K.[4] wanted them published, but I wanted the others also, & this put a stop to the business—I beg of you to attend to this for me, & give suitable notice thereof to my friends in that body.

The present is indeed an awful moment here. the change of the gov^t & the momentary suspension of aff^{rs} makes it greatly so, especially when it is known, as it is, that foreign powers are if not at the bottom, yet deeply concerned in every mov'ment. *Gardoqui when he returned to Spain settled a secret service account for six hundred thousand dollars laid out in America* and a short time after *our peace* a man (an antient *Tory*) but a friend of his, & who came from *France* for the purpose *offered Mr. Hichburn five thousand pounds sterling from Lord D—r* [5] not to influence *his opinion but presuming it would* be right, *as a proof of friendship* and who likewise told him similar tokens were intended *for others whom he named to him & who afterwards were: the first fact depends on the authority of Littlepage who told* it to *J. Barlow* sometime since on his return from *Spain* whither he was sent by the *king of Poland. Barlow adds that L. Littlepage* appeard to know nothing of the *negociation* which had been on foot *in America.* The other *fact* is from the person himself. The French have rec^d a check upon the Rhine w^h has caused a retrograde maneuvre to the Rhine. It appears that the neutrality of some of the inf[erior] powers with whom peace was made was broken by the opposit party & by w^h a wing of the French army was turned & w^h occasioned this movment—Tis not deemed a serious thing; two deputies however one of whom was in the military sect^n of the Committee of P. S. & the other suspected likewise of unf^t practices with their enemy, are arrested, as likewise is General Miranda.[6]

RC, DLC: Madison Papers. Unsigned. Words in italics written in code by JM with the deciphered text interlined by Madison.

1. JM entrusted this letter and his letter to Madison of October 23 (above) to George W. Murray, a member of the New York merchant firm, Robert Murray and Company. He shipped Madison's furniture via the same conveyance (*Madison Papers*, 16: 176-177).

2. JM to Edmund Randolph, 18 December 1794. JM enclosed this letter in his letter to Madison of the same date. The letter sent to Madison via Mr. Perkins was that of 26 July 1795 (all three, above).

3. This is the first indication that JM had learned of Edmund Randolph's resignation.

4. Rufus King.

5. Lord Dorchester.

6. Francisco de Miranda (1750-1816) was born in Caracas and served as officer in the Spanish army 1771-1782. He became a devotee of the American Revolution and an advocate for the independence of Spanish America. He left the Spanish army and went to the United States in 1783, made his way to Europe, and became a major general in the French army in 1792. He won several victories in the Netherlands, but was blamed for the French defeat at Neerwinden in 1793. Although acquitted of those charges, he was arrested during the terror and was imprisoned from July 1793 to January 1795. During the summer of 1795 he published a pamphlet in support of constitutional reform, in which he also advocated the withdrawal of French troops from foreign soil. The Committee of Public Safety, suspecting that treachery was responsible for the French reverses across the Rhine, arrested several men who had expressed opposition to French expansion, including Miranda. He was under surveillance and was in and out of prison between October 1795 and February 1796. Miranda fled France in 1798 and spent the rest of his life trying to promote the independence movement in Spanish America. He died in a Spanish prison in 1816 (Samuel Scott and Barry Rothaus, *Historical Dictionary of the French Revolution*; William Spence Robertson, *The Life of Miranda*, 1: 152-158).

To Fulwar Skipwith

Paris Br[umaire] 4. [October 26] 1795

Dear Sir

I presume it will be immaterial whether you apply for permission to export the money or myself, and therefore as it is more in y^r way shall be glad you will do it immediately, stating that it is money paid to the U States here for the interest of their loan in Holl^d for a like sum advanc'd to their agent for the F^h republick in America. If you do not obtain immediate permission, (& I wish the application to be incessantly pressed personally till you get an ans^r) I will also attend personally the suitable department in support of the demand. I think it will be best to send it by water & immediately since that is the only sure way by w^h I can act—for if bills are taken they must be bo^t & the money given up, & for which I sho^d think insurance as necessary as to secure it by water. Besides time might be lost thus by the non payment of the bills, altho' the money might not eventually be.

I wish you to send me by the bearer 50. crowns & to place for Mr George Izard in the hands of citizen Dosquit banker sur la place de chambre derriere la Cathedrale at Metz 200. immediately if convenient. I wish you also to send me by the bearer 30000^{tt} in assignats. y^{rs}

Ja^s Monroe

Dft, NN: Monroe Papers

From Joseph Fenwick

Bordeaux 28 Octo^r 1795.

Dr Sr

By a letter from Mr Skipwith our Consul general of the 18 Inst I am advised that you desired him to communicate to me the purport of an Information made against me to the President of the U. S. for having secured & protected french property shiped in the Pomona of Baltimore from this in virtue of my office & with my consular seal—As the instance is designed I trust it will be easy for me to exculpate myself from the charge.

In the first place there was not a tittle of property shiped either by me, or for my account, in the Pomona nor by any House here—Secondly all the Shippers who took certificates of neutrality from me subscribed their own names to the oath & certificate, which speak for themselves—as to myself I made no shipment, declaration, oath or certificate of property by that vessel of my own. If others who did take certificates from me, as Consul, of their own oath and declaration, subscribed by their own names, swore falsely, or made improper uses of their Certificates it is to their charge & not mine. When a Citizen of the U. S. calls on me to administer to him an oath and give a certificate thereof, the duties of my office forbid me refusing, nor have I a right, if he be a reputable man of scrutinizing into the Truth and sincerity of his affirmation or the power to pursue the application of it. Is a public officer responsible for the false oaths & declarations made before him? I believe I have before mentioned to you that I suspected there was much English property circulating in France, under false declarations in the American name. Is the officer who administers these declarations and gives certificates of them, or the person who makes & subscribes his hand thereto responsible for their truth & reality? The Directors of the Customs in America who give Registers & the President of the U. S. who issues Sea Letters, are they answerable for the false application of those papers? Yet there is too much reason not to be satisfyed that there are many foreign vessels and property protected under the American name with them. What a number of persons & property have been protected by the false application of the passports & certificates of our Ministers at London & Paris and who from the great measure of adventurers & trade as this place has been more exposed to such Impositions than myself. It will not then be extraordinary if many abuses have been made of my Certificates—nevertheless I am ready to answer for my official conduct & if any proof can be exhibited against me derogatory to the right or honor of my office I will receive without pain my suspension.

It is truly mortifying to have served with zeal thro all the Storm of the Revolution in the most difficult times & at a port that has been from the events of the war the most critical and important in the whole Consular Department of the U. S. to be thus summoned & suspected.

I will here mention to you Sir some of the presumptive motives of my being denounced, which I believe to have been done by the British Government or some of their Agents. My conduct here since coming in office, has been firm & active in preventing british subjects from profitting of the favors & privileges given to the Americans—before & since the war I have constantly endeavored to detect and counteract all measures I have suspected to be in favor british Traders to the injury of our own. This conduct has brought on me the honorable hatred of all, even the Americans that are attached to that nation, & has more than once exposed me to newspaper animadversions. Before the french war, in 1791, Mr Skipwith happend at Richmond in Virginia when a violent newspaper attack was made on my character, (to which the then Secretary of State was also privy, as his name was introduced as promoter of the measures) because I interfered to prevent the landing of American tobacco here coming thro' England, as being both contrary to the laws of France, & unfavorable to the real American Trade. This same attack was repeated in the London papers & colored in a manner attempting to have an odium on the Consul of the U. S. of acting a part contrary to the interests of his Countrymen—Several letters of mine to my friends in america since the war have been published & reprinted, which were in a language not flattering to the political conduct or military success of that nation—And I am sure there has not escaped from this place a british Spy, officer or prisoner (& there have been many) that has not carried a denunciation against me as being inimical to their projects & escape under the American name. These things small as they may be in themselves have not I am sure passed the notice of that Government & some of their Agents, who have probably seized this pretext to aim their vengeance against me, or get me out of the way. To return again to the covering of property by the Pomona in which ship I remember there were several people shiped money, some perhaps contrary to the laws of this Republic. to such I always refused administering any oath or giving any certificate; others with legal permits who took certificates of neutralization from me on their own Oath or declaration made either before me or my Chancelor (of whose probity I have never had reason to doubt and altho' I am in a degree responsible for his official conduct do not believe myself culpable for his faults if in the event there shoud be any found to his charge) and subscribed by the person deposing. That nothing was shiped by or for me in that vessel, nor no oath or certificate made to that purport under my hand or seal, to the truth of which I pledge myself, & willingly submit the honor & enjoyment of my place.

I therefore sincerely desire a strict scrutiny into the facts & that my conduct be fairly examined & judged the grounds of the information & informer made known to me. I have the honor to be Sir Your most obedient H^{ble} Servt

Joseph Fenwick

RC, ViFreJM

To James Madison

Paris Octr 29. 1795.

Dear Sir

To day the members of the Directoire are to be chosen. Yesterday the two houses were organised and the prospect is that the present will be a propitious Era in the history of the revolution. The spirit of dissention seems already to be checked by the seperation of the members into different chambers. If suitable men are put into the Directoire the happiest effects must result from the change, for hence forward the military & the police will be in their hands. The convention will have little to do with either, indeed nothᵍ at all except by legislation. But it is incertain who will be chosen into that branch; the council of 500 send up 50. names to the council of antients & who chose 5. out of them. The probability is a good choice will be made, & wʰ is much increased by the late mov'ment, for prior to that mov'ment the reaction from terrorism had greatly favored royalty. The system of terror had been carried to such an excess that it could be borne no longer. It was therefore ended first by the overthrow of Robertspere & made more complete afterwards by several legislative provisions, which introduc'd a more humane system. Those who had suffered under it became in consequence an object of compassion, & those who had contributed to their sufferings or who were even of the same political principles became in the degree an object of publick resentment. So strong indeed was the vibration in this direction, that patriotism itself in some quarters had recᵈ a sensible wound. As soon as terrorism, which was in effect the system of Rob: and wʰ was supported by law became a crime, and in which light it was considerd after his fall, all those upon whom the imputation could be fixed, were in a greater or less degree deemed criminal. In this course the question universally propounded was who were <u>terrorists</u>, who were <u>Jacobins</u>, who were <u>insurgents, anarchists</u> &ca for all these terms were synonimous. Here the friends of the revolution were put upon the defensive, & the sword, not of justice, but of revenge, put in the hands of the royalists. You will readily conceive, that the imputation of terrorism was carried to the utmost extent whilst this state of things lasted: that the list of anarchists &ca was a very comprehensive one when it was made out by the royalists: to this vibration however the 13. of Vendʳᵉ gave a finishing blow, & since which things seem to be settling fast where they shoᵈ do. By this event the spirit of royalty has recᵈ a suitable check, & that of republicanism a proportional elevation. Under these circumstances therefore the probability is that a judicious choice will be made of members for the directoire.

The eyes of the European world are turned upon yʳ branch. *If you do not act with decision your reputation is gone and with it that of our country.* Such is the state of things that *delicacy for the character of others is ruin to your own.* Perhaps if wisely *improved* you may *not only get rid* of *the treaty in question* but essentially *improve the government* especially by introducing *the principle of equal representation in the Senate. But this should begin with a state* and be proposed to the others. *The H. of R. too should ratify treaties.* Tis probable *aid may be had from my correspondence—Then call for and even publish it if necessary.*

France you will observe has continued the same friendly system of policy towards us that she adopted soon after my arrival, & notwithstanding Englᵈ has seized our vessels destined for her ports & to wʰ she thinks too much countenance is given by Mʳ Jays treaty, & notwithstanding the irritation she has felt by the manner of the negotiation & the incertain issue of that treaty. Does not this prove that if any man of sound principles had been here from the first, we shoᵈ never have had the slightest cause of complaint against her? <u>Englᵈ be assured will accomodate.</u> Indeed it is certain Bond is instructed to say so.[1] If then any change is gained for the better does it not proceed from the temper of the people being shewn to require it? does not this criminate deeply the negotiator & shew that had the negotiation been properly conducted *and the administration rested on the people* how much better terms might have been gained in the first instance *since against it they are improved*. In one of my letters I stated that if the aid of this gov^t was expected in support of our negotiation, the negotiation must be upon principles to secure its confidence, & therefore be in harmony with that of this repub^k, & carried on where its negotiation was: especially since the late one w^h had produc'd such ill effects here. This is a proposition w^h satisfies the mind of every one at first view; but if my letters are before you, it may be termed a proposition to put our councils under the influence of France, as those rascals call every thing w^h looks like an independant a liberal & confidential harmony. I mention this that you may attend to it. If my letters are called for I hope they will not be partially called for or rec^d. The business of Algiers is at an end—When Col^o H.[2] arrived here this repub^k was at war with Sp^n & Portugal—any aid therefore to be expected from it co^d not be given otherwise than directly from Marseilles. True policy also dictated an arrangment w^h wo^d embark France as deeply in the business as possible, whereby to make her the more responsible for the terms of the treaty. Col^o H: was sensible of this and immediately concurr'd in the plan of sending an agent hence who sho^d be known & respected by the French councils & if possible a citizen & in consequence coverd by a F^h passport. Thus the matter stood, Joel Barlow being nominated, & ready to depart under the patronage of France, with presents bought by her advice & every thing well arranged. Col^o H. had however left a Mr D.[3] at Alicante to correspond with the French consul at Algiers & even proceed there with power to treat in case invited by him. But he was instructed not to move without such invitation nor to act but in concert with the consul, a consideration w^h created a presumption he wo^d not move at all, untill after Col: H. sho^d return, and the greater because he, Col^o H. had come here, as he D: knew, to solicit the aid of France. Had there been a doubt on this point, I do not think we sho^d have bro^t the subject before the gov^t at all, for under the existing circumstances of Mr Jay's treaty & w^h in a great measure precluded the propriety of asking aid of France, I was satisfied if I told them that that aid was to be furnished thro the rout of Alicante and Gibralter, & thro' a man unknown to them, that nothing wo^d have been done, or if any thing so feebly as to have produc'd no effect. Discouraging too as the state of things was I knew if the arrangment was such as to promise to them full credit for the service, they wo^d embark in it with zeal. Being assured also that D. wo^d do nothing, or, if he did, in harmony with France & of course in case he previously acted, that due acknowledgm^t & respect wo^d be due to France, I proceeded to ask her aid & to accomodate the arrangm^t as above, asking for a passport and protection for D. also as a man associated with Mr Barlow, to guard agnst accidents, and because he was eventually to go to Tunis & Tripoli as Consul: Bringing him into view merely as a foundation to explain, his previous mov'ment if such was the case, before Barlow arrived, & w^h was a sufficient foundation for such expl^n in case he acted in harmony with the F^h consul. Thus as I have already said matters stood when we heard that D. had concluded a treaty, and as we have reason to suspect without any com^n with the consul. The aff^t was easily explained, by throwing the precipitancy &ca upon D. tho' it certainly chagrined this gov^t, who wished to serve us, and w^h chagrine was the greater from the consideration that the propriety of serving us whilst Mr Jay's treaty was in suspense had been discussed & decided in the affirmative. You will excuse me to Mr Beckley, Maj^r Butler, and other friends as I really am not able to write at present being much occupied.

RC, DLC: Madison Papers; unsigned. Italicized words were written code by JM and deciphered by Madison.

1. Phineas Bond, British consul at Philadelphia.

2. David Humphreys

3. Joseph Donaldson, Jr.

To Joseph Rayneval

Paris Octr 30. 1795.

Sir

By the station you held in the councils of France during the American revolution, you were not only a party in many of those transactions which contributed to that event, but acquainted with all in which this nation had any concern. From that consideration I think proper to make known to you a report which was circulated after the peace, and is still circulated in America, to the prejudice of France, respecting her conduct in the negotiation which brought about that event: and I do it for the purpose of asking of you such an explanation thereof as to enable me to determine in what light to consider that report, and of course in what degree to estimate the merits of France for the services rendered us upon that great occasion.

You will recollect that the American ministers signed a provisional treaty with those of Engl^d without the knowledge of France, & agnst the instructions of Congress, which treaty was not to take effect till a treaty between France and England sho^d be concluded. Why this was done became an object of enquiry in America & the reason given for it, as I have understood, was that France was not true to many of the objects comprized in our claims upon Britain, & which were contended for by our ministers. It was even said that France took the part of England agnst us, seeking to repress our claims upon the fisheries, the boundaries & the Missisippi, & that you went to Engl^d expressly for the purpose of fortifying the Marquess of Lansdowne agnst our demands on those points, & which trust you executed in a personal communication with that minister. It was likewise said, that our success in obtaining those claims, was owing to the liberality of the Eng^h government, in rejecting the councils of France, preferring rather to accomodate us than decline it, and when it might have declined it, being thus supported by France, as likewise to the address of our own ministers, who detecting the intrigues of France, defeated them by closing the treaty in the manner & upon the principles above stated. If it be true that the French gov^t acted as above it follows, not the treaties subsisting between the two nations are less obligatory than if it were otherwise, but that in truth France has less claim upon our gratitude as a people for such services as she did render us, than if she had observed in all cases a magnanimous and friendly policy towards us. The object of the war wo^d it is true have been partially obtained by securing independance to the territory we inhabited, but still this wo^d not justify France in taking part agnst us in favor of Engl^d, upon any points at issue during that war, & especially such as were already within our reach.

As an American citizen I will confess to you that I have felt gratitude to France for her services in our revolution, & have been mortified to hear any thing said of her conduct upon that occasion, which in a moral view ought to lessen her merit for those services ~~& which the above report has done & ought to do in case it be true~~. That the above report however has produc'd that effect cannot be doubted, nor can it be doubted that it was circulated with a view it sho^d produce that effect. But justice to France ~~and America~~ requires that the report sho^d not be credited if it be false, & whether it be true or false cannot be known unless the vindication of France is heard. For my own satisfaction therefore upon this point & perhaps eventually for that of others I have tho^t fit to state to you the above and to ask of you such explanation in relation thereto as you may be able and willing to give. I doubt not if you take up the subject you will deem it expedient to be as precise in y^r reply as I have been in stating the allegations, taking care to furnish in support of what you say such evidence as the nature of the case will admit and you are possessed of. With great respect &c

James Monroe

Dft, NHi: Rufus King Papers

Notated at bottom in JM's handwriting: "To be translated into French."

For France's role in the peace negotiations of 1783, including Rayneval's several missions to London, see Richard B. Morris, *The Peace Makers: The Great Powers and American Independence.*

From Elbridge Gerry

Cambridge 2ᵈ November 1795

My dear Sir

My object in addressing you at this time, is to request your assistance in procuring an article which is not to be procured in the United States, & which is strongly recommended as a cure for Mͬˢ Gerry's eyes. She has applied to the most eminent scientists in Boston Newyork & Philadelphia whose prescriptions have afforded her temporary relief, but have not extended to a radical cure. She has been in great danger of entirely losing her sight, & she still enjoys it in a partial degree, being unable to use it in reading writing or in any way that requires an exertion of the eyes. this will be inclosed by my particular friend Hon͇ᵇˡᵉ Thomas Russell Esqͬ of Boston[1] to his correspondent Mͬ Fenwick of Bordeaux, who will be requested to receive, defray the expense of, & transmit the article to Mͬ Russell with any directions which you may communicate respecting the application of it. the name of it is the "<u>Balm of Fioraventi</u>," & it is necessary that it should be of the best quality.[2]

Having retired to the private walks of life where the bustle & strife of politics have no admission, the gazettes are subjects of amusement, more especially when they exhibit <u>professions</u>, which a knowledge of the persons making them, discovers to be the reverse of the <u>principles</u> producing them. & the scene is heightened by the struggle of political ants to gain the summit of the mole hill, & by the exertions of each to reciprocate the fall which he has sustained by means of the others.

Mͬ Gerry joins me in sincere regards to Mͬ Monroe & be assured my dear Sir that with every sentiment of esteem & regard I remain Your affectionate friend

E Gerry

P. S. We flatter ourselves with the hope that you will return to the U States by the way of Boston, & on this event we shall depend on your making our house your head quarters.

RC, DLC: Monroe Papers

1. Thomas Russell (1740-1796) was a Boston merchant ([Boston] *Columbian Centinel*, 9 April 1796).

2. Balm of Fioravanti was a herbal compound developed by Leonardo Fioravanti (1518-1588), an Italian physician (*Enciclopedia Italiana*).

To Timothy Pickering[1]

Paris 5ᵗʰ November 1795.

Sir

On the twenty-seventh ultimo the Convention ended its career by declaring that its powers ceased and immediately afterwards the installation of the new government began, in the same hall, by a verification of the powers of its deputies and their distribution into two branches, according to the mode prescribed in the constitution, and which was completed on that and the succeeding day.[2] It was found upon inspection that the decrees heretofore noticed were universally obeyed, and that of the two thirds of its legislative branches, who were to be taken from among the members of the Convention, more than a majority were elected by the departments, so that the duty imposed on those who were elected, of supplying the deficiency by their own suffrage became proportionably more easy and less objectionable. This therefore was immediately executed by ballot; and and after which the interior organization of each branch followed and which took up a day or two only: then the members of the directoire or executive were chosen, and which was done on the 31st ultimo and whereby the new government was completely installed.[3]

When I observe that the scene which was exhibited upon this great occasion, resembled in many respects, what we see daily acted on our side of the Atlantick, in our national and State Assemblies, you will have a better idea of the tranquility and serenity which reigned throughout, than I can otherwise describe. Nor shall I be accused of an unbecoming national partiality, if I draw from the increasing Similitude in theirs and our political institutions, the most favourable hopes of the future prosperity and welfare of this Republick.

The adoption of a new constitution founded upon the equality of human rights, with its legislative powers distributed into two branches, and other improvements in the executive and judiciary departments, thou' still perhaps imperfect, yet certainly far beyond what past experiments here gave reason to expect, is an event of great importance not only to France but perhaps to mankind in general. Its complete inauguration too assures us that its merits will be tried; tho' indeed under the existing circumstances of a war with the neighbouring powers who are interested in its overthrow, of a strong party within incessantly labouring to promote the Same object, together with the derangement of the finances and other embarrassments which were inseparable from the difficulties they had to encounter, the experiment to be made, ought not to be called a fair one. If however it does succeed and the republican system is preserved here, notwithstanding the various and complicated difficulties which opposed its establishment, and still shake its foundation, it will certainly furnish a complete refutation of all those arguments which have in all ages and nations been urged against the practicability of such a government, and especially in old countries.

Revellière-Lepaux,[4] Reubell,[5] Sieyes, Letourneur[6] and Barras,[7] are elected into the directoire; and who are all distinguished for their talents, and integrity as likewise for their devotion to the revolution, a circumstance which not only furnishes reasonable ground whereon to estimate the principles of those who chose them, but which will likewise tend essentially to give stability to the revolution itself.

I write you at present only to communicate this important event, and will hereafter as heretofore keep you regularly apprized of what shall appear to me to merit communication. I have the honor to be with great respect and esteem, Sir, Your very obedient & Humble Servant

Ja^s Monroe

P. S. Sieyes has declined accepting his seat in the Directoire, and Carnot is appointed in his Stead.

Mr Fauchet has lately arrived and as he appears to be extremely dissatisfied with Mr Jay's treaty with G. Britain and is apparently well received by his government, I doubt not his communications on that head will be attended to.

RC, PP

1. This was the first dispatch that JM sent to the State Department after learning that Timothy Pickering had assumed the duties of the office.

2. The Convention dissolved on October 26, not 27 (Georges LeFebvre, *The Thermidorians and the Directory*, translated by Robert Baldrick, 239).

3. The Council of Five Hundred on 29 and 30 October drew up a list of fifty candidates for the appointment of the five-member Executive Directory. The top five receiving the most votes were Louis-Marie LaRevellière-Lépeaux; Emmanuel Sieyès, (who declined the appointment and was replaced by Lazare Carnot); Jean-François Reubell; Étienne-François-Louis Letourneur; and Paul Barras. They took office on 2 November 1795 (LeFebvre, *The Thermidorians and the Directory*, 255-256).

4. Louis-Marie LaRevellière-Lépeaux (1753-1824) was elected as a deputy to the Constituent Assembly in 1789 and to the National Convention in 1792. He served on the Committee of eleven (which drafted the Constitution of 1795) and the Committee of Public Safety. He was a member of the Directory until 18 June 1799 (Samuel Scott and Barry Rothaus, *Historical Dictionary of the French Revolution*; LeFebvre, *The Thermidorians and the Directory*, 256).

5. Jean-François Reubell (1747-1807) was an Alsatian lawyer well versed in international law and economics. He served as a member of the Directory until May 1799. During the first two years of the Directory, he played an important role in formulating France's foreign policy (Gerlof D. Homan, "Jean-François Reubell, Director," *French Historical Studies*, 1 (1960): 416-435).

6. Étienne-François-Louis Letourneur (1751-1817) was formerly an engineer and had been president of the National Convention in January 1795. He was close to Carnot (also a former engineer) and served on Directory until 26 May 1797 (www.archontology.org; accessed 10 September 2007; Georges Lefebvre, *The French Revolution from 1793-1799*, 173, 180).

7. Paul-François, vicomte de Barras (1755-1829) was from a family of the old provençale nobility. He joined a regiment of Languedoc when he was sixteen, served in India against the British, and after thirteen years attained the rank of captain. He resigned his commission and moved to Paris, where he quickly ran through his inheritance. Elected to the Convention from Var, he played a military role in crushing the Federalist Revolt in Provence, and the royalist uprising in the Paris sections. Elected last of the five-member Executive Directory, he endured the longest, 2 November 1795 to Brumaire 1799 (Martin Lyons, *France under the Directory*, 22; Jules Michelet, *Histoire de la Révolution Française*, 1222-1223; Paul Hanson, *Historical Dictionary of the French Revolution*, 27-28).

From Fulwar Skipwith

Paris 5th Novem^r 1795.

Dear Sir

In a conversation which I have just had with Mr Vanstaphorst respecting the means and mode which under present circumstances can be adopted to Place the Ingots, lodged by your Direction in my hands for account of the united States, in the hands of the united States bankers in holland, there evidently appears but two alternatives—one is to Ship the money and the other to invest it in Government bills upon Amsterdam.—To execute the First, Some Days must elapse before Permission of exportation can be obtained from Government, the Transportation then to any Seaport may be reckoned at from 10 to 15 Days, and with common luck of opportunity of Shipping 10 to 15 Days farther Delay; the Passage may be called 15 Days more and the advice of arrival 10 Days; So that little short of two months may be contemplated e'er the Specie itself could Possibly be Placed in holland; and when Placed, there would result a deduction of from 6 to 8 p^r cent of commission, freight, transportation and Insurance—on the other hand Government bills presents inconveniences; Some times they are not accepted on Presentation, and when accepted are often, from the pressure of them upon the Market, not disaccountable— upon them also would be experienced a loss of 2 p^r cent here upon the par of Exchange. The Government Paper has hitherto been regularly Paid when Due, and I do believe will continue to be, but M^r V—'s friends in holland Seem averse to receiving Such Paper, and I Presume upon the ground of its not being Negotiable.

The above information and Suggestions are the best in my priver[1] to offer you, and after taking them into Consideration I hope to be favored with your instructions of the mode to be Pursued in order to Place the Ingots or their Proceeds in holland—If to be Shipped, I should be glad to know whether you wish me to make the application to Government for Permission for exportation in behalf of the united States or would Prefer to Make Such application yourself. Respectfully. Sir, your mo. hum. Servant

RC, NN: Monroe Papers. Not signed.

1. It is not clear what Skipwith meant here.

From William Allen Deas

London 7th November 1795.

Sir,

I had the favor of yours of the 30th Sept[r] and beg leave to return you my Thanks for the Hint you have been so obliging to suggest respecting passports and for the Communications relative to the Person apprehended in France as a Spy under the Cover of a Passport in my Name. I have looked among the Entries of passports and found none in the Name of Isaacson and as I have no Recollection of any Person of that Name applying for one   I should be inclined to think the whole Business a Forgery were it not that the Channels of Information gave you reason to think the Matter finished; and from the possibility that I might have omitted entering the Passport when granted. In this latter Case you have done me the Justice to remark what I should otherwise have notic'd, that with all the Caution used on the Subject it is impossible to say but that in some Instances persons may present themselves with the Proofs that are required and yet not be entitled to a Passport, and against these Cases I dont see how it is possible to guard. The Rule at this House has been when the Parties are not personally known to require in the first place ample Documents of Citizenship and if not provided with such an Introduction from real American Citizens resident here. I notice this Regulation to observe to you that it has hitherto been customary to grant a Passport to the Person presenting yours, inserting always the same Description of a Person when checked with the Signature of the Party, but from the Circumstances you have mentioned I shall in future consider myself justified against any Appearance of Indelicacy, by requiring as full Proof to be exhibited to me as must have been presented previous to obtaining your Passport.

I am fully sensible of a rigid Attention to this Subject generally but more particularly from the Number of Persons who have become Citizens since the War for mere commercial Purposes who feel no Interest in our Country, never mean to invest there the Wealth they may acquire and many of whom in fact have permanently fixed their Residence in this Country and consider themselves as British Subjects. It appears a Contradiction that such Characters should claim the Protection of the United States and yet I do not see that a Passport can be refused them while our Laws have drawn no Line of distinction. There is another Class of Claimants from Birth previous to the War or who were banished during the War and their Descendants, but with all these, Proofs of their Residence in the United States since the Peace have been required and Certificates of Citizenship as in other Cases. In one instance indeed lately I granted a Passport to one of the latter Description presuming the Fact of Residence and Citizenship from the Companies in which I had occasionally met him but as he has never left London the Passport is now void from the Notice I found it necessary to give here and which M[r] Parker[1] who lately left London was so obliging as to say he would communicate to you & it is therefore unnecessary to guard you against it.

I have from several Quarters received similar Information to that which has been communicated to you respecting the detention of Passports at the Ports and by Cruizers and when Mr Pinckney's first Form of Passport without the description of Person was used it was only necessary to take the Name but as that form has been dis-used since the middle of March last almost all of them must be now out of Date for very few were granted for more than Six Months. I am with perfect Respect, Sir, Your most obed^t Servant

Wm Allen Deas.

LBC: ScHi: Pinckney Family Papers: Thomas Pinckney Letterbook

1. Daniel Parker (d. 1829) was a Boston merchant who provided supplies for the American and French armies during the Revolutionary War. He went to England in 1784 to escape his creditors and began working for Baring Brothers. He went to Paris in 1787 as an agent for both Barings and the Scioto Company. He remained in that city and made a great fortune by financial speculation (*The Emerging Nation: A Documentary History of the Foreign Relations of the United States Under the Articles of Confederation, 1780-1789*, 3: 718; C. Edward Skeen, *John Armstrong, Jr.*, 27, 61-62; William Stinchcombe, *The XYZ Affair*, 85-87).

From Charles Delacroix[1]

Paris, 16th Brumaire, [4th] Year of the Republic.[2] (November 7th, 1795.)

SIR,

I NOTIFY you, that the executive directory has confided to me the Ministry of Foreign Relations. Be assured, that in accepting this station, I have considered as one of its most important functions, that of keeping up the friendship which subsists between the French Republic and your government, and that I shall seize, with eagerness, every opportunity to tighten its bonds.

CH. DE LA CROIX, Minister of Foreign Affairs.

View of the Conduct, 295; the original of this letter has not been located.

1. Charles Delacroix (1741-1805) served as controller of finance under Turgot; as a deputy in the National Convention, he was a member of the Committee of Conveyance in which he rendered decrees on the property of émigrés. Delacroix served as foreign minister from 3 November 1795 to 19 July 1797. He later held diplomatic posts in Holland and Austria and several prefectures. He was the father of the renowned painter Eugene Delacroix (Roger Caratini, *Dictionnaire des Personnages de la Révolution*, 220; Kuscinski, *Dictionnaire des Constitutionnels*; Raymond Escholier, *Delacroix*, 1: 5-7).

2. The letter is misdated as Year 3.

From Timothy Pickering

War-Office Novr 7. 1795.

Sir,

I inclose a quadruplicate of my letter to you of the 27th of April last to which no answer has yet come to hand. The original was indeed long delayed here; the gentleman to whose care it was to have been committed having postponed his voyage & finally changed his mind.[1]

On the 11th of June[2] I wrote you by Col^o Vincent, a French Engineer, mentioning the utility of a skilful cannon founder to the U. States, to be employed immediately in casting cannon at private furnaces, & eventually at the arsenals of the United States. To the complete establishment of the arsenals a cannon founder will be essential. The President approves of the idea of procuring one from France: the

French are allowed, I believe, to excel all other nations in the fabrication as well as use of that instrument of war.

Col? Rochefontaine and Col? Vincent have mentioned the two Périer, brothers in Paris, who have surpassed all other founders in casting cannon.[3] Probably in this period of the war, and when the French armies and arsenals are so abundantly supplied with cannon, a complete founder from the Périer's foundery may be spared for the service of the United States. Col? R. & Col? V observed, that if those two gentlemen will recommend a founder who has been employed under them, not a mere theorist, but a practical master of the business, he may be relied on. I earnestly hope that such a skilful founder may be obtained, and disposed to come immediately to the United States. No attempts to cast large cannon have yet succeeded to our wishes: altho' I have expectations of some success from the aid of a French gentleman now employed <u>temporarily</u>: we wish to obtain more permanent and more certain aid.

If you can obtain such a skilful founder, I must request you to agree on his stipend. I cannot undertake to say that it will be an establishment for life, because Congress have not yet made provision for such an artist by name: but I have no doubt that due provision will be made. He will be useful not only to direct the casting of the cannon now wanted, but in directing the construction of a foundery in the best manner for future service. Should he not be permanently employed (which I scarcely imagine) he will be compensated for his voyages backward & forward as well as for the time he shall be employed at our founderies.

You know what salaries are given to the various public officers in the United States. The business in question seems more related to the mint than to any other department. There the director has 2000 dollars a year, & the Chief coiner & Essayer each 1500.—I just hint this referrence to present establishments as affording some guide in determining the allowance to be fixed for the founder of Cannon. Should the employment be temporary, the compensation should doubtless be greater than for a permanent establishment. With these observations I beg leave to submit the terms of compensation to your discretion. If the founder be obtained, it will be extremely desirable that he should embark with the least possible delay. I have the honour to be very respectfully Sir your ob^t servant

Timothy Pickering.

RC, NN: Monroe Papers

1. Pickering's letter of 27 April 1795 (not located), asking JM to purchase books for the War Department, had been originally entrusted to Lieutenant Noel Monvel (Pickering to JM (introducing Monvel), 27 April 1795, ViW: Monroe Papers).

2. Pickering's letter to JM of 11 June 1795 has not been located.

3. Jacques-Constantin Périer (1742-1818) was a leading French innovator in the use of steam engines for manufacturing. He and his brother Charles operated a foundry where they used steam engines for the manufacture of machinery and a grist mill that also utilized steam engines. In the 1780s they established a steam-driven water works system for the city of Paris. During the French Revolution they manufactured more than 1,200 cannon at their foundry (John Gorton, *A General Biographical Dictionary*).

To James Madison

Paris Nov.[r] 8. 1795.

Dear Sir

The gent.[n] (M.[r] Murray) by whom my letters are forwarded was detained longer by contrary winds in Engl.[d] than was expected. I endeavor however to rep.[r] the injury of delay in my other communications by adding to them what intervenes before his departure.

The gov.[t] is now completely organised in all its departments, & its effect the happiest that can be conceived upon the publick opinion. What it will be upon publick measures time only will unfold: but as the opinion is formed upon circumstances, w.[h] grow out of the organization & the apparent tone of each department, it furnishes ground for hope that its effect upon measures will not be less salutary. The division into two branches has given a check to the spirit of faction, which neither reason philosophy nor a regard for publick or personal safety could yeild. In the House of Antients you see the members sitting like those in the Senates of our respective States, quiet & without any think to do: Whilst the messengers of State keep a vigilant eye upon every Spectator, & if the slightest indecency passes, or disrespect is shewn, by wearing a hat or otherwise by any one it is immediately notic'd & corrected. As this was the chamber of the late Convention where a different style was observed the difference strikes the Spectators with amazement. And in the other house the contrast is almost as great, for the manner of debate is more formal & tranquil, & the delay in passing laws much greater, whereby more time will be given for reflection and the laws themselves be wiser of course.

Reubell, Lariveillére Lepeaux, Barras, Latourneur & Carnot are in the Directoire. Sieyes was appointed but declined as he likewise did afterwards the office of foreign aff.[rs]. The ministers are in general wise men & sound to the revolution—Merlin de Douai is minister of justice w.[h] means Home Department.[1]—Truguet of Marine,[2] LaCroix of foreign aff.[rs] Benezeck of the interior,[3] w.[h] means publick arsenals, founderies, &c &c—The minister of finance is said to be an able man in that line—his name I forget.[4]

I find by the *king of England's speech that the president has ratified the treaty. This is the only intelligence I have of it.* If the *administration had tried to get better terms it might. But to have done so would have condemned what was already done. If you mean to do anything you should call for my correspondence and publish it. It will be objected to as indelicate to me but do not regard this.* Unless it be *seen some things will never be known* which co.[d] not fail to produce an important effect. *I should be attacked* but I think not *injured and the publick essentially benefited.* Be assured *I am not anxious about my place and think the most use possible should be made of me for the publick good.* To evade it all kind of tricks & artifices will be practiced, but these it is to be presumed will not succeed. *To read a dispatch of the French minister handed by the British was not right but to be the dupe of that trick was worse let the merit of the poor victim* be what it may.[5] *I think Pinckney has succeeded in Spain in some way or other whereby the Mississippi will be opened.*[6] This I infer from *his letters to me. he was certainly duped by Jay* tho' a sensible and worthy man. *If you do not shake this party off, its caprices will hereafter pass for wisdom and the virtuous efforts of the patriots for turbulence. But you are on the ground and know best what to do.*

Your furniture, consisting of a bed of crimson damask, bedstead & mattrasses, 2 carpets & curtains for six windows have been forwarded hence sometime since for Havre—They will probably sail with this. Y.[r] china will soon be forwarded. I beg of you to send me a list of whatever you want, in furniture books &c leaving it to me to procure & send them as I find convenient. At leasure I shall make better bargains & especially as I shall buy for you when I buy for myself.

RC, DLC: Madison Papers; unsigned. Words in italics were written in code by JM and deciphered by Madison.

1. Philippe Merlin de Douai served as minister of justice from 30 October 1795 to 5 September 1797 (*Nouvelle Biographie Général*).

2. Laurent-Jean-François Truguet (1752-1839) began his career as an officer in the French navy during the American Revolutionary War. He rose to the rank of admiral and served in the French navy during the French Revolution, the Napoleonic era, and the Restoration. He was minister of the marine from 1 November 1795 to 18 July 1797 (*Nouvelle Biographie Général*).

3. Pierre Bénézech (1749-1802) held several provincial posts during the early days of the French Revolution and became director of armaments in 1794. He served as minister of the interior from 3 November 1795 until 15 July 1797. He remained in the government and held office under Bonaparte (*Dictionnaire Biographie Française*).

4. Guillaume-Charles Faipoult (1752-1817) served in the ministry of the interior 1792-1795. He held the post of minister of finance from 2 October 1795 to 13 February 1796. He later held a number of civil positions in Italy (*Dictionnaire Biographie Française*).

5. JM refers to Washington's interrogation of Secretary of State Edmund Randolph. See Thomas Jefferson to JM, 3 September 1795, above.

6. Thomas Pinckney signed a treaty with Spain on 27 October 1795. The Spanish recognized the southern boundary claims of the United States, granted navigation rights on the Mississippi through its territory, and established New Orleans as a port of deposit for American goods (*Encyclopedia of American History*).

From Constantin Volney[1]

Philadelphie 8 9bre 1795

Monsieur L'ambassadeur

Le Compte que je Vous dois de ma traversée Vous paraîtra Sans doute bien tardif: Mais Mon passage N'a été Ni aussi prompt Ni aussi heureux que je l'avais Espéré. j'ai resté 89 jours en Mer, dont 27 entre les Mains d'un corsaire qui Nous a conduit aux Bermudes: la bonne police que le gouverneur Mr Craufurd y a retablie M'a garanti du pillage de mes effets; Mais les Visites et les fouilles dans Mes malles Ne M'en ont pas moins forcé de jetter à la Mer toutes mes lettres: celles de Votre Sac ont etées decachotées, lues publiquement, et toutes les françaises retenues. j'ai regretté de ne pouvoir remplir La commission dont Vous M'aviez chargé Soit auprés de Mr Randolph Soit auprés de Vos amis. j'ai dû me borner à leur donner de Vos nouvelles Verbalement. j'ai Vu ici messieurs j. yard et mr le Dr Stephens, et j'ai ecrit à New york à Mr Livingston. d'ailleurs j'ai La Satisfaction d'avoir trouvé ici des connaissances et Même des Amis et je Vois que j'y pourrai jouir de la paix et de la liberté, que j'y Suis Venu chercher. jusqu'ici je ne puis que me louer du climat qui a reparé ma Santé si mal traitée par la mer; et je ne partage point les plaintes que des personnes bruyantes font du calme profond du dimanche. il est vrai qu'Arthur young Nous traite Nous autres français de tristes et de Silencieux; Mais je crois que dans ce jugement il N'a fait que donner la mesure de Sa loquacité. je me propose de passer ici l'hyver afin de Suivre le Congres, j'en Serai mieux préparé à Voyager au printems. J'ignore encore Si je dirigerai ma visite au Nord ou au Sud; l'habitude de Voir déranger mes projets Me les fait abandonner au Sort: Mais je ne lui livre point de même Mes Sentimens; et quoiqu'il puisse faire, il ne changera rien au Souvenir que je conserve de Vos honêtetés, et à La consideration Distinguée avec laquelle j'ai l'honneur d'être, Monsieur l'ambassadeur, Votre très obeissant Serviteur

C: Volney.

Editors' Translation

Philadelphia 8 November 1795

Mᴿ Ambassador

The account that I owe you of my crossing will no doubt appear to be tardy: but my crossing was neither as fast nor as happy as I had hoped. I was eighty-nine days at sea, of which twenty-seven were in the hands of a corsair who conducted us to Bermuda: the order imposed there by the governor, Mᴿ Craufurd,[2] protected my belongings from being pillaged; but the guards and the searches of my luggage nevertheless obliged me to throw all my letters into the sea; those in your bag were discovered, read in public, and all the French ones retained. I regretted not being able to fulfill the task with which you charged me, with respect to either Mᴿ Randolph or your friends. I was constrained to give them news of you verbally. I have seen messieurs J. Yard and Dᴿ Stephens[3] here, and I have written to Mᴿ Livingston in New York. Besides, I have the satisfaction of having found some acquaintances here and even some friends and I see that I will be able to enjoy here the peace and freedom that I came to find. Thus far, I can only congratulate myself on the climate, which has repaired my health so badly affected by the sea; and I do not share the complaints of certain noisy people about the profound quietness on Sundays. It is true that Arthur Young[4] regards us Frenchmen as gloomy and silent; but in thinking that way I believe he has merely given the moderation of loquacity. I propose to spend the winter here in order to follow events in Congress, and I will be better prepared to travel in the spring. I still do not know whether my visit will take me to the north or to the south; I am in the habit of seeing my plans derailed and so I leave them to fate; but I do not leave my sentiments to fate and whatever fate may bring, it will never change my recollection of your honesty, nor the honor I have of being, Mᴿ Ambassador, Your humble servant

C: Volney.

RC, NN: Monroe Papers

1. Constantin-François de Chasseboeuf, called Volney (1757-1820), an explorer, writer, politician, and philosopher, created his surname in 1785 based on the contraction of Voltaire and Ferney to indicate his manner of thinking. Volney made a trip to the Middle East from 1783 to 1785 and then wrote a book based on his travels, *Un Voyage en Egypte et en Syrie* (2 vols., 1787), which made him famous. At the outbreak of the French Revolution he launched himself into politics as a member of the National Assembly and as a journalist. His newspaper, *La Sentinelle du Peuple*, and his pamphlets attacked the machinations of the privileged in terms so acidic that his name became well known in Paris. He was close to the Girondists, for which he was imprisoned in 1793, but he gained his freedom after Thermidor. Before he was imprisoned Volney had prepared for a trip to the United States under the aegis of the French government. In the fall of 1795 he made arrangements for a private tour of America. In Paris he put many questions to JM and based a plan of action on the advice JM gave him. JM also provided him with the necessary documents for his trip and letters of introduction (Jean Gaulmier, *Un Grand Témoin de La Révolution et de L'Empire: Volney*, especially p. 204).

2. James Crauford was governor of Bermuda from November 1794 to October 1796 (J. Maxwell Greene, "Bermuda (alias Somers Islands). Historical Sketch," *Bulletin of the American Geographical Society*, 33 (1901): 234-235).

3. Dr. Edward Stevens.

4. Arthur Young (1741-1820) was a British agriculturist interested in advancing methods of farming. He traveled widely and observed various farming techniques, which he described in his periodical *Annals of Agriculture* (*Columbia Encyclopedia*).

To Charles Delacroix

Paris 10th November 1795

I received yesterday with pleasure the notification you were pleased to give me of your appointment by the Directoire to the office of Foreign Relations, and beg leave to assure you, that as a cultivation of the Amity and good understanding which subsists between the two Republics was a principal object of my mission here, so I shall always be happy in meeting you in all those measures, which may be deemed best calculated to promote that desirable end.

Copy, ViFreJM

To Benjamin Vaughan

Paris Novr 11. 1795

Dear Sir

Accept my acknowledgment for your several favors[1] & which be assured I always receive with pleasure. I beg you therefore to write me whenever you have leasure, classing me without chagrine among those of yr correspondents who put the highest value on yr communications & who pay you the worst for them. In truth my situation here has been an unpleasant one owing to causes you readily conceive; this consideration has laid me under some restraint & in addition to which I have had much to do but I promise you hereafter to be more punctual provided you will suggest to me wherein I can be useful to you.

I return you herewith the paper you requested & thank you for that you have plac'd in its stead. I never compared them together so that I do not know wherein they disagree. Truth only is my object & if the present one contains every thing which yr memory rejects I will most chearfully return it & take such other as it shall advise.

I see in the communication given me much reason to applaud the wisdom & liberality of the Marquiss of Lansdowne, but nothing to justify the conduct of our ministers in breaking with France & making a separate peace, or rather in signing an instrument which was neither peace nor war but so far as it changed the state of things was ostensibly in my opinion an act of perfidy on our part, and in reality so in case perfidy on the other side were not established. It behoves our people to establish this or the imputation will doubtless always rest upon them. Of this however we will confer further hereafter.

Dft, NN: Monroe Papers

1. Vaughan to JM, 15 August, 18 September and 23 September 1795, all above.

From Charles Delacroix

Paris le 24 Brumaire, an 4e [15 November 1795]

Monsieur

J'ai recu la lettre que vous m'avez écrite le 21 de ce mois, par laquelle vous demandez une autorisation de faire exporter du Territoire de la République des fonds en numéraire, lesquels Sont destinés à acquitter les intérêts dûs à la hollande pour les emprunts que les Etats-Unis d'Amérique y ont faits.

J'ai pareillement reçu la Traduction Française de cette lettre rédigée en Anglais.

Le Département des Relations Extérieures allait S'occuper des moyens de satisfaire à votre desir lorsqu'il S'est apperçu que cette Traduction non Signée n'était pas conforme à votre lettre Sur l'objet essential, celui de la valeur des fonds que vous voulez faire exporter.

Cette Traduction non Signée porte cette valeur à cent vingt mille dollars, et votre Lettre qui seule doit fixer l'attention du département puisque vous l'avez Souscrite, n'en spécifie aucune.

Le Département ne pouvant entamer d'opérations ayant pour objet l'exportation du numéraire à l'étranger sans connaître positivement la quotité des fonds à exporter, vous invite, Monsieur, à exprimer dans votre lettre la valeur des Sommes en question ou à Signer la Traduction que vous y avez jointe. Le Département vous renvoye l'un et l'autre, en vous prévenant que la réparation de ce leger oubli n'apportera que très peu de retard à l'expédition de l'autorisation que vous réclamez. Salut et Fraternité

Ch. Delacroix

Editors' Translation

Paris 24 Brumaire, Year 4 [15 November 1795]

Sir

I have received your letter of the 21st of this month in which you request authorization to export from the Republic specie destined to pay interest owed in Holland for loans taken out there by the United States of America.[1]

I have in addition received the French translation of this letter written in English.

The Department of Foreign Relations was on the point of taking measures to satisfy your request when it noticed that this unsigned translation did not accord with your letter in the essential matter of the value of the specie that you wish to export.

This unsigned translation cites a value of one hundred twenty thousand dollars, while your letter, the only copy which may be considered by the department since it is signed by you, specifies no amount.

The Department, being unable to undertake any operation to export specie overseas without knowing the amount, invites you, sir, to express in your letter the value of the sums in question, or to sign the translation which you enclosed with it. The Department returns both to you, and assures you that the correction of this minor omission will occasion only a slight delay in the expediting of the authorization you seek. Salutations and fraternity

Ch. Delacroix

RC, NN: Monoe Papers

JM's letter to Delacroix of 21 Brumaire (12 November 1795) has not been located.

To Adrienne Lafayette

Paris Nov.[r] 16th 1795

My dear Madame

I rejoice to hear that you have arrived safe and are permitted to reside with your husband, to whom I must beg you to make my most affectionate respects. He will, I doubt not, remember me as I enjoyed with him the pleasure of fighting for America, our common country. The object of this is to assure you, that you shall want nothing necessary to your support, that I will immediately answer your draft, or place in the hands of some person in Hamburgh, if more convenient to you, and subject to your order, the sum of Two hundred and fifty pounds sterling, as soon as advised by you, and according to your wishes, and that hereafter as may be necessary and as advised, I will endeavor to have you supplied with whatever you want for the accomodation of yourself and family. I beg of you therefore to dispose of me accordingly, and that you will likewise advise me in what other respect I may be servicable to you, and our most estimable friend your husband. Believe me with the utmost respect and regard to be your friend and servant.

FC, NN: Monroe Papers

On 1 September 1795 JM gave Adrienne Lafayette an American passport bearing the name of Mrs. Motier (Lafayette's surname). She and her two daughters then boarded an American packet at Dunkerque for Hamburg, Germany. A month after leaving Paris they arrived in Vienna, where Adrienne failed to obtain a pardon for Lafayette from Baron von Thurgot, the Austrian chancellor. Her party arrived at Ulmültz where Lafayette was imprisoned on October 15 (Jason Lane, *General and Madame de Lafayette*, 223-224; Harlow Giles Unger, *Lafayette*, 308-309).

To Thomas Jefferson

Paris Novr 18. 1795.

Dear Sir

Your favor of the 26. of May did not reach me till lately, owing as I presume to its having been committed to some private hand and by whom it was retained to be delivered personally till that prospect was abandoned. I was extremely gratified by it as it led me into a society which is very dear to me & often uppermost in my mind. I have indeed much to reproach myself for not having written you and others of our neighbours more frequently, but I have relied much on you not only to excuse me personally but to make my excuse to others, by assuring them how little of my time remains from publick and other duties, for those with whom by the strong claims of friendship I have a right to take liberties. Before this however you have doubtless rec.[d] mine of June last[1] and w.[h] gave a short sketch of aff.[rs] here, so that culpable as I am, still I am less so than I might have been.

I accept with great pleasure your proposal to forward my establishment on the tract adjoining you, in the expectation however that you will give yourself no further trouble in it than by employing for me a suitable undertaker who will receive from you the plan he is to execute, that you will draw on me for the money to pay him, and make my plantation one of the routs you take when you ride for exercise, at which time you may note how far the execution corresponds with the plan. With this view I shall look out for a model to be forwarded you as soon as possible, subjecting it to y.[r] correction, & give you full power to place my house orchards &c where you please, and to draw on me by way of commencment for the sum of 1.000 dol.[rs] to be paid where you please 3. months after it is presented. If to be paid without this republick tis probable the draft will be most easily disposed of in sterl.[g] money. This sum is all I can answer in the course of the ensuing year calculating always on the possible contingence of a recall & upon which I have always calculated from the moment of my introduction into the Convention, & still calculate depending on the course of events on y^r side of the Atlantick. With this sum a suitable number of hands may be hired & oxen bought to draw the stone, which with you I prefer, put the ground in order &c &c to be in readiness to proceed with greater activity the year following. These hands may plant the trees enclose and sew the ground in grass which is laid of & destined for the buildings, of which however you will best judge observing that Hogg be instructed to give occasional aids with the other hands when necessary. Believe me there is nothing about which I am more anxious than to hear that this plan is commenc'd and rapidly advancing, for be assured admitting my own discretion is my only guide much time will not intervene before I am planted there myself. I have mentioned the proposal you are so kind as make me to Mr Jones, but as tis possible my letter may unfold that item in my private aff^{ts} not to him, but to some of my good friends in a neighbring country, as my official dispatches have those of a publick nature, I beg of you likewise to communicate it to him as of my wishes in that respect.[2]

I have written La Motte and directed him to draw on me for what you owe him and have his answer saying he has drawn, for 3 or 4.00^{tt}, but yet his bill is not presented.[3] I likewise think him an honest man and deserving more than a mere official attention. I found him on my arrival under arrestation not because he had committed any positive crime but because the whole commercial class had drawn upon it, and oft not without cause, the suspicion of being unfriendly to the revolution, and which in his instance[4] was increased by the circumstance of his having married an Eng^h woman. He was however shortly afterwards set at liberty & since he has exercised his consular functions. I will also procure you the books & other articles mentioned but shall not forward them till the spring for the reason you mention. I will likewise seek out those of y^r friends who have survived the storm, remind them of y^r inquiry after their welfare & apprize you of the result. A terrible storm indeed it has been & great its havoc especially among those of a certain sphere of life, but still I doubt not I shall find many who have survived it among y^r friends.

I rejoice to hear that Short is to be our neighbour. By his last letter I am to expect him here in a week or two & with Mr Pinckney,[5] the latter having as I presume adjusted the affair of the Miss: & the boundaries. I suspect the relict of Mr Rochf:c^t forms the attraction.[6] If the Carters will take me for their paymaster for what lands they have for sale & fix a price which you approve I wo^d most willingly purchase the whole. I have western lands in possession of Mr Jones for a part of which only he has been offered £2000 Pensyl^a currency and which I should be happy to vest near me: an idea equally applicable to the case of Collé.

You[7] have I presume seen the new constitution & will I doubt not concur with me that altho defective when tested by those principles which the light of our hemisphere has furnished, yet it is infinitely superior to any thing ever seen before on this side of the Atlantick. The division of the legislature into two branches, one to consist of 500. and the other of half that number, will secure always in both due attention to the interest of the mass of the people, with adequate wisdom in each for all the subjects that may occur: The mode of election too & the frequency of it in both branches seems to render it impossible that the Executive sho^d ever gain such an influence in the legislature, as by combination, corruption, or otherwise, to introduce a system whereby to endanger the publick liberty: whilst on the other hand the Executive by its numbers & permanence, one of 5. yeilding his place to a successor annually only, seems in regard to this theatre, where the danger is always great & suspicion of course always at the height, well calculated to unite energy and system in its measures with the publick confidence, at the same time that it furnishes within itself a substantial guarantee in favor of the publick liberty. The judiciary too is better organized than heretofore. About 10. days past the constitution was completely installed in all its branches & since each has been in the exercise of its respective functions. The effect which the change has produc'd is great indeed. The Council of Antients occupies the hall lately held by the Convention, & the contrast which a tranquil body, in whose presence no person is allowed to wear his hat, or speak loud, a body who have little to do, & who discuss that little with temper & manners, is so great when compared with the scene often exhibited by its predecessor, that the Spectators look on with amazement & pleasure. The other day a demand was made by the directoire on the 500. for a sum of money & which was immediately granted & the bill in consequence sent to the 250. who upon examination discovered there was no appropriation of it & for that reason rejected the bill. The directoire then accomodated its demand to the article in the constitution as did likewise the council of 500. & whereupon the other council passed the bill. I mention this circumstance to shew the change in legislative proceedings whereby calm deliberation has succeeded a system which was neither calm nor deliberative. Since the gov^t was organized, not more than two or three laws have passed & those of no great importance, & the people go to rest of a night in tranquility consoling themselves with the grateful reflection, that now a strong impediment is opposed to the rage for legislation. They rejoice to find that their legislators have supplied the place of action by reflection. Under this gov^t too the spirit of faction seems to be curbed. Formerly when a member of any note rose and denounc'd another, it put his life in hazard let his merit or demerit be what it might. But latterly some denunciations were threaten'd in the 500., and to which the parties menac'd rose and demanded that their accusers should put in writing the allegations & sign them that they might prepare for & appear in defence, but this silencd the others, & thus tranquility seems to be established & confidence daily increasing.

The paroxisms which preceded the final dissolution of the convention & particularly that of the attack upon it, on the 13. of Vend^{re} or   of Oct^r [8] you will have heard long before this reaches you. In a few words however I will give you a general idea of it: The change of the gov^t or transmission of the powers of gov^t from one system to the other was a great experiment in the present state of affairs & which would not be made without some danger to the revolution; but yet such was the general solicitude to get rid of the revolutionary system that a refusal to make the experiment wo^d likewise be attended with danger. All France seemed to call out for a stable gov^t & this call was finally answer'd by presenting before the nation the constitution in question. But experience had shewn that each succeeding assembly had persecuted the members of the preceding one: a constituent especially was an object not less attractive of the rage of Rob^{i}sp^{re} than a cidevant Bishop or even a chouan. And reasoning from experience it was to be feared, that the deputies of the late convention would be exposed in like manner to the resentment of those who took their places, & this created in them a desire to keep their places & which was attempted by two decrees whose object was to provide for the re election of 2/3^{ds} of the legislature of the new gov^t from among the members of the convention, according to a principle of the constitution w^h applies hereafter & requires an annual change of 1/3^d only, & which decrees were submitted with the constitution for the sanction of the people. By some of the primary assemblies these decrees were adopted & by others rejected: the convention however reported & in my opinion with truth that the majority was for them & of course that they were obligatory on the Electoral assemblies. This was denied by the opponents to the decrees by whom a systematic effort was made to defeat them, first by news paper discussion, next by section: arrets which defied the authority of the convention, & finally by assembling in arms in great force to attack that body and which done on the day above mentioned.

I candidly think that this attack upon the convention as it failed was of great utility to the revolution. The system of terror was carried to such a height by Robertspiere & his associates, that in the vibration back which ensued, some danger seemed to threaten, not the overthrow of the revolution, but to put at a greater distance than there was otherwise reason to hope its happy termination: for when this vibration had gained its utmost point, it so happened that the gov^t was to be transferrd into other hands. In this stage too the royalists who were formerly persecuted more than was upon any principle justifiable, & in whose favor & upon that acc^t a general sympathy was excited, & which was of course due to humanity & had no connection with their political principles, had gained an attention which under other circumstances wo^d not have been shewn them. The probability therefore is that if the election had come on unaided by that incident, more than a majority of that description of people wo^d have been thrown into the legislature. But as the attack failed, it produc'd in a great measure the opposit effect, for in consequence the decrees were not only strictly executed, but the former censure against the royalists whose views were now completely unmasked, proportionally revived: many of whom and among those some who were candidates for the legislature & with good prospect of success, took refuge in the neighboring coun-tries or the Vendee, according as circumstances favored their escape.

On the side of the convention there were 3000. foot & 600. horse of Pichegru's army & ab^t 1000. or 1.200. of the citizens of Paris (the latter of whom were honored by their opponents with the title of terrorists) and on the opposit side there were perhaps in activity twice that number, whilst the other citizens of Paris were neutral. The battle was short for as soon as the assailants saw that opposition was made their numbers diminished, & continued to diminish by battallions, till finally none were left but those who were too marked in their characters to hope for concealment: and which latter party surrendered in a body on the next day at noon to the number of ab^t 500. In the contest 4. or 500. on both sides were killed and wounded. It was extremely complained of on the part of the assailants that the convention accepted of the service of the <u>terrorists</u>, and that it suffered cannon to be used in its defense, since they the assailants had none or but few, & whence they urged that the fight was not a fair one. You will observe that all Paris was against the decrees, 2. or 3. sections only excepted, & because as many of their own deputies were heretofore cut off they wo^d be forc'd to elect their members from among those of the Convention who belongd to other departments, & because they did not like to chose even those of them who remained. This being the temper of the city in the commencment the royalists took advantage of it first by opposing the decrees & which they did with great address, contending for the unalienable right of suffrage which they said was thereby infringed, & demanding wherefore had the good citizens of France fought & bled so freely, & otherwise sufferd so much if they were now to be enslaved, a slavery too the more odious because it was imposed by those who had assumed the mask of patriotism? one step led on to another till finally recourse was had to arms.

Before this event I doubted whether foreign powers had much agency in the interior movments & convulsions of this republick, but by it I was satisfied they had, for it was known in Engl^d Hamburg and Balse before it happened that there wo^d be a movment here at the time it took place: at which time too the c^t d'Artois approached the coast from Engl^d and between whom and the authors of that movment in Paris & the Vendee there was obviously the utmost harmony of measures. Something of the kind is to be trac'd in several preceding events but not so strongly marked, at least not to my knowledge as in the present case. Yet the ordeal thro' which France has passed and is passing in the establishment of a republican system is called an experiment of that system, whose convulsions are contrasted with the gloomy & sullen repose of the neighb'ring despotisms, by the enemies of republican gov^t & to the disadvantage of this latter species of gov^t. So often does it happen by the decrees of a blind fatality, that the authors of crimes not only succeed in exculpating themselves from the reproach they justly merit, but even in fixing the imputation of guilt upon the [innocent].

The French were lately checked on the other side of the Rhine & which caused their retreat to the Rhine: but yet they hold the two posts of Manheim & dusseldorph on the other side. Tis thought some serious rencounters will take place there soon & w^h may produce a serious effect likewise upon the war with the Emperor and on the continent. The late organization of the directoire by w^h men of real talents & integrity, & in the instances of Carnot and Barras men of great military talents, are plac'd in it, the former of whom planned the last campaign, & the latter commanded the national g[uar]ds in the great epoch of the 9th of Ther^r when the tyranny of Robertp^re was broken, and on the last event of the 13th of vend^re is well calculated to secure a wise arrangment on the part of France.

In negotiation nothing has been lately done. If any negotiations were depending they were doubtless suspended to wait the issue of the late elections & the organizat^n which ensued, in the hope on the part of the coalised powers, that something wo^d turn up from the struggles that were then expected to favor their views. But now that that prospect seems to be over tis probable they will be commenc'd, & peace their early offspring. An event which will be greatly promoted if Pichegru succeeds agnst the Austrians, and still more so if his majesty of Engl^d is agn intimidated by the unfriendly greetings of his discontented & afflicted subjects. Unhappy old man, his reign has indeed been a reign of mourning and of sorrow to the world: for we trace upon its several stages in America, the East & in Europe no other vestiges but those which are marked by the blood of the inocent, who were slaughtered in all those various climes of the world & without regard to age sex or condition. And yet we are told by many that he is a mild, an amiable and a pious man, and that the gov^t in which he presides, & by means whereof these atrocities were perpetrated, is that model of perfection of which, thro' all antiquity, Cicero & Tacitus had alone formed only a faint idea, but with which the world was never blessèd before. But you know I must not speak irreverently of dignities & therefore I will add no more on this subject at least for the present.[9]

I hear that the French have just gained a considerable advantage over the Austrians on this side of the Rhine—The Austrians crossed the R. in its neighbourhood to make a diversion there, were met by a body of French defeated & driven back. other particulars we have not. M^rs M and our child join in affectionate wishes to y^rself & whole family & pray you also to make them to my brother Joseph & all our neighbours & that you will believe me most affectionately yours

RC, DLC: Jefferson Papers. Not signed.

An incomplete version of this letter, comprising the first three paragraphs and part of the fourth, and dated 1 November 1795 is in PHi: Gratz Collection.

JM sent a variant of this letter, beginning with the fifth paragraph and omitting the last, to James McHenry. This letter has a P.S. that reads in part: "Of the forgoing I have sent a copy to two or three other friends, for you well know it is impossible for me to write a separate or rather a distinct letter to those to whom I wish to write" (JM to McHenry, 18 November 1795, DLC: McHenry Papers). An extract of the letter was printed in the (Philadelphia) *Aurora* on 20 February 1796. Other recipients, including the one who provided the extract to the *Aurora*, have not been identified.

1. JM to Jefferson, 27 June 1795, above.

2. The following sentence appears at the end of this paragraph in the November 1 version of this letter: "If the ground alloted for the enclosure around the buildings was fencd in, (the underwood being grubbed & cleared away) & sown in suitable grass it wo^d forward the business much."

3. Claude-Adam Delamotte to JM, 21 October 1795, above.

4. JM's letter to Jefferson of November 1 ends here.

5. William Short to JM, 12 October 1795, DLC: Short Papers. Short and Pinckney arrived in Paris soon after JM wrote this letter (George G. Shackelford, *Jefferson's Adoptive Son*, 109).

6. Duchess de Rochefoucauld.

7. JM's letter to McHenry starts here.

8. October 5.

9. The letter to McHenry does not include this last sentence or the subsequent paragraph. It concludes as follows:

> P. S. 21. Of the forgoing I have sent a copy to two or three other friends, for you well know it is impossible for me to write a separate or rather a distinct letter to those to whom I wish to write. I beg of you to make our affectionate regards to Mr Curson and family & to all other friends in Baltimore & that you will believe me to be sincerely yours.
>
> Ja^s Monroe

To day the foreign ministers are to be rec^d by the Directoire.

To Fulwar Skipwith

Paris Novr 19. 1795

Dear Sir

I do not distinctly understand by y^r communication to me whether this is the report which I requested you sometime since to make out for me of the cases submitted by me to y^r care, & relative to which I am to give an acc^t to the department of State & for which I requested that report, or whether it is intended as a communication of y^r own to that department, & respecting which I am consulted by you. If the former it will be proper that you address a short official note to me stating that you make this report according to my request & which note with the report I shall officially transmit as I did y^r former one soon after y^r appointm^t to the office of Consul, stating the situation of our trade within the republick. This appears to me to be the official line of proceeding & every other a departure from it: admitting that the minister has the controul of the consulate & of which I presume there is no doubt. a line too the more necessary in the present instance because I was officially charged by our gov^t with these cases, have applied to this gov^t upon them & particularly committed them to y^r care, and upon which an ans^r has long since been expected from me.

By this I do not wish to prevent y^r sending a copy of y^r report to me likewise to the Secr^y of State, or half a dozen of them if you chuse, but in case the principle above stated is true the stile of y^r commn to the Secr^y sho^d be changed, for in such case you sho^d state that to secure its reception, or for such other reason as you chuse to give, you had sent him a copy of the report you had rendered me.

Tis not for the sake of ceremony that I state & urge this to you, but really because it is the regular line of business. For the same reason and upon the same principle I shall address to you at all times hereafter any instructions & especially of a general nature which are to be executed by the Consuls under you.

In the letter of particular acknowledgment, I wo^d omit all in that paragraph after the word "particular" & [after] it thus, "by forwarding by all the means in my power the commerc^l interests of my country in general, with those of each individual in particular, & I trust in such manner as to merit his approbation." This to follow after the word offer.

I wrote some time since to Mr Fenwick requesting of him to address his letter to me & not refer me to one to you, because I think in a case upon which I am to decide, it will not look well for me to make my decision upon the copy of a letter address'd to another, unless indeed I had address'd him thro you as consul gen^l, & which was not the case as you were then not recognized. Besides I must transmit his letter to the gov^t, and I think there wo^d be a palpable impropriety for me to transmit any other than that written me, in a case where I was the judge. I shall thank you to state this to him & press his ans^r. I am y^r fr^d & serv^t

Ja^s Monroe

RC, NN: Monroe Papers

Skipwith prepared a report on the status of American claims for indemnities from France, which JM enclosed in his letter to Timothy Pickering of 6 December 1795 (below). A copy of the report could not be located.

From Timothy Pickering

Department of State Novr 23. 1795.

Sir,

The office of secretary of state is yet vacant. I write now merely to acknowledge the receipt of your several letters numbered 16, 17, 18, 19, 20 & 21.[1]

You will see an answer to the last has been anticipated by a long letter from me, dated in September, on the subject of the treaty between the United States and Great Britain.[2] By that letter you will understand that the ideas you have detailed are quite foreign to the views of the government of the United States.

Your suggestions in regard to Mr Parrish,[3] our consul at Hamburg, have led me to remind Mr Adams of a request formerly made to him, to enquire into his conduct and report the same to this department. Such I understand to be the fact; and that no report has yet been received. I am, with great respect, Sir, your ob^t servant

Timothy Pickering

RC, DLC: Monroe Papers

A note on this letter in JM's handwriting reads: "The hint had been given respecting Mr Parish sometime before not only that we might do a suitable act of our own accord, but with a view that nothing might occur from that source likely to increase the irritation it was known the British treaty had produced."

1. JM to Edmund Randolph, 14 and 26 June, 4 July, 1 and 17 August, 10 September 1795, above.

2. Pickering to JM, 12 September 1795, above.

3. JM recommended the recall of John Parish in his letter to Randolph of 4 July 1795 (above).

To Fulwar Skipwith

Novr 25. 1795.

Dear Sir

I have conferr'd with Mr Paine & he likewise is of opinion we sho^d pay the money that is lost. I have indeed from many considerations no doubt on the subject & therefore shall certainly do it.

I wish to know the result of y^r inquiries & reflections respecting the trip to Antwerp &c. I have myself no doubt that either at Antwerp or Hamburg a negotiation might be made that wo^d not only reimburse us but save some thing to the U. States. And this might be known here from many particularly Mr Lubert the partner of Dumas & upon whom I had an alternate draft from Swan in case Dallarde's was protested. The loss is so serious an one to me that if it were to be repaired I co^d wish it to be done, independant of the easy safe & quick dispatch of the money for the U. States w^h is a great object.

I hope you have plac'd or will immediately place the money under the care of the gov^t—This sho^d not be delayed a moment, it being a case in w^h y^r own as well as my character & interest are so deeply compromitted.

I shall thank you for a statment of my acc^t shewing the balance due me, after sending me by the bearer fifty thousand livres & eighty crowns in silver for M^r P's family.[1]

Ja^s Monroe

Whatever is done sho^d be done instantly.

RC, NN: Monroe Papers

Thieves broke into a locked storeroom in the American consulate at 17 Quai Voltaire, on 22 November 1795 and carried off three silver ingots worth $4,371, part of the $120,000 that Skipwith was preparing for shipment to Amsterdam as payment on the American debt. Only three people besides Skipwith and JM knew that the ingots were there: Skipwith's secretary, Thomas Davies; the doorkeeper, Jean-Charles Robert; and a Mr. Guillemard, a broker of books. The burglary was discovered by Citizen Debaune, Skipwith's coachman. Doorkeeper Robert reported it to Thomas Davies who occupied a room in the house (which Skipwith owned) (Thomas-François Violette, Police Report, 23 November 1795, NN: Monroe Papers, filed 5 November 1795).

When the news reached the United States several Federalist newspapers suggested that JM had faked the robbery in order to discredit the administration. The Federalists also suspected JM and Skipwith of using the money to speculate in real estate. In April 1796 Madison informed JM of a rumor that JM and Skipwith had purchased Chantilly, the magnificent estate of the Prince of Condé near Paris. In point of fact, Skipwith had acquired the Abbaye d'Ardenne on the outskirts of Caen for the sum of 1,200,000 livres, and JM had purchased the Pavilion Folie-Boissière, for 73,500 livres. (Henry Bartholomew Cox, *Parisian American: Fulwar Skipwith of Virginia*, 53; Irving Brant, *James Madison*, 3: 443; Ivon Bizardel, "French Estates, American Landlords," *Apollo Magazine of the Arts*, February 1975: 108-115; Lucius Wilmerding, Jr., *James Monroe Public Claimant*, 97). When JM learned of the accusations of speculation, he defended his purchase of Folie-Boissière in a letter to Aaron Burr, 25 July 1796 (below).

Madison cautioned JM that some in the cabinet were planning JM's recall and might make use of the "slightest pretext." As a consequence, JM compiled a list of Americans living in Paris who would vouch for him. Madison had first heard of the robbery from James Swan who blamed Skipwith. Aware of these accusations, Skipwith obtained affidavits from Thomas Davies, James C. Mountflorence, and other witnesses. Furthermore to prevent a default on the debt Skipwith repaid the stolen money out of his own pocket. Later, when Skipwith asked the Treasury for reimbursement, Secretary Wolcott refused. He was not repaid until May of 1802 (*Madison Papers, Secretary of State Series*, 3: 100-104; Madison to JM, 7 April 1796, below; Skipwith to Madison, 27 July 1796, *Madison Papers*, 16: 381-383; Brandt, *James Madison*, 3: 443, 504).

1. Thomas Pinckney.

To Charles Delacroix

Paris 11th Frimaire 4th year [2 December 1795]

Citizen Minister,

I observe by record of the proceedings of the Tribunal of Commerce at Havre, and of which I send you a copy, that a dispute is introduced and sustained there between Joseph Sands[1] and William Vans, two American citizens relative to a bill of exchange drawn from America, and which belongs exclusively to one of the parties. The property of Vans was arrested by Sands and condemned by the court of Havre in satisfaction of the claim above mentioned, and from which decision it was carried by appeal to the Superior Court at Rouen, where it now is. In this stage I have thought proper to call your attention to the subject, that in case the executive government of this republic should deem it proper to interfere it may be able to do it with effect.

By the 12th Article of the consular convention between France and the United States it is stipulated that all disputes which may happen between the citizens of either party in the dominions of the other shall be settled by their respective consuls and by them [only. The]² article specifies in its close some particular parties whose disputes shall be thus adjusted, but yet the true con-struction appears to include within it all disputes which may take place between citizens of either party within the jurisdiction of the other. If such then is the true construction of the article, and which I apprehend it is, it necessarily follows that the proceeding of this court is in contravention of that article, and in that view merits the attention of the executive government whose opinion will doubtless be regarded by the court.

That the article was dictated by policy, and formed for the mutual accom-odation of both parties, cannot be doubted. A principal object of it probably was to prevent suits in both countries [between]³ the same parties for the same debt and at the same time, whereby an innocent party might be doubly harassed and to the general detriment of commerce. In this light however I do not think it necessary to discuss the subject. I think it my duty only to bring it before you upon the principles of the treaty, and to ask that interfer-ence of the government in this case which it may deem suitable.

Ja⁵ Monroe.

Copy, DNA: RG 59: Dispatches from France; enclosed in JM to Timothy Pickering, 26 January 1796. *The Writings of Monroe* (2: 448) misdates this letter as 31 December 1795. The copy in NN: Monroe Papers is dated 1 December 1795. A draft of the letter is in PHi: Gratz Collection.

1. Joseph Sands (b. 1771), who arrived in France in 1794, was the son of Comfort Sands, a prominent New York merchant. Sands was arrested for espionage during the XYZ Affair in 1798 and spent a year in prison (Walter Barratt, *Old Merchants of New York*, 303; Yvon Bizardel, *Les Américains à Paris sous Louis XVI et pendant La Révolution*, 156-159).

2. The clerk who copied this letter wrote "only, the". The correct rendering is supplied by the draft in PHi: Gratz Collection.

3. The clerk who copied this letter omitted the word "between". It is supplied from the draft in PHi: Gratz Collection.

From Charles Delacroix

Paris le 12 frimaire an 4ᵉᵐᵉ De la République française.
[3 December 1795]

Citoyen

Le Directoire éxécutif m'a Chargé de vous inviter de vouloir bien Transmettre à votre Gouvernement les Plaintes que le notre à lieu de former contre Mr. Parish consul américain à Hambourg. Ce Consul se permet d'expédier des passeports à des Anglais, Sous le Titre d'anglo américains. Il leur favorise ainsi l'entrée Sur le territoire français; il est l'agent avoué de L'Angleterre pour l'equipement des émigrés. Une pareille conduite est une violation manifeste de la foi des Traités; elle a Surpris le Directoire. Fut-il en effet Jamais de moyen plus dangereux pour attaquer notre Liberté, que d'introduire en France sous les dehors Trompeurs de la Fraternité, nos ennemis les plus perfides? Qui pourrait croire qu'un consul Américain put se Souiller de ce crime aux yeux de l'Europe et trahir ainsi ses devoirs? Le Directoire est persuadé, citoyen Ministre, que vous surveillerez les Passeports qui vous Seront présentés de la Part de Mʳ. Parish et que vous reconnoitrez, par tous les moyens que sont en votre pouvoir, les fraudes coupables qui ont eu lieu dans cette Partie essentielle de la Police des Nations. Le Directoire attend de votre Patriotisme et de votre attachement pour la Republique Française alliée fidelle de la vôtre, que cet abus dangereux sera Réprimé et que vous en arreterez Sur le champs l'effet, en refusant votre attache aux passeports dont les porteurs vous parroitront suspectes. Je vous prie de m'en donner avis, afin de me mettre à même de prendre des mesures.

Je vous invite encore, par ordre exprès du Directoire de vouloir bien Transmettre cette notte officielle au gouvernement des états unis et de solliciter le prompt rappel de M^r. Parish. Notre Ministre Plénipotentiaire à Philadelphie est chargé d'en faire la réquisition formelle. Salut et Fraternité

Ch. Delacroix

Editors' Translation

Paris, 12 Frimaire, Year 4 of the French Republic. [3 December 1795]

Citizen

The Executive Directory has charged me with asking you to kindly transmit to your government the complaints our government has the right to direct toward Mr. Parish, American consul in Hamburg. This consul permits himself to send passports to Englishmen under the title of Anglo-Americans. In this way, he facilitates their entry into the French territory; he is a declared an agent of England with regard to the assistance of émigrés. Such conduct is an obvious violation to the faith of the Treaties; it surprised the Directory. Was there in fact ever a more dangerous way to attack our Liberty, than to introduce in France under the deceitful guise of Fraternity, our most treacherous enemies? Who could believe that an American Consul could sully his reputation in the eyes of Europe with this crime, and in this way betray his duties? The Directory is convinced, Citizen Minister, that you will examine the passports that M. Parish presents to you and that you will recognize, by all means in your power, the [future] guilty parties in the matters that have occurred in this essential duty of the Policing of Nations. The Directory expects from your Patriotism and your commitment to the French Republic, loyal ally of yours, that this dangerous abuse will be repressed and that you will stop its effect immediately, by refusing your consent to the passports that appear suspicious to you. I ask you to inform me of such passports so that I may prepare to take similar measures.

I invite you once more, by the express order of the Directory, to kindly transmit this official note to the government of the United States and to seek the prompt recall of M. Parish. Our Plenipotentiary Minister at Philadelphia is in charge of making a formal request. Salut and Fraternity

Ch. Delacroix

FC, DLC: FCP—France

JM enclosed this letter in his dispatch to Pickering of 22 December 1795 (below).

From William Hull[1]

Newton near Boston 3$\underline{d}$ Decemb^{r} 1795—

Dear Sir

I take the liberty of informing you of my safe arrival in this Country, and expressing my gratitude for the Attention and civilities I received from you while in France—

A sense of duty and Justice has induced me on all occasions, since my Arrival, of expressing the great Services you have rendered our Country, and the confidence which is placed in you by the French Republic—

This will be handed to you by Mr Phelps who with his Lady, expects to spend some time in Paris— Mrs Phelps is a Daugh^{r} of Mrs Leavenworth—Mr Phelps is a Young Gentleman of a very amiable Character, and in Point of fortune & expectations, equal probably to any Person in this Country[2]—Any Civilities to them will be very gratefully acknowledged by your very humble Servt

Wm Hull.

RC, DLC: Monroe Papers

1. William Hull (1753-1825) was a lawyer in Newton, Massachusetts, who had risen to the rank of lieutenant colonel in the American Revolution and who had later served as a general during the War of 1812. He served as an Indian commissioner on several occasions and held a number of state and county positions. In 1805 Jefferson appointed him governor of the newly formed Michigan Territory (*ANB*). Hull made a visit to London and Paris during the winter and spring of 1794-1795 (*New England Historical and Genealogical Register*, 47: 152).

2. Oliver Leicester Phelps (1775-1815) was the son of Oliver Phelps of Ontario County, New York. He married Betsey Law Sherman of Connecticut, the granddaughter of Roger Sherman (a signer of the Declaration of Independence), in June 1795. They sailed for Europe in December 1795 in order to visit the bride's mother, Sarah Law, and her second husband, Mark Leavenworth, who were living in Paris. They returned to the United States in the summer of 1797 (Franklin B. Dexter, *Biographical Sketches of Graduates of Yale College*, 4: 121-122; Yvon Bizardel, *Les Americains à Paris Sous Louis XVI et Pendant La Révolution*, 145-146).

Account With Gabriel Thouin

[12 Frimaire An 4 3 December 1795]

Etat des Arbres fourny à Monsieur L'Envoïé des Etats Unis de L'Amerique, Suivant Sa Demande pour le Jardin de Sa Possession rüe et Barrierre de Clichy, Par Gabriel Thoüin Entrepren^{r} rue du Jardin des Plantes N°6 Section du finistere et livré au Citoyen Son Jardinier dans le Courrant de frimaire &c. L'an 4eme de la République

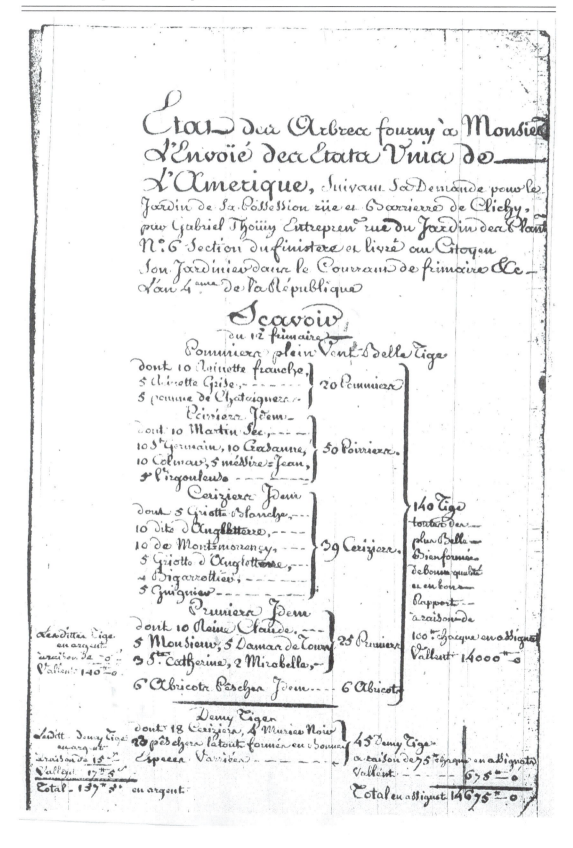

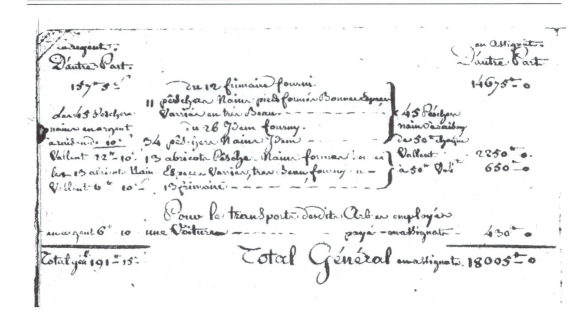

Editors Translation

[12 Frimaire An 4 3 December 1795]

Inventory of trees supplied to the gentleman, Envoy from the United States of America, Following his request for the Garden in his possession on Barriere and Clichy Street, From Entrepreneur Gabriel Thoüin,[1] Jardin des Plantes Street Nº 6 Section of Finistere and delivered to Citizen his Gardener during the current Frimaire etc. Year 4 of the Republic.

Statement
12 Frimaire

Organic Apple trees, beautiful stem
10 of which are cultivated orange Pippin
 5 gray Pippen
 5 pomme de Chataigners [chestnut trees]
20 Apple trees

        Pear trees [ditto]
10 of which are Martin Sec.,
10 St Germain,
10 Crasanne,
10 Colmar,
5 Méssire=Jean,
5 Pirgouleus.
50 Pear trees

        Cherry trees [ditto]

5 of which are Griotte Blanche,   all the

10 known as "English"   most beautiful

10 of Montmorency   well shaped

 5 English Griotte,   of good quality

 4 Bigarrottiers,   and from a good harvest

 <u>5 Guignieu</u>

39 Cherry trees

Plum Trees ditto

10 of which are Greengage (light green plums),

 5 Monsieur,

 5 Damas de Tours

 3 Ste Catherine,

 <u>2 Mirabelle</u>

25 Plum trees

<u>6 Apricot- Peach trees [ditto]</u>

6 Apricot trees

The aforementioned stems costing 20^{tt} in silver, worth 140^{tt}

140 stems of the most beautiful and well shaped, of fine quality and worth a good profit at the rate of 100^{tt} for each, in assignats valued at 14000^{tt}

Half Stems

18 Cherry trees,

 4 Blackberry bushes

<u>23 Peach trees</u>, all well shaped of mixed variety

45 Half stems.

The aforementioned half stems, in silver, at the rate of <u>15^{tt}</u>

<u>valued at 17^{tt} 5$^{~}$</u>

Total- 137^{tt} 5$^{~}$

45 half stems each at the rate of 75^{tt}

Value in assignats   675^{tt} -0

Total in assignats: 14,675^{tt} -0

From 3 December supplied

11 dwarf peach trees well shaped of mixed variety   45 dwarf peach trees

From 17 December [ditto] supplied   at the rate of

34 dwarf peach trees [ditto]   50^{tt} each

13 dwarf apricot trees well shaped, of   are worth   2250^{tt} -0

Mixed variety, very beautiful, supplied Dec. 4 each 50^{tt} valued at   650^{tt} -0

The 45 dwarf peach trees, at the rate of [10^{tt}] each are worth 22^{tt}-0.
The 13 dwarf apricot trees are worth   6^{tt}-0.
In silver: 6^{tt}-10$^{~}$
Total [gen] 191^{tt}-15.

For the transportation of the said trees, the use of a carriage

             Paid in assignats   430^{tt}-0

         General Total in assignats   18,005^{tt}-0

AD, ViFreJM

Gabriel Thouin (1747-1829) was a French gardener whose book, *Plans raisonnés de toutes les espèces de jardins* (1820), influenced subsequent garden and landscape design . Thouin introduced a system of categorizing gardens—applying a method similar to that used in plant classification—based upon four types of gardens: vegetable, fruit or orchards, botanical or medicinal gardens, and pleasure gardens (Michel Conan and John Dixon Hunt, eds., "The Coming Age of the Bourgeois Garden," in *Tradition and Innovation in French Garden Art*: *Chapters of a New History*, 160-183; Betsy G. Fryberger, *The Artist and the Changing Garden*, 14-15).

From Thomas B. Adams

The Hague 4 December 1795.

Sir

    The Bankers of the United States at Amsterdam, have called upon me to make them provision or remittances to face the sum of 270.000 florins which will become payable on behalf of the United States at Amsterdam, the first of next month.

    The reason assigned by these Gentlemen for this demand is, that the process of the Bill, drawn on Messrs Dallarde Swan & Co which they understand to be in your hands, cannot yet be forwarded to them in Specie, owing to some obstructions arising from the new order of things in France.

    They add further, that the period is fast approaching, when it has been usual for them to advertise such payments as this in question, and therefore request me to use no delay, in complying with their demand.

    As I am totally incapable of answering this call, and even doubtful of my authority to authorize the Bankers, to take any steps for securing a provision for this payment, which shall incur new burdens to the United States, I am under the necessity of representing to you Sir, the importance to the interest & credit of the United States in this Country, that a remittance of the 300.000 florins now in your hands should be affected before the first of January; & to entreat you most earnestly, to use every exertion in your power, to obtain permission from the French Government to this end. I have the honor to be &^{ca}

Copy, CtHi: Oliver Wolcott Jr. Manuscripts

Thomas Boylston Adams (1772-1832) was the third son of John and Abigail Adams. After graduating from Harvard he studied law in Philadelphia and was admitted to the bar there in 1793. In 1794 he went to Europe with his brother John Quincy Adams and served as his secretary during his missions to the Netherlands and Prussia. Thomas served as chargé d'affaires at The Hague during the interval in 1795-1796 when Quincy Adams was in London (Massachusetts Historical Society, *On-Line: The Adams Family* (www.masshist.org), accessed 26 September 2007; Walter B. Smith, *America's Diplomats and Consuls of 1776-1865*, 74).

From Charles Delacroix

Paris le 13. frimaire, l'an 4ᵉ de la République française
[4 December 1795]

Citoyen

J'ai soumis au Directoire la demande que vous avez formée d'une escorte pour conduire les Cent Vingt mille Dollars que vous avez touchés à Paris et que Vous voulez faire passer à Amsterdam. le Directoire n'a pas jugé a propos d'accorder cette escorte. D'après ses ordres, j'ai renvoyé votre Petition et le rapport qui y est joint au Ministre des Finances, afin qu'il examine S'il ne serait pas plus avantageux de garder les Cent Vingt mille dollars à Paris et de Vous donner, de votre agrement, sur la hollande une traite de pareille Valeur, qui serait payée des fonds provenant des termes échus du subside accordé aux français par le traité d'alliance avec la République des Provinces unies. Je Vous invite, Citoyen, a vouloir bien vous concerter avec le Ministre des Finances, à Ce sujet. Salut et Fraternité.

Ch. Delacroix

Editors' Translation

Paris 13 Frimaire, Year 4 of the French Republic
[4 December 1795]

Citizen

I submitted to the Directory your request for an escort for the one hundred twenty thousand dollars that you have received in Paris and wish to have transferred to Amsterdam. The Directory has not seen fit to agree to this escort. In accordance with its orders, I have forwarded your petition and the accompanying report to the minister of finance so that he can determine whether it might not be more advantageous to keep the one hundred twenty thousand dollars in Paris and, subject to your agreement, give you a bill of exchange in the same amount, to be paid when the monies awarded France by the treaty of alliance with the Republic of the United Provinces fall due. You are invited, Citizen, to consult with the minister of finance on this matter. Salutations and fraternity,

Ch. Delacroix

RC, NN: Monroe Papers

From Charles Delacroix

Paris le 13 frimaire an 4ᵉᵐᵉ de la République française.
[4 December 1795]

Citoyen

Le Directoire exécutif m'a Chargé de vous inviter de vouloir bien Transmettre à votre Gouvernement les Plaintes que le notre à lieu de former contre Mᵣ Parish consul américain à hambourg. ce Consul Se permet d'expédier des passeports à des Anglais, Sous le Titre d'anglo-américains. Et leur favorise ainsi l'entrée Sur le territoire français, il est l'agent avoué de L'Angleterre pour l'equipement des émigrés. une pareille conduite est une violation manifeste de la foi des Trâités: elle à Surprise le Directoire. fut-il en effet Jamais de moyens, plus dangereux pour attaquer notre Liberté, que d'introduire en france, sous les

dehors trompeurs de la fraternité, nos ennemis les plus perfides? qui pourrait croire qu'un consul Américain
pût se Souiller de ce crime aux yeux de l'Europe et Trahir ainsi Ses devoirs? le Directoire est persuadé,
citoyen Ministre, que vous surveillerez les Passeports qui vous Seront présentés de la Part de Mͬ Parish,
et que vous reconnoitrez, par tous les moyens que Sont en votre pouvoir, les fraudes Coupables qui ont eu
lieu dans cette Partie essentielle de la Police des Nations.

Le Directoire attend de votre Patriotisme et de votre attachement pour la République française,
alliée fidelle de la vôtre, que cet abus dangereux sera réprimé, et que vous en arrêterez l'effet, en réfusant
votre attache aux passeports dont les porteurs vous parrâitront Suspects. je vous prie de m'en donner
avis, effin de me mettre à même de prendre des mesures.

Je vous invite encore, par ordre exprès du Directoire, de vouloir bien Transmettre cette notte officielle
au gouvernement des états unis et dy solliciter le prompt rappel de Mͬ Parish, notre Ministre
Plénipotentiaire à philadelphie est chargé d'en faire la réquisition formelle. Salut et fraternité

Ch. Delacroix.

Editors' Translation

Paris, 13 Frimaire, Year 4 of the French Republic.
[4 December 1795]

Citizen,

The Executive Directory has charged me with asking you to kindly convey to your government the
complaints our government has good reason to make against Mr. Parish, the American consul in Hamburg. This consul takes the liberty of issuing passports to Englishmen under the title of Anglo-Americans, allowing their entry into France. He is a declared agent of England for equipping émigrés. Such
conduct is an obvious violation of the spirit of the treaties; it has surprised the Directory. Was there ever
a more dangerous way to attack our liberty than by introducing our most treacherous enemies into
France under the deceitful guise of friendship,? Who could believe that an American consul could sully
his reputation in the eyes of Europe with this crime, and in this way betray his duties?

The Directory is convinced, Citizen Minister, that you will examine the passports issued by Mr.
Parish and that you will identify, by all means in your power, any fraud that has occurred in this essential
part of national security.

The Directory expects from your patriotism and your attachment to the French Republic, your loyal
ally, that this dangerous abuse will be repressed and that you will stop its effect immediately, by refusing
your consent to the passports that appear suspicious. I ask you to inform me of such passports so that I
may prepare to take similar measures.

I invite you once more, by the express order of the Directory, to convey this official note to the
government of the United States and to request the immediate recall of Mr. Parish.[1] Our Minister
Plenipotentiary at Philadelphia is charged with making a formal request. Salutations and Fraternity

Ch. Delacroix.

FC, DLC: FCP—France

1. JM enclosed this letter in his dispatch to Pickering of 22 December 1795 (below).

From Andrew Masson[1]

Hambourg 6 X^bre 1795.

Sir

Mr Terrasson[2] has been so Kind as to bring a letter from you for M^de Motié.[3] That lady being no longer at hambourg, That Gentleman has been directed to me, and he will Give you the motive of it. I will Content myself with Giving you an account of the Step I Took upon me to put to the envoy of that letter for the discharge of m^r terrasson and my own. to excuse me for the liberty I took in that step, I must prove that I was obliged to advice, and do that, as it has been. I hope you'll approve of m^r terrasson's Conduct and my own.

M^de Motié after having been to Vienna Repaired to ullmutz. M^r parish and I Receiving No letter from her, Though she promised to write both of us, he Directed the letters we had each of us from different parts for her to a merchant at ullmutz in order to be Conveyed to her. that merchant instead of giving these letters, or sending them back to m^r parish, wrote to him that m^de motié was So privately Confined, that it was impossible to let her have any letter, and that he has burnt the paquet of those we had sent to him. m^r parish wrote afterwards to the Governor of ullmutz in order to inform him, and at the Same time beg of him leave to direct to himself letters for M^de motié, and the favour of an answer. The Governor has not made yet any answer since.

So was the order of things when m^r terrasson addressed himself to me. after what I told him of those events, and what he heard from Mr Parish it has been proved to him that it was quite useless to send the letter. perfectly convinced as I was that not only any letter would have Reached m^de Motié, but that they should be opened and kept. in my opinion the discovery of it would have been still worth when I know, and Consider that she has been entirely stripped of any money and any thing at the very moment she entered ullmutz.

after it has been Clearly proved that M^r terrasson's messages Could not be put at any end, and the sad Consequences which would have been the Result of it, I insisted upon m^r terrasson for keeping your letter. I engaged him in the Case of his return, to deposit it in the hands of m^r parish already connected with the particulars affairs of m^de motié, and by the Same reason with me then your letter sir, is still under your seal, and will be kept so till a particular order from ye, or from M^de Motié.

Now My most desirous wish is to see My Conduct being approved and I beg of you the favour of a line which may Confirm me in that idea.

I'll not let M^r terrasson Go away without Giving him the particulars of what may happen in that peculiar affair. we want more than ever friends and assistance. prevented as m^de motié is now from using any faculty I'll beg of you to be so kind as to Correspond some <illegible> with me concerning that unfortunate family. by my zeal to Deffend and assist him who has done every thing for liberty and his own Country, I'll try to deserve your confidence about any thing you would be Pleased to Require from me. I am With Respect Sir your Most obedient servant

Andrew Mason

RC, NN: Monroe Papers

1. Andrew Masson was an aide-de-camp to General Lafayette (André Maurois, *Adrienne, ou la Vie de Mme de Lafayette*, 345).

2. Barthélemy Terrasson had been the French consul at Baltimore and later became a merchant based in Philadelphia ("Historical News," *The American Historical Review*, 53 (1947): 205).

3. The letter that Terrasson carried to Madame Motié (Adrienne Lafayette) may have been that of 16 November 1795 (above).

To Timothy Pickering

Paris December 6th 1795.

Sir,

I was lately honoured with originals and triplicates of your favours of the 12th and 14th of September last. The duplicates are yet to be received.

By the first of these letters I learn that the President has ratified the late treaty with England, and by the second the measures taken to vindicate our territorial rights that were violated by the captain of a British Frigate, in an attempt to seize M[r] Fauchet the French minister within our jurisdiction, on his return home, and to which communications due regard shall be paid, as occasion requires.

That the treaty was ratified was a fact well established before the receipt of your favour. It was indeed generally credited before the arrival of M[r] Fauchet, by whom it was confirmed and afterwards doubted by none. As I had no reason to presume from any communication from your department that the contrary would be the case, so I had never calculated on the contrary: nor had I given this government any reason to calculate on the contrary; having left it to form its own judgment on that point according to its own lights, so that in this respect I have nothing wherewith to reproach myself on the score of discretion.

The effect which this incident produced in the councils of this country, through its several stages may be traced in my former communications and to which I beg to refer you. To these I have at present nothing material new to add. Symptoms of discontent it is true are still seen, but whether they will assume an aspect more unpleasant I know not. If they do, or any thing else occurs of sufficient importance to merit your attention I will certainly apprize you of it and without delay.

You likewise saw by my former communications that I understood and acted upon that part of my instructions which explained the object of M[r] Jay's mission to England differently from what it appears by your favour of the 12th of September and by M[r] Randolph's of the 1st of June preceding it was intended I should understand and act on it, and whereby I was placed by the course of events in a very delicate and embarrassing dilemma: from which indeed I am not perhaps yet fully extricated, though I hope and think I am. Upon this head I have only now to observe that as soon as I had reason to believe that M[r] Jay's instructions embraced objects, which I had before thought they did not, I profited of what I heard and acted accordingly, keeping out of view so far as depended on me what had before passed between the government and myself upon that subject and to which I with pleasure add that I have never heard the least intimation on it since. In reviewing this particular trait in my conduct here you will I doubt not do me the justice to observe that when I made the suggestion alluded to, it was not rashly done, nor without sufficient motive: [on the][1] contrary that, (paying due regard to the actual state of our affairs at the time) I was called on to make it by considerations the most weighty and which ought not to have been dispensed with: considerations however which I now forbear to repeat having heretofore sufficiently unfolded them.

I have the pleasure to inclose you the report of M[r] Skipwith upon the subject of the claims of many of our citizens who were heretofore injured by the occurrences of the war and in consequence entitled to indemnities, and by which you will find that many of those claims are settled, and derive useful information in respect to others.[2]

I likewise send you a letter from M[r] Fenwick explaining his conduct in regard to the charge exhibited against him in your department.[3] As M[r] Fenwick has always proved himself to be an useful indeed a valuable officer in the station he holds, and as the error imputed to him might be the effect of judgment only, and which I think it was, I have thought I could not better forward your views or the interest of my country than by continuing him in the discharge of the duties of his office, 'till the President shall finally decide in his case. He will doubtless communicate with you on the subject, so that the interval will not be great before I have the decision in question, and which will of course be duly executed.

Two days since Count Carletti minister from Tuscany was in consequence of some offence given by him to the government, ordered to depart from Paris in 48 hours, and the bounds of the Republic in eight days. 'Tis said the offence consisted in a demand made to visit the daughter of the late King, of whom he spoke in terms of extreme commiseration, and which were thought to be not only an interference in concerns exclusively their own, but to have thrown some reproach on the French government. The Count I hear departs tonight by the way of Marseilles.[4]

Soon after the government was organized the minister of foreign affairs announced a day on which the Directoire would receive the ministers of foreign powers and who were requested to rendezvous for that purpose at his house to proceed thence to that of the Directoire. We did so, and were presented without regard to precedence to that body, and whose President addressed the whole diplomatic corps in a short discourse the principal object of which was to assure it of the cordiality with which it was welcomed here by the representatives of the French people and which it contrasted with the pomp and cerimony of the ancient court which he said was neither cordial nor fraternal. I mention this latter circumstance merely to contradict the account given of the address by the journalists, and who made a particular speech for the President to each minister.

Manheim has certainly fallen again into the hands of the Austrians with the garrison, the amount of which is not known, but presumed to be several thousands.[5] But in Italy the fortune of the war is on the side of France for the same day which announced the surrender of Manheim announced likewise a great and decisive victory over the Austrians in the other quarter. The details of killed and wounded are also not yet accurately known, but it is understood that 4 or 5,000 are taken prisoners, many slain and the whole army put completely to the rout.[6]

Since the organization of the new government the character and deportment of all the departments are essentially improved. The legislative corps in both its branches exhibits in the manner of discussion, a spectacle wonderfully impressive in its favour when compared with what was daily seen in the late convention. And the executive departments begin to shew an energy which grows out of a nice partition of their duties, and the greater responsibility that belongs to each. In truth the vibration from the system of terror had by the force of moral causes gone so far, and produced so deep an effect, as to have greatly relaxed the whole machine of government. It was certainly felt in the departments, in the public councils, in foreign negotiations and in the armies. A short space of time however will now shew how far the change which has taken place in the government will furnish the means of an adequate remedy.

Mʳ Pinckney has I hear closed his business in Spain to his satisfaction and is now on his route back, intending to take Paris in his way. I trust this report is in every respect well founded, of which however you will doubtless be correctly informed before this reaches you. With great respect and esteem I have the honour to be, Sir, your most obedient and very humble serᵗ

Jaˢ Monroe.

P. S. Count Carletti has notified to the French government that he cannot depart without consent of his own.

Copy, DNA: RG 59: Dispatches from France

1. The clerk who copied this letter wrote "after". The inserted words are taken from the version of the letter published in *ASP: FR*, 1: 727-728.

2. Fulwar Skipwith's report has not been located.

3. Joseph Fenwick to JM, 28 October 1795, above.

4. Tuscan minister Francesco Saverio Carletti first attempted to see the Princess Royal in May of 1795, but was rebuffed by Merlin de Douai. Carletti ironically left Paris the same night as the Princess, whose entourage caught up with him and by order of precedence commandeered his horses (*Dizionario Biographica Degli Italiani*; Sydney Seymour Biro, *The German Policy of Revolutionary France*, 371, 450, 521-522; 524).

5. The Austrians defeated the French at Manheim on 18 October 1795. After the battle Pichegru retreated with his army to the west, leaving a 9,000 man garrison behind in the fortress at Manheim. They surrendered on 22 November 1795 (Steven T. Moss, *Historical Dictionary of the Wars of the French Revolution*, 100-101).

6. French troops under General Barthélemy Schérer defeated a combined force of Austrians and Piedmontese at Loano, Italy, on 23 November 1795. The Austrians suffered casualties of 5,500 men and the French 1,300 (Gregory Fremont-Barnes, ed., *Encyclopedia of the French Revolution and the Napoleonic Wars*, 2: 573-574).

To Charles Delacroix

Paris 9ʰ December 1795 (18ʰ frimaire l'an 4ᵉ)

and 20ʰ year of the American Republic

Citizen

I have received your favor of the 4ʰ Instant (13ᵗʰ frimaire) and hear with concern that Mʳ Parish, the american Consul at Hamburg has so far forgotten the duties of his office, and to which the intimate Connection and amity which subsists between our two governments should to have made him the more attentive, as to grant passports to English subjects whereby they are admitted here as American Citizens, to accept in any respect the employment or agency of England, or any other power at war with you, and especially in the very improper instances you mention.—Be assured Citizen Minister that I will immediately communicate your note to the government I represent and from whom you may with equal certainty confide, such conduct will receive the censure it merits. Upon this however permit me to add, as that our consular arrangement is very extensive, embracing all the european ports in many of which we have no resident Citizen, we are forced to appoint in such case, some Inhabitant of the place, as was the case in the present instance: this will account why the character of the Person is sometimes little known and of course how our government is sometimes imposed on in that respect.

I have long since and still make it an invariable rule to grant passports to none whom I do not know by satisfactory documents to be american Citizens, and no documents are admitted in case of doubt but the certificates of American Citizens. I am therefore persuaded that in the list of those now in france protected by my passports you will not find one, who is not strictly entitled to it. All those who have not my passports are of course subject to the animadversion of your police. Be assured I shall be particularly on my guard with respect to the certificates granted by Mʳ Parish.

Jaˢ Monroe

RC, DLC: FCP

To Thomas B. Adams

Paris Dec[r] 11. 1795

Sir

I was fav[d] with yours of the 4th inst[t] yesterday upon the subject of the Bill of Dallarde & Swan upon that House here in favor of the U. States for 120.000 Dols & to w[h] I give an immediate reply.

The Bill was accepted & finally paid, the Am[t] whereof is now in possession of M[r] Skipwith Consul Gen[l] for the U. States here. Demand was made for permission to export it, the moment it was rece[d] & to which an ans[r] was delayed on acc[t] of the change of the Gov[t] and temporary derangement, which followed untill the other day, when the escort which was demanded to accompany it was refused, and no notice taken of so much of the demand as respected the exportation. I am now endeavoring to obtain a decision on that point, and if obtained favorably, shall send it in the best manner possible. But this will consume time; none however that can be prevented. I sincerely wish you would draw on me for it. Money is always more valuable here than bills in foreign Countries some times 10. 15 & 20 p[r] cent; of course I should infer that bills might negotiated on me to advantage. I shall not relax my efforts but beg you to draw if possible. &[ca] &[ca] &[ca]

Copy, CtHi: Oliver Wolcott Jr. Manuscripts

From Robert R. Livingston

New York 13th Dec[r] 1795

Dear Sir

I have long since replied to your obliging favor of the 23[d] July[1] But the gen[n] who was to be the bearer of my Letters has delayed his departure to the present moment so that they will probably not reach you so early as this will.

The Session of Congress is opened & least you sh[d] not receive it by another hand I enclose you the presidents speach & the answer of the Senate which as you may easily suppose contains a full approbation of their own work while the effect of it appears in the daily capture & condemnation of our vessels I also send you Butlers speech upon the amendment which speaks the Language of the body of the people but such is the force of the stock jobbers & the British party that their voice is unattended to.[2] There is a decided majority of republicans in the lower house but they are too much fettered by the senate to be able to do any thing & indeed I cannot find any consistant system among them—You find the President has avoided laying the treaty before them till it is ratified by the King of Great Britain & many of them seem to doubt the propriety of taking notice of it till they have it officially—That is to say till it is too late to act upon it. Hamilton under the signature of Cammillus has undertaken its defence but without making many converts—I send you three or four pamphlets written by Cato which I believe speak the general sense of the people of this country on the subject. you will be pleased to present one to M[r] Le Blank & another to M[r] Jannot in my name I am Curious to know how the treaty has been rec[d] in France since it has become public

You have heard I presume that a letter of M[r] Fauchettes which was intercepted by the British has occasioned the resignation of M[r] Randolph M[r] Pickering has succeeded him & M[r] Charles Lee is Att[y] Gen[l]—The letter I allude to has some very free reflections on this Gen[n] & some intimations not very pleasing to several other republican Gen^n—It is a very curious circumstance that the president had actualy determined to withold his certification of the treaty when this letter was artfully played off upon him by Hammond in consequence of which he signed it in a fit of resentment. Thus it has twice happened that the interests of France have been materialy injured by the imprudence of her ministers. You will find by the papers I send you that King is accused of having communicated the treaty to Mr Hammond while under injunctions of secrecy[3] How the charge will be supported, or how he will refute it I know not. perhaps he may get a certificate from Jay to establish its falsity.

The British have discovered a very fine harbour in Bermuda & mean to establish dock yards there which will in time of war be extremely troublesome to us[4]—You would render an essential service to France & this country if you could induce them to possess themselves of this Island which might be very easily effected as they would take no alarm at any armament fitted out at this time as they would naturaly suppose it destined for the west indies The rascaly freebooters that inhabit it would on its reduction be as ready to cruize ag^t Britain as ag^t france I have written on this subject to Mr Fauchette turn it in your mind & see whether the Idea is not worth pursuing. I am Dear Sir with much essteem & regard &^c

RRL.

FC, NHi: Livingston Papers

1. Livingston probably refers to JM's letter of 23 June 1795 (see JM to Beckley, 23 June 1795, above). Livingston's response has been located.

2. George Washington delivered his seventh annual address to Congress on 8 December 1795, and the Senate responded on the 11th (James D. Richardson, *Messages and Papers of the President*, 1: 182-187). Stevens T. Mason thought that the Senate's response expressed too strong an approbation of the Jay Treaty and introduced a motion to strike out the offending clauses. Pierce Butler spoke in support of the motion. It was defeated (*Annals of Congress*, 5: 17-18).

3. George Hammond informed Edmund Randolph that he had seen a copy of the Jay Treaty, which had been given to him by "a member of the Senate," but he did not reveal the senator's name (*Hamilton Papers*, 18: 390).

4. Admiral George Murray, the commander of the British North American squadron from 1794 to 1796, established a naval base at Bermuda that included a shipyard (*DNB*).

From John Beckley

Philadelphia, 14th December 1795.

My dear Sir,

I take occasion to introduce to you my friend Mr James Smith, who has been about two years in our Western Country in pursuit of Lands, and now visits Europe in search of a good Market. He will come to Paris first, and then proceed to the Low Countries and Elsewhere as circumstances may direct—Any notice or countenance you can consistently afford him, will be an obligation to me.

Congress commenced its Session on Monday last, and my reelection as Clk of the H Rep^s was the first essay of party, and in the absence of 23 of my friends a vote was taken, of 30 against me, and 48 in my favor. Mr Tazewell, who lives with me during the Session, writes you very fully by an opportunity that offers thro' Mr Adet, and I refer y^o to him for explanation generally, as also for Randolphs vindication &^c &^c. [1]

The bearer hereof is an agent from Ireland in whom you may confide. His object is to obtain of France aid in favor of his distressed country. What that aid sho^d be & the manner of giving it he will mention. The French minister I am told will aid the business by a secret donation to his nation. You will act in this man as you deem best. His name is Theobald Wolfe Tone. He is the friend of Hamilton, Randolph, and a person in [whom] his country-men fully confide.[2] decypher this by our friend Madisons Cypher. Yours truly & sincerely,

John Beckley.

RC, NN: Monroe Papers. The words in iltalics were written in code by Beckley and deciphered by JM.

1. Henry Tazewell to JM, 26 December 1795, below.

2. James Smith was an alias of the Irish nationalist, Theobald Wolfe Tone (1763-1798). Tone was a leader in the Catholic emancipation movement in Ireland; when other leaders were arrested during the summer of 1795, he fled to the United States. The suppression of the reform movement persuaded Tone to pursue more radical measures, and in February 1796 he went to France to secure French support for Ireland. He became an officer in the French army and remained in that service for two years. He was captured by the British while taking part in a French naval expedition to Ireland in October 1798 and executed (*DNB*).

From Charles Delacroix

Paris le 23 Frimaire de l'an 4ᵉ de la République Française une et indivisible
[14 December 1795]

Je suis informé, citoyen, par une lettre du consul de la République Française, à Philadelphie et par le procès verbal dressé par les officiers de la Corvette de la République le Cassius, que cet vaisseau à été confisqué par le gouvernement des Etats-Unis. Il a résulté de cette mesure extraordinaire de grands dommages pour la République Française, outre la detention de la majeur partie de l'Equipage. L'Envoyé de la République Française parait avoir fait jusqu'ici de vains efforts pour obtenir la réparation [de] l'injure faite au pavillon Francais dans la corvette le Cassius. Je vous donne avis que J'ai écrit à l'envoyé de la Répᵉ pres la Répᵉ des Etats-Unis, pour qu'il poursuive avec instance ces résultats. Bien persuadé que vous employerez de votre coté vos bons offices pour fixer l'attention du gouvernement Américain sur la violation dont Je vous rends compte, Je suis convaincu que vous voudrez dans toutes les occasions concourir avec moi à tout ce qui peut maintenir, resserer même les liens de deux peuples, que l'amitié rapproche, quoique placés à deux extrémités du monde. Salut et fraternité

Le ministre des relations extérieures.
Ch. Delacroix.

Editor's Translation

Paris 23 Frimaire, year 4 of the French Republic, one and indivisible
[14 December 1795]

Citizen, I am informed in a letter from the French consul in Philadelphia and in the report of the officers of the Republic's corvette, Cassius, that this ship has been seized by the government of the United States. This extraordinary measure has greatly harmed the French Republic, over and above the detention of the greater part of the crew. The Republic's envoy appears to have made efforts that have thus far been in vain to obtain reparations for the insult to the French flag in the case of the corvette Cassius. Be advised that I have written to the Republic's envoy to the Republic of the United States, instructing him to pursue this case assiduously. Persuaded as I am that you will use your good offices to bring this violation to the attention of the American government, I trust that you will always wish to strive with me to maintain, even to improve, relations between two peoples linked in friendship, albeit located at two ends of the world. Salutations and fraternity

The Minister for Foreign Relations
Ch. Delacroix.

Copy, DNA: RG 59: Dispatches from France; enclosed in JM to Pickering, 22 December 1795.

In May 1795 the French corvette *Le Cassius* captured the *William Lindsay*, a merchant ship owned by James Yard of Philadelphia. When *Le Cassius* arrived at Philadelphia, Yard had the captain, Samuel B. Davis, arrested and the ship impounded. Criminal charges were then brought against Davis and *Le Cassius* on the grounds that the ship, originally named *Les Jumeaux*, had been outfitted in Philadelphia as a privateer, in violation of the American neutrality law. French minister Pierre Adet protested the arrest and seizure, arguing that *Le Cassius* was owned by the French government and Davis was a French naval officer, and both therefore exempt from legal proceedings in the United States. The case lingered until October 1796 when the courts, siding with France, dismissed it. It was a pyrrhic victory, however, for the long delay had had made *La Cassius* worthless to France, and it had been abandoned and dismantled in September 1796 (*ASP: FR*, 1: 629-639; *Documentary History of the Supreme Court*, 6:719-727)

To Guillaume-Charles Faipoult

Paris, le 14 X^{bre} 1795 (le 23 Frim^{re} de l'an 4e)
l'an 20. de la Rép. Américaine

Citoyen Ministre,

Le Ministre des Relations Extérieures m'avait fait espérer une réponse définitive de votre departement au sujet de la demande que J'ai adressée au gouvernement à l'effet d'obtenir son autorisation d'envoyer en Hollande la somme de 120,000 Dollars pour le service des Etats-Unis de l'Amérique, et que J'ai touché ici en remboursement d'une pareille somme dont le gouvernement des dits Etats avait fait l'avance à votre agent en Amérique. Comme il existe toujours la nécéssité la plus urgente de placer ces fonds à leur destination ce serait rendre à mon gouvernement un Service bien essentiel, s'il comporte avec les arrangements du votre d'en autoriser l'exportation, ou de fournir les moyens de les placer an Hollande de manière à en assurer l'objet. Cependant sur un dernier point Je dois vous observer que Je n'eusse point songé à démander cette autorisation si le renvoi sous protêt d'un mandat tiré par la Trésorerie de la Rép^e sur la celle des Etats-Généraux n'eut déjà occasionné un retard très préjudiciable aux interêts en question. Lorsqu'on considère que vous avez des besoins annuels de placer des fonds en Amérique, et que nous avons également besoin d'en placer en Hollande, et que c'est içi le commencement d'un arrangement qui réunit le double avantage du bénéfice et la Sécurité en faveur des deux parties J'ose me flatter, citoyen Ministre, qu'il sera facile de concilier la proposition que Je vous soumets dans ce moment avec les interêts de la Rép^e et que voudriez bien me faire l'amitié de répondre à celle-ci dans le moindre délai possible vu que chaque jour nous devient bien précieux dans l'etat ou en sont les choses. Agréez, citoyen Ministre, l'assurance de mon respect et de mon Estime.

Editors' Translation

Paris, 14 December 1795 (23 Frimaire, year 4)
Year 20 of the American Republic

Citizen Minister,

The Minister for Foreign Relations had led me to hope for a definitive response from your department on the subject of the request I made to the government for its authorization to send the sum of 120,000 dollars to Holland in the service of the United States of America, a sum I received here as reimbursement for a similar sum that the said States had advanced to your representative in America. There is still a most urgent need for the funds to be conveyed, and so it would be a great service to my government if yours could make arrangements to authorize the shipment of the funds, or supply the means of depositing them in Holland in such a way as to meet that need. On a final note, I must point out that I would not have considered requesting this authorization were it not for the failure of the Treasury of the Republic to honor the payment of a mandate drawn on the Treasury of the States General, which has already caused a delay very prejudicial to the interests in question. When one considers that every year you need to deposit funds in America, and that equally we need to deposit funds in Holland, and that herein lies the beginnings of an arrangement that offers the double advantage of profit and security for both parties. I dare to assume, Citizen Minister, that it will be easy to reconcile the proposition that I am now submitting to you with the interests of the Republic, and that you will do me the kindness of replying as soon as possible, given that every day is precious in the current state of affairs. Accept the assurance of my respect and esteem.

FC, NN: Monroe Papers

From Thomas B Adams

The Hague 17 December 1795.

Sir

Not having been favored with a reply to the letter, which I had the honor to write you on the 4ᵗʰ current, I feel an obligation dictated by my own duty & the renewed solicitations of the Bankers of the United States at Amsterdam, to address you once more upon the subject of the remittance in Specie, which has so long & so anxiously been expected to arrive from Paris.

The Bankers are already under very considerable advances for the United States in consequence of payments made by them, for which no provision has yet arrived from the Treasury Department; & they have repeatedly assured me, that unless the proceeds of the Bill on Messᵈˢ Dallarde Swan & Cᵒ shall reach them prior to the first of January, a postponement of the payment, which will fall due at that time on behalf of the United States at Amsterdam, will be inevitable.

As it is of the first importance to the Credit & Interest of our Country, that no failure whatever should take place in the punctual discharge of her pecuniary engagements in Europe, I venture to hope, that through your strenuous exertions, some expedient will yet be adopted by which the Specie in your hands may be made to reach the Bankers at Amsterdam in sufficient season to prevent the ill consequences of a delay in payment there.

Supposing all obstructions on the part of the French Government, which have hitherto impeded the transmission of the Specie to be removed, it is impossible perhaps for a person at this distance to suggest any plan to effect it, which shall have both safety & dispatch in its favor. There is reason to believe however, that the first difficulties still exist, & that the remittance is as little likely to be made now, as it has been heretofore. In this emergency, the Bill upon Mess.ʳˢ Lubbert & Dumas of Hamburg, payable at Amsterdam, occurs as a resource provided by the Secretary of the Treasury, in default of the possibility that remittances in specie from Paris, should be made.

At what sight that Bill was drawn is unknown to me, but in case a recurrence to it would probably secure a speedier realization of means for the punctual payment at Amsterdam, than by waiting for the specie in your hands, I beg leave strongly to recommend the immediate endorsement of it to our Bankers at that place.

Persuaded that the urgency of this affair will command your unwearied attention, & that due weight will be given by you to every suggestion favorable to the interests of our Country, I have the honor to be with respectful consideration Sir your very humb. & ob. serv.ᵗ

Thomas B Adams

RC, DLC: Monroe Papers

From Samuel Bayard

London 17. Dec.ʳ 1795.

Dear Sir.

There are two important questions that I expect will ere long be agitated in the High Court of appeals for prize causes, for the decision of which the fate of an immense amount of American property rests. The first respects our right to trade from the United States to the French Colonies in time of war—the second to trade from the F. Colonies to any part of Europe—

On the first question I have little apprehension G. Britain has virtually abandoned the ground they assumed in the order of Council dated the 6 Nov.ʳ 1793. by the subsequent order & instructions of the 8 Jan.ʸ 1794—Yet having lately learn'd that pains are taking on the part of this govern.ᵗ to show that our commerce with the french Islands before the war was only occasional & dependent on the will of the Governors of the respective Islands, of consequence that our present intercourse with the Islands is a departure from the permanent system of France, & therefore, under the right which G. Britain has lately assumed of permitting neutral nations to carry on the same trade only in time of war which they were allow'd in time of peace, will subject our vessels & cargoes to confiscation as <u>adopted french property</u>: In regard to the second question I fear G. B. will be tenacious, & altho' France by a <u>general</u> & <u>permanent</u> decree of the Legislature on the 19. of Feb.ʸ 1793. opened <u>all</u> the ports to the vessels of the U. S.—yet as this decree was passed subsequent to the <u>Commencem.ᵗ</u>— of the war: that this gov.ᵗ will insist on excluding our citizens from the trade between the French Colonies & any part of Europe—

If you could furnish me with any authentic documents or information on either of these points either from the public offices— or in print you w.ᵈ render an essential service to a large class of our fellow citizens who have already suffer'd much & are likely to suffer now by the illegal detention of their property.

We have accounts from Philad.ᵃ as late as the 5 Nov.ʳ but they contain nothing of importance. No Sec.ʸ of State—nor Att.ʸ Gen.ˡ had been appointed to fill the vacancies occasion'd by the resignation of M.ʳ Randolph & the death of M.ʳ Bradford.

The treaty seem'd still to be reprobated on the one side,—& advocated on the other—all parties were impatient for the meeting of Congress to know how the matter would be regarded by the House of Representatives—Their debates I have no doubt will be very animated this session—I trust however they will conduct themselves with the dignity wisdom & moderation for which they have hitherto been so much distinguished—

May the happiness, the peace & welfare of their country be the aim—& the respect of their counsels. I have the honor to be with sincere respect & esteem Dr Sir Your most obed^t serv^t

Sam Bayard

RC, PHi : Society Collection

From Willink, Van Staphorst & Hubbard

Amsterdam 17 December 1795.

Sir

We have been greatly surprized and chagrined, not to have received by the last French Mail, an answer to the very pressing and important letter we wrote you the 3 Instant more especially as Mr Jacob van Staphorst informed us under date of 11 Instant from Paris that you told him you would write us that day,[1] at same time mentioning that the French Government, had negatived your request, for a permission to forward us with an Escort the $120000 Silver you had to make over to us for account of the United States: He however was not certain, whether the Refusal was solely limited to the Escort, or if it extended to prevent in any manner the exportation of the Silver.

Be this as it may Sir, our duty prescribes us, to declare to you, most seriously and decisively, that advancing as we now are, rapidly towards the first January, little or rather no hopes at all exist of our receiving any remittances from America, or other provision, timely to discharge the Interest due here the first proximo, but from the Proceeds of the Silver in your hands, wherefore we renew our entreaties and application to you, with all the Energy we are capable of, to exert your every effort to dispatch us this Silver by express, immediately and without any delay. And if not allowable with an escort, to have it accompanied by the consul of the United States, or some other Person of confidence as far as Antwerp.

Should this Silver reach us prior to the first of January, we will on the day it falls due, discharge the January Interest. But if its arrival here be protracted after that period, we feel ourselves not in the least responsible for the effects and consequences of that tarnish that will result to the honor, credit, and Interest of the United States in Europe, solely and exclusively from the Failure of the mission entrusted to you by the Treasury of the United States, to supply us with the aforesaid Silver, to face the Engagements of your country in Holland.

Entreating you once more, to ponder well upon the extreme importance for the United States of your most vigorous and active Efforts, to preserve unsullied her hitherto unblemished Credit, we are with great Regard and Esteem.

Copy, MHi: Adams Family Papers: Letters Received

1. The letter of 3 December 1795 to JM has not been located, nor has any response written by JM. JM did write to Thomas B. Adams on the subject of the loan payment on 11 December 1795 (above).

To Charles Delacroix

[19 December 1795]

The bearer   Eldrid is a person who was arrested sometime since at Marseilles upon some charge exhibited agnst him with the com: of p: safety, & in consequence is bro⹁ to Paris detained in prison for several months & finally discharged by an arrete of the com: wʰ will be shewn you.

He had obtained my passport upon authentic documents, but being advised afterwards that he had left America before our revolution & of course ought not strictly to be considered as a citizen, I woᵈ not interfere in his behalf as an American, but at length deemed it my duty as he had my passport so far to call the attention of the govᵗ to him as to demand his trial & discharge in case he were innocent leaving it with them to dispose of him afterwards permitting him to remain or ordering him out as they thought fit.

Since his discharge however he has produc'd me the necessary documents to prove that in strict propriety he is entitled to my passport, & of course it becomes my duty to grant it. It appears likewise that he is engaged in some contracts with the govᵗ whereby it is presumed he may be useful. But as he is a person who was suspected by the govᵗ & discharged with an order to depart the country, altho' that order might be so drawn because I had not claimed him as a citizen I have thought proper to withhold my passport untill I communicated the above to you, that you might know it was not granted in case I granted it otherwise than upon mature consideration & an irresistible claim, & was not intended if granted to silence any well founded suspicion against him or protect him here agnst the wishes of the govᵗ.

Dft, PHi: Gratz Collection

There are two incomplete variants of this letter in French and one incomplete copy in English in DLC: FCP—France.

This draft is undated. The date is obtained from a copy of the letter in DLC: FCP—France.

From James Madison

Philadᵃ Decʳ 20. 1795.

Dear Sir

The last of your favors come to hand bears date Sepʳ 8. 1795, of which a duplicate has also been received. The others which it may be proper to acknowledge or reacknowledge, are of Novʳ 30ᵗʰ 1794. which was opened at Halifax, & forwarded to me in that state.—Decʳ 18, 1794. covering a copy of one of same date to Mʳ *Randolph.*—Febʸ 18. 1795. covering a copy of one of Febʸ 12. to the same.—Febʸ 25. covering a duplicate of ditto.—June 13. inclosing a copy of a letter of May 4. from Mʳ *Short.*—June 3-28-30. July 26. covering the correspondence with *Jay*—and August 15.[1]—As I cannot now give minute answers to each of these letters, & the necessity of them as to most has been superseded, I shall proceed to the object most immediately interesting to you, towit the posture of things here resulting from the embassy of Mʳ Jay. The Treaty concluded by him did not arrive till a few days after the 3ᵈ of March which put an end to the last Session of Congˢ. According to a previous notification to the Senators that branch assembled on the 28ᵗʰ of June, the contents of the Treaty being in the mean time impenetrably concealed. I understand that it was even witheld from the Secretaries at war & the Treasury, that is Pickering & Wolcot. The Senate after a few week's consultation, ratified the Treaty as you have seen. The injunction of secresy was then dissolved, by a full House, and quickly after restored sub modo, in a thin one. Mr Mason disregarding the latter vote sent the Treaty to the press, from whence it flew with an electric velocity to every part of the Union. The first impression was universally & simultaneously against it. Even the mercantile body, with an exception of Foreigners & demi-Americans, joined in the general condemnation. Addresses to the P. ag^st his ratification, swarmed from all quarters, and without a possibility of preconcert, or party influence. In short it appeared for a while that the latent party in favor of the Treaty, were struck dumb by the voice of the nation. At length however, doubts began to be thrown out in New York, whether the Treaty was as bad as was represented. The Chamber of commerce proceeded to an address to the P. in which they hinted at war as the tendency of rejecting of the Treaty, but rested the decision with the Constituted authorities. The Boston Chamber of Commerce followed the example, as did a few inland villages.[2] For all the details on this subject I refer to the Gazettes which I presume you continue to receive from the Department of State. It appears that the struggle in the public mind was anxiously contemplated by the President, who had bound himself first not to disclose the Treaty till it should be submitted to the Senate, and in the next place, not to refuse his sanction if it should receive that of the Senate. On the receipt here, however of the predatory orders renewed by G. B, the President as we gather from M^r R's pamphlet[3] was advised not to ratify the Treaty, unless they should be revoked and adhered to this resolution, from the adjournment of the Senate about the last of June till the middle of August. At the latter epoch Mr Fauchet's intercepted letter became known to him, and as no other circumstance on which a conjecture can be founded has been hinted to the public, his change of opinion, has been referred to some impression made by that letter, or by comments upon it; altho' it cannot easily be explained how the merits of the Treaty, or the demerits of the provision-order could be affected by the one or the other. As soon as it was known that the P. had yielded his ratification, the *British party* were *reinforced* by *those who bowed to* the *name of constituted authorities* and *those who are implicitly devoted to the president*. The principal *merchants of Philadelphia* with *others amounting to about four hundred* took the *lead in an address of approbation*.[4] There is good reason to believe that *many subscriptions* were *obtained by the banks whose directors solicited them* and *by the influence of British capitalists*. In *Baltimore Charlestown* & the *other commercial towns* except *Philadelphia New York and Boston* no similar *proceeding has been attainable*. *Acquiescence has been* inculcated with *more success* by *exaggerated pictures of the public prosperity* an *appeal to the popular feeling for the president* and *the bugbear of war*. Still *however there is* little *doubt that the real sentiment of the mass of the community is hostile to the treaty*. How *far it may prove* impreg-*nable* must be left *to events*. A good deal will *depend on the result of the session* & more than *ought on external contingencies*. You will see how the Session opened, in the President's Speech & the answer to it. That you may judge the better on the subject, I add in the margin of the latter, the clause expunged as not true in itself; and as squinting too favorably at the Treaty. This is the only form in which the pulse of the House has been felt. It is *pretty certain that a majority disapprove the treaty* but it is not *yet possible to ascertain their ultimate object* as *matters noware*. The *speech of the president* was *well adapted to his* view. The *answer* was from a *committee consisting of myself Sedgwick & Seagrove* in the first *instance* with the addition of *two other members* on *the recommitment*. In the first *committee my two colleagues* were *of the treaty party*. And in the *second there was a* willingness to *say all* that *truth would permit*. This explanation will assist you in comprehending the transaction.[5]—Since the *answer passed* & was *presented nothing* has been said or *done in relation to the treaty*. It is much to be *feared that the majority against the treaty* will be *broken to pieces* by *lesser & collateral differences*. Some *will say it is too soon to take up the* subject *before it is officially presented in its finished form*: others *will then say it is too late*. The opportunity of *declaring the sense of the House* in the *answer to the speech* was *sacrificed to the* opinion of *some from whom more decision* was expected than will be *experienced*, towards an *immediate consideration of the subject by itself*. The truest *policy seems to be to take up the business as soon as a majority* can be *ascertained but not to risk that* even *on a preliminary question*. What the *real state of opinions is is* now *under enquiry. I am* not *sanguine* as to *the result.* There is a clear *majority who disapprove the treaty* but it *will dwindle* under *the influence of causes well known to* you; more *especially as the states* instead of *backing the wavering* are themselves *rather giving way. Virginia* has indeed *set a firm example* but *Maryland North Carolina* & *New Hampshire* have *counteracted it* & *New York* will soon *follow with some strong proceeding* on *the same side.*[6]

I am glad to find by *your letters that France notwithstanding the late treaty* continues *to be friendly.* A magnanimous conduct will *conduce to her interest as well as ours.* It must *ultimately baffle the* in*sidious projects* for *bartering our honour* and our *trade to British pride* & *British monopoly.* The *fifteenth article of the treaty* is evidently meant to *put Britain* [on] *a better foot than France* & *prevent a* further *treaty with the latter* since it secures to *Britain gratuitously all privileges* that *may be granted to others for an equivalent* and of *course obliges France* at *her sole expence to include the* interest of *Britain in her future treaties with us.* But if the *treaty should take effect* this *abominable part* will be of *short duration* and in the mean time, something may perhaps *be done toward disconcerting the mischief in some degree.* You will *observe a navigation act is* always *in our power.* The *article relating to the Misssissippi* being *permanent* may be *more embarrassing;* yet possibly not *without some antidote for its poison.* I intended to go on in Cypher, but the tediousness obliges me to conclude the present letter, in order to seize a conveyance just known to me—Mʳ R's pamphlet is just out. Mʳ Tazewell will send that & several other things collected for you, by this conveyance—Pickering is Secretary of State—Chˢ Lee Attorney Genˡ—no Secʸ at War—The Senate have negatived Rutledge as chief Justice—Mʳ Jones keeps you informed of your private affairs. He & Mʳ Jefferson are well. I have just recᵈ your two favors of Octʳ 23 & 24, with the accompaniments, by Mʳ Murray. The articles have probably not arrived in the same ship—as Mʳ Yard has no information from N. Y. thereon. Accept from Mˢ M. & myself ten thousand thanks for your & Mˢ Monroe's goodness—which will, as general[ly] happens probably draw more trouble on you. Mʳ Yard & Mˢ Y. well. Your friends at N. Y. so too.[7]

RC, DLC: Madison Papers. Words written in italics were written in code by Madison; JM deciphered part of the code, writing the decoded text interlineally. There is an uncoded copy of this letter in DLC: Madison Papers.

1. JM to Madison, 30 November and 18 December 1795; 25 February, 13, 28 and 30 June, 26 July, and 8 September 1795; JM to Edmund Randolph, 18 December 1794; William Short to JM, 4 May 1795, all above. For the letter of 3 June 1795, see JM to Madison, 22 August 1795, above. The letter of August 15 is probably JM to Madison, 5 August 1795, above.

2. The address of the New York Chamber of Commerce to President Washington, dated 23 July 1795, and the proceedings of the 11 August 1795 meeting of the Boston Chamber of Commerce, both expressing support for the treaty, are in DLC: Washington Papers: Letterbooks.

3. Edmund Randolph's *A Vindication of Edmund Randolph's Resignation* was published in Philadelphia in December 1795. It is summarized in John J. Reardon, *Edmund Randolph*, 322-332.

4. The address of the merchants of Philadelphia to President Washington of 18 August 1795 supporting the treaty is in DLC: Washington Papers: Letterbooks.

5. The House of Representatives appointed Madison chair of a committee to draft a response to Washington's annual message of 8 December 1795. The other members of the committee were Theodore Sedgwick of Massachusetts and Samuel Sitgreaves of Pennsylvania. The text of the address, along with emendations and deletions, is in *Madison Papers*, 16: 164-167.

6. The Virginia General Assembly passed a series of resolutions in December 1795 proposing several constitutional amendments, including one that would give the House of Representatives a voice in ratifying treaties. Republicans hoped that other states would enact similar resolutions, but only South Carolina, Kentucky, and Georgia did so (Jerald Combs, *The Jay Treaty*, 172).

7. JM's friends in New York were the Kortrights.

From Guillaume-Charles Faipoult

Paris, le 30 frimaire an 4ᵉ de la République Française, une et indivisible.
[21 December 1795]

Citoyen Ministre,

Je me Suis occuppé des moyens de satisfaire a la demande que vous avez formée le 23 de ce mois relativement à l'envoi en Hollande des Cent vingt Mille Dollars destinés au service des etats unis. L'exportation de ces Valeurs métalliques ne peut être authorisée, mais Votre objet n'en sera pas moins parfaitement rempli, on Vous fournira ces traites, sur les maisons de Commerce les plus connues et en Vous donnant d'ailleurs toutes les assurances nécessaires sur la bonté de ces Traites et la certitude de leur payement. j'informe en même tems la trésorerie de cette mesure pour qu'elle fasse a cet égard toutes les dispositions Convenables.

Le Ministre des Finances
faipoult

Editors' Translation

Paris, 30 Frimaire, year 4 of the French Republic, one and indivisible.
[21 December 1795]

Citizen Minister,

I have examined the means of satisfying your request of the 23rd of this month to send the one hundred twenty thousand dollars to Holland in the service of the United States. The exportation of this metallic coin cannot be authorized, but your aims will nevertheless be fully met. We will furnish you with drafts against the most well known firms and give you besides every assurance of the trustworthiness of these drafts and the guarantee that they will be honored. I will at the same time inform the treasury of these measures so that it can make all necessary arrangements in this regard.

Minister of Finance
Faipoult

RC, NN : Monroe Papers

Following the burglary at the American consulate in November, JM and Skipwith moved the silver to the French treasury for safekeeping. Once the French had possession of the silver they were reluctant to release it and proposed instead that the United States make the payment using bills of exchange drawn on the French government (Jacob Van Staphorst to JM, 25 December 1797, NN : Monroe Papers).

To Timothy Pickering

Paris December 22ⁿᵈ 1795.

Sir,

Since my last I was favoured with yours of the 9th of October with a quadruplicate of that of the 23d of September; of which latter the original and triplicate were before acknowledged.[1]

Since my last too I have received a note from the minister of foreign affairs complaining of the conduct of Mr Parish our Consul at Hamburg in granting passports for France to British subjects, equipping the emigrants, and acting in all cases as the English agent, a copy of which note and of my reply are herewith forwarded you.[2] I hear also that his conduct was more reprehensible than is stated by the minister, for that he not only equiped the emigrants but did it in American bottoms with a view of protecting them under our flag. In calling your attention to this subject permit me to add that two American citizens Benjamin Jarvis and Thomas Randall both of New York, the former a respectable merchant as has been represented to me and the latter known to the President as captain of artillery in the late war and lately as Vice-Consul at Canton in China,[3] have requested me to communicate to you their wish to obtain appointments in the consulate in any of the respectable ports of France, or other European ports connected with the trade of France, and that I have reason to believe they would either of them be happy to accept the appointment in question. In case M[r] Parish is removed permit me further to suggest the propriety of giving to his successor two commissions, one for Hamburg the other for Altona, in the neighbourhood of Hamburg, but under the jurisdiction of Denmark: much business is done at Altona, on account of the greater freedom of its trade, for Hamburg though in some respects a free and independent city yet in others it feels the influence of the Emperor, and is therefore a less eligible port for mercantile transactions and especially those connected with France.

I sent you with my last a report of M[r] Skipwith upon the cases submitted to his care for adjustment with this government,[4] and shall continue to give him all the aid in my power in those cases which re-main unsettled and apprize you regularly of the progress. To that of Mr Gerrard due attention shall certainly be paid.[5]

At present no symptoms of an approaching peace are to be seen, unless indeed the most vigorous preparations for a continuance of war be deemed such, and which sometimes happens. The Directoire has called on the Legislature for a supply of 600 millions in specie and which was granted immediately, by a law which proposes raising it in the form of a loan, of which I send you a copy. The greatest possible exertions are making by that body, and which seem to be supported by the legislature, in putting the armies, the fleets and the interior into the best possible order: and so far as I can judge from appearances these exertions seem to produce the effects that are desired from them; for to those who are friendly to the revolution they give confidence, and from those who are not they command respect. 'Tis said that Pichegru and Jourdan have lately gained several important advantages over the Austrians, in actions which though not general were nearly so, and that in the result they have resumed their station before Mayence. The former part of this report is I believe to be depended on; the latter wants confirmation. In Italy the troops of this republic continue to reap new successes, in which quarter indeed since the victory mentioned in my last they have met with but little opposition.

Latterly the views of Prussia have become more doubtful than they were before. The conduct of Prince Hohenloe who commanded the Prussian troops at Francfort in the neighbourhood of the French and Austrian armies during the retreat of the former, and who were stationed there to preserve the line of neutrality, in favour of Prussia, 'tis said, could scarcely be deemed neutral.[6] For the civilities which were shewn by him to the Austrians upon that occasion, 'tis also said he has been rewarded since by some complimentary attention from the Emperor. The Dutch appear apprehensive that the King of Prussia will seize a suitable opportunity, if any offers, to favour the restoration of the Stadholder, and 'tis possible the conduct of the Prince Hohenloe above referred to may have increased that suspicion, by giving at least an insight into what might be the views of the Prussian cabinet, in case the retreat had continued, or any great reverse of fortune should hereafter befall the French arms. 'Tis certain however that moments of difficulty are always moments of great jealousy, and that sometimes upon such occasions suspicion is thrown upon those who do not deserve it.

The Count Carletti late Envoy &c from Tuscany left Paris for home 5 or 6 days since. He had refused going 'till he had heard from the Grand Duke, and remained notwithstanding the reiterated orders of the Directoire. Finally however he was ordered to depart in 24 hours (this was not done before as stated in my last) with intimation that force would be used to compel him in case he did not. He still held out however the flag of defiance. The 24 hours expired at which moment a commissary with a carriage &c from the government waited to receive his orders for departure, or in other words to take the Count by force and conduct him safe beyond the bounds of the Republic, and which was accordingly done. The diplomatic corps was summoned by a member either averse to this peremptory mode of proceeding, or friendly to the Count, to interfere with the Directoire in his behalf: but several of the members of that corps were of opinion that although sometimes a demand is made, on the government of a minister who gives offence, to recal him, yet there is no obligation on the goverment offended, by the law of nations to take that course; but that it may take any other, and even upon slight occasions, to rid itself of him, more prompt and summary, if it thinks fit, and in consequence no step was taken by the diplomatic corps upon the subject.

I inclose you also a note from the minister of foreign affairs complaining of the seizure and condemnation of the Corvette Cassius, which he says is in violation of the treaties between the two Republics, and to which I replied that I would present the subject to your view and doubted not I should be enabled to give a satisfactory answer thereon.[7] With sentiments of respect and esteem, I have the honour to be, Sir, your very obedient servant

Ja⁵ Monroe.

Copy, DNA: RG 59: Dispatches from France

1. The clerk who copied this letter appears to have made a mistake in writing "23ᵈ of September," for no such letter has been located. In his letter to Pickering of 6 December 1795 (above), JM acknowledged the receipt of the "originals and triplicates of your favours of the 12ᵗʰ and 14ᵗʰ of September last." It was presumably to one of these letters that JM referred.

2. Charles Delacroix to JM, 3 December 1795, and JM to Delacroix, 9 December 1795, above.

3. Thomas Randall served as a captain during the Revolutionary War and then embarked a career as a merchant in New York. He entered the China trade and made three voyages to Asia between 1784 and 1790. He was appointed vice consul for Canton in 1786, but this was only a nominal position, for he spent very little time in China (*Hamilton Papers*, 9: 38-55; 20: 70-71).

4. Fulwar Skipwith's report, enclosed in JM to Pickering, 6 December 1795 (above) could not be located.

5. Philadelphia merchant Stephen Girard wrote to JM on 7 October 1795 asking JM's assistance with a claim against France for a seized ship and cargo (*Catalogue of Monroe's Papers*, 1: 51).

6. Prince Hohenlohe-Ingelfingen commanded the Prussian troops at Frankfort. That city was supposed to be neutral, but a number of its troops were still serving with the Austrians. French General Jourdan demanded that Hohenlohe-Ingelfigen evacuate the city or suffer attack. The prince defied the French demand, but abandoned Frankfort on 24 October 1795 when he received orders to move his troops to the Polish frontier (Sydney Seymour Biro, *The German Policy of Revolutionary France*, 1: 397-399).

7. Delacroix to JM, 14 December 1795, above. A copy of JM's reply, dated 19 December 1795, is enclosed in JM to Pickering, 22 December 1795, DNA: RG 59: Dispatches from France.

From Charles Delacroix

Paris le 2 Nivose an 4<u>eme</u> de la R^e F. [23 December 1796]

Citoyen Ministre,

J'ai reçu la lettre que vous m'avez fait l'honneur de m'adresser relativement au nommé Thomas Eldred. Ce citoyen étant porteur d'un passeport signé de vous est parfaitement en sureté. Vous ne donnez point assez au hasard votre signature pour qu'elle devienne une protection insuffisante. Je n'ai au surplus aucune raison de suspecter le Citoyen Eldred et je m'empresserai de légaliser votre signature lorsqu'il se presentera. Agréez l'assurance de mon sincere attachment.

Ch. Delacroix

Editors' Translation

Paris 2 Nivose Year 4 of the French Republic [23 December 1795]

Citizen Minister,

I have received the letter with which you have honored me relating to the said Thomas Eldred.[1] Since this Citizen is a bearer of a passport signed by you, he is perfectly safe. You do not hazard to give out your signature arbitrarily, so it is a sufficient protection. In addition, I have no reason to suspect Citizen Eldred, and I will eagerly legitimize your signature when he presents himself. Please accept the assurance of my sincere affection.

Ch. Delacroix

Copy, DLC: FCP—France

1. JM to Delacroix, 19 December 1795, above.

From Aaron Burr

Philad^a 24th Decr 95

My dear Sir,

The last which I have received from you is the long one of the 18th June[1]—Happening, when it arrived at New-York to be on a Tour eastward, I had first the pleasure to read the political part of it in the Gazettes, and made, and heard, many Eulogiums upon it before I knew the Author—It is the best and most satisfactory summary we have had but the politicks of France require a new summary for Every Month—

Congress (the H. of R. I mean) are proceeding in the usual rotine of business with more temper and Calmness than was expected—How long the appearance of Moderation will continue cannot be conjectured—[2]

Your attentions to young Gelston have gratified & obliged me extremely—His father & friends are full of Gratitude to you; which they express in warm terms as often as we meet—

Some late discoveries respecting the Conduct of J. K. give me hopes of a favorable issue to those dark & mysterious transactions—Mr Knox told me that he should write you fully on that Matter—

By the Medusa I sent you Bache's paper to the 1 June—I shall endeavor herewith to send a Continuance down to this Day[3] & a parcel of others—also Randolp's Vindication—Accept the assurances of my best Wishes, & of my warmest attachment & Esteem

A. B.

RC, DLC: Monroe Papers

1. This is the same letter that JM sent to John Beckley on 23 June 1795 (above).

2. JM was involved in a dispute with John Kortright regarding the settlement of the estate of Lawrence Kortright. A letter from Thomas Knox to JM written at this time on the subject has not been located. Knox did write to James Madison on 12 December 1795 asking if JM had left any papers with Madison relating to the business (*Madison Papers*, 16: 162-163).

3. The (Philadelphia) *Aurora*.

From Willink, Van Staphorst & Hubbard

Amsterdam 24 December 1795

Sir

Your letter of the 11 Instant[1] details to us the pains you have taken, to obtain permission to send us the Silver for the Bill on Dallarde Swan & C° and under date of the 18 ditto Mr. Jacob van Staphorst informs us, the French Government had totally refused your request for leave to export it.

This is a very severe disappointment to us and could not have been expected after you informed us, we might with all safety assume any engagements on the strength of this money reaching us which induced our supplying the means to discharge the Interest due the First Instant by the United States in Antwerp.

You suggest the propriety, of our drawing upon you for the Amount of the aforegoing object. But this Sir, is impossible, no persons having at present to remit monies to France, at least for any sums of consequence, while on the contrary, the Government of that Country has immense payments to provide for both in this city and Hamburgh.

We hope and trust your thorough convictions of the necessity of Our being speedily in the possession of the Avails of the Silver will have enabled you to devise some secure good mode to have it reach us. An intelligence We are anxiously soliciting to receive from you.

We must confess to you Sir, that we are greatly surprised the French Government, should have refused to you the permission to export a small quantity of Silver to Holland to support the hitherto unblemished honor and credit of the United States more especially as you will not have failed to represent that the United States had not only paid up all the arrears of the debt due by them to France, but had likewise advanced large sums for the maintenance of the Colonies of that country, and even adopted a mode to anticipate many years the payment of the residue of that debt, to the great ease and benefit of the French Government; And if any thing was necessary to have strengthened this plea it might have been adduced, that the Bill of $120,000 was drawn by Ja[s] Swan, the person who had been employed by the French Government to negotiate and bring about the discharge by anticipation in Specie Dollars of the whole of the debt due by the United States to France, and most probably was one of the Links to the chain of operations attending that mutation.

Quite the reverse has been the conduct of the British Government to the United States. For on the first application of the <u>Chargé des affaires</u> at London for permission to remit to Holland for use of the Treasury of the United States more than Four times the value of the Bill on Dallarde Swan & Cº. A license allowing Same was unhesitatingly issued, authorizing it to be effected in Bills of Exchange, Silver, Gold, or in any other manner the Agents of the United Sates might prefer.

We are compelled to believe the refusal of the French Government to your application can but have proceeded from very cogent and imperious reasons; and consequently that its good disposition towards your Country, will induce it to do all in its power, to mitigate as it cannot entirely remedy the disappointment the United States experience, by having such a large sum of money idly locked up in your hands.

To render operative then, this goodwill, in case you should not already have adopted means to remit us the money, we recommend you to ask of the French Government, to furnish you Bills on this Republic for its amount accompanied with a strong and energetic injunction to its Agents or Ministers here, to collect the discharge of such Bills within a few days and preferently to any other object whatever.

Having however experienced that their Bills have not been promptly honored, We by all means advise you to stipulate, that the money shall remain in your hands until you will be advised by us of the discharge of the French drafts, immediately after which you will pay it, into the French Treasury, where We presume it can but be highly agreeable.

As the object and event of such a transaction would be to further the views and interests of the United States at same time the French Treasury would be reinforced by a seasonable large supply of Silver, We flatter ourselves, in case all other means shall have been tried, and proved inefficacious, that this will at last put us in possession of the property of the United States. Should this likewise miscarry the United States must continue to pay an heavy Interest on our advances, and probably be exposed to suffer its Engagements to be dishonored, while they have $120,000. Specie lying without any use or utility in your hands either to the Government of the United States or to the French Government.

Having thus discharged our duty on this occasion, We refer the matter entirely to your future direction.

Inclosed you have a letter from Mr. Pinckney Minister of the United States to the Court of Great Britain, which in his absence He has desired us to request you to open.

This Gentleman having occasion for £300. We beg of you to supply him with that Sum against his draft on us in Florins: which you will please to remit us in dimunitions of the money you have in your hands, to be forwarded to us. We are with great regard and esteem Sir Your m. ob. hb. Servants

Wilhem vanwillink
N. B. Van Staphorst & Hubbard

RC, NN: Monroe Papers

1. JM's letter to Willinck, Van Staphorst & Hubbard of 11 December 1795 has not been located.

From Henry Tazewell

Philadelphia 26. Dec[r] 1795.

My dear Sir

I have had the pleasure this morning to receive your favour, in answer to my Letter by M[r] Fauchet—Before I left Virginia, I rec[d] your former, but more lengthy communication. I now return you my thanks for both—[1]

From M[r] Fauchet you will have learned, that about the time of his leaving America, a rupture happened, between E. R.[2] & the Pres[t]. If you have rec[d] a Letter from J. Beckley written last Fall,[3] you now understand its origin—Its progress, and its present state the enclosed pamphlet will detail to you—E. R. has retired to Richmond in Virginia & is now there engaged in the practice of the Law.—The effects of his appeal to the people are not yet to be perceived—but you know his political cast not to be of that kind which promises a successful opposition to the influence which assails him. Pickering has succeeded him in the office of Secretary of State, after it was refused by P. Henry of Virginia, & others—

One of the enclosed news papers will shew you the president's communications to both Houses of Congress at the opening of the present Session. The flattering picture which he presents of our affairs, has by some been considered as a prelude to his resignation. I know not if the fact be so—Yet the continued depredations committed by G[t] B. on our Commerce, and the impudent unwarrantable impressment of our Seamen, throws a gloom over our prospects, which when added to the national degradation exhibited by M[r] Jay's Treaty presents deformities in our political situation to the Eyes of others, which the Pres[t] does not appear to have seen. Very general answers have been returned by both Houses to his communications—& therefore no precise conclusions can be drawn from either, as to the temper of the present Congress.

The Treaty with England is but slightly touched—Great address has been constantly used to keep the president's personal weight so interwoven with the questions begotten by this Treaty, as to render their discussion almost impossible, without that improper influence: Yet the subject must unavoidably soon undergo a discussion which will be pursued without yielding to any personal influences. I among others, am sorry that the president has thrown himself into such a situation. He has excited thereby much abuse in the public papers ag[t] himself, and must yet witness many disagreeable remarks applicable singly to himself from those who wish him as well as any persons in the U States—

Some of the inclosed papers will shew you the ground upon which the Treaty has been considered in Virginia—The Memorial proposed for the Virginia Legislature will particulary mark out to your view a summary of the most material objections to that degrading & injurious act. They will also inform you of the proceedings of the Virginia Legislature on that subject.[4] You may as certainly rely on the fact, that the general voice of the people of the U States is ag[t] this Compact, as you can upon any such suggestion not reduced to certainty by positive proof. To the Southward, the people are firm & almost unanimous—To the Northward the Treaty is equally condemned but an apprehension least this incident in our political career should check the growth of Executive power by the interference of the people, & so blast the wicked hopes of some who have begotten & are pursuing projects of which you are well apprized; has been so used, as to slacken the hatred to the Treaty in that quarter, but the Cloud is gathering only to make the explosion more terrible.

We anxiously expect the arrival of some intelligence from France upon the subject of this Treaty. We hope, but it is more than we have a right to expect, that the good understanding between the two Republics may not be impaired by this circumstance: We have extended towards that nation, evil for good—We hope they are better [Chris]tians & will give us good for Evil. The solicitude of the people for the success and prosperity [of] the French Republic, notwithstanding the efforts of a paper & an aristocratic faction to the contrary; is sincere & very powerful. Perhaps by looking on the present movements in America with calmness, forbearance, & temper, all may yet be well. Our administration will change soon. At no one period of the French revolution has my solicitude been greater to know the certain state of their affairs than the present. If the new Constitution can get fairly into operation, and the same republican spirit should be seen to influence their Conduct of yᵉ Governors which began & has continued the Revolution. France must soon enjoy a state of peace, & the rest of Europe must begin to profit by their example.

Internally, the affairs of the U States continue to be clouded by the acts of speculation—The paper System, begotten by avarice & ambition has afforded food for Speculation in so many various shapes, as to have reared it into a threatening Monster. The love of Country is supplanted in its votaries by the love of Gain. That Gain—with the consequence which it brings to its possessors in every corrupt political State, cannot be preserved agᵗ the just indignation of the injured people, without making the hands of yᵉ Government strong enough to resist the Complaints of those who are defrauded—Hence therefore our affairs have arrived as a crisis that is truly serious—Wealth obtained by Fraud is seeking to strengthen the hands of yᵉ Government by means which destroy at once the vital principle of free Governments, in order to secure itself, & to ensure to these defrauders a political importance which they could not derive from any other source—On the other hand, the virtuous lovers of their Country, are striving to prevent these projects, & still to preserve our Republic in its primitive purity. In proportion as a necessity is increased for destroying the means, by which this wicked speculation is conducted, the contest between the parties becomes more serious—It will terminate as it should do, so soon as the people are clearly possessed of the nature of the controversy.

It is found extremely difficult to procure proper characters to fill the confidential departments of yᵉ Government—After several overtures to others which were unsuccessful—Chˢ Lee of Virgᵃ has been appointed Attʸ Genˡ in the place of Bradford who died last Fall. The war department has not a Head and great embarassments occur in procuring one. How they will terminate I cannot tell. When Mʳ Jay was appointed Govʳ of New York—Jnᵒ Rutledge of S. C. succeeded by the President's appointmᵗ in yᵉ recess of the Senate to the office of Chief Justice—After his appointmᵗ his Sentiments which were given in a public meeting at Chˢ Town agᵗ the Treaty became known—When the Senate met the other day, the confirmation of his appointment was refused, & now the office is vacant. This incident cannot fail to add to the embarassments experienced by the Executive in filling the high offices of yᵉ Government.

As soon as I recover from a severe Cold which now afflicts me, I will write you more at large, I will therefore at the present add nothing more than an assurance of the high esteem with which I am yours

H. Tazewell.

Pray let me hear from you—Could my sonˢ get any employmᵗ with you that would bear his expenses a year or two?

RC, NN: Monroe Papers

1. Tazewell to JM, 27 June 1795. JM's response, sent via Joseph Fenwick (Fenwick to JM, 31 August 1795, above), has not been located. JM's "former" letter could not be identified.

2. Edmund Randolph.

3. John Beckley to JM, 23 September 1795, above.

4. A memorial to the Virginia General Assembly (written anonymously by James Madison) criticizing the Jay Treaty was published in the Virginia newspapers in October and November 1795 (*Madison Papers*, 16: 62-77).

5. Littleton Waller Tazewell (1774-1860) graduated from the College of William and Mary in 1791 and began the practice of law in 1796. He served several terms in the Virginia House of Delegates, was a member of Congress 1800-1801, and a U. S. Senator 1824-1832. He was governor of Virginia 1834-1836 (*ANB*).

To Thomas B. Adams

Paris Dec[r] 28th 1795

Sir

I was lately honored with your's of the 17. of Dec[r] upon the subject of the 120.000. Dolr[s], in my hands destined for our Bankers at Amsterdam. Mine to a preceding one of your's[1] stated, that an escort to conduct the money was refused—& after this, permission to export it likewise was. There remained of course no other alternative than to send it forward by Bills, & in that case either by those of the Gov[t] or individuals, the former of which I have preferr[d] as most sure, being positively assured by the Minister of Finance they shall be paid. Unhappily the term of three months is allotted for the delay upon the payment by these Bills, but a shorter term co[d] not be had in those of individuals, so that nothing better could be done.

I sho[d] have forwarded the Bill upon the House at Hamburg had I not been advised in the most satisfactory manner it wo[d] not be paid; that in truth bills on that House to a great am[t] were all ready protested, it therefore seemed best to take the money here and forward it by such opportunity or means as might occur. The other course was free from trouble to me, but it appear[d] less likely to produce the object desired by the United States.

I hope the Bankers will be bale to prevent any ill effect from this delay & especially of a sum comparatively so unimportant; they have merited well of the United States heretofore, & I trust their efforts will not be diminished or less productive than they were, when our embarrassments were much greater than they now are. With great respect &[ca]

Copy, CtHi: Oliver Wolcott Manuscripts

1. Adams to JM, 4 December 1795 and JM to Adams, 11 December 1795, above.

From Thomas B. Adams

The Hague 29 December 1795

Sir.

The letter you did me the honor to write me on the 11th Inst[t] came to hand on the 18th and Immediately addressed the Bankers at Amsterdam upon the subject of the proposal therein contained relative to the drawing upon you for the proceeds of the Bill upon Messrs Dallande Swan & C[s].

Their answer of the 25 ins[t] informs me simply that by the last Post, they acquainted you of the impossibility to comply with y[r] recommendations to draw.[1]

The Gentlemen have doubtless been more explicit in their answer to you than they have to me, as to the impediments, which forbid such a measure; but I have good reason to suppose; that its impracticability depends upon the disadvantageous rate of Exchange, between Amsterdam & Paris at this time.

A Remittance arrived from America a few days since, which enables the Bankers to advertise the punctual payment at Amsterdam; it is hoped however, that the specie, will also shortly arrive from Paris. I have the honor to be &$^{\underline{ca}}$

Copy, CtHi: Oliver Wolcott Jr. Manuscripts

1. Willink, Van Staphorst & Hubbard to JM, 24 December 1795, above.

From Fulwar Skipwith

Paris 1$^{\underline{st}}$ January 1796.

Sir,

In Conformity to your instruction respecting the bullion received from the house of Dallarde Swan & C$^{\underline{o}}$ on account of the united States, I have Paid the Same into the Treasury amounting to, 12417$^{\underline{m}}$ 6$^{\underline{on}}$ 69$^{\underline{ros}}$ Silver at the Standard of 11$^{\underline{w}}$ 10$^{\underline{grain}}$; having only retained the amount of the charges as p^{r} account you have herewith, and have received bills for the amount on amsterdam;

I informed you in due time of the Robbery that was Committed at my office of 448$^{\underline{m}}$ 7$^{\underline{on}}$ 4$^{\underline{ros}}$ of the Said Silver, but Presuming as you have Suggested that our Government may wish the whole to be Placed immediately in holland, I have made up the quantity Robb'd & Paid it into the Treasury, not doubting but that the united States on your representation of the facts, will order me to be reimbursed of that Sum, & for that Purpose & take the liberty of inclosing to you the Certificate I Procured from the American Gentlemen acquainted with the transactions, & a copy of the Proces verbal that was made up on the occasion; Respectfully Sir Your mo. hum. servant

Copy, NN: Monroe Papers; filed 5 November 1795

The enclosed certificate, dated 23 November 1795 and signed by a number of Americans resident in Paris who inspected the site of the burglary, stated that by all appearances Skipwith had taken adequate precaution to secure the silver. Skipwith also enclosed a report written by Thomas François Violette (dated 5 Frimaire An 4 or 26 November 1795), the magistrate for the district in which he resided (NN: Monroe Papers, filed 5 November 1795).

To George Washington

Paris Jany 3. 179[6].[1]

Dear Sir

Your favor of the 5 of June did not reach me till a few days past or it sho^{d} have been sooner answered. I am happy now to answer it because I am able to give you details of the lady in question[2] which will be very agreeable to you. I had advanc'd her near 2000. dol$^{\underline{rs}}$ when I was advised here by Jacob Van Staphorst that you had plac'd in the hands of his brother for Madame La Fayette the sum of two thousand three hundred & ten guilders & which had never been rec^{d}. At this time she was solicitting permission to leave France with a view of visiting & partaking with her husband the fortune to which he was exposed. I had given her a certificate that her husband had lands in America[3] & that the Congress had appropriated to his use upwards of 20.000 dol$^{\underline{rs}}$ the am^{t} w^{h} was due for his services in our revolution, & upon which basis her application was founded & granted. I made known to her the fund you had appropriated for her use & which she readily & with pleasure accepted, & which served to defray the expense of her journey. She pursued her rout by Dunkerque & Hamburg to which places I gave & procured letters of recommendation, & at the former of which she was rec^{d} in the house & entertained by our consul Mr Coffyn. I assured her when she left France there was no service within my power to render her & her husband & family that I would not with pleasure render them. To count upon my utmost efforts & command them in their favor. That it was your wish & the wish of America that I sho^d do so. To consult her husband as to the mode & measure & apprize me of his opinions thereon. She departed grateful to you & our country & since which I have not heard from her. She had thoughts of visitting in person the Emperor & endeavoring to obtain the release of her husband; but whether she did or not I cannot tell. It was reported sometime since he was released, & afterwards that she was admitted with her family into the same state of confinement with him: the latter of which I believe to be true. Before she left this I became responsible in her favor for 9000^lt upon a month's notice (in specie) the object of w^h was to free a considerable estate from some encumbrance & which was effected upon my surety. as yet I have not been called on to pay it. As soon therefore as I rec^d the draft on Holland for six thousand dol^rs in her behalf I wrote her by two different routs to assure her that I had funds for her & her husbands support & upon which she might for the present draw to the am^t of £250. ster^g, & afterwards as occasion might require & to which I have rec^d no ans^r. [4]

What may be the ultimate disposition of France towards M^r La Fayette it is impossible now to say. His integrity so far as I can find remains unimpeached, & when that is the case the errors of the head are pardoned, as the passions subside. It is more than probable I may be able to serve him with those by whom he is confined, & that I may do this without injury to the U States here; acting with candour and avowing the motive, since it is impossible that motive can be otherwise than approved, especially if the step be taken when their aff^rs are in great prosperity. For this however I shall be happy to have y^r approbation, since if I do any thing with the Emperor it must be done in y^r name, if not explicitly yet in a manner to make known to him the interest you take in the welfare of M^r La Fayette. Young La Fayette is I presume now under y^r auspices. [5]

Within a few days past a truce or armistice was concluded between Pichegru & Jourdan on the one side & Clairfayt & Wurmser on the other as it is said for three months: this was of course subject to approbation or rejection of the gov^ts on each side. I hear that it was rejected on the side of France, orders being sent by the Directoire to pursue the war without cessation. [6] Both armies are in the neighborhood of Mayence where the country is almost entirely devastated. In Italy the Austrians are completely routed & their whole army nearly demolished. 'Tis said that 8000. prisoners are brought to one of the French villages. Mrs Monroe desires her best respects to be presented to yourself & Mrs Washington, who we hope enjoy good health. If there is anything in which I can be servicable to you here, any article of curiosity or taste you wish to possess & which can be procured, I beg of you to make it known to me that I may procure it for you. With great & sincere respect and esteem I am, Dear Sir your most ob^t & very humble Servant

Ja^s Monroe

PS. There are many articles of tapestry the most beautiful that can be conceived, & w^h are intended for the walls of rooms, for chair bottoms &ca, some of which perhaps wo^d be acceptible to the com^rs of the fœderal town, & which if permitted by you or them I wo^d immediately procure & forward. [7]

RC, DLC: Washington Papers

1. JM misdated this letter 1795.

2. Adrienne Lafayette.

3. Certification of Land Granted to Lafayette, 25 July 1795, ViFreJM.

4. JM to Adrienne Lafayette, 16 November 1795, above.

5. Following her release from prison, Adrienne Lafayette visited JM and sought his assistance in making arrangements for her son, George Washington Lafayette, to get to America. JM obtained a passport for him, under the name George Motier, and he left shortly afterwards. Lafayette arrived in Boston in September 1795 and notified George Washington of his arrival. This presented a quandary for the president: he very much wanted to take the son of his old friend into his family, but he was worried about the political implications of doing so, since the Marquis de Lafayette had been declared an enemy to France. Young Lafayette resided in New York until April 1796 when Washington determined that there would be no liability in having the young man as a member of his household (Harlow G. Unger, *Lafayette*, 107, 307; James T. Flexner, *George Washington: Anguish and Farewell*, 261-264).

6. Jourdan signed an armistice on 19 December and Pichegru on 31 December 1795. Both the French and the Austrian armies were exhausted, and the armistice held until the spring (Sydney Seymour Biro, *The German Policy of Revolutionary France*, 2: 527-529).

7. The Residence Act of 16 July 1790, which provided for the establishment of a federal district on the banks of the Potomac River, created a three-member board of commissioners to supervise the development of the federal city and oversee the construction of the public buildings (Charles M. Harris, ed., *The Papers of William Thornton*, 1: xlix).

From Timothy Pickering

Department of State Jany 7. 1796.

Sir,

On the first Instant, according to a previous arrangement, the Minister of the French Republic presented to the President of the United States the colours of France. This was on Friday, and Congress did not meet again till the following Monday, when the colours were presented to the two Houses of Congress, with a message from the President and the papers mentioned in it, to wit, an address from the Committee of public safety dated the 21st of October 1794, the speech of the French Minister on presenting the colours to the President, and the President's answer; all of which copies are inclosed.[1]

After the exhibition in the House of Representatives the House passed unanimously the inclosed resolve; in pursuance of which, to make known their sentiments to the Representatives of the French people, the President has addressed a letter to the Directory of the French Republic, which you will find inclosed, and which you will take the earliest opportunity to deliver.[2]

With the resolve of the House of Representatives, the President has thought fit to communicate to the Directory the resolve of the Senate on the same subject, altho' not specially desired to do it. Thus there will be seen a concurrence of all the branches of the Government representing the people of the United States in the same affection & friendship for the French Republic.

Copies of that letter & of these resolves for your own information you will find also inclosed.[3]

In your letter of the 20th of October (the last which has been received) you say that as yet no complaints had been made against our treaty with Great Britain, nor had you heard anything from the committee on the subject, since their application relative to certain reports respecting it: yet in your postscript you express your opinion that if ratified it would excite great discontents. On this point I can only again refer you to my letter of the 25th of September,[4] in which it is demonstrated that in assenting to the terms of that treaty the United States infringe no stipulation & violate no duty towards France. And you have seen by Mr Randolph's communications last summer, that all the objections started by the French Minister were completely removed.

The treaty of peace made by General Wayne with the Indian tribes northwest of the river Ohio has been ratified by the President with the unanimous advice & consent of the Senate.[5] The Cherokees and

Creeks are also at peace with us. Such perfect tranquility on all our borders was never known since we became an independent people. But in the midst of the universal joy which this state of things excited, a few ruffians in Georgia committed some atrocious murders on about twenty creeks. This was in September. Severe retaliation is to be feared; tho' endeavours were immediately used to ward off the evil. As yet I have heard of but one family that has been struck. I have the honor to be with great respect Sir, Your Obedient Servant

Timothy Pickering.

LS, NjP. A duplicate of this letter, with slight variations, is in NhD.

1. President Washington's message to Congress, dated 4 January 1796, transmitting the letter from the Committee of Public Safety of 21 October 1795, Adet's speech, and Washington's response, dated 1 January 1796, is in *ASP: FR*, 1: 527-528.

2. House Resolution, 4 January 1796, *Journal of the House of Representatives*, 2: 397; Washington to the President of the French Directory, 7 January 1796, *Writings of Washington*, 34: 418-419.

3. Senate Resolution, 5 January 1796, *Journal of the Senate*, 2: 204; Washington to Directory, 7 January 1796, DLC: FCP—France.

4. Pickering refers to his letter to JM of 12 September 1795, above.

5. The Senate ratified the Treaty of Greenville on 22 December 1795, and Washington signed it the same day (*Territorial Papers of the United States*, 2: 525-534).

To Thomas Pinckney

Paris Jany 7. 1796.

Dear Sir

Immediately on my return I communicated to Mr P. what you requested, & was satisfied of the propriety of the precaution adopted on your part: for by several things w^h escaped him it was obvious the letter contained something of w^h you ought not to be the bearer. From what I can collect it contains some stricture or comment on Mr Jay's treaty & to w^h his name is signed to be published.[1] It is therefore in my opinion not only prudent that you send the letter back but that you sometime soon after y^r arrival confer with Johnson his book seller[2] requesting him to publish from him nothing on that subject. For altho' Mr Paines political principles are sound, & his comments upon all political subjects may be so likewise, yet I do not think that this is a suitable theatre for their publication in regard to our political transactions, especially when it is considered that he lives in my house: to which attention I thought him entitled from his services in America & especially in the present state of his health. I have intimated this to him more than once but without effect. Of the propriety of speaking to the book-seller you will judge. I only hint it for y^r consideration.

Since y^r departure we have nothing new: every thing is as when you left us. Mrs M. unites in the most affectionate wishes for yours & y^r family's welfare. I am Dear sincerely y^r friend & servt

Ja^s Monroe.

RC, NjP

1. Thomas Paine had a festering resentment towards George Washington because of what Paine perceived as Washington's unwillingness to take any action to get Paine released from prison. Paine had written a letter to Washington in February 1795 complaining of his treatment and criticizing the Jay Treaty, but JM persuaded him not to send it. Paine's resentment continued, and he began working on a longer essay on the subject. This apparently was the paper that Paine asked Pinckney to carry to

London. JM once again persuaded Paine to withhold the essay. Paine still persisted in his intention, however, and in July 1796, after he left JM's household, he sent a long public letter addressed to Washington to the United States for publication (Philip Foner, ed., *The Complete Writings of Thomas Paine*, 2: 690-723). JM was apparently unaware that Paine had a letter critical of the Jay Treaty (signed "An American") published in the (Philadelphia) *Aurora* of 2 July 1795 (*Complete Writings of Paine*, 2: 568-570).

2. Joseph Johnson (1738-1809) was a London bookseller and publisher known for his support of liberal causes. Among his better-known publications was Mary Wollstonecraft's *Vindication of the Rights of Woman*. Johnson was a sponsor of the Paine's *Rights of Man*, although he himself did not publish it (*ANB*).

From John S. Eustace[1]

Rotterdam, 10ᵗʰ January, 1796.

I have contented myself, dear Sir, since my arrival in this country, with a tribute of respectfully affectionate compliments to you and to Mʳˢ Monroe, as often as I have written to Major Mountflorence. had a single event of consequence, or a single anecdote transpired; which could have proved useful to you, in your public ministry, or capable of making you smile, amidst its laborious duties, I should not have omitted the faithful communication of either, but, (and how it happens I know not), we are not only ignorant of what passes on the Rhine (until the article of Intelligence we receive has ceased to deserve the name of news), but, at three short leagues from the seat of the provincial, and of the fœderal Governments we are even totally in the dark, <u>respecting the national politics of the day</u>! I am, however, three or four hours, every day, in a Society composed of a hundred members the first Merchants of the City, where all the news <u>they possess</u> have a free and open circulation; I dine at least five times a week with these Gentlemen, who treat me with unremitting confidence & hospitality, yet, during a residence of four months, have I constantly sought, <u>in vain</u>, for materials to compose such a letter, as might justify five minutes of intrusion: as I love this Nation—as I feel the consequence of her Independence to the political and commercial prosperity of our beloved country, I am naturally disposed to investigate the causes, which produce so censureable an apathy in all the wealthy citizens of these States; but warned by the calumny of certain public Men in France who were pleased to stile my becoming zeal in their Causes <u>Intrigue</u> <u>aristocracy</u> and even "<u>Treason</u>", I content myself with bewailing what I cannot correct. I felt the delicacy of my situation, as soon as I arrived within the hospitable walls of this charming City; yet; had determined, in case of Invasion by the Prussian or Stadholderian armies, <u>to serve as a volunteer in that of the Republic</u>: the advanced period of the Season, has alone removed my apprehensions of an <u>immediate</u> attempt; and this circumstance, united with the existence of constitutional Government in France, will hasten me to the Capital from whence I shall embark for America, as soon as I shall have obtained from the Minister of War, a confirmation of the Report of the Board of War of the Convention, and sanctioned in the Convention, by a Decree of the 26ᵗʰ September 1793 that " <u>I have rendered important services, made repeated pecuniary sacrifices, and never demerited of the Republic</u>"—for these are the express terms of the report and decree, which I had demanded of the Convention, in consequence of the tyranny of Dumouriez, and the calumnies of Marat: your uniform protection of my person and fame, against the subsequent censure of some deluded Deputies, I shall never cease to deserve, and when you shall have perused, dear Sir, the Copy of my correspondence with the French Government, and the Projects I had supplied them with (for assuring <u>increase</u> and <u>conquest</u> to their marine force and provisions to their Armies) you will not hesitate to repeat your past expressions of confidence and esteem: with this flattering testimony I shall return satisfied & well recompensed, into the private Station of a Citizen, in our beloved Country; and from this projected solitude, neither Vanity or Ambition will ever have power to withdraw me.

As a private Citizen, I shall continue a private soldier, and though we have already served, during the eight years war which assured the Independence of the United States; I shall not cease to remember with you that the Duties of a Patriot cannot close—but with his existence; and that your Services abroad supply a lesson of what there remains for me to do at home: these duties may be performed, without title or place; happily for our beloved Country, there is no lack of talent or probity; and for every Man of Education, or Travel, who may retire from public life [there are] a score of Worthies to supply the vacancy!

As to myself I really find my constitution impaired by eight hours daily study, and the constant succession of convivial & professional exercises with only four hours repose, for nearly twenty years; when we quitted together the pursuits of knowledge, for the defence of our common Liberties, I already anticipated the career of painful service in which, if I escaped its dangers, I was necessarily to persist for a number of years: General Lee had taught me to feel, that all the power of Great Britain would be employed, and perhaps exhausted, to support the tyrannic pretentions of her Sovereign; and he foresaw (as early as the alliance with France & Spain) that some European Kingdom would be republicanised after our example: he considered France, as the most likely to set this example, as really happened, from the ambition he had discovered in such of her military Nobles as served in or with, our armies; and from the acknowledged imbecility of Louis XVI in the midst of a corrupt clergy and profligate Nobility: to Spain he gave a longer period of Bondage; but he twenty times predicted that monarchy there would not live through this Century: if I owe then to my much honored & lamented Preceptor the early Knowledge I possessed of this probable Event I owe to him also any merit I may have as a patriot defender of the Rights of Mankind (for I claim no other rank) during so long a period—since without that intimate conviction, which everything he said obtained with me, I should never have hoped to realise his predictions of becoming a Colonel in America, at nineteen years of age—or a General officer in France, before I should count thirty: I have long had it on my mind, dear Sir, to sollicit an audience from you, for the communication of many circumstances important to myself, and consequently not wholly indifferent to you—since the reputation of a fellow soldier & fellow citizen must naturally interest you abroad, as a Minister, and as a Man, but your uniform kindness and Protection forbid me to do anything that might appear to aim at something more than an equal share of that becoming patronage and hospitality, which we generally enjoyed, under your auspices; or might indicate, that I considered mine as a stinted portion, when it was my duty to manifest how perfectly I was satisfied with every part of your conduct towards me. I have a favor to ask you, Sir, on the score of Information; and as I requested Mr. Whitesides to remit to you the several Brevets & other documents of my Service in the United States, it will not be difficult for you to render me this service: I wish, Sir, to know the precise terms of the act which commuted the Half pay for life of our officers into an allowance of five years full pay;[2] whether all those who served their years are entitled to it, or whether it is exclusive to those who served till the Peace, as continental Officers. As to myself, I served from the month of December 1775. till January 1783; but my last Commission from the State of Georgia, as Colonel & Adjutant General of the State Troops, gave me a local Rank & local Functions some doubts might thence arise on the source from whence I am to derive my pay, though General Wayne, on his incursion into Georgia, named me Deputy Adjutant General of the Army (then composed of Continental & State Troops); besides the assumption of the State Debts by the Union, might include the debts of each State to their respective officers—but in this Case, the accounts might be previously audited by the state auditor.

Having some small debts to discharge in Europe, (incurred by my service in France), and having an occasion to dispose of a part of my claim on the United States, I should wish to be well informed, so as to guard against even the possibility of a retard in the payment there, of the portion I might dispose of abroad: I <u>shall</u> therefore claim only as a Major which rank I held (as A D Camp to General Lee) from the 25th October 1776* to the month of January 1783: (as I left Georgia early in 1784 & never proffered any claim, I luckily escaped the snares of those speculators, who purchased at a very depreciated rate, the hard-earned wages of our Brother-officers—your private fortune, I trust, has secured you from their clutches, but how many of our comrades are there, whose Laurels <u>alone attest and recompense their glorious Services</u> in their Country's Cause!

From the table of the Pay of our officers, I find my claim stands thus (without counting the depreciation allowed on the pay received).

5 years pay as Major at 52 doll^s per month, or 600 p^r annum	3000. Dollars
D^o for rations or in lieu of Prov^s & Forage at 14 p^r mo. or 108 p^r annum	<u>840.</u>
	3840.
Interest from 1783 to 1796 at 6 pc^t	<u>2995</u>. 20/100
and this is the sum worth of my Consideration	6835. 20/100

Being forced to wait some days for a Gentleman, as a fellow traveller to Paris, I venture Sir, to sollicit a reply on the subject of the Information I have requested, if you should have leisure at the time of receiving this Letter. I beg leave Sir to [offer] my best compliments to Mrs Monroe & to assure you of the respectful consideration with which I have the honor to be your affectionate h^{ble} Servt and fellow Citizen

J. S. Eustace

*I became his volunteer adC in December 1775. Genl Washington gave me the commission of an Ensign in the 9th Reg^t of Rhode Island in June 1776, and in 8^{ber} <illegible> Genl named me his adC.

RC, NN: Monroe Papers

1. JM knew John Skey Eustace (1760-1805) from their student days together at the College of William and Mary. After serving as an officer during the Revolutionary War, Eustace settled briefly in Georgia, spent several years in the West Indies and South America, and arrived in France in 1789. He became an active proponent of the French Revolution and received an appointment as a colonel in the French army in 1792, with a promotion to maréchal de camp later that year. His term in the army proved to be short: Dumouriez arrested him for disobeying orders, and although he was exonerated, he resigned his commission in August 1793. He employed himself for the next several years as a pamphleteer; he lived mostly in the Netherlands, but traveled frequently to Paris. He fell out of favor with the French government and was expelled from the country in 1797. He traveled to England and then to the Netherlands but was expelled in turn from both those countries as well. He returned to the United States in May 1798 and after a brief foray into American politics lived in retirement in New York (Lee Kennett, "John Skey Eustace and the French Revolution," *American Society Legion of Honor Magazine*, 45 (1974): 29-43).

2. The Continental Congress enacted a law on 21 October 1780 that provided half-pay for life for officers who served in the Continental army until the end of the war. Congress amended this act in March 1783: instead of half-pay for life, officers would receive five years of full pay after the conclusion of the war. This legislation was not implemented until 1828 when Congress passed a new law allowing full pay for life (retroactive to 1826) to all surviving officers who met the qualifications of the 1780 law (Minor Myers, Jr., *Liberty Without Anarchy: A History of the Society of the Cincinnati*, 5, 15, 213-219).

To James Madison

Paris January 12ᵗʰ 1796.

Dear Sir

Yours of the 6ᵗʰ of April is the last I have received from you,[1] though since that period I have written you eight or ten at least. The theatre too on which you are, has been and probably will continue to be an interesting one, for it is presumeable the same subject which creates such solicitude among the People at large, will produce a like effect among their representatives. Certain it is, that the temper which was shewn upon that subject by the people with you, has produced a happy effect here, and moderated greatly the resentment which began to display itself, before their sentiments were known: for as soon as this government saw that the people were dissatisfied with the treaty, and that a strong motive for their dissatisfaction proceeded from the interest they took in the welfare of france, from that moment it was obvious its chagrine diminished, and that in sympathy with us again, it gradually lost sight at least to a certain degree, of its own concerns, so far as they were supposed to be affected by that treaty, and became instead of a party in, a spectator of ours. This is the external view of the effect which Mʳ Jays treaty and its incidents produced upon the Councils and people of france, and more than the external view I cannot give you, for I deemed it upon every principle most suitable for me to stand aloof upon that subject never touching on it, except when mentioned informally to me, and then confining myself strictly within the limits observed by the other party, giving such explanations only as were sought, and inculcating always good temper and moderation on the part of this government towards us as the surest means whereby to unite for ever the two republics, whether therefore the subject has been acted on by the directoire or will be, or what will be the result in case it is I cannot tell you.

The progress of this government is so far wise, steady and ene[r]getic. Its outset was distinguished by an effort to introduce into every department of the administration the most rigid œconomy, and whereby many abuses were reformed, and the public expenditure greatly diminished. The finances were in the utmost confusion, the assignats having depreciated almost to that point beyond which they would not circulate, and there was no other resource. The directoire exposed freely this state of the nation demanding funds to carry on the war, and adding without which it could not be carried on, recommending too at the same time the project of a forced loan, whereby about twenty five millions sterling in specie would be raised, and which was adopted. By this project the assignats were to be redeemed or taken in, in discharge of the loan at one hundred for one, and which would consume of it, about twelve millions sterling, rather less than one half of the loan, specie and produce only are admitted for the residue. This loan however forms a fund upon which the assignats may be circulated again, and upon which they will most probably, for a while and until some more complete system is adopted, be circulated again. By this paper I am told a great portion of the ancient debt is discharged, so that by it the war has not only been carried on to the present stage (deducting the amount of the national domains that are sold and paid for) for nothing, but the nation exonerated from a considerable portion of that debt, which depressed it before the war. This loan is now collecting and without exciting any great murmur among those upon whom it falls.[2] The forms of business too in both houses are correct and discreet, according to our ideas on the subject, and their attention seems so far to have been bestowed on the most urgent topics, and in general the result such as might have been wished. In short in every respect the character of the public councils has greatly altered for the better; the effect whereof is plainly to be discerned in the public opinion as well as public measures: for you observe among all classes an increasing opinion of personal safety, at the same time that the government displays a degree of energy that was never surpassed before. The royalists begin to despair for they know that the hopes of royalty are gone as soon as the genuine character of republican government is unfolded. Their hopes were founded in the continuance of anarchy and confusion, to promote which of course all their efforts were united. Intemperate zeal too is restrained, but the restraint is always easy, indeed it is a self one, or rather it does not exist, when the administration possesses the confidence of the People and wields the government according to their wishes. I give you the aspect up to the present time, and to which I add with pleasure that the probability is it will continue.

You will doubtless hear before this reaches you that there is a truce between france and Austria, and which was asked by the Austrian generals. When a truce is asked and granted it argues that neither party has essentially the advantage over the other, or it would neither be asked or granted, and such was I believe the fact in the present instance. The proposition from Austria was for a truce for three months, but admitted by the Directoire for one only. What the motives of Austria are, is unknown: that peace is among them, perhaps the principal one is presumeable. By some it is suspected that the Message of the English King to his Commons, was the immediate stimulus, since as the same Persons suspect, that measure was taken in haste, in accommodation with existing circumstances on the spot, and of course without the knowlege of Austria, whereby and especially as the former objects of the war were abandoned, a disposition for peace avowed, the jealousy of that power was excited.[3] Perhaps however it may be a mere financing project on the part of Austria, in the hope that by appearing to seek peace a loan for the next campaign may be more easily obtained from England. But my opinion is, there is a negociation for peace depending, and which may probably have that issue with Austria, if not with other powers and the southern more especially. The moment Austria makes up her mind to yield Belgia, the war with her is over, and the ruin of her army in italy with other events, may have inclined her to that measure, whilst the light advantages she has gained on the Rhine may have suggested the idea that now is the time to treat with some apparent credit. But with England there will probably still be difficulties, for I think france will never hear a proposal from her upon the subject of peace, that is not preceded by a declaration that she will restore every thing taken since the commencement of the war from herself and Holland, and which it is possible her present superiority at sea may prevent: certainly it would prevent it, if the discontents of the People there, and which daily in crease on account of the scarcity of bread, and the dearness of it, which latter proceeds not more from that cause, than the superabundant circulation of paper, which raises the price of every thing, and threatens more fatally to impair the manufactures and commerce of that Country, than even long and destructive wars by all their other evils.

You will also have heard of the demand of Count Carletti Minister &c from Toscany to visit the "unfortunate daughter" of Louis 16ᵗʰ who was on her departure for Basle, to be exchanged for Bournonville[4] and several of the deputies who were surrendered to the Austrians by Dumourier, and of the Manner in which that interference was resented by the directoire; suspending all intercourse with him, and ordering him forthwith without the bounds of the republic. The count explained and expostulated but without effect. The diplomatic corps convened, and by some of whom it was urged, that the count could not be Suspended, and ordered without the republic by any but his own Sovereign, except in case of conspiracy. that the order to that effect was of course a violation of the rights of nations. and by others it was urged that every government had a right to rid itself of a minister who gave offence, and by its own means: that to demand his recall, was upon trivial occasions the ordinary usage, but that it was not prescribed by the law of nations, but by that of civility and good manners only. Was this however a light occasion, a demand by the representative of a foreign power to visit the "unfortunate &c" thereby stigmatizing the revolution and reproaching france for that effort which she deems a glorious one? If demands of this kind are allowed from the representatives of other powers, what kind of demands will be inhibited? And if it be meant to check such, is it not best to do it upon such occasion, and in such manner as the present, whereby the sense of the french government being decisively pronounced, will be well understood at home and abroad? The meeting broke up without a decision; notwithstanding which it was published in all the gazettes, that the whole diplomatic corps had united in a remonstrance to the directoire against its procedure in this case without effect. Upon which another meeting was called and held for the purpose of expressing to the government, the sense which the members of that corps felt of the injury, which was done them by that misrepresentation, and to request of the Minister of foreign affairs since he knew that no such step was taken, that he would contradict the report. Upon this proposal too no decision was obtained: by it however the spirit of some of the Members of that Corps was checked, and the body itself perhaps freed from like attempts, to involve it in the interior and revolutionary politics of france, and against the spirit of the revolution, for the future. But the Count replied to this government, he would not withdraw until he had the order of his own, upon which it was notified to him if he did not commence his route within twenty four hours, he should be sent out by force, and to which a like reply was given. The twenty four hours expired at which moment a Commissary with a Carriage attended to take his orders for Basel, and by means whereof he was conducted to Basel, and with all convenient speed. The communication of this event, and its incidents was made by the french minister to the Grand Duke &ᶜ by whom it was well received: for instead of taking it in high dudgeon as was expected by many, he dispatched immediately, and upon the first intimation of it, a minister plenipotentiary (the prince of   ) for the express purpose of disavowing the demand of Carletti, and declaring his respect for the french government, and so rapid were the movements of this Envoy, that he is already on the ground, and has already made his disavowal to the Minister of foreign affairs.[5] By this measure therefore the french government has lost nothing without, and certainly within, and especially by the manner in which it has terminated, it will acquire great respect.

I am inclined to believe that *England does not mean to* execute the *treaty* & intends *to justify her evasion* by *any obstacles the H of R may throw in its* way. If then any thing is *done it is to be hoped the administration* will *immediately change* to give an opportunity to try the effect *of other councils. It is late to do it but* I think *not too late*.

of the above except the last paragʰ I have sent copies somewhat modified to Colᵒˢ Burr & Langdon.[6] you will excuse me to Tazewell, Mason, Beckley, Butler & Brown & other friends, to whom you will make my best respects.[7]

RC, DLC: Madison Papers. Written in clerk's hand except the last paragraph, which is in JM's hand. Unsigned. Words in italics were written in code by JM and deciphered by Madison.

1. Madison wrote to JM on 6 April 1795, acknowledging the receipt of letters and sending a cipher (*Madison Papers*, 15: 507).

2. Inflation, a perennial problem during the French Revolution, worsened severely during 1795, and by December assignats, the paper money of the time, were worth only one percent of their face value. The Directory responded to this problem by levying a forced loan (enacted by the assembly on 10 December 1795). The Directory hoped that the tax would not only generate revenue but also reduce the number of assignats in circulation. The loan brought in some much needed money, but it failed to halt inflation—between December 1795 and February 1796 the number of assignats in circulation increased from 29 billion to 40 billion (Eugene Nelson White, "The French Revolution and the Politics of Government Finance, 1770-1815," *Journal of Economic History*, 55 (1995): 227-255, especially 244-247; Georges LeFebvre, *The Thermidorians and the Directory*, 264-266).

3. In a speech to the House of Commons on 8 December 1795, King George III expressed his willingness to negotiate a peace treaty with France, provided "it can be effected on just and suitable terms for himself and his allies" (*Hansard's Parliamentary Debates*, 32: 569-570).

4. Pierre Riel de Beurnonville (1752-1821) entered the French army in 1774 and rose to the rank of lieutenant general. He served briefly as minister of war in 1793. Later that year he went as a deputy to the army, but was betrayed by Dumoriez to the

Austrians, who held him prisoner until 1795. In 1796 he was named commander of the northern army. Beurnonville held a number of civil posts under both Napoleon and the Restoration, including minister to Prussia 1800-1802 and minister to Spain 1802-1805 (*Dictionnaire Biographie Française*).

5. Count Neri Corsini (1771-1845) succeeded Carletti as the minister from Tuscany. He arrived in Paris on 5 January 1796 and held the post until March 1798. The wording of Corsini's disavowal of Carletti's actions was dictated by the Directory (Sydney Seymour Biro, *The German Policy of Revolutionary France*, 2: 522; *Dizionario Biografica degli Italiani*).

6. The copies of this letter to Aaron Burr and John Langdon have not been located.

7. The draft of this letter in DLC: Monroe Papers does not include this last paragraph. In its place is the following paragraph, which is struck out: "This leaves this on the 12ᵗʰ instᵗ and yet we know nothing of Mᵣ Rˢ publication nor even that the congress is convened."

To Oliver Wolcott

[Paris January 14ᵗʰ 1796][1]

When the money was received from Mᵣ Dallarde I requested Mᵣ Skipwith to take charge of it because he was our Consul and the person to whom I was to look for such a service, and because I thought it would be safer with him than any other person, and lastly because he readily undertook the safe-keeping, negotiation by bill or transportation, if Such was the case without asking any commission whatever. Unfortunately his house was broken open and a part of it stolen and which is not yet recovered tho' diligent search is made after it. I send you the documents to prove that this incident was not the effect of negligence on his part.[2] On the contrary that all due attention and care were taken by him for the preservation of it. Thinking however that you had occasion of the remittance to Holland for the precise sum specified in Mᵣ Swan's bill he offered to advance the deficit himself, in the expectation that you will pay the like amount to his order, and which I readily accepted.

Extract, DLC: Madison Papers. Fulwar Skipwith enclosed this extract in his letter to Madison of 27 July 1796 (*Madison Papers*, 16: 383). The original of this letter has not been located.

1. The date is given in the heading of the extract.

2. Certificate of Americans resident in Paris, 23 November 1795 and report of Thomas-François Violette, 26 November 1795. See Skipwith to JM, 1 January 1796, above.

From John Breckinridge

State of Kentucky, Fayette County 15ᵗʰ Janʸ 1796.

Dear Sir

When I parted with you in Albemarle, I little expected that three years would have elapsed, without my writing to you, or hearing from you. I have in general been discouraged, by the great uncertainty of Letters reaching you from this remote place, & indeed I had little to write with a conveyance of 4000 miles.

So good an oppᵒ however as at present by Colᵒ Fulton[1] I cannot omit, were I only to tell you, that my most sincere esteem & best wishes, still attend you.

I have within 12 months past removed from Lexington, & am now improving a farm, on which I mean to spend my days. I still continue in the practise of the law, & from which I hope in a few years more to be enabled "recumbere sub tegmine fagi." [2]

The western country is rising into importance, beyond any thing yet known. It was generally beleived, that the emigration last year amounted to at least 15,000; and it is now as generally beleived, that this fall & winter 30,000 have been added to our numbers. Men of character, understanding & property, are emigrating hither from all parts of the Union; and I have no doubt, that our numbers are now between 150, & 200,000.

Civilization and improvement, keep pace with the emigration. Extensive & highly cultivated farms, are to be seen every where; and in the more early settled parts of the Country, handsome & expensive buildings of brick & stone, are daily rising up. The mechanic arts flourish here, more than in any part of Virg^a with which I was acquainted. We already supply ourselves with our castings, bar iron, Salt, & paper; and from the increase of fulling mills, sheep &^{ca}, I have no doubt we might in a few years, furnish ourselves with the substantial articles of cloathing. Lands (I mean cultivated) are selling around me as high as 3 & 4 £ pr acre.

This however Sir, is the bright side of the subject. It has another, & a gloomy one. Of little ultimate avail, are all our improvements, the fertility of our soil &^{ca} &^{ca} if we are to remain cooped up, & deprived of their rational & natural enjoyment. It is true we may fill our barns with corn, & our smoke houses with meat; but without the free use of the Mississippi, our posterity in one generation more, will be content to parch & eat the one, & grease their Bodies with the other; & become as uncivilized as the savages which surround us. Without this navigation, the fertility of our soil, will prove a curse to us; for so small a portion of exertion will be necessary to procure the actual wants of Life, that in a little time, every sinew of industry will be unnerved.

I am sorry to inform you, that the people here in general, repose no confidence in the attempts of the general Gov^t, to procure the navigation of this River.

They consider the negociations now carrying on, as intirely illusory. God knows how it is, but their patience is nearly exhausted, & I suspect the accession of a few more thousands will fix the Epoch, when <u>something will be done</u>.

What that something will be, no man among us does yet pretend to scan.—We always had a strong hope from the French. We were taught to expect, they meant to turn their attention to subjugated Louisania, & that it would of course have fallen into their Hands by conquest or treaty. If so, from their liberal policy we had every thing that was reasonable to expect. But all our hopes from that Quarter are dispelled, by the late treaty with Spain.[3]—Can you give us nothing consolatory on that head? Can you tell us, if the Spaniards are not really inclined to treat for the free use of this River, what are their objections, either feigned or real? Whether in short, the prospect of obtaining it by the present negociation is such, as ought to satisfy a people, possessing all the apathy, of which human nature is capable?[4]

I know you have always been friendly to this our right, & have defended it with patriotism & firmness, when it was once in peril, for which reason, I write to you without reserve.—Perhaps your situation may have enabled you to give us some information on the subject. If it has, it would be very grateful to us.

I assure you it would give me great pleasure to hear sometimes from you; & whether you receive my letters or not, I shall now & then gratify myself by writing to you.

I am pleased that Col^o Fulton has merited the attention of the French People. He is a young man of the best Heart, & not more attached to the Western Country, than he is to the cause of our friends the French.

We wish him great success & hope he will deserve your esteem & attention.

I send you no news. Such as is worth transmitting, I presume You have at all times from the fountain head. Suffice it however to say, that Jays late treaty, is espoused here by about six persons, & damned by every body else; & that this State is among the antiministerial alias republican States. With sincere Esteem & regard I am dear Sir Your Friend & mo: Obt

J. Breckinridge

RC, DLC: Monroe Papers

1. When Edmond Genet arrived in the United States in 1793 he authorized George Rogers Clark to organize an expedition to invade Louisiana and reclaim it for France. The funds promised to finance the expedition never materialized, and in the summer of 1795 Clark sent his agent, Samuel Fulton, to Paris to seek reimbursement for the money he had expended. The Committee of Public Safety rejected the claim, and Fulton went home empty-handed. Fulton returned to Paris in 1796, but had no better luck with the Directory (James Alton James, *The Life of George Rogers Clark*, 419-436). Fulton (b. ca. 1770) served in the U. S. Army 1794-1796; he later served in the French army in Europe and in St. Domingue. He settled in Baton Rouge in 1804 and became active in the movement to annex West Florida to the United States (Francis B. Heitman, *Historical Register and Dictionary of the United States Army*; *Madison Papers*, 15: 304; *Madison Papers: Secretary of State Series*, 3: 247).

2. The quotation is a paraphrase from the opening lines of Virgil's *Eclogue*. It translates: recline beneath a broad beech canopy.

3. Breckinridge refers to the peace treaty between France and Spain.

4. A copy of the treaty between the United States and Spain arrived in Philadelphia in February 1796, and Washington submitted it to the Senate on the 26th of that month. The Senate gave its assent on March 3, and Washington signed it on March 5. The people of Kentucky learned of the ratification on March 26 (Charles Bevans, *Treaties and Other International Agreements of the United States*, 11: 516; Arthur P. Whitaker, *The Mississippi Question*, 24).

To Charles Delacroix

Paris le 16 Janvier 1796 (Le 26 Nivose de l'an 4ᵉ)
l'an 20. de la République Américaine.

Citoyen Ministre,

Plusieurs de mes compatriotes qui se trouvent actuellement à Paris ayant reçu des sommations dans leurs diverses Sections à payer leurs contingents à l'emprunt forcé viennent de me faire des reclamations là-dessus.

Je ne suis pas particulièrement instruit si la loi qui etablit l'emprunt forcé embrasse d'autres que ceux qui sont citoyens de cette République; mais s'il se trouve des cas ou des citoyens de pays étrangers y sont compris, Je suis bien persuadé que tous ceux qui sont arrivés depuis peu des Etats-Unis de l'Amérique ne sont que passagers, qu'ils n'ont aucune propriété dans ce pays-ci, et qu'ils sont généralement dans l'intention d'en sortir aussitôt de terminer les Affaires qui les y ont amenées.

Je n'avais donc d'autre conseil à donner à ceux de mes compatriotes qui ayant reçu des sommations comme J'ai dit plus haut, s'étaient adressées à moi, que de se présenter aux autorités d'où elles avaient emanées, afin de leur soumettre leurs situations respectives, et de leur exposer qu'ils sont citoyens des Etats-Unis de l'Amérique purement passagers, et sans propriété avec prière qu'on retirât les dites sommations. Cependant malgré que ces représentations avaient été généralement faites, les sommations ne sont pas retirées, et ils craignent en consequence d'être exposés sous peu de jours aux peines que la loi inflige dans les cas de non-paiement, à avoir leur effets saisis, et de se trouver eux-mêmes en lute aux embarras que le gouvernement est sans doute bien éloigné de vouloir les faire eprouver. Je l'ai donc cru convenable, Citoyen Ministre de vous soumettre cet etat des choses, en vous priant de vouloir bien prendre en considération la nécessité de faire expedier les ordres nécessaires à la police chargée de cette partie d'exempter les individus qui reclament de toute imposition injuste ou incertaine. Agréez l'assurance de mon respect et de mon estime.

Jaˢ Monroe

P. S. Je vous fais passer cy-joint un Exemplaire des sommations remises par les Sections.

Editors' Translation

Paris, 16 January 1796 (26 Nivôse Year 4)
Year 20 of the American Republic.

Citizen Minister,

Several of my countrymen who find themselves in Paris at present have received notices from their various sections to pay their share of the forced loan and have complained to me about this issue.

I am not particularly informed as to whether the law establishing taxation affects persons other than those who are citizens of this Republic; but if there were cases arising in which citizens from foreign countries are included, I am quite certain that all those recently arriving from the United States of America are here only temporarily, that they own no property in this country, and that they in general are intending to leave as soon as the business that brought them here is concluded.

Therefore, I have no other advice to offer those of my countrymen who have approached me having received such notices, than for them to report to the authorities from whom the notices originated in order that they may present their representative circumstances, and clarify their status as citizens of the United States of America, here purely for the time being and owning no property, with the plea that the aforesaid notices be withdrawn.

Nevertheless, although in general these statements have been made, the notices have not been withdrawn, and therefore they fear they will be penalized in a few days for non-payment; that they will have their possessions seized, and find themselves in financial straits, which cannot be the intention of the government. I have therefore thought it appropriate, Citizen Minister, to submit this state of affairs before you, while pleading for you to take into consideration the urgency of expediting the necessary orders for the police charged with exempting individuals, to make an exemption for such individuals who protest against all unjust or improper impositions. Accept the assurance of my respect and my esteem.

Jaˢ Monroe

P. S. I am sending you here enclosed a copy of the notices delivered by the sections.

RC, DLC: FCP—France

From Joseph Jones

Fred^g 16th Jan^ry 1796

D^r S^r

I have rec^d yours and Joes letters of the 24th October last.¹ You complain of having rec^d but few letters from me, I can in return make the same complaint.—both must ascribe our so seldom hearing from each other to the same cause the frequent miscarriage of our letters.—From June to Sepr I transmitted by various opportunities four or five only one of them it wo^d seem got to hand. I repeated in them all a rough shell of your affairs here. Your crops of wheat have proven very short of our expectation not reaching two hundred for Sale besides the seed for the next crop. I am hopes the next will be more abundant and am satisfied it wo^d have been much more so could it have been put in early but a violent storm & rain occasioned the corn to fall and a few days after another rain with high wind from a different point tumbled it in almost every direction and made it difficult to seed at any rate, and when ploughed did much injury to the corn and fodder as well as prolonged the sowing—the wheat was delivered by Hogg (except his part and that to Joe Monroe) to Mr Davies on acc^t as he had declined taking the furniture. I have not yet settled with him. Joe Monroe has bought a tract of land of two hundred acres of H. Martin² not far from Charlottesville, I apprehend merely to make him a freeholder as he has offered to represent the County.³ I was not consulted in either of the steps he has taken or probably sho^d have dissuaded him from both especially the land purchase as I do not think from what I have heard the tract was such as he sho^d have purchased. I have taken the liberty to advise his geting rid of it w^h he thinks he can effect by Dr Wardlow who Purchased the other moity and without loss. If he can there is a piece of land he tells me adjoining Mr Kerrs a place I think rented by Jones in town and w^h contains bet[ween] three & four hundred acres. this is the last year of Jones term. Joe says he is informed the land is good if I find it such as will suit him your request to aid him in the purchase shall be observed.⁴ he still is in one of your houses and is supplied as you wish. P. Marks is also dead I before informed you of the death of his wife. In consequence the Trustees have agreed to sell the negros and Lotts to raise the amount of your demand—by your direction and former engagem^t respecting that business I agreed with them to accept £1100 & the rect. for you releasing four hundred of the debt for the daughters benefit. They proposed the terms of the Sale to be for 1/3 Cash & two thirds eighteen months credit upon supposition that 1000 Cash by this way might be raised for you. Altho' these terms did not well suit your affairs here as one third of what you might purchase would lessen the prompt payment I thought it was better to accord with them than hazard the value of the security by a ready money sale or by opposition occasion delay and the dispersion of the negros by hiring out for already had two of them eloped to Richmond. The last Court day was appointed for the Sale, I attended But the business was but in part done one half of the Slaves not appearing, all except three that were present were sold and very high. It was my intention to have bought old Dick his wife and all the children as the best Characters among them but on the day of sale I found there was little hope of effecting my design as Dick had prevailed on one of the Marks to buy him and allow him the privilege of working out his freedom. Hudson Martins wife was anxious to get a boy called Dick ab^t 15 or 16 years old on acc^t of his having been bro^t up among her children and the next youngest boy Wilson I think some other had promised to buy so that the first sold for upwards of £100 and the last for upwards £95. Hannah the mother and three small Boys I have purchased for you at the price of £145. She is the mother of Jesse and esteemed a good Servant and tolerable good Cook the youngest boy ab^t a year old the eldest six or seven—Spotswood who lives with Watson⁵ and another called Charles who last year lived with Bob Jouett are yet to sell also a very likely young mulatto woman and child a Daughter of Hannahs—also an elderly man called Julius who lived last year with Hog but who was unable to attend the former Sale. I shall endeavour to buy for you Spotswood and Charles as the mother and themselves are desirous of being together but they will particularly Spotswood go very high as Watson and others want him and Watson has offered for him £100 he will sell for at least £120—Negros are near 50 p^r c^t higher than a few years past greatly I think above their worth but the late high prices of wheat corn and Tobacco have occasioned it, they hire now at 20^l p^r ann. for a man—dear as they are I shall endeavour to buy Spotswood Charles and Julius as you much want hands and having not hired any for the present year it is indispensibly necessary to add to Solomon his wife and Jesse at Hogs some others if to be got. Sukey after her quarrel with Joe Monroe has lived with Jones in Town unless she will be satisfied to live at Hogs to work for him & people and spin. I will sell her at the sale of the rest of the negros which takes place the 1st next month—these purchases will reduce the cash payment nearly if not quite a half. I have taken in your note for the purchase of Sukey—have also p^d M. Allen on acc^t your note for the hire of the Negros from Johnson 34^l the whole was £42 but have received the bal. for arbitration as the man Solomon eloped twice and the second time went to and was returned by his Master. I have paid also a former acc^t and this years Smiths acc^t to Millar amounting in the whole to 18 or 20^l a balance to Maury to <illegible> Glassell—and shall in a few days settle with Wardens acc^t a balance due the estate—Mr Miner acc^t ab^t 60 dol^s and in part for cloathing the people and other plantation supplies to Mr Kelly[6] £10.1.6 the balance of supplies were from Bell and not yet settled for. Hud: Martin claims a bal. of 50 or 60 dol^s Col Jno Nicholas ab^t £10 for Wiskey & £3 for Taxes due the Clerk—these last will of course be discounted out of the cash payment of the Sale also I expect Col Bell will look for his balance. Dr Wardlow & Meriwether and our old friend Gilmer who has lately died have claims to settle also a small demand of £5 or 6^l on acc^t. Mr Everet by order Davenport Southcomb has the £60. bond to Carter also the 166. and if the money you mention to be p^d to Madison can be got I shall apply it to him as he is very importunate the whole with the int. will be ab^t £230. I prepared a deed and bond long since and left with Joe Monroe to get Carter to execute a deed for the land he has not complied and lately I was applied to by W. Nicholas and informed the money £259 was for him and desiring to know when it wo^d be p^d. I replied as soon as possible after Mr Carter had settled and made a deed. I shall perhaps when I am up at the next Sale see them on the business. After the Sale I shall have more leisure and will give you a more full and accurate statement. The first payment of the balance of the Loudon purchase became due this month. I relied on £500 from Tayloe to enable me to make this payment but instead of payment I am compelled to a suit for the demand since the commencem^t whereof he has sold me a lott in Town for Mrs Carter to be discounted out of what I may recover and which will go in payment of the bal: of the land or 2^d paym^t out of which she was to have £500 for relinquishing her Dower in the land. The survey makes the land only 4000 acres. I am sorry to inform you I think you will loose Tenah.[7]—She brought a Child early last year and tho' she went about in June and July she complained of being unwell and in pain and said she had not been well from the time of her delivery. in Augt she went to her room and at length to her bed and has been confined and languishing ever since. Wardlow and Meriwether have attended her and used I believe their best efforts but all will I think prove ineffectual—when I left her last week she was very feeble indeed and cannot live long if she still lives. I have hired and has been constantly with her an elderly carefull black woman who resides contiguous to the plantation and has daily and I believe carefully nursed her and have furnished and directed peter to furnish any thing that she may desire or want so that I believe nothing that could administer to her relief and comfort has been neglected. I know not wh[ether] I informed you I had settled with Buckner at £70 for the Negro—such a one as the contract described could not have been bought lower and as they were rising in value I tho^t it best to close the matter at that rate than hazard consequences or delay the settlem^t of the claim. He rec^d the money from Coleman w^h had been useless and I am to pay him the balance ab[t] 35[l] this month. I shall write by this post to M[r] Madison ab[t] the money of pickering & Paine and desire him if it can be got to pay it to Philips Cramond & C[o] of Phil[a] on acc[t] Southcomb—I have written to Fowler ab[t] the pat[ent] of the Rock Castle land and shall also mention it to M[r] Madison   if it can be got I will transmit you the patent or a Copy. Jn[o] Dawson has been packing his fortune somewhat in the land way—and the other day wrote me a letter. He had determined to be in Phil[a] ab[t] the begining of Febr[y] on his way to France—I have admonished him on the subject if such is his object and shall be more pointed when I see him. I have pursued at Hogs a course similar to what you recommend, the avoiding tending the land more than once in three or four years in Corn—he is now farming his third field and the next year a fourth if to be accomplished otherwise he must return to the one he first tended—If Clover seed could be got upon any reasonable terms I should scatter seed over the chief part of the wheat but it is very scarce none to be had that I can hear of—some there was in Richmond at 16 & 18 dol[s] a bushel I got one bushel the last year for 10 dol[s] half of which I have sent up to Albemarle to be sown at last place as a clover patch to cut green for the horses in summer. I shall spend the greatest part of the Spring and Summer at your place and will attend to your request as far as can be done with the force on the place. the old fellow and the two young men I placed there last year will be continued this—sho[d] I buy Spotswood he will be there also. From all accounts of him he may be a usefull servant in the house Stable or drawing a carriage. Sukey being hired and Tenah disabled by sickness very little spining went on only enough to cloath with frocks Tenahs Children & herself and under petticoats. If Sukey continues with the estate and at Hogs I shall require the spining to go on there and with Hannah at home all that may be. I am happy to hear you are all in health and that Joe is not prone to any viscious course. I am in hopes my admonitions aided by your own and his Masters may stimulate his efforts and produce industry without which he cannot hope to make any considerable progress in learning. I must leave to Madison the communication of our political situation and the prospect and progress of our affairs in Congress whose station in Phil[a] gives a better opportunity of accurate information than I can furnish. I enclose a letter for Joe. M[r] Knox wrote to Madison for any letters you might have rec[d] from M[r] Kortright that might shew the deed to his son was not meant as an absolute conveyance or for valuable cons[ideratio]n. I have searched for such papers but cannot find such and yet I think you had some such.[8] You will I hope be able to read this letter without my transcribing it. remember me affectionately to M[rs] Monroe & Eliza. Yr friend

Jos. Jones.

RC, NN: Monroe Papers

1. Neither JM's nor Joseph Jones, Jr.'s letter of 24 October 1795 has been located.

2. Hudson Martin (1752-1830) was an Albemarle County planter who served as deputy county clerk. He sold his farm in Albemarle and moved to Amherst County (Edgar Woods, *Albemarle County in Virginia*, 265; *Marshall Papers*, 2: 326).

3. Joseph Jones Monroe was elected as one of two representatives from Albemarle County to the Virginia House Delegates for the November-December 1796 session (*Madison Papers*, 16: 281; *Register of the General Assembly of Virginia*).

4. There is no record in the Albemarle County Deed Books of Joseph J. Monroe purchasing land from Hudson Martin. Monroe at this time owned two lots in the town of Milton (which he purchased in October 1794 and sold in September 1796) and a tract of 75 acres, which he purchased from James Kerr in September 1795 (and sold back to Kerr in February 1797) (ViCCH: Deed Books, 11: 347; 12: 26, 153, 263).

5. John Watson (ca.1760-1841), a prosperous merchant in Milton, Virginia, was a longtime friend and associate of JM. Watson served as Milton's postmaster 1798-1799, justice of the peace from 1800, and sheriff of Albemarle County in 1825. (Edgar Woods, *Albemarle County*, 339; *Jefferson Papers: Retirement Series*, 3: 237-239).

6. John Kelly (d.1830) engaged in business in Charlottesville under the name of John Kelly & Co (Edgar Woods, *Albemarle County in Virginia*, 242-243).

7. Thenia Hemings.

8. Jones wrote to Madison about the payment of two bonds held by Fredericksburg merchant Thomas Southcomb on 18 January 1796. Southcomb wrote to Madison on the same subject the following April. Madison paid the bonds on 2 June 1796 (*Madison Papers*, 16: 193-194, 306).

To James Madison

Paris Jany 20. 1796.

Dear Sir

I think I mentioned to you sometime since that Mr Paine was with me. Upon my arrival I found him in prison, & as soon as I saw my application in his behalf would be attended to, I asked his release & obtained it. But he was in extreme ill health, without resource, & (aff^{ts} being unsettled) not without apprehensions of personal danger, & therefore anxious to avail himself as much as possible of such protection as I co^d give him. From motives that will readily occur to you I invited him to take a room in my house, & which he accepted. It was his intention at that time sometime in oct^r 94 to depart for America in the Spring, with which view in feb^y following, I asked permission of the Com: of p: safety for him to depart, charged with my dispatches for the department of state, a motive w^h I presumed wo^d authorize them to grant the permission asked: but was answer'd it co^d not be granted to a deputy; tho' indeed he co^d scarcely be considered as such, having been excluded [from] the convention as a foreigner, & liberated upon my application as an American citizen. His disease continued & of course he continued in my house, & will continue in it, till his death or departure for America, however remote either the one or the other event may be. I had occasion soon after Mr Paine's enlargment to intimate to him a wish, that whilst in my house, he would write nothing for the publick, either of Europe or America, upon the subject of our aff^{ts}, which I found even before his enlargment he did not entertain a very favorable opinion of. I told him I did not rest my demand upon the merit or demerit of our conduct, of which the world had a right to form & wo^d form its opinion, but upon the injury such essays wo^d do me, let them be written by whom they might & whether I ever saw them or not, if they proceeded from my house. He denied the principle, intimating that no one wo^d suppose his writings, which were consistent, were influenc'd by any one: that he was accomtomed to write upon publick subjects & upon those of America in particular, to which he now wished to turn his attention, being ab^t to depart thither & reside there for the future. But as I insisted that I owed it to the delicacy of my publick & private character to guard myself even by erroneous inferences, agnst any improper imputation or compromittment whatever, & especially as I did not wish any impression to be entertained of me which I did not create myself, being the arbiter of my own measures & the guardian of my own name, and which I knew wo^d be affected thro that door if it were opened, with many if not generally, & therefore entreated him to desist, he then accomodated, more however from an apparent spirit of accomodation, than of conviction that my demand was reasonable or my argument sound. Thus the matter ended & I flattered myself I sho^d for the future enjoy the pleasure of extending to Mr Paine, whilst he remained here, the rights of hospitality & without exposing myself to the inconvenience I so much dreaded and laboured to avert. Latterly however an incident has turned up which has again disquieted me on the same subject. He had committed to Mr Pinckney when here the other day on his return from Spain, a letter for his book seller in London, upon the propriety of carrying & delivering which unsealed Mr Pinckney asked my opinion. I frankly told him, in his place I wo^d carry nothing I did not see and approve of, & as he was of the same opinion he desired me to communicate it to Mr Paine & which I did. Mr Paine owned that his letter contained an extract of one he was writing or had written to *Frederick Muhlenburg in Philadelphia* upon Eng^h & American aff^{rs} & which he intended sho^d be published with his name. Mr Pinckney returned the letter not chusing to be the bearer of it. Upon this occasion I revived with Mr Paine the argument I had used before, expressing my extreme concern that he pursued a conduct which, under existing circumstances, gave me so much pain, & to which he made little other reply than to observe, he was surprised I continued of the same opinion I formerly was upon this subject. Whether he will send the one or the other letter I know not. I shall certainly prevent it in both cases if in my power. That to Engl^d is not sent as yet. Tis possible the one for America (is) gone or will be sent. Let me therefore entreat you to confer with the gent^n to whom it is addressed & request him in my behalf if he receives such an one, to suppress it. In any event I have thought it necessary to possess you with these facts that you may use them as occasion may require to guard me ag^{nst} any unmerited slander.

Since my last which was of the inst^t nothing new has occur'd.[1] Murmurs are heard ag^{nst} the forc'd loan but yet the collection progresses, so that there appears no reason to doubt its execution. The armies on both sides keep their respective positions near the Rhine: nor is it probable the truce will be renewed, tho' on this point nothing transpires. Tis known that Engl^d is willing to leave France in possession of the Belgic & give up every thing taken from her provided she is permitted to retain the cape of good hope &ca. I say it is known because I have it from a respectable person who has had opportunities of knowing the views of the Eng^h gov^t. But I think France will reject this with disdain, tho' indeed Holland has little claim on her to continue the war on that acc^t, having made no effort whatever in her own behalf. This latter country presents to view a curious & interesting spectacle at the present moment. Its conquest by France was at the moment when the publick mind was vibrating here from what was called terrorism to the opposit extreme: the effect of antecedent & well known causes. Under this impression the deputies in mission with the armies in Holland were appointed, and as they likewise felt & obeyed the same impulse, dreading terrorism as the worst of political evils, (altho there was no analogy in the situation of the two countries nor likely to be), it was natural they sho^d turn their attention to it where they were, as one it was more especially their duty to avoid. Such too was their conduct, by means whereof the early & flattering prospects of a complete revolution were checked. More latterly however the error of this policy has been seen thro & will doubtless be remedied so far as it depends now on the councils of France. Unless the gov^t is plac'd completely in the hands of the people there will be in the publick councils neither energy nor integrity to the cause of the people.[2]

Your china will go from hence in the course of a few days when I will send you an invoice of it. It is a plain neat service, sufficient in number & cheap. If you will permit me I will procure for you in the course of the present year furniture for a drawing room, consisting of the following articles. 1. chairs, suppose 12. or 18.—2^d Two tables or three after the taste which we prefer—3^d a sofa, perhaps 2. These all of tapestry & to suit, if to be had, the curtains we sent you, either one or the other sett. 4$^{th.}$ A clock to stand on the chimney piece, & which chimney piece I will send also, of marble, if you wish it. I wish you to send me a list of what other things you want, & especially of books & I will provide & send or bring them with me when I return home. I will procure every thing as cheap as possible, & adjust the amount when I have occasion for it. Mr Jefferson proposes to have a house built for me on my plantation near him, & to w^h I have agreed under conditions that will make the burden as light as possible upon him. For this purpose I am ab^t to send 2. plans to him submitting both to his judgment, & contemplate accepting the offer of a skilful mason here, who wishes to emigrate & settle with us, to execute the work. I wish y^{r}self & Mr Jones to see the plans & council with Mr Jefferson on the subject.

Sometime since Mr Ketland from Phil^a came here with Mr Yards recommendation & w^h disposed me to shew him & his family all the attention in my power. Indeed the circumstance of his having married M^r M's daughter who was with him was of itself a good recommendation.[3] M^r K: however brought with him his sister who was an Eng^h subject as likewise was one of his servants, & for whom also he asked my passport. I told him I co^d grant it only to American citizens. He then asked me to demand it of this gov^t & to w^h I replied that if I demanded it, I must do it as a favor: To ask a favor of this gov^t at the present time was not agreeable to me: to ask it in behalf of Eng^h subjects, in whose favor we were already suspected to be sufficiently biased was impolitick & agnst my uniform conduct; & in rejection of the solicitations of Mr Pinckney & Mr Jay in many instances, one only excepted & that when the party had his wife & family in America, his father & mother were American citizens & himself about to remove there. I told him however I wo^d take charge of the cases & obtain passports if possible without compromitting myself, & in case this co^d not be done I wo^d ask for them. I requested in consequence an American citizen to state the case & make the application in behalf of his sister & the servant, & which was done & with effect. I mentioned when Mr Ketland first called on me that we sho^d be happy to see his lady &ca when convenient &ca being sincerely disposed to shew her all the civilities in our power but she never call'd & in consequence we never saw her. It is the rule of Paris applicable in all cases, that when a stranger arrives male or female, he, or she visit those whom they wish to visit. This rule applies with greater force to publick ministers & their families & is universal throughout Europe & I believe the world, especially on the part of the people of the countries they respectively represent, & for the obvious reason that in so great a city those resident wo^d never know who arrived, if not thus advised of it. With this rule Mrs M. complied herself on her arrival, & many American Ladies who have since arrived have also complied with it, & who wo^d have cause of offense if she changed it in favor of any other. I mention these things that you may apprize Mr Yard of them, that in case misrepresentation is given he may be aware of it. I do not know it was the wish of this family to be acquainted with us or that any offense is taken: I presume the contrary is the case as I think you & M^r Y^d will upon the above statm^t: but as I know that misrepresent^n is sometimes made I have tho^t proper to give this statment. I shall write M^r Y^d & Dr Stevens in a day or two[4] to whom & their families present our best respects. Our best wishes for y^r own & Mrs M.'s health: sincerely I am y^r fn^d

Of the first parag^h of this letter I will probably send a copy to Col^o Burr to g^d agnst accidents.[5]

I am satisfied we shall never have our just weight upon the scale of nations, nor command the respect w^h is our due or enjoy the *rights* of *neutrality without a small fleet*. It is astonishing what weight a *beginning in that line* of the decent kind will have. *Let our coasts be well fortified* & such *a force of the kind be raised as will protect us from small detachments* (and *they will never send others*) and we take an imposing ground immediately. This is worthy your most serious consideration.

RC, DLC: Madison Papers. Unsigned. Words in italics were written in code by JM and deciphered by Madison.

1. JM to Madison, 12 January 1796.

2. Political discord plagued Holland during 1795. The conservative republicans who assumed power after the revolution resisted calls from the popular factions and the provinces for the meeting of a national assembly. France, eager for Holland to become an active ally in the war against Great Britain, intervened in the early months of 1796 to end the strife. The Directory sent instructions to the French minister at the Hague on 2 January 1796 to urge the government to convene an assembly, stating that France would "never recognize any government in Holland other than that which is based on the general will." The Dutch responded to this pressure and convened the National Assembly on 1 March 1796 (Simon Schama, *Patriots and Liberators: Revolution in the Netherlands, 1780-1813*, 211-247).

3. Philadelphia merchants Thomas and John Ketland were the sons of Thomas Ketland, a prominent English gunmaker. They married sisters, the daughters of Philadelphia merchant George Meade. Which Ketland visited France could not be determined (George Meade, *The Life and Letters of George Gordon Meade*, 1: 3).

4. No letters from JM to James Yard or Edward Stevens written at this time have been located.

5. JM sent the first paragraph as a letter to Aaron Burr on 10 January 1796 and to John Langdon on 12 January 1796 (JM to Burr, 10 January 1796, DLC: Monroe Papers).

From Guillaume-Charles Faipoult

Paris, le 2 Pluviose, an 4ᵉ de la République française, une et indivisible.
22 January 1796

Je vous prévient, Monsieur, que le Directoire Exécutif, par un arrêté du 29 nivose dernier a autorisé la Trésorerie Nationale, à Vous rêmettre les Cent Vingt mille Dollars en lingots, que vous y avés déposés et en échange desquels il Vous avoit été fourni des traites Sur la hollande qui n'ont point été acceptées. Le même Arrêté Vous autorise à exporter laditte somme hors le Territoire de la République. Vous pouvés en conséquence, Monsieur, dès ce moment Vous presentez à la Trésorerie pour retirer Les dits Cent Vingt mille Dollars, qui vous Seront rendus sur la remise que vous lui ferés des Effets protestés. Salut et Fraternite.

Faipoult

Editors' Translation

Paris, 2 Pluviose, year 4 of the French Republic, one and indivisible
22 January 1796

This is to inform you, sir, that the Executive Directory has, by a decree of 29 Nivôse, authorized the National Treasury to give you the one hundred twenty thousand dollars in ingots that you deposited with it in exchange for which you were supplied with drafts to be drawn in Holland, but which were not accepted. The same decree permits you to export the said sum out of the territory of the Republic. Consequently, sir, you may from this moment on, go to the Treasury in order to withdraw the said one hundred twenty thousand dollars, which will be returned upon your handing over the protested bills. Salutations and fraternity.

Faipoult

RC, NN : Monroe Papers

From David Humphreys

Lisbon Janʸ 23ᵈ 1796.

Dear Sir

It was not until yesterday that I received Mʳ Barlow's letter of the 23ᵈ of Decʳ; in which he announced that he was on the eve of his departure for Marseilles, and that he proposed to go immediately from thence to Alicant, on the business we originally concerted together. Although the preliminaries of a Treaty were actually signed at the time when we heard the rumour of that event, before my departure from France; yet there are so many complicated matters involved with the Barbary negociations, that I am very glad M.ʳ Barlow is on his way thither. Principally for two reasons, because by my last accounts M.ʳ Donaldson was confined to his bed by sickness, and the public service might suffer greatly by his death or inability to act, before a successor could arrive, and because the whole business will doubtless now be happily resumed & carried on under the mediation, good offices & in a certain degree the guarantee of the French Republic. This I conceive it would be useful for you to take all proper occasions of impressing upon its Government.

M.ʳ Donaldson's apology for having been obliged to deviate from his Instructions in some measure was, the favorable juncture for negociating, the pressing impatience of the Dey, the fear of losing the opportunity of ransoming our Citizens from Slavery, the report of the unfriendly & aristocratic disposition of the French Consul then at Algiers (confirmed by 0'Brien & others who had been uniformly friendly to us) and the absence of the French Agent General, Hercules, to whom alone (as I understood) the Instructions had been given by the Committee of Public Safety, and who has not as yet (or at least had not, a very short time ago) been himself at Algiers. M.ʳ Donaldson farther informs me that having (on his arrival) been confined to his quarters by the gout, he wrote to the French Consul; but neither receiving from him a visit (though he rec.ᵈ visits from the other Consuls) or answer; he was under an absolute necessity of proceeding directly to business, or of leaving the Regency. O'Brien (who has been here himself, & is now gone to England) confirms these particulars and assures me in very positive terms, that the French Consul endeavoured to have the demands of the Dey so much augmented as to render the conclusion of a Treaty absolutely impracticable. I give you these details, with their authority, as they come to me; because I think it is expedient you should know the facts, in order to be able to make such use of them as the circumstances shall require; and to prove to the Government of the French Republic (if necessary) that there has not been any insincerity or inconsistency in our conduct.

I enclose herewith a Memorial to the French Minister of Marine from a French Citizen, established here in commerce just at the commencement of the Revolution . . . in which he solicits a protection for a Ship he is concerned in, bound to Brazil . . . If you should find no impropriety in having it delivered, I should be much obliged by your causing it to be done accordingly . . . And, in case there should be an answer, I entreat that you would have the additional goodness to cause it to be forwarded by water . . . Otherwise, by its falling into improper hands in the Post Office, it might prove prejudicial to the Memorialist.

In begging you to offer my best Compliments to M.ʳˢ Monroe, M.ʳ Paine, M.ʳ Purveyance & our common friends with you, I have the honour to remain, my dear Sir, Your friend & h.ᵇˡᵉ Serv.ᵗ

D. Humphreys

RC, DLC: Monroe Papers

To Melancton Smith

Paris Jan.ʸ 25. 1796.

Dear Sir

I was very happy to hear from you by young M.ʳ Gelston as I always shall be whenever you find leasure to write, confiding as I do in your principles publick & private & wishing in consequence sincerely your welfare. M.ʳ Gelston son who first arrived has been for several months past in my family & to the other you may be assured I will pay the attention you & his father desire.

You have doubtless before this seen the new constitution that is adopted here, & I think will concur with me in opinion that in some respects it is an improvement upon any yet adopted. The submission of the ratification of treaties to the more numerous branch is one of its traits which merits particular commendation. This however is a subject upon which comments from me are not necessary. A representation of its progress & of the actual state of things here is more interesting & which I will concisely give. The gov^t has been in operation ab^t three months & in the course whereof it has introduc'd a reform in many branches of the adm^n, of great importance. The assignats were on the point of ceasing to circulate, the am^t thrown into circulation being so great as to render their redemption according to the sum specified impossible: and there was no specie in the treasury or other resource to supply their place. In this state of things the Directoire recommended to the legislature the project of a loan, reimbursible by instalments, but which was to be obtained by distress, upon the presumption the patriotism of all upon whom it wo^d fall was not a sufficient resource. This was imposed ab^t 5. weeks past & is now collecting with tolerable effect. The sum expected to be thus raised is 600.000.000. of livres, ab^t 25.000.000 str^g but it will certainly produce much more if generally collected, & which the present prospect authorizes the belief of. This measure therefore will supply present exigencies & give time for a more complete system & w^h is now under consideration in the council of 500.

There were in Paris many thousand young men who were comprehended in the existing requisition, & who were the instruments if not the cause of many of the commotions which took place here. These were order'd immediately to the Frontiers & in consequence actually embodied & marched off. It is said, & by respectable authority, that at least 100.000 men (including those taken from all parts) are thus raised & which you will deem no trifling reinforcement to the armies on the Rhine & in Italy.

Sometime about the middle of Decr a truce was asked by the Austrians & granted by the French generals for one month, & w^h is since prolonged by the two gov^{ts} for what term or with what view we know not. It is however suspected that a negotiation for peace is on foot, but with what prospect of success no one hazards a conjecture. It is reported that England is willing to restore every thing to France & leave her the Belgic &c provided France will leave her in possession of the cape of good hope: but this I think she will not do, tho' indeed the Dutch merit but little for any exertions yet made in the common cause, or even for themselves.

The c^t Carletti of Tuscany minister &c asked permission to see the young unfortunate daughter of Louis 16. before her departure for Balsse to be exchanged for Bournonville & several deputies surrender'd formerly by Dumourier, & for which demand his functions were suspended & himself order'd without the bounds of the Republick, & finally sent out by force, he having refused to comply. As soon as this was communicated to the G^d Duke he dispatched another Envoy to disavow the demand of Carletti & who is already on the ground.

I beg of you to make my best respects to our friend Govr Clinton who I hope has recover'd his health, as likewise to Mr Gelston, to whom I will endeavour to write, tho' as his sons are here & doubtless often write him it is of course less necessary. Believe me with real regard Dear Sir Sincerely yours

Ja^s Monroe

RC, IaU

Although not addressed, it is extremely likely that Melancton Smith was the recipient of this letter. Smith wrote to JM via Maltby Gelston on 6 August 1795 (above). This, combined with JM's reference to George Clinton's health—Smith commented on Clinton's health in his letter—points to Smith as the recipient.

From James Madison

Philadᵃ Janʸ 25. 1796

Dear Sir

The articles sent to Havre, came as you anticipated, in the same vessel with Mʳ Murray, to N. York, from whence they have safely arrived here. They lay us under very great obligations to your kindness, and are the more valuable, as we venture to consider them as bearing the sanction of Mʳˢ Monroe's taste as well as yours. The carpets, in particular, are truly important acquisitions. In the two pˢ of silk (of 25 Ells each for Curtains), charged in the Invoice as Damask at 500ᵗʰ per Ell, there has probably been some mistake or deception on the part of the vender. They are not of damask but of an inferior & cheaper sort of silk. Inclosed are samples of both pieces, that if there be error, & it be not too late, the difference of price may be refunded. It is not wished that you should otherwise rectify the error, as the articles sent are fully adequate to our purposes. The delay of the Ch[ina] till the Spring is no wise inconvenient to us. That it will be satisfactor[y we] have already abundant pledges. As to any other articles for which you so k[ind]ly offer your services, we have not at present any specific request to make. You know generally, that any little supplies accomodated to our wants & our means, of both which you are a pretty competent judge, will be acceptable—provided always that it can be done without trouble to yourself.

RC, DLC: Madison Papers. Unsigned

From James Madison

Philadᵃ January 26. 1796.

Dear Sir

Since my last[1] I have had the pleasure of your two favors of Ocᵗ 23 & 24. The business of the Treaty with G. B. remains as it stood. A copy of the British ratification has arrived; but the Executive wait, it seems, for the original as alone proper for communication. In the mean time, altho' it is probable that *the house* if brought to *say yea or nay* directly *on the merits of the treaty* will *vote against it yet* a *majority can* not be *trusted on a question* for *applying to the president for the treaty*. In the mean time also information has arrived of *the conclusion of a treaty with Spain with which the other will of course be combined*. No hint of the *terms is yet given to the public* nor are *they probably* otherwise *known to the executive* than by *the instructions*. That provision is *made for Mississippi is to be presumed*. Its *aspect on the Mississippi article* in the *British treaty* will *be particularly interesting*. Among other *attitudes* given by this *event to our situation* it is highly probable that the *Spanish treaty* will *comprise stipulations* at once *popular and similar in principle to some attacked* in *the British treaty*.

General Smith of Baltimore has offered to the House a resolution that after the ____ day of ____ no vessel shall land in the U. S. any articles not produced by the Country to which the vessel belongs.[2] It will *embarrass the eastern members* but *they will venture to oppose it as* tending to *perplex the treaty question*; and probably with *success if joined by the south members* as *hitherto from other motives*.

You will be pleased & perhaps surprised at the *scene produced by the French flag*. The *harangue of the president* must *grate the British party but they are cunning enough to be silent*. It seems that *Adet notwithstanding the complimentary* & *cordial language* of the *president and* Representatives, is *much disgusted at the deposit of the flag* elsewhere *than in the hall of Congress*. You can perhaps better *appreciate the case* than *we can*. Such a result, where other circumstances *were so propitious is unfortunate*. I send a copy of the proceeding. I also send a copy of the proceedings in the case of Randal & Whitney, which need no comment, beyond your own reflections.[3]

I send also E. R's Vindication, with a malignant attack on it, by a satirical but scurrilous writer.[4] The *latter* has *published several other pamphlets* exhibiting him in the *same character. Bond is among the putative authors*. But the *real author* is probably *some hireling* to whom *materials may be supplied. Randolph is resettled at Richmond & resumes the practice of the law* with *flattering prospects as is said*. The *effect of his pamphlet* is not yet *fully known*. His *greatest enemies* will not easily persuade *themselves that he was under a corrupt influence of France* and *his best friend can't save him* from the *self condemnation of* his *political career as explained by himself*. The "Political Observations" is *a fugitive thing of my own written at the heel of the last session* in *pure compliance with the urgency of certain friends*. It is *full of press blunders* as you will perceive.[5]

We have accounts here that Mr Paine is dead. I spoke to Mͬ Bache on the subject of the advance by you, to be repaid for Mͬ Paine, thro' my hands. He said only that he would call on me & shew me the papers, which he has not done. I inferred from his manner, that there was a deficit of funds in his hands to be explained by him. I heard nothing from Mͬ Pickering on the other pecuniary subject. Just as I am making up this packet, I have the pleasure of a letter for you from Mͬ Jones,[6] which will no doubt give you all the requisite information for which you rely on him. Mͬˢ M. seconds all the acknowledgments due to you & Mͬˢ Monroe, as well as the affectionate esteem with which I ever remain Yours

Jˢ Madison Jr.

P. S. Chˢ Lee has entered on the duties of Attʸ Genˡ. No Secr(etary) at War yet nominated—nor any Judge in the place of J. Rutlege, or (of) Mͬ Blair who has resigned.[7] Mͬ Rutledge also sent his resignation; but the Senate had previously rejected him.

RC, DLC: Madison Papers. Words in italics were written in code by Madison, a portion of which was deciphered by JM. The file copy in DLC: Madison Papers is not coded .

1. Madison's last letter preceding this one was that of 25 January 1796 (the preceding day) in which he acknowledged the receipt of household goods that JM sent from Paris. Madison probably refers to his letter of 20 December 1795.

2. Samuel Smith of Maryland introduced his resolution in the House of Representatives on 4 January 1796 (*Madison Papers*, 16: 189-190).

3. Robert Randall and Charles Whitney were partners in a land speculation scheme that aimed at obtaining pre-emption rights to 20 million acres in the Northwest Territory. Randall and Whitney attempted to secure support in Congress for the necessary legislation by offering shares in the company to members of the House of Representatives. The Speaker of the House ordered that they be brought before the House on charges of contempt of Congress and a breach of privileges. Randall was found guilty on 6 January 1796 and received a reprimand. Whitney, who engaged in lobbying activities before the House was in session, was not convicted (*Madison Papers*, 16: 175).

4. William Cobbett ("Peter Porcupine"), *A New Year's Gift to the Democrats; or, Observations on a Pamphlet, Entitled, "A Vindication of Mr Randolph's Resignation"* (Philadelphia, 1796; *Early American Imprints* #30215).

5. Madison's pamphlet, *Political Observations*, dated 20 April 1795, was written in response to attacks on the Republicans by Federalist pamphleteers (*Madison Papers*, 15: 511-534).

6. Joseph Jones to JM, 16 January 1796, above.

7. John Blair resigned from the Supreme Court in October 1795 (*ANB*).

To Timothy Pickering

Paris January 26th 1796.

Sir,

Some weeks past the property of William Vans a citizen of the United States was attached by Joseph Sands another citizen of the said States in a tribunal of France at Havre, where the cause was sustained and judgment rendered in favour of the plaintiff. From this judgment the defendant appealed to the superior tribunal of the department at Rouen, where I believe it is now depending. As soon as the suit commenced Mr Vans applied for my interference, claiming by the 12th article of the consular convention between the two republics, an exemption at the instance of a fellow citizen from the tribunals of the country, the cognizance of such controversies being as he supposed thereby exclusively vested in the consuls of each nation within the jurisdiction of the other. I examined attentively the convention and was of opinion that the construction insisted on by Mr Vans was sound, but yet as the subject was important in respect to the principle, and questionable in point of policy, I wished to decline any interference in it until I had your instruction. He continued however to press me, urging that if such was the import of the article it vested in him a right, which I ought to secure him the enjoyment of, the deprivation of which too in the present instance would be his ruin, for that the execution of the judgment by the sale of the merchandize attached at Havre where there was then no demand for it, would not only subject him in that view to a severe loss, but that he was likewise sued for the same debt in America and where judgment would likewise be probably rendered against him. Finally therefore I did apply in his behalf by a letter to the minister of foreign affairs,[1] of which I send you a copy, explaining my idea of the import of the treaty in the case in question, and requesting that the executive so far as depended on that branch, and provided it concurred with me in the construction, might cause the same to be executed and to which I have yet received no answer, though I am assured verbally that the Directoire concur with me in the construction, and that a correspondent intimation thereon will be given by the minister of justice to the court where the suit now is, and with whom it will probably be decisive. I state this case that you may apprize me, how it is the wish of the President I should act, in cases of the kind in future, and even in the present one, if not finally settled before I hear from you, and which may possibly happen. If it be wished that such controversies should be decided by the courts of the country, I doubt not such a construction and practice will be agreeable to this government; but if the contrary is preferred you will I presume see the necessity of prescribing by the suitable authority, how the consular courts are to be held, how their process is to be executed, and appeals conducted.

As connected with this subject permit me to can your attention to another, and upon which I likewise wish to be instructed. For the port of Havre there are at present two consuls, or rather a consul and a Vice Consul, both of whom Mr Cutting and Mr La Motte are recognized by this government. Was it intended the latter commission should supersede the former, and in that case should I take in the former? or is it intended that both should exist at the same time, the power of the vice Consul being dormant only when the Consul is present? I wish to know in what light I am to consider the appointments since thereby I shall know to whom I am to look for the performance of the consular duties of the port.

A third one of the same kind occurs, and which I think proper to mention to you. Sometime since Mr Pitcairn was appointed Vice Consul for Paris, and in respect to which appointment I deemed it my duty to present before you several considerations, growing out of his character as a British subject, and the actual state of things here, which made it inexpedient to demand his recognition of this government until after they were weighed, and I in consequence further instructed on that head. These were stated in my letter of 17th of May last, and to which as yet I have received no answer. As Mr Pitcairn probably expects to hear from me on the subject, I shall thank you for information what I am to say to him, and how I am to act in that respect.

The collection of the forced loan continues, and will I think succeed, but what its product will be is a point upon which there is a diversity of opinion. Some think it will fall short of the sum at which it was estimated, whilst others carry it much beyond that estimation. Certain however it is that by means thereof the embarrassments of the government will for the present be relieved, and time given for the maturity, and adoption of a more complete system of finance, which subject is now under consideration of the council of five hundred.

About the twenty-fifth of December last [a truce]² was asked by the Austrian Generals Wurmser and Clairfait, of Pichegru and Jourdan for three months, and granted subject to the will of the Directoire, by whom it is said it was allowed for one only, the report at first circulated, that it was wholly rejected, being without foundation. Whether it will be prolonged admitting the term as here stated to be correct is unknown, as likewise is the motive of Austria in asking and France in granting, it. The presumption is, it was to try the experiment of negociation in the interim, and such is the report: and it is likewise presumable that such an experiment was made or is now making: but from what I can learn there is little prospect of its producing a peace. It will be difficult to part Austria from England, whilst the latter supplies the former with money to carry on the war, and which she will probably continue to do whilst she carries it on herself. The present prospect therefore is that Europe is destined to sustain the waste and havoc of another campaign; for superior as England is at sea, with the recent conquest of the Cape of Good-Hope,³ it is not probable if she escapes an internal convulsion, the symptoms of which have diminished of late, that she will restore every thing on her part, and leave France in possession of the Belgie: and without which I think France will not make peace. A doubt indeed has latterly been circulated whether England will make any sacrifice in favor of the Emperor, whether in short she would agree to restore the possessions taken by her from France and Holland, as a consideration for the restoration of the Belgie [to]⁴ the Emperor. It is even added that intimations have been given by her, that if France will leave her in possession of her conquest from Holland, she will restore every thing taken from France, and leave her in possession of St Domingo and the Belgie. If this is true and is credited by the Emperor it will certainly tend to weaken, and perhaps absolutely to dissolve the connection between England and Austria.

I communicated to you in two preceding letters⁵ the application of Count Carletti, Minister from Tuscany for permission to visit the "<u>unfortunate young Princess &c</u>" and the displeasure which that demand gave to the Directoire, who suspended his powers immediately, ordered him to leave the Republic forthwith, and finally sent him by force beyond its limits. It was apprehended by many that this peremptory mode of proceeding would give offence to the Grand Duke: the contrary however was the case, for as soon as he heard of the transaction he dispatched another Envoy to the Directoire to disavow the demand of Carletti and declare his respect for the French government, and such was the solicitude for his hasty departure, that he actually departed without the ordinary credentials, bearing simply a letter of introduction from the Grand Duke himself. Thus therefore this business has ended without producing any injury to the French Republic, whilst it is a proof of the energy of its councils and of its decision upon the delicate subject [to]⁶ which it refers.

On the 21st instant, being the anniversary of the execution of the late king, the members of the legislative corps, of the Directoire, and all public officers [took]⁷ a new and solemn oath to support the Constitution, or rather of hatred to royalty. The directoire gave on the same day what is called a fête in the champ de Mars, where an Amphitheatre was erected and from whence the President surrounded by the other members, and all the ministers of government delivered an oration suited to the occasion to a numerous audience. It seems to be the policy of the existing government to revive the zeal of the people in favor of the republic, and of the revolution, and measures of this kind are certainly well calculated to produce that effect. With great respect and esteem, I am, Sir, y^r very humble Servant.

J^{as} Monroe.

P. S. Since writing the above I have heard through a channel that merits confidence, that the term of the truce is prolonged, and which strengthens what I intimated above, that a negociation is depending with Austria. The recent departure too of one of the Dutch Ministers for Holland, after a conference with the Directoire, and which took place about the time the truce was probably prolonged, is a circumstance which I think proper to communicate, since it gives cause to suspect if a negociation is depending it treats for a general and not a partial peace.

Copy, DNA: RG 59: Dispatches from France; a draft of this letter in PPRF lacks the postscript.

1. JM to Charles Delacroix, 31 December 1795, above.

2. The clerk who copied this letter omitted this word. It and all subsequent corrections are supplied from the draft in PPRF.

3. Shortly after fleeing the Netherlands in early 1795, the Prince of Orange urged the British to occupy the Dutch colony at the Cape of Good Hope. A British force arrived at the Cape in June 1795 but met resistance from the colonists. The British captured Cape Town in September and established a military government in the name of the Prince of Orange. They maintained control of the colony until 1803 (Henry H. Johnston, *The History of the Colonization of Africa by Alien Races* (revised edition, 1966), 135-136).

4. The clerk wrote "of".

5. JM to Pickering, 6 December and 22 December 1795, above.

6. The clerk wrote "of".

7. The clerk wrote "to".

From Thomas Pinckney

London 29 Jan^{ry} 1796

My dear Sir

I arrived at this place on the 14th of the present month after a tedious journey, and & on my arrival here found that Parliament was adjourned 'till some time in the next month; & though there were late arrivals from our Country there was no news of consequence from thence; since then the Presidents speech to the Legislature has arrived & though I think it probable you may have received it already, yet I inclose it lest that should not be the case. *I am desir'd to proceed on the negotiation on the twelfth article of the treaty & promised instructions on that subject which have not yet arrived.*

Mr Phelps who takes charge of this comes strongly recommended to me from America; & has been so obliging as to take under his care young Mr States Rutledge whom his father had recommended to your Protection & whom I presume you will place with M^r McDermot. He had only bill of thirty five pounds St^g sent for his expences, his father having relied, as he says, on a Mr Sarjeant with whom he came delivering him to you & defraying his expences but their vessel have been taken & brought here has deranged Mr Sarjeants plans & he cannot advance him money: & an elder Brother of young States[1] who was on the point of embarking for America has employed part of the £35. so that I have found it necessary to borrow for him here forty pounds which after deducting some small expences incurr'd here lately,

584 The Papers of James Monroe: Volume III

will be placed in Mr Phelps hands in order to defray his expences to Paris & to place the ballance with you & I would recommend as soon as you have calculated his years expences to draw for the whole of it once upon his father as you know our American money transactions are sometimes tedious in arranging. I say this upon the presumption that you will take charge of this youth of which circumstances you are the best Judge.

It is said not to be determined yet whether the Emperor will receive a loan from this Country or not tho' it is now confidently said that he will which circumstance will probably depend on his negociations with France.

Adieu my dear sir—be pleased to present my affectionate respects to Mrs Monroe & your daughter in which my little folks desire to unite & believe me to be sincerely yours

Thomas Pinckney

I have not had sufficient notice of Mr Phelps departure to send your books by him, but they shall be forwarded by an early opportunity.

RC, NN: Monroe Papers. The words in italics were written in code by Pinckney and deciphered by JM.

John Rutledge had three sons in Europe at this time. Charles Rutledge (b. 1773) attended school at Edinburgh and served as Pinckney's secretary during Pinckney's mission to Spain. He remained in Spain as American chargé, a post he held 1796-1799. Upon his return home he embarked on a career as a physician. William Rutledge studied in Holland 1794-1796. He later became a merchant. William was the elder brother to which Pinckney referred. States Rutledge (b. 1783) was the youngest child of John Rutledge. He attended school at St. Germain under JM's supervision. He served as a midshipman in the U. S. Navy 1798-1802 (James Haw, *John and Edward Rutledge*, 16, 229, 261; JM account books, DLC: Monroe Papers and ViFreJM; Edward Callahan, *List of Officers of the U. S. Navy and of the Marine Corps*, 1775-1900).

From Andrew Masson

2 february 1796

sir

since the letter I had the honour to direct to you dated 6 X^{bre} through M^r terrasson[1] the americans still frank and Generous in their proceedings in favour of G^{nl} Lafayette have directed an address to m^r parish in order to Render the danish Government mediator towards the course of Vienna for the liberation of that General. Mr Parish in that circumstance has distinguished himself by his Zeal as much as the concern and friendship which he has given particular proofs of. Copies of the said address have been already Sent to M^r adams at la hague M^r pinkney at london and M^r saabye at copenhagne.[2] by what I know from the americans who are here as much as those who inhabit those countries, this address is to be unanimously adopted. but it affords a peculiar importance of seeing you, sir, and the americans within your Ministry, Giving the assent to that address which serves one and indivisible cause.

then we have the honour to apply to you sir, and to Refer to your sagacity and the interest you take to the cause of that General and his family for the same adhesion which is to be given by the Citizens of the united states or [party] of them, whom you are the worthy representative at paris. M^r gregory,[3] one of the Gentlemen who have signed the said address, and M^r terrasson both gone to paris will beg of you that attention. When it is to be considered on a side that already the G^{nl} Washington has adopted the son of G^{nl} Lafayette, on the other hand the Doctor bolman[4] has been received with every mark of distinction at philadelphia for having assisted g^{nl} Lafayette in his escape, it prooves clearly that every thing which may contribute to the deliverance of that General is already approoved by the mother country. Nothing agrees better with these procedings, than those of the americans in europe concerning the address and adhesion to it specially when that liberation does not concern the french Government which has taken no part in the confinement.

I beg of you, sir, the favour of sending back that adhesion, (we submit to you to be done) to m^r parish who will be so kind as to collect all together to be forwarded to the dannemark and sweden for the intended end.

P. S. I was told that M^{de} Motié, before she quitted Vienna, has left a letter for me, by which she has appointed me to Receive all the letters which may be directed to her name, and the funds which could be sent either from her family, or from the ministry of the united states, in order to be employed to clear her debts and other wants which may occur and which I am to keep an account of. in the case of that letter Reaching me I'll let M^r parish know the contain. he has already been so kind as to advance, so I did, some money for mad^e. I have been very sensible of it. as for your letter deposited in his hands,[5] a favourable opportunity has presented itself to Give you the way of acquiting the funds mentioned in it. m^r abema who (for the wants of madame I spoke about) has already payed some money for her with a generosity which caracterises his person, has got his own counting house at paris which you are ac-quainted with. it affords you the opportunity of paying to that counting house the sum contained in your letter deposited here, or to order this letter to be remitted to M^r abema here. I had the honour to be formerly acquainted with him, and you may judge of the advantage I have to be still so. It will be a very usefull way for the money you wish to send to fill him up on account of the future advances he might be good enough to do for the present unluky circumstance.

I beg you my pardon for all the trouble I give you, sir, on these accounts, but after what Mad^e Motié told me about the peculiar kindnesses you know so well how to ally with the mission trusted to your cares, I supposed to be excused. The present occasion, though the motive very unfortunate, does however a great service to me, Giving me the opportunity of presenting to a representant of the united states the respectfull assurances of my sentiments and respects. I am, Sir, your most obed^t s^t

A. Masson

P. S. If the adhesion proposed speaks about sweden to be conjointly mediator with the dannemark, the reason is that there is no consul at stockolm; and however the hope, or rather the assurance we are in, that that government will joing the dannemark for the said mediation; it engages us to wish ardently the request of it to be made by paris's adhesion and london's to the other adhesion being already on the point to be at an end and too much advanced to mention it.

RC, NN: Monroe Papers

1. Masson to JM, 6 December 1795, above.

2. Hans Saabye was the American consul at Copenhagen 1792-1817 (Walter B. Smith, *America's Diplomats and Consuls of 1776-1865*, 74).

3. John Gregorie was a merchant from Petersburg, Virginia, who resided in Dunkirk. JM recommended him for appointment as consul at Dunkirk (JM to Pickering, 2 May 1796, below).

$. Justus-Erich Bollmann (1769-1821) was a German physician who attempted to help Lafayette escape from prison at Olmutz. Bollman established a practice in Paris, where he gained access to French society and Madame de Staël. After the September Massacres in 1792 put many of the nobility in danger, Mme de Staël implored him to get her lover, the Comte de Narbonne, to safety in London. This Bollman was able to do, but he found himself cut off from France. When the mission of rescuing Lafayette was offered to him, he seized it with enthusiasm. After his diplomatic efforts failed, Bollman determined to rescue Lafayette by force. The attempt in full daylight on 8 November 1794, almost succeeded, but Lafayette was recaptured and Bollman was arrested (*Appletons' Cyclopedia*; Andreas Latzko, *Lafayette, A Life*, 248-264; André Maurois, *Adrienne ou La Vie de*

Mme Lafayette, 3ll, 312, 329, *546)*. Masson's information on Bollman's reception at Philadelphia was erroneous. Bollmann did not arrive in the United States (at New York) until the beginning of January 1796 (*Gazette of the United States*, 13 January 1796).

5. JM to Adrienne Lafayette, 16 November 1795, above.

To Guillaume-Charles Faipoult

Paris february 4th 1796.

I have just received the inclosed Letter from the Consul General of the United States with the Republick,[1] representing the embarrassed situation of many of our citizens who have furnished supplies to the Government; and which I have thought it my duty to submit to your consideration: not doubting that you will do every thing in your power to relieve them from their embarrassment. You will readily perceive, from the delicacy of mercantile Credit, the injury they are exposed to, perhaps the ruin, by the protest of their own bills; since they were drawn in payment of the debt they had contracted in rendering such supplies to this Government; and which danger is the greater on account of the delay they had previously experienced in the adjustment of their claims. You will likewise fully appreciate the baneful effect which the example of their misfortune will produce upon the future commerce of the Country, in the discouragement of others. In this view therefore their case merits comment from me, and by submitting to you, permit me to add that all that I wish is, that you take into Consideration the circumstances of these merchants, and render them such immediate aid, in relief of their present embarrassments, by partial payments, where the cases will admit of it, (and I presume there are few, if any, that will not admit of it) as the situation of the Republick, providing for its general welfare, will authorize. In the scale of your affairs, you will observe (paying due regard to the pressure of other objects and the policy of sustaining and advancing by all practicable means the growing credit of the Government,) what attention is due to the claims of those who have embarked their Credit and their fortunes in its support; and I am well assured you will pay them all the attention they merit.

FC, NN: Monroe Papers

1. Fulwar Skipwith's letter regarding the rejection of bills drawn on the French government at Hamburg has not been located (see JM to Timothy Pickering, 16 February 1796, below).

From Jean-Jacques Cambacérès

Paris le 16 pluviose de l'an 4 [5 February 1796]

Citoyen ministre

L'intéret avec lequel vous avez bien voulu me parler de la petite cousine compagne de la citoyenne votre fille, m'autorise à vous demander pour elle une grace.

Voudriez vous permettre qu'on place dans un coin de votre voiture un paquet contenant une robe dont cette jeune personne doit se parer pour la représentation à laquelle vous devez assister.

Agréez mes excuses Si je ne viens moi- même vous demander cet acte de complaisance, mais mes occupations ne m'ont pas permis de me déplacer. Salut et fraternité.

Cambacérès

Editors' Translation

Paris 16 Pluviose year 4 [5 February 1796]

Citizen Minister

The interest you have shown in speaking of the young cousin, companion to the citizen your daughter, enables me to ask you a favor on her behalf.

Would you allow a parcel to be placed in a corner of your carriage containing a gown that this young woman is supposed to wear for the performance that you plan to attend?

Please accept my apologies if I do not come myself to request this indulgence, but my business activities have not allowed me to get away. Salutations and Fraternity.

Cambacérès

RC, NN: Monroe Papers

From Guillaume-Charles Faipoult

Paris le 16 Pluviose, an 4ᵉ de la Republique Française, une et indivisible.
[5 February 1796]

Citizen Minister

In answer to your letter of the 15 insᵗ covering another addressed to you by the consul general of the united States,[1] I have the Satisfaction to acquaint you, that sensible to the circumstances and just claims of divers American Citizens, on account of the embarrassments, which might result to them from the unpaid bills of exchange given to some and farther delays to others, in payments owed them, for sundry furnitures they have made to government, I am at this very time aiming at effectual measures, to relieve them as shortly and extensively as possible; having nothing more at heart than to strengthen and enlarge as much as lies in my power all friendly and commercial connexions between our Republics. please to be fully persuaded of these dispositions of mine and of a most Sincere regard

faipoult

RC, NN: Monroe Papers

1. JM to Faipoult, 4 February 1796, above.

From Jacob Van Staphorst

10ᵗʰ febr. 1796.

Dear Sir

It appears to me with you that the proposal of Mess. Corsange & Cᵒ is if not an advantageous at least an acceptable one, provided the Bills are not upon too long terms, which would occasion so much so much longer advances from the Bankers in Amsterdam and of consequence a loss of Interest for the United States. Besides this the only reflexion I have to make is, that they Say, that if the Cours of Exchange Should be fixed at 54 oz which is right and the Ingots at the Standard of Paris, which is the case, they can not take them at a higher price than 45# 10ˢ l'marc, Since you have received them in payment from Mess. Dallarde Swan & Cᵒ, if I am not mistaken, at 50# 17ˢ 3ᵈ which gives a loss of more than 10 pcᵗ. I am Sir, most respectfully Yours

Van Staphorst

RC, NN: Monroe Papers

JM continued to be plagued by the problem of how to transfer the funds he held in Paris to the bankers in Amsterdam. Bills of exchange proved to be unsatisfactory since they were discounted and therefore worth only a portion of actual amount. The problem was resolved when the French government agreed to take responsibility for shipping the actual silver to Amsterdam. (John H. Purviance to JM, 31 December 1796, below; Jacob Van Staphorst to JM, 25 December 1797, NN: Monroe Papers).

From Thomas Pinckney

London 15 Febʳʸ 1796

Dear Sir

I received your favor of the 27ᵗʰ of the last month by Mʳ Governeur¹ whom I regret much that I had not the pleasure of seeing during his short residence here as I happened to be from home when he brought your letter & He was engaged when I requested the favor of his company at my house—He will I believe take charge of a trunk with sundry articles which Miss Nicholson has purchased for Mʳˢ Monroe to whom Miss N: has written & inclosed the accounts.² With respect to the repeating watch you have been kind enough to bespeak for me from Lepine, I must request you to make the best bargain for me you can with respect to the price & whatever you shall agree for I will pay.

I have no late intelligence from our Government. Mʳ Adams is still in London but conceives his mission here superceded my return. It would be beneficial to Strengthen the claim of sundry of our citizens for property taken from them on the high Seas by the enemies of this nation if authenticated copies of all the arrêts of the former & present French Government reflecting our intercourse with that nation & particularly with their Colonies could be procured & speedily forwarded to this place—If it should be in your power to furnish them I have no doubt you will do so. I send herewith a copy of Mʳ Randolph's Vindication. Mʳ Pickering is confirmed in the office of Secretary of State.³ I have not heard of the nomination of a Secretary for the War department. I beg you to present my affectᵗᵉ respects & best wishes to Mʳˢ Monroe & your daughter of which my little folks beg to unite with dear Sir Your faithful and obedᵗ Servant

Thomas Pinckney

RC, NN: Monroe Papers

1. JM's letter to Pinckney, delivered by Elizabeth Monroe's brother-in-law Nicholas Gouverneur (d. 1807), has not been located.

2. Miss Nicholson has not been identified. She resided with the Monroes in Paris from July to December 1795 (Account Book, DLC: Monroe Papers). Her letter to Elizabeth Monroe has not been located.

3. Pickering was appointed on 10 December 1795 (*BDAC*).

Theobald Wolfe Tone Journal

[15 February 1796]

Went to <u>Monroe's</u>, the Ambassador's and delivered in my passport and Letters.[1] Received very politely by Monroe who inquired a great deal as to the state of the public mind in America, which I answered as well as I could, and in a manner to satisfy him pretty well as to my own sentiments. He asked me particularly whether people did not think his situation a painful one; I told him they certainly did; he interrupted me by assuring me that it was most extremely so, and spoke with a good deal of emphasis; he then asked me what people in America thought would be the conduct of France on the treaty with England and the manifest bias of the American Gov[t] in favor of the latter country? I answered that the public opinion seemed to be that France, however justly provoked, would not manifest any open discontent at the late measures. He did not make any observation on this. He then enquired how the President bore the outcry against the Treaty? I told him, with a great deal of what himself and his friends would call firmness. He then asked me did the President hold his ground with the people as formerly? I answered that he still retained a great share of his popularity, but undoubtedly it was considerably diminished, and I instanced the alteration made by the House of Rep[s] in their answer to his speech. He asked me did I think he would be re-elected, if he wished it? I answered I thought he would, undoubtedly; but that, if he was wise he would, in my opinion, never suffer himself to be proposed again. He then enquired how Pickering and Wolcott stood with the people? I answered they were looked upon as mere puppets, danced by M[r] Hamilton and that the President himself was completely under the same influence; He asked me then was it thought that himself was any wise influenced by that party? I said, by no means, but very much the reverse, and that, among other reasons, might make his situation unpleasant "<u>No</u>, said he, <u>they would cut my throat.</u>" He then, adverting to Adet's letter asked me what was his opinion of the American Government? I answered I could not pretend to say, but I did believe it was very bad, for that he seemed to me to be extremely disgusted, "<u>I believe so too</u>, answered he; <u>do You know that he has applied to be recalled?</u>" He then asked me what effect Randolph's vindication (which I had brought in my pocket, and given him) had on the public mind? I evaded answering this by saying it had only appeared a day or two before I sailed and of course I could not tell. He then asked what I thought, myself, would be the effect? I answered him that I thought it would only confirm both parties in the present way of thinking for neither would read it with impartiality; I enquired of him where I was to deliver my dispatches; he informed at the Minister for foreign Affairs, and gave me his address. I then rose and told that when he had read Beckley's letter (which was in cypher)[2] he would I hope find me excused in taking the liberty to call again; he answered he would be happy at all times to see me, and after enquiry after M[r] Hamilton Rowan,[3] how he liked America? &c. I took my leave and returned to his Office for my passport. The Secretary smoked me for an Irishman directly—<u>A la bonheur!</u>[4]

AD, Trinity College Library, Dublin

1. Tone arrived in France from the United States on 2 February 1796 and in Paris on February 12 (*Life of Theobald Wolfe Tone*, 2: 1, 7). He was using the alias James Smith, and it was under this name that he first met JM.

2. John Beckley to JM, 14 December 1795, above.

3. Archibald Hamilton Rowan (1751-1834) was an Irish nationalist. He was convicted of sedition in January 1794, but escaped from prison, fleeing first to France and then to the United States. He eventually settled in Hamburg in 1800 where he remained until 1803 when he received a pardon and returned to Ireland (Brian Lalor, *Encyclopedia of Ireland*, 944).

4. After visiting JM, Tone wrote in his diary that "I am perfectly pleased with my reception at Monroe's and at the Minister's, but can form no possible conjecture as to the event. The letter being in cypher, he could form no guess, as to whom I might be, or what might be my business. All I can say, is, that I found no difficulty in obtaining access to him; that his behavior was extremely affable and polite, and, in a word, that if I have no ground to auger any thing good, neither have I reason to expect anything bad." (*Life of Theobald Wolfe Tone*, 2: 13).

To Timothy Pickering

Paris, Feb.ʸ 16. 1796.

I think it my duty to state to you and without delay, a communication made me yesterday by the Minister of foreign affairs, of a very interesting nature. I called to represent to him the distress of several of my countrymen, occasioned by the protest at hamburgh of bills given them for supplies rendered the government; and to request his aid with the Directoire to obtain them relief. This application was intended to harmonize with one that was making informally by our Consul General with the Directoire, and which was arranged in a manner to present the demands of the claimants before that body in a forcible manner, and at the same time without wounding its feelings. But before I entered on this subject, my attention was called to another more important; and upon which he seemed pleased with the opportunity of addressing me. He observed that the Directoire had at length made up its mind, how to act in regard to our Treaty with England.—That it considered the alliance between us as ceasing to exist, from the moment the Treaty was ratified; and had or should appoint an Envoy Extraordinary to attend and represent the same to our government. That the person in view was known and esteemed in our Country, and who would be specially commissioned on this business, and whose commission would expire with it. That Mʳ Adet had asked and obtained his recall, but did not say whether any other minister would be appointed in his stead for the present; tho' as connected with Adet's resignation it is reported that Maret, lately returned from captivity in Austria, is to succeed him. The minister added some general observations on the Treaty, tending to shew that it was considered as throwing us into the scale of the coalized powers; observing that he should hand me an official note on this subject, being ordered so to do by the Directoire. As no specific objection was stated, I could make no specific reply. I expressed to him however my astonishment and concern at the measure spoken of, and inculcated in the short time I remained with him (for he was upon the point of going out) the propriety of candour in the discussion of the Treaty in its several parts, and the benefit of temper in all transactions with us, since we were certainly their best friends. To this he made no answer, and whereupon I left him. I have since heard nothing from him nor on the subject. I mean to see him however to-day; and, in case he permits me to act on the Communication, as an official one to demand an audience of the Directoire, to endeavor to divert it, if possible, from the measure contemplated; of which, and of the business generally I will write you again in a day or two.

FC, NN: Monroe Papers

Delacroix informed JM on February 15 that the Directory had decided to respond to the Jay Treaty by severing diplomatic relations with the United States and that France would send an envoy extraordinary to the United States to announce the decision. Reports that Hugues-Bernard Maret would undertake the mission proved to be false, for on February 17 the Directory announced the recall of Adet and the appointment of Colonel Charles-Humbert Vincent (who was in Paris at the time assisting in the acquisition of books and instruments for the U. S. War Department) as its special envoy. Not satisfied with a temporary rank, Vincent asked that he be appointed minister plenipotentiary to succeed Adet in the United States. Vincent's aggressiveness alienated the Directory, and this, along with JM's efforts to prevent the mission, persuaded the Directory to rescind Vincent's appointment (Albert Hall Bowman, The *Struggle for Neutrality*, 239-245; Monroe to Skipwith, January 12, 1796, NN: Monroe Papers).

Hugues-Bernard Maret (1763-1839) was the editor of *Le Moniteur Universel*. He was appointed French minister to Naples in July 1793 and was captured by the Austrians while enroute to that city. He was one of the prisoners released in late 1795 in exchange for the princess royal, and took a seat in the council of 500 after his return to Paris. He served as secretary to Napoleon throughout his reign and was minister of foreign affairs 1811-1813. He received the title duc de Bassano in 1809 (*Nouvelle Biographie Générale*).

To Charles Delacroix

Paris february 17ᵗʰ 1796.

Sir

The communication you were pleased to make me of the intention of the Directoire to appoint an Envoy extraordinary to repair to the United States to declare to our government the high dissatisfaction which the Directoire entertain in respect to the late treaty with Great Britain, and other acts which you deem unfriendly to this republic, has penetrated me with the deepest concern, because I fear from a measure so marked and conspicuous the most serious ill consequences both to you and to us. Permit me therefore to state to you with the same freedom and confidence the objections, which occur to me against this proceedure, not doubting you will pay to them all the attention they merit.

A mission of this kind is calculated not only to make an impression in america, but throughout the world. It must be intended, and will announce to the beholding nations, that you are deeply dissatisfied with us, and that even the issue of war or peace stands suspended upon the issue of the mission. Yours and our Enemies will rejoice at the event, whilst yours and our friends, if we have any beyond the bounds of each republic, will view the spectacle with horror. The mission itself will place us in a new dilemma, and which will ever afterwards be felt by both countries. Something is due in the opinion of the world to the character of the mission, its success must be brilliant, or the publick may be disappointed, and this may induce you to insist on terms that would not otherwise be thought of. If you succeed by the pressure, in things we would not otherwise grant, we are humiliated, and if you do not succeed you are humiliated or must resort to war. I state this merely to shew the dilemma in which the measure itself place us, and which ought not to be incurred if to be avoided.

The moment that the mission is known to foreign powers they will commence their intrigue both here and in Philadelphia to make it the means of separating the two republics for ever. All the other powers are interested in our separation, none in our union; and when separated where will either find a friend. Success and the terror of the french arms may diminish the number of your actual foes but as I know we have no other friend but france, so I well know you have no other real friend but America. Republics can never count upon the friendship of monarchies. If they do, they will always be deceived.

What would be the effect of a mission of this kind in all respects I cannot determine, but that it would produce certain ill consequences and no good consequences I am well satisfied. A correct view of the actual state of things in America will best demonstrate this truth.

You well know the number of your friends in America is considerable, and that this number is daily increasing. That it is of a description of Persons whose friendship is most valuable, consisting of those who are proprietors, who are grateful for services rendered us in our revolution and who feel a new and powerful motive in the establishment of your republic. What effect then would this measure have upon those who are your friends, and whose welfare must be dear to you. The first sentiment which animates the breast of every patriot is a love of liberty and of country and both of which revolt at the idea of foreign interference. These sentiments are of a generous nature and powerful when left to their free range. At the the present moment they are acting with great energy in America in your favor, all those of the description above mentioned consider this cause as their cause, and your victories as theirs. They wish to serve you but having no fleet they see not the means. But the moment you take a step of that eclat against them, denouncing as it were the whole nation to the world, for you cannot distinguish between the government and the People, and pressing a crisis in their affairs, it merits consideration whether it would not rather damp their spirits and diminish their zeal in your favor than increase it. You will readily perceive that their enemies foreign and domestic would take advantage of this measure & ascribe to it, and of course to french influence, whatever efforts they might afterwards make in your favor, and which by tarnishing the credit would lessen the force of those efforts. You recollect that this has already been charged upon them in the case of your ministers Genet and Fauchet, and when there was no kind of pretext for the imputation, and what essential injury it did to the cause of republican government with us.

Cautious as I am in hazarding an opinion which is to be regarded only from the confidence you are pleased to repose in me, yet I declare freely that in my judgment such a proceedure would do harm both to you and to us, and certainly no good. Left to ourselves every thing will I think be satisfactorily arranged, and perhaps in the course of the present year: and it is always more grateful to make such arrangements ourselves than to be pressed to it. France too will derive more credit and advantage admitting that her complaints are well founded, in acting with great delicacy towards to us than if she pursued an opposite policy, for the more magnanimous her conduct the happier the effect will be with us and the more durable its impression.

If you cast your eyes upon the United States at the present moment you will see them actually in the convulsion of a great crisis, and which is occasioned by this treaty with England and you may be sensible that the injuries we have received from England in the seizure of our vessels, and other outrages whilst you have shewn a different conduct towards us, tend greatly to increase our attachment to you, whilst it excites our indignation against her. But the moment you assume an hostile and menacing deportment towards us, does that motive diminish and the argument it furnishes begin to lose its force.

By this I would not be understood as advising that well founded complaints be withheld. On the contrary I think they should always be brought forward, as well to obtain redress where it is wished and can be given as to make known that such acts are considered as injurious. What I object to in the present instance is the manner of presenting those complaints, departing by the appointment of an Envoy extraordinary from the ordinary course of representation, and exhibiting from the nature and motive of the appointment an aspect unfriendly and menacing, and which I hope will not be done.

Before I close this letter which is written in haste permit me to assure you that I will enter with great pleasure into any explanations wished upon the several points of complaint, and which I mention for the sole purpose of possessing you of the argument to be used on our side, since you will thereby be enabled better to decide whether the complaint be well or ill founded, and of course how far it is proper to consider it in that light. With great respect & esteem I am yr. very humble servant

Jaˢ Monroe

RC, DLC: FCP—France

From Charles Delacroix

Paris le 1ᵉʳ Ventose an 4ᵉ [20 February 1796]

Monsieur

J'ai communiqué au Directoire la lettre que vous m'avez adressée le 17 février dernier (V. S.). il m'a chargé de répondre aux inquiétudes que vous y témoignez; qu'il ne croyait y avoir donné lieu, en nommant un Successeur au Citoyen Adet, qui a demandé formellement son rappel. Ce remplacement loin d'être comme Vous parroissez le craindre, le préliminaire d'une scission annonce au contraire dans le directoire, l'intention de continuer les relations amies qui ont jusqu'ici subsisté entre les deux peuples, et il a la Conscience de n'avoir rien négligé de ce qui pouvoit tendre à en resserrer les nœuds.

Peut être, comme vous paroissez l'avouer vous même, le Gouvernement fédéral n'a-t-il pas toujours concouru à ce but avec autant d'empressement. Peut être aurons nous droit de nous plaindre de quelques actes peu Conformes à la bonne harmonie qui doit exister entre d'anciens alliés; mais ce réfroidissement et ces actes ont produits dans l'Esprit du Directoire plutôt le chagrin qui regrette les écarts d'un ami que le mécontentement qui amène les ruptures. Cependant Mʳ le Directoire chargera en effet son envoyé nouveau auprès de l'Exécutif des Etats unis, de témoigner l'étonnement que lui ont causé quelques uns de ces derniers procédés, et notamment, la conclusion et la ratification du traité arreté entre les Etats unis et la Grande Bretagne en 9ʳᵉ 1794. Mais il compte encore trop sur la connaissance qui doivent avoir les Etats-Unis de leurs vrais intérets et Sur l'effet que ne manquera pas de produire sur le Gouvernement fédéral la réprobation unanime qu'a émise le peuple Américain sur ces procédés, pour ne pas attendre de la réflexion et des représentations de nos envoyés la justice que la République a droit d'Espérer des Etats-unis. Ce ne seront qu'à la dernière extrémité, qu'il employeroit les moyens contre lesquels Votre sollicitude s'éleve; pour exiger les réparations sur lesquelles l'intérêt de la république et la dignité de la nation ne lui permettroient point de transiger. Agréez, Mʳ l'assurance de ma plus parfaite estime.

Editors' Translation

Paris 1 Ventôse Year 4 [20 February 1796]

Sir

I have sent the letter you had addressed to me last February 17 (old style) to the Directory. They have given me the responsibility of responding to the concerns you have voiced; they did not realize it had caused such concerns by naming a successor to Citizen Adet who had formally requested a recall. This replacement, which is far from being a precursor to a division as you seem to fear, announces on the contrary the intention of the Directory to continue the amicable relations that have thus far subsisted between the two people; and it knows that, in good conscience, it has neglected nothing which would tend to tighten the knots of the relationship.

It may be that, as you seem to admit yourself, the federal government has not always worked toward this goal with as much eagerness. Perhaps we have the right to complain of several actions not in keeping with the good harmony that should exist between old allies. Nevertheless, in the mind of the Directory, this cooling effect and these actions have produced the sorrow that laments the lapses of a friend, rather than the discontent that leads to separation. However, sir, the Directory will instruct its new envoy to the Executive of the United States, to voice astonishment that at one of these late proceedings; notably, the completion and ratification of the treaty concluded between the United States and Great Britain in

November 1794. But it relies more on the knowledge that the United States must have of their true interests and on the effect that the unanimous disapproval of these proceeedings by the American people will have on the federal government, than upon the remarks and representations of our envoys, for the justice that the Republic has a right to expect from the United States. It will only employ the means about which you express concern as a last resort, to exact the reparations which the interests of the Republic and the dignity of the nation would scarcely permit it to compromise. Accept, sir, the assurance of my most perfect esteem.

FC, DLC : FCP—France

To Timothy Pickering

Paris, 20ᵗʰ Febʸ 1796.

Immediately after my last of the 16ᵗʰ of february was concluded, I demanded and had a conference with the minister of foreign affairs, upon the communication given in that letter.

I represented to him that the information he had given me of the intention of the Directoire to appoint an Envoy extraordinary to repair to the U. S., to declare to [our]¹ Government the dissatisfaction of this in respect to our Treaty with Great Britain, had penetrated me with the deepest concern; because I feared from a measure so marked and conspicuous, the most serious ill consequences both to them and to us. I stated to him that such a mission was calculated to make an impression in America, and throughout the world, not only that they were dissatisfied with us; but that even the issue of war and peace was Suspended on the issue of the mission: that their and our enemies would rejoice at the event; whilst theirs and our friends would behold the spectacle with horror. That the mission itself would place both Republicks in a new dilemma, and from which they could not both well extricate themselves with honor: that something was due in the opinion of the world to the caracter of the mission; its success must be brilliant, or the public would be disappointed, and this might induce them to insist on terms they would not otherwise have thought of, and which would increase their mutual embarrassments: that as soon as the mission was known to foreign powers, they would commence their intrigues to make it the means of separating us: that all were interested in our separation, none in our union: and that our separation was an evil to be deprecated by both parties: that the success and terror of their arms might diminish the number of their active enemies, but as we had never confided in the friendship of any power, but in that of France, so I was satisfied they had no real friend except America. that republicks could never count upon the friendship of monarchies; if they did count upon it, they would always be deceived. Peace there might be, but peace and friendship did not always mean the same thing.

I observed further that France had gained Credit by her late conduct towards us: for whilst England had seized our Vessels and harassed our Trade, she had pursued an opposite and more magnanimous policy; and which had produced, and would continue to produce a correspondent effect, by encreasing our resentment against England, and attachment to France. But as soon as the latter should assume an hostile or menacing deportment towards us, would this motive diminish; and the argument it furnished lose force. That by this however I did not mean to be understood, as advising that well founded complaints, if such existed, or were thought to exist, should be with-held: on the contrary I was of opinion they should be brought forward, as well to obtain redress where it was wished and could be given, as to make known in a frank and friendly manner the sentiments which each entertain'd of the conduct of the other, in cases that were interesting to it. That on my own part I was always ready to enter into such explanations when required, and would do it in the present instance with pleasure; since by being possessed of our view of the subject they would be better able to decide whether complaint was well or ill-founded, and of course how far it merited to be considered in that light. In short, I used every argument that occurred to divert the government from the measure proposed, assuring him in the most earnest manner that I was satisfied it would produce no good effect to France; on the contrary that it would produce much ill both to her and to us.

The Minister replied that France had much cause of complaint against us, independently of our Treaty with England; but that by this Treaty, ours with them was annihilated: that the Directoire considered our conduct in these respects as absolutely unfriendly to them, and under which impression that it was their duty so to represent it to us: That the mode which was proposed of making such representation had been deemed mild and respectful, and as such ought not to give offence. He admitted however that the objections I had stated against it were strong and weighty with him, and that he would immediately make them known to the Directoire, and by whom he doubted not all suitable attention would be paid to them. Since this I have not seen him, but propose seeing him again either to-day, or to-morrow, on this subject; and after which I will immediately apprize you of the State in which it may be.

This affair has given me great concern, because it opens a new æra upon us; and whose consequences, unless the measure itself be prevented, may be of a very serious kind. I shall do every thing in my power to prevent it, and in any event communicate to you and with the utmost dispatch every incident that turns up connected with it.

So far my object has been to break the measure in question; and after which, if effected, I shall most probably be called on for explanations of the Treaty complained of; and in which case I shall of course avail myself in the best manner possible of those communications, which have been heretofore received from your Department.

Copy, NN: Monroe Papers

1. The clerk wrote "your". The correction is from the draft in PHi: Gratz Collection.

From Bartholomew Terrasson

Paris february the 20th 1796.

Sir

Desiring to correspond to the confidence that on my departure for hambourg, you have shewn me, in remiting to my care one letter with duplicate to be send to Mad[e] Lafayette[1] when, once in Germany I could learn with accuracy the place where she was and that they could be forwarded safely, I think I owe you an account of my steps on that subject, more so as from the circumstances said letters have not been forwarded.

as soon I have been in hollande I have made my business to enquire where was Mad[e] Lafayette but could find nobody acquainted with her fate till my arrival at hambourg (by the beginning of December) where the first people I applied to, told me that she had been there some months before and had left in said town all her business in hands of an old aid de camp of M[r] Lafayette a m[r] masson who could answer all my enquiries about that Lady; a few days after I saw m[r] masson who really I found chiefly employed with the affairs and situation of m[r] & m[rs] Lafayette, he engaged me to call with him at the american Consul m[r] Parish & there after informing me of the situation of m[rs] Lafayette and that her confinement at olmutz was such that no letter could reach her since she was there (for the retails of what did happen to the letters send to her, I refer myself to what m[r] Masson has wrote himself to you by me)[2] they advised me both to keep your letters and if the Circumstances Should not change before my departure from hambourg, then to deposite them, what I have done in hands of the american Consul, according the receipt I have delivered to you; from the state of the things, the persuasion I was in that trusting those letters to the Post, it was to no good purpose, has made me comply with the advise of those Gentlemen and I hope, Sir, that from the same motive, you will give to it your approbation which in taking charge of the letters, has been my most earnest desire as well as of doing some thing useful for that unfortunate and interesting family, the Same wish induces me, Sir, to mention to you that during my Stay in Germany, I have been told at different time and by several Persons of respectable caracter, that when Madame Lafayette presented herself at vienna to the Emperor to beg for the liberty of her husband or the freedom to go and live with him at olmutz, She was received by him with kindness and was promised to have her correspondence allowed to her, but that she was received very differently by his ministry of foreign affairs who it is supposed generaly is influenced by the Cabinet of England for keeping so closely Mr Lafayette and by the by his Lady who since at olmutz has no more freedom than her husband; the opinion hold too, for England insisting on the detention of m^r Lafayette, is that at his return to america he could influence that Country in favor of France: I relate you all that, Sir, as I have heard it and my only aim is to assure you that I had at heart to fulfil your commission with care and to deserve the confidence you had placed in me I am with great regard Sir your Most ob^t humb. Servant

Bartholomew Terrasson.

P. S. Mr Alexander Lameth who was made Prisoner with m^r Lafayette is now free at hambourg[3]

RC, ViW: Monroe Papers

20 February 1796

1. JM to Adrienne Lafayette, 16 November 1795, above.

2. Andrew Masson to JM, 2 February 1796, above.

3. Alexandre Lameth (1760-1829) was an influential leader in the early years of the French Revolution. In the beginning Lameth supported Lafayette, but they later quarreled over the direction of the Revolution and became open enemies. Nevertheless, Lameth took flight with Lafayette and was detained with him in 1792 (André Maurois, *Adrienne ou La Vie de Mme De La Fayette*, 227, 248, 255, 555; Brand Whitlock, *Lafayette* 1: 380; Jason Lane, *General and Madame de Lafayette*,151, 164, 182).

From Joel Barlow

Alicante 23^d Feb. 1796

My dear Sir

I promised to write you from time to time such details respecting the business with which I am charged as might be interesting for you to know. I am sorry however that my first letter must be occupied with circumstances which look rather discouraging. It is almost needless to mention to you the delays I met with on my way to this place, as the story has very little connection with what is to follow, and as these delays have not at all affected the public interest, though the apprehension that they might affect it gave me some vexation at the time. At Marseilles I freighted an American Brig on which I embarked myself & the public property which I brought, to touch at Alicante & there proceed to the place of destination. This vessel arrived at Alicante, after fighting the storms & contrary winds for 21 days; but, fortunately for my poor stomach, the first violent gale forced us to take shelter in the bay of Roses, where I went on shore & pursued my journey by land.

On my arrival here I found no letters or orders from M⁣ʳ Humphreys, but instead of them I have collected, from the best information I could obtain here, the following state of facts relative to the business in question.

It appears that in the treaty made by M⁣ʳ Donaldson no precise time was fixed upon for the payment of the money stipulated to be paid by the U.S. But it was understood that it would be within about three months. The treaty I believe was signed in the early part of Sep⁣ʳ. After the expiration of the above term the Dey began to be impatient and to manifest his uneasiness that the money did not appear, & that there were no signs of its appearance, saying that he was sorry he had made the treaty, as from present circumstances it was against the interest of the regency: But as he had signed the treaty, it should be faithfully executed on his part, provided the money was paid within a reasonable time.

M⁣ʳ Donaldson being somewhat allarmed at these appearances & at hearing nothing from the money, procured a Moorish Barque & sent M⁣ʳ Sloan,¹ his interpreter, to Alicante, with dispatches for M⁣ʳ Humphreys. M⁣ʳ Sloan left Algiers about the 5ᵗʰ Jan⁣ʸ and arrived here about the 10ᵗʰ. He being obliged to perform quarantine, M⁣ʳ Montgomery,² our consul here, took the dispatches & proceeded himself to Lisbon, supposing the affair too pressing to admit of delay, & the dispatches too important to be trusted to the post. Sloan was one of the American prisoners, and had been imployed as a domestic servant to the Dey. He is now here waiting an answer from Lisbon. It is from him & from M⁣ʳ John Montgomery, brother to the consul, that I have the above information.

We will now look to the side of Lisbon, & the causes of delay in that quarter. You know the credit on which the money was to be raised was lodged in London. You know too that M⁣ʳ Humphreys, who left Havre some time in Oct⁣ʳ had a passage of above 40 days from that place to Lisbon. M⁣ʳ Donaldson had dispatched Capt. O'Brien from Algiers to Lisbon, with the treaty early in Sep⁣ʳ he probably arrived within that month. But as M⁣ʳ Humphreys did not arrive till towards the last of Nov⁣ʳ every thing must have remained inactive during that interval. I am informed that M⁣ʳ Humphreys, after his arrival, could not negotiate bills on London for more than one fourth of the sum. And it appears that on this account he did not negotiate any. Of this however I am not sure. But in consequence of his not being able to raise money in that place sufficient to fulfill the contract with the Dey, he sent Capt. O'Brien to London (not earlier than Jan⁣ʸ I believe, but I am not accurately informed as to this date) to bring the specie from thence. O'Brien went in the Brig that M⁣ʳ Humphreys had retained in the Public service. By the last letters from M⁣ʳ Montgomery at Lisbon, of the 13 inst. nothing had been heard there of O'Brien since he sailed. Indeed if no other accident has delayed him, the contrary winds must have prevented his return. They have been without packets from England for near two months. One vessel has arrived after 70 days passage.

It is now near six months since the signing of the contract, & it doubtless will be another month before the money can be paid.

But there are some other circumstances which serve to increase my apprehensions as to the result of this affair, as they convince me that the Dey is sincere in saying that the treaty is against the interest of the regency, & that he is sorry it is made. Since this was done he has had a rupture with the English, which is now settled, as it appears, much to his satisfaction. Sloan says that he told him he would rather wish that the Americans would not comply with the treaty, for since his new treaty with England he could do much better to be at war with us; but that he was ready to settle the matter either one way or the other, & it should be done immediately. The meaning of which, as I conjecture, is that he is to make a peace with Portugal if he does not conclude one with us. But if he is obliged to be at peace with us, he will not accept the terms that Portugal may offer, as a peace with that power can be of no service, unless he can cruise against us.

In consequence of this new treaty with England, he has refused to accept the same Consul who was there before the rupture, but has desired that the old one may be sent, a Mr Logge, who was there in 1793, and who persuaded him then to the truce with Portugal by holding up the advantages of going out of the straights after the Americans. Sloan says he was present at some of these conversations, and that he saw Logge, in the presence of the Dey, instructing the captains by the charts where they must cruise for the American ships, saying that he would forfeit his head if they did not catch a douzen of them within a month, provided they would follow his directions. It is certain that the most inveterate enemies we have in that place, as well as all others under heaven, are the English.

Another circumstance has been mentioned to me, how much weight it will bear I know not, that the French Consul there is rather in disgrace at present, said to be on account of a delay in the payment, on the part of the Republic, for some cargoes of grain.

This, my dear Sir, is a breif statement of facts which for some days past have lain heavy on my mind. I feel already some relief in imparting them to you. And I am not without hopes that in a few weeks more I may be able to give you more satisfactory accounts.

I ought to have told you that after receiving the above information on my arrival, I was clearly of opinion that it was best to wait here till the money should come, or be absolutely on its way. As I was well convinced that for any more of us to appear there without the means of fulfilling the contract, and without any thing new to say on the subject, would only serve to irritate the Dey. And a few days after my arrival here I received a letter from Mr Humphreys, in answer to what I wrote him from Paris, advising me to the same thing.

If you can find a moment to give me a line now and then on French politics & our own, you will oblige me very much. Address to the care of Cathalan at Marseilles, & they will come safe.

Be pleased to give my compliments to Mr Paine if he is still with you. I intended to have desired you, between ourselves before I left you, that if he should be likely to die there and soon, which God forbid, you would propose to him, in season, to leave some sketches or memoirs of his life, from which his life may be written complete. And likewise to make a list of his writings & the order in which they should be published in complete editions. Likewise it would be well that he should mention the best edition of each work, from which such new editions may be formed. Then, if you will charge yourself with executing his wishes in this respect I should be glad; if not, & he will confide them to me, I will do all in my power while I live to cherish his posthumous fame, by publishing correct editions of his works & writing a complete life, so far as he leaves it incomplete himself.

I beg you to present my best respects to Mrs Monroe. I need not ask, my dear Sir, during my absence, your particular friendship & protection to Mrs Barlow as the greatest favor you can bestow on me.[3] If you know her merit you will befriend her for her own sake sooner than for mine. I am with great respect & affection your friend & servant

Joel Barlow

RC, NN: Monroe Papers

1. Philip Sloan was an American sea captain (James Woodress, *A Yankee Odyssey: The Life of Joel Barlow*, 185).

2. Robert Montgomery was the American consul at Alicante, Spain 1793-1823 (Walter B. Smith, *America's Diplomats and Consuls of 1776-1865*, 67).

3. Acting on instructions from England, British consul Charles Logie convinced the Dey of Algiers that Portugal would pay over two million dollars for a peace treaty. As a consequence of this offer, Portugal ended its blockade, and Algerian corsairs

again freely ploughed the Atlantic. They captured eleven American merchant ships and raised the number of American captives from 13 to 117 in October and November of 1793 (*Jefferson Papers*, 27:197).

4. Barlow married Ruth Baldwin (1756-1818) in Connecticut in 1781. She remained in Paris while Barlow was in Africa and became part of the Monroes' circle of friends (*New England Quarterly*, 2 (1929): 476; Woodress, *Yankee Odyssey*, 66, 159).

Theobald Wolfe Tone Journal

[23 February 1796]

Quit Madgett,[1] who I believe <u>honest</u>, and whom I feel <u>weak</u>. Go to Monroe—received very favorably. He has had my letter decyphered and dropt all reserve. I told him I felt his situation was one of considerable delicacy, and therefore I did not at all wish to press upon him any information relative either to myself or my business, further than he might desire. He answered that the letters had satisfied him, particularly that from <u>James Thomson</u>,[2] of whom he spoke in terms of great respect, and that, as he was not responsible for what he might hear but for what he might do, I might speak freely—I then Opened myself to him, without the least reserve, and gave him such detail as I was able of the actual state of things, and of the grounds of my knowledge, from my situation. I also informed him, what I had done thus far. He then addressed me, in substance, as follows: "You must change Your plan. I have no doubt whatsoever of the integrity & sincerity of the Minister (<u>DeLaCroix</u>) nor even of Madgett, whom I believe to be honest. But in the first place, it is a subaltern way of doing business; and I the next, the Vanity of Madgett will be very likely to lead him, in order to raise his own importance in the eyes of some of his Countrymen who are here, as Patriots and of whom I have no means the same good opinion, as integrity, as I have of him, to drop some hint of what is going forward. Go at once to the <u>Directoire executif</u> and demand an audience. Explain yourself to them, and as to me, You may go so far as to refer to me for the authenticity of what You may advance and You may add, that You have reason to think that I am in a degree apprised of the outline of Your business." I mentioned <u>Carnot</u>, of whose reputation we had been long apprised & who I understood spoke English. He said nobody fitter, and that <u>La revilleire Lepaux</u> also spoke English; that either would do. I then expressed a doubt whether, as I was already in the hands of <u>Charles Delacroix</u> there might be some indelicacy in my going directly to the <u>Directoire executif</u>, and if so, whether it might not perhaps be of some disservice. He answered by no means; that, in his own function the proper person for him to communicate with was <u>DelaCroix</u>, but that nevertheless when he had any business of consequence to transact, he always went at once to the fountain head. He then proceeded to mention that in all the changes which had taken place in France, there never was an abler nor a purer set of Men at the head of affairs than at present, that they were sincere friends to Liberty and justice, and in no wise actuated by the spirit of conquest; that consequently , if they took up the business of Ireland on my motion, I would find them perfectly fair and candid; that not only the Government, but the whole people was most violently exasperated against England, and that there was no one thing that would at once command the warmest support of All parties so much as any measure which promised a reduction of her power. He then examined me pretty closely as to the State of Ireland, on which I gave him complete information as far as I was able; and we concluded by agreeing that tomorrow I should go boldly to the Luxembourg and demand an audience, either of <u>Carnot</u> or of <u>Larevilliere Lepaux</u>.[3] Monroe tells me <u>Barrere</u> (for I enquired) is yet in France, and he thought would not quit it— I told him <u>Barrere</u> would be very acceptable in Ireland as a Deputy with the Army. He answered that he did not at all doubt but it might so happen that he should be the Man; that he would not advise me to begin by bolting out the name of Barrere, but that I might take an opportunity to mention him. I remarked to him that it had fallen to Barrere's lot to make some of the most splendid reports in the

Convention, which made him well known to us, and that the people were used in a degree to associate the ideas of Barrere & Victory, which, trifling as it was, was of some consequence—On the whole, I am glad to find my Lover Barrere,[4] as I hope in no danger—<u>It would be a most extraordinary thing if I should happen to be an instrument in restoring his talents to the cause of Liberty</u>. I have always had a good opinion of him. He tells me the ground of the coolness between Pichegru and the Government is that he is supposed to be attached to too much to the Party of <u>Moderés</u>; I am glad of this; not that there is a coolness, but that the Government is not of that party. We talked of the resources of France & England. I mentioned that in my judgment France had one measure which sooner or later she must adopt and the sooner the better, and that was a <u>Bankrupty</u>. That she would then start fresh, with her immense resources against England staggering under 400.000.000 of debt. Monroe took me by the hand and said "<u>You have hit it; and I will tell You that it is a thing decided upon.</u>" If it be so, look to yourself Mr John Bull "<u>Look to Your house, Your Daughter and Your Ducats.</u>"[5] Took my leave of Monroe with whom I am extremely pleased; there is a true republican frankness about him, which is extremely interesting.

AD, Trinity College Library, Dublin

1. Nicholas Madgett (b. 1740) was an Irish-born official in the French Foreign Office who used his position to promote French support for Irish independence (Richard Hayes, *A Biographical Dictionary of Irishmen in France*).

2. Hamilton Rowan. No letter from him to JM has been located.

3. When Tone visited Carnot and Delacroix, he used JM as a reference (*Life of Theobald Wolfe Tone*, 2: 29, 32).

4. Tone uses the word lover frequently in his diary. The exact meaning is not clear, but he seems to use it to denote someone who is a friend or someone who he admires rather than a sexual partner. In this case, there is no indication that he had ever met Bertrand Barère.

5. Tone paraphrases a line from *The Merchant of Venice*.

From Joel Barlow

Alicante 26 Feb. 1796.

My Dear Sir

Since I wrote you on the 23rd inst. letters have been rec^d here from Algiers which have confirmed my worst fears and changed my determination relative to my own movements. I shall now proceed to Algiers as soon as possible, and should have set off two days ago on seeing the letters, but for contrary winds. We have had a strong Southeaster for three days, which still continues, & it seems that contrary winds, if nothing else, are to defeat our operations in that quarter. I inclose you an extract of a letter from Cathcart, an American prisoner who serves as interpreter to the Dey.[1] I should not pay so much regard to this letter, but the principal points in it are confirmed in another from Donaldson to Montgomery, of the same date, in which he says that one month is the ultimate term that the Dey will consent to the suspension of the treaty, and he advises Montgomery to expect the worst, as he no hopes of receiving the funds in that time. This month will certainty be elapsed before I can arrive. But I am determined to go on, as it can do no hurt since the affair has become so desperate, and it is possible it may save the treaty. I am confirmed in this idea by some particular information I have had that the Dey has a personal dislike to Donaldson, said to be owing to a pevish uncomplying temper in the latter. This perhaps is calumny & I mention it only between ourselves.

Letters have been rec^d this day from Montgomery at Lisbon of the 16th, which give no further news respecting the funds.

My conjecture mentioned in my former letter relative to Portugal, which at that time was meerly conjecture founded on no information, is confirmed both in the letter of Cathcart & that of Donaldson. I hope that Mr Humphreys has influence enough at this court to induce them to act in concert with us, or at least not to counteract us a second time in this troublesome business.

I write this letter, my dear Sir, principally to desire you to warn the Americans, as far as you may have it in your power, not to send their ships into the Mediterranian, untill they have better news. It would not be amiss to pass this advice to America, as I am sure that many ships are now & will be on their way to this quarter, on the strength of the news already gone to America of the peace. (The ship from Boston, mentioned in my former letter, is an instance). With great affection & respect I am My dear Sir—your friend & servant

Joel Barlow

RC, NN: Monroe Papers

1. James Leander Cathcart (1767-1843) was captured by the Algerines in July 1785 and held prisoner until 1795. During his captivity he held several administrative positions. In 1792 he became the principal Christian secretary to the dey, and as such, played a principal role in the negotiations between the United States and Algiers. Cathcart held a variety of consular posts in North Africa between 1797 and 1803. He served as U. S. consul at Madeira 1807-1815, at Cadiz 1815-1817, and upon his return to the United States he became a clerk in the Treasury Department (*DAB*).

From James Madison

Philad^a Feby 26 1796.

Dear Sir

I have written you several particular letters latterly, & now add this for a conveyance of which I am just apprised.

The British Treaty is still in the situation explained in my last. Several circumstances have indicated an intention in the Executive to lay it before the House of Rep^s but it has not yet taken place. There is reason to believe that some egregious *misconception of ideas* has disappointed the *executive* of the *original ratification*. Still however *the executive* is not to be *excused* for sacrificing *substance to form*, by *withholding the* subject *and as this* idea must gain strength with *the delay* a *call for the treaty* will become *daily more and more practicable and probable*.

The Algerine & Spanish Treaties are both before the Senate. Mr Tazewell is to make them the subject of a letter to you by the present opportunity; he being fully acquainted with them.[1] The former is stampt with *folly* & the [*most*][2] *culpable irregularities*. The latter gives *general joy*. *I* have not yet ascertained whether it *clashes with the British treaty as to the Mississippi or* is in any *point* chargeable with the *unconstitutionality alledged against the British*.

You already know that Pickering is Secretary of State, & that Charles Lee is Attorney General. The vacancy in the Secretaryship of war has been filled with Doc^r McHenry.[3] On the exclusion of Jno Rutledge, Cushing[4] was made Chief Justice, but has declined it & no successor is yet nominated. <u>Chase</u>[5] is appointed to the vacancy produced by Mr Blair's resignation. There is still a vacancy resulting from Jay's translation to the Gov^t of N. York to be filled. On these several appointments, you will make your own comments. *They are to a man of the treaty party*.

The amendments proposed by Virginia, for requiring the consent of the H. of Rep^s to Treaties, limiting the terms of Senators to three years &c. have *excited the* [*most*][6] *active party venom against that state* and the *success of the hue* and *cry has* been *greater than could have been imagined*. The *legislatures of New Hampshire Massachusets Rhode Island New York Pensylvania Delaware* have *all rejected*, and *several of them insulted the example*.

It is now pretty certain that the *president will not serve beyond his present term*. The *British party had Jay first in view* as is *believed*. It is *now said Adams is the object*. Their *second man* is not *fixt on or discovered*. It will probably be a *man who will cause a diversion of southern votes.*[7] *H. Lee* has been *conjectured* but they will hardly *think him the fittest for the purpose*. The *republicans* knowing that *Jefferson alone* can be *started with hope of success* mean to push him. *I fear much* that *he will mar the project* & *ensure the adverse election* by a peremptory and <u>*public*</u> *protest*. The *candidate for the V. P.* is *not yet designated*.

The immediate subjects before the H. of Rep^s are 1. a bill for guaranteeing a loan on a mortgage of the public lotts in the federal City, for compleating the preparations there in time, without selling the lotts below their value. The bill has been delayed by objections of various sorts urged from various motives. As the President has recommended the measure, it is probable, tho' not certain, that it will be allowed to pass.—2. a bill for selling the lands N. W of the Ohio. On this also opinions are multifarious & the issue not certain. 3. new taxes. Notwithstanding the parade with respect to our finances, there are 6,200,000 doll^rs of anticipations due to the bank now called for besides the foreign instalments, and ab^t 1,100,000 for the deferred debt which will accrue by the time plans laid now will become regularly & adequately productive. Wolcot in the spirit of his predecessor proposes to fund the anticipations &c. by selling new stock <u>irredeemable for 25 years</u>, that is, the redemption is not to commence till the end of 25 years. The new revenues contemplated are an increase of the duty on salt—a stampt tax—a tax on testamentary dispositions, an increase of the tax on Carriages—&c. A tax on leather & hats were also brought forward in a Com^e of ways & means, but will not be pressed. W^d you have supposed that a land tax & House tax as <u>indirect taxes</u>, had also a patronage?

The constitutionality of the Carriage tax has been just argued here before the federal Court of Appeals; Ch^s Lee & Hamilton on the side of the tax; Ingersoll,[8] & Campbel of Richmond, ag^st it. Lee did not distinguish himself, & took ground different from that of his co-adjutor. H. exerted himself as usual. Ingersoll appeared to advantage, & Campbel I am told, acquitted himself ably & very eloquently. The Judges on the bench were Wilson, Patterson,[9] Iredell & Chase. No decision has yet been given, but an affirmance of the law is generally anticipated.[10] The payments into the Virg^a Treas^y have also been argued at this term. Marshall & Campbel came hither for the purpose, in behalf of the debtors. They were combated by Lewis & Tilghman.[11] Marshal is said to have figured very powerfully in his argument: & it is thought the event is at least doubtful.[12]

The *birthday of the president* has been *celebrated with greater splendor than ever*. The *crisis explains the policy*. A circumstance has taken place *however more indicative in* its *nature than any display within the fashionable circle*. You will recollect the *usage of adjourning for half an hour to compliment the president on the anniversary of his birth*. Last *year there were but* <u>*thirteen*</u> *dissentients*. This *year the motion to adjourn was negatived by fifty against thirty-eight*.

It has been whispered that *you are to be recalled and Bingham to replace you*. *I* entirely *disbelieve it* but the whisper *marks the wishes of those who propagate it*.

Pickering will pay your draught on him. Bache has not yet rec^d the 2^d part of the Rights of Man, which he says is the only fund on wch Mr Payne could draw. Mrs M. offers her best regards along with mine to Mrs Monroe. A letter from Mr Jones accompanies this.[13] We are 3 months without intelligence from France. Adieu. Y^rs sincerely

J^s Madison Jr.

RC, DLC: Madison Papers. Words in italics were written in code by Madison and deciphered by JM.

1. No letter from Henry Tazewell to JM from this time has been located.

2. Miscoded as "pea".

3. James McHenry (1753-1816) of Maryland served as an officer in the Continental army, serving for a time as an aide to General Washington. He served numerous terms in the Maryland assembly, was a member of the Continental Congress 1783-1785, and was a delegate to the Constitutional Convention in 1787. McHenry was appointed secretary of war on 27 January 1796 and took office on February 6. He held the post until 1800 (*ANB*; *BDAC*).

4. William Cushing (1732-1810) was chief justice of the Massachusetts Supreme Court 1777-1789 and an associate justice of the U. S. Supreme Court 1789-1800. He served as acting chief justice while John Jay was in England (*ANB*).

5. Samuel Chase (1746-1811) was a Maryland attorney and jurist. He was a member of the Continental Congress 1774-1778 and was a signer of the Declaration of Independence. He was appointed a justice of the U. S. Supreme Court on 26 January 1796 and served until 1811 (*ANB*).

6. Miscoded as "pea".

7. Miscoded as "flow".

8. Jared Ingersoll, Jr. (1749-1822) was a Philadelphia attorney. He was a member of the Continental Congress 1780-1781 and a delegate to the Constitutional Convention in 1787. He served as attorney general of Pennsylvania 1790-1797 and 1811-1817 (*DAB*).

9. William Paterson (1745-1806) of New Jersey served as attorney general of that state 1776-1783. He was a delegate to Constitutional Convention in 1787, a member of the U. S. Senate 1789-1790, and governor of New Jersey 1790-1793. He served as a justice of the U. S. Supreme Court 1793-1806 (*ANB*).

10. *Hylton v. The United States*, heard by the Supreme Court in its February 1796 session, was a test case on the constitutionality of a law passed by Congress placing a tax on carriages. Opponents to the law argued that it was a direct tax and that it violated the provisions of the Constitution on the levying of direct taxes. Opposition was particularly strong in Virginia, and the government decided to bring the issue before the courts. Daniel Hylton, a Richmond merchant, was arrested for failure to pay the tax. After a conviction in the federal district court at Richmond, the case went to Supreme Court, which ruled that the law was constitutional. This was the first time that the court ruled on the constitutionality of a federal law (*The Documentary History of the Supreme Court of the United States*, 1789-1800, 7: 358-369).

11. William Lewis (1751-1819) was a Philadelphia attorney. He served as U. S. attorney for the eastern district of Pennsylvania 1789-1791 and as judge of the same district 1791-1792. Attorney Edward Tilghman (1750-1815) was also from Philadelphia (both *DAB*).

12. The case of *Ware v. Hylton*, argued before the Supreme Court in February 1796, centered on a Virginia law relating to the payment of pre-war debts owed to British merchants. The defense argued that the law, which allowed creditors to make deposits on the payment on their debts to the Virginia treasury, protected them from action by their British creditors. The Supreme Court ruled in March in favor of the plaintiff. Daniel Hylton, the defendant in this case, was the plaintiff in *Hylton v. United States* (*Marshall Papers*, 5: 295-329). Marshall's argument in the case is in *Marshall Papers*, 3: 4-14.

13. The letter from Joseph Jones to Monroe has not been located..

To James Madison

Paris Feby 27. 1796.

Dear Sir

This will accompany your china which is addressed to Mr Yard. I enclose also the charge by w^h you will be able to pay the duty.

About a fortnight past I was informed by *the minister of foreign affairs that the government had at length resolved* how to act *with us in respect to our treaty with England.* That *they considered it* as having *violated* or rather *annulled our treaty of alliance with them and taken part with the coalised powers. That they had rather have an open enemy than a perfidious friend.* That it was *resolved to send an envoy extraordinary to the United States to discuss this business with us* and whose *powers would expire with the execution of the trust. I was astonished with the communication and alarmed with its probable consequences.* I told him *it might probably lead to war* and *thereby separate us which was what our enemies wished.* That it *hazarded much and without a probable gain.* That from the moment a *person of that character arrived their friends would seem to act under his banner* and which circumstance would *injure their character and lessen their efforts. In truth I did everything in my power to prevent this measure* and in which I am now told by *the minister that I have succeeded* the *Directoire having resolved to continue the ordinary course of representation only.* But thro' this *I hear strong sentiments will be conveyed. The whole of this is made known to the executive by me.*

Mr Adet has sent in his resignation & pressed earnestly the acceptance of it. Of course a successor will be sent in his place.

I am astonished that I have heard nothing from you, it is now I think 9. months, altho' I have written you so often & communicated so freely. From me too there is some hasard in communicating & for reasons that will occur & w^h has been encreased by the multiplication of duplicate dispatches & w^h were forwarded merely because the originals if rec^d were not acknowledged. To me the motive for this reserve is impenetrable & therefore I repeat ag^n my astonishm^t at it.

The state of things has varied little since the organization of the new gov^t—great preparations are making for carrying on the campaign with vigor on both sides. It is said the army of the Rhine & Moselle will am^t together to 300.000 men, & that in Italy to 150.000. On the opposit side too great preparations are making, so that unless peace sho^d close the scene, a greater carnage may be expected this than in any preceding campaign. and at present there is but little prospect of peace, at least I see none.

The forced loan was less productive than was expected *and the embarrassment in the finances extreme.* Some *think another movement at hand but I see no evidence of it* at present. In all calculations on this subject *it ought to be recollected* that the *executive are sound and having the government in their hands are strong.*

There are strong symptoms of an actual rupture between us and this country. The *minister the government preferred to have us as open [enemies]*[1] *rather than perfidious friends.* Other proofs occur to shew that *this sentiment has gone deep into their councils.*

RC, DLC: Madison Papers. Not signed. Words in italics were written in code by JM and deciphered by Madison.

1. JM omitted this the code for this word.

From Fulwar Skipwith

Paris 27 Feby 1796

Dear Sir

I find that the drafts on me from Amsterdam payable <u>en espice ou valour metallique</u> must be paid here in coin or the equivalent which would incur upon the Ingots a loss of 12 a 14 pr cent—it has occurred to me therefore, and is the opinion of my Banker with whom I have been in consultation that it will be infinitely to the advantage of the United States that the Ingots be sent on, and that in order to cover me upon my acceptances I should redraw here on the United States Bankers. If you approve, I shall begin to act accordingly by writing to the Bankers and putting the Silver in motion. Waiting your answer I am very aff^y &^c

Fulwar Skipwith

RC, NN: Monroe Papers

To Charles Delacroix

28 February 1795

It gives me pleasure to explain to you in reply to your favor of 8 Vintose (27. Feb^y)[1] such circumstances as are known to me relative to one Thos Eldred and particularly upon what principles my passport was finally granted to him, since I well know from the precautions I observe that the explanation in this & all other cases where it may be asked cannot otherwise than prove satisfactory.

Soon after my arrival in this republick this man presented himself to me & obtained my passport, having produc'd the most satisfactory documents to prove that he was an american citizen. I knew nothing of him nor did I ever hear of him before; a case which often happens with me & doubtless with every other publick minister who represents an extensive territory. In such cases the only precaution that can be observed is to demand such proof of his citizenship as will satisfy the mind that his claim is just. So doing he ought to be recognized. The proof which I always ask and w^h I think proper here to communicate, is the certificate of two American citizens known to me or assured to by those who are known to merit confidence for their probity & attachment to their country, that the person claiming a passport is an American citizen: and which certificate is always deposited in my office when the passport is granted. When a passport is claimed from me upon the faith of one from any other American minister I always ask for the same proof that the passport of that minister was granted to that person, and by which precaution it rarely happens, perhaps it never happens, that I am deceived.

Some considerable time after I had granted my passport to this Eldred I heard that he was arrested upon a suspicion of the kind you mention at Toulon & soon after which that he was bro^t for trial to Paris. He now demanded my interference in his behalf to see that he had justice, & w^h I then refused upon intimation rec^d that he was not an American citizen & to w^h I was not the less [inclined] to pay attention from the suspicion to w^h he had exposed himself. Finally however as the main was detained in prison for many months, & had been protected & in the country by my passport, altho' I still doubted his claim & therefore wo^d not recognize him I thought it my duty to state the circumstances of his case to the committee of security general & request their attention to him & which was given by the arrete you mention restoring him to liberty & forthwith to depart the country. As soon as he was enlarged he presented himself to me demanding again my passport. I told him I was advised he was not an American citizen for tho born in the U States that he had left them before our decl^n of independance & therefore had lost his title. Upon this he produc'd to me the requisit proof to the contrary, declaring that the motive of the order of the committee for his departure proceeded from my not recognizing him as an American citizen, & in consequence of w^h he was included under the general law agnst foreigners & to w^h idea the stile of that arret gave some countenance as it appeared that there was no charge exhibited against him.

Upon producing proof that he was an American citizen, it became my duty to recognize him as such. His merits or demerits as a man might expose him to y^r resentment & punishment but co^d not deprive him of his rights as an American citizen: nor wo^d my recognition of him as such exempt him from the censure of y^r laws, in case he merited such censure. Still however as I had once doubted his title & so represented it to the Committee of security general, & especially as he had been suspected of some misconduct in the republick & order'd by the arret w^h enlarged him to depart the country tho' the motive of that order was doubtful I wo^d not grant the passport without previously calling y^r attention to his case that you might take such order in respect to him as you thought fit. I send you herewith a copy of my letter & of your answer by which it appears that the passport was granted with your knowledge and special approbation.[2] I likewise send you a copy of a letter from the minister of the Interior, & by which it appears ~~that it was his wish I sho^d yeild him every accomodation in my power: so that in truth in granting this man a passport I not only thought~~ there was no complaint against him[3] and as I likewise heard he was employed or had formed some contract with the gov^t I thought that in granting him a passport I was not only doing my duty to a person having a just claim on me, but that I was also doing an act of real accomodation to this gov^t.

How the man contrived to stay so long in the republick before I gave him a passport or how he obtained the confidence of this gov^t in the case you mention I know not: all that I did in his favor was to grant the passport under the circumstances above mentioned. ~~Before the passport was granted he had not the character of an American citizen, & was therefore not protected by it agnst the law w^h applies to other foreigners not residents. Nor was he by the passport agnst any well founded complaint against him of such [illegible].~~ and w^h had no relation to what preceded or followed in his respect. By those Americans who mentioned him to me I was taught to consider him as an indiscreet but not as a criminal man. ~~And I have reason to think that the motive which induc'd the minister of the interior to interpose in his behalf was that of procuring thro him considerable supplies from the African coast to Toulon & other ports on the medeteranean, but this he will be better able to explain himself~~ *and I have reason to think that the trust now repos'd in him by the gov^t; if any such is the case, is for the reason of procuring thro him supplies from Africa to the French ports on the medeteranean, of w^h however I have no knowledge & only mention to you what was said by those who applied in his favor but of w^h you will doubtless be able procure suitable information.* of this however you will doubtless be able to obtain more correct information than I possess.

Dft, DLC: Monroe Papers; undated and filed at the end of February 1795. The portion at the end in italics is from ViFreJM and is dated 28 February 1796.

1. Delacroix's letter to JM of 27 February 1796 has not been located.

2. JM to Delacroix 19 December 1795, above; Delacroix to JM, 22 December 1795, DLC: FCP—France.

3. The letter from the minister of the interior has not been located.

Theobald Wolfe Tone Journal

[28 February 1796]

Went to Monroe's about my passport, and had about an hours conversation with him—I like him very much; he speaks like a sincere republican—How came he to be an American?—He praises the Executive directory to the Skies, and De la Croix; All for the better! <u>Carnot</u> he tells me is a Military man, and one of the first Engineers in Europe. (Vide my observation touching his <u>Organising</u> about Cork harbour). <u>Le Tourneur</u> is also a Military man, so that, with <u>Barras</u>, there are three Soldiers in the Directoire—<u>I am very glad of that</u>!

AD, Trinity College Library, Dublin

From Thomas Jefferson

Mar. 2. 96.

Dear Sir

I wrote you two letters in the course of the last twelve months to wit May 26. & Sep. 6. 95. and have recieved from you those of Sep. 7. 94. & June 23. 95.[1] neither of which were late enough to inform me if either of mine had got to hand. in those I gave you all the details public & private which my situation enabled me to do. in the last I asked the delivery of a note to Frouillé for some books, particularly the sequel of the Encyclopedie, come out since he last furnished me. I hope these have got to hand.

The most remarkeable political occurrence with us has been the treaty with England, of which no man in the US. has had the effrontery to affirm that it was not a very bad one except A. H.[2] under the signature of Camillus. it's most zealous defenders only pretend that it was better than war. as if war was not invited rather than avoided by unfounded demands. I have never known the public pulse beat so full and in such universal unison on any Subject since the declaration of Independance. the House of representatives of the US. has manifested it's disapprobation of the treaty. we are yet to learn whether they will exercise their constitutional right of refusing the means which depend on them for carrying it into execution. should they be induced to lend their hand to it it will be hard swallowing with their constituents, but will be swallowed from the habits of order & obedience to the laws which so much distinguish our countrymen. the resignation or rather removal of R.[3] you will have learnt. his vindication bears hard on the executive in the opinions of this quarter, and tho' it clears him in their judgment of the charge of bribery, it does not give them high ideas of his wisdom or steadiness. the appointment of J. Rutledge to be C. J. seems to have been intended merely to establish a precedent against the descent of that office by seniority, and to keep five mouths always gaping for one sugar plumb: for it was immediately negatived by the very votes which so implicitly concur with the will of the executive. I may consign the appointment of Chace to the bench to your own knolege of him & reflections. McHenry Sec^y at war, Charles Lee Atty Genl with Pickering & Wolcott by their devotion to genuine republicanism will shew to our citizens on what principles alone they can expect to rise. the office of Sec^y of State was offered to P. H.[4] in order to draw him over & gain some popularity: but not till there was a moral certainty that he would not accept it. I presume you recieve the newspapers, & will have seen the amendments to the constitution proposed by the Virginia assembly. their reception by some of the other assemblies has been such as to call for the sacrifice of all feeling rather than ruffle the harmony so necessary to the common good. the finances are said to have been left by the late financier in the utmost derangement, and his tools are urging the funding the new debts they have contracted. thus posterity is to be left to pay the ordinary expences of our government in time of peace.

As small news may escape the notice of your other correspondents, I shall give you what occurs to me. The James river canal is now conducted into the town of Richmond & full toll is exacted. 30. Doll. a share more however are necessary to complete it.[5] the Patowmac & Norfolk canals are not in such forwardness.[6] Mayo bridge, nearly destroyed by a flood, is reestablished.[7] R. is settled again in Richmond in the business of the law.—Carter's lands on the back of yours & mr Short's have got into the hands of one of the sons, Ned, who is coming to live on them.[8] the price of wheat is 13/ here the bushel, & corn 20/ the barrel, and not to be had indeed at any price. I have been desirous of planting some fruit trees for you that they may be growing during your absence. but mr Jones's visits to the neighborhood have been so rare & short that I have not had an opportunity of asking from him the inclosure & allotment of the piece of ground which seems proper for it. the season is now passing. do not fail to send over the Abricot-peche. Bartram would recieve & plant it, and then furnish new plants.[9] Deaths are Zane, & Tho.s Pleasants of 4 mile creek.[10] mr Pendleton is also said to be all but gone. a remarkeable marriage is that of Capt. Alcock with the widow of D.r Walker. your brother[11] and family well. Derieux living in Goochland under great sufferance, and hoping a renovation of the aid promised from his aunt. my sincere affections to mrs Monroe & to yourself. Adieu.

RC, DLC: Monroe Papers. Unsigned.

1. Jefferson refers to JM's letter of 27 June 1795, above.

2. Alexander Hamilton.

3. Edmund Randolph.

4. Patrick Henry.

5. The James River Company received a charter in 1785 to improve the navigation of the river upstream from Richmond and to collect tolls on freight shipped on the river. Part of the improvements included building a canal around the falls at Richmond. The canal opened in early 1796, but the boat basin at its terminus was not finished until 1800 (Wayland F. Dunaway, *History of the James River and Kanawha Company*, 23, 28; Langhorne Gibson, Jr., *Cabell's Canal: The Story of the James River and Kanawha*, 29-30, 42-45).

6. The Potomac Company received its charter at the same time as the James River Company. Work began immediately on improving the river between Great Falls and the Shenandoah, but the biggest challenge was building a canal around Great Falls, a task that was not completed until 1802 (Cora Bacon-Foster, *Early Chapters in the Development of the Potomac Route to the West*, 53, 71-1013). The Dismal Swamp Canal Company received authorization from Virginia and North Carolina in 1790 to build a canal linking Chesapeake Bay to Albemarle Sound. Work began in 1793 but proceeded slowing: by 1796 only five miles had been dug at each end. The canal opened in 1805 (Jesse Pugh and Frank Williams, *The Hotel in the Great Dismal Swamp*, 4-5).

7. Mayo's Bridge, built in 1788 by John Mayo and operated by him as a toll bridge, spanned the James River at Richmond. It was subject to frequent flooding and was rebuilt on numerous occasions (Appletons' Cyclopedia). A bridge bearing this name still stands in Richmond.

8. Edward Carter, Jr. (b. 1750) inherited his father's Albemarle county estate, Blenheim (George Selden Wallace, *The Carters of Blenheim*, 69).

9. William Bartram (1739-1823) the renowned American botanist, resided near Philadelphia (*ANB*).

10. Isaac Zane (1743-1795) was a brigadier general in the Virginia militia and the proprietor of the Marlboro Iron works in Frederick County. He was a member of the Virginia House of Delegates 1776-1795 (*Tyler's Quarterly Historical and Genealogical Magazine*, 7: 732; *Register of the General Assembly of Virginia*; *Diary of Elizabeth Drinker*, 3: 2234). Thomas Pleasants was a planter and merchant in Henrico County, Virginia (*Jefferson Papers*, 29: 288).

11. Joseph J. Monroe.

To Charles Delacroix

Paris March 5th 1796. (15 Ventose 4th year of the french republic
and 20th of the independence of the United States of America.

Citizen Minister

Being informed by you that the Directoire executive considers the late treaty between the United States of America and Great Britain as derogating in some respects from the treaties of alliance and commerce subsisting between the two republics, and that your Minister who is about to depart hence for the United States will be instructed to represent the same to our government, I have thought it my duty to ask an audience of the Directoire executive upon that subject, not doubting that the explanations I shall be able to give upon this subject will make on that body an impression sufficiently satisfactory to merit all its attention. Permit me therefore to request Citizen Minister that you will be so obliging as to obtain for me an audience from the Directoire executive upon that subject at such time as may be most convenient for that body to receive me. Accept the assurance of my perfect esteem.

Ja[s] Monroe

RC, DLC: FCP—France

Journal

8. March 1796.

Conference with the directoire respecting the measures it proposed taking towards our gov[t] in regard to our treaty with Engl[d] & such other of our acts as are deemd unfriendly to France by that body.

I represented to them that I was told by the minister of foreign aff[rs] they had such complaints & notwithstanding the idea of sending an Envoy Extr[y] was accomodated & given up, yet they still intended some severe & potent crimination on us, perhaps the commencment of a policy little short of hostility: that before any step was taken I had deemed it my duty to ask this audience to make such representations agnst this procedure as appeared to me to be proper.

In respect to the treaty, what was the actual state & w[h] ought to be known before any step was taken?

The Senate had advised the ratification of it, upon condition that so much of the 12. article as respects our trade with the W. Indias be suspended; the President had done so, & it was not known whether the king of Engl[d] had agreed or not.—If he had & no modification was made of the trade with the W. Indias then all the articles after the 10th ended, at the expiration of 2. years after the present war. That the treaty itself depended in some of its articles for its execution on the H. of R.; that it was not before that house nor co[d] well be till its ratificat[n] was announc'd, & w[h] wo[d] be when rec[d] from Engl[d], till when it ought not truly to be consider'd as a treaty. Such the actual State.

Suppose it the wish of France ~~& of America~~ to get rid of that treaty, how do it? how can France promote the object? She can do it only by two ways. 1st by force 2. by a magnanimous policy. How by force? She cannot force us, because the great mass of our people are her friends, & because if they were not she has not the ability to do it. She must see that by pressing us she inclines us to Engl[d], & she must know that if united with Engl[d], we are secure agnst her resentment. By violence therefore, she may lose ground, but can obtain none.

2. From a magnanimous policy something may be hoped. The people are friendly to France & this sentiment must be greatly increased by the continual outrages of Engl[d] & the amicable policy of France. In the hands of the people the gov[t] is & to their wishes will its measures be accomodated.

She can however take no measure agnst that treaty without shewing she has a right [to] complain, or in other words that it violates our treaty with her. has this been shewn? no such representation has been made to me tho' I was willing to receive & expl^n according to the views of our gov^t in reply, all the objections w^h this gov^t entertains agnst that treaty &c.

The minister of foreign aff^{rs} asked to reply to me.

He said that in regard to any acts of hostility, none such were contemplated: that the Envoyship extr^y was given up in a spirit of accomodation. That the mission wo^d be as heretofore, by a minister plen^y.

That the treaty ought to be consider'd as executed—for that the Presid^t had announc'd it to the Congress & whose two chambers had replied as upon all other occasions in terms of high compliment to himself. That some mark of attention it was true was paid to the object in question, but yet it was so obscure as to mean nothing for the prominent feature in the reply of the H. of R. w^h alone contained anything of the kind was the echo of the Presidents speech & veneration for himself.

That it was true some articles in the treaty wo^d require the cooperation of that H. for the execution, & it was in the power of that house to paralize it, but of this there was no cause for hope to be derived from any circumstance that he knew of.

With respect to our friendship, he admitted the cultivators or people in the interior were the friends of France, but that our merchants and especially the most wealthy were under the dominion of Engl^d.— That our courts were partial to Engl^d & that our gov^t was as much in the interest of the coalisd powers as it co^d be without declaring war on France. That the treaty in question had injured them in several of its articles & shewd a disposition to abandon them with other observations to that effect.

After this the President of the Directoire[1] read (from what I took to be the report of the minister) a list of grievances agnst us amounting to 7. & to w^h I observ'd it was impossible for me to answer them there since I co^d not even recollect the articles from hearing them once read only—I hoped a copy of them wo^d be given me thro the official organ & to w^h I sho^d then better be able to give a suitable answer. This seemed to be assented to.

I then added I recollected some thing notic'd in the articles of complaint to w^h I co^d immediately answer. It was stated that the emigrants were well rec^d in our country. All French people were well rec^d there—that many were driven from the Islands in distress & were rec^d hospitably—we knew not whether they were royalists or republicans—we only knew that they were Frenchmen & rec^d them as our friends. That noted emigrants who were pointed out by their ministers in America, as obnoxious to this gov^t were discountenanc'd by the President & forbade his publick room.

It was likewise charged in the list read me that we had suffer'd a British frigate to take shelter in a publick bay within our jurisdiction to watch the movments of Mr Fauchet when ab^t to return home, by means whereof that minister with his publick papers had like to have been taken. To this I observ'd we had no fleet & co^d not therefore prevent such an outrage—that the President had however revoked the exequater of the British consul who gave countenance to that procedure, & complain'd to the British gov^t of it agnst the capt^n.

Carnot observed if we were unable to resent the injuries of Engl^d & said so, that was an ans^r in that case.

I then repeated what I had hinted before of my wish that the list of complaints sho^d be given me thro' the official organ with the view that no measure sho^d be taken till I gave the necessary explanations upon each & w^h agn seemed to be acceded to.

I added that my wish was to preserve the best possible understanding between the two republicks—that in pursuing this I always wish'd to respect principles. If we had injured them & it was shewn, I wo^d be among the first to urge our gov^t to do them justice. That in my station here I was a representative of the American nation, & not of any individual. That in their respective stations with us, every publick functionary was a publick servant; that the President was as much so as myself—that altho' bound to pursue his orders whilst I remain'd here, yet I wo^d not remain here to promote any object agnst my own principles.

Thus the conference ended.

It is to be observed that three days before this a private letter of Genl Washington's to G^r Morris in Engl^d was intercepted & taken by the Directoire:[2] the cover of this letter to Mr Deas in M^r W's hand writing I saw, requesting Mr Deas to deliver it without delay. The purport of the letter to Mr Morris I was told from pretty direct authority, was, to authorize an informal communicat^n between him & Ld Grenville, complaining of the treatment we had rec^d from Engl^d, who had excited the Indians, Algerines, &c to war upon us; who had seized our vessels without provocation, countenanc'd the piracies of the Bermuda privateers, w^h conduct was still continued notwithstanding all the patience we had shewn towards her. That he had signed the treaty in consequence of the advice of the Senate, & with whom he was firm tho' the sense of the great majority of the people was agnst it & by means whereof, a delicate and dangerous crisis in our aff^{ts} had arisen. But yet he tho^t the love the people had for their constit^n wo^d triumph over other considerations & secure the treaty. That under these circumstances, to continue the same irritating policy towards us was hard as it respected the friends of the treaty & impolitick. That Engl^d was deceived as to the credit & strength of America, or she wo^d not treat her as a subaltern power.

About the same time too Mr Randolph's pamphlet arrived, many passages in w^h gave extreme disgust to the French gov^t particularly the imputation w^h was attempted in the use of it by Messrs Hammond, Pickering & Walcott, to be fixed on the French gov^t of offering a bribe &c to Mr R., & thereby dishonor France, in the declaration by the President that the friends of France were the friends of war & confusion, who he says wo^d excite France to hostile measures whilst he raises no imputation agnst the partizans of Engl^d, & finally by signing the treaty shewed plainly that in case America was to take a part in the war he was for taking it on the side of Engl^d, an inference drawn from the opinion he express'd that the signing decided the alternative to w^h we were exposed, of hazarding it with the one or the other power.

These several circumstances all turned up at the same time & threw this gov^t into a ferment of the most serious kind agnst the U. States.

I think proper to observe here that untill I was advised by the minister of foreign aff^{ts} that it was intended to send an envoy &c to the U. States I had kept at some distance from the Directoire, for several reasons but particularly the following—1. I knew that this gov^t disliked our treaty with Engl^d & feared it wo^d take some measure towards us in regard to it. 2. Such was my peculiar situation & the state of parties in America that I knew in case I visited often the Directoire & was not able to prevent any improper measure, I sho^d be suspected of countenancing the measure by many persons in America, who wanting integrity themselves, deny it to others. I knew too that our adm^n had so lost ground here, that if I was not particularly cautious in my conduct, considering that I represented thro' that adm^n the American nation, I sho^d likewise lose any good opinion they might entertain of me. If then I visited them often & in consequence often spoke in favor of that treaty & of the adm^n (& w^h I must have done or admitted they were wrong & in consequence invited this gov^t to push them) I sho^d stand of course upon the same ground with the adm^n & have no weight of my own. Thus circumstanc'd I tho^t it best to follow the impulse of my own feelings, w^h were those of nature, & keep at a distance, in the belief that that was the best mode whereby to prevent any thing being done, & in the conviction that if any thing was done or intended to be done that this was the best way to retain in my power the means of proving useful to my country, if it were at all in my power to be so, w^h was always doubtful under existing circumstances.

It is also to be observed that the Presidents speech to Congress produc'd an ill effect here, by contrasting the flourishing & happy state of our country with the disorganised & unhappy state of other countries w^h was applied to that of France in particular, by the adm^n.

AD, DLC: Monroe Papers, Series 3

1. Étienne-François-Louis Le Tourneur was president of the Directory from 31 January to 30 April 1796 (www.archontology.org, accessed 15 September 2008).

2. George Washington to Gouverneur Morris, 22 December 1795 (Fitzpatrick, *Writings of Washington*, 34: 398-403).

From Charles Delacroix
9 March 1796
Version 1

Paris le 19 Ventôse 4ᵉ Année de la république française une et indivisible.

Exposé Sommaire des griefs de La république française Contre Le Gouvernement
des états unis de l'amérique

1ᵉʳ Grief. Le gouvernement fédéral a tout fait pour anéantir notre Commerce : l'art. 17 du traité de 1778 Porte: que les français Pourront Conduire les prises qu'ils auront faites, dans les ports des états unis, en <u>exemption de tous droits</u>.   Malgré cette déposition formelle, le gouvernement américain a fait prélever par les preposés de ses douanes, Ses droits ruineux Sur nos armateurs.

2ᵉ Grief. Le même article du dit traité porte que les officiers des états unis ne pourront Connaître de la validité des prîses faites par les françois. la convention Consulaire de 1788 accorde à nos marins la faculté de n'être jugés en amérique que par les Consuls de notre nation. Ce droit est Confirmé aux François par les traités de commerce Conclus entre les etats unis et la suéde, et la hollande. Les dispositions avantageuses de ces traités nous Sont devenues communes en vertu de L'art. 2 de notre traité de 1778 au mépris de ces dispositions Solennelles le gouvernement fédéral a Forcé les armateurs francais de Soumettre leurs prises aux jugements des tribunaux américains, et ces tribunaux incompetens ont fait rendre Soit aux anglois, Soit aux espagnols, les prises les plus precieuses. Plusieurs de ces prises ont même été confisquées de pleine autorité.

3ᵉ Grief. Les anglais ont Violé la neutralité stipulée Par les traités. notre ex-ministre Fauchet embarqué Sur un paquebot américain Pour retourner en france a failli etre arreté par les anglois. Le pouvoir executif des etats unis a gardé Le Silence Sur cet attentat au droit des gens, malgré La réclamation de notre agent diplomatique.

4ᵉ Grief. La Corvette française Le Cassius a été Saisie Sur la denonciation d'un anglois Comme ayant été armé aux états unis. en vain notre Ministre a reclamé Contre Cette injustice. en vain il a offert Caution pour le capitaine; le gouvernement fédéral S'est emparé de Cette Corvette et a privé nos antilles des Services qu'elle étoit destinée à leur rendre.

5ᵉ Grief. Le President Washington et les deux chambres du Congrès elles-meme ont ratifiée le traité de Jay, dont les articles 17, 18, 24 et 25 Sont destructifs des articles 17, 24 et 25 de notre traité de 1778.

Ce traité honteux ne peut Subsister Sans porter le Coup le plus Funeste à notre Commerce. il ne Sera plus permis à nos alliés d'expédier pour nous les productions de leur territoire. Ce traité est bien le premier des Griefs que nous ayons Contre les états unis.

on a Stipulé dans le traité de Jay, que les américains ne tireroient du Sucre et de Caffé des Isles françaises que Ce qui Peut Servir à la consommation des etats unis. C'étoit bien, en d'autres termes interdire à nos alliés la Faculté d'approvisioner nos Isles, puisque les américains ne tiraient Ces Sucres et ces Caffés de nos antilles, qu'on echange des Provisions qu'ils y Portaient, les habitants n'ayant pas d'autres moyens de les Payer. il est un autre avantage non moins injurieux à la France accordé Par Ce traité à l'angleterre; C'est celui de S'emparer de tous les Batimens chargés de Vivres et de Subsistances que les americains nous auront destinés. le gouvernement federal n'a-t-il pas par cet article Secondé le Sistème du Cabinet Britannique pour affamer la france? Le gouvernement fédéral a Consenti en outre que l'angleterre Confisquât Comme articles de Contrebande, S'ils étoient exportés chez ses Ennemis par les américains, toute espèce de bois de Construction, Goudron, Resine, Cuivre en Feuille, Voiles, Chauvies, Cordages, et Géneralement tout Ce qui peut Servir à l'équipement d'un Vaisseau; tandis que dans le traité de 1778 avec la france, ces mêmes articles Sont Spécialement désignés Comme Marchandises Libres. enfin l'art. 25 du traité de Jay Semble être le Comble de la perfidie. le gouvernement fédéral accorde par cet article aux anglois la faculté de Conduire leurs prises dans les ports des états unis Consent à priver les Français de Cette même Faculté qui leur étoit Garantie Par le traité de 1778. et le gouvernement S'engage à ne Conclurre aucun traité qui Soit incompatible avec Cet article.

Editors' Translation

Paris, 19 Ventôse 4ᵗʰ Year of the French Republic, one and indivisible.

Summary of Complaints of the French Republic against the Government of the United States of America.

1ˢᵗ Complaint. The federal government has done its utmost to ruin our trade; Article seventeen of the 1778 Treaty states that the French will be able to bring the prizes they have seized into the ports of the United States <u>exempt from all duties</u>. Despite this formal arrangement, the American government has had their customs employees collect ruinous duties on our ship-owners.

2ⁿᵈ Complaint. The same article of the aforementioned treaty states that the officers of the United States will not be permitted to determine the legitimacy of the prizes taken by the French. The consular agreement of 1788 grants our sailors the right to be judged in America by representatives of our nation only. The right is ratified for the French by the commercial treaty agreed upon between the United States, Sweden and Holland. The advantageous arrangements of these treaties evolved from a common understanding in accordance with Article two of our Treaty of 1778. In contempt of these official arrangements, the federal government has forced the French ship-owners to submit their prizes to the jurisdiction of the American courts, and these incompetent courts have made them return either to the English or to the Spanish the most valuable prizes; several of these prizes were even confiscated.

3ʳᵈ Complaint. The English have violated the neutrality stipulated by the treaties. Our previous Minister Fauchet, embarked on an American packet boat to return to France, was almost arrested by the English. The executive power of the United States has kept silent regarding this violation of the law of nations, despite the objection of our diplomatic representative.

4$\underline{th}$ Complaint. The French ship Le Cassius has been seized after an Englishman accused her of having been armed in the United States; our minister has argued in vain against this injustice; in vain he has offered bail for the captain. The federal government has taken possession of this ship and has deprived our islands of the services that the ship had been destined to render.

5$\underline{th}$ Complaint. President Washington and the two chambers of Congress have ratified the Jay Treaty, of which he Articles seventeen, eighteen, twenty-four, and twenty-five are detrimental to Articles seventeen, twenty-four, and twenty-five of our Treaty of 1778. This dishonorable treaty cannot remain without having the most disastrous effect on our trade. It will no longer be permitted for our allies to provision us with the products from their territories. This shameful treaty is by far the primary complaint we have against the United States.

It was stipulated in the Jay Treaty that the Americans would import from the French islands only the sugar and coffee necessary for the consumption in the United States. In other words, it was forbidden for our allies to have the right to supply our islands, since the Americans would only receive sugar and coffee from our islands in exchange for the provisions that they carried there, as the inhabitants have no other way of paying them. There is another advantage no less offensive to France that is granted to England; it is the right to seize all ships loaded with supplies and provisions that the Americans intended for France. Has not the federal government by this article seconded the scheme of the British Cabinet to starve France? Moreover, the federal government has agreed that England may confiscate as contraband, all sorts of timber, tar, resin, sheets of copper, sails, hemp, rigging, and generally all materials that could be used to equip a ship, if exported fromAmerica to France; whereas, in the Treaty of 1778 with France, the same articles are designated as free commodities. Finally, Article twenty-five of the Jay Treaty seems to be the height of treachery. In this article, the federal government grants the English the right to bring their prizes into ports of the United States, while depriving the French of the same right, which has been guaranteed to them by the Treaty of 1778. And the government is commited to not concluding any treaty that would be incompatible with this article.

Dft, DLC: FCP—France. A copy in the handwriting of John B. Prevost is in DLC: Monroe Papers.

Delacroix sent this bill of complaints to JM under cover of a note dated 11 March 1796 (21 Ventôse An 4) (NjMoHP).

From Charles Delacroix
9 March 1796
Version 2

Paris le [dix] neuf Ventôse l'an 4e de la république française.

Exposé sommaire des griefs de la République française, contre le gouvernement des Etats-unis.

1er Grief; L'inéxécution des traités.

1er. Les cours de justice des états-unis ont pris et prennent tous les jours connaissance des prises, que nos corsaires mênent dans leurs ports, Malgré la Clause expresse du traité qui le leur deffend. Nos Ministres ont proposé divers arrangements pour mettre une borne à ces usurpations; le gouvernement fédéral avait lui même proposé des mesures à cet égard. Les premières propositions n'ont point été acceptées; et les dernières mesures sont tombées en désuétude. Les dégouts, les retards, et les pertes qui résultent pour nos marins d'un pareil état de choses sont palpables, ils privent presqu'entiérement la république des avantages qu'elle devrait attendre de cet article du traité.

2ᵉ. L'admission des vaisseaux de guerre Anglaise, même dans le cas d'exclusion Stipulé par l'art 17 du traité, c'est à dire, lorsqu'ils ont fait des prîses sur la république; ou sur ses Citoyens, La Faiblesse avec laquelle le gouvernement-fédéral s'est relaché sur ce point, dans les prémiers temps, a accru les prétentions de la grande brétagne; et aujourd'hui les ports des états-unis deviennent une Station pour l'escadre de l'amiral Murray qui, depuis deux ans, S'y ravitaille, pour de là Courir sur le commerce Américain, et ravager nos propriétés. Cette division pousse même l'audace jusqu'à y mener ses prîses.

3ᵉ. La Convention Consulaire qui fait partie de nos traités, est également sans éxécution dans ses deux Clauses les plus importantes: La 1ᵉʳᵉ qui accorde à nos Consuls le droit de juger exclusivement les contestations survenues entre Français, est devenue illusoire, faute de loix qui donnent aux Consuls les moyens de faire Exécuter leurs jugements. Les Suites de cette impuissance tendent à anéantir la prérogative de nos consuls, et nuisent matériellement aux intérêts de nos Commerçants.

La Seconde donne à nos consuls le droit de faire arrêter nos marins déserteurs. L'inéxactitude de cette partie de la Convention affecte au delà de toute expression, notre service maritime, durant la relâche de nos Vaisseaux dans les ports américains. Les juges chargés par les loix de délivrer les mandats d'arrêts, ont exigés dans ces derniers temps, la présentation du rôle original d'équipages, au mépris de l'article cinq qui admet, dans les tribunaux des deux puissances, les Copies certifiées par les consuls. Les localités s'opposent en mille circonstances à la présentation du rôle original, et dans ce cas les matelots sont hors du cas d'appréhension.

4ᵉ. L'arrestation dans les ports de Philadelphie, au mois d'août 1795, du Capitaine de la Corvette le Cassius; pour faits commis par lui en haute mer; Cette mesure est contraire à l'art. 19 du traité de commerce, qui en Stipule "que les Commandants des vaisseaux publics et particuliers ne pourront être détenus un aucune maniére", et viole d'ailleurs le droit des gens le plus commun, qui met les officiers des vaisseaux publics, sous la sauve-garde de leur pavillon. Les états-unis avaient eu asséz de preuve de déférence de la part de la République, pour qu'ils comptassent sur Sa justice dans cette circonstance. Le capitaine a été emprisonné à Philadelphie, quoique le consul de la république le portât Sa caution. À peine a-t-il été élargi, que la corvette, quoique très réguliérement armée au cap par le Général Laveau, a été arrêtée, (et elle paraît l'être encore), sous le prétexte que huit mois auparavant, elle était sortie de Philadelphie et soupçonnée d'avoir été armée dans ce port.

2ᵉ Grief: L'impunité et l'outrage fait à la République, dans la personne de Son Ministre Le Cᵉⁿ Fauchet, par le Vaisseau Anglais l'affrica, de concert avec le vice consul de cette Nation.

L'arrestation dans les états-unis du paquebot qui portait le Cᵉⁿ Fauchet; la perquisition dans les malles de ce Ministre, avec le but avoué de se saisir de sa personne et de ses papiers, méritaient un éxemple. L'insulte fut commise le 1ᵉʳ aout 1795 (V. H.) Le vaisseau bloqua; tout le reste du mois; la frégate de la République, la Méduse, à Newport, et il ne reçut l'ordre de s'éloigner qu'aprés son départ, et pour un nouvel outrage fait aux états-unis par une lettre menaçante. L'exequatur n'a été retiré au vice-consul anglais, que pour avoir pris part à cette derniére insulte.

3ᵉ Grief. Le traité Conclu en novembre 1794 entre les Etats-unis, et la grande Brétagne.

Il sera facile de prouver que les états-unis, dans ce traité, ont sacriffié Sciemment et évidemment leurs liaisons avec la république; et les prérogatives les plus essentielles, et les moins contestées de la neutralité.

1ᵉ. Outre que les Etats-unis se sont départis des principes consacrés par la neutralité armée pendant la guerre, de leur indépendante, ils ont donné à l'Angleterre, au détriment de leurs premiers alliés, la marque la plus frappante, d'une condescendance sans bornes, en abandonnant la limite que mettent à la contrebande, le droit des gens; leurs traités avec toutes les autres nations, les traités même de l'angleterre avec la plus part des puissances maritimes. Sacriffier exclusivement à cette puissance les objets propres à l'équipement et à la construction des Vaisseaux. N'est ce pas s'écarter évidemment des principes de la neutralité?

2ᵉ. Ils ont été plus loin encore; ils ont consenti à étendre la dénomination et contrebande aux provisions même, au lieu de préciser, comme le font tous les traités, le cas du <u>blocus effectif</u> d'une place, comme pouvant seul faire exception à la franchise de cet article, ils ont hautement reconnu les prétentions qu'élève l'angleterre de faire éxister le <u>Blocus</u> pour nos colonies, et même pour la france <u>dans la puissance seule</u> d'une déclaration. Cet abandon qu'ils font de l'indépendance de leur commerce est incompatible avec leur neutralité. Mr. Jefferson l'a lui même reconnu par sa lettre du 7 septembre, aux Ministres plénipotentiaires des états-unis, à Londres, au sujet de l'édit du 8 juin 1793. d'après cet aveu, d'après surtout les édits tyranniques du roi de la grande Bretagne dont le commerce des états-unis, autant que leur honneur National, avait tout eu à souffrir, ou espérait un tout autre résultat, de la négociation de Mʳ Jay, il est évident, par la clause du traité qui limite l'existence de cette désertion de la neutralité, à la durée de cette guerre, que Mʳ Jay n'a point hésité à sacrifier nos colonies à la grande Bretagne, pendant le reste des hostilités présentes qui doivent décider de leur sort. On laisse à juger à M. Monroe, jusqu'à quel point ces concessions s'accordent avec l'obligation contractée par les Etats-unis, de deffendre nos possessions coloniales, et avec les devoirs non moins sacrés que leur imposent les immenses et inappréciables bénefices qu'ils ont retiré de leur commerce avec elles.

Ch. Delacroix.

Editors' Translation

Paris [1]9 Ventôse,[1] 4th year of the French Republic.

Summary Exposition of the Complaints of the French Republic against the
Government of the United States

First complaint, the failure to observe treaties.

1. The American courts of justice have been and are always taking cognizance of the prizes that our corsairs bring into their ports, despite the explicit clause in the treaty that forbids it. Our ministers have proposed several ways to limit these encroachments; the federal government had itself proposed measures that have fallen into disuse. The offences, delays, and losses suffered by our seamen as a result of this state of affairs are appreciable. They deny the republic almost entirely the advantages that it should expect from this article of the treaty.

2. The admission of English warships, even where prohibited by article seventeen of the treaty, that is to say when they have captured ships or citizens of the Republic. The weakness which the federal government has shown on this point has encouraged British pretensions, and today the ports of the United States have become a base for Admiral Murray's squadron, which for two years past was stationed there to make raids on American commerce, and devastate our property. This squadron carries its audacity even further by bringing its prizes into those ports.

3. The two most important clauses of the consular convention which forms part of our treaties are also not being enforced. The first, which gives our consuls the exclusive right to arbitrate disputes between French citizens, has become illusory from a defect in the law that would provide the means for

our consuls to enforce the laws. The consequences of this impotence tends to extinguish our prerogatives and materially affect the interests of our merchants.

The second clause gives our consuls the right to recover our sailors who desert; the failure to enforce this part of the convention has an immeasurable affect on our navy, when our ships are docked in American ports. The judges, who are charged by law with issuing the arrest warrants, have recently demanded to see the <u>original</u> ships' rosters, in contravention of article five which permits the two powers to present copies that have been certified by a consul. The local ports in every case refuse to submit the original roster, and the sailors therefore go free.

4ᵉ. The arrest in August of the captain of the corvette, <u>Cassius</u>, in the port of Philadelphia for acts committed by him on the high seas. This action contravenes article nineteen of the trade agreement which states "that the commandants of public and private vessels shall not be detained in any manner." It is also a violation of the most basic of the laws of nations which places the officers of public ships under the protection of their flag. The United States had sufficient proof of the Republic's deference for the law to recognize that it would always respect this provision. The captain was imprisoned in Philadelphia despite the warning of the French consul, and with difficulty has been released. The corvette was detained (and appears still to be so) under the pretext that eight months earlier it had left Philadelphia under suspicion of having acquired arms there, despite the fact that General Lavaux[2] armed the ship at the Cape.

> Second Complaint. The awful outrage committed against the Republic
> in the person of its minister, Citizen Fauchet, by the English ship, <u>Africa</u>,
> in concert with the vice Consul of that country.

The detention in American waters of the pacquet boat carrying Citizen Fauchet, and the search made in his luggage, with the stated aim of capturing him and his papers, serves as an example. The insult was committed on 1 August 1795. For the rest of the month, the Africa blocked the exit of the frigate, <u>Medusa</u>, which was not able to sail from Newport until after the departure of the Africa. Another outrage committed against the United States was a threatening letter from the English vice cConsul, whose credentials were withdrawn only after this latest insult in which he was involved.

> Third Complaint. The Treaty Concluded in November 1794 between the
> United States and Great Britain.

It would be easy to prove that in that treaty the United States has <u>knowingly</u> and <u>inescapably</u> sacrificed its relationship with the Republic as well as the most essential and least contested rights of neutrality.

1. The United States have not only abandoned the principles adopted by the armed neutrality during their war of independence, but have given England, to the detriment of their original allies, the most striking mark of unlimited favor, by abandoning limits imposed by the law of nations on contraband, their treaties with all other nations, and even England's treaties with most of the other maritime powers. Is not this granting to that power exclusive access to materials for equipping and building ships an obvious departure from the principles of neutrality?

2. They have gone further still. They have agreed to extend the status of contraband even to provisions. Instead of restricting it, as all treaties have done, to the conditions for effectively blockading a port which alone could constitute an exemption from this article of the treaty, they have tacitly recognized England's intentions to blockade our colonies and even France, by means of a simple declaration. This

desertion of the independence of their commerce is incompatible with their neutrality. Mr. Jefferson himself recognized this in his letter of September 7 to the minister plenipotentiary of the United States to London regarding the edict of June 8, 1793. Above all in light of the tyrannical edicts of the king of Great Britain, which took a toll on the commerce of the United States as much as on its honor, one might have hoped for a completely different result in Mr. Jay's negotiations. It is obvious from the clause in the treaty that says that this desertion of neutrality will last only until the end of the current war, which Mr. Jay did not hesitate to sacrifice our colonies to Great Britain for the remainder of the current hostilities that will determine their fate. We leave Mr. Monroe to judge the extent to which these concessions comply with the obligation undertaken by the United States to defend our colonial possessions and with the duty, no less sacred, imposed upon them from the immense and immeasurable profits they have realized through trade with these colonies.

Ch. Delacroix

FC, DLC: FCP—France; misdated 9 Ventôse 4. A copy in French is enclosed in JM to Pickering 2 May 1796, DNA: RG 59: Dispatches from France. A translation of this copy is in *ASP:FR*, 1: 732-733. An incomplete translation (first three pages only) is in NN: Monroe Papers

During his meeting with the Directory on 8 March 1796 JM requested that the French complaints against the United States be given to him in writing. Delacroix complied the following day, giving JM version one of his bill of complaints. JM responded on March 15 (below), and sometime after March 25 Delacroix asked permission to reclaim his paper so that he could revise it in light of JM's comments. JM returned Delacroix's paper and took back his own of March 15. Delacroix submitted his revised bill of complaints (version two) on April 15, and JM responded later that month. Both correspondents, however, gave their revisions the same dates as their originals (JM to Pickering 2 May 1796 and November 1796, both below).

1. The clerk who copied this letter misdated it 9 Ventôse.

2. Étienne-Maynaud-Biźe-Franc Lavaux (or Laveaux, 1751-1828) was a lieutenant-general when in 1793 he was named interim governor of Saint-Domingue (*Dictionnaire Biographie Française*).

From David Humphreys

Lisbon March 9th 1796.

(Circular)

Dear Sir.

As it appears very doubtful, whether the pecuniary arrangements on the part of the United States of America can possibly be completed at so early a period as to give satisfaction to the Dey & Regency of Algiers, & thereby prevent the renewal of Hostilities, I have thought it expedient for the interest of the public Service to address this letter to you, for the express purpose of requesting that you will be pleased to give notice to all Citizens of the United States concerned (and to whom it shall be in your power to give such notice) that they may expose themselves to great danger by attempting to proceed up the Mediterranean, before they shall be duly notified on the part of the Government of the United States, that there will be no impropriety or hazard of being captured by so doing. With Sentiments of perfect consideration & esteem I have the honour to be, D[r] Sir, Your m[o] ob. & m[o] h[ble] Serv[t]

D. Humphreys.

RC, DLC: Monroe Papers

JM received this letter on 9 April 1796. He relayed the information to Fulwar Skipwith the same day and instructed him to pass it on to the American consuls in France (JM to Skipwith, 9 April 1796, NN: Monroe Papers).

From Aaron Burr

Philadᵃ 10 Mar. 96

My dear Sir,

You will learn with some astonishment that we are now four Months without a letter of known authenticity from Paris—The most crude accounts come down no later than the 20ᵗʰ Novʳ—To this day we have not a word which can indicate the Sensations with which the french Govᵗ have received the knowledge of our Treaty with G-B. This affords room for the friends of that treaty to assert that our Allies are no way dissatisfied with it. God grant they may be right!

I send you herewith Such of the late gazettes as will suffice to shew you how Congress are occupied—I have often sent you News-papers & pamphlets, but have never had the Satisfaction to learn that one of them have come to hand.

The Motion calling on the President for the Communications will be carried—The debate has been animated, interesting & ably managed—it will Still continue for some days.[1]

A short letter from Bourdeaux of the 16 Decʳ (perhaps spurious) announces the Surrender of Manheim[2] & some internal distresses on the subject of finance—we have no idea of the projects of the Republic for raising Money since the extreme depreciation of their assignats.

your friends, as far as I can recollect, are as usual—Ellsworth Ch. Ju in the room of Cushing who resigned, really from Modesty[3]—Madison still childless, and I fear like to continue so. Very affectᵉ

A. Burr

RC, DLC: Monroe Papers

1. Edward Livingston made a motion in the House of Representatives on 2 March 1796 calling on President Washington to submit the instructions given to John Jay and correspondence with him relating to the British treaty. Extensive debate ensued and continued until March 24, when the House passed the motion (*Madison Papers*, 16: 254, 255, 263).

2. *Claypoole's American Daily Advertiser* (Philadelphia) printed two extracts on 10 March 1796 relating to the surrender of Manheim, one dated 14 December and the other 17 December 1795.

3. Oliver Ellsworth resigned his seat in the Senate on 8 March 1796 to assume the duties of chief justice (*BDAC*).

To Timothy Pickering

Paris March 11ᵗʰ 1796.

Sir

I informed you in my two last of the 16ᵗʰ and 20ᵗʰ ultimo of a communication made me by the minister of foreign affairs that the directory had resolved to send an Envoy Extraordinary to the U. S. to remonstrate against their late treaty with England and of my Efforts to prevent it and I now the pleasure of adding that I have reason to believe those efforts have been successful the minister having assured me in a late conference that the directory was disposed to accommodate in this respect & to make its representations on that subject through the ordinary channel. He repeated however, upon this occasion in terms equally strong with those he had used before, the sense which he said the directory entertained of the injury done to france by that treaty & upon which explanations were expected, and would be sought. I asked him what were his objections to the treaty, to which he replied as before, in general rather than in precise terms, urging that we had violated our treaties with france and greatly to her injury in the present war. I replied that it was not admitted by our Government that any the slightest deviation was made from our treaty with this republic, nor ought it to be so presumed until it was shewn that such was the case especially as I had before informed him and now repeated my willingness to discuss that point when he thought fit. He intimated that I should certainly hear from him on the subject & in time to receive & to attend to any observations I chose to make but being now before the directory he could not well enter on it in the manner I proposed until he had the further orders of that body in that respect. Thus therefore, the matter now stands & I have only to repeat to you my assurance that I shall continue to pay to it all the attention it deservedly merits.

The state of affairs here has not varied essentially of late either in the internal or in the external relations of the republic. The forced loan was less productive than it was expected to be and of course the relief it gives must be considered as partial and temporary only. Nor is any system yet adopted to supply what will be necessary after the amount thus raised is exhausted; though as the subject is still under discussion it is possible this may yet be done. On the other hand the Directoire by means of the organization and police seems to gain strength, and to which a late measure has essentially contributed. At the Pantheon and in other quarters there were nightly meetings of People not inconsiderable in point of numbers and who complained of various grievances, proceeding as they said from the actual government, and which ought therefore to be changed. The Directoire had its eye upon those assemblages, and as I hear gained full proof, that they were put in motion by foreign influence, and under the mask of patriotism more effectually to promote the purpose of disorganization, and in consequence shut the doors of the houses where they resorted.[1] As many of those who were at the head of those meetings were active and ferocious Agents in the popular societies during the reign of terror, and were probably then moved by the same cause, this discovery if to be relied on, tends to throw great light upon the source to which the atrocities that were then practised ought to be ascribed. Time perhaps and especially if the revolution weathers the storms it has yet to encounter, will doubtless more fully unfold the real authors of those scenes, which were so frightful to humanity, and disgraceful to man, and that they may be discovered must be the wish of all those who are the friends of truth wherever they reside.

Prussia has in the course of the winter encreased her force forty or fifty thousand men, and it is said exhibits a menacing aspect towards Holland, though her minister continues here and is apparently well received. Spain too continues her military establishment as before the peace, and whose Minister Del Campo is daily expected from England, where he has long resided.[2] The probable conjecture with respect to Spain is, that as she feared an attack from England when she made her peace with france, so she finds it necessary to guard herself against it by suitable precautions, till the war ends. Russia it is believed contemplates a blow against the Turks, in the hope now that Poland is annihilated, France otherwise sufficiently occupied, and the other powers in amity with the Empress, to wrest Constantinople from the Porte, which has long been the object of her inordinate ambition. On the other hand France seems to be collecting her forces together, and to exert every nerve her system admits of, in preparations for the war, exhibiting to her Enemies a countenance firm and independent and announcing to the beholding nations her resolution to conquer or to perish. With due respect I am Sir your most obedient and very humble servant

Ja⁵ Monroe

RC, NjP. Words in italics were written in code and deciphered by a clerk in the State Department.

1. The Jacobins took advantage of the provisions of the new constitution allowing political liberty to form new clubs from which they could promote their political and economic goals. The most prominent of these was the Pantheon Club in Paris. The Directory, fearful of a resurgence of Jacobinism, suppressed the clubs in the early months of 1796 (Isser Woloch, *Jacobin Legacy: The Democratic Movement Under the Directory*, 19-47).

2. Bernardo del Campo, y Pérez de la Serna was the Spanish minister to Great Britain 1783-1795 (*The Emerging Nation: A Documentary History of the Foreign Relations of the United States Under the Articles of Confederation, 1780-1789*, 3: 621).

To Charles Delacroix

Paris 15th of March 1796. 25 Ventose 4th year of FR

and 20th of the independence of the United States of America.

Citizen Minister

I was lately honoured with your note of the 19th Ventose (9th of March) objecting to several measures of our government that have occurred in the course of the present war and to which I presume I shall herein render you a satisfactory answer. For this purpose I shall pursue in reply the order you have observed in stating those objections, and according to the light I have on the subject give to each the answer it requires.

These objections are comprised under three distinct heads a summary of which I will first expose, that my reply to each may be better understood.

1st. Your first complaint is that we have failed to execute our treaties with you and in the following respects. 1st by submitting to our tribunals the cognizance of prizes brought into our ports by your privateers. 2^{d} By admitting english vessels of war into our ports against the stipulation of the 17th article of our treaty of commerce, even after such vessels had taken prizes from you, and in some cases with their prizes. 3^{d}. By omitting to execute the consular convention in two of its most important clauses having failed to provide as you suggest suitable means for carrying those clauses into effect the first of which secures to your consuls within the United States the exclusive jurisdiction of all controversies between french Citizens, and the second the right to pursue and recover all mariners who desert from your vessels. 4th By suffering in the port of philadelphia the arrestation of the Captain of the Corvette Cassius for an act committed by him on the high sea, and which you say is contrary to the 19th article of the treaty of commerce, which stipulates "that the Commandants of public and private vessels shall not be detained in any manner" and the rights of nations which put such officers under the protection of their respective flags: and by likewise suffering the arrestation of that Corvette though armed at the Cape upon the pretext that she was armed in the United States.

2^{d}. Your second complaint states that an outrage which was made to this republic in the Person of its Minister the Citizen Fauchet by an english vessel (the Africa) in concert with an english consul in arresting within the jurisdiction of the United States the packet boat in which he had embarked, searching his trunks, and afterwards remaining within the waters of those states for near a month to watch the movements of the vessel in which he finally sailed, was left unpunished, since you urge that the measures afterwards taken by our government in regard to that vessel and the consul were not taken in a suitable time to remedy the evil and were produced by a subsequent outrage and of a very different kind.

3^{d}. Your third and last complaint applies to our late treaty with England, and which you say not only sacrifices in favor of that power our treaty with france, but departs from that line of impartiality which as a neutral nation we were bound to observe. Particular exemplifications are given of this charge in your note, and which I shall particularly notice when I come to reply to it.

This is a summary of your complaints and to each of which I will now give a precise and I flatter myself a satisfactory answer.

1. Of the inexecution of our treaties with this republic and of the first example given of it "the submission to our tribunals of the cognizance of prizes brought into our ports by your Privateers."

Permit me in reply to this charge to ask whether you insist as a general principle that our tribunals are inhibited the right of taking cognizance of the validity of your prizes in all cases or are there exceptions to it? As a general principle without exception it cannot I think be insisted on, because examples may be given under it of possible cases, which prove it cannot be so executed and construed without an encroachment upon the inherent and unalienable rights of sovereignty in both nations, which neither intended to make, nor does the treaty warrant. Suppose for instance a prize was taken within our jurisdiction, not upon the high seas nor even at the entrance or mouths of those great rivers and bays which penetrate and fertilize our country but actually in the interior and at the wharf of some one of our cities, is this a case over which our tribunals or some other branch of our government have no right to take cognizance? Do you conceive that the true import of the treaty imposes upon us and likewise upon you in turn the obligation thus to abandon as a theatre of warfare in which you bear no part, the interior police of your country? Can it be done consistently with the dignity or the rights of sovereignty? Or suppose the privateer which took the prize and led it into port was fitted out within the United States, the act being unauthorized by treaty could we tolerate this, and refuse the like liberty to the other nation at war without departing from that line of neutrality we ought to observe? You well know that those rights which are secured by treaty form the only preference in a neutral port, which a neutral nation can give to either of the parties at war, and if these are transcended, that the nation so acting makes itself a party to the war, and in consequence merits to be considered and treated as such. These examples prove that there are some exceptions to the general principle, and perhaps there are others which do not occur to me at present. Are then the cases in question and which form the basis of your complaint within the scale of these exceptions? If they are and I presume they are, I am persuaded you will concur with me in opinion that the complaint is unfounded, and that we have only done our duty; a duty we were bound to perform as well from a respect to our rights as a sovereign and free people, as to the integrity of our character being a neutral party in the present war.

You will observe that I admit the principle, if a prize was taken upon the high sea, and by a Privateer fitted out within the republic or its dominions that in such case our courts have no right to take cognizance of its validity. But is any case of this kind alledged? I presume none is or can be shewn.

2$^\text{d}$. The second article in this charge of failing to execute our treaties with this republic, states that in contravention with the 17$^\text{th}$ article of the treaty of commerce we have admitted british vessels of war into our ports even such as have taken prizes from you, and in some cases with their prizes. The article referred to stipulates the right for your vessels of war and Privateers to enter our Ports with their prizes, and inhibits that right to your Enemies. It does not stipulate that the vessels of war belonging to your Enemies shall not enter but simply that they shall not enter with their prizes. This latter act therefore is I presume the subject of your complaint. Here too it only stipulates that in case such vessels enter yours or our ports, proper measures shall be taken to compel them to retire as soon as possible. Whether you were rightly informed with respect to the fact is a point upon which I cannot decide as I know nothing about it. Our coast is extensive, our harbours numerous and the distress of the weather may have forced them in: or they may have entered wantonly and in contempt of the authority of our government. Many outrages have been committed on us by that nation in the course of the present war and this may likewise be in the catalogue. But I will venture to affirm that no countenance was given by our government to those vessels whilst they were there, and that all suitable means were taken to compel them to retire, and without delay. You know we have no fleet and how difficult it is without one to execute a stipulation of this kind with that promptitude which your agents in our Country ardent in your cause and faithful to your interest, might expect.

3. The third article under this head states that we have omitted to execute the consular convention in two of its most important clauses, the first of which secures to the consuls of each nation in the ports of the other, the exclusive jurisdiction of controversies between their own Citizens and the second of which gives to the Consuls a right to recover such Mariners as desert from the vessels of their respective Nations.

Upon the first point, the supposed incompetency of the law provided on our part to execute the judgments of your consuls within our Jurisdiction, I can only say that as no particular defect is stated, so no precise answer can be given to the objection. And upon the second which states that the Judges charged by our law to issue warrants for arresting such of your mariners as desert from their vessels have latterly required and against the spirit of the treaty the presentation of the original registers of the vessels to which they belonged as the ground whereon to issue these warrants, I have to observe that by the clause in question (the 9th article) the originals seem to be required, and that the copies spoken of in another part of the treaty (the 5 article) obviously apply to other objects and not to this. More fully however to explain to you the conduct of our government upon this subject permit me here to add an extract from our law passed on the 14th of April 1792 expressly to carry into effect the convention in question and which applies to both cases. "The district Judges of the United States shall within their respective districts be the competent Judges for the purposes expressed in the 9th article of the said convention and it shall be incumbent on them to give aid to the consuls and vice-consuls of france in arresting and securing deserters from the vessels of the french nation, according to the tenor of the said article. And where by any article of the said convention the consuls and vice-consuls of france are entitled to the aid of the competent executive officers of the Country in the execution of any precept the marshals and their deputies shall within their respective districts be the competent officers and shall give their aid according to the tenor of the stipulations." By this extract you will clearly perceive that it was not the intention of our government to frustrate or embarrass the execution of this treaty: on the contrary that it was its intention to carry it into full effect according to its true intent and meaning, and that it has done so, so far as could be done by suitable legal provisions.

It may hereafter be deemed a subject worthy consideration whether the first of those clauses in that convention had not better be expunged from it. The principle of a foreign court established within any country, with jurisdiction independent of that country cannot well be reconciled with any correct idea of its sovereignty: nor can it exercise its functions without frequent interference with the authorities of the country, and which naturally occasions strife and discontent between the two governments. These however are not the only objections to the measure, though with me they are unanswerable. Under circumstances the most favorable it were difficult for these consular tribunals to serve their process and execute their Judgments. A limited jurisdiction to a town or village only admits of it. In the United States therefore and france where the territory is immense, and the number of citizens of each country in the other considerable, as is now the case it becomes impossible. Many of these in each country dwell perhaps in the Interior and not within one hundred leagues of any consul of their nation; how compel their attendance before him? How execute the Judgment afterwards? For the tribunals of one Country to call in the aid of the officers of another to execute its decrees or Judgments is an institution at best objectionable, but to send those officers round the country through the range of one hundred leagues is more so.

Permit me then to ask what are the motives on yours or our part for such an institution? In what respect are you or we interested that yours or our Consuls should have the exclusive jurisdiction of controversies between yours and our Citizens in each other's country? Why not submit those controversies in common with all others to the tribunals of each nation? Some considerations in favor of the institution it is true occur but yet they are light and trifling, when compared with the numerous and strong objections that oppose it. So much, however, by way of digression.

4ᵗʰ. Your fourth and last example under this head states that the Captain of the Corvette Cassius was arrested in Philadelphia for an act committed on the high sea contrary as you suggest to the 19ᵗʰ article of the treaty of commerce which stipulates "that the commandants of vessels public and private shall not be detained in any manner whatever" and of the well known rights of nations which put the officers of public vessels under the safeguard of their respective flags: and that the said Corvette was likewise seized, though armed at the Cape, upon the pretext that she was armed some time before in Philadelphia.

As you have not stated what the act was, with the commission whereof the Captain was charged, I can of course give no explanation on that head. Satisfied however I am that if the crime was of a nature to authorise our courts to take cognizance of it, he would not be exempted from their Jurisdiction by the article of the treaty in question, since that article as you perceive was intended to establish a general principle in the intercourse between the two nations, to give a priviledge to the ships of war of each to enter and retire from the ports of the other, and not to secure in favor of any particular delinquent an immunity from crimes: nor in my opinion does the law of nations admit of a different construction or give any other protection. I am happy however to hear that he is released since it furnishes an additional proof that the whole transaction was a judicial one, regular according to the course of our law and mingling nothing in it in any view that ought to give offence here.

With respect to the seizure of the corvette upon the pretext that she was armed in Philadelphia, I have only to say that if she was armed there, it was the duty of our government to seize her, the right to arm not being stipulated by treaty. And if that was alledged upon sufficient testimony as I presume was the case, there was no other way of determining the question, than by an examination into it, and in the interim preventing her sailing. It would be no satisfaction to the other party to the war, for us to examine into the case after she was gone, provided the decision was against her. On the contrary such conduct would not only expose us to the charge of committing a breach of neutrality, but of likewise doing it collusively.

2. Your second complaint states an outrage which was committed by a british frigate upon your Minister the Citizen Fauchet in concert with a british Consul, in boarding the packet in which he embarked, opening his trunks &ᶜ within the waters of the United States, and remaining there afterwards to watch the movements of the frigate in which he sailed and which you say was not resented as it ought to have been by our government, since you add the measures which were taken by it in regard to that vessel and the consul were the effect of another and subsequent outrage.

The punishment which was inflicted by our government upon the parties who committed that outrage by revoking the Exequatur of the Consul, and ordering that all supplies should be withheld from the frigate, as likewise that she should forthwith depart without the waters of the United States was, I think you will admit an adequate one for the offence. Certain it is that as we have no fleet it was the only one in our power to inflict. And that this punishment was inflicted in consequence of that outrage, you will I presume likewise admit, after you have perused the act of the President upon that subject a copy of which I herewith transmit to you,¹ and by which you will perceive that there was in truth no distinct outrage offered to the United States upon that occasion by the Parties in question, but that both the one and the other act (the attempt made upon the packet boat in which your minister had embarked by the Captain of a british frigate and which constituted the first, and the writing an insolent letter by the same

Captain to the governor of Rhode Island in concert with the british Consul there, and which constituted the second) were only several incidents to the same transaction forming together a single offence and for which that punishment was inflicted on those parties.

I think proper here to add, as a farther proof that the President was neither inattentive to what was due to your rights upon that occasion nor to the character of the United States, that he gave orders to our Minister at London to complain formally to that government of that outrage and to demand of it such satisfaction upon the parties as the nature of the insult required and which has doubtless either been given or is still expected.

3. Your third and last complaint applies to our late treaty with England and which you say has sacrificed in favor of that power our connection with france, and the rights of neutrality the most common.

1. In support of this charge you observe, that we have not only departed from the principles of the armed neutrality adopted in the course of the late war, but have abandoned in favor of England, the limits which the rights of nations and our own treaties with all other powers and even England in her treaties with many other powers have given to contraband.

2. That we have also consented that provisions should be deemed contraband not when destined to a blockaded port only, as should be the case, but in all cases by tacitly acknowledging the pretensions of England to place at pleasure and by proclamation not only your Islands but even france herself in that dilemma.

The principles of the armed neutrality set on foot by the Empress of Russia in harmony with the other neutral powers at the time you mention, and acceded to by all the powers then at war against England are extremely dear to us, because they are just in themselves, and in many respects very important to our welfare. We insert them in every treaty we make with those powers who are willing to adopt them, and our hope is that they will soon become universal. But even in the war of which you speak and when the combination against England was most formidable, all the maritime powers being arranged against her, you well know that she never acceded to them. How compel her then upon the present occasion, when that combination was not only broken, but many of the powers then parties to it, and against England, were now enlisted on her side in support of her principles. You must be sensible that under these circumstances it was impossible for us to obtain from that power the recognition of those principles, and that of course we are not culpable for having failed to accomplish that object.

I regret also that we did not succeed in obtaining a more liberal scale of contraband from that power than was obtained: for as our articles of exportation are chiefly articles of the first necessity, and always in great demand here and every where else, it was equally an object of importance to us to enlarge the freedom of commerce in that respect, by diminishing the list of contraband. Perhaps no nation on the Globe is more interested in this object than we are. But here too the same difficulty occurred that had in the preceding case, and it was in consequence deemed expedient for the time to relinquish a point we could not obtain, suffering the ancient law of nations to remain unchanged in any respect. Is it urged that we have made any article contraband that was not so before by the known and well established law of nations? which England had not a right to seize by that law, and did not daily seize when they fell in her way? This cannot be urged because the fact is otherwise: for although we have not ameliorated the law of nations in that respect, yet certainly we have not changed it for the worse, and which alone could give you just cause of complaint.

With respect to the objection stated to a clause in the eighteenth article of the treaty with England, and which presumes we are thereby prohibited bringing provisions from the United States to France, I have only to add that no such prohibition is to be found in it or other stipulation which changes the law of nations in that respect; on the contrary that article leaves the law of nations where it was before, authorizing the seizure in those cases only where such provisions are contraband "by the existing law of nations," and according to our construction when carrying to a blockaded port, and in which case payment is stipulated, but in no respect is the law of nations changed, or any right given to the british to seize other than they had before and such I presume you will agree is the true import of that article.

You will observe by the article in question that when our provisions destined for a blockaded port are seized, though by the law of nations subject to confiscation, they are nevertheless exempted from it and the owners of such provisions entitled to the payment of their value. Surely this stipulation cannot tend to discourage my countrymen from adventuring with provisions into the ports of this republic, nor in any other respect prevent their enterprises here. On the contrary was it not probable that it would produce the opposite effect, since thereby the only penalty which could deter them, that of confiscation in the case above mentioned, was completely done away?

Thus Citizen Minister I have answered according to the views of our government and the light I have upon the subject, the objections you have stated against several of its measures adopted in the course of the present war, and I hope to your satisfaction. That any occurrence should take place in the annals of the republics, which gave cause for suspicion that you doubted in any degree our sincere and affectionate attachment to your welfare, is a circumstance that cannot otherwise than give pain to our government and our People. That these however should be removed by a fair and candid examination of your complaints on both sides is the best consolation that such an occurrence can admit of. If by my feeble efforts I contribute in any degree to promote that end and preserve the harmony and affection which have so long subsisted between us, and I trust will always subsist Be assured that I accomplish an object the most grateful to my feelings that I can possibly accomplish. Permit me in concluding this letter to assure you of the respect and esteem with which I am Sir your very humble Servant.

Jaˢ Monroe

RC, DLC: FCP—France. A draft is in NN: Monroe Papers, and a copy is enclosed in JM to Pickering, 2 May 1796, DNA: RG 59: Dispatches from France. It is printed in *ASP:FR* 1: 659.

During his meeting with the Directory on 8 March 1796 JM requested that the French complaints against the United States be given to him in writing. Delacroix complied the following day, giving JM a bill of complaints (9 March 1796, above). JM responded on March 15, and sometime after March 25 Delacroix asked permission to reclaim his paper so that he could revise it in light of JM's comments. JM returned Delacroix's paper and took back his own of March 15. Delacroix submitted his revised bill of complaints on April 15, and JM responded later that month. Both correspondents, however, gave their revisions the same dates as their originals (see JM to Pickering 2 May 1796 and November 1796, both below). The letter printed here is JM's revision of his response to Delacroix. Although there are multiple copies of this document, no copies of the original have been located.

1. Revocation of exequator of Thomas Moore, British vice consul for Rhode Island, 5 September 1795; Timothy Pickering to Arthur Fenner, 5 September 1795, *ASP: FR*, 1: 665-666.

To Andrew Masson

Paris March 20. 1796.

Sir

I had the pleasure to receive your favor by M[r] Terrason[1] & a subsequent one of the 2[d] of Feb[y] last thro' M[r] Parish our consul at Hamburg.

The disposition of my letters for Madame Moutie is perfectly agreeable to me. If they wo[d] not be delivered to her it wo[d] be useless to send them, & their miscarriage might possibly do harm. Let them therefore remain where they are untill you know they can be delivered safely, & then you will of course immediately forward them to her.

I am authorised to advance Madame Moutie what will be necessary for her expences, having under my disposition a limited sum for that purpose, & upon which however she made some appropriations before she left this & for which I stand responsible, when ever the party, her relative calls for it. The residue I shall be happy to apply in such manner as she directs, & with that view (under her authority) will with pleasure always fulfill y[r] desires. There is no object more interesting to my country generally or to myself personally than the peace & happiness of that family, & of course you will always find me well disposed to harmonize with you in those measures that are calculated to promote that end.

You have inclosed me a memorial to be signed, by the Americans here for our consul M[r] Parish at Hamburg to be forwarded thence to the court of Denmark, thro' some channel not mentioned, to ask its aid in favor of the release of M[r] Moutie. Permit me to assure you that altho' I do not think this a suitable mode of procedure, & for reasons that will probably occur to you, I shall omit no opportunity w[h] presents itself to promote the liberation of the gent[n]. If the c[t] of Denmark is disposed to forward that object certainly a more eligible mode than that of petition by individuals may be adopted. Have you any reason to believe that that c[t] is so disposed? I will thank you in case you have, for the communication of it, since it may be useful in another view. I suggest the above as a motive why the projected plan sho[d] be given over, submitting it however to y[r] judgment and in the interim will keep the paper sent me, subject to such disposition as you shall direct after the rec[t] of this. The Americans who have given this proof of attachment to M[r] Moutie & M[r] Parish who has harmonised with them in that sentiment have done justice to the common feeling of America in that interesting concern, & I hope the time is not remote when their wishes will be gratified in that respect.

I shall always be happy to hear from you & to receive such details as you have respecting the situation & wishes of that most amiable family.

Dft, NN: Monroe Papers

The draft of a cover letter addressed to John Parish is appended to the bottom of this letter.

1. Masson to JM, 6 December 1795.

From Thomas Jefferson

Monticello Mar. 21. 96.

Dear Sir

I wrote you on the 2ᵈ inst. and now take the liberty of troubling you in order to have the inclosed letter to mr Gautier safely handed to him. I will thank you for information that it gets safely to hand, as it is of considerable importance to him, to the US. to the state of Virginia, and to myself, by conveying to him the final arrangement of the accounts of Grand & co. with all those parties.[1]

Mr Jones happened fortunately to come into our neighborhood a few days after the date of my last, and ordered the proper ground to be inclosed and reserved for trees for you. my gardener is this day gone to plant such as we had, which will serve for a beginning. we shall engraft more for you this spring and plant them the next.

The British treaty has been formally at length laid before Congress. all America is atip-toe to see what the H. of Representatives will decide on it. we concieve the constitutional doctrine to be that tho' the P. and Senate have the general power of making treaties yet wherever they include in a treaty matters confided by the constitution to the three branches of legislature, an act of legislation will be requisite to confirm these articles, and that the H. of Repr. as one branch of the legislature are perfectly free to pass the act or to refuse it, governing themselves by their own judgment whether it is for the good of their constituents to let the treaty go into effect or not. on the precedent now to be set will depend the future construction of our constitution, and whether the powers of legislation shall be transferred from the P. Senate and H. of R. to the P. Senate and Piamingo or any other Indian, Algerine or other chief. it is fortunate that the first decision is to be in a case so palpably atrocious as to have been predetermined by all America.—the appointment of Elsworth C. J. and Chace one of the judges is doubtless communicated to you. my friendly respects to mrs Monroe. Adieu affectionately

Th. Jefferson

RC, DLC: Monroe Papers

1. Jefferson to Jean Antoine Gautier, 17 March 1796 (*Jefferson Papers*, 29: 30-31).

To Charles Delacroix

Paris 24ᵗʰ of March 1796 (4 germinal 4ᵗʰ year of F. R.) and
20ᵗʰ of the independence of the United States of America

Citizen Minister

I have been favored with yours of the 20 ventose (18 of March) respecting two negroes American Citizens who had left their ship at Havre become objects of charity and in consequence a charge upon some of the Inhabitants there and requesting information whether those charges would be reimbursed by the United States to enable you to give instruction upon that point and upon the principle generally to the municipality of that City.[1] In reply I have the pleasure to inform you that our sailors whilst they remain attached to their vessels at home or abroad are under the particular care of the masters of such vessels, and whose duty it is in case of sickness to provide them with such necessaries as their situation may require. But when they defect their vessel such claim ceases, nor have the parties who assist them afterwards any claim for reimbursement on that account, other than on the sailors themselves. If then the two Persons in question are not Deserters the parties who assisted them will obtain their reimbursement upon application to the Consignees of that vessel in that port. And in any event I shall instruct our consul there to attend to the case and to discharge on my behalf, any well founded claims rendered from motives of humanity to two of our Citizens who were left there in distress.[2] Accept my sincere regard.

Ja^s Monroe

RC, DLC: FCP—France

1. Delacroix's letter of 18 March 1796 has not been located.

2. No letter from JM to Claude-Adam Delamotte, the American consul at Havre, on this subject has been located.

To James Madison

Paris March 24. 1796.

Dear Sir

I have not rec^d a line from you since June last altho' I have written you vol^s.

In my last[1] I communicated to you that this gov^t had resolved to send an Envoy Extr^y to the U. States to complain of our treaty &ca with Engl^d & from w^h it had been diverted (if it is diverted as I presume it is) by my earnest representations agnst it, but that it was still dissatisfied & wo^d complain in strong terms agnst several of our measures thro the ordinary channel. The publication of M^r R^s [2] defense, the Presidents Speech, & the lately acquired possession of *a letter from the president to G. Morris* said to be of an *extraordinary kind considering the parties* gave a new stimulus to discontents that existed before. I have seen in this proceedure a prospect of the probable disunion of the two countries & labour'd with the utmost efforts of w^h I was capable to prevent it, & I think with some effect. I have in consequence been led into a discussion with the minister of foreign aff^{rs} of Mr Jay's treaty & of answering the objections of this gov^t to it: a task you will readily admit not of a pleasant kind, but unavoidable in the place I hold. I hope my correspondence in this case, will not be published as was done in regard to the Jacobin Clubs,[3] & every other part of it omitted. If it is done the highest injustice will be done me, & if the other parts are not called for by the H. of R. the omission will surprize me.

I write you this in great haste & therefore cannot go into many details I otherwise wo^d by the bearer who will deliver it in person. I have written the *president the* above *incident respecting himself so that he knows it* but I have added nothing to the communication.[4]

Dr Brokenborough will deliver this, a sensible young man & to whom I refer you for further intelligence.[5]

Remember me to our Senators, to Giles & other friends in the other house, Butler & Brown &ca in the senate to Beckley to whom I have written often lately.

You have clearly proved to the whole world that y^r virtue is impregnable agnst a bribe in western lands. Whatever the calumnious may circulate in other respects, yet here you have demonstration on y^r sides.[6]

RC, DLC: Madison Papers. Unsigned. Words in italics were written in code by JM and deciphered by Madison.

1. JM to Madison, 27 February 1796, above.

2. Edmund Randolph.

3. See Edmund Randolph to JM, 8 March 1795.

4. JM to George Washington, 24 March 1796, below.

5. John Brockenbrough (1773-1852) of Essex County, Virginia graduated from Edinburgh University in 1795. Although he received a degree in medicine, Brockenbrough never followed that profession. He settled in Richmond where he became a leading a figure in business and politics (*Dictionary of Virginia Biography*).

6. JM refers to the Randall-Whitney scandal. See Madison to JM, 26 January 1796, above.

To Thomas Pinckney

Paris March 24. 1796.

Dear Sir

Your favor by M[r] Phelps has been rec[d] the only one since you left this.[1]

I have put young Rutledge with M[r] McDermot after keeping him ten days with me to break the taste for idleness he had acquired in his travels. I have done every thing for him his father co[d] wish & shall follow y[r] advice in other respects.

This gov[t] has adopted no measures respecting our commerce with its Islands since the commenc'ment of this war: is it those of ant[r] date you wish to possess? Be so kind as describe particularly what you want in this respect & if to be had I will sent it. Tell this to M[r] Bayard also: as soon as I hear from you on this head you shall have an answer.

Your watch is done & under regulation with the maker: I will send it soon.

This will be presented by D[r] Brokenborough a young man of merit of our country whom I recommend to y[r] attention, & to whom I refer you for information of political occurrences.

We are well & desire to be affec[y] remembered to y[r] family. with sincere regard I am y[r] friend & serv[t]

Ja[s] Monroe

Upon some misunderstanding with the Directoire Pichegru has sent in his resignation w[h] is accepted, & w[h] is a great loss to the nation. Clairfait has done the same so that the acc[t] is perhaps balanc'd.[2]

RC, DLC: Charles Cotesworth Pinckney Family Papers

1. Pinckney to JM, 29 January 1796, above.

2. The Directory was dissatisfied with Pichegru's performance as commander of the Army of the Rhine and determined in December 1795 to replace him. Pichegru, anticipating the removal, asked to be relieved of duty. A final decision to remove Pichegru was made in early March 1796 and was announced after Pichegru arrived in Paris on March 21 (John Hall, *General Pichegru's Treason*, 106-107, 122-123). The Comte de Clerfayt was relieved of the command of the Austrian troops in Belgium in January 1796 (*Nouvelle Biographie Générale*).

To George Washington

Paris March 24. 1796.

Dear Sir

You will decypher this by the publick cypher in the hands of the Secr^y of State.

A letter from you to G^r Morris inclosed to Mr Deas has fallen by some accident into the hands of the Directoire. It contains five or six pages. Is said to be very confidential, authorizing communications with Lord Grenville, &c. The person who told me of it and who read it, says it has produced an ill effect. He adds, that you say you have kept no copy of the letter. I mention this that you may be aware of the fact, upon the idea it may be useful and cannot be hurtful.

My publick communications are so full that I have little to add here especially as Dr Brokenborough will present this a sensible young man who has been here thro' the winter. with great respect & esteem I am dear Sir very sincerely y^r very humble Servant

Ja^s Monroe

RC, ViMtvL. The words in italics were written in code by JM, and the deciphered text was written at the bottom of the letter.

To Timothy Pickering
Version 1

Paris March 25th 1796.

Sir

Finding from the communications of the Minister of foreign affairs that the character of the mission about to be dispatched to the United States and its objects were still before the Directoire, and fearing that the ulterior communication promised me by the minister would be made at such a time as to render it impossible for me to produce any effect on the measure itself (if, indeed in any case it were so) I deemed it my duty, and accordingly demanded an audience of the Directoire on that subject, stating the information already received from the minister thereon, as the basis or motive of that demand. An audience was granted and in consequence I attended the Directoire on the 8th instant, in full council assisted by the minister of foreign affairs, and the minister of marine. As I had demanded the audience it became necessary for me to open the subject and which I did by stating what the minister had informed me, of their dissatisfaction with our treaty with England, and some other measures that had occurred during the present war, and respecting which it was contemplated to make some representation to our government by their minister who was about to depart for the United States. I told them that unless I knew distinctly what their complaints were it was impossible for me to refute or even answer them: that I did not come there to ask from that body such exposition for the purpose of discussing the subject with it, because I knew it was against rule: that I wished however the Directoire would cause the minister of foreign affairs to lay open those complaints to me, receive my answer and enter into a full discussion of them, and in the interim that it would suspend any decision in regard to the merit of those complaints, or of the mission spoken of until the result of that discussion was before it: that the discussion itself could not otherwise than throw light on the subject, and in the degree promote the interest of both countries, so far as that might be affected by their decision in the case in question. The Directoire replied that nothing was more reasonable than my demand, and that it should be complied with. Some general observations were then made by that body upon the subject of its complaints, and to which I made the answers that occurred at the time, dissipating its doubts in one or two cases at once, and particularly with respect to the countenance it heard was given in the United States to their Emigrants, by stating that we received all Frenchmen who visited us as friends: that we did not, nor could we discriminate between them generally on account of their political principles, because we did not know what their principles were: that we saw in them <u>all</u> the People of a nation, to which we were much attached for services rendered us by it in the day of our own difficulties, and treated them accordingly; and with respect to the President that he had given orders that certain distinguished Emigrants, otherwise in some respects entitled to attention, but known to be obnoxious here, should on that account be excluded his public hall which was open to all other persons. Several of the members of the Directoire reciprocated with great earnestness, professions of friendship for us, assuring me at the same time that no step should be taken in the business in question, but upon due deliberation, and after the discussion I had asked should be finished and my arguments fully weighed, and thus I left them.

On the 9ᵗʰ instant I received from the minister of foreign affairs in consequence of the demand I had made as above of the Directoire, an exposition of the complaints of this government against us in a letter which I herewith send you a copy, and on the 15ᵗʰ instant I returned him an answer to that letter and of which I likewise enclose you a copy. As you will be possessed of both these papers it will be unnecessary to make other comment on them or on the subject generally, than to observe it is probable the discussion is not ended but may yet be continued to some length: on which head however I have no authority to speak other than from the zeal heretofore shewn on the subject, having heard nothing from the minister or any other Person in the administration on it since my letter was sent in. I will write you again in a few days and especially if any thing occurs in this respect to merit your attention; it being my wish to hasten the conclusion of this for the purpose of committing it to the care of Doctor Brockenbough a young man of merit, and who departs by the route of London for America, and which channel I prefer the more effectually to guard against the seizure and inspection of my letters by the British too often practised in vessels sailing directly from the ports of france.

Upon some misunderstanding with the Directoire Pichegru has sent in his resignation and which is accepted, and which must be deemed a great misfortune to the Republic, as he is doubtless a man of great talents and integrity. Clairfait has done the same thing with the Emperor, so that each army is deprived of a great chief.

The finances here continue in derangement which is not like[ly] to be remedied by a late act calling in the Assignats, and issuing in their stead a species of paper called mandats founded on the national domains, with the right in the holder of that paper to take property for it where he likes, and where he pleases, at the ancient value. This project resembles a bank whose stock consists of, and whose credit of course depends on Land, and which never succeeded well in the lands of Individuals; the prospect therefore is worse in the hands of the public. With great respect I am Sir your obedient servant

Jaˢ Monroe

LS, NjP.

To Timothy Pickering
Version 2

Paris March 25$\underline{^{th}}$ 179[6].[1]

Sir,

Finding from the communication of the Minister of foreign affairs that the character of the mission about to be dispatched to the United States and its objects were still before the Directoire, and fearing that the Ulterior communication promised me by the minister would be made at such a time as to render it impossible for me to produce any effect on the measure itself (if indeed in any case it were so) I deemed it my duty and accordingly demanded an audience of the Directoire on that subject, stating the information already received from the Minister thereon, as the basis or motive of that demand. An audience was granted and in consequence I attended the Directoire on the 8th instant in full council assisted by the minister of foreign affairs, and the minister of marine. As I had demanded the audience it became necessary for me to open the subject, and which I did by stating what the Minister had informed me of their dissatisfaction with our treaty with England, and some other measures that had occurred during the present war, and respecting which it was contemplated to make some representation to our government by their Minister who was about to depart for the United States. I told them that unless I knew distinctly what their complaints were it was impossible for me to refute or even answer them: that I did not come there to ask from that body such exposition for the purpose of discussing the subject with it, because I knew it was against rule: that I wished however the Directoire would cause the minister of foreign affairs to lay open those complaints to me, receive my answer and enter into a full discussion of them, and in the interim that it would suspend any decision in regard to the merit of those complaints, or of the mission spoken of, until the result of that discussion was before it; that the discussion itself could not otherwise than throw light on the subject, and in the degree promote the interest of both countries so far as that might be affected by their decision in the case in question. The Directoire replied that nothing was more reasonable than my demand, and that it should be complied with. Some general observations were then made by that body, upon the subject of its complaints; and to which I made the answers that occurred at the time, dissipating its doubts in one or two instances at once, and particularly with respect to the countenance it heard was given in the United States to their emigrants, by stating that we received all frenchmen who visited us as friends: that we did not, nor could we discriminate between them generally on account of their political principles, because we did not know what their principles were; that we saw in them all the people of a nation to which we were much attached for services rendered us by it in the day of our difficulties, and treated them accordingly: and with respect to the President that he had given orders that certain distinguished Emigrants, otherwise in some respect intitled to attention, but known to be obnoxious here, should on that account be excluded his public Hall, which was open to all other persons. Several of the members of the Directoire reciprocated with great earnestness professions of friendship for us, assuring me at the same time that no step should be taken in the business in question, but upon due deliberation, and after the discussion I had asked should be finished, and my arguments fully weighed, and thus I left them.

I shall transmit to you as soon as it is closed the result of any communication which may pass between the Minister and myself and I doubt not the discussion will produce a favorable effect. I shall certainly avail myself of all the lights within my reach to do justice to a cause of so much importance to my country.

Upon some misunderstanding with the Directoire Pichegru has sent in his resignation, and obtained his dismission, an event that must be deemed unfortunate to the republic, as he is doubtless a man of great talents and integrity. Clairfait has done the same thing with the Emperor, so that each army is deprived of a great chief.

The finances here continue in derangement, which is not likely to be remedied by a late act, calling in the assignats, and issuing in their stead a species of paper called mandats, founded on the national domains, with the right in the holder of that paper to take property for it where he likes and where he pleases at the ancient value. This project resembles a bank whose stock consists of and whose credit of course depends on land, and which as it never succeeded well in the hands of individuals, will most probably never succeed well in the hands of the public.

I herewith transmit you extracts of two letters lately received from Mr Barlow;[2] and which I do with a view of giving you every information that comes to my knowledge upon the interesting topic on which they treat. With great respect I am, sir, your most obedient humble servant.

Ja^s Monroe.

Copy, DNA: RG 59: Despatches from France

During his meeting with the Directory on March 8 JM requested that the French complaints against the United States be given to him in writing. Delacroix complied the following day, giving JM a bill of complaints (9 March 1796, above). JM responded on March 15 (above), and sometime after March 25 Delacroix asked permission to reclaim his paper so that he could revise it in light of JM's comments. JM returned Delacroix's paper and took back his own. JM, however, had already sent copies of the correspondence enclosed in version one of this letter (see JM to Pickering 2 May 1796, below). JM apparently was able to recover his letter to Pickering before it was delivered to the State Department. JM then wrote and sent version two (which was received by the State Department) retaining the date of the original letter. A draft of the first version, with the second paragraph struck out, is in PHi: Gratz Collection.

1. The clerk who copied this letter misdated in 1797.

2. Joel Barlow to JM, 23 and 26 February 1796, above.

To Joseph Jones

Paris March 26. 1796.

Dear Sir

I enclose you a letter from Joseph[1] who is well & in good hands. The school in which he is, is an excellent one, & I hope he will profit considerably in it, tho' the director sometimes complains of his indolence and ill temper to his comrades. I keep him altogether there (he has not been in Paris since chr[istma]s) often write to him[2] & sometimes visit the school & examine him so that every thing is done to keep him out of the way of harm, & to advance him that can be done. Six months more under this regimen will enable me to determine what may be expected from him, & of which I will correctly inform you. He had grown much, being almost as tall as I am & promises to be much taller.

Judge Rutledge of S^o Carolina has put one of his sons here under my care & for whose disbursements I have drawn on him for five hundred dol^{rs} in favor of Mr Yard of Phil^a, to be remitted you when rec^d or answer'd to your draft. He is with Joseph, rather younger, but a well behaved youth. I had to pay on acc^t of his expenses from Engl^d, his outfit at St Germains, in beding, cloaths, advance in the school &c near 40£ of this, so that by the time this money is rec^d by you, the greater part will be exhausted here: and I think I ought not to be in advance, as care & attention are all that ought to be expected of me. If the money is rec^d Mr Yard will advise you of it & of the step necessary to place it in y^r hands.

You have I presume before this rec^d from Col^o Pickering about the like sum which was advancd for him here, & two hundred & fifty crowns that were advanc'd Mr Paine. These were to be paid to Mr Madison for you, & I hope were paid him of w^h however he has doubtless apprized you as I asked him to take that trouble for me. In addition to this bill of Mr Rutledge I shall be forc'd to advance for Col^o Pickering a further sum of five or six hundred dol^rs, & in w^h case I will direct the payment thereof to you: you will after this I hope be quite at ease. I will thank you to give me some statment of my aff^rs and in particular how Hogg proceeds &c.

You are fully possess'd of my wishes in respect to my two brothers & sister & her family & therefore I say nothing more on that subject. You will however inform me how they are according to y^r acc^ts & what is done for them. It is now eight or nine months since I heard from you, w^h induces me to conclude all letters for me miscarry, for within that time I have scarcely rec^d a letter from any one. I most sincerely wish you wo^d come over & stay with us: and certainly the care of Joseph, living with us, wo^d make the trip not ineligible or unprofitable: leaving y^r aff^rs with mine in the hands of a prudent capable person.

There is little new here. The war continues with the Emperor, Engl^d &c, & without much prospect of an early termination with either especially the latter. with the former it is possible tho' not probable soon. We are well & all desire to be affec^y remembered to y^rself, Dr B.[3] & family, Col^o Taliaferro & family & other friends. very sincerely I am y^r fn^d & serv^t

Ja^s Monroe

Josephs letter I find was sent by some other channel a few days past.

RC, ViW: Monroe Papers

1. Joseph Jones, Jr.

2. No letters from JM to Joseph Jones, Jr. written in Paris have been located.

3. William or John Bankhead.

From Thomas Pinckney

London 26 March 1796

My dear Sir

I have no letter from you since I last wrote but I am unwilling to let so favorable an opportunity as is offered by Mr Franklin to pass without enquiring after the welfare of yourself & family—though I have no intelligence to impart, being apprized of none but what you will find in the public prints—The date of my last letters from our Government were of the 26th of January consequently the business depending upon such communication remains in the State it was when I last wrote to you. Mr Liston the Envoy Extraordinary from this Court to the United States lately left England on his way to America[1]—The Chevalier de Irujo late Secretary of legation here but now Minister Plenipotentiary to our Country will also depart soon[2]—We are told a successor is nominated to Mr Adet—pray who & what is he?

The Articles for Mrs Monroe have been long purchased & packed up in a trunk ready to be sent, but except the few Articles, of which Mr Gouverneur took charge we have not been able to find any person willing to convey them. A safe opportunity will however offer in a few days by a friend of ours who has a Vessel in this River that will sail shortly by which they shall be sent. The American Papers mention the appointment of Mr Cushing of Massachussets as Chief Justice & M^r McHenry of Maryland as Secretary of War.

I beg you to make my affectionate respects united with those of my little folks to Mrs Monroe & Eliza & believe me to be Sincerely Yours

Thomas Pinckney

Salut et fraternité to our friend Short if he be with you—does there appear to be any foundation in the report of his intended marriage?

March 28

I enclose copy of a circular letter rec^d just now from Col Humphries[3] from the letter accompanying it to me it appears that there is the most imminent danger of the failure of the negociation at Algiers. I doubt not you will use all your influence with the French government to procure their good offices to prevent so calamitous a Catastrophe.

NN: Monroe Papers

1. Robert Liston (1742-1836) began his diplomatic career in 1783, holding posts in Madrid, Stockholm, and Constantinople before being appointed British minister to the United States in February 1796, a position he held until December 1800. His subsequent appointments took him to the Hague, Copenhagen, and back to Constantinople (*DNB*).

2. Carlos Martinez de Irujo (1763-1824) served as first secretary at the Spanish legation in London 1794-1795. He was the Spanish minister to the United States 1796-1809. He married Sally McKean, daughter of Thomas McKean, in 1798 (Eric Beerman, "Spanish Envoy to the United States (1796-1809): Marques de Casa Irujo and His Philadelphia Wife Sally McKean," *The Americas*, 37 (1981), 445-456).

3. David Humphreys to JM, 9 March 1796, above.

To Philippe Merlin de Douai[1]

[Paris, March 29. 1796.][2]

I have rec^d the notification you were pleased to give me in y^r favor of the 7 Germinal (27th of March)[3] that an Englishman of the name of Sommers with his family were to leave that Island for this republick under the protection of American passports, & beg to assure that I shall be on my guard ag^nst any such persons. Indeed the strict rule I have long since adopted, in requiring the evidence of two Americans known to me for their probity in all doubtful cases, in support of the claims of those who apply for passports, secures me in general from improper applications. Every intimation however you receive of this kind I shall thank you to communicate to me, since it will tend to put me more effectually on my guard & thereby enable me more easily to detect impositions notwithstanding they be covered with the utmost art.

Permit me to suggest to you the source from w^h many frauds of this kind originate, & whereby passports originally granted to proper persons get into improper hands. Knowing it you [may][4] perhaps apply a suitable remedy. At Dover my passports are frequently taken from the bearers & who never regain them. This is either done by order of the Eng^h gov^t or by the collector of the customs there of his own authority. If by order of the gov^t it may be either as a document whereon the passport of that gov^t issues in favor of the holder, or it may be for the purpose of protecting its agents under the authority of the U. States in other countries. And if done by the collector of his own authority, his motive may be, to keep up an illicit correspondence perhaps for private, perhaps for publick purposes, of the same kind. Well assured I am that Americans of good reputations & with true passports who have crossed the channel in company with Englishmen, have at one of the ports of France at least, been detained there untill they had gone thro' all the tedious forms of a communication here for permission to come to Paris on their lawful business whilst those Eng^hmen were without restraint suffered to pass into the interior where they pleased.

This however is not the only source of like imposition. By a decree of the convention, my compatriots were compelled to deposit their passports obtained from me with the sections in w^h they resided, taking in lieu thereof, a card of surety from the section. To leave Paris however it was necessary to return those cards & retake their passports: but upon application for them to the sections in many instances they co^d not be found. They were gone they knew not where. They might it is true be lost by accident; but they might likewise have been bestowed with design. I mention these circumstances to you, upon the idea that in supervising the general police of the republick & providing remedies for existing evils, they are worthy y^r attention. If they enable you to deprive all Englishmen of Passports, other than those who obtain them directly from me, & w^h I sincerely wish to see I pledge myself that this branch of your administration will have attained its utmost height of perfection, for as you justly say, none of those people get protection from me. Accept my respectful regards.

Dft, NN: Monroe Papers

1. This letter is addressed to Merlin de Douai as minister of police. Merlin, who became inister of justice in November 1795, left that post in early January 1796 for three months to help organize the new department of police, of which he became the first minister. He served in that capacity until early April 1796 (Henry Morse Stephens, *Revolutionary Europe, 1789-1815*, 182; Martyn Lyons, *France Under the Directory*, 162-163, 174; François-Alphonse Aulard, *The French Revolution, A Political History, 1789-1804*, 3: 363).

2. The draft is undated. The dateline is from an incomplete file copy of this letter that is filed with this draft.

3. Merlin's letter of 27 March 1796 has not been located.

4. JM wrote "many".

INDEX

* indicates identification

Abema, Mr. – 585

Adams, John – 136, 157, 215, 264, 267, 333, 336, 376, 434, 461, 530, 602

Adams, John Quincy – 116-117, 418, 482-483, 522, 530, 584, 588; *letters to* – 284-285, 304-305, 355; *letters from* – 156-157, 241, 269-271, 273-274, 281-282, 305-307, 398-399, 496-497

Adams, Thomas B., *letters to* – 537, 555; *letters from* – 530*, 538-539, 555-556

Adet, Pierre – 228*-229, 234, 245-246, 253, 308, 320, 365, 372, 375, 390, 400-402, 408-409, 447, 465, 538, 540, 558, 579, 589-590, 593, 604, 635; *presentation of French flag to Congress* – 558, 579

Alcock, Captain – 608

Alcudia – *see Godoy*

Algiers – 135, 157, 618, 635; *treaty with U. S.* – 21, 95, 104, 145, 194, 467-469, 474-478, 503, 576-577, 596-601; *French assistance in treaty negotiations* – 10, 21-22, 143, 145, 155, 194-195, 227, 230, 308, 394-395, 397-398, 406, 411, 423-424, 432-433, 439, 476-477, 503; *British assistance in treaty negotiations* – 194; *American prisoners in* – 95; see also, *Hasan Pasha*

Allen, Mr. – 571

Allen, Shubael – 20

Alquier, Charles-Jean-Marie – 274*

Amar, Jean-Pierre – 296

American Revolution, JM on – 81, 86-87

Ames, Fisher – 183, 260, 262, 264, 280

Amory, Mr. – 157

Anderson, Alexander – 174*

Anderson, James – 22, 87, 89*; *letter from* – 100-101

Andrews, Robert – 261

Andrews, Mr. – 432

Armour, Captain – 274

Arnoux, Abbé – 312-313

Audibert, Achille – 35*

Aufroy, Marthe – 168-170*, 249

Auguis, Pierre-Jean-Baptiste – 356, 362*

Aulagnier, Alphonse – 45

Austria, truce with France – 557-558, 564, 578, 582-583

Babeuf, François-Noël – 116

Bache, Benjamin F. – 401, 408, 495, 551, 580, 602

Bache, William – 339*, 394

Bacri, Micaiah Cohen – 474*

Balbatre, Claude-Louis – 312, 314*

Bancal des Issarts, Jean-Henri – 69

Bankhead, John – 635

Bankhead, William – 635

Barbé-Marbois, Elizabeth – 46-47*, 468

Barbé-Marbois, François – 42, 47; *letter from* – 468-469

Barère, Bertrand – 58-59*, 75-76, 112, 129, 162, 205, 254, 284-285, 292-293, 356-357, 368, 442, 599-600

Barlow, Joel – 95, 393, 395*, 474, 477-479, 499, 503, 576-577, 596-601, 634

Barlow, Ruth – 598-599*

Barney, Joshua – 17*-18, 63, 261

Barnwell, Robert – 180, 182*, 280-281

Baron, Captain – 120

Barras, Jean-Nicholas-Paul-François – 284-285, 485, 506-507*, 511, 520, 607

Barraud, Philip – 261, 263*

Barré, Jean-Baptiste-Henri – 238*-239, 373, 426, 428

Bartram, William – 608*

Bassett, Burwell – 261, 280

Bayard, Martha – 483

Bayard, Samuel – 630; *letter to* – 457-458; *letters from* – 421-422*, 481-483, 542-543

Beauchet, Marie-Josèphe-Daustry – 169-170*, 248

Beauchet, Nicholas – 169-170*, 248

Beckley, John – 164, 232, 268, 375-376, 441, 503, 538-539, 553, 565, 589, 629; *letters from* – 318-320, 464-466; *letter to* – 368-372 – *publication of* – 375-376, 550

Belgic Confederacy – 219-220

Belgium, war in – 5-6, 28-30, 54; *annexed by France* – 478

Bell, Thomas – 13, 275, 389, 391, 433, 455, 571

Bellanger, Marie-Françoise Plumard – 13, 381-382, 433-435*

Bellgarde, battle – 91-92, 114

Bendin, Madame – 249

Bénézech, Pierre – 511-512*

Benjamin, Mademoiselle – 169-170*, 248

Beresford, Mr. – 34, 38, 107, 139

Bergman, Torbern Olof – 297-298*

Bermuda – 538

Bernard, André-Antoine – 63-64*

Bernstorff, Andreas Peter – 175, 178*, 385

Berruyer, Jean-François – 485, 492*

Beurnonville, Pierre Riel – 564-566*, 578

Bézout, Etienne – 297-298*

Biard, Captain – 122

Billaud de Varennes, Jacques-Nicholas – 59, 75-76*, 112, 162, 205, 284-285, 292-293, 356-357, 368

Billom, La Société Populaire de, letter from – 36; *letter to* – 47

Binard, Mr. – 21-22

Bingham, William – 184, 264, 280, 431, 602

Bingham family – 57, 213

Bird, Henry M. – 212-213, 432

Blair, John – 580, 601

Bliss, Thomas – 453

Bloodworth, Timothy – 184*, 264, 280

Blount, William – 99

Bois-le-Duc, battle – 114, 116

Boissy D'Anglas, François-Antoine – 116, 219, 293-294, 296*, 356-357, 361, 498

Boland, Mr. – 87

Bollmann, Justus-Erich – 584-586*

Bond, Phineas – 482-483, 502, 580

Borda, Jean-Charles – 297-298*

Bordeaux, France, embargo at – 9, 11, 21, 40, 49, 51, 61, 73, 80, 87, 89, 122, 136, 174, 250

Bossut, Charles – 297-298*

Bourdon de l'Oise, François-Louis – 126, 127*, 128, 129

Bourne, Sylvanus – 306-307*

Bournonville, Mr. – 409

Bowdoin, James – 183, 185*

Boylston, Ward N. – 156-157*

Boys, William – 339, 394

Bradford, William – 88-89*, 239, 421-422, 434-435, 464, 482, 542, 554

Bradley, Stephen – 183, 264

Bréard, Jean-Jacques, letter from – 197, 198*, 199

Breckinridge, John – 275; *letter from* – 566-568

Brent, Richard – 183, 185*, 265, 276, 280, 319

Brentnall, Captain – 288

Bridport, Lord – 391

Brissot de Warville, Jacques-Pierre – 25, 113-114

Brockenbrough, John – 629, 630*-632

Brocklesby, Richard – 215-216*

Brooke, Laurence – 367, 457

Brooke, Robert – 180, 186, 260, 266; *letter from* – 223; *letter to* – 421

Brooks, Captain – 120

Brown, John – 180, 246, 384, 565, 629; *letter from* – 182-185, 239-240

Bryan, Captain – 119-120

Buchot, Philibert – 40; *letter to* – 37*, 64, 84; *letter from* – 56-57, 64-65

Buckner, Elizabeth Monroe – 15, 55-56, 217, 366-367, 456, 635

Buckner, William – 55-56*, 571
Buffington, John – 119, 299
Burnley & Co. – 455
Burr, Aaron – 1-3, 164, 181-182, 188, 246, 274, 320, 365, 384, 390, 417; *JM critical of* – 415; *letters to* – 372, 565-566, 575; *letters from* – 3-4, 5, 397, 413, 446-447, 550-551, 619
Burr, Theodosia Prevost – 4
Butler, Pierce – 164, 183, 188, 384, 441, 503, 537-538, 565, 629; *letter from* – 207-209
Cabell, Samuel J. – 319
Cambercéres, Jean-Jacques – 144, 296; *letters from* – 191-192*, 196-199, 586-587
Cambon, Pierre – 62-63*
Camillus – see Hamilton
Campan, Jeanne-Louise-Henriette – 363, 453; *letter from* – 199-200, 473
Campbell, Alexander – 261-262, 602
Cape Town, captured by British – 583
Carletti, Francesco Saverio – 217*, 220, 535-536, 549, 564-565, 578, 582
Carmichael, William – 43-44, 245
Carnes, Burrell – 21-22*
Carnot, Lazare-Nicholas – 144, 506-507, 511, 520, 599-600, 607, 610; *letter from* – 191*-192
Carpentier, Mr. – 64, 115
Carr, Eleanor – 314
Carr, John Overton – 313-314
Carr, Peter – 382
Carr, Samuel – 313-314
Carriage tax, opposition to – 260-261, 602-603
Carrichon, Père – 93*
Carrier, Jean-Baptiste – 116, 156*, 162, 205, 217, 394
Carrington, Edward – 434
Carrington, Paul – 260
Carter, Burnley C. – 275
Carter, Champe – 455
Carter, Charles – 56, 181
Carter, Edward – 16, 312
Carter, Edward, Jr. – 608*
Carter, John – 455

Carter, Mr. – 571
Carter, Mrs. – 571
Cassini, Jean-Dominique – 297-298*
Cassini de Thury, César-François – 298*
Castries, Charles-Eugène, Marquis – 324, 337*, 351
Cathalan, Stephen – 115, 143, 474-476, 478, 598; *letters from* – 94-95, 467-468
Cathcart, James L. – 600-601*
Catlet, Kemp – 312, 314*
Cato – see Livingston
Cavendish, Henry – 214, 216*
Cazeau, François – 412-413
Chambonas, Scipion-Victor-Auguste LaGarde, Marquis de – 325, 337*
Charette, François-Athanase – 273*
Charleroi, battle – 28-30, 58
Chase, Samuel – 601-603*, 607, 628
Chavaniac, Louise-Charlotte de Lafayette – 168-170*, 249, 268
Choudieu, Mr. – 296
Church, Edward – 235, 237*, 289, 303, 474
Cibon, Mr., letter from – 135*-136; *letters to* – 157-158, 475
Citizenship bill – 265, 267
Clairfayt – see Clerfayt
Clark, George Rogers – 567
Clason, Mr. – 365
Clavière, Etienne – 324, 337*
Clerfayt, François-Sebastien-Charles-Joseph, Count – 419, 557, 582, 630, 632, 634
Clinton, George – 147, 266, 268, 274, 365, 408, 416-417, 446, 464, 578; *letters to* – 18, 372; *letter from* – 60
Clopton, John – 185*, 276, 280, 319
Cobb, David – 263*
Coblentz, battle – 144-145
Coburg – see Saxe-Coburg
Cochon de Lapparent, Charles – 274*, 306
Coffyn, Francis – 21-22*, 115, 161, 314, 361
Coffyn, Francis, Jr. – 143, 361, 556; *letter to* – 314
Colchen, Jean-Victor – 364, 395; *letters to* – 286-287, 339, 380-381, 390-391, 406, 432-433, 480; *letter from* – 285-286*

Coleman, Mr. – 571

Coles, Isaac – 276*

Colliore, battle – 91-92

Collot D'Herbois, Jean-Marie – 58-59*, 75-76, 112, 205, 284-285, 292, 356-357, 368

Commerce between United States and France – 94-95, 122-123, 136, 142, 203-204, 229, 257, 308, 323-325, 371, 467; *French regulation of trade* – 49-51, 59, 61-62, 74, 158-160, 174, 196, 198-199, 429-430; *French purchases in the U. S.* – 101, 118, 124-125, 276-277; *state monopoly of trade* – 109-110, 115, 117-118, 120, 141, 250-251; *West Indies trade* – 319, 542, 630

Committee of General Security – 25, 339; *letter to* – 138-139

Committee of Public Safety – 3, 25, 99, 136-137, 141-145, 149, 151, 154, 156, 159, 163, 174-176, 189, 195, 202; *JM, "Notes on Constitution"* – 340-342; *letters to* – 49, 122-126, 145-146, 148-149, 171-172, 192-193, 195-196, 200-201, 209-211, 237, 251-252, 397-400, 402-403, 406; *letters from* – 127-128, 191-192, 196-199, 221, 404-405

Conde, battle – 75

Continental army pensions – 561-562

Cooper, John – 330, 338*

Cormontaingne, Louis – 298*

Corsange & Co. – 587

Corsica, war in – 5-6

Corsini, Neri, Count – 565-566

Couthon, Georges-Auguste – 24, 26, 29*, 48, 58, 255

Cowell, Captain – 315, 394

Coxe, Mr. – 431

Coxe, Tench – 318, 421

Crauford, James – 513*

Crèvecoeur, Guillaume-Alexandre St. John – 393, 395*

Crèvecoeur, M. G. Hector St. John – 395; *letter from* – 66; *letter to* – 86-87

Cruger, Nicholas – 87, 89*

Cummings, William – 318, 320*

Curson, Richard – 521

Cushing, William – 601, 603*, 619, 635

Cutting, Nathaniel – 581

Dalbarade, Jean – 61-62*, 102, 391, 394

D'Allarde, Pierre-Gilbert-Leroy, Baron – 374-375*, 445, 496, 522, 566

Dallas, Alexander J. – 464

Dannery, Jean-Baptiste-Thomas – 279-280*

Danton, Georges, Jacques – 5*, 25-27, 29, 113-114, 255

D'Araujo, Antonio – 200

D'Artois, Charles-Philippe, Comte – 492-493*, 498, 519

Davies, Mr. – 570

Davis, Samuel B. – 540

Davis, Thomas – 523

Dawson, John – 164, 180, 260, 264, 367, 415, 434, 457, 572

D'Ayen, Henriette Daguesseau, Duchesse – 79, 93

D'Ayen, Jean-Paul-François, Comte – 97

Dayton, Jonathan – 1*, 264

Dearborn, Henry – 183

Deas, William Allen – 83, 377-378*, 473, 483, 611, 631; *letter to* – 470-471; *letter from* – 508-509

DeBry, Jean-Antoine – 474*-476

DeButts, Captain – 18

Decator, Captain – 120

Delacroix, Charles – 511, 590, 594, 599-600, 607, 610-611, 631, 633-634; *letters to* – 514, 523-524, 536, 544, 586-569, 591-592, 605-606, 609, 621-626, 628-629; *letters from* – 509*, 514-515, 524-525, 531-532, 539-540, 550, 593-594, 612-618

Delamotte, Claude-Adam – 64*, 115, 143, 312, 433, 517, 581; *letters from* – 315, 493-494

De La Union, Count – 91-92

Del Campo, Bernardo – 620*

Delmas, Jean-François-Bertrand – 356, 362*; *letters from* – 127-128, 404-405

Democratic-Republican Societies – 88, 181-182, 260, 262; *Washington attack on* – 180-182, 266-268, 275, 311; *Randolph attack on* – 266-267; *JM comment on* – 230, 367

Denmark, alliance with Sweden – 115, 152, 175, 177-178, 258, 371, 378, 381, 383, 386, 388, 495; *ship seized by French* – 288

D'Enville, Madame – 43-44

DeRichery, Joseph – 493

DeRieux, Maria Margherita – 13*

DeRieux, Pierre – 381-382, 391, 433-434, 608; *letter from* – 12-13*

Desmanges, Mr. – 248

Dexter, Samuel – 264, 267*, 280, 319

Diplomatic corps – 535, 549, 564-565

Dismal Swamp Canal – 608

Divers, George – 16, 311, 316

Dobrée, Pierre – 21-22*, 115, 143, 161

Donaldson, Joseph, Jr. – 432-433*, 467-469, 474-477, 479, 503, 577, 597, 600-601

Dorchester, Guy Carlton, Lord – 499

Dorsai, Mr. – 312

Dubart, Louis-François – 201, 236, 244, 286-288

DuBuat, Pierre-Louis-Georges – 297-298*

Duhem, Mr. – 296

Dumont, André – 191-192*

Dumouriez, Charles François – 26, 30*, 324, 560, 562, 564-565

Duplain, Benoit-Joseph – 297-298*

D'Urtubie, Théodore-Bernard-Simon – 298*

Duvernet, Alexander – 10*-11, 40, 42, 110, 172

Eden, Frederick Morton – 305*, 309-310, 316, 367, 370, 379, 442, 496

Edwards, Enoch – 299-300*, 383, 494; *letter from* – 473-474

Edwards, Frances – 473-474*

Edwards, John – 264, 267*

Eldred, Thomas – 392, 544, 550, 605-606

Ellsworth, Oliver – 320, 619, 628

Eschasseriaux, Joseph – 144

Europe, peace overtures – 59, 115, 152, 155, 176-177, 220, 240, 411-412; *war in* – 620

Eustace, John S. – 560-562

Everett, Mr. – 571

Faipoult, Guillaume-Charles – 511-512*; *letters to* – 540-541, 586; *letters from* – 547, 576, 587

Fauchet, Jean-Antoine, Joseph – 7-11, 20-22, 79-80, 87, 89, 118, 147, 164, 173-174, 186, 230, 250, 317-319, 330-331, 366, 383-384, 397, 400, 553; *recall* – 153, 229, 253, 320; *and Jay Treaty* – 229, 258, 334, 336, 506; *and Randolph's resignation* – 378, 435, 447, 464-466, 537-538, 545; *criticized by Randolph* – 408-409; *British attempt to capture* – 426-427, 453, 534, 610, 613, 617, 621, 624-625

Faure-Conac, Gilbert-Amable – 100-101*

Fenner, Arthur – 454-455*

Fenwick, Joseph – 40, 42*, 94, 111, 115, 143, 218, 224, 364, 505, 521; *accusation against* – 318, 320, 409-410, 500-501, 534-535; *letters from* – 61-63, 202, 305, 351-352, 414, 416-417, 422-423, 430-431, 500-501

Féraud, Jean-Bertrand – 356, 361*-362, 368

Fernald, Captain – 100

Feuty, P., letter from – 187

Filicchy, Mary Cowper – 134

Filicchy, Philip – 201, 244, 290; *letter from* – 134*

Fioravanti, Leonardo – 505*

Fitzherbert, Alleyne (Lord St. Helens) – 460, 465*

Fitzhugh, Philip – 457

Fitzsimons, Thomas – 180, 182-183, 258

Fleming, Captain – 120

Forbes, Mr. – 207

Forbes, Ralph Bennet – 480*

Forbes, Robert Bennet – 480*

Forbes, Sir William – 366-367*, 389, 455

Forrest, Uriah – 224*

Fourcroy, Antoine-François, letter from – 191-192*

Fowler, John – 164-165*, 240, 352, 456, 572

France and Netherlands – see Netherlands

France, assistance in U. S. treaty negotiations – see Algiers, Great Britain, Spain, Tripoli, Tunis

France, Executive Directory – 506-507, 532, 535, 564, 576, 582, 590, 593-595, 599, 607, 609-611, 631, 633

France, complaints against U. S. – 147, 174, 279-280, 317-318, 405-406, 610-620, 629, 631-632; *objection to Jay Treaty* – 590, 593-595, 604, 610-611, 614, 617-620; *JM response* – 591-592, 594-595, 609-611, 619-626, 629, 631-633

France, constitution – 68, 295, 320; *constitution of 1793* – 356-359, 369-370, 372, 442; *constitution of 1795* – 349-350, 354, 359-360, 367, 370, 380-381, 383, 385, 412, 414, 420, 424, 435, 439, 442-443, 456, 458, 484-485, 506, 517-518, 554

France, Convention – 25-26, 34-35, 41, 58, 68, 112-113, 161-162; *display of flags* – 63, 257, 259; *attacks on* – 284-285, 292-295, 320, 355-357, 361, 368, 483-492, 496, 498, 518-520; *JM, "Notes on Constitution"* – 342-349

France, Convention, JM's address to – 30-31; *comments on* – 147, 172-173, 179, 182, 189, 199; *JM defends* – 224-227, 231, 239, 243, 245-246

France, finances – 254, 310, 563, 565, 578, 582, 604, 619, 632, 635

France, food shortages – 223, 228, 243, 246, 253-254, 269, 293-295, 304, 309, 356, 361

France, new government organized, 1795 – 502, 505-507, 511, 518, 535, 563, 578

France, peace with Portugal – 320

France, peace with Prussia – 206-207, 240, 243, 246, 253, 296, 309, 320, 367, 370

France, peace with Spain – see Spain

France, peace with Tuscany – 228, 240, 253

France, proposed loan from U. S. – 148-149, 154-155, 163-164, 177, 203, 227

France, revolutionary calendar – 33-34, 56, 79, 93

France, royalist party – 357-359, 412-413, 443, 487-490, 492, 519, 563-564

France, ships, seized by British – 616, 621; *Jean Bart* – 377

France, ships, seized by U. S. – 9, 80; *La Camille* – 9, 330; *Favorite* – 174, 330; *Cassius* – 539-540, 549, 614, 617, 621, 624

France, treaties with U. S. – *amity and commerce, 1778* – 11, 49, 52, 73-74, 122-125, 130, 132, 136, 141-142, 173, 175, 202-203, 206, 217, 227, 229, 241, 243, 323-324, 371; *military alliance, 1778* – 9, 11, 130, 132; *consular treaty* – 523-524, 581, 616-617, 621-623; *proposed* – 9, 323-328, 331

France, truce with Austria – 557-558, 564, 578, 582-583

France, war effort – 23, 28, 75-76, 151, 370, 548, 578, 604

Franklin, Benjamin – 66, 96-97, 215, 312-313, 339, 459-460

Franklin, William T. – 473, 635

Frederick Wilhelm II, king of Prussia – 5-6, 11

Fréron, Stanislaus-Louis – 356, 362*

Frestel, Felix – 46, 248-249

Frézier, Amedée-François – 297-298*

Froullés, Jean-François – 312-313*, 433

Fulton, Samuel – 566-568*

Galiano, Antonio Alcala – 102

Gallatin, Albert – 183, 185, 260

Gamble, Robert – 433-434

Gardoqui, Diego – 145-146, 149, 163, 175-176, 153-156, 235-236, 258, 435; *negotiations with Jay, 1785* – 146, 189-190, 317, 499; *letters from* – 63, 102; *letter to* – 147

Gautier, Jean-Antoine – 434-435*, 628

Gauvain, M. A. – 99*-101, 283-284, 292, 311

Gelston, David – 60*, 413, 416, 550, 577; *letter from* – 274, 365, 417-418

Gelston, John M. – 60*, 274, 311, 365, 399, 413, 417, 550, 577

Gelston, Maltby – 60*, 311, 413, 416-417, 577-578

Gem, Richard – 312-313*

Genet, Edmond – 3, 7-8, 322, 325-331, 336-337, 408, 460, 568

Geneva, Republic of – 59-60, 77

George III – 520, 564-565

Gérard, Conrad-Alexandre – 42

German States, peace with France – 418-419, 440-442

Germanicus – see Randolph

Gerrish, Captain – 120

Gerry, Ann Thompson – 505

Gerry, Elbridge – 505

Gibson, Mr. – 401

Giles, William Branch – 265, 267, 276, 312, 441, 629

Gill, Moses – 157*

Gillon, Alexander – 180, 182*, 207, 280

Gilmer, George – 313-314*, 391, 571

Gilmer, Mildred – see Wirt

Girard, Stephen – 350*, 548-549

Glad, Captain – 120

Glassell, Mr. (merchant) – 15, 571

Godoy, Manuel, Duke of Alcudia – 300-302*, 360, 428, 431, 435-436

Golofkin, Wilhelmina Mosheim – 96-97*

Goltz, Bernhard Wilhelm, Baron – 217*, 220, 243, 246

Goodrich, Jared – 84, 121; *letter from* – 86

Gouverneur, Nicholas – 588*, 635

Gracie, Archibald – 174*

Graham, William – 140*

Grammont, Rosalie – 268

Grand, Rodolphe-Ferdinand – 313-314, 434

Grant, Hary – 208

Great Britain, French aid in U. S. treaty negotiations – 148, 155, 163, 203, 227-228, 242-243, 439, 441-442

Great Britain, JM proposals for action against – 163-177, 177-178, 380, 385, 439, 441-442

Great Britain, negotiations with France – 296, 305, 309-310, 316. 360, 367, 370, 379, 420, 442, 564-565, 574, 578

Great Britain, ships, seized by French – 193; *with false American papers* – 305, 463

Great Britain, subjects detained by French – 82-83, 140-141

Great Britain, treaty with Russia – 394-395

Great Britain, treaty with U. S., 1783 – 215, 459-462, 504, 514

Great Britain, treaty with U. S., 1794 (Jay Treaty) – 1, 7, 10-11, 80, 89, 92, 158, 160, 176, 179, 183, 188-193, 202, 207, 218, 222, 227, 229, 238, 239, 246, 252-253, 256, 258, 261, 265, 268-269, 282, 287, 307, 360, 390, 408, 483, 583; *JM on* – 59, 163, 188-190, 226, 271-272, 290-292, 372-373, 423, 436-439, 456-458, 495, 498, 502-503, 511, 565; *comments on* – 17, 179, 232-234, 418, 422, 482, 545; *French reaction to* – 189, 207, 217, 240-241, 243, 310, 316-317, 353-354, 371, 381, 383-384, 409, 420, 424, 458, 465, 491-492, 506, 534, 558, 563; *ratified by Senate* – 258, 318-320, 352, 365, 375, 378, 382-384, 400, 402-403, 414, 452, 544; *signed by Washington* – 384, 390, 397, 400-404, 416, 422, 426, 428, 431, 434, 438-439, 446-447, 464, 497-498, 511, 534, 537-538, 545, 553; *House of Representatives on* – 502, 537, 543, 545-546, 565, 579, 601, 607, 619, 628; *defense of* – 258, 404, 404, 434; *defended by Randolph* – 332-336, 409; *defended by Hamilton* – 400-401, 404, 453, 537, 607; *defended by Pickering* – 447-452, 522, 558; *support of* – 537-538, 543, 545-546; *opposition to* – 384, 397, 400, 403-404, 416-417, 422-423, 426-428, 431, 434-435, 452-453, 464, 537-538, 543, 545, 553-555, 559-560, 607

Great Britain, U. S. claims against – 482, 542

Great Britain, U. S. complaints against – 331-332

Greene, George Washington – 352-353*

Greene, Nathanael – 352-353

Greenleaf, Thomas – 413*

Gregorie, John – 584-585*

Grelet, Mr. – 78-79

Grenville, William Wyndham, Lord – 332, 417-418*, 464

Grice, Captain – 120

Griffin, Cyrus – 259

Griffin, Samuel – 180, 182-183, 185, 261, 264, 276, 280, 319

Griffiths, Thomas W. – 104-105*

Grubb, James – 320

Gunn, James – 183, 208-209*, 264-265, 280

Guyton-Morveau, Louis-Bernard, letter from
 – 191-192*

Habersham, Joseph – 263, 265

Hamilton, Alexander – 35, 320, 452-453,
 498, 539, 589, 602; *resignation from treasury*
 – 181-182, 184-186, 223, 231, 238-239,
 246, 265; *and Whiskey Rebellion* – 88, 259,
 261, 311; *defends Jay Treaty* – 400-401,
 404, 453, 537, 607; *Camillus* – 401, 426,
 434, 537, 607

Hammond, George – 80, 136, 193, 215, 317,
 320, 336, 402, 408, 435, 446, 451, 464,
 538, 611

Hampton, Wade – 280-281*

Harding, William W. – 276*

Harper, Robert Goodloe – 182*

Harrison, Edmund – 264, 267*

Harvie, John, Jr. – 434

Hasan Pasha, Dey of Algiers – 433, 467-469,
 577, 597-598, 600

Haskins, Mr. – 104

Hathorn, John – 238-239*

Hawkins, Benjamin – 183-184, 264, 280, 384

Head, Mr. – 157

Hemings, Thenia – 16, 217-218, 389, 571-
 572

Hennequin, Mr. – 248

Henriot, François – 28, 32*, 255

Henry, Patrick – 264, 553, 607

Hérault Séschelles, Marie-Jean – 35*

Herculais, Louis-Alexandre d'Allois – 474*-
 475, 577

Hernley – see Harding

Heyliger, Sarah Kortright – 181

Hichborn, Benjamin – 223-224*, 236, 292,
 432-433, 439, 499; *letter from* – 282

Hoche, Louis-Lazare – 206

Hodgson, Captain – 122

Hogg, Mr. – 54, 275, 517, 570-572

Hohenloe, Prince – 548-549

Home, Rodham — 453

Hooper, Captain – 121-122

Horry, Daniel – 82-83*

Houdon, Jean-Antoine – 223

Howe, Lord Richard – 23

Hudibras (Samuel Butler) – 452-453

Hull, William – 526*

Humphreys, David, minister to Portugal –
 21-22; *negotiations with Algiers* – 21-22,
 104, 143, 145, 155, 194-195, 218, 230,
 258, 299, 308, 394, 398, 406, 411, 426,
 433, 439, 469, 476-477, 503, 597-598,
 601, 618, 636; *letters to* – 145, 474-475;
 letters from – 478-479, 576-577

Hunter, Archibald – 20

Hylton, Daniel – 603

Hylton v. U. S. – 603

Indian war – 165, 183, 559; *British assistance to*
 Indians – 80, 148, 154; *Spanish assistance to*
 Indians – 148-149, 154; *Fallen Timbers,*
 battle – 89, 183

Indian treaties – 183-184, 454-455, 558-559

Ingersoll, Jared, Jr. – 602-603*

Innes, James – 184-185, 260, 262, 434

Iredell, James – 602

Iruyo, Carlos Martinez de – 635-636*

Irvine, William – 88-89*

Italy, war in – 134, 535, 557, 564

Izard, Alice – 432

Izard, George – 211-213*, 378, 431-432, 468,
 500

Izard, Ralph – 183, 185, 208*-209, 264, 280,
 378; *letter from* – 213; *letter to* – 431-432

Jackson, James – 208-209*, 289, 384

Jackson, Jonathan – 265, 267

Jacobin clubs – 113-114, 144-145, 152-153,
 155-156, 162, 194, 230-231, 620; *publica-*
 tion of JM's comments on – 258-259, 266,
 268, 275-276, 367, 373

James River Canal – 608

Jannot, Mr. – 537

Jarvis, Benjamin – 548

Jaudenes, José de – 237, 428

Jay, John, mission to Great Britain – 1, 63,
 117, 163, 176, 188-192, 194-195, 199,
 202-203, 215-216, 218, 232, 271-272,
 290-292, 299, 353-354, 372-373, 497-498,
 511, 575, 603; *arrival in U. S.* – 318-320;

governor of New York – 266, 280, 320, 352, 365, 400, 416, 554, 601; *candidate for president* – 602; *peace commissioner, 1783* – 459-460; *negotiations with Spain, 1785* – 146, 189-190, 317, 499; *letters to* – 207; *letters from* – 37-38, 136, 158, 160, 222, 237-238

Jay Treaty – see Great Britain

Jefferson, Mary – 16, 59, 382

Jefferson, Thomas – 13, 35, 43, 52, 54, 66, 90-91, 161, 185, 217, 231, 246, 354, 367, 376, 385, 389, 405, 416, 426, 444, 455, 464, 466, 494, 546; *minister to France* – 44, 223, 421, 448; *in Paris* – 42, 53, 56, 150; *secretary of state* – 22, 136, 215, 323, 327, 330, 332-333, 336, 451, 501; *candidate for president* – 320, 400, 602; *illness*, 181, 261; *and JM's farm* – 55, 181, 574; *letters to*, 1-2, 5, 16, 58-60, 372, 381-382, 391, 516-521; *letters from* – 311-314, 433-435, 607-608, 628

Jervis, John – 80-81*

Johnson, Joseph – 559-560*

Johnson, Joshua – 273

Johnson, Mr. – 571

Jones, John Paul – 129

Jones, Joseph – 2, 18, 161, 181, 231, 269, 354, 405, 546, 580, 602; *and JM's financial affairs* – 14-15, 164, 246, 517; *and JM's farm* – 16, 59, 312-313, 433, 574, 608, 628; *letters to* – 52-56, 216-218, 366-367, 389, 414-415, 455-457, 634; *letters from* – 275-276, 352-353, 570-573

Jones, Joseph, Jr. – 17-18, 47, 53-55, 217, 232, 276, 311, 352, 367, 389, 414-415, 456, 570-572, 634-635

Jones, Meriwether – 183, 185*, 261

Jones, Mr. – 570-571

Jouett, Robert – 391*, 570

Jourdan, Jean-Baptiste – 28-30*, 58, 443-444, 456, 491, 493, 548-549, 557-558, 582

Juliers (Julich), battle – 114-116

July 4 celebration – 395-396

Justice, Captain – 122

Juttau, John – 330, 338*

Kelly, John – 571, 573*

Kensman, Captain – 122

Kentucky, settlement – 567; *discontent in* – 184-185, 262, 568

Kerr, James – 570, 572

Kerr, Walker – 98-99, 121, 275

Kervélégan, Augustin-Bernard-François – 356, 361*

Ketland, John – 575-576*

Ketland, Thomas – 575-576*

Key, Philip – 224*

Killoe, Captain – 83

King, Mr. – 258

King, Rufus – 183-184, 264 401, 404, 499, 538

Knox, Henry – 181-182, 184, 186, 231, 238, 246, 261, 265

Knox, Thomas – 550-551, 572

Kortright, John – 238, 550-551, 572

Kortright, Lawrence – 56, 134, 551, 572

Kościuszko, Tadeusz – 23, 59-60

LaBonardière, Jean-Philippe-Gaspard – 97-98*, 107, 128

Lafayette, Adrienne – 11, 258, 402; *imprisonment* – 44-46, 78-79, 93, 96, 126-127, 143-144; *release from prison* – 167, 170, 228; *family* – 46, 93, 249; *settlement of accounts* – 167-170, 247-249, 268; *financial assistance to* – 228, 268, 318, 339-340, 350, 516, 556-558, 585, 627; *in Austria* – 516, 533, 585, 595-596, 627; *letters to* – 267-268, 516; *letters from* – 44-46, 78-79, 92-93, 126-127, 165-170, 247-249

Lafayette, Anastasie – 46*

Lafayette, George Washington – 46*, 168, 249, 558, 584

Lafayette, Marquis – 67, 126-127, 170, 228, 249, 268, 556-558; *imprisonment* – 8, 11, 26, 45-46, 516, 584-585, 595-596, 627

Lafayette, Roch-Gilbert du Motier – 268

Lafayette, Virginie – 46*

LaForest, Antoine-René-Charles – 40, 42*, 408

Lalay, Pierre-Antoine – 144

Lameth, Alexandre – 596*

Lamotte – see Delamotte

Land speculation – 184, 208, 261-262, 265, 267, 580, 629

Lane, George — 100

Langdon, Eliza – 20*

Langdon, Elizabeth Sherbourne – 20*

Langdon, John – 180, 183, 187, 246, 264, 320, 384, 422; *letters from* – 20, 185, 375; *letters to* – 565-566, 575

Lansdowne, William Petty Fitzmaurice (Lord Shelbourne), Marquess – 459-462*, 504, 514

Latimer, Henry – 180, 182*, 184, 264

Latour-Foissac, Philippe-François – 297-298*

Laurence, John – 239

Laurens, Frances – 214, 216*

Laurens, Henry – 216, 459, 462-463

Laurens, John – 216

Laurens, Martha Manning – 216

Lavaux, Etienne-Maynaud-Bize-Franc – 617-618

Law, Captain – 299

Leach, Mr. – 412

Learned, Amasa – 183, 185*

Leavenworth, Mark – 526

Leavenworth, Sara – 526

LeBlanc, Georges-Pierre – 18, 23, 40, 48, 79-80, 89, 537

LeBlond, Guillaume – 297*

Lecointre, Laurent – 75-76*, 205-206

LeCompte, Mr. – 464, 466*

Lee, Charles (attorney) – 260-262, 537, 546, 554, 580, 601-602, 607

Lee, Charles (general) – 561-562

Lee, Henry – 88, 259-260, 262, 266, 434, 602; *letter to* – 14

Lee, Richard Bland – 180, 182-183, 264, 276, 280-281, 319

Legendre, Louis – 127, 356, 361

Lemoine D'Essoies, Edme-Marie-Joseph – 53, 55-56*

LeRay de Chaumont, Jacques – 22, 143, 145; *letter to* – 104

LeRevellière-Lepéaux, Louis-Marie – 506-

507*, 511, 599

Létombe, Joseph-Philippe – 137*

Letourneur, Etienne-François-Louis – 506-507*, 511, 607, 610, 612

Lewis, Nicholas – 16, 311, 313

Lewis, William – 602-603*

Lindet, Robert – 115

Liston, Robert – 635-636*

Littlepage, Lewis – 275, 499

Livermore, Samuel – 320*

Livingston, Brockholst – 426-427

Livingston, Edward – 238-239, 619

Livingston, Henry W. – 103*, 245

Livingston, John R. – 80*

Livingston, Mary – 243

Livingston, Muscoe – 218, 220*

Livingston, Robert – 377

Livingston, Robert R. – 1, 365, 513; *Cato* – 400-401, 422, 537; *letters to* – 242-243, 372, 372-373; *letters from* – 79-81, 238-239, 400-401, 426-427, 537-538

Loano, battle – 536

Logan, Deborah Norris – 376*

Logan, George, letters to – 372, 375-376*

Logie, Charles – 598*-599

Louis XVI – 321-322

Louis-Charles (Louis XVII) – 361-362*, 367

Lovett, Captain – 288

Lubbert & Dumas – 374, 445, 496, 522

Luttrell, Temple – 83

Luxemburg, siege and capture – 360-362, 370

Luzerne, Duc – 42

Lyman, William – 183, 185*

MacDonogh, Thomas – 279*

Macon, Nathaniel – 183-184*

Madgett, Nicholas – 470-471, 599-600*

Madison, Dolley – 181-182*, 232, 246, 495-496, 546, 575, 580, 602

Madison, James – 1-2, 6, 16, 19, 35, 52, 104, 129, 240, 261, 264, 275-276, 312, 318, 320, 352, 368, 382, 400, 433, 464, 523, 551, 571-573, 619; *on Jay Treaty* – 277-278, 555; *furniture* – 164, 278, 281, 424, 441, 494-497, 511, 574, 579, 604; *letters to* – 1, 24, 47-49, 161-165, 187-188, 230-

232, 245-247, 353-354, 383-384, 385, 405, 415, 423, 436-441, 494-499, 502-503, 511-512, 563-566, 573-576, 604, 629-630; *letters from* – 179-182, 268-269, 276-278, 280-281, 544-547, 579-580, 601-603

Madison, James, Bishop – 261

Madison, Thomas – 260, 262*

Maestricht, siege and capture – 115, 152-153, 155, 163

Mainz, siege and capture – 370, 372

Makouski, Dr. – 140

Malta, proposed alliance with United States – 135-136, 155, 157-158, 475

Mane, Dr. – 276

Mannheim, battle – 493, 535-536

Marat, Jean-Paul – 29-30, 69, 73*, 257, 560

Marec, Pierre – 299*

Maret, Huges-Bernard – 590-591*

Marie-Thérèse, Princess – 311, 536, 564, 578, 582

Marin, Marie Anne – 168-170*, 248-249

Marks, Joanna Sydnor – 275, 391, 435, 570

Marks, Peter – 55, 275, 366, 435, 570

Marshall, Humphrey – 264

Marshall, John – 260, 262, 434, 602

Martin, Alexander – 384

Martin, Hudson – 570-572*

Mason, Stevens T. – 6, 180, 183, 186, 232, 240, 260, 264, 400, 422, 436, 438, 452, 538, 544, 565, 629; *letter from* – 384

Masson, Andrew – 595; *letters from* – 533*, 584-586; *letter to* – 627

Mathieu, Jean-Baptiste-Charles – 356, 362*

Mauduit, Edmé – 377-378, 432

Maury, James – 16, 312, 389, 455, 571

Mazzei, Philip – 13, 314

McCarty, William – 20, 22*, 145

McDermott, Mr. – 456, 583, 630

McGhee, Captain – 122

McHenry, James – 601, 605, 607, 635; *letter to* – 520-521

McKean, Thomas – 88-89*, 259, 261

Mead, George – 193

Menou, Jacques-François, Baron – 487, 492*

Mercer, James – 269, 280

Mercer, John Fenton – 269*, 276, 280

Mercer, John Francis – 269, 280, 457; *letter from* – 17

Mercier, Pierre-Louis – 170*, 248

Merlin de Douai, Philippe – 142, 191, 231, 240, 253, 292, 511-512, 536; *letters to* – 24*, 636-637; *letters from* – 127-128, 191-192, 241

Merlin de Thionville, Antoine-Christophe – 284-285*

Mesange, Matthias – 298

Mifflin, Thomas – 2, 464

Millar, Mr. – 571

Miner, Mr. – 571

Miot, André-François, letters from – 158, 159*, 160, 161

Miranda, Francisco de – 499*

Mississippi River, U. S. claims to – 10, 148, 184-185, 189, 209-211, 221, 240-241, 252, 262-263; *British interest in* – 210, 316

Mitchell, Stephen Mix – 264, 267*

Monnoron, Louis – 478*, 492, 498

Monroe Andrew – 15, 55, 217, 366, 456, 635

Monroe, Eliza – 18, 47, 53, 56, 59, 164, 181, 186, 208, 217, 261, 266, 382, 389, 520, 572, 584, 635; *at school* – 200, 232, 311, 363, 399, 453, 456, 473, 587

Monroe, Elizabeth – 13, 16, 20, 56, 63, 116, 164, 181, 184, 186, 200, 208, 213, 217, 224, 234, 238, 261, 266, 313, 339, 363, 375, 384, 389, 419, 428, 435, 473, 483, 505, 520, 557, 559-560, 572, 575, 577, 580, 584, 588, 598, 602, 608, 628, 636; *voyage to France* – 18, 47; *in Paris* – 37, 59, 103, 127, 311, 381-382, 468-469, 494, 635; *purchase of furniture for Madison* – 278, 281, 546, 579

Monroe, Elizabeth Kerr – 313

Monroe, James, minister to France – *appointment* – 1-14, 17-20; *voyage to France* – 5-6, 16-19, 22-24, 47, 53; *reception in France* – 23-24, 30-33, 39-41, 48-49, 54, 58-59, 182, 185, 224-226, 237, 259, 371; *on conditions in France* – 27-28, 40, 203-204,

243, 246, 253-255, 368-372; *residence in Paris* – 37, 47-49, 53, 456, 473, 494, 528-530; *criticism of* – 49, 147, 224-227, 376, 522; *praise of* – 182, 185; *"Notes on Constitutions"* – 340-350; *desire to return to U. S.* – 382; *accusation of speculation* – 523; *defense of U. S.* – 575; *recall* – 376, 523, 602

Monroe, James, farms in Virginia – *Monroe Hill* – 13-14, 16, 181, 275, 414-415; *Highland* – 16, 54-56, 59, 181, 312-313, 516-517, 574, 608, 628; *Oak Hill* – 54, 56, 181, 217, 275, 312, 352, 366, 571; *crops* – 184, 570-572, 608

Monroe, James – financial matters – 14, 16, 55, 164, 217, 246, 275, 311-312, 354, 366, 389, 414, 455, 495, 516-517, 570-573, 634-635

Monroe, James, Kentucky and Ohio land – 164, 240, 246, 269, 352, 366, 455-456, 518, 572

Monroe, James, possessions – *household goods* – 15, 56; *books* – 15, 66, 86-87

Monroe, James, servants – 311; *Michael* – 18, 311; *Polly* – 18, 311

Monroe, James, slaves – 16, 55, 275, 311, 313; *Fanny* – 55, 366; *Hannah* – 570, 572; *Jesse* – 571; *Peter* – 55, 217, 218, 275; *Solomon* – 571; *Sukey* – 571-572; *Thenia Hemings* – 16, 217-218, 389, 571-572

Monroe, James, U. S. Senator – 1-2, 14, 19-20

Monroe, Joseph Jones – 13, 275, 313, 520, 570-572, 608; *JM advice to* – 15; *JM financial assistance to* – 15, 55, 217, 366, 389, 455-456, 635; *elected to House of Delegates* – 570, 572; *letter to* – 14-15

Montgomery, Janet – 243; *letter from* – 428

Montgomery, John – 597

Montgomery, Robert – 597-598*, 600

Monvel, Noel – 510

Moodie, Benjamin – 405

Moore, Thomas W. – 454-455*

Morgan, Daniel – 276, 280

Morocco, treaty with U. S. – 469

Morris, Gouverneur – 80, 82, 152, 173, 201, 207, 218, 223, 225, 271, 444-445, 611, 629, 631; *minister to France* – 1, 6-7, 10, 21-22, 24, 26, 32-32-35, 37-38, 42-43, 46-48, 52-53, 69, 71-72, 90-91, 104-105, 145, 150-151, 169-170, 189, 308, 323-327, 330; *letters from* – 46, 103

Morris, Lewis – 38-39*

Morris, Robert –183-184, 199, 264, 280

Morris, Robert, Jr. – 199*, 234

Motiè, Madame – see Lafayette, Adrienne

Mountflorence, James C. – 137, 256, 523, 560; *letters to* – 99*; *letters from* – 240, 249, 250-251, 263

Mozard, Theodore-Charles – 397

Muhlenberg, Frederick – 574

Munro, John – 100

Murray, George – 538, 616

Murray, George W. – 386*, 497, 499, 511, 546, 579

Naval war – 22-23, 29, 54, 205-207, 310, 379, 389, 391, 394, 492-493, 498

Nelson, William – 19, 261

Netherlands, war in – 76, 115, 152-153, 163, 178, 205, 216-218, 220-21, 232, 241, 245, 370, 372, *revolution* – 155, 206, 219-220, 228, 232, 241, 243, 246, 270, 281-282, 370, 575; *alliance with France* – 155, 205-206, 216, 219, 239, 241, 243, 274, 370, 383-384, 394; *French occupation* – 270, 284, 306, 574-575; *treaty with France* – 306-307, 309, 354, 360; *trade with U. S.* – 269, 273, 281

Nevers, Société Populaire de, letter to – 194

Neville, John – 79-80*, 87

Newell, Captain – 120

Nicholas, John – 571

Nicholas, Wilson Cary – 260, 264, 571

Nicholson, Miss – 452, 588

Nijmagen, battle – 152-153, 155, 163

Nivernais, Louis-Jules Mancini-Mazarini, Duc de – 488, 492*

Noailles, Alexis – 79

Noailles, Alfred – 79

Noailles, Euphémie – 79

Noailles, Louis-Marie, Viscount de – 79

Noailles, Louise – 79*

O'Brian, William – 100

O'Brien, Richard – 95*, 143, 145, 577, 597

Ochs, Peter – 215-216*

O'Hara, Charles – 140

Oliver, Robert – 17*

Orr, Alexander D. – 164-165*, 246

Oswald, Richard – 459-463*

Otto, Louis-Guillaume – 46 , 63, 102, 129, 137, 145-146, 153; *letter to* – 102-103

Oudart, Mr. – 153, 229

Paca, William – 2*

Pache, Jean-Nicholas – 257*

Page, John – 259, 261, 263, 457

Paine, Elijah – 183-184*

Paine, Thomas – 196-197, 204, 206, 258, 495, 522, 572, 580, 598, 602, 635; *imprisonment* – 33-35, 38-39, 67-73, 81-82, 97-98, 104.109, 128-134, 139-140, 143-145; *release from prison* – 82, 144; *residing with JM* – 164, 311, 456, 473, 559, 573-574, 577; *attack on George Washington* – 559-560; *letter to* – 81-82; *letters from* – 33-35, 38-39, 67-73, 97-98, 104-109, 128-134, 139-140

Parent, Mr. – 312

Paris, French Revolution in – 443; *September 1792* – 255, 257; *May 1793* – 255-256, 284-285; *Thermidor (July 1794)* – 11, 23-27, 29-30, 58, 520; *12 Germinal (1 April 1795)* – 284-285, 292-296, 308-309, 356, 361, 368-369; *1 Prairial (20 May 1795)* – 355-359, 361, 368-369; *13 Vendémiaire (5 October 1795)* – 484-492, 496, 498, 518-520

Parish, John – 393, 395*, 522, 525, 532-533, 536, 547-548, 584-585, 595, 627

Parker, Captain – 119

Parker, Daniel – 508-509*

Parker, Josiah – 261

Passports – 57, 65, 83, 103, 111-112, 151-153, 258, 363-364, 381, 390, 392, 403, 410, 470-471, 473, 508, 536, 544, 550, 575, 605-606, 636

Paterson, William – 602-603*

Patten, John – 180, 182*-183

Pelet, Jean – 144, 240, 256, 263, 295; *letter*

from – 196-197*

Pendleton, Edmund – 261, 275, 608

Pendleton, Nathaniel – 280

Périer, Jacques-Constantin – 510*

Perkins, Mr. – 497

Perkins, Thomas – 396

Peter, John – 119

Pétry, Jean-Baptiste – 40, 42*

Phelps, Betsey – 526*

Phelps, Oliver – 526*, 583, 630

Pichegru, Jean-Charles – 222, 284-285*, 295, 309, 420, 440-441, 478, 491, 493, 519-520, 536, 548, 557-558, 582, 600, 630, 632, 634

Pickering, Timothy – 183-184, 376, 572, 580, 589, 602, 611, 635; *secretary of war* – 238-239, 261, 265, 350, 427, 435, 464-465, 495, 544; *secretary of state* – 451, 521, 537, 546, 553, 588, 601, 607; *letters to* – 471-472, 505-507, 534-536, 547-549, 581-583, 590-591, 594-595, 619-620, 631-634; *letters from* – 297-298, 447-455, 481, 509-510, 522, 558-559

Pinckney, Betsy Motte – 82-83*

Pinckney, Charles – 208, 435, 453

Pinckney, Charles Cotesworth – 494

Pinckney, Mary – 494

Pinckney, Thomas – 70, 91-92, 136, 150, 211-213, 215, 304-305, 355, 421, 425, 444-445, 469, 520, 573-574; *minister to Great Britain* – 1, 218, 332, 338, 351, 388, 390, 394, 448, 470, 481, 483, 509, 551, 575, 583-584; *mission to Spain* – 229-230, 234, 236-237, 244-245, 252, 273, 289-290, 300, 303, 316-317, 360, 380, 407, 411, 424, 431, 439, 511-512, 517, 535, 584; *trip to Spain* – 363; *children* – 82-83, 140, 363, 427, 436, 452-453, 483, 523, 584, 636; *letters to* – 83-84, 199, 452-453, 483-484, 559, 630; *letters from* – 82-83, 116-117, 140-141, 232-234, 252, 363, 427-428, 435-436, 583-584, 588, 635-636

Pitcairn, Joseph – 42, 172, 256-257, 284, 307, 415, 581-582

Pitt, William – 189, 311, 459, 498

Pleasants, Thomas – 608*

Poland, war in – 6, 23, 59, 394

Portugal, peace with France – 320

Potomac Canal – 608

Preble, Edward – 84

Preble, Henry – 84*, 121; *letter from* – 85

Prentis, Joseph – 19, 260-261

Presque Isle, U. S. settlement at – 2, 454

Prevost, John B. – 4*, 5, 17, 164, 188, 283, 390, 397, 401, 415, 446

Prieur de la Marne, Pierre-Louis, letter from – 191-192*

Princess Royal – see Marie-Thérèse

Privateers, suppression of – 259-260, 262, 330, 338, 405-406, 613, 616, 621-622

Prony, Gaspard Riche de – 297-298*

Prussia, peace with France – 206-207, 240, 243, 246, 253, 296, 309, 320, 367, 370

Puller, Captain – 120

Purviance, John H. – 164-165*, 207, 218, 234, 237, 252-253, 290, 415, 430, 475, 577

Quiberon campaign – 394-395, 411-414, 423

Randall, Robert – 580, 630

Randall, Thomas – 548-549*

Randolph, Edmund, secretary of state – 1, 3-4, 16, 19, 25, 42, 55, 80, 92, 95, 104, 134, 145, 152, 164, 179, 181, 186, 187, 211-213, 217, 231, 244-246, 253, 265, 275, 276-277, 280, 283-284, 304, 320, 350-351, 354, 366, 377, 389, 399, 401, 414-416, 423, 427-428, 430-432, 455, 497, 538-539, 544; *resignation* – 378, 434-435, 443, 446-447, 451, 464-465, 478, 482, 492, 497-499, 512, 537-538, 542, 553, 558; *defense of U. S. policy on France* – 321-331; *Germanicus* – 266-267; *A Vindication of Edmund Randolph's Resignation* – 538, 546, 551, 580, 588-589, 607, 611, 629; *in Virginia* – 580, 608; *letters to* – 24-30, 39-42, 73-77, 109-116, 141-145, 153-156, 174-179, 188-190, 202-207, 218-221, 224, 228, 234, 253-257, 271-273, 290-296, 307-311, 356-362, 378-380, 392-395, 410-413, 419-421; *letters from* – 6-11, 20-22, 87-89, 98-99, 146-147, 172-174, 186, 193-

194, 229-230, 257-259, 287-288, 299-300, 317-318, 321-338, 350, 390, 401, 403-404, 408-410

Randolph, Martha Jefferson – 16, 59, 382, 391

Randolph, Thomas Mann – 16, 59, 181, 313, 382, 391, 434

Raynaval, Joseph-Matthias-Gérard – 460, 463*; *letter to* – 504-505

Read, Catherine Van Horn – 208

Read, Jacob – 185*, 208, 264, 280

Redon, Jean-Claude – 391, 395*; *letters to* – 403, 429-430, 463-464

Rehausen, Gotthard Maurits, Baron – 281-282*, 398

Reign of Terror – 8, 11, 25, 27, 29, 35, 58-59, 97, 156, 204-205, 356-357, 359, 362, 369, 502

Reubell, Jean-François – 306, 310, 506-507, 511

Reybez, Etienne-Salomon, letter to – 77; *letter from* – 77*

Rhine Valley, war in – 114, 309, 418-420, 440-441, 443-444, 456, 478, 491, 493, 499, 520, 535, 548, 557-558, 564

Richard, Joseph-Charles-Etienne – 274*; *letter from* – 127-128

Richmond, Duke of – 214-216*

Rittenhouse, David – 366, 376, 414

Roane, Spencer – 260-262

Robert, Jean-Charles – 523

Robespierre, Maximilien – 5, 8, 11, 23-27, 29*, 30, 33-35, 40, 48, 52, 58, 71, 75-76, 110, 113-114, 116, 146, 153, 161-162, 172, 185, 203, 205, 243, 254-255, 292-294, 359, 488, 502, 518, 520

Robins, Roger – 100

Robinson, Moses – 384

Rochefontaine, Stephen – 350-351*, 510; *letter to* – 472

Rochefoucauld, Charlotte Alexandrine, Duchesse (Rosalie) – 42-44*, 90-91, 149-150, 236, 245, 290, 302-303, 317, 407, 425, 517

Rockingham, Charles Watson-Wentworth,

Marquess – 463

Rohan, Louis-René-Edouard, Cardinal – 419*

Rohdes, Comte de – 466

Ross, James – 88-89*, 181, 188

Rowan, Archibald Hamilton – 589*, 599-600

Rozier, Jean-Antoine – 397

Rush, Benjamin – 376*

Russell, Mr. – 107, 140-141, 213

Russell, Thomas – 505*

Russia, treaty with Great Britain – 394-395

Rutherford, Robert – 276, 280

Rutledge, Charles – 584*

Rutledge, Edward – 208

Rutledge, John – 208, 261, 320, 435, 452-453, 546, 554, 580, 58, 601, 607, 634-635

Rutledge, States – 583-584*, 630, 634

Rutledge, William – 584*

Saabye, Hans – 584-585*

Sabatier, Raphael-Beinvenu – 473*

Sands, Joseph – 523-524*, 581

Sangro, Pablo, Prince of Castelfranco – 91-92

Saxe-Coburg, Prince Josias – 28-30, 54, 58, 76

Schérer, Barthélemy – 536

Schermehorn, Mr. – 304

Scott, Thomas – 183, 185*

Seagrove, Samuel – 545

Seaton, Elizabeth – 135

Seaton, William – 134-135*

Sedgwick, Theodore – 183, 185, 264, 545

Seldon, Miles – 261

Seybert, Adam – 339*, 394

Shays's Rebellion – 179

Sheldon, Mr. – 83

Sheldon, Mrs. – 83

Sherburne, John – 183, 185*

Sherman, Roger – 526

Short, William – 63, 134, 324, 351, 484, 636; *minister to Spain* – 42-44, 154, 209, 230, 240, 273, 286-287, 354, 360, 380, 427-428; *farm (Indian Camp)* – 312-314, 444, 517, 608; *in France* – 517, 520; *letters to* – 149-150, 302-304, 316-317; *letters from* – 42-44, 90-92, 150-151, 201, 235-237, 244-245, 288-290, 300-302, 411, 425-426, 444-445, 469

Sieyès, Emmanuel – 304, 296, 306, 310, 506-507, 511; *letter from* – 278, 279*, 280

Simcoe, John Graves – 80, 183

Simond, Mr. – 288

Simpson, James – 469

Sinclair, John – 259-260, 262*

Skipwith, Fulwar – 273, 445-446, 501, 590; *secretary to JM* – 5*, 18, 47, 53-54, 56, 165; *consul general at Paris* – 5, 84, 99, 111, 123, 136-137, 141, 151-152, 164, 174, 178, 188, 206, 220-221, 228, 257, 283-284, 286, 292, 308, 390, 397, 407, 410, 415, 426, 430, 467, 471, 500, 534, 536, 548, 566, 586, 618; *letters to* – 17, 283-284, 299, 386, 399, 427, 500, 521-523; *letters from* – 117-122, 223-224, 507, 556, 605; *see also* – U. S., *payment on Dutch loan*

Slave sale –570-571

Sloan, Philip – 597-598*

Smith, Captain – 288

Smith, Melancton – 18, 365, 417; *letter from* – 415; *letter to* – 577-578

Smith, Samuel – 579-580

Smith, William Loughton – 208, 261

Snow, Captain – 299

Southcombe, Thomas – 275, 389, 414, 455, 571-573

Spain, French assistance in U. S. treaty negotiations – 10, 148, 154-155, 163, 153-154, 195, 203, 209, 211, 221, 227-228, 230, 240, 242-243, 246, 252-253, 256-257, 263, 273, 316, 360, 380, 411, 423-424, 439, 452

Spain, JM proposals for action against – 163, 177

Spain, peace with France – 146, 149, 154, 163, 175, 206, 235-236, 243, 246, 252-253, 309, 311, 317, 320, 360, 370-371, 394, 411, 413-414, 425, 427; *U. S. mediation* – 300-302, 316, 360

Spain, treaty negotiations with U. S, 1785 – 146, 189-190, 317, 499

Spain, treaty with U. S. – 44, 89, 149, 209, 229-230, 235-237, 244-245, 289, 300-301,

303-304, 309, 316-317, 354, 360, 380,
    407, 423, 427-428, 435, 453, 511-512,
    517, 535, 567-568, 579, 601
Spain, war in – 29-30, 54, 91, 114, 144-145,
    152, 154, 163, 178, 205, 236
Spring, Captain – 355
St. Domingo, U. S. aid to – 9-11, 12, 20, 143,
    258, 308; *ceded to France* – 411, 414, 423
St. Just, Louis-Antoine – 24-26, 29*, 48, 58
Staël-Holstein, Eric Magnus, Baron – 217*,
    378, 383, 386, 394, 481; *letter from* – 386-
    388
Steele, John – 434
Stevens, Edward – 164, 181, 513, 575-576
Strachey, Henry – 460, 463*
Strange, Sir Robert – 461
Stratton, John, Jr. – 261, 263*
Strobel, Mr. – 236
Strother, George French – 19
Stuart (Stewart), David – 434
Swan, James – 100-101*, 164-165, 276-277,
    280, 352, 374-375, 385, 397, 409, 445,
    496, 522-523, 551, 556; *letter from* – 103-
    104
Swanwick, John – 180, 182*-183
Sweden, alliance with Denmark – 115, 152,
    175, 177-178, 258, 371, 378, 381, 383,
    386, 388, 394, 495; *invites U. S. to join
    alliance*– 387-388, 394, 481
Symes, Captain – 122
Talbot, William – 330, 338*
Taliaferro, John – 367, 457, 635
Tallien, Jean-Lambert – 25, 30*, 61-62, 171-
    172, 299, 411, 498
Tayloe, Mr. – 571
Taylor, George – 258-259*, 288
Taylor, John (of Caroline) – 6, 19, 164, 180,
    183, 208, 260-261, 264
Taylor, Mr. – 240, 250
Tazewell, Henry – 180, 183, 186, 224, 232,
    240, 260, 384, 430, 538-546, 565, 601,
    629; *letters to* – 6, 18-19; *letters from* – 264-
    267, 382-383, 553-555
Tazewell, Littleton W. – 554-555*
Terrasson, Barthélemy – 533*, 584, 621; *letter*

from – 595-596
Tessé, Adrienne-Catherine de Noailles – 434-
    435*
Thibaudeau, Antoine-Claire – 295*
Thompson, Henry – 17*
Thouin, Gabriel – 526-530*
Thuriot, Jacques-Alexis—142, 149
Thurlow, Edward – 461, 463*
Tilghman, Edward – 602-603*
Titcomb, Captain – 121, 288
Tomazini, Mr. – 200
Tone, Theobald Wolfe – 538-539*; *conversa-
    tions with JM* – 589-590, 599-600, 607
Toulon, insurrection – 357, 362
Towers, Captain – 120
Townshend, Thomas, Lord Sydney – 215-
    216*
Treaties – *see Algiers, Europe, France, Great
    Britain, Morocco, Prussia, Spain, Tripoli,
    Tunis, Tuscany*
Tréhourt de Beaulieu, Bernard-Thomas –
    100-101*
Treilhard, Jean-Baptiste – 142, 144; *letters
    from* – 127-128, 404-405
Trincano, Didier-Grégoire – 297*
Tripoli, U. S. treaty negotiations – 478-479,
    503; *French assistance in U. S. negotiations* –
    406, 432-433
Truguet, Laurent-Jean-François – 511-512*
Trumbull, John – 238*, 252, 282, 290-292,
    336, 353-354, 390
Trumbull, Jonathan – 264
Tucker, Leila Skipwith – 261
Tucker, St. George – 280; *letters to* – 19; *letters
    from* – 259-263
Tucker, Theodorick Tudor – 261, 263*
Tucker, Thomas Tudor – 261
Tunis, U. S. treaty negotiations – 478-479,
    503; *French assistance in U. S. negotiations* –
    406, 432-433
Tuscany, treaty with France – 228, 240, 253
Tyler, John, Sr. – 261
U. S. chief justice, appointment – 320, 554,
    601, 619
U. S. citizens, detained by France – 9, 20, 81,
    105-108, 115, 123, 138-139, 339, 392,

480, 544, 605-606

U. S. citizens, rights of citizenship – 67-72, 83-84, 111-112, 116, 129-130, 132-133, 213-215, 393, 402, 410-411

U. S. citizens in Paris, registration – 381, 390-392, 399, 402; *exemption from taxation* – 569; *pro-British* – 385

U. S. claims against France – 10, 42, 49, 51, 73-75, 174, 206, 220-221, 228, 250-251, 258, 355, 522, 534, 536, 548, 586-588

U. S. Congress, proceedings – 260-261, 265, 550, 553, 579-580, 602

U. S. consuls – 20, 22, 89, 110-111, 115, 123, 143, 145, 171, 178, 186, 240, 263, 284, 307, 392, 403, 410, 417, 429, 463, 494, 517, 522, 524, 581-582; *appointment* – 10, 21, 87, 161, 204, 256, 314, 361, 390, 393-394, 412, 415; *acceptable to France* – 64, 161, 256, 415, 525, 532, 536, 547-548; *letters to* – 314, 363-364; *letters from* – 94-95, 100-101, 134-135, 315, 493-494; *see also, Fulwar Skipwith, Joseph Fenwick*

U. S. elections – 180, 182-183, 208, 260-261, 264, 276, 280-281, 319-320

U. S. embargo – 9, 11

U. S., payment on Dutch loan – 229-230; *JM's involvement* – 374-375, 445-446, 496-497, 500, 507-508, 515, 530-531, 537-539, 543, 547, 551-552, 555-556, 566, 576, 587-588, 605; *Fulwar Skipwith's involvement* – 500, 507-508, 537, 547, 605; *theft of silver* – 522-523, 556, 566

U. S. secretary of state, letters to – 441-444, 476-578, 484-493

U. S. ships, detained in France – *Ariel* – 120; *Fabius* – 121; *Goddess of Liberty* – 120; *Iris* – 121; *Jane* – 315, 394; *Mary* – 120; *Norfolk* – 120; *Paragon* – 120; *Sally* – 120; *Susanna* – 120

U. S. ships, seized by France – 9, 21, 40, 49-52, 59, 73, 84-87, 102, 177, 119-120, 123, 146, 158-160, 175, 198, 299, 306, 392, 398; *Alexander* – 119-120; *Apollo* – 119; *Brothers* – 288; *Canton* – 122; *Catherine* – 193; *Deborah* – 288; *Fame* – 87, 89; *George*

– 122; *Hope* – 121-122; *James* – 119; *John* – 288; *Kensington* – 98-99, 121; *Lark* – 288; *Laurens* – 21-22, 87, 173, 288; *Lucy*, 288; *Mary* – 84-85, 121, 156-157, 288; *Mary Ann* – 288; *Olive Branch* – 119; *Peggy* – 122; *Polly* – 288; *Polly and Nancy* – 119-120; *President* – 288; *Robert* – 119; *Roebuck* – 122; *Ruth* – 119; *Severn* – 84-85, 121; *Theodosia* – 122; *Union* – 122; *Woodrup Sims* – 122

U. S. ships, seized by Great Britain – 11, 80, 91-92, 140, 351-352, 361, 371, 373, 378, 380-381, 383, 385-386, 401-402, 404, 423, 426-427, 436, 446-447, 498; *French reaction to* – 378, 380-381, 383

U. S. ships, seized by Spain – 430-431

U. S. War Department, *JM acquires books and supplies for* – 297-298, 350-351, 427, 471-472; *JM contracts with a cannon founder* – 471-472, 509-510

Unknown, letter to – 194-195

Vadier, Marc – 130, 254

Valenciennes, battle – 75

Vallière, Césaire-Philippe – 467-468*, 577, 598

Van Berckel, Pieter – 317, 320

Van Cortlandt, Philip – 264, 267*

Van Cortlandt, Pierre – 266-267*

Van Dorsten, Rudolph – 240-241

Van Gaasbeck, Peter – 238-239*

Vanhuele, Joseph – 107, 109*, 128

Van Staphorst, Jacob – 164-165*, 215, 219-220, 318, 340, 354, 418, 507, 543, 551, 556; *letter from* – 587-588

Van Staphorst, Nicholas – 164-165*, 556

Vans, Céleste-Rosalie – 99

Vans, William – 99, 121, 283-284*, 523, 581

Varlet, Mr. – 116

Varnum, Joseph B. – 264, 267*, 280, 320

Vauban, Sebastien LePestre – 297*

Vaughan, Benjamin – 136*; *letters from* – 213-216, 418-419, 459-462; *letter to* – 514

Vaughan, Sarah Manning – 214-216

Vendée, war in – 204, 206, 273, 492-493

Vergennes, Charles Gravier, Comte de – 459-

460

Vernier, Théodore – 357, 361-362*

Viellard, Louis-Guillaume – 312-313*

Vignola, Giocomo Barrozzio – 297-298*

Villaret-Joyeuse, Louis-Thomas – 23, 100*,
   206

Villeneuve, Jean Perny de – 297-298

Vincent, Charles-Humbert-Marie – 350-
   351*, 427, 471-472, 509-510, 590

Vincent, Mr. – 258

Violette, Thomas-François – 556

Virginia General Assembly, proposed constitutional amendments – 546, 601-602, 607

Volney, Constantin – 512-513*

Wadsworth, Jeremiah – 183

Walker, Francis – 313-314*, 319

Walker, Thomas – 313-314*

Warden, Mr. – 571.

Wardlaw, Sara – 391

Wardlaw, William – 391*, 570-571

Ware v. Hylton – 603

Warner, William – 100

Washington, Bushrod – 434

Washington, George – 20-21, 34, 74, 81, 87,
   129, 131, 143, 147, 173, 179, 184-185,
   187, 190, 211, 230, 299, 407-410, 431,
   454, 469, 481, 538, 545, 558, 602, 612;
   appointment of JM – 1-4, 6, 19; *approves
   JM's actions* – 186, 257-258; *recall of JM* –
   376; *on the French Revolution* – 6-7, 288,
   321-322, 326-327; *and the Whiskey
   Rebellion* – 79, 88, 180-181, 183, 259, 261-
   262, 266, 311; *and Democratic-Republican
   Societies* – 180-182, 266-268, 275, 311; *and
   Jay Treaty* – 189, 265, 277, 332,384, 390,
   397, 400-404, 416, 422, 426, 428, 431,
   434, 438-439, 446-447, 464, 497-498,
   511, 534, 537-538, 545, 553, 589; *and the
   Lafayettes* – 8, 143, 318, 558, 584; *and
   Randolph's resignation* – 435, 464-465, 553;
   captured letter to Gouverneur Morris – 611,
   629, 631; *on Great Britain* – 611; *statue of* –
   223, 421; *retirement* – 320, 400, 602; *letters
   to* – 4, 151-153, 556-558, 631; *letters from*
   – 2-3, 339-340

Washington, Martha – 557

Watson, John – 570, 572*

Watts, John – 238*, 264

Wayne, Anthony – 89, 163, 165, 183-184,
   188, 454-455, 558, 561

West Indies, war in – 80

Whippey, Captain – 119

Whiskey Rebellion – 79-80, 87-89, 116, 163,
   179-181, 183, 230, 259-262, 266, 276, 311

White, Alexander – 100

White, Captain – 240

Whitesides, Mr. – 561

Whitney, Captain – 100

Whitney, Charles – 580, 630

Wilkinson, James – 181, 269

William V, Prince of Orange – 216, 218

Williamson, Charles – 80

Willink, Van Staphorst & Hubbard – 46, 350,
   374, 543; *letter from* – 551-552

Willis, Captain – 288

Wilson, James – 259, 262, 265, 280, 602

Wirt, Mildred Gilmer – 313-314*, 391

Wirt, William – 313-314*

Wolcott, Oliver – 101, 238-239, 261, 265,
   414, 435, 464-465, 496, 523, 544, 589,
   607, 611; *letter from* – 374-375; *letters to* –
   445-446, 566

Wood, James – 180, 260

Woodward, Captain – 119-120

Wurmser, Dagobert – 54, 419*, 557, 582

Yard, James – 164, 181, 496, 513, 540, 546,
   575-576, 604, 634

Yates, Joseph R. – 4*

Yates, Mr. (merchant) – 15

Yates, Robert – 266-267*, 280, 320, 352

Yazoo land speculation – 265, 267, 280

Yeates, Jasper – 88-89*

Yellow fever – 88, 482-483

York, Frederick, Duke of – 76-77

Young, Arthur – 513*

Ysabeau, Claude-Alexandre – 61-62*, 63

Zane, Isaac – 608*

About the Editor

DANIEL PRESTON had 20 years of experience in historical documentary editing before joining the Papers of James Monroe Project as editor. The project is sponsored by the James Monroe Presidential Center at the University of Mary Washington in Fredericksburg, Virginia.